CARSWELL

CASES, MATERIALS AND NOTES
ON PARTNERSHIPS AND
CANADIAN BUSINESS
CORPORATIONS

Puri, Anand, Iacobucci,
Lee & MacIntosh

Sixth Edition

A cataloguing record for this publication is available from Library and Archives Canada.

ISBN 978-0-7798-7314-2 (2016 edition)

Printed in the United States by Thomson Reuters.

TELL US HOW WE'RE DOING
Scan the QR code to the right with your smartphone to send your comments regarding our products and services.
Free QR Code Readers are available from your mobile device app store.
You can also email us at carswell.feedback@thomsonreuters.com

 THOMSON REUTERS®

THOMSON REUTERS CANADA, A DIVISION OF THOMSON REUTERS CANADA LIMITED

One Corporate Plaza
2075 Kennedy Road
Toronto, Ontario
M1T 3V4

Customer Relations
Toronto 1-416-609-3800
Elsewhere in Canada/U.S. 1-800-387-5164
Fax: 1-416-298-5082
www.carswell.com
E-mail www.carswell.com/email

CASES, MATERIALS AND NOTES ON PARTNERSHIPS AND CANADIAN BUSINESS CORPORATIONS

Sixth Edition

by

Poonam Puri
Professor of Law
Osgoode Hall Law School
York University

Edward M. Iacobucci
Dean and James M. Tory
Professor of Law
Faculty of Law
University of Toronto

Anita I. Anand
Professor of Law and J.R. Kimber
Chair in Investor Protection and
Corporate Governance
Faculty of Law
University of Toronto

Ian B. Lee
Associate Professor
Faculty of Law
University of Toronto

Jeffrey G. MacIntosh
Professor and Toronto Stock Exchange
Chair in Capital Markets Law
Faculty of Law
University of Toronto

PREFACE TO SIXTH EDITION

Our primary goal in preparing this edition has been to update the materials so they reflect the important case law and statutory and doctrinal developments that have occurred over the past five years since the last edition of this casebook was published.

It is difficult to reduce the developments over this period to a short list. However, we highlight central themes that continue to be important, including: the extent to which directors' fiduciary duties extend to stakeholders in the corporation other than shareholders, the courts' use of the business judgment rule in reviewing directors' decisions, the burgeoning personal liability of directors and officers, and the continued expansion of the scope and use of the oppression remedy.

This edition has been updated to reflect significant legal changes including judicial clarification on when the derivative action should be used rather than the oppression remedy, expanded auditor liability, and the increased role of securities commissions in regulating what has historically been regarded as corporate law's domain. Although the Supreme Court of Canada found the previous attempt at a national securities regulator to be unconstitutional in 2011, the debate over the creation of a common securities regulator remains live and active, with Quebec having launched another constitutional challenge on the latest Cooperative Capital Markets Regulatory System. This edition also reviews key recommendations from a 2015 Ontario expert panel report that emerged from concerns about the lack of harmonization in corporate statutes among the provinces, territories and the federal corporate statute, and implications for competitiveness. The recommendations included expanding eligibility for limited liability status (currently only available to certain professionals in Ontario, while there are no restrictions in British Columbia) and removing residency requirements for directors (currently Ontario requires at least 25% of directors to be resident Canadians, while some other provinces and territories have no such requirements).

The global financial crisis of the late 2000s, which resulted in the fall of key businesses and many large financial institutions in the United States, emphasized the potential need for greater regulation of corporate activity, particularly in the areas of risk and compensation. Unlike in the United States, where the *Dodd-Frank Act* has provided for increased shareholder activism and governmental control of corporate activity, the legislative and judicial response to the financial crisis in Canada has been slower to develop. Whereas Canada followed the American *Sarbanes-Oxley Act* of 2002 in some significant ways, this is not the case with regards to the post-financial crisis era, perhaps because of the relative strength of Canadian financial institutions and their regulator, the Office of the Superintendent of Financial Institutions (OSFI).

All of the contributors to this edition owe a significant debt to the contributors of the previous editions: Ron Daniels, Aaron Dhir, Doug Harris, Edward Iacobucci, Ian Lee, Jeffrey MacIntosh, Poonam Puri, Ed Waitzer and Jacob Ziegel. Finally, we wish to extend our sincere appreciation to law students Tommy Leung and Andrew Mihalik for their excellent research assistance in the preparation of this edition.

Poonam Puri   Ian Lee
Anita Anand   Jeffrey MacIntosh
Edward Iacobucci

May 9, 2016

Regulating the Market for Corporate Control: A Critical Assessment of the Tender Offer's Role in Corporate Governance
Columbia Law Review

Report of the Industrial Inquiry Commission on Canadian National Railways Run-Throughs (Pursuant to Section 56 of the Industrial Relations and Disputes Investigation Act) 1965
Human Resources and Skills Development Canada
Minister of Public Works and Government Services Canada

Report of the Ontario Select Committee on Company Law (1967)
Queen's Printer (Ontario)

Report of the Royal Commission on Corporate Concentration
Minister of Public Works and Government Services, and the Privy Council Office

The Shareholders' Derivative Action
S.M. Beck
Canadian Bar Review

Share Transfer and Transmission Restrictions in the Close Corporation
D.P. Coates
University of British Columbia Law Review

Shareholders' Voting Rights and Company Control
M.A. Pickering
Stevens and Sons Limited

The Structure of the Corporation
Little, Brown and Company

Studies in Canadian Company Law Vol. II (1973)
D. Huberman
J.S. Ziegel
Butterworth & Co. (Canada) Ltd.

Unanimous Shareholder Agreements
C. Nicholls

Ultra Vires and Some Related Problems
University of British Columbia Law Review

Vicarious Liability in the Law of Torts
Butterworth's (London)

SUMMARY OF CONTENTS

TABLE OF CONTENTS

PART A — PARTNERSHIP LAW

PART B — BUSINESS CORPORATIONS LAW

Chapter 9 — Special Aspects of the Closely Held or Private Corporation

TABLE OF ABBREVIATIONS

Frequently Cited Statutes and other Legislative Sources

ABCA	Business Corporations Act, R.S.A. 2000, c. B-9
ALI SECURITIES CODE	American Law Institute, *Federal Securities Code*, May 19, 1978
BCBCA	Business Corporations Act, S.B.C. 2002, c. 57
BCCA	Company Act [Repealed], R.S.B.C. 1996, c. 62
BCSA	Securities Act, S.B.C. 2004, c. 43
BNA	Business Names Act, R.S.O. 1990, c. B.17
CBCA	Canada Business Corporations Act, R.S.C. 1985, c. C-44
CIA	Corporations Information Act, R.S.O. 1990, c. C.39
EPCA	Extra-Provincial Corporations Act, R.S.O. 1990, c. E.27
LPA	Limited Partnerships Act, R.S.O. 1990, c. L.16
MBCA	American Bar Association, Committee on Corporate Laws, *Model Business Corporations Act*, 1984
MCA	The Corporations Act, R.S.M. 1987, c. C225
OBCA	Business Corporations Act, R.S.O. 1990, c. B.16
PA	Partnerships Act, R.S.O. 1990, c. P.5
PRA	Partnerships Registration Act, R.S.O. 1980, c. 371, [repealed 1990, c. 5, s. 12; proclaimed in force May 1, 1991]
QCA	Companies Act, R.S.Q., c. C-38
QSA	Securities Act, R.S.Q., c. V-1.1
SA (or OSA)	Securities Act, R.S.O. 1990, c. S.5
SEA	Securities Exchange Act of 1934, 15 USC §78, U.S. Laws 1934, c. 404

TABLE OF CASES

Chapter 1

Partnership Law Principles

1. VARIETIES OF BUSINESS ORGANIZATION

A question all persons intending to launch a new business must ask themselves is the legal form in which the enterprise is to be conducted. Canadian law recognizes three principal types of organization for conducting a business. These are (1) a sole proprietorship, (2) a partnership and (3) a business corporation. Partnerships are further subdivided into three categories: (a) General Partnerships, (b) Limited Partnerships (LPs) and (c) Limited Liability Partnerships (LLPs).

(a) Sole Proprietorships

The sole proprietorship is both the oldest and simplest form of business organization. As its name indicates, the sole proprietorship has but one owner who has both the prerogative and responsibility of making all ultimate decisions concerning the business. There is nothing in law to prevent a sole proprietorship from becoming a large and powerful enterprise, though most sole proprietorships tend to be small and localized. Quantitatively, sole proprietorships still play an important role in the economy.

The attractions of a sole proprietorship are the ease with which such a business may be commenced and dissolved (assuming it is not subject to special municipal, provincial or federal licensing requirements) and the modest expenses involved in starting it up. Under the Ontario *Business Names Act*, R.S.O. 1990, c. B.17, s. 2(2) ("BNA"), the business name of a sole proprietorship need not be registered if the owner is using her own name.

The disadvantages are that the sole proprietor enjoys none of the advantages that accrue to a business corporation, including the one-person corporation, considered below. In particular, the unincorporated owner is fully liable for all the debts and other obligations incurred by his or her business regardless of how carefully he or she segregates it from all his or her other activities. In law the unincorporated business has no separate personality, no matter how carefully the proprietor segregates his or her business activities from his or her personal activities.

(b) Partnerships

The provincial partnerships Acts all define a partnership as the relationship subsisting between two or more persons carrying on business with a view to profit. A general partnership therefore differs from a sole proprietorship in that the former has multiple owners instead of one and, in most cases, also has a more complex organization. Ease of formation and dissolution, general lack of formalities with respect to both (other than compliance with the registration requirements under the BNA and the obligation to give notice to creditors under the *Partnerships Act* if a partner retires) and great flexibility in designing the internal managerial structure of the business are also hallmarks of the partnership.

Equally, the general partnership suffers from the same weaknesses as a sole proprietorship as compared with the business corporation, including the unlimited liability of each partner, jointly or jointly and severally, for all the debts and other obligations of the partnership. A partner can limit his or her liability by becoming a limited partner pursuant to the provisions of one of the provincial limited partnerships Acts (or the corresponding provisions in the *Partnerships Act* of those jurisdictions where both types of partnership are treated in the same Act) but this involves her or her abstention from playing any part in the direction of the business. Partners in qualifying professional firms can exclude their liability for the negligent or other described wrongful acts of a partner by registering as a Limited Liability Partnership (LLP), and meeting other statutory requirements, without losing their right to remain active partners as is true in a limited partnership. See further, *infra*, section 6. The disadvantages of unlimited liability for general partnerships can also be circumvented by forming a partnership between incorporated companies, and such partnerships are quite common. Technically speaking, an incorporated general partner is liable for all the debts of the partnership, but if the corporation has few assets the practical effect is the same as if the partner had limited liability for the partnership debts. *Cf. Haughton Graphic Ltd. v. Zivot*, *infra*, section 6.

(c) Business Corporations[1]

The history of business corporations law and the distinctive attributes of a business corporation are dealt with in Chapter 2. Here it

---

[1] "Corporation" and "Company" will be used interchangeably throughout this book to indicate an incorporated business entity unless the context indicates otherwise. "Company" or "limited company" is the term commonly used in the United Kingdom and those parts of the Commonwealth that have adopted the British-type companies legislation.

must suffice to summarize the principal features that distinguish the corporation from the unincorporated form of business enterprise. First, the corporation has its own legal personality which is separate from that of its shareholders, directors and officers. This is true even in the case of one-person corporations. The corporation can therefore sue and be sued in its own name, and equally it can enter into contracts even with its own shareholders. Second, the corporation has perpetual succession and is not affected by any changes in, or the deaths or retirements of its members. Third, shareholders are not liable for the debts or other obligations of the corporation. This last advantage alone is sufficient in many instances to make the corporation the preferred business vehicle for investors and entrepreneurs alike.

Incorporation also has some disadvantages, though none of them is serious. Incorporation must be sought from a government agency or official and requires the filing of documents and the adoption of a corporate constitution. Annual returns containing prescribed information must also be filed in many of the provinces. Further, a corporation wishing to do business in more than one province will either have to incorporate federally or obtain an extra-provincial licence to carry on business in the host province. Legal costs are involved, as are costs for business name registration under statutes such as the BNA if the corporation carries on business under an assumed name. Finally, corporations are required to hold meetings, to elect directors and to provide shareholders with information. In the case of one-person and closely held corporations modern legislation has greatly simplified these requirements and they can usually be satisfied easily.

Overall then, the advantages of incorporation greatly outweigh its disadvantages and a corporation is generally a superior business vehicle, from a legal perspective, than either the sole proprietorship or the general or limited partnership. Why then would a person or persons choose not to incorporate his or their business? We have no complete set of answers, but the following may provide a partial explanation. First, various types of professionals (*e.g.*, lawyers) are not allowed in many provinces to conduct their business in incorporated form. See further, *infra*, Chapter 3. Second, the promoters may only envisage a short term business relationship and may not think it worthwhile to incorporate. Third, partnerships, particularly those of short duration, are often formed between corporations. They may feel their corporate status already protects them adequately from unlimited liability. Fourth, the unincorporated form of business may offer tax advantages. This appears to be the dominant reason for the resurgence of interest in limited liability partnerships. See *infra*, section 6. Having offered these explanations we are bound to add a further one, and this is that many

---

"Corporation" is invariably used in the US, and is the expression now adopted in most of the provincial Acts in Canada and in the federal legislation.

small business persons may not realize how easy and relatively inexpensive incorporation is and the many advantages it can offer.

2. THE HISTORY OF PARTNERSHIP LAW

Partnership was a well known institution in Roman law (where it was known as a *societas*) and in other ancient legal systems, but partnership law itself developed only slowly in the common law. Initially, the courts of the law merchants were primarily seized of disputes between partners, and equity and the common law apparently did not play a large role until the seventeenth and eighteenth centuries. The industrial revolution and Britain's pre-eminent position as a mercantile nation gave further impetus in the nineteenth century to the development and refinement of partnership principles. The accumulation of case law made the law both uncertain and complex. The British Parliament subsequently adopted the *Partnership Act* 1890, 53 & 54 Vict. c. 39. In 1907, it also adopted the *Limited Partnerships Act* of that year, 7 Edw. 7, c. 24. However, its practical impact was negligible because the easy availability of incorporation for small businesses following the House of Lords' seminal decision in *Salomon v. Salomon & Co.* (1896), [1897] A.C. 22 (U.K. H.L.), *infra*, Ch. 2, made this a far superior business vehicle for investors concerned to exclude their liability for the enterprise's debts. In 2000, the British Parliament enacted the *Limited Liability Partnerships Act 2000*. However, unlike its Canadian counterparts, the English LLP has corporate personality and does not constitute a partnership under the *Partnership Act* 1890.

All the Canadian common law provinces have copied the 1890 Act. All of them have also adopted a limited partnerships Act or provisions dealing with limited partnerships, though not necessarily of the British variety. All of them also have requirements with respect to the registration of partnerships which may be contained in the *Partnerships Act* or in a separate Act. See further, *infra*, section 6.

The British *Partnership Act* and its Canadian counterparts are divided into the following principal parts (all the section references below and in the balance of the chapter are to the Ontario *Partnerships Act*, R.S.O. 1990, c. P.5, unless otherwise indicated):

1. Nature of Partnership (ss. 2–5);
2. Relation of Partners to Persons Dealing With Them (ss. 6–19);
3. Relation of Partners to One Another (ss. 20–31);
4. Dissolution of Partnership (ss. 32–44);
5. General (ss. 45–46).

The Act is not a complete code and s. 45 (Ont.) provides that the rules of equity and common law applicable to partnerships continue in force except so far as they are inconsistent with the express provisions of the Act.

The materials that follow are designed to expose the student to the principal characteristics of the partnership concept at common law and the modifications introduced by the LP and LLP legislation, and to enable him or her to obtain a better appreciation of the nature of corporate personality dealt with below in Chapter 2.

3. DEFINITION OF PARTNERSHIP

Section 2 of the *Partnerships Act* ("PA") defines a partnership as existing when two or more persons carry on business in common with a view to a profit. It should be noted that the term "business" is defined in ss. 1(1) as including "every trade, occupation and profession". Further, "with a view to a profit" does not mean that a profit must actually be generated. As noted by the Supreme Court of Canada in *Backman v. R.*, 2001 CarswellNat 246, 2001 CarswellNat 247, [2001] 1 S.C.R. 367 (S.C.C.) at p. 381 [S.C.R.]: "The law of partnership does not require a net gain over a determined period in order to establish that an activity is with a view to profit. For example, a partnership may incur initial losses during the start up phase of its enterprise. That does not mean that the relationship is not one of partnership, so long as the enterprise is carried on with a view to profit in the future."

Section 3 of the PA provides some important guidelines in determining whether or not a partnership exists in the prescribed situations. These rules are themselves of late origin and evolved principally from 1860 onwards. Under s. 3(1), joint tenancy or common ownership of property does not in and of itself create a partnership. This principle is discussed in the case that follows.

A.E. LePage Ltd. v. Kamex Developments Ltd.
(1977), 78 D.L.R. (3d) 223, 1977 CarswellOnt 414 (C.A.), affirmed [1979] 2 S.C.R. 155, 1979 CarswellOnt 706, 1979 CarswellOnt 706F.

BLAIR J.A.: This is an appeal from a judgment of Madam Justice Van Camp in which she allowed the claim of the respondent, a real estate agent, for commission under an exclusive listing agreement. During the term of the exclusive listing agreement the property, a large apartment building, was sold through another agent and the amount of the commission claimed was $45,000. Judgment was given against the appellants but not against the corporate defendant, Kamex Developments Limited. The question in this case is whether the appellants constituted a partnership and, if so, whether the defendant March signed the listing agreement as a partner binding the partnership.

The appellants purchased the property in question in 1970, under the name of one of them, "M. Kalmykow in trust". The defendant corporation was then incorporated to hold the property in trust for the appellants. It executed a declaration of trust and concurrently entered into a written agreement with them.

The agreement specified that the property was to be held by the defendant corporation in trust for the appellants in proportion to their interests as set forth therein. It provided that revenues and profits from the property should be paid to them in proportion to their interests and that they should be liable to pay any deficiency to the corporation in the same proportions. It provided for the sale or transfer of the interests of the appellants in the property to third parties after the other appellants named in the agreement had been given a first opportunity of refusal. The agreement also provided that any decision "regarding the sale or other dealings with the said apartment building" was to be made by a majority vote defined as the majority of the interests in the property of the appellants. The evidence disclosed that the appellants met monthly in order to discuss the operation of the property and also the possibility of its sale.

At some stage the property was listed for sale by what is called an open listing. A decision was taken by the appellants as a group that there should be no exclusive listing. Employees of the respondent approached March, one of the appellants, and as a result he executed the exclusive listing agreement. The learned trial Judge found that he signed this agreement on behalf of all the other appellants, and that he was understood to have done so by the employees of the respondent. She also found that he was not authorized by the appellants to sign the exclusive listing agreement and his act had not been approved by them.

Many issues were raised in the course of this argument but because of the nature of the pleadings, it is unnecessary to refer to all of them. The respondent's statement of claim alleged:

> On October 6, 1972, the Plaintiff entered into a written agreement (hereinafter referred to as "The Listing Agreement") with the Defendant, March. At the time of execution of the Listing Agreement, the Plaintiff was advised by March that he was a member of the partnership and had authority to enter into the Listing Agreement on behalf of the partnership. It was a term of the Listing Agreement that such Exclusive Authority was to be irrevocable until one minute before midnight on November 30, 1972.

This pleading confines the respondent to an assertion that it dealt with the appellant March as a representative of a partnership. Hence, the prime issue in this appeal is whether or not the appellants were a partnership. This involves an answer to the elementary question of whether the appellants as co-owners of the property thereby became partners.

A partnership is defined in the *Partnerships Act*, R.S.O. 1970, c. 339, s. 2, as follows:

* * *

The key words of the definition refer to "persons carrying on a business in common with a view to profit". The mere fact that property is owned in common and that profits are derived therefrom does not of itself constitute the co-owners as partners. Section 3, para. I of the *Partnerships Act* reads as follows:

> 3. In determining whether a partnership does or does not exist, regard shall be had to the following rules:
>
>   1. Joint tenancy, tenancy in common, joint property, common property, or part ownership does not of itself create a partnership as to anything so held or owned, whether the tenants or owners do or do not share any profits made by the use thereof.

Whether or not the position of co-owners becomes that of partners depends on their intention as disclosed by all the facts of the case. It is necessary to determine whether the intention of the co-owners was to "carry on a business" or simply to provide by an agreement for the regulation of their rights and obligations as co-owners of a property. The test was stated by Roach, J.A. in *Thrush v. Read*, [1950] 2 D.L.R. 392, 1950 CarswellOnt 42 (C.A.) at p. 396, as whether:

> on a true construction of the agreement, and having regard to all the circumstances, it should be held that the parties to that agreement intended to become, and thereby became, partners in a joint venture and that therefore they were not merely co-owners of the common property.

At p. 396 [D.L.R.], he said:

> In addition to the joint ownership created by the agreement, it becomes necessary therefore to find within that agreement an intention on the part of the parties thereto to carry on a business in common with a view of profit.

In that case it was clear that the purpose of a mining syndicate was not simply to hold claims as co-owners, but to carry on the business of dealing in mining claims, rights and privileges and turn the same to account. There is no such intention to carry on a business in this case.

This case is comparable to *Robert Porter & Sons Ltd. v. Armstrong*, [1926] S.C.R. 328, 1926 CarswellBC 105 where, on facts not too dissimilar from the present case, it was held that the co-owners of property were not partners. There Duff, J., dealt with the fundamental distinction between partnership and co-ownership at p. 330 [S.C.R.]:

> The real question is whether, from the evidence before us, one ought to infer an agreement in the juridical sense that the property these two persons intended dealing with was to be held jointly as

partnership property, and sold as such. Is this what they contemplated? Had they in their minds a binding agreement which would disable either of them from dealing with his share — that is to say, with his share in the land itself — as his own separate property? A common intention that each should be at liberty to deal with his undivided interest in the land as his own would obviously be incompatible with an intention that both should be bound to treat the *corpus* as the joint property, the property of a partnership. English law does not regard a partnership as a *persona* in the legal sense. Nevertheless, the property of the partnership is not divisible among the partners *in specie*. The partner's right is a right to a division of profits according to the special arrangement, and as regards the *corpus* to a sale and division of the proceeds on dissolution after the discharge of liabilities. This right, a partner may assign, but he cannot transfer to another an undivided interest in the partnership property *in specie*.

The learned trial Judge considered that the intention of the co-owners to purchase the building, hold it as an investment and sell it for profit constituted them as partners in a business carried on for profit. With respect, I am of the opinion that the mere fact that co-owners intend to acquire, hold and sell a building for profit does not make them partners. As Duff, J., said in *Robert Porter & Sons Ltd. v. Armstrong*, at p. 329 [S.C.R.], p. 341 [D.L.R.]:

> Foster and Miller unquestionably intended to buy the property, to sell it again at an enhanced price, and thereby to make profit. Indeed, the sole object of purchasing the land was to dispose of it profitably. No doubt they intended to share the outlay equally between them. As regards the purchase money, the law would, of course, give to either of them a right of contribution against the other for any payment on the joint debt in excess of his own proper share, and on a sale, each would be entitled to share in the price according to his interest. The inevitable result, if the property was held in common and sold, would be that, as between Foster and Miller themselves, the right to share in the profits and the legal responsibility for losses would be equally distributed. But these consequences all flow from the fact that these two persons were jointly responsible for the purchase money, and that each was entitled to an undivided moiety in the equitable estate vested in them, as the result of the contract of purchase.

In this case, the intention of the parties to maintain their rights as co-owners of the property is clear beyond doubt from the documents. In addition, it should be noted that the appellants wished to identify and keep separate their respective beneficial interests in the property for income tax purposes. Their intention would have been defeated if they were regarded as a partnership and the apartment building had become the property of the partnership. The fact that they are obliged by their agreement to offer a right of first refusal to the other co-owners in the event of sale is not inconsistent with their basic right to deal with their respective interests in the property . . .

* * *

Appeal allowed.

Notes

1   *Kamex* was distinguished by Murphy D.C.J. in *Lansing Building Supply (Ontario) Ltd. v. Ierullo* (1989), 71 O.R. (2d) 173, 1989 CarswellOnt 2316 (Dist. Ct.). The three individual defendants and three corporations controlled by them carried on business under a collective name. Through the corporation they held title in real property in common with a view to developing the property and selling it as condominiums. The agreement signed by the individual defendants and the corporations purported to be a co-ownership agreement and disclaimed any intention to enter into a partnership between them. One of the individual defendants ordered building materials from the plaintiff and held himself out as a partner with the other individual defendants. The plaintiff sued the individual defendants for the balance owing on the building supplies on the premise that they were in fact partners.

Murphy D.C.J. upheld the claim and distinguished *Kamex* on two grounds. The first was that the terms of the co-ownership agreement had many of the attributes associated with a partnership (*e.g.*, the provisions that the property was to be held by the defendants as tenants in common, that profits from the venture were to be distributed among the co-owners, and the fact that the right of the co-owners to deal with their interests in the land was severely restricted). The second ground was that that the conduct of the parties was consistent with the existence of a partnership. For a similar case involving the finding of a partnership among co-owners of real property, see *Volzke Construction Ltd. v. Westlock Foods Ltd.* (1986), 45 Alta. L.R. (2d) 97, reproduced below.

2   From a practical perspective, how is a third party supposed to tell the difference between a "simple" co-ownership and a partnership when the third party receives an order from one of the co-owners? To be on the safe side, must the third party obtain the signatures of all the co-owners authorizing each of them to contract on behalf of the others? Would it be better for the law to invest the co-owners of commercial property with the same type of usual authority as would be conferred on a co-owner if she were a partner? For the power of a partner to bind the partnership with respect to obligations incurred by the

partner while acting within the usual scope of the partner's authority, see PA, s. 6.

3 Where a person purports to act as agent for another, he or she is deemed to warrant his or her authority to do so. If he or she has never been appointed an agent (as apparently was true of March in *A.E. LePage Ltd. v. Kamex Developments*, *supra*), or has exceeded his or her authority as agent, the person so holding himself out is guilty of breach of warranty of authority. For the measurement of damages in such a case, see *Wickberg v. Shatsky*, *infra*, ch. 3(9).

Volzke Construction Ltd. v. Westlock Foods Ltd.
1986 CarswellAlta 94, 45 Alta. L.R. (2d) 97 (Alta. C.A.)

Moir J.A. (for the Court, allowing the appeal): — The appellant is a general contractor doing business in Northern Alberta with its headquarters in the Town of Westlock. As general contractor it undertook to build in two phases an addition to the Westlock Shopping Centre. It was not paid its final billing. It accordingly sued the respondent company alleging that the respondent was in partnership with another limited company Bonel Properties Ltd. and was liable for the debt.

* * *

The respondent had the I.G.A. franchise in the Town of Westlock. Bonel Properties Ltd. approached Horne & Pitfield, the franchisee, to take space in the expanded Westlock Shopping Centre which was to be built on to an existing mall. They were told to get in touch with David Shefsky, who was the main shareholder in the respondent Company.

Mr. Shefsky was not content to be a tenant. He wanted to be an owner. As a result he made an offer to Bonel Properties Ltd. for a 20 per cent interest in the Westlock Shopping Centre. He agreed and did pay $32,000.00 for this interest. This is clearly shown in Exhibit 10. The opening paragraph is:

> "This will confirm that Dave Shefsky is prepared to purchase an undivided twenty (20%) per cent interest of the Westlock Shopping Centre at and for a consideration of thirty two thousand ($32,000.00) dollars."

The letter closed as follows:

> "Dave Shefsky is signing this agreement as an indication of his intent to complete the purchase of an undivided twenty (20%) per cent interest in the property as at June 15, 1977."

This offer was dated June 7, 1977 and was accepted on the same letter agreement on June 8, 1977.

The plans for the expansion of the Westlock Shopping Centre had been prepared. Tenders were called for. However, Volzke went to Dave Shefsky and asked about obtaining the construction job. He was told by Shefsky that the contract would go out for tender but that Shefsky would introduce Volzke to his partners. He did so. When the tenders came in they were too high. Bonel Properties Ltd. discharged the architect. Volzke made certain suggestions to save costs. The contract was awarded to him on the basis of cost plus $30,000.00 on each of the two phases of the new construction. This led to the finding that the amount owing was $76,928.88. That finding is not challenged in this appeal.

A bank account, with printed cheques, was opened in the name of Bonel Properties Ltd. and Westlock Foods Ltd. Only the principals of Bonel Properties Ltd. had signing authority. All accounts were submitted to Bonel Properties Ltd. Each of Volzke's accounts was paid as rendered up to December 22, 1978. On that date Dave Shefsky died. The final account rendered after that date remained unpaid.

After Dave Shefsky's death Mrs. Shefsky carried on. She was refused signing authority on the bank account. She sent prospective tenants to Bonel Properties Ltd. Bonel Properties Ltd. negotiated all leases. Tenants made complaints re repairs etc. to the manager of Westlock Foods Ltd. store. Bonel Properties Ltd. arranged to complete the repairs and maintenance and paid the bills on the printed cheques of Bonel Properties Ltd. and Westlock Foods Ltd.

The interim financing of the additions to the Westlock Shopping Centre were arranged through the Treasury Branch. Both Bonel Properties Ltd. and Westlock Foods Ltd. executed the debenture in March of 1978. They were jointly and severally liable. Later a mortgage was placed with Investor's Syndicate which was signed by both companies, Bonel Properties Ltd. as to 80 per cent and the respondent as to 20 per cent.

Unhappy differences soon arose between Bonel Properties Ltd. and Westlock Foods Ltd. Apparently, Westlock Foods Ltd. as a tenant wanted things that Bonel Properties Ltd. as landlord did not want to give them. Disputes arose. Also the bank account did not provide for Westlock Foods Ltd. management as signing authorities. The title to the land on which the I.G.A. Store sat was transferred to show 80-20 ownership but title to the original Westlock Shopping Centre and the parking lot and the land on which phase 2 of the shopping centre was built, remained in the name of Bonel Properties Ltd. only.

Westlock Foods Ltd. started an action against Bonel Properties Ltd. They filed affidavits. The learned chambers judge held that there was either a partnership or joint venture between the parties. He gave to Westlock Foods Ltd. an interest in the entire operation, including the parking lot. He acted upon the affidavit of Mrs. Shefsky. When the matter went before the master to do an accounting, Mrs. Shefsky filed a further affidavit outlining her activities in aiding the business in its operation. This affidavit was put to Mrs. Shefsky in cross-examination and entered as an exhibit. It showed activities entirely consistent with the partnership.

In this case, the learned trial judge examined the cases submitted by the appellant's counsel and extracts from Lindlay on Partnership presented by the respondent's counsel. He reached the conclusion he did by finding that there was no intention to enter into a partnership and that as Westlock Foods Ltd. had no control over the business it could not be a partnership. In this, we are of the view that he erred in law.

In our respectful opinion, we think the learned trial judge should have proceeded by looking at the *Partnership Act*, R.S.A. 1980, c. P.2. Partnership is defined in that Act as follows:

"1. In this Act,

. . .

(d) 'partnership' means the relationship that subsists between persons carrying on a business in common with a view to profit;"

Nothing is said in the definition about control. We know that you can have silent partners or managing partners. Control has nothing whatever to do with the existence or non-existence of a partnership.

Secondly, there is no doubt that everyone agrees that the parties decided they would share the costs of developing the business of Westlock Shopping Centre on an 80-20 basis. Further, it was common ground that they would share the profits, if any, on an 80-20 basis. This is entirely clear.

Thirdly, we know that they spoke of each other as partners. Westlock Foods Ltd. or Mr. and Mrs. Shefsky sent tenants to Bonel Properties Ltd. They received complaints and arranged for rectification of the complaints. They were to share both the cost of expanding the mall and the profits it would make as a business.

The *Partnership Act* deals with this question in s. 4(c) which reads:

"4. In determining whether a partnership does or does not exist, regard shall be had to the following rules:

. . .

(c) the receipt by a person of a share of the profits of a business is prima facie proof that that person is a partner in the business, . . ."

Counsel for the respondent argues that there are two phases of the arrangements between the parties. The first is the construction of the shopping centre. The second is the running of the business of the shopping centre. We can find no authority for such a proposition nor is there anything in the actions of the parties or their words which leads to this highly unusual and very unfair result. This argument was not advanced before the learned trial judge and was first mentioned in oral argument before us.

On all of the facts: the letter, Exhibit 10, which says he is buying a 20 per cent interest in Westlock Shopping Centre; the introduction of the principals of Bonel Properties Ltd. as his partners; the bank account and the printed cheques; the Treasury Branch and Investors Syndicate financing; the right to be consulted about new tenants; the sending of prospective tenants; the "on the spot" looking after the construction faults and repairs; the bank account and the admission that they were to share the costs on an 80-20 basis as well as the profits being divided on that same basis; and, finally, the previous action between the parties; drives us to the conclusion that Bonel Properties Ltd. and Westlock Foods Ltd. were partners in the business of operating the Westlock Shopping Centre. . . .

Notes

The other guidelines contained in s. 3 are important to consider as well. In 1865, in *Bovill's Act*, 28 & 29 Vic. c. 86, the British Parliament sought to clarify the common law position by providing that a receipt of the share of the profits of a business by a creditor in the described circumstances was not sufficient to make him a partner of the business. These provisions were subsequently incorporated in what are now ss. 3.3(a) and (d) and 4 of the Ontario *Partnerships Act*. Sections 1 and 5 of *Bovill's Act* read as follows:

1. The Advance of Money by way of Loan to a Person engaged or about to engage in any Trade or Undertaking upon a Contract in Writing with such Person that the Lender shall receive a Rate of Interest varying with the Profits, or shall receive a Share of the Profits arising from carrying on such Trade or Undertaking, shall not, of itself, constitute the Lender Partner with the Person or the Persons carrying on such Trade or Undertaking, or render him responsible as such. . .

5. In the event of any such Trader as aforesaid being adjudged a Bankrupt, or taking the Benefit of any Act for the Relief of Insolvent Debtors, or entering into an Arrangement to pay his Creditors less than Twenty Shillings in the Pound, or dying in insolvent Circumstances, the Lender of any such Loan as aforesaid shall not be entitled to recover any Portion of his Principal, or of the Profits or Interest payable in respect of such Loan, nor shall any such Vendor of a Goodwill as aforesaid be entitled to recover any such Profits as aforesaid until the Claims of the other Creditors of the said Trader for valuable Consideration in Money or Money's Worth have been satisfied.

These provisions are critically examined below by Sir George Jessel M.R. in *Pooley v. Driver* (1876), 5 Ch. D. 458 (Eng. M.R.), another leading nineteenth-century case.

Pooley v. Driver
(1876), 5 Ch. D. 458 (Eng. M.R.)

[Borrett and Hagen, in 1868, entered into a partnership agreement to carry on a business that involved manufacturing grease, pitch and manure. The agreement provided for a division of capital in sixty equal parts. Seventeen parts were attributed to Borrett and twenty-three to Hagen. The remaining twenty parts were attributed to creditors in accordance with the funds advanced. The defendant Drivers had entered into an agreement with Borrett and Hagen. They advanced £2,500 upon the terms of a draft deed which described the Drivers as co-partners and provided terms for the repayment of the money the Drivers had advanced. Until being repaid, the Drivers held five parts of the partnership and were to share in the profits accordingly. The plaintiff Pooley held various bills of exchange from the partnership valued at approximately £5,000. The partnership was liquidated in 1873 and Pooley sought payment from the defendants of the amount owed under the bills. It was alleged that the Drivers were partners in the business. The Drivers denied this, arguing that they were simply lenders to the partnership under a written contract.]

Jessel M.R.: — The real question I have to decide in this case is, whether certain contracts, which are admitted to have been entered into, made the Defendants partners in the firm of Charles Borrett & Co. If they did, then the Plaintiff, the holder of certain bills of exchange drawn or indorsed by that firm —whether he gave value for them or not is admittedly immaterial — is entitled to the relief which he asks: if not, the action must be dismissed.

The partnership was for the term of fourteen years; the loan also was for the same term. If the partnership comes to an end sooner, the loan must come to an end sooner; so that, in fact, if you were to describe the contributors as dormant partners in the concern, liable to a limited extent to loss, and with a guarantee of their capital from the active partners, you would exactly describe their position; and I do not know of any other shorter mode of describing the position of these contributors.

Well, if that is so, is not that exactly the thing which it was intended should not take place — that a man should not put forward another to carry on the business ostensibly and himself take the profits? It is the very object and meaning of the transaction, as I understand it, to give these contributors that very position which dormant partners usually occupy, with certain collateral advantage — exceptional, perhaps, but not altogether unusual; unusual, no doubt, in the sense that I have seldom seen — I was going to say so barefaced, but, when you come to see the reason of it, I will say so palpable — an intention exhibited on the face of the documents to give the contributors all the benefits of the partnership, and if possible, to secure them from suffering from the liabilities. The reason of it was this: The framers of the instrument thought that *Bovill's Act* would protect them, and that comes again to a question of law, as to whether the Defendants who executed the deeds are in a better position than the Defendants who did not.

First of all, as to the Defendants who did not. I decided yesterday, and I merely repeat it, that Messrs. Driver, not being parties to any instrument in writing signed by them, were not parties to a "contract in writing" within *Bovill's Act*, and therefore could not have the benefit or protection afforded by that Act. But, with regard to the Defendant, who did execute the deeds, of course they would be entitled to the benefit of the Act, and then the mere question I have to try is whether they have rightly construed the Act.

It was said, and said with considerable force, by Mr. Chitty and Mr. Mathew, that they never intended to be partners. What they did not intend to do was to incur the liabilities of partner. If intending to be a partner is intending to take the profits, then they did intend to be partners. If intending to take the profits and have the business carried on for their benefit was intending to be partners, they did intend to be partners. If intending to see that the money was applied for that purpose and for no other, and to exercise an efficient control over it, so that they might have brought an action to restrain it from being otherwise applied, and so forth, was intending to be partners, then they did intend to be partners. But if it is tried by the other test, whether they intended to be protected under *Bovill's Act* from liability to third persons, then I think they did intend to be protected from liability.

But it comes back again to the same point, namely, what is the true construction of the Act? Is what they did within the provisions of the Act, or without?

I must say the Act is not so easy to construe as some Acts are, and not so difficult as some Acts are; but it seems to have been framed on an impression that the law of partnership was in a different state from what it actually was. I should be sorry to say that on my own authority, but I find it stated in pretty plain terms by the Privy Council in the case of *Mollwo, March, & Co. v. Court of Wards*, and something of the same kind was stated by other Judges, but being Judges of Courts of first instance, I do not refer to them. The Privy Council said (1): "Some reliance was placed on the statute 28 & 29 Vict. c. 86, s.1, which enacts that the advance of money to a firm upon a contract that the lender shall receive a rate of interest varying with the profits, or a share of the profits, shall not, of itself, constitute the lender a partner, or render him responsible as such. It was argued that this raised an implication that the lender was so responsible by the law existing before the passing of the Act. The enactment is no doubt entitled to great weight as evidence of the law, but it is by no means conclusive; and when the existing law is shown to be different from that which the Legislature supposed it to be, the implication arising from the statute cannot operate as a negation of its existence."

Now, I am afraid that that criticism is by no means ill-founded. The first section of the Act is this: "The advance of money by way of loan to a person engaged, or about to engage, in any trade or undertaking upon a contract in writing with such person, that the lender shall receive a rate of interest varying with the profits, or shall receive a share of the profits arising from carrying on such trade or undertaking, shall not, of itself, constitute the lender a partner with the person or the persons carrying on such trade or undertaking, or render him responsible as such.

The law was decided before the Act, by a long train of decisions before the time of Lord Eldon, who found it established. He says in Ex parte Hamper that the lending of a sum of money on a *bona fide* contract to receive a rate of interest varying with the profits, did not make a man a partner; although, I suppose, I may take it to be the equally well-established rule, though perhaps not so conclusively established, that the receiving of a share of the profits did: the two were lumped together by the statute, and therefore it was said, and rightly said, that there being, so to say, a misapprehension of the law which was supposed to be affected by the Act, you cannot look upon the Act itself as declaratory one way or the other.

That being so, what is the effect of the Act? The Act is this that the advance of money must be "by way of loan." Now what does that mean? It is not the "advance of money", but "the advance of money by way of loan". I take it to mean this, that the person advancing must be a real lender; that the advance must not only profess to be by way of loan, but must be a real loan; and consequently you come back to the question whether the persons who enter into the contract of association are really in the position of creditor and debtor, or in the position of partners, or in the only third position which I think could be suggested, that of master and servant. But the Act does not decide that for you. You must decide that without the Act; and when you have decided that the relation is that of creditor and debtor, then all the Act does is this: it says that the creditor may take a share of the profits, but, as I understand the law as laid down by the higher authorities to which I have referred, if you have once decided that the parties are in the position of creditor and debtor you do not want the Act at all, because the inference of partnership derived from the mere taking a share of profit, not being irrebuttable, is rebutted by your having come to the conclusion that they are in the position of debtor and creditor. That, in fact, was the decision in the case of *Mollwo, March, & Co. v. Court of Wards*, and in the case of *Cox v. Hickman*. Therefore you have already decided that for yourself, and the Act does not seem to me, as far as regards the first section, to do you any good at all.

Then the only other point is as to the meaning of "shall not, of itself, constitute," &c. Now there is a possible meaning to be given to the word "itself". It may mean this — though I am not sure that it does — that in construing a contract which, before the Act, by the mere circumstance of there being a share in the profits, would have raised a cogent, though not an irrebuttable inference that the so-called lender was a partner, though he professed to be a lender, the mere fact of his taking profits shall not alone raise that inference. Well, if that is the meaning — and I think Mr. Lindley attributes that meaning to it — it does not assist me very much in coming to a decision, for of course in this case there are many other circumstances besides participation in profits . . . I must decide for myself whether the parties are really in the position of creditor and debtor before I can apply the Act at all.

The words are, "advance of money by way of loan," and Mr. Lindley's note is this: "Observe these very important words. Agreements are constantly framed with all sorts of clauses, which together probably expose the lender to the risks he is desirous of avoiding" — that is, to the risk of being a partner. I do not know why those words, "of itself", were put into the Act, unless it was supposed by the framer . . . that sharing profits would otherwise have created a partnership of itself. If you take that meaning, then it is an alteration of the law; but *Cox v. Hickman* decided that that was not so, and never had been so . . .

That disposes of the law of the case as far as I am concerned. I now come to the consideration of the details of the documents, which are certainly framed in a very singular way. They seem to me to have been purposely framed with a view of giving the whole benefit which partnership could give to the contributors, and, if possible, something more than they could have obtained as partners.

* * *

The moment the contributors became parties to this deed, as I shall show they were or did become afterwards, they became entitled to shares in the capital absolutely. Then it goes on, "The capital of the said business shall be used and employed in the regular course of trade for the benefit of the partnership, and shall not be drawn out during the continuance of such partnership."

This is a very important clause, when you consider that the contributors get the benefit — as I shall show presently they do — of every covenant in the deed of partnership. The result, therefore, is this, that they became not only entitled to the shares of the capital, but entitled to compel the ostensible partners to employ that capital in the regular course of trade, and might have obtained an injunction to prevent their diverting it to any other purpose. They had therefore, to that extent, a control over the capital, namely, a control over its employment; thus they were not at all in the ordinary position of lenders.

The lender does not become entitled to any part of the assets of his debtor in specie. He has only a contract which entitles him to claim payment from the debtor as a personal demand, but this supposed creditor becomes entitled to a portion of the capital in specie, and gets the right besides to prevent the legal owners of the property from applying it to any other than a particular purpose, whether they desire to do so or not. He acquires two rights, the right to an aliquot portion of the capital itself, and a right to control the disposal of the rest of the capital.

Then there is a covenant that the partners shall conduct the business during the partnership to the best of their ability. Let us test the case by that covenant. The lender can compel these people against their will to carry on the business — I do not mean to say he can actually make them carry on the business, because that is a covenant which a Court of Equity always declines to enforce, but he could have an action for damages against them for breach of the covenant, and at all events he gets the benefit of that contract. They must carry on the business, as I shall presently, for his benefit because they have contracted to do so.

Then the 7th clause is that proper books of account and other books shall be kept in the usual way. Then there is a provision that the partners shall not sell, lend, or borrow without mutual consent; then that they shall not allow the assets to be taken in execution; and then that neither partner shall take any servants without the consent of the other. Then there is a provision as to outgoings; then a provision for one of the ostensible partners drawing out certain sums for maintenance. Then, that on the last of July in every year a general account shall be taken, and a general valuation made in the usual way, and put into a book. Then the 14th clause is this, which is very important: — [His Lordship read it.]

The moment the contributors got the benefit of this they were clearly entitled to a share of the profits as profits. Nothing can be plainer than the terms of the provision, and it shows the intention of the parties.

Then the 15th clause is this: — [His Lordship read it.] Then there is a provision to this effect, that if either of the partners becomes bankrupt the other shall have liberty to dissolve, and then the property shall become the property of the non-bankrupt partner upon his paying the value of the bankrupt partner's share to his assignees.

Then there is a provision for the widow or children of the partners; then a provision in the event of the death of either partner, which I do not think it necessary to read, and some other provisions as regards death, which precede the last clause, which is the usual arbitration clause. That is the partnership deed.

Now we come to the other deeds, which for this purpose I treat as deeds of even date. They are not exactly of even date, but they are nearly contemporaneous; the partnership dates from the 10th of October, 1868. The arrangement made with Messrs. Driver was made somewhere about the same time, and was made by a document which was never executed. It was a draft of an indenture dated the day of October 1868. I may say, in passing, that the other deeds, those executed by Bannatyne & Pye, are about the same date — one being dated the 28th of October, 1868, and the other the 7th of November, 1868 — and are in the same terms, and I will take them as having been executed shortly after the partnership.

Messrs. Driver's document recites the partnership deed; it recites some of the provisions that I have read; and then it goes on: "Whereas the said Rolles Driver and Samuel Neale Driver have agreed to advance by way of loan to the said C. Borrett and E. Hagen, under the provisions of an Act of Parliament passed in the 28th and 29th years of Her present Majesty, c. 86, entitled, "An Act to Amend the Law of Partnership", the sum of £2,500 to enable them the said C. Borrett and E. Hagen to carry on the said trade or business for the term and under and subject to the stipulations and conditions hereinafter mentioned, expressed, and declared concerning the same." Then it is witnessed, "That in consideration of the sum of £2,500," &c., the said Borrett and Hagen first of all covenant that they Borrett and Hagen, "will within six calendar months after the 1st of July, 1882, or within six calendar months after the sooner determination of the said partnership, pay unto the said Rolles Driver and Samuel Neale Driver, their executors, administrators, or assigns, the sum of £2,500."

That is a very remarkable thing for a loan. It is a loan during the continuance of the partnership. It is to be paid within six calendar months after its natural expiration, or within six months after any other expiration of the partnership. Therefore, although they call it a "loan", and although I agree that, standing alone, the fact of the duration of the loan being the duration of the partnership might not of itself be conclusive, it all tends in the same way to show that this was really intended as an advance of capital to the partnership business, made for the purpose of carrying it on, and not as an ordinary loan.

The next clause — and this is very important — is: "That the said C. Borrett and E. Hagen, their respective executors and administrators, shall in all things conform to, fulfil, and observe the covenants, clauses and agreements contained in the said recited deed of partnership of the 10th day of October, 1868, and such deed of partnership shall at all times be open to the inspection of the said Bolles Driver and Samuel Neale Driver, their executors or administrators, at the office where the said business shall be carried on." That imports the whole of the provisions of the prior deed into this deed, and makes Borrett and Hagen covenant to observe them, thus giving to the Drivers those rights both with respect to capital and profits, which I have already adverted to.

Then the next clause provides that Borrett and Hagen will, during the continuance of the loan — that is, during the maintenance of the partnership — make out accounts, and once a year, on the 1st of October, pay Messrs. Driver, on account of profits, a sum equivalent to five sixtieth parts of the profits for the year preceding the 18th of July then last past. Some argument was rested upon that, but nothing turns upon it, for this covenant never actually came into existence. If it had, I should have held that it did not vary the case in the least; that the prior clause gave them a share of proceeds as profits under the partnership, and this only makes Borrett and Hagen pay on account of the profits a sum equivalent to five sixtieth parts, showing that what they had to pay really was still profits. But that clause never came into force, because there was a proviso at the end of it to this effect, that if the sum of £10,000 was not advanced — and it was not — then Borrett and Hagen, or one of them, would "on the 1st day of October in every year during the continuance of the said loan pay to the said Rolles Driver and Samuel Neale Driver, their executors, administrators, or assigns, in lieu of the said five equal sixtieth parts of the said clear gains and profits as last aforesaid, such a proportion of the said clear gains and profits as last aforesaid as the said sum of £2,500 bears to the whole capital for the time being employed in the same business, such capital being estimated in the manner provided by the said indenture of partnership."

So that we have the interest of the loan not varying merely with the profits of the business, but varying in the proportion which the loan, which was part of the capital, bore to the whole capital, a circumstance which I think by no means immaterial in showing that it was not a genuine loan in the sense of creating the relation of debtor and creditor, but that it was indeed an advance of part of the capital.

Then the deed goes on with a very remarkable provision, "That if either the said Rolles Driver or Samuel Neale Driver shall become bankrupt or shall compound with his creditors, or in case any difference or dispute shall at anytime during the said term of fourteen years arise between the said parties hereto, or their representatives, and which differences or disputes shall be considered by arbitration, as hereinafter mentioned, to justify the determination of the arrangement hereby agreed upon, it shall be lawful for the said C. Borrett and E. Hagen, or the survivor of them, or their or his executors and administrators at any time hereafter to pay the said sum of »2,500, less any sum they shall have been overpaid on account of the said business, to the said Rolles Driver and Samuel Neale Driver, their executors, administrators, or assigns, together with the share of the said profits (if any) to which the said Rolles Driver and Samuel Neale Driver, their executors, administrators, or assigns, shall then have become entitled"; and thereupon the agreement is to be at an end.

Now that certainly is a very astonishing provision in an ordinary contract of loan. What has the bankruptcy of the creditor got to do with it? You pay the assignee, or trustee, as he is now called. It is a very remarkable thing that the bankruptcy of the creditor should put an end to the agreement, but you find it by no means remarkable if it was intended that they should really be partners. You find a similar provision in the actual partnership deed. Without attaching too much weight to this, I think it is very material.

Then there is another remarkable clause: "Within six calendar months after the expiration or sooner determination of the partnership, a final settlement of the accounts of the partnership shall be forthwith made in writing by the said C. Borrett and E. Hagen, their executors or administrators, concerning all the stock-in-trade, plant, moneys, credits, and effects then due or belonging to the said partnership estate, and also of all debts and sums of money (if any) due or owing from, and of all liabilities of the same, and a just valuation shall be made of all the particulars included in such account which shall require and are capable of valuation, and immediately after such last-mentioned account shall have been so taken and settled, the said C. Borrett and E. Hagen shall forthwith pay thereout to the said Rolles Driver and Samuel Neale Driver, their executors, administrators, or assigns, the sum of £2,500." So that the covenant is in accordance with the partnership deed to pay the £2,500 out of the assets and debts due to the partnership. I know there is another covenant to pay Messrs. Driver, which is personal, but there stands a covenant to pay out of the assets.

Then there is a provision for payment to the Drivers of "five equal sixtieth parts or shares of all the net profits of the said business." That gives them all the surplus profits that they have not yet received, including the proportion of the capital they are entitled to.

Then there is the proviso that they shall refund. It is very oddly worded, but it is agreed on all hands that it means this, that if, at the end of the partnership period, the amount already paid to the Drivers for profits shall exceed the total profits made in the business, they shall refund the excess not exceeding the £2,500. I have rather given the effect than the words, because the words are somewhat ambiguous; but it is admitted that that must be the meaning, or, in other words, that the lender, having received profit for interest, if the business afterwards makes a loss, would have to pay back, subject to the limit that he is never to be called upon to pay more than he has received, and, subject also to this, that he is never to be called upon to pay more than the total amount of his so-called loan. It is certainly a wonderful provision, if it is a *bona fide* loan, and not a mere colourable transaction to get a share of the profits without being liable to losses. Did ever any one hear of anybody lending his money on such terms, or of the notion that, after having received the profits in lieu of interest, he is to pay back the whole of them, it may be, because subsequently the business, conducted not for him, but for other people, who are really his debtors, shall have given rise to losses? It appears to me that if you want to prove that the business was conducted for him, this is cogent evidence of it. It was not conducted entirely for the benefit of the persons who were merely debtors and who stood in that relation to the supposed creditor. Then there is an arbitration clause, which is very usual in partnership articles, but not a very usual one in a mere loan deed.

These are the documents on which I am called upon to decide, and I must say that I have come to a clear conclusion that this is not a transaction of loan within the meaning of the Act of Parliament; that the true relation of the parties towards one another was that of dormant and active partners, and not of mere creditors and debtors; that in this case I need not rely on one provision or on two provisions, but on the whole character of the transaction from beginning to end. It is an elaborate device, an ingenious contrivance, for giving these contributors the whole of the advantages of the partnership, without subjecting them, as they thought, to any of the liabilities. I think the device fails; and that, looking at the law as it stands, I must hold that they are partners, and liable to the consequences of being partners, and to the whole of the engagements of the partnership, and consequently liable for the whole of its debts.

The Plaintiff is, therefore, entitled to a judgment on these bills.

Judgment accordingly.

Continental Bank of Canada v. R.
1998 CarswellNat 1496, 1998 CarswellNat 1497, (*sub nom.* Continental Bank Leasing Corp. v. Canada) [1998] 2 S.C.R. 298 (S.C.C.)

I. Introduction

Bastarache J.: — This appeal and a related appeal (Continental Bank of Canada v. R. September 3, 1998, No. 25521 [reported (1998), 98 D.T.C. 6501 (S.C.C.)], released concurrently) concern events arising out of the winding-up of Continental Bank of Canada (the "Bank") and its subsidiary, Continental Bank Leasing Corporation ("Leasing"). The broad issue is the validity of a transaction by which Central Capital Leasing ("Central") ultimately became the owner of leasing assets formerly held by the Bank and Leasing. The transaction involved the formation of a partnership into which Leasing transferred its leasing assets in return for a 99 percent interest in a partnership. Leasing transferred that partnership interest to the Bank, which subsequently sold it to Central's subsidiaries. These transactions ultimately permitted Leasing to file an election pursuant to s. 97(2) of the *Income Tax Act*, R.S.C. 1952, c. 148, as amended; this election was rejected by the Minister of National Revenue.

* * *

VI. Analysis

1. Was Leasing a member of a valid partnership with the subsidiaries of Central in December 1986 within the meaning of s. 2 of the Partnerships Act?

In order to answer this question, it is necessary to consider the various legal requirements for the proper characterization of the transactions entered into by Leasing. The sham doctrine will not be

partnership when it transferred its assets. The dispute does not surround the validity of the partnership with respect to Central's subsidiaries who entered the Partnership on December 24, 1986 and continued to operate that Partnership long after Leasing and the Bank were no longer members.

The Partnership Agreement contains most of the standard provisions that appear in partnership agreements. The agreement provides for the carrying on of "leasing services and such other businesses as the Managing Partner may from time to time determine" (Art. 2.01); it also provides for the distribution of income or loss to "those Persons who are Partners on the last day of the fiscal year of the Partnership" (Art. 5.09) and sets out the liability of the partners (Art. 3.02). The agreement further provides for the Management of the Partnership (Art. IV), Accounts and Allocations (Art. V), Dissolution (Art. VIII) and other provisions common to partnership agreements. It is not surprising that the Partnership contains all of the provisions required to form a valid partnership. The parties intended to set up a partnership that would comply with s. 2 of the *Partnerships Act* and they succeeded.

(a) Was There a Business?

By s. 1(1)(*a*) of the *Partnerships Act*, "business" includes "every trade, occupation and profession." There is no doubt that equipment leasing constitutes a business within the meaning of the *Partnerships Act*. The activities carried on by Leasing that were subsequently transferred to the Partnership included sales financing and leasing, which involved, among other things, the purchase of depreciable assets including heavy equipment and aircraft, which were then leased for a term to corporations that required the use of the assets in their business.

(b) Was the Business Carried On in Common?

If a partnership is to exist, it must be shown that two or more people carried on the business. It is also fundamental that the business is carried on in common (*Lindley & Banks on Partnership, supra*, at pp. 9-10). The respondent argues that no active business activity was conducted between December 24 and December 29, the period in which Leasing and subsequently the Bank were members of the Partnership. Therefore, according to the respondent, the Partnership did not carry on business within the meaning of s. 2 of the *Partnerships Act*. Further, s. A.9(a) of the Master Agreement set out that new transactions were prohibited between December 24 and December 29 without unanimous consent. Moreover, the three days over the 1986 Christmas holiday that were chosen for the purported involvement of Leasing in the partnership ensured that no business would be conducted.

The issue of whether an equipment leasing operation constitutes a business for the purposes of the *Income Tax Act* was before this Court in *Hickman Motors Ltd. v. R.*, [1997] 2 S.C.R. 336 (S.C.C.). In that case, L'Heureux-Dubé J., with whom the majority agreed on that point, found that a leasing business was in fact carried on by a company to which a subsidiary transferred its leasing assets, in circumstances where the parent's sole business activity was the passive receipt of rent. At p. 359, she held:

> Where machinery is rented out, the essential core operations may at times be limited to accepting rental revenue and assuming the business risk and other obligations. At any time during that period, any client could demand the execution of any of the contractual obligations, such as fixing an engine, for example. Where, because a rental business is fortunate enough to experience no mechanical breakdowns or accidents during a period of time, it "passively" accepts rental revenue and assumes business risk and obligations, it does not necessarily follow that it is not carrying on a business during that period. Holding otherwise would imply that rental businesses are "intermittent" that is, that they carry on a business only when something goes wrong in the operations. Such a proposition is unacceptable.

In the present instance, it is true that between December 24 and December 27, 1986, no meetings were held, no new transactions were entered into by the parties and no decisions were made. However, that is not determinative of the fact that no business was carried on by the Partnership. Prior to its entering the Partnership, Leasing carried on business. This business and its assets were transferred to the Partnership on December 24, 1986. There was no termination of Leasing's contracts with its customers and the contracts continued during the period of December 24 to December 27.

Evidence that the business previously carried on by Leasing was carried on by the Partnership is contained in a letter dated December 24, 1986 from Air Canada, one of the Bank's customers. In the letter, Air Canada acknowledges that "[Leasing] intends to sell and assign its interest in the Purchase Agreements, the Aircraft and the Leases to an Ontario partnership ...". Air Canada consented to the "sale and assignment of the Purchase Agreements, the Aircraft and the Leases" from the Bank to Leasing and consented "to the sale and assignment of the Purchase Agreements, the Aircraft and the Leases by [Leasing] to the Partnership".

The fact that no new business was created during the period of Leasing and the Bank's involvement in the Partnership does not negate the effect of the existing business that was continued during this time. The existence of a valid partnership does not depend on the creation of a new business. It is common that partnerships are formed when two parties agree to carry on the existing business of one of them, while the other contributes capital.

In addition, I am satisfied that the business that was carried on was carried on by the partners in common. Under the Partnership Agreement, the Partners "delegate to the Managing Partner full power and authority to manage, control, administer and operate the business and affairs of the Partnership and to represent and enter into transactions which bind the Partnership" (Art. 4.01). The fact that the management of the Partnership was given to the Managing Partner does not mandate a conclusion that the business was not carried on in common. Nor does the fact that Central, acting alone, was negotiating transactions relating to the lease portfolios prior to December 29, 1986. The respondent argues that the exclusion of Leasing and the Bank from any of those activities negates any claim that the Central entities and the Continental entities were actually carrying on business in common during that period. As *Lindley & Banks on Partnership, supra*, point out, at p. 9, one or more parties may in fact run the business on behalf of themselves and the others without jeopardizing the legal status of the arrangement.

If any of the negotiations that Central was involved in had resulted in a decision by Central's subsidiaries who were members of the Partnership during the relevant period to follow through with the transaction, under the Partnership agreement, the Partnership would have been bound by these agreements. By entering the Partnership Agreement, Leasing and the Bank recognized that any partner had the authority to bind the firm.

It is also relevant that during the brief term that Leasing and the Bank were parties to the Partnership Agreement, they held themselves out as partners. Various supporting documents, including correspondence with third parties, tax returns, financial statements and assignments of leases effected during this period, are consistent with the carrying on of a business in common. While this alone would not have the effect of validating the partnership, because holding out affects liability as against third parties and not the essential validity of the arrangement (s. 15, *Partnerships Act*), it is nonetheless evidence of the parties' intention to carry on business in common under the Partnership.

Bowman J.T.C.C. was correct in emphasizing that the members of the Partnership could not hold themselves out to third parties as not being partners. In the partnership agreement, art. 3.02 sets out the liability of the partners. It provides in part: "Subject to Article XI, the Partners shall, as between themselves, be liable for the obligations, liabilities and losses of the Partnership in the same proportion as their respective Interests." The Partnership was involved in the leasing of aircraft. If, during the period in which Leasing and the Bank were members of the Partnership, liability of the lessor was engaged because of an event involving a leased aircraft, Leasing and the Bank could not have denied that they were members of the partnership and, according to article 3.02, would have been liable for 99 percent of the loss incurred by the lessee.

The Bank and Leasing conducted themselves as partners for the duration of their memberships in the Partnership. Throughout that period, they were subject to all of the rights and obligations of partners and carried on the business of leasing in common with the other partners. There is no evidence to show that the leasing business carried on as defined in *Hickman, supra*, was not carried on by Leasing and the Central subsidiaries.

(c) Was the Business Carried On in Common with a View to Profit?

The Court of Appeal held that the parties intended to conduct a sale of assets through a device they chose to call a partnership. This intention did not include a view to profit and in fact "the idea to share profits was an afterthought when the parties originally put the deal together". This characterization by the Court of Appeal ignores the fact that the Partnership Agreement provided for the distribution of the profits from the leasing business being operated by the Partnership and that the Partnership continued to carry on the business operated for profit by Leasing. There is no evidence of any expectation other than that profits would continue to be generated during the predetermined term of Leasing's involvement in the Partnership. The Court of Appeal also relied heavily on the fact that Leasing was not legally entitled to a share of the profits of the first fiscal year because its partnership interest had already been transferred to the Bank by the time the year end was triggered on December 27, 1986. This, however, is irrelevant to the determination of the issue.

To determine whether the business was carried on with a view to profit, it is necessary to look to the provisions of the Partnership Agreement governing the distribution of profits.

5 06 *Allocation of Net Income or Loss.* The net income or loss for each fiscal year of the Partnership shall be allocated to the current accounts of the Partners in proportion to their respective average capital accounts for the period for which the allocation was made.

5 09 *Allocation of Income and Loss for Tax Purposes.* The income or loss of the Partnership for the whole of a fiscal year for the purposes of the *Income Tax Act* shall be allocated to those Persons who are Partners on the last day of the fiscal year of the Partnership in the proportions set out in section 5.06. The income or loss of the Partnership which is allocated to those Partners shall be allocated among those Partners as of the time and in the proportions set out in this article.

These provisions clearly contemplate the distribution of profits in accordance with a partner's interest in the Partnership. Profit was accumulated by the Partnership during the period of Leasing's membership in that partnership and that profit was distributed. Leasing received a cheque dated February 4, 1987 for $130,726 that was described in a financial statement dated January 11, 1988 as a 99 percent share of partnership income for the period December 24 to December 27, 1986.

Because Leasing had already transferred its partnership interest to the Bank by December 27, 1986, it was not entitled to receive the partnership income under the Partnership Agreement as it was no longer a partner at year end. This however, does not change the fact that a generation of profit and profit sharing was contemplated and effected under the Partnership Agreement. Whether the entitlement belonged to Leasing or to the Bank at the end of the year is of no consequence. The important consideration is that the 99 percent partnership interest owned initially by Leasing and then the Bank carried with it a right to share in the profits of business carried on by the Partnership.

It is not disputed that the ultimate objective of the series of transactions entered into by the parties and in particular the Partnership was to duplicate the tax consequences of the original share transaction with Central. The Bank's main intention and by extension, Leasing's main intention was to get rid of its leasing assets for the purpose of winding up. As Bowman J.T.C.C. held, at p. 2151:

> One thing is clear. Notwithstanding the pious assertions of a number of witnesses that they intended to enter into a partnership with the other parties, [the Bank's] and [Leasing's] intention was patently not to go into the leasing business in partnership with [Central] ... . The whole object of the exercise was precisely the opposite — to get out of that business. The partnership was merely a means to that end.

Simply because the parties had the overriding intention of creating a partnership for one purpose does not, however, negate the fact that profit-making and profit-sharing was an ancillary purpose. This is sufficient to satisfy the definition in s. 2 of the *Partnerships Act* in the circumstances of this case. At pp. 10-11, *Lindley & Banks on Partnership* makes the following observation:

> ... if a partnership is formed with some other predominant motive [other than the acquisition of profit], *e.g.*, tax avoidance, but there is also a real, albeit ancillary, profit element, it may be permissible to infer that the business is being carried on "with a view of profit." If, however, it could be shown that the sole reason for the creation of a partnership was to give a particular partner the "benefit" of, say, a tax loss, when there was no contemplation in the parties' minds that a profit... would be derived from carrying on the relevant business, the partnership could not in any real sense be said to have been formed "with a view of profit."

This is not a case where the disentitlement of one partner to a share of the profits was agreed to by the parties; nor is it a case where no profits were anticipated during the term of a partner's involvement. During the period in which Leasing and the Bank were partners in the business, the partnership earned a profit from its leasing operations and that profit was distributed at year end.

The respondent argues that intending to constitute a valid partnership is not the same thing as intending to carry on business in common with a view to profit. I agree. The parties in the present case, however, set up a valid partnership within the meaning of s. 2 of the *Partnerships Act*. They had the intention to and did carry on business in common with a view to profit. This conclusion is not based simply on the parties' subjective statements as to intention. It is based on the objective evidence derived from the partnership agreement entered into by the parties. As Millett L.J. held in *Orion Finance, supra,* at p. 85:

> The question is not what the transaction is but whether it is in truth what it purports to be. Unless the documents taken as a whole compel a different conclusion, the transaction which they embody should be categorised in conformity with the intention which the parties have expressed in them.

I do not see anything in the documentation that is inconsistent with the intention of the parties to create a partnership within the meaning of the *Partnerships Act.*

4. LEGAL PERSONALITY OF PARTNERSHIP

Thorne v. New Brunswick (Workmen's Compensation Board)
(1962), 33 D.L.R. (2d) 167, 48 M.P.R. 56, 1962 CarswellNB 8 (C.A.)

McNAIR C.J.N.B. (for the Court): This is a special case stated by the Workmen's Compensation Board under s. 34(8) of the *Workmen's Compensation Act*, R.S.N.B. 1952, c. 255, in which our opinion is sought on a question of law which arose on an application for compensation made to the Board by one Osborne Thorne.

The Act provides for an Accident Fund established and maintained by assessments made against employers in the industries within its scope out of which compensation may be paid by the Board to a workman and his dependents when personal injury or death is caused to him by accident arising out of and in the course of his employment in any such industry.

The facts as stated by the Board may be summarized as follows: In February 1961 Thorne and one Jules Robichaud, both residents of New Brunswick, entered into an oral agreement to carry on in partnership within the Province a combined lumbering and sawmill business. It was agreed Robichaud would have charge of the woods operations, Thorne of the milling operations, and that each partner would personally work in his branch of the undertaking at a remuneration, termed wages, of $75 per week. They commenced business in early February 1961 and, in accordance with the requirements of the Act, duly notified the Board of the new undertaking, filed with it an estimate of wages for the current year, and paid to the Board the provisional assessment applicable to the estimated payroll.

leave against them under the firm name. In the present case the facts are these. I think that it has been made out that this is a Natal firm, i.e., a colonial firm. . . For the present purpose I think that a colonial firm is in the same position as a foreign firm. . . The rules as they existed prior to the making of Order XLVIII.A have been construed to the effect that a writ such as this could not be issued without leave against a foreign firm, the members, or some of the members, of which were resident abroad. That has appeared to those conversant with the matter to involve a hardship, and it was for the purpose of getting rid of that hardship I believe that Order XLVIII.A was framed. In rule 1 of that order the words "and carrying on business within the jurisdiction" are used in addition to those which had been used in the former rules. In conjunction with that rule we have rules3 and 8 of the same order . . . Reading rule 1 of Order XLVIII.A with rules 3 and 8, it seems to me that it is now immaterial whether the writ is against an English firm or against a foreign or colonial firm . . . If the firm carries on business within the jurisdiction, then whether it is an English or a foreign firm, and whether it also carries on business in a colony or abroad or not, a writ may be issued against the partners in the firm name without leave under Order XLVIII.A r. 1.

See also by Lopes L.J., at p. 789 and Davey L.J., at pp. 790-1.

The reasons so given for the adoption in 1891 of the new provisions contained in O. 48a lend no countenance to the submission the Order constitutes a recognition of a new concept, resulting from the *Partnership Act* of 1890, of a partnership firm as a legal entity distinct from the individuals composing it. As respects New Brunswick law the proposition appears entirely fanciful in light of the fact our first *Partnership Act*, passed in 1921, post-dated by twelve years our adoption of the English O. 48a being found *in toto* in our original Rules of Court of 1909.

Support for the theory advanced by the claimant is also sought in the language of Farwell J., in his judgment in the *Taff Vale* case particularly where he says: "Now it is undoubtedly true that a trade union is neither a corporation, nor an individual, nor a partnership between a number of individuals" (p. 427), and again, "it is competent to the Legislature to give to an association of individuals which is neither a corporation nor a partnership . . . a capacity . . ." (p. 429). From such collocation of words and phrases we are asked to infer judicial recognition by this learned jurist of the new concept.

That such language was never intended by its author to denote such recognition is made clear by his later observations in *Sadler v. Whiteman*, [1910] 1 K.B. 868 (Eng. K.B.).

Our *Partnership Act*, now R.S.N.B. 1952, c. 167, is modelled on the Act of the United Kingdom. Its s. 5 reads:

5. Persons who have entered into partnership with one another are for the purposes of this Act called collectively a firm, and the name under which their business is carried on is called the firm name.

Such enactment is identical with ss. (1) of s. 4 of the Act of the United Kingdom. Its s. 4 contains however, as ss. (2), this further enactment:

(2) In Scotland a firm is a legal person distinct from the partners of whom it is composed . . .

The inclusion of those provisions in the parent Act deprives of all force the suggestion that by other provisions in the Act the Legislature intended to make of partnership firms generally legal entities or persons.

The true principles are, we feel, correctly formulated in *Pollock on Partnerships*, 15th ed., p. 24, where it is said:

The law of England knows nothing of the firm . . . as an artificial person distinct from the members composing it, though the firm is so treated by the universal practice of merchants and by the law of Scotland. In England the firm-name may be used in legal instruments both by the partners themselves and by other persons as a collective description of the persons who are partners in the firm at the time to which the description refers: and under the Rules of the Supreme Court actions may now be brought by and against partners in the firm name. An action between a partner and the firm, or between two firms having a common partner, was impossible at common law, and until 1891 it remained open to doubt whether such actions were possible since the *Judicature Acts*; but they are now expressly authorised by the Rules of Court. (Note 80 here follows reading: "Order XLVIII.A, r. 10. But not so as to enable a partner to be in substance both plaintiff and defendant: *Meyer & Co. v. Faber*, [1923] 2 Ch. 421, C.A.) . . .

Ellis v. Joseph Ellis & Co., [1905] 1 K.B. 324 (Eng. C.A.), lends support to the views we entertain. The action, brought under the *Workmen's Compensation Act* 1897 of the United Kingdom which contains a definition of "workman" corresponding closely to that found in the New Brunswick Act, was against the surviving members of a firm by the dependents of a deceased partner who under a mutual agreement worked in the colliery for wages and had, up to the time of his injury, been paid at the stipulated rate out of the proceeds of the business. It was held the Act contemplated the case of a workman employed by some other person or persons and that the deceased, having been himself one of the partners in the firm for which he was working, could not be said to have been employed by them. At p. 329 Collins M.R., says:

It seems to me obvious . . . that a person cannot for the purposes of the Act occupy the position of being both employer and employee.

And Matthew L.J., says, *ibid.*:

> The argument on behalf of the applicant . . . appears to involve a legal impossibility, namely, that the same person can occupy the position of being both master and servant, employer and employed. The deceased man in this case was a partner; and the arrangement made between him and his co-partners as to the payment of wages to him was really an agreement with regard to the mode in which accounts were to be taken between the partners, and to the share of profits to be received by him in excess of that received by the other partners in consideration of the work done by him.

Since the argument in the case at bar our attention has been drawn to two recent decisions of the English Court of Appeal in which the word "entity" was used as descriptive of a partnership firm. They are *Davies v. Elsby Brothers Ltd.*, [1960] 3 All E.R. 672 (C.A.) and *Whittam v. W.J. Daniel & Co.*, [1961] 3 All E.R. 796 (Q.B.). In our view their language falls far short of a recognition in English jurisprudence of the doctrine that as a matter of substantive law a partnership is a legal entity or *persona juridica* separate and distinct from the individuals composing it.

Question answered in the negative.

Notes

1   The decision in *Thorne* should be contrasted with the Privy Council's decision in *Lee v. Lee's Air Farming Ltd. (1960)*, [1961] A.C. 12 (New Zealand P.C.), *infra*, Ch. 2, recognizing the legitimacy of an employer-employee relationship between a corporation and its dominant shareholder.

2   Next to the absence of limited liability, the refusal of the common law to recognize its separate legal personality constitutes the weakest link in the choice of the partnership as a form of business organization as compared with the corporation. *Lindley on Partnership*, 18th ed., p. 35, summarizes the consequences as follows:

> The law, ignoring the firm, looks to the partners composing it; any change amongst them destroys the identity of the firm; what is called the property of the firm is their property, and what are called the debts and liabilities of the firm are their debts and their liabilities. In point of law, a partner may be the debtor or the creditor of his co-partners, but he cannot be either debtor or creditor of the firm of which he is himself a member.

> It should be added to the above proposition that a partner cannot be employed by his own firm, for no man can employ himself.

With minor exceptions, the provisions of the Act fully support this aggregate view of the partnership. See *e.g.*, ss. 10-11, 19 and 33.

3   Lindley, *op. cit.*, pp. 36 *et seq.* examines the current position under several heads, *viz.* (i) the partnership name; (ii) legal proceedings by and against the firm; (iii) contractual rights and liabilities; (iv) partnership disabilities; (v) sureties and securities; and (vi) revenue law. In all these cases the partnership's lack of legal personality creates serious problems. To some extent, some of the difficulties can be overcome by proper drafting of the partnership agreement and by agreement between the partnership and its employees or creditors. For example, the partnership agreement may provide that the death or retirement of a partner shall not dissolve the partnership or, in the case of an employment contract, that the contract shall not come to an end. Nevertheless, even where such difficulties have been anticipated by the drafter, there may be difficulties in interpretation. See *e.g., Bank of Montreal v. Kiwi Polish Co. (Can.) Ltd.* (1969), 9 D.L.R. (3d) 579, 1969 CarswellBC 7 (B.C. C.A.) reversed [1971] S.C.R. 991, 1971 CarswellBC 91, 1971 CarswellBC 275, and *cf. Zamikoff v. Lundy*, 9 D.L.R. (3d) 637, [1970] 2 O.R. 8, 1970 CarswellOnt 256 (C.A.). The retention of the partnership name, despite changes in the composition of the partnership, also contributes to the appearance of continuity. However, the appearance yields to reality if the partnership becomes insolvent and creditors are obliged to sue individual partners. See *infra*, s. 5(b).

4   Some real or apparent exceptions to the non-entity rule appear in the Act and in other legislation, *viz.*:

(a) PA, s. 5, recognizes the "firm" designation. See also s. 7 with respect to acts or instruments in the firm's name. However, as the judgment in *Thorne* points out, the use of the collective name is only a matter of convenience and has no substantive consequences;

(b) Section 31 limits the effect of the assignment of a partner's share, but this provision can be explained without resort to entity theories of the partnership.

(c) Section 39 of the Act deals with the application of partnership property on dissolution of the partnership and gives priority to the partnership debts.

(d) Under the *Income Tax Act*, R.S.C. 1985, c.1 (5th Suppl.) as am., s. 96, a partnership is treated as a separate person resident in Canada for the purpose of computing the partner's share of the partnership's income for the taxation year. The partnership itself, however, is not separately taxed on its notional income. It is only regarded as a conduit for the partners.

(e) Rules 8.01, 8.02 and 8.06 of Ontario's Rules of Civil Procedure provide as follows:

Rule 8.01

8.01(1) A proceeding by or against two or more persons as partners may be commenced using the firm name of the partnership.

(2) Subrule (1) extends to a proceeding between partnerships having one or more partners in common.

Rule 8.02

8.02 Where a proceeding is commenced against a partnership using the firm name, the partnership's defence shall be delivered in the firm name and no person who admits he or she was a partner at any material time may defend the proceeding separately, except with leave of the court.

Rule 8.06

8.06(1) An order against a partnership using the firm name may be enforced against the property of the partnership.

(2) An order against a partnership using the firm name may also be enforced, where the order or a subsequent order so provides, against any person who was served as provided in rule 8.03 and who,

(a) under that rule, is deemed to have been a partner;

(b) has admitted having been a partner; or

(c) has been adjudged to have been a partner,

at the material time.

(3) [OMITTED].

As noted by Chief Justice McNair in *Thorne, supra*, the English rules of practice were not intended to change the substantive law but only to remove some awkward procedural hurdles thrown up by the common law. Query whether this limited view of their effect is entirely correct of the Ontario rules and their counterparts in the other provinces? Is it true of Rule 8.01(2)? Of Rule 8.06(1)? If a new partner joins a partnership after the partnership has incurred a particular obligation, what is the effect of the creditor securing a judgment in respect of the obligation against the partnership after the new partner has joined the firm? Is the new partner liable for the partnership's old debts? (See PA, ss. 10, 18.) If he is not, why does Ontario Rule 8.06(1) permit execution against the "partnership property" without distinguishing between those who were partners at the time when the obligation was incurred and those who only subsequently became partners?

General Conclusion.

The aggregate view of the common law partnership remains substantially intact and has been only modestly affected by statutory provisions and rules of practice. The American position is more unsettled.

There was a lively debate among US scholars about the aggregate and entity theories of partnership at the time of the adoption of the *Uniform Partnerships Act* (UPA) in 1914, although the UPA itself never adopted a formal position. See *Crane & Bromberg on Partnership* (1968), pp. 16 *et seq.* A 1980s report of a subcommittee of the American Bar Association recommended a revision of the UPA and an expanded adoption of the entity approach but fell short of seeking to resolve the old controversy. See UPA Revision Subcommittee, "Should the Uniform Partnership Act be Revised?" (1987), 43 Bus. Law. 121 esp. at 124-25. The English and Scottish Law Commissions have both recommended conferring legal personality on partnerships governed by English and Scottish law.

5   Since a partnership is not a separate legal entity, a partner cannot be a creditor or employee to the partnership, because that would be akin to being a creditor or employee to oneself. This concept is clarified in *McCormick v. Fasken Martineau DuMoulin LLP*, 2014 CarswellBC 1358, 2014 CarswellBC 1359, 2014 SCC 39, [2014] 2 S.C.R. 108 (S.C.C.). The case involved a law firm with a partnership agreement that required equity partners to retire at age 65, and to divest their ownership shares at the end of that year. One partner brought a complaint to the British Columbia Human Rights Tribunal that this practice amounted to age discrimination. However, the *Human Rights Code* relied on the definition of employment. The Court of Appeal held that "because a partnership is not, in law, a separate legal entity from its partners, it is a legal impossibility for a partner ever to be 'employed' by a partnership of which he or she is a member". The Supreme Court of Canada agreed that the partner is not in an employment relationship. The Court, in reviewing anti-discrimination legislation in other countries, pointed to how partnerships were generally categorized separately from employment relationships, and usually required express statutory provisions for human rights legislation to apply to them. The Court did not go so far as to hold that a partner can never be an employee in a human rights context; a control or dependency test should be used to assess whether a partner is an employee. However, a partner is not completely deprived of protection. In a similar case, *Tim Ludwig Professional Corp. v. BDO Canada LLP*, 2016 ONSC 2225, 2016 CarswellOnt 5362 (Ont. S.C.J.), a partner facing forced retirement was protected by the terms of his partnership agreement.

5. CONDUCT OF THE BUSINESS OF THE PARTNERSHIP

(a) Relationship of the Partners to One Another

Sections 20 to 31 of the *Partnerships Act* contain the statutory presumptive rules governing the partners' relationship towards one another. Read collectively the rules lead to the conclusion that the partners' relationship is based on principles of equality, consensualism, utmost good faith and the personal character of the partnership contract.

(i) Equality

The principle of equality is reflected in the partners' right and obligation to share equally in the profits and losses of the partnership business (s. 24.1), in the right to participate in the management of the business (s. 24.5), to have access to the partnership books (s. 24.9) and in the duty to render to each other true accounts and full information of all things affecting the partnership (s. 28). All these aspects provide important contrasts with the distribution of power within a corporate structure. Particularly instructive is the right to participate in management. Modern business corporations Acts confer no inherent right in a shareholder, even a majority shareholder in a closely held corporation, to participate in the management of the corporation. If the shareholder wants to play such a role he or she must have him or herself elected as a director or enter into a "unanimous shareholder agreement." See CBCA s. 146 and, *infra*, Ch. 4.

The fact that, in the absence of a contrary agreement, every partner is entitled to participate in the management of the partnership's affairs explains the reciprocal agency basis of partnership. It also explains the fundamental rule, enshrined in s. 6 of the Act, that "the acts of every partner who does any act for carrying on in the usual way business of the kind carried on by the firm of which he or she is a member" bind the firm and the partners unless the third party allows that the partner is in fact without authority to act in the matter. The implications of these agency rules are examined more fully in ss. (ii) below.

(ii) Consensualism

The principle of consensualism in the conduct of partnership affairs is clearly evinced in several provisions. Section 20 provides that the mutual rights and duties of partners, whether ascertained by agreement or determined by the Act, may be varied by the consent of all the partners. The rule of unanimity also governs the admission of new partners (s. 24.7) and any changes in the fundamental character of the partnership business (s. 24.8). The consensual character of the partnership relation manifests itself in the rule that, unless otherwise agreed, any partner may determine the partnership at any time by giving notice of his intention to do so to the other partners (s. 26(1)). It is also reflected in the rule in s. 25 that no majority of partners can expel a partner unless the power to do so has been expressly conferred in the partnership agreement. (This does not mean that in the absence of such agreement partners are bound to each other for life even though they are very unhappy together. It means that the parties will have to seek judicial relief under PA, s. 35. They may also be entitled to terminate the partnership under one of the provisions in s. 32.)

One deviation from the unanimity rule appears in s. 24.8, which allows majority opinion to prevail in "ordinary matters" connected with the partnership business.

(iii)   Fiduciary Character

The fiduciary obligations of partners to each other are not peculiar to partnership law but apply to all persons occupying positions of trust and exercising powers for the benefit of others. As will be seen (*infra*, Ch. 6), the fiduciary obligations of directors and officers of corporations have been a fertile source of litigation.

In the partnership context, Cardozo C.J. expressed the relevant principles with particular felicity in an oft-cited passage in his judgment in *Meinhard v. Salmon*, 164 N.E. 545 (N.Y. Ct. App., 1928):

> Joint adventurers, like co-partners, owe to one another, while the enterprise continues, the duty of the finest loyalty. Many forms of conduct permissible in a workaday world for those acting at arm's length, are forbidden to those bound by fiduciary ties. A trustee is held to something stricter than the morals of the market place. Not honesty alone, but the punctilio of an honour the most sensitive, is then the standard of behaviour. As to this, there has developed a tradition that is unbending and inveterate. Uncompromising rigidity has been the attitude of courts of equity when petitioned to undermine the rule of undivided loyalty by the "disintegrating erosion" of particular exceptions. [Citations omitted.] Only thus has the level of conduct for fiduciaries been kept at a level higher than that trodden by the crowd. It will not consciously be lowered by any judgment of this court.

The fiduciary principle is given statutory expression in ss. 28, 29 and 30 of the *Partnerships Act*.

(iv)   Personal Character

Finally, the personal character of the partnership relation is evinced in s. 31 of the Act (which deals with the effect of the assignment of a partner's interest in the partnership) and in the rule adopted in s. 33 that the partnership is automatically dissolved on the death or insolvency of a partner. These features should be contrasted with the perpetual succession enjoyed by the modern corporation (see Ch. 2, s. 1) and the presumption of free transferability of its shares.

In the light of some of the aforementioned provisions, the observation has been made that a partnership is an "unstable relationship." In the statutory sense this is undoubtedly true, but it need not be true in a practical sense if the partnership agreement varies or excludes (as it usually will to some extent) the de-stabilizing provisions in the *Partnerships Act*. In particular, a well-drafted agreement will contain, *inter alia*, provisions with respect to the admission of new partners and the retirement of old ones, the effect of death or bankruptcy, the distribution of responsibilities, the provision of capital and the division of losses and profits.

(b) Relationship of the Partners to Third Parties

From a practical point of view, a person's liability for the debts or other obligations of a firm is one of the most litigated aspects of partnership law. This is not surprising, since the problem usually arises when the partnership (assuming there was a partnership to begin with) is insolvent and a creditor is trying to secure payment of its debt.

Five types of situations must be distinguished:

(i)   liabilities incurred by the partnership before the defendant became a member of it;

(ii) liabilities incurred by the partnership while the defendant was a member of it;

(iii) liabilities incurred by the business while the defendant held himself out, or allowed himself to be held out, as a partner in the business;

(iv) liabilities incurred by the business after the defendant had retired as a partner but before the creditor became aware of the change; and

(v)   posthumous liability.

Each of these situations will be briefly considered in turn.

(i) Pre-partnership Liabilities

Since partnership is a consensual relationship, it is easy to understand why PA, s. 18(1), provides that a person who is admitted as a partner into an existing firm does not thereby become liable to the creditors of the firm for anything done before he or she became a partner. The converse side of the coin is that retirement does not exonerate a partner from debts and other obligations incurred by the firm before his or her retirement, and s. 18(2) so provides.

(ii)   Liability as Partner

The elementary proposition that a partner is liable jointly with the other partners for all debts and obligations of the firm incurred while he or she is a partner is codified in s. 10 of the Act. This liability is inherent in the partnership relationship and is independent of any rights of contribution and indemnity which a partner may have against another partner under ss. 24.1 and 24.2. Another equally basic proposition, again derived from general principles of agency law, is that it is not necessary that the partner whom it is sought to hold liable actually approved or authorized the contract giving rise to the indebtedness. The firm will be liable, and therefore the partner will be liable, if his or her co-partner "does any act for carrying on in the usual way business of the kind carried on by the firm of which he or she is a member." See s. 6 of the Act. The same principles govern a partner's liability for acts performed by other agents of the firm. He or she will only have a valid defence if he or she can show that the third party knew that the person with whom he or she was dealing had no authority to bind the firm in the particular matter or did not know or believe him or her to be a partner. *Id.*

Liability of the firm, and therefore of its partners, for wrongful acts and omissions of a partner is dealt with in ss. 11–13 of the Act. Note carefully that while a partner only incurs joint liability with his or her fellow partners under s. 10, his or her liability under s. 13 is joint and several. The distinction between the two types of liability is anomalous and used to cause substantial procedural difficulties. These have largely been overcome by the means explained, *infra*, s. 6(b).

(iii)   "Holding out" Liability

A person may be held liable as a partner, even if he or she never was a partner, if the "holding out" principle of s. 15 applies to him or her. Section 15(1) provides:

> Every person, who by words spoken or written or by conduct represents himself or who knowingly suffers himself to be represented as a partner in a particular firm, is liable as a partner to any person who has on the faith of any such representation given credit to the firm, whether the representation has or has not been made or communicated to the persons so giving credit by or with the knowledge of the apparent partner making the representation or suffering it to be made.

The meaning of "knowingly suffers himself to be represented as a partner" was examined in *Tower Cabinet Co. v. Ingram*, [1949] 1 All E.R. 1033 (D.C.).

(iv)   Liability of Apparent Partner

Another aspect of the holding out principle determines the extent to which a person may continue to remain liable as a partner even after he or she has retired from the partnership. The relevant rules are set forth in PA, s. 36, and are discussed, *inter alia*, in *Ingram, supra*, and in *Dominion Sugar Co. v. Warrell*, [1927] 2 D.L.R. 198, 60 O.L.R. 169 (C.A.).

(v)   Posthumous Liability

A deceased partner's estate is not liable for any post-death partnership debts, only debts that were incurred before death. In general, see ss. 36(3).

6.   SPECIAL FORMS OF PARTNERSHIP

(a)   Limited Partnerships

(i)   Introduction

The concept of a limited partnership is foreign to the common law and is rooted in statute. In Ontario, limited partnerships are primarily governed by the *Limited Partnerships Act*, R.S.O. 1990, c. L.16.

(ii)   Important Features of the *Ontario Limited Partnerships Act*

General Features. A limited partnership is a partnership consisting of at least one general partner and one limited partner (s. 2(2)), and it is formed simply by filing a declaration under s. 3 of the LPA. As specified in s. 3(2), the declaration need only set out the name and address of the firm and the names of the general and limited partners, the general nature of the business and the contributions made by each partner. This declaration expires after five years, but the limited partnership is not dissolved by such expiry; it only has to pay an extra fee (s. 3(4)).

A limited partner is only liable to the extent of his contribution to the firm (s. 9), but this protection is lost if "he takes part in the control of the business" (s. 13(1)). Exactly what is meant by "control" is not clear, although some help is offered in s. 12(2)(a) which explicitly permits a limited partner "from time to time" to "advise as to [the firm's] management." Do you think an easy line can be drawn between advising and controlling? If a firm consistently follows the advice of a limited partner, could this be construed as amounting to control? Why should participation by a limited partner in the control of the partnership deprive him or her of his or her sheltered status? Is it because third parties are misled, or is it because the limited partner cannot have it both ways? *Cf.* the status of a shareholder-director in an incorporated company; and see the decision in *Haughton Graphic Ltd. v. Zivot* (1986), 33 B.L.R. 125 (Ont. H.C.), reproduced at the end of these notes, *infra*. However, Manitoba's *Partnership Act*, R.S.M. 1987, c. P.30, appears to be more lenient. First, a limited partner, who takes an active part in the business of the partnership, is liable as if he or she were a general partner, but only to the people he or she deals with on behalf of the partnership (s. 63(1)). Second, the people he or she deals with cannot have knowledge that he or she is a limited partner for the limited partner to be liable (s. 63(1)). Third, liability is limited to the time between the first time the limited partner dealt with the person and when the person first acquires actual knowledge that he or she is dealing with a limited partner (s. 63(2)). These provisions are more specific than Ontario's LPA, which simply states that a limited partner loses protection as soon as he or she takes control of the business.

Transferability. Section 18 gives a limited partner the right to assign his or her interest, but the assignee only has limited rights unless either all of the other partners consent in writing to the assignment or the partnership agreement gives the assignor that power. The situation is similar to selling shares in a closely held company, where the by-laws usually require the consent of the other shareholders or give them a pre-emptive right to purchase the shares before they can be sold to a third party.

Withdrawal. Aside from selling his or her interest, a limited partner has the right to receive the return of his or her contribution from the firm in four situations, as set out in s. 15: (1) on dissolution; (2) if the partnership agreement provides for it; (3) if no other procedure is specified in the partnership agreement, then after he or she has given six months notice to all other partners; or, (4) if all the partners consent to the return. However, a limited partner is not entitled to withdraw his or her contribution unless there are sufficient partnership assets to cover all of the partnership liabilities. Compare these provisions with the right of an Ontario corporation to purchase its shares under OBCA, ss. 30–36.

Dissolution. A limited partnership is dissolved upon the death, retirement or mental incompetence of a general partner or dissolution of a corporate general partner. However, by ss. 21(a) and (b), the remaining general partners can continue the business. Pursuant to s. 23(1)(b), dissolution also occurs when all of the limited partners have withdrawn from the partnership. Furthermore, under s. 15(4), a limited partner can have the partnership dissolved if, although he or she is entitled to the return of his or her contribution, it is not forthcoming on his or her demand, or if the partnership assets are insufficient under s. 14(2)(a) and he or she would otherwise be entitled to be repaid his or her contribution.

Legal Personality. In *Kucor Construction & Developments & Associates v. Canada Life Assurance Co.*, 1998 CarswellOnt 4423, 167 D.L.R. (4th) 272, [1998] O.J. No. 4733 (Ont. C.A.) at p. 289 [D.L.R.], the Court affirmed the position that a limited partnership, like a general partnership, does not have a separate legal personality.

Conclusion. We see that the limited partnership is a very specialized investment vehicle, lying somewhere in its attributes between a corporation and a regular partnership.

(iii)   Limited Partnerships and Taxation

One of the reasons for the recent popularity of limited partnerships is the fact that they combine the advantage of limited liability with the benefits of partnership tax treatment.

Avoidance of Double Taxation. Under the *Income Tax Act*, individual partners take their share of partnership income or loss into account when computing their personal income for tax purposes. This is a direct "flow through" of income as opposed to the situation where a corporate investment vehicle is used. In the latter case, the corporation pays tax on its actual or imputed profit and shareholders pay taxes on dividends received by them from the corporation, thus often resulting in "double taxation." Double taxation is said to occur whenever the same income is taxed twice. A discussion of the complexities of the corporate tax system, with its attempts to achieve varying degrees of integration for certain types and amounts of income for certain sorts of corporations is far beyond the scope of this note.

This flow-through feature has made the limited partnership particularly attractive to investors, for example, foreigners investing in Canadian real estate. The individual foreign investor has the cash generated from his or her project reduced by such deductions as CCA (capital cost allowance). Then, because income flows directly through to him or her, income for tax purposes can be reduced still further by claiming personal deductions. This contrasts with the alternative of investing through a corporation, which must pay tax based on income before the personal deductions, and at the high flat corporate rate. After that, any distribution to the foreign shareholder would be subject to withholding tax, with the rate ultimately determined by any applicable tax treaty.

For a discussion on sales tax on a limited partnership acquiring personal property, see *Edenvale Restoration Specialists Ltd. v. British Columbia*, 2013 CarswellBC 456, 2013 BCCA 85 (B.C. C.A.).

Special Incentives. In its efforts to implement specific economic policies through the taxation system, the federal government has intermittently introduced special tax incentives (some of which have since been repealed or are in the course of being phased out) designed to encourage, for example, exploration for oil and gas, Canadian feature films, construction of multiunit residential buildings (MURB's) and scientific and technologically oriented research and development. The basic incentive in these schemes is the allowance of a rapid expensing for tax purposes of the cost of items which would otherwise be capitalized and offset against income over a much longer period of time, and by allowing any resulting tax losses to offset income of the taxpayer from other sources. While a corporation can store such deductions if it does not have current income to offset the special write-offs, a partnership will normally flow them through directly to the partners. This treatment avoids any loss because of the time value of money, and ensures that the losses are actually used up rather than being eventually lost because of limitations on their storage time.

Questions

1   Can a person be a general partner and a limited partner at the same time? See LPA s. 5(1). Why would a person wish to be both?

2   Every limited partnership is required by LPA s. 2(2) to have at least one general partner. Are there any legal or policy objections to a general partner being a corporation with few assets? Would this undermine the structure of the LPA and its division between general and limited partners? Would it make a difference if the directors of the general partner corporation were elected by the limited partners? *Cf. Haughton Graphic Ltd. v. Zivot, infra.*

3   Is a limited partnership subject to the registration requirements of the BNA? Compare s. 2(3) of the BNA with s. 28 of the LPA. What incentive is there for a foreign limited partnership operating in Ontario to comply with the registration provisions of the LPA?

4   Suppose a limited partnership is formed in a jurisdiction which permits a greater amount of management participation by the limited partners than is allowed under Ontario law and that the LP conducts all or most of its business in Ontario. Would an Ontario court nevertheless hold that, because of s. 27(2), limited partner is still protected from personal liability? If the court so holds, does this mean that the policy of the Act can be defeated by the simple expedient of registering a limited partnership in the extra-provincial jurisdiction with the more favourable rules? For a discussion of this issue from an American point of view, see Note, "Regulation of Foreign Limited Partnerships" (1972), 52 Boston Univ. Law Rev. 64.

Haughton Graphic Ltd. v. Zivot
(1986), 33 B.L.R. 125 (Ont. H.C.)

EBERLE J.: In this case, the plaintiff claims for payment of a debt for printing services supplied by it to a limited partnership called Printcast Publishing Network (hereafter called "Printcast"). The existence of the debt and the amount claimed of $128,251.79 are not in dispute. The plaintiff earlier obtained a default judgment against Printcast but that judgment has remained unsatisfied.

The plaintiff sues the two named defendants as limited partners of Printcast on the ground that, in addition to exercising their rights and powers as limited partners, each took part in the control of the business of the limited partnership, within the meaning of s. 63 in Part 2 of the *Partnership Act*, R.S.A. 1980, c. P-2, as amended by R.S.A. 1980 (Supp.), c. 2; S.A. 1981, c. 28 ["the Alberta Act"]. It is common ground that the Alberta law relating to limited partnerships applies in this case.

Facts

In 1980 the defendant Gary S. Zivot (hereafter called "Zivot") promoted Printcast as a limited partnership under Alberta law, for the purpose of launching a magazine called "Goodlife" to be published in the United States. Zivot's Concept was for a structure similar to a radio or television network. The limited partnership was to be the promoter of the concept. It would sign up local affiliates and supply them with common editorial material. Each affiliate would obtain local advertising and would be responsible for addition of local material to fill out the magazine.

At the same time, Zivot incorporated Lifestyle Magazine Inc. (hereafter called "Lifestyle") to be the sole general partner in Printcast. Lifestyle was controlled by Zivot, who was the sole limited partner in the company. During subsequent financing stages, other limited partners were added, including the defendant Herbert Marshall (hereafter called "Marshall").

Lifestyle obtained the concept and the necessary development expertise for Printcast from Century Media Incorporated. That too was a company controlled by Zivot, and used by him as a vehicle for his "media development business". Century Media in turn employed Zivot, its president, as the live body to perform these services. Century Media's role in the matter is not of particular importance, the principal players being: Printcast (the limited partnership); Lifestyle (the general partner); and Zivot and Marshall (two of the limited partners).

Through Zivot's efforts, about $250,000 of seed money was obtained from investors in the latter part of 1981. At the beginning of January 1982, Printcast went into business. The first Step was to sign up affiliates in various cities. In addition, the details of the magazine and its contents had to be worked out and arrangements made with suppliers, including printing.

It is clear on the evidence and admitted by Zivot that commencing in January 1982 Zivot was known to suppliers as the "president" of Printcast. He used this title to introduce himself; he used business cards showing his relationship to Printcast; and when the magazine was published, its masthead showed Zivot as president and Marshall as executive vice-president of Printcast. Although the specific date on which Marshall joined the enterprise is unclear, there is no doubt that he played the role of executive vice-president of, and was also a limited partner in, Printcast throughout all the relevant time period.

There is no dispute about any of the above matters and I accept them as facts.

The arrangements for printing the magazine in Toronto were made between Nash, the president of the plaintiff, and Zivot, Marshall and two other employees of Printcast. I accept Nash's evidence that Zivot was introduced to him as president of Printcast and Marshall as vice-president, Nash gained the impression that Zivot was the man at the top with complete and ultimate responsibility for putting the magazine together and getting it on the market. He also gained the impression that Marshall was in charge of the administrative side of the business, including the sales and production aspects of the magazine. A deal was struck for the plaintiff to print the Toronto magazine and in late 1982, it printed the first five issues. Then Printcast went into bankruptcy, leaving the plaintiff unpaid for the printing of three issues.

Before the plaintiff did any printing, it is clear that Nash knew that he was dealing with a limited partnership. This was part of the information obtained for him about the credit worthiness of Printcast, and is recorded in Ex. 3. This information verified that the publishing venture had a capital of somewhere between $2,000,000 and $3,000,000 of which a substantial portion was held in certificates of deposit due to mature on July 1 and November 1, 1982.

Beyond this information, I am satisfied that Nash was neither given nor obtained further details about the commercial nor the legal nature of Printcast. Nash admitted that he was not familiar with the structure of a limited partnership. He was not told of the existence or identity of the general partner, Lifestyle, nor of Zivot's ownership and control of it. He was not told that both Zivot and Marshall were limited partners in Lifestyle. Thus, the contract for printing services could have been made by the plaintiff only with Printcast itself, and not with the general partner Lifestyle.

Take Part in Control

It was faintly pressed that the defendants could not be personally liable for the debt because they did not take part in the control of the limited partnership Printcast within the meaning of s. 63 of the *Partnership Act*.

The evidence, however, is all to the contrary. Zivot admitted that he was the directing mind of Printcast, that he was responsible for it, and that he managed it. Whether or not he made all of the managerial decisions, he said that he was responsible for all of them. Marshall was one of those directly under Zivot who made many of the managerial decisions in the areas of sales and administration. Zivot signed cheques on behalf of Printcast; Marshall also had the authority to do so. In fact, Zivot and Marshall were in complete control of Printcast.

In my opinion, the fact that both defendants were or may have also been acting as employees or officer of Lifestyle, all unknown to Nash, does not take the defendants outside the ambit of s. 63. The defendants' submission to the contrary must be rejected on the basis of the evidence which I accept.

* * *

Section 63 *Alberta Partnership Act*[2]

On that state of facts, and in view of the overwhelming evidence that both defendants took part in the control of the limited partnership, I come back to s. 63 of the *Alberta Partnership Act*. It reads as follows:

Liability to creditors.

63. A Limited partner does not become liable as a general partner unless, in addition to exercising his rights and powers as a limited partner, he takes part in the control of the business.

Although elaborate arguments were made as to the meaning of the section, I take a simpler view of it. If a limited partner takes part in the control of the business, he becomes liable under the statute as a general partner, i.e. unlimited liability to the extent of his assets. That is what happened in this case, and it is, effectively speaking, the end of the matter.

The elaborate arguments made only come into play if it should be found that the plaintiff somehow disclaimed reliance on that section. The arguments demonstrate that in the United States, where the limited partnership is also recognized, there are two lines of authority. One line of authority recognizes that in a statutory provision such as s. 63 of the Alberta Act, there is no room for consideration of whether or not the plaintiff relied upon the personal liability of the limited partner. It is simply a question of whether or not the limited partner took part in the control of the business and this question becomes largely a quantitative matter. An example of this line of authority is commonly taken to be *Delaney v. Fidelity Lease Ltd.*, 526 S.W. 2d 543 (Tex., 1975) in the Supreme Court of Texas.

On the other hand, there is a line of cases which espouses what is called the "specific reliance" test. An example commonly referred to is *Frigidaire Sales Corp. v. Union Properties Inc.*, 14 Wash. App. 634, 544 P. 2d 781 (Wash., 1975) in the Court of Appeals of Washington State. This view may be more fully explained by stating that "liability for a partnership's obligation to a creditor should not be imposed upon a limited partner who takes part in the control of the business unless, as a result of the limited partner's conduct, the creditor believed that the limited partner was a general partner". See Basile, "Limited Liability for Limited Partners: An Argument for the Abolition of the Control Rule" (1985), 38 Vanderbilt L. Rev. 1199, p. 1208.

---

[2]   For the corresponding section under Ontario law see s. 12(1) of the *Limited Partnership Act*, R.S.O. 1990, c. L-16.

After explaining the "specific reliance" test as above, Basile asserts that the Delaney decision, *supra*, correctly points out that the American statutory provision under discussion, which is indistinguishable from s. 63 of the Alberta Act, does not by its terms require creditor reliance as a predicate for holding a limited partner liable.

This comment identifies the problem in this case. Section 63 does not contain any requirement of reliance. If reliance was a necessary precondition to unlimited liability for a limited partner, appropriate words should be in the statute. To conclude that the words in the section require such a condition would not, in my view, be an interpretation of the words used in the section, but would be a clear addition of a second, distinct requirement to the only one currently found in the language of s. 63.

In any event, mere knowledge by the plaintiff that a magazine was being promoted and published by a limited partnership does not assist the defendants at all. What engages the liability of the limited partner is his taking part in the control of the business.

Accordingly in my view the defences must fail.

I do not think the outcome would be any different if, contrary to my findings, Zivot had explained fully to Garwood the legal particulars of the limited partnership, the legal relationship of the persons and entities concerned, the precise nature of the liability of each of them, and to whom the liabilities were owed. I say this because under s. 63 of the Alberta Act it is clear that the legal relationships can be altered by activity on the part of the limited partner. Absent some unusual situation where it might be argued that the creditor had in some way estopped himself from relying on s. 63, the result in this case would have been the same even if Mr. Zivot's evidence were to have been accepted.

In addition to the American sources cited, I was referred also to a Canadian article, "The Control Test of Investor Liability in Limited Partnerships" by R.D. Flannigan contained in (1983), 21 Alta. L. Rev. 303. This article recognizes that the reliance test is not part of the definition of taking part in the control of the business but rather that reliance is an element that is added to the control test in order to reduce the number of instances where general liability will be imposed upon limited partners. The author offers the additional test in order to allow that which is patently prohibited by the legislation, i.e., participation in control by a limited partner: see pp. 317 and 318.

There is a surprising absence of authority in Canada on the issues raised in this case. The only recent case to which I was referred is *Elevated Construction Ltd. v. Nixon* (1969), 9 D.L.R. (3d) 232 (Ont. H.C.). In his decision, Osler J. really dealt with different aspects of the *Limited Partnerships Act*, R.S.O. 1980, c. 241, but . . . in *obiter* he touched upon the question of the degree of control of the business that must be exercised by a limited partner in order to make him liable as a general partner. He pointed out that the cases are far from exhaustive, referring only to three cases from 1857 and one from 1877, all of which refer to the same limited partnership. He concluded by saying at 655 [O.R.]:

> The cases are of little assistance in determining where the line is to be drawn beyond which a limited partner is deemed to be taking part in the control of the business and each case will presumably have to be decided upon its own facts.

In opposition, the defendants relied upon s. 59 of the Alberta Act under the heading *Business dealings by partner with partnership* which commences "A Limited partner may loan money to and transact other business with the Limited partnership . . . "Emphasis was placed upon the permission to "transact other business with the limited partnership". The short answer to this submission was, I think, correctly put by counsel for the plaintiff, i.e., that, while s. 59 permits the transaction of business with the limited partnership, it does not permit the transaction of business by a limited partner on behalf of the limited partnership.

Finally it was submitted on behalf of the defendants that to hold them liable in this case means that a person who is an officer or director (or I suppose a senior employee) of the corporate general partner in a limited partnership would always be fixed with unlimited liability for the debts of the limited partnership by virtue of s. 63 of the Alberta Act on the ground that he is the person who has control of the corporate general partner. This conclusion does not logically follow. The section only applies to a person who, in addition to being an officer, director, senior employee, or other directing mind of the corporate general partner, seeks also to take advantage of personal limited liability as a limited partner in the limited partnership. In other words, s. 63 applies only if two conditions are met. One is that the person be a limited partner and the second is that he take part in the control of the business of the limited partnership. The section does not apply to someone whose sole role in, and connection with, the limited partnership is that of an officer, director or other controlling mind of the general partner. . .

Action allowed.

Questions

1   Do you agree with Eberle J.'s decision in this case? With his reasoning? Could the decision have been justified on other grounds, *viz.*, that Zivot held himself out as "president" of Printcast? Is it proper for the court to lift the corporate veil of an incorporated general partner to show that a limited partner is the directing mind of the general partner? Is this approach warranted by the language or underlying policy of s. 12(1) of the LPA?

Nordile Holdings Ltd. v. Breckenridge
(1992), 66 B.C.L.R. (2d) 183 (C.A.), aff'g [1990] B.C.W.L.D. 860 (S.C.)

GIBBS JA (orally): This appeal has its genesis in a purchase of land in 1981 pursuant to an agreement dated April 7, 1981, which I will refer to as the sale agreement. The appellant Nordile was the vendor and Arman Rental Properties Limited Partnership, a limited partnership, was the purchaser. The purchase price was payable in part by a first mortgage for $216,000 to CMHC, and in part by a second mortgage back to Nordile for $600,089.54.

Arman fell into default under the mortgages. CMHC foreclosed in 1985. Arman and Arbutus Management Ltd., the general partner of the limited partnership, were the mortgagors in the second mortgage to Nordile. On December 28, 1985 Nordile obtained judgment for $389,191 plus interest and costs against Arman and Arbutus pursuant to the terms of the second mortgage. The judgment has not been satisfied.

Nordile commenced these proceedings on March 16, 1987, claiming a right to recover the amount of the unpaid judgment and costs from John Breckenridge and Hubert Rebiffe pursuant to the *Partnership Act*, R.S.B.C. 1979, c. 312. On December 17, 1990, proceeding on an agreed statement of facts, the parties applied under Rule 33 of the Rules of Court for an opinion from the Supreme Court as to the liability of Messrs. Breckenridge and Rebiffe. On February 21, 1991 Chief Justice Esson delivered an opinion as to liability and ordered the action dismissed with costs. We have before us both an appeal and a cross appeal against that order.

It is my conclusion that the appeal fails and that the cross appeal succeeds in part. Nordile rests its case on s. 64 of the *Partnership Act* which provides:

> A limited partner is not liable as a general partner unless he takes part in the management of the business.

Breckenridge and Rebiffe were limited partners in the Arman limited partnership. They were minority shareholders in the general partner, Arbutus. They were also officers and directors of Arbutus. Breckenridge, and to a lesser extent, Rebiffe, managed Arbutus, and Arbutus managed Arman. However, paragraph 29 of the agreed statement of facts states unequivocally that when Breckenridge and Rebiffe participated in the management as directors they did so "solely in their capacities as directors and officers of the general partner, Arbutus." That agreed fact alone is sufficient to exclude liability under the "unless" provision of s. 64 of the *Partnership Act*. Acting solely in one capacity necessarily negates acting in any other capacity.

As well, I am of the opinion that liability on Breckenridge and Rebiffe is excluded, as found by Chief Justice Esson, by the wording of recital F in the sale agreement:

The parties hereto acknowledge that Arman Rental Properties Limited Partnership (the "Limited Partnership") is a limited partnership formed under the laws of British Columbia. The parties hereto agree that the obligations of the Limited Partnership shall not personally be binding upon, nor shall resort hereunder by [sic] had to, the property of any of the limited partners of the Limited Partnership or assignees of their interest in the Limited Partnership as represented by Units of the Limited Partnership but shall only be binding upon and resort may only be had to the property of the Limited Partnership or the General Partner of the Limited Partnership.

I agree with what was said by Chief Justice Esson about *Haughton Graphic (Graphics) Ltd. v. Zivot*, 1986 CarswellOnt 153, 33 B.L.R. 125 (Ont. H.C.), affirmed (1988), 38 B.L.R. xxxiii (Ont. C.A.), and with the decision of the judge in that case, and in this case, not to follow the American decisions.

The questions put to Chief Justice Esson in the stated case, and his answers to them, are as follows:

Did the Defendants, John Breckenridge and/or Hubert Rebiffe in their capacities as directors and/or officers of Arbutus and limited partners in Arman, take part in the management of Arman pursuant to section 64 of the Partnership Act so as to render them personally liable for the amounts which remain due and owing pursuant to the judgment of the Plaintiff obtained on September 27, 1985 against Arbutus and Arman?

YES.

Can the Defendants rely upon the wording of the Sale and Purchase Agreement dated April 7, 1981 entered into by the Plaintiff as vendor and Arman as investor and in particular paragraph (f) thereof which specifically excludes the personal liability of the limited partners and further restricts liability to Arman as the limited partnership, or alternatively to Arbutus as the general partner of the limited partnership?

YES.

Can the Defendants rely upon the Disclosure Statement dated March 30, 1981 wherein the personal liability of the limited partners was expressly excluded?

NO ANSWER NEEDED.

I would not disturb the answers to questions two and three. Question one is badly worded. It consists of two questions. For the answer "yes" given by the Chief Justice I would substitute yes to the part about Breckenridge and Rebiffe taking part in management in their capacities as officers and directors of Arbutus, and no to the part about them taking part in management in their capacities as limited partners and thereby rendering themselves personally liable.

For those reasons I would dismiss the appeal. I would allow the cross appeal to the extent indicated by the substitution of a yes and a no for the yes answer to question one. I would not interfere with the order dismissing the action against Messrs. Breckenridge and Rebiffe.

[Concurring judgment of McEACHERN CJBC omitted.]

Appeal dismissed;
Cross appeal is allowed to the extent mentioned by Mr. Justice Gibbs.

(b)   Limited Liability Partnerships (LLPs)

LLPs are an American innovation. The legislation was inspired by the loan and savings crisis in the US in the 1980s when law firms, especially in Texas and California, were being sued for their partners' alleged involvements in the mismanagement and wrongful diversion of loan and savings associations' funds. Partners in other law firms also came to appreciate their vulnerability to liability suits based on partnership principles of joint and several liability even though negligence was only proven against one of the partners. Partners in accounting firms quickly came to share the same concerns, since they too were exposed to similar and even greater risks because the large accounting firms are multinational in character and act for enterprises around the globe.

Texas was the first US state to adopt remedial legislation, and it did so in 1991. Similar legislation has now been adopted in many other states, but the legislation differs considerably in scope and detail. See R.W. Hamilton, "Registered Limited Liability Partnerships: Present at Birth (Nearly)" (1995), 66 Col. L. Rev. 1065. However, all the acts had a common objective, which was to restrict liability to the partner(s) directly at fault or vicariously liable for the acts of persons under his or their supervision.

In Canada, LLP legislation was first enacted in Ontario in 1998 in the form of amendments to the Ontario PA. See SO 1998, c.2, ss. 1-8. Alberta followed a year later. However, the scope of the Alberta provisions is significantly broader than the Ontario provisions. Since then various other provinces have followed suit. For a close analysis and critical evaluation of the Canadian legislation see Richard Bowes, "Limited Liability Professional Partnerships" (2000) 34 C.B.L.J. 3. Note carefully that the Ontario provisions only benefit the members of qualifying professions. So far only accountants and lawyers meet these requirements. See further, below, "Preconditions to Acquiring LLP Status". However, British Columbia allows non-professional partnerships to register as a limited liability partnership. See British Columbia's

Partnership Act, R.S.B.C. 1996, c. 348, s. 96. In response to this difference between provinces, Ontario's Ministry of Government and Consumer Services convened a panel of experts, which recommended allowing more professions and businesses to register as limited liability partnerships in Ontario than is currently the case (Business Law Agenda: Priority Findings & Recommendations Report, published in June 2015).

The United Kingdom adopted the *Limited Liability Partnership Act* in 2000. The Act has the same objectives as the North American legislation but accomplishes them by different means. See *Lindley and Banks on Partnership*, 18th ed., (2002), paras. 2–37 *et seq.* Under the British legislation the LLP is a body corporate with separate legal personality and unlimited capacity. The LLP is governed not by the *Partnership Act* 1890 but by its own provisions. Most importantly, the members of the LLP are agents of the LLP and not of each other (s. 6(1)) and are in general not liable for the LLP's debts and obligations. The members may also be employees of the LLP. In sum, the British LLP is a hybrid form of corporation and partnership.

Scope of Protection under the Ontario provisions. Section 10 of the OPA reads, in part, as follows:

> 10.(1) Except as provided in subsection (2) every partner in a firm is liable jointly with the other partners for all debts and obligations of the firm incurred while the person is a partner, and after the partner's death the partner's estate is also severally liable in a due course of administration for such debts and obligations so far as they remain unsatisfied, but subject to the prior payment of his or her separate debts.
>
> (2) Subject to subsections (3) and (3.1), a partner in a limited liability partnership is not liable, by means of indemnification, contribution, assessment or otherwise, for,
>
> (a) the debts, liabilities or obligations of the partnership or any partner arising from the negligent or wrongful acts or omissions that another partner or an employee, agent or representative of the partnership commits in the course of the partnership business while the partnership is a limited liability partnership; or
>
> (b) any other debts or obligations of the partnership that are incurred while the partnership is a limited liability partnership.
>
> (3) Subsection (2) does not relieve a partner in a limited liability partnership from liability for,
>
> (a) the partner's own negligent or wrongful act or omission;
>
> (b) the negligent or wrongful act or omission of a person under the partner's direct supervision; or

(c) the negligent or wrongful act or omission of another partner or an employee of the partnership not under the partner's direct supervision, if,

(i) the act or omission was criminal or constituted fraud, even if there was no criminal act or omission, or

(ii) the partner knew or ought to have known of the act or omission and did not take the actions that a reasonable person would have taken to prevent it.

(3.1) Subsection (2) does not protect a partner's interest in the partnership property from claims against the partnership respecting a partnership obligation.

[Subs. (4) and (5) are omitted.]

As will be seen, the operative provisions are those in s. (2) excluding a partner's direct or indirect liability arising from "negligent or wrongful acts or omissions" of another partner or an employee, agent or representative of the partnership. By including wrongful acts, along with several other changes, limited liability has changed from a "partial shield" to a "full shield". Subsection (2)(b) also excludes a partner's liability for the limited liability partnership's debts or obligations. Subsection (3) affirms a partner's liability for the partner's own negligence or the negligence of a person under the partner's direct supervision, which has been amended from "direct supervision or control" to just direct supervision. It seems, therefore, that members of an Ontario LLP continue to have joint liability for liability arising out of a partner's fraudulent or criminal conduct, and for strict liabilities arising by operation of law, *e.g.*, under employment standards legislation. Many large accounting and law firms across Canada have availed themselves of the new legislation.

Preconditions to acquiring the status of an Ontario LLP (ss. 44.1– 44.3). There are four such requirements, *viz.*: (a) there must be a written agreement between two or more persons designating their partnership as an LLP to be governed by the OPA; (b) the partnership is formed to carry on a profession governed by an act that permits practice of the profession by an LLP, and the governing body of which profession requires its members to maintain a minimum amount of liability insurance; (c) the LLP's name is registered under the OBNA; and (d) the LLP's name must include the words "limited liability partnership" or "société à responsabilité limitée" or the abbreviations "LLP", "L.L.P." or "s.r.l." as the last words or letters of the firm name. The other provincial acts have comparable provisions.

(c) Joint Ventures

A joint venture is an agreement between two parties to carry on business, usually restricted to a certain project. The elements of a joint venture are well-defined in British Columbia, as outlined in *Canlan Investment Corp. v. Gettling*, 1997 CarswellBC 1380, [1997] B.C.J. No. 1647 (B.C. C.A.): (1) A joint venture must have a contractual basis; (2) A contribution by the parties of money, property, effort, knowledge, skill or other asset to a common undertaking; (3) A joint property interest in the subject matter of the venture; (4) A right of mutual control or management of the enterprise; (5) Expectation of profit, or the presence of "adventure," as it is sometimes called; (6) A right to participate in the profits; (7) Most usually, limitation of the objective to a single undertaking or ad hoc enterprise. The same elements have also been applied in other provinces. See: *Daniels v. EOG Resources Canada Inc.*, 2014 CarswellMan 39, 2014 MBQB 19 (Man. Q.B.); *Oz Optics Ltd. v. Timbercon Inc.*, 2010 CarswellOnt 4070, 2010 ONSC 310 (Ont. S.C.J.), additional reasons 2010 CarswellOnt 5540 (Ont. S.C.J.), reversed in part on other grounds 2011 ONCA 714, 2011 CarswellOnt 12462, 107 O.R. (3d) 509 (Ont. C.A.), additional reasons 2012 CarswellOnt 13318 (Ont. C.A.).

Several other distinguishing features of a joint venture from a partnership are stated in *Blue Line Hockey Acquisition Co. v. Orca Bay Hockey Ltd. Partnership*, 2008 CarswellBC 36, 2008 BCSC 27 (B.C. S.C.), affirmed 2009 CarswellBC 177 (B.C. C.A.), leave to appeal refused 2009 CarswellBC 1861, 2009 CarswellBC 1862 (S.C.C.). For example, joint ventures can commence without actually carrying on a business, and joint venture agreements do not presumptively create fiduciary relationships. However, fiduciary obligations can arise depending on the characteristics of the particular relationship in issue using a case specific approach. See: *Chitel v. Bank of Montreal*, 2002 CarswellOnt 1824, [2002] O.J. No. 2170 (Ont. S.C.J.).

In certain instances a joint venture may be treated as a partnership and liability may be extended to participants in a joint venture based on the actions of other participants. In *Central Mortgage & Housing Corp. v. Graham*, 1973 CarswellNS 192, 43 D.L.R. (3d) 686 (N.S. T.D.), the plaintiff, Central Mortgage & Housing Corporation (CMHC) enlisted the assistance of Bras D'Or, a construction company, to build a series of homes, one of which the defendants purchased. Several defects in the home were discovered and the defendants stopped making payments on the mortgage. CMHC sued the defendants, who filed a counterclaim for damages against CMHC and Bras D'Or. The defendants claimed that the two companies were engaged in a joint venture and therefore jointly liable for damages. Jones J. found that there was a contribution by both CMHC and Bras D'Or of money, property, skill and knowledge to a common undertaking. He held that the relationship between the parties was not that of mortgagee-mortgagor, but rather a joint venture, and found both parties liable to the defendants for damages.

Part B

Business Corporations Law

Chapter 2

Evolution of Business Corporations Law and the Nature of Corporate Personality

1. INTRODUCTION

In this introductory part of the chapter, we begin with a description of the evolution of Canadian corporations law (subsection (a)) and of the constitutional basis for corporations law (b), before presenting the statutory provisions that establish the separate legal personality of corporations (c) and the classic decision of the House of Lords in *Salomon v. Salomon & Co.* (d).

(a) History of Canadian Business Corporation Law

(i) British Origins

The evolution of Canadian corporations law has been much influenced by British and American law. The British influence is the older of the two. Since knowledge of the history of British company law is also important for an understanding of the early Canadian developments, it will be appropriate to start with it here.

The common law recognizes two principal forms of incorporation, *viz.* (a) incorporation by exercise of the royal prerogative (usually referred to as incorporation by letters patent or, more colloquially, royal charter), and (b) incorporation by a private or general act of the legislature. Until well into the eighteenth century incorporation by royal charter was by far the most common method. Even it was used very sparingly until the sixteenth and seventeenth centuries to incorporate companies with commercial purposes such as the Hudson Bay Company, the London East India Company and the Levant Company for overseas trade and colonization of territories. These early charters were usually accompanied by monopolies of one description or another. Limited liability was not expressly conferred by these charters and limited liability for investors did not become a controversial issue until the early part of the nineteenth century.

By the turn of the eighteenth century there was a lively trade in royal charters of companies, and this was accompanied by frenetic speculation in the shares of these companies. The South Sea Company was the most notorious of them. It nearly collapsed in 1720 amidst much scandal and allegations of corruption in high places. That same year Parliament adopted the "*Bubble Act*" (6 Geo. 1, c. 18), an obscure piece of legislation, the only sure feature of which was that it substantially froze the development of British company law for over a century and generally cast commercial companies under a pall.

The beginning of the industrial revolution in the United Kingdom was accompanied by growing pressure for the repeal of the *Bubble Act* and a more accessible form of incorporation. The *Bubble Act* was repealed in 1825, but the first general Act for the incorporation of companies, the *Joint Stock Companies Act* (7 & 8 Vic. cc. 110 & 111), was not adopted until 1844. This Act introduced incorporation by registration, the method that has remained in dominant use in the U.K. since then and subsequently became the standard model of incorporation in most of the Commonwealth. However, the Act of 1844 still withheld the privilege of limited liability. The difficulties were compounded because the courts held that the joint stock companies were merely large partnerships and that each shareholder was a partner, even though the management of the companies was usually vested in directors or trustees.

The battle for limited liability was finally won in 1855 with the adoption of the *Limited Liability Act* (18 & 19 Vic., c. 133). This Act also introduced the requirement that incorporated companies with limited liability include the term "Limited" or "Ltd." as part of the company's name so as to warn the public of this "dangerous" new entity! The 1855 Act and earlier legislation were replaced in 1862 by the *Companies Act* (25 & 26 Vic., c. 89). This is the title by which all subsequent general companies legislation in the U.K. has come to be identified. The 1862 Act also became the model for several of the later Canadian provincial Acts.

(ii)   Early Canadian Corporations Law

None of the Canadian provinces and territories adopted general incorporation legislation before the middle of the nineteenth century. Prior to this period, incorporation by private Act was the common procedure and was used substantially for the same purposes as in the U.K.

The first general legislation consisted of two Acts, both passed in 1849, one for Upper Canada and the other for Lower Canada. These authorized the incorporation of joint stock companies for the construction of roads and bridges. Both provided for incorporation by registration of appropriate documents with the registrar of the counties through which the road was to pass or in which the work was to be situated. The 1849 Acts were followed by a more broadly aimed Act of 1850 which permitted the incorporation of companies for "manufacturing, mining, mechanical and chemical purposes." This too was a registration Act and was modelled on a New York statute of 1848.

In 1860 another general Act was adopted for the incorporation of commercial companies and this provided for incorporation by judicial decree. In 1864, a third general Act, *viz.* by Letters Patent issued under the seal of the Governor in Council. According to Wegenast (*The Law of Canadian Companies* (1931)), the idea of incorporation by letters patent pursuant to a general Act may have been suggested by an English Act of 1844 for the incorporation of joint stock banks. The letters patent method of incorporation exerted great influence on the general incorporation Acts of other provinces and on federal corporate legislation. It was not abolished in Ontario until 1970, and not by the federal government until the adoption of the *Canada Business Corporations Act* (CBCA) in 1975.

The first general incorporation Act was adopted by the federal Parliament in 1869. This repealed the pre-Confederation legislation providing for incorporation by registration and judicial decree and re-enacted the Act of 1864. The 1864 Act also served as a model for the subsequent incorporation legislation of New Brunswick, Manitoba and Prince Edward Island. The other provinces (British Columbia, Alberta, Saskatchewan and Nova Scotia) adopted at different times the British method of incorporation by registration and also adopted many of the other provisions in the British Act of 1862. One of the unfortunate consequences of this schism was that at a crucial conceptual level Canada was divided into two camps, since the method of incorporation also brought in its train important substantive differences. A further difficulty arose because it was not always easy to determine how much of the English jurisprudence, built as it was around companies incorporated by registration, was relevant to companies incorporated by letters patent.

(iii)   Modern Canadian Corporations Law

Until the 1960s, Canadian corporation law developments largely consisted of fleshing out and amending the nineteenth century legislation, and there were few basic conceptual changes. A new era in corporate legislation was introduced in 1970 with the adoption of an entirely new Act, the Ontario *Business Corporations Act* (OBCA) (R.S.O. 1970, c. 53). The Act largely implemented the recommendations of the Interim Report of the Select Committee on Company Law ("Report of the Lawrence Committee") which was published in 1967. The new Ontario Act replaced incorporation by letters patent with incorporation by registration, permitted the incorporation of one-person corporations, largely immunized third parties from the effects of the *ultra vires* doctrine, regularized pre-incorporation contracts, introduced a new regulatory framework for the issuance and transfer of investment securities, partially codified the duties of directors and officers, regulated insider trading in the corporation's securities, permitted derivative actions and improved minority shareholder protection in other important respects.

In 1971, a federal task force led by Robert Dickerson, John Howard and Leon Getz submitted to the federal government its Proposals for a New Business Corporations Law for Canada. The draft Act largely mirrored changes and concepts that had already been adopted in the Ontario Act. One major difference was that the draft Act went further than the Ontario Act in its protection of minority shareholder rights. The federal government enacted the draft Act in 1975 with only minor changes. Since then, the CBCA has become the template for many of the subsequent provincial business corporations Acts. The Act has been adopted, more or less verbatim, in Alberta, Saskatchewan and Manitoba, and has been substantially followed in New Brunswick. The Act's influence was also pronounced in important amendments adopted in Nova Scotia in 1982 and in the Quebec Act of 1980. In 1982, Ontario repealed its own Act of 1970 and replaced it with a new Act, the *Business Corporations Act*, 1982 (S.O. 1982, c. 4). With modest exceptions, the Act closely tracked the federal Act. In 1978, the Newfoundland government published the Barry Report. This likewise recommended adoption of the federal model. In 2001 the federal government adopted substantial amendments to the CBCA. See S.C. 2001, c.14, and W.D. Gray and C.W. Halladay, *Guide to the CBCA Reform: Analysis and Precedents* (Carswell 2002), and the Symposium on the amendments in (2003-4) 39 C.B.L.J. 4-137. The changes largely benefited publicly held corporations, but protection of minority shareholder interests was also enhanced in important respects. Quebec's legislation was further modernized in a 2009 overhaul.

British Columbia's position is *sui generis*. The province adopted a new *Companies Act* in 1973 which incorporated (or anticipated?) many of the features of the federal Act of 1974 but was not a carbon copy of it. British Columbia adopted an entirely new Act in 2002, the *Business Corporations Act*, SBC 2002, c. 57 (BCBCA), which came into force on March 29, 2004 and repealed the *Company Act*, RSBC 1996, c. 62. The new Act seeks to

> remedy many of the shortcomings and ambiguities in the *Company Act* and. . . introduce more modern provisions in many areas. It. . . retain[s] the contract model of incorporation and its concomitant flexibility (which will be enhanced), a decision having been made not to adopt the *Canada Business Corporations Act* model, which will continue to be available for anyone wanting to use the alternative model.

See John O.E. Lundell, "Introduction to the British Columbia Business Corporations Act," *Continuing Legal Education*, Vancouver, May 2003, §1.1.

(iv)   Securities Regulation

Even a skeletal history of modern Canadian business corporation law would be seriously incomplete without some mention of securities legislation, an area in which until recently Canada has generally led the Commonwealth. The aim of securities regulation is to provide an informed, transparent and honest market in the publicly issued and traded securities of corporations. The Canadian legislation accomplishes this by a policy of full and continuous disclosure of all relevant information and by imposing a comprehensive regime of supervision and registration of securities and members of the securities industry. The difference between corporate legislation and securities legislation is that corporate legislation is generally only concerned with corporations incorporated under the laws of the enacting province whereas securities legislation applies to corporations (and other issuers) regardless of where the issuer was incorporated[1] As a result, a corporation with publicly held securities often finds itself subject to the concurrent and, not infrequently, overlapping laws of several jurisdictions. Another important difference between corporation and securities legislation is that while rights and duties under the former are usually privately enforced (or not enforced at all), in the case of securities legislation, the investor has the assistance of a powerful watchdog with a wide range of administrative and quasi-judicial powers and, in the case of Ontario at least, with the human and financial resources to use them.

A new era in securities regulation began with the 1965 report of the Kimber Committee in Ontario. In addition to strengthening disclosure and reporting requirements, the Report recommended legislation with respect to proxies and proxy solicitations, insider trading and takeover bids. The Kimber Committee recommendations were quickly implemented in the *Securities Act*, 1966. In 1978, Ontario adopted a revised *Securities Act*, 1978, which introduced the principle of continuous disclosure and conferred new (and controversial) protection for minority shareholders in private control transactions. This is the Act which is in

---

[1]   Another distinction that is sometimes drawn is that corporation law is concerned with the organization and constitution of corporations and their internal government, whereas securities law focuses on the protection of investors in the marketplace. However, the securities legislation does not follow such neat distinctions, and there is, in fact, a good deal of overlap, as was freely admitted in several of the judgments in *Multiple Access Ltd. v. McCutcheon* (1982), 138 D.L.R. (3d) 1 (S.C.C.). In the ultimate analysis, securities law covers whatever the regulators deem necessary for the protection of investors in publicly traded issues in their jurisdictions, a position that is strongly criticized by law and economics scholars. They believe that shareholder rights should be determined by the incorporating jurisdiction and that maintenance of this distinction is essential to encourage provinces to compete for the adoption of investor-friendly corporate legislation.

force at the present time (see R.S.O. 1990, c. S-5), though it was amended in important respects in 1987. British Columbia and Quebec have also adopted new securities Acts, the former in 1985 and the latter in 1982. As noted below, the fallout from the Enron and other very recent corporate and securities market scandals in the US, leading to the Congressional adoption of the *Sarbanes-Oxley Act* and much tighter enforcement of state and federal securities regulation, has also reverberated in Canada.

Federal involvement in securities regulation has been discussed intermittently in the post-war period. In 1979, the federal government published a three-volume report on Proposals for a Securities Market Law for Canada prepared by a task force led by Philip Anisman. But it was not until 2009, after an Expert Panel appointed by the federal Minister of Finance again recommended the establishment of a national securities regulator, that the federal government moved in earnest, creating a Canadian Securities Regulator Transition Office to "lead the development of the federal Securities Act" and "lead and manage the transition to a Canadian securities regulator" (Dept. of Finance News Release 2009-064, June 22, 2009). The constitutionality of the proposed *Canada Securities Act* was referred by the governments of Quebec and Alberta to their respective Courts of Appeal, and by the federal government to the Supreme Court of Canada. All three Courts held that the proposed Act was unconstitutional on the basis that it did not come within the federal power to regulate trade and commerce. The Supreme Court characterized the draft federal legislation as an impermissible attempt to effect a "wholesale takeover of the regulation of the securities industry."[2]

In 2013, in the wake of the Supreme Court's decision, the federal government and the governments of British Columbia and Ontario opted for a different approach. Under this new approach, the participating provinces will enact a common securities act and delegate administrative and enforcement powers to a common agency. This agency will administer powers delegated to it under federal legislation concerning national data collection and the mitigation of systemic risk. As of January 2016, five provinces (Ontario, New Brunswick, British Columbia, Prince Edward Island, and Saskatchewan) are participating in this initiative.

(v)   Differences between Canada and the United States

The growing influence of American corporate and securities law on Canadian corporate and securities law should not mislead the reader into assuming that the two national regimes are interchangeable and that both operate in substantially identical political, economic and legal environments. There are many important differences between the

---

[2]   See *Reference re Securities Act (Canada)*, 2011 CarswellNat 5243, 2011 CarswellNat 5244, [2011] 3 S.C.R. 837 (S.C.C.), para. 128.

Canadian and American positions, as is shown by the following illustrations:

1. The number of publicly traded companies in the US is far larger, proportionate to population as well as in absolute terms, than the number of Canadian companies;

2. Even more importantly, the US market for publicly traded shares is much more liquid and deeper than the Canadian market. One Canadian study (Fowler & Rorke, 1988) found that only 5.3% of the securities listed on the Toronto Stock Exchange (TSX) were widely traded, that 35.3% were moderately traded, and that 59.4% were infrequently or thinly traded. These figures have important implications for the type of securities regime appropriate in the Canadian context and the need for regulatory oversight;

3. The concentration of share ownership is much higher in Canada than it is in the US. As of 1990, only 14% of the companies in the TSX 300 Composite Index were widely held among investors. 60.3% of the shares were owned by a single shareholder exercising legal control, and 25.4% were owned by one shareholder with effective control or by two or three shareholders each of whom owned 10–20% of the outstanding shares. In contrast, in the US 63% of the Fortune 500 companies were widely held, and only 18% of the companies were controlled by a single shareholder or group of shareholders with effective control. The higher concentration of Canadian share ownership leads to fewer investor-manager conflicts but increases the potential for inter-investor friction as well as triggering other consequences; and

4. The Canadian market is characterized by highly interconnected corporate relationships. Of the 100 most profitable Canadian companies in 1987, close to 45% held 10% or more of the voting shares of another company on the TSX Composite List. This familial relationship is also reflected among the directors of Canada's largest companies, many of whom hold two or more appointments.

There are also important differences at the legal level. While all the provinces and the Territories have their own business corporation legislation, with modest exceptions, Canada has not experienced the "Delaware" phenomenon.[3] Again, unlike the US, Canada does not yet have a national securities commission but, given the importance of the Ontario securities market, the Ontario Securities Commission often acts as a surrogate federal securities commission. Further, the *Ontario Securities Act* confers substantially broader powers and greater discretion on the OSC than are enjoyed by the SEC under US legislation.

---

[3] See further Wayne D. Gray, "Corporations as Winners under the CBCA Reform" (2003), 39 C.B.L.J. 4, especially Part IV and the appendix.

See further Daniels and MacIntosh, "Toward A Distinctive Canadian Corporate Law Regime" (1991) 29 O.H.L.J. 863.

(b) Constitutional Basis for Business Corporation Law

As described in the preceding section, both the federal and provincial governments have enacted general business corporation legislation and, in the case of the provinces, securities legislation as well. This short note is intended to explain the constitutional basis of their jurisdiction and to deal with some related constitutional problems.

There is no specific provision in the *Constitution Act* 1867 generally enabling the federal government to incorporate companies. However, in the leading case of *Citizens Insce. Co. of Canada v. Parsons* (1881-2) 7 A.C. 96, the Privy Council found the jurisdiction in the "Peace, Order and Good Government" clause of s. 91 of the *Constitution Act*. Sir Montague Smith reasoned that since the provinces were restricted in their jurisdiction to the "incorporation of companies with provincial objects" [*Constitution Act*, s. 92(11)] "it follows that the incorporation of companies for objects other than provincial falls within the general powers of the parliament of Canada" (*ibid.*, at p. 116). Apart from its residuary power the federal government also has ancillary incorporation powers under several of the specific heads of s. 91 (*e.g.*, s. 91(15) relating to banks and banking) and has exercised them.

The provinces enjoy express incorporation powers by virtue of s. 92(11) of the *Constitution Act*. What remained unclear, however, until the long-standing doubt was resolved by the Privy Council in *Bonanza Creek Gold Mining Co. v. R.*, [1916] 1 A.C. 566 (P.C.), was the meaning of the power to incorporate companies "with provincial objects." The Privy Council held that the words merely meant that a province could not endow a provincial corporation with the *right* to carry on its activities in another jurisdiction but that it did not preclude a province from conferring on a corporation the *capacity or power* to carry on business elsewhere if the extra-provincial jurisdiction was willing to allow it to do so. In practice, the provinces readily grant the permission subject to some modest filing or registration requirements and the payment of a fee. See further *infra*, Ch. 3, s. 2. To all intents and purposes therefore, a provincially incorporated company, *qua* company, enjoys almost as much mobility as a federally incorporated company. However, federally incorporated companies appear to enjoy greater prestige and, for reasons stated below, they cannot be prevented from commencing business in a province before they have complied with provincial registration or filing requirements and paid a fee.

Federal corporations remain subject to provincial laws of general application, such as employment standards laws, consumer protection laws and securities laws. The foregoing proposition is subject to the general principle in Canadian constitutional law that, in the event of a conflict between any valid provincial law and a valid federal law (such federal business corporations legislation), the provincial law is inoperative to the extent of the conflict. In *Multiple Access Ltd. v. McCutcheon* (1982), 138 D.L.R. (3d) 1, the Supreme Court considered whether the insider trading rules in the Ontario *Securities Act* conflicted with the similar provisions of the *Canada Business Corporations Act*, and concluded that they did not. The Supreme Court explained that mere duplication or overlap between federal and provincial provisions is not sufficient; there must be actual conflict between them to trigger the paramountcy doctrine.

For a time, there was controversy over the question whether an otherwise valid provincial law of general application might be constitutionally inapplicable to a federal corporation if its effect would be to sterilize the latter's business activity. See *John Deere Plow Co. v. Wharton*, [1915] A.C. 330, and *Great West Saddle v. R.*, [1921] 2 A.C. 91. However, it is now clear that, even in such cases, federal corporations do not enjoy immunity from otherwise valid provincial legislation. In *Canadian Indemnity Co. v. British Columbia (Attorney General)* (1976), 1976 CarswellBC 238, 1976 CarswellBC 319, [1977] 2 S.C.R. 504, 73 D.L.R. (3d) 111 (S.C.C.), the Supreme Court affirmed the validity of B.C. legislation establishing a government controlled monopoly in automobile insurance. The Court quoted, with approval, the following statement by McGillivray J.A. in *R. v. Arcadia Coal Co. Ltd.*, [1932] 2 D.L.R. 475, at 487-8:

> A provincial Legislature may enact laws, province wide, of general application (i.e., including the public generally) in respect of any of the subjects enumerated in s. 92 and in so doing may completely paralyze all activities of a Dominion trading company provided that in the enactment of such laws it does not enter the field of company law and in that field encroach upon the status and powers of a Dominion company as such.

For further discussion of the constitutional position, see P.W. Hogg, *Constitutional Law of Canada*, 5th ed. (2007), Ch. 23, Ian B. Lee, "Économie, travail et constitution," in *JurisClasseur Québec, coll. "Droit public,"* Droit constitutionnel, fasc. 17, par. 18-21 (2011); J.S. Ziegel, *Studies in Canadian Company Law* (1967), vol. 1, Ch. 5.

(c) Statutory Provisions

B.C. BUSINESS CORPORATIONS ACT
S.B.C. 2002, c. 57 as am.

3 (1)   When a company is recognized — A company is recognized under this Act,

(a) when it is incorporated under this Act,

(b) if the company results from the conversion, under this or any other Act, of a corporation into a company after the coming into force of this Act, when the conversion occurs,

(c) if the company results from an amalgamation of corporations under this Act, when the amalgamation occurs, or

(d) if the company results from the continuation into British Columbia of a foreign corporation under this Act, when the continuation occurs.

(2) A company was recognized under a former *Companies Act*

(a) when it was incorporated under that Act,

(b) if the company resulted from the conversion, under the former *Companies Act* or under any other Act, of a corporation into a company before the coming into force of this Act, when the conversion occurred,

(c) if the company resulted from the amalgamation of companies under the former *Companies Act*, when the amalgamation occurred, or

(d) if the company resulted from the continuation into British Columbia of a foreign corporation under the former *Companies Act*, when the continuation occurred.

* * *

10 (1) Formation of company — One or more persons may form a company by

(a) entering into an incorporation agreement,

(b) filing with the registrar an incorporation application, and

(c) complying with this Part.

(2) An incorporation agreement must

(a) contain the agreement of each incorporator to take, in that incorporator's name, one or more shares of the company,

(b) for each incorporator,

(i) have a signature line with the full name of that incorporator set out legibly under the signature line, and

(ii) set out legibly opposite the signature line of that incorporator,

(A) the date of signing by that incorporator, and

(B) the number of shares of each class and series of shares being taken by that incorporator, and

(c) be signed on the applicable signature line by each incorporator.

(3) An incorporation application referred to in ss. (1)(b) must

(a) be in the form established by the registrar,

(b) contain a completing party statement referred to in s. 15,

(c) set out the full names and mailing addresses of the incorporators,

(d) Set out

  (i) the name reserved for the company under s. 22, and the reservation number given for it, or

  (ii) if a name is not reserved, a statement that the name by which the company is to be incorporated is the name created,

   (A) in the case of a limited company, by adding "B.C. Ltd." after the incorporation number of the company, or

   (B) in the case of an unlimited liability company, by adding "B.C. Unlimited Liability Company" after the incorporation number of the company, and

(e) contain a notice of articles that reflects the information that will apply to the company on its incorporation.

* * *

13 (1)   Incorporation — A company is incorporated

(a) on the date and time that the incorporation application applicable to it is filed with the registrar, or

(b) subject to ss. 14 and 410, if the incorporation application specifies a date, or a date and time, on which the company is to be incorporated that is later than the date and time on which the incorporation application is filed with the registrar,

  (i) on the specified date and time, or

  (ii) if no time is specified, at the beginning of the specified date.

(2) After a company is incorporated under this Part, the registrar must issue a certificate of incorporation for the company and must record in that certificate the name and incorporation number of the company and the date and time of its incorporation.

(3) After a company is incorporated under this Part, the registrar must

(a) furnish to the company

  (i) the certificate of incorporation, and

  (ii) if requested to do so, a certified copy of the incorporation application and a certified copy of the notice of articles,

(b) furnish a copy of the incorporation application to the completing party, and

(c) publish in the prescribed manner a notice of the incorporation of the company.

* * *

17 Effect of incorporation — On and after the incorporation of a company, the shareholders of the company are, for so long as they remain shareholders of the company, a company with the name set out in the notice of articles, capable of exercising the functions of an incorporated company with the powers and with the liability on the part of the shareholders provided in this Act.

18 Evidence of incorporation — Whether or not the requirements precedent and incidental to incorporation have been complied with, a notation in the corporate register that a company has been incorporated is conclusive evidence for the purposes of this Act and for all other purposes that the company has been duly incorporated on the date and time shown in the corporate register.

* * *

30 Capacity and powers of company — A company has the capacity and the rights, powers and privileges of an individual of full capacity.

* * *

CANADA BUSINESS CORPORATIONS ACT
R.S.C. 1985, c. C-44, as am.

5 (1) Incorporators — One or more individuals not one of whom

    (a) is less than eighteen years of age,

    (b) is of unsound mind and has been so found by a court in Canada or elsewhere,

    (c) has the status of bankrupt, may incorporate a corporation by signing articles of incorporation and complying with s. 7.

(2) Bodies corporate — One or more bodies corporate may incorporate a corporation by signing articles of incorporation and complying with s. 7.

* * *

8. (1) Certificate of incorporation — Subject to subsection (2), on receipt of articles with incorporation, the Director shall issue a certificate of incorporation in accordance with section 262.

(2) Exception — failure to comply with Act — The Director may refuse to issue the certificate if a notice that is required to be sent under subsection 19(2) or 106(1) indicates that the corporation, if it came into existence, would not be in compliance with this Act.

9. Effect of certificate — A corporation comes into existence on the date shown in the certificate of incorporation. . .

15. (1)   Capacity of a corporation — A corporation has the capacity and, subject to this Act, the rights, powers and privileges of a natural person.

(2)   *Idem* — A corporation may carry on business throughout Canada.

(3)   Extra-territorial capacity — A corporation has the capacity to carry on its business, conduct its affairs and exercise its powers in any jurisdiction outside Canada to the extent that the laws of such jurisdiction permit. . .

INTERPRETATION ACT
R.S.C. 1985, c. I-21 as am.

21. (1)   Words establishing a corporation shall be construed

    (a)   as vesting in the corporation power to sue and be sued, to contract and be contracted with by its corporate name, to have a common seal and to alter or change it at pleasure, to have perpetual succession, to acquire and hold personal property for the purposes for which the corporation is established and to alienate that property at pleasure;

    (b)   in the case of a corporation having a name consisting of an English and a French form or a combined English and French form, as vesting in the corporation power to use either the English or the French form of its name or both forms and to show on its seal both the English and French forms of its name or have two seals, one showing the English and the other showing the French form of its name;

    (c)   as vesting in a majority of the members of the corporation the power to bind the others by their acts; and

    (d)   as exempting from personal liability for its debts, obligations or acts individual members of the corporation who do not contravene the provisions of the enactment establishing the corporation.

(d)   Salomon's Case

Salomon v. Salomon & Co.
[1897] A.C. 22 (H.L.)

[Aron Salomon sold his business as a leather merchant and wholesale boot manufacturer to a limited company with an authorized capital of 40,000 shares with a par value of »1 each. The only shareholders in the company were Salomon, his wife, four sons and a daughter, each of whom subscribed for one share. The sale price of the business was approximately »38,800, which was to be satisfied by the issuance to Salomon of 20,000 shares (i.e., representing a consideration of »20,000), and the payment to him either in cash or debentures, of some »16,000. In fact, at the first meeting of the directors of the company, it was decided that Salomon should be paid »6,000 in cash, and should be issued debentures amounting to »10,000, and secured upon the assets of the company.

When the company was wound up a year later it was found that if the amount realised from the assets of the company were to be first to be applied in payment of the debentures, there would be no funds left for payment of the ordinary creditors.

The liquidator claimed that the company was a mere alias or agent of Salomon, that Salomon was liable to indemnify the company against the claims of the ordinary creditors and that no payment should be made on the debentures held by Salomon until the ordinary creditors had been paid in full.

The trial judge, Vaughan Williams J., gave judgment against Salomon, and this was confirmed by the Court of Appeal. A further appeal was taken to the House of Lords.]

LORD MACNAGHTEN: My Lords, I cannot help thinking that the appellant, Aron Salomon, has been dealt with somewhat hardly in this case.

Mr. Salomon, who is now suing as a pauper, was a wealthy man in July, 1892. He was a boot and shoe manufacturer trading on his own sole account under the firm of "A. Salomon & Co." in High Street, Whitechapel, where he had extensive warehouses and a large establishment. He had been in the trade over thirty years. He had lived in the same neighbourhood all along, and for many years past he had occupied the same premises. So far things had gone very well with him. Beginning with little or no capital, he had gradually built up a thriving business, and he was undoubtedly in good credit and repute.

It is impossible to say exactly what the value of the business was. But there was a substantial surplus of assets over liabilities. And it seems to me to be pretty clear that if Mr. Salomon had been minded to dispose of his business in the market as a going concern he might fairly have counted upon retiring with at least 10,000*l.* in his pocket.

Mr. Salomon, however, did not want to part with the business. He had a wife and a family consisting of five sons and a daughter. Four of the sons were working with their father. The eldest, who was about thirty years of age, was practically the manager. But the sons were not partners: they were only servants. Not unnaturally, perhaps, they were dissatisfied with their position. They kept pressing their father to give them a share in the concern. "They troubled me," says Mr. Salomon, "all the while." So at length Mr. Salomon did what hundreds of others have done under similar circumstances. He turned his business into a limited company. He wanted, he says, to extend the business and make provision for his family. In those words, I think, he fairly describes the principal motives which influenced his action.

All the usual formalities were gone through; all the requirements of the *Companies Act*, 1862, were duly observed. There was a contract with a trustee in the usual form for the sale of the business to a company about to be formed. There was a memorandum of association duly signed and registered, stating that the company was formed to carry that contract into effect, and fixing the capital at 40,000*l*. in 40,000 shares of 1*l*. each. There were articles of association providing the usual machinery for conducting the business. The first directors were to be nominated by the majority of the subscribers to the memorandum of association. The directors, when appointed, were authorized to exercise all such powers of the company as were not by statute or by the articles required to be exercised in general meeting; and there was express power to borrow on debentures, with the limitation that the borrowing was not to exceed 10,000*l*. without the sanction of a general meeting.

The company was intended from the first to be a private company; it remained a private company to the end. No prospectus was issued; no invitation to take shares was ever addressed to the public.

The subscribers to the memorandum were Mr. Salomon, his wife, and five of his children who were grown up. The subscribers met and appointed Mr. Salomon and his two elder sons directors. The directors then proceeded to carry out the proposed transfer. By an agreement dated August 2, 1892, the company adopted the preliminary contract, and in accordance with it the business was taken over by the company as from June 1, 1892. The price fixed by the contract was duly paid. The price on paper was extravagant. It amounted to over 39,000*l*.— a sum which represented the sanguine expectations of a fond owner rather than anything that can be called a businesslike or reasonable estimate of value. That, no doubt, is a circumstance which at first sight calls for observation; but when the facts of the case and the position of the parties are considered, it is difficult to see what bearing it has on the question before your Lordships. The purchase-money was paid in this way: as money came in, sums amounting in all to 20,000*l*, were paid to Mr. Salomon, and then immediately returned to the company in exchange for fully paid shares. The sum of 10,000*l*. was paid in debentures for the like amount. The balance, with the exception of about 1000*l*. which Mr. Salomon seems to have received and retained, went in discharge of the debts and liabilities of the business at the time of the transfer, which were thus entirely wiped off. In the result, therefore, Mr. Salomon received for his business about 1000*l*. in cash, 10,000*l*. in debentures, and half the nominal capital of the company in fully paid shares for what they were worth. No other shares were issued except the seven shares taken by the subscribers to the memorandum, who, of course, knew all the circumstances, and had therefore no ground for complaint on the score of overvaluation.

The company had a brief career: it fell upon evil days. Shortly after it was started there seems to have come a period of great depression in the boot and shoe trade. There were strikes of workmen too; and in view of that danger contracts with public bodies, which were the principal source of Mr. Salomon's profit, were split up and divided between different firms. The attempts made to push the business on behalf of the new company crammed its warehouses with unsaleable stock. Mr. Salomon seems to have done what he could: both he and his wife lent the company money; and then he got his debentures cancelled and reissued to a Mr. Broderip, who advanced him 5000*l.*, which he immediately handed over to the company on loan. The temporary relief only hastened ruin. Mr. Broderip's interest was not paid when it became due. He took proceedings at once and got a receiver appointed. Then, of course, came liquidation and a forced sale of the company's assets. They realized enough to pay Mr. Broderip, but not enough to pay the debentures in full; and the unsecured creditors were consequently left out in the cold.

In this state of things the liquidator met Mr. Broderip's claim by a counterclaim, to which he made Mr. Salomon a defendant. He disputed the validity of the debentures on the ground of fraud. On the same ground he claimed rescission of the agreement for the transfer of the business, cancellation of the debentures, and repayment by Mr. Salomon of the balance of the purchase money. In the alternative, he claimed payment of 20,000*l.* on Mr. Salomon's shares, alleging that nothing had been paid on them.

When the trial came on before Vaughan Williams J., the validity of Mr. Broderip's claim was admitted, and it was not disputed that the 20,000 shares were fully paid up. The case presented by the liquidator broke down completely; but the learned judge suggested that the company had a right of indemnity against Mr. Salomon. The signatories of the memorandum of association were, he said, mere nominees of Mr. Salomon — mere dummies. The company was Mr. Salomon in another form. He used the name of the company as an alias. He employed the company as his agent; so the company, he thought, was entitled to indemnity against its principal. The counter-claim was accordingly amended to raise this point; and on the amendment being made the learned judge pronounced an order in accordance with the view he had expressed.

The order of the learned judge appears to me to be founded on a misconception of the scope and effect of the *Companies Act*, 1862. In order to form a company limited by shares, the Act requires that a memorandum of association should be signed by seven persons, who are each to take one share at least. If those conditions are complied with, what can it matter whether the signatories are relations or strangers? There is nothing in the Act requiring that the subscribers to the memorandum should be independent or unconnected, or that they or any one of them should take a substantial interest in the undertaking, or that they should have a mind and will of their own, as one of the learned Lords Justices seems to think, or that there should be anything like a balance of power in the constitution of the company. In almost every company that is formed the statutory number is eked out by clerks or friends, who sign their names at the request of the promoter or promoters without intending to take any further part or interest in the matter.

When the memorandum is duly signed and registered, though there be only seven shares taken, the subscribers are a body corporate "capable forthwith," to use the words of the enactment, "of exercising all the functions of an incorporated company." Those are strong words. The company attains maturity on its birth. There is no period of minority — no interval of incapacity. I cannot understand how a body corporate thus made "capable" by statute can lose its individuality by issuing the bulk of its capital to one person, whether he be a subscriber to the memorandum or not. The company is at law a different person altogether from the subscribers to the memorandum; and, though it may be that after incorporation the business is precisely the same as it was before, and the same persons are managers, and the same hands receive the profits, the company is not in law the agent of the subscribers or trustee for them. Nor are the subscribers as members liable, in any shape or form, except to the extent and in the manner provided by the Act. That is, I think, the declared intention of the enactment. If the view of the learned judge were sound, it would follow that no common law partnership could register as a company limited by shares without remaining subject to unlimited liability.

Mr. Salomon appealed; but his appeal was dismissed with costs, though the Appellate Court did not entirely accept the view of the Court below. The decision of the Court of Appeal proceeds on a declaration of opinion embodied in the order which has been already read.

I must say that I, too, have great difficulty in understanding this declaration. If it only means that Mr. Salomon availed himself to the full of the advantages offered by the Act of 1862, what is there wrong in that? Leave out the words "contrary to the true intent and meaning of the *Companies Act*, 1862," and bear in mind that "the creditors of the company" are not the creditors of Mr. Salomon, and the declaration is perfectly innocent: it has no sting in it.

* * *

Among the principal reasons which induce persons to form private companies, as is stated very clearly by Mr. Palmer in his treatise on the subject, are the desire to avoid the risk of bankruptcy, and the increased facility afforded for borrowing money. By means of a private company, as Mr. Palmer observes, a trade can be carried on with limited liability, and without exposing the persons interested in it in the event of failure to the harsh provisions of the bankruptcy law. A company, too, can raise money on debentures, which an ordinary trader cannot do. Any member of a company, acting in good faith, is as much entitled to take and hold the company's debentures as any outside creditor. Every creditor is entitled to get and hold the best security the law allows him to take.

If, however, the declaration of the Court of Appeal means that Mr. Salomon acted fraudulently or dishonestly, I must say I can find nothing in the evidence to support such an imputation. The purpose for which Mr. Salomon and the other subscribers to the memorandum were associated was "lawful." The fact that Mr. Salomon raised 5000*l.* for the company on debentures that belonged to him seems to me strong evidence of his good faith and of his confidence in the company. The unsecured creditors of A. Salomon and Company, Limited, may be entitled to sympathy, but they have only themselves to blame for their misfortunes. They trusted the company, I suppose, because they had long dealt with Mr. Salomon, and he had always paid his way; but they had full notice that they were no longer dealing with an individual, and they must be taken to have been cognisant of the memorandum and of the articles of association. For such a catastrophe as has occurred in this case some would blame the law that allows the creation of a floating charge. But a floating charge is too convenient a form of security to be lightly abolished. I have long thought, and I believe some of your Lordships also think, that the ordinary trade creditors of a trading company ought to have a preferential claim on the assets in liquidation in respect of debts incurred within a certain limited time before the winding-up. But that is not the law at present. Everybody knows that when there is a winding-up debenture-holders generally step in and sweep off everything; and a great scandal it is.

It has become the fashion to call companies of this class "one man companies." That is a taking nickname, but it does not help one much in the way of argument. If it is intended to convey the meaning that a company which is under the absolute control of one person is not a company legally incorporated, although the requirements of the Act of 1862 may have been complied with, it is inaccurate and misleading: if it merely means that there is a predominant partner possessing an overwhelming influence and entitled practically to the whole of the profits, there is nothing in that that I can see contrary to the true intention of the Act of 1862, or against public policy, or detrimental to the interests of creditors. If the shares are fully paid up, it cannot matter whether they are in the hands of one or many. If the shares are not fully paid, it is as easy to gauge the solvency of an individual as to estimate the financial ability of a crowd.

Notes and Questions

1   Lord Macnaghten commented that £39,000 was an "extravagant" and unrealistic valuation of the firm; why did he consider this fact irrelevant to the proper disposition of the case? Was Mr. Salomon overpaid by Salomon & Co. for his shoemaking business?

2   Nowadays *Salomon v. Salomon* is usually cited for the proposition that the corporation's legal personality is separate and independent from its members' personalities. Contemporary observers however saw the decision in a different light. To them it validated the use of the *Companies Act* 1862 (a consolidating measure) and its predecessor, the *Companies Act* of 1856, for the incorporation of private or closely held companies even if the prescribed minimum of seven shareholders were related to one another and all but one of the shareholders, as in *Salomon's* case, only held one qualifying share.

This result was by no means a foregone conclusion. As an English scholar has shown (Paddy Ireland, "The Triumph of the Company Legal Form, 1856-1914" in John Adams (Ed.), *Essays for Clive Schmitthoff*, p. 29, Professional Books Limited, 1983), in introducing the 1856 Act; the British government did not contemplate, and certainly did not intend, that it could be used to incorporate economic partnerships and sole proprietorships although there was nothing in the Act itself that precluded it being used for these purposes. The government's assumption was widely shared. Between 1856 and 1862 only 4,859 new companies were incorporated altogether and even later, according to one estimate, only 5-10% of all important business organizations were incorporated. Influential judges and members of the Bar (including Vaughan Williams J., the trial judge in *Salomon*, and Lindley L.J. in the Court of Appeal) continued to be strongly opposed to making incorporation available to economic partnerships. This explains the striking differences in approach in *Salomon* between the lower courts and the House of Lords.

3   Several factors appear to have brought about the changes in attitude. First, as already mentioned, there was no requirement in the 1862 Act for seven unconnected incorporators or a requirement that shares of the company must be offered for sale to the public. English courts have traditionally been less instrumentally oriented than their American peers in construing legislation and therefore much less reluctant to give words their ordinary meaning even if this leads to anomalous results. Second, there were prominent barristers such as Francis B. Palmer, the author of a leading company law text that is still widely used in England, who thought British partnership law constituted a trap for the unwary investor and who welcomed the 1856 Act as a solution to these difficulties. Palmer published in 1877 an influential text, *Private Companies: Their Formation and Advantages*, which did much to encourage the incorporation of private companies. Third, the "Great Depression," which hit Victorian England and lasted from 1873-1896, reminded the business community of the vulnerability of unincorporated partnerships and made incorporation and the limited liability it conferred very attractive.

These cumulative factors presumably influenced the law lords in *Salomon* in deciding to reverse the Court of Appeal's decision. The House of Lords' decision also appears to have won widespread approval. The report of the Loreburn Committee in 1906 on company law amendments recommended the formal recognition of private companies and their being relieved from several onerous requirements incumbent on public companies. These recommendations were implemented in the *Companies Act* of 1907.

2. LIMITED LIABILITY AND CREDITOR PROTECTION

(a) Statutory Provisions

In *Salomon*, the creditors of Salomon & Co. could look only to the corporation, and not to its shareholder Aron Salomon, for payment of what they were owed. The protection of their personal assets from liability is, as Lord Macnaghten observed, one of the reasons why entrepreneurs use the corporate form rather than carrying on business as an unincorporated proprietorship or partnership.

In most jurisdictions, the limited liability of shareholders is today provided for by statute. For instance, s. 45(1) of the CBCA and s. 87(1) of the BCBCA provide that, with some exceptions (discussed below), a shareholder is not liable for the obligations of the corporation. Limited liability does not inevitably flow from the proposition that the corporation is a separate entity. Some early general incorporations statutes provided for unlimited shareholder liability. Today, three jurisdictions permit the formation of companies with unlimited shareholder liability: see BCBCA, part 2.1; and *Business Corporations Act*, R.S.A. 2000, c. B-9, part 2.1; and *Nova Scotia Companies Act*, R.S., c. 81, s. 9(c).

B.C. BUSINESS CORPORATIONS ACT
S.B.C. 2002, c. 57 as am.

87 (1) Liability of shareholders — No shareholder of a company is personally liable for the debts, obligations, defaults or acts of the company except as provided in Part 2.1.

(2) A shareholder is not, in respect of the shares held by that shareholder, personally liable for more than the lesser of

    (a) the unpaid portion of the issue price for which those shares were issued by the company, and

    (b) the unpaid portion of the amount actually agreed to be paid for those shares.

(3) Money payable by a shareholder to the company under the memorandum or articles is a debt due from the shareholder to the company as if it were a debt due or acknowledged to be due by instrument under seal.

CANADA BUSINESS CORPORATIONS ACT
R.S.C. 1985, c. C-44, as am.

45. (1) Shareholder immunity — The shareholders of a corporation are not, as shareholders, liable for any liability, act or default of the corporation except under ss. 38(4), 118(4) or (5), 146(5) or 226(4) or (5).

Notes

1   Section 38(4) of the CBCA deals with reduction of capital, ss. 118(4) and (5) with the recovery of payments to shareholders in violation of the Act, s. 146(5) with shareholder agreements, and ss. 226(4) and (5) with actions against shareholders after dissolution of the corporation. For the OBCA sections corresponding to the CBCA provisions reproduced above, see ss. 4–7, 15–16, and 92(1).

2   Part 2.1 of the BCBCA provides that the incorporators may include in the notice of articles a statement that the shareholders will be liable for the obligations of the company; they would thereby establish an unlimited liability company.

(b) Policy Considerations

Limited liability is well established in corporate law, but why is it desirable? Are there countervailing considerations? The following influential article by Paul Halpern, Michael Trebilcock and Stuart Turnbull discusses the policy considerations surrounding limited liability.

Halpern, Trebilcock and Turnbull, An Economic Analysis of Limited Liability in Corporation Law
(1980), 30 U.T.L.J. 117, 147–150 (footnotes omitted)

We now attempt to derive some implications from the foregoing analysis for the form of an efficient liability regime for corporations.

First, in the case of large, widely held companies, a limited liability regime, as a general rule, is the most efficient regime. By skewing the distribution of business risks amongst different shareholders, an unlimited liability regime would create a significant measure of uncertainty in the valuation of securities and threaten the existence of organized securities markets, thus inducing costly attempts by creditors and owners to transact around the regime. The case for a limited liability regime for this class of company is very compelling. The attenuated nature of the moral hazard factor in widely held companies does not create a strong countervailing consideration.

Second, in the case of small, tightly held companies, a limited liability regime will, in many cases, create incentives for owners to exploit a moral hazard and transfer uncompensated business risks to creditors, thus inducing costly attempts by creditors to reduce these risks. An unlimited liability regime for this class of enterprise (perhaps the 'private company', recognized by mainly corporation statutes with respect to financial disclosure and securities regulation exemptions, having fewer than, say, fifty shareholders, restrictions on share transfers, and no right to make public offering) would seem to be the most efficient regime. The availability of an organized securities market is not, of course, a major countervailing factor with this class of company.

A major effect of adopting an unlimited liability regime in this context would be to shift to the corporation and its owners the onus of proposing contractual arrangements to creditors which limit the liability of the owners — (where these are desired). Requiring explicit negotiation of such arrangements is likely to improve flows to creditors about allocation of risks and sharpen the focus of creditors' incentives to monitor a corporation's activities. We acknowledge that the case for an unlimited liability regime for this class of company is not as compelling as the case for limited liability for large, widely held companies, given that in the former case, with fewer parties involved, most creditors and owners can contract around either regime at low cost, thus making the choice of liability regime relatively inconsequential. We also recognize that difficulties may be associated with attempting to distinguish by law small from large corporations for the purpose of applying different liability regimes, and that the distinction may induct some perverse and wasteful incentive effects as firms seek to manipulate internal structures to ensure compliance with the requirements of the preferred regime. However, our empirical intuition remains that, on balance, an unlimited liability regime is the most efficient regime for small, closely held companies.

Third, in cases where, as a general rule, a limited liability regime is the most efficient regime (large, widely held corporations, in our analysis), there is a case for a limited number of exceptions to the regime where some form of unlimited liability seems desirable. These exceptions might embrace the following classes of case:

A. MISREPRESENTATION

An exception is called for in the case of misrepresentations to creditors as to the legal status of a firm or its financial affairs, as in *Royal Stores v. Brown* and *Pacific Rim Installations Ltd. v. Tilt-Up Construction Ltd.* Here the party responsible for the misrepresentation should be personally liable for corporate debts induced by the misrepresentation, but, in addition, as we elaborate below, the directors of the corporation might be made personally liable (subject to offsetting insurance of compensation arrangements) to strengthen management incentives to have this form of behaviour monitored by corporate officers and employees.

B. THE INVOLUNTARY CREDITOR

In cases such as *Walkovsky v. Carlton*, transaction costs are such that a firm can transfer uncompensated business risks to this class of creditor. *Rockwell Developments Ltd. v. Newtonbrook Plaza Ltd.*, where a firm unilaterally imposed costs on another party through unmeritorious legal proceedings, involved similar considerations. Again, it can be argued that the directors of the company should be personally liable to this class of creditor. In the large, widely held corporation where this exception would apply, such a rule would minimize the information costs that owners would face in monitoring each other's wealth, would reduce creditors' transaction costs in enforcing claims, and would focus incentives to adopt cost-justified avoidance precautions on that body of persons (the directors) in such a class of corporation best able to respond to those incentives.

C. THE EMPLOYEE

Amongst corporate creditors, employees, as a class, probably face the most severe informational disabilities, have the least ability to diversify risk of business failure, and may have the strongest equity argument (in terms of relative capacity to absorb losses). This proposition is not universally true, as some employees will possess both superior information on corporate finances and high job mobility (*e.g.*, corporate executives and professional employees), while some trade creditors may be afflicted with similar disabilities to those of the less informed, less mobile corporate employees. However, fashioning a rule that clearly differentiates these situations is likely to be difficult, and present rules governing the liability of directors for limited amounts of unpaid wages of "employees" in the *Canada Business Corporation Act* may represent defensible approximations of optimal rules.

The net effect of these proposals would seem to be to obviate the need for the elaborate veil-piercing, subrogation, and consolidation rules in corporate bankruptcies advocated by Landers. In the case of small, tightly held corporations, the unlimited liability regime which we have proposed would seem responsive to many of the parent-subsidiary and affiliated company problems with which he is concerned. In the case of large, widely held companies, involuntary creditors and employees, under our proposals, receive special protection. Other creditors, prejudiced by intra-group transactions induced by moral hazard considerations, would have to rely on the misrepresentation exception. This exception is necessarily a much more limited response to creditor problems than the unlimited liability regime proposed for small, closely held corporations because any substantial move in the direction of unlimited liability in the case of large, widely held companies will engender the kind of costs that have led us generally to reject such a regime in this case. Our proposals would also contemplate as unnecessary and undesirable many of the provisions in the federal *Bankruptcy Act* and the new Bankruptcy Bill with respect to "reviewable transactions" and the liability of corporate Agents. The operational uncertainty (and consequent costs) associated with these provisions would be reduced under the relatively straightforward rules that we have proposed.

Note

The authors refer to several well known Canadian and American authorities on piercing the corporate veil. Some of these are reproduced in the section that follows. The Halpern article and the phenomenon of mass torts have provoked a strong revival of interest in the rationales of limited liability in close and publicly held corporations and in the question of when it is appropriate to deny the benefits of limited liability, particularly in the context of claims by involuntary creditors. See, *inter alia*, Easterbrook & Fischel, "Limited Liability and the Corporation" (1985), 52 U. Chi. L. Rev. 89; Hansmann & Kraakman, "Toward Unlimited Shareholder Liability for Corporate Torts" (1991) 100 Yale L.J. 1879; and Grundfest, "The Limited Future of Unlimited Liability: A Capital Markets Perspective" (1992), 102 Yale L.J. 387. On the Hansmann-Kraakman proposal, see the notes following *Walkovsky v. Carlton* in the next section of this chapter.

(b)   Alternative Sources of Creditor Protection

The judgment in *Salomon's case* implies one way in which the contractual creditors of a corporation can protect themselves from loss, given the shareholders' limited liability: as a condition for extending credit, they can demand a security interest in the corporation's assets as collateral. Creditors can also insist upon a guarantee from the shareholders, demand a higher interest rate as compensation for the risk assumed, or simply refuse to lend to the corporation.

In addition to the above contractual devices, the law provides creditors with several other types of protection in their dealings with corporations.

(i)   Cautionary Suffix

The Canadian Acts invariably require the addition to the corporation's name of one of the words "Corporation," "Limited,"

"Incorporated" or the abbreviations "Inc.," "Ltd." and "Corp.," (or their equivalents in French) to warn creditors that they are dealing with a limited liability entity. See *e.g.*, CBCA s. 10(1), BCBCA, s. 23, OBCA, s. 10(l). Legislation also frequently requires a corporation to set out its name in legible characters "in all contracts, invoices, negotiable instruments and orders for goods or services". See *e.g.*, CBCA, s. 10(5), *Business Names Act*, R.S.O. 1990, c. B.17, s. 2(6), and BCBCA s. 27(1). Note also that a corporation is not precluded from adopting a trade name so long as it continues to comply with s. 10(5): CBCA s. 10(6), and registers the assumed name under the *Business Names Act*, R.S.O. 1990, c. B.17 as am., s.2(1). It has been held in Ontario that failure to comply with the OBCA disclosure requirements imposes no personal civil liability on the corporation's officers or directors since the OBCA (and the same is true in the CBCA) only treats non-disclosure as an offence under s. 252: *Watfield International Enterprises Inc. v. 655293 Ontario Ltd.* (1995), 21 B.L.R. (2d) 158, 1995 CarswellOnt 540 (Gen. Div.). Failure to comply with the OBN requirements gives rise to a criminal penalty under s. 10 and the corporation's inability to maintain proceedings in Ontario without the court's leave: s. 7(1) and (2).

Nevertheless, there are many reported cases where the officer or director of a corporation has been held personally liable for non-disclosure of the fact that he was contracting on behalf of a corporation, especially where he had previously dealt with the other party in an individual capacity before the incorporation of the company. In *Turi v. Swanick*, 2002 CarswellOnt 3041, 30 B.L.R. (3d) 118 (Ont. S.C.J.), Spiegel J. also held that a lawyer who incorporates a company for a small business person is under a contractual and common law duty to inform his client, first, that the client must be careful to use the company's legal name in entering into contracts on behalf of the company and, second, of the legal consequences of the client failing to follow this procedure.

In a still more telling case, *Wolfe v. Moir* (1969), 69 W.W.R. 70, 1969 CarswellAlta 36 (T.D.), the defendant Gordon L. Moir was held personally liable for injuries suffered by the plaintiff while skating on a roller skating rink in Lethbridge ("Fort Whoop-Up") owned by Chinook Sport Shop Ltd. Gordon L. Moir and his wife were the company's shareholders and officers and Gordon Moir apparently also acted as manager of the skating rink. The skating rink was advertised in the *Lethbridge Herald* in the following fashion:

Roller Skating
Tonight
8:00 to 10:30 p.m.
Moir's Sportland
(Fort Whoop-Up)
Special Group Rates.

Moir had previously served as recreation director for the city of Lethbridge and his name was well known in the community. Sinclair J. also found that the names "Fort Whoop-Up" or "Moir's Sportland" had not been registered by Moir or his company under s. 72 of the Alberta *Partnership Act*, R.S.A. 1955, c. 230, s. 21(1) requiring a company or partnership carrying on business under an assumed name to file a declaration disclosing the assumed name. Similarly, Moir's company had failed to comply with s. 82(1)(c) of the *Companies Act*, R.S.A. 1955, c. 53, Alberta's then-counterpart to OBCA s. 10(5).

On the strength of these facts, Sinclair J. held Moir personally liable for the plaintiff's injuries. He reasoned, *inter alia*, as follows:

> In the present case, as I have already pointed out, other than for the evidence of Mr. and Mrs. Moir that the business was operated by Chinook Sport Shop Ltd. of which they were, respectively, secretary and president, there was nothing to indicate that the usual corporate formalities were gone through. It seems to me that for a person to successfully rely upon what is, after all, the extraordinary protection from personal liability granted to an individual by *The Companies Act*, it is incumbent upon him to establish that at least the formalities prescribed by the statute have been complied with. This he has failed completely to do.

> Further, in my view, the effect of sec. 82 (1) (*b*) of *The Companies Act* is that if a person chooses to advertise and to hold himself out to the public without identifying the name of a company with which he is associated, he runs the risk of being held personally liable. There are many cases in which an individual has been held personally responsible for an obligation because he did not make it clear when the obligation was incurred that he was acting on behalf of a company.

Sinclair J. did not examine the Partnership and Companies Acts provisions to determine what sanctions they imposed for non-compliance with the registration and disclosure provisions and, of course, *Wolfe v. Moir* was decided before Watfield, *supra*. Nor apparently did the plaintiff give evidence that he thought his admission contract to the skating rink was with Moir personally. Nevertheless, it seems clear that Sinclair J.'s decision was based, in part at least, on liability by estoppel.

(ii)   Capital Maintenance Requirements

Corporations statutes contain provisions designed to ensure that the corporation receives cash or its true equivalent for its issued shares, and prohibiting the corporation from declaring dividend or redeeming or purchasing the corporation's shares when the corporation is insolvent or if this would make it insolvent. See CBCA ss. 34-36, 42. The idea behind the latter provisions is to ensure that payments are not made to shareholders if this would leave the corporation with insufficient assets to meet its obligations to creditors.

On the other hand, there is no obligation under the CBCA, the OBCA, or (it seems) the BCBCA for a corporation to have a minimum paid up capital. The purpose of such requirements, which one finds in many Western European countries, is to ensure that a corporation begins its existence with a surplus of assets over liabilities.

(iii)   Publicity

All the Acts require the filing of information in a public office stating the location of the corporation's head office or registered office and giving the names of its current directors. See *e.g.*, BCBCA, ss. 10-11, 407 and Form 1; CBCA s. 19 and Forms 3 and 6, s. 263 and Form 22; and the *Corporations Information Act*, R.S.O. 1990, c. C.39. Prescribed records must also be maintained at the corporation's head office or at any other place designated by the directors or (in B.C.'s case) the corporation's records office and made accessible there to shareholders and creditors or (in B.C.'s case) to any person. See BCBCA, ss. 42, 46; CBCA, ss. 20-21; OBCA, ss. 140, 145.

In addition, the CBCA (s. 160(1)) requires a "distributing corporation" (this includes a corporation with securities traded on a stock exchange) to file annual financial statements. Corporations with publicly traded securities also have periodic filing obligations under the various Securities Acts.

(iv)   Officers' and Directors' Liability

A corporation is managed by or under the supervision of its board of directors, who typically delegate authority to one or more officers they appoint. As a result, where creditors are unable to obtain satisfaction of the corporation's obligations from the assets of the corporation, they might attempt to establish the liability of officers or of members of the board of directors. Moreover, many statutes that create obligations for corporations impose liability on officers or directors of a corporation as a means of encouraging corporate compliance. A few of the more common examples are described in the following paragraphs.

Unremitted taxes. Sec. 227.1 of the *Income Tax Act*, introduced in 1981, provides that directors are jointly and severally liable with the corporation for failure to deduct or withhold required taxes or to remit such taxes to Revenue Canada. A due diligence defence is available to directors under s. 227.1(3) and, predictably, it has attracted much litigation. See Lynn Campbell, "Directors' Diligence under the Income Tax Act" (1990) 16 C.B.L.J. 480.

Unpaid wages. Directors are liable for unpaid wages owing to the corporation's employees, whether or not the directors have been negligent. See CBCA, s. 119 and OBCA, s. 131, and *Mesheau v. Campbell* (1983), 141 D.L.R. (3d) 155 (Ont. C.A.) (excerpted below). In *Allard c. Myhill*, 2012 CarswellQue 12026, 2012 QCCA 2024 (C.A. Que.), the court held that in a case where a unanimous shareholders' agreement removed all powers from directors, the individuals who made decisions for the corporation, the de facto directors, would be held liable under CBCA s. 119.

Occupational health and safety. In several provinces and at the federal level, directors and officers have duties under occupational health and safety legislation. In Ontario, for example, directors and officers must take reasonable care to ensure that the corporation complies with the *Occupational Health and Safety Act*. See *Occupational Health and Safety Act,* R.S.O. 1990, c. O.1, s. 32. A director or officer who violates this duty commits an offence under the Act: s. 66. In B.C., an officer, director or agent of a corporation who "authorizes, permits or acquiesces in the commission of" an occupational health and safety offence is also guilty of an offence. See *Workers Compensation Act*, R.S.B.C. 1996, c, 492, s. 213(2).

Environmental protection. In many jurisdictions, environmental protection legislation imposes obligations on directors and officers of corporations. See, for instance, *Environmental Protection Act,* R.S.O., c. E-19, s. 194 (duty to take all reasonable care to prevent contravention of Act by corporation); *R. v. Bata Industries Ltd.*, 1992 CarswellOnt 211, 9 O.R. (3d) 329 (Ont. Prov. Div.) (directors convicted of offence for failure to ensure compliance with Act).

Tort committed by director, officer or employee. It was already settled by the early 1920s that the representative character of the defendant as an officer, director, or employee of a company did not shield him from personal liability for such traditional torts as trespass, assault, libel, and at least some types of negligence even if the officer or director was acting in the normal course of his duties. See Atkin L.J.'s judgment in *Performing Rights Society Ltd. v. Ciryl Theatrical Syndicate Ltd.*, [1924] 1 K.B. 1 at 14-15. In *London Drugs Ltd. v. Kuehne & Nagel International Ltd.*, 1986 CarswellBC 98, 2 B.C.L.R. (2d) 181 (B.C. S.C.), reversed 1990 CarswellBC 74 (B.C. C.A.), affirmed 1992 CarswellBC 913, 1992 CarswellBC 315 (S.C.C.), Trainor J., at first instance, went so far as to assert that the B.C. courts now recognize that "there is no general rule that an employee cannot be sued for tort committed in the course of carrying out the very services for which the plaintiff had contracted with his employer", but he cast the net too widely. One important exception was carved out in McCardie J.'s well known judgment in *Said v. Butt*, [1920] 3 K.B. 497 (Eng. K.B.), which continues to be treated as good authority in Canada, as well as in England. This case held that an officer of a company could not be sued for procuring breach of contract between the company and the other contracting party. Subsequent Ontario courts interpreted the judgment to mean that officers and directors could not be sued generally for committing economic torts if they were acting within the normal scope of their office. However, this notion was firmly scotched by Carthy J.A. in *ADGA Systems International Ltd. v. Valcom Ltd.*, 1999 CarswellOnt 29, 43 O.R. (3d) 101 (Ont. C.A.), leave to appeal refused 2000 CarswellOnt 1160, 2000 CarswellOnt 1161 (S.C.C.), in delivering the unanimous judgment of the Ontario Court of Appeal. In his opinion, the principle in *Said v. Butt* only applies to subsisting contracts between the company and the plaintiff; it does not apply where, as in *ADGA Systems*, the officer is accused of procuring breach of contract between the plaintiff company and its own employees. Although the court stated that the "*Said v. Butt* exception" does not apply in *ADGA Systems*, it appears to apply in the tort of negligence. The court's comments in *ADGA Systems* were further explored in a recent Alberta case, *Hogarth v. Rocky Mountain Slate Inc.*, 2013 CarswellAlta 189, 2013 ABCA 57 (Alta. C.A.), additional reasons 2013 CarswellAlta 835 (Alta. C.A.), leave to appeal refused 2013 CarswellAlta 1119, 2013 CarswellAlta 1120 (S.C.C.). Rocky Mountain Slate Inc. created a limited partnership for the development of a quarry. Promotional materials were distributed, but the court found them to be negligently misrepresented. The plaintiff investors sued the officers of the corporation, but the court held that the officers were not personally liable, and emphasized the policy importance for entrepreneurs to use limited liability structures to promote ventures, even if they are risky ventures. The name Rocky Mountain Slate, and not the officers', was on the promotional materials. As a result, the court stated if the investors, "know they are dealing with a corporate structure, the corporation should be presumptively responsible for any misrepresentations".

(v)   The Oppression Remedy

The statutory oppression remedy was designed to overcome restrictive common law rules making it very difficult for minority shareholders to sue management. See BCBCA, s. 227, CBCA, s. 241 and OBCA, s. 248. However, the definition of "complainant" in CBCA s. 238(c) and (d) includes the Director of the CBCA[4] and "any other person who, in the discretion of a court, is a proper person to make an application under this Part." When these provisions were first adopted it was not envisioned that they would apply to general creditors and that creditors could seek relief from allegedly oppressive or unfairly prejudicial conduct by a corporation and its management. However, the contrary has been held in a series of cases beginning with *First Edmonton Place Ltd. v. 315888 Alberta Ltd.* (1988), 40 B.L.R. 28 (Alta.

---

[4]   The Director of the CBCA is a federally appointed official responsible for the administration of the CBCA and is not an officer or agent of any corporation.

Q.B.), stayed on appeal (1989), 45 B.L.R. 110 (Alta. C.A.), and allowing relief directly against the offending officers or directors. See further Ziegel (1993), 43 U.T.L.J. 511, 526-29 and *Downtown Eatery (1993) Ltd. v. Ontario* (2001), 54 O.R. (3d) 161, 2001 CarswellOnt 1680 (C.A.). From a creditor's point of view, these precedents provide a possible avenue for avoiding the restrictive impact of shareholders' limited liability.

(vi)   Duties in the Vicinity of Insolvency

It is basic common law doctrine, now codified in the Canadian business corporations Acts, that directors must act in the best interests of the corporation. *Cf.* CBCA s. 122(1)(a). In many jurisdictions, this duty has been interpreted so as to require the directors to put the interests of creditors ahead of those of the shareholders when the corporation was insolvent or near insolvency. See, e.g., *Credit Lyonnais Bank Nederland N.V. v. Pathe Communications Corporation*, 1991 Del. Ch. LEXIS 215 (Del. Ch. Dec. 30. 1991) and Ziegel, *supra*, at 517–21. Sec. 214 of the English *Insolvency Act* ("wrongful trading provision") now holds directors personally liable if the company continues to trade at a time when the directors ought to realize that it is unlikely that the company will be able to meet its new obligations. Similar legislation has been adopted in Australia and New Zealand.

The doctrine that the directors' duties shift towards creditor protection as a corporation nears insolvency was judicially endorsed in Canada for the first time by the Quebec Superior Court in *People's Department Stores Ltd. (1992) Inc., Re*, 1998 CarswellQue 3442, 23 C.B.R. (4th) 200 (Que. S.C.), reversed 2003 CarswellQue 145, 224 D.L.R. (4th) 509 (Que. C.A.), leave to appeal allowed 2003 CarswellQue 3487, 2003 CarswellQue 3488 (S.C.C.), affirmed 2004 CarswellQue 2862, 2004 CarswellQue 2863, [2004] 3 S.C.R. 461 (S.C.C.), reversed 2003 CarswellQue 146 (Que. C.A.).

(vii)   Piercing the Corporate Veil

Another strategy for overcoming limited liability involves arguing that a court should disregard the corporation's separate legal personality, i.e., that it should pierce the corporate veil. This doctrine is the subject of separate treatment in Part 3 of this chapter, below.

(viii)   Cases

In the remainder of this section, we reproduce excerpts from two cases discussed above, concerning directorial liability for unpaid wages and director and officer tort liability, respectively.

Mesheau v. Campbell

1982 CarswellOnt 777, 39 O.R. (2d) 702, 141 D.L.R. (3d) 155 (Ont. C.A.)

WEATHERSTON J.A. (for the court): Section 114 of the *Canada Business Corporations Act*, S.C. 1975, c. 33 provides in part as follows:

114(1) Directors of a corporation are jointly and severally liable to employees of the corporation for all debts not exceeding six months wages payable to each such employee for services performed for the corporation while they are such directors respectively.

(2) A director is not liable under subsection (1) unless

(a) the corporation has been sued for the debt within six months after it has become due and execution has been returned unsatisfied in whole or in part;

(b) the corporation has commenced liquidation and dissolution proceedings or has been dissolved and a claim for the debt has been proved within six months after the earlier of the date of commencement of the liquidation and dissolution proceedings and the date of dissolution; or

(c) the corporation has made an assignment or a receiving order has been made against it under the *Bankruptcy Act* and a claim for the debt has been proved within six months after the date of the assignment or receiving order.

The issue in this appeal is whether the directors are liable to an employee for an unsatisfied judgment debt against a corporation on a claim for wrongful dismissal. In my opinion, they are not.

The plaintiff says he has complied with all the conditions of the section. He sued his employer, Emblem Mat Corporation, for damages within six months after his wrongful dismissal. The action was not defended. The plaintiff proved his claim and obtained a judgment, execution of which has been returned unsatisfied in whole. The defendants are, and were at all material times directors of the employer.

A cause of action similar to that created by s. 114 of the *Canada Business Corporations Act* was created by s. 52 of the *Ontario Joint Stock Companies Letters Patent Act*, S.O. 1874, c. 35 whereby it was enacted:

52. The Directors of the Company shall be jointly and severally liable to the labourers, servants and apprentices thereof, for all debts not exceeding one year's wages, due for services performed for the Company whilst they are such Directors respectively; but no Director shall be liable to an action therefor, unless the Company has been sued therefor within one year after the debt became due, nor yet unless such Director is sued therefor within one year from the time when he ceased to be such Director, nor yet before an execution against the Company has been returned unsatisfied in whole or in

part; and the amount due on such execution shall be the amount recoverable with costs against the Directors.

As to that section, Osler J.A. said in *Welch v. Ellis* (1895), 22 O.A.R. 255 at 258 that:

> Our enactment would appear to have been borrowed from some of the laws of the State of New York, which provide that the stock-holders of the company in the events contemplated, shall be liable for all debts that may be due and owing to their "labourers, servants and apprentices" for services performed for the corporation. . .

The Ontario section limits the liability of directors to one year's wages, but otherwise follows the form of the New York statute. The liability is for services performed for the corporation. Section 114 follows precisely the same form, except that the benefit of the section has been extended to all employees, not merely to "labourers, servants and apprentices", and the temporal limit is six months.

In *Zavitz v. Brock et al.* (1974), 3 O.R. (2d) 583, 46 D.L.R. (3d) 203, the question was whether the plaintiff came within the class of persons entitled to the benefit of the section of the Ontario *Corporations Act*, R.S.O. 1960, c. 71 [now R.S.O. 1990, c. C.38] then in force, namely, clerks, labourers, servants, apprentices and other wage earners. Arnup J.A. said at p. 590 [O.R.]:

> Some further limited assistance is gained from the fact that the right of a person in the prescribed class to sue is a right to claim "for all debts due . . . for services performed for the company, not exceeding six months wages, and for the vacation pay . . .".

Mr. Brown argued for the plaintiff that the arrangement of phrases in the Ontario statute made it significantly different from s. 114 of the *Canada Business Corporations Act*, and that under the latter act the directors are liable for all debts, however created, subject to a quantitative limit equal to six months' wages. I do not agree. The history of the section and its manifest purpose make it perfectly clear that the words "all debts" are modified by the phrase "for services performed for the corporation" and are subject to the quantitative limit of six months' wages payable to each such employee.

A claim for damages for wrongful dismissal is a claim for unliquidated damages. It is not a debt, nor is it "for services performed for the corporation". In *Mullen v. Millar* (1924), 55 O.L.R. 563 [affirmed 56 O.L.R. 345, [1925] 2 D.L.R. 321], it was held that the plaintiffs could not succeed under the Ontario statute then in force because they had not yet entered the employ of the company. In the present case, the plaintiff's cause of action arose after his employment was terminated. In neither case was the debt "for services performed for the corporation".

Appeal allowed; cross-appeal dismissed.

Notes

1   Section 114(1) of CBCA 1975 is s. 119(1) in the current Act. The corresponding provision in the OBCA is s. 131(1). *Mesheau v. Campbell* is only one of a larger number of divided cases dealing with the issue whether a claim for termination pay can be characterized as a "debt". The conflict was resolved by the Supreme Court of Canada in *Crabtree (Succession de) c. Barrette*, [1993] 1 S.C.R. 1027, 1993 CarswellQue 25, 1993 CarswellQue 155, discussed by Bryan C.G. Haynes in (1994) 23 C.B.L.J. 283. The Court supported the *Mesheau* line of cases.

2   There are more than one hundred federal and provincial statutes imposing personal liability on directors as a means of ensuring the corporation's compliance with regulatory requirements.. In a number of high profile cases directors have resigned en masse on the eve of a company's bankruptcy because of the spectre of personal liability (it is probably too late at that stage); lawyers are also cautioning clients about the downside of becoming directors. Indemnity insurance ("D & O insurance") is available to protect officers and directors against personal liability, but it is expensive. See further Ron Daniels, "Must Boards Go Overboard? An Economic Analysis of the Effect of Burgeoning Statutory Liability on the Role of Directors in Corporate Governance" (1995), 24 C.B.L.J. 229.

3   Employees' pursuit of directors for unpaid wages reflects in part the low preference which unpaid wages have historically enjoyed in bankruptcy. In particular, wages claims were, until recently, subordinated to security interests in favour of lenders and others granted by a company prior to its bankruptcy. To remedy the position, in 2005, Parliament enacted a "Wage Earners Protection Program" (WEPP) with two significant features. First, employees receive a priority charge over the employers' assets in respect of claims for unpaid wages earned during the six months preceding the insolvency, in an amount up to $2,000 (*Bankruptcy and Insolvency Act*, s. 81.3). Second, employees are entitled to receive up to $3,000 from the WEPP in respect of unpaid wages (*Wage Earner Protection Program Act*, s. 7). To the extent that any payments are made to the employee from the WEPP, the Crown is subrogated to the employee's rights against the employer (*WEPPA*, s. 26) and, in particular, can assert the employee's priority charge over the employer's assets.

ADGA Systems International Ltd. v. Valcom
(1999), 43 O.R. (3d) 101, 1999 CarswellOnt 29 (C.A.)

CARTHY J.A. (for the Court): This appeal presents for consideration once again the troublesome issue of the liability of officers and directors of a corporation for acts done in pursuance of a corporate purpose.

The plaintiff, ADGA Systems International Ltd., has claimed that a competitor, the defendant Valcom Ltd., raided its employees and caused the plaintiff economic damage. The plaintiff also claims against three of its own employees for breach of fiduciary duty in acceding to the importunes of Valcom Ltd. The issue in controversy on this particular appeal is the claim by the plaintiff against the director and two employees of Valcom Ltd. for their personal involvement in this recruitment program. Those three defendants brought a motion for summary judgment seeking to dismiss the claim against them. The motion was dismissed by Mercier J. The Divisional Court then heard an appeal from that order, allowed the appeal, and dismissed the claim against those three defendants. The plaintiff now appeals to this court and seeks to justify proceeding to trial against MacPherson, the Director of Valcom Ltd. and Ewing and McKenzie, senior employees of Valcom Ltd. The question is whether the respondents can be sued for their actions as individuals, assuming those actions were genuinely directed to the best interests of their corporate employer. In my view a cause of action does exist against the respondents and a trial is required to determine the merits of that action.

* * *

Analysis

* * *

My first observation is that I recognize the policy concern expressed by the Divisional Court, and other General Division judges, over the proliferation of claims against officers and directors of corporations in circumstances which give the appearance of the desire for discovery or leverage in the litigation process. This is a proper concern because business cannot function efficiently if corporate officers and directors are inhibited in carrying on a corporate business because of a fear of being inappropriately swept into lawsuits, or, worse, are driven away from involvement in any respect in corporate business by the potential exposure to ill-founded litigation. That being said, it is not appropriate to extend the reasoning of *ScotiaMcLeod*[5] beyond its intended application by reading it as protecting all conduct by officers and employees in pursuit of corporate purposes. The common law should not develop on an ad hoc basis to put out fires. When a policy issue arises, here from modern business realities, the courts must proceed on a principled basis to establish a framework for further development which recognizes the new realities but preserves the fundamental purpose served by that area of law. For this reason I intend to analyze the development of law in this field from its beginnings.

---

[5] *Montreal Trust Co. of Canada v. ScotiaMcLeod Inc.* (1995), 26 O.R. (3d) 481 (C.A.).

That beginning is found in the House of Lords' decision in *Salomon v. Salomon & Co. Ltd.*, [1895-9] All E.R. 33 (H.L.), which established that a company, once legally incorporated, must be treated like any other independent person, with rights and liabilities appropriate to itself. From time to time, litigants have sought to lift this "corporate veil", by seeking to make principals of the corporation liable for the obligations of the corporation. However, where, as here, the plaintiff relies upon establishing an independent cause of action against the principals of the company, the corporate veil is not threatened and the *Salomon* principle remains intact.

The distinction between an independent cause of action and looking through the corporation was confirmed by the subsequent case of *Said v. Butt*, [1920] 3 K.B. 497. This is a King's Bench decision but has been adopted in Canada and throughout the United States. (See, for instance, *Kepic v. Tecumseh Road Builders* (1987), 18 C.C.E.L. 218 at p. 222, 23 O.A.C. 72; and *Golden v. Anderson*, 64 Cal.Rptr. 404 (1967) at p. 408.)

In *Said v. Butt*, the plaintiff was engaged in a dispute with an opera company which refused to sell him tickets to a performance. The plaintiff purchased a ticket through an agent and when he appeared at the opera the defendant, an employee of the opera company recognized him and ejected him. The plaintiff sued the employee for wrongfully procuring the company to break a contract made by the company to sell the plaintiff a ticket.

The court held that there was no contract because the company would not knowingly have sold a ticket to the plaintiff. Nevertheless, on the assumption that there was a contract, the court considered the implications to the defendant employee. McCardie J. stated at p. 504:

> It is well to point out that Sir Alfred Butt possessed the widest powers as the chairman and sole managing director of the Palace Theatre, Ld. He clearly acted within those powers when he directed that the plaintiff should be refused admission on December 23. I am satisfied, also, that he meant to act and did act *bona fide* for the protection of the interests of his company. If, therefore, the plaintiff, assuming that a contract existed between the company and himself, can sue the defendant for wrongfully procuring a breach of that contract, the gravest and widest consequences must ensue.

After detailing the mischief that would flow from permitting such claims to be made McCardie J. concluded at p. 506:

> I hold that if a servant acting *bona fide* within the scope of his authority procures or causes the breach of a contract between his employer and a third person, he does not thereby become liable to an action of tort at the suit of the person whose contract has thereby been broken . . . Nothing that I have said to-day is, I hope, inconsistent with the rule that a director or a servant who actually

takes part in or actually authorizes such torts as assault, trespass to property, nuisance, or the like may be liable in damages as a joint participant in one of such recognized heads of tortious wrong.

For present purposes, I extract the following from McCardie J.'s reasons. First, this is not an application of Salomon. That case is not mentioned anywhere in the reasons. Second, it provides an exception to the general rule that persons are responsible for their own conduct. That exception has since gained acceptance because it assures that persons who deal with a limited company and accept the imposition of limited liability will not have available to them both a claim for breach of contract against a company and a claim for tortious conduct against the director with damages assessed on a different basis. The exception also assures that officers and directors, in the process of carrying on business, are capable of directing that a contract of employment be terminated or that a business contract not be performed on the assumed basis that the company's best interest is to pay the damages for failure to perform. By carving out the exception for these policy reasons, the court has emphasized and left intact the general liability of any individual for personal conduct.

The third point of interest arises from this excerpt from the reasons at p. 505:

> The explanation of the breadth of the language used in the decisions probably lies in the fact that in every one of the sets of circumstances before the Court the person who procured the breach of contract was in fact a stranger, that is a third person, who stood wholly outside the area of the bargain made between the two contracting parties. If he is in the position of a stranger, he will be prima facie liable, even though he may act honestly, or without malice, or in the best interests of himself; or even if he acts as an altruist, seeking only the good of another. . .

The court was there referring to the stranger as the wrongdoer but the same principle might be applied in the converse situation where the stranger is the victim. This suggestion, was picked up later in the dissenting reasons of La Forest J. in *London Drugs Ltd. v. Kuehne & Nagel International Ltd., infra*, to the effect that a jurisprudential division line might be drawn between those who contract with the company, or voluntarily deal with it, and can be taken to have accepted limited liability, and strangers to the company whose only concern is not to be harmed by the conduct of others. On that theory, those harmed as strangers to the corporate body naturally look for liability to the persons who caused the harm and those who have in some manner accepted limited liability in their dealings with the company would be limited in recourse to the company. As evidenced by the decision in *London Drugs v.*

Kuehne that theory of demarcation of liability has not been adopted in Canada.

The consistent line of authority in Canada holds simply that, in all events, officers, directors and employees of corporations are responsible for their tortious conduct even though that conduct was directed in a *bona fide* manner to the best interests of the company, always subject to the *Said v. Butt* exception.

In *Lewis v. Boutilier* (1919), 52 D.L.R. 383 at p. 389 (S.C.C.), the president of a company was held personally liable for negligently putting a boy to work in a dangerous area of a sawmill where he was killed. It was held to be no defence to the president that the corporation that owned the sawmill might also be liable.

In *Berger v. Willowdale A.M.C.* (1983), 41 O.R. (2d) 89 at p. 98, 145 D.L.R. (3d) 247 (C.A.) . . . this court dealt with a claim by an employee against the president of her employer corporation for damages arising from slipping on an icy sidewalk. Under the *Workmen's Compensation Act*, employees could not be sued for such workplace accidents. However, executives were excluded from the definition of employees under the *Workmen's Compensation Act*. The court held that, given the existence of a duty of care owed by the president to this employee, and a failure to respond appropriately to that duty, damages against the president were recoverable even though the action against the company was barred by the provisions of the *Workmen's Compensation Act*. The fact that the duty of care coexisted in the employer and president did not constitute a bar to a claim against the executive officer.

In *Sullivan v. Desrosiers* (1986), 76 N.B.R. (2d) 271 (C.A.) . . . the plaintiffs were surrounding landowners of a hog farm who claimed that their lands had been polluted by a manure lagoon on the site of the farm. The issue before the Court of Appeal was whether the owner of the company could be held personally liable.

At p. 277 Hoyt J.A. stated:

> The question here is whether Mr. Sullivan, who was the manager and principal employee of the company that committed the nuisance, may be responsible along with the company. I see no reason why, because of his involvement in creating and maintaining the nuisance, Mr. Sullivan should not also be responsible.

And at p. 278:

> Nor am I attracted to the submission that Mr. Sullivan is protected by reason of the rule in *Salomon v. Salomon & Co.*, [1897] A.C. 22. The question here, as I have pointed out, is not whether Mr. Sullivan was acting on behalf of or even if he "was" the company, but whether a legal barrier, here a company, can be erected between a person found to be a wrongdoer and an injured party thereby relieving the wrongdoer of his liability. In my opinion, once it is

determined that a person breaches a duty owed to neighbouring landowners not to interfere with their reasonable enjoyment of their property, liability may be imposed on him and he may not escape by saying that as well as being a wrongdoer he is also a company manager or employee.

The Supreme Court of Canada again considered the issue of an employee's liability for acts done in the course of his duties on behalf of the employer in *London Drugs Ltd. v. Kuehne & Nagel International Ltd.*, [1992] 3 S.C.R. 299, 97 D.L.R. (4th) 261. The plaintiff delivered a transformer to a warehouse company for storage. An employee of the warehouse company negligently permitted the transformer to topple over, causing extensive damage. Even though there was a contractual relationship between the company and the customer, the majority held in favour of the claim against the employee.

Iacobucci J. stated at pp. 407-08:

> There is no general rule in Canada to the effect that an employee acting in the course of his or her employment and performing the "very essence" of his or her employer's contractual obligations with a customer does not owe a duty of care, whether one labels it "independent" or otherwise, to the employer's customer . . .

> The mere fact that the employee is performing the "very essence" of a contract between the plaintiff and his or her employer does not, in itself, necessarily preclude a conclusion that a duty of care was present.

La Forest J. dissented on this issue and was prepared to relieve the employee from personal liability in tort where the tort occurred in the context of a breach of contract between the employer and the customer, and so long as the employee's tort was in the course of duties. His analysis of the distinction between the voluntary and involuntary creditor is, and will continue to be, of interest as policy questions impact upon the evolving jurisprudence in this area. At p. 349 he stated:

> The distinction between voluntary and involuntary creditors is also useful in this area. As commentators have pointed out (Halpern, Trebilcock and Turnbull, "An Economic Analysis of Limited Liability in Corporation Law" (1980), 30 U.T.L.J. 117), different types of claimants against the corporation have differing abilities to benefit from being put on notice with respect to the impact of the limited liability regime. At one end, creditors like bond holders and banks are generally well situated to evaluate the risks of default and to contract accordingly. These "voluntary" creditors can be considered to be capable of protecting themselves from the consequences of a limited liability regime and the practically systematic recourse by

banks to personal guarantees by the principals of small companies attests to that fact.

At the other end of the spectrum are classic involuntary tort creditors exemplified by a plaintiff who is injured when run down by an employee driving a motorcar. These involuntary creditors are those who never chose to enter into a course of dealing with the company and correspond to what I have termed as the classic vicarious liability claimant.

These Canadian authorities at the appellate level confirm clearly that employees, officers and directors will be held personally liable for tortious conduct causing physical injury, property damage, or a nuisance even when their actions are pursuant to their duties to the corporation.

* * *

Although the jurisprudence on this subject has followed a very straight path since the decisions in *Salomon v. Salomon* and *Said v. Butt*, in recent years in this jurisdiction judges hearing motions to dismiss claims have tended to smudge these principles, inspired, in my view, and as expressed by them, by the legitimate concern as to the number of cases in which employees, officers, and directors are joined for questionable purposes. The assumption has filtered into reasons for judgment that the employee is absolved if acting in the interests of the corporation, the employer, even in cases that do not raise the *Said v. Butt* defence.

An immediate example is found in the reasons of the Divisional Court in this case where at p. 214 of the reasons it is stated:

> There was no evidence to show that what these appellants did was to further their own interests in any respect. All evidence points to the fact that their actions were done as part of their duties of employment and to further the interests of Valcom.

The judgment then proceeds to analyze the jurisprudence in support of the above conclusion. Dealing with the appellate authorities referred to by the Divisional Court, the first is *Craik v. Aetna Life Insurance Co. of Canada*, [1995] O.J. No. 3286 (Gen. Div.), Court File No. 95-CQ-64403, affirmed by the Court of Appeal [1996] O.J. No. 2377. The facts are somewhat similar to those before this court, but the decision of Cumming J. and the oral endorsement of this court appear to pivot on the fact that the pleadings asserted that the corporation acted tortiously but did not assert that the employees acted in any personal capacity. The claim against the employees was struck out.

* * *

The Divisional Court placed its prime reliance on the judgment in *ScotiaMcLeod Inc.* and in doing so created a much broader canvass for the reasoning of this court than it was, by its language, intended to fill. That case concerned whether a reasonable cause of action was pleaded against certain individual directors of the defendant company. The plaintiff's complaint was that, as a result of certain filing statements, it had been misled into making investments in the defendant corporation's debentures.

The dismissal of the claim against what I will call a group of non-active directors was upheld because the pleading did not allege any negligence against them. The plaintiff sought to hold those directors vicariously liable for the negligence of the corporation, and no attempt was made in the pleading to single out their activities as individuals. This is similar to the situation in *Craik v. Aetna, supra.* On the other hand, two of the directors who had attended and made representations at a due diligence meeting were alleged to have been directly and personally involved in the marketing of the debentures and to have made representations which were relied upon by the plaintiffs. The action against those active directors was permitted to go to trial.

An excerpt from the reasoning of Finlayson J.A. in *ScotiaMcLeod Inc.*, at pp. 490-91 O.R., pp. 720-21 D.L.R., has been quoted from time to time by General Division judges and, here, by the Divisional Court, as suggesting some limitation on the liability of directors and officers who are acting in the course of their duties:

> The decided cases in which employees and officers of companies have been found personally liable for actions ostensibly carried out under a corporate name are fact-specific. In the absence of findings of fraud, deceit, dishonesty or want of authority on the part of employees or officers, they are also rare. Those cases in which the corporate veil has been pierced usually involve transactions where the use of the corporate structure was a sham from the outset or was an afterthought to a deal which had gone sour. There is also a considerable body of case-law wherein injured parties to actions for breach of contract have attempted to extend liability to the principals of the company by pleading that the principals were privy to the tort of inducing breach of contract between the company and the plaintiff: see *Ontario Store Fixtures Inc. v. Mmmuffins Inc.* (1989), 70 O.R. (2d) 42 (H.J.C.), and the cases referred to therein. Additionally there have been attempts by injured parties to attach liability to the principals of failed businesses through insolvency litigation. In every case, however, the facts giving rise to personal liability were specifically pleaded. Absent allegations which fit within the categories described above, officers or employees of limited companies are protected from personal liability unless it can be shown that their actions are themselves tortious or exhibit a separate identity or interest from that of the company so as to make the act or conduct complained of their own.

The operative portion of this paragraph is the final sentence which confirms that, where properly pleaded, officers or employees can be liable for tortious conduct even when acting in the course of duty. That this is clearly the intent of what was being stated is evidenced by the conclusion that the action should proceed against two defendants; against whom negligent conduct had been properly pleaded. The reasoning of *ScotiaMcLeod* has been recently applied by this court in decisions which confirm my interpretation.

* * *

Conclusion

It is my conclusion that there is no principled basis for protecting the director and employees of Valcom from liability for their alleged conduct on the basis that such conduct was in pursuance of the interests of the corporation. It may be that for policy reasons the law as to the allocation of responsibility for tortious conduct should be adjusted to provide some protection to employees, officers or directors, or all of them, in limited circumstances where, for instance, they are acting in the best interests of the corporation with parties who have voluntarily chosen to accept the ambit of risk of a limited liability company. However, the creation of such a policy should not evolve from the facts of this case where the alleged conduct was intentional and the only relationship between the corporate parties was as competitors. Any such evolution should await facts which are apposite to the policy concerns and should probably be articulated as a definitive extension of the defence in *Said v. Butt*. Such a development would be in the direction indicated by La Forest J. in his dissenting reasons in London Drugs and thus may have to await further consideration by the Supreme Court. In the meantime the courts can only be scrupulous in weeding out claims that are improperly pleaded or where the evidence does not justify an allegation of a personal tort. A principled development of jurisprudence is the tradition and the strength of the common law and must take precedence over incidental attempts to abuse the law as it develops.

* * *

Appeal allowed.

Notes and Questions

1   For a searching examination of the reasoning in *ADGA Systems* see "Workshop Presentations: Directors' and Officers' Liability" (2001) 35 C.B.L.J. 1-71. Given Carthy J.A.'s explanation of the basis of McCardie J.'s decision in *Said v. Butt*, why was the same reasoning not also applied by the Supreme Court in *London Drugs* to exempt the negligent employee from personal liability? From a policy perspective, is there a difference between protecting a director against liability for causing the company to breach its contract and protecting an employee who accidentally drops goods in a warehouse belonging to a customer of his employer? If the underlying concern is that the

employer may be judgment-proof and that holding the employee liable will encourage an employer to carry insurance, why does the same reasoning not apply to the director in *Said v. Butt*?

2   In *Williams v. Natural Life Health Foods Ltd.*, [1998] 1 W.L.R. 830 (H.L.), the plaintiff acquired a franchise from the defendant company for the operation of a health food shop. Prior to signing the contract, the company sent the plaintiffs detailed financial projections in the preparation of which the second defendant had played a prominent part. The plaintiffs did not know the second defendant and had little contact with him before the contract was signed. The turnover from the plaintiffs' franchise was much less than predicted by the company and the plaintiffs sued both the company and the second defendant for negligent representation relying on the rule in *Hedley Byrne*. The action against the second defendant failed. The House of Lords held, reversing the Court of Appeal, that to establish the liability of a director or employee for negligent representation a plaintiff had to show an assumption of personal responsibility by the director or employee. That burden had not been discharged in the present case. Does the judgment have wider implications or is it only further evidence of the House of Lords' reluctance to expand the scope of liability for economic torts?

3.   PIERCING THE CORPORATE VEIL

(a)   What is Piercing the Corporate Veil?

The expression "piercing the corporate veil" or "lifting the corporate veil" can refer to two distinct legal phenomena each of which may be described, loosely, as "disregard[ing] the separate legal personality of a corporation" (*642947 Ontario Ltd. v. Fleischer*, 2001 CarswellOnt 4296, 56 O.R. (3d) 417 (Ont. C.A.)). First, the expression can refer to the imposition of liability upon the shareholders of a corporation for the obligations of the corporation. A person wronged by an impecunious corporation might ask a court to hold the corporation's shareholders liable for her loss — that is, to pierce the corporate veil.

Second and more generically, the expression can refer to the non-recognition of the separate personality of a corporation where the correct construction of a statutory or other legal standard so requires. Sometimes, for instance, in construing words that might be thought to refer to a single legal person (such as "owner," or "employer" or "taxpayer"), a court will decide that the relevant unit of analysis is not a corporation in isolation but a corporation together with other entities such as its parent, subsidiary or shareholders. For instance, in *De Salaberry v. Minister of National Revenue*, excerpted below, the Federal Court took into account the conduct of a group of corporations under common ownership in characterizing the actions of one of them of tax purposes, rather than viewing the taxpayer's conduct in isolation.

(b)   What is the Basis for Piercing the Corporate Veil?

Corporations statutes are clear in providing that the corporation is a legal person separate and distinct from its shareholders and that the latter are not liable for the obligations of the former. For instance, the CBCA provides, at s. 45, that "the shareholders of a corporation are not, as shareholders, liable for any liability, act or default of the corporation" (except in four specific circumstances not relevant here). Nevertheless, courts have repeatedly stated that, sometimes, the legal personality of the corporation may be disregarded for the purpose of imposing liability directly upon shareholders or if necessary for the correct construction or application of a legal standard.

What is the legal justification for doing so? The jurisprudence has been criticized (including by judges themselves) for incoherence — in *Clarkson Co. Ltd. v. Zhelka*, excerpted below, Thompson J. stated that the cases on veil-piercing "illustrate no consistent principle." He went on to offer, as an approximation of the underlying principle, that the separate personality of a corporation will not be upheld where it would produce results "flagrantly opposed to justice." But "justice" is a vague concept. As you study the decisions excerpted in this part of the chapter, try to flesh the concept out by (i) identifying the facts that courts have treated as material in determining that the corporation's personality should, in a particular case, be disregarded, and (ii) searching for standards more specific than "justice" which they have articulated and followed.

In particular, consider what difference it makes (or should make) whether (a) the party seeking to pierce the corporate veil is an involuntary, rather than a voluntary creditor (consider *Walkovsky v. Carlton, Rockwell v. Newtonbrook*); or (b) the court is being asked to disregard the corporation's legal personality for a purpose other than holding the shareholders liable for the corporation's obligations to its contractual creditors and tort victims (consider *Dole v. Patrickson, Lee v. Lee's Air Farming; De Salaberry v. M.N.R.*).

(c)   Cases

(i)   General

Clarkson Co. v. Zhelka
1967 CarswellOnt 144, [1967] 2 O.R. 565, 64 D.L.R. (2d) 457 (Ont. H.C.)

[Selkirk promoted, incorporated and controlled several companies, including St. George Developments Ltd., Langstaff Land

Developments Ltd., Fidelity Real Estate Ltd., and Industrial Sites and Locations Ltd. In 1959, Industrial bought some land, and being without money or other assets at that time, paid for it in part with cash advanced by Langstaff and St. George. In 1960, Industrial conveyed the land to Zhelka, the sister of Selkirk, in return for a $120,000 promissory note. In 1961 Zhelka mortgaged the land to Gelberg, and when Gelberg began foreclosure action, part of the land was sold, and the cash applied to pay off the mortgage and a Province of Ontario tax lien. Interest adjustments paid to Zhelka somehow found their way into the bank account of Fidelity Real Estate.

Selkirk was adjudged a bankrupt in 1960, and the Clarkson Co. Ltd. was appointed as trustee in bankruptcy. Clarkson sought a declaration that the land, registered in the name of Zhelka, was held by Zhelka or by Industrial as trustee for Selkirk, alleging that Industrial was a mere agent and the alter ego of Selkirk, directed by Selkirk to the prejudice and confusion of his personal creditors.]

THOMPSON J. (after stating the facts, continued): I unhesitatingly conclude that the conveyance to Miss Zhelka and the entire transaction with her was without consideration and voluntary and entered into with the intention of protecting the lands against resort thereto by the creditors and others having claims against Industrial. Undoubtedly, Selkirk was the moving factor behind the whole plan.

* * *

It is my view that there is a resulting trust in Industrial and that it never was intended that Miss Zhelka should take any beneficial interest in the property conveyed; and that despite the fact that she subsequently mortgaged the lands to Gelberg for the convenience of one of the associated companies.

I have no doubt that the conveyance is open to attack by the creditors of Industrial under the Statute of Elizabeth, 13 Eliz., c. 5, now the *Fraudulent Conveyances Act*, R.S.O. 1960, c. 154. The Court would not lend its assistance, however, to the grantor in the recovery of the property, were it sought by Industrial upon the principle of the maxim *in pari delicto, potior est conditio possidentis*. . .

Even if the plaintiff were successful in its contention that Industrial is merely the agent or the *alter ego* of Selkirk, it is doubtful whether the plaintiff claiming through Selkirk, the bankrupt, could acquire any greater rights than he could in the face of the maxim quoted. It is also questionable as to whether, in that event, it could avoid the transaction under the general policy of the bankruptcy law or as a "settlement" within the meaning of s. 60 of the *Bankruptcy Act*, R.S.C. 1952, c. 14. It would, however in such event, be open to attack by the trustee as a conveyance fraudulent as against creditors of the debtor.

These considerations, however, become academic by reason of the fact that the plaintiff does not attack the transaction as a settlement or otherwise under the *Bankruptcy Act,* nor as a conveyance fraudulent against the debtor's creditors. The case is framed upon the premise that the property is held by the defendants or one of them as agent or trustee for the debtor and that it constitutes part of his estate or property passing to the plaintiff upon bankruptcy.

Such considerations become still more academic in the light of the view I ultimately adopt as to the relationship between the debtor Selkirk and Industrial.

There can be little doubt that the companies forming Selkirk's corporate structure were interrelated in the sense that there were transfers of assets from one to another or advances of money as between them, although none of them was a subsidiary of another in the true sense of the word.

It equally appears from the evidence that the only person to benefit financially from or to receive moneys arising from their operation was Selkirk himself.

The picture as to their procedures, however, is not altogether clear. The absence of records leaves substantial gaps in the evidence. Selkirk, himself, the one who, if he would, could have thrown much light upon the scene, was not called as a witness. Too much has been left to unsafe conjecture and frequently that which might have developed into proof has become arrested on the border of suspicion.

* * *

The evidence clearly demonstrates that George A. Selkirk always had and retained in fact complete control over all these companies upon which the evidence touches. He dictated the corporate policy in each case and was the moving and directing force in all of their business operations. The directors and officers, and particularly in the case of Industrial, were his nominees, including members of his immediate household and family, and were subject to his influence and I have no doubt to his domination. To all intents and purposes Industrial and its associated companies were one-man companies.

In reaching such conclusions, I am, I may say, quite uninfluenced by any alleged admissions or statements said to have been made by Selkirk. There are instances throughout the evidence of statements alleged to have been made to others by him. He is not a party to the action and such could not form admissible evidence for the plaintiff. Either one must consider them as entirely hearsay or as self-serving statements.

We are here, of course, primarily concerned only with Selkirk's relationship to Industrial. His connection with the other companies and their interconnection with Industrial is only of importance in so far as it may tend to establish a pattern of conduct. Industrial, despite its default in Government returns and irregularity in its proceedings, was regularly incorporated and has been kept alive as a corporate entity. Its charter has not been revoked under s. 326 [am. 1964, c. 10, s. 8] of the *Corporations*

Act, R.S.O. 1960, c. 71, although, apparently, it has been under departmental investigation. In 1963, it was still being taxed and some $14,000 levied against it under the *Corporations Tax Act* (ex. 21).

There is no evidence to indicate that when Industrial was incorporated in 1958, that Selkirk was insolvent; and nowhere is evidence to be found tracing any of Selkirk's personal assets into the hands of Industrial. The only indication that any of his personal assets passed into any of his companies is in the dictum in *Selkirk v. M.N.R.* earlier referred to. There is no intimation that at that time Selkirk was insolvent or that the transfer was in any way irregular or questionable. It does appear that later the Langstaff company advanced moneys to Industrial, but by the same token, it appears that Industrial still later advanced or repaid to Langstaff an approximately equal sum. I can see nothing unlawful or illegal per se, as against the personal creditors of Selkirk, in these interchanges of funds between companies. Even if there were an unlawful element, the only persons who were injured or damnified would be the shareholders or creditors of the companies involved. It is true that Selkirk has benefited personally from activities of his companies in dealings or transactions of questionable validity.

Industrial seldom had a bank account. Rental from the buildings upon the lands in question was received by his nominee or nominees rather than by Industrial. None of it, however, has been traced into his own hands, although one might suspect that some of it at least did reach him. In any event, only a small portion of it accrued due and was paid before his bankruptcy.

Fidelity Real Estate Ltd. appears recently to be the only one of the companies operating with a bank account and Industrial was indirectly the recipient of some of its funds.

The moneys paid to Miss Zhelka upon the settlement of the Gelberg action, some $9,249, went into the Fidelity bank account. These were really the funds of Industrial. Out of that account were paid some of Selkirk's personal bills for clothing, a retaining fee to a solicitor acting for him upon a criminal charge or charges of fraud pending against him and a sum offered by him by way of restitution in connection with such charge.

Whether Selkirk was entitled to moneys by way of salary or otherwise from Fidelity does not appear. If he was, at the time of such payments, a director of Fidelity as he once was, and the moneys were merely a loan or an advance to him, the transaction of course would fall within the prohibition of the *Corporations Act* respecting loans to shareholders.

The sum and substance of all this is that Selkirk has received some comparatively minor benefits from the operation of his companies and at times in a manner which, so far as regularity is concerned, is questionable. An aura of suspicion has been cast about him. I have no doubt that where his personal advantage is concerned he would go a long way.

But the question remains, in what way has his association with his corporate offspring injured, defeated or prejudiced his personal creditors? Apart from a small portion of the rents which he may have received, if any, from the buildings on the Steeles Ave. lands, it would appear that all benefits have accrued since his bankruptcy and really fall into the category of after-acquired property, to which recourse by the trustee is under the provisions of the *Bankruptcy Act.*

This is not a case where a debtor or a prospective debtor has transferred his own assets to a corporation of his making for the purpose of avoiding existing personal liabilities or obligations; nor is it a case where he has personally made a secret or clandestine profit by such a transfer.

There is here no claim of complaint by any creditor, if such there now be, of Industrial or its associated companies, nor by any director or shareholder.

In a critical analysis of the situation, one asks oneself just where is any fraud upon Selkirk's personal creditors being perpetrated by the operation of his companies and his conduct with relation thereto? To me the evidence falls short of establishing that.

No doubt his creditors are disappointed at their inability to have access to his corporate assets and particularly where he himself is reaping some financial benefit therefrom. But that must of necessity be, so long as the Legislature provides for and encourages the formation of private corporations. Without such, of course, enterprise and business adventure would be stifled. Limited liability is one of the landmarks of incorporation.

The plaintiff as trustee in bankruptcy for some reason apparently has not seen fit to follow any funds reaching the hands of his debtor as after-acquired property nor to intervene with respect thereto.

The cases in which the Courts, both in this Province and in England, have seen fit to disregard the corporate entity or personality, and instead to consider the economic realities behind the legal facade, fall within a narrow compass. The Legislature, in the fields of revenue and taxation, and particularly with respect to true subsidiaries, has made much greater departure in this respect. Such cases as there are, illustrate no consistent principle. The only principle laid down is that in the leading case of *Salomon v. Salomon & Co., Ltd.,* [1897] A.C. 22; and in general such principle has been rigidly applied. Briefly stated, it is that the legal persona created by incorporation is an entity distinct from its shareholders and directors and that even in the case of a one man company, the company is not an alias for the owner.

The exceptions would appear to represent refusals to apply the logic of the *Salomon* case where it would be flagrantly opposed to justice.

Counsel have presented me with an exhaustive review of these authorities. I can see no useful purpose in here reiterating it. The conclusions to be drawn from the cases as a whole were well stated by Mr.

Justice Masten in his article on " 'One Man Companies' and their Controlling Shareholders" at 14 Can. Bar Rev. 663 (1936), where he discusses the authorities.

In questions of property and capacity, of acts done and rights acquired or liabilities assumed, the company is always an entity distinct from its corporators. It is not an alias or a sham and the principle of the *Salomon* case stands unimpaired.

If a company is formed for the express purpose of doing a wrongful or unlawful act, or, if when formed, those in control expressly direct a wrongful thing to be done, the individuals as well as the company are responsible to those to whom liability is legally owed.

In such cases, or where the company is the mere agent of a controlling corporator, it may be said that the company is a sham, cloak or *alter ego*, but otherwise it should not be so termed.

Whether an individual has constituted the company his agent is a question of fact in each case. A controlling or total share interest does not in itself establish such agency. Due regard must be had to law of principal and agent relating to the formation of the relationship.

Although the instant case may be close to the line, the plaintiff has failed to satisfy me that I should declare Industrial to be his *alter ego* or his mere agent for the conduct of his personal business or for the purposes of the conveyance in question to the defendant Zhelka. In the result, the action must be dismissed.

As I have previously intimated, I think the defendant Zhelka has invited these proceedings. I fail to see how the plaintiff, as trustee for the creditors of Selkirk, could afford to stand idly by in the face of her earlier statement in the Gotfried action that she was holding the lands in question for her brother. It was, as events have proven, a false statement, or at least a totally irresponsible one; but the plaintiff in my view on the strength of it was justified in seeking judicial investigation of the whole matter.

In view of the relationship between the defendants and of the fact that the alternative plea by the corporate defendant that Miss Zhelka holds the lands in trust for it is virtually a plea asserting its own fraud against its creditors, I do not feel that it should have costs.

Judgment for defendant.

Notes and Questions

1   Does the decision contain any statement or statements more specific than the "flagrantly opposed to justice" standard as to the legal conditions under which the *Salomon* principle will not operate and the shareholders will incur personal liability for liabilities of the corporation?

2   What facts did the judge treat as most relevant in deciding not to pierce the corporate veil?

3   In a typical veil-piercing case, the corporation's creditors seek to hold the shareholders liable for the corporation's obligations. It is, in other words, a contest between the corporation's creditors and its shareholders. Does this case fit that mold?

4   For a more recent case dealing with an individual acting as the directing mind of multiple corporations, where one corporation failed to perform its obligations, another corporation was also found to be bound through an agency relationship, see *1196303 Ontario Inc. v. Glen Grove Suites Inc.*, 2015 CarswellOnt 12741, 2015 ONCA 580 (Ont. C.A.).

Transamerica Life Insurance Co. of Canada v. Canada Life Assurance Co.
1996 CarswellOnt 1699, 28 O.R. (3d) 423 (Ont. Gen. Div.), affirmed 1997
CarswellOnt 3496, [1997] O.J. No. 3754 (Ont. C.A.)

Sharpe J.: In the period 1983 to 1989, the plaintiff, Transamerica Life Insurance Company of Canada, made 54 mortgage loans which were arranged by the defendant Canada Life Mortgage Services Ltd. ("C.L.M.S."). A number of the mortgages have fallen into default, resulting in an alleged loss of some $60 million. Transamerica asserts that C.L.M.S. owed it a duty to do the underwriting (due diligence, risk assessment and analysis) for these loans, that C.L.M.S. failed in that regard, and that Transamerica has suffered loss as a consequence. In its claim against C.L.M.S., Transamerica pleads breach of contract, breach of fiduciary duty, fraud, misrepresentation and negligence. C.L.M.S. denies that it owed Transamerica any duty to underwrite the loans, asserts that it acted throughout simply as a mortgage broker, and contends that it was for Transamerica to do its own underwriting and due diligence with respect to the loans in question.

C.L.M.S. is the wholly owned subsidiary of the Canada Life Assurance Company. Transamerica asserts that Canada Life is liable for the wrongs of C.L.M.S. on a variety of grounds and has joined Canada Life as a defendant to this lawsuit. Canada Life asserts that it had nothing to do with the mortgages in question and that there is no basis for the claim that it is legally responsible for the alleged wrongs of its wholly owned subsidiary, C.L.M.S. Canada Life brings this motion for summary judgment on the grounds that Transamerica had failed to show that there is a triable issue as to Canada Life's liability and asks that the action against it be dismissed.

ISSUES

Transamerica bases its claim against Canada Life on three grounds which, it asserts, permit the court to look behind the separate corporate existence of C.L.M.S. and attach liability to its sole shareholder, Canada Life. These assertions give rise to the following issues on this motion for summary judgment.

1. Is there a basis for "piercing the corporate veil" and holding Canada Life liable for the acts of its wholly owned subsidiary, C.L.M.S.?

    [.. .]

FACTS

C.L.M.S. was incorporated in 1974 to carry on business as a mortgage correspondent and general financial agent. Before the creation of C.L.M.S., Canada Life had regularly invested in mortgages originated by its branch offices. The branches produced more mortgage investment opportunities than Canada Life could handle and Canada Life decided to incorporate C.L.M.S. to carry on the business of mortgage correspondent and to deal with both Canada Life and other institutional investors. As C.L.M.S. was to be a wholly owned subsidiary, governing legislation required Canada Life to obtain the consent of the Department of Insurance, now Office of the Superintendent of Financial Institutions ("O.F.S.I."), to its incorporation. The Department of Insurance was satisfied that the proposed business of C.L.M.S. was ancillary to the business of insurance as required by s. 65 of the Canadian and British Insurance Companies Act, R.S.C. 1985, c. I-12. Henry Heft, the employee of the Department of Insurance who dealt with the C.L.M.S. matter, testified that under the legislation, the Department was not interested in the way in which C.L.M.S. carried on its business, but only that it was ancillary to the business of insurance, that Canada Life's investment was not unreasonable and properly accounted for, and that C.L.M.S. did not exceed the powers it was given under its letters patent. It was Heft's understanding that the activity of a mortgage correspondent was to "be there for the service of people wanting to invest funds, and also for the service of people looking for the funds". The Department took no interest in whether the borrower or the lender paid C.L.M.S. a fee and knew that C.L.M.S. would be dealing with borrowers in all aspects of the proposed mortgage business. Paragraph (a)(ii) of the C.L.M.S. objects provides:

> . . . to assist in the development, financing, construction and promotion of various real and immoveable properties, including research and feasibility studies relating to commercial, industrial, residential and public and private undertakings.

Heft understood this to refer to providing or obtaining financing for owners of real estate, in other words, borrowers.

It was Heft's evidence that the Department was not concerned about C.L.M.S. engaging in the business of assisting borrowers. Heft also testified that the Department did not address the particular matter of whether the due diligence review, analysis and risk assessment was the function of the insurance company lender or C.L.M.S. as mortgage broker. It was, however, his own personal understanding that this would be the responsibility of the lender.

In March 1981, Transamerica and C.L.M.S. established a "Master Agreement" to govern their relationship, and in the period to 1989, Transamerica invested in 54 mortgages originated by C.L.M.S. pursuant to this agreement. The terms of this agreement do not specifically provide that C.L.M.S. is to perform any underwriting function on Transamerica's behalf. C.L.M.S. takes the position that the agreement excludes this duty and asserts that it does not engage in the business of underwriting mortgage loan proposals for any lender. C.L.M.S. has an agreement with Canada Life in terms virtually identical to the Transamerica agreement and Canada Life does its own due diligence, review and risk assessment of proposed loans and does not look to C.L.M.S. to perform this function. The interpretation of the agreement and the nature of the relationship between C.L.M.S. and Transamerica is hotly disputed as Transamerica takes the position that C.L.M.S. was responsible for the underwriting function with respect to the loans it made.

The relationship between C.L.M.S. and Canada Life is as follows. C.L.M.S. has its own head office and branch offices distinct from those of Canada Life. C.L.M.S. has its own bank accounts. It is and was managed and operated independently of Canada Life. C.L.M.S. management exercises independent discretion in conducting the business of C.L.M.S. Apart from the president, the senior management of C.L.M.S. is independent of Canada Life. Two vice-presidents have overall responsibility for the affairs of C.L.M.S. The president of C.L.M.S. is a Canada Life employee. He spends a very small percentage of his time on C.L.M.S. business and he plays no role in the day-to-day management of C.L.M.S. While his salary is paid by Canada Life, the portion of it attributable to the time he spends on C.L.M.S. business is charged back to C.L.M.S. Canada Life does provide C.L.M.S. with certain administrative services, including payroll, salary records and legal services. The cost of these services is billed to C.L.M.S. by Canada Life, and responsibility for hiring, promotion and remuneration of C.L.M.S. employees remains that of C.L.M.S. management. All members of the C.L.M.S. board of directors and the president of C.L.M.S. are senior executives of Canada Life.

Canada Life and C.L.M.S. take the position that the exigencies of the market required there to be an arm's-length relationship between the two companies. They contend that prospective lenders, including Transamerica, were concerned that Canada Life would be in a favoured position and "cherry-pick" the best investments, and for that reason C.L.M.S. was operated as a business entirely separate and independent of Canada Life.

The individual who dealt directly with Transamerica during the relevant period, Stuart Pearson, was the branch manager of the Toronto Regional Branch. He reported to Tom Deegan, one of the two vice-presidents. Pearson and Deegan were both employees of C.L.M.S. and neither had any duties or responsibilities to Canada Life. The affidavit of

J. Gordon Fleming, President and Chairman of the Board of C.L.M.S.
from 1984 to 1994 describes the involvement, or lack thereof, of Canada
Life in the dealings between C.L.M.S. and Transamerica:

> All business dealings between CLMS and Transamerica were
> conducted by CLMS employees directly with Transamerica employ-
> ees. There has been absolutely no involvement in the business
> dealings between CLMS and Transamerica by directors, officers or
> employees of Canada Life other than the presence of representatives
> of Canada Life in discussion with Transamerica about this litigation
> commencing in 1992. There was never any involvement in the actual
> business dealings between CLMS and Transamerica that gives rise to
> this litigation by the directors, officers or employees of Canada Life
> nor indeed was there even any knowledge of it by them.

There is no evidence, subject to what follows relating to certain
meetings in 1989, that Mr. Fleming or any other Canada Life officer or
employee were involved in any way in the dealings between C.L.M.S. and
Transamerica. The relationship between C.L.M.S. and Transamerica was
not discussed by the Board of Directors of C.L.M.S. Apart from six
letters from the legal department of Canada Life, acting in the capacity of
solicitors for C.L.M.S., there is no evidence of any communication
whatsoever between Canada Life and Transamerica in relation to the
transactions at issue in this suit prior to the initiation of proceedings.
As noted already, the president of C.L.M.S., Mr. Fleming and his
predecessor, R.D. Radford, were the only officers of C.L.M.S. who were
also officers of Canada Life. There is no evidence to suggest that Mr.
Radford was aware of or involved with Transamerica. Fleming's
involvement prior to the initiation of proceedings was as follows. In
1989, senior officers from Transamerica's parent came to Toronto to
conduct a review of the mortgage investment practices and procedures of
Transamerica. The inferences to be drawn from this review is a matter of
dispute between C.L.M.S. and Transamerica. Transamerica takes the
position that this review should have made it apparent to C.L.M.S. that
Transamerica was relying on C.L.M.S. for underwriting advice in relation
to the mortgages in which it was investing. C.L.M.S. takes the position
that the review suggested otherwise and points to the fact that a report of
the review recognized that Transamerica should not be relying on
C.L.M.S. for underwriting but rather should ensure it had internal
capacity to perform that function. The significance of this review will be
an issue for trial as between C.L.M.S. and Transamerica. For the
purposes of this motion, Transamerica argues that there is evidence that
Fleming became aware of the review and that his failure to set the record
straight as to the nature of the service being provided by C.L.M.S. to
Transamerica is sufficient to fix liability on Canada Life. The only
evidence of Fleming's awareness is as follows. The defendants have
produced an extract from a minute of a C.L.M.S. management meeting of

June 28, 1989, of Fleming and the two vice-presidents, Curtin and Deegan:

> Mr. Fleming was advised of a visit from the Senior Vice-President of Transamerica who was conducting an "underwriting audit" of their mortgage dealings in Canada. Attending the meetings were Joseph Barbieri, Bob Clarke and myself.

> Transamerica was interested in mortgage financing in Canada and their questions were mainly directed to types of financings, building construction, appraisals, etc. There was no criticism of our services either from the branch or head office.

Transamerica takes the position that this is sufficient to fix Fleming, and through Fleming, Canada Life, with knowledge of the breach of contract, breach of fiduciary duty, and misrepresentations alleged against C.L.M.S. In my view, this assertion reads far more into the minute than is warranted by the minute itself and by the balance of the evidence surrounding the meetings of the visiting Transamerica executives. Fleming denies that he was told that Transamerica thought that C.L.M.S. was doing the underwriting. It was his evidence that during the course of a meeting that lasted about two minutes, he was told that C.L.M.S. had had a visit from Transamerica. He stated that he is almost certain that this was the first time he learned that C.L.M.S. was doing business with Transamerica and that he considered it to be a routine matter for an investor to come to learn more about the mortgage market in Canada. He agreed that if he had been made aware that Transamerica was operating under the mistaken impression that C.L.M.S. was doing the underwriting for the loans, he would have instructed the C.L.M.S. staff to set the matter straight, but the information he was given did not convey that information.

ANALYSIS

1. Is there a basis for "piercing the corporate veil" and holding Canada Life liable for the acts of its wholly owned subsidiary, C.L.M.S.?

On behalf of Transamerica, Mr. Bates submits that the applicable legal test for piercing the corporate veil can be stated no more precisely than this: the corporate veil will be pierced when it is "just and equitable" to do so. As authority for that proposition, reliance is placed on the following passage from the judgment of Wilson J. in *Kosmopoulos v. Constitution Insurance Co. of Canada*, 1987 CarswellOnt 132, 1987 CarswellOnt 1054, [1987] 1 S.C.R. 2 (S.C.C.) at pp. 10-11 and 34 [S.C.R.]:

> As a general rule a corporation is a legal entity distinct from its shareholders: Salomon v. Salomon & Co. [1897] A.C. 22 (H.L.). The law on when a court may disregard this principle by "lifting the corporate veil" and regarding the company as a mere "agent" or "puppet" of its controlling shareholder or parent corporation

follows no consistent principle. The best that can be said is that the "separate entities" principle is not enforced when it would yield a result "too flagrantly opposed to justice, convenience or the interests of the Revenue": L.C.B. Gower, Modern Company Law (4th ed. 1979) at p. 112. I have no doubt that theoretically the veil could be lifted in this case to do justice. . . But a number of factors lead me to think it would be unwise to do so.

If accepted, the argument advanced by Transamerica would represent a significant departure from the principle established in Salomon v. Salomon & Co., [1897] A.C. 22 at p. 51, [1895-9] All E.R. Rep. 33 (H.L.), per Lord Macnaghten:

> The company is at law a different person altogether from the subscribers to the memorandum; and, though it may be that after incorporation the business is precisely the same as it was before, and the same persons are managers, and the same hands receive the profits, the company is not in law the agent of the subscribers or trustee for them. Nor are the subscribers as members liable, in any shape or form, except to the extent and in the manner provided by the Act.

In my view, the argument advanced by Transamerica reads far too much into a dictum plainly not intended to constitute an in-depth analysis of an important area of the law or to reverse a legal principle which, for almost 100 years, has served as a cornerstone of corporate law.

It was conceded in argument that no case since Kosmopoulos has applied the preferred "just and equitable" test. In Kosmopoulos itself, the Supreme Court, including Wilson J., rejected the submission that the corporate veil be lifted. Moreover, it will be noted that Wilson J. does not use the phrase "just and equitable" but rather quotes a passage from an English text which describes the test in much more stringent terms.

Two recent judgments of this court have refused to read the Kosmopoulos dictum as granting carte blanche to lift the corporate veil absent fraudulent or improper conduct: *W.D. Latimer Co. v. Dijon Investments Ltd.*, 1992 CarswellOnt 724, 12 O.R. (3d) 415 (Ont. Gen. Div.); *801962 Ontario Inc. v. MacKenzie Trust Co.* (March 22, 1994), Doc. 92-CQ-28502, B31/92A, [1994] O.J. No. 2105 (Ont. Gen. Div.). In the MacKenzie case, Spence J. reviewed the case-law in detail and concluded:

> These decisions do not support a claim that the test in Salomon v. Salomon has been superseded by a new "business entity" or "single business entity" test. They merely illustrate the principle that, in particular fact situations, where the nature of the legal issue in dispute makes it appropriate to have regard to the larger business entity, the court is not precluded by Salomon v. Salomon from doing so. In a few cases, there are statements that the court will lift the

corporate veil "where injustice would otherwise result". I am not able to conclude that such statements are intended to remove the authority of the Salomon principle. I think they may be more in the nature of a shorthand formulation reflecting the approach of the courts in the cases discussed above.

The proposition that the dictum of Wilson J. in Kosmopoulos suggests a fundamental shift in the law was also rejected by the British Columbia Court of Appeal in *B.G. Preeco I (Pacific Coast) Ltd. v. Bon Street Holdings Ltd.*, 1989 CarswellBC 104, 37 B.C.L.R. (2d) 258, 60 D.L.R. (4th) 30 (B.C. C.A.). Seaton J. observed (at p. 267) that the passage quoted in Kosmopoulos (at p. 138) from Gower, Modern Company Law, 4th ed. (1979), concluded with a passage which disapproved of the free-wheeling "just and equitable" approach:

> The most that can be said is that the courts' policy is to lift the veil if they think that justice demands it and they are not constrained by contrary binding authority. The results in individual cases may be commendable, but it smacks of palm-tree justice rather than the application of legal rules.

Seaton J.A. went on to quote a Canadian text, Welling, Corporate Law in Canada (1984), at p. 129, which disapproved of the approach of some American cases to adopt a general fairness test:

> Little need be said about this rationale, other than that it simply will not do. There are, so far as we know, no such broadly enforceable standards of "fair play and good conscience," at least in Canadian corporate law.

It should also be noted that the most recent edition of Gower, Modern Company Law, 5th ed. (1992) puts the test for lifting the corporate veil in much more stringent terms. The authors review the decision of the English Court of Appeal in Adams v. Cape Industries plc, [1991] 1 All E.R. 433, which, they state (at p. 125) "subjected lifting the veil to the most exhaustive treatment that it has yet received in the English (or Scottish) courts". The authors conclude that the Adams decision significantly attenuates the grounds for lifting the veil, and they make no suggestion, as they did in the earlier edition cited in Kosmopoulos, that the test is anything like a "just and equitable standard" (at pp. 132-33):

> There seem to be three circumstances only in which the courts can do so. These are:
>
> (1) When the court is construing a statute, contract or other document.
> (2) When the court is satisfied that a company is a "mere facade" concealing the true facts.

(3) When it can be established that the company is an authorized agent of its controllers or its members, corporate or human.

In a recent judgment of the Ontario Court of Appeal, *Gregorio v. Intrans-Corp.*, 1994 CarswellOnt 237, 18 O.R. (3d) 527, 115 D.L.R. (4th) 200 (Ont. C.A.) at p. 536 [O.R.], additional reasons at 1994 CarswellOnt 3827 (Ont. C.A.), Laskin J.A. restated the legal principles relating to the liability of a parent company for the acts of its subsidiary as follows:

> Generally, a subsidiary, even a wholly owned subsidiary, will not be found to be the alter ego of its parent unless the subsidiary is under the complete control of the parent and is nothing more that a conduit used by the parent to avoid liability. The alter ego principle is applied to prevent conduct akin to fraud that would otherwise unjustly deprive claimants of their rights.

There are undoubtedly situations where justice requires that the corporate veil be lifted. The cases and authorities already cited indicate that it will be difficult to define precisely when the corporate veil is to be lifted, but that lack of a precise test does not mean that a court is free to act as it pleases on some loosely defined "just and equitable" standard. There may be a principal-agent relationship between two related corporations which leads to liability despite separate legal personalities: see Gower, supra; *Clarkson Co. v. Zhelka*, 1967 CarswellOnt 144, [1967] 2 O.R. 565, 64 D.L.R. (2d) 457 (Ont. H.C.) at p. 578 [O.R.]. It is also the case that the courts will look behind corporate structures where necessary to give effect to legislation, especially taxation statutes: see Gower, supra; *Jodrey Estate v. Nova Scotia (Minister of Finance)*, 1980 CarswellNS 78, 1980 CarswellNS 82, (sub nom. *Covert v. Nova Scotia (Minister of Finance)*) [1980] 2 S.C.R. 774, 41 N.S.R. (2d) 181 (S.C.C.). Neither of these two exceptions applies to the situation of the case at bar.

As just indicated, the courts will disregard the separate legal personality of a corporate entity where it is completely dominated and controlled and being used as a shield for fraudulent or improper conduct. The first element, "complete control", requires more than ownership. It must be shown that there is complete domination and that the subsidiary company does not, in fact, function independently: *Aluminum Co. of Canada v. Toronto (City)*, 1944 CarswellOnt 71, [1944] S.C.R. 267, [1944] 3 D.L.R. 609 (S.C.C.) at p. 271 [S.C.R.]; *Bank of Montreal v. Canadian Westgrowth Ltd.*, 1990 CarswellAlta 29, 72 Alta. L.R. (2d) 319 (Alta. Q.B.), affirmed 1992 CarswellAlta 57 (Alta. C.A.). The evidence before me indicates that the relationship between Canada Life and C.L.M.S. was that of a typical parent and subsidiary. While C.L.M.S. is wholly owned by Canada Life and its board of directors is comprised of Canada Life executives, I have found that it does have an independent management and conducts a business separate and distinct from that of its parent.

There is, in my opinion, no evidence sufficient to give rise to a triable issue that C.L.M.S. is the mere puppet of Canada Life.

The second element relates to the nature of the conduct: is there "conduct akin to fraud that would otherwise unjustly deprive claimants of their rights"? In my view, while Transamerica has alleged fraud against C.L.M.S., there is no evidence to suggest that Canada Life has any involvement in that alleged fraud, apart from the fact that C.L.M.S. is its wholly owned subsidiary. The officers and employees of Canada Life were not involved in the dealings between C.L.M.S. and Transamerica, and no evidence has been advanced sufficient to give rise to a triable issue that Canada Life is somehow using C.L.M.S. as a shield for some nefarious purpose.

It is submitted that this is a developing area of the law, and that it would be wrong for me to grant summary judgment and thereby preclude having the issue fully considered at trial in light of all the evidence. As I have already indicated, it is my view that the law in this area is not developing at anything close to the extent submitted by Mr. Bates. Moreover, there is nothing in the facts of this case to suggest that this would be a case where the court might be tempted to lift the corporate veil in the interest of doing justice between the parties. Transamerica has simply not been able to make out a triable issue or arguable case that the court should look behind the corporate veil. There has been extensive discovery, cross-examination on affidavits and this motion has been pending for almost an entire year. Transamerica has had the fullest possible opportunity to advance its case. It is clearly established that on a motion for summary judgment, a party is no longer entitled to sit back and rely on the possibility that more favourable facts may develop at trial. To avoid summary judgment, a party is required to put its best foot forward. The onus remains on the moving party to show that there is no genuine issue for trial, but the responding party must "lead trump or risk losing": *Pizza Pizza Ltd. v. Gillespie*, 1990 CarswellOnt 408, 75 O.R. (2d) 225, 33 C.P.R. (3d) 515 (Ont. S.C.J.); *1061590 Ontario Ltd. v. Ontario Jockey Club*, 1995 CarswellOnt 63, 21 O.R. (3d) 547, 43 R.P.R. (2d) 161 (Ont. C.A.). In my view, Transamerica has failed to present evidence to indicate that there is a triable issue on this point and Canada Life has met the onus of showing that it should be granted summary judgment on this issue.

* * *

CONCLUSION

For the foregoing reasons, I conclude that the moving party, Canada Life, has met the onus of demonstrating that there is no genuine issue for trial. The responding party, Transamerica, has had full opportunity to come forward with evidence to show that there is a genuine issue for trial but has failed to do so. Accordingly, Canada Life is entitled to summary judgment dismissing the action against it. The remaining defendant C.L.M.S. is hereby granted leave to amend the statement of defence to plead the limitation defence pursuant to s. 36(4) of the Competition Act. I may be spoken to with respect to costs.

Motion granted.

(ii)   Involuntary Creditors

Rockwell Developments Ltd. v. Newtonbrook Plaza Ltd.
1972 CarswellOnt 902, [1972] 3 O.R. 199, 27 D.L.R. (3d) 651 (Ont. C.A.)

ARNUP J.A. (for the Court): Samuel Kelner, a solicitor in Toronto, appeals from the order of Parker J., dated November 5, 1971, whereby Kelner was ordered to pay personally the defendant's costs of the action brought against it by Rockwell Developments Ltd. (hereafter "Rockwell"), which action, by a judgment of Parker J., dated March 19, 1970, was dismissed with costs payable by Rockwell to the defendant. The defendant moves to quash Kelner's appeal on the ground that no appeal lies to this Court from an order of Parker J., as to costs only, save by his leave, and an application made to Parker J., for leave to appeal was dismissed.

The appeal and the motion to quash do not fall into neat separate compartments. The power of Parker J., to make the order as to costs against Kelner is involved also in the question of whether there is a right to appeal from that order. I therefore state the facts which are involved in the consideration of both the motion to quash and the appeal itself.

For a number of years prior to 1967 Kelner, while practicing law with Mr. Irwin Cooper, had been interested in the purchase and development of real estate in Metropolitan Toronto. It was his practice to incorporate separate limited companies for each separate real estate development in which he became interested. Rockwell was a private Ontario company incorporated "in the 1950s" and "did a variety of business transactions from that time, from time to time". In 1967 it had outstanding 26 common shares, one held by Kelner, one by Cooper, one by a girl in their law office, and 23 by Planet Development Corporation Limited. It is Kelner's evidence that the shares held by the three individuals, who were also the directors, were held in trust for Planet Development Corporation Ltd., and that he in turn was the beneficial owner of all of the shares of Planet.

In 1967 Kelner became interested in lands in the Town of Markham, owned by Newtonbrook Plaza Ltd. a company which (in the language of Parker J., in his judgment after the trial) was "owned by" one Abraham Parsham. An offer to purchase was made by Rockwell, signed by Kelner as its secretary, to Newtonbrook Plaza Ltd., accepted by the latter, the acceptance being signed on its behalf by Parsham as president. Because of a difficulty respecting the zoning of the land, Rockwell asserted a right to close the transaction with an abatement in the purchase price, while Newtonbrook asserted that Rockwell could either close the transaction in accordance with its terms, or call it off.

Rockwell executed and registered some form of document described as an "assignment". Following tenders by each side upon the other, Rockwell sued Newtonbrook for specific performance with an abatement in price, and Newtonbrook in a separate action sued Rockwell for a declaration that the original agreement of purchase and sale was null and void, claimed an order expunging the registration of the assignment, and further claimed damages for slander of title. These two actions were tried together, over a period of five days. In a reserved judgment dated March 19, 1970, Parker J., dismissed the action of Rockwell with costs, directed in the second action that the Rockwell assignment be expunged from the Registry Office, and since it was admitted by counsel for Newtonbrook that the property had greatly increased in value since July, 1967, Parker J., granted that company no other relief and directed that there be no costs in the action it had brought.

The costs of Newtonbrook in Rockwell's action were taxed at $4,800 and were not paid by Rockwell. Kelner was examined as an officer of the judgment debtor corporation, following which a substantive motion was made to Parker J., by Newtonbrook for an order directing that Kelner pay personally the costs directed by the original judgment to be paid by Rockwell to Newtonbrook. Kelner made an affidavit on that motion and was cross-examined thereon.

From the material filed on such motion a number of additional facts emerged. There was no resolution of the directors of Rockwell authorizing Kelner to enter into the offer to purchase on its behalf; the deposit of $10,000 was advanced by Kelner and his partner Cooper from their own funds, direct to Newtonbrook or its agent, and did not go through the bank account of Rockwell nor was there any entry in Rockwell's books of account respecting it. The tendered sum of $28,000 which preceded the action was also advanced by Kelner and Cooper, and did not go through the bank account or books of Rockwell. In due course both the deposit of $10,000 and the tendered amount of $28,000 found its way back to Kelner and Cooper. There was no resolution of the directors authorizing the institution of Rockwell's action against Newtonbrook, nor the defence of the action of Newtonbrook against Rockwell. There was no resolution respecting the retainer of solicitors, although solicitors were retained to prosecute Rockwell's action and to defend Newtonbrook's action against it.

Both in 1967 and subsequently, Rockwell had literally no assets except a small bank account, which had dwindled from about $400 in 1964 to $31.85 in October, 1970, when Kelner was examined as an officer of Rockwell in aid of the judgment. On the last-mentioned date Rockwell's solicitors had not been paid; by the time the motion was heard they had been paid, by Kelner and Cooper, against the moneys going direct from Kelner and Cooper to the solicitors, with no entry in the books of account of the company.

Kelner described the putting up of the deposit, the tender money, and the amount required to pay Rockwell's solicitors as being "shareholders' loans", and stated that "our accountant would pick this up in due course". There is no reference anywhere in the books or records of Rockwell to any shareholders' loans. . . .

* * *

Turning to the merits of the appeal, it would appear that while he did not discuss the cases apart from the *Sturmer* and *Curry* decisions, Parker J., was addressing his mind to the issues as I have expressed them herein. As already indicated he found that "Kelner was the actual contracting party and the person who set this process in action . . . he was the actual litigant and Rockwell was only a nominee to hold title".

With great respect, I am unable to agree with these conclusions. The use of a "one man company" for the carrying on of business transactions, authoritatively recognized and expressed in *Salomon v. Salomon & Co.*, [1897] A.C. 22, and the correlative propositions that the property of the company is distinct from that of its members, and its transactions create legal rights and obligations vested in the company itself as opposed to its members, continue today. The subject is discussed in Gower, *Modern Company Law*, 2nd ed. (1957), at pp. 62-6.

I can find no basis for the finding that Mr. Kelner was the "actual contracting party". He was undoubtedly the individual who would ultimately benefit, in whole or in part, from the contract, but the contract was made with the company alone. Mr. Kelner could not have sued upon it, nor could he himself have been sued. Both he and Mr. Parsham were pursuing the same course of action; they were quite content to enter into contracts made by the companies which they respectively controlled.

It was undoubtedly the fact that Kelner was "the person who set this process in action", in the sense that he was the individual who, on behalf of the company, gave instructions to its solicitors, but this does not, in my view, justify a finding that he was "the actual litigant". Nor can I find justification for the finding that "Rockwell was only a nominee to hold title". This seems to imply that Rockwell was a trustee for Kelner, but it is contrary to all established principles of company law to suggest that a corporation is a trustee for its shareholders, or even for its single shareholder. On the evidence, there were to be other shareholders — certainly Mr. Cooper, according to Kelner's evidence — and there is a reference in the judgment of Parker J., at trial to the real estate agent who negotiated the transaction, and who was known to Kelner, and to the evidence that "at the time the deposit was paid there was an agreement between (the agent) and Mr. Kelner that (the agent) could have up to fifty per cent of the deal".

In argument Mr. Rolls conceded that "if this was a true corporate transaction, my case would be difficult or impossible". He sought to avoid the *Salomon* principle by reference to the fact that there was nothing in the minute book or the books of account of the company concerning the transaction and indeed, apart from the fact that the company had made the offer to purchase, there was nothing in the corporate records as such, respecting the purchase.

Unquestionably, the handling of the corporate records, both as to the minute book and as to the books of account, was slipshod, but no one connected with Rockwell was in a position to complain except Kelner himself. There was no allegation of fraud on the part of Kelner except one suggestion, not seriously pressed, that Kelner had "facilitated a fraudulent preference" by seeing to the payment of the account of the company's solicitors, after the motion herein had been launched, so that those solicitors were paid in preference to "other creditors". As already indicated, these fees were paid by Kelner and Cooper from their own funds, allegedly as an advance on behalf of the corporation. If this was a fraudulent preference, it is still open to Newtonbrook to attack it if so advised.

Notes and Questions

1   Halpern, Trebilcock and Turnbull, *supra*, cite this case as an example of a situation involving an involuntary creditor. Do you see why? How might Newtonbrook alternatively be viewed as a voluntary creditor?

2   What facts did counsel for Newtonbrook rely upon in seeking to avoid the *Salomon* principle? Why might those facts have been legally relevant?

3   The cost decision in *Rockwell Developments* did not sit well with legislators or with other courts. See now Ontario Rules of Civil Procedure, Rule 56, Security for Costs (Rule 56.01(d), below), and the decision in *269335 Alberta Ltd. v. Starlite Investments Ltd.*, 1987 CarswellAlta 148, 18 C.P.C. (2d) 161 (Alta. Q.B.).

Rules of Civil Procedure

56.01 (1) The court, on motion by the defendant or respondent in a proceeding, may make such order for security for costs as is just where it appears that,

(a) the plaintiff or applicant is ordinarily resident outside Ontario;

(b) the plaintiff or applicant has another proceeding for the same relief pending in Ontario or elsewhere;

(c) the defendant or respondent has an order against the plaintiff or applicant for costs in the same or another proceeding that remain unpaid in whole or in part;

(d) the plaintiff or applicant is a corporation or a nominal plaintiff or applicant, and there is good reason to believe that the plaintiff or applicant has insufficient assets in Ontario to pay the costs of the defendant or respondent;

(e) there is good reason to believe that the action or application is frivolous and vexatious and that the plaintiff or applicant has insufficient assets in Ontario to pay the costs of the defendant or respondent; or

(f) a statute entitles the defendant or respondent to security for costs.

4   Can the facts in *Rockwell Developments* be distinguished from the situation that confronted the Ontario Court of Appeal in *642977 Ontario Ltd. v. Fleischer* (2001), 56 O.R. (3d) 417 (C.A.)? In the latter case, a corporation named Sweet Dreams Corporation was involved in litigation with another party. Two individuals named Halasi and Krauss controlled Sweet Dreams. As a condition to obtaining an interim injunction from the trial judge, Sweet Dreams gave an undertaking with respect to costs if the injunction was discharged and its case was unsuccessful. The injunction was discharged and the trial judge held Halasi and Krauss personally liable on Sweet Dreams' undertaking. Halasi and Krauss appealed.

Speaking for the Court, Laskin J.A. reversed the trial judge on Sweet Dreams' liability on the undertaking. However, he also made it clear that had Sweet Dreams been liable on its undertaking the trial judge would have been justified in lifting the corporate veil to hold H and K personally liable. Laskin J.A. reasoned, in part, as follows:

> Typically, the corporate veil is pierced when the company is incorporated for an illegal, fraudulent or improper purpose. But it can also be pierced if when incorporated "those in control expressly direct a wrongful thing to be done": *Clarkson Co. v. Zhelka* at p. 578. Sharpe J. set out a useful statement of the guiding principle in *Transamerica Life Insurance Co. of Canada v. Canada Life Assurance Co.*, 1996 CarswellOnt 1699, 28 O.R. (3d) 423 (Ont. Gen. Div.) at pp. 433-34 [O.R.], affirmed 1997 CarswellOnt 3496, [1997] O.J. No. 3754 (Ont. C.A.): "the courts will disregard the separate legal personality of a corporate entity where it is completely dominated and controlled and being used as a shield for fraudulent or improper conduct."

These authorities indicate that the decision to pierce the corporate veil will depend on the context. They also indicate that the separate legal personality of the corporation cannot be lightly set aside. Yet, however restrictive corporate law principles for piercing the corporate veil may be, in the context of an undertaking to the court, the trial judge's findings support going behind Sweet Dreams and imposing personal liability.

She found that Sweet Dreams had no assets to honour its undertaking, that Halasi and Krauss controlled Sweet Dreams and that when Halasi and Krauss tendered the undertaking for Sweet Dreams they knew it had no assets. All of these findings are reasonably supported by the evidence. Moreover, Halasi was a sophisticated developer and Krauss was a lawyer. They tendered an undertaking to the court, which they knew was worthless, to gain an advantage. When called on to honour the undertaking, they tried to hide behind a shell company, which they controlled, to escape liability. In the words of Sharpe J. in Transamerica Life, Sweet Dreams was "completely dominated and controlled" by Halasi and Krauss, and used by them "as a shield for . . . improper conduct".

5   The *Fleischer* test of "those in control expressly direct a wrongful thing to be done" was explored in the recent Ontario Court of Appeal Case, *Shoppers Drug Mart Inc. v. 6470360 Canada Inc.*, 2014 CarswellOnt 1133, 2014 ONCA 85 (Ont. C.A.), leave to appeal refused 2014 CarswellOnt 8632, 2014 CarswellOnt 8633 (S.C.C.). Michael Wayne Beamish was the sole officer, director and shareholder of 6470360 Canada Inc. (647). His corporation collected utility bills for Shoppers Drug Mart (Shoppers), and periodically sent one remittance summary for the total amount during that period. Shoppers would transfer the amount to 647's clearing account that was in the joint names of Beamish and 647. Some of the funds were misappropriated, and not used to pay Shoppers' utility bills. The court found that 647 was unjustly enriched by the misappropriation. The court stated that since Beamish was the directing mind, the sole shareholder of the company that holds the accounts, and had sole signing authority over the accounts, he expressly directed and caused the wrongful act. Therefore, the corporate veil was pierced, and Beamish was held personally liable.

Walkovsky v. Carlton
223 N.E.2d 6 (N.Y.C.A., 1966)

FULD J.: This case involves what appears to be a rather common practice in the taxicab industry of vesting the ownership of a taxi fleet in many corporations, each owning only one or two cabs.

The complaint alleges that the plaintiff was severely injured four years ago in New York City when he was run down by a taxicab owned by the defendant Seon Cab Corporation and negligently operated at the time by the defendant Marchese. The individual defendant, Carlton, is claimed to be a stockholder of 10 corporations, including Seon, each of which has but two cabs registered in its name, and it is implied that only the minimum automobile liability insurance required by law (in the amount of $10,000) is carried on any one cab. Although seemingly independent of one another, these corporations are alleged to be "operated . . . as a single entity, unit and enterprise" with regard to financing, supplies, repairs, employees and garaging, and all are named as defendants. The plaintiff asserts that he is also entitled to hold their stockholders personally liable for the damages sought because the multiple corporate structure constitutes an unlawful attempt "to defraud members of the general public" who might be injured by the cabs.

The defendant Carlton has moved, pursuant to CPLR 3211(a)7, to dismiss the complaint on the ground that as to him it "fails to state a cause of action". The court at Special Term granted the motion but the Appellate Division, by a divided vote, reversed, holding that a valid cause of action was sufficiently stated. The defendant Carlton appeals to us, from the non-final order, by leave of the Appellate Division on a certified question.

The law permits the incorporation of a business for the very purpose of enabling its proprietors to escape personal liability . . . but, manifestly, the privilege is not without its limits. Broadly speaking, the courts will disregard the corporate form, or, to use accepted terminology, "pierce the corporate veil", whenever necessary "to prevent fraud or to achieve equity" . . . In determining whether liability should be extended to reach assets beyond those belonging to the corporation, we are guided, as Judge Cardozo noted, by "general rules of agency". (*Berkey v. Third Ave. Ry. Co.*) In other words, whenever anyone uses control of the corporation to further his own rather than the corporation's business, he will be liable for the corporation's acts "upon the principle of *respondeat superior* applicable even where the agent is a natural person". . . Such liability, moreover, extends not only to the corporation's commercial dealings . . .

In the Mangan case. . . (*supra*), the plaintiff was injured as a result of the negligent operation of a cab owned and operated by one of four corporations affiliated with the defendant Terminal. Although the defendant was not a stockholder of any of the operating companies, both the defendant and the operating companies were owned, for the most part, by the same parties. The defendant's name (Terminal) was conspicuously displayed on the sides of all of the taxis used in the enterprise and, in point of fact, the defendant actually serviced, inspected, repaired and dispatched them. These facts were deemed to provide sufficient cause for piercing the corporate veil of the operating company — the nominal owner of the cab which injured the plaintiff — and holding the defendant liable. The operating companies were simply instrumentalities for carrying on the business of the defendant without imposing upon it financial and other liabilities incident to the actual ownership and operation of the cabs . . .

In the case before us, the plaintiff has explicitly alleged that none of the corporations "had a separate existence of their own" and, as indicated above, all are named as defendants. However, it is one thing to assert that a corporation is a fragment of a larger corporate combine which actually conducts the business. (See Berle, The Theory of Enterprise Entity, 47 Col.L.Rev. 343, 348–350.) It is quite another to claim that the corporation is a "dummy" for its individual stockholders who are in reality carrying on the business in their personal capacities for purely personal rather than corporate ends. . .Either circumstance would justify treating the corporation as an agent and piercing the corporate veil to reach the principal but a different result would follow in each case. In the first, only a larger *corporate* entity would be held financially responsible . . . while in the other the stockholder would be personally liable . . . Either the stockholder is conducting the business in his individual capacity or he is not. If he is, he will be liable; if he is not, then, it does not matter — insofar as his personal liability is concerned — that the enterprise is actually being carried on by a larger "enterprise entity". (See Berle, "The Theory of Enterprise Entity", 47 Col.L.Rev. 343.)

* * *

The individual defendant is charged with having "organized, managed, dominated and controlled" a fragmented corporate entity but there are no allegations that he was conducting business in his individual capacity. Had the taxicab fleet been owned by a single corporation, it would be readily apparent that the plaintiff would face formidable barriers in attempting to establish personal liability on the part of the corporation's stockholders. The fact that the fleet ownership has been deliberately split up among many corporations does not case the plaintiff's burden in that respect. The corporate form may not be disregarded merely because the assets of the corporation, together with the mandatory insurance coverage of the vehicle which struck the plaintiff, are insufficient to assure him the recovery sought. If Carlton were to be held individually liable on those facts alone, the decision would apply equally to the thousands of cabs which are owned by their individual drivers who conduct their businesses through corporations organized pursuant to s. 401 of the Business Corporation Law, Consol. Laws, c. 4 and carry the minimum insurance required by subdivision 1 (par. [a]) of s. 370 of the Vehicle and Traffic law, Consol. Laws, c. 71. These taxi owner-operators are entitled to form such corporations . . . and we agree with the court at Special Term that, if the insurance coverage required by statute "is inadequate for the protection of the public, the remedy lies not with the courts but with the Legislature." It may very well be sound policy to require that certain corporations must take out liability insurance which will afford adequate compensation to their potential tort victims. However, the responsibility for imposing conditions on the privilege of incorporation has been committed by the Constitution to the Legislature (N.Y. Const. art. X, §1) and it may not be fairly implied, from any statute, that the Legislature intended, without the slightest discussion or debate, to require of taxi corporations that they carry automobile liability insurance over and above that mandated by the Vehicle and Traffic Law.

This is not to say that it is impossible for the plaintiff to state a valid cause of action against the defendant Carlton. However, the simple fact is that the plaintiff has just not done so here. While the complaint alleges that the separate corporations were undercapitalized and that their assets have been intermingled, it is barren of any "sufficiently particularized statements" . . . that the defendant Carlton and his associates are actually doing business in their individual capacities, shuttling their personal funds in and out of the corporations "without regard to formality and to suit their immediate convenience" . . . Such a "perversion of the privilege to do business in a corporate form" . . . would justify imposing personal liability on the individual stock-holders . . . Nothing of the sort has in fact been charged, and it cannot reasonably or logically be inferred from the happenstance that the business of Seon Cab Corporation may actually be carried on by a larger corporate entity composed of many corporations which, under general principles of agency, would be liable to each other's creditors in contract and in tort.

In point of fact, the principle relied upon in the complaint to sustain the imposition of personal liability is not agency but fraud. Such a cause of action cannot withstand analysis. If it is not fraudulent for the owner-operator of a single cab corporation to take out only the minimum required liability insurance, the enterprise does not become either illicit or fraudulent merely because it consists of many such corporations. The plaintiff's injuries are the same regardless of whether the cab which strikes him is owned by a single corporation or part of a fleet with ownership fragmented among many corporations. Whatever rights he may be able to assert against parties other than the registered owner of the vehicle come into being not because he has been defrauded but because, under the principle of *respondeat superior*, he is entitled to hold the whole enterprise responsible for the acts of its agents.

In sum, then, the complaint falls short of adequately stating a cause of action against the defendant Carlton in his individual capacity . . .

* * *

KEATING J. (dissenting): The defendant Carlton, the shareholder here sought to be held for the negligence of the driver of a taxicab, was a principal shareholder and organizer of the defendant corporation which owned the taxicab. The corporation was one of 10 organized by the defendant, each containing two cabs and each cab having the "minimum liability" insurance coverage mandated by s. 370 of the Vehicle and Traffic Law. The sole assets of these operating corporations are vehicles themselves and they are apparently subject to mortgages.

From their inception these corporations were intentionally undercapitalized for the purpose of avoiding responsibility for acts which were bound to arise as a result of the operation of a large taxi fleet having cars out on the street 24 hours a day and engaged in public transportation. And during the course of the corporations' existence all income was continually drained out of the corporations for the same purpose.

The issue preceded by this action is whether the policy of this State, which affords those desiring to engage in a business enterprise the privilege of limited liability through the use of the corporate device, is so strong that it will permit that privilege to continue no matter how much it is abused, no matter how irresponsibly the corporation is operated, no matter what the cost to the public. I do not believe that it is.

Under the circumstances of this case the shareholders should all be held individually liable to this plaintiff for the injuries he suffered . . . At least the matter should not be disposed of on the pleadings by a dismissal of the complaint. "If a corporation is organized and carries on business without substantial capital in such a way that the corporation is likely to have no sufficient assets available to meet its debts, it is inequitable that shareholders should set up such a flimsy organization to escape personal liability. The attempt to do corporate business without providing any sufficient basis of financial responsibility to creditors is an abuse of the separate entity and will be ineffectual to exempt the shareholders from corporate debts. It is coming to be recognized as the policy of law that shareholders should in good faith put at the risk of the business unencumbered capital reasonably adequate for its prospective liabilities. If capital is illusory or trifling compared with the business to be done and risks of loss, this is a ground for denying the separate entity privilege." (Ballantine, *Corporations* [rev. ed., 1946] §129, pp. 302-303.)

In *Minton v. Cavaney* . . . the Supreme Court of California had occasion to discuss this problem in a negligence case. The corporation of which the defendant was an organizer, director and officer operated a public swimming pool. One afternoon the plaintiffs' daughter drowned in the pool as a result of the alleged negligence of the corporation.

Justice Roger Traynor, speaking for the court, outlined the applicable law in this area. "The figurative terminology 'alter ego' and 'disregard of the corporate entity,'" he wrote, "is generally used to refer to the various situations that are an abuse of the corporate privilege . . . The equitable owners of a corporation, for example, are personally liable when they treat the assets of the corporation as their own and add or withdraw capital from the corporation at will . . . when they hold themselves out as being personally liable for the debts of the corporation . . . or *when they provide inadequate capitalization and actively participate in the conduct of corporate affairs*". . . (italics supplied).

Examining the facts of the case in light of the legal principles just enumerated, he found that "[it was] undisputed that there was no attempt to provide adequate capitalization. [The corporation] never had any substantial assets. It leased the pool that it operated, and the lease was forfeited for failure to pay the rent. Its capital was 'trifling compared with the business to be done and the risks of loss'" . . .

It seems obvious that one of "the risks of loss" referred to was the possibility of drownings due to the negligence of the corporation. And the defendant's failure to provide such assets or any fund for recovery resulted in his being held personally liable.

In *Anderson v. Abbott*, the defendant shareholders had organized a holding company and transferred to that company shares which they held in various national banks in return for shares in the holding company. The holding company did not have sufficient assets to meet the double liability requirements of the governing Federal statutes which provided that the owners of shares in national banks were personally liable for corporate obligations "to the extent of the amount of their stock therein, at the par value thereof, in addition to the amount invested in such shares" (U.S. Code, tit. 12, former §63).

The court had found that these transfers were made in good faith, that other defendant shareholders who had purchased shares in the holding company had done so in good faith and that the organization of such a holding company was entirely legal. Despite this finding, the Supreme Court, speaking through Mr. Justice Douglas, pierced the corporate veil of the holding company and held all the shareholders, even those who had no part in the organization of the corporation, individually responsible for the corporate obligations as mandated by the statute . . .".

The policy of this State has always been to provide and facilitate recovery for those injured through the negligence of others. The automobile, by its very nature, is capable of causing severe and costly injuries when not operated in a proper manner. The great increase in the number of automobile accidents combined with the frequent financial irresponsibility of the individual driving the car led to the adoption of s. 388 of the Vehicle and Traffic Law which had the effect of imposing upon the owner of the vehicle the responsibility for its negligent operation. It is upon this very statute that the cause of action against both the corporation and the individual defendants is predicated.

In addition the Legislature, still concerned with the financial irresponsibility of those who owned and operated motor vehicles, enacted a statute requiring minimum liability coverage for all owners of automobiles. The important public policy represented by both these statutes is outlined in s. 310 of the Vehicle and Traffic Law. That section provides that:

> The legislature is concerned over the rising toll of motor vehicle accidents and the suffering and loss thereby inflicted. The legislature determines that it is a matter of grave concern that motorists shall be financially able to respond in damages for their negligent acts, so

that innocent victims of motor vehicle accidents may be recompensed for the injury and financial loss inflicted upon them.

The defendant Carlton claims that, because the minimum amount of insurance required by the statute was obtained, the corporate veil cannot and should not be pierced despite the fact that the assets of the corporation which owned the cab were "trifling compared with the business to be done and the risks of loss" which were certain to be encountered. I do not agree.

The Legislature in requiring minimum liability insurance of $10,000, no doubt, intended to provide at least some small fund for recovery against those individuals and corporations who just did not have and were not able to raise or accumulate assets sufficient to satisfy the claims of those who were injured as a result of their negligence. It certainly could not have intended to shield those individuals who organized corporations, with the specific intent of avoiding responsibility to the public, where the operation of the corporate enterprise yielded profits sufficient to purchase additional insurance. Moreover, it is reasonable to assume that the Legislature believed that those individuals and corporations having substantial assets would take out insurance far in excess of the minimum in order to protect those assets from depletion. Given the costs of hospital care and treatment and the nature of injuries sustained in auto collisions, it would be unreasonable to assume that the Legislature believed that the minimum provided in the statute would in and of itself be sufficient to recompense "innocent victims of motor vehicle accidents . . . for the injury and financial loss inflicted upon them".

* * *

The defendant contends that a decision holding him personally liable would discourage people from engaging in corporate enterprise.

What I would merely hold is that a participating shareholder of a corporation vested with a public interest, organized with capital insufficient to meet liabilities which are certain to arise in the ordinary course of the corporation's business, may be held personally responsible for such liabilities. Where corporate income is not sufficient to cover the cost of insurance premiums above the statutory minimum or where initially adequate finances dwindle under the pressure of competition, bad times or extraordinary and unexpected liability, obviously the shareholder will not be held liable (Henn, *Corporations*, p. 208, n. 7).

The only types of corporate enterprises that will be discouraged as a result of a decision allowing the individual shareholder to be sued will be those such as the one in question, designed solely to abuse the corporate privilege at the expense of the public interest . . .

[Desmond C.J. and Van Voorhis, Burke and Scileppi JJ. concurred with Fuld J. Bergan J. concurred with Keating J.]

Note Re Adams v. Cape Industries
[1990] 1 Ch. 433 (Eng. C.A.)

In this leading modern English case, the Court of Appeal unambiguously reaffirmed the legitimacy of a parent company establishing subsidiaries even if its purpose in doing so is to shield the parent company from tort liability. The defendant Cape Industries, an English company, presided over a group of subsidiary companies that mined asbestos in South Africa and marketed it in various countries and subdivisions thereof, including Texas in the US. Employees of a Texas company using the asbestos products claimed to have been injured by them and brought a class action against the subsidiaries and Cape Industries. Cape did not defend the action and default judgment was entered against it in Texas. Cape did not carry on business and had no office in Texas when the action was instituted against it.

The plaintiffs sought to enforce the Texas judgment in England. Under English conflict of laws rule, a foreign judgment is only enforceable in England if the defendant has either submitted to the jurisdiction of the foreign court or was present in the foreign jurisdiction when the action was instituted. Since Cape had not submitted to the Texas jurisdiction and had no office in Texas at any material time, the plaintiffs had to persuade the Court of Appeal either that the subsidiaries were only a façade or that it was appropriate to lift the corporate veil between Cape and its subsidiaries in order to do justice between the parties. Scott J., at trial, and the Court of Appeal on appeal were satisfied that the subsidiary involved in the distribution of the asbestos in Texas (and inferentially elsewhere in the US) had a genuine existence and emphatically rejected the notion that English law permits the corporate veil to be lifted among members of a group of companies even where the plaintiff is an involuntary creditor. The Court of Appeal said:

> We do not accept as a matter of law that the court is entitled to lift the corporate veil as against a defendant company which is the member of a corporate group merely because the corporate structure has been used so as to ensure that the legal liability (if any) in respect of particular future activities of the group (and correspondingly the risk of enforcement of that liability) will fall on another member of the group rather than the defendant company. Whether or not this is desirable, the right to use a corporate structure in this manner is inherent in our corporate law. Mr. Morison urged on us that the purpose of the operation was in substance that Cape would have the practical benefit of the group's asbestos trade in the United States of America without the risks of tortious liability. This may be so. However, in our judgment, Cape was in law entitled to organise the group's affairs in that manner and . . . to expect that the court would apply the principle of *Salomon v. A. Salomon & Co. Ltd.* [1897] A.C. 22 in the ordinary way.

Note Re Prest v. Petrodel Resources Ltd.
[2013] U.K.S.C. 34

In recent decisions, the United Kingdom Supreme Court has adopted a similarly cautious approach to piercing the corporate veil. For example, in *Prest,* Lord Sumpton observed that the "separate personality and property of a company is [though] a fiction . . . the whole foundation of English company and insolvency law." Nevertheless, he continued, there is a common law jurisdiction to pierce the corporate veil where "legal personality is being abused for the purpose of some relevant wrongdoing." Specifically, "if there is a legal right against the person in control of [the company] which exists independently of the company's involvement, and a company is interposed so that the separate legal personality of the company will defeat the right or frustrate its enforcement," the veil may be pierced. For further discussion, see Thomas G. Heintzman and Brandon Kain, "Through the Looking Glass: Recent Developments in Piercing the Corporate Veil" (2013), 28 B.F.L.R. 525.

Note Re Shareholder Liability for Corporate Torts: The Hansmann-Kraakman Proposal

Dissatisfaction with the limited liability shield and its impact on tort victims has encouraged commentators to search for solutions. We saw earlier (*supra*, this chapter) the solution offered by Halpern *et al.* A more recent proposal, which has provoked much discussion, is one by Professors Hansmann and Kraakman ("Toward unlimited shareholder liability for corporate tort" (1991), 100 Yale L.J. 1879) involving the imposition of *pro rata* liability on shareholders rather than full individual liability for the torts of their corporation. The authors reason that the threat of even *pro rata* liability will give the market an incentive to monitor a corporation's risky activities and impound the risk in the reduced price of the shares without significantly impairing the functioning of securities markets.

(iii)   Statutory Construction Outside Commercial/Torts Context

Lee v. Lee's Air Farming Ltd.
[1961] A.C. 12 (P.C.)

[The appellant's husband formed the respondent company for the purpose of carrying on the business of aerial top dressing. He held all the issued shares of the company with the exception of one. He was appointed governing director of the company for life and, pursuant to the company's articles of association, was appointed chief pilot of the company at a salary arranged by him. Article 33 also provided that in respect of such employment the relationship of master and servant should exist between him and the company.

The husband was killed while piloting the company's aircraft in the course of aerial top dressing. His widow, the appellant, claimed compensation under the New Zealand *Workmen's Compensation Act*, 1922. On a case stated for its opinion on a question of law, the New Zealand Court of Appeal held that since the deceased was the governing director in whom was vested the full government and control of the company, he could not also be a servant of the company. The widow appealed.]

LORD MORRIS: . . .The substantial question which arises is, as their Lordships think, whether the deceased was a "worker" within the meaning of the *Workers' Compensation Act*, 1922, and its amendments. Was he a person who had entered into or worked under a contract of service with an employer? The Court of Appeal thought that his special position as governing director precluded him from being a servant of the company. On this view it is difficult to know what his status and position was when he was performing the arduous and skilful duties of piloting an aeroplane which belonged to the company and when he was carrying out the operation of top-dressing farm lands from the air. He was paid wages for so doing. The company kept a wages book in which these were recorded. The work that was being done was being done at the request of farmers whose contractual rights and obligations were with the company alone. It cannot be suggested that when engaged in the activities above referred to the deceased was discharging his duties as governing director. Their Lordships find it impossible to resist the conclusion that the active aerial operations were performed because the deceased was in some contractual relationship with the company. That relationship came about because the deceased as one legal person was willing to work for and to make a contract with the company which was another legal entity. A contractual relationship could only exist on the basis that there was consensus between two contracting parties. It was never suggested (nor in their Lordships' view could it reasonably have been suggested) that the company was a sham or a mere simulacrum. It is well established that the mere fact that someone is a director of a company is no impediment to his entering into a contract to serve the company. If, then, it be accepted that the respondent company was a legal entity their Lordships see no reason to challenge the validity of any contractual obligations which were created between the company and the deceased . . .

Nor in their Lordships' view were any contractual obligations invalidated by the circumstance that the deceased was sole governing director in whom was vested the full government and control of the company. Always assuming that the company was not a sham then the capacity of the company to make a contract with the deceased could not be impugned merely because the deceased was the agent of the company in its negotiation. The deceased might have made a firm contract to serve the company for a fixed period of years. If within such period he had retired from the office of governing director and other directors had been appointed his contract would not have been affected. The circumstance that in his capacity as a shareholder he could control the course of events would not in itself affect the validity of his contractual relationship with the company. When, therefore, it is said that "one of his first acts was to appoint himself the only pilot of the company," it must be recognised that the appointment was made by the company, and that it was none the less a valid appointment because it was the deceased himself who acted as the agent of the company in arranging it. In their Lordships' view it is a logical consequence of the decision in *Salomon's* case that one person may function in dual capacities. There is no reason, therefore, to deny the possibility of a contractual relationship being created as between the deceased and the company. If this stage is reached then their Lordships see no reason why the range of possible contractual relationships should not include a contract for services, and if the deceased as agent for the company could negotiate a contract for services as between the company and himself there is no reason why a contract of service could not also be negotiated. It is said that therein lies the difficulty, because it is said that the deceased could not both be under the duty of giving orders and also be under the duty of obeying them. But this approach does not give effect to the circumstance that it would be the company and not the deceased that would be giving the orders. Control would remain with the company whoever might be the agent of the company to exercise it. The fact that so long as the deceased continued to be governing director, with amplitude of powers, it would be for him to act as the agent of the company to give the orders does not alter the fact that the company and the deceased were two separate and distinct legal persons. If the deceased had a contract of service with the company then the company had a right of control. The manner of its exercise would not affect or diminish the right to its exercise. But the existence of a right to control cannot be denied if once the reality of the legal existence of the company is recognised. Just as the company and the deceased were separate legal entities so as to permit of contractual relations being established between them, so also were they separate legal entities so as to enable the company to give an order to the deceased. . .

Appeal allowed.

Notes and Questions

In *Buchan and Ivey v. Secretary of State for Employment*, [1997] IRLR 80, a U.K. administrative tribunal held that an "employee" was not entitled to unemployment insurance when his corporate employer went into receivership and laid him off, because he was also the majority stockholder and sole director of the corporation. Is this result inconsistent with *Lee* or can the cases be distinguished? If the two results are inconsistent, which is more defensible?

De Salaberry Realties Ltd. v. Minister of National Revenue
(1974), 46 D.L.R. (3d) 100, 74 D.T.C. 6235, 1974 CarswellNat 166
(Fed. T.D.)

DECARY J.: The appeal is from income tax assessments for the years 1963, 1964, and 1965, confirmed by a judgment of the Tax Appeal Board on September 3, 1970, and pertaining to the profit realized by the appellant in selling land alleged to be purchased only for shopping center purposes.

At the opening of the hearing the Court refused to permit that the transcript of evidence before the Tax Appeal Board be put as exhibit on the ground that the appeal is a trial *de novo* and that such a way of proceeding would prevent the Court from questioning the witnesses and judging their credibility. The Court requested counsel to establish the chain of authority for the final policy and decision-making for the two ultimate beneficial owners, the Bronfman and the Steinberg families . . .

The evidence discloses that, during the pertinent years, the way of proceeding for each group, was to cause to have a company incorporated per one or few purchases. It would be naive to believe that the multiplicity of companies ensuing was wanted for business reasons and not for tax reasons. Indeed each company sells one or a few parcels of land whereas the group sells many.

The Court cannot confine itself, for passing judgment on the course of conduct, to the one of the appellant but must resort to the one of the groups. I do not conceive a medical doctor having to make a diagnosis on the general state of health of a patient that would examine only his right arm. Complete examination is required for the medical doctor and so is it needed in the present instance: the appellant is a member of the body of the Bronfmans and of the Steinbergs.

Considering that finding, the rule of *Salomon v. A. Salomon & Co. Ltd.*, [1897] A.C. 22 (H.L.), cannot be invoked for refraining the Court from passing judgment on the course of conduct of the groups of the sister companies and of the parent companies of the appellant.

The Steinberg group had a case in this Court that was decided by my learned brother Heald J., where the facts were, in substance, similar to those of the present case inasmuch as the finding of law was concerned. That case is the one of *Wilderton Shopping Centre Inc. v. M.N.R.*, [1972] C.T.C. 319, [1972] D.T.C. 6277, which is on appeal to the Appeal Division of this Court. In view of the fact that I consider the course of conduct of the group rather than the one of the appellant I do not consider that I should wait for the judgment of the Appellate Division. I agree with the result of the judgment of my learned brother Heald.

It is in evidence that Cemps Investments Ltd. is owned and controlled by trusts settled by the Bronfman family and that Steinberg's Ltd. is owned and controlled by the Steinberg family.

As to the Bronfman family, the Cemps Investments Ltd. owns all the shares of Cemps Holdings Ltd., now the Fairview Corporation of Canada Limited. The business of Cemps Holdings Ltd. is, *inter alia*, to manage the dealing in land of its wholly owned or partly owned subsidiaries which are subsidiaries or grandchildren corporations of Cemps Investments Ltd. The sub-subsidiaries are the legal owners of land at the times relevant to this appeal.

As to the Steinberg family, Steinberg's Limited owns all the shares of Ivanhoe Corporation. The business of Ivanhoe Corporation is the same as the one of Cemps Holdings Ltd., it owns shares of subsidiaries that are legal owners of land at the times relevant to this appeal.

After a careful study of the market possibility and the population growth, Cemps Holdings Ltd. or Ivanhoe Corporation causes a company to be incorporated to purchase a parcel of land. No attention is given to the matter of zoning before purchasing because it is assumed that any difficulty in that respect can be overcome.

Plans are prepared that are in fact pre-plans, costing $3,000 to $5,000, whereas definite plans, blues, would cost close to $50,000. These facts are in evidence. The officers and directors of each of these sub-subsidiaries, sister companies, are the same persons; the objects of the companies are similar; they are managed by their parent company which in turn, on a general policy level, is governed by their grandparent company. The structure is the same in the Bronfman and in the Steinberg group.

Though there may be only one or two purchases, the area being large, too big for the needs, there are many sales made by the sub-subsidiaries, sister companies of the appellant; in fact, it is in evidence that the two parent companies, Cemps Holdings Ltd. and Ivanhoe Corporation are often approached by people wanting to buy land though no advertisement is made by them. I deduce that it has to be known that their subsidiaries have excess land and that they are willing to sell. Notice should be taken that it is not the sub-subsidiaries that are approached but the subsidiaries, Cemps Holdings Ltd. and Ivanhoe Corporation. That indicates that the centre of policy and decision-making is not at the level of the sub-subsidiaries but closer to the grandparent companies, Cemps Investments Ltd. and Steinberg's Ltd. The directors of Cemps Holdings Ltd. and Ivanhoe Corporation are nominees of their parent company and therefore under their influence.

By purchasing, even if forced to, more land than reasonably required, it is evident that the appellant, like the group, has the intention to sell the excess which is of no other use. It is inventory for the appellant. The appellant is an instrument of his parent company and its grandparent company in purchasing and selling land.

I do regard the appellant as a legal entity distinct from the other companies of each group but I look at each group to find out the course of conduct which stamps the one of the appellant, an instrument of the group.

That the appellant is an instrument of the group is revealed by its thin capitalization: $1,000 divided in 100 shares of a par value of $10 each. With such a thin capitalization the appellant made two purchases amounting to nearly two millions. Funds had to be obtained from the two groups. That is a strong clue that the appellant is nothing but an instrument of its grandparent companies of the two families, but a liability of such an amount warrants a certainty of available funds from the groups.

The little, if any, attention paid to zoning and the assumption that any difficulty in that regard could be overcome, have been proven wrong in the present case for the two purchases of the appellant. In my opinion, such carelessness about zoning indicates strongly that the main objective is to acquire land that can always be disposed of if the plans are frustrated. To me, that and the thin capitalization are the birth of a sham or of a docile instrument. Primarily there is a slight desire of building a shopping centre and secondarily there is an intention to sell land. Such a way of doing, in my opinion, is not serious and is prompted only for possible tax advantages. To grasp the magnitude of the Bronfman and the Steinberg groups, I think it is required to know of the corporations of each group.

In the Bronfman group, there are the trusts owning all the shares of Cemps Investments Limited and that company owns all the shares of Cemps Holding Limited at times relevant to this appeal, now the Fairview Corporation of Canada Limited, and Cemps Holdings Limited owned 50% of the shares of the appellant at the time of purchase and sale of land by the appellant.

The Fairview Corporation of Canada Limited owns all the shares of the Fairview Corporation Limited which, in turn owns all the shares in two other companies; 51% of the shares of one company; 50% of the shares of five companies; 33-1/3% to 30.1% of the shares of three companies. There were 13 companies in the Bronfman group in 1972 after many subsidiaries were amalgamated during the years 1967 to 1969. There were about 10 companies so amalgamated. At the times relevant to this case the total of the companies in the Bronfman group was over 10 companies.

In the Steinberg group, the family owns all the shares of Steinberg's Limited which in turn owns all the shares of Ivanhoe Corporation. The latter company in turn owned all or a substantial part of the shares of 18 companies in the Montreal district.

In the Bronfman group, we have a great-grandparent corporation, a grandparent corporation, a parent corporation and two wholly owned sub-subsidiary corporations and eight companies where the interest of the parent corporation, Ivanhoe, is 50% or more. In the Steinberg group, there are the grandparent corporation, the parent corporation and 18 companies wholly or partially owned by the parent company.

It is my opinion that such pyramiding of corporations, in each group, demonstrates the extent of the need not to restrict the scrutiny of the course of conduct to the one of the appellant which is only an instrument in the hands of the groups.

In each group the directors of the subsidiaries, of the sub-subsidiaries and of the sub-sub-subsidiaries are nominees of the great-grandparent or grandparent corporation from where emanates the general policy-making and decision-taking of the group.

The Court takes note that the sister companies, those in each group of the same level as the appellant, do not deal with each other but deal only with their respective parent company, that is, Cemps Holdings Ltd. for those of the Bronfman group and Ivanhoe Corporation for those of the Steinberg group. Each of these sister companies has the same general objects and their business is essentially similar. Each one buys and sells land. If one is isolated from its sister companies there are only one or two purchases and a few more sales. When they are reunited, then their dealings are impressive and indicate that their business includes buying and selling in the ordinary course of events.

Furthermore, these sister companies are all instruments of their parent companies, Cemps Holdings Ltd. and Ivanhoe Corporation, which have caused them to be incorporated; have determined their thin capitalization; have made the market and population growth surveys; have seen that pre-plans of architects be drafted that could be used for any supermarket: the said pre-plans cost at most $5,000 whereas blues would cost $50,000; have been approached by people wanting to buy land owned by the appellant and its sister companies; have authorized the sale of land of the appellant and its sister companies; have dictated the course of conduct of the sister companies; have received and have obeyed the policy-making and the decision-taking of Cemps Investments Ltd. or Steinberg's Limited, their parent company, and grandparent or great-grandparent of the sister companies.

In such a pattern there is no room for any free will on the part of the appellant and its sister companies; they are, directly, instruments of their parent corporation and, indirectly, of their grandparent or great-grandparent corporation.

In view of these facts the course of conduct of the appellant must not be viewed in an isolated way but in taking into account the activities of its group. In such a light there is no doubt that the course of conduct of the appellant is the one of trader in land, and even in isolating the appellant, which should not be done, the course of conduct, then, is also that of a trader in land.

I have perused the activities of both groups to ascertain their course of conduct and also to ascertain the course of conduct of one of their instruments, the appellant.

I have disregarded the entity of the appellant in having recourse to the activities of both groups in order to judge the course of conduct of the appellant. There are precedents and authors that justify my collecting of the evidence.

In Palmer and Prentice, *Cases and Materials on Company Law (1969)*, we find these remarks at p. 49:

An attempt was made to specify the criteria which, if satisfied, would indicate that a subsidiary company was carrying on the business of the parent company by Avory J. [sic] in *Smith, Stone and Knight Ltd. v. Birmingham Corporation*, [1939] 4 All E.R. 116, noted (1939), 3 Mod. L. Rev. 226:

Were the profits treated as profits of the company? — When I say "the company" I mean the parent company — secondly, were the persons conducting the business appointed by the parent company? Thirdly, was the company the head and brain of the trading venture? Fourthly, did the company govern the adventure, decide what should be done and what capital should be embarked on the venture? Fifthly, did the company make the profits by its skill and direction? Sixthly, was the company in effectual and constant control?

Applying these criteria it can be said that the profits were treated as profits of the parent company: a prospectus for the issue of shares in the Ivanhoe company reveals that fact; the appointments of the persons conducting the business of the appellant were made by the two parent companies and are the same people and they also act in the parent company; the parent company is the head and brain of the trading venture; the policy is established by the parent company; the capital to be brought in the venture was decided by the parent company, whether or not, once and for all, or in each instance, and that makes no difference; it is by the skilled direction of the parent company that the profit was made; the parent company is in effectual and constant control of the appellant or the said officers of both companies are the same people paid by the parent.

Ibid., on the same page, we read:

In a similar vein the decision *City of Toronto v. Famous Players Canadian Corporation Ltd.*, [1935] 3 D.L.R. 685, [1935] 3 D.L.R. 327 (C.A.), established that the business of one company can embrace the apparent or normal business of another where it can be said "that the second company is in fact the puppet of the first; when the directing mind and will of the former reaches into and through the corporate facade of the latter and becomes, itself, the manifesting agency. In such a case it is not accurate to describe the business as being carried on by the puppet for the benefit of the dominant company. The business is in fact that of the latter.

In the present instance, the appellant is the puppet of the two parent companies, it being owned 50-50; the mind and will of the parent companies reach through the facade of the appellant. The parent companies carry [on], in fact, the business of the appellant.

* * *

The business of the appellant is not apparent unless recourse is to be had to the group to ascertain the overall course of conduct, otherwise only a part of the course of conduct is apparent, the appellant being a shield; the appellant, being a subsidiary, has to be reckoned with as to the ownership of the land but its conduct must be ascertained by the course of conduct of the whole group; the appellant's parent companies are in fact in an intimate and immediate domination of the appellant which has no independent functioning of its own.

* * *

In Gower, *Principles of Modern Company Law*, 3rd ed. (1969), we read at pp. 194-5 as to holding and subsidiary companies:

The most striking limitation imposed by the Companies Acts on the recognition of the separate personality of each individual company is, however, in connection with associated companies within the same group enterprise. As we have seen, it has become a habit to create a pyramid of inter-related companies, each of which is theoretically a separate entity but in reality part of one concern represented by the group as a whole.

In the present case we have a pyramid of corporations and the appellant is part of the group of companies.

Ibid., at p. 200, we read:

It may therefore be said that not only has the veil been lifted in the interests of the Revenue but further steps have been taken in the interests of members towards recognizing "enterprise entity" rather than corporate entity.

As to group enterprises, which is the case we are concerned with we read, *ibid.*, at p. 213:

Consideration of the cases in which the courts have treated a company as the agent of its controlling shareholder suggests that they are more ready to do so where the shares are held by another company. In other words, they are coming to recognize the essential unity of a group enterprise rather than the separate legal entity of each company within the group.

There is, in the present case, an essential unity of group enterprise which, for purposes of evidence of course of conduct, I recognize rather than the course of conduct of the separate legal entity of the appellant.

[Decary J. proceeded to consider American doctrine, and concluded]:

Upon the evidence adduced, I find that the appellant, being a member of a horizontal group of sister companies incorporated for the same object and a member of a vertical group, there being a parent and a grandparent company for the Bronfman family and for the Steinberg family, must have its course of conduct determined by the one of its sister companies, its parent companies and its grandparent company because the appellant is only an instrument in the carrying on of the business of its parent companies and of its grandparent company, whose business of the parent and grand-parent companies include, *inter alia*, directly or indirectly, the real estate one, under many forms and shapes, and the course of conduct of the appellant is hereby determinated to be the one of a trader in land as a member of the horizontal business group and of the vertical business group of the member-companies, and the membership not being, in fact, for business reason as shown, *inter alia*, by the thin capitalization of the appellant and its dominance by its parent companies, consequently the profit realized in 1963, 1964 and 1965 on the sale of parcels of land is one made in the turning into account of inventory and is income of the appellant under the provisions of ss. 3 and 4 of the *Income Tax Act*.

Appeal dismissed.

[Decary J.'s judgment was affirmed on appeal to the Federal Court of Appeal (1976), 70 D.L.R. (3d) 706.]

Notes

1   In *Jodery Estate v. Nova Scotia (Minister of Finance)*, [1980] 2 S.C.R. 774, 1980 CarswellNS 78, 1980 CarswellNS 82, the issue was whether 12 grandchildren, the beneficiaries under the will of Roy A. Jodrey, were liable to pay succession duties under the Nova Scotia *Succession Duties Act*. The deceased who, prior to his death, was resident and domiciled in Nova Scotia, had sought to avoid the impact of the Act by incorporating three companies under Alberta law. (1) The JBH company was the parent company and issued each of the grand-children 100 shares at $1 per share paid by the grandchildren; (2) JCG was a subsidiary company and issued 100 common shares, all of which were beneficially owned by the parent company; (3) WRI was the third company but was not related to the first two companies. It issued two common shares, both of which were owned by the deceased. The deceased transferred to WRI his shares in a Nova Scotia investment company in exchange for a promissory note for $3,735,200. He also added a codicil to his will revoking an earlier bequest to his grandchildren and substituting a bequest to the subsidiary company including the note of WRI.

A majority of the Supreme Court of Canada (Martland, Pigeon, Beetz, and Chouinard JJ.), affirming the decision of the Nova Scotia Court of Appeal, held that the grandchildren were "beneficially entitled" to the deceased's estate and therefore subject to succession duties. Martland J., referring to the relationship between the parent company and its subsidiary, said:

> Both companies were incorporated on the same day in the same office by the same lawyers. Neither the parent company nor the subsidiary company engaged in any business activity between their dates of incorporation and the date of Mr. Jodrey's death. Neither of them had any creditors. Both of them had the same directors. Both had the same officers.

> This is eminently a case in which the court should examine the realities of the situation and conclude that the subsidiary company was bound hand and foot to the parent company and had to do whatever its parent said. It was a mere conduit pipe linking the parent company to the estate.

Dickson J., supported by Ritchie and McIntyre JJ., dissented vigorously and reaffirmed his confidence in the fundamental soundness of the *Salomon* principle:

> There is a tendency to think loosely in terms of a parent owning the assets of its wholly owned subsidiary but that is not so in law. No one would suggest that a person owning 100 shares of Canadian Pacific is the owner of, or has a beneficial interest in, the assets of Canadian Pacific. No distinction can be made in principle between ownership of 100 shares in a major corporation and ownership of all of the issued shares in a small company. In neither case does the shareholder own any asset other than shares. And the situation is unaffected by the fact that one or more shareholders may have voting control and thereby be in a position to acquire the assets or a portion thereof on wind-up, or upon a distribution of assets other than on wind-up. If shareholders are beneficially entitled to the property of a corporation in which they hold shares, then s. 2(5) would not have been necessary.

> It is fundamental that a company as a body corporate is in contemplation of law an entity separate and distinct from shareholders who compose it. The principle of *Salomon v. Salomon & Co. Ltd.*, *supra*, is still very much part of our law and in general the courts have rigidly applied it.

2. In *Stubart Investments Ltd. v. R.*, [1984] 1 S.C.R. 536, 1984 CarswellNat 222, 1984 CarswellNat 690, the question was whether a corporate affiliate, established solely for tax planning purposes, should be ignored on the ground that the new corporate structure

served no *bona fide* business purpose. The business purpose test was
adopted in the US as far back as 1934 (see *Gregory v. Helvering*, 293
U.S. 465 (S.C., 1935)) and is an established doctrine of US tax law. It
was belatedly embraced by the House of Lords in *W.T. Ramsay Ltd.
v. Inland Revenue Commissioners*, [1981] 2 W.L.R. 449 (U.K. H.L.).
In *Stubart*, the Supreme Court was urged to follow suit. The Supreme
Court refused to do so on the grounds that a taxpayer's right to
organize its affairs was deeply entrenched in Canadian law and
implicitly recognized in the *Income Tax Act*, and that adoption of the
business purpose test would create too much uncertainty.

Dole Food Co. et al. v. Patrickson et al.
(2003), 123 S. Ct. 1655 (U.S.)

[The plaintiffs (Patrickson and others) filed a state-court action against
Dole Food Company and others, alleging injury from chemical exposure.
Dole joined ("impleaded") the Dead Sea Bromine Co. and Bromine
Compounds Ltd. (the "Dead Sea Companies") as defendants. The latter
two companies argued that they were entitled to have the case transferred
("removed") to federal court, on the ground that they were
"instrumentalities of a foreign state" (Israel) within the meaning of the
Foreign Sovereign Immunities Act of 1976. The Ninth Circuit Court of
Appeals disagreed. The Dead Sea Companies appealed to the Supreme
Court of the United States.]

Justice KENNEDY delivered the opinion of the Court.

II

A

Title 28 U.S.C. § 1441(d) governs removal of actions against foreign
states. It provides that "[a]ny civil action brought in a State court against
a foreign state as defined in [28 U.S.C. § 1603(a)] may be removed by the
foreign state to the district court of the United States for the district and
division embracing the place where such action is pending." See also 28
U.S.C. § 1330 (governing original jurisdiction). Section 1603(a), part of
the FSIA, defines "foreign state" to include an "agency or
instrumentality of a foreign state." "[A]gency or instrumentality of a
foreign state" is defined, in turn, as:

"[A]ny entity—

"(1) which is a separate legal person, corporate or otherwise, and

"(2) which is an organ of a foreign state or political subdivision
thereof, or a majority of whose shares or other ownership interest is
owned by a foreign state or political subdivision thereof, and

"(3) which is neither a citizen of a State of the United States . . . nor created under the laws of any third country." § 1603(b).

B

The Court of Appeals resolved the question of the FSIA's applicability by holding that a subsidiary of an instrumentality is not itself entitled to instrumentality status. Its holding was correct.

The State of Israel did not have direct ownership of shares in either of the Dead Sea Companies at any time pertinent to this suit. Rather, these companies were, at various times, separated from the State of Israel by one or more intermediate corporate tiers. For example, from 1984-1985, Israel wholly owned a company called Israeli Chemicals, Ltd.; which owned a majority of shares in another company called Dead Sea Works, Ltd.; which owned a majority of shares in Dead Sea Bromine Co., Ltd.; which owned a majority of shares in Bromine Compounds, Ltd.

The Dead Sea Companies, as indirect subsidiaries of the State of Israel, were not instrumentalities of Israel under the FSIA at any time. Those companies cannot come within the statutory language which grants status as an instrumentality of a foreign state to an entity a "majority of whose shares or other ownership interest is owned by a foreign state or political subdivision thereof." § 1603(b)(2). We hold that only direct ownership of a majority of shares by the foreign state satisfies the statutory requirement.

Section 1603(b)(2) speaks of ownership. The Dead Sea Companies urge us to ignore corporate formalities and use the colloquial sense of that term. They ask whether, in common parlance, Israel would be said to own the Dead Sea Companies. We reject this analysis. In issues of corporate law structure often matters. It is evident from the Act's text that Congress was aware of settled principles of corporate law and legislated within that context. The language of § 1603(b)(2) refers to ownership of "shares," showing that Congress intended statutory coverage to turn on formal corporate ownership. Likewise, § 1603(b)(1), another component of the definition of instrumentality, refers to a "separate legal person, corporate or otherwise." In light of these indicia that Congress had corporate formalities in mind, we assess whether Israel owned shares in the Dead Sea Companies as a matter of corporate law, irrespective of whether Israel could be said to have owned the Dead Sea Companies in everyday parlance.

A basic tenet of American corporate law is that the corporation and its shareholders are distinct entities. A corporate parent which owns the shares of a subsidiary does not, for that reason alone, own or have legal title to the assets of the subsidiary; and, it follows with even greater force, the parent does not own or have legal title to the subsidiaries of the subsidiary. The fact that the shareholder is a foreign state does not change the analysis.

Applying these principles, it follows that Israel did not own a majority of shares in the Dead Sea Companies. The State of Israel owned a majority of shares, at various times, in companies one or more corporate tiers above the Dead Sea Companies, but at no time did Israel own a majority of shares in the Dead Sea Companies. Those companies were subsidiaries of other corporations.

The veil separating corporations and their shareholders may be pierced in some circumstances, and the Dead Sea Companies essentially urge us to interpret the FSIA as piercing the veil in all cases. The doctrine of piercing the corporate veil, however, is the rare exception, applied in the case of fraud or certain other exceptional circumstances, and usually determined on a case-by-case basis. The Dead Sea Companies have referred us to no authority for extending the doctrine so far that, as a categorical matter, all subsidiaries are deemed to be the same as the parent corporation. The text of the FSIA gives no indication that Congress intended us to depart from the general rules regarding corporate formalities.

Where Congress intends to refer to ownership in other than the formal sense, it knows how to do so. Various federal statutes refer to "direct and indirect ownership." See, e.g., 5 U.S.C. § 8477(a)(4)(G)(iii) (referring to an interest "owned directly or indirectly"); 12 U.S.C. § 84(c)(5) (referring to "any corporation wholly owned directly or indirectly by the United States"); 15 U.S.C. § 79b(a)(8)(A) (referring to securities "which are directly or indirectly owned, controlled, or held with power to vote"); § 1802(3) (" The term 'newspaper owner' means any person who owns or controls directly, or indirectly through separate or subsidiary corporations, one or more newspaper publications"). The absence of this language in 28 U.S.C. § 1603(b) instructs us that Congress did not intend to disregard structural ownership rules.

The FSIA's definition of instrumentality refers to a foreign state's majority ownership of "shares or other ownership interest." § 1603(b)(2). The Dead Sea Companies would have us read "other ownership interest" to include a state's "interest" in its instrumentality's subsidiary. The better reading of the text, in our view, does not support this argument. The words "other ownership interest," when following the word "shares," should be interpreted to refer to a type of interest other than ownership of stock. The statute had to be written for the contingency of ownership forms in other countries, or even in this country, that depart from conventional corporate structures. The statutory phrase "other ownership interest" is best understood to accomplish this objective. Reading the term to refer to a state's interest in entities lower on the corporate ladder would make the specific reference to "shares" redundant. Absent a statutory text or structure that requires us to depart from normal rules of construction, we should not construe the statute in a manner that is strained and, at the same time, would render a statutory term superfluous.

The Dead Sea Companies say that the State of Israel exercised considerable control over their operations, notwithstanding Israel's indirect relationship to those companies. They appear to think that, in determining instrumentality status under the Act, control may be substituted for an ownership interest. Control and ownership, however, are distinct concepts. The terms of § 1603(b)(2) are explicit and straightforward. Majority ownership by a foreign state, not control, is the benchmark of instrumentality status. We need not delve into Israeli law or examine the extent of Israel's involvement in the Dead Sea Companies' operations. Even if Israel exerted the control the Dead Sea Companies describe, that would not give Israel a "majority of [the companies'] shares or other ownership interest." The statutory language will not support a control test that mandates inquiry in every case into the past details of a foreign nation's relation to a corporate entity in which it does not own a majority of the shares.

The better rule is the one supported by the statutory text and elementary principles of corporate law. A corporation is an instrumentality of a foreign state under the FSIA only if the foreign state itself owns a majority of the corporation's shares.

* * *

The judgment of the Court of Appeals in No. 01-594 is affirmed, and the writ of certiorari in No. 01-593 is dismissed.

It is so ordered.

Justice BREYER, with whom Justice O'CONNOR joins, concurring in part and dissenting in part.

Unlike the majority, I believe that the statutory phrase "other ownership interest . . . owned by a foreign state," 28 U.S.C. § 1603(b)(2), covers a Foreign Nation's legal interest in a Corporate Subsidiary, where that interest consists of the Foreign Nation's ownership of a Corporate Parent that owns the shares of the Subsidiary.

* * *

The statute's language, standing alone, cannot answer the question. That is because the words "own" and "ownership"—neither of which is defined in the FSIA—are not technical terms or terms of art but common terms, the precise legal meaning of which depends upon the statutory context in which they appear.

Thus, this Court has held that "shipowne[r] "can include a corporate shareholder even though, technically speaking, the corporation, not the shareholder, owns the ship. *Flink v. Paladini*, 279 U.S. 59, 62-63, 49 S.Ct. 255, 73 L.Ed. 613 (1929). Moreover, this Court has held that a trademark can be "owned by "a parent corporation even though, technically speaking, a subsidiary corporation, not the parent, registered and thus owned the mark. *K mart Corp. v. Cartier, Inc.*, 486 U.S. 281, 292, 108 S.Ct. 1811, 100 L.Ed.2d 313 (1988) (opinion of KENNEDY, J.) Similarly, here the words "other ownership interest" might, or might not, refer to the kind of majority-ownership interest that arises when one owns the shares of a parent that, in turn, owns a subsidiary. If a shareholder in Company A is an "owner" of Company A's ship . . . then why should the shareholder not be an "owner" of Company A's subsidiary? If Company A's trademark can be said to be "owned by" its shareholder, . . . then why should Company A's subsidiary not be said to be "owned by" its shareholder? And, at the very least, can we not say that the shareholder has an "ownership interest" in the subsidiary?

Neither do the various linguistic indicia to which the majority points help resolve the question. As the majority points out, the statute's use of the word "shares" leans in favor of reading "ownership" as incorporating formal, technical American legal requirements. But any resulting suggestion of formal technical limitation is neatly counterbalanced by the fact that the "statute had to be written for the contingency of ownership forms in other countries, or even in this country, that depart from conventional corporate structures." And given this latter necessity, there is no reason to read the phrase "shares or other " as if those words meant to exclude from the scope of "other" any kind of mixed, say, debt/ equity, ownership arrangement that might involve shares only in part.

* * *

The majority's "veil piercing" argument is beside the point. So is the majority's reiteration of the separateness of a corporation and its share-holders, a formal separateness that this statute explicitly sets aside. . . .

Statutory interpretation is not a game of blind man's bluff. Judges are free to consider statutory language in light of a statute's basic purposes. And here, . . . an examination of those purposes sheds considerable light. The statute itself makes clear that it seeks: (1) to provide a foreign-state defendant in a legal action the right to have its claim of a sovereign immunity bar decided by the "courts of the United States," i.e., the federal courts, 28 U.S.C. § 1604; see § 1441(d); and (2) to make certain that the merits of unbarred claims against foreign states, say, states engaging in commercial activities, see § 1605(a)(2), will be decided "in the same manner" as similar claims against "a private individual," § 1606; but (3) to guarantee a foreign state defending an unbarred claim certain protections, including a prohibition of punitive damages, the right to removal to federal court, a trial before a judge, and other procedural rights (related to service of process, venue, attachment, and execution of judgments). §§ 1330, 1391(f), 1441(d), 1606, 1608-1611.

Most important for present purposes, the statute seeks to guarantee these protections to the foreign nation not only when it acts directly in its own name but also when it acts through separate legal entities, including corporations and other "organ[s]." 28 U.S.C. § 1603(b).

Given these purposes, what might lead Congress to grant protection to a Foreign Nation acting through a Corporate Parent but deny the same protection to the Foreign Nation acting through, for example, a wholly owned Corporate Subsidiary? The answer to this question is: In terms of the statute's purposes, nothing at all would lead Congress to make such a distinction.

* * *

I believe that the Court should decide this issue just as it decided *Flink*. There, the Court unanimously determined that, in light of "[t]he policy of the statutes" in question, a corporate shareholder was an "owner" of a ship, which, technically speaking, belonged to the corporation. Justice Holmes wrote, in his opinion for the Court:

> "For th[e] purpose [of these statutes] no rational distinction can be taken between several persons owning shares in a vessel [here, a subsidiary] directly and making the same division by putting the title in a corporation and distributing the corporate stock. The policy of the statutes must extend equally to both . . . t We are of [the] opinion that the words of the acts must be taken in a broad and popular sense in order not to defeat the manifest intent. This is not to ignore the distinction between a corporation and its members, a distinction that cannot be overlooked even in extreme cases . . ., but to interpret an untechnical word ['owner'] in the liberal way in which we believe it to have been used . . .."

No more need be said.

Question

The majority approaches the case from the standpoint of "basic tenet[s] of American corporate law" whereas the minority approaches the case from the standpoint of the policy underlying the FSIA. What reasons are there for preferring one approach or the other?

Lynch v. Segal
2006 CarswellOnt 7929, 82 O.R. (3d) 641 (Ont. C.A.), leave to appeal refused 2007 CarswellOnt 4425, 2007 CarswellOnt 4426 (S.C.C.)

[The appellant corporations appeal from an order transferring to S.'s wife, L., certain lands beneficially owned by them.

The order arises in the context of an application by L. against S. for child and spousal support. S did not defend the application (he fled the jurisdiction), but had no assets in his name. Consequently, L. sought an order against the appellant corporations under 34(1)(c) of the Family Law Act, R.S.O. 1990, c. F.3 requiring that the issued capital of both corporations or, alternatively, the land owned by them, be transferred to her.]

Blair J.A.: Central to this action, and appeal, are what [counsel for L.] referred to as the "extraordinary lengths [to which Mr. Segal went] to set up legal formulations which would have the effect of distancing himself in every possible way from any assets, corporations or trusts which could be connected to him". Mr. Segal's carefully honed practice is to set up intermediary vehicles in order to screen himself from creditors, including his spouses, and to use various aliases and pseudonyms to that end. . . .

The appellants were incorporated by an Ontario solicitor, Mr. Dolson, shortly before the acquisition of the respective tracts of land they hold, on instructions from Mr. Segal, who said he was representing a group of investors. They were incorporated on behalf of unnamed beneficial owners, with no reporting letter, little correspondence and no notes in the file. Mr. Dolson was instructed to appoint himself to be the sole shareholder, president and director of the corporations; to prepare and execute blank Nominee Agreements providing that the corporations held the Lands in trust for an undisclosed beneficial owner; to endorse the Share Certificates and Share Transfers in blank; and to execute resignations in respect of his positions as officer and director. He was then instructed to send the incorporating documents, the Share Certificates, Share Transfers and Nominee Agreements, completed in blank form, together with the signed resignations, to [Mr. Segal's solicitor on the Isle of Guernsey]. Shares of the appellants were issued in blank and held by unnamed nominees supposedly fronting for mysterious high-end foreign investors operating through the medium of international trusts.

This was the same ploy utilised by Mr. Segal in respect of the corporation holding title to the parties' matrimonial mansion on Warren Road, and in respect of a further corporation (Sondol Wireless Connectivity Inc.) holding title to a third development tract of land in the Milton area. In both of these cases, he was able to have the corporate structure of the companies altered quickly to make himself the president and controlling officer; he then effected the sale of the assets and transferred the sale proceeds into untouchable overseas accounts. . . .

[The appellants submitted that the trial judge erred in finding that S. was the beneficial owner of their share capital or of the lands.] Rather, the appellants submitted, they are owned by mysterious but not-to-be-named high net worth individuals and families operating through international trust vehicles out of the Isle of Guernsey. At most, they contended, the vesting order should have been made in respect of the shares of the corporations. Alternatively, the trial judge should have imposed some other more suitable remedy such as a charging order against the Lands or the shares.

There was ample evidence, however, to support the trial judge's findings that Moses Segal and the appellant corporations "are one and the same", that he is the beneficial owner of the shares of [both corporations] and that he is also the beneficial owner of the Lands.

* * *

The well-known corporate law principle, first enunciated in *Salomon v. Salomon & Co.*, [1897] A.C. 22 (H.L.), that the shareholders of a corporation are separate and distinct from the corporate legal entity is — as MacPherson J.A. recently noted in *Wildman v. Wildman*, 2006 CarswellOnt 6042, [2006] O.J. No. 3966 (Ont. C.A.) at para. 23 — "an important one" but not, however, "an absolute principle". There is a line of jurisprudence establishing in very general terms that the courts will not enforce the "separate entities" notion where "it would yield a result too flagrantly opposed to justice, convenience or the interests of the Revenue'": *Kosmopoulos v. Constitution Insurance Co. of Canada*, 1987 CarswellOnt 132, 1987 CarswellOnt 1054, [1987] 1 S.C.R. 2 (S.C.C.) at p. 10 [S.C.R.], citing L.C.B. Gower, *Principles of Modern Company Law*, 4th ed. (London: Stevens & Sons, 1979) at 112. See also *Debora v. Debora*, 2006 CarswellOnt 7633, [2006] O.J. No. 4826 (Ont. C.A.) at para. 24; *Transamerica Life Insurance Co. of Canada v. Canada Life Assurance Co.*, 1996 CarswellOnt 1699, 28 O.R. (3d) 423 (Ont. Gen. Div.) at p. 432-434 [O.R.], affirmed 1997 CarswellOnt 3496, [1997] O.J. No. 3754 (Ont. C.A.); and *642947 Ontario Ltd. v. Fleischer*, 2001 CarswellOnt 4296, 56 O.R. (3d) 417 (Ont. C.A.) at paras. 67-69.

A more flexible approach is appropriate in the family law context, particularly where - as here - the corporations in question are completely controlled by one spouse, for that spouse's benefit, and no third parties are involved. The same situation arose in *Wildman, supra*. In that case, Mr. Wildman operated a successful high-end landscaping business through a corporation and several sole proprietorships. There were no third-party investors in the companies and Mr. Wildman controlled them completely. In order to enforce the other parts of his order requiring Mr. Wildman to pay large sums of money for spousal and child support, the trial judge in that case directed that the amounts owing were to be secured by way of a charge not only against the appellant personally, but also against his companies.

In rejecting Mr. Wildman's appeal from the latter disposition, Mac-Pherson J.A. said, at paras. 48-49:

> This is matrimonial litigation, not commercial litigation. Importantly, the record establishes that *the appellant and his companies are one and the same*. No third party has any interest in any of the companies. . .

> In the end, although a business person is entitled to create corporate structures and relationships for valid business, tax and other reasons, *the law must be vigilant to ensure that permissible corporate arrangements do not work an injustice in the realm of family law. In appropriate cases, piercing the corporate veil of one spouse's business enterprises may be an essential mechanism for ensuring that the other spouse and children of the marriage receive the financial support to*

which, by law, they are entitled. The trial judge was correct to recognize that this was such a case. [Emphasis added.]

In my view, Justice Paisley, like the trial judge in *Wildman*, was correct in recognizing that this case is one in which it is appropriate to pierce the corporate veil. During argument he observed that Mr. Segal was not using the appellant corporations for permissible corporate arrangements, but rather "was using the corporate structure for one sole purpose, to disguise his property so that his spouse and children would have no claim against him should he ever have to defend against a claim." In his reasons for judgment he referred to Mr. Segal's scheme "to conceal his assets", "to disguise [them] through every means possible", and to create the impression that "someone other than he owned his property." The record supported these observations and findings. In the circumstances, piercing the corporate veil, and finding that both the corporate shares and the Lands are beneficially owned by Mr. Segal, was - to adopt the language of MacPherson J.A. above - "an essential mechanism for ensuring that [Ms. Lynch] and [the] children of the marriage receive the financial support to which, by law, they are entitled."

The "beneficial ownership" findings are central, because they provide the foundation upon which the trial judge was able to make the vesting order that is challenged on appeal. It is not because Mr. Segal was found to be the beneficial owner of the shares of [the appellants] that the order may stand; it is because the trial judge found Mr. Segal to be the beneficial owner *of the Lands*. Once it is accepted that *the Lands* belong to Mr. Segal, they become a fair target for a vesting order under section 34(1)(c) of the *Family Law Act* or section 100 of the *Courts of Justice Act*, if such an order is otherwise appropriate in the circumstances.

(d)   Purpose of the Corporate Veil

It can be tempting to conflate the corporate veil — its separate legal personality — with the principle of limited liability, given the interaction between the two principles in situations such as that in *Salomon v. Salomon*. And of course, a core meaning of "piercing the corporate veil" is to hold the shareholders responsible for the obligations of a corporation, despite the shareholders' statutory immunity from such responsibility.

But the two principles are conceptually distinct. The corporation's legal personality is its capacity to acquire, hold and dispose of property, to enter into contracts, and to sue and be sued, incurring rights and obligations that are its own and are distinct from those of any other person (such as its shareholders). The implications of this personality go well beyond shareholders' limited liability, and shareholders are far from the only beneficiaries of the principle. In particular, the corporation's ownership of its own assets protects the reliance interest of the corporation's employees and other creditors, who know that the assets will be available to meet obligations to them and cannot be diverted from the business to pay the shareholders' own creditors. It has been said that this, rather than limited liability, is the "truly essential function of organizational law": Henry Hansmann and Reinier Kraakman, "The Essential Role of Organizational Law" (2000) 110 Yale L.J. 387.

In a case currently before the Ontario courts, tort plaintiffs of a U.S. parent company seek to enforce the debt against assets owned by the U.S. company's Canadian subsidiary. *Yaiguaje v. Chevron Corp.*, 2013 ONCA 758, 118 O.R. (3d) 1, 370 D.L.R. (4th) 132, 2013 CarswellOnt 17574 (Ont. C.A.), affirmed 2015 SCC 42, 2015 CarswellOnt 13353, 2015 CarswellOnt 13354 (S.C.C.). Unlike in a typical veil-piercing case, such cases do not represent a contest between a corporation's creditors and its shareholder, but between the interests of two sets of creditors: the creditors of the U.S. parent, and the creditors of the Canadian subsidiary. If a subsidiary's assets can, by disregarding the corporate veil, be used to meet obligations of the parent, there will be less available to meet obligations owed to the subsidiary's creditors.

4.   THEORIZING CORPORATE PERSONALITY

What is the nature of the personality that *Salomon v. Salomon* tells us is brought into being on incorporation? There are three principal schools of thought.

The subscribers to the *fiction* theory argue that corporate personality is a legal creation and that, as Chief Justice Marshall of the US Supreme Court observed in *Dartmouth College v. Woodward*, (1819) 4 Wheat. 518, at 636, a corporation is "an artificial being, invisible, intangible, and existing only in contemplation of law." A similar sentiment is reflected in Coke's report of the *Sutton Hospital Case* (1613), 10 Co. Rep. 23a, where it was said that "a corporation aggregate of many is invisible, immortal and rests only in intendment and consideration of the law." This view emphasizes the role of the state, through its law, in permitting corporations to exist and operate. It is sometimes said by adherents of this view that corporate personality is a "concession" from the state.

The supporters of the *real entity* school, on the other hand, assert that "when a group reaches a sufficient level of organization, when it can make decisions and when it has a continuity of experience, then a new personality has actually come into existence, regardless of whether the state accords it legal recognition." Bonham & Soberman, "The Nature of Corporate Personality" in *Studies in Canadian Company Law* (Ziegel ed.), vol. 1, at p. 6; see also F.W. Maitland, "Moral Personality and Legal Personality," in *The Collected Works of Frederic William Maitland* (1911).

A third and especially influential approach is adopted by members of the *contractarian* school, of which Judge Easterbrook and Daniel Fischel are leading exponents. See *The Economic Structure of Corporate Law*, ch.

1(1991). Contractarians agree with the fiction theorists that corporate personality is a fiction; however, rather than emphasizing the role of the state in bringing corporations into existence, contractarians view the corporation as a web of transactions, or "contracts", among shareholders, creditors of the corporation, employees, management and the board of directors. For contractarians, the corporation's legal personality is neither a special privilege nor the reflection of a metaphysical group personality, but a mere notational convenience in the context of multilateral contracting. In Easterbrook & Fischel's words, "[it] would be silly to attach a list of every one of Exxon's investors to an order for office furniture just to ensure that all investors share their percentage of the cost."

The theories of corporate personality are often brought to bear on questions of principle and policy in corporate law. Consider, for instance, the longstanding debate about whether the law should require boards of directors to pursue stockholder profits exclusively, or whether it should permit them to sacrifice profits in the public interest. It is sometimes said, in favour of an affirmative answer, that the state is entitled to expect of corporations, in exchange for bringing them into existence, that they will conduct themselves responsibly. To this, the proponents of an exclusive focus on profits reply that the corporate form is not a special privilege, but an incident of the ordinary commercial freedom of the many people who participate in incorporated ventures.

As we shall see in the concluding section of this chapter, theories of corporate personality also surface in the debate as to whether and, if so, why corporations ought to be subject to liability under the criminal law.

5. CORPORATE CRIMINAL RESPONSIBILITY

Given the predominance of business corporations as the preferred form of business organization, it is not surprising that much attention has focussed on the problems that arise in seeking to apply traditional criminal law concepts and penological theories to offences committed by corporations. Two major issues have dominated the debate. The first is, why should corporations be held criminally responsible at all? The second is, under what circumstances should criminal responsibility be ascribed to corporations, particularly in the case of *mens rea* offences?

So far as the first issue is concerned, scholars, law reform committees and judges have long debated the rationale of imposing criminal sanctions on an artificial body existing only in contemplation of law and that, to quote Lord Chancellor Thurlow's oft-quoted epigram, has "no soul to damn: no body to kick". Starting from these premises, it was long supposed that *mens rea* could not be attributed to a corporation and, equally, that of the traditional aims of criminal punishment — deterrence, incapacitation, rehabilitation and retribution — only deterrence made any sense in the case of corporations. Even that has been questioned on the ground that deterrence can be accomplished just as effectively by civil and administrative law remedies. Moreover, given that corporations can only act through human beings, wouldn't it be more logical to identify and punish those individuals rather than delude ourselves by punishing an artificial person? Indeed, a meaningful fine usually hits the pockets of many who are not to blame, including the shareholders of the convicted corporation or the corporation's employees if the sanction is severe enough to force layoffs.

There is, of course, another side to the coin. Large corporations exert enormous influence over the economic, and frequently social, welfare of the communities in which they are located. In some cases, corporations also cause real harms in a manner which society ought to treat as criminal: antitrust violations, racketeering, drug money laundering, financial frauds, and industrial pollution. Civil sanctions in such cases, it is argued, are not sufficient and the stigma of a criminal conviction is as telling for a corporation as it is for an individual accused.

For comprehensive discussions of these themes, see *inter alia*, Brent Fisse, "Reconstructing Corporate Law: Deterrence, Retribution, Fault and Sanctions" (1982), 56 So. Cal. L. Rev. 1141; John Coffee Jr., "'No Soul to Damn: No Body to Kick': An Unscandalized Inquiry into the Problem of Corporate Punishment" (1981), 79 Mich. L. Rev. 386; Jennifer A. Quaid, "The Assessment of Corporate Criminal Liability on the Basis of Identity" (1998) 43 McGill L.J. 67; and Ian B. Lee, "Corporate Criminal Responsibility as Team Member Responsibility" (2011) 31 Oxford J. Leg. Stud. 755.

So far as the second issue is concerned (on what basis criminal liability should attach to corporations), so far as offences requiring *mens rea* are concerned, the established Anglo-Canadian doctrine is that only the mental state of those directing the corporation's affairs will be ascribed to the corporation (the so-called "identification" or "organic" theory of corporate criminal liability). The seminal case is *Canadian Dredge & Dock v. R.*, although a major change in the law was effected in 2003 by the enactment of Bill C-45.

Canadian Dredge & Dock Co. Ltd. v. The Queen
(1985), 19 D.L.R. (4th) 314, 1985 CarswellOnt 939, 1985
CarswellOnt 96 (S.C.C.), affirming (1981), 56 C.C.C. (2d) 193,
1981 CarswellOnt 1243 (C.A.)

[A number of corporations were charged with conspiracy to defraud contrary to ss. 338(1) and 423(1)(d) [now ss. 380(1) and 465(1)(c) respectively] of the *Criminal Code*. The allegations arose out of the rigging of bids for dredging contracts in Hamilton harbour. Senior officers of the corporate accused (in each case, a general manager, vice-president or president) agreed in advance which company would submit the low (and hence winning) bid, in every case at an inflated price. The losing bidders (and co-conspirators) received payments from the winning bidder and/or occasionally a profitable subcontract. In some cases, the senior officers who orchestrated the fraudulent scheme kept for themselves the side payments which, under the agreement, were to have been paid to their corporation.

Four corporate defendants appealed their convictions on these charges and the dismissal of their appeals by the Ontario Court of Appeal. The grounds of appeal were as follows:

(i)   One corporate defendant challenged the doctrine that a corporation could be convicted for a *mens rea* offence under the "identification" theory of corporate criminal liability;

(ii) Two of the defendants argued that a corporation is not criminally liable where the directing mind of the corporation "is, at the material time:

(a)   acting in fraud of the corporation;
(b)   acting wholly or partly for his or her own benefit, or
(c)   acting contrary to instructions that he not engage in illegal actions in the course of his duties." (*Ibid.*, DLR, at 319).

Speaking for a unanimous Supreme Court, Estey J. affirmed the correctness of the "identification" theory of corporate criminal liability. The following lengthy extract from his judgment (*ibid.*, at 322-332) relates both the history of corporate criminal liability in Anglo-Canadian law and the policy choices that faced the common law courts]

ESTEY J. The position of the corporation in criminal law must first be examined. Inasmuch as all criminal and quasi-criminal offences are creatures of statute the amenability of the corporation to prosecution necessarily depends in part upon the terminology employed in the statute. In recent years there has developed a system of classification which segregates the offences according to the degree of intent, if any, required to create culpability.

(a) Absolute liability offences

Where the Legislature by the clearest intendment establishes an offence where liability arises instantly upon the breach of the statutory prohibition, no particular state of mind is a prerequisite to guilt. Corporations and individual persons stand on the same footing in the face of such a statutory offence. It is a case of automatic primary responsibility. Accordingly, there is no need to establish a rule for corporate liability nor a rationale therefor. The corporation is treated as a natural person.

(b) Offences of strict liability

Where the terminology employed by the Legislature is such as to reveal an intent that guilt shall not be predicated upon the automatic breach of the statute but rather upon the establishment of the *actus reus*, subject to the defence of due diligence, an offence of strict liability arises: see *R. v. City of Sault Ste. Marie* [1978] 2 S.C.R. 1299. As in the case of an absolute liability offence, it matters not whether the accused is corporate or unincorporate, because the liability is primary and arises in the accused according to the terms of the statute in the same way as in the case of absolute offences. It is not dependent upon the attribution to the accused of the misconduct of others. This is so when the statute, properly construed, shows a clear contemplation by the Legislature that a breach of the statute itself leads to guilt, subject to the limited defence above noted. In this category, the corporation and the natural defendant are in the same position. In both cases liability is not vicarious but primary.

(c) Offences requiring *mens rea*

These are the traditional criminal offences for which an accused may be convicted only if the requisite *mens rea* is demonstrated by the prosecution. At common law a corporate entity could not generally be convicted of a criminal offence. Corporate criminal immunity stemmed from the abhorrence of the common law for vicarious liability in criminal law, and from the doctrine of *ultra vires*, which regarded criminal activities by corporate agents as beyond their authority and beyond corporate capacity. At the other extreme in the spectrum of criminal offences there are certain crimes which cannot in any real sense be committed by a corporate as a principal, such as, perjury and bigamy, whatever the doctrine of corporate criminal liability may be. As a corporation may only act through agents, there are basically only three approaches whereby criminal intent could be said to reside or not reside in the corporate entity:

(i)   a total vicarious liability for the conduct of any of its agents whatever their level of employment or responsibility so long as they are acting within the scope of their employment;

(ii) no criminal liability unless the criminal acts in question have been committed on the direction or at the request, express or clearly implied, of the corporation as expressed through its board of directors;

(iii) a median rule whereby the criminal conduct, including the state of mind, of employees and agents of the corporation is attributed to the corporation so as to render the corporation criminally liable so long as the employee or agent in question is of such a position in the organization and activity of the corporation that he or she represents its *de facto* directing mind, will, centre, brain area or ego so that the corporation is identified with the act of that individual. There is said to be on this theory no responsibility through vicarious liability or any other form of agency, but rather a liability arising in criminal law by reason of the single identity wherein is combined the legal entity and the natural person; in short, a primary liability. This rule stands in the middle of the range or spectrum. It is but a legal fiction invented for pragmatic reasons.

* * *

At common law there was no difficulty in finding liability in a corporation in the law of torts, even though the state of mind of the corporation was established by imputing to that corporation the intentions and the conduct of its servants and agents. Thus, in the law of torts, the courts from the earliest times found vicarious liability in the corporation on the principles of agency. On the other hand, the common law of England has shrunk back from the application of the doctrine of vicarious liability for the determination of corporate liability in criminal law for the acts of its agents (with the four exceptions already noted). This led to an irrational result, namely: general corporate immunity from liability under the criminal law at a time when the corporation, for a variety of reasons, had become the principal vehicle of commerce in the community. The State itself, through corporate and taxation legislation particularly, had actually promoted or at least facilitated this result. Early in the century the courts began to dismantle the principle of corporate immunity in the criminal law. Procedural and other obstacles to the imposition of corporation criminal liability were overcome: see Leigh, "Criminal Liability of Corporations and Other Groups", 9 Ott. L.R. (No. 2) 247 at pp. 248-9 (1977). Perhaps the last major procedural impediment, the impossibility, as seen by some courts, of punishing a corporation when the only statutory sanction imposed was imprisonment . . . was removed in 1909 by the *Criminal Code Amendment Act*, 1909 (Can.), c. 9, s. 2 (the predecessor to the present s. 647 of the *Criminal Code*) which allowed the substitution of a fine in lieu of any punishment where a corporation is convicted. Ironically, the destruction of the most difficult barrier, the attribution of *mens rea* to a corporation, began in earnest in a case in civil law: *Lennard's Carrying Co., Ltd. v. Asiatic Petroleum Co., Ltd.*, [1915] A.C. 705. The House of Lords was concerned with a corporation's civil liability for damages under a statute which afforded a defence where such loss occurred without its "fault or privity". At issue was whether the "fault" of a director, who was active in the operations of the corporation, was in law the fault of the corporation itself. The Lord Chancellor, Viscount Haldane, laid down the general principle of corporate liability which is still the guiding principle in United Kingdom law (at pp. 713-4):

a corporation is an abstraction. It has no mind of its own any more than it has a body of its own; its active and directing will must consequently be sought in the person of somebody who for some purposes may be called an agent, but who is really the directing mind and will of the corporation, the very ego and centre of the personality of the corporation. That person may be under the direction of the shareholders in general meeting; that person may be the board of directors itself, or it may be, and in some companies it is so, that that person has an authority co-ordinate with the board of directors given to him under the articles of association, and is appointed by the general meeting of the company, and can only be removed by the general meeting of the company . . .

Convictions were thereafter sustained under a variety of statutes including those establishing offences requiring proof of the element of *mens rea*, the courts applying the words of the House of Lords in *Lennard's* case, *supra*, in attributing to the accused corporation the actions of the "directing mind". See *Director of Public Prosecutions v. Kent and Sussex Contractors, Ltd.*, [1944] K.B. 146 at pp. 155-6, where Viscount Caldecote L.C.J. said:

The offences created by the regulation are those of doing something with intent to deceive or of making a statement known to be false in a material particular. There was ample evidence, on the facts as stated in the special case, that the company, by the only people who could act or speak or think for it had done both these things . . .

These general principles found application in the courts of this country in a series of cases. In *R. v. Fane Robinson Ltd.*, [1941] 3 D.L.R. 409, the Court of Appeal of Alberta set aside an acquittal of two companies where two of its directors and officers conspired with another to defraud an insurance company by inflating the charges made by the defendant company to the insurance company for automobile repairs. Ford J.A., for the court, found . . . that the two officers were the:

acting and directing will of [the accused corporation] generally and in particular in respect of the subject-matter of the offenses with which it is charged, that their culpable intention (*mens rea*) and their illegal act (*actus reus*) were the intention and the act of the company and that conspiracy to defraud and obtaining money by false pretenses are offenses which a corporation is capable of containing.

In so doing the court followed the United Kingdom authorities, including *Lennard's*, *supra*, and found the company criminally liable stating . . . :

if the act complained of can be treated as that of the company, the corporation is criminally responsible for all such acts as it is capable of committing and for which the prescribed punishment is one which it can be made to endure.

The court expressly avoided finding criminal liability through the doctrine of *respondeat superior*.

* * *

The transition from virtual corporate immunity from criminal liability to virtual equality with humans in like circumstances under the criminal law is traced in greater detail by Jessup J., as he then was, in *R. v. J.J. Beamish Construction Co. Ltd.*, *supra*. Three years later, Schroeder J.A., of the Court of Appeal of Ontario, in *R. v. St. Lawrence Corp. Ltd.*, *supra*, . . . again reviewed this transition. In the end, Schroeder J.A. adopted the same statement of the governing principle as Jessup J. had in *Beamish*, *supra*, although the earlier case is not cited . . .

This rule of law was seen as a result of the removal of the officer or managerial-level employee from the general class of "inferior servants or agents" for whose acts the corporate employer continued (as in the case of the human employer) to be immune from vicarious liability in criminal law. This result is generally referred to as the "identification" theory. It produces the element of *mens rea* in the corporate entity, otherwise absent from the legal entity but present in the natural person, the directing mind. This establishes the "identity" between the directing mind and the corporation which results in the corporation being found guilty for the act of the natural person, the employee. Such is the power of legal reasoning. It is the direct descendant of Blackstone's famous theorem: "The husband and the wife in law are one and that one is the husband." It is a full brother of the *dictum* in corporate law that merging corporations cease to exist but find a continuance in the amalgamated company. In order to trigger its operation and through it corporate criminal liability for the actions of the employee (who must generally be liable himself), the actor-employee who physically committed the offence must be the ego, the "centre" of the corporate personality, the "vital organ" of the body corporate, the *alter ego* of the employer corporation or its "directing mind". Schroeder J.A. in *St. Lawrence*, *supra*, for example, refers to the officer or senior management employee as the corporation's "primary representative . . . through whom the company acts, speaks, and thinks" . . . The terminology "primary representative" comes from, or is coincidentally used in, C.R.N. Winn., "Criminal Responsibility of Corporations", 3 Camb. L.J. 398 (1929), where it is stated, at p. 404:

> the conspiring minds are in fact the minds of the directors, or other primary representatives. It is submitted that no mere conspiracy of inferior agents could affect the corporation with criminal guilt. If the guilty intention in the minds of the primary representatives is attributed to the corporation in this case where, more than any- where, it is the vital element of the offence, it seems that it will always

be proper to attribute to a corporation the guilty state of its primary representatives when they do criminal acts on its behalf in the exercise of its powers.

At p. 407 the learned author continues:

It is clear, on the one hand, that to seek to hold a corporation criminally liable for the acts of all its servants within the scope of their employment would be an innovation. The criminal law has never applied the maxim *"respondeat superior,"* and to seek to ingraft from without what has not taken spontaneous growth might prove an experiment foredoomed to failure.

* * *

The principle of attribution of criminal actions of agents to the employing corporate principal in order to find criminal liability in the corporation only operates where the directing mind is acting within the scope of his authority *Beamish, supra,* . . . and *St. Lawrence, supra,* in the sense of acting in the course of the corporations' business . . . Scattered throughout the submissions on behalf of the four appellants, was a translation of the directing-mind rule to a requirement that for its application the directing mind must, at all times, be acting in the scope of his employment. Conversely, the argument went, if the directing mind was acting totally outside the "scope of the employment", the attribution of the acts of the directing mind to the corporate employer would not occur. The terminological problems arise from the fact that the concept of vicarious liability in the law of torts has been traditionally fenced in by the concept of the employee acting within "the scope of his employment" and not, in the classic words, "on a frolic of his own". The identification theory, however, is not concerned with the scope of employment in the tortious sense. "Scope of employment" in the *St. Lawrence* judgment, *supra,* and the other discussions of that term in Canadian law have reference to the field of operations delegated to the directing mind.

* * *

Notes

1   So far as the scope of the identification doctrine was concerned, Estey J. gave it considerable elasticity (*ibid.,* at 336-337):

The identity doctrine merges the board of directors, the managing director, the superintendent, the manager or anyone else delegated by the board of directors to whom is delegated the governing executive authority of the corporation, and the conduct of any of the merged entities is thereby attributed to the corporation. In *R. v. St. Lawrence Corp. Ltd.* and nineteen other corporations, [1969] 3 C.C.C. 263, 5 D.L.R. (3d) 263, [1969] 2 O.R. 305 (Ont. C.A.), and other authorities, a corporation may, by this means, have more than one directing mind. This must be particularly so in a country such as Canada where corporate operations are frequently geographically widespread. The transportation companies, for example, must of necessity operate by the delegation and subdelegation of authority from the corporate centre; by the division and subdivision of the corporate brain, and by decentralizing by delegation the guiding forces in the corporate undertaking. The application of the identification rule in *Tesco, supra*, may not accord with the realities of life in our country, however appropriate we may find to be the enunciation of the abstract principles of law there made.

2   *Acting in Fraud of the Corporation*. Once it was established that the corporations constituted part of the corporate mind and will, the defendant corporations were obliged to raise this defence because the Ontario Court of Appeal, reaffirming earlier Anglo-Canadian precedents, had held that it made no difference that the delinquent corporate executive was using his office to defraud the corporation. This curious doctrine, apparently based on the analogy of a corporation's tortious liability for the acts of its agents committed in the course of their ostensible employment, had been strongly criticized by commentators and Estey J. had no difficulty in exposing its weaknesses. However, in delineating what he described as "the outer limit of the delegation doctrine" (sic), he added some new wrinkles which are bound to create difficulties in future cases. He said (*ibid.*, at 351):

> In my view, the outer limit of the delegation doctrine is reached and exceeded when the directing mind ceases completely to act, in fact or in substance, in the interests of the corporation. Where this entails fraudulent action, nothing is gained from speaking of fraud in whole or in part because fraud is fraud. What I take to be the distinction raised by the question is where all of the activities of the directing mind are directed against the interests of the corporation with a view to damaging that corporation, whether or not the result is beneficial economically to the directing mind, that may be said to be fraud on the corporation. Similarly, but not so importantly, a benefit to the directing mind in single transactions or in a minor part of the activities of the directing mind is in reality quite different from benefit in the sense that the directing mind intended that the corporation should not benefit from any of its activities in its undertaking. A benefit of course can, unlike fraud, be in whole or in part, but the better standard, in my view, is established when benefit is associated with fraud. The same test then applies. Where the directing mind conceives and designs a plan and then executes it whereby the corporation is intentionally defrauded, and when this is the substantial part of the regular

activities of the directing mind in his office, then it is unrealistic in the extreme to consider that the manager is the directing mind of the corporation. His entire energies are, in such a case, directed to the destruction of the undertaking of the corporation. When he crosses that line he ceases to be the directing mind and the doctrine of identification ceases to operate. The same reasoning and terminology can be applied to the concept of benefits.

Where the criminal act is totally in fraud of the corporate employer and where the act is intended to and does result in benefit exclusively to the employee-manager, the employee-directing mind, from the outset of the design and execution of the criminal plan, ceases to be a directing mind of the corporation and consequently his acts could not be attributed to the corporation under the identification doctrine. This might be true as well on the American approach through *respondeat superior*. Whether this is so or not, in my view, the identification doctrine only operates where the Crown demonstrates that the action taken by the directing mind (a) was within the field of operation assigned to him; (b) was not totally in fraud of the corporation, and (c) was by design or result partly for the benefit of the company.

On the facts, the defence did not prevail because "the appellants received benefits in the form of contracts and subcontracts, direct payouts and other benefits." Further, "the directing minds were acting partly for the benefit of the employing appellant and partly for their own benefit." (*Ibid.*, at 352-353.) It could not be said that any of the corporations had been defrauded in the narrow sense used above, even though some of the benefits of the illicit scheme were diverted to individuals who were the directing mind and will.

3 *Effect of Corporate Officer Acting in Violation of Express Orders.* Estey J. was much less sympathetic to this defence and rejected it summarily on the ground that (p. 341): "If the law recognized such a defence, a corporation might absolve itself from criminal consequence by the simple device of adopting and communicating to its staff a general instruction prohibiting illegal conduct and directing conformity at all times with the law." (*Ibid.*, at 341). However, cognizant of the distinction between offences of "strict liability" i.e. offering a due diligence defence: see *R. v. Sault Ste. Marie (City)* (1978), 40 C.C.C. (2d) 353, 85 D.L.R. (3d) 161, 1978 CarswellOnt 24, 1978 CarswellOnt 594 (S.C.C.), and those requiring *mens rea* (as at bar), he noted that such a communication would be relevant with reference to offences of strict liability. In respect of offences of *mens rea*, it was irrelevant.

Criminal Code, R.S.C. 1985, c. C-46, as amended by S.C. 2003, c. 21.

1. (1) The definition "every one, person, owner " in section 2 of the Criminal Code is replaced by the following:

every one, person and owner, and similar expressions, include Her Majesty and an organization;

(2) Section 2 of the Act is amended by adding the following in alphabetical order:

organization means

(a) a public body, body corporate, society, company, firm, partnership, trade union or municipality, or

(b) an association of persons that

(i) is created for a common purpose,

(ii) has an operational structure, and

(iii) holds itself out to the public as an association of persons;

[. . .] "representative", in respect of an organization, means a director, partner, employee, member, agent or contractor of the organization;

[. . .] "senior officer" means a representative who plays an important role in the establishment of an organization's policies or is responsible for managing an important aspect of the organization's activities and, in the case of a body corporate, includes a director, its chief executive officer and its chief financial officer;

[. . .]

22.1 In respect of an offence that requires the prosecution to prove negligence, an organization is a party to the offence if

(a) acting within the scope of their authority

(i) one of its representatives is a party to the offence, or

(ii) two or more of its representatives engage in conduct, whether by act or omission, such that, if it had been the conduct of only one representative, that representative would have been a party to the offence; and

(b) the senior officer who is responsible for the aspect of the organization's activities that is relevant to the offence departs — or the senior officers, collectively, depart — markedly from the standard of care that, in the circumstances, could reasonably be expected to prevent a representative of the organization from being a party to the offence.

22.2 In respect of an offence that requires the prosecution to prove fault — other than negligence — an organization is a party to the offence if, with the intent at least in part to benefit the organization, one of its senior officers

    (a) acting within the scope of their authority, is a party to the offence;

    (b) having the mental state required to be a party to the offence and acting within the scope of their authority, directs the work of other representatives of the organization so that they do the act or make the omission specified in the offence; or

    (c) knowing that a representative of the organization is or is about to be a party to the offence, does not take all reasonable measures to stop them from being a party to the offence.

[. . .]

718.21 A court that imposes a sentence on an organization shall also take into consideration the following factors:

    (a) any advantage realized by the organization as a result of the offence;

    (b) the degree of planning involved in carrying out the offence and the duration and complexity of the offence;

    (c) whether the organization has attempted to conceal its assets, or convert them, in order to show that it is not able to pay a fine or make restitution;

    (d) the impact that the sentence would have on the economic viability of the organization and the continued employment of its employees;

    (e) the cost to public authorities of the investigation and prosecution of the offence;

    (f) any regulatory penalty imposed on the organization or one of its representatives in respect of the conduct that formed the basis of the offence;

    (g) whether the organization was — or any of its representatives who were involved in the commission of the offence were — convicted of a similar offence or sanctioned by a regulatory body for similar conduct;

    (h) any penalty imposed by the organization on a representative for their role in the commission of the offence;

(i) any restitution that the organization is ordered to make or any amount that the organization has paid to a victim of the offence; and

(j) any measures that the organization has taken to reduce the likelihood of it committing a subsequent offence.

[. . .]

732.1 (3.1) The court may prescribe, as additional conditions of a probation order made in respect of an organization, that the offender do one or more of the following:

(a) make restitution to a person for any loss or damage that they suffered as a result of the offence;

(b) establish policies, standards and procedures to reduce the likelihood of the organization committing a subsequent offence;

(c) communicate those policies, standards and procedures to its representatives;

(d) report to the court on the implementation of those policies, standards and procedures;

(e) identify the senior officer who is responsible for compliance with those policies, standards and procedures;

(f) provide, in the manner specified by the court, the following information to the public, namely,

(i) the offence of which the organization was convicted,

(ii) the sentence imposed by the court, and

(iii) any measures that the organization is taking — including any policies, standards and procedures established under paragraph (*b*) — to reduce the likelihood of it committing a subsequent offence; and

(g) comply with any other reasonable conditions that the court considers desirable to prevent the organization from committing subsequent offences or to remedy the harm caused by the offence.

(3.2) Before making an order under paragraph (3.1)(*b*), a court shall consider whether it would be more appropriate for another regulatory body to supervise the development or implementation of the policies, standards and procedures referred to in that paragraph.

Notes and Questions

1   Under the 2003 amendments, reproduced above, criminal liability may be incurred not only by a corporation but also by other types of association. The amendments do not make it a prerequisite for liability that the association be constituted by a statute that confers legal personality upon it, as corporations are. Has Parliament implicitly endorsed the "real entity" view of corporate personality?

2   Is the "senior officer" concept in s. 22.1 identical to the "directing mind" concept under the identification doctrine?

3   Sec. 22.1(a)(ii) introduces the concept of cumulative negligence into Canadian criminal law. Where responsibilities are dispersed in an organization, it is sometimes difficult to find a single wrongdoer, since several people might have done things that, although individually innocent, actually create great risk when considered as a whole.

4   Do the 2003 amendments preserve without modification the fraud-on-the corporation defence established in *Canadian Dredge*?

5   There are few reported cases under the 2003 amendments. See *R. v. Metron Construction Corp.*, 2012 ONCJ 506, 2012 CarswellOnt 9497 (Ont. C.J.), reversed 2013 CarswellOnt 12217 (Ont. C.A.) (corporation convicted of criminal negligence (guilty plea)); *R. c. Pétroles Global Inc.*, 2013 QCCS 4262, 2013 CarswellQue 9172 (C.S. Que.), leave to appeal allowed 2013 CarswellQue 9268 (C.A. Que.) (corporation convicted of conspiracy to fix prices).

6   For commentary on the 2003 amendments, see Todd Archibald, Ken E. Jull and Kent Roach, "The Changed Face of Corporate Criminal Liability" 48 Crim. L.Q. 367 (2004).

7   The 2003 amendments introduced sentencing provisions specific to organizations (s. 718.21 and s. 732.1). For discussion of sentencing issues relating to corporations, see Poonam Puri, "Sentencing the Criminal Corporation" 39 Osgoode Hall Law Journal 611-653 (2001).

Chapter 3

The Process of Incorporation

1. INTRODUCTION

In this chapter we consider a number of issues associated with the incorporation and classification of corporations and the conceptual difficulties presented by pre-incorporation contracts.

2. PLACE OF INCORPORATION

The federal government, the provinces and the territories have concurrent jurisdiction to incorporate corporations. Incorporators therefore can elect to incorporate under federal, provincial or territorial law. Moreover, they generally have a choice of fourteen laws since none of the corporations Acts require the incorporators to be resident in the province or territory of incorporation.

Some of the Acts impose Canadian nationality and/or residency requirements for directors, however. See *e.g., CBCA* s. 105(3) and *OBCA* s. 118(3).Case law has clarified that the *OBCA* requirements are directed specifically at residency requirements, rather than at loss or termination of directors. In cases where a corporation only has one director and he or she is a non-resident of Canada, that director may not conduct business or the affairs of the corporation until a quorum is restored, and that quorum meets residency requirements (*International Baslen Enterprises Ltd. v. Kirwan*, 2006 CarswellOnt 395, 12 B.L.R. (4th) 169, 207 O.A.C. 21 (Ont. C.A.)).

The Acts in Quebec, British Columbia, New Brunswick, Nova Scotia, Nunavut, Prince Edward Island, Northwest Territories, and Yukon are all silent on the residency requirements of directors. Ontario's Ministry of Government and Consumer Services Expert Panel recommended removing residency requirements for directors in Ontario (Business Law Agenda: Priority Findings & Recommendations Report, published in June 2015).

If the incorporators see an advantage in doing so, they may even incorporate offshore (a choice usually dictated by tax reasons) since the normal conflict of laws rule is that the validity of the incorporation, the status of the corporation and its general personal law will be governed by the law of its incorporation. See Janet Walker, *Canadian Conflict of Laws*, 6th ed. (2005) 30.1. However, the conflict of laws rule must be applied with caution. Section 302(2) of the US *Restatement of the Law, Conflict of Laws*, 2d ed. (St Paul, MN: American Law Institute, 1971) 3 at 306 indicates that the local law of the state of incorporation will not be applied "in the unusual case where, with respect to the particular issue, some other state has a more significant relationship to the occurrence and the parties." Some American courts have refused to apply the law of incorporation to closely held corporations in determining management-shareholder relationships where there was no significant link between the jurisdiction of incorporation, the corporation's place of business and the shareholders' places of residence. Furthermore, certain provisions of California and New York corporations statutes apply to corporations with a close connection to the state, even if they are incorporated elsewhere.

In Ontario, the *Not-for-Profit Corporations Act*, S.O. 2010, c. 15 provides an alternative means of incorporation for organizations that promote not-for-profit objectives. These include charitable organizations (including religious organizations), social clubs, service clubs, sporting and athletic organizations, professional and trade associations, ratepayers' associations, and other community organizations. The purpose of the statute is to simplify the incorporation procedure, enhance corporate governance, give more rights to members, and better protect directors and officers from liability. The Act received Royal Assent on October 25, 2010, and is still subject to Royal Proclamation from the Lieutenant Governor. However, it has not come into force as of April 2016. Similar legislation has been enacted by the federal government in the *Canada Not-for-Profit Corporations Act* 2009, c. 23, which provides a streamlined incorporation procedure and corporate governance framework for federally incorporated not-for-profit corporations.

The Competition for State and Provincial Charters: the Delaware Phenomenon

In the U.S., the "full faith and credit" clause in the U.S. Constitution requires states to recognize extra-state corporations and, starting at the turn of the century, this led to keen competition among several states to attract new incorporations (and subsequent reincorporations of existing corporations) by offering flexible corporations Acts favourable to management. The race was won by Delaware. The Delaware government claims that over half of all U.S. publicly traded corporations, and 64% of Fortune 500 companies are incorporated in the state (online: < http://corp.delaware.gov/aboutagency.shtml >, figures that are consistent with earlier data compiled by Roberta

Romano in *The Genius of American Corporate Law* (Washington: AEI Press, 1993).

Early commentators generally interpreted the Delaware phenomenon as a competition in laxity (a "race to the bottom") and urged federal intervention. The seminal exposition of this thesis was published in 1974 by Columbia University law professor and former SEC commissioner Professor William Cary. See "Federalism and Corporate Law: Reflections upon Delaware" (1974), 83 Yale L.J. 663, and Nader, Green & Seligman, *Constitutionalizing the Corporation: The Case for the Federal Chartering of Giant Corporations* (1976).

Cary's thesis was strongly attacked by "law and economics" practitioners. Professor Ralph K. Winter Jr., formerly of the Yale Law School and now a federal Senior Circuit Judge on the Second Circuit Court of Appeals, was one of the first to question Cary's thesis, and, along with Cary, is considered one of the titans of this debate. See "State Law, Shareholder Protection, and the Theory of the Corporation" (1977), 6 J. Legal Stud. 251. Professor Winter argued that the market for state charters is no different than the market for any other competitive product and that a corporation's managers would not choose a 'more lax' jurisdiction unless it was in the shareholders' interest. In his view, management would be restrained from sacrificing shareholder interests by the same competitive forces — capital markets, product markets, employment markets and the market for corporate control — that deter managerial rent-seeking and abuses in general.

Some scholars have attempted to quantify the claimed benefits of Delaware incorporation: Robert Daines' analysis ("Does Delaware Law Improve Firm Value?" (2001), 62 J.Fin.Econ. 559) suggests that Delaware firms were, all else equal, worth more than non-Delaware firms in the majority of years during his sample period from 1981 to 1996. Others, however, dispute both the significance and persistence of this effect. See Lucian Bebchuk, Alma Cohen and Allen Ferrell, "Does the Evidence Favour State Competition in Corporate Law" (2002), 90 Cal. L. Rev. 1775, Guhan Subramanian, "The Disappearing Delaware Effect" (2002) Harvard Law and Economics Discussion Paper No. 391, and Feng Chen and Kenton Yee "Are Delaware Firms Oranges? Fundamental Attributes and the Delaware Effect" (2006) 1st Annual Conference on Empirical Legal Studies Paper.

Recent contributions to the US debate question the extent to which Delaware is subject to actual competition for incorporations: if Delaware faces no real threat from any single other state, should we question the extent to which competitive forces in fact discipline the production of state corporate law? See Lucian Bebchuk and Assaf Hamdani, "Vigorous Race or Leisurely Walk: Reconsidering the Competition Over Corporate Charters" (2002), 112 Yale L.J. 553, update online: SSRN < http:// papers.ssrn.com/sol3/papers.cfm?abstract_id = 325520 >, Robert Daines, "The Incorporation Choices of IPO Firms" (2002), 77 N.Y.U.L. Rev.

1559, and Marcel Kahan and Ehud Kamar "The Myth of State Competition in Corporate Law" (2002), 55 Stanford L. Rev. 679. Perhaps a greater discipline on Delaware's corporate law-making power is from federal law, such as the Sarbanes-Oxley Act and Dodd-Frank Report. See Mark Roe "Delaware and Washington as Corporate Law Makers" (2009) 34 Del. J. Corp. L. 1. Among out-of-state incorporations, however, Delaware is dominant, leading some scholars to conclude that the actual competition is between in-state incorporation and Delaware incorporation.

Bebchuk & Cohen have found that states offering a proliferation of antitakeover statutes are significantly more successful in the incorporations market than states that do not offer these statutes. (Lucian Bebchuk & Alma Cohen, "Firms' Decisions Where to Incorporate" (2003) 46 J.L.Econ. 383.)

Some have questioned the effect of antitakeover devices on shareholder value, suggesting that they effectively diminish target shareholder value by hampering hostile takeover bids. See, *e.g.*, Lucian Arye Bebchuk, John C. Coates IV, and Guhan Subramania, "The Powerful Force of Staggered Boards: Theory, Evidence, and Policy" (2002) 54 Stan. L. Rev. 887; Lucian Bebchuk, "The Case Against Board Veto Power In Corporate Takeovers" (2002) 69 U. Chicago L. Rev. 973; John C. Coates IV & Guhan Subramanian, "A Buy-Side Model of M&A Lockups: Theory and Evidence" (2000) 53 Stan. L. Rev. 307; Robert B. Thompson & D. Gordon Smith, "Toward A New Theory of the Shareholder Role: "Sacred Space" in Corporate Takeovers" (2001) 80 Tex. L. Rev. 261. However, Lynn Stout argues that evaluating the effectiveness of antitakeover devices by looking only at potential lost share premiums does not consider the value of these devices prior to a takeover bid. (Lynn A. Stout, "Do Antitakeover Defenses Decrease Shareholder Wealth? The Ex Post/Ex Ante Valuation Problem" (2002) 55 Stan. L. Rev. 845, online: SSRN < http://papers.ssrn.com/sol3/ papers.cfm?abstract_id = 338601 > .) She argues that antitakeover devices can enhance shareholder value; for example, in the case of startup or young corporations, as these devices provide a measure of stability, particularly in terms of retaining managers. Fuel has recently been added to the debate about the effects of regulatory competition on corporate governance since European public limited-liability companies (Societas Europaea) were given the freedom to choose their EEC country of incorporation in 2001. (*Statute for a European Company (SE)*, OJ L 294, 10 November 2001, p. 1–21, Art. 8.1, online: EUR-lex < http://eur-lex.europa.eu/LexUriServ/LexUriServ.do?uri = CELEX:32001R2157:EN :HTML > .)

Shopping for favourable corporation laws has never been a prominent feature in Canada nor have the provinces and the federal government actively competed for incorporations. The Canadian tradition, in fact, has been in the opposite direction: many have argued that provincial and federal administrators are more interested in promoting greater uniformity among provincial and federal corporation laws than in widening the gap between them. See Ziegel, *Studies in Canadian Company Law*, vol. 2 (1973), 62–67. There are probably many reasons for the absence of a Canadian Delaware. One of them undoubtedly is that, until the early 1970s, the differences among the provincial Acts and between the provincial and federal Acts were not as pronounced as were those among the various state laws in the US (although this does not explain why one of the provinces or the federal government did not strike out on its own with a view to capturing a larger share of the corporations market). Another reason may be the greater conservatism of Canadian corporate lawyers and their unwillingness to expose their clients to an unfamiliar corporate law regime. Whatever the true explanation, the general practice is to incorporate provincially in the province where the corporation expects to carry on its business, provided no significant extra-provincial operations are envisioned, and to incorporate federally if the corporation expects to conduct business in several provinces.

Douglas Cumming and Jeffrey MacIntosh examined the Canadian market in 2000 and concluded that theory and empirical evidence indicated that institutional barriers had limited the extent of competitive corporate law production. They also argued that Canadian legislators sought to maximize uniformity, as opposed to revenues derived from a competitive incorporation business ("The Role of Interjurisdictional Competition in Shaping Canadian Corporate Law" (2000), 20 Int'l. Rev. L. & Econ. 141). In a subsequent study ("The Rationales Underlying Reincorporation and Implications for Canadian Corporations" (2002), 22 Int'l. Rev. L. & Econ. 277), the same authors found evidence that interprovincial reincorporations tended to be prompted by the transaction costs of carrying on business, while federal reincorporations had a more substantive law-shopping component, and that reincorporation in some cases enhanced and in other cases diminished firm value. The same authors found that venture capital entrepreneurs favoured federal incorporation over provincial ("Crowding Out Private Equity: Canadian Evidence" (2006), 21 J. Bus. Venturing 569).

3. EXTRA-PROVINCIAL LICENSING AND FILING REQUIREMENTS

Under the Ontario *Extra-Provincial Corporations Act*, R.S.O. 1990, c. E.27 (*EPCA*), corporations incorporated in a Canadian province other than Ontario ("Class 1 Corporations") or in a territory of Canada or under the *CBCA* ("Class 2 Corporations") are not required to obtain a licence under the act to carry on business in Ontario. Corporations incorporated under the laws of a jurisdiction outside Canada ("Class 3

Corporations") (*Ont. EPCA* s. 2(1)) are subject to the full force of the provincial requirements applicable to extra-provincial corporations. The requirements for corporations required to be licenced as extra-provincial corporations differ considerably in detail among provinces but share several basic features. First, it is an offence for such corporations to carry on business in the province without a licence, although prosecutions for non-compliance are rare. Second, an unlicenced extra-provincial corporation is usually incapable of maintaining an action or other proceeding before a provincial court or tribunal "in respect of a contract made by it." (*Ont. EPCA* s. 21 (1)). However, the defect can usually be cured retroactively by obtaining a licence. Third, the granting of a licence is usually discretionary with the designated official (although refusals apparently are rare), and the official is authorized to attach conditions. (*Ont. EPCA* s. 5(5)). Fourth, in common with domestic corporations, extra-provincial corporations are usually required to make annual filings of pertinent information. See *e.g.*, the *Corporations Information Act*, R.S.O. 1990, c. C.39, s. 3.1.

A critical feature of the licensing requirements is that they are triggered only if the extra-provincial corporation is "carrying on business" in the province. The definition of "carrying on business" has provoked a considerable volume of litigation. See *e.g.*, *Weight Watchers International Inc. v. Weight Watchers of Ontario Ltd.* (1972), [1973] 1 O.R. 549, 31 D.L.R. (3d) 645, 1972 CarswellOnt 295 (H.C.); *Success International Inc. v. Environmental Export International of Canada Inc.*, 1995 CarswellOnt 25, 23 O.R. (3d) 137, 123 D.L.R. (4th) 147 (Ont. Gen. Div.). Section 1(2) of *Ont. EPCA* makes it clear that an extra-provincial corporation will be deemed to carry on its business in Ontario if, *inter alia*, it has a "resident agent, representative, warehouse, office or place where it carries on its business in Ontario". *Ont. EPCA* s. 1(3), however, is also a common provision, providing that an extra-provincial corporation does not carry on its business in Ontario by reason only that, "(a) it takes orders for or buys or sells goods, wares or merchandise; or (b) offers or sells services of any type, by use of travelers or through advertising or correspondence."

4. CONTINUANCE UNDER THE LAW OF ANOTHER JURISDICTION

An important feature of the *CBCA* and its provincial counterparts is the ability of a corporation "to continue" its corporate existence under the law of another jurisdiction (referred to in the US as "reincorporation"). See *CBCA* ss. 187-188 and *OBCA* ss. 180-81. A corporation may wish to do so for one of a number of reasons: because of tax advantages, because it has shifted its business operations to the new jurisdiction, because of a desire to amalgamate with a corporation in the other jurisdiction or simply because the corporate climate is more hospitable in the second jurisdiction.

Whatever the reason, every continuance involves a two-step procedure. First, the emigrating corporation must obtain the consent of the authorities in the jurisdiction of its incorporation (the "export" step). Second, it must meet the requirements of the federal or provincial Act under which it seeks to be continued (the "import" step). Not surprisingly, it is easier to meet the requirements of the immigrating jurisdiction (can you see why, perhaps based on the discussion of regulatory competition earlier in this chapter?) than it is to meet the requirements of the emigrating jurisdiction — an interesting reversal of the hurdles normally confronting immigrating individuals. Note carefully that, as in the case of mergers and amalgamations within the same jurisdiction, continuance under the law of another jurisdiction does not affect the migrating corporation's prior obligations, property rights and involvement in all prior civil, criminal and administrative proceedings pending before continuance. See *CBCA* s. 187(7) and *OBCA* s. 181(9). Does this mean that continuance involves no change in the status of the corporation?

In *Canada (Director appointed under s. 260 of the Business Corporations Act), Re* (1991), 80 D.L.R. (4th) 619, 1991 CarswellOnt 128 (C.A.), the substantive issue was whether the *CBCA* "export" provisions can be successfully evaded by a "three-cornered amalgamation" which, in that case, involved Varity Corporation amalgamating with a newly incorporated *CBCA* corporation, resulting in the publicly held shares of Varity being exchanged for shares in a Delaware corporation. The Ontario Court of Appeal held that s. 185 of the *CBCA* could not be interpreted to confer on the Director (of Varity) under the Act wide discretionary power to veto a proposed amalgamation on the grounds of inadequate protection of shareholders or creditors.

5. CLASSIFICATION OF CORPORATIONS

Many different types of classification exist for corporations. The following notes are limited to those types that are relevant for the purposes of modern business corporations Acts.

(a) Publicly traded vs. privately held corporations

Corporations vary widely in the number of shareholders, value of assets and involvement in the securities market; a statutory framework that may be appropriate for a corporation with widely dispersed shareholders may be quite inappropriate for a closely held corporation ("CHC") with few shareholders. Chapter 9 provides an historical overview of the comparatively recent process by which Canadian corporations law has meaningfully addressed the distinction, although the process of adaptation is still incomplete. The *CBCA* and the *OBCA* differ in their definitional approach, as well in the substantive consequences, of the definitional criteria.

The present *OBCA* distinguishes between a "non-offering corporation" and an "offering corporation". *OBCA* s. 1(1) defines an "offering corporation" as a corporation that is offering its securities to the public within the meaning of subsection (6) and that is not the subject of an order of the [Ontario Securities] Commission deeming it to have ceased to be offering its securities to the public". *OBCA* s. 1(6) deems a corporation to be "offering its securities to the public only where,

(a) in respect of any of its securities a prospectus or statement of material facts has been filed under the *Securities Act* or any predecessor thereof, or in respect of which a prospectus has been filed under *The Corporations Information Act* . . . or any predecessor thereof, so long as any of such securities are outstanding or any securities into which such securities are converted are outstanding; or

(b) any of its securities have been at any time since the 1st day of May, 1967, listed and posted for trading on any stock exchange in Ontario recognized by the Commission regardless of when such listing and posting for trading commenced".

The distinction between offering and non-offering corporations is material under the *OBCA* for the purposes of: ss. 40 (lien on shares), 42 (restrictions on transfer, etc.), 111 (mandatory solicitation of proxy), 112 (information circular), 115(2) and (3) (minimum number of directors and outside directors), 138(1) (insider liability), 148 (exemption from audit requirements), 154 (information to be laid before annual meeting), 158(1) (audit committee) and Part XV (compulsory acquisitions).

The *CBCA* does not provide a single distinction for all purposes under the Act, but rather relies on different distinctions in different contexts. For example, the *CBCA* Regs. Pt. 2(1) defines a "distributing corporation" as a corporation that is a "reporting issuer" under provincial securities legislation that provide that definition (B.C., Alberta, Saskatchewan, Manitoba, Ontario, Quebec, New Brunswick, Nova Scotia, and Newfoundland), and, in the case of a corporation that is not a "reporting issuer", a corporation

(i) that has filed a prospectus or registration statement under provincial legislation or under the laws of a jurisdiction outside Canada,

(ii) any of the securities of which are listed and posted for trading on a stock exchange in or outside Canada, or

(iii) that is involved in, formed for, resulting from or continued after an amalgamation, a reorganization, an arrangement or a statutory procedure, if one of the participating bodies corporate is a corporation to which subparagraph (i) or (ii) applies.

The following are the material provisions of the *CBCA* that rely on the definition of "distributing corporation": ss. 2(1) (definition of "squeeze-out transaction"), 21 (access to corporate records), 49(9) (limits on restriction on transfer of shares), 102(2) (number of directors), 135(1.1) (notice of meeting), 149(2) (mandatory solicitation of proxies), 160(1) (distribution of financial statements), 163(1) (dispensing with auditor), 171 (audit committee), 174 (constraints on shares), Part XI (insider trading) and Part XVII (compulsory and compelled acquisitions).

In other contexts, the *CBCA* refers to a corporation engaged in a "distribution to the public", as in s. 82(2) (applicability of trust indenture provisions). Finally, in still other contexts, the *CBCA* relies on other *indicia* of closely-held corporations, as in ss. 149(2)(b) (number of shareholders required for mandatory solicitation of proxies) and 160(1) (filing of financial statements).

(b)   One-person Corporations

The only significant substantive issue associated with the legal validity of one-person corporations concerns the holding of meetings. Etymologically, a meeting requires two or more persons and that is also the general corporate law rule: *Cowichan Leader Ltd., Re* (1963), 42 D.L.R. (2d) 111, 45 W.W.R. 57, 1963 CarswellBC 149 (S.C.). Most Acts accordingly provide that, where a corporation only has one shareholder, he or she alone may constitute a meeting. The same rule applies to a corporation that has only one director. See *CBCA* ss. 114(8) and 139(4), *OBCA* ss. 101(4) and 126(12). These provisions should be read in conjunction with the equally common provisions recognizing the validity of unanimous resolutions in writing. See *CBCA* s. 142(1) and *OBCA* s. 104(1).

(c)   Constrained Share Corporations

Federal and provincial legislation permit corporations with publicly issued shares to restrict their transfer to comply with Canadian ownership and control requirements. See *CBCA* s. 174, Regs., Pt. 9 and *OBCA* s. 42(2).

(d)   Professional Corporations

The 1967 Lawrence Report favoured permitting members of professions to incorporate themselves, subject to safeguards for the protection of the public, reasoning that carrying on a professional practice in corporate form permits classification of the legal relationships between shareholders of the company and third parties; simplifies or eliminates difficulties arising by virtue of the withdrawal, retirement or death of members of a professional partnership; expedites transfer of interests in the practice from one person to another or to incoming members of the practice; and permits the accumulation of partnership profits for the purpose of re-investing in fixed assets or for other purposes. In addition, there are, under existing law, very real income tax advantages which would accrue to the professional person or partnership on incorporation of the practice. There seems to be no reason why all these advantages should not be available to those who are active in professional life. (*Ontario Select Committee on Company Law, Interim Report* (1967), para. 2.2.4.)

OBCA s. 3.1(2) permits a professional corporation to practice a profession governed by an act if (i) that act expressly permits the practice of that profession by a corporation, or (ii) if the act is one of those listed in s. 3.1(2)(b) (which includes legislation relating to accountants and lawyers). The *Law Society Act*, R.S.O. 1990, c. L.8 was amended in 1991 and updated in 2006 to permit lawyers to practice through corporations. The *OBCA* makes it clear that the liability of a member of a profession for a professional liability claim is not affected by the fact that he or she is practising through a professional corporation and that shareholders of professional corporations remain liable under their governing legislation for acts of employees and agents of the corporation. Section 61.0.5(1) of the *Law Society Act* further provides that the professional, fiduciary and ethical obligations of persons practising law (or providing legal services) are not diminished by the fact that they are practising law through a professional corporation and apply equally to the corporation and its directors, officers, shareholders, agents and employees. For applications of similar provisions, see *Corkery v. Foster Wedekind* (1987), 45 D.L.R. (4th) 159, 1987 CarswellAlta 262 (Q.B.) and *Sandilands v. Powell*, 2003 ABCA 162, 2003 CarswellAlta 956, 330 A.R. 92 (Alta. C.A.).

It appears that interest in professional corporations in Canada is (or was) largely motivated by tax considerations. Fundamentally, the benefits associated with professional corporations versus limited liability partnerships vary by type of professional, size of firm, and objective of incorporation (Vern Krishna, "Professional Corporations" (2005) 25:9 Lawyers Weekly (QL)).

(e) Unlimited Liability Companies

Three Canadian jurisdictions, Alberta, British Columbia, and Nova Scotia, permit the incorporation of "unlimited liability companies" or "unlimited liability corporations" ("ULCs"), which are corporations without limits on the liability of their members (see *Companies Act*, R.S.N.S. 1989, c. 81, s. 9(c), *Business Corporations Act*, R.S.A. 2000, c. B-9, s. 15.2 (*"ABCA"*), *Business Corporations Act*, S.B.C. 2002, c. 57, s. 51.11 (*"BCBCA"*)). A ULC's name, in Nova Scotia, may not include the words "limited" or "incorporated", although it can use the words "company" or "Co." and identify itself as a ULC. In Alberta and British Columbia, the name shall end with "Unlimited Liability Corporation" or the abbreviation "ULC". In Nova Scotia, the liability of members of a ULC is unlimited, but, unlike partners who bear direct liability to creditors on an ongoing basis, the liability of ULC members arises only on the winding up of the ULC in the event that its assets are insufficient to meet its obligations. In Alberta, shareholders have unlimited liability for any liability, and it is joint and several in nature. In British Columbia, shareholders, and former shareholders, are liable jointly and severally regardless of whether the company liquidates or dissolves. In Nova Scotia, members can limit their personal liability to third parties by contract, and there are numerous limitations on the liability of former members (*Companies Act*, s. 135). In Alberta, former shareholders are not liable if the liability, act, or default of unlimited liability existed after the shareholder ceased to be one (*ABCA*, s. 15.2(3)). British Columbia has a similar limitation, along with other limitations on liability for former members (*BCBCA*, s. 51.3(2)). In addition, investors in a ULC typically insulate themselves from unlimited personal liability by interposing a limited liability corporation or limited partnership between themselves and the ULC. In 2015, a panel appointed by Ontario's Ministry of Government and Consumer Services recommended that Ontario should permit the incorporation of Unlimited Liability Corporations (Business Law Agenda: Priority Findings & Recommendations Report, published in June 2015).

The principal reason for using a ULC is the fact that US tax rules permit the ULC to elect to be taxed as a partnership in the US, even though it is a corporation for all purposes (including tax) in Canada.

6. CORPORATE NAMES

One of the more important matters that must be decided upon in the incorporation process is the selection of a corporate name. The legislation in all jurisdictions seeks to regulate the use of corporate names, primarily with a view to ensuring that the public will not be misled by confusingly similar corporate names. The statutory provisions vary from province to province, both in the degree of their complexity and in the detail of their requirements. The relevant statute must be consulted in each case to determine the appropriate requirements. See, for example, *CBCA* ss. 10–13 and *OBCA* ss. 8–12. There may be additional statutory requirements outside of the corporation law statutes. For example, in Ontario, a corporation must comply with the *Business Names Act* R.S.O. 1990 c. 17 (*BNA*) in order to register its name. Per s. 7(1) of the *BNA*, a corporation must comply with the *BNA* in order to maintain a court proceeding in Ontario in connection to its business, unless it obtains leave from the court. Where the incorporator does not care for a specific name, *CBCA* s. 11(2) and *OBCA* s. 8 allow the use of assigned unique number names.

Whether by detailed statutory provision, regulation or administrative practice, a common theme in the regulation of corporate names is the protection of the public against deception. See, for example, *OBCA* ss. 9(l)(b) and *CBCA* s. 12(1) and *Canada Business Corporations Regulations*, Part 2. The statutes and regulations generally speak of a likelihood of deception, confusion, etc. See *F.P. Chapple Co., Re*, 1960 CarswellOnt 26, 25 D.L.R. (2d) 706 (Ont. C.A.). If there is no evidence to deceive, public policy tends to look past the usage of an improper name, and favour validating contracts made under such name. See *Hurley Corp. v. Canadian IPG Corp.*, 2010 ONSC 681, 2010 CarswellOnt 629 (Ont. S.C.J.). To prevent deception, *BCBCA* s. 27(1) requires the full legal name of the corporation to be displayed on all official publications, contracts, invoices, and its seal, etc. Failing to do so can create personal liability for the agent (*Out West Windows Glass Home Maintenance Ltd. v. Tilley*, 2014 CarswellBC 3700, 2014 BCPC 296, [2014] B.C.J. No. 3063 (B.C. Prov. Ct.)). This is especially true if the agent does not identify the company as limited liability, because the onus to do so is on the agent (*Pageant Media Ltd. v. Piche*, 2013 CarswellBC 3766, 2013 BCCA 537, 22 B.L.R. (5th) 65 (B.C. C.A.)).

The specific characteristics (*e.g.*, knowledge and skill) of the class of purchasers will be taken into account in assessing potential for deception (*CC Chemicals Ltd., Re*, 1967 CarswellOnt 37, [1967] 2 O.R. 248, 63 D.L.R. (2d) 203 (Ont. C.A.)). For a more comprehensive discussion of regulation of corporate names, see Iacobucci, Pilkington & Prichard, *Canadian Business Corporations* (1977).

Apart from the protection accorded to corporate names (and any goodwill associated with them) under corporate legislation, there is also the protection accorded by the common law concerning passing off and federal trademark legislation. For a discussion of the relationship between these forms of protection, see *Fastening House Ltd. v. Fastway Supply House Ltd.*, 1974 CarswellOnt 440, 3 O.R. (2d) 385, 45 D.L.R. (3d) 505 (Ont. H.C.).

Where a lawyer is advising an unsophisticated or high-risk client, and fails to convey the importance of using the full corporate name, including the legal element, and the consequences in terms of personal liability for the failure to do so, the lawyer will be liable to this client for breach of the duty of care. (*Turi v. Swanick*, 2002 CarswellOnt 3041, 61 O.R. (3d) 368 (Ont. S.C.J.)).

7. INCORPORATION TECHNIQUES

Historically there were major differences in the methods of incorporation employed in various jurisdictions. Generally speaking, in the Western provinces (excluding Manitoba), Nova Scotia and Newfoundland, incorporation was effected by delivery to the incorporating official, commonly known as the Registrar of Companies, of two documents entitled, respectively, the memorandum of association and the articles of association. The former constituted the basic constitutional document of the company, containing its name, capital structure and a statement of its proposed business.

These jurisdictions are generally referred to as "registration" or "memorandum" jurisdictions. It has been held that the duty of the incorporating officer is to ensure that the documents filed comply with the provisions of the statute, and in particular, that the proposed company has no objects which are illegal, and that there is no objection to the use of the proposed name. Upon being satisfied of this, he or she is bound to accept the documents and issue a certificate of incorporation. The incorporating officer cannot decline to register the documents if the Act has been complied with and, at common law, *mandamus* would lie to compel him to do so: *R. v. Companies Registrar, ex parte Bowen*, [1914] 3 K.B. 1161; and *Crown Lumber Co., Re*, 1943 CarswellAlta 55, [1943] 4 D.L.R. 415 (Alta. T.D.).

In the remaining provinces, and federally, incorporation was effected by making an application to a public official for a grant of Letters Patent of Incorporation. The letters patent contained information approximately equivalent to the contents of the memorandum, but there was no requirement to file the by-laws which corresponded to the articles of association and contained the internal regulations of the corporation.

In these letters patent jurisdictions, a grant of letters patent creating a corporation was an act of the executive, and the Minister involved could, in his absolute and uncontrolled discretion, refuse to grant letters patent or impose arbitrary terms for their issue.

The Lawrence Report concluded that the letters patent system was "a historical anachronism which ought not to be preserved; and that modern public policy no longer requires that a corporation can come into being only by ministerial Act" (*Ontario Select Committee on Company Law, Interim Report* (1967) para. 1.1.6).

Ontario and the other former letters patent jurisdictions, other than PEI, have all now moved towards a system involving a minimum of administrative discretion with respect to the grant of corporate status. Under this regime, incorporation is effected by delivering to the incorporating officer a document called "articles of incorporation". See *e.g.*, *CBCA* ss. 6-9 and *OBCA* ss. 4-7. There is no requirement to file the by-laws; however, it is possible to entrench in the articles of incorporation provisions which would otherwise be proper subject matter for by-laws.

See *CBCA* s. 6(2) and *OBCA* s. 5(3). As is true in memorandum jurisdictions, if the documents are in order, the incorporating officer is required to issue a certificate of incorporation. An appeal lies from the officer's refusal to do so. See *CBCA* ss. 245-246 and *OBCA* ss. 251-252.

Three of the former memorandum jurisdictions — Alberta, Saskatchewan, and Newfoundland — have also adopted the terminology and incorporation techniques of the federal Act, consistent with their general adoption of that Act. The other memorandum jurisdictions (B.C. and Nova Scotia) have so far retained the British legacy, although with some modifications in the case of the new *BCBCA*. Under the *BCBCA* s. 10, the memorandum is replaced by a document called the "notice of articles", the articles will no longer be publicly filed, and the incorporators will enter into a brief "incorporation agreement" intended to preserve the contractual basis of the memorandum corporation.

8. THE NATURE OF THE CORPORATE CONSTITUTION

The differences between the memorandum and letters patent, and now *CBCA* type jurisdictions go well beyond the methods of incorporation to some important conceptual distinctions. Although their significance has been reduced by legislation, an understanding of the distinctions remains important in studying the British jurisprudence and in considering the residual differences not resolved by the modern Canadian Acts.

(a) Pre-CBCA Distinctions

Before the adoption of the *CBCA* and its provincial counterparts, the most relevant distinctions relating to the nature of the corporate constitution were the following:

(1) In the absence of statutory restrictions, a letters patent corporation was deemed to have the capacity and powers of a natural person; a memorandum company, on the other hand, was subject to the doctrine of *ultra vires* as a result of the decision in *Riche v. Ashbury Ry. Carriage & Iron Ore Co.* (1875), L.R. 7 H.L. 653 (H.L.).

(2) In memorandum jurisdictions, the articles of association constituted a public document and outsiders were deemed to have constructive notice of its contents. Conversely, the by-laws were never required to be filed in the letters patent jurisdictions and accordingly the doctrine of constructive notice did not apply to them.

(3) In the memorandum jurisdictions, the memorandum and articles of association constitute a contract between the shareholders and, as construed by the courts, a mutually enforceable contract between the

shareholders and the company. There was no corresponding provision in the letters patent Acts. This did not, of course, mean that the letters patent and by-laws were not binding on the corporation and its members, but it meant that the source of their binding character, and its extent, depended on the express or implied terms of the statute.

(4) The deemed consensual character of the constitution of a memorandum company brought important resulting consequences which have survived to some extent to the present day. First, the allocation of powers between the directors and shareholders was regarded as an internal question to be resolved by the company's constitution. Accordingly, *BCBCA* s. 136(1) provides, "The directors of a company must, subject to this Act, the regulations and the memorandum and articles of the company, manage or supervise the management of the business and affairs of the company". Second, although its scope remains unclear, there is ample authority for the proposition that residual authority remains with the shareholders in a general meeting to break a deadlock among directors (*Barron v. Potter*, [1914] 1 Ch. 895, 83 L.J. Ch. 646), to ratify *ultra vires* acts of the directors (*Irvine v. Union Bank of Australia* (1877), 2 A.C. 366; *Bamford v. Bamford*, [1970] Ch. 212, [1969] 1 All E.R (1969)), and to commence action in the company's name (*Marshall's Valve Gear Co. v. Manning, Wardle & Co.*, [1970] 1 Ch. 267, 78 L.J. Ch. 46). This conception also underlies the rule in *Foss v. Harbottle* (1843), 2 Hare 461, 67 E.R. 189.

The position for the most part was very different in the letters patent jurisdictions. To begin with, it is clear that the directors derive their managerial authority from the Act and not from the corporation's constitution. See Wegenast, *supra*, pp. 353-4, *Kelly v. Electrical Construction Co.* (1907), 16 O.L.R. 232, and *infra*, Ch. 4. Typically, the letters-patent Acts provided (as the *CBCA* s. 102(1) and *OBCA* s. 115(1) now provide) that "Subject to any unanimous shareholder agreement, the directors shall manage, or supervise the management of, the business and affairs of a corporation."

The directors' exclusive managerial authority was also emphasized in letters patent jurisdictions in the usual statutory provision giving directors the exclusive power to adopt bylaws, albeit subject to a requirement for shareholder approval at the next annual meeting of the corporation. On the other hand, in interpreting the statutory by-law making powers, the Canadian courts were not willing to construe them as broadly as the British courts were in reviewing the validity of amendments to articles of association. *Cf. Hutchings v. Can. National Fire Ins. Co.* (1917), 27 Man. R. 496, 33 D.L.R. 752 (C.A.), affirmed [1918] A.C. 451, 39 D.L.R. 401 (P.C.) with *Sidebottom v. Kershaw, Leese & Co. Ltd.*, [1920] 1 Ch. 154, 89 L.J. Ch. 113 (C.A.). The Canadian courts apparently also reserved the general common law right, applied originally to municipal institutions, to test the reasonableness of the by-laws of letters patent corporations. This supervisory jurisdiction was never extended to memorandum companies, although the position has now been changed by statute. See *Edmonton Country Club Ltd. v. Case*, [1975] 1 S.C.R. 534, and the discussion of the "oppression remedy," *infra*, Ch. 10.

Finally, the residual authority of the shareholders in a letters patent jurisdiction has never been clearly defined or put on a sound conceptual footing. Many cases established that the rule in *Foss v. Harbottle* (with its implication of shareholders' power of ratification) applied to letters patent as well as memorandum companies, but beyond this one cannot speak with any assurance. See Wegenast, *supra*, pp. 267, 352, and S.M. Beck, "An Analysis of Foss v. Harbottle" in Ziegel (Ed.), *Studies in Canadian Company Law* (1967), vol. 1, Ch. 18 at pp. 552–556.

For further discussions of the above issues, see M. Neuman, "Letters Patent and Memorandum of Association Companies" in *Studies, supra*, vol. 1, Ch. 3, and B. Slutsky, "The Division of Power between the Board of Directors and the General Meeting," *ibid.*, vol. 2, Ch. 4 (1973).

(b) Current Position

The significant changes in the differences between memorandum and letters patent jurisdictions introduced in the 1970s federal and provincial legislation are the following:

(1) The doctrine of *ultra vires*, so far as it affects the position of third parties, and the doctrine of constructive notice with respect to the contents of public corporate documents, have been abolished in the *CBCA*, the *OBCA* and the *BCBCA*. See, *infra*, Ch. 4.

(2) The entrenched nature of the directors' power is confirmed in *CBCA* s. 102(1), *OBCA* s. 115(l) but subject to important qualifications involving unanimous shareholder agreements (*CBCA* s. 146, *OBCA* s. 108), shareholder proposals (*CBCA* s. 137, *OBCA* s. 99), shareholders' concurrent powers to initiate by-law changes (*CBCA* ss. 103, 137, *OBCA* ss. 99, 116) and a trust agreement between the shareholders and management. (*Piikani Investment Corp. v. Piikani First Nation*, 2008 ABQB 775, 2008 CarswellAlta 2070, [2008] A.J. No. 1470 (Alta. Q.B.)) *People's Department Stores Ltd. (1992) Inc., Re*, 2004 SCC 68, 2004 CarswellQue 2862, 2004 CarswellQue 2863, [2004] 3 S.C.R. 461, 49 B.L.R. (3d) 165 (S.C.C.) affirmed that, subject to any unanimous shareholder agreement to the contrary, it is the duty of the directors, rather than the duty of the shareholders who elected them, to manage the company.

(3) Both the *CBCA* s. 120(7.1), and *OBCA* s. 132(8), confirm the shareholders' power to ratify a voidable contract in which an officer or director has a material interest. See *Joy Estate v. 1156653 Ontario Ltd.*, 2007 CarswellOnt 3762, [2007] O.J. No. 2315 (Ont. S.C.J.), additional reasons at 2007 CarswellOnt 7323 (Ont. S.C.J.), additional reasons at 2007 CarswellOnt 7739 (Ont. S.C.J.).

(4) The courts are given an explicit power in favour of shareholders and other "complainants" to enjoin the corporation and its officers from violating the Act, its regulations or the corporation's constitution and to require compliance with their provisions. See *CBCA* s. 247, *OBCA* s. 253(1) and, *infra*, Ch. 10(5). This power does not apply to the actions of a director acting as a shareholder. (*Polar Star Mining Corp. v. Willock*, 2009 CarswellOnt 1416, 96 O.R. (3d) 688 (Ont. S.C.J.)) Courts may, pursuant to CBCA s. 247, go so far as to appoint an inspector, or ensure that the corporation discharges its financial disclosure obligations to its shareholders. (*Pandora Select Partners, LP v. Strategy Real Estate Investments Ltd.*, 2007 CarswellOnt 1567, 27 B.L.R. (4th) 299 (Ont. S.C.J. [Commercial List])).

Note that differences that may appear important in law often are much less so in practice, particularly according to accounts of the corporation asserting that shareholders have ceased to exercise a meaningful managerial or supervisory role in the affairs of the corporation.

(c) Note on the Scope of the Contract Created by the Memorandum and Articles of Association in Memorandum Jurisdictions

(1) It is clearly established in the common law that the memorandum and articles do not constitute a contract between the company and a nonmember. In *Eley v. Positive Government Security Live Assce. Co.* (1876), 1 Ex. D. 88, 45 L.J.Q. B. 451 (C.A.), the articles, which were prepared by Eley, provided that he should be the company solicitor. He subsequently became a member; his employment was later terminated, and he sued for breach of contract. It was held that the articles could not be relied upon to support his claims, since he was not a party to them at the critical time of incorporation.

(2) Statutory exceptions to the common law exist in two Canadian jurisdictions. *BCBCA* s. 19(3) does not expressly provide that each member is deemed to contract with the company, though this has been held to be its effect: *Hickman v. Kent or Romney Marsh Sheepbreeders' Association*, [1915] Ch. 881, 84 L.J. Ch. 688.The Nova Scotia *Companies Act* s. 24(1) is similar in this regard. See *Sumner v. PCL Constructors Inc.*, 2010 ABQB 536, 2010 CarswellAlta 1637, [2010] A.J. No. 948 (Alta. Q.B.), reversed in part 2011 CarswellAlta 1934 (Alta. C.A.), leave to appeal refused 2012 CarswellAlta 1115, 2012 CarswellAlta 1116 (S.C.C.).

It follows, in principle, that not only are the members bound to the company but that the company is also bound to the members: *Wood v. Odessa Waterworks Co.* (1889), 42 Ch. D. 636, 58 L.J. Ch. 628 (Ch. Div.).

It is also clear that a contract exists between the members *inter se*. Finally, there is abundant authority for the view that the contractual force of the memorandum and articles is, so far as members are concerned, limited to contractual rights or imposing burdens upon them in their capacity as members.

(3) In *Hickman v. Kent or Romney Marsh Sheepbreeders' Association* [1915] 1 Ch. 881, 84 L.J. Ch. 688, it was suggested that for a right to be conferred upon a member *qua* member, it must be part of the provisions applicable to all members. In *Rayfield v. Hands*, [1960] Ch. 1, the articles required every member who intended to transfer his shares to notify the directors who were then required to take the shares at a fair value. The plaintiffs duly gave notice, but the defendant denied liability to take up and pay for the shares, and plaintiff sought to compel them to do so, and succeeded. It was held that the obligation to acquire the shares was imposed upon the directors as members. Would the result have been different if the directors had not been required by the articles to be members?

(4) It is generally considered that the remedy available to a member who complains of a breach of the articles is a declaration or injunction, but not damages. There is authority for the proposition that a shareholder cannot sue a company for damages in respect of his position as shareholder unless he or she is also in a position to rescind his membership contract, and does so: *Houldsworth v. City of Glasgow Bank* (1880), 5 App. Cas. 317, and *Philipzyk v. Edmonton Real Estate Board Co-operative Listing Bureau Ltd.*, 1975 CarswellAlta 34, 55 D.L.R. (3d) 424 (Alta. C.A.). Do *BCBCA* s. 228, *OBCA* s. 253, and *CBCA* s. 247, permit damages to be awarded? *Cf. Goldhar v. Quebec Manitou Mines Ltd.* (1976), 9 O.R. (2d) 740, *infra*, Ch. 10 and *Sumner v. PCL Constructors Inc.*, *supra*.

(5) There is an ongoing debate with respect to the relationship between s. 14 of the English Act and the rule in *Foss v. Harbottle*. It is often said that directors' and officers' duties lie only to the company, although there is a growing body of case-law debating what exactly this means (discussed more fully in Chapter 6). Nevertheless, it is now recognized, both in the memorandum and letters patent jurisdictions, that there may be a concurrent breach of duty to the shareholders and to the company. However, the principle is somewhat differently formulated in the two systems. *Cf. Gower, op. cit.*, pp. 120, with *Goldex Mines Ltd. v. Revill* (1975), 7 O.R. (2d) 216, 54 D.L.R. (3d) 672 (C.A.), *infra*, Ch. 10.

(6) Given the unclear British position, the Alberta Law Reform Institute felt that "There is no need to resort to the artificial implication of a contract, and indeed, the notion that there is a contract is likely to interfere with the proper working out of rights and obligations which arise because of relationships, the nature of which is determined by law." (*Proposals for a New Alberta Business Corporations Act* (1980), vol. 1, p. 21.)

Does *CBCA* s. 239 make it any easier to distinguish between individual and derivative rights of a shareholder, and to determine the circumstances when an action can only be brought by, or on behalf of, the corporation? See *Re Goldhar & Quebec Manitou Mines Ltd.* (1977), 9 O.R. (2d) 740, 61 D.L.R. (3d) 612 (Div. Ct.), *infra*, Ch. 10.

9. ALTERATION OF THE CORPORATE CONSTITUTION

All corporate legislation includes provisions of varying degrees of comprehensiveness and complexity governing the method by which the constitution of the corporation may be altered. See, *e.g.*, *CBCA* ss. 173–180 and *OBCA* ss. 168–173. It is impossible here to summarize in any useful way the details of the mechanisms prescribed by the various statutes for effecting an alteration, or the extent to which the corporate constitution is, in each jurisdiction, subject to alteration.

Three general characteristics of the statutory requirements are common, however. First, alteration of the constitution requires, in each case, a special procedure, generally in the form of a shareholders' resolution that must be agreed to by more than a mere majority of the shareholders. Second, if rights are attached to the shares of a particular group or class of shareholders (*e.g.*, preferred shares) that are, in some sense, unique, provision is generally made for the shareholders holding those shares to give their consent separately to any alteration of those rights. Third, modern corporate legislation commonly provides that shareholders who disagree with, and vote against, certain proposed alterations are entitled to have their shares bought from them at a valuation. This so-called "appraisal remedy" is examined in Ch. 10.

The limitations imposed by these provisions are principally procedural in character and must, of course, be observed if the alteration is to be effective. In addition, however, there are substantive limitations.

First, a shareholder cannot, without his or her consent, be required to take or subscribe for more shares or have his or her liability to contribute to the assets of the company increased:

> The doctrine of limited liability operates to protect the holders of fully-paid shares not only from the claims of creditors of the company, but also from obligations, financial or other, sought to be imposed by other shareholders of the company. It would be a strange thing and contrary to all jurisprudence, if the purchaser of shares in a public company could be required all of a sudden and against his will, at the instance of the company or a majority of its shareholders, to contribute to the operating expenses, or capital requirement needs of the company.

Per Dickson, J. in *Edmonton Country Club Ltd. v. Case*, [1975] 1 S.C.R. 534, 44 D.L.R. (3d) 554, 565.

Second, the principle that a majority may not exercise its powers in fraud of, or so as to oppress, a minority also operates as a limitation upon the power to alter the constitution.

10.   PRE-INCORPORATION CONTRACTS

The fact that Anglo-Canadian law does not recognize the existence of a corporation until a certificate of incorporation has been issued or other prescribed conditions have been met creates significant legal and practical difficulties, usually when a promoter concludes a contract on behalf of a proposed corporation. This may happen in a variety of circumstances: the promoter may feel it important to get the commitment of the other party to the pre-incorporation contract before he or she has an opportunity to change his or her mind; the other party may insist on the pre-incorporation contract being concluded by a given date; the existence of the pre-incorporation contract may be a pre-condition of the promoter being able to attract other investors to the corporation, and so forth. The promoter often wants to avoid personal liability on the pre-incorporation contract and, since most promoters are not lawyers, she probably believes she can secure this immunity by signing the pre-incorporation contract in a representative capacity. Frequently the promoter is also under the mistaken impression that the corporation has already been incorporated or that compliance with the statutory incorporation requirements is only a minor inconsequential formality.

Part (a) of the following materials explores the common law status of pre-incorporation contracts, while Part (b) deals with the important statutory reforms introduced in the business corporations acts that have changed the historic common law position. In considering the legal position, it will be helpful to distinguish between the following situations:

1.   Both parties to the pre-incorporation contract (the promoter and the contracting party) know that the company has not yet been incorporated.
2.   The promoter knows that the company has not yet been incorporated but the contracting party does not.
3.   Neither party to the pre-incorporation contract knows that the company has not yet been incorporated; the promoter mistakenly believes that the company has been incorporated and the contracting party relies on the promoter's representations.

Where the company is eventually incorporated, consider also the differences between the situations where the corporation purports to ratify or adopt the pre-incorporation contract, and where it does not ratify or adopt the contract.

Finally, as you read these materials and the claims that each contracting party is making, consider whether or not it should matter if the contracting party (i.e., the party that is not the promoter) made any inquiry, prior to concluding the pre-incorporation contract, into the assets or solvency of the corporation purporting to enter into the contract. Is there an element of a windfall if the promoter is held personally liable on the pre-incorporation contract where the contracting party made no such inquiries?

(a) Common Law Position

Kelner v. Baxter
(1866), L.R. 2 C.P 174 (Common Pleas)

[The plaintiff was a wine merchant and the proprietor of the Assembly Rooms at Gravesend. In August, 1865, it was proposed that a company should be formed for establishing a joint-stock hotel company at Gravesend to be called The Gravesend Royal Alexandra Hotel Company, Limited; the plaintiff and a number of other gentlemen were to be directors. Further, the plaintiff was to be the manager of the proposed company, and Mr. Dales (one of the defendants) was to be the permanent architect. One part of the scheme was that the company should purchase the premises of the plaintiff for the sum of »5,000, of which »3,000 was to be paid in cash, and »2,000 in paid up shares. This agreement was carried into effect and completed, with Mr. Baxter (another defendant) being the nominal purchaser on behalf of the company. In December a prospectus was settled. On the 9th of January, 1866, a memorandum of association was executed by the plaintiff and the defendants and others.

Pending the completion of the sale, the plaintiff continued to carry on the business and for that purpose purchased additional stock (i.e. wine). On the 27th of January, 1866, an agreement was entered into for the transfer of this additional stock to the company on the following terms:

"January 27th, 1866.

"To John Dacier Baxter, Nathan Jacob Calisher, and John Dales, on behalf of the proposed Gravesend Royal Alexandra Hotel Company, Limited.

"Gentlemen, — I hereby propose to sell the extra stock now at the Assembly Rooms, Gravesend, as per schedule hereto, for the sum of »900, payable on the 28th of February, 1866.

(Signed) "John Kelner."

Then followed a schedule of the stock of wines, etc., to be purchased, and at the end was written as follows:

To Mr. John Kelner.

"Sir, — We have received your offer to sell the extra stock as above, and hereby agree to and accept the terms proposed.

(Signed)   "J.D. Baxter,
"N.J. Calisher,

"J. Dales,
"On behalf of the Gravesend Royal Alexandra
Hotel Company, Limited."

Pursuant to this agreement the goods in question were handed over to the company and consumed by it in the business of the hotel. On February 1st a meeting of the directors took place at which the following resolution was passed: "That the arrangement entered into by Messrs. Calisher, Dales, and Baxter, on behalf of the company, for the purchase of the additional stock on the premises, as per list taken by Mr. Bright, the secretary, and pointed out by Mr. Kelner, amounting to »900, be, and the same is hereby ratified." There was a subsequent ratification by the company, on April 11th, but this was after the commencement of the action.

The articles of association of the company were stamped on the 13th of February and on the 20th the company obtained a certificate of incorporation under the *Companies Act* 1862.

The company collapsed, and this action was brought against the defendants, based on the agreement of January 27th.

Erle C.J. rendered judgment for the plaintiff for »900.]

ERLE, C.J.: I am of opinion that this rule should be discharged. . . . A difficulty has arisen because the plaintiff has at the head of the paper addressed it to the plaintiffs [*sic*: read defendants?] on behalf of the proposed Gravesend Royal Alexandra Hotel Company, Limited," and the defendants have repeated those words after their signatures to the document; and the question is, whether this constitutes any ambiguity on the fact of the agreement, or prevents the defendants from being bound by it. I agree that if the Gravesend Royal Alexandra Hotel Company had been an existing company at this time, the persons who signed the agreement would have signed as agents of the company. But, as there was no company in existence at the time, the agreement would be wholly inoperative unless it were held to be binding on the defendants personally. The cases referred to in the course of the argument fully bear out the proposition that, where a contract is signed by one who professes to be signing "as agent," but who has no principal existing at the time, and the contract would be altogether inoperative unless binding upon the person who signed it, he is bound thereby: and a stranger cannot by a subsequent ratification relieve him from that responsibility. When the company came afterwards into existence it was a totally new creature, having rights and obligations from that time, but no rights or obligations by reason of anything which might have been done before. . . The plaintiff parted with his stock upon the faith of the defendants' engagement that the price agreed on should be paid on the day named. It cannot be supposed that he for a moment contemplated that the payment was to be contingent on the formation of the company by the 28th of February. The paper expresses in terms a contract to buy. And it is a cardinal rule that no oral evidence shall be admitted to shew an intention different from that which appears on the face of the writing. I come, therefore, to the conclusion that the defendants, having no principal who was bound originally, or who could become so by a subsequent ratification, were themselves bound, and that the oral evidence offered is not admissible to contradict the written contract.

WILLES J.: I am of the same opinion. Evidence was clearly inadmissible to shew that the parties contemplated that the liability on this contract should rest upon the company and not upon the persons contracting on behalf of the proposed company. The utmost it could amount to is, that both parties were satisfied at the time that all would go smoothly, and consequently that no liability would ensue to the defendants. . . Who is to pay? The company, if it should be formed. But, if the company should not be formed, who is to pay? That is tested by the fact of the immediate delivery of the subject of sale. If payment was not made by the company, it must, if by anybody, be by the defendants. . .

Both upon principle and upon authority, therefore, it seems to me that the company never could be liable upon this contract: and, as was put by my Lord, construing this document *ut res magis valeat quam pereat*, we must assume that the parties contemplated that the persons signing it would be personally liable. Putting in the words "on behalf of the Gravesend Royal Alexandra Hotel Company," would operate no more than if a person should contract for a quantity of corn "on behalf of my horses." As to the suggestion that there should have been a special count, that is quite a mistake. There need not be a special count unless there was a person existing at the time the contract was made who might have been principal. The common count perfectly well represents the character of the liability which these defendants incurred. It is quite out of the question to suppose that there was any mistake. The document represents the real transaction between the parties. I think that the course taken at the trial was perfectly correct, and that the rule should be discharged.

Rule Discharged.

[The concurring judgments of Byles and Keating JJ. are omitted.]

Notes

1   Do you agree with Willes J.'s reasoning that "we must assume that the parties contemplated that the persons signing the pre-incorporation contract would be personally liable"? If the defendants anticipated this result, why did they sign the contract "on behalf of" the proposed company? The evidence at trial was that the plaintiff was to be the manager of the proposed company and that the company was in fact incorporated on February 20, 1866, i.e., before the agreed date for the payment of the stock.

2   Can you suggest how, in the realm of pre-incorporation contracts, the court could have overcome or distinguished the common law rule that a contract cannot be made with a non-existent principal? In view of the fact that the court treated the purported ratification of the pre-incorporation contract by the Hotel Company as a total nullity, what obligations, if any, did the company assume with respect to the stock received by it, and to whom?

3   It was established at common law that the "non-ratification" rule cannot be avoided by recourse to such devices as "adopting" the pre-incorporation contract (*Relpetti Ltd. v. Oliver-Lee Ltd.*, 52 O.L.R. 315, [1923] 3 D.L.R. 1400 (C.A.)) or resort to a "provisional contract" (*Hudson-Mattagami Exploration Mining Co. v. Wettlatufer Bros. Ltd.*, 62 O.L.R. 387, [1928] 3 D.L.R. 661 (C.A.)). What is required at common law is a fresh contract, a requirement which, in the absence of a new written document, presents considerable difficulties. See generally, Getz, "Pre-incorporation Contracts: Some Proposals" (1967), U.B.C. L. Rev. 381, 382–387. For examples of cases in which the requirement has been satisfied, see *Howard v. Patent Ivory Mnfg. Co.* (1888), 38 Ch. D. 156; *Heinhuis v. Blacksheep Charters Ltd.* (1988), 46 D.L.R. (4th) 67 (B.C.C.A.); *Brown Brothers Motor Lease Canada Ltd. v. Kirkpatrick* (1992), 67 B.C.L.R. (2d) 141, 1992 CarswellBC 127 (C.A.); and *Phelps Holdings Ltd. v. Strata Plan VIS 3430*, 2010 BCCA 196, 2010 CarswellBC 1247 (B.C.C.A.). The latter cases indicate contemporary Canadian courts' willingness to relax the strict common law requirements.

4   Since the decision in *Kelner v. Baxter* was based on the assumed intention of the parties, it is of course open to the promoter in other cases to show that he or she had expressly excluded his personal liability. A Canadian common law decision where this defence succeeded is *Dairy Supplies v. Fuchs* (1959), 18 D.L.R. (2d) 408, 28 W.W.R. 1 (Sask.).

5   It is important to note that *Kelner v. Baxter* has been overruled by statute (*CBCA* s. 14(2)).

Black v. Smallwood
[1966] A.L.R. 744 (High Court of Australia)

[The appellants purported to enter into a contract for the sale of land to Western Suburbs Holdings Pty. Ltd. The contract was signed as follows:

Western Suburbs Holdings Pty. Ltd.

Robert Smallwood	}	Directors.
J. Cooper		

It was subsequently found that Western Suburbs Holdings Pty. Ltd. had not at that time been incorporated but it is common ground that both the appellants and the respondents believed that it had been and that the latter were directors of the company. Thereafter the appellants instituted a suit for specific performance against the respondents in accordance with the terms of the contract, alleging that the respondents as agents contracting on behalf of a principal not yet in existence are bound.

Upon the trial the appellants were successful in obtaining a decree for specific performance but on appeal to the Full Court the decree was set aside and the suit dismissed. The appellants further appealed to the High Court.]

BARWICK C.J., KITTO, TAYLOR AND OWEN JJ: *Kelner v. Baxter* was cited as an authority for the proposition that there is a rule of law to the effect that where a person contracts on behalf of a nonexistent principal he is himself liable on the contract. But we find it impossible to extract any such proposition from the decision. In that case it appears from the contract itself that the defendants had no principal; they had purported to enter into a contract, on behalf of the "proposed Gravesend Royal Alexandra Hotel Company," and the fact that they had no principal was obvious to both parties. But it was not by reason of this fact alone that the defendants were held to be liable; the court proceeded to examine the written instrument in order to see if, in these circumstances, an intention should be imputed to the defendants to bind themselves personally, or perhaps, to put it another way, whether, the intention being sufficiently clear that a binding contract was intended, there was anything in the writing inconsistent with the conclusion that the defendants should be bound personally. The decision was that, in the circumstances, the writing disclosed an intention that the defendants should be bound . . ."

* * *

WINDEYER J.: . . . In many cases courts have had to decide whether an agent had, in the particular case, incurred a personal liability on a contract in writing made by him on behalf of a principal. And these decisions have sometimes turned upon narrow differences in wording, which seem to be the progeny by miscegenation of early technical rules relating to the form of the execution of deeds . . . But here that question does not really arise, for the document which the respondents signed does not purport to be a contract made by them as agents for the supposed company. They thought that the company existed and that they were in fact directors. It is therefore impossible to regard them as having used the name of the company as a mere pseudonym or firm name or as having intended to incur a personal liability. The reason for the formation of the company may have been to ensure that they would not be personally liable. It is however suggested that, notwithstanding the form of the document, a personal obligation to perform the contract has been imposed upon them by law, because at the time they inserted the name of the company as purchaser there was no such company in existence.

So far as this proposition is based upon *Kelner v. Baxter* it must fail. The facts of this case differ essentially from the facts of that. Some statements in textbooks and in judgments that abbreviate the effect of that decision can be at least misleading, unless they be read with the facts well in mind. For example, Latham C.J. said that there "the intention was . . . evident that the proposed company and not the persons purporting to act as agents should be the contracting parties, and yet the court found no difficulty in substituting the agents for the supposed principal as the contracting party": *Summergreene v. Parker* [(1950) 80 C.L.R. 304 at 314]. But it is wrong to read this as meaning that whenever a person contracts professedly on behalf of a principal not yet in existence or already gone out of existence, the so-called agent is "substituted" as the contracting party and becomes personally liable to perform the contract or pay damages for non-performance. Doubtless in *Kelner v. Baxter* both the plaintiff and the defendants expected that payment for the goods would be made from the funds of the company that was in process of being formed. That, however, was not a term of the contract. And when the goods were bought it was well-known to all concerned that the company had not yet been formed. ... The defendants in *Kelner v. Baxter* therefore contracted as principals. They were not substituted as principals. They were the principals. The contrast with this case is obvious. Here, instead of both parties knowing that the company was not in existence, they both, appellants and respondents, thought that it was. . . .

It would, I think, be contrary to now-established principle to hold a man personally liable on a contract when he did not intend personally to contract and when, the transaction being in writing, the writing could not upon its true construction, when read in the light of what both parties took to be the facts, mean that he had done so. The purported contract in this case was a nullity, for the supposed purchaser did not exist when it was made. The suit for specific performance therefore must fail.

Appeal dismissed.

Note

In *Newborne v. Sensolid (Great Britain) Ltd.*, [1953] 1 All E.R. 708, [1954] 1 Q.B. 45, a pre-incorporation contract was concluded between Leopold Newborne (London) Ltd. and the defendant for the supply of goods to the defendant. The contract was signed "Leopold Newborne (London) Ltd." and underneath appeared the plaintiff's name "Leopold Newborne." The defendant repudiated the contract and an action was commenced in the name of Leopold Newborne (London) Ltd. It was then discovered that the company had not been incorporated at the time of the making of the contract. Newborne then sought to enforce the pre-incorporation contract personally, relying on the decision in *Kelner v. Baxter*. He failed both before Parker J. and the Court of Appeal on the ground that the pre-incorporation contract was made, not with the plaintiff, whether as agent or as principal, but with a limited company which at the date of the contract was non-existent, and that therefore the contract was a total nullity.

In *Phonogram Ltd. v. Lane* [1981] 3 All E.R. 182 (C.A.),a case which was concerned with the construction of s. 9(2) of the U.K. *European Communities Act*, 1972, Lord Denning M. R., deprecated the fine common law distinction between a contract signed "for" and a contract signed "as agent." Oliver J. thought the real question in every case was the true intention of the parties and that the liability of a person who signed did not turn on the distinction drawn in *Newborne's*.

Wickberg v. Shatsky & Shatsky
(1969), 4 D.L.R. (3d) 540 (B.C. S.C.)

[In 1965 the two defendants purchased an interest and became directors of a corporation by the name of Rapid Addressing Systems Ltd., which was carrying on business in Vancouver selling and servicing business machines and supplies. The defendants decided to carry on business under the name Rapid Data (Western) Ltd., although no company was ever incorporated under that name. The defendants hired the plaintiff to be manager of the corporation, and executed a contract on the letterhead of Rapid Data (Western) Ltd. and signed by the defendant L. Shatsky as president, saying that he was hired as general manager of the company at a salary of $15,000 *per annum*, "to be reviewed six months from this date". The defendants subsequently instructed the plaintiff that the company should drop the "Ltd." from its name and continue as Rapid Data (Western). The business was not successful and on August the 26, 1966, the plaintiff, after refusing to work on straight commission, was given a notice terminating his services.]

DRYER J.: The plaintiff now brings this action against the two defendants. Counsel for the plaintiff contends (1) that the defendant Lawrence Shatsky is liable as a party to the contract, ex. 1, since it was signed by him as agent for a nonexistent principal; and (2) that Lawrence Shatsky and Harold Shatsky are each liable for breach of warranty of authority in that they warranted the existence of Rapid Data (Western) Ltd. and warranted Lawrence Shatsky's authority to sign the contract on behalf of Rapid Data (Western) Ltd.; and (3) that the business by which the plaintiff was employed was a firm in which Lawrence Shatsky and Harold Shatsky were partners and that consequently each of them is liable for the losses suffered by the plaintiff arising from the nonperformance of the contract, ex. 1.

The first contention, *viz.*, that Lawrence Shatsky is liable since he signed ex.1 on behalf of Rapid Data (Western) Ltd., a non-existent corporation, is based upon the principle said to be established by *Kelner v. Baxter* (1866), L.R. 2 C.P 174. In my opinion the plaintiff's claim under this heading cannot succeed by reason of the principle laid down in *Black et al. v. Smallwood* (1966), 39 A.L.J.R. 405. In *Kelner v. Baxter* both parties knew that the company was not in existence. In *Black v. Smallwood* both parties thought that the company in question was in existence. In the case at bar the plaintiff thought that Rapid Data (Western) Ltd. was in existence and the defendants knew that it was not. Counsel for the plaintiff contends that that distinction makes the rule laid down in *Black et al. v. Smallwood* inapplicable. No authority is cited in support of this distinction. In my opinion, the distinction between *Kelner v. Baxter* and *Black et al. v. Smallwood* is that in *Kelner v. Baxter* the decision was that in the circumstances the writing disclosed an intention that the defendant should be bound whereas that was not the case in *Black et al. v. Smallwood*. (See *Black et al. v. Smallwood* at p. 406.) It follows that, in my opinion, the reasoning in *Black et al. v. Smallwood* is not inapplicable to the case at bar. Here the parties did not have the same view as to the facts at the time the contract was entered into. Nevertheless it was not the intention of the parties or either of them when the contract was made that Lawrence Shatsky who signed as a director should be personally liable on the contract and therefore, on the principle laid down in *Black et al. v. Smallwood*, he cannot be held liable on the contract. That does not mean, of course, that he could not be liable for breach of warranty of authority or for fraud if they were pleaded and proven. Breach of warranty of authority is pleaded and I will deal with it now.

In my opinion, the defendants undoubtedly so acted as to warrant to the plaintiff that Rapid Data (Western) Ltd. was a legal entity and that they had the power to represent it and to speak for it when entering into ex. 1 with the plaintiff. At the same time I feel that the plaintiff knew very shortly after the date of ex. 1 that the business was not being carried on by an incorporated company known as Rapid Data (Western) Ltd. . . ..

However, at the time of entering into ex. 1, the plaintiff did not know that Rapid Data (Western) Ltd. was not incorporated and the defendants did, but, I can see no causal connection between the damage suffered by the plaintiff and the breach of the warranty as to its existence. The fact that Rapid Data (Western) Ltd. was not incorporated and the fact that Rapid Data (Western) Ltd. was not the operator of the business did not cause the plaintiff's loss. Moreover, as pointed out above, shortly after he commenced working and shortly after the date of Ex.1 the plaintiff knew that the business was being carried on under the name Rapid Data (Western) which should have alerted any normal businessman to the fact that it was a firm rather than a corporation. If, as he says, he attached little significance to the omission of the word "Ltd.", he would surely have attached little significance to the presence of that word in the name of the operator of the business originally presented to him. His loss, as I see it, resulted from the fact that the business was not a success, not from the breach of warranty. . .

The plaintiff is therefore, as I see it, entitled only to nominal damages for this breach of warranty. He is entitled to such nominal damages against both defendants . . .

Judgment for plaintiff.

Notes

1   What was the effect of the plaintiff being told by the defendant Shatsky, a few days after he had received the written contract of employment, "to stop using the name Rapid Data (Western) Ltd. and to carry on under the name Rapid Data (Western)", i.e., that the word "Ltd." was to be dropped? Did it mean that from that date onwards there was a new implied contract of employment between the plaintiff and the principals of Rapid Data (Western) unincorporated? Who were the principals, and would it have been in the plaintiff's interest to have relied on the second contract rather than the first?

2   A judgment similar to *Shatsky* was rendered in another pre-incorporation case, *Delta Construction Co. Ltd. v. Lidstone* (1979), 96 D.L.R. (3d) 457, 29 Nfld. & P.E.I.R. 70 (Nfld., S.C. T.D.). The defendants, wishing to form Algo Enterprises Limited, instructed a solicitor and, on April 2, 1975, signed the memorandum and articles of association. The documents were left with the solicitor in the belief that he was to be the third subscriber and that he would complete the incorporation. About a month later, needing the company's seal, Lidstone went to the solicitor's office and received a seal from a clerk. The seal was used in connection with banking *documents*, a bank account was opened, and, later, the seal was passed to a solicitor for Central Mortgage and Housing Corporation to be used in connection with a real estate transaction. In August, 1975, the defendants became aware, through the solicitor for CMHC, that the company had not been incorporated. Their solicitor was contacted and he advised that the company would be incorporated without delay. It was not incorporated until October 22, 1975.

In the meantime, in May, 1975, Lidstone requested the plaintiff to do work for Algo Enterprises Limited. He was well known to the plaintiff's manager as the plaintiff had done work for companies in which Lidstone had an interest. The value of the work done was $17,845. Approximately $3,200 was paid, before the company was incorporated, by cheques drawn on a bank account in the name of Algo Enterprises Limited. The project foundered and the balance, approximately $14,645, was not paid. Noel J. said (at p. 463):

Did the plaintiff suffer damages as a result of Lidstone's breach of warranty?

At most Lidstone represented that an existing company, Algo Enterprises Limited, required work to be done by the plaintiff. The plaintiff was, clearly, expected to extend credit to the company but Lidstone did not warrant that the company had any assets, that it was solvent, or that the plaintiff's account would be paid. The decision to extend credit was made by the plaintiff. Since the project foundered, it is reasonable to suppose that if the plaintiff is successful in this suit for the balance of its account, assuming the defendants to be solvent, it would be in a better position than it would have been in had the company been in existence as the parties believed. In short, the non-existence of the company would be a windfall to the plaintiff. If the defendants are obliged to pay the plaintiff's account, in effect, they would be guarantors of the account which neither they nor the plaintiff intended should be the case.

3   What should be the measure of damages for false warranty of authority where the company has never been incorporated and, unlike in *Wickberg v. Shatsky*, has never done any business? How can one tell whether or not the incorporated company would have been successful? In the interests of contract performance and greater care in the use of the corporate form, should a court make every presumption against the defendant and assume that the corporation would have been properly financed and properly managed?

4   Apart from the liability of the purported agent for false warranty of authority, what liability is incurred by the person who has actually received the benefit of the plaintiff's work? What is the common law position where the party contracting with the assumed corporation refuses to pay for benefits conferred by the corporation?

(b) Statutory Reforms

In 1967, the Ontario Select Committee on Company Law released an interim report with recommendations for reform in the law of pre-incorporation contracts. They found that the rule in *Kelner v. Baxter* did not consistently protect the parties to a pre-incorporation contract. They also observed that the majority of States of the United States rejected *Kelner v. Baxter*. Based on these findings, the Committee recommended that the law be amended to allow a corporation, through a unilateral act, to adopt a pre-incorporation contract, thereby relieving the promoter of any liability. The Committee also recommended that, where it is just and equitable to the interests of the contracting party, application could be made to the High Court of Ontario for an order that the promoters and the company will be jointly and severally liable under a pre-incorporation contract. The Select Committee's recommendations were implemented in

s. 20 of the 1970 Ontario *Act*, and repealed in 2006. The current provisions are reproduced below:

21. (1) Except as provided in this section, a person who enters into an oral or written contract in the name of or on behalf of a corporation before it comes into existence is personally bound by the contract and is entitled to the benefits thereof.

(2) A corporation may, within a reasonable time after it comes into existence, by any action or conduct signifying its intention to be bound thereby, adopt an oral or written contract made before it came into existence in its name or on its behalf, and upon such adoption,

(a) the corporation is bound by the contract and is entitled to the benefits thereof as if the corporation had been in existence at the date of the contract and had been a party thereto; and

(b) a person who purported to act in the name of or on behalf of the corporation ceases, except as provided in subsection (3), to be bound by or entitled to the benefits of the contract.

(3) Except as provided in subsection (4), whether or not an oral or written contract made before the coming into existence of a corporation is adopted by the corporation, a party to the contract may apply to a court for an order fixing obligations under the contract as joint or joint and several or apportioning liability between the corporation and the person who purported to act in the name of or on behalf of the corporation, and, upon such application, the court may make any order it thinks fit.

(4) If expressly so provided in the oral or written contract referred to in subsection (1), a person who purported to act in the name of or on behalf of the corporation before it came into existence is not in any event bound by the contract or entitled to the benefits thereof.

* * *

The federal provisions appear in *CBCA* s. 14.

14. (1) Subject to this section, a person who enters into, or purports to enter into, a written contract in the name of or on behalf of a corporation before it comes into existence is personally bound by the contract and is entitled to its benefits.

(2) A corporation may, within a reasonable time after it comes into existence, by any action or conduct signifying its intention to be bound thereby, adopt a written contract made before it came into existence in its name or on its behalf, and on such adoption

(a) the corporation is bound by the contract and is entitled to the benefits thereof as if the corporation had been in existence at the date of the contract and had been a party thereto; and

(b) a person who purported to act in the name of or on behalf of the corporation ceases, except as provided in subsection (3), to be bound by or entitled to the benefits of the contract.

(3) Subject to subsection (4), whether or not a written contract made before the coming into existence of a corporation is adopted by the corporation, a party to the contract may apply to a court for an order respecting the nature and extent of the obligations and liability under the contract of the corporation and the person who entered into, or purported to enter into, the contract in the name of or on behalf of the corporation. On the application, the court may make any order it thinks fit.

(4) If expressly so provided in the written contract, a person who purported to act in the name of or on behalf of the corporation before it came into existence is not in any event bound by the contract or entitled to the benefits thereof.

Notes and Questions

1   For the purposes of imposing liability, the distinction between a corporation that has not yet incorporated and one that has lost its corporate status may be irrelevant (*Peak Mechanical Ltd. v. Lewko*, 2005 SKQB 83, 2005 CarswellSask 214, 3 B.L.R. (4th) 75 (Sask. Q.B.)).

2   Borins J.A. provided an extensive review of the legislative history and evolution of OBCA s. 21 in *Sherwood* Design *Services Ltd. v. 872935 Ontario Ltd.* (1998), 39 O.R. (3d) 576, 1998 CarswellOnt 1739 (C.A.) at pp. 593–600 [O.R.].

3   Another approach is represented by the Alberta statute, which uses the concept of a "deemed warranty" from the promoter to the other party that (i) the corporation will come into existence within a reasonable time and (ii) that the corporation will adopt the contract within a reasonable time after the corporation is incorporated. The promoter is liable to the other party for damages for a breach of this warranty, and the measure of damages for a breach of the warranty is the same as if the corporation existed when the pre-incorporation contract was made, the promoter had no authority to make the contract on the corporation's behalf, and the corporation refused to ratify the contract. See the Alberta *Business Corporations Act*, RSA 2000, c. B-9, s. 15(2) and *BCBCA* s. 20, which follows this deemed warranty approach.

4 What steps are necessary for a corporation to adopt a pre-incorporation contract? Courts have held the wording of the *OBCA* to be permissive enough that formal adoption is not required, so long as some action is taken to signify intent to be bound. See *Design Home Associates v. Raviv*, 2004 CarswellOnt 1660, 44 B.L.R. (3d) 124 (Ont. S.C.J.), affirmed 2006 CarswellOnt 125 (Ont. C.A.). Courts have held that the wording of the *CBCA* is also similarly permissive. See *Shoppers Drug Mart Inc. v. 6470360 Canada Inc.*, 2014 CarswellOnt 1133, 2014 ONCA 85 (Ont. C.A.) at paras. 31-37, leave to appeal refused 2014 CarswellOnt 8632, 2014 CarswellOnt 8633 (S.C.C.).

5 The Ontario Court of Appeal further explored the question of formal adoption in *TMD Investments Ltd. v. Fiddlehead's Cafe Inc.*, 2007 CarswellOnt 3737, 2007 ONCA 428 (Ont. C.A.). Although formal adoption is not required, the action to signify intent to be bound must be made within a reasonable time according to *OBCA* s. 21(2). In this case, the trial judge held that the only act signifying intent were certain rental payments, but they were made almost one year after incorporation, which the trial judge held was not within a reasonable time. What factors should be considered in determining reasonable time? In your view, does modern technology, increasing both ease and speed of communication, significantly reduce what is considered to be reasonable time?

6 Why should a promoter be held personally liable if the pre-incorporation contract is not adopted by the corporation and the other party to the contract was not aware at the time of its conclusion that the corporation did not yet exist? The Federal Proposals (paras. 69-70) rationalized the new rule on the ground that the common law distinctions between the personal liability of a promoter and his liability on other grounds (principally for breach of warranty of authority) are difficult to apply and that the latter are not always adequate substitutes for contractual remedies. A further reason given by the Proposals is that "as a matter of business reality, the promoter is usually in control of the pre-incorporation and immediate post-incorporation process and is able to protect himself." Do you find these reasons convincing?

7 Why does *CBCA* s. 14(2) only enable a corporation to adopt a written pre-incorporation contract? (Note carefully that the *OBCA* s. 21(2) does not adopt this restriction). The Federal Proposals justified the requirement of a written pre-incorporation contract on the ground that "this seems the only way of ensuring full disclosure of the terms of the contract, which is an essential protection for the corporation" (para. 71). Do you agree? What is the promoter's position when there is no written pre-incorporation contract?

8   Does *CBCA* s. 14(2) prevent the promoter from assigning the pre-incorporation contract to the corporation? Would such an assignment relieve him or her from personal liability?

9   Why should the court be empowered under the above provisions to impose personal liability on the promoter even though the pre-incorporation contract has been adopted by the corporation? The Federal Proposals thought the power was necessary to prevent a promoter evading liability "by procuring the adoption of a contract by a shell corporation with insufficient assets to meet its obligations under the contract" (para. 72). Do you find this explanation convincing? For a reported case in which the court refused to exercise its discretion under the Ontario Act to impose liability on the promoter, see *Bank of N.S. v. Williams* (1976), 12 O.R. (2d) 709, 70 D.L.R. (3d) 108.

10   Under what circumstances is a court likely to hold a corporation liable for a pre-incorporation contract not adopted by it? Do you agree with the Federal Proposals (para. 72) that the appropriate conditions may exist if a fraudulent promoter seeks to evade his obligations "by hiding behind a corporation that he in fact dominates"? What "obligations" has he in fact assumed? Are the Federal Proposals consistent in holding the promoter personally liable where the corporation is not incorporated, on the ground that he has it in his power to make sure that it is incorporated, and to continue to hold him or her liable even if the corporation is incorporated?

11   What is the effect of contractual exclusion of the promoter's personal liability on the promoter's ability to enforce the pre-incorporation contract personally where the company is never incorporated? In *Guido v. Swail*, [1987] O.J. No. 63, 1987 CarswellOnt 2636 (Ont. H.C.) the defendants orally agreed to sell to the plaintiff certain shares. A draft purchase agreement in writing evidenced the plaintiffs' intention to contract on behalf of a corporation to be incorporated and without incurring personal liability. The defendants subsequently repudiated the agreement and the plaintiffs brought an action for specific performance. Smith J. dismissed the action on the ground that, having excluded their personal liability, the plaintiffs could not now rely on *OBCA* ss. 21(1) and (2) to make the pre-incorporation contract binding where no incorporation had occurred. Do you agree with this reasoning and, if you do, does this mean that there is no binding agreement where the promoter has excluded his or her personal liability unless and until a corporation is formed and ratified the agreement?

12   What significance attaches to the fact that *CBCA* s. 14(1) speaks of a person entering into a "contract" on behalf of a corporation not yet in existence? In *Westcom Radio Group Ltd. v. MacIsaac* (1989), 70 O.R. (2d) 591 (Div. Ct.), the defendant was sued on an advertising contract that she had signed on behalf of her employer. Unknown to the both the defendant and the plaintiff, the business had never been incorporated.

In the Divisional Court, Austin J. upheld the lower court's ruling that the defendant was not liable on the contract. This resulted in a 2-stage test in which it must first be established that the pre-incorporation "contract" was a valid contract at common law, and if it is, then the statutory rules are applied.

Professor Ziegel argued ((1990) 16 Can. Bus. L.J. 341, at p. 345) that "It is abundantly clear that the drafters were only using the word [contract] in a colloquial sense and that they fully appreciated that there was no binding contract with the corporation . . . The result of [*Westcom's*] reading of s. 21(1) of the *OBCA* . . . is to make nonsense of the whole subsection and to deprive it of all meaning."

In *Szecket v. Huang* (1998), 42 O.R. (3d) 400 (C.A.), the Ontario Court of Appeal apparently sided with Professor Ziegel. Although the Court declined to overrule *Westcom*, it characterized the *Westcom* two-step inquiry as "unnecessarily complex" and stated that the lower court judge's analysis based on *Westcom* "represented one of the problems arising from the common law of pre-incorporation contracts, which the legislature intended to remedy by the enactment of s. 21." *Szecket v. Huang* was a case where both parties knew that the company purporting to contract had yet to be incorporated.

In *1080409 Ontario Ltd. v. Hunter* (2000), 50 O.R. (3d) 145, 2000 CarswellOnt 2399 (S.C.J.), Pepall J. resolved the dilemma of the apparent conflict between *Westcom* and *Szecket v. Huang* by distinguishing both prior cases based on the state of knowledge of the parties as to the incorporated status of the company. On the facts before her, however, she reached a result consistent with the analysis in *Szecket v. Huang* following what she described as "the undeniable legislative intent" of *OBCA* s. 21.

The third treatment of *OBCA* s. 21 by the Ontario Court of Appeal is in *1394918 Ontario Ltd. v. 1310210 Ontario Inc.*, 2002 CarswellOnt 8, 57 O.R. (3d) 607 (Ont. C.A.).

The court adopted the approach in *Szecket v. Huang*, clarifying that *OBCA* s. 21 will apply to all pre-incorporation contracts regardless of knowledge of incorporation status as between the contracting parties, and further clarifying that the two-stage analysis in *Westcom* is unnecessary.

See also Poonam Puri, "The Promise of Certainty in the Law of Pre-Incorporation Contracts" (2001), 80 Can. Bar Rev. 1051.

Landmark Inns of Canada Ltd. v. Horeak
1982 CarswellSask 139, 18 Sask. R. 30, [1982] 2 W.W.R. 377
(Sask. Q.B.)

The defendant sought to establish an optometry business in Regina, and intended to form a corporation to operate the business. He entered into a lease agreement with the plaintiff company in October 1979, and signed the agreement as "South Albert Optical and Contact Lenses Ltd.", appointing himself chairman of the company. The lease agreement required the plaintiff to perform renovations to the property, which the plaintiff did. The defendant eventually decided to lease a different property. By letter on November 22 1979, the defendant's solicitor advised the plaintiff that the leasing of the premises would not proceed, which the defendant confirmed in a phone call to the plaintiff.

On February 25 1980, South Albert Optical and Contract Lenses Ltd. was incorporated, and adopted the lease between the plaintiff and defendant. The plaintiff commenced action against the defendant for lost rent and the cost of the renovations.

MAURICE J.: The action involves the interpretation of s. 14 of the Business Corporations Act of the province of Saskatchewan, R.S.S. 1978, c. B-10. . . .

Section 14 of the Business Corporations Act read as follows [see *OBCA* s. 21 (Eds.)]. Subsection (1) codifies the law on pre-incorporation contracts, as stated in the leading case of *Kelner (Kelmer) v. Baxter* (1866), L.R. 2 C.P 174; also see *Dairy Supplies Ltd. v. Fuchs* (1959), 28 W.W.R. 1, 18 D.L.R. (2d) 408 (Sask. C.A.).

The defendant, having entered into a written contract in the name of South Albert Optical and Contact Lenses Ltd. before it came into existence, is personally bound by the contract unless the provisions of s. 14(2) or (4) of the Act apply to the transaction.

The defendant says that the purported adoption of the lease by South Albert Optical and Contact Lenses Ltd. on 19th March 1980 has the effect of ceasing to make him bound by the lease in accordance with s. 14(2). I cannot agree with this contention. The lease was repudiated when the defendant's solicitor wrote to the plaintiff on 22nd November 1979 advising that the lease would not be proceeded with. The defendant confirmed this in a telephone conversation with Kornberg.

Martin C.J.S., in the case of *Can. Doughnut Co. Ltd. v. Can. Egg Products Ltd.*, 11 W.W.R. 193, [1954] 2 D.L.R. 77, affirmed [1955] S.C.R. 398, [1955] 3 D.L.R. 1, stated at p. 86:

> The authorities are to the effect that an express declaration by one party made either before or at the date fixed for performance that he refuses to recognize the contract as binding discharges the other party from further liability: the latter is freed from further performance and may sue for damages.

The plaintiff accepted the repudiation and obtained a new lease for the premises. The contract having been repudiated, which repudiation was accepted, the contract was at an end. It could not therefore be adopted by the company at a later date.

The defendant says that, as the lease shows the name of the tenant to be South Albert Optical and Contact Lenses Ltd. and it was signed by the defendant as chairman under the seal of the company, the contract expressly provides that the defendant was not to be bound by the contract in accordance with s. 14(4) of the Act.

I cannot agree with this contention either. The section clearly contemplates that the contract will be entered into by a person in the name of or on behalf of a corporation. In this case the lease was entered into in the name of South Albert Optical and Contact Lenses Ltd. To relieve a person of personal responsibility, the contract must contain something more. As the section says, it must contain an express provision that a person who enters into a written contract in the name of a company before it comes into existence is not personally bound by the contract. The lease contains no such provision . . .

Judgment for plaintiff.

Notes and Questions

1   Does Saskatchewan's section 14(1) (which is substantially the same as *CBCA* s. 14) distinguish between the situations where the other party to the pre-incorporation contract knows the corporation is not yet in existence at the time of the making of the contract and those where he or she does not know? Ought it to?

2   Was Maurice J. correct in stating that s. 14(1) "codifies the law on pre-incorporation contracts" in *Kelner v. Baxter*?

3   Can a promoter effectively repudiate a pre-incorporation contract before the company is incorporated? If he or she can, was there an effective repudiation by the defendant in the present case? Is the company bound by such a repudiation?

4   In *Okinczyc v. Tessier* (1979), 8 R.P.R. 249 (Ont. H.C.), a contract for the purchase of a parcel of land was signed between the plaintiff (vendor) and the defendant Tessier. The agreement included the following provision:

> It is understood between the parties that the purchaser is buying above described property in trust for a limited company which is to be incorporated.

The corporation, the Niagara Montrose Apartment Corporation, was incorporated on December 30, 1978, its first directors being Tessier and Blenkarn. Blenkarn was Tessier's solicitor. The project was abandoned and Tessier failed to close on the agreed date.

The plaintiff sought to hold Tessier personally liable on the pre-incorporation contract. Steele J. found (at p. 256) that "there were no organizational resolutions or minutes of any meetings [of the company] and that there was never a shareholders' or directors' meeting of the company and the company has no assets."

Is the absence of a formal resolution adopting a pre-incorporation contract fatal in the case of a one-person corporation? See *OBCA* ss. 104 and 129, and *cf. Eisenberg v. BNS*, [1965] S.C.R. 681, *infra*, Ch. 10. Do the *CBCA* and *OBCA* pre-incorporation provisions apply to a contract signed "in trust" for a corporation still to be incorporated? What would be sufficient evidence of the adoption of a contract by a one-person corporation whose sole beneficial shareholder is the person who signed the pre-incorporation contract?

5   Defendants, real estate developers in Oregon, applied for a loan through the plaintiff for the purpose of developing a parcel of land. The plaintiff was in the business of lending money and securing loans from other sources. The plaintiff informed the defendants that any loan would have to be made to a corporation so as to overcome the usury restrictions under the then Oregon law on loans to individuals. As a prerequisite to seeking a loan commitment for defendants, the plaintiff required a "good faith" deposit from the defendants. The deposit took the form of a note made payable to the plaintiff. When the plaintiff was preparing the note he asked the defendants which corporation would borrow the money and execute the good faith deposit note. The defendants did not have a corporation but told the plaintiff the corporation's name would be "Iron Mountain Invest-ment Co., Inc." The note was so prepared and signed by the personal defendant for the corporation. The plaintiff knew at this time that there was no corporate entity. The corporation was never incorpo-rated and the defendant defaulted on the note. Assuming the relevant facts had occurred in Canada, would the defendant be held liable under the *CBCA* or the *OBCA*? *Cf. Sherwood and Roberts-Oregon, Inc. v. Alexander* (1974), 525 P 2d 135 (Ore.).

Chapter 4

Management and Control of the Corporation

1. CORPORATE GOVERNANCE: THE ROLE OF LEGAL AND MARKET INSTRUMENTS

(a) Introduction

This chapter (and following chapters) of the casebook explore the governance structure of the corporation. In particular, the mechanisms by which managerial action is facilitated, monitored and controlled are discussed. At the core of these chapters is the problem of ensuring the accountability of managers to the goals of the corporation. That is, irrespective of the particular goals to which the corporation is devoted, there is a natural propensity for corporate actors to deviate from these goals in an effort to maximize their own welfare. Corporate law, in conjunction with a variety of other instruments, can serve to limit the scope for such opportunism.

(b) The Challenge of Berle and Means

The concern over opportunism by corporate managers has been a central theme of corporate law scholarship ever since the publication of Berle and Means' seminal treatise on the subject of corporate governance in 1932, Adolf A. Berle and Gardiner C. Means, *The Modern Corporation and Private Property*, rev. ed. 1967. The central subject of their work was the considerable scope for unfettered discretion that managers of the largest corporations in America enjoyed because of the separation of ownership and control in these corporations. The high degree of separation of ownership and control in American corporations during the 1920s and 1930s was marked by the growing level of dispersion of share ownership of the largest industrial corporations. For instance, in 1929, 88 of the 200 largest corporations in the United States were found not to have a controlling shareholder, and only 22 were corporations privately owned or controlled. By the time a second edition of their study was prepared in 1967, Berle and Means could report that, as of 1963, 169 of the 200 largest U.S. corporations had dispersed ownership, while only 5 were privately owned or controlled. According to Berle and Means, the effect of this growing dispersion of share ownership was to dull the incentive for any particular shareholder to assume the responsibility for controlling the affairs of the corporation. In essence, the growing dispersion of share ownership transformed shareholders into passive principals of the corporations they owned.

If shareholders were unable to exercise control over the modern corporation, where did control over these large enterprises reside? Berle and Means asserted that the members of a new managerial elite filled the vacuum left by the failure of scattered shareholders to exercise control. But, in contrast to the shareholders of the corporation, the members of this elite held only minor ownership interests in the capital of the corporation. The obvious implication of the separation of ownership and control was that management, because it lacked a direct stake in the corporation, would not be motivated to advance the welfare of the corporation and its owners. The legacy, therefore, of the separation of ownership and control was to submerge the profit motive as the primary force motivating corporate action. The conception of corporate America that Berle and Means held was of large aggregations of capital being directed by managers who were virtually unaccountable to any constituency but themselves.

(c) Enter the Contractarians

(i)   Introduction to the Corporate Contract

The analysis fashioned by Berle and Means has had a profound effect on the way in which subsequent scholars, judges and policy-makers have viewed the corporation. But while their prognosis of corporate governance remained virtually unchallenged for almost four decades after the original publication of *The Modern Corporation and Private Property*, by the 1970s their analysis received close scrutiny by scholars belonging to the law and economics movement. At one level, the work of the new scholars built on the original work by Berle and Means. At another level, it deepened and, sometimes, contradicted it. Essentially, by expanding the analysis of Berle and Means, these scholars have been able to evaluate a broad range of conflicts that beset the modern corporation. Among the most notable works in this genre is a book by Frank Easterbrook and Daniel Fischel, *The Economic Structure of Corporate Law* (1991), and the following articles: Michael Jensen and William H. Meckling, "Theory of the Firm: Managerial Behaviour, Agency Costs and Ownership Structure" (1976), 3 J. Fin. Econ. 305; Eugene Fama, "Agency Problems and the Theory of the Firm" (1980), 88 J. Pol. Econ. 288; Eugene Fama and Michael Jensen, "Separation of Ownership and

Control" (1983), 26 J. Law and Econ. 301 and "Agency Problems and Residual Claims" (1983), 26 J. Law and Econ. 327; Frank Easterbrook and Daniel Fischel, "Corporate Control Transactions" (1982), 91 Yale L.J. 698; Ronald Gilson, "A Structural Approach to Corporations: The Case Against Defensive Tactics in Takeovers" (1981), 33 Stan. L.R. 819; and Jonathan Macey, *Promises Kept, Promises Broken* (2008).

At the core of the law and economics analysis of the corporation is the conception of the corporation as a nexus of contractual relationships among the corporation's shareholders, creditors, managers, employees and suppliers. Implicit in these contractual relationships is the delegation from principal to agent of functional authority over corporate affairs. Although this delegation allows for specialization of tasks, it entails the danger that the delegates (the agents) will use their delegated authority to pursue their own goals at the expense of those goals favoured by the delegators (the principals). The conflicts ("agency conflicts") that arise naturally from the delegation of authority are the principal unit of analysis of these theorists. More specifically, from the law and economics perspective, the purpose of corporate law is to achieve the cost-effective reduction of agency costs.

The agency conflict of greatest relevance to Berle and Means' concern is, of course, that occasioned by the delegation of authority from shareholders to managers in the corporation. Jensen and Meckling, *supra*, modeled the problems inherent in this relationship by first examining the case where ownership and control are concentrated in a single person — the owner-manager. Obviously, when corporations are controlled by owner-managers, there is no scope for agency conflict. If the owner-manager engages in "diversion," by diverting corporate assets to his or her personal use, or in "shirking", by failing to render his or her maximum effort in the performance of her duties *qua* manager (by slacking on the job or by opting for a quieter life by pursuing relatively safe investment projects that do not maximize profits), then he or she will bear the full costs of such behaviour in the form of reductions in the amount of profit he or she realizes as a shareholder. As a general matter, therefore, when ownership and control are fused, the prospect of debilitating agency conflicts is minimized because the costs of opportunistic behaviour are reflected back onto the party engaging in such behaviour.

When, however, the connection between ownership and management is severed, or, at least, attenuated, the probability of agency conflict and its accompanying costs increase. Take, for example, the case of a small family-run firm that has as its sole asset a local corner variety store. Assume that the only shareholders of the company are a husband and wife. The couple provide the initial capital that facilitates the acquisition of the store, the purchase of its opening inventory, and the payment of sundry operational expenses. The husband and wife are also the only managers of the store, and, in conjunction with their role in providing capital, are owner-managers. Also, the store lacks any significant creditors.

Now assume that the couple decides that it wants to establish a chain of variety stores and requires sources of outside capital to facilitate this growth. If the couple sells 40% of the firm to raise the necessary capital for expansion, it can be seen that the calculus governing the decision whether or not to engage in opportunistic behaviour is altered by their diminished ownership interest. Prior to the sale, a dollar of income expended on generating some level of personal benefit, in the form of lavish office facilities, exotic "business" travel, expensive cars, corporate jets, *etc.*, cost the couple a full dollar in terms of the final profit they will realize from the store's operation. After the sale, however, a dollar of firm revenue used to pay expenses incurred by the couple only costs the couple 60 cents. If the amount of personal benefit received exceeds 60 cents per dollar of expenditure, the couple will have benefited from this outlay. As a consequence, they have an incentive to increase the amount of expenses they incur in the execution of their managerial duties because they bear only a portion of the costs entailed by that expenditure. Similarly, the sale of the ownership interest will also increase the propensity of the couple to shirk more than they would have if they were the exclusive owner-managers. Simply put, the greater the ownership stake sold by the couple to outside investors, the greater the incentive facing the couple to engage in opportunistic behaviour.

It can be seen that the analysis invoked by Jensen and Meckling is simply a formal way of modeling the problem of the separation of ownership and control originally described by Berle and Means. That is, the problem of separation of ownership and control gives rise to the agency conflict. It is important to note, however, that in contrast to Berle and Means' dim prognosis on the capacity of shareholders to control endemic agency conflicts, several economic theorists share confidence in the capacity of shareholders, even those in widely held corporations, to anticipate and control agency conflicts. This optimism flows to some extent from the contractual conception of the corporation: it does not make sense for a party to enter into a disadvantageous contract; hence, the fact that outsiders are willing to enter into the corporate contract suggests that there is some assurance of agency fidelity. Contractarians would predict that agency conflicts are controlled to the point where an additional dollar spent in inducing a certain kind of managerial behaviour is exactly equivalent to the benefit thereby generated.

There are two foundations for the conclusion that corporations will be structured so as to minimize agency costs. First, there are important incentives for private actors to choose a corporate framework that provides investors with assurance that managerial agency problems will be cost-effectively minimized. Second, there exist several legal and market mechanisms that corporate actors can rely on to discipline managers.

On the question of incentives, return to the example of the family-owned corner store. The family, who initially owns the entire firm, decides to sell 40% of the firm to outside investors. They have the choice between two corporate law rules. One, the "permissive" rule, would allow them discretion to use corporate funds to buy themselves a house. The other, the "restrictive" rule, would prevent them from making such a purchase. Prior to selling a share of the firm, the family chooses the relevant corporate law rule. If the family chooses the permissive rule, investors will anticipate that the family is likely to divert corporate funds to buy themselves a house, even if they would not otherwise have done so, since this, in effect, gives the family a 40% discount on the purchase (paid for by outside investors). Investors confronted with the permissive rule therefore will lower their estimate of the value of a 40% share of the firm. The family, by choosing the permissive rule, realizes a smaller amount in the sale of an ownership stake in the firm; they are punished financially for choosing the permissive rule. In contrast, if the family chooses the restrictive rule, investors would be willing to pay more for the stake; the family would be rewarded for their decision.

Incentives thus exist for corporations to choose sensible governance structures. But this is not to say that very strict legal rules are always optimal. If, for example, the restrictive rule in the example not only prevented the acquisition of the house, but it also prevented the family from earning a salary, which would in turn induce the family not to work for the store, the costs of the rule may exceed its benefits — if so, the family would have an incentive not to choose such a regime. In addition, the wisdom of a strict legal rule must be weighed against alternative market mechanisms that may create a better combination of strictness on certain dimensions and laxity on others.

What are the mechanisms identified by contractarian theorists to control agency conflicts in corporations? Theorists point to a number of market and legal instruments. Legal instruments typically restrain managerial opportunism by imposing *ex post* costs on managers engaging in such activities. The statutory and common law duties enumerated in the following chapters set out standards against which managerial conduct will be evaluated. If detected, departures from these duties impose significant *ex post* penalties.

Market instruments operate at two levels. Like legal rules, market mechanisms can, by direct intervention, impose significant costs on self-serving management. But markets play a second role in furnishing information to the corporation's principals, which enhances the quality of supervision by corporate owners. If market signals furnish owners with information of managerial shirking or diversion, then owners can discipline managers in a variety of ways.

(ii)   Voting — Independent and Instrumental Value

Overview

At the core of many of the legal and market control mechanisms used by owners to constrain managerial self-interest is the institution of shareholder voting. Voting is a powerful control mechanism that may be useful in itself or it may, in an instrumental fashion, be used to facilitate the operation of other mechanisms. On its own, the institution of shareholder voting vests owners with the ability to determine the membership of the board of directors of the corporation. Although some corporate constitutions articulate rules for determining the composition of corporate boards that depart from simple majority rule, for the most part, majority rule is the dominant decision rule for board elections. As numerous commentators have observed, corporate boards often do not manage the corporation, they are vested with the responsibility of appointing and supervising the managers of the corporation. If management fails to perform as expected, then it is the responsibility of the board to instigate changes to management. Thus, if shareholders, as owners of the corporation, are dissatisfied with the board's vigilance in ensuring optimal managerial performance, it is within the power of shareholders to alter the composition of the board.

In addition to voting for positions on corporate boards, most corporate statutes provide that shareholders are entitled to vote on the occurrence of enumerated events. Generally speaking, these events involve substantial changes to the structure of the corporation. Amalgamations, change of incorporating jurisdiction, sale of substantially all of the company's assets and various changes to the rights and obligations of investor constituencies are events that trigger the voting mechanism. In contrast to the simple majority voting rules that govern election of board members, voting on fundamental corporate changes is typically subject to supra-majority (greater than 50%) voting rules. It is useful to note that the initial position of the supra-majority voting rules triggered by the initiation of substantial corporate changes fetters not only management's ability to generate agency costs for the owners of the firm, but also limits the capacity of various investor constituencies to impose agency costs on each other. For instance, supra-majority rules constrain the ability of majority shareholders to adopt changes that augment their own wealth at the expense of minority shareholders.

Information Provision and Collective Action Problems

The independent capacity of shareholder voting to constrain agency costs is a function of the magnitude and quality of information that is available to shareholders. The greater the information available to shareholders concerning the performance of corporate agents, the more rational and effective their voting. But while information is of unequivocal value to shareholders, it cannot be produced, assimilated and disseminated without cost. As a result, the optimal level of information investment by a firm's principals is a function of the costs and benefits of information generation. Rationally, shareholders should, on an aggregate basis, invest in information activities to the point where the benefits that are received from such expenditure are equal to the costs.

Unfortunately, the likelihood of generating an optimal level of information provision by corporate shareholders is undermined by the presence of various coordination problems. These problems arise because, in economic jargon, shareholder information possesses "public good" attributes — the good must be produced jointly, and once supplied, it is difficult, if not impossible, to exclude others from consuming it. (The theory of public goods is developed by Samuelson, "The Pure Theory of Public Expenditure" (1954), 36 Rev. of Econ. Statistics 386.) Because an investment in the provision of a public good cannot be recouped, these goods will normally be undersupplied by the private market. In the case of corporate information, its public goods character means that shareholders must overcome endemic collective action problems in order to produce collectively an amount of information commensurate with the importance of the issue subject to the vote. Shareholders will reason that, since the benefits from an investment in information activities will accrue to all shareholders irrespective of their individual contribution, it is better to "free ride" on the investment of other shareholders than to contribute oneself. Of course, if this is a rational strategy for one shareholder, it is equally rational for all similarly situated shareholders, and, predictably, investment in information-related activities will be sub-optimal. (Collective action problems are discussed at length in Robert Clark, *Corporate Law* (1986), pp. 389–400 and Easterbrook and Fischel, "Voting in Corporate Law" (1983), 26 Journal of Law and Economics 395.) There are two reasons why corporations may not be vulnerable to the most acute collective action problems. First, an individual shareholder may own a sufficiently large percentage of shares that the collective action problem is not insuperable. Collective action problems arise if each shareholder anticipates that his or her behaviour has only a trivial impact on corporate activities. But large shareholders will anticipate that their actions, including gathering information and voting sensibly, could affect outcomes. At the extreme, a "controlling shareholder", that is, a shareholder that can elect a majority of the board of directors by virtue of votes from his or her shares alone, anticipates that his or her decisions will with certainty affect a vote. Controlling shareholders therefore have incentives to monitor managers closely and govern behaviour accordingly. Canada, in contrast to the United States and the United Kingdom, has a significant number of large corporations with controlling shareholders, which diminishes concern about collective action problems: see R. Daniels and J. MacIntosh, "Towards a Distinctive Canadian Corporate Law Regime" (1991) 29 Osgoode Hall L.J. 863; R. Daniels and E. Iacobucci, "Some of the Causes and Consequences of Corporate Ownership Concentration in Canada" in R. Morck, Ed., *Concentrated Corporate Ownership* (2000). Note, however, that controlling shareholders, while overcoming collective action problems, do not eliminate concerns about self-interested, sub-optimal governance. Controlling shareholders may take advantage of minority shareholders by causing the corporation to take actions that benefit the controller while harming minority shareholders. Later chapters discuss these problems.

Aside from controlling shareholders, large but non-controlling shareholders may also be able to overcome collective action problems. Shares in Canada and other market economies are increasingly owned not by individuals, but rather by various kinds of large aggregations of capital. These "institutional investors" include private and public pension funds, mutual funds, insurance companies and banks. Such shareholders do not fit the Berle and Means model of atomistic shareholders each with trivial share ownership, but rather may own a significant number of shares that induce them to invest in information. Moreover, the recent emergence of large "hedge funds" may also be influential in assessing collective action problems. Some of these funds adopt a strategy of buying a significant block of shares, actively seeking to influence management in a manner that they predict will add value to the corporation, and profiting from the appreciation of their shares. For example, the spin-off of Tim Horton's from its parent corporation Wendy's resulted in significant part because of pressure on management from hedge funds. For more on hedge funds and corporate management, see M. Kahan and E.Rock, "Hedge Funds and Corporate Governance and Control" (2007) 155 U.Penn.L.Rev. 1021.

Second, aside from the role of large shareholders in overcoming collective action problems, markets themselves can address such problems by providing information to shareholder-voters. If, for example, markets, through their natural operation, are able to furnish shareholders with reliable information concerning agency cost levels, then it is possible that pervasive collective action problems can be overcome. (For a further discussion of the operation of equity markets with particular attention to the control of managerial agency costs, see: Ronald Gilson and Reinier Kraakman, "The Mechanisms of Market Efficiency" (1984) 70 Va. L. Rev. 549.)

Markets and Information Provision

I. The Capital Market. Of the various markets whose operation furnishes shareholders with valuable information, the most important is the capital market. The capital market comprises numerous bond and equity markets that are located in countries throughout the world. Although these markets are located within distinct domestic boundaries, the rapid advances in technology, combined with diminished barriers to capital mobility, permit commentators to speak realistically of one global capital market. Although only a very small minority of Canadian corporations have shares that are traded on a stock market, these companies are the largest and most profitable in the country.

Capital markets play a central role in controlling agency costs. At the time that a shareholder makes his or her initial investment, capital markets, if perfectly efficient, will ensure that the price that is paid for securities of a corporation fully reflects the magnitude of expected costs generated by agency conflicts. This means that shareholders will not suffer reductions in their wealth by managerial shirking or diversion because these costs were anticipated at the time of initial investment and were impounded into the price paid for their shares.

Of course, there are limits to the extent to which managerial opportunism can be accurately anticipated at the time of initial investment. Foresight is not perfect, and management may embark on a course of action that was not foreseeable when the shareholder made his or her initial investment. By incorporating the consequences of management misconduct into share prices, capital markets furnish shareholders with a signal of corporate performance. Accordingly, if the price of a corporation's securities increases at a rate that compares favourably with the securities of corporations having similar characteristics, the investor can be reasonably confident that the corporation in which he or she has invested is being well managed. Conversely, if the share price of the corporation underperforms industry competitors, the spectre of managerial incompetence is raised.

How efficient are capital markets in pricing agency conflicts? At the outset it is important to note that efficient pricing is not predicated on every investor being fully informed of the magnitude of these costs; efficient pricing only requires (i) that some subset of fully-informed investors, i.e., "marginal investors", be able to accurately price the magnitude of expected agency costs, and (ii) that the price paid by marginal investors not diverge significantly from the price paid by less informed investors for shares purchased within the same time frame on the market.

The accuracy of capital market pricing is a subject that has attracted considerable and sustained scholarly attention in the corporate finance literature. Essentially, the efficiency of capital markets is determined in relation to different types of data. The conclusion that the market is "efficient" with respect to a certain data set is just a shorthand way of saying that there are no opportunities for dedicated stock analysts and traders to realize long term abnormal positive returns from devising and executing trading strategies based on a given data set. (The focus is on "*abnormal* positive returns" because all investors expect positive returns in the normal course of events — this is why they invest.) The theory underlying market efficiency is that competition to invest in capital markets ought to drive returns to normal levels; that is, there are too many investors and too many potential investments for a given investor to systematically (as opposed to episodically) beat the market. Ultimately the challenge of empirical tests of market efficiency is that there is no way to know what the "true" value of a share is at any point in time, and hence no way to have certainty whether a given price of a share is equal to its value. There is, however, implicit evidence of market efficiency. For example, studies have found that capital markets rapidly respond to publicly available information, i.e., information that is disclosed in the financial press and in various publicly available offering documents. Not surprisingly, the empirical evidence also demonstrates that markets are not efficient with respect to "insider information", i.e., information respecting the performance of the company that is not publicly available. (For a discussion of empirical tests of capital market efficiency, see, e.g., E. Fama, "Efficient Capital Markets II" (1991) 46 J. Finance 1575).

II. The Product Market. Another market that provides useful information to shareholders is the product market. This market is the market in which the corporation's goods are bought and sold. The success or failure of a company's goods on the product market is governed by the price, quality, and service characteristics of the corporation's products. If a company supplies a product that is superior to competing products, then the company's profits should increase. Conversely, if a company's product fails to earn the patronage of a sufficient range of consumers, then a powerful, but crude, information signal will be made to the principals of the corporation. Dismal product market performance sends a signal to investors about managerial performance, particularly if a corporation is performing poorly while its industry peers are thriving. Shareholders can threaten to alter the composition of the board through their voting power if the board refuses to discipline senior management. Increasingly in the last several years, the threat of shareholder discipline has provoked a number of boards in leading North American corporations to initiate the ouster of reigning senior managers.

Direct Control of Agency Costs through Markets

So far, we have only considered shareholder voting as an independent agency cost control mechanism. In this vein, the operation of various markets works to enhance the quality of shareholder voting by increasing the amount of information available to shareholders. Other markets exert a powerful impact on managerial behaviour by imposing direct penalties on opportunistic managerial behaviour. The effectiveness of these markets is not contingent upon the ability of shareholders to overcome collective action problems.

I. The Managerial Market. The managerial market is the market where the services of corporate managers are traded. The threat of having to compete in the managerial market encourages managers to act in their principals' best interests. A manager who shirks or diverts will, if the managerial market is efficient, suffer reductions in the pay he or she may have otherwise received corresponding to the magnitude of the agency costs he or she is expected to generate for present or future employers. Clearly, if these costs are fully impounded into an opportunistic manager's expected pay, then the manager derives no net benefit from engaging in opportunistic behaviour. Any immediate gain from opportunism is offset by reductions in the value of the manager's human capital. Of course, the effectiveness of this mechanism turns on the ability of the market to evaluate the performance of the manager under consideration in isolation from his or her team. But linking even crude measures of managerial performance, like share price, to managerial pay can offer valuable incentives to managers to perform their duties diligently.

II. The Product Market. As discussed, the product market can discipline managers indirectly, by providing information to shareholders about performance. The product market can also sanction managers directly for inferior performance. *In extremis*, an egregious failure of the company to compete successfully in the product market will result in the bankruptcy of the firm. Even if the corporation successfully reorganizes and continues to operate after bankruptcy, management is replaced following most bankruptcies. Thus, managers have an incentive to avoid failure in the product market.

III. The Market for Corporate Control. The final, and, perhaps, the most powerful market safeguard against the generation of agency costs, is the "market for corporate control". Essentially, this mechanism, which was first identified by Henry Manne (Manne, "Mergers and the Market for Corporate Control" (1965), 73 J. Pol. Econ. 110), operates by transferring control of mismanaged corporations (i.e., corporations beset by high levels of agency costs) to owners more willing or able to discipline self-serving managers. The transfer of control is effected by the use of the hostile takeover bid. The principal attraction of the hostile bid is that it can operate independently of the consent of target management. Once control is amassed by an acquirer (51% of voting stock is necessary for legal control but a smaller percentage is often sufficient for *de facto* control), he or she can exercise the voting rights conferred by control and oust existing management by electing new directors. The acquirer of control profits by purchasing shares at a price that reflects significant agency problems, reducing those problems once in control, and then realizing the greater value of the shares. For example, private equity funds may seek to acquire the shares of underperforming publicly traded companies and make a profit by improving their performance and selling the securities back to the public in the future. (But see discussion of other possible motivations for takeovers, including value transfers from other constituencies, in Chapter 6, *infra*.)

There is considerable empirical evidence that supports this rather crude description of the market for corporate control. Scholars have found strong evidence that many corporations that are the subject of hostile takeovers are poorly managed companies, and that successful takeovers increase the aggregate value of target corporations (see discussion, *infra*, in Chapter 6).

Significantly, like legal rules and the managerial market, the market for corporate control is effective in both discouraging deviations from shareholder wealth maximization before they occur, and penalizing such behaviour if it does indeed occur. The fear of a possible takeover, and consequent threat of job loss, serves as a powerful countervailing force on management shirking and diversion. The more credible the threat from the control market, the more willing incumbent managers will be to adopt strategies that reduce the risk of a takeover. Perhaps the most potent defensive tactic is self-imposed restraint on shirking and diversion; by diminishing opportunistic behaviour, the share price of the corporation will rise and attenuate the gains accruing to an acquiror from a control shift.

(d)   The Role of Corporate Law in the Contractarian Model of the Corporation

In any contract, parties have an economic incentive to adopt value-maximizing rules. For example, if a warranty is worth $10 to a customer, but would only cost a seller $5, then the parties can *both* be made better off by including a warranty in a contract. They will each try to capture a larger share of the value by haggling over a price, but including a warranty at any price greater than $5 and less than $10 makes both better off. Similarly, if corporations are simply a nexus of contracts, it makes sense to conclude that investors and entrepreneurs (managers) would agree on a set of corporate law rules that maximize value and minimize agency costs. This analysis then invites the question: if a corporation is simply a nexus of contracts, what role is there for corporate law as a body of law distinct from contract law? That is, does acceptance of the contractarian view of the corporation abolish the need for corporate law? There is further reason to question the justification for corporate law. We have reviewed how markets discipline managers in a variety of ways. If these markets work to align the interests of managers and shareholders, is corporate law redundant? Lest the reader fear that this casebook was written (and purchased) in vain, let us quickly reassure you that corporate law can serve a vital role despite these important considerations. First, many of the markets we describe only work successfully *because* of the law. For example, the market for corporate control depends on the ability of an acquirer of shares to vote to oust directors; voting rules are a matter of corporate law. Capital markets depend on the rules that corporate law establishes for determining how investors realize returns. For example, it takes corporate law to establish many of the rights associated with share ownership that in turn make shares valuable.

Second, there are important advantages from having the rules operate as a matter of corporate law rather than simple contract. Whenever parties enter into a contract, there are costs associated with reaching agreement; economists refer to these as "transaction costs." Under the contractarian model, corporate law reduces transaction costs by providing a "standard form contract" that offers private actors an off-the-rack set of corporate rules that represent what most parties would want. Entrepreneurs can offer investors this "contract" simply by incorporating. This saves parties (and society) considerable transaction costs given the large number of incorporations that occur in any given period of time. Moreover, many corporate law rules are complicated, and it would be very difficult (and costly) for parties themselves to specify their content in a contract. For example, incorporation gives rise to fiduciary duties that have been refined over 150 years of company law. Incorporation also gives rise to a corporation with a separate legal personality, as we have seen in Chapter 2, which in turn suggests, amongst other things, that a debt obligation of the corporation is not (generally) a debt of the shareholder, and equally, a debt of a shareholder is not that of the corporation. Replicating such rules through private contract would be complicated and costly: see H. Hansmann and R. Kraakman, "The Essential Role of Organizational Law" (2000) 110 Yale L. J. 439; E. Iacobucci and G. Triantis, "Legal and Economic Boundaries of the Firm" (2007) 93 Virginia L. Rev. 515.

The contractarian view does not, therefore, lead to a conclusion that corporate law serves no meaningful purpose; rather, it suggests that corporate law can facilitate the contracting process by providing a standard form contract and legal personality. This in turn has implications for the kind of corporate law we should observe. In particular, corporate law under the contractarian view should strive to offer parties terms that they would want, but should give private parties the option to contract around a particular term if they prefer to do so. Corporate law under this view ought to play an "enabling" role that facilitates contracting by offering a set of default rules, and should generally avoid a "mandatory" role that requires parties to adopt particular rules. Unless there is some kind of market failure that engenders mistrust of private contracting, corporate law should seek to give parties what they want and allow them something different if they so choose.

(e) Critique of the Contractarian Model of the Corporation

Criticism of the agency theorists' model of corporate governance can be pitched at two distinct levels. The first and most obvious criticism is to express skepticism with the capacity of markets to effectively control agency costs. In this respect, the criticism against the model reflects not different underlying values or ideologies, but only different perceptions regarding empirically testable hypotheses. Critics of the idea of leaving corporate law to private parties would, for example, emphasize the string of spectacular failures of large, public corporations, like Enron and WorldCom in North America and Satyam and Parmalat globally, and contend that regulators must step in to fill the corporate governance void. Critics would also argue that the global financial crisis of 2007-2009 was brought about in part by the failure of directors and managers to appropriately manage both risk and compensation. Contractarians are likely to respond that these failures, spectacular though they may have been, pale beside the successes resulting from the private choice of corporate governance regimes.

Criticisms of contractarianism seem most potent in relation to the claims made by the most strident proponents of the model, who assert that the cost of all agency conflicts is anticipated and reflected back onto managers by the mechanisms enumerated above. But in order for this extreme claim to be valid, the various instruments set out above must operate with a high degree of efficiency. We know, however, that this is unlikely: product and managerial markets often suffer from various structural imperfections, capital markets are not efficient in relation to certain sets of information, the corporate control market only operates above certain threshold levels of agency cost and, finally, legal rules may be incorrectly articulated and applied.

Given that market imperfections clearly exist, is the managerial model of corporate governance propounded by Berle and Means validated? To concede some scope for uncontrolled agency costs is not to accept the strong claim that management is unfettered by any external constraint. Clearly, the various mechanisms enumerated above serve to impose some limitations on managerial discretion, although the precise contours of the domain accorded managerial discretion by these limitations is far from settled. Furthermore, to the extent that agency costs are left uncontrolled by the corporate governance regime, it is important to compare these costs with the benefits that are achieved from the separation of ownership and control, and with the existing regulatory alternatives. In terms of the former, the benefits from disentangling ownership and control are substantial and are related to specialization; owners are freed from selecting managers on the basis of factors unrelated to managerial skill, i.e., wealth and risk preferences. In terms of the latter, the recognition that agency costs are not fully addressed by the current corporate governance regime does not support its rejection. To do so would require the critic to propose some alternative set of institutional arrangements that permit the same benefits as the current regime but at lower cost. As always, the question is not "Is this system flawless?" but rather, "How does this system compare to others?" Are government officials drafting mandatory rules likely to choose better rules than entrepreneurs and investors, who, after all, invest their own money and time in the corporation?

In contrast to the empirical nature of the criticisms canvassed above, the second major set of criticisms levelled against the contractarian model is normative in character. For instance, Victor Brudney's reservations regarding the model relate to the implications of the contractual metaphor for corporate law reform ("Corporate Governance, Agency Costs, and the Rhetoric of Contract" (1985), 85 Col. L. Rev. 1403). According to Brudney (at p. 1404):

> the rhetoric of contract proceeds on doubtful assumptions about the circumstances of the parties, imports inappropriate normative consequences to govern the relationships thus assumed, and serves the ideological function of legitimating substantially unaccountable managerial discretion to determine corporate activities and to serve itself at the expense of investors.

Brudney is concerned, in particular, with the hostility of the model to regulatory intervention. If parties have, through their autonomous and fully informed conduct, created a mutually acceptable bargain, then the scope for state intervention is greatly confined.

A similar line of argument is developed by Robert Clark. He finds the contractual metaphor "troublesome" because it fails to accurately depict reality, engenders facile optimism about the optimality of existing rules and institutions, deflects attention from underlying value judgments, and is highly indeterminate in application. Clark also criticizes the advisability of viewing shareholders as principals of the corporation. Clark compares the power of principals in "pure" agency relationship with shareholders in the modern corporation and finds that shareholders lack many of the rights routinely accorded legal principals. (Robert Clark, "Agency Costs Versus Fiduciary Duties," in *Principals and Agents: The Structure of Business*, Pratt and Zeckhauser, Eds. (1985), Ch. 3.)

Finally, Bruce Chapman argues that the contractual theory of the corporation is impoverished for its failure to take into account other values unrelated to contract ("Trust, Economic Rationality, and the Corporate Fiduciary Obligation", (1993) 43 University of Toronto Law Journal 547). He notes that adepts of the law and economics approach construe the corporate fiduciary obligation as being properly owed to shareholders "only because all efficient corporate contractors would recognize that shareholders, as residual claimants, put the highest value on control of the corporation" (at 548). He then proceeds to challenge this view on the basis that:

competitive corporate contracting cannot achieve all that this view promises unless it is aided by the very value that a contractual understanding of the fiduciary obligation denies, namely, the duty of loyalty and trust. Trust plays an essential role in modern economics, and without it, or without the coordination that is provided by institutional loyalty, even efficient wealth-maximizing corporate contracting can make us all worse off. That too, unfortunately, is the stuff of competition. Nor can the concept of trust be very easily accommodated into the contractual model of the corporation. Properly interpreted, the concepts of trust and loyalty present a deep challenge not only to the contractual model, but also to the very conventions of instrumental rationality upon which the model is based (at 549).

2. AN INTRODUCTION TO THE LEGAL MODEL OF THE CORPORATION

(a) Introduction

The remainder of this chapter examines the basic structure of corporate governance that is set out in the CBCA and its cognate legislation. First, we consider the effect of an apparent tension, if not conflict, between a corporation's internal choice of rules and an apparently mandatory provision in the relevant corporate statute. How does one's view of the appropriate role of corporate law affect the outcome in *Bushell v. Faith*? Second, we turn to questions of how to interpret potentially ambiguous corporate rules. Are the interpretations of the courts consistent with the contractarian perspective, or do they instead suggest the Berle and Means description of the clear primacy of corporate managers over investors? Third, we review how a regime of privately chosen corporate rules interacts with those who were not party to those choices. In particular, we examine how third parties entering into contracts with the corporation are affected by the failure of a corporation to live up to its internal code of conduct. We also examine the significance of the private choice of corporate objectives. This raises important questions of corporate social responsibility: is there a duty, or even a capacity, of corporate actors to account for constituencies seemingly outside at least a narrow view of the "corporate contract"? Again, in all these cases, ask how the alternative conceptions of corporate law as either facilitating contracting or regulating behaviour affect legal outcomes.

(b) Mandatory versus Enabling Interpretations of Corporate Statutes

Absent a statutory right or a power in the corporate constitution, shareholders have no right to remove a director prior to the expiration of his term of office (*Imperial Hydropathic Hotel Co., Blackpool v. Hampson* (1882), 23 Ch. D. 1 (C.A.)). The power to remove directors can be an important exercise of ultimate control by the shareholders, and the CBCA makes provision for removal in s. 109 by ordinary resolution at a special meeting. The CBCA s. 6(4) further stipulates that the articles cannot provide for removal of a director by a greater number of votes than provided in s. 109 — an ordinary resolution.

A way around a similar, though not identical, U.K. statute was sanctioned by the House of Lords in the following case. How does one's conception of the role of corporate law affect one's evaluation of the outcome in this case?

Bushell v. Faith
[1970] A.C. 1099, [1970] 1 All E.R. 53 (H.L.)

[The articles of association of Bush Court (Southgate) Ltd provided that "in the event of a Resolution being proposed at any General Meeting of the Company for removal from office of any Director, any shares held by that Director shall on a poll in respect of such Resolution carry the right to three votes per share . . ." The company had an issued capital of 300 shares, held as to 100 by the appellant Bushell, and as to 100 each by the respondent Faith and his sister Bayne. Bushell & Bayne proposed an ordinary resolution at a general meeting of the Company to remove Faith as a director. On a show of hands the resolution was passed 2-1; Faith demanded a poll and the resolution was defeated 300-200. At trial an injunction was issued restraining Faith from acting as a director. The Court of Appeal reversed ([1969] 1 All E.R. 1002) and Bushell appealed to the House of Lords.]

LORD UPJOHN: My Lords, this appeal raises a question of some importance to those concerned with the niceties of company law, and the relevant facts, which are not in dispute, can be very shortly stated. The respondent company Bush Court (Southgate) Ltd (a formal party to the proceedings) was incorporated on 19th September 1960, and at all material times had an issued capital of 300 fully paid-up shares of »1 each held as to 100 shares each by a brother and his two sisters namely the appellant Mrs. Bushell, the respondent Mr. Faith and their sister Dr. Kathleen Bayne.

The respondent was a director but his conduct as such displeased his sisters who requisitioned a general meeting of the company which was held on 22nd November 1968, when a resolution was proposed as an ordinary resolution to remove him from his office as director. On a show of hands the resolution was passed, as the sisters voted for the resolution; so the brother demanded a poll and the whole issue is how votes should be counted on the poll having regard to special art. 9 of the company's articles of association.

The company adopted Table A in Sch I to the *Companies Act 1948*, with variations which are immaterial for present purposes. The relevant articles of Table A are:

2. Without prejudice to any special rights previously conferred on the holders of any existing shares or class of shares, any share in the company may be issued with such preferred, deferred or other special rights or such restrictions, whether in regard to dividend, voting, return of capital or otherwise as the company may from time to time by ordinary resolution determine.

62. Subject to any rights or restrictions for the time being attached to any class or classes of shares, on a show of hands every member present in person shall have one vote, and on a poll every member shall have one vote for each share of which he is the holder.

Special art.9 is as follows:

In the event of a Resolution being proposed at any General Meeting of the Company for the removal from office of any Director, any shares held by that Director shall on a poll in respect of such Resolution carry the right to three votes per share and regulation 62 of Part I of Table A shall be construed accordingly.

Article 96 of Table A, which empowers a company to remove a director by ordinary resolution, is excluded by the articles of the company so that the appellant relies on the mandatory terms of s. 184(1) of the *Companies Act 1948*, which so far as relevant is in these terms:

A company may by ordinary resolution remove a director before the expiration of his period of office, notwithstanding anything in its articles or in any agreement between it and him . . .

It is not in doubt that the requirements of sub-s. (2) have been satisfied. So the whole question is whether special art 9 is valid and applicable, in which case the resolution was rejected by 300 votes to 200, or whether that article must be treated as overridden by s. 184 and therefore void, in which case the resolution was passed by 200 votes to 100. So to test this matter the appellant began an action for a declaration that the respondent was removed from office as a director by the resolution of 22nd November 1968, and moved the court for an interlocutory injunction restraining him from acting as a director. This motion comes by way of appeal before your Lordships.

The appellant argues that special art 9 is directed to frustrating the whole object and purpose of s. 184 so that it can never operate where there is such a special article and the director in fact becomes irremovable. So she argues that, having regard to the clear words "notwithstanding anything in its articles" in s. 194, special art 9 must be rejected and treated as void. The learned judge, Ungoed Thomas J, so held. He said: "It would make a mockery of the law if the courts were to hold that in such a case a director was to be irremovable", and later he concluded his judgment by saying: "A resolution under art 9 is therefore not in my view an ordinary resolution within s. 184. The [appellant] succeeds in the application."

The respondent appealed, and the Court of Appeal (Harman, Russell and Karminski L.JJ.) allowed the appeal. Harman LJ did so on the simple ground that the 1948 Act did not prevent certain shares or classes of shares having special voting rights attached to them and on certain occasions. He could find nothing in the 1948 Act which prohibited the giving of special voting rights to the shares of a director who finds his position attacked. Russell L.J. in his judgment gave substantially the same reasons for allowing the appeal and he supported his judgment by reference to a number of recent precedents particularly those to be found in Palmer's Company Precedents [17th ed., 1956] but, with all respect to the learned Lord Justice, I do not think these precedents which, so far as relevant, are comparatively new can be said to have the settled assent and approbation of the profession, so as to render them any real guide for the purposes of a judgment; especially when I note the much more cautious approach by the learned editors of 5 Ency Forms & Precedents (4th ed.) 1966, p. 428, where in reference to a form somewhat similar to special art 9 they state in footnote 14:

> The validity of such a provision as this in relation to a resolution to remove a director from office remains to be tested in the courts.

My Lords, when construing an Act of Parliament it is a canon of construction that its provisions must be construed in the light of the mischief which the Act was designed to meet. In this case the mischief was well known; it was a common practice, especially in the case of private companies, to provide in the articles that a director should be irremovable or only removable by an extraordinary resolution; in the former case the articles would have to be altered by special resolution before the director could be removed and of course in either case a three-quarters majority would be required. In many cases this would be impossible, so the Act provided that notwithstanding anything in the articles an ordinary resolution would suffice to remove a director. That was the mischief which the section set out to remedy; to make a director removable by virtue of an ordinary resolution instead of an extraordinary resolution or making it necessary to alter the articles.

An ordinary resolution is not defined nor used in the body of the 1948 Act although the phrase occurs in some of the articles of Table A in Sch I to the Act. But its meaning is, in my opinion, clear. An ordinary resolution is in the first place passed by a bare majority on a show of hands by the members entitled to vote who are present personally or by proxy and on such a vote each member has one vote regardless of his shareholding. If a poll is demanded then for an ordinary resolution still only a bare majority of votes is required. But whether a share or class of shares has any vote on the matter and, if so, what is its voting power on the resolution in question depends entirely on the voting rights attached to that share or class of shares by the articles of association.

I venture to think that Ungoed Thomas J. overlooked the importance of art 2 of Table A which gives to the company a completely unfettered right to attach to any share or class of shares special voting rights on a poll or to restrict those rights as the company may think fit. Thus, it is commonplace that a company may and frequently does preclude preference shareholders from voting unless their dividends are in arrear or their class rights are directly affected. It is equally commonplace that particular shares may be issued with specially loaded voting rights which ensure that in all resolutions put before the shareholders in general meeting the holder of those particular shares can always be sure of carrying the day, aye or no, as the holder pleases.

Counsel for the appellant felt, quite rightly, constrained to admit that if an article provided that the respondent's shares should, on every occasion when a resolution was for consideration by a general meeting of the company, carry three votes such a provision would be valid on all such occasions including any occasion when the general meeting was considering a resolution for his removal under s. 184.

My Lords, I cannot see any difference between that case and the present case where special voting rights are conferred only when there is a resolution for the removal of a director under s. 184. Each case is an exercise of the unfettered right of the company under art 2 whereby:

> any share in the company may be issued with such . . . special rights . . . in regard to . . . voting . . . as the company may from time to time by ordinary resolution determine.

Parliament has never sought to fetter the right of the company to issue a share with such rights or restrictions as it may think fit. There is no fetter which compels the company to make the voting rights or restrictions of general application and it seems to me clear that such rights or restrictions can be attached to special circumstances and to particular types of resolution. This makes no mockery of s. 184; all that Parliament was seeking to do thereby was to make an ordinary resolution sufficient to remove a director. Had Parliament desired to go further and enact that every share entitled to vote should be deprived of its special rights under the articles it should have said so in plain terms by making the vote on a poll one vote one share. Then, what about shares which had no voting rights under the articles? Should not Parliament give them a vote when considering this completely artificial form of ordinary resolution? Suppose there had here been some preference shares in the name of the respondent's wife, which under the articles had in the circumstances no vote; why in justice should her voice be excluded from consideration in this artificial vote? I only raise this purely hypothetical case to show the great difficulty of trying to do justice by legislation in a matter which has always been left to the corporators themselves to decide.

I agree entirely with the judgment of the Court of Appeal, and would dismiss this appeal.

LORD DONOVAN: My Lords, the issue here is the true construction of s. 184 of the *Companies Act 1948*; and I approach it with no conception of what the legislature wanted to achieve by the section other than such as can reasonably be deduced from its language.

Clearly it was intended to alter the method by which a director of a company could be removed while still in office. It enacts that this can be done by the company by ordinary resolution. Furthermore, it may be achieved notwithstanding anything in the company's articles, or in any agreement between the company and the director.

Accordingly any case (and one knows there were many) where the articles prescribed that a director should be removable during his period of office only by a special resolution or an extraordinary resolution, each of which necessitated, *inter alia*, a three to one majority of those present and voting at the meeting, is overridden by s. 184. A simple majority of the votes will now suffice; an ordinary resolution being, in my opinion, a resolution capable of being carried by such a majority. Similarly any agreement, whether evidenced by the articles or otherwise, that a director shall be a director for life or for some fixed period is now also overreached.

The field over which s. 184 operates is thus extensive for it includes, admittedly, all companies with a quotation on the Stock Exchange. It is now contended, however, that it does something more; namely, that it provides in effect that when the ordinary resolution proposing the removal of the director is put to the meeting each shareholder present shall have one vote per share and no more; and that any provision in the articles providing that any shareholder shall, in relation to this resolution, have "weighted" votes attached to his shares, is also nullified by s. 184. A provision for such "weighting" of votes which applies generally, i.e. as part of the normal pattern of voting, is accepted by the appellant is unobjectionable; but an article such as the one here under consideration which is special to a resolution seeking the removal of a director falls foul of s. 184 and is overridden by it.

Why should this be? The section does not say so, as it easily could. And those who drafted it and enacted it certainly would have included among their numbers many who were familiar with the phenomenon of articles of association carrying "weighted votes". It must therefore have been plain at the outset that unless some special provision were made, the mere direction that an ordinary resolution would do in order to remove a director would leave the section at risk of being made inoperative in the way that has been done here. Yet no such provision was made, and in this Parliament followed its practice of leaving to companies and their shareholders liberty to allocate voting rights as they pleased.

When therefore it is said that a decision in favour of the respondent in this case would defeat the purpose of the section and make a mockery of it, it is being assumed that Parliament intended to cover every possible case and block up every loophole. I see no warrant for any such assumption. A very large part of the relevant field is in fact covered and covered effectively. And there may be good reasons why Parliament should leave some companies with freedom of manoeuvre in this particular matter. There are many small companies which are conducted in practice as though they were little more than partnerships, particularly family companies running a family business; and it is, unfortunately, sometimes necessary to provide some safeguard against family quarrels having their repercussions in the boardroom. I am not, of course, saying that this is such a case; I merely seek to repeal the argument that unless the section is construed in the way the appellant wants, it has become "inept" and "frustrated".

I would dismiss the appeal.

LORD MORRIS OF BORTH-Y-GEST. My Lords, it is provided by s. 184(1) of the *Companies Act 1948* that a company may by ordinary resolution remove a director before the expiration of his period of office. The company may do so notwithstanding anything to the contrary in its articles. So if an article provided that a director was irremovable he could nevertheless be removed if any ordinary resolution to that effect was passed. So also if an article provided that a director could only be removed by a resolution carried by a majority greater than a simple majority he would nevertheless be removed if a resolution was passed by a simple majority.

Some shares may, however, carry greater voting power than others. On a resolution to remove a director shares will therefore carry the voting power that they possess. But this does not, in my view, warrant a device such as special art 9 introduces. Its unconcealed effect is to make a director irremovable. If the question is posed whether the shares of the respondent possess any added voting weight the answer must be that they possess none whatsoever beyond, if valid, an *ad hoc* weight for the special purpose of circumventing s. 184. If special art 9 were writ large it would set out that a director is not to be removed against his will and that in order to achieve this and to thwart the express provision of s. 184 the voting power of any director threatened with removal is to be deemed to be greater than it actually is. The learned judge thought that to sanction this would be to make a mockery of the law. I think so also.

I would allow the appeal.

[Lord Reid and Lord Guest where also of the opinion that the appeal should be dismissed.]

Question

Is the decision in *Bushell* explicable on the basis that it involved a small, private company? Is this a case where the statute should differentiate between the private and public company in terms of what is permissible? For a comment on *Bushell*, see Prentice, (1969), 32 Mod. L. Rev. 693.

(c) Directorial Power and Interpreting the Corporate "Contract"

In the following cases there is a dispute over the interpretation of legal rules concerning directors. Are the results consistent with a contractarian view that sees shareholders as principals and directors as their agents, or do they confirm the Berle and Means view that directors can exercise virtually unfettered discretion? Where the cases limit director power, is this the result of a concern that the law should impose regulatory restrictions on the scope of director power, or simply the result of the court's attempt to interpret the corporate contract implicitly adopted by the parties?

Kelly v. Electrical Construction Co.
1907 CarswellOnt 248, 16 O.L.R. 232 (Ont. C.P.)

[Action to set aside the election of the board of directors of the defendant company which was an Ontario corporation. At the annual meeting, four absent shareholders, who were represented by proxy, were not allowed to vote. The evidence showed that the directors had adopted a by-law in 1897 stating that "all instruments appointing proxies shall be deposited at the head office of the company at least one day before the date at which they are to be used". This by-law was not confirmed at the next annual meeting of shareholders but was confirmed at a shareholders' meeting in 1905.]

MULOCK C.J.: The first question to determine is whether the by-law respecting proxies passed by the board of directors on May 13th, 1897, or any by-law, was in force at the election of directors held on February 5th, 1907.

Section 47 of the *Companies Act* declares that the directors may from time to time make by-laws . . . to regulate "(e) the requirements as to proxies . . . but every such by-law . . . unless in the meantime confirmed at a general meeting of the company duly called for that purpose, shall only have force until the next annual meeting of the company, and in default of confirmation thereat shall at, and from that time only, cease to have force, and in that case no new by-law to the same or the like effect shall have any force until confirmed at a general meeting of the company."

The directors' by-law of May 13th, 1897, was not confirmed at the next annual meeting after its passage, and thus it ceased "to have force." The only kind of by-law capable of confirmation by the shareholders under the provisions of sec. 47 is one in force at the time of such annual meeting. Thus the by-law in question not being in force at the time of the annual meeting of May 16th, 1905, was not capable of confirmation, but the shareholders at their annual meeting of May 16th, 1905, purported to pass a by-law in the exact language of that of May 13th, 1897, respecting proxies, and it was contended that if the shareholders' by-law did not operate as a confirmation of the directors' by-law it could be supported as a by-law originating in the first instance at a shareholders' meeting, and that, irrespective of the statute, the shareholders had inherent power to pass it as a piece of domestic legislation necessary for the proper carrying on of the affairs of the company.

This contention, I think, cannot prevail. The presumption that a corporation has implied power to pass by-laws necessary for the proper management of its affairs arises only in the absence of express power. Here the *Companies Act* declares what powers, in respect of proxies, shall be enjoyed by a corporation subject to its provisions, and therefore the question here is not what powers arise by implication, but what are the powers of the corporation having regard to its express statutory powers.

Section 63 of the *Companies Act* enacts that "at all general meetings of the company every shareholder shall be entitled to as many votes as he holds shares in the company, and may vote by proxy," and sec. 47 declares that the board of directors may pass by-laws regulating the requirements as to proxies. These two sections must be read together, their effect being that each shareholder is entitled to the right to vote by proxy subject to the one qualification, namely, compliance with the requirements of a directors' by-law, which, if not confirmed within the time limited for that purpose, ceases to exist.

Section 47, empowering directors to pass by-laws respecting proxies, impliedly withholds such power from the general body of shareholders. As stated by Vaughan, B., in *Rex v. Westwood* (1830), 7 Bing. 1, at p. 29:

> Wherever a charter confers an express power of making by-laws, as to a particular subject, on a certain part of the corporation (more especially where, as in this case, those terms are very general and comprehensive), there is no ground on which a presumption can be raised of an implied power existing in the body at large; but that such power is expressly taken from that body according to the rule, *Expressum facit cessare tacitum.*

Were the rule otherwise there might in the present case be in existence at the same time previous to the election two inconsistent by-laws, one passed by the board of directors, the other by the shareholders, prescribing conflicting regulations respecting proxies. It cannot, I think, be seriously argued that the statute contemplated such a possibility. I am therefore of opinion that the express power conferred by sec. 47 upon the board of directors to pass by-laws respecting proxies deprives the body at large of any inherent power to deal with that subject, and therefore the shareholders' by-law of May 16th, 1905, if regarded as originating with that body, is null and void. Then the directors' by-law of May 13th, 1897, not having been confirmed by the shareholders within the time fixed by sec. 47, also became null and void. The plaintiffs did not, by their statement of claim, attack the by-law on the ground that it was merely a shareholders' by-law. Nevertheless this point came up for consideration at the trial, and the defendants unsuccessfully endeavored to discover a directors' by-law to serve as foundation for the shareholders' by-law.

Note

1   The by-laws, like articles of association, are the rules for the internal governance of the corporation. Control over their initiation is an important allocation of power. Section 103 of the CBCA vests the power to make by-laws in the directors subject to the articles, by-laws or a unanimous shareholder agreement providing otherwise. Thus, the corporate constitution may provide for a sharing of power, may give the power exclusively to one group, or may simply leave the statutory allocation in place. In one sense the power is always shared, as s. 103(2) of the CBCA requires shareholder approval of all by-laws, and any amendment or repeal. Section 103(5) is an alternate route, through a shareholder proposal in s. 137, for initiation of a by-law. This will be discussed further in Chapter 8.

2   In *Northern Minerals Investment Corp. v. Mundoro Capital Inc.*, 2012 BCSC 1090, 2012 CarswellBC 2153 (B.C. S.C. [In Chambers]), the board of directors adopted a policy that required nominations for directors to be made by a certain date in advance of an annual meeting. A shareholder sought a declaration that this policy was invalid as the board did not have authority to adopt it. The court dismissed the petition, holding that "[t]he residual power to manage a corporation's affairs rested with the directors. As a matter of contractual interpretation, the directors' powers flowed from the Act and articles in which the directors were in fact granted residual powers. . . As for the Policy itself, neither the Act nor the articles expressly precluded directors from creating such a policy. [The objecting shareholder] did not establish that the Policy infringed shareholders rights."

Automatic Self-Cleansing Filter Syndicate Co. Ltd. v. Cuninghame
[1906] 2 Ch. 34, 7 5 L.J. Ch. 437 (C.A.)

[The articles of association of the Automatic Self-Cleansing Co., provided that "the management of the business and the control of the company shall be vested in the directors, subject nevertheless . . . to such regulations . . . as may from time to time be made by extraordinary resolution" (a vote of three quarters of the shareholders). At a general meeting called by the directors at the request of a major shareholder who had arranged for the sale of the company's assets, a resolution approving the sale was passed by a simple majority and the directors were instructed to carry the transaction into effect. The directors were of the opinion that the sale on the terms set out was not for the benefit of the company and refused to do so.] COLLINS M.R.: This is an appeal from a decision of Warrington J., who has been asked by the plaintiffs, Mr. McDiarmid and the company, for a declaration that the defendants, as directors of the company, are bound to carry into effect a resolution passed at a meeting of the shareholders in the company on January 16 . . .

[At the trial] Arington J. held that the majority could not impose that obligation upon the directors, and that on the true construction of the articles the directors were the persons authorized by the articles to effect this sale, and that unless the other powers given by the memorandum were invoked by a special resolution, it was impossible for a mere majority at a meeting to override the views of the directors. That depends, as Warrington J. put it, upon the construction of the articles. First of all there is no doubt that the company under its memorandum has the power in clause 3(k) to sell the undertaking of the company or any part thereof. In this case there is some small exception, I believe, to that which is to be sold, but I do not think that that becomes material. We now come to clause 81 of the articles, which I think it is important to refer to in this connection. [His Lordship read the clause.] Then come the two clauses which are most material, 96 and 97, whereby the powers of the directors are defined. [His Lordship read clause 96 and clause 97(1).] Therefore in the matters referred to in article 97(1) the view of the directors as to the fitness of the matter is made the standard; and furthermore, by article 96 they are given in express terms the full powers which the company has, except so far as they "are not hereby or by statute expressly directed or required to be exercised or done by the company", so that the directors have absolute power to do all things other than those that are expressly required to be done by the company; and then comes the limitation on their general authority — "subject to such regulations as may from time to time be made by extraordinary resolution". Therefore, if it is desired to alter the powers of the directors that must be done, not by a resolution carried by a majority at an ordinary meeting of the company, but by an extraordinary resolution. In these circumstances it seems to me that it is not competent for the majority of the shareholders at an ordinary meeting to affect or alter the mandate originally given to the directors, by the articles of association. It has been suggested that this is a mere question of principal and agent, and that it would be an absurd thing if a principal in appointing an agent should in effect appoint a dictator who is to manage him instead of his managing the agent. I think that the analogy does not strictly apply to this case. No doubt for some purposes directors are agents. For whom are they agents? You have, no doubt, in theory and law one entity, the company, which might be a principal, but you have to go behind that when you look to the particular position of directors. It is by the consensus of all the individuals in the company that these directors become agents and hold their rights as agents. It is not fair to say that a majority at a meeting is for the purposes of this case the principal so as to alter the mandate of the agent. The minority also must be taken into account. There are provisions by which the minority may be over-borne, but that can only be done by special machinery in the shape of special resolutions. Short of that the mandate which must be obeyed is not that of the majority — it is that of the whole entity made up of all the shareholders. If the mandate of the directors is to be altered, it can only be under the machinery of the memorandum and articles themselves. I do not think I need say more. . .

[The judgment of Cozens-Hardy L.J. has been omitted.]

Note

1   In *Scott v. Scott*, [1943] 1 All E.R. 582 (Ch.D.), a resolution authorizing a dividend to be paid to each preference shareholder was passed at the general meeting. The company's articles provided that: "The directors may from time to time pay to the members such interim dividends as appear to the directors to be justified by the profits of the company." In an action brought by the defendants challenging the validity of the resolution, Lord Clauson speaking for the court stated:

> I do not think it is suggested that if this resolution is a resolution for the payment of an interim dividend that it could possibly be held to be valid, it having been passed by the company in general meeting. If it was, then the annual general meeting impugned upon the sphere of activity which, in the most express terms, is confined to the directors . . . How the directors can manage the business if they are to be interfered with in such an ordinary financial matter . . . I cannot conceive. It seems to me it is quite clear that this resolution, if it is not aimed at declaring an interim dividend, is aimed at interfering with the management of the business by the directors and, as such, it is in my view wholly inoperative, and the general meeting had no power to pass it.

2   In *Macson Dev. Co. Ltd. v. Gordon* (1959), 19 D.L.R. (2d) 465 (N.S. S.C.), the president of the plaintiff company, having obtained the resignation of his fellow directors in order, as he told them, to facilitate the company's liquidation, held a meeting at which he appointed a second director and shortly thereafter convened a meeting of directors which passed a resolution authorizing a law suit. Subsequently, at a special general meeting of the shareholders who were the "resigned" directors, a resolution was passed disapproving of the action and authorizing its discontinuance. A notice of motion was brought to strike out the name of the company as plaintiff on the ground that the institution of the action was unauthorized.

McDonald J. held that, as sole remaining director, the president had the power under the Articles to fill up a vacancy, as he and the newly appointed director constituted a quorum. By virtue of another Article which delegated the entire management of the company into the hands of the directors, the shareholders' resolution was invalid and could not overrule the decision of the directors. Accordingly, the action was properly brought.

3   The Court in *Bioartificial Gel Technologies (Bagtech) Inc. (Syndic de) c. R.*, 2012 TCC 120, 2012 CarswellNat 1209, 2012 CarswellNat 5313 (T.C.C. [General Procedure]), affirmed 2013 CarswellNat 2049, 2013 CarswellNat 3309 (F.C.A.), a tax case, invoked the principle that "shareholders, even acting unanimously, may not fetter the board's power to manage or supervise the management of the business and affairs of the corporation or prevent it from performing its legal duty to do so."

4   Gower states in *Modern Company Law* (4th ed.), p. 146:

> [T]he result of the cases appears to be that the directors have ceased to be mere agents of the company . . . Both they and the members in general meeting are primary organs of the company between whom the company's powers are divided. The general meeting retains ultimate control, but only through its powers to amend the articles (so as to take away, for the future, certain powers from the directors) and to remove the directors and to substitute others more to its taste. Until it takes one or other of these steps the directors can, if they are so advised, disregard the wishes and instructions of the members in all matters not specifically reserved (either by the Act or the articles) to a general meeting. And, as we shall later see, the practical difficulties in the way of effectively exercising even this measure of supervision are very great owing to the directors' control over the proxy-voting machinery. The old idea that the general meeting alone is the company's primary organ and the directors merely the company's agents or servants, at all times subservient to the general meeting, seems no longer to be the law as it is certainly not the fact.

Hayes v. Canada-Atlantic & Plant S.S. Co.
181 F. 289 (1st Cir. 1910)

[At common law, the directors had no authority to delegate their powers without special authority from either the relevant companies Act or the by-laws. This rule was said to arise from the principle of *delegatus non potest delegare*. Whether the board should be considered a delegate, particularly when its powers derive from the statute and not by grant from the shareholders, is problematic. The maxim has been altered both in corporate statutes and in most corporate constitutions. The reality in the public company is that directors can only operate by delegating discretionary authority to committees, officers and agents.

Section 115 of the CBCA authorizes the directors, subject to the articles or by-laws, to appoint one of their number as managing director, or to appoint a committee of directors and delegate to it "any" of the powers of the directors. The open-ended power of delegation is cut down extensively by s. 115(3) of the CBCA, which withholds powers of particular importance, such as issuing securities, declaring dividends, adopting by-laws and approving a take-over bid circular. In those instances, and the others listed, only the board can act. In sum, the delegation is limited to the ordinary course of business. In most public companies, delegation to an executive committee is the rule.

The attitude of the courts to such delegation is illustrated by the decision in *Hayes v. Canada-Atlantic & Plant S.S. Co.*, a case which may well have influenced the drafting of s. 115(3) of the CBCA.]

PUTNAM, CIRCUIT JUDGE: [W]e might leave the case here, but it is perhaps better to open the record in some respects quite fully. The charter provides as follows:

> (2) The directors may annually appoint from among themselves an executive committee for such purposes and with such powers and duties as the directors or by-laws determine; and the president shall be *ex officio* a member of such executive committee.

The formal by-laws of the corporation provide as follows:

> Sec. 8. The directors shall annually appoint from among themselves two directors, who, with the president, shall form an executive committee, and said committee shall have full powers of the board of directors when said board is not in session.

Section 8 is expressed literally in very broad terms, in that it purports to vest the committee with the "full powers" of the board of directors. Hayes maintains that this expression, "full powers" has no limitation whatever, while a true construction limits it to the ordinary business operations of the corporation. It must be so limited, as we will see on further examination of the charter and by-laws. Also, although Perry had a majority interest, absolute or contingent, and was the treasurer of the corporation, and although it appears that the proceedings attempted at the alleged meetings of the executive committee and of the directors were hostile to his interests in a fundamental way and to such an extent as to deprive him of the treasurership, and although also it is said that all this does not bear directly on the case; nevertheless, we should exhibit what was attempted to be done by Hayes and Gale for the purpose of showing in a concrete way that it is not tolerable that the by-law in question should have the construction which Hayes claims for it.

The Canadian joint-stock companies act (32-33 Victoria, Chapter 15) directs that the affairs of a corporation shall be managed by a board of directors, and that, in the absence of other provisions in a special way or in the by-laws of the company, the directors shall elect the president and shall regulate the allotment of stock, and the forfeiture of stock for nonpayment, and the transfer of stock. It also provides among other things, for by-laws regulating the number of the directors, their term of service, the amount of their stock qualification, and their remuneration, if any, and "the appointment, functions, duties and removal of all agents, officers and servants of the company, the security to be given by them to the company and their remuneration." In addition to the above, we have already quoted the by-law under which the executive committee was constituted, in effect that the directors should annually appoint from among themselves two directors who with the president should constitute such committee.

Hayes and Gale, at the alleged meeting held on June 6, 1904, undertook to transact the following matters: They removed Perry from his office of treasurer and appointed Gale in his place. They directed payment to Hayes of the salary, and of the $506.33 in dispute, although his salary had never before been fixed or authorized. They fixed an annual salary for Gale as managing director at $1,854.20. They amended the by-laws so that special meetings of the shareholders could be called only by the president. They amended, as we have said, the by-law establishing the executive committee so that the committee should consist of only one director besides the president; and they amended the by-law providing for meetings of the directors so that they could be called only by the president.

It is not worthwhile to follow all through the meeting of the executive committee held June 24, 1904. A crucial matter which we need in this connection is that all the proceedings were in the pecuniary interests of Hayes and Gale, and they were the only persons who were voting in relation thereto. These two persons, when they undertook to amend the by-law by virtue of which they were constituted a committee, so tied up the corporation that no special meeting of the stockholders or directors could be called except by one of themselves; that is, the president. In other words, they proceeded in such a way that, if their action had been effectual, the two men, acting in their own pecuniary interests, would have absorbed the entire powers of the corporation for an indefinite period. The two also assumed, by implication, the power of issuing stock, thus shutting out, if they saw fit, the possibility of the existing shareholders obtaining control of the stock at any meeting thereof which any of them might find some legal method of calling. It is certainly intolerable to maintain that the words "full powers", in the provision for the appointment of the executive committee, practically divested the directors of all their functions, and built up a new foundation for it in lieu of that formally established. Such an assumed absorption of the powers of the creator by the created is too absurd to receive the approbation of any court of law. We recite these facts because they exhibit in a concrete way, by illustration, the impossibility of giving force to the words "full powers" in the by-law referred to except with limitations restricting them to the ordinary business transactions of the corporation. Having in mind that neither the president nor any director of a corporation is entitled to compensation for his services without some special provision of statute or some action of the stockholders or other directors, and having in view the limitations necessarily implied for the reasons we have stated, we must hold that the matter of such compensation was specifically retained for the personal action of the directors by the particular enumeration thereof, notwithstanding that there were other powers, of a general nature, which might well have vested in the executive committee, which would fully satisfy the call of the words "full powers" . . .

Sherman & Ellis v. Indiana Mutual Casualty
41 F.2d 588 (7th Cir. 1930)

[A prudent management decision in some cases may be to contract for the management services of third parties who possess particular expertise. This is often the case in the realm of services such as hotel management, entertainment, and restaurants. The important legal question is the extent to which management may be vested in third parties. The matter has been left to the courts to sort out, with the line between permissible and impermissible delegation often being a very fine one. In *Sherman & Ellis*, the defendant insurance company granted its management to the plaintiff insurance company for a period of twenty years. The contract contained the following term:

> That for and during a period of twenty years from the date hereof, it will supply without compensation other than the payment specified in article II, paragraph First, hereof, the underwriting and executive management for the Mutual Company in the person of its President, Frank H. Ellis, or such other of its officers as it may from time to time designate, who shall be competent to perform the services of chief executive head and underwriting manager of the Mutual Company, to the end that the same competent management which the Indiana Manufacturers Reciprocal Association has enjoyed in the past may continue uninterrupted for the benefit of the Mutual Company policy holders. . .]

EVANS CIRCUIT JUDGE: The line of demarcation between cases which recognize the right of officers of a corporation to delegate certain managerial duties to a stranger and cases which deny such authority is not entirely clear or easy to follow. That corporations may, at least for a limited period, delegate to a stranger certain duties usually performed by the officers, is clear.

On the other hand, it is equally well settled that there are duties, the performance of which may not be indefinitely delegated to outsiders . . .

The case of *Jones v. Williams*, 40 S.W. 353, is as strong as any that appellant has cited, and illustrates, perhaps as well as any, the extent to which the courts have gone in upholding such delegations of authority. There the Board of Directors gave an outsider the position of editor and manager of a large daily paper for a period of five years, during which time said outsider was to determine the editorial policy of the paper. But the facts in that case fall short of those presented in the instant suit. The period of control there fixed was five years. Here it is twenty years. There a larger part of the board's official duties was undelegated. Here nothing of importance was left for the board of directors, but the unimportant, the ministerial duties.

It is true the statutes of most of the states authorizing the organization of corporations are of general application and are easily complied with. Yet we cannot believe that the requirements therein found or the official duties therein prescribed are mere formalities or only directory in character. This is particularly true of insurance companies upon whose conservative management and financial responsibility a multitude of policyholders are dependent. The grant of corporate power by a state is upon the hypothesis that these powers shall be exercised by the corporation's officers, annually elected by the stockholders and not by the officers of another corporation.

Reverting to the language of this agreement for a moment, it appears "that for and during the period of twenty years from the date hereof it [appellant] will supply . . . the underwriting and executive management . . . in the person of its president, Frank H. Ellis, or such other officer as it may from time to time designate," and that "during said twenty-years period" the casualty company shall elect the officer furnished by appellant for its underwriting manager who "shall have general supervision and charge of the underwriting affairs of the corporation."

Such an agreement negatives the thought that appellant was merely the soliciting agent of the casualty company. It contemplated the substitution of appellant for the officers of the casualty company. What was the casualty company's business? To write casualty insurance and adjust the losses growing out of such insurance. If there existed a conflict of opinion between the board and appellant, whose voice under this contract would control? Obviously, appellant's. The length of time during which the agreement was to operate likewise indicated that not only managerial powers were delegated, but the entire policy of the casualty company business was to be fixed and determined by appellant. No other conclusion can be drawn from this agreement and the evidence than that the casualty company was to be merely an instrumentality through which appellant was to conduct a casualty insurance business in the state of Indiana. The agreement which accomplished this result transcends the spirit and theory upon which corporate franchises are based, and is void.

Kennerson v. Burbank Amusement Co.
260 P. 2d 823 (Calif. C.A. 1953)

PETERS J.: Inasmuch as the directors must exercise and maintain control over corporate affairs in good faith, they are prohibited from delegating such control and management to others and any contract so providing is void. By this contract with Kennerson the Board has attempted to confer upon him the practical control and management of substantially all corporate powers. The sole asset of this corporation was the management of, and the fixtures in, the Manor Theatre building. By the contract the Board has attempted to transfer all control over bookings, personnel, admission prices, salaries, contracts, expenses and even fiscal policies to Kennerson. While the contract provides that moneys are to be banked in the name of Burbank, Kennerson is authorised to book "other forms of entertainment" so that he could, without restraint, change the very nature of the enterprise, and could even assign his powers to others. The fact that Kennerson is under a duty to make periodic reports to the Board does not constitute a sufficient retention of control over discretionary corporate policy to comply with the rule.

Kennerson admits that it is the law that a board cannot divest itself of its fundamental powers by contract, but contends that the requirements that Kennerson must report and account saves this contract from violating this rule . . . as long as the corporation exists, its affairs must be managed by the duly elected Board. The Board may grant authority to act, but it cannot delegate its function to govern. If it does so, the contract so provided is void . . .

A case quite similar to the instant one is *Long Park v. Trenton-New Brunswick Theatres Co.* 77 N.E. 2d 633. There the New York Court of Appeals held invalid, as at matter of law, a contract to manage a theatre business, which contract was somewhat similar to the one here involved. There the board delegated to another corporation the right to manage all the theatres leased or to be leased by the granting corporation. As in the instant case, full and uncontrolled authority over books, policies, admission prices and personnel was granted. The court held that by such a contract "the powers of the directors over the management of its theatres, the principal business of the corporation, were completely sterilized". Such restrictions and limitations upon the powers of the directors are clearly in violation of s. 27 of the General Corporation Law ("The business of a corporation shall be managed by its board of directors.").

The court in *Long Park* was also influenced by the fact that the management contract could not be changed by the directors but could only be changed pursuant to a decision of an arbitrator. As Peters J. noted in *Kennerson*, the problem is one of degree. If substantially all corporate powers are delegated, the contract will be held void and unenforceable. An example of a valid management contract is contained in *Cullen v. Governor Clinton Co.*, 110 N.Y.S. 2d 614 (1952). A management contract was entered into by the owners of the Governor Clinton Hotel. When the contract was challenged, the court ruled as follows:

> Whether the hotel could better be operated through the medium of a management company presented a question of business judgment. If the decision had been arrived at as the result of an honest, prudent and careful belief of the directors that it was for the best interest of the hotel company, then that determination would not be subject to interference by the courts, even though an error in judgment may have been committed.

Question

The result of the cases seems to be that the directors may make a valid decision to enter into a management contract to have the business operated by a third party as long as in so doing they still continue to function as a board of directors with ultimate control over the business.

What if, in *Kennerson*, the board had decided to lease the theatres in return for a percentage of the profits? Is there any difference between that undoubtedly valid act and what took place in *Kennerson* or in *Long Park?*

Realty Acceptance Corp. v. Montgomery
51 F.2d 636 (3rd Cir. 1930)

[An important question in the context of the employment of a senior officer or a service director is the relationship between the individual's contractual rights and the company's rights to amend or repeal its by-laws or articles of association. American and Commonwealth courts have upheld the validity of individual contracts in the face of the corporation's undoubted power to amend its by-laws or articles of association or to not re-elect or to remove a director.]

JUDGE MORRIS: By this action of covenant tried to the court without the intervention of a jury under R.S. §649 (28 USCA §773), Henry G. Montgomery, the plaintiff, seeks to recover from Realty Acceptance Corporation, the defendant, damages for the breach of its contract under seal, of September 23, 1924, employing plaintiff as its president and as the president of the Stuyvesant Corporation, all of whose capital stock was owned by the defendant, from the date of the contract to December 31, 1929, at a salary, from October 1, 1924, to December 31, 1929, at the rate of $25,000 a year, payable in equal monthly installments. The main breaches alleged are the removal of the plaintiff from the presidency of each corporation by the respective boards of directors in December 1926, and the nonpayment of any salary for the years 1927 to 1929, inclusive.

Defendant, a Delaware corporation, admits the contract and that, prior to its execution, it was authorized by its board of directors. It likewise admits the ouster and the nonpayment of salary for the three years. It makes no claim that plaintiff was incompetent. It asserts, however, in avoidance of liability, that its by-laws and those of the Stuyvesant Corporation, chartered under the laws of New York, both provided, at the time the contract was made, that the president:

> shall be chosen annually by the Board of Directors and shall hold his office until his successor shall have been duly chosen and qualified or . . . he . . . shall have been removed in the manner hereinafter provided, and . . . may be removed, either with or without cause, by the vote of a majority of the whole Board of Directors . . .

that plaintiff's removal by both companies was carried out in strict conformity with the by-laws; that the by-laws were valid and nullified or became by implication a part or condition of the contract; and that the contract was void for the further reason that it was against public policy.

Plaintiff does not deny that the by-laws were in existence at the time the contract was entered into; that they were valid; that he had knowledge thereof; or that the removal proceedings were had in strict conformity therewith. He takes the position, however, that, as there was no statutory inhibition against the employment of officers of Delaware or New York corporations for a fixed term, as the by-laws were amendable, article X, "by the affirmative vote of a majority of the whole Board of Directors . . ." and as the making of the contract employing plaintiff for a fixed term was expressly authorized by more than a majority of defendant's board of directors, the contract was a *pro tanto* supersession of the by-laws, and must prevail over them.

Many cases deal with the relation of by-laws and contracts under varying circumstances. The Superior Court of New York ruled, in *Martino v. Commerce Fire Ins. Co.*, 47 N.Y. Super. Ct. 520, that a contract of employment for a definite time prevailed over a by-law declaring that certain employees of the class to which plaintiff belonged should hold office during the pleasure of the board. The Appellate Division of the Supreme Court of that state decided in *Reiss v. Usona Shirt Co.*, 159 N.Y.S. 1031, 1033, that:

> the fact that the by-laws of the defendant, as known to the plaintiff, provided that the treasurer should be elected each year, and that he could be removed with or without cause by the directors, did not necessarily render such an agreement as was asserted by the plaintiff *ultra vires* the corporation.

Cuppy v. Stollwerck Bros., 216 N.Y. 591, III N.E. 249, 251, was an action to recover salary due, under a contract of employment, for one year, from which plaintiff was discharged at the end of four months under the authority of a by-law providing "the Board of Directors by a majority

vote may . . . remove a director or officer and by like vote fill the vacancy
. . ." The court held that, "while the by-law empowered the board of
directors to remove a director or officer, it did not authorize them to
terminate a contract with one whom they had employed for a definite
term. The fact that the plaintiff had been elected a director in no way
alters the situation. His election as director was in pursuance of his
contract of employment. It did not supersede the contract and render his
contract which was for a definite term terminable at will . . ."

In *Nelson v. James Nelson & Sons, Limited*, [1913] 2 K.B. 471, the
facts were that plaintiff was elected managing director of the defendant
for the term of four years. Before the expiration of that term, the directors
revoked the appointment. The defendant contended that the article of
association providing that the directors might revoke the appointment of
any managing director appointed by them became by implication a part
of the contract and authorized plaintiff's removal. The court denied this
contention, saying:

> Is there any prohibition in the articles against the directors
> appointing a managing director for a fixed term, provided he
> remains a director and performs his duty satisfactorily? If there is
> one it is to be extracted from the words "and may revoke such
> appointment". But I think sufficient meaning is given to these words
> if they are read "and may exercise the power of revoking the
> appointment when the company or directors may legally do so" . . .
> Article 85(b) is, I believe, a very ordinary one in articles, and it would
> seem greatly to the prejudice of the company if, while they could
> employ a clerk for a fixed term, they could not offer so important an
> official as a managing director any security of tenure, but only an
> appointment at will or pleasure.

If the by-law may not be read into the contract of employment, it
would seem to be of no importance that the by-law of the defendant
provides for removal "either with or without cause" . . .

To read into a contract of employment for a definite period,
expressly authorized by the board of directors, a by-law amendable by a
majority of the board, and thus nullify the contract, would sacrifice
substance and straightforwardness for form and procedure. Defendant's
further contention that, if the contract be upheld at the expense of the by-
law, boards of directors may by contract of employment for terms of
years perpetuate their business policy and deprive succeeding boards of
the power to afford relief, is not convincing. It sticks in the bark, for the
evil possibilities suggested have their true foundation, not in the
supremacy of contract over by-law, but in the futility of a limitation
which rests solely upon a by-law amendable by a majority of the board.
Were there doubt of the board's power to amend by necessary implication
through solemnly authorized, inconsistent acts, the limitation would
constitute no barrier to the commission of the suggested acts by a board

so disposed, for the board could formally and expressly repeal the by-law containing the limitation and thereupon with all regularity authorize the contracts for terms of years.

I am of the opinion and find that the contract made by the defendant pursuant to the express authority of its board of directors, which had express power to amend at will the by-laws of the defendant, modified, in its legal effect, all inconsistent by-laws and prevails over them.

Nor was the contract one against public policy. It was not tainted with fraud. The restraint thereby placed upon the future freedom of action of defendant's board of directors cannot be said to have been in fact or principle injurious to the public interest. The term of office therein fixed was neither permanent, unlimited nor for life, but, in view of plaintiff's relation to defendant and his familiarity and grasp of its business, was for a reasonable period only. The contract was in conflict with no statute . . .

The defendant takes the position, however, that the contract, even if valid, was subject to the implied condition that the plaintiff should remain a duly qualified director, and shows that, pursuant to the authority of the by-laws of the two companies, he was removed as a director of each by their respective boards on December 31, 1926. His salary was paid to the end of 1926. But these facts are of no avail to the defendant. The contract was breached by the defendant while plaintiff was still a director of each company. Upon defendant's breach, plaintiff's cause of action was complete, and he was under no obligation longer to keep himself qualified for the presidency. Moreover, the contract contained an implied condition that the defendant would do nothing to defeat the rights of plaintiff under the contract, would do nothing to render his performance thereunder impossible. Yet defendant, the sole stockholder of the Stuyvesant Corporation, through its representatives, the directors of Stuyvesant, removed plaintiff's qualification for the presidency of that corporation by removing him from its board. That act constituted neither a defense to the prior breach nor a termination of defendant's liability under the contract. If of any legal effect, it was a further breach of the contract by the defendant.

The contract was not only valid, it was breached by the defendant.

Southern Foundries (1926) Ltd. v. Shirlaw
[1940] 2 All E.R. 445, [1940] A.C. 701 (H.L.)

[Shirlaw was appointed managing director of Southern Foundries Ltd. for a period of ten years. The articles of the Company provided for the appointment of a managing director and also provided that he be subject to the same provisions as to removal as the other directors but "subject to the provisions of any contract between him and the company." The article also provided that if the managing director ceased to be a director "he shall *ipso facto* and immediately cease to be a managing director."

When Federated Foundries acquired control of Southern it adopted a new set of articles. Pursuant to the new articles, it removed Shirlaw as a director who then ceased to be managing director.]

LORD PORTER: It is common ground, and, indeed, long-established law, that a company cannot forgo its right to alter its articles, but it does not follow that the alteration may not be, or result in, a breach of contract. The principle is perhaps most clearly enunciated first in *Allen v. Gold Reefs of West Africa Ltd.* [1900] 1 Ch. 656, a case in which a company was held entitled to alter its articles so as to obtain a lien on fully paid shares, though before the alteration it had a lien only upon partially-paid shares. Lindley M.R. states the position thus:

> A company cannot break its contracts by altering its articles, but, when dealing with contracts referring to revocable articles, and especially with contracts between a member of the company and the company respecting his shares, care must be taken not to assume that the contract involves as one of its terms an article which is not to be altered. . . . It is easy to imagine cases in which even a member of a company may acquire by contract or otherwise special rights against the company, which exclude him from the operation of a subsequently altered article: [1900] 1 Ch. at 673-4.

The principle was also clearly enunciated in *Bailey v. British Equitable Assurance Co.* [1904] in 1 Ch. 374, in which a participating policyholder had taken out a policy which the Court of Appeal thought entitled him to have the whole of the profits distributed, and he was held entitled to a declaration that the assurance company ought to distribute the whole of such profits. The action was necessitated because the company, which, when the policy was taken out, had been formed, and was operating under a deed of settlement providing for the distribution of the whole of the profits, at a later date proposed to register itself with limited liability, to substantiate a memorandum and articles for the deed of settlement, and, under the terms of the articles, to carry part of the profits to a reserve fund. The Court of Appeal affirmed a declaration by Kekewich J. that the company ought to continue to distribute the entire profits arising from the participating branch of its business, and Cozens Hardy M.R. said:

> But the case of a contract between an outsider and the company is entirely different, and even a shareholder must be regarded as an outsider in so far as he contracts with the company otherwise than in respect of his shares. It would be dangerous to hold that in a contract of . . . service . . . validly entered into by a company there is any greater power of variation of the rights and liabilities of the parties than would exist if, instead of the company, the contracting party had been an individual: [1904] 1 Ch. at 385.

The general principle, therefore, may, I think, be stated thus. (i) A company cannot be precluded from altering its articles thereby giving itself power to act upon the provisions of the altered articles, but so to act may nevertheless be a breach of contract if it is contrary to a stipulation in a contract validly made before the alteration. (ii) Nor can an injunction be granted to prevent the adoption of the new articles. In that sense, they are binding on all and sundry, but for the company to act upon them all none the less render it liable in damages if such action is contrary to the previous engagements of the company. If, therefore, the altered articles had provided for the dismissal without notice of a managing director previously appointed, the dismissal would be *ultra vires* the company, but would nevertheless expose the company to an action for damages if the appointment had been for a term of (say) 10 years and he were dismissed in less. Once it is established that the appointment is for a time certain and the dismissal before its termination, the result follows, and I do not understand the appellants to contend to the contrary. The complication lies in the facts (i) that the respondent has been dismissed, not from his office of managing director, but has been removed from his position of director, and (ii) that the removal has been effected, not by the Southern company, but by the Federated Company. So far as the first matter is concerned, the decision must, I think, be reached by applying the well-known principle laid down by Cockburn C.J. in *Stirling v. Maitland* (1864) 5 B & S 841 at 852:

> I look on the law to be that, if a party enters into an arrangement which can only take effect by the continuance of a certain existing state of circumstances, there is an implied engagement on his part that he shall do nothing of his own motion to put an end to that state of circumstances under which alone the arrangement can be operative. I agree that if the company had come to an end by some independent circumstance, not created by the defendants themselves, it might very well be that the covenant would not have the effect contended for; but if it is put an end to by their own voluntary act, that is a breach of covenant for which the plaintiff may sue. The transfer of business and the dissolution of the company was certainly the act of the company itself, so that they have by their act put an end to the state of things under which alone this covenant would operate.

If, therefore, the Southern company had altered their articles in such a way as to enable them to remove the respondent from his directorship at will, and had so removed him, I, in common, I believe, with all your Lordships, would regard their action as coming under the dictum of Cockburn C.J. as an actionable breach of contract.

In reaching this conclusion I find myself unable to accept the dissenting judgment of Sir Wilfrid Greene M.R., who took the view that under the contract the plaintiff was expressly appointed managing director, not for 10 years, but only for such a period not exceeding 10 years as he remained a director, and that no term could be implied which would prevent the company from terminating the respondent's directorship, with the result that he ceased to be capable of retaining his position as managing director.

However, no such alteration was made. The new articles did away with all former grounds of removal and termination of the director's office, and left it to the Federated company at their absolute discretion to keep or remove a director of the Southern company. That change, it is said, is no breach, or, at any rate, is not contended to be a breach, of the respondent's contract, and his later removal is the act of Federated, and not of the Southern company, and one, therefore, for which the latter company is not responsible. This contention was negatived by Sir Wilfrid Greene M.R., as well as the other two members of the Court of Appeal. As, however, the main argument appears to have been grounded upon the question of the true construction of the contract the matter now under consideration was treated as subsidiary, with the consequence that it was dealt with very shortly in the Court of Appeal.

I cannot say that I have found the solution an easy one, and obviously, having regard to the divergence of view in your Lordship's House, the matter is one which tends itself to a conflict of opinion. Some support for the appellants' contention was sought in *Bluett v. Stutchbury's Ltd.* (1908) 24 T.L.R. 469. The case is very shortly reported, and the exact grounds of the decision are not easy to ascertain, but they lend some countenance to the appellants' argument, inasmuch as in that case, as in this, the articles had been altered so that the retention or dismissal of the director from his directorship was left to the determination of a third party. Cozens Hardy MR is reported to have said that, in such circumstances, if the third party deprived the managing director of his directorship, and, he necessarily ceased to be managing director, the company could not prevent that action, and were in no sense the authors of the dismissal.

If the true view be that the only action taken by the company was the alteration of the articles, and if, indeed, thereafter they were in no way implicated in the act of the Federated company in removing the respondent, and could not help themselves, then the appeal must succeed. However, though it is true that ultimately the Southern company could not prevent the Federated company from removing the respondent from his directorship, the act of removal is not, I think, solely the act of the Federated company. Rather it is the combined act of both, an act impossible to the latter but for the act of the former, and not resulting in a breach of contract until the power of dismissal given by the former was acted upon by the latter. To say that the Southern company could have helped themselves if they removed the respondent from his directorship, but could not do so where they authorized the removal by another, would seem to me to treat what is at best a technicality as if it were the substance of the case. It is the Southern company's act which has resulted in the respondent's removal, and none the less so though his dismissal required two acts, and not one, for its accomplishment. I would affirm the judgment of the Court of Appeal.

Note

1   In *Shindler v. Northern Raincoat Co.*, [1960] 2 All E.R. 239, [1960] 1 W.L.R. 1038 Shindler was not voted to be a director, which rendered him ineligible to be a managing director despite a contract appointing him to this position for ten years. The House of Lords stated, citing, *Stirling v. Maitland* (1864) 5 B &S at p. 852, that:

> if a party enters into an arrangement which can only take effect by the continuance of a certain existing state of circumstances, there is an implied engagement on his part that he shall do nothing of his own motion to put an end to that state of circumstances, under which alone the arrangement can be operative.

> Applying that respectable principle to the present case, there is an implied engagement on the part of the defendant company that it will do nothing of its own motion to put an end to the state of circumstances which enables the plaintiff to continue as managing director. That is to say, there is an implied undertaking that it will not revoke his appointment as a director. . .

2   In *Kidder v. Photon Control Inc.*, 2011 BCSC 1016, 2011 CarswellBC 2044 (B.C. S.C.), affirmed 2012 CarswellBC 2352 (B.C. C.A.), leave to appeal refused 2013 CarswellBC 1576, 2013 CarswellBC 1577 (S.C.C.), Kidder brought an action for wrongful dismissal against Photon. For 13 years, Kidder was a director, president, and CEO of the companies that merged to become Coldswitch, which later became Photon. In June 2001 Kidder was not re-elected as a director. In July 2001, his employment was terminated, allegedly for just cause. Photon claimed, among other things, that the employment contract was frustrated because, under Photon's articles and the *B.C. Company Act*, s. 134, Kidder could not be president if he was no longer a director. The court held that the doctrine of frustration did not apply and that Kidder had a valid claim for wrongful dismissal. It reasoned that while Kidder was required to be a director of the company in order to be president, Kidder was in fact both president and CEO. Even though his position as president was terminated, his position as CEO was not. The court held in the alternative that even if Kidder were required to be a director to be president and CEO, the contract was not frustrated as the board of directors could itself have relied on its authority in the company's articles and the statutes to

appoint Kidder to the board. Is this case consistent with *Montgomery, supra* and *Southern, supra*?

3.   THE SCOPE OF THE "CORPORATE CONTRACT"

This section asks which parties are properly the subject of concern under corporate law, as opposed to other areas of law. In particular, in the following cases the question arises of how constituencies other than managers and investors interact with the corporation. Should private choices by managers and investors on how initially to structure the corporation prevail over the interests of other parties that come into important contact with the corporation? In reading the cases, again consider how one's view of corporate law might affect outcomes. Are the cases explained by a regulatory view of corporation law that mistrusts private choices of objectives? Or are the cases better explained by a contractual view of corporations? We examine agency doctrines and how parties entering into explicit contracts with the corporation are affected by internal corporate rules, and then examine important questions of corporate goals and social responsibilities. We begin with a brief description of the *ultra vires* doctrine.

(a)   Note on the *Ultra Vires* Doctrine

The "*ultra vires* doctrine" is referred to at various points in this chapter. This was a rule that held that a corporation, particularly one in a memorandum jurisdiction, had no legal capacity to act in any way that was not specifically authorized by its incorporating documents. Only if an act was *intra vires*, or within the powers of the corporation, did the corporation have the capacity to pursue it. The doctrine has been dramatically limited, indeed virtually eliminated, by modern corporate law statutes: unless corporate powers are explicitly restricted, it is assumed that the corporation has the powers of a natural person. Consider the following provisions of the CBCA:

15. (1) A corporation has the capacity and, subject to this Act, the rights, powers and privileges of a natural person.

(2) A corporation may carry on business throughout Canada.

(3) A corporation has the capacity to carry on its business, conduct its affairs and exercise its powers in any jurisdiction outside Canada to the extent that the laws of such jurisdiction permit.

16. (1) It is not necessary for a by-law to be passed in order to confer any particular power on the corporation or its directors.

(2) A corporation shall not carry on any business or exercise any power that it is restricted by its articles from carrying on or exercising, nor shall the corporation exercise any of its powers in a manner contrary to its articles.

(3) No act of a corporation, including any transfer of property to or by a corporation, is invalid by reason only that the act or transfer is contrary to its articles or this Act.

Question

Why would a corporation, or its promoters, ever seek to limit corporate powers?

(b) Agency Doctrines and the Corporation

Since a corporation is only an artificial entity in the contemplation of law, it must act through natural persons to conclude contracts and enter into transactions generally. This section deals with the rules governing a corporation's liability for the acts of its agents.

A natural principal is liable for the acts of an agent if the agent had actual, usual, apparent or ostensible authority to commit the acts from the principal. "Usual" authority means authority ascribed to the agent by common or trade understanding by virtue of the particular office held by him. "Apparent" or "ostensible" authority means the authority with which the agent has been clothed as a result of the principal's express or implied representations. Such representations may be implied from the principal's conduct or acquiescence as well as from his spoken or written words. See *Freeman and Lockyer v. Buckhurst Park Properties (Manager) Ltd.*, [1964] 2 Q.B. 480, per Diplock L.J.

These basic agency rules also apply to corporations, but they are greatly complicated by a number of factors. The first is that many corporations have complex organizations — there are many "agents" and many "principals" — and it may not be easy to determine which superior manager or officer in the chain of command is entitled to make representations with respect to the apparent authority of an inferior agent. Again, at the same level of authority, the "principal" may in fact comprise a group of individuals of greater or smaller size. This will be true, for example, where the question is whether the board of directors have held out one of their number as president or managing director although he was never formally appointed to this position. Or again the question may arise whether the corporation is bound by the acts of *de facto* directors because the shareholders knew of, and acquiesced, in their assumption of office.

A second complication is that the courts superimposed special corporate rules on the normal agency rules. The most important of these was the constructive notice rule, usually associated with *Ernest v. Nicholls*

(1857), 6 H.L. Cas. 401, 10 E.R. 1351, that outsiders are deemed to be familiar with the contents of those of the corporation's constitutional and related documents that are filed in a public office. Consequently, if these documents impose restrictions on an agent's authority (by which is included the authority of organs such as the board of directors or a committee of directors) the outsider will be bound even though the agent was acting within his usual authority or was clothed with apparent authority. The outsider will not be allowed to plead his ignorance of the restrictions.

Almost simultaneously with the constructive notice rule, the English courts also introduced an important qualification to it, generally referred to as the "indoor management" rule or the rule in *Royal British Bank v. Turquand* (1856), 6 E. & B. 327, 119 E. R. 886, after the case which gave it birth. In the latter case, Jervis C.J. explained the qualification as follows:

> We may now take for granted that the dealings with these companies are not like dealings with other partnerships and that the parties dealing with them are bound to read the statute and the deed of settlement. But they are not bound to do more. And the party, here, on reading the deed of settlement, would find not a prohibition from borrowing, but a permission to do so on certain conditions. Finding that the authority might be made complete by a resolution, he would have a right to infer the fact of a resolution authorising that which on the face of the document appeared to be legitimately done.

In other words, the constructive notice doctrine was confined to actual restrictions on a corporate agent's authority; it did not require an outsider to satisfy himself that the internal regulations of the corporation had actually been complied with. In this way, as Prof. Prentice has pointed out, the courts sought to balance the corporation's interest not to have its assets dissipated by unauthorized acts of its agents with the interests of outsiders to be able to conduct business with the corporation's agents without undue restrictions. Prentice, "The Indoor Management Rule" in Ziegel (Ed.), *Studies in Canadian Company Law*, vol. 1, p. 309 (1967).

(c) The Indoor Management Rule

The indoor management rule in Canada is now largely found in corporate statutes. The following provisions of the CBCA are representative:

> 17. No person is affected by or is deemed to have notice or knowledge of the contents of a document concerning a corporation by reason only that the document has been filed by the Director or is available for inspection at an office of the corporation.

18. (1) No corporation and no guarantor of an obligation of a corporation may assert against a person dealing with the corporation or against a person who acquired rights from the corporation that

(a) the articles, by-laws and any unanimous shareholder agreement have not been complied with;

(b) the persons named in the most recent notice sent to the Director under section 106 or 113 are not the directors of the corporation;

(c) the place named in the most recent notice sent to the Director under section 19 is not the registered office of the corporation;

(d) a person held out by a corporation as a director, an officer or an agent of the corporation has not been duly appointed or has no authority to exercise the powers and perform the duties that are customary in the business of the corporation or usual for a director, officer or agent;

(e) a document issued by any director, officer or agent of a corporation with actual or usual authority to issue the document is not valid or not genuine; or

(f) a sale, lease or exchange of property referred to in subsection 189(3) was not authorized.

(2) Subsection (1) does not apply in respect of a person who has, or ought to have,knowledge of a situation described in that subsection by virtue of their relationship tothe corporation.

Sherwood Design Services Inc. v. 872935 Ontario Ltd.
(1998), 39 O.R. (3d) 576, 1998 CarswellOnt 1739 (Ont. C.A.)

[The following case deals with the purpose and meaning of the statutory indoor management rule. Two of the judges discuss s. 19 of the OBCA, which is analogous to s. 18 of the CBCA reproduced above.]

ABELLA J.A.: An agreement to buy the assets of Sherwood Design Services Inc. was signed by [K, M and P] "in trust for a corporation to be incorporated". The purchase price was $300,000. In addition, [K, M and P] signed a promissory note in the amount of $45,000. This amount was payable on demand in the event that the transaction did not close. There was no reference to a company to be incorporated in the promissory note. At the request of the purchasers, Sherwood informed its major clients that the business was being sold, causing Sherwood to lose its contracts with them.

A numbered company, 872935 Ontario Limited, was incorporated on December 15, 1989. A partner in the law firm retained by the purchasers, gave evidence that it was his responsibility to incorporate shell companies for use by the firm's clients as the need arose. 872935 Ontario Limited was to be used for the benefit of [K, M and P] in connection with their purchase of Sherwood's assets.

Several days before the scheduled closing, on January 11, 1990, the solicitor for the purchasers sent a letter to the vendor's lawyer stating:

> I wish to advise that 872935 Ontario Limited which was incorporated on December 15, 1989 has been assigned by [our law firm] as the corporation that will complete the asset purchase from Sherwood Design Services Inc.

Accompanying this letter were unsigned copies of a certified copy of the directors' resolution adopting the asset purchase agreement, a certificate of incumbency, and an undertaking to re-adjust "for your review and consideration".

The transaction was not completed. On the closing date, January 22, 1990, no one attended on behalf of the purchasers. Sherwood eventually sold the business for $125,000. The numbered company was assigned by the purchasers' law firm to other clients in April 1990 for the purpose of completing a different commercial real estate transaction, purchasing a commercial building. The numbered company thus became a company with assets able to answer any liability the earlier transaction may have attracted.

* * *

[Abella J.A. relied on the rules governing pre-incorporation contracts in s. 21 of the OBCA to decide the case. She held in favour of the appellants (i.e., the original plaintiffs who had sued the numbered company).]

[CARTHY J.A., concurring, agreed with Abella J.A. on s. 21, but offered the following observations about the importance of the indoor management rule found in s. 19 of the OBCA:]

The core of the trial judge's findings and of the reasons of Borins J.A. is that the January 11, 1990 letter written by Mr. Nichols did not represent the act of the corporation. I disagree with this basic premise. Nichols had the authority of the law firm and the sole director, Fuller, and his individual clients, to utilize the corporation in the transaction. His letter speaks both as an agent for the corporation and as reflecting instructions from the individual clients. However, none of this has any significance in light of the indoor management rule which prevents the corporation from disputing the ostensible authority held out by the letter of January 11. The recipients of that letter were entitled to adopt its terms at face value and, in this case, to approach the closing of the transaction expecting to deal with the corporation.

Section 19 of the Ontario *Business Corporations Act, 1982*, S.O. 1982, c. 4, reads in part:

a corporation . . . may not assert against a person dealing with the corporation, or with any person who has acquired rights from the corporation that . . . a person held out as . . . agent of the corporation . . . does not have authority to exercise the powers . . . that are usual for such. . . agent.

The vendor was a person dealing with the corporation when it received the letter from Nichols, and it now purports to have acquired rights from the corporation. The solicitor certainly held out the authority to speak on behalf of the corporation when he referred to it as the creature of his legal firm, with the clear inference that a member of the firm is the nominal director. The solicitor also had ostensible authority to speak for his individual clients.

The company cannot, therefore, dispute the authority of the solicitor to write the letter of January 11 and is bound by whatever legal implication arises from the words "has been assigned by Miller Thompson as the Corporation that will complete the asset purchase from Sherwood Design Services Inc."

* * *

[BORINS J.A. dissented, holding that the corporation was not bound by the contract under s. 21, nor was the indoor management rule relevant. His comments on the latter issue are as follows:]

I have also had the opportunity to read the concurring reasons of Carthy J.A. I am respectfully unable to agree with his conclusion that the appellant, Sherwood, is entitled to the protection afforded by s. 19 of the O.B.C.A.

The relevant language of s. 19 reads as follows:

19. A corporation or a guarantor of an obligation of a corporation may not assert against a person dealing with the corporation or with any person who has acquired rights from the corporation that . . .

(d) a person held out by a corporation as a director, an officer or an agent of the corporation has not been duly appointed or does not have authority to exercise the powers and perform the duties that are customary in the business of the corporation or usual for such director, officer or agent . . .

except where the person has or ought to have, by virtue of the person's position with or relationship to the corporation, knowledge to that effect.

Section 19 is the codification of the indoor management rule. It is derived from *Royal British Bank v. Turquand* (1856), 119 E.R. 886, 6 E. & B. 327 (Ex. Ch.), which stands for the proposition that a person contracting with a corporation, and dealing in good faith, may assume that acts within its constitution and powers have been properly and duly performed and is not bound to inquire into whether acts of internal management have been regular.

For the purpose of this appeal, the "person" referred to in s. 19(d) is Sherwood. In my view, s. 19(d) does not apply for the reason that, when Mr. Nichols wrote to Sherwood's solicitors on January 11, 1990, Sherwood had not had any contractual dealings with the respondent corporation. Its contract was with the individual respondents "in trust for a corporation to be incorporated". This is not a case where a party is seeking to enforce against a corporation a contract entered into on its behalf by an agent who the corporation alleges had no authority to contract on its behalf, where the corporation would be foreclosed by s. 19(d) from asserting the agent's lack of authority. Rather, it is a case where a party is seeking to enforce against a corporation a contract entered into on behalf of a non-existent corporation which it is alleged was adopted by the corporation, subsequent to its incorporation, within the meaning of s. 21(2). Section 21, directed as it is to pre-incorporation contracts, is premised on the circumstance that the contracting party did not deal with the corporation against whom it seeks to enforce the contract, but dealt with a person who contracted on behalf of a corporation to be incorporated. On the other hand, s. 19 is premised on the circumstance that the "person" seeking to enforce rights against a corporation had direct dealings with the corporation through "a director, an officer or an agent of the corporation".

The application of s. 19(d) was not before the trial judge for consideration. Consequently, he made no express finding of fact relative to the applicability of the indoor management rule. The findings of fact of the trial judge are reviewed in paras. 45–49 [pp. 591–92 *ante*]. He found that Mr. Nichols' letter of January 11, 1990, did not constitute an act of the corporation, and that Mr. Nichols was not acting on behalf of the corporation when he wrote the letter. In my respectful view, the trial judge's findings of fact do not support the conclusion that, in writing the letter, Mr. Nichols was an agent of the corporation, or had been held out by it as its agent.

If I am wrong in my opinion that s. 19(d) does not apply to the circumstances of this case and that the findings of fact of the trial judge do not support its application, there is a further reason why Sherwood is not entitled to the protection of s. 19(d). At common law, a person contracting with a corporation was precluded from relying on the indoor management rule if the circumstances were such as to put him or her on inquiry which they failed to make: see *Morris v. Kanssen*, [1946] A.C. 459 at p. 475, [1946] 1 All E.R. 586 (H.L.); *Rolled Steel Products (Holdings) Ltd. v. British Steel Corp.*, [1986] Ch. 246 at pp. 284-85. In my view, the closing language of s. 19 reflects this principle.

Sherwood cannot presume in its own favour that the letter of January 11, 1990, was an act of the corporation signifying its intention to be bound by the pre-incorporation contract, if an inquiry that it ought to have made would have disclosed that the corporation was unaware of the contract at that time. As I have pointed out, the unsigned draft resolution of the directors adopting the contract was sufficient to place Sherwood's solicitors on notice that the corporation had not adopted the contract. This document, together with the other unsigned documents sent with the letter, made it obvious that the corporation had not been formed, and, thus, had not had the opportunity to direct its mind to whether it would adopt, or reject, the pre-incorporation contract. . .

Appeal allowed.

(d) Corporate Goals and Social Responsibilities

Since at least the 1930s there has been a growing debate about the role of the business corporation in modern society. There are many approaches to the question, but two principal schools of thought. The contractarian view is neutral about the *content* of the goals that a corporation or any other organization might choose to pursue. However, this view further holds that once the choice has been made and the (metaphorical) contract entered into, a single party should not be granted the power to modify unilaterally the corporate contract. Given that the goal of investors in for-profit corporations is to realize a positive return on their investment, it is a reasonable assumption under the contractarian view that the goal of a corporation is to make profit. If a person saves for retirement by investing in a share rather than gives to charity, it is presumably because he or she hopes to realize gains that will help support his or her in retirement. Once such an objective is chosen, a contractarian would view it as opportunistic for any given agent to choose to pursue a different goal. On the other hand, if a goal other than profit were explicitly adopted from the start, any investor or contributor to the enterprise would have no grounds for complaint.

The other school of thought rejects the contractarian model, particularly given its focus on profit maximization, as much too narrow and as divorced from the realities of modern society. Its adherents contend that business corporations, both individually and collectively, have an enormous influence on the welfare of employees, consumers and the communities in which they operate and that responsible corporate managers have long recognized this fact in seeking to strike a reasonable balance between the interests of shareholders and the other constituencies affected by corporate behaviour. These debates are not simply academic. They have a direct bearing on the outcome of litigation, as will be seen both from the cases reproduced in this section and in later chapters. Acceptance of one or other of these contending philosophies also affects such seemingly unrelated questions as whether employees and other non-shareholder constituencies should be represented on the board of directors, whether directors may use their legal powers to frustrate takeover bids on the ground that a new management would be unsettling to the corporation's employees, and whether corporations should desist from investing in countries with oppressive regimes. The present section begins with some case law which places these conflicts in context, and concludes with extracts from the writings of scholars and others discussing the role of the modern corporation in a broader context. Again, ask yourself how one's view of the appropriate role of corporate law affects one's view of the outcomes in this case.

Dodge v. Ford Motor Company
204 Mich. 459, 170 N.W. 668, 3 A.L.R. 413 (1919)

[The Ford Motor Company was incorporated in 1903 under the laws of Michigan with authorized capital stock of $150,000 of which $100,000 was then issued, $49,000 for cash, $40,000 for patents and $11,000 for other property. In 1908, the authorized and issued capital was increased to $2,000,000 by the declaration of a stock dividend out of accumulated profits. Thereafter its directors regularly declared cash dividends at the rate of 60 per cent per year on the increased capital of $2,000,000 and between December, 1911, and October, 1915, also declared additional special cash dividends from time to time amounting in all to $41,000,000. Thereafter no special dividends were declared except one of $2,000,000 declared on November 8, 1916, before the answers in the present case were filed, and Henry Ford, who controlled the board of directors, had stated that no more special dividends would be declared at present and that the greater portion of the profits should be put back into the business in order to expand it, thereby increasing employment and selling a larger number of cars at a lower price per car. The surplus of the corporation at July 31, 1916, was $112,000,000 and it had cash and municipal bonds amounting of nearly $54,000,000. On November 2, 1916, the directors voted to expend $11,325,000 to erect blast furnaces and other plant in which to manufacture iron and other products for use in the manufacture of cars, and also $5,150,000, out of a program calling for $9,895,000 for a substantial duplication of existing plant. Thereupon, two minority stockholders, owning one tenth of the company's stock, brought suit to compel the declaration of an additional dividend of not less than 75 per cent of the accumulated cash surplus. The court ordered the declaration of a dividend of $19,275,385.96. Defendants appealed.]

OSTRANDER J.: When plaintiffs made their complaint and demand for further dividends the Ford Motor Company had just concluded its most prosperous year of business. The demand for its cars at the price of the preceding year continued. It could make and could market in the year beginning August 1, 1916, more than 500,000 cars. Sales of parts and repairs would necessarily increase. The cost of materials was likely to advance, and perhaps the price of labour, but it reasonably might have expected a profit for the year of upwards of $60,000,000 . . .

In justification, the defendants have offered testimony tending to prove, and which does prove, the following facts. It had been the policy of the corporation for a considerable time to annually reduce the selling price of cars, while keeping up, or improving, their quality. As early as in June, 1915, a general plan for the expansion of the productive capacity of the concern by a practical duplication of its plant had been talked over by the executive officers and directors and agreed upon, not all of the details having been settled and no formal action of directors having been taken. The erection of a smelter was considered, and engineering and other data in connection therewith secured . . .

The plan, as affecting the profits of the business for the year beginning August 1, 1916, and thereafter, calls for a reduction in the selling price of the cars . . . In short, the plan does not call for and is not intended to produce immediately a more profitable business but a less profitable one; not only less profitable than formerly but less profitable than it is admitted it might be made. The apparent immediate effect will be to diminish the value of shares and the returns to shareholders.

It is the contention of plaintiffs that the apparent effect of the plan is intended . . . to continue the corporation henceforth as a semi-eleemosynary institution and not as a business institution. In support of this contention they point to the attitude and to the expressions of Mr. Henry Ford . . .

"My ambition," said Mr. Ford, "is to employ still more men to spread the benefits of this industrial system to the greatest possible number, to help them build up their lives and their homes. To do this we are putting the greatest share of our profits back in the business."

With regards to dividends, the company paid sixty per cent on its capitalization of two million dollars, or $1,200,000, leaving $58,000,000 to reinvest for the growth of the company. This is Mr. Ford's policy at present, and it is understood that the other stockholders cheerfully accede to this plan . . .

He had made up his mind in the summer of 1916 that no dividends other than the regular dividends should be paid, "for the present".

The record, and especially the testimony of Mr. Ford, convinces that he has to some extent the attitude towards shareholders of one who had dispensed and distributed to them large gains and that they should be content to take what he chooses to give. His testimony creates the impression, also, that he thinks the Ford Motor Company has made too much money, has had too large profits, and that although large profits might be still earned, a sharing of them with the public, by reducing the price of the output of the company, ought to be undertaken. We have no doubt that certain sentiments, philanthropic and altruistic, creditable to

Mr. Ford, had large influence in determining the policy to be pursued by the Ford Motor Company — the policy which has been herein referred to.

It is said by his counsel that:

> Although a manufacturing corporation cannot engage in humanitarian works as its principal business, the fact that it is organized for profit does not prevent the existence of implied powers to carry on with humanitarian motives such charitable works as are incidental to the main business of the corporation . . .

In discussing this proposition, counsel have referred to decisions [citations omitted]. These cases, after all, like all others in which the subject is treated, turn finally upon the point, the question, whether it appears that the directors were not acting for the best interests of the corporation . . . There should be no confusion (of which there is evidence) of the duties which Mr. Ford conceives that he and the stockholders owe to the general public and the duties which in law he and his co-directors owe to protesting, minority shareholders. A business corporation is organized and carried on primarily for the profit of the stockholders. The powers of the directors are to be employed for that end. The discretion of directors is to be exercised in the choice of means to attain that end and does not extend to a change in the end itself, to the reduction of profits or to the non-distribution of profits among stockholders in order to devote them to other purposes . . .

As we have pointed out, and the proposition does not require argument to sustain it, it is not within the lawful powers of a board of directors to shape and conduct the affairs of a corporation for the merely incidental benefit of shareholders and for the primary purpose of benefiting others, and no one will contend that if the avowed purpose of the defendant directors was to sacrifice the interests of shareholders it would not be the duty of the courts to interfere.

We are not, however, persuaded that we should interfere with the proposed expansion of the business of the Ford Motor Company. In view of the fact that the selling price of products may be increased at any time, the ultimate results of the larger business cannot be certainly estimated. The judges are not business experts . . . We are not satisfied that the alleged motives of the directors, in so far as they are reflected in the conduct of the business, menace the interests of shareholders. It is enough to say, perhaps, that the court of equity is at all times open to complaining shareholders having a just grievance . . .

The large sum appropriated for the smelter plant was payable over a considerable period of time. So that, without going further, it would appear that, accepting and approving the plan of the directors, it was their duty to distribute on or near the first of August, 1916, a very large sum of money to stockholders . . .

It is obvious that an annual dividend of sixty per cent upon $2,000,000 or $1,200,000 is the equivalent of a very small dividend upon $100,000,000, or more.

The decree of the court below fixing and determining the specific amount to be distributed to stockholders is affirmed . . .

[Steere, Fellows, Brooke and Stone JJ. concurred with Ostrander J.]

Notes

1   The reasoning in *Dodge v. Ford Motor Co.* should be compared with Plowman J.'s reasoning in *Parke v. Daily News, Ltd., infra,* this chapter. Does the court in *Dodge* exclude the possibility of a Michigan corporation engaging in any type of public welfare activity not linked to profit maximization, or is it only the directors' conscious decision to limit a corporation's profits that attracted the court's censure?

2   As will be noted, it was part of the plaintiff's complaint in *Dodge* that the directors were under a duty to distribute so much of a company's profits as were not required for legitimate business purposes. The general Anglo-Canadian rule is that directors are not obliged to declare dividends unless the corporation's constitution so provides or the corporation has lawfully bound itself to do by the terms of issue of a particular security. Typically the by-laws leave the declaration of dividends to the directors' discretion. The modern American view appears to be that "-
the mere existence of an adequate corporation surplus is not sufficient to invoke court action to compel . . . a dividend. There must also be bad faith on the part of the directors." William S. Stewart, "Judicial Review of Dividend Policy in Suits by Minority Shareholders" (1974), 12 Am. Bus. L. J. 43, 45, cited in Frey, Choper *et al., Cases and Materials on Corporations,* 2nd ed., p. 1067.

Miles v. Sydney Meatpreserving Co. (Ltd.)
16 C.L.R. 50 (HCA 1912), affirmed 17 C.L.R. 639 (Privy Council 1913)

[A company had originally been established by deed of settlement for the purpose of carrying on the business of meat preserving, and as an exporter of processed meat. It was subsequently incorporated by special Act, with the same purposes. The Act provided that the regulations might be altered, but not in opposition to the general scope or true intent and meaning of the deed of settlement, and that no dividends should be paid except out of profits. By the deed of settlement it was provided that the clear *bona fide* net profits arising from the operations of the company should be applied in payment to the shareholders of a dividend in proportion to the number of shares held by them, and that the directors should every half year determine upon such dividend or dividends or bonus out of such clear profits (if any) as they in their judgment, conforming to the provisions of the deed, should see fit; and that the directors might in their discretion out of the profits of each half year set apart and appropriate such sum as they might think advisable for increasing the works or plant or to a reserve fund, and that after such appropriation the balance (if any) should be available for payment of dividends. A majority of the shareholders were graziers.

No dividends were ever paid by the company, but it was the settled policy of the company, which was approved by a majority of the shareholders and was publicly announced, to carry on their operations, not with a view to paying dividends to the members, but with a view to benefiting the pastoral industry generally, although such a policy involved the benefiting of such of the members as were interested in that industry, and the affairs of the company were conducted in accordance with that policy. The plaintiff, a shareholder and director of the company, sought: a declaration that the defendant company and its directors were not entitled to carry on the business of the company in the interest only of those members concerned to maintain the price of cattle, or in the interest of squatters and graziers generally; and an injunction restraining that carrying on of the business of the company otherwise than with a view to earning profits for distribution among all members, regardless of whether they were graziers or squatters.

A majority of the High Court of Australia dismissed the claim, Griffiths C.J. saying, in the course of his judgment (p. 64):]

> [The plaintiff's] whole case is based upon the conduct of the directors in not trying to earn a profit for the purpose of immediate distribution. He contends that in the case of every company which is established for gain, in the sense that dividends may be declared out of profits, an implied contractual duty is imposed upon the directors of endeavouring to earn profits so as to be able to distribute them. If this is so, the duty must surely extend to making the largest possible profits, and to distributing the profits when earned. This last obligation is expressly negatived by *Burland v. Earle* In my opinion, no such contractual duty is known to the law. In the case of a great many companies the practical question arises whether they shall be carried on for the purpose of earning immediate profits or with the motive of indirectly achieving some ulterior object which the members may consider beneficial. Take, for instance, the case of a company formed to establish communication by water or land with a new suburb or newly settled locality. If the contention of the appellant is sound, the company would be bound to charge such tolls and dues as would produce the largest immediate profit, without regard to the encouragement of settlement in the new locality. Again, a trading company which thought fit to expend part of its income upon providing good and wholesome residences for its employees instead of distributing it in dividends could be enjoined from doing

so. In my judgment, such matters are entirely matters of internal management with which the Court has no authority to interfere.

Isaacs J., dissenting, observed (p. 68):

It was urged that the decision in this point would have an important bearing on ordinary trading corporations under the Companies Acts. To this I assent, but I think it would be regarded as a new idea if shareholders were told that companies formed to carry on business operations, were never bound to try and make a profit, in other words, that such a company is not intended to make its trading operations a commercial success. If the respondents are right, a bank would be justified in devoting its capital to bolstering up the outside business concerns of such of its shareholders as could control the management, and, as fast as profits came in, appropriate them to extending its facilities for further assistance to those enterprises, telling the rest of the shareholders that dividends were expressly provided for in the articles yet that paying dividends was no part of its scheme, and would never be countenanced.

Questions

Is the majority's reasoning in *Miles* consistent with the court's reasoning in *Dodge v. Ford Motor Co.* and the English case law reviewed in Plowman J.'s judgment in *Parke v. Daily News Ltd., infra*? What is the significance of majority shareholder approval of directors' non-dividend policy?

Parke v. Daily News Ltd.
[1962] 1 Ch. 927, [1962] 2 All E.R. 929 (Ch. D.)

[Daily News Ltd. (D.N.), as a major part of its business, owned two well-known London newspapers. The newspapers employed about 2,800 persons. Two wholly owned subsidiaries owned the copyrights to the newspapers. The newspapers were not profitable and, in order to salvage their value before it was too late, the directors of D.N. decided to look for a purchaser for the newspapers, including their plant, premises and copyrights.

Associated Newspapers Ltd. (A.N.) eventually agreed to purchase the newspapers for »1,925,000 together with a small additional sum to be determined subsequently. The sale was completed on October 17, 1960. Prior to the sale the board of directors of D.N. had decided that, after meeting all the necessary expenses arising from the cessation of the newspaper, the balance of the sale price should be used exclusively for the benefit of the staff and pensioners of the newspapers, and more particularly for (1) payments in lieu of notice, (2) payment of a third week's holiday to each employee entitled to it, (3) provision for pensioners of the newspapers, and (4) compensation for those employees who would lose their jobs based on their length of service with the company. The agreement between D.N. and A.N. expressly provided that A.N. was not to be responsible for any liabilities incurred or other obligations owing by D.N. to its former employees.

The agreement between D.N. and A.N. was not made contingent on its approval by the shareholders of A.N. D.N. first advised its shareholders of the agreement on October 17, 1960. On January 20, 1961, D.N. sent the shareholders notice of a meeting at which the shareholders were to be asked, *inter alia*, to approve disbursement of the balance of the sale price of the newspaper assets as described above. Shortly afterwards the plaintiff, who held a substantial number of shares in D.N., commenced a representative action against D.N. and its directors seeking a declaration that the proposed resolution was *ultra vires* the defendant company and illegal, and enjoining D.N. from disposing of the assets as proposed.

Plowman J. stated the facts and, after finding that D.N. was not contractually bound to its former employees to pay them compensation for the loss of their jobs and had not obligated itself to do so in its agreement with A.N., continued as follows:]

PLOWMAN J.: It is the plaintiff's submission that in these circumstances the proposed payment of compensation is gratuitous and *ultra vires* the defendant company. Mr. Finer, on behalf of the plaintiff, referred me to a large number of authorities, but it will be sufficient for me to refer to two or three of them. The first is the well-known case of *Hutton v. West Cork Railway Co.* [(1883) 23 Ch. D. 654 C.A.]. That was a case where a company had transferred its undertaking to another company and was going to be wound up. After completion of the transfer, a general meeting of the transferor company was held at which a resolution was passed to apply (among other sums) a sum of 1,000 guineas in compensating certain paid officials of the company for their loss of employment, although they had no legal claim for compensation. It was held by the Court of Appeal (Baggallay L.J. dissenting) that the resolution was invalid, as the company was no longer a going concern and only existed for the purpose of winding up. On the facts, of course, it differs from the present case in that (among other things) here the defendant company has transferred only part (albeit the main part) of its undertaking and is proposing, not to wind up, but to continue trading. In an oft-cited judgment, Bowen L.J. said:

> Now the directors in this case have done, it seems to me, nothing at all wrong. Let us clear the ground, because my sympathies are rather with the judgment of Fry L.J., if one could really exercise sympathy in a case where questions of law have to be decided. Not only have they done nothing wrong, but I confess I think the company have done what nine companies out of ten would do, and do without the least objection being made. They have paid, perhaps liberally,

perhaps not at all too liberally, persons who have served them faithfully. But that, of course, does not get rid of the difficulty. As soon as a question is raised by a dissentient shareholder, . . . sympathy must be cut adrift, and we have simply to consider what the law is. In this particular instance the plaintiff is a person who stands *prima facie* in the condition of those who are bound by the vote of a general meeting acting within the powers of a general meeting, but he complains that the majority propose to expend certain purchase money which the company are receiving from the Bandon company in two ways which he thinks are beyond their powers. In the first place he says that the majority are going to spend money in compensating the managing director and other officials, who are being extinguished by this transfer to the Bandon company, for the loss of their places. Now the compensation which is to be awarded is not compensation for any legal loss they have sustained: because I understand that these gentlemen could always have been discharged, and have received notice amply sufficient to prevent them from having any cause of legal grievance, and they simply have been asked in the usual way to cease to serve the masters who have no further cause for their services. In the second place, the plaintiff complains that money is sought to be paid for remuneration of the directors.

After dealing at that point with the question of remuneration of directors, with which I am not concerned, Bowen L.J. went on to say:

Now can a majority compel a dissentient unit in the company to give way and to submit to these payments? We must go back to the root of things. The money which is going to be spent is not the money of the majority. That is clear. It is the money of the company, and the majority want to spend it. What would be the natural unit of their power to do so? They can only spend money which is not theirs but the company's, if they are spending it for the purposes which are reasonably incidental to the carrying on of the business of the company. That is the general doctrine. *Bona fides* cannot be the sole test, otherwise you might have a lunatic conducting the affairs of the company, and paying away its money with both hands in a manner perfectly *bona fide* yet perfectly irrational. The test must be what is reasonably incidental to, and within the reasonable scope of carrying on, the business of the company. Applying that kind of view, what is the character of these payments? First of all, I ask myself what is the kind of touchstone or test to apply if the company was an ordinary going concern; and, secondly, whether this company is still in the same position as an ordinary railway, or whether it has not become a railway company of a very limited kind, a business adventure of a very exceptional sort, and its business contracted accordingly within very narrow and easily defined units.

After dealing further with the question of directors' remuneration, Bowen L.J. goes on to say:

Directors, under those circumstances, often do get money. But whenever they get it it is in the nature of a gratuity voted. That does not get rid of the difficulty, because one must still ask oneself what is the general law about gratuitous payments which are made by the directors or by a company so as to bind dissentients. It seems to me you cannot say the company has only got power to spend the money which it is bound to pay according to law, otherwise the wheels of business would stop, now can you say that directors who have got all the powers of the company given to them by section 90 of the *Companies Clauses Consolidation Act*, are always to be limited to the strictest possible view of what the obligations of the company are. They are not to keep their pockets buttoned up and defy the world unless they are liable in a way which could be enforced at law or in equity. Most businesses require liberal dealings. The test there again is not whether it is *bona fide*, but whether, as well as being done *bona fide*, it is done within the ordinary scope of the company's business, and whether it is reasonably incidental to the carrying on of the company's business for the company's benefit. Take this sort of instance. A railway company, or the directors of the company, might send down all the porters at a railway station to have tea in the country at the expense of the company. Why should they not? It is for the directors to judge, provided it is a matter which is reasonably incidental to the carrying on of the business of the company, and a company which always treated its employees with Draconian severity, and never allowed them a single inch more than the strict letter of the bond, would soon find itself deserted — at all events, unless labour was very much more easy to obtain in the market than it often is. The law does not say that there are to be no cakes and ale, but there are to be no cakes and ale except such as are required for the benefit of the company. Now that I think is the principle to be found in the case of *Hampson v. Price's Patent Candle Co*. The Master of the Rolls there held that the company might lawfully expend a week's wages as gratuities for their servants; because that sort of liberal dealing with servants eases the friction between masters and servants, and is in the end, a benefit to the company. It is not charity sitting at the board of directors, because as it seems to me charity has no business to sit at boards of directors *qua* charity. There is, however, a kind of charitable dealing which is for the interest of those who practise it, and to that extent and in that garb (I admit not a very philanthropic garb) charity may sit at the board, but for no other purpose.

Then a little later Bowen L.J. repeats:

[T]he ultimate test is not *bona fides*, but what is necessary for carrying on business. That is the test which Fry L.J. has not applied to this case. Such is the general view of the law I should take about a company which was a going concern. Now let us see whether this company is a going concern in the same sense, and whether we have the same limit with regard to the payment of money.

After considering that matter Bowen L.J. said:

Compensation, and a gratuity for past services generally, without reference to such services as were rendered during the winding up, can no longer be charges or expenditure reasonably incident to the carrying on — not the business of the old company — but what the business of the company would be for the purposes of its continued existence. It was moribund, and would only want to die in peace and distribute its assets, and it would not, as it seems to me, be proper to carry to the revenue account of such a company the money it voted to directors in a liberal spirit for what they had done in past years, or to a managing director for the disappointment and vexation of being deprived of an office for which he had been amply paid. The revenue debts and charges of the company must be viewed with reference to the qualified nature of its existence still left. That being so, I think the resolution as to compensation is clearly wrong. The directors have no right to give it. It might in some instances be worth the while of a company to compensate a meritorious, but dismissed officer, but that kind of justification cannot exist in the case of a dying company. I think that makes the resolution bad, and I think it also renders it necessary to pass some fresh resolution, because I agree with Cotton L.J. that if the meeting has given over to the directors generally a surplus on the assumption that »1,050 can be expended upon officials (which is not a correct assumption), and that the surplus would accordingly have to be increased by the »1,050, it does not at all follow that it meant the directors to have that »1,050. It seems to me, however, that the meeting has not considered it in the right view, and not measured it in the right measure. I do not understand Cotton L.J. to say that no remuneration can be granted to the directors out of the purchase money which is reasonably measured by the services they have rendered in winding up this company and in connection with the completion of the dissolution and transfer; but this resolution is couched in much wider terms and is evidently based upon the idea that they might be charitable with reference to past services done for the company at the time it was a going company, and I think a willing majority has no right to bind a dissentient minority by any resolution so conceived.

The second authority to which I wish to refer is the equally well-known case of *In re Lee, Behrens & Co. Ltd*. That case was concerned with the legality of a deed of covenant entered into by a company at a time when it was a going concern by which it granted a pension of £500 per annum to the widow of a former managing director. Eve J. said:

> But whether they be made under an express or implied power, all such grants involve an expenditure of the company's money, and that money can only be spent for purposes reasonably incidental to the carrying on of the company's business, and the validity of such grants is to be tested, as is shown in all the authorities, by the answers to three pertinent questions; (i) Is the transaction reasonably incidental to the carrying on of the company's business? (ii) Is it a *bona fide* transaction? and (iii) Is it done for the benefit and to promote the prosperity of the company?

In the event, the conclusion (or one of the conclusions) which Eve J. reached is:

> The conclusion to which in my opinion such evidence as is available irresistibly points is that the predominant, if not the only, considerations operating in the minds of the directors, was a desire to provide for the applicant, and that the question, what, if any, benefit would accrue to the company never presented itself to their minds. If there were nothing more in the case than what I have just indicated, I should feel myself bound in the circumstances to support the liquidator's rejection of this lady's proof,

and the primary ground on which the liquidator had rejected the proof was that the payment was *ultra vires* the company.

The conclusions which, I think, follow from these cases are; first, that a company's funds cannot be applied in making *ex gratia* payments as such; secondly, that the court will inquire into the motives actuating any gratuitous payment, and the objectives which it is intended to achieve; thirdly, that the court will uphold the validity of gratuitous payments if, but only if, after such inquiry, it appears that the tests enumerated by Eve J. are satisfied; fourthly, that the onus of upholding the validity of such payments lies on those who assert it.

Mr. Finer submits that the proposal to pay compensation in the present case was actuated by motives of generosity towards employees, by philanthropy, by a wish to undermine the financial sacrifice being made by the Cadbury family as shareholders, by a desire to ward off criticism and to avoid political repercussions, and that the rights of the shareholders were entirely overlooked. He therefore submits that the payment will not pass the tests laid down by Eve J. [Plowman J. discussed at length *Kaye v. Croydon Tramways Co.*, [1898] 1 Ch. 358, distinguished it, and then continued:]

It is, of course, conceded that if a transaction is *ultra vires*, the mere fact that the failure to carry it out would involve a breach of faith cannot make it *intra vires*. But it is said that the test of *ultra vires* is not whether the obligation entered into is legally binding (and I accept that) and that by reason of the matters set out in paragraph 19 it was in the company's interest to give the undertaking at the time it was given, or believed by the directors to be so.

The defendants have failed to satisfy me that there is any substance in this. Paragraph 19 is, I think, merely an attempt to justify *ex post facto* a transaction actuated by motives which, and the propriety of which, I must now consider. At this point I want to make it quite clear that the integrity of the defendants is unchallenged, and I am satisfied that their motives have been honourable throughout. But at the end of the day I am not satisfied that the decision to distribute this enormous sum of money was taken simply in the interests of the company as it would remain after the transfer of the newspaper enterprise.

That the decision to dispose of the newspaper business before it became insolvent, so as to leave the other assets intact, was a decision taken in the interests of the shareholders I have no doubt. But the decision embodied in the formula, and I quote it again:

> Subject to the inevitable costs arising to devote the whole of the purchase price to our staff and pensioners by giving compensation or pension benefits as well as the notice money that every employee will receive

was a different decision which was, in my judgment, motivated by other considerations. Predominant among such other considerations was, I think, the desire to treat the employees generously, beyond all entitlement, and to appear to have done so.

I reach this conclusion not only from a perusal of the correspondence and other documents that I have already read, but also from the evidence given in the witness-box, limited as it was, and it is right that I should give one or two instances which I have not hitherto mentioned of the sort of evidence I have in mind. [His Lordship examined the evidence and continued:] These and other passages appear to me to show that the view was taken that in respect of the proceeds of an enterprise which they had helped to build, the employees had claims to consideration to which it was proper for the defendant company to pay regard, and that the interests of the shareholders would be satisfied by ensuring that the other assets of the company remained intact for their benefit. The view that directors, in having regard to the question what is in the best interests of their company, are entitled to take into account the interests of the employees, irrespective of any consequential benefit to the company, is one which may be widely held. Traces of it appeared in Mr. Redhead's evidence, and Mr. Leach, an accountant of great experience, said in examination-in-chief:

I think that although obviously the prime duty of directors is to their shareholders to conserve the assets, they also have these days a very practical obligation to their employees.

Mr. Leach was cross-examined about that statement:

(Q) One of the matters which affected the conclusion, at least in your mind, as I understand it, was that a company's duty these days must be regarded as one not only to the shareholders, but also to the employees?

(A) Yes. I think I said that the prime duty must be to the shareholders; but boards of directors must take into consideration their duties to employees in these days.

But no authority to support that proposition as a proposition of law was cited to me; I know of none, and in my judgment such is not the law.

In *Greenhalgh v. Arderne Cinemas Ltd.* Lord Evershed M.R. said, in a different context, that the benefit of the company meant the benefit of the shareholders as a general body, and in my opinion that is equally true in a case such as the present.

In my judgment, therefore, the defendants were prompted by motives which, however laudable, and however enlightened from the point of view of industrial relations, were such as the law does not recognise as a sufficient justification. Stripped of all its side issues, the essence of the matter is this, that the directors of the defendant company are proposing that a very large part of its funds should be given to its former employees in order to benefit those employees rather than the company, and that is an application of the company's funds which the law, as I understand it, will not allow.

If this is right, then it appears to me to follow from the *Hutton* case that the proposal to pay compensation is one which a majority of shareholders is not entitled to ratify. The *Hutton* case was followed on this point in *Stroud v. Royal Aquarium and Summer and Winter Garden Society Ltd.*

Declaration accordingly.

Notes

1 Many of the pre-CBCA Canadian corporation statutes conferred explicit powers on corporations to establish funds or trusts for present or former employees and to make philanthropic contributions generally. For example, OBCA 1970, s. 15(2), provided that "A corporation has power as incidental and ancillary to the objects set out in its articles:

8. to establish and support or aid in the establishment and support of associations, institutions, funds or trusts for the benefit of employees or former employees of the corporation or its prede-

cessors, or the dependents or connections of such employees or former employees, and grant pensions and allowances, and make payments towards insurance or for any object similar to those set forth in this paragraph, and to subscribe or guarantee money for charitable, benevolent, educational or religious objects or for any exhibition or for any public, general or useful objects . . ."

How would *Parke v. Daily News* have been decided under such a provision? How would the case be decided under CBCA, s. 15, which deals with the capacity of a corporation, in the absence of express restrictions on the corporation's business pursuant to s. 6(1)(f)? Does s. 15(1) entitle the corporation to disburse its funds as it sees fit? When reading *BCE, infra,* consider whether gratuitous payments would be in breach of directors' fiduciary duties.

2   Section 247 of the U.K. *Companies Act 2006* provides as follows:

(1) The powers of the directors of a company include (if they would not otherwise do so) power to make provision for the benefit of persons employed or formerly employed by the company, or any of its subsidiaries, in connection with the cessation or the transfer to any person of the whole or part of the undertaking of the company or that subsidiary.

(2) This power is exercisable notwithstanding the general duty imposed by section 172 (duty to promote the success of the company).

(3) In the case of a company that is a charity it is exercisable notwithstanding any restrictions on the directors' powers (or the company's capacity) flowing from the objects of the company.

(4) The power may only be exercised if sanctioned—
    (a) by a resolution of the company, or
    (b) by a resolution of the directors,

in accordance with the following provisions.

(5) A resolution of the directors—
    (a) must be authorised by the company's articles, and
    (b) is not sufficient sanction for payments to or for the benefit of directors, former directors or shadow directors.

(6) Any other requirements of the company's articles as to the exercise of the power conferred by this section must be complied with.

(7) Any payment under this section must be made—
    (a) before the commencement of any winding up of the company, and

(b) out of profits of the company that are available for dividend.

Does this provision go far enough? Does it go too far?

3   In *Teck Corporation Limited v. Millar*, [1973] 2 W.W.R. 385, 33 D.L.R. (3d) 288 (B.C. S.C.), Berger J. said (at p. 314):

> A classical theory that once was unchallengeable must yield to the facts of modern life. In fact, of course, it has. If today the directors of a company were to consider the interests of its employees no one would argue that in doing so they were not acting *bona fide* in the interests of the company itself. Similarly, if the directors were to consider the consequences to the community of any policy that the company intended to pursue, and were deflected in their commitment to that policy as a result, it could not be said that they had not considered *bona fide* the interests of the shareholders.

Is he suggesting that *Parke v. Daily News* would have been decided differently in Canada? And if he is, would you agree with him? Berger J.'s views should be compared with those expressed by Mr. Justice Freedman in the CNR "Run-Throughs" Report, *infra*. This passage in *Teck* assumes prominence in Supreme Court jurisprudence on directors' and officers' fiduciary duties. When reading *Peoples* and *BCE* below, consider their consistency with *Teck* and *Parke*.

Peoples Department Stores Ltd. (1992) Inc., Re
2003 CarswellQue 145, 2003 CarswellQue 145 (Que. C.A.), leave to appeal allowed 2003 CarswellQue 3487, 2003 CarswellQue 3488 (S.C.C.), affirmed 2004 CarswellQue 2862, 2004 CarswellQue 2863 (S.C.C.)

[Wise Stores Inc. acquired Peoples Department Stores Inc. from Marks and Spencer Canada Inc. in a "leveraged buy-out": Wise Stores effectively borrowed much of the purchase price from Marks and Spencer. The integration of Peoples within Wise Stores did not go smoothly. Inventory records, for example, were often incorrect as the companies' systems were poorly integrated. The three principal shareholders, officers and directors of Wise Stores were the Wise brothers. One brother consulted the vice-president of administration and finance of both Wise Stores and Peoples about solutions to the integration problems. On his recommendation, the Wise brothers decided to implement a joint inventory procurement policy whereby the two firms would divide responsibility for purchasing. Peoples would make all purchases from North American suppliers and Wise would make all purchases from overseas suppliers. Peoples would transfer inventory to Wise and vice-versa, with each company incurring a debt obligation to the other. Within a year of the implementation of the new inventory procurement system, both Wise and Peoples declared bankruptcy.

Peoples' trustee filed a petition against the Wise brothers. Amongst other things, the trustee claimed that they had favoured the interests of Wise Stores over Peoples to the detriment of Peoples' creditors, in breach of their duties as directors under s. 122(1) of the Canada Business Corporations Act ("CBCA"). The trial judge found the Wise brothers in breach of their fiduciary duties, holding that directors owed such duties to creditors in the vicinity of insolvency. The Court of Appeal set aside the trial judge's decision.]

MAJOR, DESCHAMPS J.J.: The principal question raised by this appeal is whether directors of a corporation owe a fiduciary duty to the corporation's creditors comparable to the statutory duty owed to the corporation. For the reasons that follow, we conclude that directors owe a duty of care to creditors, but that duty does not rise to a fiduciary duty. We agree with the disposition of the Quebec Court of Appeal. The appeal is therefore dismissed. . .

This case came before our Court on the issue of whether directors owe a duty to creditors. The creditors did not bring a derivative action or an oppression remedy application under the CBCA. Instead, the trustee, representing the interests of the creditors, sued the directors for an alleged breach of the duties imposed by s. 122(1) of the CBCA. The standing of the trustee to sue was not questioned. . .

Although the shareholders are commonly said to own the corporation, in the absence of a unanimous shareholder agreement to the contrary, s. 102 of the CBCA provides that it is not the shareholders, but the directors elected by the shareholders, who are responsible for managing it. This clear demarcation between the respective roles of shareholders and directors long predates the 1975 enactment of the CBCA: see *Automatic Self Cleansing Filter Syndicate Co. v. Cunninghamef*, [1906] 2 Ch. 34 (Eng. Ch.); see also art. 311, C.C.Q. . .

Considerable power over the deployment and management of financial, human, and material resources is vested in the directors and officers of corporations. For the directors of CBCA corporations, this power originates in s. 102 of the Act. For officers, this power comes from the powers delegated to them by the directors. In deciding to invest in, lend to or otherwise deal with a corporation, shareholders and creditors transfer control over their assets to the corporation, and hence to the directors and officers, in the expectation that the directors and officers will use the corporation's resources to make reasonable business decisions that are to the corporation's advantage.

The statutory fiduciary duty requires directors and officers to act honestly and in good faith vis-à-vis the corporation. They must respect the trust and confidence that have been reposed in them to manage the assets of the corporation in pursuit of the realization of the objects of the corporation. They must avoid conflicts of interest with the corporation. They must avoid abusing their position to gain personal benefit. They must maintain the confidentiality of information they acquire by virtue of their position. Directors and officers must serve the corporation selflessly, honestly and loyally: see K.P. McGuinness, The Law and Practice of Canadian Business Corporations (1999), at p. 715. . .

In our opinion, the trial judge's determination that there was no fraud or dishonesty in the Wise brothers' attempts to solve the mounting inventory problems of Peoples and Wise stands in the way of a finding that they breached their fiduciary duty. . .

This appeal does not relate to the non-statutory duty directors owe to shareholders. It is concerned only with the statutory duties owed under the CBCA. Insofar as the statutory fiduciary duty is concerned, it is clear that the phrase the "best interests of the corporation" should be read not simply as the "best interests of the shareholders". From an economic perspective, the "best interests of the corporation" means the maximization of the value of the corporation: see E.M. Iacobucci, "Directors' Duties in Insolvency: Clarifying What Is at Stake" (2003), 39(3) Can. Bus. L.J. 398, at pp. 400-1. However, the courts have long recognized that various other factors may be relevant in determining what directors should consider in soundly managing with a view to the best interests of the corporation. For example, in Teck Corp. v. Millar, 1972 CarswellBC 284, 33 D.L.R. (3d) 288 (B.C. S.C.), Berger J. stated, at p. 314:

> A classical theory that once was unchallengeable must yield to the facts of modern life. In fact, of course, it has. If today the directors of a company were to consider the interests of its employees no one would argue that in doing so they were not acting *bona fide* in the interests of the company itself. Similarly, if the directors were to consider the consequences to the community of any policy that the company intended to pursue, and were deflected in their commitment to that policy as a result, it could not be said that they had not considered *bona fide* the interests of the shareholders.

> I appreciate that it would be a breach of their duty for directors to disregard entirely the interests of a company's shareholders in order to confer a benefit on its employees: *Parke v. Daily News Ltd.*, [1962] Ch. 927. But if they observe a decent respect for other interests lying beyond those of the company's shareholders in the strict sense, that will not, in my view, leave directors open to the charge that they have failed in their fiduciary duty to the company.

The case of *Olympia & York Enterprises Ltd. v. Hiram Walker Resources Ltd.*, 1986 CarswellOnt 1050, 59 O.R. (2d) 254 (Ont. Div. Ct.), approved, at p. 271, the decision in *Teck*, supra. We accept as an accurate statement of law that in determining whether they are acting with a view to the best interests of the corporation it may be legitimate, given all the circumstances of a given case, for the board of directors to consider, inter alia, the interests of shareholders, employees, suppliers, creditors, consumers, governments and the environment.

The various shifts in interests that naturally occur as a corporation's fortunes rise and fall do not, however, affect the content of the fiduciary duty under s. 122(1)(a) of the CBCA. At all times, directors and officers owe their fiduciary obligation to the corporation. The interests of the corporation are not to be confused with the interests of the creditors or those of any other stakeholders.

The interests of shareholders, those of the creditors and those of the corporation may and will be consistent with each other if the corporation is profitable and well capitalized and has strong prospects. However, this can change if the corporation starts to struggle financially. The residual rights of the shareholders will generally become worthless if a corporation is declared bankrupt. Upon bankruptcy, the directors of the corporation transfer control to a trustee, who administers the corporation's assets for the benefit of creditors.

Short of bankruptcy, as the corporation approaches what has been described as the "vicinity of insolvency", the residual claims of shareholders will be nearly exhausted. While shareholders might well prefer that the directors pursue high-risk alternatives with a high potential payoff to maximize the shareholders' expected residual claim, creditors in the same circumstances might prefer that the directors steer a safer course so as to maximize the value of their claims against the assets of the corporation.

The directors' fiduciary duty does not change when a corporation is in the nebulous "vicinity of insolvency". That phrase has not been defined; moreover, it is incapable of definition and has no legal meaning. What it is obviously intended to convey is a deterioration in the corporation's financial stability. In assessing the actions of directors it is evident that any honest and good faith attempt to redress the corporation's financial problems will, if successful, both retain value for shareholders and improve the position of creditors. If unsuccessful, it will not qualify as a breach of the statutory fiduciary duty.

For a discussion of the shifting interests and incentives of shareholders and creditors, see W.D. Gray, "Peoples v. Wise and Dylex: Identifying Stakeholder Interests upon or near Corporate Insolvency — Stasis or Pragmatism?" (2003), 39 Can. Bus. L.J. 242, at p. 257; E. M. Iacobucci & K.E. Davis, "Reconciling Derivative Claims and the Oppression Remedy" (2000), 12 S.C.L.R. (2d) 87, at p. 114. In resolving these competing interests, it is incumbent upon the directors to act honestly and in good faith with a view to the best interests of the corporation. In using their skills for the benefit of the corporation when it is in troubled waters financially, the directors must be careful to attempt to act in its best interests by creating a "better" corporation, and not to favour the interests of any one group of stakeholders. If the stakeholders cannot avail themselves of the statutory fiduciary duty (the duty of loyalty, supra) to sue the directors for failing to take care of their interests, they have other means at their disposal. . .

In light of the availability both of the oppression remedy and of an action based on the duty of care, which will be discussed below, stakeholders have viable remedies at their disposal. There is no need to read the interests of creditors into the duty set out in s. 122(1)(a) of the CBCA. Moreover, in the circumstances of this case, the Wise brothers did not breach the statutory fiduciary duty owed to the corporation.

Appeal Dismissed.

Notes and Questions

1   Is there a principled basis for treating the fiduciary duty to creditors as arising in the vicinity of insolvency? While the Supreme Court rejected the notion in *Peoples*, other jurisdictions have accepted it. Consider the following excerpt from the trial judge in *Peoples*:

We were invited by counsel for the Trustee-Petitioner to consider the notion of creditors as "stakeholders" in a corporation.

Over the past 20 years or so . . .British, Australian and New Zealand courts have repeatedly held, at least where a company is insolvent or near to insolvency, that the directors' duties lies not only towards the company's shareholders, but that they are also bound to act in the best interests of the company's creditors . . . The aggregate effect of these developments is to change radically the traditional corporate law doctrine that the directors' duty is to promote the welfare of the company's shareholders and that creditors must be expected to look after themselves. ("Creditors as corporate stakeholders: The Quiet Revolution — an Anglo-Canadian Perspective" (1993), 43 University of Toronto Law Journal 511; Jacob G. Ziegel, Faculty of Law, University of Toronto.) In *Nicholson v. Parmakraft (N.Z.) Ltd.*, [1985] 1 N.Z.L.R. 242, Cooke J. wrote a landmark opinion where he declared at p. 249:

The duties of directors are owed to the company. On the facts of particular casesthis may require the directors to consider *inter alia* the interests of creditors. Forinstance creditors are entitled to consideration, in my opinion, if the company isinsolvent, or near-insolvent or of doubtful solvency, or if a contemplated paymentor other course of action would jeopardise its solvency.

This would appear to closely describe the status of Peoples as it was plunged headlong into the new domestic inventory procurement policy.

I would respectfully adopt the approach of Cumming-Bruce and Templeman L.J. in *Re Horsley & Weight Ltd.* [1982] Ch. 442, 454-456. Both Lord Justices favoured an objective test: whether at the time of the payment in question the directors "should have appreciated" or "ought to have known" that it was likely to cause loss to creditors or threatened the continued existence of the company. . .

The Courts of Australia echoed that holding in Nicholson and also recorded judgments to the same effect even prior to Nicholson.

In *Kinsela v. Russel Kinsela PTY Ltd.*, [1986] 4 N.S.W.L.R. 722, Street C.J. wrote at p. 732:

> The obligation by directors to consider, in appropriate cases, the interests of creditors has been recognized also in the High Court of Australia. In *Walker v. Wimborne* (1976) 137 CLR 1 Mason J. said (at 6-7): . . . it should be emphasized that the directors of a company in discharging their duty to the company must take account of the interest of its shareholders and its creditors. Any failure by the directors to take into account the interests of the creditors will have adverse consequences for the company as well as for them.

Barwick C.J. concurred in the judgment of Mason J.:

> It is, to my mind, legally and logically acceptable to recognise that, where directors are involved in a breach of their duty to the company affecting the interests of the shareholder, then shareholders can either authorise that breach in prospect or ratify it in retrospect. Where, however, the interests at risk are those of creditors I see no reason in law or in logic to recognise that the shareholders can authorise the breach. Once it is accepted, as in my view it must be, that the directors' duty to a company as a whole extends in an insolvency context to not prejudicing the interest of creditors (*Nicholson v. Permakreft (NZ) Ltd. and Walker v. Wimborne*) the shareholders do not have the power or authority to absolve the directors from that breach.

In England, the House of Lords put its stamp of approval on this concept in *Winkworth v. Edward Baron Development Co., Limited et al.*, [1987] 1 All E.R. 114, by Lord Templeman, at p. 118.

But a company owes a duty to its creditors, present and future. The Company is not bound to pay off every debt as soon as it is incurred and the company is not obliged to avoid all ventures which involve an element of risk, but the company owes a duty to its creditors to keep its property inviolate and available for the repayment of its debts. The conscience of the company, as well as its management, is confided to its directors. A duty is owed by the directors to the company and to the creditors of the company to ensure that the affairs of the company are properly administered and that its property is not dissipated or exploited for the benefit of the directors themselves to the prejudice of the creditors.

Even though in Winkworth the directors' actions were motivated by the wish to benefit themselves, and that was not the case with the Wise Brothers here, the general rationale of that judgment applies in the present case.

We agree with the thrust of those judgments and find that Canadian Corporate Law should evolve in that direction.

2 What guidance does *Peoples* offer directors in making decisions when confronted with a clash of shareholder and creditor interests?

3 *Peoples* cites *Teck*, which in turn cites *Parke*, with approval. Are these cases consistent with one another?

BCE Inc., Re
2008 SCC 69, 2008 CarswellQue 12595, 2008 CarswellQue 12596, [2008] 3
S.C.R. 560 (S.C.C.)

[From SCC Headnote: At issue is a plan of arrangement that contemplates the purchase of the shares of BCE Inc. ("BCE") by a consortium of purchasers (the "Purchaser") by way of a leveraged buyout. After BCE was put "in play", an auction process was held and offers were submitted by three groups. All three offers contemplated the addition of a substantial amount of new debt for which Bell Canada, a wholly owned subsidiary of BCE, would be liable. BCE's board of directors found that the Purchaser's offer was in the best interests of BCE and BCE's shareholders. Essentially, the arrangement provides for the compulsory acquisition of all of BCE's outstanding shares. The price to be paid by the Purchaser represents a premium of approximately 40 percent over the market price of BCE shares at the relevant time. The total capital required for the transaction is approximately $52 billion, $38.5 billion of which will be supported by BCE. Bell Canada will guarantee approximately $30 billion of BCE's debt. The Purchaser will invest nearly $8 billion of new equity capital in BCE.

The plan of arrangement was approved by 97.93 percent of BCE's shareholders, but was opposed by a group of financial and other institutions that hold debentures issued by Bell Canada. These debentureholders sought relief under the oppression remedy under s. 241 of the *Canada Business Corporations Act* ("*CBCA*"). They also alleged that the arrangement was not "fair and reasonable" and opposed court approval of the arrangement under s. 192 of the *CBCA*. The crux of their complaints is that, upon the completion of the arrangement, the short-term trading value of the debentures would decline by an average of 20 percent and could lose investment grade status.

The Quebec Superior Court approved the arrangement as fair and dismissed the claim for oppression. The Court of Appeal set aside that decision, finding the arrangement had not been shown to be fair and held that it should not have been approved.]

THE COURT:

Overview of Rights, Obligations and Remedies Under the CBCA

An essential component of a corporation is its capital stock, which is divided into fractional parts, the shares: *Bradbury v. English Sewing Cotton Co.*, [1923] A.C. 744 (H.L.), at p. 767; *Zwicker v. Stanbury*, 1953 CarswellNS 25, [1953] 2 S.C.R. 438 (S.C.C.). While the corporation is ongoing, shares confer no right to its underlying assets.

A share "is not an isolated piece of property . . . [but] a 'bundle' of interrelated rights and liabilities": *Sparling v. Québec (Caisse de dépôt & placement)*, 1988 CarswellQue 29, 1988 CarswellQue 147, [1988] 2 S.C.R. 1015 (S.C.C.) at p. 1025 [S.C.R.], *per* La Forest J. These rights include the right to a proportionate part of the assets of the corporation upon winding-up and the right to oversee the management of the corporation by its board of directors by way of votes at shareholder meetings.

The directors are responsible for the governance of the corporation. In the performance of this role, the directors are subject to two duties: a fiduciary duty to the corporation under s. 122(1)(*a*) (the fiduciary duty); and a duty to exercise the care, diligence and skill of a reasonably prudent person in comparable circumstances under s. 122(1)(*b*) (the duty of care). The second duty is not at issue in these proceedings as this is not a claim against the directors of the corporation for failing to meet their duty of care. However, this case does involve the fiduciary duty of the directors to the corporation, and particularly the "fair treatment" component of this duty, which, as will be seen, is fundamental to the reasonable expectations of stakeholders claiming an oppression remedy.

The fiduciary duty of the directors to the corporation originated in the common law. It is a duty to act in the best interests of the corporation. Often the interests of shareholders and stakeholders are co-extensive with the interests of the corporation. But if they conflict, the directors' duty is clear — it is to the corporation: *Peoples Department Stores*.

The fiduciary duty of the directors to the corporation is a broad, contextual concept. It is not confined to short-term profit or share value. Where the corporation is an ongoing concern, it looks to the long-term interests of the corporation. The content of this duty varies with the situation at hand. At a minimum, it requires the directors to ensure that the corporation meets its statutory obligations. But, depending on the context, there may also be other requirements. In any event, the fiduciary duty owed by directors is mandatory; directors must look to what is in the best interests of the corporation.

In *Peoples Department Stores*, this Court found that although directors *must* consider the best interests of the corporation, it may also be appropriate, although *not mandatory*, to consider the impact of corporate decisions on shareholders or particular groups of stakeholders. As stated by Major and Deschamps JJ., at para. 42:

> We accept as an accurate statement of law that in determining whether they are acting with a view to the best interests of the corporation it may be legitimate, given all the circumstances of a given case, for the board of directors to consider, *inter alia*, the interests of shareholders, employees, suppliers, creditors, consumers, governments and the environment.

As will be discussed, cases dealing with claims of oppression have further clarified the content of the fiduciary duty of directors with respect to the range of interests that should be considered in determining what is in the best interests of the corporation, acting fairly and responsibly.

In considering what is in the best interests of the corporation, directors may look to the interests of, *inter alia*, shareholders, employees, creditors, consumers, governments and the environment to inform their decisions. Courts should give appropriate deference to the business judgment of directors who take into account these ancillary interests, as reflected by the business judgment rule. The "business judgment rule" accords deference to a business decision, so long as it lies within a range of reasonable alternatives: see *Pente Investment Management Ltd. v. Schneider Corp.*, 1998 CarswellOnt 4035, (sub nom. *Maple Leaf Foods Inc. v. Schneider Corp.*) 42 O.R. (3d) 177 (Ont. C.A.); *Kerr v. Danier Leather Inc.*, 2007 SCC 44, 2007 CarswellOnt 6445, 2007 CarswellOnt 6446, [2007] 2 S.C.R. 331 (S.C.C.). It reflects the reality that directors, who are mandated under s. 102(1) of the *CBCA* to manage the corporation's business and affairs, are often better suited to determine what is in the best interests of the corporation. This applies to decisions on stakeholders' interests, as much as other directorial decisions. . .

The Section 241 Oppression Remedy

The debentureholders in these appeals claim that the directors acted in an oppressive manner in approving the sale of BCE, contrary to s. 241 of the *CBCA*. . .

Determining whether a particular expectation is reasonable is complicated by the fact that the interests and expectations of different stakeholders may conflict. The oppression remedy recognizes that a corporation is an entity that encompasses and affects various individuals and groups, some of whose interests may conflict with others. Directors or other corporate actors may make corporate decisions or seek to resolve conflicts in a way that abusively or unfairly maximizes a particular group's interest at the expense of other stakeholders. The corporation and shareholders are entitled to maximize profit and share value, to be sure, but not by treating individual stakeholders unfairly. Fair treatment — the central theme running through the oppression jurisprudence — is most fundamentally what stakeholders are entitled to "reasonably expect". . .

The fact that the conduct of the directors is often at the centre of oppression actions might seem to suggest that directors are under a direct duty to individual stakeholders who may be affected by a corporate decision. Directors, acting in the best interests of the corporation, may be obliged to consider the impact of their decisions on corporate stakeholders, such as the debentureholders in these appeals. This is what we mean when we speak of a director being required to act in the best interests of the corporation viewed as a good corporate citizen. However, the directors owe a fiduciary duty to the corporation, and only to the corporation. People sometimes speak in terms of directors owing a duty to both the corporation and to stakeholders. Usually this is harmless, since the reasonable expectations of the stakeholder in a particular outcome often coincide with what is in the best interests of the corporation. However, cases (such as these appeals) may arise where these interests do not coincide. In such cases, it is important to be clear that the directors owe their duty to the corporation, not to stakeholders, and that the reasonable expectation of stakeholders is simply that the directors act in the best interests of the corporation. . .

Fair Resolution of Conflicting Interests

As discussed, conflicts may arise between the interests of corporate stakeholders *inter se* and between stakeholders and the corporation. Where the conflict involves the interests of the corporation, it falls to the directors of the corporation to resolve them in accordance with their fiduciary duty to act in the best interests of the corporation, viewed as a good corporate citizen.

The cases on oppression, taken as a whole, confirm that the duty of the directors to act in the best interests of the corporation comprehends a duty to treat individual stakeholders affected by corporate actions equitably and fairly. There are no absolute rules. In each case, the question is whether, in all the circumstances, the directors acted in the best interests of the corporation, having regard to all relevant considerations, including, but not confined to, the need to treat affected stakeholders in a fair manner, commensurate with the corporation's duties as a responsible corporate citizen.

Directors may find themselves in a situation where it is impossible to please all stakeholders. The "fact that alternative transactions were rejected by the directors is irrelevant unless it can be shown that a particular alternative was definitely available and clearly more beneficial to the company than the chosen transaction": *Maple Leaf Foods, per* Weiler J.A., at p. 192.

There is no principle that one set of interests — for example the interests of shareholders — should prevail over another set of interests. Everything depends on the particular situation faced by the directors and whether, having regard to that situation, they exercised business judgment in a responsible way. . .

Application to These Appeals

It is apparent that the directors considered the interests of the debentureholders and, having done so, concluded that while the contractual terms of the debentures would be honoured, no further commitments could be made. This fulfilled the duty of the directors to consider the debentureholders' interests. It did not amount to "unfair disregard" of the interests of the debentureholders. As discussed above, it may be impossible to satisfy all stakeholders in a given situation. In this case, the Board considered the interests of the claimant stakeholders. Having done so, and having considered its options in the difficult circumstances it faced, it made its decision, acting in what it perceived to be the best interests of the corporation.

What the claimants contend for on this appeal, in reality, is not merely an expectation that their interests be considered, but an expectation that the Board would take further positive steps to restructure the purchase in a way that would provide a satisfactory purchase price to the shareholders and preserve the high market value of the debentures. . .

The difficulty with this proposition is that there is no evidence that it was reasonable to suppose it could have been achieved. BCE, facing certain takeover, acted reasonably to create a competitive bidding process. The process attracted three bids. All of the bids were leveraged, involving a substantial increase in Bell Canada's debt. It was this factor that posed the risk to the trading value of the debentures. There is no evidence that BCE could have done anything to avoid that risk. Indeed, the evidence is to the contrary. . .

Conclusion

We conclude that the debentureholders have failed to establish either oppression under s. 241 of the *CBCA* or that the trial judge erred in approving the arrangement under s. 192 of the *CBCA*.

For these reasons, the appeals are allowed, the decision of the Court of Appeal set aside, and the trial judge's approval of the plan of arrangement is affirmed with costs throughout. The cross-appeals are dismissed with costs throughout.

Appeals allowed; cross-appeals dismissed.

Notes and Questions

1   The Court speaks of a conflict between stakeholders on the one hand and the corporation on the other. What does this mean?

2   Is there a fiduciary obligation for directors to consider creditors? Shareholders? Other stakeholders? Should there be such obligations? Why?

3 What does conceiving the corporation as a "good corporate citizen" imply for directors' fiduciary duties?

4 Concern has been expressed that directors' duties under *BCE* are indeterminate. In E. Iacobucci, "Indeterminacy and the Canadian Supreme Court's Approach to Corporate Fiduciary Duties" (2009) 48 Canadian Business Law Journal 232, the author provides the following analogy. Is it apt?

> Imagine that you are a bus driver. You are instructed to drive a number of passengers from City A to City B. You are told that there are at least two groups of passengers. One subset wants to take a scenic, hilly route. Another group of passengers gets motion sickness very easily and prefers a flat, boring route. Suppose that you do not have a specific contract telling you what route to take. You are puzzled over which route to take: scenic and potentially nauseating, or boring and benign? You are told that your conduct is governed by a fiduciary duty. Seeking guidance there, you are told that you have a fiduciary duty to act in the best interests of the bus. *BCE* and *Peoples* establish that boards of directors have a duty to act in the interests of a fictional being. This is. . . as useful a piece of guidance to directors as the duty to act in the interests of a motor vehicle is to the bus driver.

5 The Court states that, "at a minimum," directors have a fiduciary obligation to ensure that the corporation complies with its statutory obligations. Why is this? If personal liability of directors and officers is appropriate where there is a breach of a statutory obligation, why does the statute not establish this itself?

6 A good deal of attention focused in the 1970s upon the subject of political and other contributions by corporations, and upon various forms of payments, broadly described as "bribery", designed to secure competitive advantages for those making them. In some situations such payments, if made to public officials, may constitute criminal offences. In the present context, a question of greater interest is how they will be treated in corporate law. The affair of Polysar Ltd., a Canadian Crown corporation, and its wholly owned marketing subsidiary, Polysar International S.A. (PISA), is a case in point. In 1976, the Honourable J.B. Aylesworth, Q.C., and Mr. David Stanley were requested by the directors of Polysar to investigate the payment practices of PISA. Their Report is included as an appendix to the Proceedings of the House of Commons Standing Committee on Public Accounts (1977).

The Report found a number of practices engaged in by PISA which, though perhaps not illegal by Canadian law, were nonetheless questionable. For example, in one case PISA gave quantity discounts, in themselves perfectly proper, to one customer, but instead of paying the discount directly to the customer, the payment was credited to a numbered account in a Swiss bank, the beneficial owner of which was unknown to PISA. The authors of the Report concluded that the customer was almost certainly engaged in tax evasion, and may have been defrauding a minority shareholder. In another case, unusually large, and probably unjustified, volume rebates were granted, which were paid to foreign subsidiaries of the customer. The Report concluded that the rebates were in fact "add-ons", "the real sale price being artificially inflated and the difference between real price and invoice price being credited, on the customer's instructions, to a foreign affiliate". The authors of the Report were of the opinion that the purpose of the customer was to evade foreign exchange regulations. The Report also observed (p. 19A: 14):

> It was drawn repeatedly to our attention that the sole criterion applied by PISA management to the acceptability of any given manner of doing business was whether or not it was consistent with Swiss Law. We cannot report to you that we approve of a criterion that what is acceptable is what one can get away with. In our experience, any business corporations must set certain standards as to what classes of business it is prepared to transact. Again in our experience, we believe that the corporations with the highest standards in this regard are normally those which are most successful. We are not able to commend to you the business standards with which PISA has been content.

7   Consider s. 172 of the U.K. *Companies Act 2006*, titled duty to promote the success of the company:

   (1) A director of a company must act in the way he considers, in good faith, would be most likely to promote the success of the company for the benefit of its members as a whole, and in doing so have regard (amongst other matters) to—

      (a) the likely consequences of any decision in the long term,

      (b) the interests of the company's employees,

      (c) the need to foster the company's business relationships with suppliers, customers and others,

      (d) the impact of the company's operations on the community and the environment,

      (e) the desirability of the company maintaining a reputation for high standards of business conduct, and

      (f) the need to act fairly as between members of the company.

(2) Where or to the extent that the purposes of the company consist of or include purposes other than the benefit of its members, subsection (1) has effect as if the reference to promoting the success of the company for the benefit of its members were to achieving those purposes.

(3) The duty imposed by this section has effect subject to any enactment or rule of law requiring directors, in certain circumstances, to consider or act in the interests of creditors of the company.

Is s. 172 consistent with *BCE*? Is it consistent with *Parke* or *Hutton*?

CNR "Run-Throughs" Report

[In 1964, Mr. Justice Freedman, then of the Manitoba Court of Queen's Bench, was appointed a Commissioner under section 56 of the *Industrial Relations and Disputes Investigation Act* to inquire into the industrial situation arising from the running of certain trains of the Canadian National Railways through the terminals of Nakina, Ontario and Wainwright, Alberta. In his *Report of the Industrial Inquiry Commission on Canadian National Railways "Run-Through"* (Ottawa: Queen's Printer, 1965) he discussed the company's responsibility towards communities in the run-through situation based on its being a publicly-owned corporation:]

THE COMMISSIONER: One ground on which Canadian National was alleged to have a responsibility towards communities in the run-through situation was that it was a publicly owned corporation. More than once the Commission heard the statement that because Canadian National was a government enterprise owned by the people of Canada it owed a special duty to communities. The Commission feels bound to say that this argument has little merit. In the first place, Canadian National, within the framework of statutory controls and public policy applicable to railways in general, was always expected to be operated as an ordinary commercial concern. It is proper that it should today be operated in the same way. In the second place, it would be entirely unfair to impose on Canadian National a burden towards communities from which its competitors, chief among them the Canadian Pacific Railway, would be free. It might perhaps be argued that the company's competitors should also be subject to the same burden. But to say that is to acknowledge the barrenness of the claim that a special responsibility rests on the C.N. by virtue of its being publicly owned.

Another source from which responsibility was said to derive was parentage. Canadian National, it was argued, owed a special duty to a community which it had fathered. This approach, it may incidentally be noted, would exclude from the range of the company's responsibility all communities other than those which it had created. But with regard to this latter group it was submitted that the company's parental status fixed it with a continuing obligation which it was bound to honour. There is a certain plausibility to this argument. At first blush it seems to have considerable value. A moral quality is imparted to it from the concept of the parent-child relationship and the natural duty linked with that relationship. But closer examination reveals that this contention has its limitations. Does the fact of creation impose on the company an obligation from which it can never be freed? At what stage does community infancy come to an end? The Commission was told that Melville was a creation of the company or of one of its predecessors. But this happens to have occurred several decades ago. Must the company still bear a responsibility for the perpetuation of that community, even if sound economic considerations dictated policies for the company in another direction? Then too one company may create a town and be relatively inactive in it, while a second company may later enter upon the scene and be responsible for its real development. Would it be fair to say that the first company, as its creator, owed a special duty to the town which the second did not? Clearly parentage of itself is an unsafe ground upon which to fix liability. It may play some role, but a limited one, and one which should be applied with caution.

A third ground urged upon the Commission was that railroading was traditionally an instrument of national policy, that it was characterized by much regulation and control on the one hand and by government subsidies on the other, and that a railway company would therefore be under a greater duty to a community than would an ordinary commercial enterprise. At least this submission has the merit of putting the railway companies on the same footing and not exposing Canadian National to a liability not shared by Canadian Pacific. It is true that historically railroads have been assigned a role somewhat different from the ordinary mercantile concern. It is also true that over the years this difference in function and treatment has in varying degrees been maintained. But that condition of affairs is the result of public policy. Its source is government action, not company duty. If in an industry already subject to much regulation it should be deemed in the public interest to add a new regulation on the matter of run-throughs, well and good; but that would primarily be a matter for the concern and determination of government. The Commission is therefore of the view that this alleged ground of duty on the part of the company is better dealt with as an aspect of government responsibility — a subject which is considered below — and it will be reserved for such treatment accordingly.

Perhaps the true ground of company responsibility to communities was indicated by the company itself. It is the ground of good corporate citizenship. It has no basis in law, it is unenforceable, and it has very distinct limits. But in the context of a good society it does exist, and it can function as an operating principle. What it consists of and how far it extends were set forth in a brief submitted in the testimony of Mr. W.T. Wilson, the company's Vice-president of Personnel and Labour Relations. In that brief the following preliminary statement was contained:

> It should be emphasized at the outset that Canadian National has no legal obligation toprovide assistance to a community adversely affected by its action, far less to perpetuatethe existence of that community. Company policy on this matter reflects a desire to be agood corporate citizen by recognizing the interests of communities in the manner ofintroducing changes which affect them.

The Commission would say at once that it knows no basis in law, in the absence of express contract or government regulation, for imposing responsibility on a company towards a community. A company is not obliged to remain in a town or to continue an uneconomic operation there. It has the right to leave, or to alter or reduce the nature of its activity there. The result of its action may be to prejudice the interests of a community or even to imperil its future, but the company would in no way be answerable.

Not only is that the legal position but it is the economic one as well, except to the extent that a company is prepared to accept a self-imposed duty to act otherwise. It may be that with regard to communities which it created a company would be more readily disposed to accept such a duty. But if this should be so it would still be no more than the expression of good corporate citizenship. Parentage may strengthen a company's sense of obligation. But of itself it does not constitute a separate or independent ground of duty. What force it possesses is merged in the larger ground of good corporate citizenship. Unless that larger ground is actively present, other considerations will be of little avail.

Report of the Royal Commission on Corporate Concentration (1978)

[In 1975, the federal government appointed a Royal Commission to inquire into and report upon "(a) the nature and role of major concentrations of corporate power in Canada; (b) the economic and social implications for the public interest of such concentrations; and (c) whether safeguards exist or may be required to protect the public interest in the presence of such concentrations." The Report of the Royal Commission on Corporate Concentration (the "Bryce Commission") was published in 1978. In chapter 16, entitled "Business and Society", the Report deals with the social responsibilities of large corporations and expresses the following cautionary views:]

THE COMMISSION: We move now to a discussion, in slightly more specific terms, of what society may legitimately expect from corporations in terms of social responsibility, and how we think corporations should respond. Society's values are continuously changing, and thus the burden of relieving (or of not relieving) various harmful or otherwise undesirable effects for which corporations may in part be responsible will be in constant flux among corporations and the society in which they operate. It is not that long ago that a vista of smoking factory chimneys signalled prosperity: "Where there's muck there's money." The same scene today attracts condemnation. Other examples of this kind of change in public attitude are given by R.W. Ackerman and R.A. Bauer in Corporate Social Responsiveness: The Modern Dilemna [sic] (1976):

> Well within the memory of the older of the two authors, women were criticized for "taking a job that a man needs." Disposable containers were desirable until quite recently. Cheap and profligate (we can afford it) use of energy was eulogized. Plastics were a triumph of our civilization rather than non-biodegradable solid waste. In the market place, the doctrine of let the buyer beware has been replaced by the doctrine of let the seller beware. Employers were only recently forbidden by law to keep records of the race of their employees. Now it is required in order to develop affirmative action plans. One could go on, but we believe the point is made.

This phenomenon suggests to us first, that, whatever obligations business managers may have to respond to social change, they should not be expected always to be at the forefront of change. Although a business corporation may innovate in economic matters, in the social field it is probably better suited to meet challenges than to foresee and lead social change. Our conclusion in this respect is also, in part, a recognition of the force behind one of the critical arguments we summarized earlier in this chapter.

Second, society should be careful about the *kinds* of social obligations it asks business to assume, and business should be equally cautious in accepting them. In particular, we suggest that social problems within the third category we described earlier, that is those that lie essentially outside business activity, should normally not be treated as things to which corporations can respond (except perhaps through traditional philanthropy). Put another way, business should properly be concerned only with things that are direct consequences of economic activity; it should not undertake external "good works". The line between the two will not be easy to draw, but a recognition that there is a line should help to develop attainable objectives.

That the warning is apposite is shown by the experience of corporations in the United States. According to what we have read, many of the more innovative and ambitious social action programs, such as the establishment of businesses in the ghettos and other schemes of urban redevelopment, were generally unsuccessful. Of course, we do not know all the details of those programs, and the reasons for their apparent failure are no doubt many and varied. Nevertheless, it would be folly to ignore the findings of those who have studied and commented upon them.

Most of these attempts originated in the late 1960s, at a time when social criticism of all kinds was at a peak. There was a popular argument that the skills of business people could be deployed in almost any field of activity and to the solution of almost any problem. Not a few business leaders joined the chorus. While to some the projects were probably little more than public relations exercises with nothing substantive behind them, many no doubt believed sincerely that they could supply the talent and energy that was lacking in government and elsewhere.

At all events, disillusion resulted when business so often failed to solve problems outside its experience and ability. In addition, the widespread assumption that the problems of economic growth and universal affluence had been mastered was shattered in the 1970s, and with it many of the ambitious programs of social reform to which business was expected to commit itself.

Richard A. Posner, Economic Analysis of Law
3rd ed. (1986), pp. 394–97

While some people criticize the modern corporation for not trying assiduously enough to maximize profits, others criticize it for making profit maximization its only goal. Corporations have long made charitable donations. Why, then, should they not devote a portion of their revenues to other social needs such as controlling pollution or training members of disadvantaged minorities? But charitable donations are not a strong precedent; especially when they are made in the places where the corporation's plants or headquarters are located, they can usually be justified to shareholders as efficient advertising or public relations expenses.

There are economic reasons for questioning both the feasibility and appropriateness of major corporate commitments to social goals other than profit maximization. In competitive markets, a sustained commitment to any goal other than profitability will result in the firm's shrinking, quite possibly to nothing. The firm that channels profits into pollution control will not be able to recoup its losses by charging higher prices to its customers. The customers do not benefit as customers from such expenditures; more precisely, they benefit just as much from those expenditures if they purchase the lower-priced product of a competing firm that does not incur them. Thus the firm will have to defray the expenses of pollution control entirely out of its profits. But in a competitive market there are no corporate profits, in an economic sense, other than as a short-run consequence of uncertainty (the shareholders being the residual claimants of any excess of corporate revenues over costs). Accounting profits in a competitive market will, in the long run, tend to equality with the cost of attracting and retaining capital in the business. If these profits decline, the firm will, in all likelihood, eventually be forced out of business. True, if it has the usual upward-sloping marginal cost curve at its current output, it may be able to continue in business for a time by reducing its output — but not forever. At its lower output, it will not be able to pay the owners of whatever resources it uses in the production of its output as much as those owners could obtain elsewhere: monopsony is rarely a long-run game (see § 10.9, *supra*). The only exception would be if the owners of these resources (who might be the firm's shareholders) were altruists who received utility from the firm's practice of social responsibility. How likely is that? [Judge Posner considers the position in monopolistic markets and concludes:]

Thus in neither a competitive nor a monopolistic market is it realistic to expect much voluntary effort to subordinate profit maximization to social responsibility. Is this regrettable? Maybe not. There are problems of:

(1) Suboptimization: The manager who tries both to produce for the market at lowest cost and to improve society is likely to do neither very well.

(2) Standard: How are managers to decide what is a politically or ethically correct stance?

(3) Distributive justice: Is it proper that the costs of social responsibility be borne (mainly) by consumers in the form of higher product prices, a form of taxation that is usually regressive? And

(4) Substitution: The exercise of social responsibility by the corporation reduces the ability of the shareholders to exercise social responsibility themselves, while profit maximization increases their wealth and with it the resources they can devote to political contributions, charitable gifts, and the like.

Henry Hansmann and Ranier Kraakman, "The End of History for Corporate Law"
(2001) 89 Georgetown L. J. 439

Much recent scholarship has emphasized institutional differences in corporate governance, capital markets, and law among European, American, and Japanese companies. Despite very real differences in the corporate systems, the deeper tendency is toward convergence, as it has been since the nineteenth century. The basic law of corporate governance — indeed, most of corporate law — has achieved a high degree of uniformity across developed market jurisdictions, and continuing convergence toward a single, standard model is likely . . .

[T]here is today a broad normative consensus that shareholders alone are the parties to whom corporate managers should be accountable, resulting from widespread disenchantment with a privileged role for managers, employees, or the state in corporate affairs. This is not to say that there is agreement that corporations should be run in the interests of shareholders alone — much less that the law should sanction that result. All thoughtful people believe that corporate enterprise should be organized and operated to serve the interests of society as a whole, and that the interests of shareholders deserve no greater weight in this social calculus than do the interests of any other members of society. The point is simply that now, as a consequence of both logic and experience, there is convergence on a consensus that the best means to this end (that is, the pursuit of aggregate social welfare) is to make corporate managers strongly accountable to shareholder interests and, at least in direct terms, only to those interests. It follows that even the extreme proponents of the so-called "concession theory" of the corporation can embrace the primacy of shareholder interests in good conscience. Of course, asserting the primacy of shareholder interests in corporate law does not imply that the interests of corporate stakeholders must or should go unprotected. It merely indicates that the most efficacious legal mechanisms for protecting the interests of nonshareholder constituencies — or at least all constituencies other than creditors — lie outside of corporate law. For workers, this includes the law of labor contracting, pension law, health and safety law, and antidiscrimination law. For consumers, it includes product safety regulation, warranty law, tort law governing product liability, anti-trust law, and mandatory disclosure of product contents and characteristics. For the public at large, it includes environmental law and the law of nuisance and mass torts.

Creditors, to be sure, are to some degree an exception. There remains general agreement that corporate law should directly regulate some aspects of the relationship between a business corporation and its creditors. Conspicuous examples include rules governing veil-piercing and limits on the distribution of dividends in the presence of inadequate capital. The reason for these rules, however, is that there are unique problems of creditor contracting that are integral to the corporate form, owing principally to the presence of limited liability as a structural characteristic of that form. These types of rules, however, are modest in scope. Outside of bankruptcy, they do not involve creditors in corporate governance, but rather are confined to limiting shareholders' ability to use the characteristics of the corporate form opportunistically to exploit creditors . . .

An important source of the success of the standard model is that, in recent years, scholars and other commentators in law, economics, and business have developed persuasive reasons . . . to believe that this model offers greater efficiencies than the principal alternatives. One of these reasons is that, in most circumstances, the interests of equity investors in the firm — the firm's residual claimants — cannot adequately be protected by contract. Rather, to protect their interests, they must be given the right to control the firm. A second reason is that, if the control rights granted to the firm's equity-holders are exclusive and strong, they will have powerful incentives to maximize the value of the firm. A third reason is that the interests of participants in the firm other than shareholders can generally be given substantial protection by contract and regulation, so that maximization of the firm's value by its shareholders complements the interests of those other participants rather than competing with them. A fourth reason is that, even where contractual and regulatory devices offer only imperfect protection for nonshareholder interests, adapting the firm's governance structure to make it directly responsible to those interests creates more difficulties than it solves. . .

Kent Greenfield, "Reclaiming Corporate Law in a New Gilded Age"
2 Harv. L. & Pol'y Rev. (2008)

This question—whether corporate governance should be adjusted to take into account the interests of non-shareholder stakeholders—depends primarily on the answer to another question: whether it is more efficient to regulate corporations from the "outside" or from the "inside." In other words,. . . the question is simply whether it would be more efficient to use corporate law to oblige businesses to consider the interests of non-equity investors or to continue to use. . . regulatory initiatives external to the corporate form.

[This] "external" versus "internal" dichotomy is too simple. Regulations of corporations come in a multitude of forms. Even ones that are seen as external—tax law, for example—often have as a goal the adjustment of behavior within the firm. It is more correct. . . to characterize the regulation of the corporation as falling into three categories: (1) regulation requiring or encouraging certain results (e.g., pollution laws that prohibit the discharge of certain effluents); (2) regulation requiring or encouraging certain processes or actions (e.g., disclosure laws, nondiscrimination laws); and (3) regulation requiring or encouraging certain internal structures (e.g., a board that is elected by shareholders). When characterized this way, it becomes clear that the non-equity investors in corporations typically are forced to depend on regulatory initiatives that focus on results and on procedures. The only stakeholder that has any significant structural protection within the corporate form is the shareholder.

[It may be questioned whether the] interests of stakeholders [are] adequately protected by [regulatory efforts of the first two types.] [In addition, it should be considered] whether the corporation's structure can be adjusted so that its distinctive abilities can be put to greater use in protecting non-shareholder stakeholders. . . . It is often cheaper to avoid a problem than to rectify it later, and it is often better to give the responsibility to avoid a problem to the person who knows most about it and can avoid it at the least expense. As such, corporate law may have comparative advantages over other kinds of law in addressing the concerns of its stakeholders.

For example, because the central purpose of the corporation is to create wealth, broadly defined, it is likely to be more efficient to have the corporation distribute this wealth among those who contribute to its creation rather than having government redistribute wealth after the fact through tax and welfare laws. A fair distribution of corporate profit to employees, for example, will likely have significant positive multiplier effects (such as workers being more productive because they feel they are being fairly treated) that would not likely occur with later governmental redistribution initiatives.

Moreover, in dealing with issues such as economic well-being or environmental sustainability, corporate managers may have expertise that government bureaucrats do not, and there may be efficiencies in a corporate setting that do not exist in a governmental setting. Broadening corporate responsibilities would allow corporations and their management to be proactive in addressing issues of social concern, which in turn might be more efficient than relying on the mostly reactive power of government regulation.

In the end, if non-shareholder stakeholders need more regulatory protection than they now receive, it is foolish and inefficient as a matter of public policy to leave corporate law as an untapped resource."

Chapter 5

The Duty of Care Owed by Managers and Directors to the Corporation

1. INTRODUCTION

Canadian corporate law requires directors and officers of a corporation to abide by two duties: a duty of care and a duty of loyalty. This chapter addresses the duty of care owed by directors and officers to a corporation (the duty of loyalty will be discussed in Chapter 6). We begin with a review of the historically lax common law requirements of the duty of care, followed by a discussion of the statutory reform that has affected the area. We conclude with a discussion of the business judgment rule and the ability of directors and officers to seek indemnification for violations of their duty of care.

2. COMMON LAW

City Equitable Fire Insurance Co. Ltd.
[1925] 1 Ch. 407

[An order was made for the winding-up of an insurance company that was at one time very profitable. An investigation showed a deficit of some £1,200,000 at the time there were large trading profits. The losses were the result of investments in securities which had depreciated and of diversion of funds by the managing director into another company in which he was interested. The managing director was jailed for fraud. The liquidator brought action against the directors and auditors [pursuant to a power equivalent to s. 215(1)(b) of the CBCA] alleging negligence and breach of duty.]

ROMER J.: It has sometimes been said that directors are trustees. If this means no more than that directors in the performance of their duties stand in a fiduciary relationship to the company, the statement is true enough. But if the statement is meant to be an indication by way of analogy of what those duties are, it appears to me to be wholly misleading. I can see but little resemblance between the duties of a director and the duties of a trustee of a will or of a marriage settlement. It is indeed impossible to describe the duty of directors in general terms, whether by way of analogy or otherwise. The position of a director of a company carrying on a small retail business is very different from that of a director of a railway company. The duties of a bank director may differ widely from those of an insurance director, and the duties of a director of one insurance company may differ from those of a director of another. In one company, for instance, matters may normally be attended to by the manager or other members of the staff that in another company are attended to by the directors themselves. The larger the business carried on by the company the more numerous, and the more important, the matters that must of necessity be left to the managers, the accountants and the rest of the staff. The manner in which the work of the company is to be distributed between the board of directors and the staff is in truth a business matter to be decided on business lines. To use the words of Lord Macnaghten in *Dovey v. Cory*:

> I do not think it desirable for any tribunal to do that which Parliament has abstained from doing — that is, to formulate precise rules for the guidance or embarrassment of business men in the conduct of business affairs. There never has been, and I think there never will be, much difficulty in dealing with any particular case on its own facts and circumstances; and, speaking for myself, I rather doubt the wisdom of attempting to do more.

In order, therefore, to ascertain the duties that a person appointed to the board of an established company undertakes to perform, it is necessary to consider not only the nature of the company's business, but also the manner in which the work of the company is in fact distributed between the directors and the other officials of the company, provided always that this distribution is a reasonable one in the circumstances, and is not inconsistent with any express provisions of the articles of association. In discharging the duties of his position thus ascertained a director must, of course, act honestly; but he must also exercise some degree of both skill and diligence. To the question of what is the particular degree of skill and diligence required of him, the authorities do not, I think, give any very clear answer. It has been laid down that so long as a director acts honestly he cannot be made responsible in damages unless guilty of gross or culpable negligence in a business sense. But as pointed out by Neville J. in *In re Brazilian Rubber Plantations and Estates, Ltd.*, one cannot say whether a man has been guilty of negligence, gross or otherwise, unless one can determine what is the extent of the duty which he is alleged to have neglected. For myself, I confess to feeling some difficulty in understanding the difference between negligence and gross negligence, except in so far as the expressions are used for the purpose of drawing a distinction between the duty that is owed in one case and the duty that is owed in another. If two men owe the same duty to a third person, and neglect to perform that duty, they are both guilty of negligence, and it is not altogether easy to understand how one can be guilty of gross negligence and the other of negligence only. But if it be said that of two men one is only liable to a third person for gross negligence, and the other is liable for mere negligence, this, I think, means no more than that the duties of the two men are different. The one owes a duty to take a greater degree of care than does the other: see the observations of Willes J. in *Grill v. General Iron Screw Collier Co.* If, therefore, a director is only liable for gross or culpable negligence, this means that he does not owe a duty to his company, to take all possible care. It is some degree of care less than that. The care that he is bound to take has been described by Neville J. in the case referred to above as "reasonable care" to be measured by the care an ordinary man might be expected to take in the circumstances on his own behalf. In saying this Neville J. was only following what was laid down in *Overend & Gurney Co. v. Gibb* as being the proper test to apply, namely:

> Whether or not the directors exceeded the powers entrusted to them, or whether if they did not so exceed their powers they were cognisant of circumstances of such a character, so plain, so manifest, and so simple of appreciation, that no men with any ordinary degree of prudence, acting on their own behalf, would have entered into such a transaction as they entered into?

There are, in addition, one or two other general propositions that seem to be warranted by the reported cases: (1.) A director need not exhibit in the performance of his duties a greater degree of skill than may reasonably be expected from a person of his knowledge and experience. A director of a life insurance company, for instance, does not guarantee that he has the skill of an actuary or of a physician. In the words of Lindley M.R.:

> If directors act within their powers, if they act with such care as is reasonably to be expected from them, having regard to their knowledge and experience, and if they act honestly for the benefit of the company they represent, they discharge both their equitable as well as their legal duty to the company: [See *Lagunas Co. v. Lagunas Syndicate*].

It is perhaps only another way of stating the same proposition to say that directors are not liable for mere errors of judgment. (2.) A director is not bound to give continuous attention to the affairs of his company. His duties are of an intermittent nature to be performed at periodical board meetings, and at meetings of any committee of the board upon which he happens to be placed. He is not, however, bound to attend all such meetings, though he ought to attend whenever, in the circumstances, he is reasonably able to do so. (3.) In respect of all duties that, having regard to the exigencies of business, and the articles of association, may properly be left to some other official, a director is, in the absence of grounds for suspicion, justified in trusting that official to perform such duties honestly. In the judgment of the Court of Appeal in *In re National Bank of Wales, Ltd.*, the following passage occurs in relation to a director who had been deceived by the manager, and managing director, as to matters within their own particular sphere of activity:

> Was it his duty to test the accuracy or completeness of what he was told by the general manager and the managing director? This is a question on which opinions may differ, but we are not prepared to say that he failed in his legal duty. Business cannot be carried on upon principals of distrust. Men in responsible positions must be trusted by those above them, as well as by those below them, until there is reason to distrust them. We agree that care and prudence do not involve distrust; but for a director acting honestly himself to be held legally liable for negligence, in trusting the officers under him not to conceal from him what they ought to report to him, appears to us to be laying too heavy a burden on honest business men.

That case went to the House of Lords, and is reported there under the name of *Dovey v. Cory.* Lord Davey, in the course of his speech to the House, made the following observations:

> I think the respondent was bound to give his attention to and exercise his judgment as a man of business on the matters which were brought before the board at the meetings which he attended, and it is not proved that he did not do so. But I think he was entitled to rely upon the judgment, information and advice, of chairman and general manager, as to whose integrity, skill and competence he had no reason for suspicion. I agree with what was said by Sir George Jessel in *Hallmark's Case*, and by Chitty J. in *In re Denham & Co.*, that directors are not bound to examine entries in the company's books. It was the duty of the general manager and (possibly) of the chairman to go carefully through the returns from the branches, and to bring before the board any matter requiring their consideration; but the respondent was not, in my opinion guilty of negligence in not examining them for himself, notwithstanding that they were laid on the table of the board for reference.

These are the general principles that I shall endeavour to apply in considering the question whether the directors of this company have been guilty of negligence. But in order to determine whether any such negligence, if established, renders the directors liable in damages, it is necessary to consider the provisions of art. 150 of the company's articles of association . . .

The importance of the article for the present purpose is to be found in the later part, which provides that the directors are not to be answerable for insufficiency or deficiency of any security or for any other loss, misfortune, or damage which may happen in the execution of their respective offices or trusts or in relation thereto "unless the same shall happen by or through their own wilful neglect or default respectively." . . . [His Lordship discussed the meaning of wilful default in the above context and then entered into an extensive review of the evidence, finding that some of the directors and the auditor had been guilty of negligence but were protected by Article 150, which required wilful misconduct. The case was appealed to the Court of Appeal so far as the decision absolved the auditors, where the decision of Romer J. was affirmed ([1925] 1 Ch. 500). Article 150 would now be invalidated by s. 205 of the *Companies Act* (1948). Section 122(3) of the CBCA is to the same effect.]

Note

Romer J.'s judgment is considered the *locus classicus* on directors' duty of care. In failing to establish a professional standard for a director, his judgment ensured that an action for breach of duty would rarely succeed. The standard was that of the reasonable person given the individual director's expertise. Moreover, a director was not bound to give his full time to the job and was entitled to rely on the company's officers.

Re Brazilian Rubber Plantations and Estates, Ltd.
[1911] 1 Ch. 425 (C.A.)

[The directors of a company, Sir Arthur Aylmer Bart., Henry William Tugwell, Edward Barber and Edward Henry Hancock were all induced to become directors by Harboard or persons acting with him in the promotion of the company. Sir Arthur Aylmer was absolutely ignorant of business. He only consented to act because he was told the office would give him a little pleasant employment without his incurring any responsibility. H.W. Tugwell was partner in a firm of bankers in a good position in Bath; he was seventy-five years of age and very deaf; he was induced to join the board by representations made to him in January, 1906. Barber was a rubber broker and was told that all he would have to do would be to give an opinion as to the value of rubber when it arrived in England. Hancock was a man of business who said he was induced to join by seeing the names of Tugwell and Barber, whom he considered good men. The four directors relied on a report for the acquisition of a rubber plantation that contained an exaggeration of the acreage of the plantation.]

NEVILLE J.: The evidence in this case has been brought before the Court in a somewhat inconvenient manner, the public examination having been followed by affidavits upon which no cross-examination has taken place. Inasmuch, however, as the liquidator does not charge the respondents with dishonesty, but with negligence based in the main upon undisputed facts, this state of the evidence is of the less consequence. In my opinion it would have been impossible to sustain a charge of dishonesty against any of the respondents. They were, in my opinion, honest men, who performed what they supposed to be their duty as directors, whether or not they fell short in fact of the obligations imposed upon them by their office. Unfortunately for themselves, they fell into the toils of dishonest men. I have not the promoters of the company before me, and I am unable, therefore, to separate the knaves from their dupes; but it appears clear from the evidence that the report upon which the directors were asked to, and did, act was concocted in London, from the particulars furnished by the original vendors, who appear to have been straightforward men. . .

I have to consider what is the extent of the duty and obligation of directors towards their company. It has been laid down that so long as they act honestly they cannot be made responsible in damages unless guilty of gross negligence. There is admittedly a want of precision in this statement of a director's liability. In truth, one cannot say whether a man has been guilty of negligence, gross or otherwise, unless one can determine what is the extent of the duty which he is alleged to have neglected. A director's duty has been laid down as requiring him to act with such care as is reasonably to be expected from him, having regard to his knowledge and experience. He is, I think, not bound to bring any special qualifications to his office. He may undertake the management of a rubber company in complete ignorance of everything connected with rubber, without incurring responsibility for the mistakes which may result from such ignorance; while if he is acquainted with the rubber business he must give the company the advantage of his knowledge when transacting the company's business. He is not, I think, bound to take any definite part in the conduct of the company's business, but so far as he does undertake it he must use reasonable care in its despatch.

Such reasonable care must, I think, be measured by the care an ordinary man might be expected to take in the same circumstances on his own behalf. He is clearly, I think, not responsible for damages occasioned by errors of judgment. . . .

In this case, therefore, I must consider whether the directors acted without reasonable prudence in adopting the contract on the information which they possessed. I entirely concur in the view that this must not be tested by considering what the Court itself would think reasonable. The gravamen of the charge of negligence is based upon the absence of an independent report or opinion. Now, in my opinion, men in general take a very different view of the importance of independent testimony from that obtaining in the Courts. Business men have very frequently to act on information derived from interested persons. In so doing the wise men amongst them no doubt make an allowance for exaggeration, but exaggeration and fraud are not the same thing. If the report had been merely exaggerated, there was no fear of the company making a bad bargain; there was ample margin to allow for exaggeration. The directors did make inquiries, but they were from persons whom, it is said, they ought to have known to be interested. One of them, Webb, was a person in a position entitling his opinion and word to great weight, and though reflection would have shewn the directors that he could not have been instructed to act on behalf of the company by persons independent of the promoters, I think the directors were not to be blamed for placing considerable reliance upon his assurances. A certain Lord B., who was at first proposed as a director, was by arrangement to consult his solicitors and to communicate the result to the others — Barber said only in case the report was unfavorable. He did not make any communication, but though he did not join the board himself, he put, as the directors supposed, his cousin upon it. Upon the whole I come to the conclusion that the directors believed that the contract was a beneficial one for the company, and that, notwithstanding the discrepancy in prices and the absence of an independent report, this conclusion was not arrived at by negligence on their part as directors. . . .

Notes

1 In the *Re City Equitable* case, the Court stated that the responsibility of the directors varied with the nature of the company on whose board they served. In which ways should a director's role vary across corporation types? Do different sized corporations implicate fundamentally different roles in the nature of director supervision or only in the intensity of supervision?

2 *Re Brazilian* clearly sets the bar at a low level for directors. However, it at least seems clear that directors who blindly do all that they are asked to do will be held accountable. In *Selangor United Rubber Estates Ltd. v. Cradock*, [1968] 2 All E.R. 1073 (Ch. Div.), Ungoed-Thomas J. held that two nominee directors of a company who blindly sanctioned the conveyance of all of the assets of the plaintiff company to another company, thereby enabling one of the principals of the latter company to gain control of the plaintiff company with the plaintiff company's own assets, were liable in equity for the wrongful conversion of the plaintiff company's funds. This arrangement also had the effect of looting minority shareholders of their proportionate interest in the assets of the corporation.

During the trial, one of the directors, Mr. Barlow-Lawson, stated that once he became the nominee director of Cradock, the person who would ultimately gain control of the plaintiff company, "he gave no service to any [other] in the company". The second director, Mr. Jacob, who was an employee of Cradock, stated that he never made any enquiries about the resolutions he voted for (facilitating the arrangement) nor did he consider the interests of shareholders other than Cradock. Instead, he simply did what Cradock requested of him. In the course of the Court's judgment, Ungoed-Thomas J. stated that:

> It seems to me, however, that both Mr. Barlow-Lawson and Mr. Jacob were nominated as directors of the plaintiff company to do exactly as they were told by Mr. Cradock, and that is in fact what they did. They exercised no discretion or volition of their own and they behaved in utter disregard of their duties as directors in the general body of stockholders or creditors or anyone but Mr. Cradock. They put themselves in his hands, not as their agent or adviser, but as their controller. They were puppets which had no movement apart from the strings and those strings were manipulated by Mr. Cradock. They were voices without any mind but that of Mr. Cradock; and with that mind they are fixed in accordance with the view which I have already expressed on the law. They doubtless hoped for the best but risked the worst; and that worst has now befallen them. ([1968] 2 All E.R. 1073 (Ch. Div.), at 1123).

3   Director liability for breach of the duty of care is predicated on personal negligence. Gower suggests (*Gower's Principles of Modern Company Law*, 5th ed., 588 fn. 30) that reform is occurring in the proposed Fifth Company Law Directive and the proposed Statute for a European Company that all members of the board would be jointly and severally responsible for a breach of duty, leaving it to the courts to provide individual relief where it is justified. Do you agree?

4   Under s. 130 of the Ontario *Securities Act*, the directors' failure in *Brazilian Rubber* to identify the misstatements in the prospectus would have rendered them, *prima facie*, liable to buyers of the securities for damages. Section 130(3) does, however, provide a number of so-called "due diligence" defences for liability. The due diligence defences give the impugned directors the ability to demonstrate that they were not negligent in the preparation of the prospectus. In respect of portions of the prospectus that were prepared by an "expert" (or that summarize an expert report) the standard that the directors must meet to escape liability is that they "had no reasonable grounds to believe and did not believe that there had been a misrepresentation" in the prospectus (s. 130(3)(c)). In the case of other parts of the prospectus (the so-called "non-expertised" parts) the directors are not liable unless they "failed to conduct such reasonable investigation as to provide reasonable grounds for a belief that there had been no misrepresentation." (s. 130(5)). On the facts of *Re Brazilian*, the prior owner's report on the property would *not* be considered to be an expert's report. Thus, the higher standard would apply, and the directors would be required to make a reasonable investigation to confirm the facts in the report or face liability.

3. NOTE ON STATUTORY REFORM AND JUDICIAL INTERPRETATION OF THE STATUTORY DUTIES OF CARE

Much criticism was heaped on the lax standard prescribed in the common law explored above. The result is s. 122(1)(b) of the CBCA, s. 134(1)(b) of the OBCA, and s. 142(1)(b) of the BCBCA. The history of the legislative changes in Ontario is reviewed in *Soper v. R.* (1997), [1998] 1 F.C. 124, 1997 CarswellNat 853, 1997 CarswellNat 2675 (C.A.), while the history of the federal reforms is reviewed in the excerpt from *People's Department Stores Ltd. (1992) Inc., Re*, 2003 CarswellQue 145, [2003] Q.J. No. 505 (Que. C.A.), leave to appeal allowed 2003 CarswellQue 3487, 2003 CarswellQue 3488 (S.C.C.), affirmed 2004 CarswellQue 2862, 2004 CarswellQue 2863 (S.C.C.). Interestingly enough, however, in both cases, the court uses this legislative history to support the view that the Ontario and federal statutory provisions essentially *adopt* the common law standard of care. Do you agree with the courts' interpretation of the statutory standard? Was the phrase "in comparable circumstances" really meant to embrace the skill and knowledge of the individual director? Are there other aspects of these provisions that would allow the importation of subjective factors?

You should note that these statutory provisions cover more than just Romer J.'s first proposition from *Re City Equitable* (and ancillary statements regarding the standard of care). Romer J.'s second proposition states, *inter alia*, that a director "is not . . . bound to attend all [directors'] meetings, though he ought to attend whenever, in the circumstances, he is reasonably able to do so." None of the Canadian statutory provisions *require* that directors attend meetings. However, the CBCA, the OBCA, and the BCBCA all draw a distinction between the director who attends a meeting and one who does not. Section 123 of the CBCA is typical of what the statutes require. It provides that "[a] director who is present at a meeting of directors or committee of directors is deemed to have consented to any resolution passed or action taken at the meeting" unless his or her dissent is entered in the minutes of the meeting or, within seven days after he or she becomes aware of the resolution, sends his or her written dissent to the secretary of the company. However, suppose that a director who fails to attend a meeting and does not subsequently become aware of a resolution (either by accident or design) learns of the resolution only upon receiving a statement of claim suing her *qua* director for a corporate resolution taken in her absence. Can that director, within seven days of receiving the statement of claim, still send a written notice to the company dissenting from the resolution? For similar provisions, see the OBCA, s. 135 and the BCBCA, s. 154(5).

Romer J,'s third proposition states that "a director is, in the absence of grounds for suspicion, justified in trusting [an] official [with delegated authority] to perform such duties honestly." The CBCA, by contrast, states:

> 123.(5) A director has complied with his or her duties under subsection 122(1) [the duty of loyalty and the duty of care] if the director relied in good faith on
>
> (a) financial statements of the corporation represented to the director by an officer of the corporation or in a written report of the auditor of the corporation fairly to reflect the financial condition of the corporation; or
>
> (b) a report of a person whose profession lends credibility to a statement made by the professional person.

The statutory provision is notably different from Justice Romer's proposition. In one respect, it is broader. The CBCA requires only *good faith* reliance; it does not, as Justice Romer's proposition does, require that the reliance be in any way *reasonable* or *non-negligent*. However, in another respect the CBCA is narrower. It does *not* allow for reliance on "officials" (which appears to mean internal managers), but only in respect of financial statements and reports of professionals or "a person whose profession lends credibility to a statement made by that professional person". It is possible that a court might interpret the scope of that provision to include an officer or other employee of the corporation, although that interpretation is by no means obvious. As a matter of statutory interpretation, can the common law rule stand side-by-side the statutory rule? The cases that follow explore the meaning of the statutory duty of care provisions.

4. STATUTORY REFORM: CORPORATE LAW

Peoples Department Stores Ltd. (1992) Inc., Re
2003 CarswellQue 145, [2003] Q.J. No. 505 (Que. C.A.), leave to appeal
allowed 2003 CarswellQue 3487, 2003 CarswellQue 3488 (S.C.C.),
affirmed 2004 CarswellQue 2862, 2004 CarswellQue 2863 (S.C.C.), 2004
S.C.C. 68, [2004] 3 S.C.R. 461

[The Wise brothers (Lionel, Ralph, and Harold) were the sole shareholders of Wise Inc. ("Wise"), which owned a chain of department stores in Quebec. Marks and Spencer ran another chain of department stores, owned and operated by Peoples Department Stores Inc. ("Peoples"). Both companies were incorporated under the CBCA. Marks and Spencer sold the Peoples chain to Wise. However, the contract between the two companies forbade Wise from merging its operations with those of Peoples until the purchase price was paid, presumably in order that Marks and Spencer could more easily resume control of Peoples should there be a default in the payment of the purchase price.

Thus, while Wise ended up owning all of the shares in Peoples, it had to continue to run Peoples as a subsidiary corporation.

This contractual stipulation caused enormous grief to Wise. Both Wise and Peoples were in parlous financial condition, and the Wise brothers sought ways to cut costs. One of the biggest headaches they had was in relation to the purchase of goods for resale; each company had its own administrative purchasing and inventory apparatus and this was causing major mix-ups in ordering, excess inventory at some stores, and deficient inventory at others. In response, David Clément, Wise's vice-president for administration and finance, developed a solution. He proposed the integration of the management of the inventories of Wise and Peoples Inc. into a single computer file, as if the two entities constituted only one company that operated some 125 stores. Peoples Inc. would be entrusted with all the purchases required to run the two chains, at least so-called local purchases, i.e., those made in North America. Wise would pay Peoples Inc. upon receipt of the merchandise in its stores. Wise would be given responsibility for purchases made abroad for the two chains, since, before the acquisition, Peoples Inc. did not purchase supplies outside North America and did not have the financial tools required for that type of operation. Around December 1993, the brothers submitted Clément's proposal to the buyers. They saw it as the solution to their problem. Given how the proposal was received, the brothers accepted it without studying the indirect impact it could have. In short, they relied on Clément's skills and decided that the proposal would be implemented as of February 1994.

Pelletier J.A. then described how the implementation of this policy resulted in Wise running up large debts to Peoples. This was because Peoples paid for all the inventory that was put on the shelves in *both* stores, and billed Wise for its share. This resulted in Wise constantly owing money to Peoples, however, since it had trouble paying its debts. Ultimately, both Wise and Peoples failed and went into bankruptcy proceedings, with Wise owing Peoples a sum of money that the trial judge fixed at something in excess of $4 million. This inter-corporate debt resulted in prejudice to the creditors of Peoples, since the creditors of Peoples, in effect, had to stand in line with all of the creditors of Wise for this $4 million, rather than having exclusive access to the $4 million (which it would have done had the money been in the till at Peoples). A trustee in bankruptcy was appointed for Peoples, and the trustee commenced action against the Wise brothers *qua* directors of Peoples. Note that in bankruptcy proceedings, the trustee in bankruptcy replaces the board of directors. Thus, the trustee's action is the formal equivalent of an action taken by Peoples Inc. against its own directors. While this action is not formally a *derivative* action (because it was not undertaken by a shareholder in the name of the corporation, but rather by the corporation directly), everything that the court says below regarding the duties of directors is equally applicable to derivative actions.

Substantively, the trustee alleged that in adopting the new inventory procurement policy, the Wise brothers had breached both their duty of loyalty to Peoples under CBCA s. 122(1)(a) and their duty of care under CBCA s. 122(1)(b). In respect of the former, the court noted that the trial judge had found that the directors had acted in good faith, and that there was no fraud or dishonesty in their adoption of the inventory procurement policy. Hence, there could be no breach of the duty of loyalty. The following excerpts deal solely with the issue of the duty of care.]

That directors must satisfy a duty of care is a long-standing principle of the common law, although the duty of care has been reinforced by statute to become more demanding. Among the earliest English cases establishing the duty of care were *Dovey v. Cory*, [1901] A.C. 477 (H.L.); *In re Brazilian Rubber Plantations and Estates, Ltd.*, [1911] 1 Ch. 425 (C.A.); and *In re City Equitable Fire Insurance Co.*, [1925] 1 Ch. 407 (C.A.). In substance, these cases held that the standard of care was a reasonably relaxed, subjective standard. The common law required directors to avoid being grossly negligent with respect to the affairs of the corporation and judged them according to their own personal skills, knowledge, abilities, and capacities. See McGuinness, *supra*, at p. 776: "Given the history of the case law in this area, and the prevailing standards of competence displayed in commerce generally, it is quite clear that directors were not expected at common law to have any particular business skill or judgment."

The 1971 report entitled *Proposals for a New Business Corporations Law for Canada* (1971) ("Dickerson Report") culminated the work of a committee headed by R.W.V. Dickerson which had been appointed by the federal government to study the need for new federal business corporations legislation. This report preceded the enactment of the CBCA by four years and influenced the eventual structure of the CBCA.

The standard recommended by the Dickerson Report was objective, requiring directors and officers to meet the standard of a "reasonably prudent person" (vol. II, at. p. 74):

9.19

(1) Every director and officer of a corporation in exercising his powers and discharging his duties shall

   (b) exercise the care, diligence and skill of a reasonably prudent person.

The report described how this proposed duty of care differed from the prevailing common law duty of care (vol. I, at p. 83):

242. The formulation of the duty of care, diligence and skill owed by directors represents an attempt to upgrade the standard presently required of them. The principal change here is that whereas at present the law seems to be that a director is only required to demonstrate the degree of care, skill and diligence that could reasonably be expected from him, having regard to his knowledge and experience — *Re City Equitable Fire Insurance Co.*, [1925] Ch. 425 — under s. 9.19(1)(b) he is required to conform to the standard of a reasonably prudent man. *Recent experience has demonstrated how low the prevailing legal standard of care for directors is, and we have sought to raise it significantly.* We are aware of the argument that raising the standard of conduct for directors may deter people from accepting directorships. The truth of that argument has not been demonstrated and we think it is specious. The duty of care imposed by s. 9.19(1)(b) is exactly the same as that which the common law imposes on every professional person, for example, and there is no evidence that this has dried up the supply of lawyers, accountants, architects, surgeons or anyone else. It is in any event cold comfort to a shareholder to know that there is a steady supply of marginally competent people available under present law to manage his investment. [Emphasis added.]

The statutory duty of care in s. 122(1)(*b*) of the CBCA emulates but does not replicate the language proposed by the Dickerson Report. The main difference is that the enacted version includes the words "in comparable circumstances", which modifies the statutory standard by requiring the context in which a given decision was made to be taken into account. This is not the introduction of a subjective element relating to the competence of the director, but rather the introduction of a contextual element into the statutory standard of care. It is clear that s. 122(1)(*b*) requires more of directors and officers than the traditional common law duty of care outlined in, for example, *Re City Equitable Fire Insurance, supra.*

The standard of care embodied in s. 122(1)(*b*) of the CBCA was described by Robertson J.A. of the Federal Court of Appeal in *Soper v. Canada*, [1998] 1 F.C. 124, at para. 41, as being "objective subjective". Although that case concerned the interpretation of a provision of the *Income Tax Act*, it is relevant here because the language of the provision establishing the standard of care was identical to that of s. 122(1)(*b*) of the CBCA. With respect, we feel that Robertson J.A.'s characterization of the standard as an "objective subjective" one could lead to confusion. We prefer to describe it as an objective standard. To say that the standard is objective makes it clear that the factual aspects of the circumstances surrounding the actions of the director or officer are important in the case of the s. 122(1)(*b*) duty of care, as opposed to the subjective motivation of the director or officer, which is the central focus of the statutory fiduciary duty of s. 122(1)(*a*) of the CBCA.

The contextual approach dictated by s. 122(1)(*b*) of the CBCA not only emphasizes the primary facts but also permits prevailing socioeconomic conditions to be taken into consideration. The emergence of stricter standards puts pressure on corporations to improve the quality of board decisions. The establishment of good corporate governance rules should be a shield that protects directors from allegations that they have breached their duty of care. However, even with good corporate governance rules, directors' decisions can still be open to criticism from outsiders. Canadian courts, like their counterparts in the United States, the United Kingdom, Australia and New Zealand, have tended to take an approach with respect to the enforcement of the duty of care that respects the fact that directors and officers often have business expertise that courts do not. Many decisions made in the course of business, although ultimately unsuccessful, are reasonable and defensible at the time they are made. Business decisions must sometimes be made, with high stakes and under considerable time pressure, in circumstances in which detailed information is not available. It might be tempting for some to see unsuccessful business decisions as unreasonable or imprudent in light of information that becomes available *ex post facto*. Because of this risk of hindsight bias, Canadian courts have developed a rule of deference to business decisions called the "business judgment rule", adopting the American name for the rule.

Directors and officers will not be held to be in breach of the duty of care under s. 122(1)(*b*) of the CBCA if they act prudently and on a reasonably informed basis. The decisions they make must be reasonable business decisions in light of all the circumstances about which the directors or officers knew or ought to have known. In determining whether directors have acted in a manner that breached the duty of care, it is worth repeating that perfection is not demanded. Courts are ill-suited and should be reluctant to second-guess the application of business expertise to the considerations that are involved in corporate decision making, but they are capable, on the facts of any case, of determining whether an appropriate degree of prudence and diligence was brought to bear in reaching what is claimed to be a reasonable business decision at the time it was made.

The trustee alleges that the Wise brothers breached their duty of care under s. 122(1)(*b*) of the CBCA by implementing the new procurement policy to the detriment of Peoples' creditors. After considering all the evidence, we agree with the Court of Appeal that the implementation of the new policy was a reasonable business decision that was made with a view to rectifying a serious and urgent business problem in circumstances in which no solution may have been possible. The trial judge's conclusion that the new policy led inexorably to Peoples' failure and bankruptcy was factually incorrect and constituted a palpable and overriding error.

In fact, as noted by Pelletier J.A., there were many factors other than the new policy that contributed more directly to Peoples' bankruptcy. Peoples had lost $10 million annually while being operated by M & S. Wise, which was only marginally profitable and solvent with annual sales of $100 million (versus $160 million for Peoples), had hoped to improve the performance of its new acquisition. Given that the transaction was a fully leveraged buyout, for Wise and Peoples to succeed, Peoples' performance needed to improve dramatically. Unfortunately for both Wise and Peoples, the retail market in eastern Canada had become very competitive in the early 1990s, and this trend continued with the arrival of Wal-Mart in 1994.

* * *

The Wise brothers treated the implementation of the new policy as a decision made in the ordinary course of business and, while no formal agreement evidenced the arrangement, a monthly record was made of the inventory transfers. Although this may appear to be a loose business practice, by the autumn of 1993, Wise had already consolidated several aspects of the operations of the two companies. Legally they were two separate entities. However, the financial fate of the two companies had become intertwined. In these circumstances, there was little or no economic incentive for the Wise brothers to jeopardize the interests of Peoples in favour of the interests of Wise. In fact, given the tax losses that Peoples had carried forward, the companies had every incentive to keep Peoples profitable in order to reduce their combined tax liabilities.

Arguably, the Wise brothers could have been more precise in pursuing a resolution to the intractable inventory management problems, having regard to all the troublesome circumstances involved at the time the new policy was implemented. But we, like the Court of Appeal, are not satisfied that the adoption of the new policy breached the duty of care under s. 122(1)(b) of the CBCA. The directors cannot be held liable for a breach of their duty of care in respect of the creditors of Peoples.

* * *

When faced with the serious inventory management problem, the Wise brothers sought the advice of the vice-president of finance, David Clément. The Wise brothers claimed as an additional argument that in adopting the solution proposed by Clément, they were relying in good faith on the judgment of a person whose profession lent credibility to his statement, in accordance with the defence provided for in s. 123(4)(b) (now s. 123(5)) of the CBCA. The Court of Appeal accepted the argument. We disagree.

The reality that directors cannot be experts in all aspects of the corporations they manage or supervise shows the relevancy of a provision such as s. 123(4)(b). At the relevant time, the text of s. 123(4) read:

123. . . .

(4) A director is not liable under section 118, 119 or 122 if he relies in good faith on

(*a*) financial statements of the corporation represented to him by an officer of the corporation or in a written report of the auditor of the corporation fairly to reflect the financial condition of the corporation; or

(*b*) a report of a lawyer, accountant, engineer, appraiser or other person whose profession lends credibility to a statement made by him.

Although Clément did have a bachelor's degree in commerce and 15 years of experience in administration and finance with Wise, this experience does not correspond to the level of professionalism required to allow the directors to rely on his advice as a bar to a suit under the duty of care. The named professional groups in s. 123(4)(*b*) were lawyers, accountants, engineers, and appraisers. Clément was not an accountant, was not subject to the regulatory overview of any professional organization and did not carry independent insurance coverage for professional negligence. The title of vice-president of finance should not automatically lead to a conclusion that Clément was a person "whose profession lends credibility to a statement made by him". It is noteworthy that the word "profession" is used, not "position". Clément was simply a non-professional employee of Wise. His judgment on the appropriateness of the solution to the inventory management problem must be regarded in that light. Although we might accept for the sake of argument that Clément was better equipped and positioned than the Wise brothers to devise a plan to solve the inventory management problems, this is not enough. Therefore, in our opinion, the Wise brothers cannot successfully invoke the defence provided by s. 123(4) (*b*) of the CBCA but must rely on the other defences raised.

Notes

1   For a thoughtful critique of the lower court judgment in *Peoples* (which confused the duty of care and the duty of loyalty), see Edward M. Iacobucci, "A *Wise* Decision? An Analysis of the Relationship Between Share Ownership Structure and Directors' and Officers' Duties" (2002) 36 Can. Bus. L.J. 337.

2   The issue of environmental obligations of directors and officers is dealt with in *R. v. Bata Industries Ltd.* (1992), 9 O.R. (3d) 329 (Prov. Div.). In the yard of the defendant Bata Ltd.'s shoe factory, there was a large chemical waste storage site that stored several decaying, rusting and uncovered containers. Several of the containers held chemicals which were known carcinogens. The Court found that the storage of the containers and the disposal of their contents had been a matter of concern for interested persons for several years prior to

1989, when charges were brought against the company and three of its directors.

The directors were charged with failing to take all reasonable care to prevent a discharge contrary to s. 75(1) of the *Ontario Water Resources Act* and s. 147(a) of the *Environmental Protection Act*. Among other things, the directors argued that they could not be convicted under these sections, as they had met the prescribed due diligence standard. In his decision, Ormston Prov. Div. J. held that:

(a) The directors are responsible for reviewing the environmental compliance reports provided by the officers of the corporation, but are justified in placing reasonable reliance on reports provided to them by corporate officers, consultants, counsel or other informed parties.

(b) The directors should substantiate that the officers are promptly addressing environmental concerns brought to their attention by government agencies or other concerned parties including shareholders.

(c) The directors should be aware of the standards of their industry and other industries which deal with similar environmental pollutants or risks.

(d) The directors should immediately and personally react when they have notice the system has failed.

He exculpated one of the three directors, and convicted the other two. The exculpated director, Thomas G. Bata, was found to have little operational impact on the activities of the shoe factory, and acted appropriately and promptly when alerted to the environmental violations. The first convicted director, Douglas Marchant, was found to have knowledge of the violations six months before taking any action, and was held to have not acted in a timely or appropriate manner. The second convicted director, Keith Weston, was the on-site manager of the plant, and was found to have failed to discharge his duty to "walk-about" on a regular basis to ensure no violations occurred.

5.   THE SECURITIES REGULATORS' PUBLIC INTEREST DUTY OF CARE

One of the most important developments in the corporate law field in the past 30 years is the steadily increasing intrusion of the securities regulators into the corporate law domain. Thus, for example, takeover bids are regulated partly as a matter of corporate law and partly as a matter of securities law — although increasingly it is the activities of the securities regulators that are pivotal in contested takeover bids, rather than the courts. For example, in 2016, the Canadian Securities

Administrators (CSA) adopted a 50% mandatory minimum tender condition, and a 10-day extension period when certain bid conditions are met. However, regulators still take into account corporate statutes in creating rules. For example, in addition to the above changes, the CSA reduced the proposed 120-day minimum bid period to a 105-day period to accommodate compulsory acquisition provisions in corporate statutes that squeeze out non-tendering shareholders under certain circumstances. Ontario regulators have also promulgated detailed rules governing both "going private" and "related party" transactions — matters that traditionally fell within the corporate law domain. Perhaps most importantly, securities regulators have taken jurisdiction over a wide variety of corporate matters under the "public interest" powers. These powers are so-named because the securities regulators may exercise them when, in their opinion, they believe it is in the public interest to do so. Section 127 of the Ontario *Securities Act* (R.S.O. 1990, c. S.5) is typical and provides:

> 127 (1) The Commission may make one or more of the following orders if in its opinion it is in the public interest to make the order or orders:
>
> 1.   An order that the registration or recognition granted to a person or company under Ontario securities law be suspended or restricted for such period as is specified in the order or be terminated, or that terms and conditions be imposed on the registration or recognition.
>
> 2.   An order that trading in any securities by or of a person or company cease permanently or for such period as is specified in the order.
>
> 2.1   An order that the acquisition of any securities by a particular person or company is prohibited permanently or for the period specified in the order.
>
> 3.   An order that any exemptions contained in Ontario securities law do not apply to a person or company permanently or for such period as is specified in the order.
>
> 4.   An order that a market participant submit to a review of his, her or its practices and procedures and institute such changes as may be ordered by the Commission.
>
> 5.   If the Commission is satisfied that Ontario securities law has not been complied with, an order that a release, report, preliminary prospectus, prospectus, return, financial statement, information circular, take-over bid circular, issuer bid circular, offering memorandum, proxy solicitation or any other document described in the order,

     i.   be provided by a market participant to a person or company,

     ii. not be provided by a market participant to a person or company, or

     iii. be amended by a market participant to the extent that amendment is practicable.

6.   An order that a person or company be reprimanded.

7.   An order that a person resign one or more positions that the person holds as a director or officer of an issuer.

8.   An order that a person is prohibited from becoming or acting as a director or officer of any issuer.

8.1 An order that a person resign one or more positions that the persons holds as a director or officer of a registrant.

8.2 An order that a person is prohibited from becoming or acting as a director or officer of a registrant.

8.3 An order that a person resign one or more positions that the person holds as a director or officer of an investment fund manager.

8.4 An order that a person is prohibited from becoming or acting as a director or officer of an investment fund manager.

8.5 An order that a person or company is prohibited from becoming or acting as a registrant, as an investment fund manager or as a promoter.

9.   If a person or company has not complied with Ontario securities law, an order requiring the person or company to pay an administrative penalty of not more than $1 million for each failure to comply.

10. If a person or company has not complied with Ontario securities law, an order requiring the person or company to disgorge to the Commission any amounts obtained as a result of the non-compliance.

If staff believes that the public interest has been violated, then it may refer the matter to "the Commission" (a defined term that formally excludes the staff, and includes only the appointed Commissioners), who typically sit in panels of three. One of the most common sanctions meted out under the public interest powers is a "cease trade" order (s. 127(1)2), pursuant to which the Commission may effectively stop any transaction that involves trading of securities in its tracks. Another common sanction is a "denial of trading exemptions" (s. 127(1)3), which, when applied to individuals, means that those individuals cannot trade in their personal securities portfolios for the duration of the order. In the following case, a hearing was commenced to determine whether a denial of exemptions order should be made against the directors and officers of Standard Trustco for failing to disclose vital information to the public. Although the Commission might have framed the issue solely as one of a failure to carry out statutory disclosure obligations, it chose quite a different path, enunciating for the first time a "duty of care" that springs entirely from the regulators' public interest jurisdiction.

Standard Trustco Ltd., Re
(1992), 6 B.L.R. (2d) 241, 1992 CarswellOnt 140 (Securities Comm.)

[Standard Trustco was a holding company that held substantially all of the shares of Standard Trust ("Standard"), a trust company. Representatives of the Office of the Superintendent of Financial Institutions ("OSFI", the trust company federal regulator) had expressed extreme concerns to the board of Standard about its financial condition. Despite this, on July 24, 1990, the board summarily approved the release of a press release to the public (drafted by management) that completely glossed over the company's difficulties and failed to mention most of OSFI's serious concerns about the company's condition. The board also approved payment of the company's periodic dividend to shareholders. OSFI informed the Ontario Securities Commission (OSC) of what had taken place, and the OSC informed Standard that unless appropriate disclosure was forthcoming, it would issue a cease trade order barring all trading in Standard shares. OSFI also threatened to seize control of the company. A press release with appropriate disclosure was put out on July 27, indicating (*inter alia*) that the interim financial statements would be audited. This audit showed an enormous ($50 million) loss, as opposed to a $5 million profit as previously reported. Standard subsequently went into bankruptcy and was liquidated.

While the OSC did not, in 1992, have court-like powers (its powers have since been increased substantially), it did (and still does) have the power to make various orders "in the public interest" against participants in securities markets. One of these is a "denial of exemptions" order, pursuant to which individuals or companies are forbidden from trading any securities that they might own for a stated period of time. In this case, an OSC hearing was commenced to determine whether a denial of exemptions order should be made in respect of any of the directors and/or managers of Standard Trustco and Standard Trust. Note that a denial of exemptions order is a relatively trivial sanction — it merely prevents named persons from trading their personal portfolios of securities. However, at the time, it was the only sanction available to the OSC.

The decision in *Standard Trustco* marks a watershed in the application of the public interest powers. The usual threshold for the issuance of a public interest order is a finding that there has been some "abuse of the capital markets". In *Standard Trustco*, for the very first time, securities regulators suggested that in determining whether there had been such abuse, they would apply their very own "standard of care". As will be seen from the excerpts below, this standard of care may go beyond the standard of care that the courts have enunciated.]

ONTARIO SECURITIES COMMISSION:

Under the OBCA, directors and officers in exercising their powers and discharging their duties must act honestly and in good faith with a view to the best interests of the corporation and must exercise the care, diligence and skill that a reasonably prudent person would exercise in comparable circumstances. The standard set out in the LTCA [the *Ontario Loan and Trust Corporations Act*, to which Standard was also subject] is similar except that it substitutes "a reasonably prudent director or officer" for "a reasonably prudent person". In the commentary which accompanied the draft LTCA when it was released for consultation in 1985, it was noted that the "prudent director" test was intended to reflect a greater standard necessary for deposit-taking institutions.

In making our decision in this matter we had to go beyond considering whether the Respondents complied with the OBCA and the LTCA. We had to determine whether the conduct of the Respondents was contrary to the public interest.

Responsibility of Directors

(i)   General

As against the Respondent directors it was alleged that they acted contrary to the public interest on July 24, 1990 by voting to approve the Standard Trust unaudited interims and the issuance of the Standard Trustco unaudited interims without making appropriate inquiries in relation to the concerns of OSFI and its requirement for an audit. We believe that this, together with the allegation relating to the misleading press release, was the most serious allegation in this hearing.

Counsel for the Respondent directors submitted that it was appropriate for the directors to approve the financial statements of Standard Trustco and Standard Trust prepared by management as they did and to then have members of management, two of whom were also directors, seek the advice of the company's lawyer and auditor on whether disclosure should be made of OSFI's concerns and whether a note should be added to the financial statements. Counsel for the Respondent directors took the position that there was a basis for the directors to have confidence in management. We are of the opinion that, in relying on management to the extent they did and only taking the steps they did, the Respondent directors failed to exercise the kind of prudence and due diligence that they ought to have exercised, given the information they had about the financial condition of Standard Trust and Standard Trustco on July 24, 1990, and the seriousness of the concerns expressed by OSFI which were shared by CDIC. In reaching this conclusion, we have taken into account the fact that almost all of the directors, if not all, had backgrounds which suggested that they were a relatively sophisticated group. It was not appropriate in the circumstances for the Respondent directors to have placed as much reliance on management as they did, both in terms of relying on management's financial statements and relying on management to consult with the outside lawyer and auditor. Directors should not rely on management unquestioningly where they have reason to be concerned about the integrity or ability of management or where they have notice of a particular problem relating to management's activities. As of July 24, 1990, there was reason for the Respondent directors to question management. First, the Superintendent of Financial Institutions, Standard Trust's senior financial institution regulator, had taken the unusual step of attending a Standard Trust Board meeting together with the Chairman of CDIC and raised very serious concerns calling into serious question management's financial statements involving management's accounting policy and appraisals for which management was responsible.

Second, the Respondent directors were in possession of information on July 24, 1990, which, particularly when considered together with the concerns expressed by Mr. Mackenzie, should have caused them not to rely on management to the extent they did and to make further inquiries. . .

In our view, in the circumstances, it was incumbent upon all of the Respondent directors to make a number of inquiries directly of various people to obtain the necessary information and advice in order to satisfy themselves about the integrity of the interim financial statements before they made the decision to approve and issue the financial statements. We agree that the directors ought to have consulted the auditor and counsel. At the very least, the directors ought to have given management specific direction on the inquiries that were to be made of the outside lawyer and the auditor and insisted that management report back to the Boards with the results of the inquiries so that the Boards could then consider the advice and exercise their judgment on whether to issue the financial statements or make additional disclosure or make further inquiries. Given the seriousness of the issue at hand, the directors should not have felt that they could rely on advice provided by the outside lawyer and auditor to management, when the directors did not even hear or consider the advice prior to exercising their judgment with respect to the financial statements. In addition, the Boards ought to have made a number of other inquiries. Some such inquiries which occurred to us included making inquiries of OSFI and CDIC at the Standard Trust Board meeting; asking the Audit Committees what inquiries they made and discussions they had, particularly in light of their qualified recommendation to the Boards;

asking Mr. Hammond about the problems in the mortgage portfolio, such as questions relating to the level of arrears, the loan loss calculation, the loans to Owl Developments, the property appraisals and Standard Trust's experience in collecting on arrears; asking Mr. Howe about the appropriateness of the accrual policy and the reserves, particularly when at least some of the directors knew he had recently expressed some concern about those matters, and perhaps asking Mr. Howe about the accounting practices of other financial institutions; consulting with another accounting firm, for example about the accrual policy, in light of the fact that a longstanding policy which had been followed by the company and accepted by Peat Marwick was put in serious question; providing Mr. Smith or another outside corporate securities lawyer with complete background information and asking for advice relating to the materiality of OSFI's concerns and the course of action they should follow in respect of the financial statements from a legal perspective; asking Mr. Gray, the company's in-house lawyer, for his advice on the same legal matters; asking Mr. Seago whether he had reviewed OSFI's concerns and calculations and had an opinion on them in relation to management's calculations; and perhaps seeking advice from independent property appraisers, particularly in respect of the properties involving Owl Developments. The Boards should have considered having such people attend meetings of the Boards at which time the directors could have made the inquiries. In the circumstances, the directors should have also asked to see the press release which was to accompany the release of the financial highlights of Standard Trustco and should have reviewed it carefully to ensure that it was not misleading. . .

[NOTE: The respondents also argued that they could shelter behind OSFI, in two ways. First, OSFI did not specifically object to the release of the interim financial statements. Second, OSFI recommended that the board seek outside legal advice about their disclosure obligations, which they did. The OSC decided that a board is responsible for making its own decisions, and may not rely on those of the regulator.]

Counsel for the non-management directors argued that we should not make any finding against his clients because the Notice of Hearing does not specifically allege that they "authorized or permitted the issuance by Trustco of a press release which was materially misleading." He submitted that there was no nexus between the behaviour of his clients and the capital markets. We are of the view that the non-management directors knew or ought to have known that once they approved the subject financial statements a press release would be issued releasing the financial information. To put it another way, if the directors had not approved the financial statements on July 24, 1990, the misleading press release would not have been issued. We are therefore of the view that by approving the financial statements without making the appropriate inquiries they should bear some of the responsibility for the subsequent release of the misleading information to the public, which provided the nexus to the capital market. In addition, as we discussed, we believe that one of the inquiries they should have made was in relation to the contents of the press release.

As a result, we have found that the Respondent directors failed to exercise the care, diligence and skill that reasonably prudent persons would have exercised in comparable circumstances and that they acted contrary to the public interest on July 24, 1990, by voting to approve the Standard Trust and Standard Trustco unaudited interim financial statements without making appropriate inquiries in relation to the concerns of OSFI. We are of the view that their conduct was abusive of the capital markets.

(ii)   Responsibility of Audit Committee Members

[I]n our opinion the members of the Audit Committees should bear somewhat more responsibility than the other directors for what occurred at the Board meetings on July 24, 1990, not because there was a greater standard of care imposed on them, but rather because their circumstances were different. As members of the Audit Committees, they had a greater opportunity to obtain knowledge about and to examine the affairs of the company than non-members had. As a result, more was expected of them in respect of overseeing the financial reporting process and warning other directors about problems.

* * *

(iii)   Responsibility of Mrs. Roman-Barber [the Chairman of the Board of Directors of both Standard Trustco and Standard Trust] and Mr. O'Malley [the President, Chief Executive Officer and a director of Standard Trustco and Standard Trust]

Mrs. Roman-Barber and Mr. O'Malley should bear the greatest responsibility among the directors for what transpired on July 24, 1990 because, similar to the case of the members of the Audit Committees, their circumstances were different. First, they came to the meeting with more information than some of the other directors. For example, Mr. O'Malley was aware that MFI had been sufficiently concerned about the condition of Standard Trust that MFI had conducted an examination of Standard Trust in May, 1990. Mr. O'Malley and Mrs. Roman-Barber were both aware of the problems that Standard Trust and Standard Trustco were experiencing with their mortgage loans to Owl Developments. They had both also heard the concerns expressed by Mr. Di Giacomo after Manulife personnel had conducted a brief due diligence on Standard Trustco. Notwithstanding that Mr. O'Malley and Mrs. Roman-Barber had such additional information, they do not appear to have passed it on to the other directors.

Second, the evidence suggested that Mrs. Roman-Barber and Mr. O'Malley were largely in control of the Board meetings on July 24, 1990.

They both had responsibility for setting the order in which matters would be dealt with. Mr. O'Malley told the directors in essence that they should not question Mr. Mackenzie about his comments. Mrs. Roman-Barber terminated the meeting before there appeared to be a decision about what ought to be done in respect of an audit or releasing the financial statements. Also, Mrs. Roman-Barber did not propose that the Board reconvene after the lawyer and auditor were consulted or that the Board reconvene to make appropriate inquiries of others about the financial statements.

Third, Mr. O'Malley and Mrs. Roman-Barber appeared to be the ones who determined that the financial statements should be released on July 24, 1990.

(iv)   Responsibility of Outside Directors

Outside directors should play an important and effective role on a Board because of their separation and independence from management. They should ask questions of management and others in order to properly oversee the company's operations and disclosure, particularly where they have notice that the company may have serious financial problems. In some cases it is appropriate for outside directors to make inquiries and have discussions in the absence of management where they have a concern about something which management has done. In this case, the outside directors failed to fulfil their role.

Responsibility of Officers

We are of the view that the officers did not do all that they ought to have done in the circumstances. Notwithstanding that, with the exception of the conduct of Mr. O'Malley in issuing the press release, we were not satisfied that the evidence presented at the hearing was sufficient for us to find that the conduct of the officers in respect of the allegations against them was abusive of the capital markets such as to warrant our intervention.

Notes

1   Note that the Commission did not feel bound to cite any corporate law precedent at all in enunciating its public interest duty of care. Rather, it simply stated that the securities regulatory duty of care sprang from its jurisdiction to protect the public interest. In short, there are now *two* duties of care that practitioners must worry about — the corporate duty and the securities regulatory duty, which may or may not be the same. This is likely to create uncertainty for corporate legal advisors. This uncertainty is only exacerbated by the fact that, unlike a court, a securities regulatory tribunal is not subject to the doctrine of precedent. Thus, even if the Commission had cited

and followed applicable judicial authorities, it could subsequently depart from those standards.

2   The Commission's decision in *Standard Trustco* has been harshly criticized by Jeffrey MacIntosh ("Standard Trustco Case Signals Expansion of the 'Public Interest' Powers of Securities Regulators" (1993), 1 Corporate Financing 38). His concerns focus not only on the uncertainty that the case creates for corporate managers and their legal advisors, but on the manner in which *Standard Trustco* constitutes an unwarranted expansion of the Commission's public interest powers.

3   A series of recent cases illustrates contrasting approaches by the securities commissions of the different provinces in exercising their public interest duty of care power regarding a poison pill defence by a target board in response to a hostile takeover. A poison pill provides shareholders of a target company the opportunity to purchase shares of the company at a deeply discounted price when there is a hostile takeover offer for the company, making it impossible for the hostile bidder to obtain control. The policy rationale for regulating poison pills is to allow the target's board additional time to seek other bidders and increase shareholder value. However, pills can also be used to entrench self-interested management, contrary to the intent of the policy reasons behind a poison pill (Poonam Puri (Winter 2010/ 2011). There Oughta Be a Rule, *Listed Magazine*, 17).

The Alberta Securities Commission in *Pulse Data Inc., Re*, 2007 ABASC 895, 2007 CarswellAlta 1667 (Alta. Securities Comm.) and the Ontario Securities Commission in *Neo Material Technologies Inc., Re*, 2009 CarswellOnt 5084, 32 O.S.C.B. 6941 (Ont. Securities Comm.) both allowed a poison pill to remain indefinitely even though the directors of the respective corporations were not seeking a superior transaction for shareholders. The Ontario Securities Commission, in its reasons stated:

> As discussed above, in this case, Pala submits that the only proper use of a shareholder rights plan in the face of a take-over bid is to allow a board of directors sufficient time to seek out alternative bidders. Consistent with the Supreme Court's statements in *BCE* and the established body of corporate case law it is our view that, shareholder rights plans may be adopted for the broader purpose of protecting the long-term interests of the shareholders, where, in the directors' reasonable business judgment, the implementation of a rights plan would be in the best interests of the corporation.

The British Columbia Securities Commission followed a different approach in *Icahn Partners LP, et al., Re*, 2010 BCSECCOM 233 (B.C. S.C.). They held that a poison pill is only acceptable when used temporarily by directors in an attempt to maximize shareholder wealth in the face of a hostile takeover bid.

The different approaches are highlighted by the Ontario Securities Commission (OSC) in *Baffinland Iron Mines Corp., Re*, 33 OSCB 11385. The OSC stated that there is no one test or consideration that constitutes the "holy grail" when deciding whether a rights plan should remain in place or be cease traded. The decision depends on the specific facts and circumstances as to whether cease trading is in the public interest.

Which of the two approaches do you prefer? Should the regulation of poison pills and other defensive tactics be determined by securities regulators under the public interest power or by the courts? Professor Poonam Puri, *supra*, has argued in favour of reform in poison pill regulation.

* * *

The following case provides a recent example of the Ontario Securities Commission's treatment of the public interest power in the context of the elimination of a dual class share structure:

Magna International Inc., Re
2010 CarswellOnt 10322, 34 O.S.C.B. 1290 (Ont. Securities Comm.)

[A statement of allegations was brought by the Staff of the Ontario Securities Commission regarding a proposed plan of arrangement by Magna International Inc. Magna International had a dual class share structure; it consisted of 112,072,348 Class A subordinate voting shares carrying one vote per share, and 726,829 Class B shares owned entirely by the Stronach Trust that carried 300 votes per share. The Class B shares were not publically traded and represented 66% of the voting power of all shares. The Class A shares did not have a coattail provision attached to them (put in place for the protection of minority shareholders in change of control transactions), nor were there any "sunset" provisions that would terminate the control of the Class B shares after a specified period of time. Magna International proposed a plan of arrangement to eliminate its dual class of shares by having Magna International purchase the Class B shares and replace them with 9,000,000 newly issued Class A shares and $300 million, for a total consideration of approximately $860 million. The objective of the plan of arrangement was to create a single class of shares that would result in the shares being traded at a higher market value. Magna International sought to conduct a shareholder vote regarding the proposed transaction. Before the vote, the Ontario Securities Commission issued a notice of hearing alleging that the proposed transaction was against the public interest.]

The decision of the Ontario Securities Commission:

The Commission has jurisdiction under subsection 127(1) of the Act to intervene in a transaction where it concludes that it is in the public interest to do so *Re Canadian Tire*, supra at p. 29 (QL), *Re H.E.R.O.* and *Committee for Equal Treatment of Asbestos Minority Shareholders v. Ontario (Securities Commission)*, 2001 CarswellOnt 1959, 2001 CarswellOnt 1960, [2001] 2 S.C.R. 132 (S.C.C.) ("Asbestos") at para. 39 (SCC).

The Commission's public interest jurisdiction is animated by the purposes set out in subsection 1.1 of the Act, namely (i) to provide protection to investors from unfair, improper or fraudulent practices, and (ii) to foster fair and efficient capital markets and confidence in capital markets. As a result, the Commission must consider the fair treatment of investors, capital market efficiencies and public confidence in capital markets when exercising its public interest jurisdiction (*Asbestos*, supra at para. 41).

The Act states that these purposes are achieved by having regard to:

> requirements for timely, accurate and efficient disclosure of information; restrictions on fraudulent and unfair market practices and procedures; and requirements for the maintenance of high standards of fitness and business conduct to ensure honest and responsible conduct by market participants.

The Supreme Court of Canada has confirmed the Commission's broad jurisdiction to intervene on public interest grounds where doing so would further the purposes of the Act. However, the Court noted that the Commission's jurisdiction is constrained by the purposes of the Act and the regulatory nature of section 127. The primary purpose of an order under section 127 is to restrain future conduct that is likely to be prejudicial to the public interest in fair and efficient capital markets (*Asbestos*, supra at paras. 42, 43 and 45; see also *Patheon*, supra at para. 114).

The Commission has held that it is entitled to intervene on public interest grounds in conduct that is technically in compliance with securities law requirements but that is inconsistent with the animating principles underlying those requirements or is abusive of investors or the capital markets. The Commission may find conduct to be abusive if a proposed transaction is artificial and defeats the reasonable expectations of investors or shareholders (*Re Canadian Tire*, supra; *Re H.E.R.O.*, supra at p. 3776; *Financial Models Co., Re*, 2005 CarswellOnt 748, 28 OSCB 2184 (Ont. Securities Comm.) and *Patheon*, supra at para. 116).

The Commission recognized in *Re Canadian Tire* that it should act to restrain a transaction that is clearly abusive of shareholders and of the capital markets, whether or not that transaction constitutes or involves a breach of Ontario securities law. The Commission's mandate under section 127 is not, however, to intervene in transactions under some rubric of ensuring fairness. To invoke its public interest jurisdiction, in the absence of a demonstrated breach of securities law or the animating principles underlying that law, a transaction must be demonstrated to be abusive of shareholders in particular, or of the capital markets in general. A showing of abuse is something different from, and must go beyond, a complaint of unfairness (See *Re Canadian Tire*, supra and *Canfor Corp., Re*, 1995 CarswellOnt 385, 18 O.S.C.B. 475 (Ont. Securities Comm.) at p. 487 [O.S.C.B.]).

Analysis

While the Commission has a broad public interest jurisdiction, that jurisdiction must be exercised for appropriate regulatory purposes and with some caution and restraint. Where there is no breach of Ontario securities law, the Commission should generally act under its public interest jurisdiction only where there is conduct inconsistent with Ontario securities law or the animating principles underlying that law, or an abuse of shareholders or the capital markets. It was held in *Cablecasting Ltd., Re*, [1978] O.S.C.B. 37 (Ont. Securities Comm.) that the Commission will be less reluctant to exercise its public interest authority where the principle of a new policy ruling is foreshadowed by principles already enunciated under Ontario securities law or in existing policy statements. The Commission stated:

> Another relevant consideration in assessing whether to act against a particular transaction is whether the principle of the new policy ruling that would be required to deal with the transaction is foreshadowed by principles already enunciated in the Act, the regulations or prior policy statements. Where this is the case the Commission will be less reluctant to exercise its discretionary authority than it will be in cases that involve an entirely new principle.

In *Re Canadian Tire*, the issue before the Commission was whether a take-over bid that was made in compliance with applicable Ontario securities law was nonetheless abusive of shareholders and the capital markets. In *Re Canadian Tire*, the transaction was structured by an offeror to avoid triggering a coat-tail provision for the benefit of the holders of Class A non-voting shares of Canadian Tire Corporation, Limited ("Canadian Tire"), while paying a huge control premium for the common shares of Canadian Tire. The Commission found that the transaction was grossly abusive of shareholders and should be cease traded in the public interest.

In our view, the key finding in *Re Canadian Tire* was that the public holders of Class A non-voting shares of Canadian Tire had a reasonable expectation, as a result of the coat-tail protection contained in Canadian Tire's articles, that they would share in any control premium being paid for the common shares. That reasonable expectation was being frustrated by an artificial transaction structured specifically to avoid triggering the coat-tail protection. The holders of common shares, including the controlling shareholders of Canadian Tire, were receiving an offer for their shares at a huge premium to the market price of those shares. Public holders of Class A non-voting shares were not receiving any offer for their shares and they were not being given any right to vote on or approve the offer made to the holders of common shares. In those circumstances, the Commission concluded that the offer being made to the holders of common shares was grossly abusive, undermined confidence in the capital markets and should be restrained.

The circumstances before us in this matter were quite different. There was no "coat-tail" protection available to the Class A Shareholders and there was no sunset provision applicable to Magna's dual class share structure. As a result, the Stronach Trust was legally entitled to sell its Class B Shares to any purchaser at whatever price it negotiated. Holders of Subordinate Voting Shares knew when they purchased their shares that they had no right to participate in any such offer (see paragraph 66 of these reasons for an example of the public disclosure made in this respect). As a result, in our view, the Class A Shareholders had no reasonable expectation that they would share in any control premium being paid for the Class B Shares. In addition, and most importantly, the Class A Shareholders were being given the right to vote on and approve the Proposed Transaction. There is a financial rationale why the Class A Shareholders might wish to vote in favour of that transaction. If Class A Shareholders did not vote to approve the Proposed Transaction, it would not proceed.

If approval by a majority vote of the minority Class A Shareholders had not been a requirement for proceeding with the Proposed Transaction, we have little doubt that we would have restrained it as an abusive related party transaction.

It seemed to us that the primary complaint of the Opposing Shareholders was that the price proposed to be paid by Magna to the Stronach Trust for the Class B Shares was excessive and unprecedented. In our view, a transaction is not abusive simply because certain investors or shareholders consider the price proposed to be paid to be outrageous. There are other Class A Shareholders who see the financial benefits to them of the Proposed Transaction and support proceeding with it. It is not our role as securities regulators to assess the desirability of the Proposed Transaction from a financial or economic standpoint. That is ultimately for the Class A Shareholders to determine.

The Class A Shareholders will suffer the dilution from the Proposed Transaction and will have some portion of the potential benefits arising from it. In our view, the Class A Shareholders should be entitled to decide for themselves whether the Proposed Transaction proceeds. They will make that decision through the proposed majority of the minority shareholder vote.

Accordingly, in our view, once the issue of adequate disclosure was addressed, there were no valid grounds for us to conclude in the circumstances that the Proposed Transaction was abusive of Class A Shareholders or should be restrained on other grounds. It is clear from Commission decisions that any view or perception that we may have as to the possible unfairness of a transaction is not a sufficient ground upon which we can or should intervene in the public interest.

All of the Class A Shareholders would have no doubt preferred that the Stronach Trust sell its Class B Shares to Magna at a lower price. However, such a transaction does not appear to have been available. A controlling shareholder is entitled to decide whether and on what terms it is prepared to sell its control block (see *Benson v. Third Canadian General Investment Trust Ltd.*, 1993 CarswellOnt 166, 14 O.R. (3d) 493 (Ont. Gen. Div. [Commercial List])). The Court concluded in that case that:

> The AGF bid stirred up the pot and got some (and possibly many) shareholders drooling for an opportunistic one-time value bump. However, this dessert was not on the menu. . .

We would simply add for clarity that we should not be taken to be suggesting that shareholder approval can remedy a transaction or circumstances that are abusive of shareholders or the capital markets. To the contrary, if a transaction is abusive, then shareholder approval will not be sufficient.

Conclusion

Based on the evidence before us, and given the requirement for majority of the minority Class A Shareholder approval of the Proposed Transaction, we were not persuaded that the Proposed Transaction was abusive or that we should intervene in the public interest on other grounds.

Note

Nonetheless, the Ontario Securities Commission did not allow the proposed transaction on the basis that the disclosure provided by Magna to its shareholders regarding the transaction was inadequate. Do you agree with the decision of the Ontario Securities Commission? Was the ability of the shareholders to vote on the transaction the primary consideration? What is the appropriate role of independent directors in a situation like this, where the corporation is a controlled corporation? What are the boundaries for securities regulators? Are they inappropriately encroaching into the territory of corporate law regulators? For a further discussion, see *infra* Chapter 6.

6. THE EXPLOSIVE EXPANSION OF STATUTORY DUTIES FOR DIRECTORS

In addition to some of the liabilities sketched out above, there are hundreds of Canadian statutes that impose liabilities of one kind or another on directors. This proliferation of liabilities has been harshly criticized for the deleterious impact that they have on board decision-making, particularly when companies are in the vicinity of insolvency. In 1992, in two notorious cases, the directors of two financially distressed companies, Westar Mining Ltd. and Canadian Airlines International Ltd., resigned *en masse* in order to avoid exposure to employee related financial liabilities (see the following section). In the following article, Daniels and Morgan voiced concern with the proliferation of legislated liability on the operation of the Canadian system of corporate governance.

Ron Daniels and Ed Morgan
"Directors Face Grab-Bag of Liabilities"
(Financial Post, August 12, 1992, at 40)

In the past decade, directors have been made personally liable for corporate misdeeds under a wide range of legislation. By one lawyer's count, more than 106 different federal and provincial statutes, covering subjects as diverse as environmental protection and funeral services, impose civil and criminal liability on the boards of companies operating within Ontario. Significantly, these liabilities seldom work to ensure director fidelity to shareholder interest, but focus on aligning the efforts of directors with other, broader societal goals.

The sheer volume of law undermines the traditional legal assumption that individuals appointed to corporate boards "know the law" prior to or even after their election. The orgy of legislative activity also does violence to the standard model of corporate governance. Because these statutes foist liability on directors for not preventing certain types of corporate action for instance, failure to remit various corporate taxes, or the discharge of environmental waste, directors are forced to abandon their traditional advisory role in favour of another, more alien role that insinuates them deeply into day-to-day corporate operations.

For instance, under the *British Columbia Employment Standards Act*, directors are responsible not only for wages owing to employees, but for severance benefits as well. It is one thing to make directors oversee the prompt payment of wages for services currently provided to the corporation; it is quite another to insist that directors be able to predict the likelihood of massive future terminations, and then to secure the creation of a treasure trove to meet these obligations.

Another difficulty with the grab-bag of liabilities imposed on directors is the tension which all of this creates with the liberal notion that individuals be held accountable only for their own wrongs. The erosion of any causal relationship between liability and individual responsibility is found in the courts' evisceration of the statutory due-diligence defence.

A final problem is the difficulties directors face in securing insurance. Like other specialized lines of insurance, directors and officers liability insurance is subject to fluctuations in capacity that make it hard for companies to assure directors they will be protected for as long as they serve.

Even if a policy can be obtained, D&O insurers frequently exclude coverage for these non-corporate law risks. For instance, the Wyatt Company's 1987 survey on Canadian D&O insurance reported that 91% of the policies excluded coverage for pollution and environmental damage, while 17% excluded coverage for actions taken by regulatory agencies.

Given these insurance, limits, liability-shy individuals invited to serve on corporate boards are left with two basic options: Either decline the invitation or insist as a precondition of appointment that the company agree to refrain from any activity — no matter how productive or worthwhile — that risks inviting some liability.

What accounts for the continued allegiance of legislatures to the statutory liability device? One argument is that conventional forms of liability that are imposed directly on the corporation itself and the actual wrongdoers just don't do the trick. Consequently, innocent bystanders must be enlisted in the crusade against corporate wrongs.

If so, the legislature must show there is a lot of undeterred corporate wrongdoing going on in society, and this wrongdoing derives from defects in quaint systems of fault-based liability.

Legislatures would no doubt be hard-pressed to do so. Indeed, this proliferation of liability likely is an attempt to off-load many of the core responsibilities of the modern welfare system onto the backs and into the pockets of directors.

If a legislature decides that corporations should have greater responsibility for the impact of their activities on the environment, shouldn't it be the legislature that establishes and pays for the monitoring necessary to enforce these goals? Similarly, if the legislature determines that workers dislocated by industrial decline should receive compensation or retraining assistance, then shouldn't the funds for such programs be paid from the consolidated revenue fund, not from the consolidated personal assets of directors and their families?

Ultimately, if the limited liability corporation is to continue to serve as our primary engine of wealth creation, making possible the rich range of social welfare programs to which we are accustomed, legislatures are going to have to signal a retreat from their addiction to unconstrained directorial liability. Otherwise, in our zeal to expand the social welfare agenda and clean up corporate wrong, we will continue to risk tossing out the board with the legislative bath.

Notes

1   A more academic treatment of the effect of legislated liabilities on Canadian corporate governance is provided in R. J. Daniels: "Must Boards Go Overboard?: An Economic Analysis of the Effects of Burgeoning Statutory Liability on the Role of Directors in Corporate Governance", (1994) 24 Can. Bus. L.J. 229.

2   In 1993, in response to mounting concern over the quality of the Canadian corporate governance regime, the Toronto Stock Exchange established a committee to consider corporate governance issues. The committee was headed by former Ontario Securities Commission Chair Peter Dey. In 1994, the committee published its final report, "Where Were the Directors?". Among other matters, the report expressed concern with the growth of legislated directorial liabilities, especially those employee related liabilities that did not provide a due diligence defence. The committee called for a comprehensive governmental review of statutory liability provisions in order to ensure their necessity and effectiveness. The call to action was taken up by federal corporate regulators in their review of the CBCA, culminating in the introduction of a number of due diligence defences for what had before been offences of absolute liability.

7.   OTHER STATUTORY DIRECTOR LIABILITIES IN CORPORATE LAW

Directors are subject to a variety of liabilities in corporate law other than the duty of loyalty (CBCA s. 122(1)(a), OBCA s. 134(1)(a)) and duty of care (CBCA s. 122(1)(b), OBCA s. 134(1)(b)). In particular, CBCA s. 118(1) and OBCA s. 130(1) make directors liable when the corporation sells shares for consideration other than money, "to make good any amount by which the consideration received is less than the fair equivalent of the money that the corporation would have received if the share had been issued for money on the date of the resolution". CBCA s. 118(2) (and OBCA s. 130(2)) prescribe further liabilities relating to various wrongful corporate payments. CBCA, s. 119 (OBCA, s. 131) renders directors jointly and severally liable to employees for all debts not exceeding six months' wages payable to each such employee for services performed for the corporation while they serve as directors. In order to bring a claim against directors, employees must have first obtained judgment against the corporation or have proved a claim against it. If this judgment or claim is not satisfied in full, then the employee is entitled to sue the directors personally for the amount of the shortfall. In the case of the CBCA, suit must be initiated against the directors within two years of the time that the director ceased to serve the corporation (s. 119(3)).

These sections are further explored in *Englefield v. Wolf*, 33 B.L.R. (4th) 288, 2006 CarswellOnt 1962.

You will note that both CBCA s. 118(6) and OBCA s. 130(6) allow the director to escape liability by proving that he "did not know and could not reasonably have known that the share was issued for a consideration less than the fair equivalent of the money that the corporation would have received if the share had been issued for money".

In addition, however, pursuant to the most recent round of amendments to the CBCA, directors have been given a due diligence defence with respect to all of the s. 118 and s. 119 liabilities in addition to the pre-existing statutory defence of reliance on financial statements or expert reports (see CBCA s. 123(4)). The OBCA has followed the same wording in regards to a reasonable diligence defence with respect to s. 130 (see OBCA s. 135(4)).

8.   THE BUSINESS JUDGMENT RULE

In the United States, the duty of care standard has been subject to judicial modification by the so-called "business judgment rule". The rule may be stated as follows: When there is no evidence of fraud, illegality or conflict of interest in respect of a given corporate action involving business judgment, the directors are *presumed* to have acted in good faith and on a reasonable basis (*Shlensky v. Wrigley*, 95 Ill. App. 2d 173, 237 N.E.2d 776 (1968)). Thus, there will be no liability for breach of *either* the duty of loyalty (CBCA s. 122(1)(a)) or the duty of care (CBCA s. 122(1)(b)). It is important to note some common confusion that surrounds the business judgment rule. The correct way of stating the US rule is as an *onus* shifting device, and not a *burden* shifting device. The onus of proof determines who must prove their case — the plaintiff or the defence. Thus, in a civil case, the onus of proof is usually on the plaintiff. The burden of proof, on the other hand, describes the height of the evidentiary hurdle that the plaintiff must surmount to succeed. In a civil case, this is a balance of probabilities. By contrast, in a criminal case, the Crown must prove its allegations beyond a reasonable doubt. Under the US business judgment rule, the rule *shifts* the onus to the plaintiff and off the shoulders of the directors, tempering prior law stating that there is an onus on a person accused of having been a faithless fiduciary to demonstrate the entire fairness of the transaction. However, if the plaintiff can show some evidence of fraud, illegality, or conflict of interest, then under the US rule the onus of proof shifts onto the shoulders of the fiduciaries to demonstrate the entire fairness of the transaction.

By contrast, in Canada the initial onus of proof is *always* on the plaintiff. Thus, there is no need to shift the initial onus of proof off the shoulders of the directors. However, the question still remains whether the onus ought to shift onto the shoulders of the directors once the plaintiff has adduced evidence sufficient to raise an issue of fraud, illegality, or conflict of interest. The excerpt from *Schneider*, below, suggests that there will be *no* onus shifting (although the excerpt from *Brant* suggests that, as a practical matter, it may not make any difference). Thus, lacking the onus-shifting feature of the US "business judgment rule", the Canadian rule is somewhat *sui generis*.

In addition, you will note that the business judgment rule fuses the duty of care and the duty of loyalty. It gives directors a presumption of having acted in good faith and with due care. We will return to the business judgment rule in Chapter 6, and examine a special variant of the rule that applies in the context of takeover bids.

With respect to the US case of *Smith v. Van Gorkum*, note the emphasis that the court places on the *procedures* by which the decision was arrived at. This case is emblematic of one of the more important changes in corporate law jurisprudence in the past several decades — namely, the proceduralization of the duties of loyalty and care. That is, if all appropriate procedures are taken in corporate decision-making — and, in particular, referring the matter to an independent committee of the board, securing an outside valuation or other professional outside advice, and making sure that the board wrings its hands for a sufficient amount of time — liability becomes unlikely.

The basis for the business judgment rule is clear: the courts are reluctant to engage in extensive *ex post facto* review of the substantive merits of judgments made by directors. This reluctance is rooted in the concern that an environment characterized by the prospect of judicial "second-guessing" is inhospitable to effective business decision-making. Basically, obtrusive judicial scrutiny of decisions made in good faith by a board of directors is deemed inimical to the models of corporate governance upon which corporate law is constructed.

Why is judicial scrutiny of substantive decisions so incompatible with effective corporate governance? The most obvious concern is the gulf between the nature of managerial and judicial decision-making, and the implications of this divergence upon the institutional competence of the judiciary to undertake meaningful review of business decisions. Because there is no strong *a priori* basis for believing that the courts will be better able than the directors to make decisions that are in the best interests of the corporation, the role of the judiciary in reviewing complex business judgments, which are themselves the culmination of a host of complex judgments, is highly suspect. Even a seemingly straightforward judgment to expand a corporation's line of business into a new market may, in fact, be the culmination of a myriad discrete judgments regarding the capacity of the corporation to produce and market a new product, the anticipated reaction of rival corporations to the new product, the expected response of consumers to the new product, and the likely impact of macro-economic variables on the strength of market demand. In this respect, it is difficult to make a strong case that judges, with their background in legal analysis, are able to effectively assimilate the kinds of detail involved in a given business decision, and then to arrive at a decision that is clearly superior to the one generated by the directors.

But even if the judiciary were able to effectively evaluate the substantive merits of decisions made by directors, it is still not clear that they should do so. This is because of the inherent unfairness to directors that may result from *ex post* evaluation of *ex ante* decisions. Hindsight is twenty-twenty, and there is the danger that courts will dismiss the very real constraints that beset the process of business decision-making in reviewing directorial competence. Business decisions are, by their very nature, made in an environment where less-than-optimal information and time is available to decision-makers. In this environment of constrained decision-making, there is the real possibility that business decisions may be adopted that will, in time, prove to have been deeply flawed. Nevertheless, the fact that these decisions generate disappointing results does not necessarily implicate the legitimacy or the integrity of the decision-making that generated them. Whether courts are able to muster the expertise and sensitivity that will allow them effectively to simulate the impact of the constraints that impaired managerial foresight at the time that a decision was made is extremely unlikely. And, even if they could, how could judges possibly evaluate the appropriateness of *ex ante* decisions, given the inherent tradeoffs that have to be made by directors in choosing between risk and return? It is simply inconceivable that a court is equipped to decide whether a director is correct in selecting between two competing projects, one of which has a greater expected value and risk than the other. To say that a director erred in selecting either one of the projects is implicitly to impose a risk-return criterion on business decision-making that possesses only tenuous force.

Finally, apart from the capacity of courts to "second-guess" business judgments, it is clear that any dilution of the business judgment rule will have the effect of substantially increasing the level of care that directors must meet. This, in turn, will, because of the increased risk of personal liability, dissuade some directors from accepting board positions, and will deprive shareholders of the talents and experience of qualified individuals.

Smith v. Van Gorkom
488 A.2d 858 (Del. S.C. 1985)

[Van Gorkom was the Chairman of Trans Union. Trans Union was entitled to certain tax credits and deductions under US tax law, but did not have enough income to take full advantage of them. In August, 1980, Trans Union's board of directors began to consider the sale of the company to a purchaser who had enough income to take advantage of Trans Union's deductions. Donald Romans, Chief Financial Officer for Trans Union, reported to the board that a rough feasibility investigation he had done as to whether a leveraged buy-out of Trans Union was possible suggested a price of $50 or $60 per share. Van Gorkom remarked that he would be willing to take $55 for his shares.

In September, Van Gorkom approached Pritzker, a corporate takeover specialist, to interest him in buying Trans Union for $55 per share. On September 18, Pritzker agreed to make such an offer. Trans Union's shares had a market value at the time of $37.25. On September 20, Van Gorkom met with Trans Union's senior management, of whom only two supported the takeover proposal. Nonetheless, Van Gorkom took the proposal to a meeting of Trans Union's directors the same day. He gave a twenty-minute presentation on the proposal, but did not explain how the figure of $55 per share had been arrived at. Copies of the drafted Merger Agreement arrived too late for the directors to study them. Romans explained to the board how he had looked at $50 and $60, and later $55 and $65, to see if a leveraged buy-out could be arranged at those prices, but that this did not amount to a valuation of the company. However, he told the board that $55 per share was in the fair price range, although at the beginning of it. Trans Union's attorney advised the board that they might be sued if they turned down Pritzker's offer, and that a fairness letter from an investment banker was not required by law for them to accept the offer. After two hours, the board approved the proposed Merger Agreement.

Five of Trans Union's directors were "inside" directors and five were "outside" directors. Of the five outside directors, four were corporate chief executive officers and one was the former Dean of the University of Chicago Business School.

The majority of the Court found that the directors did not act in an informed manner and could not be protected by the business judgment rule. The following excerpts deal with the actions of the directors at the meeting of September 20]

HORSEY, JUSTICE (for the majority): We turn to the issue of the application of the business judgment rule to the September 20 meeting of the Board.

The Court of Chancery concluded from the evidence that the Board of Directors' approval of the Pritzker merger proposal fell within the protection of the business judgment rule. The Court found that the Board had given sufficient time and attention to the transaction, since the directors had considered the Pritzker proposal on three different occasions, on September 20, and on October 8, 1980 and finally on January 26, 1981. On that basis, the Court reasoned that the Board had acquired, over the four-month period, sufficient information to reach an informed business judgment on the cash-out merger proposal. The Court ruled:

> that given the market value of Trans Union's stock, the business acumen of the members of the board of Trans Union, the substantial

premium over market offered by the Pritzkers and the ultimate effect on the merger price provided by the prospect of other bids for the stock in question, that the board of directors of Trans Union did not act recklessly or improvidently in determining on a course of action which they believed to be in the best interest of the stockholders of Trans Union.

* * *

Under Delaware law, the business judgment rule is the offspring of the fundamental principle, codified in 8 Del.C. §14(a), that the business and affairs of a Delaware corporation are managed by or under its board of directors. . .

In carrying out their managerial roles, directors are charged with an unyielding fiduciary duty to the corporation and its shareholders. *Loft, Inc. v. Guth*, Del.Ch., 2 A.2d 225 (1938), aff'd. Del.Supr., 5 A.2d 503 (1939). The business judgment rule exists to protect and promote the full and free exercise of the managerial power granted to Delaware directors. *Zapata Corp. v. Maldonado, supra* at 782. The rule itself "is a presumption that in making a business decision, the directors of a corporation acted on an informed basis, in good faith and in the honest belief that the action taken was in the best interests of the company." *Aronson, supra* at 812. Thus, the party attacking a board decision as uninformed must rebut the presumption that its business judgment was an informed one. *Id.*

The determination of whether a business judgment is an informed one turns on whether the directors have informed themselves "prior to making a business decision, of all material information reasonably available to them." *Id.*

Under the business judgment rule there is no protection for directors who have made "an unintelligent or unadvised judgment." *Mitchell v. Highland-Western Glass*, Del.Ch., 167 A. 831, 833 (1933). A director's duty to inform himself in preparation for a decision derives from the fiduciary capacity in which he serves the corporation and its stockholders. *Lutz v. Boas*, Del.Ch., 171 A.2d 381 (1961). See *Weinberger v. UOP, Inc., supra*; *Guth v. Loft, supra*. Since a director is vested with the responsibility for the management of the affairs of the corporation, he must execute that duty with the recognition that he acts on behalf of others. Such obligation does not tolerate faithlessness or self-dealing. But fulfillment of the fiduciary function requires more than the mere absence of bad faith or fraud. Representation of the financial interests of others imposes on a director an affirmative duty to protect those interests and to proceed with a critical eye in assessing information of the type and under the circumstances present here.

* * *

Thus, a director's duty to exercise an informed business judgment is in the nature of a duty of care, as distinguished from a duty of loyalty. Here, there were no allegations of fraud, bad faith, or self dealing, or proof thereof. Hence, it is presumed that the directors reached their business judgment in good faith, *Allaun v. Consolidated Oil Co.*, Del.Ch., 147 A. 257 (1929), and considerations of motive are irrelevant to the issue before us.

The standard of care applicable to a director's duty of care has also been recently restated by this Court. In *Aronson, supra*, we stated:

> While the Delaware cases use a variety of terms to describe the applicable standard of care, our analysis satisfies us that under the business judgment rule director liability is predicated upon concepts of gross negligence. (footnote omitted)

We again confirm that view. We think the concept of gross negligence is also the proper standard for determining whether a business judgment reached by a board of directors was an informed one.

In the specific context of a proposed merger of domestic corporations, a director has a duty under 8 Del.C. 251(b), along with his fellow directors, to act in an informed and deliberate manner in determining whether to approve an agreement of merger before submitting the proposal to the stockholders. Certainly in the merger context, a director may not abdicate that duty by leaving to the shareholders alone the decision to approve or disapprove the agreement. See *Beard v. Elster*, Del.Supr., 160 A.2d 731, 737 (1960). Only an agreement of merger satisfying the requirements of 8 Del.C. §251(b) may be submitted to the shareholders under §251(c) . . .

It is against those standards that the conduct of the directors of Trans Union must be tested, as a matter of law and as a matter of fact, regarding their exercise of an informed business judgment in voting to approve the Pritzker merger proposal.

* * *

The issue of whether the directors reached an informed decision to "sell" the Company on September 20, 1980 must be determined only upon the basis of the information then reasonably available to the directors and relevant to their decision to accept the Pritzker merger proposal. This is not to say that the directors were precluded from altering their original plan of action, had they done so in an informed manner. What we do say is that the question of whether the directors reached an informed business judgment in agreeing to sell the Company, pursuant to the terms of the September 20 Agreement presents, in reality, two questions: (A) whether the directors reached an informed business judgment on September 20, 1980; and (B) if they did not, whether the directors' actions taken subsequent to September 20 were adequate to cure any infirmity in their action taken on September 20. We first consider the directors' September 20 action in terms of their reaching an informed business judgment.

On the record before us, we must conclude that the Board of Directors did not reach an informed business judgment on September 20, 1980 in voting to "sell" the Company for $55 per share pursuant to the Pritzker cash-out merger proposal. Our reasons, in summary, are as follows:

The directors (1) did not adequately inform themselves as to Van Gorkom's role in forcing the "sale" of the Company and in establishing the per share purchase price; (2) were uninformed as to the intrinsic value of the Company; and (3) given these circumstances, at a minimum, were grossly negligent in approving the "sale" of the Company upon two hours' consideration, without prior notice, and without the exigency of a crisis or emergency.

As has been noted, the Board based its September 20 decision to approve the cash-out merger primarily on Van Gorkom's representations. None of the directors, other than Van Gorkom and Chelberg, had any prior knowledge that the purpose of the meeting was to propose a cash-out merger of Trans Union. No members of Senior Management were present, other than Chelberg, Romans and Peterson; and the latter two had only learned of the proposed sale an hour earlier. Both general counsel Moore and former general counsel Browder attended the meeting, but were equally uninformed as to the purpose of the meeting and the documents to be acted upon.

Without any documents before them concerning the proposed transaction, the members of the Board were required to rely entirely upon Van Gorkom's 20-minute oral presentation of the proposal. No written summary of the terms of the merger was presented; the directors were given no documentation to support the adequacy of $55 price per share for sale of the Company; and the Board had before it nothing more than Van Gorkom's statement of his understanding of the substance of an agreement which he admittedly had never read, nor which any member of the Board had ever seen.

Under 8 Del.C. §141(e), "directors are fully protected in relying in good faith on reports made by officers." . . .

The term "report" has been liberally construed to include reports of informal personal investigations by corporate officers, *Cheff v. Mathes*, Del.Supr., 199 A.2d 548, 556 (1964). However, there is no evidence that any "report," as defined under §141(e), concerning the Pritzker proposal, was presented to the Board on September 20. Van Gorkom's oral presentation of his understanding of the terms of the proposed Merger Agreement, which he had not seen, and Romans' brief oral statement of his preliminary study regarding the feasibility of a leveraged buy-out of Trans Union do not qualify as §141(e) "reports" for these reasons: The former lacked substance because Van Gorkom was basically uninformed as to the essential provisions of the very document about which he was talking. Romans' statement was irrelevant to the issues before the Board since it did not purport to be a valuation study. At a minimum for a report to enjoy the status conferred by §141(e), it must be pertinent to the subject matter upon which a board is called to act, and otherwise be entitled to good faith, not blind, reliance. Considering all of the surrounding circumstances — hastily calling the meeting without prior notice of its subject matter, the proposed sale of the Company without any prior consideration of the issue or necessity therefor, the urgent time constraints imposed by Pritzker, and the total absence of any documentation whatsoever — the directors were duty bound to make reasonable inquiry of Van Gorkom and Romans, and if they had done so, the inadequacy of that upon which they now claim to have relied would have been apparent.

The defendants rely on the following factors to sustain the Trial Court's finding that the Board's decision was an informed one: (1) the magnitude of the premium or spread between the $55 Pritzker offering price and Trans Union's current market price of $38 per share: . . . (3) the collective experience and expertise of the Board's "inside" and "outside" directors; and (4) their reliance on Brennan's legal advice that the directors might be sued if they rejected the Pritzker proposal. We discuss each of these grounds *seriatim*:

(1)

A substantial premium may provide one reason to recommend a merger, but in the absence of other sound valuation information, the fact of a premium alone does not provide an adequate basis upon which to assess the fairness of an offering price. Here, the judgment reached as to the adequacy of the premium was based on a comparison between the historically depressed Trans Union market price and the amount of the Pritzker offer. Using market price as a basis for concluding that the premium adequately reflected the true value of the Company was a clearly faulty, indeed fallacious, premise, as the defendants' own evidence demonstrates.

The record is clear that before September 20, Van Gorkom and other members of Trans Union's Board knew that the market had consistently undervalued the worth of Trans Union's stock, despite steady increases in the Company's operating income in the seven years preceding the merger. The Board related this occurrence in large part to Trans Union's inability to use its ITCs as previously noted. Van Gorkom testified that he did not believe the market price accurately reflected Trans Union's true worth; and several of the directors testified that, as a general rule, most chief executives think that the market undervalues their companies' stock. Yet, on September 20, Trans Union's Board apparently believed that the market stock price accurately reflected the value of the Company for the purpose of determining the adequacy of the premium for its sale.

In the Proxy Statement, however, the directors reversed their position. There, they stated that, although the earnings prospects for Trans Union were "excellent," they found no basis for believing that this would be reflected in future stock prices. With regard to past trading, the Board stated that the prices at which the Company's common stock had traded in recent years did not reflect the "inherent" value of the Company. But having referred to the "inherent" value of Trans Union, the directors ascribed no number to it. Moreover, nowhere did they disclose that they had no basis on which to fix "inherent" worth beyond an impressionistic reaction to the premium over market and an unsubstantiated belief that the value of the assets was "significantly greater" than book value. By their own admission they could not rely on the stock price as an accurate measure of value. Yet, also by their own admission, the Board members assumed that Trans Union's market price was adequate to serve as a basis upon which to assess the adequacy of the premium for purposes of the September 20 meeting.

* * *

Indeed, as of September 20, the Board had no other information on which to base a determination of the intrinsic value of Trans Union as a going concern. As of September 20, the Board had made no evaluation of the Company designed to value the entire enterprise, nor had the Board ever previously considered selling the Company or consenting to a buy-out merger. Thus, the adequacy of a premium is indeterminate unless it is assessed in terms of other competent and sound valuation information that reflects the value of the particular business.

Despite the foregoing facts and circumstances, there was no call by the Board, either on September 20 or thereafter, for any valuation study or documentation of the $55 price per share as a measure of the fair value of the Company in a cash-out context. It is undisputed that the major asset of Trans Union was its cash flow. Yet, at no time did the Board call for a valuation study taking into account that highly significant element of the Company's assets.

* * *

Here, the record establishes that the Board did not request its Chief Financial Officer, Romans, to make any valuation study or review of the proposal to determine the adequacy of $55 per share for sale of the Company. On the record before us: The Board rested on Romans' elicited response that the $55 figure was within a "fair price range" within the context of a leveraged buyout. No director sought any further information from Romans. No director asked him why he put $55 at the bottom of his range. No director asked Romans for any details as to his study, the reason why it had been undertaken or its depth. No director asked to see the study; and no director asked Romans whether Trans Union's finance department could do a fairness study within the remaining 36-hour period available under the Pritzker offer.

Had the Board, or any member, made an inquiry of Romans, he presumably would have responded as he testified: that his calculations were rough and preliminary; and, that the study was not designed to determine the fair value of the Company, but rather to assess the feasibility of a leveraged buy-out financed by the Company's projected cash flow, making certain assumptions as to the purchaser's borrowing needs. Romans would have presumably also informed the Board of his view, and the widespread view of Senior Management, that the timing of the offer was wrong and the offer inadequate.

The record also establishes that the Board accepted without scrutiny Van Gorkom's representation as to the fairness of the $55 price per share for sale of the Company — a subject that the Board had never previously considered. The Board thereby failed to discover that Van Gorkom had suggested the $55 price to Pritzker and, most crucially, that Van Gorkom had arrived at the $55 figure based on calculations designed solely to determine the feasibility of a leveraged buy-out. No questions were raised either as to the tax implications of a cash-out merger or how the price for the one million share option granted Pritzker was calculated.

We do not say that the Board of Directors was not entitled to give some credence to Van Gorkom's representation that $55 was an adequate or fair price. Under §141(e), the directors were entitled to rely upon their chairman's opinion of value and adequacy, provided that such opinion was reached on a sound basis. Here, the issue is whether the directors informed themselves as to all information that was reasonably available to them. Had they done so, they would have learned of the source and derivation of the $55 price and could not reasonably have relied thereupon in good faith.

None of the directors, Management or outside, were investment bankers or financial analysts. Yet the Board did not consider recessing the meeting until a later hour that day (or requesting an extension of Pritzker's Sunday evening deadline) to give it time to elicit more information as to the sufficiency of the offer, either from inside Management (in particular Romans) or from Trans Union's own investment banker, Salomon Brothers, whose Chicago specialist in merger and acquisitions was known to the Board and familiar with Trans Union's affairs.

Thus, the record compels the conclusion that on September 20 the Board lacked valuation information adequate to reach an informed business judgment as to the fairness of $55 per share for sale of the Company.

* * *

(2)

The directors' unfounded reliance on both the premium and the market test as the basis for accepting the Pritzker proposal undermines the defendants' remaining contention that the Board's collective experience and sophistication was a sufficient basis for finding that it reached its September 20 decision with informed, reasonable deliberation. Compare *Gimbel v. Signal Companies, Inc.*, Del. Ch., 316 A.2d 599 (1974), aff'd *per curiam*, Del.Supr., 316 A.2d 619 (1974). There, the Court of Chancery preliminary enjoined a board's sale of stock of its wholly-owned subsidiary for an alleged grossly inadequate price. It did so based on a finding that the business judgment rule had been pierced for failure of management to give its board "the opportunity to make a reasonable and reasoned decision." 316 A.2d at 615. The Court there reached this result notwithstanding the board's sophistication and experience; the company's need of immediate cash; and the board's need to act promptly due to the impact of an energy crisis on the value of the underlying assets being sold — all of its subsidiary's oil and gas interests. The Court found those factors denoting competence to be outweighed by evidence of gross negligence; that management in effect sprang the deal on the board by negotiating the asset sale without informing the board; that the buyer intended to "force a quick decision" by the board, that the board meeting was called on only one-and-a-half days' notice; that its outside directors were not notified of the meeting's purpose; that during a meeting spanning "a couple of hours" a sale of assets worth $480 million was approved; and that the Board failed to obtain a *current* appraisal of its oil and gas interests. The analogy of *Signal* to the case at bar is significant.

(3)

Part of the defense is based on a claim that the directors relied on legal advice rendered at the September 20 meeting by James Brennan, Esquire, who was present at Van Gorkom's request . . .

Several defendants testified that Brennan advised them that Delaware law did not require a fairness opinion or an outside valuation of the Company before the Board could act on the Pritzker proposal. If given, the advice was correct. However, that did not end the matter. Unless the directors had before them adequate information regarding the intrinsic value of the Company, upon which a proper exercise of business judgment could be made, mere advice of this type is meaningless; and, given this record of the defendants' failures, it constitutes no defense here.

We conclude that Trans Union's Board was grossly negligent in that it failed to act with informed reasonable deliberation in agreeing to the Pritzker merger proposal on September 20; and we further conclude that the Trial Court erred as a matter of law in failing to address that question before determining whether the directors' later conduct was sufficient to cure its initial error.

A second claim is that counsel advised the Board it would be subject to lawsuits if it rejected the $55 per share offer. It is, of course, a fact of corporate life that today when faced with difficult or sensitive issues, directors often are subject to suit, irrespective of the decisions they make.

However, counsel's mere acknowledgement of this circumstance cannot be rationally translated into a justification for a board permitting itself to be stampeded into a patently unadvised act. While suit might result from the rejection of a merger or tender offer, Delaware law makes clear that a board acting within the ambit of the business judgment rule faces no ultimate liability. *Pogostin v. Rice, supra.* Thus, we cannot conclude that the mere threat of litigation, acknowledged by counsel, constitutes either legal advice or any valid basis upon which to pursue an uninformed course.

* * *

We hold, therefore, that the Trial Court committed reversible error in applying the business judgment rule in favor of the director defendants in this case.

* * *

McNEILLY, JUSTICE, dissenting: The majority opinion reads like an advocate's closing address to a hostile jury. And I say that not lightly. Throughout the opinion great emphasis is directed only to the negative, with nothing more than lip service granted the positive aspects of this case. In my opinion Chancellor Marvel (retired) should have been affirmed. The Chancellor's opinion was the product of well reasoned conclusions, based upon a sound deductive process, clearly supported by the evidence and entitled to deference in this appeal. Because of my diametrical opposition to all evidentiary conclusions of the majority, I respectfully dissent.

It would serve no useful purpose, particularly at this late date, for me to dissent at great length. I restrain myself from doing so, but feel compelled to at least point out what I consider to be the most glaring deficiencies in the majority opinion. The majority has spoken and has effectively said that Trans Union's Directors have been the victims of a "fast shuffle" by Van Gorkom and Pritzker. That is the beginning of the majority's comedy of errors. The first and most important error made is the majority's assessment of the directors' knowledge of the affairs of Trans Union and their combined ability to act in this situation under the protection of the business judgment rule.

Trans Union's Board of Directors consisted of ten men, five of whom were "inside" directors and five of whom were "outside" directors. The "inside" directors were Van Gorkom, Chelberg, Bonser, William B. Browder, Senior Vice-President-Law, and Thomas P. O'Boyle, Senior Vice-President-Administration. At the time the merger was proposed the inside five directors had collectively been employed by the Company for 116 years and had 68 years of combined experience as directors. The "outside" directors were A. W. Wallis, William B. Johnson, Joseph B. Lanterman, Graham J. Morgan and Robert W. Reneker. With the exception of Wallis, these were all chief executive officers of Chicago based corporations that were at least as large as Trans Union. The five "outside" directors had 78 years of combined experience as chief executive officers, and 53 years cumulative service as Trans Union directors.

The inside directors wear their badge of expertise in the corporate affairs of Trans Union on their sleeves. But what about the outsiders? Dr. Wallis is or was an economist and math statistician, a professor of economics at Yale University, dean of the graduate school of business at the University of Chicago, and Chancellor of the University of Rochester. Dr. Wallis had been on the Board of Trans Union since 1962. He also was on the Board of Bausch & Lomb, Kodak, Metropolitan Life Insurance Company, Standard Oil and others.

William B. Johnson is a University of Pennsylvania law graduate, President of Railway Express until 1966, Chairman and Chief Executive of I.C. Industries Holding Company, and member of Trans Union's Board since 1968.

Joseph Lanterman, a Certified Public Accountant, is or was President and Chief Executive of American Steel, on the Board of International Harvester, Peoples Energy, Illinois Bell Telephone, Harris Bank and Trust Company, Kemper Insurance Company and a director of Trans Union for four years.

Graham Morgan is a chemist, was Chairman and Chief Executive Officer of U.S. Gypsum, and in the 17 and 18 years prior to the Trans Union transaction had been involved in 31 or 32 corporate takeovers.

Robert Reneker attended University of Chicago and Harvard Business Schools. He was President and Chief Executive of Swift and Company, director of Trans Union since 1971, and member of the Boards of seven other corporations including U.S. Gypsum and the Chicago Tribune.

Directors of this caliber are not ordinarily taken in by a "fast shuffle". I submit they were not taken into this multi-million dollar corporate transaction without being fully informed and aware of the state of the art as it pertained to the entire corporate panorama of Trans Union. True, even directors such as these, with their business acumen, interest and expertise, can go astray. I do not believe that to be the case here. These men knew Trans Union like the back of their hands and were more than well qualified to make on the spot informed business judgments concerning the affairs of Trans Union including a 100% sale of the corporation. Lest we forget, the corporate world of then and now operates on what is so aptly referred to as "the fast track". These men were at the time an integral part of that world, all professional business men, not intellectual figureheads . . .

At the time of the September 20, 1980 meeting the Board was acutely aware of Trans Union and its prospects. The problems created by accumulated investment tax credits and accelerated depreciation were discussed repeatedly at Board meetings, and all of the directors understood the problem thoroughly. Moreover, at the July, 1980 Board meeting the directors had reviewed Trans Union's newly prepared five-year forecast, and at the August 1980 meeting Van Gorkom presented the results of a comprehensive study of Trans Union made by The Boston Consulting Group. This study was prepared over an 18 month period and consisted of a detailed analysis of all Trans Union subsidiaries, including competitiveness, profitability, cash throw-off, cash consumption, technical competence and future prospects for contribution to Trails Union's combined net income.

* * *

I have no quarrel with the majority's analysis of the business judgment rule. It is the application of that rule to these facts which is wrong. An overview of the entire record, rather than the limited view of bits and pieces which the majority has exploded like popcorn, convinces me that the directors made an informed business judgment which was buttressed by their test of the market.

At the time of the September 20 meeting the 10 members of Trans Union's Board of Directors were highly qualified and well informed about the affairs and prospects of Trans Union. These directors were acutely aware of the historical problems facing Trans Union which were caused by the tax laws. They had discussed these problems *ad nauseam*. In fact, within two months of the September 20 meeting the board had reviewed and discussed an outside study of the company done by The Boston Consulting Group and an internal five year forecast prepared by management. At the September 20 meeting Van Gorkom presented the Pritzker offer, and the board then heard from James Brennan, the company's counsel in this matter, who discussed the legal documents. Following this, the Board directed that certain changes be made in the merger documents. These changes made it clear that the Board was free to accept a better offer than Pritzker's if one was made. The above facts reveal that the Board did not act in a grossly negligent manner in informing themselves of the relevant and available facts before passing on the merger. To the contrary, this record reveals that the directors acted with the utmost care in informing themselves of the relevant and available facts before passing on the merger . . .

Notes and Questions

1   Following the decision of the Delaware Supreme Court, the directors settled with the approval of the Delaware Chancery Court. According to Cary and Eisenberg, the settlement involved the payment of $23.5 million. Of this amount, $10 million was covered by the directors' insurance policies (Cary and Eisenberg, *Corporations, Cases and Materials*, 5th ed., 1987 Supplement, pages 102-103). The balance was, interestingly enough, paid by the Pritzker group on behalf of the Trans Union directors, even though the group was not a defendant to the action.

2   Is the judgment in the *Trans Union* case consistent with the rationale of the business judgment rule? Is the Court's conclusion that the directors breached the duty of care justified by the facts of the case? In particular, what impact should the premium over market price that the shareholders received on their Trans Union shares have had on the Court's conclusion? In view of the efficient capital markets hypothesis, what role should be accorded judicial determinations of "intrinsic value"? Should these values be permitted to trump prices generated by the market? Finally, what effect will the decision have on the incentive for managers to engineer transactions that facilitate shifts in corporate control? For a discussion of these issues, see Daniel Fischel, "The Business Judgment Rule and the *Trans Union* Case" (1985), 40 Business Lawyer 1437; Herzl and Katz, "*Smith v. Van Gorkom*: The Business of Judging Business Judgment" (1986), 41 Business Lawyer 1187; Chittur, "The Corporate Director's Standard of Care: Past, Present, and Future" (1985), 10 Del. J. Corp. L. 451.

3   In terms of the importance of certainty and predictability for business planning, what effect do you think the decision had and will have? See Bayless Manning, "Reflections and Practical Tips on Life in the Boardroom After *Van Gorkom*" (1985), 41 Business Lawyer 1 at 1, who states that the *Trans Union* case:

> exploded a bomb . . . Stated minimally, the court there pierced the business judgment rule and imposed individual liability on independent (even eminent) outside directors of Trans Union because (roughly) the court thought they had not been careful enough, and had not enquired enough, before deciding to accept and recommend to Trans Union's shareholders a cashout merger at a per-share that was less than the "intrinsic value" of the shares . . . The corporate bar generally views the decision as atrocious. Commentators predict dire consequences as directors come to realize how exposed they have become.

See also Macey and Miller, "*Trans Union* Reconsidered" (1988), 98 Yale L.J. 127.

4   Is the *Trans Union* court's faith in independent valuation of corporations via fairness opinions merited? Are these opinions clearly superior to the good faith review of an offer for shares of a corporation by the corporation's board of directors? In view of the fact that valuations are commissioned by the board of directors, do you think the exercise will contribute much information to shareholders? Fischel, *supra*, at page 1446, argues that:

> The benefit of comparing the price Pritzker was willing to pay with the trading price of Trans Union's shares is that both reflected market transactions — what willing buyers pay to willing sellers.

The same cannot be said of the results of valuation studies . . .
Indeed, anyone familiar with valuation techniques divorced from
market transactions recognizes how uncertain, almost random, the
whole process is: how slightly different estimates of future earnings
or changes in the capitalization rate applied to such earnings can
produce significantly different numbers; how different appraisers
typically reach radically different conclusions.

In a similar vein, Manning, *supra*, argues that the *Trans Union* decision
constituted "the Investment Bankers' Relief Act of 1985" (at 3).

5   The *Trans Union* judgment exhibits faith in the capacity of rigorous
procedural review to ensure that substantively fair outcomes are
generated. Is this assumption merited? In the realm of fiduciary
duties, how much latitude should courts have to substitute procedural
review for substantive review without compromising shareholder
welfare?

6   Following the judgment of the Delaware Supreme Court in *Trans
Union* the Delaware legislature responded by introducing the following provision into its corporate code:

102(b) . . . the certificate of incorporation may . . . contain any or
all of the following matters . . .

(7) A provision eliminating or limiting the personal liability of
a director to the corporation or its stockholders for monetary
damages for breach of fiduciary duty as a director, provided that
such provision shall not eliminate or limit the liability of a director:
(i) for any breach of the director's duty of loyalty to the
corporation or its stockholders; (ii) for acts or omissions not in
good faith or which involve intentional misconduct or a knowing
violation of the law; (iii) under ss. 174 of this title [Liability of
Directors for Unlawful Payment of Dividend or Unlawful Stock
Purchase or Redemption]; or (iv) for any transaction from which
the director derived an improper personal benefit. No such
provision shall eliminate or limit the liability of a director for
any act or omission occurring prior to the date when such
provision becomes effective.

What effect will s. 102(b)(7) have on the performance of directors? Is
the section consistent with the various models of corporate govern-
ance? Should a provision limiting the duty of care be a mandatory or
permissive term in corporate articles? See: Coffee, "No Exit?: Opting
Out, The Contractual Theory of the Corporation and the Special
Case of Remedies" (1988), 53 Brooklyn Law Rev. 919; Schaffer,
"Delaware's Limit on Director Liability: How the Market for
Incorporation Shapes Corporate Law" (1987), 10 Harv. Journal of
Law and Public Policy 665.

How extensive is the protection afforded by s. 102(b)(7)? First, the provision does not limit liability with respect to a breach of the director's duty of loyalty to the corporation. In view of the overlap that exists in the United States between the duty of care and the duty of loyalty, it is likely that plaintiffs will simply recast actions claiming breach of the former as actions for breach of the latter. Second, s. 102(b)(7) does not apply to acts or omissions not in good faith, or which involve intentional misconduct, or a knowing violation of the law, or for any transaction from which the director derived an improper personal benefit. It would seem therefore that the additional protection s. 102(b)(7) affords is limited to directorial negligence which, it can be argued, most directors would be indemnified against under the general indemnification provisions. Third, the provision only protects directors from monetary liability and preserves alternative remedies such as injunctive or declaratory relief. Furthermore, the section does not shield directors from liability for actions taken in their capacity as officers of the corporation. For an amplification of these issues, see: Veasey, Finkelstein, and Bigler, "Delaware Supports Directors with a Three Legged Stool of Limited Liability, Indemnification, and Insurance" (1987), 42 Business Lawyer 399; Hanks, "Evaluating Recent State Legislation on Director and Officer Liability Limitation and Indemnification" (1988), 43 Business Lawyer 1207.

Interestingly, since 1986, half of the state legislatures in the United States have adopted legislative amendments that shield corporate directors from liability for breach of the duty of care. See: Investment Responsibility Research Center, IRRC Corporate Governance Bulletin, vol. IV, no. 5, (Sept./Oct. 1987), at 155.

UPM-Kymmene Corp. v. UPM-Kymmene Miramichi Inc.

2002 CarswellOnt 2096, 27 B.L.R. (3d) 53, 32 C.C.P.B. 120 (Ont. S.C.J. [Commercial List]), additional reasons at 2002 CarswellOnt 3579 (Ont. S.C.J. [Commercial List]), leave to appeal refused 2004 CarswellOnt 691 (Ont. C.A.)

[In *UPM-Kymmene Corp. v. UPM-Kymmene Miramichi Inc.* (commonly referred to as the *Repap* decision), the board of directors of Repap approved the compensation agreement for a proposed chairman, Mr. Berg. The board relied on the opinion of the compensation committee, who in turn relied on the opinion of a compensation consultant in approving the agreement. However, the compensation consultant was under the impression that she was providing advice on a non-contentious agreement; unbeknownst to her, the compensation agreement was opposed by management and was resisted by previous directors, who had resigned in protest. The agreement was approved without further investigation by the board of directors. The agreement provided for a very generous salary with a large bonus structure, and included a change of control provision (a so-called "golden parachute") that, if effected, would bankrupt Repap. A shareholder brought an action to set aside the compensation agreement as a failure of the directors' fiduciary duties. In setting aside the agreement, Lax J. discussed the business judgment rule]:

Lax J.: It is settled law that the duty of due care requires that where directors make decisions likely to affect shareholder welfare, their decision must be made on an informed and reasoned basis. In CW Shareholdings, Mr. Justice Blair expressed it in this way:

> In the end, they must make a decision and exercise their judgment in an informed and independent fashion, after a reasonable analysis of the situation and acting on a rational basis with reasonable grounds for believing that their actions will promote and maximize share-holder value: see, *820099 Ontario Inc. v. Harold E. Ballard Ltd.*, 1991 CarswellOnt 142, 3 B.L.R. (2d) 123 (Ont. Gen. Div.), additional reasons at (May 7, 1991), Doc. RE 1305/90 (Ont. Gen. Div.), affirmed 1991 CarswellOnt 141 (Ont. Div. Ct.); *Olympia & York Enterprises Ltd. v. Hiram Walker Resources Ltd.*, 1986 CarswellOnt 1050, 59 O.R. (2d) 254, 37 D.L.R. (4th) 193 (Ont. Div. Ct.) at pp. 270-273 [O.R.].

A Board is entitled, indeed encouraged, to retain advisors, but this does not relieve directors of the obligation to exercise reasonable diligence. In Hanson Trust PLC v. ML SCM Acquisition Inc., the United States Court of Appeals for the Second Circuit was asked to determine if directors' approval to grant a lock-up option of substantial corporate assets in a takeover struggle was protected by the business judgment rule. As Pierce J. stated, in duty of care analysis, a presumption of propriety inures to the benefit of directors, who enjoy wide latitude under the business judgment rule in devising strategies. However, as he noted:

> The proper exercise of due care by a director in informing himself of material information and in overseeing the outside advice on which he might appropriately rely is, of necessity, a pre-condition to performing his ultimate duty of acting in good faith to protect the best interests of the corporation..

* * *

The business judgment rule protects Boards and directors from those that might second-guess their decisions. The court looks to see that the directors made a reasonable decision, not a perfect decision. This approach recognizes the autonomy and integrity of a corporation and the expertise of its directors. They are in the advantageous position of investigating and considering first-hand the circumstances that come before it and are in a far better position than a court to understand the affairs of the corporation and to guide its operation.

However, directors are only protected to the extent that their actions actually evidence their business judgment. The principle of deference presupposes that directors are scrupulous in their deliberations and demonstrate diligence in arriving at decisions. Courts are entitled to consider the content of their decision and the extent of the information on which it was based and to measure this against the facts as they existed at the time the impugned decision was made. Although Board decisions are not subject to microscopic examination with the perfect vision of hindsight, they are subject to examination.

. . . Repap did not require, nor could it afford, Mr. Berg's services. With a minimum of effort, the Compensation Committee and the Board could have learned this and everything else they needed to know to make an informed decision on a reasonable basis. This did not occur. Instead, the Agreement was approved on the recommendation of a Compensation Committee that never met to discuss it and had no substantive involvement in the process that led to it.

The business judgment rule cannot apply where the Board of Directors acts on the advice of a director's committee that makes an uninformed recommendation. Although it was not unreasonable for the Board to assume the Committee had done a careful job, this did not relieve the directors of their independent obligation to make an informed decision on a reasonable basis. In order to act in the best interests of the shareholders of Repap, each director was required to understand the terms and meaning of the Agreement and to consider it carefully against the circumstances of Repap at the time. They were required to review the [consultant] opinion carefully and evaluate it thoughtfully against the circumstances of Repap at the time. This did not happen.

A contract, such as the one in issue between the Chairman and the Company, should be the subject of careful, objective analysis, and it was not. The process leading up to the March 23, 1999, meeting and the proceedings there fall far short of the exercise of prudent judgment in the interests of the shareholders that is expected of directors. In the space of thirty minutes . . . the Board of Directors of Repap approved an Agreement that gave someone it did not know, had not recruited, and had just met, a generous salary with a lengthy term of employment, an unprecedented bonus structure, termination and change of control protection inconsistent with the employment objective, and stock options amounting to 13.4% of the company. The directors did not fulfil their duties to Repap. Their decision was not an informed or reasoned one. The business judgment rule cannot be applied in these circumstances to protect their decision from judicial intervention.

Brant Investments Ltd. v. KeepRite Inc.
(1991), 3 O.R. (3d) 289, 1991 CarswellOnt 133 (C.A.)

[In *KeepRite*, a parent corporation (Inter-City Manufacturing Ltd., or "ICM") had a number of subsidiaries. One of these, which was 65% owned by a subsidiary of the parent, was KeepRite. KeepRite was a publicly held corporation, and the balance of the shares were in the hands of public shareholders. ICM decided to use its powers of control to merge KeepRite with two of its wholly-owned subsidiaries. It struck an independent committee of the board of directors to review the proposed terms of the transaction and to determine whether the transaction was fair to the public shareholders of KeepRite. The committee indicated that it would not endorse the merger unless (*inter alia*) the price paid to the public shareholders was increased. The full board approved the transaction on the basis of the changes recommended by the committee. A group of minority shareholders nonetheless sued, claiming that the transaction was oppressive to the interests of the minority shareholders.]

MCKINLAY J.A.:

Onus of proof

The appellants submit that, in an application for relief under s. 234 (now s. 241), once a dissenting shareholder has shown that an impugned transaction involves benefits to one group of shareholders in which dissenting shareholders do not share, and a corresponding detriment to the dissenting shareholders which the other group of shareholders do not suffer, then the burden of proof rests upon the majority shareholders to demonstrate that: (a) the impugned transaction is at least as advantageous to the company and to all shareholders as any available alternative transaction; (b) that no undue pressure was applied to the company, its officers and directors, to accept the impugned transaction as proposed; and (c) that the substance of the impugned transaction and the process of decision-making leading to its acceptance were intrinsically fair to the dissenting shareholders.

No case was cited to us that would substantiate such broad and onerous legal requirements. In any event, the learned trial judge in his very careful reasons dealt with each question raised. He did not consider that there were benefits to ICG which were not shared by the dissenting shareholders, nor did he consider that the dissenting shareholders suffered a detriment which ICG did not suffer. A review of the evidence and of the trial judge's decision makes it clear that there was substantial evidence on which he could base such findings. That being so, the burden of proof which the appellants would have shifted to the respondents on the above-mentioned bases does not arise.

Anderson J. pointed out that possible solutions to KeepRite's problems suggested by the dissenting shareholders were considered and rejected by KeepRite management and by the independent committee. To suggest that directors are required, when entering into a transaction on behalf of the corporation, to consider every available alternative transaction is unrealistic. Any number of considerations may be relevant, if not vital, to the carrying out of a particular transaction at a particular time. In many cases, there will not be obvious or immediate alternatives. The extent to which directors should inquire as to alternatives is a business decision, which, if made honestly in the best interests of the corporation, should not be interfered with.

The appellants also take the position that the single fact that this was a non-arm's-length transaction shifts the burden of proof to the respondent. The only example of such a shift of onus cited to us was in *Sinclair Oil Corp. v. Levien*, 280 A.2d 717 (1971). The facts in that case were much stronger than the facts in this case. Sinclair Oil Corporation allegedly caused damage to its subsidiary, Sinclair Venezuelan Oil Company (Sinven), as a result of numerous acts, including causing the subsidiary to pay substantial dividends, denying industrial development to the subsidiary and causing breach of contract between that subsidiary and a wholly owned subsidiary of Sinclair. The case involved a derivative action by minority shareholders of Sinven for losses suffered by it as a result of its parent's actions. In that case, the fiduciary duty owed by the parent to the subsidiary resulted in a shifting of the burden of proof to Sinclair to show "intrinsic fairness" in the dealings between it and its subsidiary.

As pointed out by the appellants, courts in this jurisdiction have held that where a party who owes a fiduciary duty deals with trust property to his own personal benefit, a burden of proof, the nature of which will depend on the circumstances of the case, will rest on the fiduciary. There are undoubtedly other cases where proof of basic preliminary facts would warrant a shift of onus. Whether or not this is one of those cases we need not decide since, as pointed out by Anderson J., the respondents in this case assumed from the outset the burden of adducing evidence as to the nature of the transaction, the manner in which it was carried out, and the result. It was not merely the non-arm's-length nature of the transaction that made it, in the trial judge's words, "tactically sound" to do so. As many of the necessary facts were solely in the knowledge of the respondents, the burden of adducing evidence on those facts would have been theirs in any event.

Independent committee

The appellants attack the role of the independent committee on the basis, first, that it was not, in fact, independent, and second, that the advice given by the committee to the directors of KeepRite was not in the best interests of the company and its shareholders.

With respect to the makeup of the committee, the evidence discloses that all of its members were outside members of the board of KeepRite.

None was an officer or director of ICG. The three-member committee comprised H. Purdy Crawford and John Edison, both solicitors, and Ross Hanbury, a former partner of Wood, Gundy. Mr. Crawford became involved with KeepRite in the winter of 1979 when the Odette Group retained him and the law firm in which he was a senior partner in connection with the possible acquisition of KeepRite. That group eventually became owners of approximately 50 per cent of the shares of KeepRite. It was at the request of the Odette Group that Mr. Crawford became a director of KeepRite. His first encounter with ICG was at the time of its failed take-over bid for KeepRite. He continued as a member of the board after ICG acquired its interest in KeepRite in 1981. Mr. Edison had acted as legal adviser to the founder of KeepRite from its inception, and had also acted for the company over a number of years. He was a long term member of the KeepRite board. Mr. Hanbury had been involved with KeepRite since the 1960s, when Wood, Gundy was involved in a public offering of KeepRite shares. There is no evidence of any involvement with ICG by any of these individuals.

The trial judge found as a fact that the members of the committee were truly independent in the sense that they "felt at all times free to deal with the impugned transaction upon its merits" (*Brant Investments, supra,* at p. 756 O.R.). There was more than adequate evidence to substantiate such a finding.

* * *

The real complaint of the appellants on this appeal is that, rather than making his own assessment of the value to KeepRite of the transaction, the learned trial judge relied on the decision of the independent committee that the transaction was of value to KeepRite because of the synergies and economics of scale involved. The appellants argue that, although reliance on investigations carried out by such a committee may be appropriate in some cases, it is not appropriate in this case where, they argue, the committee itself did not adequately assess the benefits of the transaction to KeepRite. The appellants criticize work of the independent committee on the following bases:

  (a) the committee did not consider whether there were alternative transactions open to KeepRite;

  (b) the committee approved the transaction based upon assurances that certain "synergistic" benefits could be achieved by combining the businesses — they were aware of the need for a strategic plan to realize these benefits but proceeded without obtaining one;

  (c) the committee never received a final report from the consultants retained to review management's assumptions concerning the anticipated synergies; and

(d) the committee did not commission a valuation of the Inter-City businesses on a going concern basis.

(a)   Possible Alternative Transactions

The appellants argue that there were a number of alternative transactions available to KeepRite which were not considered by the independent committee, and they point specifically to three. First, they say that Wood, Gundy, KeepRite's financial advisers, and Mr. McKay, KeepRite's chief executive officer, believed that equity could be raised in the absence of an asset purchase. Mr. S.A. Jarislowsky, called by the appellants, testified that the dissenting shareholders would have looked favourably at supporting such an offering. I do not consider that Mr. Jarislowsky's after-the-fact evidence of such a position is of assistance. There was some evidence that an alternative suggestion was made by Mr. Jarislowsky on behalf of the dissenting shareholders prior to the carrying out of the transaction. However, it is not for the minority shareholders to dictate to corporate officers the manner in which they should deal with corporate problems. Whether or not the directors or the independent committee looked favourably on any suggestion by Mr. Jarislowsky is irrelevant unless it could be shown that he presented an alternative which was definitely available and clearly more beneficial to the company than the chosen transaction. However, the suggestion made by Mr. Jarislowsky was nothing more than that — a mere suggestion.

[The court reviewed the specific suggestions and concluded that the independent committee had canvassed these.]

It is clear from the evidence that the independent committee did consider some alternative possibilities for solving KeepRite's problems. It did so, however, in the context of a concrete proposal for the purchase of assets from the ICG companies. The evaluation of that proposal was the purpose for which the committee was struck. I agree with the words of the trial judge where he stated at pp. 757-58 O.R.:

> There is nothing inherently wrong in a parent company making such a proposal to a subsidiary. Any difficulty arises because the transaction, if carried forward, will not be at arm's length. It was because of that aspect of the transaction, and to protect against the vices which may be involved, that the Independent Committee was called into existence. In my view, the committee was not thereupon called to make a wide-ranging search for alternatives, or in other words, to determine whether the proposal which had been made was the best possible solution to the problem. Its function was to determine whether the proposed transaction was fair and reasonable and of benefit to KeepRite and its shareholders.

(b) Strategic Plan

The appellants argue that, although the independent committee was aware of the need for a strategic plan to realize the synergistic benefits of the transaction, they proceeded without obtaining such a plan. First of all, the evidence referred to by the appellants on this point does not reveal that the committee considered that a comprehensive "strategic plan" to realize synergistic benefits was necessary. Mr. Purdy Crawford, a witness with broad experience in corporation matters, indicated in his evidence that it is not unusual for decisions to be made with respect to very substantial acquisitions without any previously existing strategic plan. However, in this case, the committee and the directors of KeepRite considered it absolutely necessary in the situation in which KeepRite found itself that some action be taken which would alleviate the concerns of KeepRite's bankers.

Early in 1983 a task force comprised of representatives of both KeepRite and ICG was appointed to study and report on the merits of combining the air-conditioning business of KeepRite and the heating business of the Inter-City companies. In the process of the work of that task force, a background financial paper was prepared which analyzed the financial impact of combining the businesses. This financial analysis was filed as an exhibit at trial. It analyzed the anticipated synergies from the integration of the two operations, and the anticipated effect on the resulting balance sheet of KeepRite — both of which were very important for the purposes of KeepRite's bankers.

It is clear from the evidence that KeepRite did have a plan to realize the proposed benefits of the transaction, which was reviewed by the independent committee. There does not appear to have been a minutely detailed plan setting out projected day-by-day actions to be followed after closing of the transaction, but no one suggests that such a detailed plan was necessary, or even desirable.

(c) Consultants' Report

The independent committee retained the firm of Crosbie, Armitage as consultants to assess the benefits of the proposed transaction to KeepRite. Crosbie, Armitage did, in fact, make an assessment of the anticipated synergistic benefits of the transaction. Allan Crosbie presented a report dated March 23, 1983 to a meeting of the independent committee on that same date. His report contained an appendix setting forth the main elements of the proposed business plan arising out of the transaction and a reasonably detailed financial analysis of the proposed acquisition. He made it clear in his report that the assumptions on which it was based were developed by KeepRite and ICG senior operating personnel in several working sessions in which Crosbie, Armitage participated. Thus, the underlying assumptions used in the financial analysis represented a consensus view of the senior management of the two companies. On the basis of the information contained in the report, it was Mr. Crosbie's opinion that:

Not only are there important cost savings as a result of rationalization of the businesses, but in addition there are substantial increased sales opportunities.

At the meeting of the independent committee, Mr. Crosbie informed its members that the transaction appeared to him and his associates to make business sense. Mr. McKay informed the committee that senior management could successfully carry out the integration and business plan as set out in the Crosbie, Armitage report.

The appellants criticize the independent committee because it did not obtain a further final report from Crosbie, Armitage establishing their confirmation of some of the assumptions on which their original report was based. In my opinion, the fact that the committee did not require such a report in no way invalidates the opinion contained in the original report and conveyed orally to the committee by Mr. Crosbie. The learned trial judge considered it completely appropriate that the assumptions on which the report was based were developed by senior operating personnel of KeepRite and ICG, along with personnel of Crosbie, Armitage. I agree. Those individuals were not only the persons who had access to and familiarity with the relevant information, but many of them were also the officers who would be implementing the integrated business plan after the completion of the transaction. There was no suggestion that any of the information presented was inaccurate or misleading.

(d) Valuation of the Inter-City Business on a Going-Concern Basis

The appellants complain that:

The Committee did not commission a valuation of the Inter-City businesses on a going-concern basis, even though Mr. McKay expressed concern about their profitability. The Inter-City businesses had substantial losses in 1982, and budgeted further losses for 1983. They were reviewed by Inter-City, KeepRite and at least two members of the Committee as only marginally profitable, if at all.

None of these allegations is disputed by the respondents. The two Inter-City businesses, the major assets of which were to be purchased by KeepRite, had not recently been profitable. KeepRite itself had suffered substantial losses in the 1982 fiscal year, was experiencing a decrease in its share of the market in its field, and was under substantial pressure from its bankers to acquire new equity financing. It was not the profitability of the businesses as separate entities that was of concern to the independent committee, but the benefits to KeepRite of combining their operations. It is probably worth while at this point to quote from the summary business plan included in the Crosbie, Armitage report, since it very concisely indicates what the expected benefits to KeepRite would be:

1. KeepRite would acquire the assets and liabilities of the businesses of ICG Manufacturing and ICG Energy respectively, exclusive of the St. Catharines facility and deferred taxes.

2. ICG's sheet metal business would be wound up on an orderly basis.

3. The significant portion of ICG's St. Catharines manufacturing business would be integrated into KeepRite's Brantford manufacturing facility.

4. KeepRite and ICG's sales and distribution components would be rationalized. Also, as part of this rationalization, ICG would terminate its existing distribution business and sell direct or through other distributors in a manner similar to KeepRite. As part of the restructuring of ICG's sales and marketing network, this should enable reductions in sales personnel and the amounts of finished goods inventory that would have to be carried.

5. With the rationalization of the KeepRite and ICG selling and distribution networks, it is anticipated that sales of certain product lines in Canada, the US and offshore markets would be expanded slightly. In particular, in Canada, with the rationalization of KeepRite's and ICG's sales forces, domestic sales increases are projected; in the US, utilizing KeepRite's existing sales and distribution network, sales increases of selected ICG products are projected.

6. As part of this overall program, provision is to be made for establishing a senior marketing group.

7. As part of the rationalization program, KeepRite and ICG Manufacturing and Engineering personnel requirements would be rationalized with attendant savings in costs.

8. As part of the rationalization program, KeepRite and ICG corporate administration, finance and EDP departments would be rationalized with attendant savings in costs.

The independent committee retained Price, Waterhouse, KeepRite's auditors, to review the statement of net book values of ICG assets as at March 31, 1983. Price, Waterhouse held discussions with Coopers & Lybrand, who had completed an audit of the Inter-City companies as at December 31, 1982. Price, Waterhouse presented its opinion to the committee that the net book values were appropriate and appeared to have been arrived at in accordance with generally accepted accounting principles.

Since KeepRite was purchasing assets for the purpose of combining the two operations, the committee did not consider a going-concern valuation to be necessary.

The trial judge was satisfied that the independent committee was aware of its mandate, was at all times conscious that this was not an arm's-length transaction, and appropriately carried out its function of assessing the benefits of the transaction to KeepRite. He was completely satisfied on the evidence that the committee carried out its function in an appropriate and independent manner. I see no reason whatever to doubt the correctness of that finding. Neither the evidence nor the argument persuades me that his findings were anything other than appropriate.

Business judgment and the oppression remedy

The appellants argue strongly that since the enactment of s. 234 (now s. 241) of the CBCA, it is no longer appropriate for a trial judge to delegate to directors of a corporation, or to a committee such as that established in this case, judgment as to the fairness of conduct complained of by dissenting shareholders. This is particularly important, they argue, because the persons to whom that judgment is delegated are the very persons whose conduct is under scrutiny. They argue that the trial judge in this case erred in his approach to the exercise of his jurisdiction under s. 234, when he stated, at pp. 759-60 O.R.:

> the court ought not to usurp the function of the board of directors in managing the company, nor should it eliminate or supplant the legitimate exercise of control by the majority . . . Business decisions, honestly made, should not be subjected to microscopic examination.

This, they argue, indicates that the trial judge declined to exercise independent judgment with respect to the fairness of essential aspects of the impugned transaction. Such a submission is, in my view, patently unfounded. The portion of the trial judge's reasons quoted above should be placed in context. The relevant portion of the reasons is quoted below (pp. 759-60 O.R.):

> The jurisdiction is one which must be exercised with care. On the one hand the minority shareholder must be protected from unfair treatment; that is the clearly expressed intent of the section. On the other hand the court ought not to usurp the function of the board of directors in managing the company, nor should it eliminate or supplant the legitimate exercise of control by the majority. In *Re Bright Pine Mills Pty. Ltd.*, 1969 V.R. 1002 (Supreme Court of Victoria), analogous legislation to s. 234 was under consideration. At p. 1011 O'Bryan J., writing for the full court, says:
>
> > It is true to say, however, that it was not intended . . . to give jurisdiction to the Court (a jurisdiction the courts have always been loath to assume) to interfere with the internal management of a company by directors who in the exercise of the powers conferred upon them by the memorandum and articles of association are acting honestly and without any purpose of advancing the interests

of themselves or others of their choice at the expense of the company or contrary to the interests of other shareholders.

Although the statute there under consideration was confined to "oppression", I consider the caveat there expressed to apply with equal force to the wider language of s. 234. Business decisions, honestly made, should not be subjected to microscopic examination. There should be no interference simply because a decision is unpopular with the minority.

There can be no doubt that on an application under s. 234 the trial judge is required to consider the nature of the impugned acts and the method in which they were carried out. That does not mean that the trial judge should substitute his own business judgment for that of managers, directors, or a committee such as the one involved in assessing this transaction. Indeed, it would generally be impossible for him to do so, regardless of the amount of evidence before him. He is dealing with the matter at a different time and place; it is unlikely that he will have the background knowledge and expertise of the individuals involved; he could have little or no knowledge of the background and skills of the persons who would be carrying out any proposed plan; and it is unlikely that he would have any knowledge of the specialized market in which the corporation operated. In short, he does not know enough to make the business decision required. That does not mean that he is not well equipped to make an objective assessment of the very factors which s. 234 requires him to assess. Those factors have been discussed in some detail earlier in these reasons.

It is important to note that the learned trial judge did not say that business decisions honestly made should not be subjected to examination. What he said was that they should not be subjected to microscopic examination. In spite of those words, the learned trial judge did, in fact, scrutinize, in a very detailed and careful manner, the nature of the transaction in this case and the manner in which it was executed. Having carefully reviewed the major aspects of the appellants' criticisms of the transaction, he came to the conclusion that it in no way, either substantively or procedurally, offended the provisions of s. 234. Having carefully reviewed all of the exhibits and transcribed evidence to which we were referred, I have no hesitation in agreeing with the correctness of his assessment.

The appellants refer specifically to two areas where they say the trial judge declined to exercise independent judgment with respect to the fairness of essential aspects of the transaction. These were:

(1) whether the impugned transaction was, in fact, for the benefit of KeepRite as a whole, or rather beneficial to Inter-City and detrimental to KeepRite; and

(2) whether the "earnings dilution" caused by the disparity in historical earnings between KeepRite and the Inter-City businesses resulted in unfairness to the dissenting shareholders.

With respect to the first argument, I can only say that the reasons of the trial judge indicate exactly the reverse. If anything, he took an excess of care in exercising independent judgment with respect to the fairness of the transaction.

With respect to the second, the trial judge in his reasons dealt with the question of the disparity in historical earnings between the ICG subsidiaries and KeepRite. He stated that the members of the independent committee and the directors were aware of these problems and considered that they had been overcome. The learned trial judge was of the view that this was a matter of business judgment and he was not disposed to intervene. The appellants argue that the disparity in historical earnings would inevitably result in an earnings dilution to the shareholders of KeepRite. Such a result was by no means inevitable. A large proportion of the assets transferred consisted of inventory and accounts receivable, the book value of which were guaranteed by ICG, and no interest was payable on the note given by KeepRite to ICG covering payment of the purchase price. The cash resulting from realization of the receivables and inventory would have the effect of reducing the bank borrowings of KeepRite, and the transaction was very favourably viewed by KeepRite's bankers. If, in addition, the anticipated synergies were realized (which it appears in retrospect they were) there would likely be an earnings enhancement per share rather than the "earnings dilution" alleged by the dissenting shareholders.

Notes and Questions

1   There are clearly contrasting elements in the degree of deference afforded the board in *Brant* and *Van Gorkom*. Which do you prefer?

2   The Supreme Court addressed the business judgment rule in relation to disclosure requirements under the Ontario *Securities Act* in *Kerr v. Danier Leather Inc.*, 2007 CarswellOnt 6445, 2007 CarswellOnt 6446, [2007] S.C.J. No. 44, 286 D.L.R. (4th) 601 (S.C.C.). The court found that the legal obligation of disclosure could not be subordinated to the business judgment rule, as the quality of disclosure is something the court must evaluate itself. What other legal obligations would not be subject to the business judgment rule?

Pente Investment Management Ltd. v. Schneider Corp.
(1998), 42 O.R. (3d) 177, 1998 CarswellOnt 4035 (C.A.)

[In *Pente Investment Management Ltd.*, Maple Leaf made a takeover bid for the Schneider Corp., which the directors of Schneider thwarted by entering into a lock-up arrangement with another bidder (with the express approval of the company's controlling shareholders). The court dealt the issue of the onus of proof as follows:]

WEILER J.A.: The duty of directors when dealing with a bid that will change control of a company is a rapidly developing area of law and, as I have indicated, Canadian authorities dealing with the question of the onus, or burden of proof, have not been uniform. In Brant Investments, *supra*, the issue whether the burden of proof is on the directors to justify their actions as being in the best interests of the company or on the shareholders challenging the actions of the company was also raised. McKinlay J.A., at pp. 311-12, found it unnecessary to decide the question because the trial judge had dealt with the issues on a substantive basis, and his decision did not turn on which party had the onus or burden of proof. The same is true in the present case. I would add, however, that it may be that the burden of proof may not always rest on the same party when a change of control transaction is challenged. The real question is whether the directors of the target company successfully took steps to avoid a conflict of interest. If so, the rationale for shifting the burden of proof to the directors may not exist. If a board of directors has acted on the advice of a committee composed of persons having no conflict of interest, and that committee has acted independently, in good faith, and made an informed recommendation as to the best available transaction for the shareholders in the circumstances, the business judgment rule applies. The burden of proof is not an issue in such circumstances.

Note

In *BCE Inc., Re*, 2008 CarswellQue 12595, 2008 CarswellQue 12596, [2008] 3 S.C.R. 560, 52 B.L.R. (4th) 1 (S.C.C.) the Supreme Court stated the business judgment rule as follows:

> In considering what is in the best interests of the corporation, directors may look to the interests of, inter alia, shareholders, employees, creditors, consumers, governments and the environment to inform their decisions. Courts should give appropriate deference to the business judgment of directors who take into account these ancillary interests, as reflected by the business judgment rule. The "business judgment rule" accords deference to a business decision, so long as it lies within a range of reasonable alternatives: see *Pente Investment Management Ltd. v. Schneider Corp.*, 1998 CarswellOnt 4035, 42 O.R. (3d) 177 (Ont. C.A.); *Kerr v. Danier Leather Inc.*, 2007 SCC 44, 2007 CarswellOnt 6445, 2007 CarswellOnt 6446, [2007] 2 S.C.R. 331 (S.C.C.). It reflects the reality that directors, who are mandated under s. 102(1) of the CBCA to manage the corporation's business and affairs, are often better suited to determine what is in the best interests of the corporation. This applies to decisions on stakeholders' interests, as much as other directorial decisions.

Unique Broadband Systems Inc., Re
2014 CarswellOnt 9327, 2014 ONCA 538, 121 O.R. (3d) 81, 13 C.B.R.
(6th) 278, 242 A.C.W.S. (3d) 80, 322 O.A.C. 122

[UBS had in place an incentive-driven share appreciation rights plan ("SAR Plan") for its directors and senior management. Upon certain triggering events, a SAR unit holder would be paid an amount equal to the difference between the market trading price of a UBS share and a strike price specified in the SAR Plan. In 2003, UBS acquired a controlling 51.8% equity interest in Look Communications Inc. ("Look"), a telecommunications company. Mr. McGoey also served as a director and CEO of Look. Look's primary asset was a band of telecommunications spectrum. In early 2009, Look engaged in a process to sell the spectrum through a court-supervised plan of arrangement. Ultimately the spectrum was sold for $80 million on May 4, 2009 to Inukshuk Wireless Partnership, a consortium of Rogers Communications Inc. ("Rogers") and Bell Canada (the "Spectrum Sale"). The board of directors of UBS (the "UBS Board") resolved to treat the Spectrum Sale as a triggering event pursuant to the SAR Plan. After the Spectrum Sale, the UBS Board's compensation committee, which consisted of Mr. McGoey and two other UBS Board members, began reviewing the SAR Plan. Each member of the compensation committee had a considerable number of SAR units. UBS' outside legal counsel advised that, while s. 3.15 of National Policy 58-201 (which deals with the Corporate Governance Guidelines) says that a board should appoint a compensation committee entirely of independent directors, this was a guideline only and was not a requirement either pursuant to securities law or TSX Rules. At the meeting, each director disclosed his conflict of interest regarding their SAR unit holdings. The directors then unanimously resolved to cancel the SAR units and establish a SAR cancellation payment pool of $2,310,000, based on a fixed unit price of $0.40 per share. The UBS Board met on July 8 and 9, 2009, and the directors considered the issue of awarding bonuses for certain personnel. The UBS Board then approved the establishment of a bonus pool in the amount of $3.4 million (the "Bonus Pool"). On July 5, 2010, a special shareholders' meeting was held, and Mr. McGoey and the other directors were removed as directors. Mr. McGoey then resigned as CEO of UBS, took the position that he was terminated without cause, and sued UBS. The trial judge held that Mr. McGoey and the other members of the UBS board breached their fiduciary duties to the company. Below is the Court of Appeal's decision affirming the trial court's decision that the directors breached their fiduciary duty in implementing the SAR Cancellation Awards and the Bonus Pool.]

Analysis

(i) Breach of Fiduciary Duty

As mentioned above, Mr. McGoey asserts that the trial judge erred in finding that he had breached his fiduciary duties. At the heart of Mr. McGoey's submission is that the decisions he made with respect to the SAR Cancellation Awards and the Bonus Award were done with the advice of experienced legal counsel and are protected by the business judgment rule.

In my view, the trial judge's finding that Mr. McGoey's breached his fiduciary duties to UBS was well supported in the evidence before her and by the lack of any clear explanation from Mr. McGoey as to how the UBS Board decided to establish the SAR Cancellation Awards and the Bonus Pool. For the reasons set forth below, I see no error in the trial judge's reasoning and in her conclusion that Mr. McGoey's actions were driven by self-interest, unsupported by any reasonable or objective criteria, and contrary to the best interests of UBS.

Below I consider the general principles of the law of fiduciary duties, an analysis of the trial judge's decision regarding the SAR Cancellation Awards and Bonus Pool, and the defences raised by Mr. McGoey.

General Principles

It is undisputed that, Mr. McGoey, as a director and CEO of UBS, owed the company fiduciary duties. The imposition of fiduciary duties on directors and officers of a corporation is consistent with the origins of the doctrine in trust law. A director or senior officer of a corporation is in a position of trust. He or she is charged with managing the assets of a corporation honestly and in a manner that is consistent with the objects of the corporation. Courts will be loath to interfere with the legitimate exercise of corporate duties, but they will intervene where a fiduciary breaches the trust reposed in him or her.

Mr. McGoey's fiduciary duties included an obligation to act in good faith and in the best interests of the corporation. He had a specific obligation to scrupulously avoid conflicts of interest with the corporation and not to abuse his position for personal gain: *People's Department Stores Ltd. (1992) Inc., Re*, 2004 SCC 68, [2004] 3 S.C.R. 461 (S.C.C.), at paras. 35 and 42; and *BCE Inc., Re*, 2008 SCC 69, [2008] 3 S.C.R. 560 (S.C.C.), at paras. 39 and 89.

As Granger J. stated in *Moffat v. Wetstein* (1996), 29 O.R. (3d) 371 (Ont. Gen. Div.), at p. 390:

Subsumed in the fiduciary's duties of good faith and loyalty is the duty to avoid a conflict of interest. The fiduciary must not only avoid a direct conflict of interest but must also avoid the appearance of a possible or potential conflict. The fiduciary is barred from dividing loyalties between competing interests, including self-interest.

Disclosure of a directors' interest in a transaction is just the first step. Disclosure does not relieve a director of his or her obligation to act honestly and in the best interests of the corporation: *UPM-Kymmene Corp. v. UPM-Kymmene Miramichi Inc.* (2002), 214 D.L.R. (4th) 496(Ont. S.C.J. [Commercial List]), aff'd (2004), 183 O.A.C. 310 (Ont. C.A.).

It is against these standards that the trial judge was obliged to consider the actions of Mr. McGoey.

SAR Cancellation Awards

With respect to the SAR Cancellation Awards, the trial judge concluded that there was no evidence as to how the UBS Board arrived at the non-market price of $0.40 per unit and how it determined that it was in the best interests of the corporation. The UBS Board provided no credible analysis to justify why they considered that these payments, which represented a significant percentage of UBS market capitalization, were fair and reasonable in the circumstances.

In considering the reasonableness of the UBS Board's actions in this regard, I find that the following facts are germane.

As of May 4, 2009, when the UBS Board resolved to treat the Spectrum Sale as a triggering event pursuant to the SAR Plan, it anticipated that the trading price of UBS shares would rise from $0.15 to a range of $0.30 to $0.50 per share.

On June 17, 2009, the shares of UBS were still trading at $0.15 per share. Thus, the anticipated gains between the strike price and the trading price had not materialized. It was in these circumstances that the UBS Board decided to implement the SAR Cancellation Awards without the benefit of any independent or third party advice that could speak to the reasonableness of their decision.

As found by the trial judge, the potential Rogers share transaction never went beyond the negotiation stage and was completely off the table by July 20, 2009 and could not serve as a justification for the $0.40 unit price.

Mr. McGoey's SAR Cancellation Award was allocated to him on August 28, 2009, pursuant to which he was entitled to receive a payment from UBS of $600,000, whereas, under the SAR Plan, he would have been entitled to a payment of $75,000.

Given these facts, and in the absence of any credible evidence regarding the *bona fides* of the SAR Cancellation Awards or the process by which they were created, the trial judge reached the reasonable conclusion that the decision to implement the new scheme was driven by UBS Board's self-interest. I see no error in that conclusion.

I also agree with the trial judge's conclusion that the $0.40 unit value was unjustified and unrealistic. It was notionally based on a transaction with Rogers that was far from certain and which had been terminated at the time when the SAR Cancellation Awards were allocated. What the SAR Cancellation Awards really achieved was the removal of the uncertainty that was part of the SAR Plan. Under this new scheme, the recipients' awards were not dependant on an increase in the share price, the awards would be granted regardless of the trading price of the shares. This removal of the uncertainty was to the benefit of the recipients and was of no benefit to the corporation.

Bonus Pool

The trial judge rejected the position of Mr. McGoey that there was a reasonable rationale for the establishment of the Bonus Pool and his allocation of $1.2 million. This finding was well supported by the evidence at trial, including the following.

The UBS Board did not seek or receive any expert advice on an appropriate bonus structure. Nor did they have any comparable or other data regarding executive compensation in the marketplace.

There was no documentation that stipulated the performance factors or criteria by which Mr. McGoey's performance would be evaluated. The trial judge rejected Mr. McGoey's evidence that the services he provided for Look qualified as the criteria under which he could be awarded a bonus by UBS. She concluded that, when the UBS bonus was awarded, there were, in fact, no criteria.

Similarly, there was no documentation that showed how the Bonus Pool was quantified. The best evidence we have is that Mr. McGoey went to a UBS Board meeting seeking to establish a $7 million bonus pool but the UBS Board found that amount "too high" and established a $3.4 million bonus pool instead.

In my view, on these facts, the trial judge was correct to conclude that Mr. McGoey's establishment of the Bonus Pool and the allocation of a part of the Bonus Pool to him breached his fiduciary duties to UBS.

Defences

I do not accept Mr. McGoey's rather novel argument that there can be no finding of a breach of fiduciary duty because, before he could be paid under the SAR Cancellation Awards or the Bonus Pool, he was removed from office by the shareholders of UBS. Counsel for Mr. McGoey suggests that the breach is incomplete because no damages have been suffered.

This submission is not correct at law. As stated by Mark Ellis in his text, *Fiduciary Duties in Canada*, in the context of discussing conflicts of interest:

Entering into a *potential* conflict of interest is a breach whether or not the conflict is operative; once such a conflict becomes operative to jeopardize the beneficiary or his property, the fiduciary breach would then give rise to the remedies available in law. The point is important: to wait until damage or prejudice actually occurs is to prejudice the beneficiary's right to utmost loyalty and avoidance of conflict. If such a schism in theory is allowed, the law would be encouraging a finding that the duty "piggy-backs" the damage caused rather than premising damage on the basis of duty. [Emphasis in original.]

Similarly, in *Canson Enterprises Ltd. v. Boughton & Co.*, [1991] 3 S.C.R. 534 (S.C.C.), at p. 553, McLachlin J. (as she then was) stated that "[a] breach of fiduciary duty is a wrong in itself, regardless of whether a loss can be foreseen".

It would be a remarkable result if a fiduciary could be allowed to act in a manner contrary to his duty with impunity, on the basis that he was prevented by the beneficiary's vigilance from receiving a personal benefit.

Mr. McGoey's counsel also argued that the trial judge erred in simply comparing the payments under the SAR Plan and the SAR Cancellation Awards, without considering that the SAR Cancellation Awards also required the recipients to execute releases and were contingent upon Look receiving the full payment of funds from the Spectrum Sale and UBS having sufficient resources.

I do not find this argument persuasive. The last payment under the Spectrum Sale was received on September 11, 2009. Mr. McGoey's release was executed four days later. It is true that the funds from the Spectrum Sale had not been paid over to UBS; however, it was hardly a doubtful proposition that the money would have found its way to UBS, given Mr. McGoey and his associates' control over Look's board.

The trial judge also rejected Mr. McGoey's argument that his actions were undertaken with the assistance of independent legal advice from Mr. McCarthy and, therefore, could not constitute a breach of his fiduciary duties. I agree with the trial judge's conclusion on this issue. The UBS Board never sought an opinion from Mr. McCarthy regarding the reasonableness of the changes to the SAR Plan and the bonuses. Indeed, the evidence is clear that Mr. McCarthy did not have any information during the relevant time regarding the quantity of the Bonus Award or the SAR Cancellation Awards allocated to Mr. McGoey or to any other director or officer of UBS.

Finally, the trial judge carefully considered Mr. McGoey's argument that his actions were protected by the business judgment rule. She reviewed the law and identified the critical issue at para. 122 of her reasons:

I must now examine the board's and Mr. McGoey's actions and decide whether business judgment is what was exercised here, or whether it was self help, or worse, breach of fiduciary duty, dressed in business judgment's clothes.

The trial judge properly concluded that the business judgment rule was of no assistance to Mr. McGoey because he did not satisfy the rule's preconditions of honesty, prudence, good faith, and a reasonable belief that his actions were in the best interests of the company: *Corporacion Americana de Equipamientos Urbanos S.L. v. Olifas Marketing Group Inc.* (2003), 66 O.R. (3d) 352 (Ont. S.C.J.), at paras. 13 and 14.

It must be remembered that the business judgment rule is really just a rebuttable presumption that directors or officers act on an informed basis, in good faith, and in the best interests of the corporation. Courts will defer to business decisions honestly made, but they will not sit idly by when it is clear that a board is engaged in conduct that has no legitimate business purpose and that is in breach of its fiduciary duties. In the present case, there was ample evidence upon which the trial judge could base her conclusion that the presumption had been rebutted.

In summary, I conclude that the trial judge did not err in finding that Mr. McGoey breached his fiduciary duties to UBS.

9. INDEMNIFICATION AND INSURANCE

Ronald J. Daniels and Susan M. Hutton,
"The Capricious Cushion: The Implications of the
Directors' and Officers' Insurance Liability Crisis on
Canadian Corporate Governance"
(1993), 22 Can. Bus. L.J. 182

* * *

In this article we explore the dynamics of the Canadian directors' and officers' insurance market by focusing on the crisis that afflicted that market in the mid-1980s (the "D&O crisis"). The crisis involved a dramatic and unanticipated contraction in the availability of D&O insurance. By understanding the roots of that crisis, one can make some informed predictions respecting the availability and pricing of directors' and officers' insurance in Canada. Our conclusions are somewhat troubling for enthusiasts of enhanced legal liabilities for directors. Close examination of the D&O crisis reveals that the market is vulnerable to cyclical industry-wide fluctuations in capacity and pricing that greatly undermine the ability of directors to insure against the future costs of legal liability. These problems are exacerbated by market conventions which limit the effective duration of coverage (short policy and post-policy discovery periods).

Although a number of different independent theories have been proffered to explain the occurrence of the mid-1980s crisis in liability insurance, following Romano's study of the American D&O crisis, we prefer a multifactorial explanation that draws on an amalgam of endogenous (industry) and exogenous (legal and market) components. This approach is congenial to the determination of the extent to which linkages between the American and Canadian economies affected the Canadian crisis. While we find evidence that American trends are being used to inform risk prediction in the Canadian D&O market, we argue that this is not evidence of undue market power possessed by American insurers (essentially a story positing cross subsidies from Canadian to American consumers), but is simply the result of statistical imperatives which limit the predictive significance of the Canadian loss experience.

* * *

II. THE RATIONALE FOR AND STRUCTURE OF D&O LIABILITY INSURANCE

By and large, most liberal scholars are willing to support government intervention designed to internalize the non-negotiated external costs of a given activity pursuant to Kaldor-Hicks notions of efficiency. Typically, this intervention takes the form of either property rights or liability rules that attempt to reconstruct the allocation of resources that fully informed parties would conclude through their transaction-costs-free bargaining. However, when the party generating external costs is a corporation, special problems are posed for courts and legislatures in determining the extent to which individual parties within the corporation should be held legally responsible for this activity, and the way in which this responsibility should interact with enterprise liability.

The issue of the appropriate scope for enterprise and personal liability is heightened in the case of directors who may not have been directly responsible for ordering the corporation to engage in certain socially undesirable types of activity, but are nevertheless held legally responsible for the consequences of this activity by virtue of their corporate status. This liability is commonly referred to as "gatekeeper liability", and is found in the various common law and statutory duties that officers and directors owe to shareholders, employees, creditors, suppliers and communities. The rationale for gatekeeper liability is based on the belief that the existing array of traditional sanctions and rewards pinpointing liability on the enterprise and on the actual wrongdoer within the enterprise are incapable of reducing the level of corporate wrongdoing to socially optimal levels. It is therefore necessary to enlist the services of third-party monitors, albeit under the threat of personal liability, to score further reductions in corporate wrongdoing.

Like other forms of civil liability, gatekeeper liability for corporate delicts will affect both the care and activity levels of targeted individuals. This is both the intended and obvious effect of deterrence-based liability rules. However, there is a danger that the rules imposing this liability will be given overly zealous interpretation by the courts, resulting in excessive levels of deterrence. This is of particular concern in the corporate case given managerial risk aversion and the prospect that the application of gatekeeper liability will be governed by compensatory rather than deterrence objectives.

To temper excessive care and activity level reactions to potential gatekeeper liability, modern corporate law statutes permit a corporation to indemnify a director for any expense reasonably incurred in defending, settling or satisfying a judgment for any action, provided that the director's fiduciary duty to act "honestly and in good faith and with a view to the best interests of the corporation" has been fulfilled. For indemnity with respect to criminal or administrative actions enforceable by fines, there must also have been reasonable grounds for believing that the conduct was lawful. This option to indemnify becomes an obligation if the director is substantially successful on the merits of the defence to any action, again so long as he or she acted honestly and in good faith with a view to the best interests of the corporation; and had reasonable grounds for believing that his or her conduct was lawful. The quality of corporate governance is upheld by this obligation since winning on a technicality, such as the expiration of a limitation period barring the action in question, does not give rise to a mandatory duty for the corporation to indemnify the successful director.

Modern corporations statutes also permit a corporation to purchase insurance for the benefit of a director against any liability which may be incurred in his or her capacity as a director, provided always that such liability does not result from a failure to act honestly and in good faith with a view to the best interests of the corporation. Corporations can, therefore, purchase insurance for directors with coverage for a wider range of behaviour than that for which direct corporate indemnification is allowed. Actions which are insurable but not indemnifiable include those for which objectively reasonable grounds did not exist, but in respect of which the director none the less acted honestly and in good faith; an example would be a successful shareholders' derivative action for negligence where the court refuses to permit indemnification.

Due to the different coverages of indemnification and D&O insurance, corporations typically purchase two types of D&O liability insurance coverage: Corporate Reimbursement Coverage, to cover losses to the corporation arising from the corporation's indemnification of a director, and Personal Coverage to cover the liability of a director for which he or she is not indemnified by the corporation and would otherwise be personally responsible. In addition to coverage for legal liabilities not permitted at law to be covered through corporate indemnification, Personal Coverage assures directors that they will not be forced to bear costs for which the corporation may lawfully indemnify them, but owing to financial hardship (*e.g.*, insolvency) cannot. Such coverage will also protect the officer and director against the failure of the corporation to remit withheld taxes to Revenue Canada or to pay employee wages that are due.

The supply side of the D&O insurance market is two-tiered, with "primary" insurers writing the policies and then reselling the coverage in excess of a certain designated loss liability (the so-called "excess" layer) to what are known as "reinsurers". The reinsurers are liable for a particular claim only after the original insurer has paid a designated amount — this retained amount is known as the "primary" layer. The reinsurers receive a portion of the premium commensurate to their portion of the risk, but also pay what is known as a "ceding" commission to the insurer that brings them the business. The capacity of the reinsurance market to underwrite risks has a profound effect upon the capacity of the primary insurers, particularly for such large and specialized risks as D&O policies, since it is through reinsurance that insurers themselves spread their risks and limit their potential liability.

* * *

(3) Summary

When one considers the proliferation of non-corporate law directorial duties, it may be that there was a greater expansion of Canadian directors' and officers' liability during the "crisis" years of the mid-1980s than there was in the United States. However, there are simply not enough reported cases in Canada on which to form a statistically sound evaluation, and claims data is of only minor assistance. Thus, the lack of sufficient claims experience prevented the industry from forming a conclusion as to how D&O policies would be interpreted by Canadian courts in the early crisis year of 1985.

Therefore, while Romano argues that an "anti-insurance" bias on the part of U.S. courts when interpreting D&O policies led to non-diversifiable risk and uncertainty and undermined the insurance function, the very lack of opportunity to interpret such documents in Canadian courts meant that no independent analysis of the risks of that or any other bias could be formed. D&O insurers have no choice but to apply the U.S. example to Canada, tempered of course by Canadian claims experience and such judgments as are in fact generated by the Canadian courts. With the trends in the United States in 1985-86 towards a stricter application of the negligence and fiduciary standards applicable to directors, towards increased statutory duties of directors, and towards strict interpretations of D&O policies against the insurer, D&O insurers operating in Canada raised the premiums here in anticipation of a similar, albeit more "Canadian" (that is, subdued), judicial trend.

The foregoing analysis of the nature and causes of the most recent crisis in Canadian D&O liability insurance lays to rest any fears that the crisis was the artificial creation of collusion or of foreign insurers seeking to cross-subsidize their losses in foreign markets. Rather, the evidence corresponds with Winter's theory of competitive insurance cycles operating in a climate of restrictions on costless equity infusions. As Winter concludes:

> in general a crisis will be characterized by an increase in premiums that is greater — possibly much greater — than could be "justified" by any increase in expected claims. This increase and the consequent increase in profits is consistent with a competitive market. The marketwide increase in profits does not imply collusion.

The Canadian D&O liability insurance crisis can thus be seen in the context of a crisis in liability insurance generally. After years of surplus supply, the investment income underwriting, and cheap and abundant reinsurance, a trend towards higher tort awards and more stringent standards of care in the United States and several severe storms in Europe caused the global reinsurance market to contract — seemingly overnight. The severe contraction of the supply of reinsurance, and the inability of the Canadian capital markets to finance independently the larger risks such as D&O coverage, had the most severe impact on the most uncertain lines. As Winter says, "The most uncertain lines will bear the brunt of shocks to the capacity of the entire market, absorbing and releasing capacity over the cycle."

The small and undeveloped nature of the Canadian D&O market means that the law of large numbers is inoperative and Canadian D&O policies cannot be underwritten as a completely separate market. Thus, the uncertainty generated by the changing application of directors' negligence standards in the United States and the policy of interpreting D&O contracts against the interests of the insurer had a profound impact on expected claims in Canada and discouraged a uniquely Canadian expansion in reinsurance supply. This impact was in addition to the direct influence warranted by the trading and corporate links between the two countries. The failure to see the Canadian D&O market separately from that in the U.S. is not the result of investor or consumer myopia but of the statistical requirements of the insurance industry and the relative lack of applicable judicial precedents in Canada.

Notes and Questions

1   What difficulties might you foresee in arrangements that allow a corporation to furnish compensation for suits brought by or on behalf of the corporation against directors and officers without any judicial supervision?

2 If the rationale for indemnification and insurance arrangements is tied to the impact of lawsuits on legitimate business decisions, is it not more appropriate to recommend amendments to corporate law statutes and judicial doctrines that give rise to liability in such circumstances in the first place? Several jurisdictions have introduced amendments to their corporate statutes in an effort to circumscribe the scope of liability. See, for example, the discussion surrounding Delaware's adoption of s. 102(b)(7), *supra*.

3 In *UBS*, Mr. McGoey sought indemnification for his legal fees in suing UBS. However, the trial judge held that Mr. McGoey was not entitled to indemnification, since he breached his fiduciary duty. The Court of Appeal decision affirming this finding is provided below.

Unique Broadband Systems Inc., Re
2014 CarswellOnt 9327, 2014 ONCA 538, 121 O.R. (3d) 81, 13 C.B.R. (6th) 278, 242 A.C.W.S. (3d) 80, 322 O.A.C. 122

* * *

(ii) Eligibility for Indemnification

The trial judge noted that UBS' indemnity obligations arise under various sources and documents: the Jolian Management Services Agreement; Article 7 of the UBS by-laws; specific indemnity agreements between Mr. McGoey and UBS; and s. 134(4.1) of the *OBCA*.

The trial judge also referred to Marrocco J.'s finding that the indemnification provisions under the UBS by-laws are "only available if the director or officer acted honestly and in good faith with a view to the best interests of the Corporation": at para. 183.

The trial judge concluded that, given her finding of a breach of fiduciary duty, the indemnity obligations were not operative.

I see no error in this finding. The purpose of statutory and contractual indemnity provisions is to ensure that officers and directors who are acting in good faith and in the best interests of a corporation are not exposed to legal costs. It is commercially sensible and good public policy to offer this protection. The rationale for offering the protection is eliminated, however, where the officer or director has not acted in good faith and in the best interests of the corporation.

In a related case, this court upheld an application judge's decision to refuse advanced funding for the legal costs of Look's directors and officers because the corporation had established a strong *prima facie* case of bad faith on the part of the parties seeking the funding: *Cytrynbaum v. Look Communications Inc.*, 2013 ONCA 455, 116 O.R. (3d) 241 (Ont. C.A.), leave to appeal refused, (2014), [2013] S.C.C.A. No. 377 (S.C.C.).

In the present case, while the trial judge did not specifically state that Mr. McGoey acted in bad faith, she did conclude that he was ineligible to receive indemnification because he had not met the standard of acting honestly and in good faith. This decision was open to the trial judge to make on the evidence before her and there is no basis for appellate interference.

Chapter 6

Fiduciary Duties Owed by Directors and Managers to the Corporation

1. INTRODUCTION TO FIDUCIARY DUTIES

Fiduciary duties are legal norms that are imposed on directors and managers in relation to their conduct with the corporation and shareholders. Fiduciary duties may also affect the relationship between different shareholders of the corporation or between the shareholders and the corporation. These duties ensure that the myriad corporate actors carry out their respective duties with the utmost good faith, do not put themselves in a position where their duty may conflict with self-interest, and do not derive a secret profit from their office.

(a) The Importance of Fiduciary Duties

The chapter is both descriptive and normative. That is, we wish not only to develop doctrinal fluency with the basic nature of fiduciary duties, but also to stimulate thought about what the fiduciary duty of directors and officers (referred to collectively below as "managers") *ought to be*. It is not an overstatement to say that fiduciary duties are the heart and soul of corporate law and at the very core of our conception of the role and functions of the corporation in modern society. It is thus not surprising that there is much disagreement about how such duties ought to be defined.

Economists and those who adhere to a "law and economics" conception of the world tend to view the corporation primarily as an organ of wealth generation. In this worldview, the shaping of corporate law is therefore very much a question of how to define the fiduciary duty in such as way as to ensure that it performs that function effectively and efficiently. From this perspective, it is usually thought that a shareholder-centric duty is appropriate; i.e., that directors and officers should be charged with the task of maximizing shareholder wealth, and that departures from that goal should count as breaches of fiduciary duty.

This might at first seem counter-intuitive. Maximizing the wealth generated by a corporation means maximizing the *aggregate wealth of each and every constituency that is affected by corporate behaviour*. This accounting should include, for example, employees, financial creditors (such as bondholders and banks), trade creditors, the government as tax collector, consumers, and all constituencies affected by corporate externalities, such as pollution.

There are a number of reasons, however, why economists have tended to reject such a broadly defined duty. For one thing, it is very difficult to put into operation. It is difficult enough for a board to determine how shareholders will be affected by any given decision. Is it realistic to expect a board to gather information about the affect of its decisions on each and every corporate constituency, and weigh them all together? And if a board must take into account all of these different constituencies, how are their interests to be traded off where there is conflict? Adopting a duty-at-large seems to make an unrealistic assumption about the information available to the average boards, and the time that boards can afford to devote to decision-making. It also creates the spectre of irresolvable uncertainty about what will and what will not lead to liability, since judges will be confronted with the same questions. Liability may end up being as much a function of the judge's politics as an objective weighing of interests, even if the latter was actually feasible.

Alternatively, if courts chose to exercise a light hand and defer to the business judgment of managers in deciding the issue of liability, many have suggested that a duty owed to all degenerates into a duty owed to none. If sued, the managers will always be able to avoid liability by inventing some plausible story about which constituencies they thought were most deserving of attention — being those that adventitiously benefitted from the corporate action.

In this view, the way in which we define the fiduciary duty is really a question of second best. If we can't realistically define a duty that ensures global wealth maximization (i.e., that of all constituents added together), then what duty is likely to come closest to ensuring a global maximum in the widest range of situations? On this score, shareholder wealth maximization comes out on top because shareholders are the only constituency with a "residual" interest in corporate profits. Maximizing the size of the residual claim will tend, in a plurality of situations, to maximize the aggregate value of all claims.

Conversely, if the duty is defined in terms of maximizing the value of the fixed claims, there is a concern that this will strike a fatal blow to the spirit of risk and innovation that is a primary driver of a vibrant private sector. The best way to maximize the value of the fixed claims is to manage conservatively, avoid risk, and "stay the course," rather than searching for new and innovative ways of doing things (which engender a higher risk of failure).

But what about those situations in shareholder primacy will fail to achieve a global maximum? It is certainly not a novel proposition to suggest that directors may choose actions that simply transfer wealth from one or more fixed claimants (e.g., employees, creditors, consumers, the local community, etc.) to the shareholders. The shareholder primacy view recognizes this danger, but would consign protection of non-shareholder constituencies to the matrix of private and public laws that lie outside fiduciary duties. For example, employees are protected by, *inter alia*, contract law, employment law, and health and safety laws. The local community is protected by zoning laws, environmental laws, and various private law doctrines such as nuisance and negligence. Creditors are protected by contract law, commercial law, banking laws, securities laws, and the like. Thus, non-shareholder welfare is not forgotten. It is simply relegated to *other* protective mechanisms.

Proponents of the shareholder primacy view of the world buttress their view by asserting that fiduciary duties, at their core, serve a "gap filling" function. In general, gap filling doctrines are those that the law specifies where complete contracting is not possible. By "complete contracting," we mean entering into a contract that stipulates the rights, duties, obligations, and liabilities of all parties in every possible state of the world. Because the world is very complex, complete contracting is definitionally impossible. Nonetheless, the idea is that there are some situations in which the contract between the parties will be more open-ended than others (i.e., less amenable to contractual allocation of risk), and these are the situations in which the law should specify a "gap filling" doctrine. In the corporate context, it is argued that shareholders, not having an explicit "contract" with the corporation, *and* being residual claimants, are the most exposed of all corporate constituencies to the danger of managerial perfidy. They cannot protect themselves, as many fixed claimants are able to do, via contractual means. Thus, the law should fill the gap in shareholders' rights with a fiduciary duty owed to the shareholders alone.

What is the content of this duty? According to Easterbrook and Fischel, "Corporate Control Transactions" (1982), 91 Yale L.J. 698, at p. 702:

> [Fiduciary] rules (should) approximate the bargain that investors and agents would strike if they were able to dicker at no cost. Such rules preserve the gains resulting from the delegation of authority and the division of labor while limiting the ability of agents to further their own interests at the expense of investors.

Easterbrook and Fischel's conception of fiduciary duties has been strongly criticized by Victor Brudney ("Corporate Governance, Agency Costs, and the Rhetoric of Contract" (1985), 85 Col. L. Rev. 1403) and by Robert Clark ("Agency Costs Versus Fiduciary Duties," in Pratt and Zeckhauser, Eds., *Principals and Agents: The Structure of Business* (1985), Ch. 3).

Needless to say, there are other views of the corporation in society that would see the fiduciary duty defined more broadly. Variations include giving shareholders a primary role in managers' deliberations, but requiring that the managers at least "consider" the welfare of other constituencies; allowing the government to add "public interest" directors to boards; and empowering at least some fixed claimants — usually employees — to elect a minority of directors to the board. Those who reject the economist's view of the corporation and fiduciary duty generally see the corporation as imbued with a richer job description than just wealth maximization. These people point to the instrumental role of the corporation in modern society. Corporations are the largest employers in the private sector. In addition, corporate behavior affects us all in a myriad of ways, often deleterious. These include dangerously manufactured products, negligent or fraudulent claims about product quality, externalities such as pollution, discriminatory hiring practices, abusive behavior to employees in the workplace, and so on.

In the end, what we choose as the content of the fiduciary duty is as much a political question as an economic one. Those who favour a broader duty than simple shareholder primacy may be quite willing to trade off some measure of wealth generation for distributional goals based on their notions of what constitutes a good, fair or just society.

As we shall see, the traditional conception of fiduciary duties is that such duties are owed to the corporation, but that the corporation means, in effect, the shareholders (i.e., the shareholder primacy view). However, two recent cases in the Supreme Court of Canada (excerpted below) reject this notion, holding that "the corporation" does *not* mean the shareholders — or any other corporate constituency. Rather, the managers should seek to make the corporation a "better corporation," which they may do without regard to any particular corporate constituency, or even the body of corporate constituents in their entirety. Thus, in a short period of time, we have moved from one end of the normative spectrum to the other. It is up to you to decide which you prefer.

(b) A Moving Target

You should be aware when you read cases dealing with the fiduciary duties of directors and officers that wholesale change has taken place over the past hundred and fifty years, rendering older cases of questionable authority. In general, the substantive content of the duty has passed through at least four phases:

1   Initially, corporate fiduciary duties were borrowed from trust law and reflected the severity and uncompromising nature of the fiduciary duty in trust law. Under the "conflict rule," if a director or officer acted with the least conflict of interest, or even in the presence of a

potential conflict of interest, the contract or transaction was voidable at the instance of the corporation. Similarly, under the "profit rule", if the director or officer made even a nominal profit as a result of his or her position in the corporation, again the fiduciary duty was breached, with similar consequences. This strict view of fiduciary duties was based in part on the evidentiary difficulty of producing objective evidence to contradict typically self-serving statements of motive by directors and officers.

2   It gradually became apparent, however, that wholesale adoption of fiduciary principles from the law of trusts, did not work very well in corporate law. It is very common in private corporations, for example, for directors or officers to sell assets to, or purchase assets from, the corporation. Moreover, many directors have diverse business interests which may, from time to time, create conflicts or potential conflicts of interest. Thus, it became the practice to include in a company's primary constating document a clause that allowed directors and officers to enter into contracts with their company, or to have material interests in other parties with whom the company was dealing, so long as full disclosure was made and the interested party refrained from voting on any matter involving his or her conflict of interest. In time, the courts got the hint and started to move away from the conflict and profit rules and toward a more flexible standard that simply required directors and officers to act in good faith and with a view to the best interests of the company.

This new standard was based squarely on shareholder primacy. While the courts held that the managers' fiduciary duties were owed to the corporation, they also equated "the corporation" with the share-holders (see e.g., *v. Daily News, infra* Chapter 6). This was, in no small part, due to the fact that shareholders were seen as the "owners" of the corporation, and relatedly, corporations were seen as organs of wealth generation. Managers were thus viewed as agents of the shareholders (at least in the sense indicated in *Automatic Self-Cleansing Filter Syndicate v. Cunninghame*), charged with the duty of maximizing shareholder wealth.

3   The third age involved the incorporation of the common law into an explicit provision in the statute outlining the fiduciary duty. Thus, the modern CBCA reads:

122. (1) Every director and officer of a corporation in exercising their powers and discharging their duties shall

(*a*) act honestly and in good faith with a view to the best interests of the corporation. . .

The statutory standard was formulated by the Dickerson Committee, empanelled by the federal government in the early 1970s to undertake the first major review of federal corporate law in nearly 40 years. According to the report of the Dickerson Committee, the committee intended that the statutory standard (somewhat modified by Parliament prior to its adoption) reflect the extant common law. The standard reflected in the federal legislation was ultimately adopted in virtually every corporate law statute in Canada.

It is noteworthy that the Dickerson Committee expressed the view not only that the common law standard reflect shareholder primacy, but that the new statutory standard would do so as well (while also expressing reservations about this).

4   Two recent Supreme Court of Canada cases (excerpted below) have greatly transformed the statutory standard content by rejecting shareholder primacy. Thus, for example, *Peoples* states:

> At all times, directors and officers owe their fiduciary obligation to the corporation. The interests of the corporation are not to be confused with the interests of the creditors or those of any other stakeholders.

It should be noted that this articulation of the managers' fiduciary duty is *not* equivalent to saying that the fiduciary duty is owed to each and every constituency that has some interest in corporate behavior. Rather, in *Peoples* and *BCE*, the Supreme Court effectively treats "the corporation" as an abstract entity, and requires that managers determine what course of conduct is in the best interest of that entity. That course of conduct may be coincident with the interests of one or more constituencies — or it may be coincident with the interests of *no* constituency.

This view of the managers' fiduciary duty has been subject to much criticism. In particular, it has been suggested that it is conceptually incapable of any sensible interpretation. Professor Iacobucci, for example, suggests that the Supreme Court's formulation is no less problematic than a tour bus operator seeking to determine his bus' route by asking "what is in the best interest of the bus?" rather than querying his customers (see Chapter 4). There are many other potential problems that stem from such a conceptually indeterminate standard. Not the least of these is whether it is actually possible for managers and courts to define the law of fiduciary duties in a systematic and predictive way, so as to offer some modicum of certainty in guiding corporate conduct. We hope that you will spend some time thinking about this when we get to *Peoples* and *BCE*.

(c)   Common Law Cases Involving Conflict and Profit Rules

The evolution from strict trust law principles to the more flexible good faith standard did not take place overnight. Rather, it reflected a gradual migration from the one to the other. Thus, for example, in the Supreme Court of Canada's decision in *Canadian Aero Service Ltd. v. O'Malley* (1973), 1973 CarswellOnt 236, 1973 CarswellOnt 236F, [1974] S.C.R. 592, 40 D.L.R. (3d) 371 (S.C.C.), excerpted below, Justice Laskin stated that the common law fiduciary principle "in its generality betokens loyalty, good faith and avoidance of a conflict of duty and self-interest." Justice Laskin's decision is thus reflective of *both* the older and the newer law. Nonetheless, as noted, the nearly contemporaneous report of the Dickerson Committee opted in favour of the good faith standard, at the expense of the conflict and profit rules.

Understanding older corporate law cases does, however, require some understanding of these rules. An illustrative case involving the conflict rule (which was applied far more often than the profit rule) is *Aberdeen Railway Co. v. Blaikie Bros.* [1843-60] All E.R. Rep. 249, 2 Eq. Rep. 1281 (H.L.), Blaikie was both a director of Aberdeen Railway and a partner in Blaikie Bros., a firm that had sold a quantity of "railway chairs" to Aberdeen. As director of Aberdeen, Blaikie had an interest in seeking the lowest possible price for the chairs. However, as a partner in Blaikie Bros., he had an interest in securing the highest price possible — a clear conflict of interest. The House of Lords had no difficulty in finding that the transaction was voidable at the option of the corporation.

While the conflict was patent in *Aberdeen*, it was rather more subtle in *Transvaal Lands Co. v. New Belgium (Transvaal) Land and Development Co.* [1914] 2 Ch. 488, 84 L.J. Ch. 94 (C.A.). In that case, Harvey was one of two directors of Transvaal Lands (the plaintiff company). He and another director had voted to purchase shares in Lydenberg (Transvaal) Gold Exploration Company from the defendant, New Belgium. It turned out that Harvey owned 1000 shares of the selling company — not as the beneficial owner, but as trustee under his father-in-law's will. In addition, his wife was beneficially interested in one tenth of the shares (subject to her mother's life interest). In allowing the plaintiff company to avoid the transaction, the Court of Appeal held that "the validity or invalidity of a transaction cannot depend upon the extent of the adverse interest of the fiduciary." In other words, any conflict of interest, no matter how small, would be sufficient to render the transaction voidable.

As noted, the other common law principle borrowed from trust law was the profit rule, which stated that a fiduciary could not earn a profit from his or her office (other than agreed-upon remuneration). While formulated in somewhat different terms, it is difficult to think of situations where the profit rule would apply where the conflict rule would not, and vice-versa, since any profit realized from a fiduciary's office will usually betoken a conflict of interest. In like manner, where there is a conflict of interest, there will usually be a profit made. But whether or not the conflict and profit rules are two sides of the same coin, both were enforced with zealous strictness (as can be seen from the *Regal* case below).

(d)   The Hydra-Headed Fiduciary Duty

Unfortunately, despite the articulation of a single statutory standard that nominally applies in *all* contexts, the Canadian courts have tended to apply different standards in different contexts. Justice Laskin's decision in *Canadian Aero Services*, for example, appears to have created a duty in the context of corporate opportunities that differs from that applied in other contexts. Managers appropriate a "corporate opportunity" when they take for themselves the benefit of a business opportunity that ought to have gone to the corporation. In *Canadian Aero Services*, for example, the president and vice-president of the company resigned their positions in order to incorporate their own company, which bid for and won a contract to do topographical mapping in Guyana. The court found that they two had appropriated a corporate opportunity, and ordered the two managers to hand over the profit that they had made from the contract.

In fixing the legal standard, Justice Laskin mixed together the older "conflict" and "profit" rules with the more modern "good faith" standard. In fact, a material portion of the decision consists of a discussion of the nature and application of the profit and conflict rules. No doubt because the decision emanates from the highest court in the land, and devoted much ink to the conflict and profit rules, lower court judges have often made use of these rules in deciding cases involving corporate opportunities.

We will also see that in respect of the issue of "competition," the common law took a radical departure from the usual conflict and profit rules, and permitted a person to serve as a director of two competing corporations. Remarkably, in such cases, and in spite of the unitary statutory standard, this anomalous common law still pops up — although more often than not, simply to be rejected by the court.

The case of hostile takeover bids presents another anomaly — and one that appears to have had the effect of swallowing the statutory standard whole. As noted, the statutory standard requires that directors and officers "act honestly and in good faith with a view to the best interests of the corporation." This standard is facially subjective. However, in defining the duty of directors and officers in the context of a hostile takeover bid, the Canadian courts (like their U.S. counterparts) require that there be some *objective* evidence to back up the managers' normally self-serving statements that they were acting in the best interest of the corporation.

This actually makes good sense. A takeover bid is an offer by a person or company, made to all shareholders, to purchase shares in a target corporation. The purpose of the offer is almost invariably to acquire control of the target. A "hostile" bid is one made without the approbation of management. Importantly, when a hostile bid succeeds, the target directors and officers often lose their jobs. There is therefore what might be called a "structural" conflict of interest, insofar as the target managers will be tempted to fight off a hostile bid, even if it is in the best interests of the shareholders. Because of this structural conflict, it makes sense to define the fiduciary duty in somewhat more exacting terms than in other contexts.

English and Canadian courts initially responded to this structural conflict by enunciating an "improper purpose rule", pursuant to which any attempt by the managers to influence control of the corporation was *per se* a breach of fiduciary duty. However, in the watershed case of *Teck Corp. v. Millar* (1972), 1972 CarswellBC 284, [1973] 2 W.W.R. 385, 33 D.L.R. (3d) 288 (B.C. S.C.), Justice Berger indicated that his preference was for a rule that was more in keeping with the "good faith" standard applicable in most other contexts. Nonetheless, recognizing the built-in conflict of interest, Justice Berger stated:

> If the directors have the right to consider the consequences of a takeover, and to exercise their powers to meet it, if they do so *bona fide* in the interests of the company, how is the Court to determine their purpose? In every case the directors will insist their whole purpose was to serve the company's interest. And no doubt in most cases it will not be difficult for the directors to persuade themselves that it is in the company's best interests that they should remain in office. Something more than a mere assertion of good faith is required.

> How can the Court go about determining whether the directors have abused their powers in a given case? How are the Courts to know, in an appropriate case, that the directors were genuinely concerned about the company and not merely pursuing their own selfish interests?. . .

> I think the Courts should apply the general rule in this way: The directors must act in good faith. Then there must be reasonable grounds for their belief. If they say that they believe there will be substantial damage to the company's interests, then there must be reasonable grounds for that belief. If there are not, that will justify a finding that the directors were actuated by an improper purpose.

Despite being only a lower court decision, Justice Berger's articulation of the fiduciary duty in the context of a hostile takeover bid was subsequently adopted by courts right across the country. More recent decisions (such as *Pente*, below) articulate the standard in somewhat more precise terms — based in no small measure on procedural steps that the board is normally expected to take to deal with the structural conflict. But in so doing, they have continued (and expanded) the requirement for an objective element that goes beyond the statutory standard.

Another anomaly arises insofar as self-dealing transactions are covered by their own code of conduct in the CBCA and similar statutes. Self-dealing transactions (or directors' and officers' interested transactions, or related party transactions) arise when a corporate fiduciary enters into a contract or transaction with the corporation, or has a material interest in a party entering into a contract or transaction. The corporate law (e.g., CBCA s.120) effectively specifies a safe harbour rule that applies only in the context of these transactions.

(e) Interaction between Fiduciary Duties and the Business Judgment Rule

In recent years, Canadian courts have adopted a "business judgment rule" that colours the determination of liability in the context of both the fiduciary duty and the duty of care. The business judgment rule is, in essence, a "safe harbour" rule. By this we mean that if the directors and officers fulfill certain conditions — mostly involving the procedural integrity of the decision-making process — they will tend to escape liability. Indeed, if the business judgment rule is found to apply, then it usually follows as a matter of course that the court will find no breach of duty. Thus, the focal point of most contemporary adjudication of disputes involving alleged breaches of fiduciary duty is whether the directors or officers may claim the benefit of the rule.

Above, we suggested that the anomalous treatment of takeover bid cases in the Canadian courts (i.e., the departure from the statutory standard) may have swallowed the rule whole. The reason for this is the Canadian business judgment rule has been largely worked out in cases involving hostile takeover bids, and applied without differentiation in other cases.

To more fully understand this, it is useful to contrast the American position. As we noted, the structural conflict of interest in the takeover bid context supplies a very good reason to specify a more demanding fiduciary duty in that context. Based on this, the American courts have defined a variation on the business judgment rule that applies *only* in the takeover bid context (as we shall see in the *Unocal* and *Revlon* cases excerpted below). In other cases, they apply a more relaxed ruled.

For some reason, the Canadian courts have not made this differentiation. The business judgment rule worked out in takeover bid cases has been applied by the courts in many different types of cases involving alleged breaches of fiduciary duty.

(f) Overlap with the Oppression Remedy

A particularly unsatisfying aspect of contemporary Canadian corporate law is the overlap, of still undetermined extent, between the statutory fiduciary duty and the statutory oppression remedy (e.g. CBCA s. 241). The oppression remedy allows a complainant to complain about conduct of the corporation or its directors that is oppressive, unfairly prejudicial to, or which unfairly disregards the interests of the complainant. The oppression remedy creates an overlap with the fiduciary duty in referring specifically to conduct of the directors. Thus, on the face of the statute, where a director is alleged to have misbehaved, a complainant may have resort *either* to a derivative action alleging breach of fiduciary duty, *or* an action under the oppression remedy.

What is a derivative action? Both at common law and under the various Canadian statutes, managers' fiduciary duties are owed to the corporation. This makes the corporation the proper plaintiff to complain about any wrongdoing by directors or officers. However, there is an obvious danger: the wrongdoing directors will likely refrain from suing themselves when there is an alleged wrong, and the shareholders will be left out in the cold. To address this danger, the statutes (e.g., CBCA s. 239) allow a shareholder (or more generally, "complainant") to commence an action *"in the name and on behalf of a corporation"*. Thus, if the directors refuse to bring an action, a shareholder may (with the permission of a court, pursuant to s. 239) commence the action himself or herself. Thus, actions to redress alleged breaches of fiduciary duty are virtually always derivative actions.

To understand this, we need to understand the difference between a *derivative* and a *personal* action. The traditional hallmark of a derivative action is that all shareholders are affected by the complained-of conduct equally, and all are affected indirectly. Thus, for example, if the managers are alleged to have overpaid themselves, that affects all shareholders both co-equally and indirectly. (The decision of the Supreme Court in *BCE* greatly clouds this definition, but we'll leave that for later.) By contrast, a *personal* action traditionally lies when a shareholder or shareholders have some complaint that is *not* shared by all the other shareholders. A classic example is the wrongful refusal of the directors to allow certain shareholders to vote their shares in a corporate election. That is a wrong that is unique to the complaining shareholders.

In fact, the drafters of the provision (the Dickerson Committee) intended that the oppression remedy be largely *personal* in nature. The committee envisioned that the oppression remedy could be used in derivative-type disputes (i.e., when the corporation as a whole is harmed) only in cases involving private corporations in which the dispute, though facially derivative in nature, is substantively personal in nature. For example, suppose that there are two shareholders in a corporation - a majority shareholder and a minority shareholder. Further suppose that the majority shareholder uses his or her power to appoint himself or herself and his or her cronies to the board, and then instructs the board to vote that the corporation pay him or her clearly excessive remuneration. The harm that is done is formally a harm to *the corporation*. All shareholders are harmed indirectly and co-equally. Thus, the payment of excessive remuneration should, as in other corporate contexts, result in a *derivative* and not a *personal* action. However, the reality is that the majority shareholder benefits, while the minority shareholder loses. In other words, it's really a dispute of a personal flavour between the two shareholders. Despite formally being a derivative wrong, substantively it is a personal wrong.

The Dickerson Committee envisioned that the oppression remedy would cover mostly personal actions — but also derivative actions that, as in the above example, have a strongly personal flavor. Despite this, as we will see below, with some variation as between provinces, the courts have allowed all manner of derivative complaints to be litigated under the oppression remedy. It is not difficult to find oppression cases of every stripe that traditionally would have been litigated as fiduciary duty cases. This has greatly added to the overlap between the fiduciary duty of directors and officers and the oppression remedy. It has also created parallel streams of jurisprudence in which two plaintiffs with virtually identical facts may realize different legal outcomes, depending on the doctrinal slot into which the case was thrown. This does little to enhance the impression of even-handed justice that is so essential to the operation of any legal system.

In fact, most litigators will plead *both* breach of fiduciary duty *and* the oppression remedy in any case involving director misconduct. However, the balance of the plaintiff's argument in court will typically focus on the oppression remedy. This is because the oppression remedy has a broader substantive trigger (in essence, "fairness") and broader remedies, and is thus more plaintiff friendly. But it is nonetheless somewhat odd — if not in fact downright inconvenient for both litigators and judges - that there should be two corporate doctrines that overlap so profoundly.

In *BCE*, the Supreme Court of Canada appears to have made an attempt to run the two standards together. This, unfortunately, has only muddied the waters even further. If a breach of fiduciary duty is alleged, can (or must) the court apply oppression remedy cases willy-nilly? Are the two statutory standards really one, as against decades of decisions that suggest otherwise? To complicate things further, large parts of the *BCE* decision are *obiter dictum*, including the court's remarks concerning the relationship between the oppression remedy and the fiduciary duty. But there is no separation in the decision of those matters that are *ratio* and those parts that are *obiter*. It is unclear how the lower courts will respond to this confusion.

Despite this overlap between the fiduciary duty and the oppression remedy, by its wording, the oppression remedy only allows the complainant to complain about conduct of the directors — and not the officers. This is a further anomaly that needs to be ironed out.

2. BASIC SELF-DEALING TRANSACTIONS

(a) Introduction to Basic Self-Dealing

Examination of basic self-dealing transactions provides a useful starting point for studying the appropriate scope of fiduciary duties. Essentially, self-dealing transactions involve contracts or transactions concluded between the directors and officers of a corporation, either directly or through their interest in another entity, and the corporation itself. The dangers entailed by self-dealing transactions are obvious: whenever an insider contracts with the corporation, the risk of diversion of corporate wealth is clear. That is, insiders contracting with the corporation operate under a strong incentive to cause the corporation to enter into transactions on terms that favour the insider. Although requiring directors to hold a direct stake in the corporation will dull the incentive to appropriate wealth via self-dealing, it will not eradicate it. This is because when unfair self-dealing occurs, the loss that the director sustains on his or her investment in the corporation from an interested transaction is likely to be more than offset by the gains he or she realizes in his or her personal capacity.

The simplest form of self-dealing transaction is the sale of an asset to the corporation by a director or officer at a price that exceeds the asset's fair market value (or, its converse, the purchase of an asset from the corporation by an officer or director at a price that is below fair market value). The price differential at the corporation's expense constitutes an "unbargained for" diversion of wealth from shareholders to the interested party. As such, the costs occasioned by self-dealing transactions constitute a form of agency cost.

Initially, the strict conflict and profit rules were applied to self-dealing transactions. However, the context in which this caused the most strain was self-dealing transactions, prompting legislatures to specify a special code for such transactions several decades before the statutes were amended to incorporate a more general fiduciary duty. The current statutory provisions governing self-dealing transactions in the CBCA and OBCA enshrine judicial review of a procedural and substantive nature.

In considering the evolution of legal rules in this area, you should be sensitive to the arguments favouring the adoption of different legal rules. To the extent that retreat from a categorical rule against self-dealing transactions is predicated on a recognition that certain benefits may be derived from self-dealing transactions, what are those benefits? Are they likely to be concentrated in certain types of contexts or corporations, and, if so, can legal rules be structured and applied such that beneficial self-dealing transactions are upheld, while unfair self-dealing transactions are invalidated? What are the costs to corporate actors of employing a selective or differential rule to evaluate self-dealing transactions, in terms of predicting the legal status of self-dealing transactions? What differences are involved in the nature of the inquiry implicated by the adoption of different rules, and are all the rules equally compatible with judicial expertise? Finally, what role, if any, is there for market forces in controlling or evaluating self-dealing transactions?

(b)   The Legislative Provisions

Section 120 of the CBCA is a legislative attempt to regulate contracts with directors or officers through a full disclosure mechanism. Compare s. 132 of the OBCA, especially ss. (7), (8), and (9). The legislation raises a number of issues, including the following:

1   When is a contract "material"? What is a "material" interest? While there is no guidance in the statute as to what is "material", some guidance is provided in the requirements for a "management information circular." Under Part VIII of the CBCA (s. 149(1)), management is required to solicit proxies from all shareholders in connection with any shareholders meeting. Further, (under s. 150(1)), management must send shareholders a "management proxy circular in prescribed form." When we turn to the regulation passed under the CBCA (Canada Business Corporations Act Regulations, 2001, SOR 2001-512, s. 55), it states that a management information circular "shall be in the form provided for in Form 51-102F5 (Information Circular) of NI 51-102." The acronym "NI" signifies a "national instrument", which is a regulatory instrument adopted by *all* of the securities regulatory authorities across Canada (in most cases, as a rule under each provincial securities enactment). NI 51-102 is entitled "Continuous Disclosure Obligations", and Form 51-102F5 ("Information Circular"), which is effectively part of NI 51-102, sets out the content requirements for management information circulars (the same thing as a "management proxy circular"). Item 11 of Form 51-102F5 is titled "Interest of Informed Persons in Material Transactions" and states:

> Describe briefly and, where practicable, state the approximate amount of any material interest, direct or indirect, of any informed person of the company, any proposed director of the company, or any associate or affiliate of any informed person or proposed director, in any transaction since the commencement of the company's most recently completed financial year or in any proposed transaction which has materially affected or would materially affect the company or any of its subsidiaries.

The definitions part of the instrument defines "informed person" as:

(a)   a director or executive officer of a reporting issuer;

(b)   a director or executive officer of a person or company that is itself an informed person or subsidiary of a reporting issuer;

(c)   any person or company who beneficially owns, directly or indirectly, voting securities of a reporting issuer or who exercises control or direction over voting securities of a reporting issuer or a combination of both carrying more than 10 percent of the voting rights attached to all outstanding voting securities of the reporting issuer other than voting securities held by the person or company as underwriter in the course of a distribution; and

(d)   a reporting issuer that has purchased, redeemed or otherwise acquired any of its securities, for so long as it holds any of its securities.

While on its face this would seem to indicate that shareholders are to be made aware of each and every material contract or transaction, it turns out that this may not be the case. The "Instructions" for Form 51-102F5 state:

(v)   You do not need to disclose the information required by this Item for any transaction or any interest in that transaction if:

(A)   the rates or charges involved in the transaction are fixed by law or determined by competitive bids,

(B)   the interest of the specified person in the transaction is solely that of director of another company that is a party to the transaction. . .

(C)   the transaction does not directly or indirectly, involve remuneration for services, and

(I)   the interest of the specified person or company arose from the beneficial ownership, direct or indirect, of less than 10 per cent of any class of voting securities of another company that is a party to the transaction,

(II)   the transaction is in the ordinary course of business of the company or its subsidiaries, and

(III)   the amount of the transaction or series of transactions is less than 10 per cent of the total sales or purchases, as the case may be, of the company and its subsidiaries for the most recently completed financial year.

(vi) Provide information for transactions not excluded above which involve remuneration, directly or indirectly, to any of the specified persons or companies for services in any capacity unless the interest of the person arises solely from the beneficial ownership, direct or indirect, of less than 10 per cent of any class of voting securities of another company furnishing the services to the company or its subsidiaries.

The OBCA requirements are to essentially the same effect. Do you think that this is perhaps too generous to directors and officers? Note also that s. 120(6.1) allows shareholders to examine the minutes of directors' meetings at which a disclosure of interest was made (an exception to the usual rule that shareholders do not have access to the minutes of directors' meetings). Does this cure the problem?

You will notice that under CBCA s. 120(6), "a general notice to the directors" that a party "is to be regarded as interested" in various matters is a sufficient declaration of interest to avoid liability. How can this be squared with the requirement in the first subsection of the "nature and extent" of the interest? The puzzle deepens when one examines the common law. For example, in *The Liquidators of the Imperial Mercantile Credit Association v. Edward John Coleman and John Watson Knight* [1873] L.R. 7 E. & I. App. 189 (H.L.), Coleman was a director of the Imperial Mercantile Credit Association ("MCA"). He was also a stock broker, and in that capacity had agreed to underwrite (i.e., sell on commission) a large issuance of debentures from a company called Peto. Coleman lobbied the board of MCA to, in effect, sub-contract with him to sell most of the debentures. He pocketed the difference between the 5% commission that Peto had agreed to pay him, and the 1.5% commission that he agreed to pay MCA. But while company's articles of association required that any interested director "declare his interest", Coleman disclosed to the board of MCA only that he had "an interest" in the transaction. The House of Lords found Coleman liable, holding that he this was insufficient disclosure to satisfy the company's articles. In the course of his judgment, Lord Chelmsford stated:

> If the directors had been fully informed of the real state of things, would they have accepted the proposal, and ought they to have done so as trustees for the shareholders?

A similar result is found in *Gray v. New Augarita Porcupine Mines Ltd.*, [1952] 3 D.L.R. 1 (Ontario P.C.) (a Privy Council case from Ontario). The company's by-laws allowed a director to avoid liability in respect of a contract in which the director was interested by disclosing to the company "the nature of his interest". At a meeting of the board, Gray (the controlling shareholder) made a proposal that all his liabilities to the Company be extinguished in return for the payment of a fixed sum. Despite the fact that he never told the board the exact quantum of his debts to the company, the board approved the settlement (from which he benefitted handsomely). The Privy Council had little difficulty in holding that disclosure that he had an interest was insufficient to discharge his obligation to disclose "the nature of his interest".

2   Section 120(7.1) requires that, if shareholders are to approve a contract or transaction, "disclosure of the interest was made to the shareholders in a manner sufficient to indicate its nature." Once again, is a general disclosure of interest sufficient? Or must it be particularized in the manner indicated in the two aforementioned decisions?

3   Section 120(5) provides that "a director required to make a disclosure under subsection (1) shall not vote on any resolution to approve the contract or transaction". Does "any resolution" mean just a director's resolution? Or does it include a shareholder resolution under ss. (7.1)? What interpretation is best supported by sound policy considerations?

4   Why do you suppose directors are allowed to vote on certain matters under s. 120(5)?

5   May a director improperly vote on an interested transaction, in violation of s. 120(5), and still be absolved from liability under s. 120(7)? While it might seem silly to contemplate that this could be the case, consider that the specific requirements to escape liability in (a), (b) and (c) do *not* include *not voting* (note that while ss. 7(a) requires that "disclosure of the interest was made in accordance with subsections (1) to (6)," s. 120(5) is not a disclosure section).

6   Note that under ss. 120(7) and ss. 120(7.1) the court is given discretion to overturn a contract or transaction if it does not satisfy the requirement that "the contract or transaction was reasonable and fair to the corporation when it was approved". Does this supplement or replace the court's more general discretion with respect to fiduciary matters under ss. 122(1)(a)?

7   Relatedly, you will notice that in order to be absolved from liability under ss. 120(7.1), the director or officer must have been "acting honestly and in good faith". This is different from the standard indicated in ss. 122(1)(a) that each director and officer must act "act honestly and in good faith *with a view to the best interests of the corporation*". Under conventional statutory interpretation, we would conclude that a under ss. 120(7.1) a director or officer need not have been acting with a view to the best interest of the corporation to escape liability. This raises a broader question: what does acting "with a view to the best interests of the corporation" add to acting

honestly and in good faith? Does either ss. 120(7.1) or ss. 123(a)(a) require amendment?

3.   CORPORATE OPPORTUNITIES

(a)   Introduction to Corporate Opportunities

In the normal course of their activities, directors and managers of the corporation are required to evaluate a range of projects in order to determine whether the corporation should invest in them. In the normal course of affairs, a project will be recommended to the corporation if the project's benefits exceed its costs. The materials in the following section deal with the problems that arise when persons operating in a fiduciary relationship to the corporation independently invest in a project that could have been acquired by the corporation. Like self-dealing transactions, investment by a director or manager in such projects is problematic because valuable opportunities may be diverted from the corporation to directors and officers acting in a personal capacity.

One way to control such conduct is to impose fiduciary duties upon directors and officers that limit their ability to "take" opportunities belonging to the corporation. The difficulty, however, is that there is no clear agreement on the criteria that determine when a transaction "belongs" to the corporation. Must the project be in the corporation's line of business for a conflict to arise? Does an opportunity belong to the corporation solely on the basis of the profiteer having been made aware of the opportunity because of his or her connection with the corporation? What effect does a corporation's inability to exploit an opportunity (owing to financial, legal or managerial impediments) have on determining whether the project belongs to the corporation? Does an opportunity still "belong" to the corporation if it has been considered and rejected by the corporation? Finally, as in the case of self-dealing transactions, is there an argument for imposing different rules on directors and managers depending on the context in which the transaction arises?

The theory used to evaluate these cases is, of course, similar to the theory utilized to analyze other conflict transactions. At heart, the issue is simply one of determining whether the director or manager has usurped the authority granted to her by the shareholders of the corporation in order to acquire some "unbargained for" personal benefit. As such, corporate opportunities represent another instance of agency costs, and invite control through judicial sanction.

We noted earlier that corporate opportunities seem to present a doctrinal anomaly, since Justice Laskin in the *Canadian Aero Services* case (below) fused the older common law (the conflict and profit rules) with the more modern "good faith" standard. In addition, lower courts still apply this fused standard, even though it is at odds with the statutory fiduciary duty. For this reason, it is useful to have a reasonably good understanding of how the courts dealt with corporate opportunities under the older trust-derived standards.

(b) The Common Law

Regal (Hastings) Ltd. v. Gulliver
[1942] 1 All E.R. 378 (H.L.)

[The appellant company was the owner of a cinema in Hastings. With a view to the sale of the property of the company as a going concern they were anxious to acquire two other cinemas in Hastings. For this purpose they formed a subsidiary company with a capital of £50,000 in £1 shares. They were offered a lease of the two cinemas, but the landlord required a guarantee of the rent by the directors unless the paid-up capital of the subsidiary company was £5,000. The intention of the directors of the appellant company was that the appellant company should hold all the shares in the subsidiary company, and, since the appellant company at that time was unable to provide more than £2,000, it seemed that the directors would be obliged to give the required guarantee. The directors wished to avoid giving this guarantee, and the matter was arranged in this way. The appellant company was to take up 2,000 shares at par; the chairman of the directors promised to find £500; the other directors promised to do the same; and Garton, who was the solicitor to the appellant company, also promised to provide £500. This arrangement was made at a board meeting to which the directors and Garton were called by two notices, one of a board meeting of the appellant company and the other of a board meeting of the subsidiary company. Both meetings were to be held at the same time and place. In fulfillment of the arrangement 2,000 shares were allotted to the appellant company; 500 to each of the directors and Garton, but the shares in respect of the £500 "found" by the chairman of the directors were allotted to and paid for by two companies and one private individual, so that the companies and the individual took as beneficial owners and not as nominees of the chairman. At the same meeting, the board accepted a £92,500 offer for its interest in the three theatres, £77,500 being allocated to Regal's theatre and £5,000 to the leasehold interest in the other two. Ultimately the transaction was not carried through by the sale of the property of the company as a going concern, but by the sale of all the shares in the appellant company and in the subsidiary company. The 3,000 shares in the subsidiary company which were allotted to or on behalf of the directors of the appellant company and Garton were sold at a profit of £2 16s. 1d. per share. It was found as a fact that all the transactions were *bona fide*.

As a sequel to the sale of the shares in Regal, the company came under the management of a new board of directors, who caused to be issued the writ which initiated the litigation. By this action Regal sought to recover from its five former directors and its former solicitor a sum of £8,142, 10s. either as damages or as money had and received to the plaintiffs' use. The action was tried by Wrottesley J., who entered judgment for all the defendants with costs. An appeal by the plaintiffs to the Court of Appeal was dismissed with costs]

LORD RUSSELL OF KILLOWEN: The rule of equity which insists on those, who by use of a fiduciary position make a profit, being liable to account for that profit, in no way depends on fraud, or absence of *bona fides*; or upon such questions or considerations as whether the profit would or should otherwise have gone to the plaintiff, or whether the profiteer was under a duty to obtain the source of the profit for the plaintiff, or whether he took a risk or acted as he did for the benefit of the plaintiff, or whether the plaintiff has in fact been damaged or benefitted by his action. The liability arises from the mere fact of a profit having, in the stated circumstances, been made. The profiteer, however honest and well-intentioned, cannot escape the risk of being called upon to account.

The leading case of *Keech v. Sandford* is an illustration of the strictness of this rule of equity in this regard, and of how far the rule is independent of these outside considerations. A lease of the profits of a market had been devised to a trustee for the benefit of an infant. A renewal on behalf of the infant was refused. It was absolutely unobtainable. The trustee, finding that it was impossible to get a renewal for the benefit of the infant, took a lease for his own benefit. Though his duty to obtain it for the infant was incapable of performance, nevertheless he was ordered to assign the lease to the infant, upon the bare ground that, if a trustee on the refusal to renew might have a lease for himself, few renewals would be made for the benefit of *cestuis que trust*. Lord King L.C., said at p. 62:

> This may seem hard, that the trustee is the only person of all mankind who might not have the lease: but it is very proper that the rule should be strictly pursued, and not in the least relaxed. . .

One other case in equity may be referred to in this connection, *viz.*, *Ex p. James*, decided by Lord Eldon L.C. That was a case of a purchase of a bankrupt's estate by the solicitor to the commission, and Lord Eldon L.C., refers to the doctrine thus, at p. 345:

> This doctrine as to purchases by trustees, assignees, and persons having a confidential character, stands much more upon general principles than upon the circumstances of any individual case. It rests upon this: that the purchase is not permitted in any case however honest the circumstances; the general interests of justice requiring it to be destroyed in every instance; as no court is equal to the examination and ascertainment of the truth in much the greater number of cases.

Let me now consider whether the essential matters, which the plaintiff must prove, have been established in the present case. As to the profit being in fact made there can be no doubt. The shares were acquired at par and were sold three weeks later at a profit of £2 16s. 1d. per share. Did such of the first five respondents as acquired these very profitable shares acquire them by reason and in course of their office of directors of Regal? In my opinion, when the facts are examined and appreciated, the answer can only be that they did. The actual allotment no doubt had to be made by themselves and Garton (or some of them) in their capacity as directors of Amalgamated; but this was merely an executive act, necessitated by the alteration of the scheme for the acquisition of the lease of the two cinemas for the sole benefit of Regal and its shareholders through Regal's shareholding in Amalgamated. That scheme could only be altered by or with the consent of the Regal board. Consider what in fact took place on Oct. 2, 1935. The position immediately before that day is stated in Garton's letter of Sept. 26, 1935. The directors were willing to guarantee the rent until the subscribed capital of Amalgamated reached £5,000. Regal was to control Amalgamated and own the whole of its share capital, with the consequence that the Regal shareholders would receive their proportion of the sale price of the two new cinemas. The respondents then meet on Oct. 2, 1935. They have before them an offer to purchase the Regal cinema for £77,500, and the lease of the two cinemas for £15,000. The offer is accepted. The draft lease is approved and a resolution for its sealing is passed in anticipation of completion in five days. Some of those present, however, shy at giving guarantees, and accordingly the scheme is changed by the Regal directors in a vital respect. It is agreed that a guarantee shall be avoided by the six respondents bringing the subscribed capital up to £5,000. I will consider the evidence and the minute in a moment. The result of this change of scheme (which only the Regal directors could bring about) may not have been appreciated by them at the time; but its effect upon their company and its shareholders was striking. In the first place, Regal would no longer control Amalgamated, or own the whole of its share capital. The action of its directors had deprived it (acting through its shareholders in general meeting) of the power to acquire the shares. In the second place, the Regal shareholders would only receive a largely reduced proportion of the sale price of the two cinemas. The Regal directors and Garton would receive the moneys of which the Regal shareholders were thus deprived. This vital alteration was brought about in the following circumstances — I refer to the evidence of the respondent Garton. He was asked what was suggested when the guarantees were refused, and this is his answer:

> Mr. Gulliver said "We must find it somehow. I am willing to find £500. Are you willing," turning to the other four directors of Regal, "to do the same?" They expressed themselves as willing. He said,

"That makes £2,500," and he turned to me and said, "Garton, you have been interested in Mr. Bentley's companies; will you come in to take £500?" I agreed to do so.

My Lords, I have no hesitation in coming to the conclusion, upon the facts of this case, that these shares, when acquired by the directors, were acquired by reason, and only by reason of the fact that they were directors of Regal, and in the course of their execution of that office.

It now remains to consider whether in acting as directors of Regal they stood in a fiduciary relationship to that company. Directors of a limited company are the creatures of statute and occupy a position peculiar to themselves. In some respects they resemble trustees, in others they do not. In some respects they resemble agents, in others they do not. In some respects they resemble managing partners, in others they do not. . .

[After reviewing the authorities:]

In the result, I am of opinion that the directors standing in a fiduciary relationship to Regal in regard to the exercise of their powers as directors, and having obtained these shares by reason and only by reason of the fact that they were directors of Regal and in the course of the execution of that office, are accountable for the profits which they have made out of them. The equitable rule laid down in *Keech v. Sandford* and *Ex p. James*, and similar authorities applies to them in full force. It was contended that these cases were distinguishable by reason of the fact that it was impossible for Regal to get the shares owing to lack of funds, and that the directors in taking the shares were really acting as members of the public. I cannot accept this argument. It was impossible for the *cestui que* trust in *Keech v. Sandford* to obtain the lease, nevertheless the trustee was accountable. The suggestion that the directors were applying simply as members of the public is a travesty of the facts. They could, had they wished, have protected themselves by a resolution (either antecedent or subsequent) of the Regal shareholders in general meeting. In default of such approval, the liability to account must remain. The result is that, in my opinion, each of the respondents Bobby, Griffiths, Bassett, and Bentley is liable to account for the profit which he made on the sale of his 500 shares in Amalgamated.

The case of the respondent Gulliver, however, requires some further consideration, for he has raised a separate and distinct answer to the claim. He says: "I never promised to subscribe for shares in Amalgamated. I never did so subscribe. I only promised to find others who would be willing to subscribe. I only found others who did subscribe. The shares were theirs. They were never mine. They received the profit. I received none of it". If these are the true facts, his answer seems complete. The evidence in my opinion establishes his contention. Throughout his evidence Gulliver insisted that he only promised to find £500, not to subscribe it himself. The £500 was paid by two cheques in favour of

Amalgamated, one a cheque for £200 signed by Gulliver as director and on behalf of the Swiss company Seguliva, the other a cheque for £300 signed by Gulliver as managing director of South Downs Land Co., Ltd. They were enclosed in a letter of Oct. 3, 1935, from Gulliver to Garton, in which Gulliver asks that the share certificates be issued as follows, 200 shares in the name of himself, Charles Gulliver, 200 shares in the name of South Downs Land Co., Ltd., and 100 shares in the name of Miss S. Geering. The money for Miss Geering's shares was apparently included in South Down Land Co.'s cheque. The certificates were made out accordingly, the 200 shares in Gulliver's name being, he says, the shares subscribed for by the Swiss company. . .

There remains to consider the case of Garton. He stands on a different footing from the other respondents in that he was not a director of Regal. He was Regal's legal adviser; but, in my opinion, he has a short but effective answer to the plaintiffs' claim. He was requested by the Regal directors to apply for 500 shares. They arranged that they themselves should each be responsible for £500 of the Amalgamated capital, and they appealed, by their chairman, to Garton to subscribe the balance of £500 which was required to make up the £3,000. In law his action, which has resulted in a profit, was taken at the request of Regal, and I know of no principle or authority which would justify a decision that a solicitor must account for profit resulting from a transaction which he has entered into on his own behalf, not merely with the consent, but at the request of his client. . .

One final observation I desire to make. In his judgment Lord Greene M.R. stated that a decision adverse to the directors in the present case involved the proposition that, if directors *bona fide* decide not to invest their company's funds in some proposed investment, a director who thereafter embarks his own money therein is accountable for any profits which he may derive therefrom. As to this, I can only say that to my mind the facts of this hypothetical case bear but little resemblance to the story with which we have had to deal . . .

LORD PORTER: My Lords, I am conscious of certain possibilities which are involved in the conclusion which all your Lordships have reached. The action is brought by the Regal company. Technically, of course, the fact that an unlooked for advantage may be gained by the shareholders of that company is immaterial to the question at issue. The company and its shareholders are separate entities. One cannot help remembering, however, that in fact the shares have been purchased by a financial group who were willing to acquire those of the Regal and the Amalgamated at a certain price. As a result of your Lordships' decision that group will, I think, receive in one hand part of the sum which has been paid by the other. For the shares in Amalgamated they paid £3 16s. 1d. per share, yet part of that sum may be returned to the group, though not necessarily to the individual shareholders by reason of the enhancement in value of the shares in Regal — an enhancement brought about as a result of the receipt by the company of the profit made by some of its former directors on the sale of Amalgamated shares. This, it seems, may be an unexpected windfall, but whether it be so or not, the principle that a person occupying a fiduciary relationship shall not make a profit by reason thereof is of such vital importance that the possible consequence in the present case is in fact as it is in law an immaterial consideration. . .

LORD SANKEY: As to the duties and liabilities of those occupying such a fiduciary position, a number of cases were cited to us which were not brought to the attention of the trial judge. In my view, the respondents were in a fiduciary position and their liability to account does not depend upon proof of *mala fides*. The general rule of equity is that no one who has duties of a fiduciary nature to perform is allowed to enter into engagements in which he has or can have a personal interest conflicting with the interests of those whom he is bound to protect. If he holds any property so acquired as trustee, he is bound to account for it to his *cestui que* trust. The earlier cases are concerned with trusts of specific property: *Keech v. Sandford*, per Lord King L.C. The rule, however, applies to agents, as, for example, solicitors and directors, when acting in a fiduciary capacity. . .

It is not, however, necessary to discuss all the cases cited, because the respondents admitted the generality of the rule as contended for by the appellants, but were concerned rather to confess and avoid it. Their contention was that, in this case, upon a true perspective of the facts, they were under no equity to account for the profits which they made. I will deal first with the respondents, other than Gulliver and Garton. We were referred to *Imperial Hydropathic Hotel Co., Blackpool v. Hampson*, where Bowen L.J., at p. 12, drew attention to the difference between directors and trustees, but the case is not an authority for contending that a director cannot come within the general rule. No doubt there may be exceptions to the general rule, as, for example, where a purchase is entered into after the trustee has divested himself of his trust sufficiently long before the purchase to avoid the possibility of his making use of special information acquired by him as trustee (see the remarks of Lord Eldon, in *Ex p. James* at p. 352) or where e purchases with full knowledge and consent of his *cestui que* trust. *Imperial v. Hampson* makes no exception to the general rule that a solicitor or director, if acting in a fiduciary capacity, is liable to account for the profits made by him from knowledge acquired when so acting.

It was then argued that it would have been a breach of trust for the respondents, as directors of Regal, to have invested more than £2,000 of Regal's money in Amalgamated, and that the transaction would never have been carried through if they had not themselves put up the other £3,000. Be it so, but it is impossible to maintain that, because it would have been a breach of trust to advance more than £2,000 from Regal and that the only way to finance the matter was for the directors to advance the balance themselves, a situation arose which brought the respondents outside the general rule and permitted them to retain the profits which accrued to them from the action they took. At all material times they were directors and in a fiduciary position, and they used and acted upon their exclusive knowledge acquired as such directors. They framed resolutions by which they made a profit for themselves. They sought no authority from the company to do so, and, by reason of their position and actions, they made large profits for which, in my view, they are liable to account to the company. . .

LORD MACMILLAN: The point was not whether the directors had a duty to acquire shares in question for the company and entered into the transaction lawfully, in good faith and indeed avowedly in the interests of the company. However, that does not absolve them from accountability for any profit which they made, if it was by reason and in virtue of their fiduciary office as directors that they entered into the transaction.

The equitable doctrine invoked is one of the most deeply rooted in our law. It is amply illustrated in the authoritative decisions which my noble and learned friend Lord Russell of Killowen has cited. I should like only to add a passage from *Principles of Equity*, by Lord James, which puts the whole matter in a sentence (3rd ed., 1778, Vol. 2, p. 87): "Equity", he says, "prohibits a trustee from making any profit by his management, directly or indirectly".

The issue thus becomes one of fact. The plaintiff company has to establish two things: (i) that what the directors did was so related to the affairs of the company that it can properly be said to have been done in the course of their management and in utilization of their opportunities and special knowledge as directors; and (ii) that what they did resulted in a profit to themselves. The first of these propositions is clearly established by the analysis of the whole complicated circumstances for which the House is indebted to my noble and learned friend who has preceded me. The second proposition is admitted, except in the case of Gulliver, in whose case I agree that, on the evidence, he is not proved to have made any profit personally. The conditions are, therefore, in my opinion, present which preclude the four directors who made a personal profit by the transaction from retaining such profit. . .

LORD WRIGHT: [The] question can be briefly stated to be whether an agent, a director, a trustee or other person in an analogous fiduciary position, when a demand is made upon him by the person to whom he stands in the fiduciary relationship to account for profits acquired by him by reason of his fiduciary position, and by reason of the opportunity and the knowledge, or either, resulting from it, is entitled to defeat the claim upon any ground save that he made profits with the knowledge and the assent of the other person. The most usual and typical case of this nature is that of principal and agent. The rule in such cases is compendiously expressed to be that an agent must account for net profits secretly (that is, without the knowledge of his principal) acquired by him in the course of his agency. The authorities show how manifold and various are the applications of the rule. It does not depend on fraud or corruption.

The Courts below have held that it does not apply in the present case, for the reason that the purchase of the shares by the respondents, though made for their own advantage, and though the knowledge and opportunity which enabled them to take the advantage came to them solely by reason of their being directors of the appellant company, was a purchase which, in the circumstances, the respondents were under no duty to the appellant to make, and was a purchase which it was beyond the appellant's ability to make, so that, if the respondents had not made it, the appellant would have been no better off by reason of the respondents abstaining from reaping the advantage for themselves. With the question so stated, it was said that any other decision than that of the Courts below would involve a dog-in-the-manger policy. What the respondents did, it was said, caused no damage to the appellant and involved no neglect of the appellant's interests or similar breach of duty. However, I think the answer to this reasoning is that, both in law and equity, it has been held that, if a person in a fiduciary relationship makes a secret profit out of the relationship, the Court will not inquire whether the other person is damnified or has lost a profit which otherwise he would have got. The fact is in itself a fundamental breach of the fiduciary relationship. Nor can the Court adequately investigate the matter in most cases. The facts are generally difficult to ascertain or are solely in the knowledge of the person who is being charged. They are matters of surmise; they are hypothetical because the inquiry is as to what would have been the position if that party had not acted as he did, or what he might have done if there had not been the temptation to seek his own advantage, if, in short, interest had not conflicted with duty . . .

It is suggested that it would have been mere quixotic folly for the four respondents to let such an occasion pass when the appellant company could not avail itself of it; but Lord King faced that very position when he accepted that the person in the fiduciary position might be the only person in the world who could not avail himself of the opportunity. It is, however, not true that such a person is absolutely barred, because he could by obtaining the assent of the shareholders have secured his freedom to make the profit for himself. Failing that, the only course open is to let the opportunity pass. To admit of any other alternative would be to expose the principal to the dangers against which James L.J. in the passage I have quoted uttered his solemn warning. The rule is stringent and absolute because "the safety of mankind" requires it to be absolutely observed in the fiduciary relationship. In my opinion, the appeal should be allowed in the case of the four respondents . . .

Notes and Questions

1   Do Lords Russell, Sankey, Macmillan and Wright all base their judgments on the same legal principles? Is there truly such a thing as "financial inability" when a corporation has the chance to invest in a profitable enterprise? If the purpose in *Regal* was to package the three properties for immediate resale, was that not a venture that could have been financed in the normal way?

2   Do you agree with Lord Russell's decision as to Gulliver? On what basis did he escape liability? Is there a case for treating the solicitor, Garton, differently?

3   The Supreme Court of Canada adopted the principle of *Regal* in *Zwicker v. Stanbury* (1953), [1954] 1 D.L.R. 257, [1953] 2 S.C.R. 438, 1953 CarswellNS 25, and in *Midcon Oil & Gas Co. v. New British Dominion Oil Co.*, [1958] S.C.R. 314, 12 D.L.R. (2d) 705, 1958 CarswellAlta 70.

4   Lord Porter's concern with the windfall that would be obtained by the new shareholders of Regal formed the basis of McDermid J.A.'s dissent in *Abbey Glen Property Corp. v. Stumborg*, 85 D.L.R. (3d) 35, [1978] 4 W.W.R. 28, 1978 CarswellAlta 236 (C.A.). He agreed that there had been a breach of fiduciary duty, but declined to give judgment for the plaintiff corporation as it had paid a price for the shares calculated on an estimate of the corporation's assets and without reference to possible liability of former directors. Clement J.A., for the majority, held that "a change in shareholders of itself cannot diminish the rigour of the obligation to account to the company . . ." For a comment see Braithwaite, "Unjust Enrichment and Directors' Duties: *Abbey Glen Property Corp. v. Stumborg*" (1979), 3 Can. Bus. L.J. 210. See also s. 240(c) of the CBCA and s. 247(c) of the OBCA, which provide for payment of a judgment to former as well as present security holders rather than to the corporation itself in a shareholders' derivative action.

Peso Silver Mines Ltd. v. Cropper
[1966] 56 D.L.R. (2d) 117, 59 W.W.R. 329 (B.C. C.A.); affirmed, [1966] S.C.R. 673, 56 W.W.R. 641

[Peso Silver Mines Ltd. was incorporated as a private company in British Columbia in March, 1961, to take over a group of silver mining claims in the Yukon. The defendant Cropper, along with his associates Walker and Verity, was instrumental in incorporating Peso. Cropper, Walker and Verity were Peso's first directors, and Cropper was the managing director. In September, 1961, Peso was converted to a public company and shares were sold to the public, the proceeds being used to finance development of the claims. Peso acquired further claims and by March,

1962, held 362 claims covering 20 square miles, the purchase and development of which had put a considerable strain on its finances.

In late March, 1962, Peso, through Cropper and Verity, was offered three groups of claims (the Dickson claims), one of which was contiguous to its Yukon holdings. The Peso board, which by this time had been enlarged to six, turned the offer down because of strained finances and because it felt that Peso had enough ground under control. Approximately six weeks later, in May, 1962, Cropper, Walker, Verity and Dr. Aho, Peso's consulting geologist, formed a private company, Cross Bow, to take up the Dickson claims. Cross Bow was then converted to a public company with its shares being sold to finance development. Because of this, Walker, the President of Peso, wrote to the B.C. Superintendent of Brokers explaining the transaction. In the course of that letter, Walker explained that the Peso board was not interested in the company acquiring any more ground because of its financial position and because of the number of claims it already held. Walker went on to say that "... other parties however were interested in acquiring ground in this district, and we felt that some control might be maintained if we joined these groups. Our first interest is for the Peso shareholders and the continued and extensive development of the Peso ground, and it is to this end that our main interest must lie. We do feel, however, that if we do not become part of this new additional ground control, other people would be participating and acquiring regardless."

In December, 1963, control of Peso was purchased by Charter Oil. The president of Charter then demanded that Cropper, Walker and Verity turn over their interest in the company that held the Dickson claims to Peso. Walker and Verity agreed to do so but Cropper refused. The president of Charter then used his majority control position on the board of Peso to have Peso commence an action against Cropper for an accounting and declaration of trust and dismissed him as managing director.

Cropper claimed damages against the company for wrongful dismissal. The trial judge dismissed the company's claim and allowed Cropper's counterclaim for damages in the amount of $10,000.]

BULL, J.A.: . . . Notwithstanding, in this modern day and country when it is accepted as commonplace that substantially all business and commercial undertakings, regardless of size or importance, are carried on through the corporate vehicle with the attendant complexities involved by interlocking, subsidiary and associated corporations, I do not consider it enlightened to extend the application of these principles [of fiduciary duties] beyond their present limits. That the principles, and the strict rules applicable to trustees upon which they are based, are salutory cannot be disputed, but care should be taken to interpret them in the light of modern practice and way of life.

I now turn to the question of whether or not the acquisition by the respondent of the Cross Bow and Mayo shares in the one transaction and the Dayton shares in the other, fall within the first principle that no one who has fiduciary duties must be allowed to retain a profit from an engagement where his personal interest conflicts or may conflict with those of the principal to whom the duties are owed. There is no question whatsoever that the respondent as managing-director of the appellant was in a fiduciary relationship to it. Also there is no doubt that the respondent acted in the best of faith in both transactions and that there was no thought or intent on his part to profit himself at the expense of the appellant. The appellant had no interest in those of the Peso claims offered to it by Dickson before such offer was made, and, in fact, there is no evidence as to whether or not it knew the claims even existed. It did have a very definite interest in the properties while it was considering whether it could or would purchase them, but that interest ceased to exist when, by admittedly *bona fide* decision of its full board of directors made after professional advice was received, the offer was rejected by the appellant. It was only after this temporary interest of the appellant had ceased and after "it had been out of his mind", did the respondent participate in the impugned transaction. If the transaction had taken place when and as it did, but without the offer of these contiguous properties being before the appellant's directors for decision or during the time the appellant was considering the matter, the situation would have been entirely different, and the respondent might well have had to account to the appellant for his participation. But that is not the case here, and I cannot conclude that because offers of properties are continuously put before a mining company and rejected, henceforth any personal dealing with any of them by a director raises a conflict of personal interests with the interests of the company. On the contrary, it would seem that an out-and-out *bona fide* rejection by the company would be the best evidence that any later dealings with the property by anyone would not be against its interests. This is not a case like *Keech v. Sandford*, where a trustee took unto himself property that had been trust property but which was impossible, although desired, to be continued as such. Nor is the situation found in the *Regal (Hastings), Ltd.* case, where the full acquisition of the property was conceived and wanted by the company but other circumstances made it impossible to take that portion which the directors personally took. The interests of the trustee in the one case and of the directors in the other remained always in conflict with those of the principal. With regard to the second transaction involving the Dayton properties, the evidence is extremely unsatisfactory as to what these were, where they were, and whether or not they, or some of them, were rejects of the appellant. It does seem, however, that none of the claims were contiguous or adjacent to those of the appellant, and the evidence given by witnesses for the appellant would seem to show that the appellant was not interested in them for one reason or another. I do not think that the appellant has adduced evidence sufficient to support a finding that the interests of the appellant were in conflict at any time with the personal interests of the respondent so far as his holdings in Dayton are concerned.

It was the second principle of law as set out in the *Regal (Hastings), Ltd.* case that the appellant most strongly urged to support his submission that the respondent should be held accountable. It was said, with respect to the Cross Bow and Mayo transaction, that, as these properties were put up for sale to the appellant in the first instance the subsequent acquisition by the respondent and the two other directors was by reason of the fact that they acquired the knowledge of and about the properties *qua* directors and that therefore their personal transaction was one made by "reason of being directors" and "in the course of execution of that office". I cannot agree. I consider that the authorities require that to come within the rule, the impugned transactions must, as stated by Lord Russell, be by reason of the fact, and *only by reason* of the fact, that they were directors and in the *course of the execution* of that office. That clearly was the situation in the *Regal (Hastings), Ltd.* case where the whole transaction was implemented by the directors carrying out their duties as required by their company in a company transaction but in which they were personally involved. In the case of *Zwicker v. Stanbury*, supra, the directors were charged with the duty of and were carrying out a financial reorganization of a company which was in difficulties and took unto themselves in an allegedly private capacity securities which were or could form a very part of the refinancing processes being considered. In the case at bar, undoubtedly the knowledge of the Cross Bow properties came to the respondent and others because they were directors of the appellant. Also it cannot be questioned that these directors were acting only as such and in execution of that office when they considered and rejected the offer to the company of the properties in question. But their later negotiation for and acquisition of the mineral claims, although based on such knowledge acquired as aforesaid, could not, in my respectful opinion, be said to have been done "only" in their capacity as directors and "in the execution of that office". Once again, these properties were not something the appellant had brought within the ambit of its business or plans. They, along with others, were simply offered to it and rejected. I cannot think that the mere acquisition of knowledge in a directors' meeting qua director in itself would bring any subsequent dealing with the subject matter into the realm of being in the execution of that office.

In the *Regal (Hastings), Ltd.* case, Greene, M.R., said in the Court of Appeal in his unreported judgment dated February 15, 1941 (and with which Mackinnon, L.J., and du Parcq, L.J., agreed), that:

> To say that the Company was entitled to claim the benefit of those shares would involve this proposition: Where a Board of Directors

considers an investment which is offered to their company and *bona fide* comes to the conclusion that it is not an investment which their Company ought to make, any Director, after that Resolution is come to and *bona fide* come to, who chooses to put up money for that investment himself must be treated as having done it on behalf of the Company, so that the Company can claim any profit that results to him from it. That is a proposition for which no particle of authority was cited; and goes, as it seems to me, far beyond anything that has ever been suggested as to the duty of directors, agents, or persons in a position of that kind.

Although the judgment of the Court of Appeal was reversed by the House of Lords as cited above, the above-quoted hypothetical case suggested by the Master of the Rolls did attract the comment of Lord Russell when he said at p. 391:

One final observation I desire to make. In his judgment Lord Greene, M.R., stated that a decision adverse to the directors in the present case involved the proposition that, if directors *bona fide* decide not to invest their company's funds in some proposed investment, a director who thereafter embarks his own money therein is accountable for any profits which he may derive therefrom. As to this, I can only say that to my mind the facts of this hypothetical case bear but little resemblance to the story with which we have had to deal.

As Greene, M. R., was found to be in error in his decision, I would think that the above comment by Lord Russell on the hypothetical case would be superfluous unless it was intended to be a reservation that he had no quarrel with the proposition enunciated by the Master of the Rolls, but only that the facts of the case before him did not fall within it. Apparently this view also has been taken by Denning, M.R., where, in *Phipps v. Boardman*, [1965] 1 All E.R. 849 at p. 856, [1965] 2 W.L.R. 839, a case involving the liability of trustees, he said:

Likewise with *information or* knowledge which he has been employed by his principal to collect or discover, *or which he has otherwise acquired*, for the use of his principal, then again if he turns it to his own use, so as to make a profit by means of it for himself, he is accountable (see *Lamb v. Evans*, [1893] 1 Ch. 218 at pp. 226, 230, *Regal (Hastings), Ltd. v. Gulliver*, [1942] 1 All E. R. 378) for such information or knowledge is the property of his principal, just as much as an invention is (see *Triplex Safe Glass Co. v. Scorah*, [1937] 4 All E.R. 693 at p. 698; [1938] Ch. 211 at p. 217, *Sterling Engineering Co., Ltd. v. Patchett*, [1955] 1 All E.R. 369 at pp. 374, 376; [1955] A.C. 534 at pp. 544, 547). It is otherwise when the information or knowledge is not the property of his principal. There are several cases which show that you cannot prevent an agent from taking advantage of an opportunity of earning money, even though it is an opportunity which comes his way in consequence of his employment, so long as he does not use his master's property, or break his contract by so doing; see *Whitney v. Smith* (1869), L.R. 4 Ch. App. 513 at 521, *Re Corsellis*, Lawton v. Elwes (1883), (1887), 34 Ch. D. 675, *Aas v. Benham*, [1891] 2 Ch. 244 at p. 258 per Bowen, L.J., and the instance given by Lord Greene, M.R., in *Regal (Hastings), Ltd. v. Gulliver*.

Accordingly, I have come to the conclusion that the appellant cannot succeed upon the circumstances here present.

I would, therefore, dismiss the appeal from the judgment dismissing the appellant's action against the respondent.

[On appeal, the unanimous judgment of the Supreme Court was delivered by:]

CARTWRIGHT, J.: Counsel for the appellant founded his argument on the decision of the House of Lords in *Regal (Hastings), Ltd. v. Gulliver et al.*, in which the principles of equity relating to the liability of a person who acquires property in regard to which a fiduciary relationship exists are considered and the leading cases are reviewed. The judgment in *Regal* has been followed by this Court in *Zwicker v. Stanbury* and in *Midcon Oil & Gas Ltd. v. New British Dominion Oil Co. Ltd. et al.* Counsel for the respondent accepts the statements of the law contained in *Regal* and submits that their application to the facts of the case at bar does not result in imposing liability on the respondent.

It is not necessary to review the somewhat complicated facts of the *Regal* case. While each of the Law Lords stated his reasons in his own words, there was no difference in substance between their statements of the test to be applied in determining whether or not the directors were liable to account for the profit which they personally had made on the purchase and resale of shares in a subsidiary of *Regal*. It will be of assistance to consider the actual words which were used. . . .

[Cartwright, J. then quoted from the various opinions in *Regal*, most notably that of Lord Russell who stressed that the directors obtained these shares "by reason and only by reason of the fact that they were directors of Regal and in the course of execution of that office. . .".].

. . .The phrases which I have italicized in some of the passages quoted above appear to me to state in varying words the principle which Lord Russell of Killowen laid down, at p. 389 of the *Regal* judgment, in the passage quoted above which was adopted by Locke J. in the *Midcon* case.

On the facts of the case at bar I find it impossible to say that the respondent obtained the interests he holds in Cross Bow and Mayo by reason of the fact that he was a director of the appellant and in the course of the execution of that office.

If the members of the House of Lords in *Regal* had been of the view that in the hypothetical case stated by Lord Greene the director would have been liable to account to the company, the elaborate examination of the facts contained in the speech of Lord Russell of Killowen would have been unnecessary.

The facts of the case at bar appear to me in all material respects identical with those in the hypothetical case stated by Lord Greene and I share the view which he expressed that in such circumstances the director is under no liability. I agree with the conclusion of the learned trial judge and of the majority in the Court of Appeal that the action fails.

Notes and Questions

1   In a dissenting judgment in the Court of Appeal, Norris, J.A. looked to the principles set out in *Regal* to show that the intentions of the directors were irrelevant and that a strict application of the principles laid out in *Keech v. Sandford* was required. He then went on to discuss the policy upon which his decision was based, in contrast to the policy preference enunciated by Bull, J.A:

> Some argument was presented to the effect that because of the complexity of modern business, modern practice and the modern way of life, the strict rule laid down in the *Regal* and other cases should not be applied. . . . With the greatest respect, it seems to me that the complexities of modern business are a very good reason why the rule should be enforced strictly in order that such complexities may not be used as a smoke screen or shield behind which fraud might be perpetrated. The argument is purely and simply an irrelevant argument of expediency as to what the law should be, not what it is. It might as well be said that such an argument if given effect to would open the door to fraud, and weaken the confidence which ordinary people should have in dealing with corporate bodies. In order that people may be assured of their protection against improper acts of trustees it is necessary that their activities be circumscribed within rigid limits. The language used and referred to with approval in the *Regal* case, e.g., "the inflexible rule", "the inexorable rule", "The rule is stringent and absolute, because 'the safety of mankind' requires it to be absolutely observed in the fiduciary relationship" indicate how strict the rule is. The history today of the activities of many corporate bodies has disclosed scandals and loss to the public due to failure of the directors to recognize the requirements of their fiduciary position. No great hardship is imposed on directors by the enforcement of the rule, as a very simple course is available to them which they may follow [approval by the shareholders].

2   Do you agree that *Peso* is different from *Regal* because the directors of *Peso* turned down the Dickson claims? In both *Peso* and *Regal* did not both companies want to acquire property (mining claims, a lease) which they could not afford? What decision might have been reached in *Regal* if the directors had taken the lease in their own names rather than purchase the shares themselves? Would it have been possible to have received the fully informed consent of an independent board in *Peso*, or should the directors have sought the permission of the shareholders? For an analysis and criticism of the case, see Stanley M. Beck, "The Saga of Peso Silver Mines: Corporate Opportunity Reconsidered" (1971), 49 Can. Bar Rev. 80; Note (1967), 30 Mod. L. Rev. 450.

Canadian Aero Services Ltd. v. O'Malley
(1973), [1974] S.C.R. 592, 40 D.L.R. (3d) 371

[The plaintiff-appellant company, Canaero, claimed that the defendants had improperly taken the fruits of a corporate opportunity in which the corporation had a prior and continuing interest. The main business of Canadian Aero (Canaero) was topographical mapping and geographical exploration. The defendants were assigned to Guyana for the purpose of developing and procuring a contract for the mapping of that country. The defendants thereafter resigned from Canaero, and unknown to the plaintiff, they incorporated a company (Terra Surveys Inc.) to perform identical work to that of their previous employer. Terra's proposal to map the terrain of Guyana was accepted in competition with a proposal submitted by Canaero. Canaero alleged that O'Malley and Zarzycki had wrongfully taken the benefit of the corporate opportunity in breach of a fiduciary duty owed to the corporation.

In an action for an accounting and payment of profits, both the trial court and the Ontario Court of Appeal found against the plaintiff. However, the reasoning of the Court of Appeal was different from that of the trial judge in that the Court of Appeal was of the view that the relationship of the parties was that of employer and employee involving no fiduciary obligations.]

LASKIN, J.: . . . There are four issues that arise for consideration on the facts so far recited. There is, first, the determination of the relationship of O'Malley and Zarzycki to Canaero. Secondly, there is the duty or duties, if any, owed by them to Canaero by reason of the ascertained relationship. Thirdly, there is the question whether there has been any breach of duty, if any is owing, by reason of the conduct of O'Malley and Zarzycki in acting through Terra to secure the contract for the Guyana project; and, fourthly, there is the question of liability for breach of duty if established.

Like Grant, J., the trial judge, I do not think it matters whether O'Malley and Zarzycki were properly appointed as directors of Canaero or whether they did or did not act as directors. What is not in doubt is that they acted respectively as president and executive vice-president of Canaero for about two years prior to their resignations. To paraphrase the findings of the trial Judge in this respect, they acted in those positions and their remuneration and responsibilities verified their status as senior officers of Canaero. They were "top management" and not mere employees whose duty to their employer, unless enlarged by contract, consisted only of respect for trade secrets and for confidentiality of customer lists. Theirs was a larger, more exacting duty which, unless modified by statute or by contract (and there is nothing of this sort here), was similar to that owed to a corporate employer by its directors. I adopt what is said of this point by Gower, *Principles of Modern Company Law*, 3rd ed. (1969), at p. 518 as follows:

> . . .these duties, except in so far as they depend on statutory provisions expressly limited to directors, are not so restricted but apply equally to any officials of the company who are authorized to act on its behalf, and in particular to those acting in a managerial capacity.

The distinction taken between agents and servants of an employer is apt here, and I am unable to appreciate the basis upon which the Ontario Court of Appeal concluded that O'Malley and Zarzycki were mere employees, that is servants of Canaero rather than agents. Although they were subject to supervision of the officers of the controlling company, their positions as senior officers of a subsidiary, which was a working organization, charged them with initiatives and with responsibilities far removed from the obedient role of servants.

It follows that O'Malley and Zarzycki stood in a fiduciary relationship to Canaero, which in its generality betokens loyalty, good faith and avoidance of a conflict of duty and self-interest. Descending from the generality, the fiduciary relationship goes at least this far:a director or a senior officer like O'Malley or Zarzycki is precluded from obtaining for himself, either secretly or without the approval of the company (which would have to be properly manifested upon full disclosure of the facts), any property or business advantage either belonging to the company or for which it has been negotiating; and especially is this so where the director or officer is a participant in the negotiations on behalf of the company. . . .

[Laskin, J. then went on to discuss *Regal Hastings* and quote passages from the judgment.]

I need not pause to consider whether on the facts in *Regal (Hastings) Ltd. v. Gulliver* the equitable principle was over-zealously applied; see, for example, Gower, *op. cit.*, at pp. 535-7. What I would observe is that the principle, or, indeed, principles, as stated, grew out of older cases concerned with fiduciaries other than directors or managing officers of a modern corporation, and I do not therefore regard them as providing a rigid measure whose literal terms must be met in assessing succeeding cases. In my opinion, neither the conflict test, referred to by Viscount Sankey, nor the test of accountability for profits acquired by reason only of being directors and in the course of execution of the office, reflected in the passage quoted from Lord Russell of Killowen, should be considered as the exclusive touchstones of liability. In this, as in other branches of the law, new fact situations may require a reformulation of existing principle to maintain its vigour in the new setting.

The reaping of a profit by a person at a company's expense while a director thereof is, of course, an adequate ground upon which to hold the director accountable. Yet there may be situations where a profit must be disgorged, although not gained at the expense of the company, on the ground that a director must not be allowed to use his position as such to make a profit even if it was not open to the company, as for example, by reason of legal disability, to participate in the transaction. An analogous situation, albeit not involving a director, existed for all practical purposes in the case of *Boardman et al. v. Phipps*, [1967] 2 A.C. 46 which also supports the view that liability to account does not depend on proof of an actual conflict of duty and self-interest. Another, quite recent, illustration of a liability to account where the company itself had failed to obtain a business contract and hence could not be regarded as having been deprived of a business opportunity is *Industrial Development Consultants Ltd. v. Cooley*, [1972] 2 All E.R. 162,a judgment of a Court of first instance. There, the managing director, who was allowed to resign his position on a false assertion of ill health, subsequently got the contract for himself. That case is thus also illustrative of the situation where a director's resignation is prompted by a decision to obtain for himself the business contract denied to his company and where he does obtain it without disclosing his intention.

What these decisions indicate is an updating of the equitable principle whose roots lie in the general standards that I have already mentioned, namely, loyalty, good faith and avoidance of conflict of duty and self-interest. Strict application against directors and senior management officials is simply recognition of the degree of control which their positions give them in corporate operations, a control which rises above daily accountability to owning shareholders and which comes under some scrutiny only at annual general or at special meetings. It is a necessary supplement, in the public interest, of statutory regulation and accountability which themselves are, at one and the same time, an acknowledgement of the importance of the corporation in the life of the community and of the need to compel obedience by it and by its promoters, directors and managers to norms of exemplary behaviour. . . . [Laskin, J. went on to review case law from Australia, England, New Zealand and the United States to demonstrate his point.]

Submissions and argument were addressed to this Court on the question whether or how far Zarzycki copied Canaero's documents in preparing the Terra proposal. The appellant's position is that Zarzycki was not entitled to use for Terra what he compiled for Canaero; and the respondents contended that, although Zarzycki was not entitled to use for Terra the 1965 report or proposal as such that he prepared for Canaero, he was entitled to use the information therein which came to him in the normal course and by reason of his own capacity. It was the respondents' further submission that Zarzycki did not respond in 1966, on behalf of Terra on the basis of the 1965 report as an officer of and for Canaero; and they went so far as to say that it did not matter that O'Malley and Zarzycki worked on the same contract for Terra as they had for Canaero, especially when the project was not exactly the same.

In my opinion, the fiduciary duty upon O'Malley and Zarzycki, if it survived their departure from Canaero, would be reduced to an absurdity if it could be evaded merely because the Guyana project had been varied in some details when it became the subject of invited proposals, or merely because Zarzycki met the variations by appropriate changes in what he prepared for Canaero in 1965, and what he proposed for Terra in 1966. I do not regard it as necessary to look for substantial resemblances. Their presence would be a factor to be considered on the issue of breach of fiduciary duty but they are not a *sine qua non*. The cardinal fact is that the one project, the same project which Zarzycki had pursued for Canaero, was the subject of his Terra proposal. It was that business opportunity, in line with its general pursuits, which Canaero sought through O'Malley and Zarzycki. There is no suggestion that there had been such a change of objective as to make the project for which proposals were invited from Canaero, Terra and others a different one from that which Canaero had been developing with a view to obtaining the contract for itself.

Again, whether or not Terra was incorporated for the purpose of intercepting the contract for the Guyana project is not central to the issue of breach of fiduciary duty. Honesty of purpose is no more a defence in that respect than it would be in respect of personal interception of the contract by O'Malley and Zarzycki. This is fundamental in the enforcement of fiduciary duty where the fiduciaries are acting against the interests of their principal. Then it is urged that Canaero could not in any event have obtained the contract, and that O'Malley and Zarzycki left Canaero was an ultimate response to their dissatisfaction with that company and with the restrictions that they were under in managing it. There was, however, no certain knowledge at the time O'Malley and Zarzycki resigned that the Guyana project was beyond Canaero's grasp. Canaero had not abandoned its hope of capturing it, even if Wells was of opinion, expressed during his luncheon with O'Malley and Zarzycki on August 6, 1966, that it would not get a foreign aid contract from the Canadian Government. Although it was contended that O'Malley and Zarzycki did not know of the imminence of the approval of the Guyana project, their ready run for it, when it was approved at about the time of their resignations and at a time when they knew of Canaero's continuing interest, are factors to be considered in deciding whether they were still under a fiduciary duty not to seek to procure for themselves or for their newly-formed company the business opportunity which they had nurtured for Canaero.

Counsel for O'Malley and Zarzycki relied upon the judgment of this Court in *Peso Silver Mines Ltd. (N.P.L.) v. Cropper* (1966), 58 D.L.R. (2d) 1, [1966] S.C.R. 673, 56 W.W.R. 641, as representing an affirmation of what was said in *Regal (Hastings) Ltd. v. Gulliver* respecting the circumscription of liability to circumstances where the directors or senior officers had obtained the challenged benefit by reason only of the fact that they held those positions and in the course of execution of those offices. In urging this, he did not deny that leaving to capitalize on their positions would not necessarily immunize them, but he submitted that in the present case there was no special knowledge or information obtained from Canaero during their service with that company upon which O'Malley and Zarzycki had relied in reaching for the Guyana project on behalf of Terra.

There is a considerable gulf between the *Peso* case and the present one on the facts as found in each and on the issues that they respectively raise. In *Peso*, there was a finding of good faith in the rejection by its directors of an offer of mining claims because of its strained finances. The subsequent acquisition of those claims by the managing director and his associates, albeit without seeking shareholder approval, was held to be proper because the company's interest in them ceased. There is some analogy to *Burg v. Horn* because there was evidence that Peso had received many offers of mining properties and, as in *Burg v. Horn*, the acquisition of the particular claims out of which the litigation arose could not be said to be essential to the success of the company. Whether evidence was overlooked in *Peso* which would have led to the result reached in *Regal (Hastings) Ltd. v. Gulliver* (see the examination by Beck, "The Saga of Peso Silver Mines: Corporate Opportunity Reconsidered", 49 Can. Bar Rev. 80 (1971), at p. 101) has no bearing on the proper disposition of the present case. What is before this Court is not a situation where various opportunities were offered to a company which was open to all of them, but rather a case where it had devoted itself to originating and bringing to fruition a particular business deal which was ultimately captured by former senior officers who had been in charge of the matter for the company. Since Canaero had been invited to make a proposal on the Guyana project, there is no basis for contending that it could not, in any event, have obtained the contract or that there was any unwillingness to deal with it.

It is a mistake, in my opinion, to seek to encase the principle stated and applied in *Peso*, by adoption from *Regal (Hastings) Ltd. v. Gulliver* in the straight-jacket of special knowledge acquired while acting as directors or senior officers, let alone limiting it to benefits acquired by reason of and during the holding of those offices. As in other cases in this developing branch of the law, the particular facts may determine the shape of the principle of decision without setting fixed limits to it. So it is in the present case. Accepting the facts found by the trial Judge, I find no obstructing considerations to the conclusion that O'Malley and Zarzycki continued, after their resignations, to be under a fiduciary duty to respect Canaero's priority, as against them and their instrument Terra, in seeking to capture the contract for the Guyana project. They entered the lists in the heat of the maturation of the project, known to them to be under active Government consideration when they resigned from Canaero and when they proposed to bid on behalf of Terra.

In holding that on the facts found by the trial Judge, there was a breach of fiduciary duty by O'Malley and Zarzycki which survived their resignations I am not to be taken as laying down any rule of liability to be read as if it were a statute. The general standards of loyalty, good faith and avoidance of a conflict of duty and self-interest to which the conduct of a director or senior officer must conform, must be tested in each case by many factors which it would be reckless to attempt to enumerate exhaustively. Among them are the factor of position or office held, the nature of the corporate opportunity, its ripeness, its specificness and the director's or managerial officer's relation to it, the amount of knowledge possessed, the circumstances in which it was obtained and whether it was special or, indeed, even private, the factor of time in the continuation of fiduciary duty where the alleged breach occurs after termination of the relationship with the company, and the circumstances under which the relationship was terminated, that is whether by retirement or resignation or discharge. . . .

Liability of O'Malley and Zarzycki for breach of fiduciary duty does not depend upon proof by Canaero that, but for their intervention, it would have obtained the Guyana contract; nor is it a condition of recovery of damages that Canaero establish what its profit would have been or what it has lost by failing to realize the corporate opportunity in question. It is entitled to compel the faithless fiduciaries to answer for their default according to their gain. Whether the damages awarded here be viewed as an accounting of profits or, what amounts to the same thing, as based on unjust enrichment, I would not interfere with the quantum. The appeal is, accordingly, allowed against all defendants save Wells, and judgment should be entered against them for $125,000. The appellant should have its costs against them throughout. I would dismiss the appeal as against Wells with costs.

Questions

Has the Supreme Court implicitly overruled *Peso*? Does Laskin's judgment allow a lawyer to give a director viable guidelines for his conduct? Would the flexibility urged by Laskin C.J. in applying fiduciary standards cut both ways? That is, would it (should it) lead to a different result in *Phipps*? See also Beck, "The Quickening of Fiduciary Obligation: Canadian Aero Services v. O'Malley", *supra*.

Notes on US Cases

1   In *Burg v. Horn*, 380 F.2d 897 (C.A. 2nd Cir., 1967) the plaintiff was a one-third shareholder and director of Darand Realty Corp. She sued derivatively the two other shareholder-directors, alleging that they took advantage of corporate opportunities by purchasing for themselves and for their profit several low-rent rooming and apartment buildings which should have been purchased for Darand. Prior to and after the formation of Darand by these three share-holders, the defendants were indirectly (through solely owned corporations) involved in the real estate business themselves. This was known to the plaintiff when she became a shareholder in Darand. There was no agreement or discussion as to whether defendants should continue their real estate business as before but the plaintiff and her husband had "expected" the defendants to offer any low-rent properties they found in Brooklyn to Darand. While the defendants were purchasing and selling real estate of this character on their own account, Darand was operating similarly. The plaintiff's action sought an accounting for receipts and expenditures and the imposi-tion of a constructive trust on the alleged corporate opportunities over several years. In ruling in favour of the defendants, Chief Judge Lumbard canvassed the three basic approaches taken by the US courts in corporate opportunity cases. The first is the "interest" or "expectancy" test, which is applied by asking whether the corporation needs or was seeking the opportunity in question. As Judge Lumbard noted in his decision, this test has been criticized as being vague and unhelpful, but is nonetheless the one most often applied. The second approach is to ask whether the opportunity is in the "line of business" of the corporation. The leading case is *Guth v. Loft, Inc.*, 5 A.2d 503 (S.C. Del., 1939), in which the Supreme Court of Delaware expressed the point as follows (at p. 514):

> Where a corporation is engaged in a certain business, and an opportunity is presented to it embracing an activity as to which it has fundamental knowledge, practical experience and ability to pursue . . . and is one that is consonant with its reasonable needs and aspirations. . . it may be properly said that the opportunity is in the line of the corporation's business.

In *Burg*, this test was rejected by Judge Lumbard as "too broad a generalization." Rather, he said that the relationship between the director and his corporation had to be examined in each case to determine if all opportunities within its line of business had to be offered to it. The third test is the more general one of "fairness" — a test that echoes in Laskin C.J.'s judgment in *Canaero*. Judicial expression of this test is found in *Durfee v. Durfee & Canning*, 80 N.E.2d 522 (S.C. Mass., 1948), at p. 529:

> [T]he true basis of the doctrine [of corporate opportunity] should not be found in any expectancy or property interest concept, but in the unfairness on the particular facts of a fiduciary taking advantage of an opportunity when the interests of the corporation justly call for protection.

This is the standard ultimately adopted by Chief Justice Lumbard in *Burg*. On the facts of the case, he held that no implied duty could be found that would have required the Horns to funnel all of their business through Darand. Moreover:

> a person's involvement in more than one venture of the same kind may negate the obligation which might otherwise be implied to offer similar opportunities to any one of them, absent some contrary understanding. Thus we affirm Judge Dooling's holding that the properties acquired by defendants were not corporate opportunities of Darand.

The judgment has been criticized for allowing lower standards of fiduciary duties to govern directorial behaviour when directors enjoy multiple directorships. This is argued to be undesirable because it enhances the scope for unscrupulous conduct in settings where this danger is already high. See, for instance, "Note on Corporate Opportunity" (1968), 43 N.Y.U.L. Rev. 187, in which it was argued that the court erred in considering the fact of multiple directorships to be a factor favouring the defendants in *Burg v. Horn*. The court was also criticized for failing to impose the burden of proof on the defendants:

> The *Burg* court. . . misplac(ed) the burden of proof, for the Horns were not required to show that they had fully disclosed all their acquisitions to Mrs. Burg, nor that they had offered Darand the opportunity of acquiring these properties. Rather than infer from the lack of an agreement that the Horns were free to acquire the properties, it would have been preferable for the court to have imposed upon the Horns a duty to fully disclose these properties and to offer them to Darand unless the Horns could prove an agreement with Mrs. Burg allowing them to operate independently of Darand (at 193).

Chief Justice Lumbard's "fairness" approach may find resonance in Laskin C.J.'s statement in *Canaero* that he was "not to be taken as laying down any rule of liability to be read as if it were a statute." Rather, the general standards of loyalty and good faith "must be tested in each case by many factors . . ." To similar effect is the holding of the Delaware Supreme Court in the leading case of

Johnston v. Green, 121 A.2d 919 (1956): "whether [an investment opportunity offered to a director becomes a corporate opportunity] in any particular case, depends on the facts — upon the existence of special circumstances that would make it unfair for him to take the opportunity for himself."

2   The burden of proof in corporate opportunity cases in the US is most often placed on the person taking the opportunity, by analogy to the "interested transaction" cases where the fiduciary has the burden of establishing the inherent fairness of the contract. The position of directors and senior officers, as well as of parent corporations, would seem to call for the inherent fairness standard in all corporate opportunity cases.

Brudney and Clark, "A New Look at Corporate Opportunities"
(1981), 94 Harv. L. Rev. 997 at 998–1006 (footnotes deleted)

The law of corporate opportunities is among the least satisfactory limbs of doctrine in the corpus of corporate law. Not only are the common formulations vague, but the courts have articulated no theory that could serve as a blueprint for constructing meaningful rules. In part, this situation reflects the fact that the vast bulk of corporate opportunity cases have involved close corporations. Open-ended rules are often suitable for close corporations and the essentially contractual relationships of their investors and managers. But sharper doctrinal responses are called for by the claims of investors in public corporations against their executives, directors, and parent corporations. In this Article, we examine the theoretical underpinning of the corporate opportunity doctrine, and suggest relatively clear rules to implement it.

We begin by asking why there is any need for a corporate opportunity doctrine. According to the formulation of most courts, if a business opportunity is determined to be a corporate opportunity, then a corporate fiduciary — such as a director, officer, or controlling shareholder — may not take or "usurp" it for his own benefit, unless proper consent is given. Thus, a corporate opportunity is defined to be, as against fiduciaries, a corporate asset. The reasons for forbidding its appropriation are the same as those for generally forbidding corporate agents and fiduciaries from unilaterally taking corporate property for themselves. An essential reason is that a generalized fiduciary duty of loyalty is efficient . . .

In our examination of the problem of identifying corporate opportunities, we suggest what we think are relevant considerations and feasible rules. Our study rests upon two assumptions that are not generally reflected in the present doctrine. First, we submit that different considerations and rules should be employed for close corporations than for publicly held corporations. Second, we believe that in the latter case, rules should depend upon whether the appropriator is (1) a full-time officer or executive, (2) only an outside director or a part-time executive of more than one corporation, or (3) a parent corporation.

* * *

Relevant Differences between Close and Public Corporations

The basic choice to be made when importing the fiduciary principle from the law of trusts to define the corporate opportunity doctrine is between a categorical approach and a selective approach. The former forbids all personal gains to the trustee from dealings relating to trust property, even if the transaction would deprive the beneficiary of nothing, and even if it might produce benefits for both him and the trustee. The latter forbids only behavior that in particular circumstances creates a serious probability of injury to the beneficiary; it would not prohibit transactions merely because the trustee as well as the beneficiary may gain from them. The categorical approach would define corporate opportunity in sweeping terms to include all possible active modes of making a profit, and would take a strict stance towards proposed exceptions and defenses. It would prohibit an officer or executive, for example, from taking any other active business opportunity — at least without the consent of the corporation. The selective approach would define corporate opportunity more narrowly, by criteria that relate each opportunity to the operations, needs, or expectations of the firm. It would require the fiduciary to show only that the opportunity he took does not fall within the criteria. On this approach, insiders would be denied some active business opportunities, but permitted to accept others.

In our view, it is desirable to use the selective approach for close corporations and the categorical approach for public corporations. Fundamentally, the stockholders of public corporations are more like the beneficiaries of trusts, for whom the stricter rule was fashioned, than are the participants in private ventures. Certainly this appears true when we consider stockholders in their role as selectors and monitors of their fiduciaries. And other relevant differences between the two types of enterprise also support our view.

The ability of the stockholders of private corporations to select the fiduciaries to whom they have entrusted their capital, and to police their management's contributions to (and diversions from) the enterprise is much greater than the selecting and monitoring capacities of shareholders in public corporations. Investors in public corporations are usually passive and widely scattered contributors of money to be managed by pre-selected officers to whom they effectively delegate full decision making power over operating matters. In contrast, investors in private ventures are fairly small in number and tend to know one another. They make more conscious choices when selecting managers from among themselves. They are likely to be active participants rather than merely passive contributors of funds. And they can consent in a more meaningful way to diversions of corporate assets by fellow participants, either when they form or join enterprises, or on the occasion of the diversion. Accordingly, such investors have less need of categorical strictures on such diversions.

Moreover, both the scope of the duties and the nature of the compensation of the managers differ between the two types of corporation. The duties of the executives of a public corporation normally require full-time application of their managerial talents and energies and leave no room for active participation in the development or operation of other businesses. Correspondingly, their compensation arrangements are such that neither equity nor efficiency requires them to be allowed to take covert indirect compensation as they see fit. But for many close corporations, other expectations may be more reasonable. The participants may sometimes agree, or assume in the initial arrangements, that their managing colleagues are not to work only for the particular corporation, but are free to engage in other activities. In any event, it is feasible in close corporations (as it is *not* in public corporations) to obtain the consent of all participants to such part-time employment by the managing participants. And such consent may well be inferred in close corporations when some participants are under compensated in relation to other participants. The formal compensation arrangements may not adequately separate the role of a participant's talents and efforts from the role of his capital contributions in determining his returns. In this context, a claim of under compensation might be plausible when the participants in the close corporation agreed or understood — or probably would have agreed, had they thought of the matter — that their financial rewards should reflect variations in their continuing active efforts as well as their initial capital contributions.

Finally, differences between the opportunity sets of the two types of enterprise imply different constraints on their managers. A publicly held enterprise may fairly be treated as large and flexible enough to accept any new investment opportunities that offer an appropriate return per unit of risk. Hence, its opportunity set embraces virtually any business in which its executives might want to invest and take an active role. The opportunity set of a close corporation is not nearly so broad. Market imperfections and transaction costs may preclude or impede such corporations' efforts to accept projects unrelated to their existing experience or talent or beyond their existing financial capacity. There may be many businesses that the officers of a closely held enterprise may seek to develop on their own time, but that would not deprive the enterprise of any opportunity it could reasonably hope to exploit.

All these differences between close and public corporations — in the investors' abilities to select and monitor managers and to contract with one another, in the managers' duties and compensation arrangements, and in the size of opportunity sets — are mainly a consequence of differences in size. They suggest that lawmakers *generally* ought to construct corporate law doctrines with a different jurisprudential orientation in the two contexts. As a rough but fair generalization, the basic characteristics of the corporate form of organization and the related statutory rules are best suited for large-scale enterprises owned by numerous public investors. In this context, legal rules can and should be uniformly applicable even when they are fairly precise and specific. The rules of corporate law, which define the relationships of stockholders to each other and to management, constitute something like a "standard contract" to which all the actors who play the standard roles of shareholder, director, and officer automatically agree merely by virtue of their assuming these roles. The outcome of legal disputes governed by public corporation law should leave little play for the vagaries of particular understandings and arrangements.

But the notion that corporate participants should be viewed as entering voluntarily into a "standard contract," or prefixed set of roles and relationships, has much less relevance to close corporations. The close corporation "deal" simply does not have to be the same for all close corporations. The roles of the investor and the manager are more likely to be mixed and shared by the participants, and the range of variations in the terms of participation is likely to be greater. As indicated, this is a straightforward consequence of size differences. The small number of players in the typical close corporation makes possible a far greater amount of real communication and agreement among all players about their particular situations and objectives. As the number of players increases, however, the number of communication channels needed to connect them all with each other increases astronomically. Publicly held corporations simply cannot have a meaningful system of "open" communications and particularized agreements among all their players.

Of course, commentators, courts, and lawmakers have long recognized that the special traits of close corporations made it desirable to modify some of the original formal rules in corporate statutes, at least with respect to such corporations. But our analysis of the differences between the two types of corporation also has implications for the judge-made fiduciary principle. It suggests that rules explicating the principle for specific recurring situations — rules like those governing corporate opportunities — should leave more room in the close corporation context for results to turn on the special facts, arrangements, and understandings of each situation. Lawmakers should assume that the parties in close corporations are better able than those in public ones to make individual bargains. Hence, less rigid rules than the categorical ones we shall propose in later Parts of this Article should govern participants in close corporations. What those less rigid rules should be is another question. In general, we believe that in this context only modest alterations are needed in the guidelines provided by existing law.

4. COMPETITION

The rubric of "competition" actually implicates a number of discrete fact patterns. These include:

1   A director serving on the boards of two competing corporations.

2   A director or officer operating a business that competes with the corporation.

3   A director or officer having a material interest in an entity that competes with the corporation.

Each of these fact patterns involves a conflict of interest. Thus, one might suppose that the common law would historically have applied the conflict and profit rules and found a breach of fiduciary duty. For reasons that are not well understood, the *London and Mashonaland* case that immediately follows took a very different tact, allowing a person to sit on the boards of two competing companies without breaching their duty to either. And, as we will see in the *Slate* case that follows *London and Mashonaland*, the influence of this common law anomaly lives on even in the face of a unitary statutory standard that nominally applies to all alleged breaches of fiduciary duty.

Before we get started, however, you should note both the similarities and differences between this section and the section on "Basic Self-Dealing Transactions" earlier in this chapter. The latter encompasses situations where there is a contract or transaction between a director or officer and the corporation, or where the director or officer is a director of, or has a material interest in an entity contracting with the corporation. This section, on the other hand, deals with situations in which a director or officer *competes* with the corporation (or is a director or officer of a competitor).

Another thing to note is that there is a significant overlap between cases falling under the "competition" rubric and the "corporate opportunities" rubric. Indeed, arguably the doctrinal distinction between them is somewhat artificial.

London and Mashonaland Exploration Company, Limited v. New Mashonaland Exploration Company, Limited
[1891] W.N. 165

CHITTY, J.: Motion on behalf of the plaintiff company to restrain the defendant company from publishing any announcement that Lord Mayo was one of its directors, and to restrain Lord Mayo from authorizing or permitting any such publication, and from acting as director of the defendant company.

The above-named companies were incorporated for the same object, and were rival companies. The plaintiff company was registered in

March, 1891, and in the following month a resolution was passed at a meeting of the directors appointing Lord Mayo a director and chairman. The plaintiff company alleged that Lord Mayo accepted the appointment, and approved of a prospectus privately circulated, wherein his name appeared as director and chairman, and that numerous applications for shares had been received upon the faith of such prospectus. In July the prospectus of the defendant company was circulated with the name of Lord Mayo at the head of its list of directors. It was admitted that Lord Mayo had never acted as a director, nor attended any board meeting of the plaintiff company, and that he had never agreed, either expressly or by the articles of association, not to become a director of any similar company.

Even assuming that Lord Mayo had been duly elected chairman and director of the plaintiff company, there was nothing in the articles which required him to give any part of his time, much less the whole of his time, to the business of the company, or which prohibited him from acting as a director of another company; neither was there any contract express or implied to give his personal services to the plaintiff company and not to another company. No case had been made out that Lord Mayo was about to disclose to the defendant company any information that he had obtained confidentially in his character of chairman: the analogy sought to be drawn by the plaintiff company's counsel between the present case and partnerships was incomplete: no sufficient damage had been shown, and no case had been made for an injunction: the application was wholly unprecedented, and must be dismissed with costs.

Questions

1   Mr. Justice Chitty's brief judgment on a motion in *London and Mashonaland*, might never have been elevated into a judicial principle if it had not been picked up and repeated in the *dicta* of Lord Blanesburgh L.C. in *Bell v. Lever Bros. Ltd.*, [1932] A.C. 161 (H.L.):

> And this brings me to the position of a director in relation to contracts of the second class, with which we are here alone concerned. The principle will be found in the case usually cited in relation to it, although reported only in the Weekly Notes, of *London and Mashonaland Exploration Co. v. New Mashonaland Exploration Co.* where it was held that, it not appearing from the regulations of the company that a director's services must be rendered to that company and to no other company, he was at liberty to become a director even of a rival company, and it not being established that he was making to the second company any disclosure of information obtained confidentially by him as a director of the first company he could not at the instance of that company be restrained in his rival directorate. What he could do for a rival company, he could, of course, do for himself.

The "second class" of contract to which Lord Blanesburgh referred was one in which the director's company had no interest. Thus, the holding of *London and Mashonaland* that a director could become interested in a rival concern was used simply to emphasize the point in issue — that the director could be a party to a contract in which his company was not interested. Notwithstanding this use of *London and Mashonaland*, Lord Blanesburgh's *dicta* in *Bell v. Lever Bros. Ltd.* have been cited ever since as authority for the proposition that a director may engage in a competing business. For a case that ignores *Aberdeen Railway* and follows *London and Mashonaland*, see *Waite's Auto Transfer Ltd. v. Waite*, [1928] 3 W.W.R. 649 (president and director of one company allowed to set up a rival concern that canvassed customers of the first company). Would the holding in *Waite's Auto Transfer* survive the decision of the Supreme Court in *Canaero*?

2   A director who joins a rival concern and prefers its interests to those of the first company would likely face an application under s. 241 of the CBCA or s. 248 OBCA, with respect to the conduct of the first company. The use of the oppression remedy in such a case has been considered by the House of Lords. In *Scottish Co-Operative Whole-sale Society Ltd. v. Meyer*, [1959] A.C. 324 (H.L.), Lord Denning was referred to Lord Blanesburgh's dicta in *Bell v. Lever Bros.* that a director could join the board of a rival company, to which he replied: "That may have been so at that time. But it is at the risk now of an application under s. 210 [the statutory oppression remedy] if he subordinates the interest of the one company to those of the other". Professor Gower, *Principles of* Modern Company Law (1997, 6th ed.), p. 622, comments as follows:

> It has been recognized that one who is a director of two rival concerns is walking a tight-rope and at risk if he fails to deal fairly with both.

3   In *Abbey Glen Property Corp. v. Stumborg*, [1976] 2 W.W.R. 1, McDonald J., in dealing with the defendant's argument that since the directors owed a fiduciary duty to another company they could not be in breach of their fiduciary duty to the plaintiff if what they did was in furtherance of their duty to the other company, indicated that he did not agree with the decision in *London and Mashonaland*. McDonald, J. said that although it was not strictly necessary to decide the point:

> I do not hesitate to express my opinion that the sweeping proposition for which the *London and Mashonaland* case and Lord Blanesburgh's dicta is cited is not the law. Even where there is no question of a director using confidential information, there may well be cases in which a director breaches his fiduciary duty to Company A merely by acting as a director of Company B. This

will particularly be possible when the companies are in the same line of business and where acting as a director of Company B will harm Company A. Beyond that I need go no further than to say that the question whether there has been a breach of a director's duty to Company A must be determined upon the basis of the factors enumerated in *Canadian Aero Services v. O'Malley* and *Regal (Hastings) Ltd. v. Gulliver*, and a negative answer will not necessarily be produced by the mere fact that a director is also a director of Company B and owes it a like fiduciary duty.

Note

Suppose that a director or officer starts up a business that competes with his or her corporation, and earns a profit thereby. In such as case, we could apply *either* the doctrine of corporate opportunities, *or* doctrines related to competition. This might initially seem like a trivial distinction. After all, we have a unitary statutory standard that should, on its face, apply to all fact patterns equally. However, after *London and Mashonaland*, it may make a big difference which doctrine we apply. While merely a lower court English case decided over a hundred years ago, the endorsement given *London and Mashonaland* by the House of Lords in *Bell v. Lever Bros. Ltd.*, [1932] A.C. 161 (H.L.) has given the case legs even to this day. While the following case is a corporate opportunities case, it nonetheless illustrates the important interplay between *London and Mashonaland* and the doctrine of corporate opportunities.

Slate Ventures Inc. v. Hurley

1996 CarswellNfld 64, 139 Nfld. & P.E.I.R. 235, 433 A.P.R. 235, 27 B.L.R. (2d) 41 (Nfld. T.D.), affirmed 1997 CarswellNfld 203 (Nfld. C.A.)

[Newfoundland Slate Inc. ("Newfoundland Slate") operated slate quarries. Hurley, a director of Newfoundland Slate, purchased a slate quarry (the Allison Quarry) for his own account without informing the company. The pertinent corporate law statute (Corporations Act, R.S.N. 1990, c. C-36) contained a statutory fiduciary duty (in s. 203) copied from the CBCA. Barry J. discussed the applicable law as follows:]

BARRY J.: Despite this clearly expressed rule [the conflict rule], Chitty, J., in *London & Mashonaland Exploration Co. v. New Mashonaland Exploration Co.*, [1891] W.N. 65, dismissed a company's application to restrain its chairman and director from acting as director of a rival company, on the ground the chairman had no contract, express or implied, to give his personal services to the applicant. *London & Mashonaland* was applied in *Bell v. Lever Bros. Ltd.*, [1932] A.C. 161 (H.L.). Then in Scottish Co-op Wholesale Soc. Ltd. v. Meyer, [1958] 3 All E.R. 66 (H.L.), Denning L.J. stated, at 88:

> Your lordships were referred to *Bell v. Lever Brothers Ltd.*, where Lord Blanesburg said that a director of one company was at liberty

to become a director also of a rival company. That may have been so at that time. But it is at the risk now of an application under section 210 [the oppression remedy] if he subordinates the interests of the one company to those of the other.

At 400-07, Welling [Bruce Welling, *Corporate Law in Canada* (Butterworths, 1984)] summarizes his review of the case law by rejecting the "corporate opportunity doctrine" as an unnecessary complication. He suggests the two "touchstones" are conflict of interest and connection with the fiduciary position. He sets out the following propositions as the current law on fiduciaries' liability in Canada:

(i)   Where there is an actual conflict of duty and interest and the information or opportunity is acquired by virtue of the fiduciary's position, the fiduciary is clearly liable to account for any profit.

(ii) Where there is a potential conflict of duty and interest and the information is acquired by virtue of the fiduciary's position, the fiduciary is accountable for any profit.

(iii) Where there is no conflict of duty and interest, real or potential, and the information or opportunity is acquired independently, the fiduciary is clearly not accountable.

(iv) Where there is a potential conflict of duty and interest, but the information or opportunity is acquired independently, the fiduciary is not accountable.

(v)   Where there is an actual conflict of duty and interest, but the information or opportunity is acquired independently, the fiduciary is accountable.

(vi) Where there is no conflict of duty and interest, but the information or opportunity is acquired by virtue of the fiduciary position, the fiduciary is accountable.

The evidence clearly establishes in the present case Hurley did not acquire the information about the opportunity to purchase the Allison Quarry by virtue of his position as director of Newfoundland Slate. Therefore, only propositions (iii), (iv) and (v) are relevant here.

I accept that the facts in proposition (iv) may logically arise. I accept, also, that proposition (iv) correctly states the current law. I find support for it in *Tombill* [*Tombill Gold Mines Ltd. v. Hamilton (City)*, 1956 CarswellOnt 80, 5 D.L.R. (2d) 561 (S.C.C.)] not mentioned by Welling, which supports his view that corporate directors are not prohibited from competing with their corporations. He correctly points out, at 404, that such competition would be impossible if the director's general fiduciary duty required the director to turn over all information and opportunities in which their corporations might be interested. Inter-locking boards of directors would disappear. I agree with Welling that a proper dividing line between the director's right to compete with the corporation and the corporation's right to have fiduciaries' personally acquired opportunities is the factual distinction between propositions (iv) and (v). Where information or an opportunity is acquired independently, directors may compete, though there is a potential conflict of duty and interest, but must account if there is an actual conflict.

So the question for determination in the present case becomes whether there was any conflict between Hurley's duty as director and his interests in the present case and, if so, was that conflict actual or potential. Consideration of two of the factors set out in *Canaero* will assist here.

Barry J. found that since Newfoundland Slate had a general interest in acquiring new slate quarries, the Allison Quarry "meets the 'interest' and 'line of business' tests for corporate opportunities." This gave rise, however, only to a "potential" conflict of interest. As in *Peso*, Hurely argued that there was no *actual* conflict because the company could not afford to buy the Allison property. Barry J. rejected this assertion on the facts, on the basis that "the president of Newfoundland Slate testified the Allison property was important to the corporation because it would add to slate reserves, provide a different colour slate needed for meeting customer needs, and prevent competitors from getting a foothold within Newfoundland" (and there was objective evidence to support this assertion). He thus found that there was an actual conflict of interest and went on to hold Hurely liable to account to Newfoundland Slate.

The result would have been different if Newfoundland Slate had not shown, by the circumstances surrounding the purchase of the Bryant property, that it had an active interest in acquiring slate properties on Random Island. Without this, Hurley's situation would have been one of only *potential* conflict of duty and interest. . .

Having found Hurley in breach of his common law fiduciary duty, I need not apply the provisions of s. 203(1) of the *Corporations Act*. These, in any event, do not add anything to the duties already required by the common law.

Slate Ventures Inc. v. Hurley
1997 CarswellNfld 203, 156 Nfld. & P.E.I.R. 304, 483 A.P.R. 304, 37 B.L.R. (2d) 138 (Nfld. C.A.)

[The Newfoundland Court of Appeal affirmed the trial judgment on the basis that Hurley did indeed have an actual conflict of interest in respect of the Allison Quarry.]

Following [Justice Laskin's] examination of the authorities [in *CanAero*], the statement (already quoted earlier in this decision) is made that the "norms of exemplary behaviour" expected of promoters, directors and managers of a corporation are "general standards of loyalty, good faith and avoidance of a conflict of duty and self-interest to which the conduct of a director or senior officer must conform". Thus the starting point for a director may be analogized as being not unlike a strict liability situation which may be varied by many factors. (See also the second quote from Laskin in the early part of this judgment.)

It would appear in this matter that the trial judge would not have found Hurley in breach of his duty as a director had not Newfoundland Slate been able to demonstrate, by its expressed interest in the Bryant property, that it had an active interest in acquiring slate properties on Random Island (and the financial means to exercise that interest), included in which would obviously have to be the Allison Quarry. The judge states that a potential conflict of duty and interest would not have been sufficient.

With respect, I am unable to agree with that conclusion. In stating that a potential conflict is insufficient on the facts of this case, it seems to me that the trial judge is operating from a much less onerous threshold than is espoused by *Canaero* and other authorities. I do not wish to read more into his finding than necessary, but his reasoning appears to lead to a conclusion that, in the absence of a contractual stipulation to the contrary, a director has an *ab initio* right to compete with the corporation of which he or she is a director, but that that right could be displaced by evidence establishing an actual conflict and thus a breach. If that is what Welling's proposition (4) is saying, I do not subscribe to it. In other words, a minimalist approach is taken which in my view runs counter to the ratio of *Canaero*. I am not unaware that a right to compete may exist in certain cases, but I think it unnecessary to get into such discussion here.

Appeal Dismissed.

The approach of the appeals court in *Slate* was adopted in the following case.

Cranewood Financial Corp. v. Norisawa
2001 BCSC 1126, 2001 CarswellBC 1790 (B.C. S.C.)

Cohen J.: The decision in *Canaero* seems to contradict the proposition that a director is not generally prohibited from serving as a director or officer of a competing corporation and is at liberty to compete in business on their own. For example, in *London & Mashonaland Exploration Co. v. New Mashonaland Exploration*, [1891] W.N. 65, the court dismissed a company's application to restrain its chairman and director from acting as director of a rival company. *Slate Ventures Inc. v. Hurley*, 1996 CarswellNfld 64, 139 Nfld. & P.E.I.R. 235 (Nfld. T.D.), affirmed 1997 CarswellNfld 203, 156 Nfld. & P.E.I.R. 304 (Nfld. C.A.) deals with the apparent discrepancy between *Canaero* and the general principle that a director is not restrained from engaging in competition with the company to which he or she owes a fiduciary duty. Because the issue in this case focussed on the question of when it is permissible for a director to compete with the corporation, I rely extensively on the *Slate* decision, *supra*. . .

Neither the decision of the Supreme Court or the Court of Appeal considered the issue of a director who acquired the information or opportunity by virtue of his or her position as a director of the company because it was clear from the facts of *Slate, supra,* that Hurley came by the information regarding the quarry independently of his position as a director. Other cases, however, have focussed on how fiduciaries came to acquire the corporate opportunity. In *Regal (Hastings) Ltd. v. Gulliver,* [1942] 1 All E.R. 378 (U.K. H.L.) the court held that the corporate opportunity clearly came to the directors of Regal "by reason of the fact that they were directors of Regal and in the course of their execution of that office" (at p.387). In comparison, the court in *Peso Silver Mines Ltd. v. Cropper,* 1966 CarswellBC 90, [1966] S.C.R. 673 (S.C.C.), held that the director who participated in an investment group which had previously been offered to the corporation, was not in breach of his fiduciary duty because he was "not approached in his capacity as a director. . . but as an individual member of the public" (at p. 682).

In summary, a determination of whether there has been a breach of fiduciary duty in the case at bar comes down to two questions: 1) was there either an actual or potential conflict of interest by virtue of Kim incorporating ETI and EBMR to pursue telecommunication and biomedical opportunities, and 2) were the telecommunication and biomedical investment opportunities pursued by ETI and EBMR acquired by Kim by virtue of his position as a director and officer of EMI? If there is either a potential or actual conflict of interest with the company, Kim will be liable to account. Even where there is no actual or potential conflict of interest, but the information or opportunity was acquired by virtue of his position as a director of EMI, Kim will be liable to account.

Notes

1   The trial and appeals court decisions in *Slate* are illustrative of the legal uncertainty created by the very different attitudes evinced by the Supreme Court in *Peso* and *CanAero.* Recall that in *CanAero,* Justice Laskin distinguished *Peso* in the following way:

> There is a considerable gulf between the *Peso* case and the present one on the facts as found in each and on the issues that they respectively raise. In *Peso,* there was a finding of good faith in the rejection by its directors of an offer of mining claims because of its strained finances. The subsequent acquisition of those claims by the managing director and his associates, albeit without seeking shareholder approval, was held to be proper because the company's interest in them ceased. There is some analogy to *Burg v. Horn* because there was evidence that Peso had received many offers of mining properties and, as in *Burg v. Horn,* the acquisition of the

particular claims out of which the litigation arose could not be said to be essential to the success of the company.

It is this distinction that is the foundation of much of the present uncertainty in the law. Distinguishing *Peso* on this basis, rather than overruling it, accepts that there is indeed a line between the illegal appropriation of a corporate opportunity and permissible competition. That line is whether the opportunity was "essential to the success of the company". However, when one reads the balance of the decision in *CanAero*, the attitude evinced by Justice Laskin makes it difficult to believe that he would have decided *Peso* in the same way. The sense that one gets reading Justice Laskin's decision is that he embraces the law that we see enunciated in *Regal (Hastings)* — and if he would change it in any respect, it would be to make it *stricter* (e.g., by jettisoning the profit rule limitation that any profit made in the course of, and by reason only of the fiduciary's position).

The two *Slate* decisions are illustrative of the very different interpretations that the law is capable of bearing. The lower court decision is largely consistent with *Peso* (although admittedly it draws the line between permissible competition and impermissible appropriation of a corporate opportunity in a slightly different way, based primarily on two factors: i) was there an actual or merely potential conflict of interest? ii) did the defendant acquire knowledge of the opportunity via his or her position with the company?) It cedes a fairly wide scope to fiduciaries to engage in permissible competition. By contrast, the appeals court decision, and that in *Cranewood*, are at odds with *Peso* and finds its inspiration in the strict words of Justice Laskin's in *CanAero*. It would appear to cede little room to fiduciaries to engage in competition.

2   The above decisions are a remarkable illustration of the siren song of the common law in the face of a clear statutory standard. Barry J. devotes almost all of his decision to an examination of the common law standard, concluding summarily at the end that the statutory standard does "not add anything to the duties already required by the common law." Perhaps he ought to have considered whether it *subtracted from* those duties, given that there is no hint of the conflict rule in the statutory standard. The appeals court did not quibble with Barry J.'s holding on this point. Neither court seems to have been aware (or to have found it important) that *CanAero* was a purely common law case, having been decided in a jurisdiction that did not have a statutory fiduciary duty. Could it really be the case that the statutory standard changes nothing? While, from a policy point of view, there is much to recommend the stricter common law approach, there is nonetheless a tension between the expression of legislative will

in CBCA s. 122(1)(a), and a fair and/or efficient resolution of these cases.

3   One mistake often made by students is to apply CBCA s. 120 (OBCA s. 132) to situations involving competition. Consider the following: Where a director or officer of Corporation XYZ operates a business that competes with Corporation XYZ, CBCA s. 120 and OBCA s. 132 *do not apply*, since there will be no "contract or transaction" between the competing corporations. Nor will these sections apply if a director or officer has a material interest in a party that is competing with the corporation — AGAIN unless there is a contract or transaction between the two entities (which is unlikely if they are competitors).

5.   TO WHOM IS THE FIDUCIARY DUTY OWED?

As we noted in our introductory note, two recent Supreme Court of Canada decisions have altered the foundation of fiduciary duties in rejecting the shareholder primacy view, and embracing what might be styled a more "pluralistic" view. The first of these, *People's Department Stores Ltd. (1992) Inc., Re*, 2004 CarswellQue 2862, 2004 CarswellQue 2863, [2004] 3 S.C.R. 461, 244 D.L.R. (4th) 564 (S.C.C.), was decided in 2004. We have drawn excerpts from the second of these cases, the *BCE* case, which immediately follows.

When you read the excerpts from *BCE* in this chapter, it might be helpful to keep the following in mind. The subject matter of the litigation was a transaction that BCE Inc. proposed to carry out under s. 192 of the CBCA. That section permits a corporation to undertake a wide variety of corporate fundamental changes as a so-called "arrangement". Each and every one of the transactions that may be carried out under s. 192(1) can also be effected via some other section or sections in the statute. For example, a corporation may effect an amalgamation either under s. 192, or pursuant to ss. 181-183. It may change its articles via an arrangement, or pursuant to ss. 173-179. Why the overlap? Section 192(2) allows a transaction to be completed as an arrangement only "[w]here it is not practicable for a corporation that is not insolvent to effect a fundamental change in the nature of an arrangement under any other provision of this Act." Typically, complicated transactions with multiple steps are carried out as arrangements. It might be possible to carry out these transactions purely under other sections of the statute, but to do so would cause great additional inconvenience, expense, and/or time. In such situations, the courts are willing to hold that it would not be "practicable" to carry out the transaction under any other section of the statute. Such was the case in the BCE transaction.

In order to effect a transaction by way of an arrangement, a corporation must first go to court to secure the court's assent. In this first hearing, the most important job of the court (aside from determining if the transaction is not "practicable" to be carried out under other provisions of the statute) arises under ss. 192(4)(c), which allows the court to make "an order requiring a corporation to call, hold and conduct a meeting of holders of securities or options or rights to acquire securities in such manner as the court directs." It is standard practice for the court to require that shareholders approve the transaction by a special resolution. If a corporation has more than one class of shares, it is also very common for a court to require that each of those classes approve the transaction by an ordinary resolution. Under the corporate arrangement provisions, it is not very common for a court to order that non-shareholder constituencies vote on the arrangement. In fact, ss. 192(4)(c) only permits a court to call a meeting of "holders of securities" or options or rights to acquire securities. The definition of "security," and the associated definition of "debt obligation" strongly suggest that only shareholders and financial creditors are security holders — i.e., not employees, trade creditors, or others.

Once the requisite approvals have been secured, then the corporation returns to court a second time to obtain final approval of the arrangement. Pursuant to common law grafted on to ss. 192(4)(e) of the statute (empowering the court to approve the arrangement), the court will hold a hearing to determine if the arrangement is "fair and reasonable." Once this determination is made, the court will grant final approval.

In *BCE*, Mr. Justice Silcoff of the Quebec Superior Court required that shareholders vote on the transaction. More than 97% voted in favour. While the debentureholders were not allowed to vote, Mr. Justice Silcoff nonetheless granted them standing to assert that the arrangement was not "fair and reasonable." The debenture holders also alleged that the transaction was oppressive under the statutory oppression remedy (CBCA s. 241), and constituted a violation of the directors' fiduciary duty under CBCA s. 122(1)(a). The gist of the debentureholders' argument was that the announcement of the transaction had caused the value of the debentures to decrease by about 20%, and that the directors had violated their duty (under any or all of the above-mentioned provisions) to protect the economic interests of the debenture holders, or to at least *consider* their interests. After an extended hearing, Justice Silcoff held that the transaction was fair and reasonable, that the directors had not breached their fiduciary duties, and that the transaction was not oppressive. The Quebec Court of Appeal reversed the decision, holding that under the Supreme Court of Canada's decision in *People's Department Stores Ltd. (1992) Inc., Re*, 2004 CarswellQue 2862, 2004 CarswellQue 2863, [2004] 3 S.C.R. 461, 244 D.L.R. (4th) 564 (S.C.C.), the directors had a duty to at least consider the interests of the debentureholders, which they had not done. That decision was appealed to the Supreme Court of Canada. The excerpt which follows deals with the issue of to whom the directors and officers fiduciary duty is owed to.

You will note that part of the excerpt deals with the oppression remedy. This is because the Supreme Court seems to compress the fiduciary duty and the oppression remedy into a single liability — i.e., the nature of the one informs the interpretation of the other. This creates some difficulties that are discussed following the excerpt (together with other difficulties created by the judgment).

For a detailed review of the facts of the case, see Chapter 4.

BCE Inc., Re

2008 CarswellQue 12595, 2008 CarswellQue 12596, [2008] 3 S.C.R. 560, 301 D.L.R. (4th) 80 (S.C.C.)

Overview of Rights, Obligations and Remedies under the CBCA

[T]his case does involve the fiduciary duty of the directors to the corporation, and particularly the "fair treatment" component of this duty, which, as will be seen, is fundamental to the reasonable expectations of stakeholders claiming an oppression remedy.

The fiduciary duty of the directors to the corporation originated in the common law. It is a duty to act in the best interests of the corporation. Often the interests of shareholders and stakeholders are co-extensive with the interests of the corporation. But if they conflict, the directors' duty is clear — it is to the corporation: *Peoples Department Stores*.

The fiduciary duty of the directors to the corporation is a broad, contextual concept. It is not confined to short-term profit or share value. Where the corporation is an ongoing concern, it looks to the long-term interests of the corporation. The content of this duty varies with the situation at hand. At a minimum, it requires the directors to ensure that the corporation meets its statutory obligations. But, depending on the context, there may also be other requirements. In any event, the fiduciary duty owed by directors is mandatory; directors must look to what is in the best interests of the corporation.

In *Peoples Department Stores*, this Court found that although directors *must* consider the best interests of the corporation, it may also be appropriate, although *not mandatory*, to consider the impact of corporate decisions on shareholders or particular groups of stakeholders. As stated by Major and Deschamps JJ., at para. 42:

> We accept as an accurate statement of law that in determining whether they are acting with a view to the best interests of the corporation it may be legitimate, given all the circumstances of a given case, for the board of directors to consider, *inter alia*, the interests of shareholders, employees, suppliers, creditors, consumers, governments and the environment.

As will be discussed, cases dealing with claims of oppression have further clarified the content of the fiduciary duty of directors with respect to the range of interests that should be considered in determining what is in the best interests of the corporation, acting fairly and responsibly.

In considering what is in the best interests of the corporation, directors may look to the interests of, *inter alia*, shareholders, employees, creditors, consumers, governments and the environment to inform their decisions. Courts should give appropriate deference to the business judgment of directors who take into account these ancillary interests, as reflected by the business judgment rule. The "business judgment rule" accords deference to a business decision, so long as it lies within a range of reasonable alternatives: see *Pente Investment Management Ltd. v. Schneider Corp.*, 1998 CarswellOnt 4035, 42 O.R. (3d) 177 (Ont. C.A.); *Kerr v. Danier Leather Inc.*, 2007 SCC 44, 2007 CarswellOnt 6445, 2007 CarswellOnt 6446, [2007] 2 S.C.R. 331 (S.C.C.). It reflects the reality that directors, who are mandated under s. 102(1) of the *CBCA* to manage the corporation's business and affairs, are often better suited to determine what is in the best interests of the corporation. This applies to decisions on stakeholders' interests, as much as other directorial decisions. . .

The Section 241 Oppression Remedy

The debentureholders in these appeals claim that the directors acted in an oppressive manner in approving the sale of BCE, contrary to s. 241 of the *CBCA*.

Security holders of a corporation or its affiliates fall within the class of persons who may be permitted to bring a claim for oppression under s. 241 of the *CBCA*. The trial judge permitted the debentureholders to do so, although in the end he found the claim had not been established. The question is whether the trial judge erred in dismissing the claim.

We will first set out what must be shown to establish the right to a remedy under s. 241, and then review the conduct complained of in the light of those requirements.

[The court noted that the concept of "reasonable expectations" underlies the oppression remedy. See Chapter 10.]

Determining whether a particular expectation is reasonable is complicated by the fact that the interests and expectations of different stakeholders may conflict. The oppression remedy recognizes that a corporation is an entity that encompasses and affects various individuals and groups, some of whose interests may conflict with others. Directors or other corporate actors may make corporate decisions or seek to resolve conflicts in a way that abusively or unfairly maximizes a particular group's interest at the expense of other stakeholders. The corporation and shareholders are entitled to maximize profit and share value, to be sure, but not by treating individual stakeholders unfairly. Fair treatment — the central theme running through the oppression jurisprudence — is most fundamentally what stakeholders are entitled to "reasonably expect".

The fact that the conduct of the directors is often at the centre of oppression actions might seem to suggest that directors are under a direct duty to individual stakeholders who may be affected by a corporate decision. Directors, acting in the best interests of the corporation, may be obliged to consider the impact of their decisions on corporate stakeholders, such as the debentureholders in these appeals. This is what we mean when we speak of a director being required to act in the best interests of the corporation viewed as a good corporate citizen. However, the directors owe a fiduciary duty to the corporation, and only to the corporation. People sometimes speak in terms of directors owing a duty to both the corporation and to stakeholders. Usually this is harmless, since the reasonable expectations of the stakeholder in a particular outcome often coincides with what is in the best interests of the corporation. However, cases (such as these appeals) may arise where these interests do not coincide. In such cases, it is important to be clear that the directors owe their duty to the corporation, not to stakeholders, and that the reasonable expectation of stakeholders is simply that the directors act in the best interests of the corporation. . .

[On the facts of the case, the court ruled in favour of BCE, on the basis that the debenture holders had failed to establish a reasonable expectation that the directors would protect either the investment grade rating or the market value of the debentures.]

Commercial practice — indeed commercial reality — undermines the claim that a way could have been found to preserve the trading position of the debentures in the context of the leveraged buyout. This reality must have been appreciated by reasonable debentureholders. More broadly, two considerations are germane to the influence of general commercial practice on the reasonableness of the debentureholders' expectations. First, leveraged buyouts of this kind are not unusual or unforeseeable, although the transaction at issue in this case is noteworthy for its magnitude. Second, trust indentures can include change of control and credit rating covenants where those protections have been negotiated. Protections of that type would have assured debentureholders a right to vote, potentially through their trustee, on the leveraged buyout, as the trial judge pointed out. This failure to negotiate protections was significant where the debentureholders, it may be noted, generally represent some of Canada's largest and most reputable financial institutions, pension funds and insurance companies. . .

Finally, the claim must be considered from the perspective of the duty on the directors to resolve conflicts between the interests of corporate stakeholders in a fair manner that reflected the best interests of the corporation.

The best interests of the corporation arguably favoured acceptance of the offer at the time. BCE had been put in play, and the momentum of the market made a buyout inevitable. The evidence, accepted by the trial judge, was that Bell Canada needed to undertake significant changes to continue to be successful, and that privatization would provide greater freedom to achieve its long-term goals by removing the pressure on short-term public financial reporting, and bringing in equity from sophisticated investors motivated to improve the corporation's performance. Provided that, as here, the directors' decision is found to have been within the range of reasonable choices that they could have made in weighing conflicting interests, the court will not go on to determine whether their decision was the perfect one.

Considering all the relevant factors, we conclude that the debentureholders have failed to establish a reasonable expectation that could give rise to a claim for oppression. As found by the trial judge, the alleged expectation that the investment grade of the debentures would be maintained is not supported by the evidence. A reasonable expectation that the debentureholders' interests would be considered is established, but was fulfilled. The evidence does not support a further expectation that a better arrangement could be negotiated that would meet the exigencies that the corporation was facing, while better preserving the trading value of the debentures.

Given that the debentureholders have failed to establish that the expectations they assert were reasonable, or that they were not fulfilled, it is unnecessary to consider in detail whether conduct complained of was oppressive, unfairly prejudicial, or unfairly disregarded the debentureholders' interests within the terms of s. 241 of the *CBCA*. Suffice it to say that "oppression" in the sense of bad faith and abuse was not alleged, much less proved. At best, the claim was for "unfair disregard" of the interests of the debentureholders. As discussed, the evidence does not support this claim.

Notes

The Supreme Court's decision in *BCE* creates a number of difficulties for directors, officers, legal advisors to corporations, and judges. Some of these are the following:

1   "May"? Or "Must"?

There are conflicting passages in *BCE* concerning whether directors "may" take the interests of affected corporate constituencies into account, or whether they "must" do so. Quoting *Peoples*, the judgment initially subscribes to the view that the consideration of various constituencies is *not mandatory*, but permissive. But on the facts of the case, the Supreme Court concluded that the directors of *BCE* had a *duty* to consider the best interests of the debenture holders. Thus, the judgment leaves us with conflicting pronouncements on this important issue.

2   Confounding Fiduciary Duties and the Oppression Remedy: The Legal Standard?

Another difficulty with the Supreme Court's decision is that it treats the directors' fiduciary duty under s. 122(1)(a) and the directors' duties under the oppression remedy as if they were a single liability, borrowing concepts from one to illuminate the extent of the other. It has been commonplace in the past for the courts to hold that the standard of liability under the oppression remedy (effectively, "fairness") includes and goes beyond directors' fiduciary duties. However, no court has ever adopted the reverse reasoning: that is, that what is oppressive ipso facto constitutes a breach of fiduciary duty. This is problematic for a number of reasons. One is that the directors' and officers' fiduciary duty is a subjective standard — acting "honestly and in good faith with a view to the best interests of the corporation". By contrast, the courts have held that the legal standard under the oppression remedy is objective. That is, under the oppression remedy, it is an unfair result that matters, and oppression may occur even if the directors have acted in good faith. How can the two liabilities be viewed as one, if the legal standard is so different?

3   Confounding Fiduciary Duties and the Oppression Remedy: To Whom Is the Duty Owed?

Yet another difficulty is that the court holds that the fiduciary duty is owed to "the corporation," and the corporation "is not to be confused with" the interests of any particular corporate constituency. The court seems to assume that the scope of the oppression remedy is similarly defined. And yet, s. 241(3) allows a complainant to complain only about conduct that is "oppressive or unfairly prejudicial to or that unfairly disregards the interests of any security holder, creditor, director or officer." Thus, by its terms, the oppression remedy envisions a much more limited set of plaintiffs. Again, how is it then that the oppression jurisprudence is informative of the legal standard for the fiduciary duty?

4   What Survives of the Existing Fiduciary Duty Jurisprudence?

Another difficulty arises in that the status of all jurisprudence dealing with fiduciary duties has now been rendered of questionable value. Are the courts to give oppression jurisprudence its full sway under s. 122(1)(a), or do the words of s. 122(1)(a) still mean something?

5   What is the Fiduciary Duty of Directors and Officers of Target Companies When There Is a Hostile Takeover Bid?

Jurisprudence prior to *BCE* uniformly assumes that the duty of directors of target corporations (i.e., those that are subject to a hostile takeover bid) is owed to shareholder alone. In addition, the securities regulators have required — and still require — target directors to look only to the welfare of shareholders. Thus, *BCE* has created great confusion among business people, their legal advisors, and courts as to what standard is to be applied in this context. This issue is dealt with more fully in the section on Takeover Bids.

6   How Does the Business Judgment Rule Operate Within Connection With a Pluralistic Fiduciary Duty?

As we will see below, the "business judgement rule" is a rule of judicial deference to the business decisions of corporate fiduciaries, as long as they fall within a "range of reasonableness." The procedural integrity of the decision-making process is central to securing the benefit of the business judgment rule. In turn, obtaining advice from outside, disinterested parties is often a key part of demonstrating procedural propriety. Before *BCE*, outside experts were typically called upon to evaluate the effect of a corporate action on shareholders. After *BCE*, must a board of directors secure advice on each and every constituency that stands to be affected by corporate action, if they are to demonstrate procedural propriety? If not, then what must they do to show that they at least considered the welfare of different constituencies? The judgment in *BCE* does not shed any light on these important issues.

7   How Do We Define a Derivative Action as Opposed to a Personal Action?

A derivative action has traditionally been defined as one in which all shareholders are harmed both equally and indirectly. It is essentially an adjunct to the shareholder primacy view of the corporation. If the fiduciary duty is owed to "the corporation," and the corporation is not to be confused with the interests of any particular constituency, then how do we define a derivative action?

8   What Evidence Must a Complainant Adduce to Win its Case in a Derivative Action?

Relatedly, what evidence must a complainant adduce to succeed in a derivative action? In a shareholder-focused universe, it is clear that the plaintiff must show prejudice to the shareholders. In a universe in which the fiduciary duty is owed to the corporation, and the corporation is not to be confused with the interest of any particular constituency, then what evidence must a plaintiff adduce to succeed? In theory, since the corporation is seen as an entity distinct from any of its constituents, even showing net prejudice to the entirety of all corporate constituents is not enough. But what is?

9   What Is the Status of the Court's Comments on the Oppression Remedy?

One of the difficulties in determining the legal scope of the Supreme Court's decision arises from the fact that, while the issue of oppression is argued in all of the various factums, the plaintiffs formally abandoned their oppression argument at the hearing. The case was thus argued before the court only on the basis of the directors' fiduciary duty and the "fair and reasonable" standard for the approval of an arrangement. Thus, the court's extended comments about the oppression remedy are actually obiter dicta.

The jurisprudence suggests that there are two critical factors for lower courts to use in deciding whether to follow a Supreme Court obiter. One is whether the issue was argued before the court. The other is whether the issue was dealt with in a sufficiently detailed manner to suggest that the court intended to outline a detailed code for the lower courts to follow. In *BCE*, these factors cut in precisely opposite directions (since the oppression claims were abandoned at the start of the appeal hearing).

For further discussion on the impact of the *BCE* decision, see Poonam Puri, "The Future of Stakeholder Interests in Corporate Governance" (2010) 48 Can. Bus. L. J. 427 and Edward Waitzer "*People's, BCE*, and the Good Corporate Citizen" (2009) 47 Osgoode Hall L. J. 439.

6. HOSTILE TAKEOVERS AND DEFENSIVE TACTICS BY TARGET MANAGEMENT

(a) Introduction to Hostile Takeovers and Defensive Tactics

By far the most contentious subject area for the study of fiduciary duties relates to management defensive tactics in response to a hostile takeover bid. A hostile takeover bid enables an outside acquirer to obtain control of a target corporation without having to obtain the assent of target management. Simply put, an acquirer will make a bid (almost always at some premium above the market price of the shares) to the target shareholders for some or all of the voting shares of the target company. If, within the prescribed time period, the requisite number of shares are tendered by target shareholders into the bid, then the shares will be "taken up" by the acquirer and the bid completed.

It is the ability of a new owner to sidestep target management in obtaining control of the corporation that renders the hostile takeover bid so threatening to target management. According to the management discipline hypothesis, takeovers are motivated by the gains that an acquirer can realize from displacing opportunistic management with more dedicated and efficient managers, perhaps even the acquirer herself, once control is obtained. Under this hypothesis, the gains from the takeover of a corporation directly vary with the severity of agency problems besetting the target corporation. The more opportunistic target management has been, in terms of their levels of diversion and shirking, the greater the benefit, and corresponding incentive, to an acquirer to obtain control and oust target management.

If the management discipline hypothesis is accepted as being the exclusive, or even a contributory, motive for takeovers, the tendency for target management to fiercely resist takeovers is not surprising. Target management, fearing the loss of their jobs and reputational capital, will do their best to stave off a hostile takeover by using a range of defensive tactics. These tactics may make a control acquisition more expensive to an acquirer, or may even deter the takeover altogether. In either case, management resistance dulls the incentive for takeovers, and, because any reduction in the level of takeover activity will increase the scope for managerial opportunism, resistance by target management will harm target shareholders. As Henry Manne pointed out several decades ago, any constraint on the takeover market will exacerbate the problems occasioned by the separation of ownership and control in the modern corporation (Henry Manne, "Mergers and the Market for Corporate Control" (1965), 73 J. Pol. Econ. 110 at 113). This is because "[o]nly the takeover scheme provides some assurance of competitive affairs among corporate managers and thereby affords strong protection to the interests of vast numbers of small, non-controlling shareholders." (The management discipline hypothesis is currently most strongly associated with the work of Easterbrook and Fischel, *infra*.)

If the management discipline hypothesis is correct, then the analysis of defensive tactics falls neatly within the scope of fiduciary duty doctrine: since the spectre of self-interested behaviour is omnipresent when managers fend off takeovers, courts should, as in other conflict situations, enforce a blanket prohibition against such conduct. The first difficulty, however, is that it is far from settled that managerial discipline is always the sole or dominant motive for takeover activity. Commentators have claimed that a number of competing motives for takeovers exist, some of which will result in transactions that are entirely bereft of economic value. But once competing motives for takeovers are acknowledged to exist, the efficacy of employing a blanket prohibition against all defensive tactics becomes suspect. Arguably, defensive tactics should be permitted where transactions are harmful to shareholders or to society. Here again, the issue of categorical versus selective rules becomes important, as does the ancillary issue of the judiciary's ability to effectively delineate between "desirable" and "undesirable" takeovers.

Adding another layer of complexity to the determination of the appropriate scope of managerial defensive tactics is the issue of auctions. That is, even if it is assumed that takeovers are motivated by desirable goals, some scholars (like Gilson, *infra*), have argued that target management should be able to engage in certain types of conduct aimed at establishing an auction that will raise the price of target shares to the acquirer. Whether auctions should be permitted or, indeed, encouraged, must be considered at normative and positive levels. In terms of the former, a decision to promote auctions indicates a desire to confer much of the benefit from takeover transactions on target shareholders. But why should the law deliberately favour target shareholders over acquirers? What are the equitable arguments in support of this position? In terms of the latter, if it is agreed that target shareholders should be the principal beneficiaries of takeover activity, what are the costs to societal welfare (because of reduced takeover activity) that are entailed by this commitment?

The following materials canvass the issue of the appropriate scope of defensive tactics from a number of different perspectives. First, several different theoretical perspectives are presented on the takeover debate — in particular, the issues of competing takeover motives and the appropriate role of auctions is discussed. Second, empirical evidence relating to various theoretical motives for takeover bids is presented. The response of Anglo-Canadian and American courts to defensive tactics is then documented.

Last, but certainly not least, the status of the jurisprudence that follows has been thrown into a state of doubt by *BCE* decision. The Canadian courts, following their U.S. counterparts, had previously defined the directors' and officers' fiduciary duty as a duty to seek the best value reasonably available *to the shareholders* in the circumstances. On the basis of questionable secondary (rather than primary) authority, the Supreme Court rejected this shareholder focus. This is bound to create considerable confusion among directors and officers (and their legal advisors) as well as judges in determining the scope of the fiduciary duty in this context.

The difficulty is exacerbated by the court's holding that "[w]here the corporation is an ongoing concern, [the fiduciary duty] looks to the long-term interests of the corporation." Again, following the U.S. example, Canadian courts had previously held that the duty is to secure the best value *immediately* available. The danger in redefining the temporal focus is that if we look to long-term value, virtually any plausible story will pass muster under the "business judgement rule", rendering the duty of little practical value. It also raises the spectre of a "just say no" defence, in which the directors adopt defensive measures that foreclose the possibility that a hostile bid might succeed, rather than letting shareholders ultimately decide the issue. Prior to *BCE*, it was widely assumed that neither the courts nor the securities regulators would permit a "just say no" defence. However, since a bid will either succeed or fail in the *short* term, allowing directors to resist on the basis of long-term considerations necessarily entails the possibility of such a defence. Did the Supreme

Court appreciate the consequences of its statement that directors must pursue the long-term interests of the corporation?

Finally, as we see below, securities regulators are frequently called upon to adjudicate takeover bid contests under their "public interest" powers. In employing these powers in relation to hostile takeover bids, they have consistently held that directors' duties are owed to shareholders alone. They have also consistently held that, under the public interest powers, they may define standards of conduct in a manner that departs from the applicable corporate law. Counsel advising a board of directors is thus caught between a rock and a hard place. Does counsel advise directors to obey the dictates of the newly pluralistic corporate law, or those of shareholder-centred securities law?

(b) Theoretical and Empirical Perspectives

Jeffrey MacIntosh,
"The Poison Pill: A Noxious Nostrum for Canadian Shareholders"
(1993), 15 Canadian Business Law Journal, p. 276 (footnotes deleted)

The purpose of this article is straightforward. By reviewing the empirical literature on the effects of poison pills on shareholder wealth, I will construct an argument that poison pills are not in the best interests of shareholders. Shareholders would be well advised not to vote in favour of them. I will also suggest that courts and administrators should sanction such plans only when approved by shareholders. Securities regulators should block any attempt to put a pill in place when shareholders are asked to consider more than one issue in a single vote, as Inco shareholders were recently asked to do. Where shareholders approve poison pill plans, the courts should carefully supervise their deployment in order to enhance the likelihood that pills are used in the best interests of shareholders and not simply to entrench target managers.

What Is the Function of Poison Pills?

There are two competing accounts of the function and purpose of poison pills. These may be described as the "shareholder interest" and "managerial entrenchment" hypotheses.

Shareholder Interest Hypothesis

The germ of this explanation is that a hostile acquirer is able to employ coercive tactics that effectively force target shareholders to tender into a low bid, even though shareholders as a group would prefer to hold out for more. The poison pill is the antidote to this coercion. By making an acquisition prohibitively expensive without the co-operation of management, the pill enables holders. So empowered, management may either defeat a bid that is too low, force the acquirer to make a more generous offer, or shop the company around for a better bid. Alternatively, management may use the breathing space accorded them by the pill to put together a competing proposal, like a "self-tender" (issuer bid), recapitalization, divestiture of assets or the like resulting in greater value for the target shareholders. In this way, shareholders will receive "full and fair value" for their shares.

Proponents of this view typically identify two types of "coercive" activity by bidders. The first is the two-tier bid. A two-tier bid is a 100% share acquisition effected in two stages. The bidder initially makes a takeover bid for sufficient shares to give the acquirer control of the firm. Remaining shareholders are then forced out in a second step amalgamation or similar transaction. The second step cashout price is lower than that offered shareholders on the first step takeover bid. Although shareholders as a group may share the determination that the price offered is too low, this two-tier arrangement ostensibly offers each individual shareholder a powerful incentive to tender into the first step partial bid. If the shareholder fails to tender, and the bid is successful, that shareholder is struck with the lower second-tier price for all her shares. This element of compulsion may also result in a lower valued two-tier bid beating out a higher valued any-or-all bid.

The second form of compulsion is said to be a partial bid for less than all the shares of the corporation. By reducing the public float of shares available for trading, a partial bid creates a condition of illiquidity in the market for those shares remaining in public hands after the conclusion of the bid. This effectively transforms a partial bid into the equivalent of a two-tier bid, with a similar element of compulsion.

As noted, the poison pill is supposed to counter these coercive influences.

The Management Entrenchment Hypothesis

When a successful hostile takeover bid occurs, the end result may be, and often is, loss of employment for the incumbent managers. This creates a potent conflict of interest for target managers, who may be more tempted to preserve their jobs at all costs than to act in the best interests of shareholders. Thus, the power given target management by the pill may be used abusively, rather than beneficially, to deter or thwart hostile bids and preserve managerial tenure. Because takeover bids usually result in the payment of large premiums to target shareholders, foreclosing a bid will result in a loss of potential takeover premiums with a corresponding diminution in share values. Moreover, incumbent managers will be insulated from the market for corporate control; shareholders may therefore find themselves stuck with inefficient managers, resulting in further losses in share value.

* * *

Summary of the Empirical Evidence

The available evidence on the effects of poison pills, taken in its totality, is highly consistent with the managerial entrenchment hypothesis. On the announcement of the adoption of poison pill plans, share prices on average decline. The decline is more pronounced where the firm is already the subject of takeover speculation or an ongoing takeover battle. It is also greater where the pill in question has an ownership discrimination feature characteristic of the most form of flip in pill, like that adopted by Inco. Additional evidence supporting the management entrenchment hypothesis is garnered from the behaviour of stock prices around court decisions regarding poison pills. Decisions upholding pills lead to share price declines, and decisions striking them down lead to price increases, on average. Firms adopting pills typically have lower profitability than industry cohorts and lower average share holdings by managers, further supporting the management entrenchment hypothesis. Although managers often state that the pill is designed to thwart coercive two-tier and partial offers, the evidence points strongly away from any such coercive effect. In a majority of cases, the pill is used not against these supposedly coercive forms of offers, but against any-or-all offers, suggesting that managers may simply appeal to the coercion argument as a matter of convenience rather than conviction.

(c) Defensive Tactics and the Theory of Takeovers

Easterbrook and Fischel,
"The Proper Role of a Target's Management in Responding
to a Tender Offer"
(1982), 94 Harv. L. Rev. 1161

Tender offers are a method of monitoring the work of management teams. Prospective bidders monitor the performance of managerial teams by comparing a corporation's potential value with its value (as reflected by share prices) under current management. When the difference between the market price of a firm's shares and the price those shares might have under different circumstances becomes too great, an outsider can profit by buying the firm and improving its management. The outsider reduces the free riding problem because it owns a majority of the shares. The source of the premium is the reduction in agency costs, which makes the firm's assets worth more in the hands of the acquirer than they were worth in the hands of the firm's managers.

All parties benefit in this process. The target's shareholders gain because they receive a premium over the market price. The bidder obtains the difference between the new value of the firm and the payment to the old shareholders. Non-tendering shareholders receive part of the appreciation in the price of the shares.

More significantly for our purposes, shareholders benefit even if their corporation never is the subject of a tender offer. The process of monitoring by outsiders poses a continuous threat of takeover if performance lags. Managers will attempt to reduce agency costs in order to reduce the chance of takeover, and the process of reducing agency costs leads to higher prices for shares.

If the company adopts a policy of intransigent resistance and succeeds in maintaining its independence, the shareholders lose whatever premium over market value the bidder offered or would have offered but for the resistance or the prospect of resistance. This lost premium reflects a foregone social gain from the superior employment of the firm's assets.

* * *

The Arguments Supporting the Right of Target Management to Adopt a Defensive Strategy

Our analysis cuts against the grain of many cases and a substantial amount of commentary. The rationales offered to support the right of target management to resist tender offers can be grouped in four categories: (1) tender offers do not increase welfare; (2) the target's shareholders benefit from price increases when tender offers are defeated; (3) the target's management has obligations to non-investor groups that may be adversely affected by a tender offer; and (4) the target's management is obligated to prevent unlawful conduct. In the sections that follow, we consider and reject each of these rationales as a basis for resistance.

The Arguments That Tender Offers Do Not Increase Welfare

Our argument relies on the premise that tender offers increase social welfare by moving productive assets to higher-valued uses and to the hands of better managers. Numerous commentators, however, have reached a contrary conclusion. It has been observed, for instance, that many target companies are "well run," have substantial amounts of cash from successful operations, and that the offeror retains the target's management after acquiring control. These observations are invoked to support an assertion that the acquired firms were not doing poorly; consequently, the argument concludes, tender offers do not move assets to better managers.

This is unpersuasive. It amounts to second-guessing the market. Unless the acquirer is giving away its money, the premium price paid for the shares indicates a real gain in the productivity of the assets. If General Motors is willing to bid $100 for a ton of steel owned by General Electric, and GE sells, we would count this as a value-increasing transaction despite the fact that GE otherwise would have put the steel to "good use" (perhaps $90 worth). The highly subjective observation that acquired firms are well run does not exclude the possibility that, in new hands, the firms would be better run. Only proof that markets are not efficient in pricing shares could support the argument that tender offers do not improve the use of resources.

That acquired firms often are cash rich, perhaps implying successful past operations, also does not demonstrate that takeovers are undesirable. To the contrary, that a firm holds a substantial cash position indicates agency costs. Cash can be invested. The acquirer usually invests the cash it obtains in the takeover, thus putting idle resources to work. The retention of the target's management after a takeover also is not significant. Although the management may keep their old titles, they often lose effective control to officers of the acquirer. Retention in office may be a form of bribe, paid to secure acquiescence in the takeover, rather than a signal of satisfactory performance.

Martin Lipton has advanced a related argument: Tender offers decrease social welfare because they "adversely affect long-term planning and thereby jeopardize the economy." But he fails to demonstrate how long-term planning is "adversely affected," let alone the economy jeopardized. The threat of takeovers does not prevent managers from engaging in long-range planning. If the market perceives that management has developed a successful long-term strategy, this will be reflected in higher share prices that discourage takeovers. To be sure, the risk of a tender offer ensures that corporate managers will be unable to assume that they can continue in office indefinitely. But this risk of displacement does not reduce welfare. Precisely the opposite is true; some insecurity of tenure is necessary to spur managers to their best performance. Society benefits from an active takeover market, therefore, because it simultaneously provides an incentive to all corporate managers to operate efficiently and a mechanism for displacing inefficient managers.

Harold Williams, former Chairman of the Securities and Exchange Commission, has argued that tender offers decrease welfare because they divert resources that otherwise could be used for capital investments and instead are used only to rear-range the ownership of existing corporate assets. The answer to this argument is that funds used to finance a tender offer are not necessarily diverted from investment to consumption. They are merely shifted from the acquiring corporation to the target's shareholders. The acquiring corporation could equally well have distributed these funds as dividends or put them to other non-investment uses. There is also no reason to assume that the target's shareholders will use these funds for consumption rather than capital investment. The shareholders may reinvest what they receive from the tender offeror. There is, therefore, no reason to conclude a priori that an active takeover market diverts funds from capital investment.

Tender offers have also been characterized as "raids" in which the offeror pays a premium for a working majority of the shares in order to loot the firm to the detriment of the minority shareholders. It is unlikely, however, that any tender offer for a substantial percentage of a company's shares will be motivated by a desire to loot the acquired corporation. A looter generates no new value, and thus cannot afford to pay a premium price for all shares. Even if a bidder seeks less than all shares, it cannot pay a significant premium for those it obtains. If, for example, the offeror acquires for $15 per share 70% of a firm whose shares had been trading for $10, it cannot hope to make a profit by looting. Also, looting from minority shareholders violates established rules, and a bidder would not be likely to escape detection if it violated these rules.

Another argument against tender offers portrays them as reducing the welfare of the shareholders of the acquirers by more than the premium paid to the target's shareholders. In this view, tender offers represent self-aggrandizing empire building by acquiring managers who err in deciding what firms to acquire or what price to pay. The difficulty with this view is its implicit assumption that product and labor market constraints (and the tender offer process itself) do not discipline managers. A corporation headed by an empire-building management team that did not maximize profits would fare poorly in the product market and would have lower share prices; its managers would fare poorly in the employment market. The corporation itself would become a takeover candidate.

Finally, it has been suggested that takeovers create monopolies. Profit increases that come about because of monopolization produce reductions in social welfare. This view, however, is contradicted by the evidence. Most tender offers raise no antitrust problems, and one careful study has shown that takeovers generally reduce concentration in the acquired firms' markets.

The raider, managerialist, and monopolist models of tender offers are also contradicted by data on stock price movements. Most of the movement in the price of a stock is correlated with movement in the market as a whole and depends on general economic conditions. But the movements in individual stock prices net of movements in the market give a rough picture of the fortunes of the issuing companies — called cumulative average residuals, or CARs — are powerful indicators of a company's performance.

* * *

The Argument That Share Price Increases Justify Resistance from Target's Management

Several commentators have noted that even if a tender bid fails, the share price of the target often rises, sometimes to more than the tender offer price. If shareholders so benefit, the argument goes, then management is justified in resisting tender offers. Although the data marshalled to support this point varies in quality, the premiums offered in unsuccessful offers appear to be less than the appreciation after the offer is defeated. This fact calls for explanation.

The most plausible reason for a price increase following the tender offer's defeat is that the market sees the defeat as simply one round in an extended auction. The market anticipates that in the future another offeror — one not saddled with the first offeror's higher costs of information — will acquire the target. Many management-induced withdrawals are followed by higher offers, and share prices increase as the eventual acquisition becomes more likely.

Another possible explanation for the price increase following a defeated tender offer is that the offer itself served to rouse the target's management to action. The offer warned management to improve its performance, and either the offer or the accompanying public disclosure may have provided the target's management with the information to do so.

Regardless of the cause of the price increase, shareholders in general have little cause for rejoicing. The price rise comes about because someone is taking a free ride on information generated by the first offeror. Free riding of this sort reduces the incentive to make the first offer, and, for the reasons we have developed earlier, decreases the amount of monitoring, decreases the number of offers, and harms shareholders in the long run.

* * *

Defensive Tactics and the Business Judgment Rule

In view of the recognized limits on the scope of the business judgment rule, it is surprising that courts have invoked the rule so freely as a basis for refusing to review the defensive conduct of managers faced with a hostile tender offer. A frequent consequence of a successful takeover attempt is the replacement of incumbent managers. For acquirers, replacement of target management is typically a significant motive for making the tender offer in the first place; for the target's shareholders, such offers present the most effective means of manifesting disapproval of management. Given the serious and unavoidable conflict of interest that inheres in any decision on one's own ouster, courts ought not to make available to a manager resisting a tender offer — and, in effect, fighting against his own replacement — the same deference accorded to the decisions of a manager in good standing.

Indeed, unlike transactions involving a conflict of managerial interest outside the realm of tender offers, efforts undertaken by target management primarily to resist a takeover bid should not even be susceptible of the justification that they happen to benefit the target. Such efforts to resist should instead be proscribed completely. Conflicts transactions outside the realm of tender offers are not similarly interdicted because they typically involve corporate decisions that shareholders, as a practical matter, simply cannot make. But in deciding whether to accept or reject a tender offer, managers enjoy no particular comparative advantage over shareholders. The decision does not involve management of the corporation's affairs in any meaningful sense and thus can be made by shareholders even though they are not involved in those affairs to any significant degree.

Moreover, the rationales underlying the policy of judicial restraint embodied in the business judgment rule in no way counsel against implementation of a rule of managerial passivity. The deference accorded managerial decisions under the business judgment rule reflects, in part, the inability of courts to make better business decisions than managers and, in part, the inefficiency that would result were managers encouraged to disregard the costs of gathering information and making decisions. A rule of managerial passivity does not require courts to make business decisions at all, let alone better decisions than managers. To implement a rule of passivity, all a court need do is determine whether managers were passive. It need not gather costly information nor induce managers to incur inefficiently large costs of decision making to stave off litigation. Under a rule of passivity, managerial decisions would be subject to attack only if designed to defeat takeover bids, and not for being inadequately researched.

* * *

The Meaning of Managerial Passivity

Although we have concluded that shareholders would want management to be passive in the face of a tender offer, we have not attempted to define precisely what we mean by passivity. Doubtless, managers must carry out the corporation's ordinary business. Perhaps, too, management should be able to issue a press release urging shareholders to accept or reject the offer. The offeror also will convey its views to the shareholders, who can act on these messages in light of the self-interest of both the management and the offeror. But almost any other defensive actions expend the target's resources and produce no gain to investors. Thus, management should not propose anti-takeover charter or bylaw amendments, file suits against the offeror, acquire a competitor of the offeror in order to create an antitrust obstacle to the tender offer, buy or sell shares in order to make the offer more costly, give away to some potential "white knight" valuable corporate information that might call forth a competing bid, or initiate any other defensive tactic to defeat a tender offer.

Our proposal for managerial passivity does not mean, however, that managers must go to sleep when they suspect an imminent tender offer. A requirement of managerial somnolence would deprive the corporation of valuable business opportunities and might give firms a device for hindering their competitors' operations. Yet many legitimate business decisions could have the effect of making the corporation less attractive to the bidder and thus could be called resistance. It is also possible, however, that many business decisions, ostensibly taken for the purpose of seizing valuable business opportunities, are actually undertaken for the purpose of defeating the tender offer. Distinguishing resistance from passivity will be simple in some cases and hard in others.

The timing of managerial action provides a useful, if imperfect, basis for resolving this dilemma. On the one hand, courts could simply presume, subject to rebuttal by a litigant who established the contrary, that any plans or programs set in motion before target managers had reason to believe that there would be a takeover attempt were not undertaken with a view to resisting the tender offer. Such plans would presumptively comply with the rule of passivity and would thus enjoy the freedom from judicial scrutiny otherwise available under the business judgment rule. On the other hand, if actions that materially hindered either the offer or the acquisition were taken immediately after management first had reason to know of an impending offer, then courts could presume that the actions were undertaken with a view to defeating the offer. The target's managers could be allowed to overcome the presumption, but only by a substantial demonstration that their actions were undertaken for the economic benefit of the target rather than for the purpose of defeating the offer.

This allocation of burdens places on the management — which has a clear conflict of interest and superior access to information about the reasons for and consequences of its deeds — the responsibility of justification. It meets two essential criteria: it does not incapacitate management from seizing profitable business opportunities just because another firm is attempting to acquire the target, and it also does not freely allow defensive stratagems.

Roberta Romano,
"A Guide to Takeovers: Theory, Evidence and Regulation"
(1992), 9 Yale Journal on Regulation 119

Theories of Takeovers and Related Transactions

One important, and undisputed, datum about acquisitive transactions should be noted from the outset: acquisitions generate substantial gains to target company shareholders. All studies find that target firms experience statistically significant positive stock price responses to the announcement of takeover attempts or merger agreements. On average, there is a 20% increase over the pre-announcement market price for mergers and a 30% increase for tender offers in the period around the takeover announcement. Abnormal returns in going-private transactions (leveraged buyouts) are of similar magnitude, ranging across studies between 20% and 37%. Without question, the announcement of a bid is good news for target shareholders.

The different explanations of acquisitions that will be examined are efforts at explaining the source of these gains.

The data are more ambiguous, however, concerning acquiring firms' returns. Depending on the sample and time period, acquirers experience positive, negative, or zero abnormal returns on a bid's announcement and completion. From the acquirer's perspective, there are two classes of explanations or motivations for a takeover: value-maximizing and non-value-maximizing ones. Value-maximizing explanations view takeovers as undertaken in order to increase the equity share price of the acquiring firm. Non-value-maximizing explanations consider takeovers in diametrically opposite terms, as transactions that maximize managers' utility rather than shareholder wealth. These two explanations therefore predict a different stock price reaction, positive and negative, respectively.

Value-maximizing explanations can be subdivided into efficiency, expropriation (wealth transfer), and market inefficiency explanations. This division is pivotal for policy analysis, but has no differential impact on the acquirer's expected return from the transaction. It will be positive in each case. Each non-value-maximizing explanation can be characterized as a distinct expropriation story, in which wealth is transferred from the acquiring firm's shareholders to the target firm (as well as to the managers). These transactions will thus have a negative stock price effect. To preview the classification schema, see Table 1.

There are, however, theoretically plausible reasons for not finding positive abnormal returns to bidders even when acquisitions are value-maximizing transactions. First, acquiring firms are typically much larger than target firms, making it more difficult to measure abnormal returns. Second, a bid may reveal information about the bidding firm unrelated to the particular acquisition, confounding the stock price effect. Third, if the takeover market is competitive, then bidders will earn only normal returns, as abnormal profits are competed away. Finally, for acquiring firms that have an active mergers and acquisitions program, the gain from a specific acquisition may have been anticipated in the bidder's stock price at the time the mergers and acquisitions program was announced.

Despite these interpretative subtleties concerning acquirers' stock price reactions, one may draw some generalizations from the data. The price movement for acquirers is small in percentage terms and less statistically significant than that for target firms. In addition, acquirers' returns have decreased over time and, in the 1980s, may have been negative. Moreover, even when acquirers earn negative returns, when their losses are aggregated with the targets' gains, acquisitions still net a positive abnormal return. Thus, because the division of the gain is skewed toward targets, takeovers that appear to be non-value-maximizing transactions for bidders may be socially beneficial (that is, aggregate wealth increases).

Studies of the performance of target firms after acquisition also shed light on whether acquisitions are value-maximizing or non-value-maximizing transactions. Here, stock price data are less reliable indicators for, as the interval over which the price is examined increases, changes can no longer be readily attributed to the event in question (the takeover) because it will be confounded with other events. Most of these studies therefore use accounting data to determine long-term changes in performance. As with event studies of the announcement effects on acquirers, the ex-post performance findings are also mixed. While earlier studies find no operating improvements in merged firms, more recent sophisticated studies find that performance improves post-merger.

One difficulty in assessing post-merger performance is in determining the appropriate comparison, which entails constructing a counterfactual benchmark — what the two firms' performances would have been had they not merged. In an important paper, Jarrell compares post-merger performance to analysts' pre-merger forecasts of the firms' performance. She finds that five years post-merger, the merged firms perform significantly better (9%) than the benchmark, although one to two years immediately after the merger the performance was worse than the benchmark. The capital market also accurately anticipates long-term performance: using regression analysis, Jarrell finds that the abnormal stock price effects upon a bid's announcement are significantly positively related to the merged firm's subsequent profitability. These data indicate that acquisitions are, indeed, value-maximizing, for the long-term performance of the combined firms improved. They also suggest that negative findings of earlier studies are, in all likelihood, the product of failure to use an appropriate benchmark.

Value-Maximizing Efficiency Explanations

There are two efficiency explanations of takeovers: to realize synergy gains and to reduce agency costs.

Value-Maximizing Expropriation Explanations

Expropriation explanations of takeovers focus on four distinct groups: taxpayers, bondholders, employees, and consumers.

Expropriation from Labor

The expropriation explanation of takeovers that attracts the most attention involves labor as the victim. The most sophisticated version of this explanation is Shleifer and Summers' breach of implicit contract explanation of hostile takeovers.

In Shleifer and Summers' scenario, shareholders initially hire trustworthy individuals as managers, in order to make credible long-term contract commitments to workers. The long-term commitments are implicit, rather than explicit contracts. After employees are hired, shareholders will want to breach the implicit contract, in order to increase their returns by lowering labor's share. A trustworthy management prevents them from doing so by honoring the informal agreements. A hostile takeover will, however, permit shareholders to behave opportunistically because, unlike trustworthy incumbents, a raider will not hesitate to break implicit contracts, cutting costs and releasing the pent-up value of the firm to shareholders.

Implicit contracts protect workers who have invested in transaction-specific human capital. By breaking these contracts, shareholders, through the raider, expropriate the quasi-rent value of the workers' investments. But, as shareholders benefit from workers who make such investments, the implicit contracts are ex ante efficient and it is hence undesirable that they be violated ex post. We then need a device to prevent the contracts from being broken, and trustworthy managers are posited to perform that function.

Shleifer and Summers' thesis is clever but not convincing. A key problem with their explanation is that it is questionable whether workers, particularly unionized workers, would opt to protect such extremely vulnerable investments as firm-specific capital through an implicit contract rather than some other explicit governance structure. As Williamson details, if contracts cannot be specified to avoid opportunism, other mechanisms will be devised to protect the vulnerable party's investment. The difficulty with the analysis is that Shleifer and Summers misuse the concept of an implicit contract. As Schwartz has observed, an implicit contract is a contract whose terms are observable to the contracting parties, but not to third parties, such as courts, and hence, not verifiable. An explicit contract is, correspondingly, one whose terms are both observable and verifiable. The choice of contact type depends upon the characteristics of the relevant contracting terms; if certain information is observable and verifiable, then it can be the basis of an explicit contract term, for performance of the contract can be conditioned on such a term and its breach can be enforced in court. The terms of concern to Shleifer and Summers — pension benefits, pension fund assets, wages, employment levels — are observable and verifiable. Thus they will be subject to explicit, and not implicit, contracting.

Finally, Shleifer and Summers offer no compelling reason why a hostile bidder can so easily do what incumbent management cannot, bargain for wage concessions. Many firms, including other airlines, engage in concession bargaining, and such efforts are typically independent of any hostile takeover threat. While it is not in the shareholders' interest to overpay workers, it is also not in their interest to underpay them.

Holmstrom suggests an alternative explanation to Shleifer and Summers' implicit contract story, which builds upon reputation. In this view, managers may be burdened with a reputation for weakness from past practices of capitulating to labor demands in order to make their jobs as managers more comfortable, and this reputation affects their credibility as bargainers in hard times. Thus, unlike raiders, who bring no such baggage to the negotiating table, incumbent management cannot obtain concessions. While interesting, I do not find this reputational explanation persuasive. It would be in labor's interest to grant concessions to the management it knows, rather than to a hardnosed raider, because past experience indicates that when financial conditions improve, the incumbents will be likely to seek comfort and return to the old regime of worker quasi-rents, whereas there is no basis to expect such favorable treatment from a raider.

Rosett tests Shleifer and Summers' breach of contract explanation more directly by examining union wage contracts before and after takeovers. He finds no support for their thesis: there is, in fact, a positive *gain* in union wealth levels after hostile acquisitions. Although there are losses after friendly acquisitions, even then the losses are insignificant relative to the premiums (when measured over 18 years after the takeover, the union losses in friendly acquisitions equal approximately 5% of the shareholders' gain). Bhagat, Shleifer, and Vishny also find that layoffs occur infrequently, affect high-level white collar workers, are higher when management successfully defeats a bid (either by remaining independent or by finding a white knight) than when a hostile bidder succeeds and, most important, result in losses that are small compared to takeover premiums (10-20%). In sum, while we would need counterfactual data to test the labor expropriation hypothesis fully — we need to know how many workers would have been laid off or what the wage profile would have looked like if the firm had not been acquired — what we do know suggests that expropriation from labor does not motivate takeovers.

Value-Maximizing Market Inefficiency Explanations

The final value-maximizing (that is, beneficial to acquirers' shareholders) explanation of takeover gains is premised on market inefficiency, the view that stock prices do not reflect firms' "fundamental value." According to this explanation, which is probably as widely-circulated in the popular press as the labor expropriation explanation, acquirers exploit market inefficiency by identifying undervalued firms, and presumably capture a large share of the gains by paying premiums below the correct valuation. There are two distinct market inefficiency explanations: general underpricing of stocks and myopia (overvaluation of current profits and excessive discounting of future profits).

Non-Value-Maximizing Expropriation Explanations

There are four non-value-maximizing explanations of takeovers. The first three are related, as they are all forms of managerialism: diversification, self-aggrandizement and free cash flow excesses by acquirers. The fourth, the hubris hypothesis, is a non-value-maximizing explanation ex post (once the bid is made) and not necessarily ex ante: managers may intend to maximize equity share prices by an acquisition but they overvalue the transaction's gains.

Summary and Conclusion

The preceding discussion — the explanations of takeovers and supporting empirical evidence — is summarized in Table 1. There is a substantial body of research that is consistent with agency cost reduction or synergy gain explanations of takeovers. There is, however, scant support for any of the expropriation explanations, whether the hypothetical victims are bondholders, labor, consumers or the government. There is even less support for market inefficiency explanations.

The data are more ambiguous regarding non-value-maximizing explanations. Manager-controlled firms engage in more diversifying mergers than owner-controlled firms and some acquirers earned negative abnormal returns in the 1980s. But these data can also be interpreted as consistent with value-maximization: firm-level diversification may lower executive compensation costs, and competition (auctions) reduces bidders' returns and may lead to overpayment (winner's curse). Most important, the net gains of acquisitions remain positive when bidder and target returns are matched. This finding undercuts the non-value-maximizing interpretation because it indicates that the gain from acquisitions is more than a simple transfer of wealth from acquirers to targets.

Table 1

Explanations of Takeovers

Explanation	Evidence
VALUE MAXIMIZING	
Efficiency	
1. Synergy Gains	
a. Operating	- positive correlation between bidder and target returns in pure conglomerate and product extension mergers; smaller bidding banks experience higher returns than larger bidding banks; higher returns in bank mergers the smaller the target bank relative to the acquiring bank; related acquisitions more profitable than unrelated acquisitions; substantial portion of gains from hostile takeovers due to reallocation of target assets to purchasers in related industries.
b. Financial	- capital expenditure planning shifted to central headquarters; higher premiums when acquirer's cash flow rate higher than target's; increased capital outlays after acquisitions; accounting conventions have no stock price effects.
c. Diversification	- low stock return correlation bank mergers

associated with significantly higher abnormal returns than high stock return correlation bank mergers; target bank stock return variability decreases after merger.

2. Reduced Agency Costs

a. Inefficient Management

- high management turnover after takeover; bidders have higher rates of return than targets; targets have low Tobin's q ratios; hostile takeover targets are poor performers; targets whose managers are replaced had negative returns pre-takeover; bad bidders make good targets; significant cash flow improvements after both unrelated and related-firm acquisitions.

b. Free Cash Flow

- probability of going private directly related to free cash flow and inversely related to growth; premiums correlated with free cash flow; targets have low Tobin's q ratios.

c. Improved Incentives from Ownership Increase (MBOs)

- productivity and operating improvements post-buyout; returns on going public (post-buyout value increase) directly related to management's equity stake.

Expropriation

1. Taxes

- interest deduction explains significant portion of MBO premium, other tax benefits not important; net tax effect from MBO estimated as positive and debt shield value reduced by rapid repayment; post-buyout investors earn very high return in reverse buyouts.

2. Bondholders

- small negative or no significant impact on bondholder wealth; size of gain not correlated with amount of outstanding debt; protective covenants increasingly used in industries where LBOs more likely.

3. Labor

- no significant negative impact on employment levels, except for top and middle managers; some evidence that employment increases with control changes; no significant wage effect; overfunded pension reversions not significant factor.

4. Monopoly Power

- no effect on competitors' stock prices; unrelated acquisitions less profitable than related acquisitions in the 1980s; hostile takeovers reallocate assets to related buyers.

Market Inefficiency

1. Underpricing	- stock prices of targets that are not acquired return to pre-bid levels; event studies generally supportive of market efficiency.
2. Market Myopia	- stock prices respond positively to increases in research and development (R&D) and capital investment expenditures; post-acquisition R&D expenditures do not decrease; targets in low intensity R&D industries and tend to spend less on R&D than industry; firms reduce R&D expenditures after adopting defensive charter amendments.

NON-VALUE-MAXIMIZING

1. Diversification	- manager controlled firms more likely to engage in diversifying mergers than owner-controlled firms.
2. Self-Aggrandizement	- bidder and target return correlations in pure conglomerate and product extension mergers are positive and not negative; positive relation between acquirers' abnormal returns and management stock ownership; bad bidders make good targets; acquirers' returns less negative when board is independent.
3. Free Cash Flow	- bad bidders are more likely to be acquired than good bidders; acquirers have positive abnormal returns before acquisition; acquirers have low Tobin's q ratios; free cash flow explains variance in returns across bidders; increases in free cash flow associated with decreases in bidders' gain from a takeover.
4. Hubris	- negative returns to acquirers in 1980s; bad bidders make good targets; bidders overpay in auctions.

I therefore read the literature as most consonant with the value-maximizing, efficiency-enhancing explanations of takeovers. However, different takeover theories each explain best only subsets of acquisitions and, though empirical studies might point in a particular direction, none are conclusive. There may be, then, instances of non-value-maximizing acquisitions as well as acquisitions which transfer wealth from particular groups to target shareholders, but these should be viewed as the exception, rather than the rule.

Notes

The debate over takeover policy and the appropriate scope of management defensive tactics is dealt with in the following articles. The argument for complete managerial passivity in response to a takeover bid is made in: Easterbrook and Fischel, "The Proper Role of a Target's

Management in Responding to a Tender Offer", *supra*; Easterbrook and Fischel, "Auctions and Sunk Costs in Tender Offers" (1982), 35 Stan. L.R. 1; and Schwartz, "The Fairness of Tender Offer Prices in Utilitarian Theory" (1988), 18 Jour. Legal Studies 165.

Critical evaluation and modification of Easterbrook and Fischel's argument from within an economic analysis paradigm is found in: Bebchuk, "The Case for Facilitating Competing Tender Offers" (1982), 95 Harv. L.R. 1028; Bebchuk, "The Case for Facilitating Competing Tender Offers: A Reply and Extension" (1982), 35 Stan. L. Rev. 23; Coffee, "Regulating the Market for Corporation Control: A Critical Assessment of the Tender Offer's Role in Corporate Governance" (1985), 84 Colum. L. Rev. 1145; Gilson, "A Structural Approach to Corporations: The Case Against Defensive Tactics in Tender Offers", *supra*; Gilson, "The Case Against Shark Repellent Amendments: Structural Limitations on the Enabling Concept" (1982), 34 Stan. L. Rev. 775; Gilson, "Seeking Competitive Bids Versus Pure Passivity in Tender Offer Defense" (1982), 35 Stan. L. Rev. 51; Roll, "The Hubris Hypothesis of Corporate Takeovers" (1986), 59 J. Bus. 197. Analysis and criticism from outside the economic paradigm is found in: Lipton, "Takeover Bids in the Target's Boardroom" (1979), 35 Bus. Law. 101; Lipton, "Takeover Bids in the Target's Boardroom: An Update After One Year" (1980), 36 Bus. Law. 1017; Lipton, "Takeover Bids in the Target's Boardroom: A Response to Professors Easterbrook and Fischel" (1980), 55 N.Y.U.L. Rev. 1231; Lowenstein, "Pruning Deadwood in Hostile Takeovers: A Proposal for Legislation" (1983), 83 Colum. L. Rev. 249.

Canadian evidence on the gains from corporate control transactions is considered by B. Espen Eckbo, "Mergers and the Market for Corporate Control: The Canadian Evidence" (1986), 19 Cdn. Jour. of Econ. 236 (which is now, regrettably, quite out of date).

(d)   The Common Law

(i)   An Introduction to Takeover Defences

Forgetting the directors' fiduciary duties and the oppression remedy for a moment, there is a wide variety of defensive tactics that management of a target company may take when confronted with a "hostile" takeover bid (i.e., one not made with the assent of the management of the target company). In the older cases, one finds that the defensive measure of choice was almost always an issuance of shares into friendly hands (e.g., the directors themselves, or their close business associates). The idea was to ensure that there was a large rump of shares that would *not* be tendered into the bid. If that rump was large enough, a hostile bid would necessarily fail. Under current legislation, directors have retained the power to issue shares at any time: CBCA, s. 25 and OBCA, s. 23. In the

United States, the issuance of shares is still employed in some cases as a takeover defence. This is often done by using so-called "blank check preferred" shares. Blank check preferred shares are issued long before any takeover bid occurs, and allow the board to fix the terms of issuance. If a hostile takeover bid occurs, the directors may then issue the shares on whatever terms they choose — and these terms of issuance may invest the holders with various rights that make a transfer of control difficult (or various follow-on transactions that an acquirer might choose to do, such as a sale of major assets).

As takeover bids became more frequent in the 1970s, 80s, and 90s, the menagerie of takeover defences was enormously expanded, replete with its own lexicon of colourful names — the totality of which is generally referred to as "shark repellent." Thus, for example, if the bidder sought to acquire a key asset possessed by the target, the directors might sell that asset to someone else — a so-called "sale of the crown jewels" (note that under the CBCA and OBCA, this may require a shareholder vote: see CBCA s. 189(3), OBCA s. 184(3)). Likewise, a "scorched earth" defence may involve liquidating the crown jewels, ensuring that the firm's debt becomes immediately due and payable upon a change in control (also called a "poison put"), or taking other steps to make the target unattractive. A "Pac-Man" defence consists of turning the tables and seeking to acquire control of the bidder. A "white knight" is an alternative bidder sought by target management — often one that is more sympathetic to keeping management on, or that will be more generous in showing them out the door. There are many more colourful terms of this ilk.

In the mid-1980s, a revolutionary defence, called the "poison pill," was invented by New York corporate lawyer Martin Lipton (of Wachtell, Lipton, Rosen & Katz). It was first used in Canada by Inco Corp. (now known as Vale) in 1989. The poison pill (also known by its more pedestrian name of "shareholder rights plan") has come to dominate the field of takeover defences both in Canada and the United States. While there are many types of poison pills, Canadian pills tend to have a number of features in common. The pill starts with an issuance of "rights" to the company's shareholders (a right being an option to buy more shares in the company). Typically, one right will be issued for each share held by a given shareholder, so that if I have 100 shares, I will be issued 100 rights. Each right entitles the holder to purchase one additional share in the company (from the company) at half the market price of the company's stock at the time the right is exercised. However, rights only become exercisable should any shareholder (the "acquiring person") obtain more than a stated percentage of the company's stock — typically 20%, but in some cases 10% or (rarely) even 5%. When the ownership threshold is crossed, securities lawyers often refer to this as a "flip-in" event.

What makes the poison pill a potent takeover defence is that the only shareholder that cannot exercise its rights is the "acquiring person". Thus, if I want to make a takeover bid that will result in my owning more than 20% of the corporation's stock, I must take into account the fact that all of the other shareholders of the corporation will be able to buy one share for every share that they hold — at half the market price.

This has a dramatic effect on the bidder, as illustrated by the following example. Suppose that a corporation has 100 shares outstanding that trade in the market at $100 per share. This means that the total value of the corporation is $100 x 100, or $10,000. The corporation has a poison pill, with the attributes described immediately above, that is triggered when anyone acquires more than 20% of the corporation's shares. Now suppose that I make a bid for the company's shares at $120 per share, and I succeed in purchasing 40 shares. My total acquisition cost is $4800 ($120 x 40). But because my ownership triggers the pill, the non-tendering shareholders, holding 60 shares, all exercise their pill rights such that 60 new shares are issued by the target. Now, there are 160 shares outstanding. Instead of owning 40% of the target firm's shares, I now own only 40/160, or 25%. Worse, the market price of the shares will have dropped. Assuming for the sake of simplicity that the market price at the time of exercise is $100 per share, each right entitles the holder to purchase a share from the corporation at $50. Thus, the issuance of shares raises $50 x 60, or $3000 in cash. We will assume that the post-bid value of the corporation (not counting the money raised) is the same as the pre-bid value, or $10,000. Then, taking into account the money raised, the post-bid value is $13,000. But since there are 160 shares outstanding, the market price will be only $81.25 ($13,000/160).

Where does this leave the bidder? The bidder paid $4,800 for shares that are now worth only $3,250 in the market. In effect, this means that instead of paying a 20% premium over market, the bidder effectively pays nearly 48% ($1550, the dollar premium over market, divided by $3250, the post-bid market price of the shares). In addition, the bidder sees its 40% holding diluted to only 25%. It is little wonder that the bidders virtually never trigger a poison pill (there is only one recorded case): it simply makes a takeover bid too expensive. In its net effect, a poison pill is equivalent to writing a dividend cheque to every shareholder of the corporation except the bidder (can you see how?).

Canadian poison pills usually have a "permitted bid" feature, which allows a bidder to cross the triggering ownership threshold without triggering the pill, as long as certain requirements are met. These conditions usually require that the bidder; i) hold the bid open for a longer period of time than that required by the securities legislation (e.g. 60 or 120 days, versus 35 days); ii) to proceed only if 50% or more of the shares not already held by the bidder are tendered into the bid; iii) allow shareholders to withdraw their tenders at any time before the shares are taken up by the bidder and paid for; iv) extend the bid for a further 10 days once 50% of the shares are tendered. In addition, the permitted bid feature may require the bidder to make an "any-or-all" offer (i.e., impose no ceiling on the number of shares that will be purchased), rather than a "partial bid."

The incentive to use a "permitted bid" feature, and indeed the incentive to use a pill at all, have arguably been greatly diminished by changes to the Canadian takeover bid regime that took effect on May 9, 2016 (via National Instrument 62-104, "Take-Over Bids and Issuer Bids"). The new rules replicate the first, third, and fourth requirements of a typical permitted bid clause (as discussed in the previous paragraph), arguably rendering a permitted bid clause redundant. Moreover, since one of the main purposes of the pill is to give target management time to secure a better deal for target shareholders (whether by negotiating with the bidder(s), seeking a white knight, or by some other means), this obviously diminishes the incentive to adopt any kind of poison pill.

One final feature of the typical pill is worthy of note. The board of directors may, at any time, "waive" the pill in favour of any acquirer. That is, they may declare that the rights will not be exercisable should that bidder trigger what would otherwise be a "flip-in" event (i.e., cross the stated ownership threshold).

As noted earlier, the ostensible purpose of the pill is to force any acquirer to negotiate directly with management if they wish to purchase control of the firm. The idea is that management, representing the shareholders, can negotiate a better deal or find a more attractive alternative transaction (and/or that the delay occasioned by the pill will allow other bidders to join the fray). The "dark side" of the pill, however, is that even where management cannot engage in a "just say no" defence, deploying a pill can raise the cost of an acquisition to the point where it will materially lower the probability that any bid will ever materialize.

(ii)   *Teck v. Millar*, a Canadian Watershed

The earliest English and Canadian cases regulated very closely any attempt by the board of the target company to prevent someone from gaining control by buying up shares. Virtually all of these cases involved an issuance of shares into friendly hands to defeat an intended acquisition of control. Under the "improper purpose" doctrine, the courts held it was *per se* an improper purpose for the directors to issues shares to defeat a control position, even if they were acting honestly in what they thought was the best interests of the company. Thus, if shares were issued contemporaneously with someone's attempt to gain control by buying up shares, the courts would carefully examine the motive behind the issuance of shares. If there was a *bona fide* reason not connected with the issue of control (basically, the need to raise money), the issuance could stand. However, if the issuance was done with a view to influencing who controlled the company, the issuance was made with an improper purpose and was struck down.

For example, in *Bonisteel v. Collis Leather Co.* (1919), 45 O.L.R. 195 (H.C.), the court found that an issuance of shares was in good faith and in what the directors perceived to be the best interests of the company. Nonetheless, the court held that the issuance was made with an improper purpose — the purpose of defeating the intended acquisition of a control block by a shareholder that the board did not approve of. Thus, while in *Bonisteel* the directors did not, strictly speaking, violate their fiduciary duty to the company, they nonetheless acted in an illegal manner. While in *Bonisteel* the court held that the issuance was void, in most other improper purpose cases, the courts have held that an issuance of shares for the purpose of influencing control of the company was merely voidable.

Then, in 1972, everything changed as a result of the watershed ruling in *Teck Corp. Ltd. v. Millar* 33 D.L.R. (3d) 288, [1973] 2 W.W.R. 385 (B.C. S.C.). In the mining industry in B.C., a "junior" mining company will typically seek to enter into an "ultimate deal" with a much larger company (the "major"). The ultimate deal involves the issuance of a controlling block of shares to the major sufficient to allow for the full development of the junior's mining properties. In *Teck*, Afton Mines was a junior company that held attractive mining properties. For this reason, two different suitors were anxious to complete an ultimate deal with Afton: Canadian Explorations Ltd. (Canex), and Teck Corp. Millar, the moving force behind Afton, strongly favoured Canex, which he felt was the more capable of the two companies and the better partner in an ultimate deal. While he felt that the company was not quite ready for an ultimate deal, Afton nonetheless needed operating funds. Millar and the board thus caused Afton to sell a non-controlling block of shares to Canex at $3.00 per share, even though Teck had offered $4.00.

Teck then began to purchase Afton's shares in the market, and by the end of May, 1972 they had obtained a majority of the shares of Afton at a cost of some $16,000,000, at an average price of $13 per share. During this period (April-May) Millar held many meetings with Placer, a subsidiary of Canex, and Teck representatives, as well as with officials of two other majors, concerning an ultimate deal. Towards the end of May, Millar knew that Teck was close to acquiring control — as did Placer. Millar then proposed a 70% (Afton) — 30% (Placer) ultimate deal to Placer which was accepted on May 30th and signed on June 1st, after approval by Placer's board. Under the terms of the contract, Placer was to receive 30% of Afton's outstanding share capital if it chose to put the property into production after further exploration and development work.

Teck meanwhile was concerned that Afton would make an ultimate deal with another major and sent a letter on May 29th to the Afton directors saying that no ultimate deal should be made yet and that Teck could arrange better terms than anyone else. On May 30th, Teck requisitioned a shareholders' meeting of Afton. On May 31st Teck delivered a letter to Millar and the Afton directors saying no ultimate deal should be made without consultation and legal action would be taken if a deal was made involving the issuance of shares. On the same day, Teck's solicitors delivered a letter to Afton's solicitors stating that Teck owned a controlling position and that Afton should take no action outside the ordinary course of business until the requisitioned shareholders' meeting was held. Despite the letter, Afton's solicitor advised the board that they could enter into the deal with Placer provided they genuinely thought such action to be in the best interests of Afton. The ultimate deal was signed on June 1st and Teck launched its action on June 2nd.

Teck Corp. v. Millar
(1972), 1972 CarswellBC 284, [1973] 2 W.W.R. 385, 33 D.L.R. (3d) 288
(B.C. S.C.)

BERGER, J.: . . . Now counsel for Teck does not accuse the defendant directors of a crass desire merely to retain their directorships and their control of the company. Teck acknowledges that the directors may well have considered it to be in the best interests of the company that Teck's majority should be defeated. Even so, Teck says, the purpose was not one countenanced by the law. Teck relies upon *Hogg v. Cramphorn Ltd.*, [1967] Ch. 254. . . [In *Hogg v. Cramphorn.*] Buckley, J., takes the view that the directors have no right to exercise their power to issue shares, in order to defeat an attempt to secure control of the company, even if they consider that in doing so they are acting in the company's best interests. . .

[I]f *Hogg v. Cramphorn Ltd., supra*, is right, directors may not allot shares to frustrate an attempt to obtain control of the company, even if they believe that it is in the best interests of the company to do so. This is inconsistent with the law as laid down in *Re Smith & Fawcett Ltd.* How can it be said that directors have the right to consider the interests of the company, and to exercise their powers accordingly, but that there is an exception when it comes to the power to issue shares, and that in the exercise of such power the directors cannot in any circumstances issue shares to defeat an attempt to gain control of the company? It seems to me this is what *Hogg v. Cramphorn Ltd.* says. If the general rule is to be infringed here, will it not be infringed elsewhere? If the directors, even when they believe they are serving the best interests of the company, cannot issue shares to defeat an attempt to obtain control, then presumably they cannot exercise any other of their powers to defeat the claims of the majority or, for that matter, to deprive the majority of the advantages of control. I do not think the power to issue shares can be segregated, on the basis that the rule in *Hogg v. Cramphorn Ltd.* applies only in a case of an allotment of shares.

The impropriety lies in the directors' purpose. If their purpose is not to serve the company's interest, then it is an important purpose. Impropriety depends upon proof that the directors were actuated by a collateral purpose, it does not depend upon the nature of any shareholders' rights that may be affected by the exercise of the directors' powers.

My own view is that the directors ought to be allowed to consider who is seeking control and why. If they believe that there will be substantial damage to the company's interests if the company is taken over, then the exercise of their powers to defeat those seeking a majority will not necessarily be categorized as improper.

If the directors have the right to consider the consequences of a takeover, and to exercise their powers to meet it, if they do so *bona fide* in the interests of the company, how is the Court to determine their purpose? In every case the directors will insist their whole purpose was to serve the company's interest. And no doubt in most cases it will not be difficult for the directors to persuade themselves that it is in the company's best interests that they should remain in office. Something more than a mere assertion of good faith is required.

I think the Courts should apply the general rule in this way: The directors must act in good faith. Then there must be reasonable grounds for their belief. If they say that they believe there will be substantial damage to the company's interests, then there must be reasonable grounds for that belief. If there are not, that will justify a finding that the directors were actuated by an improper purpose. . .

I am not prepared therefore to follow *Hogg v. Cramphorn Ltd.*, *supra*. I think that directors are entitled to consider the reputation, experience and policies of anyone seeking to take over the company. If they decide, on reasonable grounds, a take-over will cause substantial damage to the company's interests, they are entitled to use their powers to protect the company. That is the test that ought to be applied in this case. [Stating that "[t]he whole case, in my view, turns on the question of Millar's motivation", the court went on to find that Millar, and the other directors, genuinely believed that Canex was the better development partner. While Millar was aware that entering into an ultimate deal with Canex would frustrate Teck's intended acquisition of control and its ability to enter into an ultimate deal with Afton, his purpose was not to frustrate that acquisition of control. Rather it was to strike the best deal he could for the company. In addition, in a passage that is reminiscent of *Automatic Self-Cleansing Filter Syndicate* (*supra*, p. x), Berger J. stated:]

The defendant directors were elected to exercise their best judgment. They were not agents bound to accede to the directions of the majority of the shareholders. Their mandate continued so long as they remained in office. They were in no sense a lame duck board. So they acted in what they conceived to be the best interests of the shareholders, and signed a contract which they knew the largest shareholder, holding a majority of the shares, did not want them to sign. They had the right in law to do that.

[Berger J. also held that "[t]he onus of proof is on the plaintiff. . .]

Notes

1   On defensive tactics, see generally see Frank Iacobucci, "Planning and Implementing Defences to Take-Over Bids: The Directors' Role", (1981), 5 Can. Bus. L.J. 131; Jeffrey G. MacIntosh, "The Poison Pill: A Noxious Nostrum for Canadian Shareholders" (1989) 18 Can. Bus. L.J. 276; Edward Iacobucci, "Directors and Corporate Control Contests: Reconciling Frank Iacobucci's Views from the Academy and the Bench" (2007) 57 University of Toronto Law Journal 251.

2   The core of Berger J.'s test is that:

> [t]he directors must act in good faith. Then there must be reasonable grounds for their belief. If they say that they believe there will be substantial damage to the company's interests, then there must be reasonable grounds for that belief. If there are not, that will justify a finding that the directors were actuated by an improper purpose . . .

> By comparison, as we noted earlier, the statutory fiduciary duty in the CBCA and other cognate statutes requires that the directors "act honestly and in good faith with a view to the best interests of the corporation." One curiosity about *Teck* and its progeny is that while the statutory test makes no mention of "reasonable grounds" for the directors' belief, the courts have nearly uniformly imported the requirement for reasonable grounds into the test for the propriety of directors' conduct on the occurrence of a takeover bid. Is there any warrant for a court to disregard a statutory test in favour of a common law test?

3   In *Teck*, Berger J. stated:

> The classical theory is that the directors' duty is to the company. The company's shareholders are the company: Boyd, C., in *Martin v. Gibson*, 1907 CarswellOnt 27, 15 O.L.R. 623 (Ont. H.C.), and therefore no interests outside those of the shareholders can legitimately be considered by the directors. But even accepting that, what comes within the definition of the interests of the shareholders? By what standards are the shareholders' interests to be measured?

> In defining the fiduciary duties of directors, the law ought to take into account the fact that the corporation provides the legal framework for the development of resources and the generation of wealth in the private sector of the Canadian economy: Bull, J.A., in

Peso Silver Mines Ltd. v. Cropper, 1965 CarswellBC 144, 56
D.L.R. (2d) 117 (B.C. C.A.) at pp. 154-5 [D.L.R.], affirmed 1966
CarswellBC 90, 58 D.L.R. (2d) 1 (S.C.C.).

> ". . .the corporation has become almost the unit of organization
> of our economic life. Whether for good or ill, the stubborn fact
> is that in our present system the corporation carries on the bulk
> of production and transportation, is the chief employer of both
> labor and capital, pays a large part of our taxes, and is an
> economic institution of such magnitude and importance that
> there is no present substitute for it except the State itself."

Jackson J., in *State Tax Commission v. Aldrich et al.* (1942), 316
U.S. 174 at p. 192.

> A classical theory that once was unchallengeable must yield to
> the facts of modern life. In fact, of course, it has. If today the
> directors of a company were to consider the interests of its
> employees no one would argue that in doing so they were not
> acting *bona fide* in the interests of the company itself. Similarly,
> if the directors were to consider the consequences to the
> community of any policy that the company intended to pursue,
> and were deflected in their commitment to that policy as a
> result, it could not be said that they had not considered *bona
> fide* the interests of the shareholders.

> I appreciate that it would be a breach of their duty for directors to
> disregard entirely the interests of a company's shareholders in
> order to confer a benefit on its employees: *Parke v. Daily News
> Ltd.*, [1962] Ch. 927. But if they observe a decent respect for other
> interests lying beyond those of the company's shareholders in the
> strict sense, that will not, in my view, leave directors open to the
> charge that they have failed in their fiduciary duty to the company.
> In this regard, I cannot accept the view expressed by Professor E.
> E. Palmer in *Studies in Canadian Company Law*, c. 12, "Directors
> Power and Duties", pp. 371-2.

You will note that this statement is *obiter dictum*, since it forms no
part of the *ratio*. Nonetheless, it was the foundation for the Supreme
Court of Canada's rejection of shareholder primacy in *People's
Department Stores Ltd. (1992) Inc., Re*, 2004 CarswellQue 2862, 2004
CarswellQue 2863, [2004] 3 S.C.R. 461, 244 D.L.R. (4th) 564
(S.C.C.).

4 Berger J. drew extensively upon American authority in crafting the
standard to be applied to directors. In particular, he cited with
approval the approach taken in *Cheff v. Mathes*, 199 A.2d 548 (Del.
S.C., 1964) and *Kors v. Carey*, 158 A.2d 136 (Del. Ch., 1960). These
cases not only specify the standard of behaviour applicable to

directors, but represent the first application of the "business judgment rule" in the context of contested takeovers. You will recall that we introduced the business judgment rule in Chapter 5 (dealing with the duty of care). In the United States, the business judgment rule is both a rule of deference to managerial expertise *and* an onus-shifting device. It arose out of the fact that in the United States, the courts had held that when a fiduciary was sued for an alleged breach of fiduciary duty, an onus fell on the defendant directors to show the intrinsic fairness of the transaction. Feeling that this was too onerous, the courts fashioned the business judgment rule, pursuant to which an initial onus lay on the plaintiff to show facts suggesting that the action in question involved fraud, illegality, dishonesty of purpose, self-dealing or, more generally, a conflict of interest. Only then would an onus shift to the directors to show the fairness of the transaction. However, beginning with *Cheff v. Mathes*, and more fully expressed in the American cases explored below, the American courts' takeover jurisprudence has been coloured by the fact that the case of contested takeover bids is inherently different from many other cases involving an allegation of breach of fiduciary duty. When a takeover bid occurs, a potent conflict of interest arises. The duty of the directors is to act in the best interest of the shareholders. This may well involve accepting a premium takeover bid. However, hostile takeovers often result in directors and senior officers losing their jobs. Thus, the directors (and particularly the inside directors) will often be tempted to fend off a hostile takeover bid that is in the shareholders' best interests, in order to preserve their jobs. For this reason, the American courts have held that in cases involving hostile takeovers, an initial onus of proof (described in the *Unocal* case which immediately follows) falls upon the directors. They may then shift the onus back to the plaintiff by satisfying the *Unocal* test.

You will note that, in contrast to the onus-shifting that is an intrinsic part of the American business judgment rule, in *Teck*, Berger J. stated that the onus of proof was on the plaintiff throughout. Keep the issue of the onus of proof in mind in reading the Canadian takeover cases that follow the American authorities below, to see whether the Canadian cases have now come into line with US authority.

5   In any case involving allegations of director and/or officer misconduct, and extending well beyond the issue of hostile takeover bids, it is a virtual certainty that the plaintiff will allege not only that there has been a breach of fiduciary duty under CBCA s. 122 (or its equivalent in other jurisdictions), but also that there has been oppressive conduct under CBCA s. 241 (or its equivalent elsewhere). You will note that a suit alleging director or officer misconduct is a suit of a derivative nature. That is, the nature of the alleged wrong is one done to the entire body of shareholders, and not merely some

subset of shareholders (which would ground only a personal action: see Chapter 10 for further details). While on its face it is not entirely clear that the oppression remedy was intended to embrace suits of an inherently derivative nature, the balance of authority favours the view that a derivative-type suit may be commenced under the oppression remedy. See Jeffrey G. MacIntosh, "The Oppression Remedy: Personal or Derivative?" (1991) 70 Can. Bar Rev. 29. In particular, the courts have not balked at allowing oppression claims in cases involving hostile takeovers. See, e.g., *Canada (Director appointed under s. 253 of Canada Business Corporations Act) v. Royal Trustco Ltd.* (1984), 6 D.L.R. (4th) 682, 1984 CarswellOnt 90 (C.A.), appeal dismissed by Supreme Court, [1986] 2 S.C.R. 537, 1986 CarswellOnt 1010, 1986 CarswellOnt 1488, and the *Schneider* case, below. There are certain advantages and potential disadvantages to claiming oppression. One possible advantage is that an oppression suit may be begun by the "application" procedure, rather than as a full blown "action." The application procedure involves affidavit rather than *viva voce* evidence, and dispenses with potentially expensive discovery proceedings. However, in most cases this potential advantage is more illusion than reality. If there are contested facts (as there almost invariably are in cases involving alleged breaches of fiduciary duty or oppression), then the court will convert the application into an action involving the normal trial procedures. The real advantages of an oppression suit are two-fold. First, the substantive standard ("fairness") is broader than either the common law or statutory fiduciary duty standard. For example, even if the directors act honestly and in good faith, with a view to the best interests of the corporation, they may act in a manner that yields a *result* that is unfair and, therefore, oppressive. See, e.g., *Ferguson v. Imax Systems Corp.* (1983), 43 O.R. (2d) 128, 150 D.L.R. (3d) 718, 1983 CarswellOnt 926 (C.A.), leave to appeal to the Supreme Court of Canada refused (1983) 52 N.R. 317n, (1983) 2 O.A.C. 158n; and see generally Jeffrey G. MacIntosh, Janet Holmes, and Steve Thompson, "The Puzzle of Shareholder Fiduciary Duties" (1991), 19 Can. Bus. L.J. 86; Jeffrey G. MacIntosh, "Minority Shareholder Rights in Canada and England: 1860–1987" (1989) 27 Osgoode Hall L.J. 561. In addition, the oppression provisions give the court a much wider remedial jurisdiction than is available under either common law or equitable principles. See, *e.g.*, CBCA s. 241(3). In addition, as explored in Chapter 7, the oppression remedy gives the plaintiff more freedom to draw the conduct of a controlling shareholder into the action. For these reasons, prudent counsel will almost always allege oppression in any case involving alleged breach of fiduciary duty.

The judgment of the Supreme Court on Canada in *BCE* introduces a further complication, explored above, of running the fiduciary duty and the oppression remedy together, making it difficult to know how the courts will interpret either provision, whether in the context of a hostile takeover bid or otherwise.

6 In *Bernard v. Valentini* (1978), 18 O.R. (2d) 656, 83 D.L.R. (3d) 440 (H.C.), Cory J. held that on an application for an interim injunction to restrain the directors of a company from issuing shares for the alleged purpose of maintaining control, it was not incumbent upon an applicant to establish a strong *prima facie* case:

> It is sufficient if the applicant satisfies the court that the case is not a frivolous one and that there are substantial issues to be tried. Once the applicant has satisfied that prerequisite, then the granting of relief will be dependent upon a consideration of other matters, including the threatened harm to the applicant which might not be adequately compensated by way of damages, the preponderance of convenience and the effect of the injunction upon the parties.

On the facts, Cory J. held that it was a proper case to issue an injunction conditional upon the plaintiff giving the usual undertaking as to damages. The shares in fact had been issued and the injunction restrained the individual defendants from exercising any rights that flowed from the shares.

See also *Shield Development Co. v. Snyder* (1975), [1976] 3 W.W.R. 44 (B.C. S.C.) and *Exco Corp. v. Nova Scotia Savings & Loan Co.* (1987), 35 B.L.R. 149 (N.S. S.C.).

7 Under s. 34 of the CBCA and s. 30 of the OBCA, a corporation is given power to purchase its own shares. Should the same considerations apply to a repurchase of shares as to an allotment? Does it make a difference that on a repurchase, shareholders may not be able to sell their shares at an increased price as they would on a takeover? Is there greater potential for abuse of fiduciary duty on a repurchase? The Ontario *Securities Act* R.S.O. 1990 c. S.5, Part XX, coupled with various rules adopted by the Ontario Securities Commission and other regulators across the country specially regulate issuer bids.

8 In *Sparling v. Royal Trustco* (1984), 6 D.L.R. (4th) 682, appeal dismissed by Supreme Court, [1986] 2 S.C.R. 537, Cory J.A. of the Ontario Court of Appeal held that the oppression remedy in the CBCA can be invoked by the Director (the administrative official who oversees the application of the Act) to protect minority shareholders. In *Royal Trustco*, the directors of the target company (Royal Trustco) were not informed of defensive tactics being used by their management to fend off a takeover bid. In particular, the directors failed to inform shareholders that they had arranged for shares to be purchased on the open market by investors that were "friendly" to management (thereby greatly lowering the likelihood that the bidder, Campeau Corporation, would be able to amass enough stock to gain control of Royal Trustco). This was a material omission in the information circular sent to shareholders regarding the bid. This omission allowed the Director to seek damages from the company and its directors under the oppression remedy. The Court rejected the argument that the Director was precluded from bringing such an action as it would amount to the creation of a new remedy, i.e., a class action on behalf of aggrieved shareholders for which there was insufficient statutory authority. The Court held that failing to allow the Director to bring the action would deny shareholders a remedy that Parliament sought to confer under the Act. In support of its conclusion, the Court held that "[i]n the C.B.C.A. there is a clear indication that the Director is a protector of the public's interest in corporate affairs."

9   Because Canadian takeover jurisprudence is in some respects derivative of American takeover jurisprudence, in the following section we examine the American situation. We then compare other Canadian cases to see the ways in which Canadian takeover cases have tracked this US jurisprudence, and the ways in which they have not.

(iii)   American Jurisprudence on Defensive Tactics

As the *Teck* case illustrates, the Canadian jurisprudence on takeover bids has been heavily influenced by the U.S. cases — so much so that in order to fully appreciate the Canadian position, it is necessary to have a good understanding of U.S. cases. In the U.S. jurisprudence, there are two foundational cases (*Unocal* and *Revlon*) upon which all subsequent jurisprudence is founded.

The approach in *Unocal* and *Revlon* is based on the earlier judgment of the Delaware Chancery court in *Cheff v. Mathes*, 199 A.2d 458, 41 Del. Ch. 494 (1964), which is the beginning of modern American jurisprudence regarding the response of directors to a takeover bid (as well as the basis for Justice Berger's decision in *Teck*). *Cheff* involved a share re-purchase by a corporation at a premium above market price, from a shareholder who threatened to acquire control of the corporation. The re-purchase was held to be a permissible exercise of directorial discretion. In the course of his reasons, Carey J. stated that the test for evaluating the conduct of directors was

> whether or not defendants satisfied the burden of proof of showing reasonable grounds to believe a danger to corporate policy and effectiveness existed by the presence of . . . (the potential acquirer's) . . . stock ownership. It is important to remember that the directors satisfy their burden by showing good faith and reasonable investigation; the directors will not be penalized for an honest mistake of

judgment, if the judgment appeared reasonable at the time the decision was made.

The test developed in *Cheff* underwent modification in *Unocal Corp. v.* Mesa Petroleum Co., 493 A.2d 946 (Del. S.C. 1985). In *Unocal,* a third party made a two-tier tender offer for Unocal. In a two-tier offer, the acquirer (in this case Mesa Petroleum) begins with a "partial" takeover bid for a stated percentage of the target firm's equity. A partial bid will typically involve the intended acquisition of 20–40% of the target's shares — just sufficient to give the acquirer *de facto* control (shares that are tendered into the bid are taken up *pro rata* by the acquirer until it reaches its acquisition target). Once the bid has been completed and the acquirer has control, it will then use its power of control to effect a "second step" transaction in which the remaining public shareholders are forced out of the company (i.e., a "going private", "squeezeout", "freezeout" or "force out" transaction). The squeezeout transaction will be effected at a lower price than that which was offered in the first step (i.e., the takeover bid), and it is for this reason that the two steps taken together are referred to as a "two-tier" offer. In order to defend against the two-tier bid, Unocal management offered to repurchase shares of Unocal at a premium price from all shareholders *except* Mesa Petroleum. This gave shareholders an alternative transaction at a higher price than the Mesa bid, and had the effect of stopping Mesa's attempt to gain control of Unocal. As noted above, the test applied to assess the propriety of the directorial conduct was based on a standard of review that was more onerous than the business judgment rule that usually applies in cases alleging breach of fiduciary duty, but less demanding than a full-blown fairness test. The following extract from the case discusses this "intermediate standard", in the context of a takeover bid found by the court to be highly coercive.

Unocal Corp. v. Mesa Petroleum Co.
493 A.2d 946 (Del. S.C. 1985)

MOORE J.:

The issues we address involve these fundamental questions: Did the Unocal board have the power and duty to oppose a takeover threat it reasonably perceived to be harmful to the corporate enterprise, and if so, is its action here entitled to the protection of the business judgment rule?

Mesa contends that the discriminatory exchange offer violates the fiduciary duties Unocal owes it. Mesa argues that because of the Mesa exclusion the business judgment rule is inapplicable, because the directors by tendering their own shares will derive a financial benefit that is not available to *all* Unocal stockholders. Thus, it is Mesa's ultimate contention that Unocal cannot establish that the exchange offer is fair to *all* shareholders, and argues that the Court of Chancery was correct in concluding that Unocal was unable to meet this burden.

Unocal answers that it does not owe a duty of "fairness" to Mesa, given the facts here. Specifically, Unocal contends that its board of directors reasonably and in good faith concluded that Mesa's $54 two-tier tender offer was coercive and inadequate, and that Mesa sought selective treatment for itself. Furthermore, Unocal argues that the board's approval of the exchange offer was made in good faith, on an informed basis, and in the exercise of due care. Under these circumstances, Unocal contends that its directors properly employed this device to protect the company and its stockholders from Mesa's harmful tactics.

We begin with the basic issue of the power of a board of directors of a Delaware corporation to adopt a defensive measure of this type. Absent such authority, all other questions are moot. Neither issues of fairness nor business judgment are pertinent without the basic underpinning of a board's legal power to act.

The board has a large reservoir of authority upon which to draw. Its duties and responsibilities proceed from the inherent powers conferred by 8 *Del. C.* §141(a), respecting management of the corporation's "business and affairs". Additionally, the powers here being exercised derive from 8 *Del. C.* § 160(a), conferring broad authority upon a corporation to deal in its own stock. From this it is now well established that in the acquisition of its shares a Delaware corporation may deal selectively with its stockholders, provided the directors have not acted out of a sole or primary purpose to entrench themselves in office.

Finally, the board's power to act derives from its fundamental duty and obligation to protect the corporate enterprise, which includes stockholders, from harm reasonably perceived, irrespective of its source.

Thus, we are satisfied that in the broad context of corporate governance, including issues of fundamental corporate change, a board of directors is not a passive instrumentality.

When a board addresses a pending takeover bid it has an obligation to determine whether the offer is in the best interests of the corporation and its shareholders. In that respect a board's duty is no different from any other responsibility it shoulders, and its decisions should be no less entitled to the respect they otherwise would be accorded in the realm of business judgment. *See also* Johnson v. Trueblood, 629 F.2d 287, 292-293 (3d Cir. 1980). There are, however, certain caveats to a proper exercise of this function. Because of the omnipresent spectre that a board may be acting primarily in its own interests, rather than those of the corporation and its shareholders, there is an enhanced duty which calls for judicial examination at the threshold before the protections of the business judgment rule may be conferred.

This Court has long recognized that: We must bear in mind the inherent danger in the purchase of shares with corporate funds to remove a threat to corporate policy when a threat to control is involved. The directors are of necessity confronted with a conflict of interest, and an objective decision is difficult.

In the face of this inherent conflict directors must show that they had reasonable grounds for believing that a danger to corporate policy and effectiveness existed because of another person's stock ownership.

However, they satisfy that burden "by showing good faith and reasonable investigation. . ."

Furthermore, such proof is materially enhanced, as here, by the approval of a board comprised of a majority of outside independent directors who have acted in accordance with the foregoing standards.

In the board's exercise of corporate power to forestall a takeover bid our analysis begins with the basic principle that corporate directors have a fiduciary duty to act in the best interests of the corporation's stockholders.

As we have noted, their duty of care extends to protecting the corporation and its owners from perceived harm whether a threat originates from third parties or other shareholders. But such powers are not absolute. A corporation does not have unbridled discretion to defeat any perceived threat by any Draconian means available.

A further aspect is the element of balance. If a defensive measure is to come within the ambit of the business judgment rule, it must be reasonable in relation to the threat posed. This entails an analysis by the directors of the nature of the takeover bid and its effect on the corporate enterprise. Examples of such concerns may include: inadequacy of the price offered, nature and timing of the offer, questions of illegality, the impact on "constituencies" other than shareholders (i.e., creditors, customers, employees, and perhaps even the community generally), the risk of nonconsummation, and the quality of securities being offered in the exchange.

While not a controlling factor, it also seems to us that a board may reasonably consider the basic stockholder interests at stake, including those of short term speculators, whose actions may have fueled the coercive aspect of the offer at the expense of the long term investor. Here, the threat posed was viewed by the Unocal board as a grossly inadequate two-tier coercive tender offer coupled with the threat of greenmail.

Specifically, the Unocal directors had concluded that the value of Unocal was substantially above the $54 per share offered in cash at the front end. Furthermore, they determined that the subordinated securities to be exchanged in Mesa's announced squeeze out of the remaining shareholders in the "back-end" merger were "junk bonds" worth far less than $54. It is now well recognized that such offers are a classic coercive measures designed to stampede shareholders into tendering at the first tier, even if the price is inadequate, out of fear of what they will receive at the back end of the transaction. Wholly beyond the coercive aspect of an inadequate two-tier tender offer, the threat was posed by a corporate raider with a national reputation as a "greenmailer".

In adopting the selective exchange offer, the board stated that its objective was either to defeat the inadequate Mesa offer or, should the offer still succeed, provide the 49% of its stockholders, who would otherwise be forced to accept "junk bonds", with $72 worth of senior debt. We find that both purposes are valid.

However, such efforts would have been thwarted by Mesa's participation in the exchange offer. First, if Mesa could tender its shares, Unocal would effectively be subsidizing the former's continuing effort to buy Unocal stock at $54 per share. Second, Mesa could not, by definition, fit within the class of shareholders being protected from its own coercive and inadequate tender offer.

Thus, we are satisfied that the selective exchange offer is reasonably related to the threats posed. It is consistent with the principle that "the minority stockholder shall receive the substantial equivalent in value of what he had before."

This concept of fairness, while stated in the merger context, is also relevant in the area of tender offer law. Thus, the board's decision to offer what it determined to be the fair value of the corporation to the 49% of its shareholders, who would otherwise be forced to accept highly subordinated "junk bonds", is reasonable and consistent with the directors' duty to ensure that the minority stockholders receive equal value for their shares.

Mesa contends that it is unlawful, and the trial court agreed, for a corporation to discriminate in this fashion against one shareholder. It argues correctly that no case has ever sanctioned a device that precludes a raider from sharing in a benefit available to all other stockholders. However, as we have noted earlier, the principle of selective stock repurchases by a Delaware corporation is neither unknown nor unauthorized.

Thus, while the exchange offer is a form of selective treatment, given the nature of the threat posed here the response is neither unlawful nor unreasonable. If the board of directors is disinterested, has acted in good faith and with due care, its decision in the absence of an abuse of discretion will be upheld as a proper exercise of business judgment.

In conclusion, there was directional power to oppose the Mesa tender offer, and to undertake a selective stock exchange made in good faith and upon a reasonable investigation pursuant to a clear duty to protect the corporate enterprise. Further, the selective stock repurchase plan chosen by Unocal is reasonable in relation to the threat that the board rationally and reasonably believed was posed by Mesa's inadequate and coercive two-tier tender offer. Under those circumstances the board's action is entitled to be measured by the standards of the business judgment rule. Thus, unless it is shown by a preponderance of the evidence that the directors' decisions were primarily based on perpetuating themselves in office, or some other breach of fiduciary duty such as fraud, overreaching, lack of good faith, or being uninformed, a Court will not substitute its judgment for that of the board.

In this case that protection is not lost merely because Unocal's directors have tendered their shares in the exchange offer. Given the validity of the Mesa exclusion, they are receiving a benefit shared generally by all other stockholders except Mesa. In this circumstance the test of *Aronson v. Lewis*, 473 A.2d at 812, is satisfied. *See also* Cheff v. Mathes, 199 A.2d at 554. If the stockholders are displeased with the action of their elected representatives, the powers of corporate democracy are at their disposal to turn the board out.

With the Court of Chancery's findings that the exchange offer was based on the board's good faith belief that the Mesa offer was inadequate, that the board's action was informed and taken with due care, that Mesa's prior activities justify a reasonable inference that its principle objective was greenmail, and implicitly, that the substance of the offer itself was reasonable and fair to the corporation and its stockholders if Mesa were included, we cannot say that the Unocal directors have acted in such a manner as to have passed an "unintelligent and unadvised judgment".

The decision of the Court of Chancery is therefore REVERSED, and the preliminary injunction is VACATED.

Note

The *Revlon* case, which follows, modifies *Unocal* in some important respects.

Revlon Inc. v. MacAndrews & Forbes Holdings Inc.
506 A.2d 173 (Del. S.C., 1985)

[*Revlon Inc. v. MacAndrews & Forbes Holdings Inc.*, 506 A.2d 173 (Del. Super, 1985) plays a special role among the cases announcing Delaware's "intermediate standard" of review. In addition to contributing to the development of the proportionality test, the opinion also sets out the limits of the test's application. Once the company's sale has become "inevitable", *Revlon* decrees that resistance under the aegis of *Unocal's* proportionality test must end, and management's duty shifts from canvassing alternatives to a sale to determining how the sale should take place.

In this case, the court determined that the Revlon directors had breached their duty of care by entering into a series of transactions with Forstmann Little & Co. that had the effect of thwarting the efforts of Pantry Pride Inc. to acquire Revlon. These transactions included an option granted Forstmann to purchase certain assets (the lock-up option),a promise by Revlon to deal exclusively with Forstmann (the no-shop option) and the payment of a $25 million cancellation fee to Forstmann if the transaction was aborted. The court analysed the genesis of these transactions in light of the history of the Pantry Pride takeover bid, and determined that they represented unwarranted concessions granted to Forstmann in an attempt by the directors to avoid liability for debt incurred during a previous round of defensive tactics designed to thwart Pantry Pride's bid. The following extract from the case describes the history of this deal, and demonstrates the point at which defensive tactics fail the *Unocal* test.]

MOORE J.: On August 19, the Revlon board met specially to consider the impending threat of a hostile bid by Pantry Pride. At the meeting, Lazard Freres, Revlon's investment banker, advised the directors that $45 per share was a grossly inadequate price for the company. Felix Rohatyn and William Loomis of Lazard Freres explained to the board that Pantry Pride's financial strategy for acquiring Revlon would be through "junk bond" financing followed by a break-up of Revlon and the disposition of its assets. With proper timing, according to the experts, such transactions could produce a return to Pantry Pride of $60 to $70 per share, while a sale of the company as a whole would be in the "mid 50" dollar range. Martin Lipton, special counsel for Revlon, recommended two defensive measures: first, that the company repurchase up to5 million of its nearly 30 million outstanding shares; and second, that it adopt a Note Purchase Rights Plan. Under this plan, each Revlon shareholder would receive as a dividend one Note Purchase Right (the Rights) for each share of common stock, with the Rights entitling the holder to exchange one common share for a $65 principal Revlon note at 12% interest with a one-year maturity. The Rights would become effective whenever anyone acquired beneficial ownership of 20% or more of Revlon's shares, unless the purchaser acquired all the company's stock for cash at $65 or more per share. In addition, the Rights would not be available to the acquirer, and prior to the 20% triggering event the Revlon board could redeem the rights for 10 cents each. Both proposals were unanimously adopted.

Pantry Pride made its first hostile move on August 23 with a cash tender offer for any and all shares of Revlon at $47.50 per common share and $26.67 per preferred share, subject to (1) Pantry Pride's obtaining financing for the purchase, and (2) the Rights being redeemed, rescinded or voided.

The Revlon board met again on August 26. The directors advised the stockholders to reject the offer. Further defensive measures also were planned. On August 29, Revlon commenced its own offer for up to 10 million shares, exchanging for each share of common stock tendered one Senior Subordinated Note (the Notes) of $47.50 principal at 11.75% interest, due 1995, and one-tenth of a share of $9.00 Cumulative Convertible Exchangeable Preferred Stock valued at $100 per share. Lazard Freres opined that the notes would trade at their face value on a fully distributed basis. Revlon stockholders tendered 87 percent of the outstanding shares (approximately 33 million), and the company accepted the full 10 million shares on a pro rata basis. The new Notes contained covenants which limited Revlon's ability to incur additional debt, sell assets, or pay dividends unless otherwise approved by the "independent" (non-management) members of the board.

At this point, both the Rights and the Note covenants stymied Pantry Pride's attempted takeover. The next move came on September 16, when Pantry Pride announced a new tender offer at $42 per share, conditioned upon receiving at least 90% of the outstanding stock. Pantry Pride also indicated that it would consider buying less than 90%, and at an increased price, if Revlon removed the impeding Rights. While this offer was lower on its face than the earlier $47.50 proposal, Revlon's investment banker, Lazard Freres, described the two bids as essentially equal in view of the completed exchange offer.

The Revlon board held a regularly scheduled meeting on September 24. The directors rejected the latest Pantry Pride offer and authorized management to negotiate with other parties interested in acquiring Revlon. Pantry Pride remained determined in its efforts and continued to make cash bids for the company, offering $50 per share on September 27, and raising its bid to $53 on October 1, and then to $56.25 on October 7.

In the meantime, Revlon's negotiations with Forstmann and the investment group Adler & Shaykin had produced results. The Revlon directors met on October 3 to consider Pantry Pride's $53 bid and to examine possible alternatives to the offer. Both Forstmann and Adler & Shaykin made certain proposals to the board. As a result, the directors unanimously agreed to a leveraged buyout by Forstmann. The terms of this accord were as follows: each stockholder would get $56 cash per share; management would purchase stock in the new company by the exercise of their Revlon "golden parachutes"; Forstmann would assume Revlon's $475 million debt incurred by the issuance of the Notes; and Revlon would redeem the Rights and waive the Notes covenants for Forstmann or in connection with any other offer superior to Forstmann's.

When the merger, and thus the waiver of the Notes covenants, was announced, the market value of these securities began to fall. The Notes, which originally traded near par, around 100, dropped to 87.50 by October 8. One director later reported (at the October 12 meeting) a "deluge" of telephone calls from irate noteholders, and on October 10 the Wall Street Journal reported threats of litigation by these creditors.

Pantry Pride countered with a new proposal on October 7, raising its $53 offer to $56.25, subject to nullification of the Rights, a waiver of the Notes covenants, and the election of three Pantry Pride directors to the Revlon board. On October 9, representatives of Pantry Pride, Forstmann and Revlon conferred in an attempt to negotiate the fate of Revlon, but could not reach agreement. At this meeting Pantry Pride announced that it would engage in fractional bidding and top any Forstmann offer by a slightly higher one. It is also significant that Forstmann, to Pantry Pride's exclusion, had been made privy to certain Revlon financial data. Thus, the parties were not negotiating on equal terms.

Again privately armed with Revlon data, Forstmann met on October 11 with Revlon's special counsel and investment banker. On October 12, Forstmann made a new $57.25 per share offer, based on several conditions. The principal demand was a lock-up option to purchase Revlon's Vision Care and National Health Laboratories divisions for $525 million, some $100-$175 million below the value ascribed to them by Lazard Freres, if another acquirer got 40% of Revlon's shares. Revlon also was required to accept a no-shop provision. The Rights and Notes covenants had to be removed as in the October 3 agreement. There would be a $25 million cancellation fee to be placed in escrow, and released to Forstmann if the new agreement terminated or if another acquirer got more than 19.9% of Revlon's stock. Finally, there would be no participation by Revlon management in the merger. In return, Forstmann agreed to support the par value of the Notes, which had faltered in the market, by an exchange of new notes. Forstmann also demanded immediate acceptance of its offer, or it would be withdrawn. The board unanimously approved Forstmann's proposal because: (1) it was for a higher price than the Pantry Pride bid, (2) it protected the noteholders, and (3) Forstmann's financing was firmly in place. The board further agreed to redeem the rights and waive the covenants on the preferred stock in response to any offer above $57 cash per share. The covenants were waived, contingent upon receipt of an investment banking opinion that the Notes would trade near par value once the offer was consummated.

Pantry Pride, which had initially sought injunctive relief from the Rights plan on August 22, filed an amended complaint on October 14 challenging the lock-up, the cancellation fee, and the exercise of the Rights and the Notes covenants. Pantry Pride also sought a temporary restraining order to prevent Revlon from placing any assets in escrow or transferring them to Forstmann. Moreover, on October 22, Pantry Pride again raised its bid, with a cash offer of $58 per share conditioned upon nullification of the Rights, waiver of the covenants, and an injunction of the Forstmann lock-up.

On October 15, the Court of Chancery prohibited the further transfer of assets, and eight days later enjoined the lock-up, no-shop, and cancellation fee provisions of the agreement. The trial court concluded that the Revlon directors had breached their duty of loyalty by making concessions to Forstmann, out of concern for their liability to the noteholders, rather than maximizing the sale price of the company for the stockholders' benefit.

We turn first to Pantry Pride's probability of success on the merits. The ultimate responsibility for managing the business and affairs of a corporation falls on its board of directors.

* * *

In discharging this function the directors owe fiduciary duties of care and loyalty to the corporation and its shareholders.

* * *

These principles apply with equal force when a board approves a corporate merger . . . and of course they are the bedrock of our law regarding corporate takeover issues.

* * *

While the business judgment rule may be applicable to the actions of corporate directors responding to takeover threats, the principles upon which it is founded — care, loyalty and independence — must be satisfied.

If the business judgment rule applies, there is a "presumption that in making a business decision the directors of a corporation acted on an informed basis, in good faith and in the honest belief that the action taken was in the best interests of the company."

* * *

However, when a board implements anti-takeover measures there arises "the omnipresent specter that a board may be acting primarily in its own interests, rather than those of the corporation and its shareholders . . ."

* * *

This potential for conflict places upon the directors the burden of proving that they had reasonable grounds for believing there was a danger to corporate policy and effectiveness, a burden satisfied by a showing of good faith and reasonable investigation. . . . In addition, the directors must analyze the nature of the takeover and its effect on the corporation in order to ensure balance — that the responsive action taken is reasonable in relation to the threat posed.

* * *

The Revlon directors concluded that Pantry Pride's $47.50 offer was grossly inadequate. In that regard the board acted in good faith, and on an informed basis, with reasonable grounds to believe that there existed a harmful threat to the corporate enterprise. The adoption of a defensive measure, reasonable in relation to the threat posed, was proper and fully accorded with the powers, duties, and responsibilities conferred upon directors under our law.

However, when Pantry Pride increased its offer to $50 per share, and then to $53, it became apparent to all that the break-up of the company was inevitable. The Revlon board's authorization permitting management to negotiate a merger or buyout with a third party was a recognition that the company was for sale. The duty of the board had thus changed from the preservation of Revlon as a corporate entity to the maximization of the company's value at a sale for the stockholders' benefit. This significantly altered the board's responsibilities under the

Unocal standards. It no longer faced threats to corporate policy and effectiveness, or to the stockholders' interests, from a grossly inadequate bid. The whole question of defensive measures became moot. The directors' role changed from defenders of the corporate bastion to auctioneers charged with getting the best price for the stockholders at a sale of the company.

This brings us to the lock-up with Forstmann and its emphasis on shoring up the sagging market value of the Notes in the face of threatened litigation by their holders. Such a focus was inconsistent with the changed concept of the directors' responsibilities at this stage of the developments. The impending waiver of the Notes covenants had caused the value of the Notes to fall, and the board was aware of the noteholders' ire as well as their subsequent threats of suit. The directors thus made support of the Notes an integral part of the company's dealings with Forstmann, even though their primary responsibility at this stage was to the equity owners.

The original threat posed by Pantry Pride — the break-up of the company — had become a reality which even the directors embraced. Selective dealing to fend off a hostile but determined bidder was no longer a proper objective. Instead, obtaining the highest price for the benefit of the stockholders should have been the central theme guiding director action. Thus, the Revlon board could not make the requisite showing of good faith by preferring the noteholders and ignoring its duty of loyalty to the shareholders. The rights of the former already were fixed by contract.

* * *

The noteholders required no further protection, and when the Revlon board entered into an auction-ending lock-up agreement with Forstmann on the basis of impermissible considerations at the expense of the shareholders, the directors breached their primary duty of loyalty.

The Revlon board argued that it acted in good faith in protecting the noteholders because *Unocal* permits consideration of other corporate constituencies. Although such considerations may be permissible, there are fundamental limitations upon that prerogative. A board may have regard for various constituencies in discharging its responsibilities, provided there are rationally related benefits accruing to the stockholders. *Unocal,* 493 A.2d at 955. However, such concern for non-stockholder interests is inappropriate when an auction among active bidders is in progress, and the object no longer is to protect or maintain the corporate enterprise but to sell it to the highest bidder.

Revlon also contended that . . . it had contractual and good faith obligations to consider the noteholders. However, any such duties are limited to the principle that one may not interfere with contractual relationships by improper actions. Here, the rights of the noteholders were fixed by agreement, and there is nothing of substance to suggest that any of those terms were violated. The Notes covenants specifically contemplated a waiver to permit sale of the company at a fair price. The Notes were accepted by the holders on that basis, including the risk of an adverse market effect stemming from a waiver. Thus, nothing remained for Revlon to legitimately protect, and no rationally related benefit thereby accrued to the stockholders. Under such circumstances we must conclude that the merger agreement with Forstmann was unreasonable in relation to the threat posed.

A lock-up is not *per se* illegal under Delaware law. . . . Options can entice other bidders to enter a contest for control of the corporation, creating an auction for the company and maximizing shareholder profit. Current economic conditions in the takeover market are such that a "white knight" like Forstmann might only enter the bidding for the target company if it receives some form of compensation to cover the risks and costs involved.

* * *

However, while those lock-ups which draw bidders into the battle benefit shareholders, similar measures which end an active auction and foreclose further bidding operate to the shareholders' detriment.

* * *

The Forstmann option had a similar destructive effect on the auction process. Forstmann had already been drawn into the contest on a preferred basis, so the result of the lock-up was not to foster bidding, but to destroy it. The board's stated reasons for approving the transactions were: (1) better financing, (2) noteholder protection, and (3) higher price. As the Court of Chancery found, and we agree, any distinctions between the rival bidders' methods of financing the proposal were nominal at best, and such a consideration has little or no significance in a cash offer for any and all shares. The principal object, contrary to the board's duty of care, appears to have been protection of the noteholders over the shareholders' interests.

While Forstmann's $57.25 offer was objectively higher than Pantry Pride's $56.25 bid, the margin of superiority is less when the Forstmann price is adjusted for the time value of money. In reality, the Revlon board ended the auction in return for very little actual improvement in the final bid. The principal benefit went to the directors, who avoided personal liability to a class of creditors to whom the board owed no further duty under the circumstances. Thus, when a board ends an intense bidding contest on an insubstantial basis, and where a significant by-product of that action is to protect the directors against a perceived threat of personal liability for consequences stemming from the adoption of previous defensive measures, the action cannot withstand the enhanced scrutiny which *Unocal* requires of director conduct.

* * *

In conclusion, the Revlon board was confronted with a situation not uncommon in the current wave of corporate takeovers. A hostile and determined bidder sought the company at a price the board was convinced was inadequate. The initial defensive tactics worked to the benefit of the shareholders, and thus the board was able to sustain its *Unocal* burdens in justifying those measures. However, in granting an asset option lock-up to Forstmann, we must conclude that under all the circumstances the directors allowed considerations other than the maximization of shareholder profit to affect their judgment, and followed a course that ended the auction for Revlon, absent court intervention, to the ultimate detriment of its shareholders. No such defensive measure can be sustained when it represents a breach of the directors' fundamental duty of care. . . . In that context the board's action is not entitled to the deference accorded it by the business judgment rule. The measures were properly enjoined. The decision of the Court of Chancery, therefore, is

AFFIRMED.

Paramount Communications Inc. v. QVC Network Inc.
637 A.2d 34 (Del. S.C., 1994)

Veasey Chief Justice:

Applicable Principles of Establish Delaware Law

The General Corporation Law of the State of Delaware (the "General Corporation Law") and the decisions of this Court have repeatedly recognized the fundamental principle that the management of the business and affairs of a Delaware corporation is entrusted to its directors, who are the duly elected and authorized representatives of the stockholders.

* * *

Under normal circumstances, neither the courts nor the stockholders should interfere with the managerial decisions of the directors. The business judgment rule embodies the deference to which such decisions are entitled.

Nevertheless, there are rare situations which mandate that a court take a more direct and active role in overseeing the decisions made and actions taken by directors. In these situations, a court subjects the directors' conduct to enhanced scrutiny to ensure that it is reasonable. The decisions of this Court have clearly established the circumstances where such enhanced scrutiny will be applied. . . . The case at bar implicates two such circumstances: (1) the approval of a transaction resulting in a sale of control, and (2) the adoption of defensive measures in response to a threat to corporate control.

* * *

The Significance of a Sale or Change of Control

* * *

Because of the intended sale of control, the Paramount-Viacom transaction has economic consequences of considerable significance to the Paramount stockholders. Once control has shifted, the current Paramount stockholders will have no leverage in the future to demand another control premium. As a result, the Paramount stockholders are entitled to receive, and should receive, a control premium and/or protective devices of significant value. There being no such protective provisions in the Viacom-Paramount transaction, the Paramount directors had an obligation to take the maximum advantage of the current opportunity to realize for the stockholders the best value reasonably available.

The Obligations of Directors in a Sale or Change of Control Transaction

The consequences of a sale of control impose special obligations on the directors of a corporation. In particular, they have the obligation of acting reasonably to seek the transaction offering the best value reasonably available to the stockholders. The courts will apply enhanced scrutiny to ensure that the directors have acted reasonably. The obligations of the directors and the enhanced scrutiny of the courts are well-established by the decisions of this Court. The directors' fiduciary duties in a sale of control context are those which generally attach. In short, "the directors must act in accordance with their fundamental duties of care and loyalty." . . .

It is basic to our law that the board of directors has the ultimate responsibility for managing the business and affairs of a corporation. In discharging this function, the directors owe fiduciary duties of care and loyalty to the corporation and its shareholders. This unremitting obligation extends equally to board conduct in a sale of corporate control.

* * *

In determining which alternative provides the best value for the stockholders, a board of directors is not limited to considering only the amount of cash involved, and is not required to ignore totally its view of the future value of a strategic alliance. . . . Instead, the directors should analyze the entire situation and evaluate in a disciplined manner the consideration being offered. Where stock or other non-cash consideration is involved, the board should try to quantify its value, if feasible, to achieve an objective comparison of the alternatives. In addition, the board may assess a variety of practical considerations relating to each alternative including: [an offer's] fairness and feasibility; the proposed or actual financing for the offer, and the consequences of that financing;

questions of illegality; . . . the risk of non-consummation; . . . the bidder's identity, prior background and other business venture experiences; and the bidder's business plans for the corporation and their effects on stockholder interests.

* * *

These considerations are important because the selection of one alternative may permanently foreclose other opportunities. While the assessment of these factors may be complex, the board's goal is straightforward: Having informed themselves of all material information reasonably available, the directors must decide which alternative is most likely to offer the best value reasonably available to the stockholders.

Enhanced Judicial Scrutiny of a Sale or Change of Control Transaction

Board action in the circumstances presented here is subject to enhanced scrutiny. Such scrutiny is mandated by: (a) the threatened diminution of the current stockholders' voting power; (b) the fact that an asset belonging to public stockholders (a control premium) is being sold and may never be available again: and (c) the traditional concern of Delaware courts for actions which impair or impede stockholder voting rights.

* * *

The key features of an enhanced scrutiny test are: (a) a judicial determination regarding the adequacy of the decisionmaking process employed by the directors, including the information on which the directors based their decision; and (b) a judicial examination of the reasonableness of the directors' action in light of the circumstances then existing. The directors have the burden of proving that they were adequately informed and acted reasonably.

Although an enhanced scrutiny test involves a review of the reasonableness of the substantive merits of a board's actions, a court should not ignore the complexity of the directors' task in a sale of control. There are many business and financial considerations implicated in investigating and selecting the best value reasonably available. The board of directors is the corporate decisionmaking body best equipped to make these judgments. Accordingly, a court applying enhanced judicial scrutiny should be deciding whether the directors made a reasonable decision, not a perfect decision. If a board selected one of several reasonable alternatives, a court should not second-guess that choice even though it might have decided otherwise or subsequent events may have cast doubt on the board's determination. Thus, courts will not substitute their business judgment for that of the directors, but will determine if the directors' decision was, on balance, within a range of reasonableness.

Revlon and Time-Warner Distinguished

The Paramount defendants and Viacom assert that the fiduciary obligations and the enhanced judicial scrutiny discussed above are not implicated in this case in the absence of a "break-up" of the corporation, and that the order granting the preliminary injunction should be reversed. This argument is based on their erroneous interpretation of our decisions in Revlon and Time-Warner.

* * *

The decisions of this Court following reinforced the applicability of enhanced scrutiny and the directors' obligation to seek the best value reasonably available for the stockholders where there is a pending sale of control, regardless of whether or not there is to be a break-up of the corporation.

* * *

Under Delaware law there are, generally speaking and without excluding other possibilities, two circumstances which may implicate Revlon duties. The first, and clearer one, is when a corporation initiates an active bidding process seeking to sell itself or to effect a business reorganization involving a clear breakup of the company. However, Revlon duties may also be triggered where, in response to a bidder's offer, a target abandons its long-term strategy and seeks an alternative transaction involving the breakup of the company.

* * *

The Paramount defendants' position that both a change of control and a break-up are required must be rejected. Such a holding would unduly restrict the application of Revlon, is inconsistent with this Court's decisions in Barkan and Macmillan, and has no basis in policy. There are few events that have a more significant impact on the stockholders than a sale of control or a corporate break-up. Each event represents a fundamental (and perhaps irrevocable) change in the nature of the corporate enterprise from a practical standpoint. It is the significance of each of these events that justifies: (a) focusing on the directors' obligation to seek the best value reasonably available to the stockholders; and (b) requiring a close scrutiny of board action which could be contrary to the stockholders' interests.

Accordingly, when a corporation undertakes a transaction which will cause: (a) a change in corporate control; or (b) a break-up of the corporate entity, the directors' obligation is to seek the best value reasonably available to the stockholders. This obligation arises because the effect of the Viacom-Paramount transaction, if consummated, is to shift control of Paramount from the public stockholders to a controlling stockholder, Viacom. Neither Time-Warner nor any other decision of this Court holds that a "break-up" of the company is essential to give rise to this obligation where there is a sale of control.

Note

The *Unocal* test has been applied in so many cases that they are now too numerous to mention. In some of these cases, defensive tactics have been found to be reasonable under the *Unocal* test: see, *e.g.*, *Polk v. Good*, 507 A.2d 531 (Del. S.C. 1986); *Moran v. Household International Inc.*, 500 A.2d 1346 (Del. S.C. 1985); *Newmont Mining Corp. v. Pickens*, 831 F.2d 1448 (9th Cir. 1987); *Grand Metropolitan PLC v. Pillsbury Co.*, Civ. No. 10323 (Del. Ch., 1988); *Desert Partners, L.P v. USG Corp.*, 686 F. Supp. 1289 (N.D. Ill, 1988). In other cases, defensive tactics have been found to be unreasonable under the *Unocal* test: see, *e.g.*, *Phillips v. Instituform of North America, Inc.*, C.A. No 9173 (Del. Ch. Aug. 27, 1987); *AC Acquisition Corp. v. Anderson, Clayton & Co.*, 519 A.2d 103 (Del. Ch. 1986); *Dynamics Corp. of America v. CTS Corp.*, 637 F. Supp. 406 (N.D. Ill. 1986), aff'd, 794 F.2d 250 (7th Cir. 1986), rev'd on other grounds, 107 S. Ct. 1637 (1987); *Robert M. Mass Group, Inc. v. Evans*, Fed. Sec. L. Rep. (CCH) para. 93,924 (Del. Ch. July 14, 1988); *City Capital Associates Ltd. Partners v. Interco Inc.*, Civ. No. 10105 (Del. Ch. Nov. 1, 1988).

(iv)   Developments in Canadian Jurisprudence after *Unocal* and *Revlon*

Pente Investment Management Ltd. v. Schneider Corp.
(1998), 42 O.R. (3d) 177, 1998 CarswellOnt 4035 (C.A.)

WEILER J.A.: Schneider is a 108 year-old company now governed by the *Business Corporations Act (Ontario)* ("OBCA") which went public three decades ago. The Family, consisting of the third and fourth generations, through Holdings retained control through a two class share structure. The Family held 70.5% of the voting common shares representing 7.6% of the total equity of Schneider and 17.2% of the non-voting A Shares representing 15.3% of the equity; thus the Family held 22.9% of the equity but a control block of the votes that was sufficient to pass a special majority if only the common shares were taken into account. However, in the tradition of fair dealing espoused by the founder J.M. Schneider, when the sharing of premium previously attributable to multiple voting shares as opposed to single shares became an issue in the Canadian Tire case *Re Canadian Tire Corp.* (1987), 35 B.L.R. 117 (Ont. Div. Ct.), the Family was instrumental in adopting a coattails provision in amending Schneider articles of incorporation in 1988 even though it was not required to do so at that time as it was not issuing any further shares then. There were pronouncements made that the A shareholders would be treated equally and equitably as if they were partners with the common shareholders.

[In order to ensure the fair treatment of the non-voting A shares, the Schneider family took the initiative in proposing that a "coattail" provision be inserted in the company's articles, and this was duly passed by the requisite majority of shareholders. The coattail aimed at ensuring equal treatment of the voting shares and the non-voting A shares in the event of a takeover bid, and it did so in the following manner: Suppose that an acquirer sought to gain control of Schneiders. It need only make a takeover bid for the voting common shares, and not for the Class A shares, since holding Class A shares will add nothing to its power to control the company. The coattail, however, specified that on the occurrence of an offer for the voting shares alone (an "exclusionary" offer), the Class A shareholders would have the right to convert their shares into voting common shares. That way, an acquirer would effectively be forced to extend the takeover bid to the Class A shares. If it did not, then it could not be sure of gaining control of the company, since presumably on the making of an "exclusionary offer" for the common shares, all Class A shares would be converted into common shares, and the acquirer would hold only a small percentage of the total votes.

However, the Schneider family was concerned to retain a veto over any takeover bid that occurred. The coattail was thus drafted so that if there was an exclusionary offer for the common shares, the Class A shares would *not* be convertible into common shares *if* the holders of 50 per cent or more of the common shares filed a certificate with the company's transfer agent and secretary indicating that they would not accept an exclusionary offer. This certificate could even be filed as a "standing certificate" before any offer was made, and the Schneider family duly filed a standing certificate. This effectively gave the Schneider family a veto over any takeover bid. While an acquirer might still make an exclusionary bid for the common shares, it could never gain control of a majority of the common shares, since the family held a majority block and could simply decide not to tender. In addition, it could not gain control of the company by buying up Class A shares, making an "exclusionary offer" for the common shares, and converting its Class A shares into common shares, because the anti-conversion certificate would prevent the Class A shares from being converted into common shares. Despite these protections, Maple Leaf Foods believed that it could acquire control of Schneiders by making simultaneous takeover bids that were not entirely identical for the two classes of shares, thus making an "exclusionary offer" that would trigger the coattail provision, giving all of the Class A shares a vote. The court continued:]

On November 5, 1997, Maple Leaf, a competitor of Schneider, announced its intention to make an unsolicited take-over bid for [Schneider's common shares] at $19 a share, through its holding company SCH. In response, the Board established a special committee consisting of the independent non-family directors to review the Maple Leaf offer and to consider other alternatives. Subsequently Maple Leaf itself made an offer of $22 a share, but this offer was rejected by the Family. Ultimately, the Family told the special committee that the only offer it would accept was an offer made by Smithfield Foods, an American company that, at the time, was equal to $25 a share. In order for the Family to accept the Smithfield offer, which would have had the effect of enabling Smithfield to "lock-up" control of Schneider, the Board had to take certain steps which, on the advice of the special committee, it took. Despite this, and after the Family had agreed to the Smithfield offer, on December 22, 1997, Maple Leaf made a further offer of $29 a share to Schneider's common and Class A shareholders.

[Despite this, the Schneider family continued to refuse to lift its certificate of anti-conversion for any bid other than the Smithfield bid. The family apparently had mixed motives for favouring the Smithfield bid. Mr. Justice Farley, the trial judge, observed that: "In particular, the Schneider Family advised the Board of Directors that it had reviewed the various proposals in terms of three factors: financial value, continuity of the Corporation in a manner consistent with the Schneider family's desires, and the effect of any transaction on the Corporation's various stakeholders, including shareholders, employees, suppliers, and customers." However, as indicated in the Court of Appeal judgment, the consideration offered in the three different bids had different tax consequences — and, hence, different value — in the hands of the Schneider family. In particular, the Maple Leaf and Booth Creek offers were cash offers, and the Smithfield offer was a share exchange offer. Smithfield's share exchange offer would yield a tax saving to the Schneider family of $4 per share. Weiler J.A. continued:]

While the appellants have challenged Farley J.'s finding that the Family would not sell to Maple Leaf, there is ample evidence to support this finding. Even at $29 a share, when tax considerations were factored in, the Maple Leaf offer was only as advantageous as the Smithfield offer to the Family, not more advantageous. Apart from financial criteria, Maple Leaf did not meet the Family's expressed concern about the effect of a change of control on the continuity of employment for Schneider's employees, the welfare of suppliers, and the relationship with its customers, whereas Smithfield did . . .

At a subsequent meeting of the Special Committee that night, Nesbitt Burns advised that while the Smithfield proposal was within the $25–29 fair price range, the risk associated with adverse share price movement and exchange rate movement during the short period until the offer could be formally accepted should be reflected by applying a 6% discount to the offer so that its present value was $23.50. Nesbitt Burns also told the Special Committee that, in its view, if the Smithfield offer were permitted to expire and no other change of control transaction involving Schneider were consummated, the shares of Schneider would settle in a trading range between $18 and $20 a share.

The Special Committee then recessed and Dodds [the CEO] made enquiries of Smithfield as to whether it would raise its offer. Smithfield refused to pay more but Dodds was successful in negotiating a slight improvement in the exchange rate aspect of the offer.

The original proposal, as submitted by Smithfield, contemplated that the transaction would proceed by way of a plan of arrangement or merger. That is, the Board would approve of the Family entering into a lock-up agreement for its shares with Smithfield, then the merger proposal would be voted upon by all shareholders and approved by the court. Before asking the shareholders and the court to approve the merger the Board would have had to provide an opinion that the transaction was fair. In light of Nesbitt Burns' discounted valuation of the Smithfield proposal, the Board was unwilling to do so.

To avoid the Board having to issue an opinion that the proposed transaction was fair, Smithfield made offers by way of take-over bids to acquire any and all common voting shares and all Class A shares of Schneider on the condition that the Family agree to tender its shares. The shares of Schneider were to be exchanged for .5415 of a share in a newly incorporated, wholly-owned Canadian subsidiary of Smithfield. Each whole exchangeable share would then be exchangeable for one common share in Smithfield. The structure of this second transaction meant that Smithfield might not be able to acquire two-thirds of the Class A shares and, therefore, might not be able to take Schneider private.

In order for the Family to accept the offer from Smithfield, it was still necessary for the Board to waive the standstill provision in the confidentiality agreement Smithfield signed and to remove the rights plan. The Family asked the board to do this. Upon the recommendation of the special committee, the Board did so. On December 18, 1997, the Family entered into the lock-up agreement.

On December 22, 1997, Maple Leaf announced that, despite the Family's lock-up agreement with Smithfield, it was increasing its offer to $29 per share, cash, conditional on obtaining two-thirds of each class of share. Prior to this, Maple Leaf entered into deposit agreements with two funds to buy Maple Leaf's shares at $29, no matter what the outcome of its latest bid was. On December 30, 1997, five Class A shareholders, holding in aggregate 675,000 shares, representing more than 10 per cent of the total Class A shares outstanding, wrote a letter to Schneider's Board of Directors complaining that "the actions or inaction of the Special Committee, together with those of the Schneider family have in effect, contaminated the value maximization process outlined by the board in its directors' circular and in its public statements".

Determining Whether the Directors Have Acted in the Best Interests of the Corporation

The mandate of the directors is to manage the company according to their best judgment; that judgment must be an informed judgment; it must have a reasonable basis. If there are no reasonable grounds to support an assertion by the directors that they have acted in the best interests of the company, a court will be justified in finding that the directors acted for an improper purpose: *Teck Corp. v. Millar* (1973), 33 D.L.R. (3d) 288 (B.C.S.C.) at pp. 315-16, adopted as the law in Ontario by Montgomery J. in *Olympia & York Enterprises Ltd. v. Hiram Walker Resources Ltd.* (1986), 59 O.R. (2d) 255, 37 D.L.R. (4th) 194 (H.C.J.), affirmed (1986), 59 O.R. (2d) 254, 37 D.L.R. (4th) 193 (Div. Ct.).

One way of determining whether the directors acted in the best interests of the company, according to Farley J., is to ask what was uppermost in the directors' minds after "a reasonable analysis of the situation": *820099 Ontario Inc. v. Harold E. Ballard Ltd.* (1991), 3 B.L.R. (2d) 123 at p. 176 (Ont. Gen. Div.), affirmed (1991), 3 B.L.R. (2d) 113 (Ont. Div. Ct.); *CW Shareholdings Inc. v. WIC Western International Communications Ltd.*, No. 98-CL-2821 (May 17, 1998), Toronto (Gen. Div.) [reported 39 O.R. (3d) 755, 160 D.L.R. (4th) 131]. It must be recognized that the directors are not the agents of the shareholders. The directors have absolute power to manage the affairs of the company even if their decisions contravene the express wishes of the majority shareholder: *Teck Corp. Ltd. v. Millar, supra,* at p. 307. However, acting in the best interests of the company does not necessarily mean that the directors must act in the best interests of one of the groups protected under s. 234. There may be a conflict between the interests of individual groups of shareholders and the best interests of the company: *Brant Investments Ltd. v. Keep Rite Inc.* (1987), 60 O.R. (2d) 737, 42 D.L.R. (4th) 15 (H.C.J.), affirmed (1991), 3 O.R. (3d) 289 at p. 301, 3 O.R. (3d) 289 (C.A.). Provided that the directors have acted honestly and reasonably, the court ought not to substitute its own business judgment for that of the Board of Directors: *Brant Investments v. Keep Rite Inc., supra,* which deals with the analogous section of the *Canadian Business Corporations Act*, R.S.C. 1985, c. C-44. If the directors have unfairly disregarded the rights of a group of shareholders, the directors will not have acted reasonably in the best interests of the corporation and the court will intervene: *820099 Ontario Inc. v. Harold E. Ballard Ltd., supra.*

The appellants have urged this court to consider the actions of the directors pursuant to a standard which is derived from statute law in the State of Delaware known as "enhanced scrutiny". The key features of the enhanced scrutiny test are a judicial determination of the adequacy of the decision-making process employed by the directors and a judicial examination of the reasonableness of the directors' actions in light of the circumstances then existing: *Paramount Communications v. QVC Network Inc.*, 637 A.2d 34 at p. 45 (Del. 1934). The directors have the onus of satisfying the court that they were adequately informed and acted reasonably. Some Canadian authorities such as *Exco Corp. v. Nova Scotia Savings & Loan Co.* (1987), 35 B.L.R. 149, 78 N.S.R. (2d) 91 (S.C.) and *347883 Alberta Ltd. v. Producers Pipelines Inc.* (1991), 80 D.L.R. (4th) 359, 92 Sask. R. 81 (C.A.) have adopted a proper purpose test, which is similar to enhanced scrutiny in that it shifts the burden of proof to the directors to show that their acts are consistent only with the best interests of the company and inconsistent with any other interests. These cases recognize that there may be a conflict between the directors who manage the company and the interests of certain groups of shareholders, particularly those s. 248 is designed to protect, and have espoused shifting the burden of proof as a method of overcoming the potential conflict.

The law as it has evolved in Ontario and Delaware has the common requirements that the court must be satisfied that the directors have acted reasonably and fairly. The court looks to see that the directors made a reasonable decision, not a perfect decision. Provided the decision taken is within a range of reasonableness, the court ought not to substitute its opinion for that of the board even though subsequent events may have cast doubt on the board's determination. As long as the directors have selected one of several reasonable alternatives, deference is accorded to the board's decision: Paramount, *supra*, at p. 45; *Brant Investments*, *supra*, at p. 320; *Themadel Foundation v. Third Canadian General Investment Trust Ltd.* (1998), 38 O.R. (3d) 749 at p. 754 (C.A.). This formulation of deference to the decision of the Board is known as the "business judgment rule". The fact that alternative transactions were rejected by the directors is irrelevant unless it can be shown that a particular alternative was definitely available and clearly more beneficial to the company than the chosen transaction: *Brant Investments*, *supra*, at pp. 314-15.

A common method used to alleviate concerns that a conflict of interest exists between directors, who may be major shareholders, and the interests of a minority or non-voting group of shareholders, is the creation of a special committee from among the independent members of a board who do not have a conflict. The purpose of a special committee is to advise the Directors and to make a recommendation as to what the Board should do. It appears that under the law of Delaware, where a Board acts on the recommendation of a special committee, the decision will be accorded respect under the business judgment rule, provided that the special committee has discharged its role independently, in good faith, and with the understanding that in a situation where a change of control transaction is contemplated, the special committee can only agree to a transaction that is fair in the sense of being the best available in the circumstances: *In re First Boston, Inc. Shareholders Litigation*, [1990] Fed. Sec. L. Rep., para. 95, 322 (Del. 1990).

The duty of directors when dealing with a bid that will change control of a company is a rapidly developing area of law and, as I have indicated, Canadian authorities dealing with the question of the onus, or burden of proof, have not been uniform. In *Brant Investments*, *supra*, the issue whether the burden of proof is on the directors to justify their actions as being in the best interests of the company or on the shareholders challenging the actions of the company was also raised. McKinlay J.A., at pp. 311-12, found it unnecessary to decide the question because the trial judge had dealt with the issues on a substantive basis, and his decision did not turn on which party had the onus or burden of proof. [See Note 3 at end of document.] The same is true in the present case. [See Note 4 at end of document.] I would add, however, that it may be that the burden of proof may not always rest on the same party when a change of control transaction is challenged. The real question is whether the directors of the target company successfully took steps to avoid a conflict of interest. If so, the rationale for shifting the burden of proof to the directors may not exist. If a board of directors has acted on the advice of a committee composed of persons having no conflict of interest, and that committee has acted independently, in good faith, and made an informed recommendation as to the best available transaction for the shareholders in the circumstances, the business judgment rule applies. The burden of proof is not an issue in such circumstances.

The members of the committee acted in good faith in the sense that they acted honestly. The committee's decision was also informed, in the sense that the committee was aware that any offer for Schneider's shares might be bettered by Maple Leaf, and that the Family would not sell to Maple Leaf. While the appellants have challenged Farley J.'s finding that the Family would not sell to Maple Leaf, there is ample evidence to support this finding. Even at $29 a share, when tax considerations were factored in, the Maple Leaf offer was only as advantageous as the Smithfield offer to the Family, not more advantageous. Apart from financial criteria, Maple Leaf did not meet the Family's expressed concern about the effect of a change of control on the continuity of employment for Schneider's employees, the welfare of suppliers, and the relationship with its customers, whereas Smithfield did. Once again, the real questions are whether the committee was independent and whether the process undertaken by the special committee was in the best interests of Schneider and its shareholders in the circumstances. While *Paramount, supra*, indicates that non-financial considerations have a role to play in determining the best transaction available in the circumstances, here it was conceded that the court should only have regard to financial considerations.

Should members of Schneider's senior management, particularly Dodds, have been permitted to have a significant role in the sale negotiations with potential bidders?

The appellants submit that Dodds had a conflict of interest because he had an interest in continued employment with Schneider and a further conflict arising out of his loyalty to the Family.

A potential conflict of interest arises because as a director of a target company, the senior executive has a duty to act in the best interests of the shareholders, but as a member of senior management the executive retains an interest in continued employment. In actively negotiating with a potential bidder the executive is negotiating with his potential boss or executioner. The appellants rely on the decision of Blair J. in *CW Shareholdings Inc.*, supra, for the proposition that no senior executive of a company being sold should be permitted to have a significant role in the sale process.

The *raison d'être* of a special committee independent of management and the controlling shareholder is to protect the interests of minority shareholders and to bring a measure of objectivity to the assessment of bids. If, as was the case in *CW Shareholdings*, senior management in the target company is a member of the special committee, the purpose in setting up the special committee might be compromised and less reliance placed on its assessment of a particular bid than if the committee were truly independent. Blair J. recognized this and he was critical of the role played by senior management in *CW Shareholdings*. In the end, however, he concluded that the involvement of management in the special committee did not so taint its approval of the Shaw Communications bid as to undermine the transaction. He also found that the committee had conducted itself in a fashion that enabled the directors to carry out their objective of maximizing shareholder value. In that case, Blair J. upheld the Board's decision, based upon the special committee's recommendation to enter into an agreement with Shaw that provided for a break fee and asset agreement in the event that its bid was not accepted.

A major distinction between the *CW Shareholdings* decision and this case is that senior management, including Dodds, was not part of the special committee that was set up, and consequently had no vote as to whether to recommend a bid. A potential conflict of interest still existed, however, because of the active role Dodds played in negotiating with the bidders.

Farley J. recognized that in allowing Dodds and, to a lesser extent, Hooper, the chief financial officer of Schneider, to deal with bidders directly, a potential conflict of interest existed but that this had to be balanced against the benefits to be obtained. He stated:

> It would be appropriate, however, to comment as well [th]at the use of the two management directors, Dodds and Hooper, in dealing with the bidders and advisors directly, would not seem inappropriate. Potentially there could be conflict, but that must be balanced against the reasonable benefits to be obtained. They knew the operations of the business — what the bidders would be interested in and they were guided by the advisors. They reported to the special committee which could make the "final" decisions and give directions. Potential conflict was minimized by the bail-out packages granted them. From the material before me it would not appear that these management persons acted or behaved inappropriately overall. It would be undesirable to subject each step they took to isolated microscopic inspection. I note in passing that Dodds would have

received approximately $1,000,000 in stock and options value extra if the Maple Leaf $29 offer had been accepted as opposed to the Smithfield one; of course no one but Maple Leaf knew how much it would have offered if it had been solicited on December 17.

[Weiler J.A. held that, on the facts, Dodd not have a significant conflict of interest, since Maple Leaf Foods had promised to treat him generously if the Maple Leaf bid was successful (and for a number of other reasons).]

Should the special committee have been created?

The appellants submit that by creating a special committee, hiring advisers, and setting up a data room, the Family used Schneider's money to better the offer from Maple Leaf, which it was not entitled to do. In addition to being rejected by Farley J., a similar argument was rejected by Montgomery J. in *Olympia & York, supra,* at p. 272. The reason is obvious: the appointment of a special committee is intended to ensure that the interests of those the oppression remedy is intended to protect are not unfairly disregarded or prejudiced. It is clearly in the interests of a company, and of all shareholders, for alternatives to an unsolicited takeover offer to be explored. It might give the shareholders a higher price for their shares. The creation of a special committee was part of the process undertaken by the Board to obtain the best transaction available in the circumstances.

Should the special committee have created a data room?

The appellants' submission that proprietary confidential information obtained from the data room was a valuable corporate asset that was either given away to the acquiring company or dissipated must also fail. As Farley J. pointed out, access to the data room was essential in order to conduct a market canvass for alternative offers. Other bidders, particularly those who had not operated in the Canadian market, needed to gain an appreciation of market conditions, and of Schneider's business. That could only be obtained with access to Schneider's confidential information. No alternative bid would have been elicited without access to Schneider's confidential information. Maple Leaf, as a competitor of Schneider for many years, had an appreciation of market conditions and of Schneider's business and did not require further information in order to make its bid.

The decision to establish a data room at the company's expense was that of the special committee, made with full knowledge of the Family's position that it was not committed to selling. The Board did not seek the approval or the consent of the Family to establish the data room for the use of information or for the nature of the confidentiality agreements that were signed with prospective bidders.

In creating a data room the special committee acted independently and reasonably. The creation of a data room made confidential information available to all bidders as part of a process to get the best transaction available to the shareholders in the circumstances. I see no merit in this ground of appeal.

Flawed committee process

The appellants submit that the trial judge ignored or failed to appreciate the evidence given by Ruby, the chairman of the special committee, to the effect that the special committee had no involvement in any negotiations with prospective bidders, that Dodds conducted the negotiations, and that the special committee did not consider whether Dodds had any conflict of interest. After considering the circumstances under which Dodds acted, I have already concluded that Dodds did not have a conflict of interest.

The special committee had no prior experience in dealing with a take-over bid and did not have the in-depth knowledge of Schneider that Dodds did. It was therefore appropriate for the special committee not to conduct the negotiations with potential bidders directly. Farley J. found that although the special committee did try to determine the views of the Family "recognizing its gatekeeper and veto role", there was no evidence that the approval of the Family was sought with respect to any decision taken by the special committee. The evidence supports the conclusion that the members of the special committee acted independently in the sense that they were free to deal with the impugned transaction on its merits. This ground of appeal also fails.

Should the special committee have insisted that Maple Leaf and any other interested party be given an opportunity to make their best and final offer prior to the board of directors of Schneider taking the steps that it did on December 17, 1997 to commit its shares to Smithfield?

The appellants submit that the Board was obliged to keep the bidding process alive by going back to Maple Leaf after it received the Smithfield bid on December 17. This submission has two alternative premises: (1) the directors could only discharge their duty to act in the best interests of the corporation by conducting an auction of the shares of Schneider; (2) a public expectation had been created by the comments made by the Schneider family that an auction would be held and, therefore, both the Family and the Board were under a duty to ensure that an auction was conducted.

The appellant's first premise is wrong in law. The second is contrary to Farley J.'s findings of fact and those findings are supported by the evidence.

Was there a duty to conduct an auction of the shares of Schneider?

The decision in Revlon v. McAndrews & Forbes Holdings, Inc., 506 A.2d 173 (Del. 1986), stands for the proposition that if a company is up for sale, the directors have an obligation to conduct an auction of the company's shares. *Revlon* is not the law in Ontario. In Ontario, an auction need not be held every time there is a change in control of a company.

An auction is merely one way to prevent the conflicts of interest that may arise when there is a change of control by requiring that directors act in a neutral manner toward a number of bidders: *Barkan v. Amsted Industries Inc.*, 567 A.2d 1279 at p. 1286 (Del. 1989). The more recent *Paramount* decision in the United States, *supra*, at pp. 43–45 has recast the obligation of directors when there is a bid for change of control as an obligation to seek the best value reasonably available to shareholders in the circumstances. This is a more flexible standard, which recognizes that the particular circumstances are important in determining the best transaction available, and that a board is not limited to considering only the amount of cash or consideration involved as would be the case with an auction: *Paramount, supra,* at p. 44. There is no single blueprint that directors must follow. Although the decision in *Paramount* and the other decisions of the courts in Delaware to which I have referred are not the law of Ontario, they can offer some guidance.

When it becomes clear that a company is for sale and there are several bidders, an auction is an appropriate mechanism to ensure that the board of a target company acts in a neutral manner to achieve the best value reasonably available to shareholders in the circumstances. When the board has received a single offer and has no reliable grounds upon which to judge its adequacy, a canvass of the market to determine if higher bids may be elicited is appropriate, and may be necessary: *Barkan, supra,* at p. 1287, citing *In re Fort Howard Corp. Shareholders Litig.*, Del. Ch., C.A. No. 991, 1988 WL 83147.

The Family did not seek to sell its controlling interest in Schneider. The Board received an offer from Maple Leaf that it felt was inadequate, but, in the final analysis, the best way to judge its adequacy was to determine if higher bids could be elicited through a market canvass. The fact that a market canvass was conducted did not mean that the Family would agree to sell its stake. Indeed, Farley J. found as a fact that the Family's decision to sell was highly conditional on a satisfactory offer being received.

The appellant submits that there was considerable evidence indicating that the Schneider Family had by December 17, if not before, concluded that a sale of its shares was inevitable. Having undertaken a market canvass, however, there was no obligation on the special committee to turn this canvass into an auction, particularly because to do so was to assume the risk that the competing offers that the market canvass had generated might be withdrawn. There was no obligation on the special committee or the Board to go back to Maple Leaf on December 17 and ask it to make another offer. A market canvass and not an auction was being conducted; the special committee and the Board only had a short time within which to consider Maple Leaf's offer;

Maple Leaf had already been asked to make an appropriate offer, and there was no certainty it would make a higher bid. There was an obligation on the special committee and the directors to consider the bids which their market canvass had realized in addition to Maple Leaf's bid. Farley J. found Maple Leaf knew, or should have known, that the bidding process was almost over when it made its $22 per share bid. Maple Leaf's board had authorized the issuance of enough Maple Leaf shares to finance a $29 a share bid for Schneider before the bidding process entered its final stage. Maple Leaf was nonetheless content to let its $22 bid stand despite knowing that there were competing bids that might be accepted in preference to its own, and despite the fact that Maple Leaf's board had authorized a higher $29 bid. This was a risk Maple Leaf chose to assume.

Was there a public expectation created by the Family that an auction would be held? While s. 248 protects the legitimate expectations of shareholders, those expectations must be reasonable in the circumstances, and reasonableness is to be ascertained on an objective basis. [Find Note 5 at end of document.] The interests of the shareholders of a company are intertwined with the expectations that have been created by the company's principals: Naneff v. Con-Crete Holdings Ltd. (1995), 23 O.R. (3d) 481, 23 B.L.R. (2d) 286 (C.A.). Therefore, the question is whether the statements made by the Family, and widely reported in press releases issued in response to Maple Leaf's bids, created a reasonable expectation that an auction would be held. Whether or not a reasonable expectation has been created is a question of fact: Arthur v. Signum Communications Ltd., [1993] O.J. No. 1928 (Div. Ct.), Campbell J., for the court, at paras. 6-7. After examining the press releases and the evidence, Farley J. found that any expectations of the claimants, who were non-Family shareholders, were not reasonable or founded in fact.

A summary of his findings on this point is as follows:

- The Family's position on selling its controlling shareholding in Schneider was always conditional to a high degree. The Family only said that they "might consider" selling. The conditional nature of the Family's position was always clearly expressed by the Board in its public statements.

- It was inappropriate for Maple Leaf to ignore the plain meaning of the public statements made by the Family and the Board. Maple Leaf "wished" that there was an unrestricted auction for Schneider but in fact there never was.

- The claimants had not proved that their reasonable expectations were thwarted. "When the gatekeeper shareholder merely indicates that it 'might consider' accepting a more financially attractive offer, then the shareholders are speculating that a deal on that basis may come to pass in which they could participate".

There was more than adequate evidence to support these findings and they cannot be disturbed.

In as much as there was no reasonable expectation on the part of the non-Family shareholders that an auction would be held after receiving the last Smithfield bid, the special committee was not obliged to give Maple Leaf an opportunity to make a third bid for Schneider's shares.

[The court then discussed allegations that the special committee had favoured the family rather than non-family shareholders. The court held that the special committee did what it could do given that the Schneider family refused to tender into any bid other than the Smithfield bid. The passage that deals with this issue may be found in Chapter 7.]

I would dismiss the first main ground of appeal.

Note

1   A further aspect of the judgment deals with the coattail provision attached to the non-voting shares. Weiler J.A. described the function of a coattail as follows:

> Coattail provisions are designed to ensure that if the common voting shareholders wish to accept an offer that will lead to a change in control and if the price or terms offered to the common voting shareholders are more favourable than those offered to the holders of non-voting shares, the non-voting shareholders get an equal opportunity to participate in any change of control premium.

> The provisions work in the following way. If the holders of restricted shares, such as non-voting shares, are excluded from participating in the common voting share takeover bid, they will then be given a right of conversion of their restricted or non-voting shares into common voting shares. Coattail provisions are intended to encourage non-exclusionary bids. When triggered, the non-voting shareholders then have the opportunity to participate in the take-over bid.

The articles of Schneider Corp. defined the coattail in the following terms:

> "Exclusionary Offer" means an offer to purchase common shares of the Corporation that... is not made concurrently with an offer to purchase Class A Non-Voting shares that is identical to the offer to purchase common shares in terms of price per share and percentage of outstanding shares to be taken up exclusive of shares owned immediately prior to the offer by the Offeror and in all other material respects and that has no condition attached other than the right not to take up and pay for shares tendered if no shares are tendered pursuant to the offer for common shares.

Weiler J.A. noted that:

> If the word acquired or purchased had been used in the definition of "exclusionary offer" instead of tendered there would not have been a problem with coattail provision. But Maple Leaf's lawyers recognized the problem. Maple Leaf's offer to purchase the common shares of Schneider was made concurrently with its offer to purchase the Class A shares. The offer to the Class A shareholders contained a condition entitling Maple Leaf not to take up and pay for any Class A shares deposited if Maple Leaf did not acquire any common shares pursuant to the offer to purchase common voting shares. This was not the condition permitted under the coattail provisions. The coattail provisions gave the right not to take up and pay for Class A shares if no common shares were tendered. Because the condition attaching to its Class A shares was different, Maple Leaf submits that its offer to the common shareholders was an exclusionary one.

Thus, Maple Leaf hoped that no one would notice that that it was making an exclusionary offer that would trigger the coattail — least of all the Schneider family, who could then file an anti-conversion certificate to cause the coattail *not* to be activated. Maple Leaf's hope was thus that they would receive a large number of Class A shares in their takeover bid for the Class A's, that the Class A shares would become voting shares, and that they would then have enough votes to displace the Schneider family as controllers of Schneiders.

Despite the wording of the coattail, both the lower court and the court of appeal held that the coattail was not triggered. Weiler J.A. held that:

> The words of a statute to be interpreted are to be read in their entire context and in their grammatical and ordinary sense harmoniously with the scheme of the Act, the object of the Act, and the intention of Parliament: *Rizzo v. Rizzo Shoes Ltd.*, [1998] 1 S.C.R. 27, 154 D.L.R. (4th) 193. (This decision holds that although the literal reading of the words in the *Employment Standards Act* entitling an employee to severance, termination, or vacation pay upon termination by the employer would not include the employer's bankruptcy, when the words are examined in their entire context they must be interpreted to include a termination resulting from the bankruptcy of the employer.) So, too, here, the wording of the coattail provision must be given an interpretation which accords with its object and the intention of the framers of the provision.

> The interpretation of a coattail provision must be viewed objectively and as a reasonably prudent business person would

view it: *Saunders v. Cathton Holdings Ltd.* (1997), 88 B.C.A.C. 264 at p. 272, 36 B.L.R. (2d) 151.

When the public interest is involved, evidence with respect to the understanding and intention of the provision is admissible to assist in determining whether a proposed interpretation is consistent with the public interest: *Re Canadian Tire Corp.* (1987), 35 B.L.R. 117 (Ont. Div. Ct.) at pp. 143-44.

The purpose of adopting a coattail provision is to discourage exclusionary offers, whereas a literal reading of Schneider's coattail provision gives the opposite effect. Certainty of meaning is of paramount importance in commercial transactions that affect the public. Those considering whether or not to tender to an offer to purchase their shares must know what investment decision they are making: see *Saunders, supra*, at pp. 272-73. In this instance, it appeared to the shareholders that the offers were the same because the amount to be paid to both classes of shareholders was the same. Maple Leaf understood how its offers would be perceived. If, instead, Maple Leaf was of the opinion that its offer was exclusionary, it could have said in its offering circular that it intended to apply to the appropriate authorities to have the issue of whether or not the offer was exclusionary determined in court as was done in *CW Shareholdings, supra*. Maple Leaf did not.

The interpretation of Maple Leaf's offers adopted by Farley J. is consistent with the way a reasonably prudent business person would construe the offer. The outcome he reaches is consistent with public expectations and is commercially sound. It employs a purposive approach. Farley J. did not err in holding that the Maple Leaf offer for common shares was not an "exclusionary offer" and that the coattail provisions in Schneider's articles had not been triggered.

(v)   The Powers of Securities Regulators in Policing Defensive Tactics

The securities regulators have the power to make orders "in the public interest." For example, the Ontario *Securities Act* (R.S.O. 1990, c. S-5) grants the Ontario Securities Commission the power to make orders "in the public interest" in section 127, excerpted in Chapter 5.

These powers give the securities regulators a great deal of discretion to regulate takeover bids. In particular, s. 127(1)2, the so-called "cease trade" power, allows the Ontario Securities Commission ("OSC") to effectively enjoin any transaction that it finds contrary to the public interest. Thus, for example, the Ontario Securities Commission issued a cease trade order to enjoin a takeover bid in *Canadian Tire Corp. v. C.T.C. Dealer Holdings Ltd.* (1987), 35 B.L.R. 56, 10 O.S.C.B. 857, 1987 CarswellOnt 128 (Securities Comm.), affirmed (1987), 59 O.R. (2d) 79, 23

Admin. L.R. 285, 35 B.L.R. 117, 37 D.L.R. (4th) 94, 21 O.A.C. 216, 1987 CarswellOnt 1733 (Div. Ct.), leave to appeal to Ont. C.A. refused (1987), 35 B.L.R. xx (Ont. C.A.), which appears in the chapter immediately following.

The regulators have issued National Policy 62-202 (which has been adopted in concert by all the various Canadian regulatory authorities) that indicates the manner in which regulatory discretion will be exercised in relation to defensive tactics associated with takeover bids.

National Policy 62-202: Take-Over Bids — Defensive Tactics

Part 1: Defensive Tactics

1.1 Defensive Tactics

(1) The Canadian securities regulatory authorities recognize that take-over bids play an important role in the economy by acting as a discipline on corporate management and as a means of reallocating economic resources to their best uses. In considering the merits of a take-over bid, there is a possibility that the interests of management of the target company will differ from those of its shareholders. Management of a target company may take one or more of the following actions in response to a bid that it opposes:

  1. Attempt to persuade shareholders to reject the bid.

  2. Take action to maximize the return to shareholders including soliciting a higher bid from a third party.

  3. Take other defensive measures to defeat the bid.

(2) The primary objective of the take-over bid provisions of Canadian securities legislation is the protection of the *bona fide* interests of the shareholders of the target company. A secondary objective is to provide a regulatory framework within which take-over bids may proceed in an open and even-handed environment. The take-over bid provisions should favour neither the offeror nor the management of the target company, and should leave the shareholders of the target company free to make a fully informed decision. The Canadian securities regulatory authorities are concerned that certain defensive measures taken by management of a target company may have the effect of denying to shareholders the ability to make such a decision and of frustrating an open take-over bid process.

(3) The Canadian securities regulatory authorities have determined that it is inappropriate to specify a code of conduct for directors of a target company, in addition to the fiduciary standard required by corporate law. Any fixed code of conduct runs the risk of containing provisions that might be insufficient in some cases and excessive in others. However, the Canadian securities regulatory authorities wish to advise participants in the capital markets that they are prepared to

examine target company tactics in specific cases to determine whether they are abusive of shareholder rights. Prior shareholder approval of corporate action would, in appropriate cases, allay such concerns.

(4) Without limiting the foregoing, defensive tactics that may come under scrutiny if undertaken during the course of a bid, or immediately before a bid, if the board of directors has reason to believe that a bid might be imminent, include

   (a) the issuance, or the granting of an option on, or the purchase of, securities representing a significant percentage of the outstanding securities of the target company,

   (b) the sale or acquisition, or granting of an option on, or agreeing to sell or acquire, assets of a material amount, and

   (c) entering into a contract other than in the normal course of business or taking corporate action other than in the normal course of business.

(5) The Canadian securities regulatory authorities consider that unrestricted auctions produce the most desirable results in take-over bids and they are reluctant to intervene in contested bids. However, they will take appropriate action if they become aware of defensive tactics that will likely result in shareholders being deprived of the ability to respond to a take-over bid or to a competing bid.

(6) The Canadian securities regulatory authorities appreciate that defensive tactics, including those that may consist of some of the actions listed in subsection (4), may be taken by a board of directors of a target company in a genuine attempt to obtain a better bid. Tactics that are likely to deny or limit severely the ability of the shareholders to respond to a take-over bid or a competing bid may result in action by the Canadian securities regulatory authorities.

(7) As a general rule, the Canadian securities regulatory authorities will not advise parties as to the propriety of proposed action in a particular case except in the context of a meeting or proceeding of which interested parties have been given notice.

Part 2: Effective Date

2.1 Effective Date — This National Policy comes into force on August 4, 1997.

Note

The issue of poison pills has come before the securities regulators in a number of cases. Until recent developments (discussed below) created some doubt, the following case was thought to be representative of the attitude of the regulators toward pills.

Chapters Inc., Re
(2001), 24 O.S.C.B. 1657, 2001 CarswellOnt 903 (Securities Comm.)

[In *Chapters Inc.*, Trilogy (a company formed by Heather Reisman, owner of Indigo, and Gerry Schwartz to acquire Chapters) approached Chapters with a view to negotiating a friendly takeover of Chapters by Trilogy. These overtures were rebuffed, and the board of Chapters adopted a "tactical" poison pill (i.e., one adopted in anticipation of a specific bid being made). The pill had a "permitted bid" feature with the usual provisions (outlined in the note above), except that in order to be a permitted bid, the bid had to remain open for 45 days. Trilogy went ahead and made a hostile bid. Chapters search for a "white knight" bidder located another bidder — Future Shop ("FS") — which announced that it too would make an offer for the shares of Chapters. The board of Chapters strongly preferred the FS bid, publicly recommending it to shareholders and indicating that it would waive the pill in favour of the FS bid. Further facts of note are recounted in the Ontario Securities Commission's decision, below]:

Ontario Securities Commission:

The Shareholder Rights Plan

   . . . Our analysis should be considered against the background of the following brief summary. Chapters has had nearly two months since the Trilogy unsolicited cash bid, to secure the emergence of Future Shop — colloquially a white knight. Not only have management shares of approximately thirty percent (30%) of the target shareholders, including management, locked up to the white knight, but the target has also entered into a support agreement with Future Shop providing for a five percent (5%) break fee and a no-shop clause. The target has also waived the pill with respect to Future Shop but to no other bidder. In this context, Chapters sought to keep the shareholder Rights Plan in place, at least until mid-march, despite the above efforts to end the auction. We cannot agree with Chapter's position in this regard.

[The Commission quoted extensively from National Policy 62-202, indicating that shareholders must ultimately decide the fate of competing takeover bids.]

   The authority of the Canadian securities administrators to exercise this mandate has resulted in a series of decisions that serve to guide the Commission's approach with respect to defensive tactics. The starting point is the decision in *Re Canadian Jorex Ltd.* (1992), 15 O.S.C.B. 257.

   In *Jorex*, the Commission established the overriding principle governing the consideration of poison pills, that is "there comes a time when the pill has to go". As a result of *Jorex*, the question becomes not whether, but "when does the pill go."

In order to make this determination, the Commission is guided by the decision in *Re Consolidated Properties* (2000), 23 O.S.C.B. 7981. In Consolidated, the Commission referred to the test used in *Re MDC Corporation and Regal Greetings & Gifts Inc.* (1994), 17 O.S.C.B. 4971, to determine whether or not the pill should go:

> As the Commission said in the *Matter of MDC Corporation and Regal Greetings & Gifts Inc.* . .
>
> If there appears to be a real and substantial possibility that, given a reasonable period of further time, the board of the target corporation can increase shareholder choice and maximize shareholder value, then, absent some other compelling reason requiring the termination of the plan in the interests of shareholders, it seems to us that the Commission should allow the plan to function for such further period, so as to fulfil their fiduciary duties.
>
> On the basis of the decisions since Regal, "reasonable possibility" would appear to us to be a more appropriate description than "real and substantial possibility", although both may in practice amount to the same thing.

Implicit in this assessment is a balancing of interests. When applying the Regal test, the Commission must consider and balance the duties of management against the interests of shareholders. This approach was adopted in *Argentina Gold Corp.*, [1999] 6 B.C.S.C. Weekly Summary 23, where the British Columbia Securities Commission stated:

> In determining whether a poison pill should stay or go, there is a natural tension between the objectives of letting the shareholders decide for themselves, as described in *Jorex*, and of letting management and the board fulfil what they see as their fiduciary duties, as set out in *Regal*. Striking a balance between these objectives in any particular case is highly dependent on the specific facts.

As recognized by the Commission in *Argentina Gold*, the individual result of a poison pill case depends on the specific facts. All relevant factors must be considered when determining whether or not the pill has outlived its purpose. *Royal Host Real Estate Investment Trust* (1999), 22 OSCB 7819, a decision of the Alberta, British Columbia and Ontario Securities Commissions, provides the following list of factors:

While it would be impossible to set out a list of all of the factors that might be relevant in cases of this kind, they frequently include:

- whether shareholder approval of the rights plan was obtained;

- when the plan was adopted;

- whether there is broad shareholder support for the continued operation of the plan;

- the size and complexity of the target company;

- the other defensive tactics, if any, implemented by;

- the number of potential, viable offerors;

- the steps taken by the target company to find an alternative bid or transaction that would be better for the shareholders;

- the likelihood that, if given further time, the target company will be able to find a better bid or transaction;

- the nature of the bid, including whether it is coercive or unfair to the shareholders of the target company;

- the length of time since the bid was announced and made;

- the likelihood that the bid will not be extended if the rights plan is not terminated.

This is the approach that was taken in *Jorex* and that served as the starting point for the analysis in the subsequent decisions.

The principal factors which, in our view, were relevant to the determination that it was time for the Chapters pill to go are as follows:

(a) The Rights Plan was adopted on April 16, 2000, by Chapters' Board of Directors and was confirmed by Chapters' Shareholders on September 13, 2000. Although the pill is not strictly tactical, it was adopted subsequent to the March 2000 meeting between Gerald Schwartz and Larry Stevenson where Mr. Schwartz expressed an interest in a friendly merger of Chapters and Indigo.

When shareholders approve a pill it does not mean that they want the pill to continue indefinitely. A company's board of directors is not permitted to maintain a shareholder rights plan indefinitely to prevent a bid's proceeding, but may do so as long as the board is actively seeking alternatives and if there is a real and substantial possibility that the board can increase shareholder choice and maximize shareholder value. It was submitted by counsel for Trilogy that the Support Agreement confirmed that Chapters is no longer seeking alternative bids.

(b) Outside of the Shares locked-up by the Future Shop Support Agreement, there has been no demonstration of broad shareholder support for the continuance of the pill. Moreover, counsel for Trilogy has provided support from two institutional shareholders indicating that they wanted to be free to tender to the offer.

(c) Chapters is neither large in size, nor complex in nature. As such, a potential bidder should be able to assess the company in a relatively short period of time.

(d) As a result of the Trilogy Offer, Chapters has engaged in a number of defensive tactics. On January 18, 2001, the Chapters Board announced that it had entered into a support agreement with Future Shop under which Future Shop would be making an offer. The Support Agreement waives the pill with respect to Future Shop and disallows Chapters the ability to remove the pill for competitive bids without breaching the Support Agreement.

The Support Agreement contained a number of typical terms and conditions. Firstly, the agreement contained a covenant requiring Chapters to support the Future Shop Proposed Offer and also provided for a break fee of approximately 5% of the aggregate transaction price. Secondly, the Support Agreement contained a non-solicitation term, commonly known as a "no-shop provision", whereby Chapters would not participate in or encourage any unsolicited written acquisition proposal by a third party. Thirdly, the Support Agreement also precluded Chapters from releasing any third party, aside form Future Shop, from confidentiality obligations.

The Support Agreement also contained some not so typical terms. One of such terms required the Rights Plan to remain in place in order that the proposed offer by Future Shop could be prepared and mailed, and that the Rights Plan be waived in respect of the Future Shop Proposed Offer at a point in time when Future Shop is in a position to take up and pay for deposited Shares. In effect, this term equalizes the timing of all bids and is discussed below.

Additionally, the Rights Plan included a provision under which the plan would terminate with respect to all bids upon the waiver of the rights plan (the "waive-for-one-waive-for-all" clause). The traditional use for such a clause is to remove management's ability to use discretionary powers in a manner that waives the application of a pill to a bid that it is prepared to recommend, while requiring a competing bid to wait out the full permitted bid period.

Under a typical "waive-for-one-waive-for-all" clause, once management waives the pill for one bid, the pill is automatically waived for all bids. These clauses are used to accentuate the auction process. The Chapters Board, however, has agreed to include a clause in the Future Shop Support Agreement so that the pill is only waived for competing bids upon the take-up of Chapters Shares by Future Shop. This places a significant amount of control in the hands of Future Shop.

It is highly unlikely that a competing bidder, such as Trilogy, would continue an offer for such an extended period of time and assume the risks associated with the modified clause in the Future Shop Support Agreement. The longer the bid is open increases the bid's sensitivity to market risks and the time value of money. Also, as it stands, if shareholders, other than the locked-up shareholders, chose to tender to a competing bid, Future Shop could frustrate that choice by declining to take up any shares under its bid and therefore avoid triggering the deemed waiver clause. The use of the clause in this manner eliminates shareholder choice and subverts the very purpose for which a deemed waiver clause was intended.

Finally, Chapters has entered into an agreement with Future Shop not to waive the pill in favour of any other bid. While the parties are free to enter into a support agreement, its terms cannot trump a determination by the Commission that it is in the public interest that the pill be cease traded.

(e) Chapters and Indigo are the major players in the Canadian retail book industry. The likely absence of synergies with companies outside the book industry result in the existence of few potential, viable offerors.

(f) The plan was firmly in place on November 28, 2000 when Trilogy announced its bid to acquire the Chapters Shares. During the 54 days the plan has been in effect, Chapters commenced a search for alternatives that resulted in the emergence of a proposed offer from Future Shop on January 18, 2001, 51 days after the announcement of the Trilogy Offer.

(g) Given the Lock-Up and Support Agreements that now exist between Chapters and Future Shop, it is unlikely that extending the pill will result in a competing bid.

(h) The current offer by Trilogy is a $15.00 all cash bid for 4,888,000 of the 11,374,704 outstanding Shares of Chapters. This represents a significant premium over the market value of the stock at the time of the bid. The bid is also partial in that it is for only 43% of the outstanding Shares of Chapters. As such, it was argued that it was coercive. If one factors out the shares subject to the Lock-Up Agreement, each non-locked up Chapters shareholder who tenders would receive a 75.4 percent take-up, translating into $11.31 in cash per share.

Moreover, the Proposed Enhancement announced on January 20, 2001 is also an all cash offer at $17.00 per share for all of the Shares outstanding less the locked-up Shares and the Shares already owned by Trilogy.

(i) The Rights Plan has been in effect for 54 days. This time period is significantly longer than the minimum 21-day period currently required in the Act.

(j) Trilogy submitted that it had no intention of extending its current bid beyond the January 24, 2001, expiration date unless the pill was cease traded by the Commission. Although counsel for Chapters submitted that in many cases where this assertion has been made, the bid was nevertheless extended, we prefer the approach adopted by the British Columbia Securities Commission in *Argentina Gold, supra*, as follows:

> Although an offeror's assertions in these circumstances that it will not extend must be assessed with caution, we could not discount the possibility that Barrick would decide to stand back and see what happened on the property with a view to returning with a lower bid

or abandoning its interest altogether if exploration results turned out to be less promising than they appeared.

Argentina Gold's shareholders might well have been willing to take the risk of letting the Barrick bid fall away (indeed later events showed they were), but that was a decision for them to make "without undue hindrance from defensive tactics that may have been adopted by the target board with the best of intentions" (to quote *Jorex*).

We do not consider it unreasonable that Trilogy might have withdrawn its offer. Mr. Wright testified as to the costs and risks associated with keeping an offer outstanding for a longer period of time. As a result, it was unlikely that an extension of the pill would lead to an increase in either the Future Shop Proposed Offer, or the Trilogy bid. In fact, the evidence demonstrated that the maintenance of the pill was precisely the obstacle preventing Trilogy from increasing its offer. Consequently, Trilogy chose not to amend its offer unless the pill was removed. Instead, Trilogy announced its intention to enhance its offer if and when the Commission cease traded the shareholders rights plan.

Accordingly, we conclude that there was no reasonable possibility that, given a reasonable period of time, the Chapters Board would be able to increase shareholder choice or value. Indeed we were satisfied that shareholders would not receive the benefit of the Proposed Enhancement unless the pill was cease traded.

Note

The approach of the Ontario Securities Commission to bar a "just say no" defense (echoed in decisions of other provincial commissions across Canada) was thought to be well-settled policy. However, in *Re Neo Material Technologies Inc.*, the OSC took a sharp turn in the road. The target's board had essentially adopted a "just say no" stance to a hostile bid, employing the pill to block a bid without seeking any other bid or value-maximizing transaction. Despite this, the OSC declined to cease trade the company's poison pill. The decision is also noteworthy in greatly enhancing the importance of the target directors' fiduciary duty in the determination of whether the public interest was violated. Finally, the decision borrows heavily from *BCE* in abandoning prior judicial and regulatory pronouncements that directors are to act solely in the interest of target shareholders. It also borrows the view from *BCE* that target directors are entitled (or perhaps compelled) to consider the long term interests of the corporation in crafting an appropriate response to a hostile bid.

Neo Material Technologies Inc., Re
2009 CarswellOnt 5084, 32 O.S.C.B. 6941, 63 B.L.R. (4th) 123 (Ont. Securities Comm.)

[In the *Neo* case, Neo Technologies ("Neo") had a poison pill with a "permitted bid" feature in place, pursuant to which the poison pill rights would not be triggered as long as i) the offer was open for 60 days; ii) at least 50% of Neo's shares (other than those held by the offeror) tendered their shares into the bid (the "Minumum Tender Condition"); and iii) once the 50% tender threshold was met, the bid was extended for a further 10 day. Pala Investments Holdings Limited ("Pala"), Neo's largest shareholder, with a bit more than 20% of Neo's shares, made a partial bid (through a wholly-owned numbered company, referred to below as "083") to acquire 20% of the shares of Neo that it did not already have. The bid was designed to comply with the permitted bid feature of the pill. (Note carefully that a minimum tender condition does not require that 50% of the target's shares be *purchased* by the bidder; only that 50% be *tendered* into the bid. Under applicable securities legislation, if more shares are tendered than the bidder wishes to purchase, the bidder need only purchase a *pro rata* portion of each shareholder's tender.) Neo responded by adopting a *second* poison pill which was essentially identical to the first, except that the definition of "permitted bid" was amended to require that the offer be made to all of Neo's shareholders for all of their shares. Neo indicated that it would seek shareholder approval of this pill at its upcoming annual general meeting of shareholders ("AGM"). The management proxy stated that the purpose of the second pill was:

> [T]o prevent the acquisition of control of, or a creeping takeover bid for, the Company by means of a partial bid. The [second pill] requires that any offer to acquire shares of the Company be made to all shareholders for all of their shares to ensure that all shareholders of the Company are treated equally and fairly in connection with any take-over bid for the company. The [second pill] is being adopted to discourage discriminatory, coercive or unfair attempts to take over the Company.

Pala responded by *lowering* the percentage of shares sought to 12%, and making its bid conditional on the first pill being waived and the second pill withdrawn from the annual shareholders meeting. Neo declined to do so, declaring that the Pala offer was inadequate "from a financial point of view". Pala then announced that it would again lower the percentage of shares sought to about 10%, but at a higher price ($1.70, versus $1.40 per share).

At the AGM, slightly more than 81% of Neo's shareholders, other than Pala (representing about 83% of the shares that Pala did not hold) voted in favour of the second pill. Nonetheless, at a hearing before the

Commission (held two weeks after Neo shareholders approved the second pill), Pala sought an order that the second Neo pill be cease traded (an order effectively equivalent to an injunction). The central issue was (in the words of the *Chapters* decision) "whether or not the pill should go"]:

Ontario Securities Commission

Under what circumstances generally should the Commission exercise its public interest jurisdiction to cease trade a shareholder rights plan?

When dealing specifically with shareholder rights plans, the Commission has historically taken the approach of balancing the public interest regarding the right of the shareholders of the target to tender their shares to the bidder of their choice against the duties of the target board to maximize shareholder value (Re Falconbridge Limited (2006), 29 O.S.C.B. 6783 ("Falconbridge") at para. 33).

In Lac Minerals, the Commission stated:

> [T]he Commission will only make an order under section 127 of the Act when it is in the public interest to do so. In considering whether to make an order in this case, the real issue the Commission has to determine was whether, the extent to which, and when the Commission should interfere with the conduct of the Lac Board, professed to be directed at maximizing shareholder value, in the interests of allowing the shareholders of Lac to respond to one of the two outstanding take-over bids.

> This issue involved interesting questions about the relationship between securities law and corporate law. It raised the tension between (i) the board's duty to manage the corporation honestly and in good faith with a view to the best interests of the corporation; and (ii) the shareholders' "right" to decide whether to sell their shares in response to a take-over bid.

> (*LAC Minerals Ltd., Re*, 1994 CarswellOnt 1097, 17 O.S.C.B. 4963 (Ont. Securities Comm.) ("Lac Minerals") at 4968-4969)

. . .In deciding whether interference with a decision of a board of directors is necessary to protect the *bona fide* interests of target shareholders, the Commission may consider any number of factors. These factors include but are not limited to:

[The Commission reproduced the same list of factors as appear in the *Chapters* case, *supra*]

Which factors are relevant will vary from case to case since all shareholder rights plans are unique to the circumstances of the bid (Falconbridge at para. 36). The Commission has made it clear that:

> [I]t is fruitless to search for the "holy grail" of a specific test, or series of tests, that can be applied in all circumstances. Take over bids are

fact specific; the relevant factors, and the relative importance to be attached to each, will vary from case to case. As a result, a test that focuses on certain factors to the exclusion of others will almost certainly be inappropriate in some cases to which we attempt to apply it.

As the Commission stated in *Cara Operations Ltd., Re*, 2002 CarswellOnt 4033, 25 O.S.C.B. 7997 (Ont. Securities Comm.) ("Re Cara") at para. 65:

> [I]f a plan does not have shareholder approval, it generally will be suspect as not being in the best interest of the shareholders; however, shareholder approval of itself will not establish that a plan is in the best interests of shareholders.

Further, it is not simply that shareholder approval has been given that is an influential factor; rather, such approval ought to be informed, provided freely and fairly, and in the absence of coercion or undue pressure (*Pulse Data Inc., Re*, 2007 ABASC 895, 2007 CarswellAlta 1667 (Alta. Securities Comm.) ("Pulse Data") at para. 101 and *MDC Corp., Re*, 1994 CarswellOnt 1098, 17 O.S.C.B. 4971 (Ont. Securities Comm.) ("Regal") at para. 11). . .

In the circumstances of this case, are there good and sufficient reasons for this Commission to exercise its public interest jurisdiction to set aside Neo Board's adoption of the Second Shareholder Rights Plan?

. . .We are in agreement with the position taken by the Alberta Securities Commission [in *Pulse Data Inc., Re*, 2007 ABASC 895, 2007 CarswellAlta 1667 (Alta. Securities Comm.)] that, as a general matter, recent and informed shareholder ratification of a rights plan, erected in the face of the hostile take-over bid is suggestive of a finding that the continuation of the shareholder rights plan is in the *bona fide* interest of a target's shareholders.

Turning to the case at hand, in deciding that it is not in the public interest to cease trade the Second Shareholder Rights Plan at this time, we were influenced by the following considerations:

[The shareholder rights plan was adopted as a direct response to the Pala offer: it was approved by an overwhelming majority of shareholders; the shareholders were sufficiently informed]

We are therefore of the opinion that by voting for the Second Shareholder Rights Plan, Neo's shareholders knew, or ought reasonably to have known, that they were voting against the Pala Offer and we have not been presented with any evidence to suggest otherwise.

This being said, we endorse Staff's position that a fully informed shareholder approval of a rights plan implemented in the face of a hostile bid is not determinative where:

1. There is evidence that the board process in evaluating and responding to the bid, including the decision to implement a shareholder rights plan, was not carried out in the best interest of the corporation and the target's shareholders, as a whole; or

2. There is evidence to suggest that management or the board of directors coerced or unduly pressured the target's shareholders to approve the shareholder rights plan. ..

[The OSC found no evidence that the board had not acted in the best interest of the corporation, nor that shareholders had been coerced or unduly pressured to vote in favour of the pill. With respect to the former, the Commission borrowed heavily from jurisprudence on the operation of the "business judgment rule", putting a great deal of weight on the procedures that were adopted by the board. In particular, the Commission held that "[b]oard process will be compromised where: (i) advisors to the special committee are not independent; or (ii) decisions by the target board or special committee suggest entrenchment. On the facts it found no evidence of either. In this respect, the OSC also stated:]

Staff agrees with Neo's submissions that the Neo Board discharged its fiduciary obligations by: (i) establishing an independent special committee; and (ii) retaining independent legal and financial advisors to assist the independent special committee in reviewing the Pala Offer.

A review of the case law supports the position that in ascertaining whether a board of directors has discharged its fiduciary obligations, the Commission must give effect to the business judgment rule. ..

[The Commission took from *Pente v. Schneider* the proposition that the board's decision must be within a "range of reasonableness".]

We are therefore left to consider whether the Neo Board exercised reasonable business judgment in furtherance of its fiduciary obligations: (i) in adopting the Second Shareholder Rights Plan in the face of the Pala Offer; and (ii) in subsequently deciding not to trigger an auction in order to maximize shareholder value at that time. In other words, were these decisions within the range of reasonable alternatives?

In our view, the Neo Board was entitled to adopt the Second Shareholder Rights Plan in the face of the Pala Offer. Such defensive tactics ". . . are neither novel nor exotic" (Falconbridge at para. 36) and their adoption has been explicitly recognized for legitimate business purposes in NP 62-202. Based on the evidence before us, we find that the Neo Board undertook a rigorous process to evaluate its response to the Pala Offer and identified a number of concerns, as identified above. The principal concern was that the Pala Offer would have constituted or facilitated a creeping take-over.

We acknowledge that in many instances a primary purpose for adopting a shareholder rights plan is to allow the board to pursue alternative value-enhancing transactions, which includes seeking an alternate bid. In fact, we recognize that in the circumstances of many of the cases referred to, and considered by us, that obligation may have crystallized. However, we do not see this as the only legitimate purpose for a shareholder rights plan. As stated above, Canadian law imposes and recognizes a fiduciary duty owed by a board to the corporation as a whole. The so-called "business judgment" rule properly permits directors to make appropriate decisions sufficient to fulfill their fiduciary obligations. To the extent that the scope and content of these duties were not clear in the context of a hostile take-over bid, they have been better amplified by the recent statements of the Supreme Court of Canada in *BCE Inc., Re*, 2008 CarswellQue 12595, 2008 CarswellQue 12596, [2008] 3 S.C.R. 560 (S.C.C.) ("BCE"). In that case, the Supreme Court discussed the fiduciary duty of directors as follows:

[The Commission quoted from *BCE* paras. 37-39 and 66, which are excerpted in *BCE, supra*.]

In our view, these statements make it clear that there is no specific formula to apply on directors in every case, including an obligation to permit and facilitate an auction of company shares each and every time an offeror makes a bid. In fact, Canadian courts have historically not imposed such duty on directors to the corporation. As the Ontario Court of Appeal stated in Schneider:

[T]he decision in Revlon v. MacAndrews & Forbes Holdings, Inc., 506 A.2d 173 (Del. 1986), stands for the proposition that if a company is up for sale, the directors have an obligation to conduct an auction of the company's shares. Revlon is not the law in Ontario. In Ontario, an auction need not be held every time there is a change of control of a company.

(Schneider at para. 61)

We also defer to the comments of the Supreme Court of Canada in BCE where the Court noted:

What is clear is that the Revlon line of cases has not displaced the fundamental rule that the duty of directors cannot be confined to particular priority rules, but is rather a function of business judgment of what is in the best interest of the corporation, in the particular situation it faces. . . .

(BCE at para. 87)

We are bound by this principle as a matter of law, and have a duty to apply it in cases such as these. However, we add that in our view this articulation is not a deviation from past Commission determinations but is consistent with them.

As discussed above, in this case, Pala submits that the only proper use of a shareholder rights plan in the face of a take-over bid is to allow a board of directors sufficient time to seek out alternative bidders. Consistent with the Supreme Court's statements in BCE and the established body of corporate case law it is our view that, shareholder rights plans may be adopted for the broader purpose of protecting the long-term interests of the shareholders, where, in the directors' reasonable business judgment, the implementation of a rights plan would be in the best interests of the corporation.

Based on the evidence before us, we find that after assessing the offer the Neo Board concluded that: (i) the current economic circumstances are, if not unique, a once in a lifetime event and have depressed the market prices of shares in a broad range of public companies, including Neo; (ii) Neo has little debt, strong cash reserves and solid business relationships and so, at present, is well positioned not only to survive the current economic situation but also to emerge a stronger and more valuable enterprise upon the eventual return of more normal conditions; (iii) now is an absolutely inappropriate time for the collectivity of Neo's shareholders to run an auction or allow effective control of Neo to be acquired by any one shareholder as that would be an impediment to such a transaction in the future; and (iv) the effect of a bid by a financial investor such as Pala would not be advantageous at this time for either Neo as an enterprise or the collectivity of Neo shareholders.

It is evident that, in the view of the Neo Board, avoiding an auction at this time was in the long-term best interest of the corporation and of the shareholders, as a whole. This decision reflects the business judgment of the Neo Board, and there is no evidence to suggest that it was made in any manner other than in furtherance of its fiduciary obligations to the corporation.

Notes and Questions

1   Following the above excerpts, the Commission added an additional section entitled "If the Second Shareholder Rights Plan is allowed to stand, has the time come for it to be terminated by the Commission?" The Commission then went on to state: "We acknowledge that case law supports both Pala's and Staff's submissions that there comes a time when a rights plan must go." Further:

> In light of our findings above, we are not convinced that the time has come to "cease trade" the Second Shareholder Rights Plan. The Second Shareholder Rights Plan stands in the way of the Pala Offer and has continued to provide the Neo Board the opportunity to act in a manner which, based on the reasonable business judgment of the Neo Board and management, protects the long-term interests of Neo and the shareholders, as a whole.

Is it logically possible to allow a target board to "just say no" while simultaneously declaring that there is a time when the pill must go?

2   In prior decisions, such as *Standard Trustco* (*supra*, Chapter 5) the Commission had clearly stated that the purview of the public interest powers is different from that of corporate law. In particular, the Commission may define its own extra-corporate-law standards upon which the public interest rests. Why then, in *Neo*, does the Commission declare that it is bound by *BCE* "as a matter of law, and have a duty to apply it in cases such as these"?

3   The Commission cites the decision of the Ontario Court of Appeal in *Schneider* to support the view that there is no duty to auction in Ontario. But what of the paragraphs following the excerpted part of *Schneider* that state that there is a duty on directors to "seek the best value reasonably available to shareholders in the circumstances"?

4   The Commission quotes *BCE* to the effect that "the Revlon line of cases has not displaced the fundamental rule that the duty of directors cannot be confined to particular priority rules." Is this an accurate representation of *Revlon*?

5   The Commission asserts that the view of fiduciary duty expressed in *BCE* "is not a deviation from past Commission determinations but is consistent with them." Is this accurate?

6   While there are prior regulatory decisions that refer to the directors' fiduciary duty in determining what is in the public interest, both the emphasis placed on this duty, and the role of the duty are quite different than in *Neo*. For example, in the entire decision in *Chapters*, the word "fiduciary" crops up but twice. Both times it is used when there is a tension between allowing shareholders to decide if they wish to tender into a bid, and allowing management to use a pill (or other measure) to prevent shareholders from tendering in order to fulfill its fiduciary duty to get the best value for shareholders. It is clear from *Chapters* and other previous decisions (as well as NP 62-202) that this view of the fiduciary duty does extend to permitting a "just say no" defence. By contrast, in *Neo* the very focal point of the inquiry is whether directors have complied with their fiduciary duty in corporate law. Moreover, that duty is now interpreted to permit a "just say no" defence. Thus, the "tension" between shareholders and directors was previously resolved by allowing directors some room to keep a pill in place, but ultimately allowing shareholders to decide the issue. In *Neo*, the "tension" is resolved by entirely turning the issue over to the directors — at least in cases where shareholder have voted overwhelmingly in favour of the pill.

7   Is shareholder approval of a poison pill equivalent to shareholders ultimately deciding the issue of how the bid should fare by either

tendering or not tendering into a bid? Note that shareholder approval is a *collective* action that binds the minority, while allowing shareholders to tender permits an individualized decision.

8   NP 62-202 states that the regulators will take appropriate action *"if they become aware of defensive tactics that will likely result in shareholders being deprived of the ability to respond to a take-over bid or to a competing bid."* Is that subject to the ability of the majority of shareholders to declare that a minority shall not tender?

9   For a further discussion on poison pills, see Poonam Puri (Winter 2010/2011). There Oughta Be a Rule, *Listed Magazine*, 17.

The subsequent decision of the Ontario Securities Commission in *Re Baffinland Iron Mines Corp.*, 2010 LNONOSC 904 (December 3, 2010), with a different panel of commissioners, seems to repudiate *Neo*. In this decision, the word "fiduciary" appears only 5 times.

Re Baffinland Iron Mines Corp.
2010 LNONOSC 904

[As in *Neo*, there were two suitors for the target, Baffinland Iron Mines Corp. ("Baffinland"); Nunavut Iron Ore Acquisition Co. ("Nunavut") and ArcelorMittal S.A. ("ArcelorMittal"). Management of Baffinland favoured the ArcelorMittal bid, and had entered into a support agreement that, *inter alia*, contained a "no shop" clause, a break fee of $11 million, and which required Baffinland to keep the poison pill in place until just prior to the expiry of the ArcelorMittal bid. Contrary to the result in *Neo*, the Commission cease traded the Baffinland pill. The key factors for doing this were similar to those in *Chapters*, and included: the pill had been in place for a long period of time (57 days), allowing Baffinland directors sufficient time to find a competing offer: no Baffinland shareholders expressed any view on whether the pill should be left in place; Nunavut stated that the only impediment to it raising its offer was the pill; and leaving the pill in place would give ArcelorMittal an advantage by forcing Nunavut, the first bidder, to undergo the risk and expense of keeping its bid open for a long period of time.]

Ontario Securities Commission

The decision in *Canadian Jorex Ltd., Re*, 1992 CarswellOnt 127, 15 O.S.C.B. 257 (Ont. Securities Comm.) ("Canadian Jorex") was the first decision in which Canadian securities commissions considered the circumstances in which they would cease trade a shareholder rights plan or "poison pill". The Commission held in *Canadian Jorex* that there comes a time when a shareholder rights plan "has got to go". In our view, it is generally time for a shareholder rights plan "to go" when the rights plan has served its purpose by facilitating an auction, encouraging competing bids or otherwise maximizing shareholder value. A rights plan will be cease traded where it is unlikely to achieve any further benefits for shareholders.

[As in *Neo*, the Commission stated that "there is no one test or consideration that constitutes the "holy grail" when deciding whether a rights plan should remain in place or be cease traded", and again reproduced the list of factors that we see in *Chapters*. It stated "[a]lmost all of those considerations are relevant, to one extent or another, in the circumstances before us." The Commission noted that the auction seemed to have come to an end, and continued.]

Accordingly, in our view, it is not necessary for the Rights Plan to remain in place in order to facilitate an auction; there are now two competing bids on the table. To us, the most important consideration in these circumstances is that Baffinland has agreed in the Support Agreement not to solicit further offers and, accordingly, it needs no further time to do so. That suggests that the auction process is coming to an end. It seems unlikely that the Rights Plan will achieve more for shareholders in terms of inducing a further offer from a new bidder.

Based on the evidence before us, we have concluded that there is no real and substantial possibility that Baffinland will be able to increase shareholder choice by keeping the Rights Plan in place (see *Re MDC Corp.*, 1994 LNONOSC 211). . .

It is clear that one of the effects of the Support Agreement is to eliminate the timing advantage of the Nunavut Offer by maintaining the Rights Plan in the face of that offer. In effect, Nunavut cannot take up common shares under its offer until the expiry of the ArcelorMittal Offer. In our view, Nunavut is entitled as the first bidder to the timing advantage its offer has under our take-over bid regime. . . .

Deference to the Business Judgment of the Baffinland Board

Baffinland has also submitted that we should consider the factors discussed in *Royal Host* (see paragraph 30 of these reasons) "through the lens of deference to the reasonable business judgment of the target company's directors" as contemplated in *Neo Material Technologies Inc., Re*, 2009 CarswellOnt 5084, 63 B.L.R. (4th) 123 (Ont. Securities Comm.) ("*Neo*"). We do not agree.

In *Neo*, the Commission concluded that it would defer to the wishes of shareholders who had overwhelmingly voted to keep the relevant rights plan in place in the face of the specific bid that was before shareholders at the time of the vote. The vote was held only two weeks before the hearing. NP 62-202 states that "prior shareholder approval of corporate action would, in appropriate cases, allay" concerns with respect to a defensive tactic. In *Neo*, the Commission concluded that it should defer to the wishes of shareholders as expressed by the recent shareholder vote. . .

Accordingly, in our view, *Neo* does not stand for the proposition that the Commission will defer to the business judgment of a board of directors in considering whether to cease trade a rights plan, or that a board of directors in the exercise of its fiduciary duties may "just say no" to a take-over bid. Such a conclusion would have been inconsistent with the provisions of NP 62-202 and the relatively long line of regulatory decisions that began with *Canadian Jorex*. To the contrary, the Commission in *Neo* deferred to the wishes of shareholders as contemplated by NP 62-202. Neo suggests only that whether or not the board of directors of a target issuer is acting in the best interests of that issuer and its shareholders, and is complying with its fiduciary duties, is a relevant, although secondary, consideration for the Commission in deciding whether to cease trade a rights plan. Whether a board of directors is complying with its fiduciary duties does not determine the outcome of a poison pill hearing.

Notes

1   In *Re Icahn Partners LP and Lions Gate Entertainment Corp.*, 2010 BCSCCOM 432, the B.C. Securities Commission rejected *Neo*, stating "shareholder approval is not relevant where there are no alternatives to the bid and the target board has no intention of seeking any." Thus, on the facts of *Neo*, the B.C. Commission would have cease traded the pill. How the *Baffinland* panel would have ruled on this is subject to some doubt. Thought it characterizes *Neo* as a case involving regulatory deference to shareholders (rather than to the board), it also says that there is no "just say no" defence. How do you think the *Baffinland* panel would have decided *Neo*?

2   The Delaware Court of Chancery in *Air Products & Chemicals, Inc. v. Airgas, Inc.*, C.A. No. 5249-CC (Del. Ch. Feb. 15, 2011) was recently asked to invalidate a poison pill put in place by Airgas Inc. The principle argument against the poison pill was that the directors did not consult with shareholders regarding the takeover offer the pill was designed to counter. Nevertheless, the Supreme Court declined to invalidate the pill. Chancellor Chandler stated:

> As this case demonstrates, in order to have any effectiveness, pills do not — and cannot — have a set expiration date. To be clear, though, this case does not endorse 'just say never.' What it does endorse is Delaware's long-understood respect for reasonably exercised managerial discretion, so long as boards are found to be acting in good faith and in accordance with their fiduciary duties (after rigorous fact-finding and enhanced scrutiny of their defensive actions). The Airgas board serves as a quintessential example.

3   *Baffinland* does not directly repudiate *Neo's* adoption of *BCE's* broad notion of to whom the fiduciary duty is owed. Nonetheless, the decision focuses entirely on the welfare of shareholders, and thus seems by strong implication to repudiate *Neo* and restore the Commission's historical focus on shareholders. Perhaps it would have been better if the *Baffinland* panel expressly dealt with this point.

4   In like fashion, *Baffinland* does not expressly repudiate *Neo's* adoption of the view in *BCE* that directors can or should take a "long term" view in applying their fiduciary duties. But again, the tenor of the decision, coupled with the denial of a "just say no" defence could be taken as a repudiation of *Neo* on this point.

7.   SANCTION BY SHAREHOLDERS OF FIDUCIARY BREACH

(a)   Introduction to Ratification

One of the most troubled areas in company law is that of shareholder approval — ratification — of an act by the board or individual directors that constitutes a breach of fiduciary duty. In such disparate areas as the issuance of shares, self-interested contracts, corporate opportunity, duty of care, and compensation, the question of legitimation through shareholder sanction arises. In particular, which breaches of duty may be ratified and which may not, and what is the logic of the distinction? Assuming that a given fiduciary breach is subject to ratification, what form of ratification, i.e., unanimous, supra-majority, or bare majority, is required? Does the form of required ratification differ across contexts? What impact does interested shareholder voting have on the effect of ratification? What is the effect of properly executed ratification — i.e., validation of the transaction, immunization of the transaction from judicial review on certain grounds, or a shift in the burden for establishing some defect in the transaction to the plaintiff? The treatment in the cases of these issues is far from satisfactory.

Arguably, any attempt to deal on a principled basis with ratification must begin with a realization that shareholder ratification is subject to many of the same "collective action" problems that beset shareholder voting in other more benign situations, i.e., election of directors. These collective action problems emanate from the free rider problems that are endemic to shareholder voting in the corporation. Because there is little reason to expect that shareholders of widely held corporations will examine ratification issues any more closely than other corporate action requiring their approval (i.e., voting for directors in the normal course of affairs), the value of ratification, especially when it is in the form of a bare shareholder majority, is suspect.

If shareholder ratification in the form of simple or bare shareholder majorities is vulnerable, should the rules governing ratification be altered? An obvious and extreme cure for shareholder apathy would be a rule of unanimity. Under such a rule, the vote of even a shareholder with a single share is important because she retains the power to "hold-up" any proposed action by her refusal to vote in favour of it. Consequently, the shareholder will find that, given that she has clear causal impact on corporate activity, it is in her rational interest to invest in information generation and assimilation activities to the extent of the pro-rated value of the proposed corporate activity on her particular shareholding. Whether a more stringent voting rule is desirable turns on a comparison of the costs and benefits it occasions. For it is indeed possible that the benefits from more widespread and active shareholder voting on ratification are eclipsed by the costs that accompany a more stringent rule in terms of delay and minority shareholder opportunism. These costs may be so high as to effectively bar a corporation from concluding an interested transaction, irrespective of its intrinsic merits. Therefore, in considering the materials in this section, you should bear in mind the consequences entailed by the adoption of different ratification regimes, and, in particular, the effects on a corporation's capacity to adopt transactions that are only available to the corporation on the basis that they are accompanied by a self-interested element.

Finally, in considering the following materials, you should be cognizant of the roots of the ratification power: the power is derived from memorandum corporate law jurisdictions, where shareholders hold residual power in the corporation. The adoption of the ratification power by the courts in letters patent jurisdictions (e.g., Ontario and the western provinces, except for B.C.) where there was *no* such residual power, was of highly questionable legal pedigree (if you are not sure why, you might want to revisit *Kelly v. Electrical Construction, supra*, Chapter 4).

In what follows, we explore ratification in a chronological sequence from the early days of corporate law to the present. A full understanding of the different ages of ratification is not of mere historical value: it will help you to place more recent cases (and statutory provisions) in a helpful interpretive context.

(b)   The Common Law

In its early days, corporate law exhibited a very strongly majoritarian bias. By this we mean that the courts believed that, in respect of matters of corporate policy as well as internal disputes between the shareholders and the corporation's directors and officers, a majority of shareholders should have final say. The *locus classicus* of this view is a case called *Foss v. Harbottle* (1843) 67 ER 189. In *Foss*, two minority shareholders alleged that the five directors of the company had committed various breaches of their fiduciary duty to the company — including fraudulent appropriation of assets. However, when they sought to hold the directors accountable, the court declined to give them standing. The *ratio* of *Foss* is well summarized by the Jenkins L.J. in *Edwards v. Halliwell*, [1950] 2 All ER 1064 (C.A.):

> The rule in Foss v Harbottle, as I understand it, comes to no more than this. First, the proper plaintiff in an action in respect of a wrong alleged to be done to a company or association of persons is *prima facie* the company or the association of persons itself. Secondly, where the alleged wrong is a transaction which might be made binding on the company or association and on all its members by a simple majority of the members, no individual member of the company is allowed to maintain an action in respect of that matter for the simple reason that, if a mere majority of the members of the company or association is in favour of what has been done, then *cadit quaestio* [i.e., that is the end of the matter].

The rule established that where the company suffers harm, the company itself is the true and proper claimant. Therefore the shareholders cannot generally sue for wrongs done to the company.

Foss is the foundation of the common law relating to shareholder ratification. If a majority of shareholders either *had* ratified a corporate wrong, or might at some point in the future ratify the wrong, then an individual shareholder had no standing to assert any breach of fiduciary duty. In essence, *Foss* stands for the proposition that there is no common law derivative action.

The case that follows, *North-West Transportation*, illustrates the unbending nature of this predisposition to majority rule, insofar as the Privy Council allowed a majority of shareholders to sanction what would otherwise have been their own breaches of duty. This principal of ratification, and the absence of a common law derivative action, left minority shareholders in a most unenviable position. As long as a majority of shareholders ratified an alleged wrong, an individual shareholder had no legal means of redress for any alleged breach of duty by a director or officer.

North-West Transportation Company, Limited v. Beatty
(1887), 12 App. Cas. 589 (P.C.)

SIR RICHARD BAGGALLAY: The action, in which this appeal has been brought, was commenced on the 31st of May, 1883, in the Chancery Division of the High Court of Justice of Ontario. The plaintiff, Henry Beatty, is a shareholder in the North-West Transportation Company, Limited, and he sues on behalf of himself and all other shareholders in the company, except those who are defendants. The defendants are the company and five shareholders, who, at the commencement of the action, were the directors of the company. The claim in the action is to set aside a sale made to the company by James Hughes Beatty, one of the directors, of a steamer called the *United Empire*, of which previously to such sale he was sole owner.

The general principles applicable to cases of this kind are well established. Unless some provision to the contrary is to be found in the charter or other instrument by which the company is incorporated, the resolution of a majority of the shareholders, duly convened, upon any question with which the company is legally competent to deal, is binding upon the minority, and consequently upon the company, and every shareholder has a perfect right to vote upon any such question, although he may have a personal interest in the subject-matter opposed to, or different from, the general or particular interests of the company.

On the other hand, a director of a company is precluded from dealing, on behalf of the company, with himself, and from entering into engagements in which he has a personal interest conflicting, or which possibly may conflict, with the interests of those whom he is bound by fiduciary duty to protect; and this rule is as applicable to the case of one of several directors as to a managing or sole director. Any such dealing or engagement may, however, be affirmed or adopted by the company, provided such affirmance or adoption is not brought about by unfair or improper means, and is not illegal or fraudulent or oppressive towards those shareholders who oppose it.

The material facts of the case are not now in dispute. .. .

At a meeting of the directors held on the 10th of February, 1883, and at which all the directors except the defendant William Beatty were present, it was resolved that a by-law, which was read to the meeting, for the purchase of the *United Empire*, should pass. It is unnecessary to refer in detail to the terms in which this by-law was expressed; it is sufficient to state that, after reciting an agreement between the company and the defendant James Hughes Beatty, that the company should buy and the defendant should sell the steamer *United Empire* for the sum of $125,000, to be in part paid in cash and in part secured, as therein mentioned, it was enacted that the company should purchase the steamer from the defendant upon those terms, with various directions for giving effect to the terms of the contract.

The agreement recited in the by-law was executed at the same meeting.

At a meeting of shareholders, held, as arranged, on the 16th of February, 1883, the by-law which had been enacted by the directors was read by the secretary, and, after being modified in its terms, with respect to the price, was adopted by a majority of votes.

The *United Empire*, on her completion, was delivered to the company, and has ever since been employed in the ordinary business of the company. . . .

It is proved by uncontradicted evidence, and is indeed now substantially admitted, that at the date of the purchase the acquisition of another steamer to supply the place of the *Asia* was essential to the efficient conduct of the Company's business; that the *United Empire* was well adapted for that purpose; that it was not within the power of the Company to acquire any other steamer equally well adapted for its business; and that the price agreed to be paid for the steamer was not excessive or unreasonable.

. . . Had there been no material facts in the case other than those above stated, there would have been, in the opinion of their Lordships, no reason for setting aside the sale of the steamer; it would have been immaterial to consider whether the contract for the purchase of the *United Empire* should be regarded as one entered into by the directors and confirmed by the shareholders, or as one entirely emanating from the shareholders; in either view of the case, the transaction was one which, if carried out in a regular way, was within the powers of the company; in the former view, any defect arising from the fiduciary relationship of the defendant James Hughes Beatty to the company would be remedied by the resolution of the shareholders, on the 16th of February, and, in the latter, the fact of the defendant being a director would not deprive him of his right to vote, as a shareholder, in support of any resolution which he might deem favourable to his own interests.

There is, however, a further element for consideration, arising out of the following facts, which have been relied upon in the arguments on behalf of the plaintiff, as evidencing that the resolution of the 16th of February was brought about by unfair and improper means. . . .

[Sir Richard Baggallay went on to show that the by-law which adopted the Beatty contract was passed by votes which Beatty himself either possessed or controlled.]

. . .it follows that the majority of votes in favour of the confirmation of the by-law was due to the votes of the defendant J.H. Beatty.

These last-mentioned facts were stated by the plaintiff in his claim in the action, and he not only insisted that the defendant J.H. Beatty was in such a fiduciary relation to the company that it was not competent for him, under any circumstances, to enter into the contract for the sale of his steamer to the company, but he made various charges of fraud and collusion against the defendant directors, other than the defendant J.D. Beatty, who was also the secretary of the company.

These charges of fraud and collusion were abandoned at the trial of the action, but the facts before referred to were pressed upon the judges, before whom, in succession, the action came, and afforded to those judges who were of opinion that the sale should be set aside the substantial grounds for their decisions.

The action first came on to be heard before the Chancellor of Ontario, who, on the 6th of May, 1884, ordered the sale to be set aside, with the usual consequential directions. All charges of fraud and collusion being discarded, the Chancellor treated the question as one of "purely equitable law," and held that the threefold character of director, shareholder, and vendor, sustained by the defendant J. H. Beatty, involved a conflict between duty and interest, and that, being so circumstanced, he could not be permitted, in the conduct of the company's affairs, to exercise the balance of power which he possessed, to the possible prejudice of the other shareholders.

The defendants appealed against the order of the Chancellor, and, on the 17th of April, 1885, the Court of Appeal of Ontario allowed the appeal, and ordered that the plaintiff's bill should be dismissed, with costs. In the opinion of the members of that Court, the resolution to purchase the steamer was a pure question of internal management, and the shareholders had a perfect right, either to ratify the act of the directors, or to treat the matter as an original offer to themselves, and to assent to and complete the purchase.

From the order of the Court of Appeal the plaintiff appealed to the Supreme Court of Canada, and on the 9th of April, 1886, the Supreme Court reversed the order of the Court of Appeal, and affirmed that of the Chancellor. It appears to have been the opinion of the judges of the Supreme Court that the case turned entirely on the fiduciary character of the defendant J. H. Beatty as a director: that, if the acts or transactions of an interested director were to be confirmed by the shareholders, it should be by an exercise of the impartial, independent, and intelligent judgment of disinterested shareholders and not by the votes of the interested director, who ought never to have departed from his duty; that the course pursued by the defendant J. H. Beatty was an oppressive proceeding on his part; and that, consequently, the vote of the shareholders, at the meeting of the 16th of February, 1883, was ineffectual to confirm the by-law which had been enacted by the directors. The nature of the transaction itself does not appear to have been taken into consideration by the judges in their decision of the case.

From this decision of the Supreme Court of Canada the appeal has been brought with which their Lordships have now to deal. The question involved is doubtless novel in its circumstances, and the decision important in its consequences; it would be very undesirable even to appear to relax the rules relating to dealings between trustees and their beneficiaries; on the other hand, great confusion would be introduced into the affairs of joint stock companies if the circumstances of shareholders, voting in that character at general meetings, were to be examined, and their votes practically nullified, if they also stood in some fiduciary relation to the company.

It is clear upon the authorities that the contract entered into by the directors on the 10th of February could not have been enforced against the company at the instance of the defendant J.H. Beatty, but it is equally clear that it was within the competency of the shareholders at the meeting of the 16th to adopt or reject it. In form and in terms they adopted it by a majority of votes, and the vote of the majority must prevail, unless the adoption was brought about by unfair or improper means.

The only unfairness or impropriety which, consistently with the admitted and established facts, could be suggested, arises out of the fact that the defendant J.H. Beatty possessed a voting power as a shareholder which enabled him, and those who thought with him, to adopt the by-law, and thereby either to ratify and adopt a voidable contract, into which he, as a director, and his co-directors had entered, or to make a similar contract, which latter seems to have been what was intended to be done by the resolution passed on the 7th of February.

It may be quite right that, in such a case, the opposing minority should be able, in a suit like this, to challenge the transaction, and to shew that it is an improper one, and to be freed from the objection that a suit with such an object can only be maintained by the company itself.

But the constitution of the company enabled the defendant J.H. Beatty to acquire his voting power; there was no limit upon the number of shares which a shareholder might hold, and for every share so held he was entitled to a vote; the charter itself recognized the defendant as a holder of 200 shares, one-third of the aggregate number; he had a perfect right to acquire further shares, and to exercise his voting power in such a manner as to secure the election of directors whose views upon policy agreed with his own, and to support those views at any shareholders' meeting; the acquisition of the *United Empire* was a pure question of policy, as to which it might be expected that there would be differences of opinion, and upon which the voice of the majority ought to prevail; to reject the votes of the defendant upon the question of the adoption of the by-law would be to give effect to the views of the minority and to disregard those of the majority.

The judges of the Supreme Court appear to have regarded the exercise by the defendant J.H. Beatty of his voting power as of so oppressive a character as to invalidate the adoption of the by-law; their Lordships are unable to adopt this view; in their opinion the defendant was acting within his rights in voting as he did, though they agree with the Chief Justice in the views expressed by him in the Court of Appeal, that the matter might have been conducted in a manner less likely to give rise to objection.

Notes and Questions

1   You will note that, in the words of the Privy Council, the Supreme Court of Canada held that "if the acts or transactions of an interested director were to be confirmed by the shareholders, it should be by an exercise of the impartial, independent, and intelligent judgment of disinterested shareholders and not by the votes of the interested director." This type of voting approval is now typically referred to as a "majority of the minority" approval. It reflects the rather sensible principle that people ought not to deflect legal liability by ratifying their own wrongs. Nonetheless, the Privy Council rejected the

majority of the minority ratification requirement on the ground that "great confusion would be introduced into the affairs of joint stock companies if the circumstances of shareholders, voting in that character at general meetings, were to be examined, and their votes practically nullified, if they also stood in some fiduciary relation to the company." In fact, there are now a variety of majority of the minority approval requirements built into various corporate and securities law statutes in order to restrain the possible excesses of those who are both fiduciaries and controlling shareholders (we discuss some of these *infra*). This may have marginally increased the cost of securing shareholder approval for certain corporate actions, but it has not resulted in the "great confusion" that the Privy Council anticipated.

2   As illustrated by *North-West Transportation*, the only limit to the common law principle of ratification was that the ratification was "such affirmance or adoption is not brought about by unfair or improper means, and is not illegal or fraudulent or oppressive towards those shareholders who oppose it." This, in fact, is commonly recognized as the "fraud on the minority" exception to the rule in *Foss v. Harbottle* (*supra*). Following *Foss*, the courts realized that perhaps they had erred on the side of excessive deference to majority rule. That rule allowed directors or officers who were also majority shareholders (individually or collectively) to steal assets from the corporation, and suffer no private law consequences, by the simply calling a shareholder meeting and passing a resolution approving their own conduct. The "fraud on the minority" exception to the rule in *Foss* was meant to address this danger. If a court found that the corporate conduct in question fell within the exception, the transaction was said to be *void ab initio* (and not merely voidable). Since you can't ratify a legal nullity, ratification — by any majority or super-majority ceased to have any legal effect.

Unfortunately, as the excerpts from the Beck articles (*infra*, Chapter 10) make clear, the "fraud on the minority" exception was not given a lot of scope. It was essentially limited to those situations in which fiduciaries appropriated corporate assets (including the taking of corporate opportunities). Minority shareholders thus continued to be exposed to the danger that corporate fiduciaries could escape liability for their wrongs by ratifying their own conduct. It was for this reason, as discussed in the next section, that the Dickerson Committee (the drafters of the CBCA) recommended that the statute include provisions that blunted the force of the common law rule.

(c) Ratification Provision in Corporate and Securities Law

In 1971, at the behest of the federal government, the Dickerson Committee, undertook a comprehensive review of the federal corporate law and produced a draft statute for Parliamentary review (Robert W.V. Dickerson, John L. Howard, Leon Getz, *Proposals for a New Business Corporations Law for Canada*, 1971). This draft statute forms the basis for the current CBCA and almost every other corporate law statute in Canada. The committee drafted two sections in this regard, which (without material alteration) became what are now s. 122(3) and s. 242(1) of the CBCA, The first of these provides:

> 122 (3) Subject to subsection 146(5), no provision in a contract, the articles, the by-laws or a resolution relieves a director or officer from the duty to act in accordance with this Act or the regulations or relieves them from liability for a breach thereof.

The second provides:

> 242 (1) An application made or an action brought or intervened in under this Part shall not be stayed or dismissed by reason only that it is shown that an alleged breach of a right or duty owed to the corporation or its subsidiary has been or may be approved by the shareholders of such body corporate, but evidence of approval by the shareholders may be taken into account by the court in making an order under section 214, 240 or 241.

You'll notice that s. 122(3) applies to all provisions in the Act, and therefore covers both derivative actions and oppression applications. By its terms, s. 242(1) also applies to both. This creates a bit of a contradiction, insofar as s. 122(3) simply says that a ratification does not have the effect of relieving a director or officer from the duty to comply with the Act, while s. 242(1) states that the court may take evidence of such approval into account. But in any case, the Dickerson Committee hoped that the courts would employ s. 242(1) to fashion a common law "majority of the minority" voting principle. The committee stated (in para. 487):

> Rather than set out a specific rule declaring how an act of the directors may be ratified, we think it better to characterize share-holder ratification or waiver as an evidentiary issue, which in effect compels the court to go behind the constitutional structure of the corporation and examine the real issues. If, for example, the alleged misconduct was ratified by majority shareholders who were also the directors whose conduct is attacked, evidence of shareholder ratification would carry little or no weight. If, however, the alleged misconduct was ratified by a majority of disinterested shareholders after full disclosure of the facts, that evidence would carry much more weight indicating that the majority of disinterested share-

holders condoned the act or dismissed it as a mere error of business judgment.

The courts have not been perhaps as vigorous in developing a common law "majority of the minority" standard as the committee would have liked. While there are examples of courts employing such a standard, it cannot be claimed that it has become common.

Note that there is another shareholder ratification provision in the CBCA: s. 120(7.1). That section provides that, even if a director or officer fails to comply with the procedural code in s. 120 relating to interested transactions, the shareholders may affirm the transaction *by a special resolution* and hold the director or officer not liable. In addition to shareholder ratification, however, the fiduciary must have been acting honestly and in good faith (why not also "with a view to the best interests of the corporation" as in s. 122(1)(a)?), and the court must be satisfied that the transaction was "reasonable and fair to the corporation". The Dickerson Committee stated:

> Particularly noteworthy is the overriding criterion that the contract be "reasonable and fair to the corporation", which is necessary to preclude mutual "back-scratching" by directors who might otherwise tacitly agree to approve one another's contradicts with the corporation."

Can an interested officer or director vote on such a resolution? The Dickerson Report would only have forbidden a director from voting in respect of a *directors' resolution* (Proposals for a New Business Corporations Law for Canada, v.2, s. 9.17(4) (draft statute)). The CBCA as enacted (s. 120(5)) states that "[a] director required to make a disclosure under subsection (1) shall not vote on any resolution to approve the contract or transaction." "Any resolution" in s. 120(5) can easily be interpreted to include a *shareholder* resolution. However, that would permit an *officer* who is not a director to vote his or her shares to approve his or her own transaction. That peculiarity suggests either that "any resolution" in s. 120(5) does in fact mean any *directors'* resolution. That interpretation is given force by the fact that at least two of the exceptions to the prohibition on voting in s. 120(5) relate to situations in which *all* of the directors may simultaneously be interested. Without the exceptions in s. 120(5), there could never be a quorum of directors to approve the named types of resolutions. If that interpretation is correct, the federal statute recreates the inequities of the common law standard in allowing interested parties to sanction their own wrongs.

One case that employs a majority of the minority standard is *Wedge v. McNeill* (1981), 126 D.L.R. (3d) 596 (P.E.I. S.C.), Mr. Justice Large held that it was "contrary to law for the defendants to vote ... in the circumstances of unfair and inequitable contracts with a failure to disclose exorbitant profits" where the defendant directors had used their votes as shareholders to approve a contract with another company in which they were the majority shareholders. The Prince Edward Island Court of Appeal reversed the trial court decision (1982), 142 D.L.R. (3d) 133 (P.E.I. C.A.), on the basis that "not sufficient facts were set out for the trial judge to come to a proper conclusion". Chief Justice Nicholson did note that there could be circumstances "which would prohibit them [the directors] from voting [as shareholders]."

There are other cases in which a majority of the minority approval has been given some weight. For example, approval by a majority of the minority has sometimes been required by a court in connection with a statutory arrangement, or taken to be an *indicium* that a statutory arrangement should be approved as "reasonable and fair": *see e.g., Audax Gas & Oil Ltd., Re*, 1985 CarswellAlta 284, 42 Alta. L.R. (2d) 353 (Alta. Q.B.); *Gold Texas Resources Ltd., Re*, 1989 CarswellBC 1397, [1989] B.C.J. No. 167 (B.C. S.C. [In Chambers]). In similar fashion, it has been taken as evidence of the fairness of an amalgamation: *see e.g. Triad Oil Holdings Ltd. v. Manitoba (Provincial Secretary)*, 1967 CarswellMan 11, 59 W.W.R. 1 (Man. C.A.).

Another case flirting with a majority of the minority standard is *Universal Explorations Ltd. v. Petrol Oil & Gas Co.* (1982), 1982 CarswellAlta 211, [1983] 1 W.W.R. 542, 23 Alta. L.R. (2d) 57 (Alta. Q.B.), in which Universal Explorations purchased 65% of the shares of another company called Petrol with a view to amalgamating the two companies. Under Alberta legislation, the amalgamation required the approval of 75% of the shareholders of each amalgamating company. While the requisite majorities were secured, 69.2% of the minority shareholders of Petrol voted again the transaction. Moore A.J.C. held that "this court is of the opinion that it is significant, although not determinative, that in the case at bar a majority of the minority are opposed to the amalgamation," He refused to give his approval to the amalgamation on other grounds.

In some circumstances, both corporate law and securities law require a majority of the minority shareholder approval in order for the corporation to proceed with certain types of transactions. The archetypical case is a "going private" transaction, in which, in essence, all of the public shareholders are evicted from the company, concentrating share ownership in the hands of a small number of shareholders and transforming the company into a private company. Under the CBCA, a going private transactions may only be effected with the affirming votes or each class of shares affected, *excluding* the votes of "affiliates" (which would include a parent corporation), and "holders of shares that would, following the squeeze-out transaction, be entitled to consideration of greater value or to superior rights or privileges than those available to other holders of shares of the same class." Ontario Securities Commission Multilateral Instrument 61-101 ("Protection of Minority Security Holders in Special Transactions") also requires a majority of the minority vote for a "business combination" (which includes a going private transaction and any other transaction involving a related party that forcibly terminates the ownership of a shareholder), and any "related party transaction". The Rule states:

Part 8: Minority Approval

8.1 General

(1) If minority approval is required for a business combination or related party transaction, it shall be obtained from the holders of every class of affected securities of the issuer, in each case voting separately as a class.

(2) In determining minority approval for a business combination or related party transaction, an issuer shall exclude the votes attached to affected securities that, to the knowledge of the issuer or any interested party or their respective directors or senior officers, after reasonable inquiry, are beneficially owned or over which control or direction is exercised by

(a) the issuer,

(b) an interested party,

(c) a related party of an interested party, unless the related party meets that description solely in its capacity as a director or senior officer of one or more persons that are neither interested parties nor issuer insiders of the issuer, or

(d) a joint actor with a person referred to in paragraph (b) or (c) in respect of the transaction. The term "related party" is fairly complex, but includes (*inter alia*) a director or senior officer, a shareholder holding a "control block" (defined as "a person or company... that, whether alone or with joint actors, beneficially owns or exercises control or direction over securities of the entity sufficient to affect materially the control of the entity", and which presumes that control of "more than 20 per cent of the votes attached to all the outstanding voting securities of the entity is considered sufficient to affect materially the control of the entity); and a person or company excising control or direction over shares carrying more than 10 per cent of the voting rights of the issuer. The definition of "related party transaction" is also complex, but generally includes "a transaction between the issuer and a person or company that is a related party of the issuer at the time the transaction is agreed to".

Where one or more persons that are interested parties hold in excess of 90% of the shares of the corporation, however, the regulators will allow a minority of shareholders to be forcibly evicted from a corporation without a majority of the minority vote. See Ontario Securities

Commission MI 61-101, Part 4.6(1)(a), and see *Ford Motor Co. of Canada v. Ontario (Municipal Employees Retirement Board)*, 2006 CarswellOnt 13, 79 O.R. (3d) 81 (Ont. C.A.), additional reasons at 2006 CarswellOnt 1526 (Ont. C.A.), leave to appeal refused 2006 CarswellOnt 5134, 2006 CarswellOnt 5135 (S.C.C.).

In some cases, the Toronto Stock Exchange may require a majority of the minority vote. This is the case, for example in connection with the creation of multiple classes of voting shares. See TSX Venture Exchange, Corporate Finance Manual, Policy 3.5 (Restricted Shares), Part 5.2.

There are other situations in which the courts have held that statutory powers are not available in circumstances in which the power was enlisted by a majority shareholder in a manner that was unfair to the minority. For a (now somewhat dated) summary, see Jeffrey G. MacIntosh, "Minority Shareholder Rights in Canada and England: 1860-1987" (1989) 27 Osgoode Hall L.J. 561.

Chapter 7

Regulating the Exercise of Power by Controlling Shareholders

1. THE CONCEPT OF "CONTROL"

Controlling shareholders fall into two camps; those with "*de jure*" control and those with "*de facto*" control. Shareholders with *de jure* control hold (or have the power to vote) 50% plus 1 of the votes and are thus able to secure the passage of an ordinary resolution without the cooperation of any other shareholder. A shareholder possessing *de jure* control is also referred to as a "majority" shareholder. The concept of *de facto* control arises out of the fact that, under our corporate statutes, only those shares that are actually voted (whether in person or by proxy) count in determining whether corporate resolutions are passed. Thus, for example, under the CBCA, "ordinary resolution" means "a resolution passed by a majority of the votes cast by the shareholders who voted in respect of that resolution" (CBCA, s. 2(1)). Typically, in a public corporation, not all shareholders will vote (many consign their forms of proxy to the "circular file," i.e., the waste bin). Thus, a shareholder holding perhaps 20%, or even 10% or less, can be confident of securing the passage of an ordinary resolution. Such a shareholder possesses the power of *de facto* control, and is thus a "controlling" (although not a "majority") shareholder. Below, we use the phrase "controlling shareholder" to refer to *all* shareholders possessing *de jure* or *de facto* control.

(Note, however, that while *de facto* control is usually defined in terms of the votes necessary to secure an ordinary resolution without the cooperation of any other shareholder, it may also be defined as the power to secure a *special* resolution (two-thirds of the votes cast).)

We sometimes also speak of the power of "negative" control — that is, the power to *block* the passage of a special resolution. A shareholder (or coalition of shareholders) can possess either a *de jure* or a *de facto* power of negative control. Thus, a shareholder holding 34% of the shares possesses the *de jure* power to block a special resolution, while a shareholder holding perhaps 10% of the shares might have sufficient shares, as a practical matter, to block a special resolution (and therefore has a *de facto* power of negative control).

2. WHY SHOULD WE WORRY ABOUT THE EXERCISE OF POWER BY CONTROLLING SHAREHOLDERS?

Jeffrey G. MacIntosh, "Corporations"
Law Society of Upper Canada, Special Lectures,
1990: Fiduciary Duties, 189, at xx (footnotes omitted)

Fiduciary duties are commonly imposed in situations in which one person — who for convenience I will refer to as the "agent" — undertakes to perform a task on behalf of another, who for convenience I will refer to as the "principal." The agent upon whom fiduciary duties are imposed will typically have incentives to act at odds with her duty to further the interests of the principal. There will thus be a "conflict of interest." Moreover, through the exercise of discretionary powers ceded to her by the principal, the agent will have the ability to favour her interests over those of the principal. It is this combination of incentives and power to effect the economic welfare of another that are the impetus for the imposition of fiduciary duties.

Corporate directors and officers (who I will refer to collectively as "managers") furnish an obvious example. Directors and officers are essentially agents of the corporation's shareholders. Although their *legal* duty is formally owed to *the corporation*, the courts have often said that "the corporation" means, in effect, the body of shareholders as a whole, and indeed creditors and other fixed claimants who one might have thought of as an integral part of "the corporation" have no standing at common law to enforce the fiduciary duties of the managers. Although it may not be doctrinally accurate to think of shareholders as principals, it is an analytically helpful construct in the sense that directors and officers are charged with the task of maximizing corporate value, and the achievement of this objective will also maximize shareholder wealth. But whether we think of "the corporation" or the shareholders as the principal matters not. What is important is that fiduciary duties are imposed on corporate managers both because they have incentives to favour their own interests at the expense of those whom they serve, and because they have wide-ranging powers that can be used to achieve this end. For example, the directors set their own remuneration, and might easily be tempted to siphon off the corporation's assets by setting an extraordinary level of remuneration. Corporate officers might use the corporation's funds to buy an unneeded company jet, rather than using the money for new investments. There are innumerable other ways in which the managers might divert corporate funds to serve their own purposes, rather than those of the firm.

All of this seems rather obvious. But if this is so, then certainly the case in favour of imposing fiduciary duties on controlling shareholders must be equally obvious. They too have incentives to favour themselves at the expense of other corporate claimants — including minority shareholders. Equally importantly, majority or controlling shareholders will have the ability to accomplish this objective. The primary means for effecting such harm is through the exercise of the voting powers ceded shareholders both by the corporation's constating documents and by the governing legislation. For example, the controllers might vote to amend the articles to expropriate minority shareholders at an undervalue. Or, they might vote to transfer the corporation's assets to themselves at an undervalue. Given the wide range of matters upon which shareholders are empowered to vote, the controllers will not lack for opportunities to elevate their own interests over those of the minority.

It is clear, however, that shareholders need not always resort to exercise of their voting powers to accomplish the objective of favouring themselves at the expense of the minority. Where the controlling shareholders and the managers are the same (or substantially the same) persons, the controllers may use their managerial powers as the instrumentality for effecting a transfer of wealth from minority to majority. But even without an identity of controlling shareholders and managers, the controllers' power to appoint and dismiss directors and officers is certain to result in a management that is highly attentive to the wishes of the controller. Thus, the ability to work harm to minority interests arises whether or not controlling shareholders themselves formally participate in the management of the company.

* * *

For a further exegesis of some of the problems that can arise as between controlling and minority shareholders, see Ronald J. Daniels and Jeffrey G. MacIntosh, "Toward a Distinctive Canadian Corporate Law Regime" (1992) 29 Osgoode Hall L. J. 863; David Strangeland, Ronald J. Daniels and Randall Morck, in "In High Gear: A Case Study of the Hees-Edper Corporate Group," in Ronald J. Daniels and Randall Morck, Eds., *Corporate Decision-Making in Canada* (1995). Indeed, Daniels and MacIntosh suggest that because Canadian capital markets are heavily dominated by corporations that have a controlling shareholder (including many that are part of extended corporate empires controlled by extremely wealthy families), the question of controlling shareholder conduct is one of the central issues in the regulation of Canadian capital markets.

While, however, a good *prima facie* case exists for imposing a fiduciary duty on controlling shareholders or regulating controlling shareholder conduct by other means, there is another side to the story. While in many cases benefits will result either from impressing controlling shareholders with duties to other shareholders (or otherwise constraining their conduct), we must always weigh these benefits against the *costs* of regulation. For example, impressing controlling shareholders with a fiduciary duty may deter some transactions that are purely redistributive (i.e., that transfer wealth from minority to majority shareholders) and which are therefore wasteful from a social perspective. Moreover, creating such duties will create new costs associated with litigating disputes about the propriety of shareholder conduct. While such suits may reduce the probability of opportunistic shareholder conduct, not all suits will be meritorious. Those that are not will not only create direct costs that are a deadweight social loss, but also opportunity costs associated with tying up various shareholders and corporate personnel in the litigation process. We further examine the costs and benefits of controlling shareholders at the end of the chapter.

3.   THE STRONGLY MAJORITARIAN TEMPERAMENT OF EARLY ANGLO-CANADIAN COMMON LAW

The strongly majoritarian temperament of early English and Canadian company law is described by Jeffrey G. MacIntosh, "Minority Shareholder Rights in Canada and England: 1860–1987" (1989) 27 Osgoode Hall L.J. 561 (footnotes omitted):

> The wellspring of the principle of majoritarianism in company law is undoubtedly the 1843 holding in the case of *Foss v. Harbottle* [(1843), 2 Hare 461]. In that case it was decided that in respect of any wrong done to the company, the decision of whether or not to undertake an action was a matter for the majority of shareholders to decide. Thus, an individual shareholder could not sue in respect of a wrong done *to the corporation* if a majority of shareholders either *had* ratified the wrong, or simply *could* ratify the wrong (whether or not such ratification had actually occurred). [Note: In *Foss*, the company had purchased land from some of its directors at an inflated price, and minority shareholders sought to overturn the transaction.]
>
> The holding clearly suggests that, within the sphere in which a majority of shareholders is competent to act, the will of the majority is absolute.
>
> The holding in *Foss v. Harbottle* is not only a rule about the decision making structure of the corporation and the relative positions of majority and minority; it is also a statement of the jurisdictional limits of judicial intervention in corporate affairs. Thus, according to Lord Davey in *Burland v. Earle* [[1902] A.C. 83 (P.C.), at 93]:
>
> > it is an elementary principle of the law relating to joint stock companies that the Court will not interfere with the internal

*management of companies acting within their powers, and in fact has
no jurisdiction to do so.*

The rule can be justified on a number of grounds: the prevention of a
multiplicity of shareholder actions; the avoidance of futile litigation
(where an individual shareholder suit is derailed by subsequent
shareholder ratification); or the impropriety of judicial interference in
matters which involve business or investment judgment and which are
properly within the province of shareholders to decide. However, this
ostensibly procedural rule is clearly not without substantive effect: it
creates a significant danger (particularly where the directors are majority
or controlling shareholders) of the diversion of corporate resources by
majority shareholders without minority shareholder redress. The obvious
dangers of the rule in *Foss v. Harbottle* generated exceptions to the rule.
One of these exceptions was more or less mechanical in its application: an
individual shareholder could sue in respect of matters requiring the assent
of some special majority of shareholders. A second exception allowed a
shareholder to sue to restrain an act *ultra vires* the corporation. Two
other exceptions were anything but mechanical; a shareholder could sue
in respect of matters which constituted a "fraud on the minority" of
shareholders (where the wrongdoers were in control) or in respect of
those harms which were a wrong to the shareholder *personally*, rather
than merely *derivatively*. The exceptions to the rule are tied together by a
common thread; in none of these cases could a majority of shareholders
ratify the wrong. The exceptions to the rule are in a sense the obverse of
those matters which are in essence matters relating to the internal
management of the company. If, for example, a corporate act constituted
a fraud on the minority, it could not be said to constitute merely a matter
of internal management to be resolved according to the will of a majority
of shareholders.

As has been pointed out by a number of commentators, the
substance of what constituted a "fraud on the minority" was limited
essentially to appropriation of corporate assets or the grossest sort of
overreaching by majority shareholders. As the famous case of *Northwest
Transportation Co. v. Beatty* made clear, a mere conflict of interest was
insufficient, by itself, to call the fraud principle into action. What was
required was a truly egregious interference with clearly defined minority
shareholder rights. The courts adopted the posture that shareholders
owed no duties of a fiduciary character — either to the company, or to
fellow shareholders.

At least part of the reason for the reluctance to impose fetters on the
exercise of majority power appears to have been the result of the
nineteenth century conception of the nature of the property interest
represented by holding shares in a company. Shares are a species of
property. And, as was said by Jessel M.R. in *Pender v. Lushington* [(1877),
6 Ch. D. 70 (C.A.)]:

where men exercise their rights of property, they exercise their rights from some motive adequate or inadequate, and I have always considered the law to be that those who have the rights of property are entitled to exercise them, whatever their motives may be for such exercise.

Therefore, a shareholder might vote as he please, though he be "actuated in giving his vote by interests entirely adverse to the interests of the company as a whole."

For Lord Jessel, the vote which accompanies the share is an inseparable incident of the property entitlement; *ergo*, there must be as few fetters on its exercise as possible. This conclusion is far from inevitable; indeed, it is fundamentally tautological. The unspoken (and unsupported) premise is that once the characterisation of "property" has been established, the right must be as nearly absolute as possible. Reasoning from first principles, it is just as easy to imagine that the voting right accompanying share ownership is impressed with duties of a fiduciary character owed to fellow shareholders or to the company. Lord Jessel's essentially question-begging definition of the nature of the property interest associated with share ownership, however, no doubt had an intuitive appeal to nineteenth century jurists more used to dealing with "property" rights as *a priori* constructs than as mere instrumentalities.

This relatively unencumbered spirit of majoritarianism which had gained ascendency by the turn of the century, invaded all the cracks and recesses of company law, including jurisprudence dealing with corporate fundamental changes. So far as the minority shareholder was concerned, a sort of corporate *caveat emptor* was the rule of the day.

Few passages illustrate the position of the minority shareholder quite so graphically as this quotation from a 1928 judgment of Middleton J.A. in respect of a minority shareholder's winding-up application, holding that:

> [the plaintiff] is a minority shareholder and must endure the unpleasantness incident to that situation. If he choose to risk his money by subscribing for shares, it is part of his bargain that he will submit to the will of the majority. In the absence of fraud or transactions *ultra vires*, the majority must govern, and there should be no appeal to the Courts for redress.

North West Transportation Co Ltd v Beatty (1887), L.R. 12 App. Cas. 589 (P.C.), *supra* Chapter 6 (and which is referred to in the above excerpt) is a good illustration of just how far the courts were prepared to defer to the will of the majority.

4.   EARLY ENGLISH JUDICIAL ATTEMPTS TO CREATE A FIDUCIARY DUTY

While early company law was strongly majoritarian in flavour, there is ample evidence of a constant rearguard action on the part of a non-trivial number of judges to impress at least *majority* shareholders with a fiduciary duty. While these attempts ultimately proved abortive, the seeds of the duty that these cases *would have* planted in the common law have now become important in understanding the nature of the quasi-fiduciary duty that the courts have created under the oppression remedy.

Jeffrey G. MacIntosh,
"Minority Shareholder Rights in Canada and England: 1860–1987"
(1989) 27 Osgoode Hall L.J. 561 (footnotes omitted)

The first tentative steps towards a generalized fiduciary duty of shareholders can be seen in those cases which impressed upon shareholders a duty to exercise their voting powers in good faith. This duty of good faith, enunciated around the turn of the century, was substantially toothless for the first fifty years of its existence: nonetheless, it provided a toehold for later important developments.

The grandfather of all these cases is *Allen v. Gold Reefs of West Africa, Limited* [[1900] 1 Ch. 656 (C.A.)]. Zuccani, a shareholder, held large quantities of both partly and fully paid shares. [NOTE: At the time when *Allen* was decided, when shareholders purchased shares from the company, they were not required to pay the full price (as they are today). Only part of the price could be paid, with the balance being a debt owed to the company. In this case, it was said that the shareholder held "partly paid" shares.] The articles allowed the directors to make calls on the partly paid shares [i.e., the directors could require that shareholders holding partly paid shares pay off some or all of their debt to the company], and also furnished the company with a lien in respect of unpaid calls, extending to the partly paid, but not the fully paid shares. When Zuccani died, he left a large sum owing in respect of unpaid calls on his partly paid shares. When it appeared that the assets of the estate would be insufficient to pay all claimants, the shareholders passed a special resolution amending the articles so that the fully paid shares, in addition to the partly paid shares, were subject to the lien. As Zuccani was the only holder of fully paid shares, there can be little doubt that the action of the company was aimed at the shares held by Zuccani's estate; indeed, counsel for the company admitted as much. Zuccani's estate argued that the alteration was oppressive, in bad faith and amounted to a retrospective alteration of the articles of the company.

In a holding which echoes decisions canvassed earlier as to the defeasible nature of shareholders' rights, Lindley M.R. noted that the statute appeared to allow for any type of variation of the articles, and held that "[t]he power thus conferred on companies to alter the regulations contained in their articles is limited only by the provisions contained in the statute and the conditions contained in the company's memorandum of association". The "contractual" rights of shareholders bestowed by the articles were said to be "limited as to their duration by the duration of the articles which confer them". Nevertheless, Lindley M.R. also held that:

> Wide, however, as the language of s. 50 is, the power conferred by it must, like all other powers, be exercised subject to those general principles of law and equity which are applicable to all powers conferred on majorities and enabling them to bind minorities. It must be exercised, not only in the manner required by law, but also *bona fide for the benefit of the company as a whole*, and it must not be exceeded. [Emphasis added.]

The Court of Appeal was, however, not persuaded that the modification had been undertaken in bad faith: the amendment was allowed to stand.

The outcome by itself might be enough to persuade an observer of average perception that the good faith principle did not, at its inception, have very sharp teeth.

Note carefully how closely the *Allen* duty parallels the fiduciary duty owed by directors and officers. In the CBCA, s. 122 states:

> 122. (1) Every director and officer of a corporation in exercising their powers and discharging their duties shall
>   (a) act honestly and in good faith with a view to the best interests of the corporation . . .

In *Allen*, the court would have impressed shareholders with the duty to act "*bona fide for the benefit of the company as a whole*".

Nonetheless, MacIntosh indicates two ways in which the courts substantially eviscerated this fiduciary duty. First, in *Shuttleworth v. Cox Brothers*, [1927] 2 K.B.9 (C.A.), the English Court of Appeal held that the issue of whether the shareholders had acted in good faith was to be judged, subject to strict limits, from the viewpoint of the shareholders themselves. In the words of Bankes L.J.:

> the test is whether the alteration of the articles was *in the opinion of the shareholders* for the benefit of the company. By what criterion is the Court to ascertain the opinion of the shareholders upon this question? The alteration may be so oppressive as to cast suspicion on the honesty of the persons responsible for it, or so extravagant that no reasonable men could really consider it for the benefit of the company. In such cases . . . the alteration of the company's articles shall not stand . . .

This sharply circumscribed the *Allen* principle. Second, as noted by MacIntosh:

> The *Allen* court had suggested not only that shareholders must act in good faith, but that they must act *for the benefit of the company as a whole*. In *Greenhalgh v. Arderne Cinemas (No.2)* [[1951] 1 Ch. 286 (C.A.)], Evershed M.R. said,
>
> > the phrase "the company as a whole", does not (at any rate in such a case as the present) mean the company as a commercial entity, distinct from the corporators: it means the corporators as a general body, that is to say the case may be taken of an individual hypothetical member and it may be asked whether what is proposed is in the honest opinion of those who voted in its favour, for that person's benefit.

In the view of Lord Evershed, this is the functional equivalent of a principle of non-discrimination:

> I think that the matter can, in practice, be more accurately and precisely stated by looking at the converse and by saying that a special resolution of this kind would be liable to be impeached if the effect of it were to discriminate between the majority shareholders and the minority shareholders, so as to give to the former an advantage of which the latter were deprived.

However, as MacIntosh notes, *Greenhalgh* and other decisions interpreted the meaning of "discriminate" very narrowly. As long as a change in the articles affected all shareholders in a *formally* equal manner, the resolution would not be interpreted to be discriminatory. This is illustrated by the facts of *Allen* itself; the majority clearly acted in a manner that was "discriminatory" insofar as the resolution in that case was passed only to get more money out of Zuccani's estate. It was aimed at affecting, and did in fact affect, only a single shareholder. Since most shareholder resolutions are crafted to have the same legal impact on all shareholders of a class or classes, this restrictive definition of "discrimination" severely circumscribed the good faith principle.

In addition, as noted above, in *Pender v. Lushington* Lord Jessel M.R. held that "a shareholder may vote his shares from whatever motive, though he be 'actuated in giving his vote by interests entirely adverse to the interests of the company as a whole.'" As noted by MacIntosh, this is simply inconsistent with the anti-discrimination principle in *Allen*.

To summarize, the *Allen* principle — which seems to be essentially a fiduciary duty — was substantially eviscerated by subsequent judicial developments. However, as discussed below, *Allen* is nonetheless important, as it has recently been revived under the oppression remedy. The oppression remedy thus substantially incorporates the typically statutory fiduciary standard (acting in good faith and in the best interests of the company) and, as we shall see, extends this duty to include a duty of *fairness*.

5. MORE RECENT CANADIAN JUDICIAL ATTEMPTS TO CREATE A FIDUCIARY DUTY

The courts' schizophrenic attitude toward the issue of shareholders fiduciary duties is evident in the Canadian cases. Writing in 1990, MacIntosh noted that:

> In four lower court holdings in three different provinces (one affirmed by the Ontario Court of Appeal), the principle that shareholders owe no fiduciary duty has been reaffirmed. And in *Wotherspoon v. Canadian Pacific Ltd.* [(1981), 35 O.R. (2d) 449, 129 D.L.R. (3d) 1 (C.A.)], the Ontario Court of Appeal in *obiter* has suggested that if shareholders owe any fiduciary duty, it would be owed only to the company, and not to other shareholders.

See Jeffrey G. MacIntosh, "Corporations", in *Law Society of Upper Canada, Special Lectures, 1990: Fiduciary Duties*, 189 (footnotes omitted). However, MacIntosh also noted:

> But to go no further than these cases would be a grave mistake, for the adventurous researcher can discover a solid handful of cases that insist that shareholders do owe fiduciary duties, either to the company or to other shareholders. There are no less than three lower court holdings in Ontario of this ilk. Perhaps even more astonishing, there are five (or perhaps even six) Ontario Court of Appeal judgments that support the existence of shareholder fiduciary duties.

The most commonly cited of these is *Goldex Mines Ltd. v. Revill* (1975), 7 O.R. (2d) 216, 54 D.L.R. (3d) 672 (C.A.). As summarized by MacIntosh (*ibid.*):

> In *Goldex Mines Ltd. v. Revill* the Court of Appeal again appears to have signalled the existence of shareholder fiduciary duties. A struggle for control of Probe Mines Limited led (*inter alia*) to charges that the directors of the company had violated the proxy rules governing public corporations. A key issue before the Court of Appeal was whether a violation of the proxy rules constituted a derivative action (for which leave of the court would be necessary) or a personal action. The court held that any misrepresentation or failure to make proper disclosure to shareholders would give rise to *both* a derivative and a personal action. It is in this context that the court stated that:
>
> > The principle that the majority governs in corporate affairs is fundamental to corporation law, but its corollary is also important — that the majority must act fairly and honestly. Fairness is the

touchstone of equitable justice, and when the test of fairness is not met, the equitable jurisdiction of the Court can be invoked to prevent or remedy the injustice which misrepresentation or other dishonesty has caused. The category of cases in which fiduciary duties and obligations arise is not a closed one.

The action contemplated by the Court of Appeal was a personal action. Thus, the fiduciary duty posited by the court would flow from the "majority" of shareholders to minority shareholders, rather than to the company.

6. THE CURRENT CANADIAN POSITION WITH RESPECT TO FIDUCIARY DUTIES OF SHAREHOLDERS AT COMMON LAW

Brant Investments Ltd. v. KeepRite Inc.
(1991), 3 O.R. (3d) 289, 80 D.L.R. (4th) 161 (C.A.)

[The important facts of *Brant* are fairly simple. Inter-City Gas Corporation (ICG, incorporated in Manitoba) stood atop the pyramid of companies involved in the transactions in question. ICG owned all of the shares in Inter-City Manufacturing Ltd. (ICM, also incorporated in Manitoba). In turn, ICM owned all of the shares of ICG Energy Products Ltd. (Energy Products), a federally incorporated company. ICM also owned 65% of the shares of Keeprite Inc. Thus, Keeprite, ICM, and Energy Products were all under common control. It was decided by ICG that it would be useful to integrate the operations of Keeprite, ICM and Energy Products. Thus, the board of Keeprite was approached with a view to approving a purchase of substantially all of assets of the other two companies. The board of Keeprite set up a committee of independent directors (i.e., directors who were not officers of Keeprite and not otherwise connected with Keeprite) to investigate the fairness of the transaction to Keeprite. The committee met a number of times and recommended a substantial reduction in the purchase price, from $24 million to about $20 million. This was done, and the transaction was approved by the full board and the asset purchase was completed.

Certain minority shareholders of Keeprite commenced an oppression action, arguing that the asset purchases were oppressive to the interests of the minority interests of Keeprite. This action failed at trial and was appealed to the Ontario Court of Appeal.

Note that in order to raise the money to effect the asset purchases, Keeprite made a "rights" offering (rights are securities which entitle the holder to purchase further shares in the company, at some future date) to its shareholders. Because exercise of the rights would result in the issuance of more common shares than the articles permitted, the articles of incorporation had to be amended to accommodate the rights offering.

This required shareholder approval by a special resolution, and also allowed shareholders voting against the amendment to the articles to dissent and claim the "fair value" of their shares, under what is now CBCA s. 190. The plaintiff shareholders dissented and asked the court to fix a fair value for their shares. While the following excerpts deal only with the issue of oppression, the plaintiffs are referred to below as the "dissenting shareholders".]

The judgment of the Court was delivered by McKinlay J.A.:

MCKINLAY J.A.: The learned trial judge dismissed the oppression action on the basis that the record did not establish any of the grounds on which an oppression remedy may be granted pursuant to s. 234(2), and that no prejudicial effect on or disregard of the interests of the minority had been shown. The appellants argued three grounds of appeal:

(a) the trial judge erred in concluding that there is no fiduciary duty owed by a majority shareholder to the minority, particularly in respect of a transaction in which the majority shareholder has a clear conflict of interest with the minority;

(b) the trial judge misdirected himself with respect to the onus of proof of oppression; and

(c) the trial judge erred in failing to apply an objective test of fairness in considering whether the impugned transaction consisted of or resulted in oppression of the dissenting shareholders, and in particular:

(i) he erred in concluding that some "want of probity" or bad faith of the respondents is requisite to a finding of oppression; and

(ii) he erred in suggesting that allegations of oppressive corporate conduct can be disposed of on the basis of judicial deference to the business judgment of corporate officers and directors.

The trial judge, while recognizing that the categories of fiduciary relationships are not closed and have recently been broadened, was of the view that majority shareholders owe no fiduciary duty to minority shareholders, first, because no such duty is currently recognized by Canadian authority or learned opinion and, second, because the relationship between the majority and the minority lacks any of the *indicia* which have traditionally led courts of equity to find such a duty.

The appellants cite three Ontario cases to support their position that the common law recognizes a fiduciary duty owed by a majority shareholder to the minority: *Goldex Mines Ltd. v. Revill* (1974), 7 O.R. (2d) 216, 54 D.L.R. (3d) 672 (C.A.), at pp. 223-24 O.R.; *Ontario (Ontario Securities Commission) v. McLaughlin*, Ont. H.C.J., Henry J., December 20, 1987 [summarized at 10 A.C.W.S. (3d) 270]; and *Re Canadian Tire Corp.* (1987), 35 B.L.R. 56, 10 O.S.C.B. 857 (Securities Commission), affirmed (1987), 59 O.R. (2d) 79 sub nom. *Re C.T.C. Dealer Holdings Ltd. and Ontario Securities Commission*, 23 Admin. L.R. 285, 35 B.L.R.

117, 37 D.L.R. (4th) 94, 21 O.A.C. 216 (Div. Ct.) [leave to appeal to Ont. C.A. refused (1987), 35 B.L.R. xx].

In *Goldex Mines,* the Ontario Court of Appeal dismissed an appeal from the Divisional Court which had set aside the writs in two actions because, in the opinion of the Divisional Court [*Probe Mines Ltd. v. Goldex Mines Ltd.,* [1973] 3 O.R. 869, 38 D.L.R. (3d) 513], the actions were derivative in nature and the requisite leave had not been granted prior to the issuing of the writs. The proposed actions were based on allegedly false and misleading information disseminated by the company to shareholders. In the process of dismissing the appeal, the Court of Appeal made the following comment at p. 224 [O.R.]:

> The principle that the majority governs in corporate affairs is fundamental to corporation law, but its corollary is also important — that the majority must act fairly and honestly. Fairness is the touchstone of equitable justice, and when the test of fairness is not met, the equitable jurisdiction of the Court can be invoked to prevent or remedy the injustice which misrepresentation or other dishonesty has caused. The category of cases in which fiduciary duties and obligations arise is not a closed one: *Laskin v. Bache & Co. Inc.,* [1972] 1 O.R. 465 at p. 472, 23 D.L.R. (3d) 385 at p. 392.

The Court of Appeal in that case did not hold that a fiduciary duty was owed by directors or majority shareholders to the minority shareholders, but merely commented that the category of cases in which fiduciary duties arise is not closed.

[McKinlay J.A. then noted that in *Laskin v. Bache* (referred to immediately above) the Ontario Court of Appeal held that "[s]uch a special [fiduciary] duty may arise from the circumstances and relations of the parties. These may give rise to an implied contract at law or to a fiduciary obligation in equity." She thus implied that the holding in *Goldex* stands for no more than that relatively modest proposition.]

Ontario (Ontario Securities Commission) v. McLaughlin, supra, involved motions by the defendants pursuant to rules 20.01 and 21.01 of the Rules of Civil Procedure, O. Reg. 560/84, for orders striking out statements of claim as showing no triable issue. The plaintiffs, in their statements of claim, had asserted an alternative claim for injuries they suffered as minority shareholders, through diminution of the value of their shares by reason of an alleged breach of fiduciary duty owed to them by the majority shareholders. In considering whether or not to strike this claim, Henry J. referred to the Court of Appeal decision in the *Goldex* case and also to the decision of Anderson J. in the case at bar. He concluded that there were differing views on this issue requiring legal clarification, and that the matter should be left to the trial judge. Consequently, he refused to strike the claim based on breach of fiduciary duty.

The last case cited by the appellants on this issue was *Re Canadian Tire Corp.*, *supra*, in which the Ontario Securities Commission decided to issue, pursuant to the provisions of s. 123 of the *Securities Act*, R.S.O. 1980, c. 466, a cease-trading order on a take-over bid and on the trade in common shares owned by the majority shareholders. In its reasons, the Commission stated that the vendors on the take-over bid were "in a fiduciary position in at least two categories — as directors of Tire and as Tire's controlling shareholders" (at p. 954 [O.S.C.B.], p. 110 [B.L.R.]), but did not explain to whom the fiduciary duty was owed. In its comments, the Commission purported to rely on the decision of the Ontario Court of Appeal in the *Goldex Mines* case. However, the Commission stated that its decision to impose a cease-trading order did not depend on finding a fiduciary duty, and that the Commission was not the proper forum "particularly in a s. 123 proceeding, to determine the question of whether or not there has been a breach of fiduciary duty" (at p. 955 O.S.C.B., p. 111 [B.L.R.]). What the Commission did determine in its reasons in that case was that the majority shareholders failed to act fairly and honestly and that their unfair and dishonest conduct supported facts which in themselves would have been sufficient to warrant a cease trading order under s. 123. On appeal, the Divisional Court quite properly rejected the appellant's argument that the Commission had usurped the functions of a court in finding a breach of fiduciary duty on the part of the selling shareholders, since the Commission did not so find.

It is clear that none of the foregoing authorities imposes a fiduciary duty on majority shareholders or directors in favour of minority shareholders. The case that comes closest to doing so is the *Goldex Mines* case, which was decided prior to the coming into force of the CBCA in December of 1975, and involved facts which, if they arose at the present time, would appropriately lead to an application under s. 234 of the CBCA or its counterpart, s. 247(2) of the *Ontario Business Corporations Act*, 1982, S.O. 1982, c.4 (the OBCA). The enactment of these provisions has rendered any argument for a broadening of the categories of fiduciary relationships in the corporate context unnecessary and, in my view, inappropriate.

Question

1   Did the court canvass the full range of available precedent? Are you persuaded by the court's reading of the *Goldex* case?

7. DUTIES OWED BY SHAREHOLDERS UNDER THE OPPRESSION REMEDY

While *Brant* appears to completely foreclose the issue of a shareholder fiduciary duty, the last paragraph from the above excerpt from *Brant* arguably gives back what the court purports to take away.

The court appears to suggest that if a shareholder fiduciary duty need be crafted, then this can be done under the oppression remedy. The oppression remedy allows a shareholder to bring an action where they have been treated unfairly or improperly, and will be discussed in greater detail in Chapter 10. The following section indicates that courts have, in fact, fashioned a fiduciary duty under the oppression remedy, although they have more commonly styled the duty as one of "equitable rights" or simply "fairness" (the overarching general standard under the oppression remedy). The grandfather of all these cases — the *Ebrahimi* case that follows — is arguably the most important corporate law decision in modern times. It not only holds that shareholders may owe each other equitable duties, but that such duties are grounded in shareholder *expectations* (although as subsequent holdings have made clear, these expectations must be reasonable). You will note that *Ebrahimi* is not an oppression case, but a case arising under an English statutory provision that allows a court to wind up a company if it is "just and equitable" to do so. Nonetheless, as indicated further below, the "equitable rights" and "expectations" principles from *Ebrahimi* have been imported into scores of Canadian oppression cases.

Ebrahimi v. Westbourne Galleries Ltd.
(1972), [1972] 2 All E.R. 492, [1973] A.C. 360 (H.L.)

LORD WILBERFORCE: My Lords, the issue in this appeal is whether the respondent company, Westbourne Galleries Ltd., should be wound up by the court on the petition of the appellant who is one of the three shareholders, the personal respondents being the other two. The company is a private company which carries on business as dealers in Persian and other carpets. It was formed in 1958 to take over a business founded by the second respondent (Mr. Nazar). It is a fact of cardinal importance that since about 1945 the business had been carried on by the appellant and Mr. Nazar as partners, equally sharing the management and the profits. When the company was formed, the signatories to its memorandum were the appellant and Mr. Nazar and they were appointed its first directors. Of its issued share capital, 500 shares of »1 each were issued to each subscriber and it was found by the learned judge, after the point had been contested by Mr. Nazar, that the appellant paid up his shares out of his own money. Soon after the company's formation the third respondent (Mr. George Nazar) was made a director, and each of the two original shareholders transferred to him 100 shares, so that at all material times the appellant held 400 shares, Mr. Nazar 400 and Mr. George Nazar 200. The Nazars, father and son, thus had a majority of the votes in general meeting. Until the dispute all three gentlemen remained directors. The company made good profits, all of which were distributed as directors' remuneration. No dividends have ever been paid, before or after the petition was presented.

On 12th August 1969 an ordinary resolution was passed by the company in general meeting, by the votes of Mr. Nazar and Mr. George Nazar, removing the appellant from the office of director, a resolution which was effective in law by virtue of s. 184 of the *Companies Act 1948* and art. 96 of Part I of Table A. Shortly afterwards the appellant presented his petition to the court.

This petition was based in the first place on s. 210 of the *Companies Act 1948*, the relief sought under this section being an order that Mr. Nazar and his son be ordered to purchase the appellant's shares in the company. In the alternative it sought an order for the winding-up of the company. The petition contained allegations of oppression and misconduct against Mr. Nazar which were fully explored at the hearing before Plowman J. The learned judge found that some were unfounded and others unproved and that such complaint as was made out did not amount to such a course of oppressive conduct as to justify an order under s. 210. However, he made an order for the winding-up of the company under the "just and equitable" provision. I shall later specify the grounds on which he did so. The appellant did not appeal against the rejection of his case under s. 210 and this House is not concerned with it. The company and the individual respondents appealed against the order for winding-up and this was set aside by the Court of Appeal. The appellant now seeks to have it restored.

My Lords, the petition was brought under s. 222(f) of the *Companies Act 1948*, which enables a winding-up order to be made if "the court is of opinion that it is just and equitable that the company should be wound up". This power has existed in our company law in unaltered form since the first major Act, the *Companies Act 1862*. Indeed, it antedates that statute since it existed in the *Joint Stock Companies Winding-up Act 1848*. For some 50 years, following a pronouncement by Lord Cottenham LC in 1849, the words "just and equitable" were interpreted so as only to include matters *ejusdem generis* as the preceding clauses of the section, but there is now ample authority for discarding this limitation. There are two other restrictive interpretations which I mention to reject. First, there has been a tendency to create categories or headings under which case must be brought if the clause is to apply. This is wrong. Illustrations may be used, but general words should remain general and not be reduced to the sum of particular instances. Secondly, it has been suggested, and urged on us, that (assuming the petitioner is a shareholder and not a creditor) the words must be confined to such circumstances as affect him in his capacity as shareholder. I see no warrant for this either. No doubt, in order to present a petition, he must qualify as a shareholder, but I see no reason for preventing him from relying on any circumstances of justice or equity which affect him in his relations with the company, or, in a case such as the present, with the other shareholders.

One other signpost is significant. The same words "just and equitable" appear in the *Partnership Act 1892*, s. 25, as a ground for dissolution of a partnership and no doubt the considerations which they reflect formed part of the common law of partnership before its codification. The importance of this is to provide a bridge between cases under s. 222(f) of the *Companies Act 1948* and the principles of equity developed in relation to partnerships.

The winding-up order was made following a doctrine which has developed in the courts since the beginning of this century. As presented by the appellant, and in substance accepted by the learned judge, this was that in a case such as this, the members of the company are in substance partners, or quasi-partners, and that a winding-up may be ordered if such facts are shown as could justify a dissolution of partnership between them. The common use of the words "just and equitable" in the company and partnership law supports this approach. Your Lordships were invited by the respondents' counsel to restate the principle on which this provision ought to be used; it has not previously been considered by this House. The main line of his submission was to suggest that too great a use of the partnership analogy had been made; that a limited company, however small, essentially differs from a partnership; that in the case of a company, the rights of its members are governed by the articles of association which have contractual force; that the court has no power or at least ought not to dispense parties from observing their contracts; that, in particular, when one member has been excluded from the directorate or management, under powers expressly conferred by the *Companies Act 1948* and the articles, an order for winding-up whether on the partnership analogy or under the just and equitable provision, should not be made. Alternatively, it was argued that before the making of such an order could be considered the petitioner must show and prove that the exclusion was not made *bona fide* in the interests of the company.

My Lords, I must first make some examination of the authorities in order to see how far they support the respondents' propositions and, if they do not, how far they rest on a principle of which this House should disapprove. I will say at once that, over a period of some 60 years, they show a considerable degree of consistency, and that such criticism as may be made relates rather to the application of accepted principle to the facts than to the statements of principles themselves . . .

[Lord Wilberforce then reviewed several authorities, and continued:]

My Lords, in my opinion these authorities represent a sound and rational development of the law which should be endorsed. The foundation of it all lies in the words "just and equitable" and, if there is any respect in which some of the cases may be open to criticism, it is that the courts may sometimes have been too timorous in giving them full force. The words are a recognition of the fact that a limited company is more than a mere judicial entity, with a personality in law of its own: that there is room in company law for recognition of the fact that behind it, or amongst it, there are individuals, with rights, expectations and obligations inter se which are not necessarily submerged in the company structure. That structure is defined by the *Companies Act 1948* and by the articles of association by which shareholders agree to be bound. In most companies and in most contexts, this definition is sufficient and exhaustive, equally so whether the company is large or small. The "just and equitable" provision does not, as the respondents suggest, entitle one party to disregard the obligation he assumes by entering a company, nor the court to dispense him from it. It does, as equity always does, enable the court to subject the exercise of legal rights to equitable considerations; considerations, that is, of a personal character arising between one individual and another, which may make it unjust, or inequitable, to insist on legal rights, or to exercise them in a particular way.

It would be impossible, and wholly undesirable, to define the circumstances in which these considerations may arise. Certainly the fact that a company is a small one, or a private company, is not enough. There are very many of these where the association is a purely commercial one, of which it can safely be said that the basis of association is adequately and exhaustively laid down in the articles. The superimposition of equitable considerations requires something more, which typically may include one, or probably more, of the following elements: (i) an association formed or continued on the basis of a personal relationship, involving mutual confidence — this element will often be found where a pre-existing partnership has been converted into a limited company; (ii) an agreement, or understanding, that all, or some (for there may be "sleeping" members), of the shareholders shall participate in the conduct of the business; (iii) restriction on the transfer of the members' interest in the company — so that if confidence is lost, or one member is removed from management, he cannot take out his stake and go elsewhere.

It is these, and analogous, factors which may bring into play the just and equitable clause, and they do so directly, through the force of the words themselves. To refer, as so many of the cases do, to "quasi-partnerships" or "'in substance partnerships" may be convenient but may also be confusing. It may be convenient because it is the law of partnership which has developed the conceptions of probity, good faith and mutual confidence, and the remedies where these are absent, which become relevant once such factors as I have mentioned are found to exist: the words "just and equitable" sum these up in the law of partnership itself. An in many, but not necessarily all, cases there has been a pre-existing partnership the obligations of which it is reasonable to suppose continue to underlie the new company structure. But the expressions may be confusing if they obscure, or deny, the fact that the parties (possibly former partners) are now co-members in a company, who have accepted, in law, new obligations. A company, however small, however domestic, is a company not a partnership or even a quasi-partnership and it is through the just and equitable clause that obligations, common to partnership relations, may come in.

My Lords, this is an expulsion case, and I must briefly justify the application in such cases of the just and equitable clause. The question is, as always, whether it is equitable to allow one (or two) to make use of his legal rights to the prejudice of his associate(s). The law of companies recognizes the right, in many ways, to remove a director from the board. Section 184 of the *Companies Act 1948* confers this right on the company in general meeting whatever the articles may say. Some articles may prescribe other methods, for example a governing director may have the power to remove (*cf. Re Wondoflex Textiles Pty Ltd.*). And quite apart from removal powers, there are normally provisions for retirement of directors by rotation so that their re-election can be opposed and defeated by a majority, or even by a casting vote. In all these ways a particular director-member may find himself no longer a director, through removal, or non-re-election: this situation he must normally accept, unless he undertakes the burden of proving fraud or *mala fides*. The just and equitable provision nevertheless comes to his assistance if he can point to, or prove, some special underlying obligation of his fellow member(s) in good faith, or confidence, that so long as the business continues he shall be entitled to management participation, an obligation so basic that if broken, the conclusion must be that the association must be dissolved. And the principles on which he may do so are those worked out by the courts in partnership cases where there has been exclusion from management (see *Const v. Harris*) even where under the partnership agreement there is a power of expulsion (see *Blisset v. Daniel* and *Lindley on Partnership*).

I come to the facts of this case. It is apparent enough that a potential basis for a winding-up order under the just and equitable clause existed. The appellant after a long association in partnership, during which he had an equal share in the management, joined in the formation of the company. The inference must be indisputable that he, and Mr. Nazar, did so on the basis that the character of the association would, as a matter of personal relation and in good faith, remain the same. He was removed from his directorship under a power valid in law. Did he establish, a case which, if he had remained in a partnership with a term providing for expulsion, would have justified an order for dissolution? This was the essential question for the judge. Plowman J. dealt with the issue in a brief paragraph in which he said:

> while no doubt the petitioner was lawfully removed, in the sense that he ceased in law to be a director, it does not follow that in removing him the respondents did not do him a wrong. In my judgment, they did do him a wrong, in the sense that it was an abuse of power and a breach of good faith which partners owe to each other to exclude one of them from all participation in the business on which they have embarked on the basis that all should participate in its management. The main justification put forward for removing him was that he was

perpetually complaining, but the faults were not all on one side and, in my judgment, this is not sufficient justification. For these reasons, in my judgment, the petitioner therefore has made out a case for a winding-up order.

Reading this in the context of the judgment as a whole, which had dealt with the specific complaints of one side against the other, I take it as a finding that the respondents were not entitled, in justice and equity, to make use of their legal powers of expulsion and that, in accordance with the principles of such cases as *Blisset v. Daniel*, the only just and equitable course was to dissolve the association. To my mind, two factors strongly support this. First, Mr. Nazar made it perfectly clear that he did not regard the appellant as a partner; but did regard him as an employee. But there was no possible doubt as to the appellant's status throughout, so that Mr. Nazar's refusal to recognize it amounted, in effect, to a repudiation of the relationship. Secondly, the appellant, through ceasing to be a director, lost his right to share in the profits through directors' remuneration, retaining only the chance of receiving dividends as a minority shareholder. True that an assurance was given in evidence that the previous practice (of not paying dividends) would not be continued, but the fact remains that the appellant was henceforth at the mercy of the Messrs. Nazar as to what he should receive out of the profits and when. He was, moreover, unable to dispose of his interest without the consent of the Nazars. All these matters lead only to the conclusion that the right course was to dissolve the association by winding-up.

I must deal with one final point which was much relied on by the Court of Appeal. It was said that the removal was, according to the evidence of Mr. Nazar, *bona fide* in the interests of the company, that the appellant had not shown the contrary, that he ought to do so or to demonstrate that no reasonable man could think that his removal was in the company's interest. This formula, "*bona fide* in the interests of the company" is one that is relevant in certain contexts of company law and I do not doubt that in many cases decisions have to be left to majorities or directors to take which the courts must assume had this basis. It may, on the other hand, become little more than an alibi for a refusal to consider the merits of the case, and in a situation such as this it seems to have little meaning other than "in the interests of the majority". Mr. Nazar may well have persuaded himself, quite genuinely, that the company would be better off without the appellant but the appellant disputed this, or thought the same with reference to Mr. Nazar, what prevails is simply the majority view. To confine the application of the just and equitable clause to proved cases of mala fides would be to negative the generality of the words. It is because I do not accept this that I feel myself obliged to differ from the Court of Appeal.

I would allow the appeal and restore the judgment of Plowman J. I propose that the individual respondents pay the appellant's costs here and in the Court of Appeal.

Appeal allowed.

Notes

1   The "just and equitable" ground for winding up is a common statutory provision that appears, for example, in the CBCA (s. 214(1)(b)(ii)). As noted by Lord Wilberforce, the courts have fashioned a number of doctrinal categories that justify a "just and equitable winding up": "loss of substratum", "justifiable lack of confidence", "deadlock" and "the partnership analogy". In *Ebrahimi*, Lord Wilberforce granted the winding up on the basis of the partnership analogy.

2   You will note that while Lord Wilberforce recognizes that in small or private corporations "equitable considerations" may arise that alter the strict legal bargain of the parties, he is careful to confine this to the context of a just and equitable winding up. Canadian courts have simply ignored this limitation and have transposed the expectations principle holus bolus to the oppression remedy, although mostly with respect to *private* rather than *public* companies.

3   Lord Wilberforce also suggested that to invoke the expectations principle, "the superimposition of equitable considerations" will typically require that the association be formed or continued on the basis of a personal relationship involving mutual confidence, an agreement that some or all of the shareholders participate in the conduct of the business, and restrictions on the transferability of the shares. While Canadian courts will typically take these and similar factors into account in deciding whether there has been oppression in the case of a private company, they are not regarded as essential *indicia* of oppression.

4   The following case indicates the extent to which early judicial attempts to create a fiduciary duty for shareholders have been revived under the oppression remedy.

Ferguson v. Imax Systems Corp.
(1983), 150 D.L.R. (3d) 718 (Ont. C.A.)

BROOKE J.A.: The appellant seeks relief under s. 234 of the *Canada Business Corporations Act*, 1974-75-76 (Can.), c. 33. She alleges that Imax Corporation (the company), in attempting by a special resolution to amend its articles to reorganize its capital, is acting in a manner that is oppressive, unfairly prejudicial, or that unfairly disregards her interests as a security holder. She alleges that the powers of the directors of the company have been exercised in a similar fashion with the same results.

As a result the appellant sought an injunction to restrain the company from holding a special meeting to vote on the resolution, or failing that, other similar relief. She contends that the effect of the resolution would be the redemption of her class B non-redeemable shares and that the resolution was designed to, and would, in fact, put her out of the company because she was the only holder of class B shares without any other share interest through which she could participate in the company's growth which now seems certain.

Hollingworth J. dismissed her application: see 12 B.L.R. 209. He reviewed the evidence, made few findings of fact, and dismissed the application holding that a case of oppression had not been made out. However, pursuant to s. 184(4) of the Act he appointed an appraiser to assist the court in fixing fair value for the class B shares. Both parties appealed. The company appealed to the Divisional Court from the order appointing the appraiser and the appellant cross-appealed from the order dismissing her application for injunction.

The facts are as follows. The company was incorporated in 1967 to exploit a patented film projection system. On the evidence, the promoters of the company were Ivan Graeme Ferguson, R. Kerr, R. Kroiter, and Betty June Ferguson, the appellant, who was the wife of Ivan Graeme Ferguson. The first shareholders were three couples, Mr. and Mrs. Ferguson, Mr. and Mrs. Kroiter, and Mr. and Mrs. Kerr. Mrs. Kroiter was Mr. Ferguson's sister and Mr. Kerr had been Mr. Ferguson's friend from school days.

Shares were issued and allotted equally among the three couples so that each family's holdings were the same. Each husband received 700 shares of the common stock of the company and each wife received 700 shares of the class B stock of the company. The shares of the class B stock were nonredeemable and entitled the holder to receive in priority to the common shares a non-cumulative cash dividend at the rate of 5¢ per share per year and thereafter the class B shares participated equally as to dividends with the common shares and in the event of liquidation, dissolution or winding-up. However, the class B shares were non-voting unless the company failed to pay the 50 dividend for two consecutive years. The capital structure of the company also provided for class A preference shares, none of which was ever issued.

It is of some importance to the appellant that, unlike the other two wives who apparently at no time did any work for the company, she worked hard in the company's interest and was one of its founders together with the three men. It is really not disputed that in the early days of the company the three men were each employed in other endeavors and could not devote their full time to the company.

The appellant was a film editor and had knowledge of the film business. Her evidence is that she took part with the three men in the decision to buy the patent and after the company was incorporated, participated in its management and administration. During those years, unlike the other two wives, the appellant participated in the day-to-day administration of the business. Indeed, she assumed full responsibility for an office that the company operated in New York City from the date of the company's incorporation until that office was closed in 1970. To a large extent she was not compensated for her work and efforts but carried on to help the company in which she had an ownership-interest.

During those years there were apparently agreements entered into between the members of the three families. The effect of the agreements was that in the event that a wife predeceased her husband her shares would pass to him, and in the event of his death that his shares and those of his wife would be sold to the surviving male shareholders. The appellant said that she signed the agreement because her husband told her that the company was near bankruptcy and that the agreement was needed to satisfy financiers. However, the agreements also secured the control of the company within the three families.

After the office in New York was closed, some of its records were moved to the appellant's home here and thereafter she did some of the company's business from there and, at the same time, worked as a film editor on a feature film produced by the company.

About this time each of the husbands and the wives agreed to reduce their shareholding and each transferred 70 shares of his or her stock to a valued employee, Mr. William Shaw, as an incentive for him to remain with the company. During that period Mrs. Kerr transferred her shares to her husband and the company issued further shares to some small investors but significantly each investor, as in the case of each family, held an equal number of both common and class B shares. The result was that at the time material to these proceedings, the company had issued an outstanding 2,069.57 shares of both classes of stock. . . In 1972 the appellant and her husband separated. In 1974 they were divorced. At that time the company was emerging from its financial difficulties and in 1974 made a profit of some $72,000. . .

It is the appellant's contention that from the time of her separation Mr. Ferguson set out to put her out of the company, to get her shares and to see to it that she did not participate in any benefits from the growth of the company. He was unwilling to permit her to continue as a shareholder and, she contends, as the dominant person in the control group and as the company's president and a director, he put pressure on the others in the group and the directors to squeeze her out.

The fact is that shortly after Ms. Ferguson separated from her husband she was discharged by the company. It is her evidence that during negotiation of their separation agreement her husband tried to get her to sell or transfer her shares to him but she refused. She said, and it is not denied, that he took the position in negotiations that it would not be in the interests of the company to have non-working shareholders. The contention was obviously untenable having regard to the share position of each of Mrs. Kroiter and Mrs. Kerr at that time.

It was the appellant's evidence that Mr. Ferguson put heavy pressure on the company not to declare dividends and that by virtue of his close friendship with his fellow officers, directors and shareholders, Mr. Kerr, Mr. Shaw, and Mr. Kroiter, he was able to prevent the declaration of dividends and so her participation in the financial growth of the company. It is a fact that, save for the 50 per share preferred dividend on the class B shares, no dividends were declared or paid by the company down to the date that the notice of the meeting to alter the corporation's share structure was delivered although, on the evidence of its earnings and the financial statements, it seems probable that the company was in a position to pay dividends.

It was the appellant's evidence, and it was uncontested, that in 1977 she was told by Mr. Kerr, who was then a director, that the company would not declare dividends because Mr. Ferguson refused to have her share equally with him in corporate distributions. Subsequently, in 1978, she says she was told by Mr. Breukelman and Mr. Kerr that she should sell her shares as her husband would prevent a declaration of dividends so long as she remained a shareholder. On being pressed on this issue in cross-examination she said:

Q. Can you recall anything else that occurred at that conversation?
A. Yes, it was a very long conversation.
Q. What else can you recall?
A. Well, I told him, I did not want to sell my shares and I said, did I have to in order for William to get more percentage of the company. He said, no, that the company could issue more shares, which they have done. It was very long. Do you want to hear it all, the whole conversation. It went on for a very long time. I'd be happy to go through it. Anyway, he said, that the company — he wanted the company to issue dividends because there were people that did not work in the company, for instance his close friend Jim Chaplin who had invested in the company, and the company wanted to issue dividends, but they couldn't because I would share equally in the same amount of money that Graeme got. That made him very unhappy.
Mr. Manes: Made who unhappy?
The Deponent: Graeme Ferguson, unhappy that I would get equal amount of dividends that he got. Therefore, he was putting pressure on Robert and everybody not to issue dividends. That they wanted to issue dividends because people like Daymond and his close friend Jim Chaplin were not getting anything out of the company for their investments because they were not paying dividends. He said, he didn't personally care about the difference between class B and Preference Shares because he held both Class B and Common Shares and everybody else in the company also held both Class B and Common Shares. Graeme's sister held only Class B, Preferred

Shares, but her husband held the Common Shares so everybody else in that company it does not effect what happens to the Class B shares because they will get the money out of the company through the Common Shares. And he said, you know, if we don't pay dividends we can take it out in salaries or expense accounts, but that it wasn't — he felt badly about Jim Chaplin not getting any money for his investment in the company, if the company would not pay dividends and that is why they wanted me to sell my shares.

By Mrs. Block:

Q. Are you saying, that in order to sell, in order to give Shaw more shares, Kerr was proposing that you sell all of your 630 shares to Shaw?

A. He did not put it that way, no. He said, would I sell my Imax Shares and the gist of the conversation was, would I sell because Graeme would not allow the company to pay dividends. You know, he said they could issue more shares to Bill Shaw and they could, but they didn't need my shares in order to give Bill Shaw more shares. The reason they wanted me to sell out was because they wanted to be able to pay dividends and Graeme did not want any dividends being paid because I would share equally with him. He worked in the company. He felt he worked very hard in the company. I was no longer working in the company. I said, "Look Robert, when I divorced Graeme", and I had to divorce him. He brought a young woman home and committed adultery in my living room and it was damaging to my children.

Mr. Manes: I don't think we have to go through that.

The Deponent: That's why I had to divorce him and them I'm not loose, I'm forced from the company for divorcing him. Now they're saying I'm not entitled to dividends because I'm not working in the company, but you know Jim Chaplin doesn't work in the company and they want to see him get dividends. Roman Kroiter is at the film board. You know, his shares are in, what do you call it, escrow or they're being held because he works for the government, but they don't mind him getting a part of the company, it's only me that isn't. That they don't want to pay dividends to.

By Mrs. Block:

Q. In respect of the contribution of shares to Shaw, what did Kerr say to you about giving some of your shares to Shaw? Was he talking about giving all of your shares or some of your shares to Shaw?

A. He didn't say anything about giving shares to Bill Shaw.

Q. I mean selling.

A. He said, would I sell my Imax shares, that they wanted to issue Bill Shaw some more shares in the company and I said, "Well do I have to sell my shares in order for Bill to get more shares in the company", and he said, no that the company could issue more shares, and they have as far as I understand it. You can look that up, it's right in there that they issued him more shares.

Q. So you say that you were never asked to sell part of your shares as the other shareholders were willing to do to give Bill Shaw participation?

A. I was never told that other shareholders were willing to do that. I was asked if I would sell my shares. I said, no I absolutely did not want to sell my shares. I would not.

This evidence is not denied. Having regard to the whole of the cross-examination and the affidavit material, I am satisfied that what she says is true. The company could pay dividends. Mr. Ferguson set out to stop the payment because he did not want Mrs. Ferguson to share in the benefits in the growth of the company and wanted to force her to sell her shares to him or to one of the other men in the company. It was argued that he was but one shareholder and one director and alone could not stop the company from the payment of dividends. But the fact is that he did so. Mr. Kerr, Mr. Shaw, and Mr. Kroiter were his friends and close to him and from the evidence of Mrs. Ferguson it is clear that they yielded to the pressure that he brought on them to bring about this result. In my opinion this conduct was oppressive and unfair to her.

The event leading to this litigation was the delivery of a notice of a special meeting of shareholders which the plaintiff received on November 16, 1979. The resolution proposed to be voted on at the special meeting was one that in effect would cancel and convert all of the class B non-redeemable shares into class A shares. Those shares would, until 1984, be non-voting and limited to 9% cumulated dividends. Thereafter the shares would be redeemed by the company at a designated value of $175 per share plus any unpaid cumulated dividends. That value was set as of November 9, 1979, and was based on an evaluation prepared for the company. The resolution also provided for removing the limitation on the number of shares that might be issued by the company.

In the notice of the meeting the company explained the purpose of the resolution and said in an information circular that the purpose of the change was:

> The amendment of the Corporation's articles as contemplated by the special resolution is being proposed in order to enable the Corporation to more effectively plan for future growth, through the provision of a simpler equity structure, while providing to the holders of preference shares of the Corporation a predictable and substantial cash flow — both by way of cumulative cash dividends and by way of redemption of shares — over the period through to February 29, 1984. The share provisions will also afford the holders of preference shares the opportunity to sell such shares to the Corporation at a specified price in the event of certain changes in control of the Corporation.

There was no evidence by way of affidavit or otherwise from the president or a director of the company or anyone as to why the resolution had been put before the shareholders. However, there was an affidavit by an expert in corporation management finance who said that five benefits which might flow from such a resolution were:

(a) it removes limits on the number of common shares which may be issued and the consideration for which they may be issued resulting in increased financing flexibility;

(b) it provides the Respondent with "a cleaner capital structure";

(c) it provides Class B Preference shareholders with a certain and very attractive return on their investment;

(d) it permits the orderly retirement of non-participating shares, assuring new investors that their equity participation will be equal to their voting power;

(e) the new capital structure facilitates the use of equity participation incentives as a means of attracting middle and upper management people to the Respondent.

This evidence, although giving a possible explanation for the corporate reorganization, does not give the reasons that motivated those in management and so does not refute the inference of unfairness.

A review of the finances of the company as revealed by the evidence indicates that it is profitable and should continue to be so and that it may be timely for the company to redeem some of its equity holding. Nevertheless, in my opinion, these facts do not insulate the company from dealing fairly with the appellant who is a minority shareholder.

The policy of the law to ensure just and equitable treatment of minorities can be traced back to early cases. In *Allen v. Gold Reefs of West Africa, Ltd.*, [1900] 1 Ch. 656 at p. 671, Lindley M.R., speaking of the powers of a corporation to amend its articles, said:

it must, like all other powers, be exercised subject to those general principles of law and equity which are applicable to all powers conferred on majorities and enabling them to bind minorities. It must be exercised, not only in the manner required by law, but also *bona fide* for the benefit of the company as a whole, and it must not be exceeded.

In *Goldex Mines Ltd. v. Revill et al.* (1974), 7 O.R. (2d) 216 at p. 224, 54 D.L.R. (3d) 672 at p. 680, Arnup J.A. for this court, after considering the earlier cases, said:

The principle that the majority governs in corporate affairs is fundamental to corporation law, but its corollary is also important — that the majority must act fairly and honestly. Fairness is the touchstone of equitable justice and when the test of fairness is not met, the equitable jurisdiction of the court can be invoked to prevent or remedy the injustice which misrepresentation or other dishonesty has caused.

But s. 234 must not be regarded as being simply a codification of the common law. Today one looks to the section when considering the interests of the minority shareholders and the section should be interpreted broadly to carry out its purpose: see the *Interpretation Act*, R.S.C. 1970, c. I-23, s. 11. Accordingly, when dealing with a close corporation, the court may consider the relationship between the shareholders and not simply legal rights as such. In addition, the court must consider the *bona fides* of the corporate transaction in question to determine whether the act of the corporation or directors effects a result which is oppressive or unfairly prejudicial to the minority shareholder. Counsel has referred us to a number of decisions. They establish primarily that each case turns on its own facts. What is oppressive or unfairly prejudicial in one case may not necessarily be so in the slightly different setting of another.

Here we have a small close corporation that was promoted and is still controlled by the same small related group of individuals. The appellant's part in that group and her work for the corporation is important. Further, the attempt to force her to sell her shares through non-payment of dividends was not simply the act of Mr. Ferguson, but was also the act of the others in the group including the present director, in concert with him. Having regard to the intention of that group to deny the appellant any participation in the growth of the company I think the resolution authorizing the change in the capital of the company is the culminating event in a lengthy course of oppressive and unfairly prejudicial conduct to the appellant. In my opinion the company has not acted *bona fides* in exercising its powers to amend. By the payment of moneys now as a capital payment, which moneys on the evidence ought to have been by way of dividends over the years the appellant's non-redeemable shares are now to be redeemed and those in control of the company will be rid of her. She is the only one so affected. All of the other class B shareholders hold an equal number of common shares personally or through their spouses. The appellant cannot be considered like someone who came to the company lately and took a minority position in one of several classes of stock. Like the Kroiters and the Kerrs, her investment must be regarded as being in the shares which she and her husband held. The agreements as to the disposition of family shares in the event of the death of the husband or the wife confirm that this was really a family venture not only in the case of the Fergusons but for each of the three couples.

Viewed in this way, and as all of the other class B shareholders held an equal number of common shares either personally or with their spouses, it is idle to suggest that the vote on the resolution would be anything other than a means to get moneys which they had eagerly sought by way of dividends but were denied because of the appellant's presence and as a means to end her presence as an obstacle to further payment. I doubt if any corporate purpose would enter the minds of the class B shareholders when the resolution was put to them to vote on. The resolution was a final solution to the problem of the ex-wife shareholder.

In my opinion the appellant satisfied the onus upon her when relying on s. 234 of the Act and she was entitled to the relief sought in the first instance. We have been advised that a motion to prohibit the company from proceeding with the meeting of shareholders to vote on the resolution was dismissed by Holland J. and accordingly the vote was held and its outcome was as predicted. In the circumstances the appeal is allowed. The order of Hollingworth J. dismissing the appellant's claim and appointing an assessor pursuant to s. 184(4) of the Act is set aside and an order will go forever prohibiting the company from implementing the resolution.

The appellant will have her costs in this court and in all of the proceedings below.

Appeal allowed.

Notes

1   One of the difficulties that courts have encountered under the oppression remedy has been how to fit majority or controlling shareholders into a section that deals nominally only with the conduct of "the corporation" and "the directors". *Ferguson* is illustrative of one of the ways in which courts have finessed this issue. While, strictly speaking, a shareholder resolution does not amount to *corporate* conduct, once the corporation acts upon that resolution, it converts shareholder conduct into corporate conduct — which falls squarely within the purview of the oppression remedy. This device is implicitly used in *Ferguson*. While the court consistently refers to the unfair conduct that occurred as conduct of the *company*, it is clear that the court is effectively discussing the conduct of the coalition of shareholders that comprised a controlling interest.

2   Note also that, however the court arrives at its finding of oppression, the oppression remedy specifically allows the court to make orders against a controlling shareholder. See, *e.g.*, CBCA ss. 241(3)(f), (g). In fact, the most common remedy given under the oppression remedy is an order that a controlling shareholder purchase the shares of the complaining minority. See, e.g., *Miller v. F. Mendel Holdings Ltd.* (1984), 26 B.L.R. 85 (Sask. Q.B.); *National Building Maintenance Ltd. v. Dove*, [1972] 5 W.W.R. 410 (B.C. C.A.). Since "the court may make any interim or final order it thinks fit", a judge may make other orders against controlling shareholders as well. See generally Jeffrey

G. MacIntosh, "Corporations", in *Law Society of Upper Canada, Special Lectures, 1990: Fiduciary Duties*, 189.

3   Under the oppression provision, a complainant may complain about conduct not only of the corporation, but "of any of its affiliates". Thus, *corporate* controllers that possess *de jure* control (and, hence, qualify as "affiliates") fall directly within the purview of the oppression remedy.

4   As an exercise, work through the interlocking set of definitions in the CBCA defining the term "affiliate", to see how they restrict the concept of affiliate to *de jure* controlling corporations.

5   Corporations that are not *de jure* controllers (and, hence, affiliates) can be brought within the oppression provision by any of the other means indicated in these cases and notes. However, the case that immediately follows these notes suggests yet another way in which controlling shareholder conduct can be attacked — via the conduct of interlocking directors.

6   Note also how *Ferguson* relies on both *Allen v. Gold Reefs of West Africa* and *Goldex Mines v. Revill* in holding that Betty Ferguson had been treated *unfairly*. This demonstrates the extent to which the courts have used the oppression remedy to revive doctrines that *Brant v. Keeprite* otherwise appears to have put to rest. More generally, the oppression remedy has served the function of breaking the old pro-majoritarian paradigm of shareholder relations and substituting a new, more balanced view of controller/minority relations. See generally Jeffrey G. MacIntosh, Janet Holmes, and Steve Thompson, "The Puzzle of Shareholder Fiduciary Duties" (1991) 19 Can. Bus. L.J. 86.

7   Under the oppression remedy, however, *Allen* has been revived with a twist. Recall that in *Allen*, the court imposed a duty of "good faith" on the majority shareholder. In *Ferguson*, the court found that the company had not acted in good faith and so had breached the *Allen* duty. However, the balance of authority favours the view that a showing of bad faith is not a prerequisite to demonstrating oppression. All that is required that the conduct in question *effect a result* that is unfair. See, e.g., *Brant v. Keeprite, supra*. Thus, the same result that is achieved in *Ferguson* could be reached even without a finding of bad faith conduct. However, *Ferguson* suggests that a showing of *bad faith* is almost certain to lead to a finding of oppression. See generally Jeffrey G. MacIntosh, "Bad Faith and the Oppression Remedy: Uneasy Marriage or Amicable Divorce?" (1990) 69 Can. Bar Rev. 276.

8   Note also how in *Ferguson* the court sidesteps the limitations (noted above in the excerpt from MacIntosh) that the courts had placed on the good faith principle in *Allen*. The first was that the court was to decide the issue of whether the shareholders had acted in good faith from the point of view of the shareholders themselves, unless the conduct was "so oppressive as to cast suspicion on the honesty of the persons responsible for it, or so extravagant that no reasonable men could really consider it for the benefit of the company". By contrast, it is now clear that the fairness standard under the oppression remedy is to be judged objectively, from the court's perspective (hence, the absence of a need to show bad faith). As the Ontario Court of Appeal stated in *Pente Investment Management Ltd. v. Schneider Corp.* (1998), 42 O.R. (3d) 177, 1998 CarswellOnt 4035 (C.A.), "[w]hile s. 248 protects the legitimate expectations of shareholders, those expectations must be reasonable in the circumstances and reasonableness is to be ascertained on an objective basis".

9   Note also that after *Allen*, the idea that shareholder "discriminatory" conduct could be set aside was restricted to situations in which there was some *legal* difference in the manner in which the controller and the majority were treated. However, in *Imax*, Betty Ferguson was affected in precisely the same *legal* manner as every other shareholder — even though the economic effect on her of the change in the articles was unique. The court thus effectively adopts a definition of discrimination that parallels that in the human rights cases, i.e., formally identical legal treatment may amount to illegal discrimination if it has a disparate impact on different individuals or groups.

10   *Ferguson* also imports the idea from *Ebrahimi* that (in Mr. Justice Brooks' words) "when dealing with a close [i.e., private] corporation, the court may consider the relationship between the shareholders and not simply legal rights as such". In essence, *Ferguson* fuses Lord Wilberforce's "equitable considerations" with the idea of "fairness" under the oppression remedy. This fusion is made even more explicit in the decision of the Ontario Court of Appeal in *Pente Investment Management Ltd. v. Schneider Corp.* (1998), 42 O.R. (3d) 177, 1998 CarswellOnt 4035 (C.A.). The court stated:

> Conduct which disregards the interests of any shareholder and not simply a shareholder's legal rights will infringe s. 248 of the OBCA [the oppression remedy]. This is because the oppression remedy is basically an equitable remedy and the court has jurisdiction to find an action is oppressive, unfairly prejudicial, or unfairly taken in disregard of the interests of a security holder if it is wrongful, even if it is not actually unlawful: *Fair Foods Ltd. v. Watt* (1990), 4 W.W.R. 685 (Alta. Q.B.), aff'd (1991) 4 W.W.R. 695 (Alta. C.A.), leave to appeal refused [1991] 2 S.C.R. viii.

Scottish Co-operative Wholesale Society Ltd. v. Meyer
(1958), [1959] A.C. 324, [1958] 3 All E.R. 66 (H.L.)

[Scottish Co-operative, the parent company, formed a subsidiary to enter the rayon business. In organizing the business, the parent employed Meyer, making him managing director of the subsidiary and one of its substantial stockholders in order to have the benefit of his expertise and business contacts. The parent, however, retained fifty-one percent of the shares and control of the board of directors. At the end of five years, Meyer was no longer needed for the successful operation of the business, and the parent, in an effort to force him out, established its own department to perform the subsidiary's tasks. At the same time, the parent's nominees on the subsidiary's board passively supported the parent by allowing the subsidiary's traditional activities to decline.]

LORD DENNING: My Lords, I had myself prepared a summary of the material facts in this case but, in view of the comprehensive statement by my noble and learned friend, Lord Keith of Avonholm, I will not burden your Lordships with what I had written. I would only say that I am sorry that the events of 1952 were excluded as irrelevant. Dr. Meyer and Mr. Lucas from the very beginning put those events in the forefront of their complaints. They did so in the first letter of their solicitors dated February 19, 1953, and in the original petition lodged on July 14, 1953. The burden of their complaints was that, when there was a recession in 1952 in the rayon trade, they — Dr. Meyer and Mr. Lucas — tried, on behalf of the textile company, to develop trade in other goods: particularly in the export of woollen materials to Germany (where they had valuable trade connections) and in a large export order for »60,000: but that they were thwarted in their efforts by the actions of two of the nominee directors, who tried to get the trade for the Scottish Co-operative Wholesale Society itself. Whether these complaints be true or not your Lordships cannot know — because these allegations were excluded from probation. But your Lordships have, I think, sufficient material to decide the case on the other facts which were proved.

The complaints which were established were, I think, these: The cooperative society set up a competing business. It established its own merchant converting department, engaged in the rayon trade itself, and quoted more favorable terms to its own department than it did to the textile company. It is said that the co-operative society did this with intent to injure the textile company — to depress the value of its shares so that the co-operative society could get them cheap — but I would not myself go as far as this. It seems to me that the co-operative society all the time was seeking to promote its own interests. It was ready in 1946 to enlist the co-operation of Dr. Meyer and Mr. Lucas when they were useful to it — so as to get an introduction into the rayon trade — but it was ready to throw them over when they were no longer useful. By which I mean that it was ready to withdraw all support from them. That was, I think, the state of mind of the co-operative society right from the moment in November, 1951, when Dr. Meyer and Mr. Lucas refused to realign the shares at par. At that time the rayon trade was in a recession and Dr. Meyer and Mr. Lucas were not of so much use to the society as they had been. By the time the rayon trade revived, the controls were off and the co-operative society was able to engage in rayon production itself — and it had no further need of Dr. Meyer and Mr. Lucas or of the textile company. It had its own department for rayon. So the textile company could go to the wall. It had "served its purpose" — or rather the purpose of the co-operative society — and could be let go into liquidation. The cooperative society had not the voting power to put it into voluntary liquidation. But liquidation might come about by sheer inanition. So it came about that, when Dr. Meyer and Mr. Lucas in January, 1953, offered to sell their shares to the co-operative society at a price to be negotiated (mentioning 96s.), the co-operative society refused "at the present time." The co-operative society thought, perhaps, that, if they waited, sooner or later liquidation would come about, or that terms of purchase would be arranged later more favorable to the co-operative society than paying 96s. a share.

Such being "the matters complained of" by Dr. Meyer and Mr. Lucas, it is said: "Those are all complaints about the conduct of the co-operative society. How do they touch the real issue — the manner in which the affairs of the textile company were being conducted?" The answer is, I think, by their impact on the nominee directors. It must be remembered that we are here concerned with the manner in which the affairs of the textile company were being conducted. That is, with the conduct of those in control of its affairs. They may be some of the directors themselves, or, behind them, a group of shareholders who nominate those directors or whose interests those directors serve. If those persons — the nominee directors or the shareholders behind them — conduct the affairs of the company in a manner oppressive to the other shareholders, the court can intervene to bring an end to the oppression.

What, then, is the position of the nominee directors here? Under the articles of association of the textile company the co-operative society was entitled to nominate three out of the five directors, and it did so. It nominated three of its own directors and they held office, as the articles said, "as nominees" of the co-operative society. These three were therefore at one and the same time directors of the co-operative society — being three out of 12 of that company — and also directors of the textile company — three out of five there. So long as the interests of all concerned were in harmony, there was no difficulty. The nominee directors could do their duty by both companies without embarrassment. But, so soon as the interests of the two companies were in conflict, the nominee directors were placed in an impossible position. Thus, when the realignment of shareholders was under discussion, the duty of the three directors to the textile company was to get the best possible price for any new issue of its shares (see *per* Lord Wright in *Lowry v. Consolidated African Selection Trust Ltd.*), whereas their duty to the co-operative society was to obtain the new shares at the lowest possible price — at par, if they could. Again, when the co-operative society determined to set up its own rayon department, competing with the business of the textile company, the duty of the three directors to the textile company was to do their best to promote its business and to act with complete good faith towards it; and in consequence not to disclose their knowledge of its affairs to a competitor, and not even to work for a competitor, when to do so might operate to the disadvantage of the textile company (see *Hivac Ltd. v. Park Royal Scientific Instruments Ltd.*), whereas they were under the selfsame duties to the co-operative society. It is plain that, in the circumstances, these three gentlemen could not do their duty by both companies, and they did not do so. They put their duty to the cooperative society above their duty to the textile company in this sense, at least, that they did nothing to defend the interests of the textile company against the conduct of the cooperative society. They probably thought that "as nominees" of the cooperative society their first duty was to the co-operative society. In this they were wrong. By subordinating the interests of the textile company to those of the co-operative society, they conducted the affairs of the textile company in a manner oppressive to the other shareholders.

It is said that these three directors were at most only guilty of inaction — of doing nothing to protect the textile company. But the affairs of a company can, in my opinion, be conducted oppressively by the directors doing nothing to defend its interests when they ought to do something — just as they can conduct its affairs oppressively by doing something injurious to its interests when they ought not to do it.

The question was asked: "What could these directors have done?" They could, I suggest, at least on behalf of the textile company, have protested against the conduct of the co-operative society. They could have protested against the setting up of a competing business. But then it was said: "What good would that have done?" Any protest by them would be sure to have been unavailing, seeing that they were in a minority on the board of the cooperative society. The answer is that no one knows whether it would have done any good. They never did protest. And it does not come well from their mouths to say it would have done no good, when they never put it to the test. See the decision of this House in *Morison, Pollexfen & Blair Ltd. v. Walton*, as described by Scrutton L.J. in *Coldman v. Hill.* Even if they had protested, it might have been a formal gesture, ostensibly correct, but not to be taken seriously.

Your Lordships were referred to *Bell v. Lever Brothers Ltd.*, where Lord Blanesburgh said that a director of one company was at liberty to become a director also of a rival company. That may have been so at that time. But it is at the risk now of an application under s. 210 if he subordinates the interests of the one company to those of the other.

So I would hold that the affairs of the textile company were being conducted in a manner oppressive to Dr. Meyer and Mr. Lucas. The crucial date is, I think, the date on which the petition was lodged — July 14, 1953. If Dr. Meyer and Mr. Lucas had at that time lodged a petition to wind up the company compulsorily, the petition would undoubtedly have been granted. The facts would plainly justify such an order on the ground that it was "just and equitable" that the company should be wound up: see *In re Yenidje Tobacco Co. Ltd.* But such an order would unfairly prejudice Dr. Meyer and Mr. Lucas because they would only recover the break-up value of their shares. So instead of petitioning for a winding-up order, they seek to invoke the new remedy given by s. 210 of the *Companies Act 1948.* But what is the appropriate remedy? It was said that s. 210 only applies as an alternative to winding up and that an order can only be made under s. 210 if the company is fit to be kept alive: whereas in this case the business of the company was virtually at an end when the petition was lodged, and there was no point in keeping it alive. If the co-operative society were ordered, in these circumstances, to buy the shares of Dr. Meyer and Mr. Lucas, this would amount, it was said, to an award of damages for past misconduct — which is not the remedy envisaged by s. 210.

Now, I quite agree that the words of the section do suggest that the legislature had in mind some remedy whereby the company, instead of being wound up, might continue to operate. But it would be wrong to infer therefrom that the remedy under section 210 is limited to cases where the company is still in active business. The object of the remedy is to bring "to an end the matters complained of", that is, the oppression, and this can be done even though the business of the company has been brought to a standstill. If a remedy is available when the oppression is so moderate that it only inflicts wounds on the company, whilst leaving it active, so also it should be available when the oppression is so great as to put the company out of action altogether. Even though the oppressor by his oppression brings down the whole edifice — destroying the value of his own shares with those of everyone else — the injured shareholders have, I think, a remedy under s. 210.

One of the most useful orders mentioned in the section — which will enable the court to do justice to the injured shareholders — is to order the oppressor to buy their shares at a fair price: and a fair price would be, I think, the value which the shares would have had at the date of the petition, if there had been no oppression. Once the oppressor has bought the shares, the company can survive. It can continue to operate. That is a matter for him. It is, no doubt, true that an order of this kind gives to the oppressed shareholders what is in effect money compensation for the injury done to them: but I see no objection to this. The section gives a large discretion to the court and it is well exercised in making an oppressor make compensation to those who have suffered at his hands.

True it is that in this, as in other respects, your Lordships are giving a liberal interpretation to s. 210. But it is a new section designed to suppress an acknowledged mischief. When it comes before this House for the first time it is, I believe, in accordance with long precedent — and particularly with the resolution of all the judges in *Heydon's* case — that your Lordships should give such construction as shall advance the remedy. And that is what your Lordships do today.

I would dismiss the appeal.

Appeal dismissed.

Notes and Questions

1   In his judgment, Viscount Simmonds would appear to be willing to go even farther than Lord Denning in applying the oppression remedy to the conduct of shareholders. He said that:

> it is not possible to separate the transactions of the society [the majority shareholder] from those of the company. Every step taken by the latter was determined by the former ... [I]t appears to me incontrovertible that the society behaved to the minority shareholders of the company in a manner which can justly be described as "oppressive". They had the majority power and they exercised their authority in a manner "burdensome, harsh and wrongful"— I take the dictionary meaning of the word.

See also *Re H.R. Harmer Ltd.*, [1959] 1 W.L.R. 62 (C.A.). The English Court of Appeal has also applied the oppression remedy quite explicitly to the conduct of shareholders, as evidenced by the following passage from *Re Jermyn Street Turkish Baths Ltd.*, [1971] 3 All E.R. 184 (C.A.). Buckley L.J. held that:

> In our judgment, oppression occurs when shareholders having a dominant power in a company, either (1) exercise that power to procure something that is done or not done in the conduct of the company's affairs or (2) procure by an express or implicit threat of an exercise of that power that something is not done in the conduct of the company's affairs...

Thus, it may be quite unnecessary to use the device employed by Lord Denning (the interlocking dictatorships) to bring shareholder conduct within the oppression remedy.

8. THE DUTY OF A CONTROLLING SHAREHOLDER WHEN TENDERING A TAKEOVER BID

Pente Investment Management Ltd. v. Schneider Corp.
(1998), 40 B.L.R. (2d) 244, 1998 CarswellOnt 2156 (Gen. Div.
[Commercial List]), affirmed (1998), 42 O.R. (3d) 177, 1998 CarswellOnt
4035 (C.A.)

[In *Maple Leaf*, Maple Leaf Foods wished to acquire a controlling interest in Schneider Corp. However, Schneider Corp. had been set up with two classes of shares — the common shares, which were voting, and the Class A shares, which were essentially identical to the common shares except that they did not vote. The Schneider family held 70.5% of the common shares and therefore controlled the company (even though they held only 7.6% of the total equity of the company when the Class A shares were factored in). The Schneider family thus effectively held a veto over any takeover bid for Schneider Corp. The articles of Schneider Corp., however, contained a "coattail" provision that allowed the Class A shareholders to convert their shares into common shares on the occurrence of an "exclusionary offer" for the common shares (i.e., an offer to the common shareholders alone). However, the articles also allowed shareholders holding 50% or more the common shares to file a "non-conversion" certificate, indicating that they would refuse to tender their shares into a takeover bid. If such a certificate was filed, then even if there was an "exclusionary offer" for the common shares, the Class A shareholders could not convert their shares into common shares. This certificate could be filed as a "standing certificate" that applied to *any* takeover bid that might occur, and the family duly filed a standing certificate. This effectively gave them a veto over any takeover bid that occurred. Despite this, Maple Leaf Foods made simultaneous takeover bids for *both* the common shares and the Class A shares, taking the view that they had made an exclusionary offer for the common shares, because their bid for the Class A shares contained slightly different conditions than the bid for the common shares. If the offer was indeed "exclusionary", it would trigger the coattail, and by triggering the coattail, Maple Leaf hoped to acquire a controlling interest in Schneider Corp. via their holdings of Class A shares, which, pursuant to the exclusionary offer, they thought would all be converted into voting common shares, diluting the family's control position. The Maple Leaf bid prompted Schneider Corp. to look for other offers, and two were forthcoming — from Booth Creek and Smithfield. The family ultimately decided that it only would tender its shares into the Smithfield bid. Why did the family favour the Smithfield bid? According to Farley J.:]

FARLEY J.: In particular, the Schneider Family advised the Board of Directors that it had reviewed the various proposals in terms of three factors: financial value, continuity of the Corporation in a manner consistent with the Schneider family's desires, and the effect of any transaction on the Corporation's various stakeholders, including shareholders, employees, suppliers and customers . . .

At the Board meeting which commenced approximately one hour later, Fontana, as the spokesperson for the Family, read the following statement, apparently verbatim:

The family has supported the effective process that the Board and the Special Committee have pursued in response to the original MLF bid that came unexpectedly six weeks ago. We believe that not it would be important to that process for the family to state its opinion at this time.

We also think that it is important to reiterate that we as a family did not seek to sell this company but that through the process of the last 6 weeks we have come to the conclusion that now is the time to sell the control of the company.

During the last six weeks we have recognized the following points.

1. The 108 year history of this company results in a strong feeling with this family. It always has been and we hope that it can continue in the future.

2. We recognize that the meat packing industry has been evolving into larger players that can withstand the financial vagaries of commodity markets and that have the financial resources to invest in the business.

3. For a Canadian company to takeover our company we believe that there would have to be significant rationalization of our company and that J.M. Schneider Inc. would essentially disappear and that the Schneider brands may be eroded over the long term.

4. We would like to see Schneiders grow and take advantage of the opportunities that we believe are available to the pork industry and that J.M. Schneiders tried to take advantage of on their own in their business plans.

5. We would like to see a healthy pork industry evolve with several large players in Canada. This would be good for the many stakeholders of the Canadian pork industry.

These general issues are important to the family but all offers must be considered from a financial perspective as well.

There are essentially three offers on the table:

The $22 MLF offer has been rejected by the Family but we recognize that why (it) will top any bid [sic].

The Gillett deal at $25.50 is a straight cash offer. We believe that this deal could satisfy many of the other issues that we have raised but for the family there are tax considerations that make this offer less attractive than the other offers. In addition the conditions of the offer are such that it amounts to option [*sic*] to decide later rather than commit now to the company and the pork industry. Only the family is required to commit now. These conditions are on the extreme end in favour of the buyer rather than the seller.

The last offer is from Smithfield. It offers the family the ability to take all shares therefore allowing us to continue to participate in the growth of the pork industry. It also allows the family to take advantage of tax considerations. These conditions are available in the MLF offer but we, as a family, believe that the following points support the Smithfield offer:

1. The opportunity for share growth and value enhancement is greater with the Smithfield share.

2. For family shareholders wanting to diversity [*sic*] in the future, the liquidity of this stock is attractive.

3. Smithfield/JMS company will be a dominant North American player that is growing in international markets.

4. The family will have a representative in the Smithfield board.

5. There is greater opportunity in the Smithfield offer for the Schneider brands and the company to grow.

6. We know that Smithfield has been active in the past purchasing other companies. We understand that after these purchases, they have allowed the companies to continue to operate and grow relatively independently.

In conclusion, the family has unanimously agreed that we will support the Smithfield bid. (Emphasis added.)

[The case raises three issues of interest for the purposes of this chapter; 1. did the Schneider family, as shareholders, owe the company or the other shareholders a fiduciary duty in deciding to whom to tender, or could they act solely out of selfish self-interest? 2. can shareholders consider the best interests of constituencies other than shareholders in deciding how to tender? 3. does the existence of a controlling shareholder change the role of the board of directors?

Farley J. addressed the first of these issues as follows:]

It must be appreciated that the Family as controlling shareholders did not have to sell to anyone or to any bid, no matter how lucrative that bid may be seen on any objective basis. They could say at any time "Thank you but NO!" or words to that equivalence. They could act in what they perceived as their interests (and logically even against their interests if they chose to do so). Did the Family at any time do anything — or omit to do something which they ought to have done — which would preclude them from maintaining that position — or preclude them from selling to someone else on a basis that may not be as financially attractive a deal as a third party may be offering? While this latter concept may jar against the view that persons should act in their best financial interests — that is, that one should be rational in a dollar sense — there is, to my view, no obligation to do so in these circumstances.

[In so holding, however, Farley J. appears to have drawn a distinction between a shareholder's decision about whether to tender into a takeover bid, and a shareholder's decision about how to vote. In respect of the latter, Farley J. embraces the *Allen* good faith limitation in the following passage:]

I pause to note that if one however gets into a situation where one is voting in a corporate situation and the vote effects the class within which one is voting, then Viscount Haldane in *British America Nickel Corp. v. M.J. O'Brien Ltd.*, [1927] A.C. 369 (Ontario P.C.) would appear to place a restriction on a shareholder's discretion to act in his own interests when he observed at pp. 371-3:

> They must be exercised subject to a general principle, which is applicable to all authorities conferred on majorities of classes enabling them to bind minorities; namely, that the power given must be exercised for the purpose of benefiting the class as a whole, and not merely individual members only. Subject to this, the power may be unrestricted. It may be free from the general principle in question when the power arises not in connection with a class, but only under a general title which confers the vote as a right of property attaching to a share. . .
>
> But their Lordships do not think that there is any real difficulty in combining the principle that while usually a holder of shares or debentures may vote as his interest directs, he is subject to the further principle that where his vote is conferred on him as a member of a class he must confirm to the interest of the class itself when seeking to exercise the power conferred on him in his capacity of being a member.

[The second issue noted above — may shareholders take non-shareholder interests into account when deciding how to tender — was not explicitly addressed by the court. However, by necessary implication, Farley J.'s decision suggests that this is permissible. For this and other reasons, Farley J. ultimately held in favour of the defendants and dismissed the suit.]

Note

1   In upholding Farley J.'s decision, the Court of Appeal did not comment on the above-noted aspects of Farley J.'s judgment. See *Pente Investment Management Ltd. v. Schneider Corp.* (1998), 42 O.R. (3d) 177, 1998 CarswellOnt 4035 (C.A.) (other aspects of which are explored in the following section).

9.   THE DUTY OF THE BOARD OF DIRECTORS WHEN THERE IS A CONTROLLING SHAREHOLDER

Pente Investment Management Ltd. v. Schneider Corp.
(1998), 42 O.R. (3d) 177, 1998 CarswellOnt 4035 (C.A.)

[NOTE: In view of the fact that the Schneider family refused to tender into any bid except the Smithfield bid, as discussed in the preceding judgment, the board of Schneider Corp. took certain measures to favour the Smithfield bid over the other bids. In particular, Smithfield and Booth Creek had been required, as a condition for reviewing the firm's books, to enter into a "standstill" agreement whereby they agreed not to make an offer for Schneider Corp. within two years except with the written consent of the board of Schneider Corp. In order to allow the Smithfield (but not the Booth Creek) bid to proceed, the board waived the standstill agreement in favour of Smithfield. The board had also put in place a poison pill, which it also withdrew in favour of Smithfield. This allowed the Schneider family to enter into a contractual "lock-up" arrangement in which the Schneider family agreed to tender into the Smithfield bid and no other bid.]

WEILER J.A.: It must be recognized that the directors are not the agents of the shareholders. The directors have absolute power to manage the affairs of the company even if their decisions contravene the express wishes of the majority shareholder: *Teck Corporation Ltd. v. Millar et al.* (1973), 33 D.L.R. (3d) 288 (B.C. S.C.) at 307 . . .

The appellants allege that the advice given by the special committee to the Board of Schneider was not in Schneider's best interests or those of its shareholders. They submit that the special committee should have refused to waive the standstill provisions in the confidentiality agreement with Schneider, thereby preventing the agreement between the Family and Smithfield. The appellants also submit that if the Board of Schneider could not enter into a share exchange with Smithfield because of fairness concerns it could not agree to a takeover bid. These submissions are really alternative ways of saying that the transaction with Smithfield was unfair to the non-Family shareholders, that it was not in the best interests of the company.

If the Smithfield offer can reasonably be considered to be the best available offer in the circumstances, then the Smithfield offer was not unfair or contrary to the best interests of the company. This is also essentially a fact driven question on which Farley J. made the following findings:

- The Smithfield offer was solicited by Schneider. Smithfield, a reluctant suitor, had to be "coaxed" to make a bid. Smithfield imposed a "no-shop" condition on its offer to the Schneider Family and did not want to haggle.

- There was no breach of confidence in the communications between Smithfield, and the Schneider Board and the Family. The spirit of the standstill provision between Smithfield and Schneider was honoured. Confidential information was used appropriately in the best interests of the shareholders. At all times the Schneider Board remained in control of the process dealing with the Smithfield offer.

- It was reasonable for the Board to accommodate a transaction between Smithfield and the Family by waiving the standstill provision contained in the Smithfield confidentiality agreement in view of advice received that the share price of Schneider would fall back to a range of $18 to $20 per share in the absence of a change of control transaction.

- Maple Leaf could not have made an offer that would have been satisfactory to the Schneider Family at that time.

- The Board exercised their powers and discharged their duties honestly and in good faith.

- The Board pursued all available opportunities to maximize shareholder value and achieved reasonable results for all of the shareholders of Schneider.

- It was unfair to say that the special committee had the Family's interests uppermost in its mind not those of the shareholders generally, or the non-Family shareholders specifically. It was beyond the power of the special committee to insist that the Family give up its veto power and the special committee realized this.

As Farley J. emphasized, one of the particular circumstances having a bearing on a board of directors' attempts to obtain the best deal available in the circumstances is whether the company has a controlling shareholder. For example, in *Paramount*, *supra*, control of the corporation was not vested in a single person, entity, or group, but was widely held by a number of unaffiliated shareholders. In that case, the proposed sale of shares represented a premium for the change and consolidation of control of the company in a group that would have the power to materially alter the interests of the widely dispersed shareholders. In *Pente*, the control premium for the shares of Schneider belonged to the Family. By contrast, the unaffiliated shareholders do not own, and are not giving up, the power to control the company's future.

Notes

1   The Court of Appeal's judgment indicates that while the existence of a controlling shareholder does not alter the board's duty to act in the best interests of the company (i.e., *all* of the shareholders), it might well condition the options that are available to the board. On the facts, the board simply could not force the Schneider family to tender into any particular bid. It had to accept this reality, and do what was in the best interest of all of the shareholders, given this constraint. On the facts, it did so. A very similar holding is found in *Benson v. Third Canadian General Investment Trust Ltd.* (1993), 14 O.R. (3d) 493, 1993 CarswellOnt 166 (Gen. Div. [Commercial List]).

2   The board of Schneider Corp. convened a special committee of the board of directors (often simply called an "independent committee") to report to the full board on the various takeover bids. In general, the convening of a special committee, *especially one that is made up of independent directors*, is now a standard board procedure and one that is given a good deal of weight by the courts in deciding whether the directors acted appropriately. In any case in which there is a controlling shareholder, failing to appoint an independent committee to opine on major transactions will seriously raise the probability of director liability. The greater the extent to which the committee has independent directors (or, better still, "unrelated" directors — i.e., those who have no relationship to the corporation other than as directors) will significantly influence the degree of deference that the courts will accord the committee. Further excerpts from *Schneider* in Chapter 6, however, indicate that there is no absolute requirement that *all* committee members be independent. See also *CW Shareholdings Inc. v. WIC Western International Communications Ltd.* (1998), 39 O.R. (3d) 755, 1998 CarswellOnt 1891 (Gen. Div. [Commercial List]).

10.   "MAJORITY OF THE MINORITY" VOTING

Imposing fiduciary or fiduciary-like duties on controlling shareholders is not the only way to protect minority interests against the over-reaching of controlling shareholders. Another way is by "majority of the minority" voting. The term is not a term of art. However, the general idea is to condition corporate action on the approval of shareholders, *excluding* either the controlling shareholder(s), any shareholder that stands to benefit from the corporate action or both. Majority of the minority voting is explored in Chapter 6 ("Fiduciary Duties") and Chapter 8 ("Shareholders' Rights").

11.   THE ROLE OF THE SECURITIES REGULATORS

As noted earlier, the securities regulators have the power to make orders "in the public interest." Please re-read the Ontario *Securities Act* (R.S.O. 1990, c. S-5), s. 127, which is reproduced in Chapter 5 of this casebook.

Note that subsection 127(1)2, the so-called "cease trade" power, allows the Ontario Securities Commission ("OSC") the power to effectively enjoin any transaction that it finds contrary to the public interest, at least if the transaction involves "trading" (a term that is very broadly defined in the legislation to include acts in furtherance of a trade, even if there is no consummated trade). A wide variety of transactions that may involve improper conduct on the part of a controlling shareholder involve trading. These include a takeover bid, an "issuer bid" (in which the corporation makes a public offer to repurchase its own securities), an amalgamation (which involves the cancellation of existing securities and the issuance of new securities to take their place), and a "going-private" transaction, pursuant to which public shareholders are effectively evicted from the corporation, turning the corporation from a public to a private corporation. The OSC further protects minority shareholders in these sorts of transactions with procedural requirements in Multilaterial Instrument 61-101. If the transaction involves the use of an exemption under the securities legislation, ss. 127(1)3 allows the OSC to bar access to the exemption, again effectively enjoining the transaction. This can be used, for example, to prevent a controlling shareholder from adding to its shareholdings, if the shareholder's acquisition of shares will either drive its holdings above the 20% ownership threshold, or add to its holdings, if it started out with more than 20% (*vide* the overlap with ss. 127(1)2.1). The OSC might also use its power to order that a person resign one or more positions that the person holds as a director or officer of an issuer, to loosen the grip that a controlling shareholder might exercise by virtue of a directorial or management position. The discretionary powers also give the OSC the muscle to deter transactions before they ever come to fruition, simply by threatening to convene a hearing to determine whether one or more of the discretionary powers will be exercised.

The following case is an example of a transaction that was stopped not by the courts, but by the Ontario Securities Commission using its cease trade power.

Re Canadian Tire
(1987), 10 O.S.C.B. 857 (Securities Comm.), affirmed by Divisional
Court (1987), 10 O.S.C.B. 1771 (Div. Ct.)

[Canadian Tire had two classes of shares — voting common shares and "Class A" non-voting common shares that were essentially identical to the voting shares save for the absence of a vote. The voting common shares constituted only 4% of the total equity of the company. This so-called "dual class" share structure is common in Canada, because of the large number of family-controlled corporations; the dual class structure enables the family to control the company by holding only a small part of the total equity. Indeed, in 1983, the Billes family had used its control to cause the company to enter into a reorganization pursuant to which the existing common shares were divided into two parts — the voting commons and the non-voting Class A shares. Existing shareholders were given fixed proportions of each. The Billes family subsequently sold off its non-voting shares and used the proceeds to purchase additional voting commons, allowing them to sell a substantial fraction of their equity while remaining in control of the company. In the end, three children of the founding shareholders of Canadian Tire — Fred, David, and Martha Billes — owned 60.9% of the outstanding voting common shares of Canadian Tire. Both the voting common shares and the Class A shares traded on the Toronto Stock Exchange.

In order to secure shareholder and regulatory approval of the reorganization, the Billes family agreed to attach a coattail provision to the Class A shares. This coattail stated that if there was a takeover bid for the voting common shares, *and* a majority of the voting shares were tendered into the takeover bid, then the Class A shares would become voting shares. This would give any acquiror an incentive to make a takeover bid for *both* the voting shares and the Class A shares.

The coattail was leaky, however, insofar as there could be a premium takeover bid for the voting shares that would *not* trigger the coattail as long as fewer than 50% of the voting shares were tendered into a bid. Because the Billeses owned more than 50% of the Class A shares, they could effectively keep the coattail from being triggered by refusing to tender some or all of their shares into a takeover bid.

As it turned out, some years later Fred and David (but not Martha) decided that they wanted to sell their voting shares, but only if they could get an average of $100 per share for them. In order to do this, they made a deal with the independently owned dealers of Canadian Tire (which were not owned by Canadian Tire, but which purchased all of their goods from Canadian Tire, as well as support services). Under the deal, the independent dealers would make a bid for the voting common shares at $160 per share (when the shares were trading for about $25 in the public market). However, so as not to trigger the coattail, the bid would be a "partial" takeover bid for only 49% of the common shares. The brothers would tender all of their shares into the takeover bid and (under applicable securities laws) would have 49% of their shares taken up and paid for at the premium price, and the rest returned to them. Following the takeover bid, they planned to sell off the remaining 51% of their holdings into the public market, thus disposing of all of their shares. Since under this arrangement the coattail would not be triggered, the Class A shareholders would fail to participate in the takeover premium. The Class A shares (which, prior to the takeover bid, had traded at about a 25–30% discount to the voting shares) were mostly held by institutional shareholders. These institutional shareholders prompted the Ontario Securities Commission to call a hearing into whether a cease trade order should be issued (effectively enjoining the transaction), in order to protect the interests of the Class A shareholders.]

Ontario Securities Commission:

The Public Interest

In these circumstances, we have no hesitation in saying that this transaction is contrary to the public interest, as that term is used in section 123 of the Act. When the public market is sold some $100 million of Class A non-voting shares consequent upon a reorganization that, among other things, provides takeover protection to those shares and the controlling shareholders, some three years later, devise a scheme in conjunction with those who wish to obtain control of the Corporation, to circumvent the coattail while, in effect, receiving the full price for their shares, regulatory intervention to stop an abusive transaction is called for. A transaction such as is proposed here is bound to have an effect on public confidence in the integrity of our capital markets and on public confidence in those who are the controllers of our major corporations. If abusive transactions such as the one in issue here, and this is as grossly abusive a transaction as the Commission has had before it in recent years, are allowed to proceed, confidence in our capital markets will inevitably suffer and individuals will be less willing to place funds in the equity markets. That can only have a deleterious effect on our capital markets and, in that sense, it is in the public interest that this Offer be cease traded along with the Billeses' tendering of their common shares to the Offer.

The Proper Forum

Counsel for the Billeses and the Dealers also argued that the Commission is not the proper forum for this case. The contention was that this is a private matter between the Class A shareholders and the controlling shareholders. Accordingly, the Class A shareholders should pursue their remedies in the courts where the issues can more properly be sorted out through the trial process. This contention is supported by the fact that the Notice of Hearing in para. 14 alleges breaches of fiduciary duty, and such breaches are properly matters to be tried in the courts, either under the oppression remedy or in a derivative action.

The contention that the issue here is a private one between two classes of shareholders is far wide of the mark. A purported sale of control in the circumstances set out above, where the rights of the holders of some 83 million Class A shares are concerned, is not a private matter, although individual rights in terms of a particular shareholding are involved. This is demonstrably a public matter involving a major public company and one that concerns and impacts on the public marketplace. In the sense in which counsel were using the idea of a private *lis*, any takeover bid would, according to their analysis, be a private matter between shareholders. Yet it is well known that takeover bids, the rules applying to them and how they are conducted, are very much a public matter in the sense of their concern to, and impact on the marketplace and its perceived integrity. The Commission, accordingly, has always played a major role in overseeing such transactions.

Moreover, the argument that this matter more properly belongs before the courts, mistakes the respective roles of the courts and the Commission in overseeing the management and actions of public companies and protecting shareholders' interests. The Commission is vested with the power to regulate the capital markets in the public interest and is given broad powers to do so. The power to intervene includes the power to cease trade and to do so, at least initially, without a public hearing if satisfied of the necessity. In carrying out its regulatory function, the Commission necessarily impacts on the rights and obligations of companies, directors and shareholders. But it does so from the perspective of the regulation of the public markets and their fair and efficient operation. The subjecting of takeover bids to an elaborate code of rules and regulations, backed by the power to issue a cease trade order, if conduct during the course of a bid calls for it, is perhaps the best known example of this regulatory function.

The courts, on the other hand, adjudicate rights between shareholders and their companies. In so doing, the judicial process has the advantage of the refinement of issues provided by pleadings, examinations for discovery and the trial process. Moreover, the courts are able to provide remedies appropriate to the individual case. What the courts are not structured to do, is to move quickly to regulate public markets through regulating shareholder and/or corporate conduct. To be sure, the injunction remedy is available in the proper case, but it is not a remedy designed to be used as a regulatory tool.

The line between when Commission action or judicial process is appropriate in shareholder and corporate matters is, of course, not so clearly marked as the foregoing comments would indicate. There is bound to be overlap as there is no clear line between securities and corporate matters and many issues before the Commission involve the conduct of fiduciaries. But the role of the Commission is not to determine breaches of fiduciary duty, or to deal with a breach of a corporate statute, in order to provide a private remedy. Rather, it is to regulate shareholder and corporate conduct in the context of, and for the purpose of, regulating the public securities markets. Again, the line will not always be clear as intervention in matters that from one aspect are of a private nature will, from another aspect, be seen to have public market implications. If the Commission should mistake its role in a particular case, or act beyond the jurisdiction granted, the courts can rectify the matter and set out a new balance through the appeal procedure granted under s. 9 of the Act [allowing for appeal of any Commission decision to the Divisional Court].

Breach of Fiduciary Duty

As to the allegations of breach of fiduciary duty here, we agree that in most cases, that is a matter best left to the courts to determine. Indeed, we declined to hear evidence on the allegation in para. 14(v) of the Notice of Hearing on just that basis. Our decision to impose a cease trading order does not depend on a finding of breach of fiduciary duty. However, an allegation of breach of fiduciary duty, and evidence which clearly concerns the conduct of those who are fiduciaries, can be important in supporting facts which otherwise would support a s. 123 [public interest] order. That is the case here. The Billeses are in a fiduciary position in at least two categories; as directors of Tire and as Tire's controlling shareholders.

While the law in Canada is still developing with respect to the fiduciary duty that controlling shareholders owe to the minority, the courts in Ontario have clearly signalled that duty of fairness to the minority is imposed upon those who are in a controlling shareholder position. The judgment of the Ontario Court of Appeal in *Goldex Mines Ltd. v. Revill* (1974), 54 D.L.R. (3d) 672 (Ont. C.A.) is much in point. In dealing with the developing jurisprudence with respect to fiduciary duties, the Court made the following statement:

> The principle that the majority governs in corporate affairs is fundamental to corporation law, but its corollary is also important, that the majority must act fairly and honestly. Fairness is the touchstone of equitable justice, and when the test of fairness is not met, the equitable jurisdiction of the Court can be invoked to prevent or remedy the injustice which misrepresentation or other dishonesty has caused. The category of cases in which fiduciary duties and obligations arise is not a closed one: *Laskin v. Bache & Co., Inc.,* [1972] O.R. 465 at p. 472, 23 D.L.R. (3d) 385 at p. 392.

That statement by the Court of Appeal provides guidance to the Commission with respect to the conduct of controlling shareholders when that conduct is in question in a case where Commission staff seeks a cease trade order. To repeat, the Commission is not the proper forum, particularly in a s. 123 proceeding, to determine the question of whether or not there has been a breach of fiduciary duty. But an allegation and a *prima facie* showing of such a breach can be useful evidence to support facts which otherwise call for intervention by the Commission under s. 123.

Here, the relationship of the Billeses as controlling shareholders to the minority is clear. And it is equally clear that their conduct, particularly seen in light of the events of 1983, in seeking now to avoid the takeover bid protection that was inserted for the protection of the Class A shareholders is a failure on their part to act fairly and honestly. In that sense, their conduct supports the facts here which otherwise call for the invocation of a cease trade under s. 123.

Notes

1   The Class A shares consistently traded in the market at a substantial (25–30%) discount to the voting common shares. It has been argued that the price of a share consists of two components — the first reflecting the value of the company under current management and the second reflecting the likelihood that an acquirer will make a takeover bid for the shares at a premium above market. See Frank H. Easterbrook and Daniel R. Fischel, "The Proper Roles of a Target's Management in Responding to a Tender Offer" (1981), 94 Harv. L. Rev. 1161. If so, the difference in price between voting and non-voting shares that are otherwise substantially identical results from the likelihood that any takeover bid will be made only for the voting shares. In similar fashion, if non-voting shares are protected by an airtight coattail, voting and non-voting shares should trade at similar prices. Thus, if the market regarded the Canadian Tire coattail as binding in all situations, presumably the price of the voting shares and the Class A shares would have been much closer than it was. This suggests that the institutional Class A shareholders were quite aware that they were buying shares with questionable takeover bid protection and the receipt of a takeover premium by the Class A shares would have been a windfall. There was in fact testimony before the Commission to the effect that the market was well aware of the leaky nature of the coattail. Indeed, while an investment banker from one large firm had testified that the market had not been aware of the terms of the coattail, it turned out that his own firm had sent clients a memorandum detailing the deficiency in the Canadian Tire coattail (i.e., the fact that it could be circumvented by a bid for less than 50% of the voting common shares). Thus, both theory and evidence cast some doubt on the wisdom of the *Canadian Tire* ruling.

2   Regardless of whether the Commission got it right, however, the effect of the *Canadian Tire* decision (upheld by the Divisional Court) is clear — the securities regulators will apply fiduciary standards of conduct in determining whether controlling shareholders have breached the public interest. Thus, the situation is something like

this. First, the courts have held that controlling shareholders owe no fiduciary duty either to other shareholders or to the corporation. Second, nonetheless, the courts appear to have created a quasi-fiduciary duty (if not an outright fiduciary duty) under the oppression remedy. Third, the securities regulators will apply fiduciary standards of conduct in determining whether to apply their public interest powers. Since securities regulators are not bound by judicial precedent, however, (and are not bound by their own prior rulings) these fiduciary standards may differ materially from those applied by the courts.

12. ARE CONTROLLING SHAREHOLDERS GOOD FOR CANADIAN CAPITAL MARKETS?

It is very common for Canadian corporations to have a controlling shareholder. For example, R. Morck and D. Strangeland, in "Corporate Performance and Large Shareholders: An Empirical Analysis", in D. Strangeland, Ph.D. Thesis, Faculty of Business, University of Alberta, 1995, found that fewer than 16% of the largest 550 Canadian corporations had no shareholder holding 20% or more of the stock. Someshwar Rao and Clifton R. Lee-Sing, in "Governance Structure, Corporate Decision-Making and Firm Performance in North America", in Ronald J. Daniels and Randall Morck, Eds., *Corporate Decision-Making in Canada* (Calgary: University of Calgary Press, 1995), 43, found that 55.5% of a very large sample of Canadian firms had a *de jure* controller, 21.4% had a *de facto* controller (defined as having a shareholder with 20–49.9% ownership), and 23.1% were widely held (defined as having no shareholder with as much as 20% ownership). Comparable figures are reported in Ronald J. Daniels and Jeffrey G. MacIntosh, "Toward a Distinctive Canadian Corporate Law Regime" (1992) 29 Osgoode Hall L. J. 863, and Rafael La Porta, Florencio Lopez-de-Silanes and Andrei Shleifer, "Corporate Ownership Around the World" (1999) 54 J. Fin. 471. This is not atypical of relatively small capital markets like Canada's. By contrast, large capital markets like those in the United States are dominated by "manager controlled" or "widely held" companies; i.e., companies lacking a controlling shareholder. This divergence of corporate type between Canada and the US prompted Daniels and MacIntosh ("Toward a Distinctive Canadian Corporate Law Regime" (1992) 29 Osgoode Hall L. J. 863) to suggest that in Canada, corporate disputes will more often consist of minority/controlling shareholder disputes rather than shareholder/manager disputes. This is because a controlling shareholder will tend to closely monitor managers but may be tempted to engineer transactions or corporate payouts in a manner that favours its interests over those of the minority. This speculation now has some empirical footing. In particular,

MacIntosh and Schwartz (Jeffrey G. MacIntosh and Lawrence P. Schwartz, "Do Institutional and Controlling Shareholders Increase Corporate Value?", in Ronald J. Daniels and Randall Morck, Eds., *Corporate Decision-Making in Canada* (Calgary: University of Calgary Press, 1995, 303)) found that:

> [t]here is fairly strong support for the hypothesis that the presence of a controlling shareholder resulted in a lower price to book ratio. However, there is even stronger support for the hypothesis that the presence of a controlling shareholder resulted in both higher return on assets and return on equity, although there was no discernible effect on sales growth.
>
> Save for the absence of an affect on sales growth, however, these results are consistent with our hypotheses about the effect of a controlling shareholder on firm value. We earlier hypothesized that the presence of a controlling shareholder should result in better monitoring of managers. This in turn should result in higher ROA [return on assets] and ROE [return on equity] (which we assume are not as likely to be affected by redistributive transactions as price to book). However, in an efficient market, where controllers regularly engage in some redistribution of profits at the expense of non-controlling interests, the price of firms with controlling shareholders will be discounted to reflect this risk. The fact that the price to book ratio is less when there is a controlling shareholder thus suggests that, even though such corporations generate higher profits, these profits are siphoned off by controlling shareholders.

This does not mean, however, that we can expect all shareholder-controlled enterprises to be run more efficiently than non-shareholder controlled companies. The above study looked at *averages*. As in any statistical population, there will be considerable variation around the average. In particular cases, the controlling interest may adopt policies that lead to *lower* corporate value. A case study on point is provided by David Strangeland, Ronald J. Daniels and Randall Morck, in "In High Gear: A Case Study of the Hees-Edper Corporate Group", in Ronald J. Daniels and Randall Morck, Eds., *Corporate Decision-Making in Canada* (Calgary, University of Calgary Press, 1995), 223. The authors of this study examined what was once an extremely large corporate conglomerate controlled by a single family (the Bronfmans) — the "Hees-Edper" group of companies. At its height, this conglomerate consisted of over 100 companies that comprised approximately 15% of the value of the companies traded on the Toronto Stock Exchange. In order to motivate the managers of the various companies in the conglomerate, managers were given low salaries but were required to borrow money from their companies in order to buy company stock. In addition, the companies were organized in a pyramidal structure, such that the parent company would own 51% of another company, which would own 51% of another company, which would own 51% of another company, and so on. Many of the subsidiary companies were public companies. Using this technique, the Bronfmans were able to command a vast empire of companies even though their indirect ownership of firms in the middle and bottom of the pyramid was extremely small. Strangeland *et al.* compared the performance of these companies with those that were not part of a similar corporate group. They found that their performance was, at best, no better than these other companies. Indeed, there were indications that the Hees-Edper group of companies experienced inferior performance despite having higher levels of risk.

This study should be used with caution in interpreting the effect of a controlling shareholder on firm performance, however. The authors attributed the poor performance of the conglomerate companies to the practice of paying senior managers small salaries coupled with mandatory share ownership. This encouraged the managers to take inefficient risks with their companies in order to cause the stock price to appreciate. In addition, the use of conglomerate structure, now widely discredited (because it spreads management expertise too thin), appears to have played a role in the poor performance. The authors speculate that the conglomerate structure both contributed to, and facilitated the taking of inefficient risks. Finally, it should also be noted that while the later performance of the Hees-Edper group was not particularly impressive, judging from the early success of the conglomerate, a very high level of management expertise was presumably applied at earlier stages.

Another study that shows a more ambiguous effect of control on performance than the MacIntosh/Schwartz study is Vijay Jog and Ajit Tulpule, "Control and Performance: Evidence from the TSE 300", in Ronald J. Daniels and Randall Morck, Eds., *Corporate Decision-Making in Canada* (Calgary: University of Calgary Press, 1995), 105. The authors summarize their findings as follows:

> This analysis allows us to draw some reasonably robust conclusions based on the overall results and associated statistical tests. First, it is clear that the relationship between control and stock market performance is sector-specific, with the non-manufacturing sector being more sensitive to the effects of control than the manufacturing sector. In the manufacturing, an investor would have been better off simply investing in large Canadian manufacturing firms — which did better than the overall manufacturing sector portfolio. There was little, if any, use in investing in securities, based on the degree of control of a firm within that sector or within a specific size group. However, in the nonmanufacturing sector, investment based on control does have performance implications . . . [A]ccounting-based measures fail to detect any differences in firm performance based on the associated degree of control, either for a given year or over the entire time period. Overall, none of our results shows any consistent

differences between widely held firms and closely held firms belonging to the TSE 300.

Someshwar Rao and Clifton R. Lee-Sing, in "Governance Structure, Corporate Decision-Making and Firm Performance in North America", in Ronald J. Daniels and Randall Morck, Eds., *Corporate Decision-Making in Canada* (Calgary: University of Calgary Press, 1995) 43, also found no relationship between either the rate of return in equity or the return on assets and concentration of corporate ownership. However, the rate of return was higher for firms with a *de facto* controller.

The results in these studies may be a product of the fact (as suggested by the MacIntosh/Schwartz study) that controlling shareholders have both positive and negative effects on corporate value. While controlling shareholders police management more efficiently, increasing corporate value, they are also frequently able to use their powers of control to favour their interests over those of the minority. There is in fact an abundance of other evidence that is consistent with this proposition. See Ronald J. Daniels and Paul Halpern, "Too Close for Comfort: The Role of the Closely Held Public Corporation in the Canadian Economy and the Implications for Public Policy" (1996), 26 Can. Bus. L. J. 11.

One particular case of ownership concentration merits discussion. Studies have been conducted to examine the effect of *managerial* ownership on corporate performance. The seminal theoretical work in this regard is that by Michael Jensen and William Meckling, "Theory of the Firm: Managerial Behavior, Agency Costs and Ownership Structure" (1976), 3 J. of Fin. Econ. 305. Jensen and Meckling speculated that as manager ownership increases, the value of the firm should also monotonically increase. This is because the interests of the managers are more fully aligned at high levels of managerial ownership. For example, when a manager owns 75% of a company with no debt, for every dollar she takes out of the company in the form of perquisite consumption and/or shirking, she indirectly bears (through diminution in the value of her equity claims) 75% of the cost. However, if the manager owns 1% of the firm, for every dollar she takes out of the company, she indirectly bears only 1% of the cost. Thus, managerial incentives to consume perquisites and to shirk diminish as ownership increases.

This view of the "agency costs" of the separation of ownership and control, however, overlooks the fact that as managers accrue larger ownership interests, they become harder to displace through the mechanism of a hostile takeover or a proxy contest. They can therefore consume private benefits of control (such as enjoying the prestige that accompanies control of a major public corporation) without fear of being displaced.

Empirical investigations on the value of managerial share ownership have yielded interesting results. Randall Morck, Andrei Schliefer and Robert W. Vishny, in "Management Ownership and Market Valuation:

An Empirical Analysis" (1988), 20 J. of Fin. Econ. 293, found that as ownership rises from 0 to 5%, market valuation increases. However, from 5% to 25%, market valuation decreases. From 25% upwards, it increases again. This changing relationship may well reflect the trade-off of the alignment effect of higher ownership with the entrenchment effect. However, looking at a sample of much smaller companies, J.J. McConnell and H. Servaes, in "Additional Evidence on Equity Ownership and Corporate Value" (1990) 27 J. Fin. Econ. 595 found that there was an increase in corporate value up to about 40–50% ownership, and a decrease thereafter. Both of these studies, however, strongly suggest that *managerial* ownership is an important determinant of corporate value.

Both the causes of concentrated ownership in Canada and other potential problems associated with concentrated ownership are examined in detail in Ronald J. Daniels and Paul Halpern, "Too Close for Comfort: The Role of the Closely Held Public Corporation in the Canadian Economy and the Implications for Public Policy" (1996), 26 Can. Bus. L. J. 11; Randall K. Morck, in "On the Economics of Concentrated Ownership" (1996), 26 Can. Bus. L. J. 63; and Ronald J. Daniels and Edward M. Iacobucci, "Some of the Causes and Consequences of Corporate Ownership Concentration in Canada", in R. Morck, Ed., *Concentrated Corporate Ownership* (Chicago: University of Chicago Press, 2000), 81. These include: market power and protectionism, the effect of concentrated ownership on corporate growth, efficiency consequences associated with control by founders and subsequently by their heirs, and effects on banking regulation and investment rules.

Interestingly, in a study of the 49 largest economies in the world, La Porta *et al.* find that the kind of concentrated ownership structure that prevails in Canada is the norm, rather than the exception. See Rafael La Porta, Florencio Lopez-de-Silanes and Andrei Shleifer, "Corporate Ownership Around the World" (1999) 54 J. Fin. 471. Controlling shareholders often accentuate their control through the use of pyramidal ownership structures in which the controlling shareholder controls corporation A, which owns a controlling interest in corporation B, which owns a controlling interest in corporation C, and so on (just as in the Hees-Edper group of companies, *supra*). Through this device, the ultimate controller can control a huge empire of companies via an equity interest at the top of the pyramid that is small compared to the total assets under control. While the study found that there were pyramidal ownership structures in Canada, the number of such structures was not disproportionate to other developed countries in the sample. The most significant finding of this study is that when shareholder rights are strong, ownership tends to be *less* concentrated. This is because when shareholder rights are weak, the private benefits of control escalate. That is, when controlling shareholder conduct is relatively unchecked, the controller can divert more of the corporation's earnings stream into its own pocket.

This creates a potent incentive for those with the means to acquire — and exploit — control.

In a companion piece also examining corporations with controlling shareholders, La Porta *et al.* find that when shareholder rights are weak, corporations had lower valuations. Thus, the expropriation effected by controlling shareholders does more than simply transfer wealth from minority shareholders to controlling shareholders; it also impairs the efficiency of the corporate sector. See Rafael La Porta, Florencio Lopez-De-Silanes, Andrei Shleifer and Robert Vishny, "Investor Protection and Corporate Valuation" (2002) 57 J. Fin. 1147.

Chapter 8

Shareholders' Rights

1. INTRODUCTION

This chapter will begin a focus on the role of shareholders in the corporation. Canadian corporation statutes reflect an enabling philosophy in that the formation and activities of corporations have been encouraged by placing very few hurdles to achieving incorporation. Indeed society generally has provided many inducements in support of corporations, such as preferential income tax treatment. As a subject, corporation law is a form of constitutional law that is set against this enabling philosophy and that attempts to regulate the rights and duties of those who participate in the corporation and, to a limited degree, those who relate to or are greatly affected by it. In this respect, normative rules of corporation law are in many cases difficult to prescribe or articulate on many of the various issues that are studied in this book.

Many popular generalizations or assumptions that have been made about shareholders are especially in need of re-examination in the light of the major social, economic and political changes that have occurred in Western societies generally and in Canadian society in particular. One of the general assumptions is that shareholders are the owners of the corporation, but this statement begs further analysis to ask what does ownership mean in this context, and compared to what; or put another way, what property or rights are owned by the shareholder? It is also said that shareholders are primarily if not exclusively interested in the growth or return on their investment. Is this in fact the case? What, if anything, happens to this assertion of shareholder expectations when the state becomes the sole or dominant shareholder of the corporation or when religious, charitable or other interest-based institutions are the shareholders?

Numerous significant developments have taken place in the size and type of corporation and the nature of the shareholder constituency. A fairly unique feature of the Canadian corporate landscape (as against the US or UK for example) is that the vast majority of corporations in Canada are closely held, and it is often said that the needs and expectations of shareholders in these entities differ materially from those of their counterparts in widely held corporations. As a result, many argue for correspondingly different statutory and judicial rules. Indeed, some aspects of the closely held corporation will receive special attention in the Chapter 9.

At the same time, the mix of shareholders has become extremely complicated and varied. The emergence of institutional shareholdings has been profound when one thinks of the portfolio investments of mutual funds, pensions, insurance companies, credit unions and other financial intermediaries. It is most appropriate to ask whether corporation law has kept properly abreast of these developments. In this connection, the role of provincial securities commissions under securities legislation is very relevant since these bodies have greatly affected, and in turn have been influenced by, shareholder concerns on various issues traditionally left to corporation law. However, following a report by an Expert Panel on Securities Regulation, the federal Ministry of Finance formed the Canadian Securities Transition Office to establish a national securities regulatory authority. The focus has now shifted to establishing a common regulator on a cooperative basis. The proposed Cooperative Capital Markets Regulatory System, along with the *Capital Markets Act*, will create a single regulator applying one set of rules in participating jurisdictions. It will be interesting to see how the relationship between Canadian corporate and securities law will change if and when a common regulatory authority is established. As evidenced by the introduction of the *Sarbanes-Oxley Act* of 2002 in the US, the corresponding Canadian response, and the introduction of the *Dodd—Frank Wall Street Reform and Consumer Protection Act*, securities regulators are increasingly regulating in the area of corporate governance. See discussion, *infra*.

Against this background, we examine briefly what rights are or should be given to shareholders by corporation statutes in the modem context. To the extent there are rights assigned, there must also be means of enforcing these rights through effective remedies, and this subject is explored in Chapter 10.

At this stage, it might be concluded that as long as shareholders have reasonable protection for their interests, they are content to leave to others the management of the business affairs of the corporation. As this argument goes, shareholders, at least in the widely held corporation, have neither the expertise nor the interest to run the corporation. The reasonable protection will, *inter alia*, include the imposition of duties of care and skill and fiduciary fair dealing on corporate management as outlined in previous chapters. However, where the matter under consideration by the corporation comes closer to affecting the nature of the shareholders' investment or is a decision on who will run the corporation, it is more likely the shareholders will wish to have a voice on the matter. (See generally an analysis of the criteria for shareholder involvement in corporate decision making in Eisenberg, "The Legal Roles of Shareholders and Management in Modern Corporate Decision

Making" (1969), 57 Cal. L. Rev. 1; Iacobucci, Pilkington, and Prichard, *Canadian Business Corporations* (1977), 132–48).

The next issue is how such shareholder opinion gets expressed. Here the pervasive majority rule of corporation law is directly encountered. In the context of examining shareholder rights, one has to determine which rights are individually conferred and which are subject to majority support. Checks and balances for the protection of minority shareholders have been recognized by courts and legislators for some time; whether they have been effectively recognized is another question.

2. PRE-EMPTIVE RIGHTS

Pre-emptive rights require that the corporation must offer existing shareholders the opportunity to subscribe for a new share offering in the proportion that their shareholdings bear to the total number of shares issued and outstanding. We have already seen that the company's managers may be tempted (whether for good or bad motives) to issue shares to defeat a current or anticipated takeover bid, or to alter the distribution of control. See *supra*, Chapter 6. The existence of a pre-emptive right makes it much more difficult for managers to do so, since all shareholders must be offered their *pro rata* allotment.

A pre-emptive right can serve another function: share issuance at an undervalue will result in the "dilution" of the interests of current shareholders, with concomitant diminution in the value of their investments. Suppose, for example, that there are 100 shares in ABC Inc., a company with a steady net profit of $1,000 per year, which is paid out annually as dividends on the shares. Earnings per share are $10, and hence the annual dividend amounts to $10 per share. Based on a price/earnings ratio (or "multiplier") of 10, each share will trade for $100. (Note that in practice, this price/earnings ratio is determined by the market.) The total value of the company is $10,000 (100 shares worth $100 each). Suppose now that the controlling shareholder in the company causes 50 shares to be issued to herself at $40 each (i.e., at a $60 discount from actual value). This will result in $2000 flowing into the corporate treasury, which the company will then invest. We will make the assumption that net profits rise in proportion to the cash infusion; that is, they go to $1200 per year. Now what are the shares worth? There are 150 shares outstanding, and net profits of $1200 to be divided among them. This means that earnings per share are $8 per annum. Using the same price/earnings ratio as before, each share is now worth only $80. Every minority shareholder loses $20 per share held. While the value of the holdings of the majority shareholder decreases by an identical amount, she nonetheless gains overall by virtue of having purchased the shares issued at an undervalue. The share issuance at an undervalue has resulted in a transfer of wealth from the minority shareholders to the majority shareholder. A pre-emptive right would have given every minority shareholder the opportunity to purchase the underpriced shares, resulting in protection from dilution.

In the United States, prior to the enactment of statutory provisions dealing with the matter, the courts recognized the pre-emptive right as a means of shareholder protection against dilution of their interests without their consent (see Drinker, "The Pre-emptive Right of Shareholders to Subscribe to New Shares" (1930), 43 Harv. L. Rev. 586).

Under Canadian common law, the issuance of shares by a corporation does not give rise to a pre-emptive right. See *Harris v. Sumner* (1909), 39 N.B.R. 204 (C.A.). However, under the older "improper purpose" test (still current in England) an issuance of shares designed to alter or influence control could be struck down as a breach of the fiduciary duty of the directors. See *Bonisteel v. Collis Leather Co.*, *supra*, at Chapter 6. The Canadian courts seem to have jettisoned this test in favour of the test of acting honestly on reasonable grounds enunciated by Berger J. in *Teck v. Millar*, *supra*, at Chapter 6. The *Teck* test was adopted by the Manitoba Court of Appeal in *Olson v. Phoenix Industrial Supply Ltd. et al.*, noted, *supra*, at Chapter 6, and has also been adopted by the lower courts of several provinces, including Ontario. In that case, an issuance of shares designed expressly to deprive the majority shareholder of control was approved on the grounds that the evidence established that the directors were acting honestly, in good faith and in the best interests of the company in issuing shares, and that they did so on reasonable grounds. See also *Hiram Walker*, *supra*, at Chapter 6.

It is no longer sufficient to have regard only to the common law; the enactment of the oppression remedy has brought about wholesale change in the law of business corporations, and there are at least three cases that have considered the question of pre-emptive rights. The English case *Re a Company*, [1985] B.C.L.C. 80 (Ch. D.) involved a small corporation with only two shareholders; Lewis owned 1/3 of the shares, and the Boltons owned 2/3. When disagreements arose between the parties, a resolution was brought forward by the Boltons to increase the capital of the company and to give the directors authority to issue shares. Lewis sought an injunction under the English oppression provision to prevent the Boltons from voting their shares in favour of the resolution. The Boltons testified that it was their intention to issue shares only on the basis of a *pro rata* rights offering ("rights" are securities that entitle the holder to purchase shares; a rights offering is usually made to the company's shareholders on a *pro rata* basis). The court granted the injunction, holding that even a *pro rata* offering could operate in an unfairly prejudicial manner

> if it could be shown, for example, that it was known that although the offer would be *pro rata* yet the member would be unable by reason of his own circumstances to take it up, and that the

knowledge was a factor leading to the making of an offer which was in truth illusory because it could never be accepted. (*Ibid.*, at 82.)

Similarly, in *Re Sabex Int. Ltee* (1979), 6 B.L.R. 65 (Que. S.C.), a corporation was formed through the combination of one business owned by the applicants and another owned by the respondents. The respondents held 54% of the shares and the applicants 44%. The corporation sought further funds to expand operations; however, its bankers insisted that an additional $100,000 of share equity be invested before they would expand the company's line of credit. In order to satisfy this requirement, the company put forward a rights offering to all shareholders. The applicants objected under s. 234 of the CBCA (now CBCA s. 241) on the ground that the offering was oppressive because it forced them to participate in order to avoid diluting their interests. Although acknowledging the legitimate need for additional equity, the fact that the plan treated all shareholders in a formally equal manner and the presence of good faith, the court nonetheless granted the injunction prohibiting the rights offering, seemingly because the effect of the offering would dilute the minority's interest if it did not subscribe. Do you think this is an appropriate result? See also *Mazzotta v. Twin Gold Mines* (1987), 37 B.L.R. 218 (Ont. H.C.) (reaching a similar result).

The Ontario Securities Commission has taken steps to combat the potential abuses associated with non-*pro rata* share offerings. OSC National Instrument 45-101, which deals with rights offerings, provides (in part):

Part 7 Additional Subscription Privilege

7.1

Additional Subscription Privilege — An issuer shall not grant an additional subscription privilege to a holder of a right unless the issuer grants the additional subscription privilege to all holders of rights.

7.2

Stand-by Commitment — If there is a stand-by commitment for a rights offering, the issuer shall grant an additional subscription privilege to all holders of rights.

7.3

Number or Amount of Securities

(1) Under an additional subscription privilege, each holder of a right shall be entitled to receive, on exercise of the additional subscription privilege, the number or amount of securities that is equal to the lesser of

    (a) the number or amount of securities subscribed for by the holder under the additional subscription privilege; and

    (b) $x(y/z)$ where

x = the aggregate number or amount of securities available through unexercised rights,

y = the number of rights previously exercised by the holder under the rights offering, and

z = the aggregate number of rights previously exercised under the rights offering by holders of rights that have subscribed for securities under the additional subscription privilege.

(2) Any unexercised rights shall be allocated on a *pro rata* basis to holders who subscribed for additional securities based on the additional subscription privilege up to the number of securities subscribed for by a particular holder.

7.4

Price of Securities — The subscription price under an additional subscription privilege or a stand-by commitment shall be the same as the subscription price under the basic subscription privilege.

A "stand-by commitment" can include an agreement to purchase all the rights not taken up by shareholders on the rights offering. The National Instrument recognizes the fact that not all shareholders will purchase rights even where the offering is below market price; thus, if a party related to (and acting in concert with) a major or controlling shareholder gives a standby commitment, the major or controlling shareholder will be able to increase its proportionate ownership in the company, and hence its ability to control the company.

Section 26 of the OBCA expressly allows a pre-emptive restriction to be written into the company's articles, or be adopted by unanimous shareholder agreement. Section 28 of the CBCA is similar in this regard, although it makes no mention of a unanimous shareholder agreement, and specifies certain exceptions where pre-emptive rights are impossible, such as for consideration other than money.

The U.K. *Companies Act*, 1980 introduced pre-emptive rights because of the European Common Market directives on company law harmonization (see now *Companies Act*, 1985, s. 89). For a discussion of the U.K. provisions, see Daniel D. Prentice, *Companies Act 1980* (Toronto: Butterworths 1980), pp. 23–31. The statutory treatment in the US is even more varied: denying pre-emptive rights in some jurisdictions, denying them unless expressly granted, expressly granting them and authorizing limitations on them. (See Iacobucci, Pilkington, and Prichard, *Canadian Business Corporations* (1977), 147–150).

Which approach do you prefer?

3. SHAREHOLDER VOTING

(a) Introduction

The separation of ownership and control in the modern corporation gives rise to potential problems that have already been alluded to; managers may not pay attention to the interests of shareholders as much as their own interests. Usually, a significant portion of a manager's personal wealth will be tied to the firm, not only in the form of stock and stock options, but also in the form of the manager's salary. By comparison, shareholders usually hold diversified portfolios of securities and are less concerned about the risk of any single investment as they are about the riskiness of the portfolio as a whole. As a result, managers may select investment projects that are less risky, and therefore less rewarding financially, in an effort to protect their own interests (whether intentionally or not).

In a now very famous work written in 1932 (*The Modern Corporation and Private Property*), Adolf Berle and Gardiner Means suggested that the separation of ownership and control in the modern public corporation spelled the end of effective shareholder oversight of corporate managers. In their view, management had become a virtually autonomous organ of the corporation, therefore it was inevitable that managers would engage in a significant level of non-profit maximizing behaviour.

Aside from legal controls over the behaviour of the corporate managers, there are a variety of market mechanisms that serve to constrain managerial behaviour and ensure that managers do not depart too far from profit maximizing behaviour. These have already been alluded to, and include the market for corporate control, the market for managers, and the product markets in which the firm sells its wares.

One type of legal restraint has already been examined; managerial duties of a fiduciary nature.

Shareholder voting is both a device for registering shareholder preferences relating to important business decisions in the life of the corporation and for controlling managerial diversion, slack and risk-shifting. Shareholders are statutorily empowered to vote for directors and to vote in respect of an enumerated set of transactions that are often referred to as "fundamental changes." These include (*inter alia*) amalgamation (CBCA s. 183, OBCA s. 176); sale of all or substantially all the assets of the corporation (CBCA ss. 189(3)–(8), OBCA ss. 184(3)–(8)); continuance in another jurisdiction (CBCA s. 188, OBCA s. 181); and changes to the corporation's articles of incorporation (CBCA s. 173, OBCA s. 168).

Shareholder voting seems a natural answer to the problems of managerial excess, ineptitude and risk-shifting. If managers fail to perform adequately, then shareholders may replace the directors (and through them, the managers). Enfranchising shareholders can lead to oversight of management in a number of important ways. First, there may be shareholders with large blocks of shares, particularly institutional investors like insurance companies, pension and mutual funds, banks and other financial intermediaries. A high percentage of all shares traded in the market are now controlled by such investors. These investors will have much better incentives to use their voting power (and powers of suasion) effectively to ensure that individuals with proven track records are elected as directors. The old "Wall Street" (or "Bay Street") rule under which institutional investors simply sold their holdings if dissatisfied with management is on its way to becoming an anachronism. See Jeffrey G. MacIntosh, "The Role of Institutional and Retail Investors in Canadian Capital Markets" (1993), 31 Osgoode Hall L.J. 371; and Brian R. Cheffins, "Michaud v. National Bank of Canada and Canadian Corporate Governance: A 'Victory' for Shareholder Rights?" (1998), 30 C.B.L.J. 20.

Second, the existence of a voting class of security holders facilitates replacement of management through the mechanism of the "hostile" takeover bid (i.e., one that is not sanctioned by management). There are business circumstances in which it may become profitable for an acquiror to mount a takeover bid for the company's voting equity, and if successful, use its aggregated voting power to appoint a new managerial team. This could not occur but for the existence of a class of security holders possessing the power to elect directors.

Lastly, the existence of a voting class of security holders facilitates the replacement of management by means of a proxy battle. In such a contest, a dissident shareholder (or, more frequently, group of shareholders) attempts to replace management by securing the proxies of shareholders and using these proxies to vote for an alternate slate of directors nominated by the dissidents.

Thus, empowering at least one class of security holders to elect directors serves as a useful check on the potential tendency of management to depart, at least to a degree, from their assigned role of maximizing corporate profits.

Notwithstanding the apparent positive effects of shareholder voting, some empirical evidence suggests that shareholder voting has little to no positive effect on corporate activity (See Roberta Romano "Less Is More: Making Shareholder Activism A Valued Mechanism Of Corporate Governance" (2000) Yale J. L. & Econ 241; and Yair Listoken "If You Give Shareholders Power, Do They Use It? An Empirical Analysis" (2009) Yale Law & Economics Research Paper No. 383) Since in the typical case few shareholders will actually be able to attend the shareholders' meeting, most shareholders who vote do so by "proxy"; that is, they nominate someone else (the proxyholder) to vote for them at the meeting by means of a written instrument (the form of proxy). Under the CBCA and OBCA, the management of most corporations is required to send shareholders a form of proxy on which management designates its nominations for directors. The form of proxy also allows the shareholder to endorse management's slate of candidates by nominating as proxyholder a person designated by management and indicated on the form, who will vote for management's choices. It will be beyond the reach of most shareholders to nominate alternate candidates for directors before the meeting, since both the CBCA and OBCA allow only shareholders holding 5% of the shares or 5% of a class of shares entitled to vote at the meeting to make nominations for directors (CBCA s. 137(4); OBCA s. 99(4)). Although shareholders may make nominations at the meeting itself, such nominations will almost always be doomed to failure where management has solicited proxies for its nominees in advance. Thus, in the usual case (unless a shareholder or group of shareholders has mounted a proxy battle) the slate of candidates nominated by management will run unopposed — and will be elected to office (See Lucien Bebchuk "The Myth of the Shareholder Franchise" (2007) 3:Virg. L. Rev. 675).

Further, there is the problem of "rational shareholder apathy" (a phrase coined by Robert Clark in his article "Vote Buying and Corporate Law" (1979), 29 Case West. L. Rev. 776). In the modern public corporation share ownership is often fragmented amongst a large number of shareholders, particularly in the US and UK. (This problem is less prevalent in Canada, as we have more closely held corporations, dual class share structures, and cascading ownership, all of which concentrate voting power in the hands of a few shareholders.) The costs of becoming sufficiently informed to vote effectively are quite large. Shareholders must familiarize themselves with the records of those standing for election, and such information may be difficult to come by, if available at all. For the average shareholder, the benefits are tenuous; the probability that votes wielded by shareholder will influence the outcome is small. Further, to the extent that benefits accrue from using one's votes carefully, the benefits are distributed amongst all shareholders, creating a classic "free rider" effect. As a result, many shareholders simply fail to return the proxy material sent to them by management. Many others who choose to exercise their voting franchise will do so by endorsing without investigation management's team of nominees. See *The Proxy System*, *infra*, and see generally Raymond Crete, *The Proxy System in Canadian Corporations* (1986), Clark, *supra*, and Easterbrook and Fischel, "Voting in Corporate Law" (1983), 26 J. Law & Econ. 395.

Shareholder voting is far from costless; there are considerable costs associated with the preparation and mailing of proxy materials to shareholders, especially in very large public corporations, not to mention the cost of the meeting itself. Since the benefits of shareholder voting (at least in the larger public corporation) appear to be minimal, is shareholder voting an anachronism?

In a recent discussion paper, Carol Hansell et al. identified five key criteria that must be satisfied in order to have effective shareholder proxy voting. ("The Quality of the Shareholder Vote in Canada" Discussion Paper, online < http://www.dwpv.com/shareholdervoting/ > .) These criteria are: (i) investors must be in a position to make an informed decision; (ii) the rules of the voting system must be sufficiently explained to shareholders; (iii) an investor's vote must have full weight at the shareholder meeting; (iv) votes attached to securities must be cast by those who have an economic interest attached to the security; and (v) the system must be transparent enough to inspire confidence. The authors suggest that the Canadian shareholder voting system is flawed and must address these five criteria in order to be effective. The Canadian Securities Administrators have attempted to address these issues. In 2013, the CSA consulted the public on making relevant changes to the proxy voting infrastructure. This led other provincial regulators to hold roundtable discussions considering the issues with proxy voting in Canada. In 2015, the CSA released a progress report focusing on accurate, reliable, and accountable vote reconciliation. See Canadian Securities Administrators, "CSA Staff Notice 54-303 Progress Report on Review of the Proxy Voting Infrastructure," online < https://www.osc.gov.on.ca/documents/ en/Securities-Category5/csa_20150129_54-303_progress-report.pdf > .

(b)   Note on Statutory and Judicial Voting Entitlements

The right to vote is a fundamental right of shareholders and is one feature that distinguishes shareholders from creditors. Voting rights are enshrined in the corporate legislation of each Canadian jurisdiction. Section 24(3) of the CBCA provides that at least one class of shares must be voting, entitled to receive dividends, and to receive the assets remaining on dissolution. To a similar effect is section 22(3) of the OBCA, except that this section requires only that there be a class of shares having voting rights and the entitlement to receive the remaining property of the corporation upon dissolution. In each statute, if the articles are silent about voting rights, then each share carries one vote (CBCA s. 140(1), OBCA s. 102(1)).

Since only one class of the corporation's shares must have the right to vote, and since it is possible to create a capital structure with many different classes of shares, it is clear under the CBCA and OBCA (and the legislation of the other provinces) that shares may be created with no voting rights at all. It is usual, for example, to create preferred shares that do not vote (although preferred shares may have a contingent vote that comes into play if, say, preferred dividends are not paid for 6 of any 8 consecutive quarters). It became increasingly common in the 1980s to create "common" shares that do not possess the right to vote. Sometimes these common shares are identical in all respects, save voting rights, to a class of voting common shares. More often, they will possess a higher dividend rate or a preferential dividend as a "sweetener" to induce purchase of the shares.

Where one or more classes of shareholders do not vote (either for directors or to approve corporate fundamental changes) clear dangers of opportunistic behaviour are created. For example, suppose holders of the voting class of shares resolved to amend the articles of incorporation to remove a preferential dividend attaching to a class of preferred shares. There is nothing, save perhaps a suit for breach of fiduciary duty or an oppression action, that would prevent this from occurring. There are two distinct forms of statutory response to the dangers of abuse that arise from the unequal distribution of voting rights. One is to mandatorily enfranchise shares that would not otherwise carry the right to vote. This is done in the CBCA, for example, in connection with an amalgamation (s. 183(3)), sale, lease or exchange of all or substantially all the assets of the corporation (s. 189(6)) and continuance in another jurisdiction (s. 188(4)). See *Magna International Inc., Re*, 2010 CarswellOnt 5916, [2010] O.J. No. 3454 (Ont. S.C.J.), affirmed 2010 CarswellOnt 6651 (Ont. Div. Ct.).

Another form of response also seen in the CBCA is the requirement that certain fundamental transactions be approved separately by every class of shareholders, whether or not the class would otherwise carry the right to vote. This is done, for example, in connection with an amalgamation (s. 183(4)), sale, lease or exchange of all or substantially all the assets of the corporation (s. 189(7)) and amendments to the articles of incorporation (s. 176) (in each case, note the limitations imposed upon the furnishing of a class vote). The OBCA employs only the latter technique. See, *e.g.*, OBCA ss. 170, 176(3), 184(6).

Voting rights can serve as a check on opportunistic behaviour: recall the facts of *Northwest Transportation v. Beatty* (*supra*, Chapter 6). A major shareholder in the company sold a steamship to the company. That same shareholder then used his votes to "ratify" the sale to the company. Clearly, a ratification secured only by the votes of an interested shareholder is not a very effective means of ensuring the fairness of the transaction. One would have a much higher degree of confidence in the fairness of the transaction if it was ratified by at least a majority of the uninterested shareholders (that is, shareholders having no particular interest in the subject matter of the transaction). The same applies to shareholder approval of fundamental transactions.

There are as yet few statutory requirements for approval of transactions by a majority of disinterested shareholders (or a "majority of the minority"). Such a requirement is found in the OBCA in section 190, however (dealing with "going private"; that is, evicting the "public" shareholders and concentrating ownership in the hands of a relative few shareholders). Moreover, there appears to be a growing trend at common law to require that shareholder approvals or ratifications be given by a majority of the minority of shareholders. See, e.g., *Wedge v. McNeil* (1981), 126 D.L.R. (3d) 596 (P.E.I. S.C.), reversed on evidentiary grounds by (1982), 142 D.L.R. (3d) 133 (P.E.I.C.A.); *Re Northwest Forest Products Ltd.*, *infra*, Chapter 10; *Clemens v. Clemens Bros. Ltd.*, [1976] 2 All E.R. 268 (Ch. D.). See generally, *supra*, Chapter 6.

Increasingly, the securities regulators of the various provinces are requiring approval of certain transactions either by a majority of shareholders or, in some cases, by a majority of the minority. Also, where an existing class of equity securities is broken up into voting and non-voting (or restricted voting) components by a change in the articles or otherwise, the Ontario Securities Commission (Rule 56-501) requires approval of the transaction by a majority of shareholders, not counting any shareholders who form part of a controlling group (i.e., a majority of the minority). Similarly, OSC Multilateral Instrument 61-101 requires that a majority of the minority vote be held to approve transactions with interested parties, including going private transactions and "related party transactions" (major transactions involving interested parties). See *Magna International Inc., Re*, 2010 CarswellOnt 4416, 72 B.L.R. (4th) 235 (Ont. Securities Comm.), additional reasons 2010 CarswellOnt 10322 (Ont. Securities Comm.).

The stock exchanges are also involved. The Toronto Stock Exchange, for example, may require approval of an issuance of shares where a substantial block of shares is issued or where the issuance materially affects the control of the issuer. The required approval may be of all shareholders, or of a majority of the minority. In *HudBay Minerals Inc., Re*, 2009 CarswellOnt 352, 32 O.S.C.B. 1089 (Ont. Securities Comm.), on a proposal to acquire outstanding shares of Lundin Mining Corporation, which required the approval of Lundin's shareholders, but not the approval of HudBay's shareholders. Although, the TSX generally requires shareholder approval for acquisitions involving dilution in excess of 25%, the TSX exempted approval by Hudbay's shareholders in this case. However, the OSC held that to maintain the quality of the marketplace, the shareholders of the acquirer were entitled to vote on the proposal. See TSX Company Manual Sec. 604. But see also *Re Torstar Corporation and Southam Inc.* [6 June 1986] O.S.C.B. 3033 and *Re Canada Malting*, [27 June 1986] O.S.C.B. 3565.

(c) Note on Classification of Shares

Rule 56-501 of the Ontario Securities Commission, noted above, creates a scheme for the classification of shares according to their voting rights. The purpose of the scheme is to ensure that buyers and sellers of publicly traded securities fully understand the nature of the voting rights attaching to the securities being traded.

1.1 Definitions

In this Rule

* * *

"class" includes a series of a class;

"common shares" means equity shares to which are attached voting rights exercisable in all circumstances, irrespective of the number or percentage of shares owned, that are not less, on a per share basis, than the voting rights attaching to any other shares of an outstanding class of shares of the issuer, unless the Director makes a determination under section 4.1 that the shares are restricted shares;

* * *

"equity shares" means shares of an issuer that carry a residual right to participate in the earnings of the issuer and, upon the liquidation or winding up of the issuer, in its assets;

* * *

"non-voting shares" means restricted shares that do not carry the right to vote generally, except for a right to vote that is mandated in special circumstances by law;

"preference shares" means shares to which are attached a preference or right over the shares of any class of equity shares of the issuer, but does not include equity shares;

* * *

"restricted share term" means each of "non-voting shares", "subordinate voting shares", "restricted voting shares" and every other term designated by the Director under subsection 4.1(2);

"restricted shares" means
  (a) equity shares that are not common shares, and
  (b) equity shares determined to be restricted shares under subsection 4.1(1);

"restricted voting shares" means restricted shares that carry a right to vote subject to a restriction on the number or percentage of shares that may be voted by a person, a company or any combination of persons and companies, except to the extent the restriction or limit is permitted or prescribed by statute and is applicable only to persons or companies that are not citizens or residents of Canada or that are otherwise considered as a result of any law applicable to the issuer to be non-Canadians;

* * *

"subject securities" means shares that have the effect, or would have the effect if and when issued, of changing a class of outstanding equity shares into restricted shares;

"subordinate voting shares" means restricted shares that carry a right to vote, if there are shares of another class of shares outstanding that carry a greater right to vote on a per share basis

Under this Rule, if an issuer has restricted shares, or securities that are convertible, exchangeable, or exercisable into restricted shares, then the shares must be described using the classification scheme. The appropriate term must be used in documents sent by the issuer to its shareholders.

(d) Permissible Limitations on the Right to Vote in the Corporation's Constitution

Jacobsen v. United Canso Oil & Gas Ltd.
11 B.L.R. 313, [1980] 6 W.W.R. 38 (Alta. Q.B.)

[The defendant, United Canso Oil & Gas Ltd., was incorporated pursuant to the *Companies Act* on April 15, 1954. On March 16, 1964, United Canso enacted a by-law (By-Law No. 6), which provided that no person shall be entitled to vote more than 1,000 shares of the defendant notwithstanding the number of shares actually held by him. United Canso was subsequently reincorporated, first under the *Canada Corporations Act* and eventually under the *CBCA*. The plaintiff brought an action to determine, as a preliminary point of law, whether or not the by-law contravened the *Companies Act*, *Canada Corporations Act*, and *CBCA*.]

FORSYTH J.: The issue before the Court raises certain fundamental questions with respect to the rights of shareholders of a corporation. It was argued by the plaintiff that there is a presumption of equality between shareholders and the voting restriction in question contravenes this presumption. In this regard reference was made to *Palmer's Company Law* (22nd ed., 1976), vol 1, p. 334, where the learned author states:

> Prima facie the rights carried by the shares rank *pari passu i.e.*, the shareholders participate in the benefits of membership equally. It is only when a company divides its share capital into different classes with different rights attached to them that the prima facie presumption of equality of shares must be displaced.

Gower, on *Modern Company Law* (3rd ed., 1969) at p. 349, expresses a similar sentiment where the learned author states:

> The typical company — one limited by shares — must issue some shares, and the initial presumption of the law is that all shares confer equal rights and impose equal liabilities. As in partnership equality is assumed in the absence of evidence to the contrary. Normally the shareholders' rights will fall under three heads: (i) dividends, (ii) return of capital on a winding up (or authorised reduction of capital), and (iii) attendance at meetings and voting, and unless there is some indication to the contrary all the shares will confer the like rights to all three. So far as voting is concerned this is a comparatively recent development, for, on the analogy of the

partnership rule, it was long felt that members' rights to control through voting should be divorced from their purely financial interests in respect of dividend and capital, so that the equality should be between members rather than between shares. . . It is now recognised that *if voting rights are to vary, separate classes of shares must be created so that the different number of votes can be attached to the shares themselves and not to the holder.* (The italics are mine.)

It is to be noted that the learned author of course was dealing with the development of company law in England, but nevertheless there are many parallels to be drawn between the evolution of company law in England and that in Canada. . .

It appears to me clear on a reading of the by-law [By-law No. 1] that it was contemplated that it was only when different classes of shares were created that a change in the voting rights of one vote for each share might be established. It does not follow, however, that that by-law in effect in itself restraints the corporation from subsequently duly passing the amending By-law No. 6 containing the restriction of voting rights in respect of the one class of shares. I would note here that there was no argument advanced and indeed it was conceded that that by-law was properly passed insofar as the formalities are concerned, that is, notice to shareholders and the requisite number of shareholders being present.

The first question to be addressed is, however, whether By-law No. 6, although duly ratified by the shareholders of United Canso, was nevertheless passed in accordance with the then provisions of the *Companies Act.*

At first blush, ss. 102 and 103 of the *Companies Act,* as they then were, would seem to support the validity of a by-law limiting the number of votes a shareholder might have regardless of the number of shares held. Sections 102 and 103 as they read at the time of enactment of By-law No. 6, provided in part as follows:

102. Subject to the provisions of any by-law of the company duly enacted under the provisions of this Act, each share of the capital stock of any company issued and allotted, shall, subject to the provisions of this Part, carry voting rights and entitle the shareholder to one vote for each such share owned by him.

103. In the absence of other provisions in that behalf in the letters patent, supplementary letters patent or by-laws of the company.

* * *

(b) at all meetings of shareholders every shareholder is entitled to give one vote for each share then held by him; . . .

However, those sections must be read in the context of the Act as a whole and not in isolation. . . In considering the issues to be determined in the relevant provisions of the *Companies Act*, it is important to remember that United Canso has only one class of shares, these being par value shares.

Part I of the Act, and in particular those sections dealing with formation of new companies, sets forth, *inter alia*, the information to be set forth in an application for letters patent including the nature and number of shares, including classes of shares it is proposed to issue. Section 12 deals with different classes of shares and subs. (1) of s. 12 provides in part as follows:

> 12.(1) The letters patent or supplementary letters patent of a company may provide for shares of more than one class and for any preferred, deferred or other special rights, restrictions, conditions or limitations attaching to any class of shares; . . .
>
> (2) The shares of all series of the same class carrying voting rights shall not carry the right to more than one vote for each share, and when any fixed cumulative dividends or amounts payable on a return of capital are not paid in full, the shares of all series of the same class shall participate rateably in respect of such dividends including accumulations, . . .
>
> (5) The authorized capital of a company having shares with a nominal or par value shall, with respect to those shares, be the total nominal amount of those shares.

* * *

> (8) Each share of the capital stock without nominal or par value shall be equal to every other such share of the capital stock subject to the preferred, deferred or other special rights or restrictions, conditions or limitations attached to any class of shares.

As already noted the one class of shares of United Canso are par value shares and accordingly the provisions of subs. (8) are not directly applicable, but only no doubt due to the ramifications which flow from the issuance of par value rather than non-par value shares including the provisions of subs. (5) previously quoted.

> (14) In no case shall shares of a public company of any class or any subdivision of any class, whether with or without par value, be issued and allotted to which shall attach any exclusive right to control the management of the business or affairs of the company by the election or removal of the board of directors thereof or otherwise.
>
> (15) Nothing in subsection (14) shall be deemed to prevent the issue, under authority of provision therefor either by letters patent or by-law, of any preferred shares to which are attached preferential voting rights, exercisable in a stated event only, although, in the stated

event, an exclusive right to control or manage is attached to or is an incident to such preferred shares.

In short, s. 12 recognizes the establishment of different classes of shares which may contain restrictions, conditions or limitations attaching to such classes of shares. There is no comparable section in the Act suggesting such restrictions, conditions or limitations where there is only one class of shares.

Section 33(4) of the *Companies Act* is interesting in that it states:

(4) Where the capital stock of the company consists of more than one class of shares every certificate of each class shall contain a statement of the rights and conditions attaching to such class of shares.

Surely Parliament could not have intended that where there was only one class of shares that class could contain rights and conditions which need not be evidenced on the share certificate itself and that the holder would be presumed to know the by-laws or the provisions of the letters patent of the company and that it is only when there are several classes of shares that such rights and conditions must be set forth in the statement on the certificate.

Section 59 of the *Companies Act* also seems to be supportive of this position. Section 59(1) provides in part as follows:

59.(1) When no provision is made by the letters patent or supplementary letters patent for shares of more than one class, the directors of a company may from time to time make by-laws.

(a) for the creating and issuing of any shares as preferred shares with such preferred or other special rights, restrictions, conditions or limitations, whether in regard to dividend, voting, return of capital, or otherwise as may be set out in any such by-law, but no limitations shall be imposed upon the right to vote;

In short, I am satisfied that the provisions of ss. 102 and 103 previously quoted relating to the altering of the one vote for one share provision must be read, in considering the Act as a whole, as contemplating the issuance of different classes of shares carrying rights and restrictions, and conditions including voting restrictions with respect to such class of shares. In my view, the *Companies Act* in force at the time of the enactment of the by-law recognized the presumption of law quoted by the authorities previously referred to that all shares confer equal rights and impose equal liabilities and that if voting rights are to vary separate classes of shares must be created so that the different numbers of votes can be attached to the shares by themselves and not to the holder. It follows that By-law No. 6 at the time it was first enacted, contravened the provisions of the *Companies Act* and was invalid.

However, as noted, supplementary letters patent for United Canso were issued on July 25, 1974, amending the letters patent of United Canso by adding thereto the voting limitations contained in By-law No. 6. These supplementary letters patent were issued under the provisions of the *Canada Corporations Act* which Act replaced the *Companies Act*. The *Canada Corporations Act* while replacing the *Companies Act* nevertheless contains substantially the same provisions previously referred to in the *Companies Act*. . .

The provisions of s. 33(4) of the *Companies Act* previously quoted has its counterpart somewhat expanded in s. 36(4) of the *Canada Corporations Act* which provides as follows:

> (4) Where a company has more than one class of shares
>
> (a) the preferences, rights, conditions, restrictions, limitations or prohibitions attaching to any class of shares shall be stated in legible characters
>> (i) on every share certificate representing that class of shares, or
>> (ii) by a writing permanently attached to the share certificate; or
> (b) there shall be inscribed on each such share certificate, in legible characters, a statement that there are preferences, rights, conditions, restrictions, limitations or prohibitions attached to such class of shares, and that the full text thereof is obtainable on demand, and without fee, from the secretary of the company.

* * *

At the time of the enactment of the *Canada Corporations Act*, s. 104 [re-en. R.S.C. 1970 (1st Supp.), c. 10, s. 8] of that Act read as follows:

> 104. Subject to the provisions of any by-law of the company duly enacted under this Act, each share of the capital stock of a company issued and allotted, shall, subject to this Part, carry voting rights and entitle the shareholder to [one] vote for each share owned by him.

That section was [re-enacted] however, to read as follows:

> 104. Subject to section 105, and in the absence of other provisions in that behalf in the letters patent or supplementary letters patent, at all meetings of shareholders every shareholder is entitled to give one vote for each share then held by him, but no shareholder in arrears in respect of any call is entitled to vote at any meeting.

Thus, it became necessary if a change was contemplated with respect to voting rights for shares to obtain such change by applying for and obtaining supplementary letters patent rather than simply by amending the by-laws of the company. However, again bearing in mind the provisions of the *Canada Corporations Act* previously referred to which carried forward from the *Companies Act*, it appears this section, referring to a change in the basic provision of one share one vote, can only have been contemplated to come into effect where more than one class of shares was established and not, as in the case of United Canso, where there is only one class of shares.

The question arises as to whether or not the fact that supplementary letters patent were in fact issued changes this situation. I do not see how the administrative act of having caused the supplementary letters patent to issue can validate and render enforceable a provision which appears to be clearly contrary to the intent of the Act under which the supplementary letters patent were issued.

Section 4 of the *Canada Corporations Act* should be noted which provides as follows:

> 4. The provisions of this Part relating to matters preliminary to the issue of the letters patent or supplementary letters patent are directory only, and no letters patent or supplementary letters patent issued under this Part shall be held void or voidable on account of any irregularity or insufficiency in respect of any matter preliminary to the issue of the letters patent or supplementary letters patent.

I do not think, however, that this provision in any way changes that position as clearly as what was being dealt with here was not an irregularity or insufficiency but rather a fundamental provision attaching to the one class of shares of United Canso which as already mentioned clearly appears to be contrary to the overall provisions of the *Canada Corporations Act.*

I am, accordingly, satisfied notwithstanding the issuance of supplementary letters patent incorporating By-law No. 6 and limiting the right of a holder of shares to no more than 1000 votes regardless of the number of shares that such by-law and the supplementary letters patent issued in 1974 were invalid.

This does not end the matter. A certificate of continuance for United Canso was issued on October 24, 1979, pursuant to s. 181 of the *Canada Business Corporations Act* and the articles of continuance contained, attached as Sched. 2, the same voting restriction previously set forth in By-law No. 6. Accordingly, it is necessary to consider the provisions of the *Canada Business Corporations Act* and, in particular, whether or not by virtue of the fact that the limitation was contained in the articles of continuance, that limitation became effective on the issuance of the certificate of continuance and is, accordingly, still in force.

It should be first noted that the authority for continuance of United Canso under the *Canada Business Corporations Act* is contained in s. 261.

Section 181 [am. 1978-79, c. 9, s. 57] of the *Canada Business Corporations Act* provides in part as follows:

> "181(1.1). A body corporate that applies for continuance under subsection (1) may, without so stating in its articles of continuance, effect by those articles any amendment to its Act of incorporation,

articles, letters patent or memorandum or articles of association if the amendment is an amendment a corporation incorporated under this Act may make to its articles.

. . . [I]t is clear pursuant to sub s. (1.1) of s. 181 that an amendment to the letters patent can be effected in the articles of continuance with respect to any corporation applying for continuance under the *Canada Business Corporations Act*, if the amendment is an amendment a corporation incorporated under this Act may make to its articles. Does the *Canada Business Corporations Act* contemplate an amendment of the nature set forth in the articles of continuance?

* * *

Again it is to be noted that particular provisions come into play where there are two or more classes of shares requiring the setting forth of rights, privileges, *etc.*, attaching to such shares. Thus, the distinction is clearly made between that situation and the situation where there is only one class of shares where it must be assumed there are no rights, restrictions, etc., attaching to such shares. Section 134(1) is similar to the previously quoted provisions of the *Canada Corporations Act* and the *Companies Act* and provides as follows:

134.(1) Unless the articles otherwise provide, each share of a corporation entitles the holder thereof to one vote at a meeting of shareholders.

However, that section must [be] read in relation to s. 24 [am. 1978-79, c. 9, s. 9] of the Act which provides as follows [subss. (3), (4)]:

(3) Where a corporation has only one class of shares, the rights of the holders thereof are equal in all respects and include the rights.

(a) to vote at any meeting of shareholders of the corporation;

(b) to receive any dividend declared by the corporation; and

(c) to receive the remaining property of the corporation on dissolution.

(4) the articles may provide for more than one class of shares and, if they so provide,

(a) the rights, privileges, restrictions and conditions attaching to the shares of each class shall be set out therein; and

(b) the rights set out in subsection (3) shall be attached to at least one class of shares but all such rights are not required to be attached to one class.

It seems abundantly clear on a reading of s. 24(3) as well as the reading of the entire Act that again Parliament has even more clearly specified that it is only when there is more than one class of shares that different rights, privileges, restrictions and conditions attaching to shares may arise.

It is argued that subs. (3) of s. 24 must be read as being subject to subs. 168(5)(c) of the Act which reads as follows:

> (5) Subject to subsections 254(2) and (3), the Governor in Council may make regulations with respect to a corporation that constrains the issue or transfer of its shares prescribing
>
> * * *
>
> (c) the limitations on voting rights of any shares held contrary to the articles of the corporation;

In short, s. 24(3) must not be read in the absolute sense but is subject to other provisions in the Act which may change the basic position established by s. 24. Section 168(5)(c), however, clearly has a very restricted application and only applies to corporations which constrain the issue or transfer of their shares for the particular purposes as set out in s. 168.

It is also argued that s. 24(3) is not inconsistent with the provisions of Bylaw No. 6 as continued under the articles of continuance of United Canso in that it deals with the right to vote but not in any way with the number of votes. The voting limitations in the articles of continuance clearly do not affect the right of a shareholder to vote and apply equally to all shareholders. It is only when their shareholdings exceed 1,000 shares that they are restricted from voting any shares in excess of 1,000. I am not satisfied this is an interpretation which can be put on s. 24(3). In effect it is argued that the rights of the holders of the shares are equal in that all shareholders can only vote a maximum of 1,000 shares regardless of the number of shares held. It might similarly be argued that they would be equal if all shareholders could only receive dividends to a maximum of 1,000 shares regardless of the number of shares held or receive the remaining property of the corporation on the basis of a 1,000 share maximum regardless of the number of shares held. It seems to me reading s. 24 as a whole, each shareholder has the right to vote at any meeting of shareholders on the basis of the number of shares held where the corporation only has one class of shares and that this presumption can only be upset where there are more [than] one class of shares established in which case the provisions of subs. (4) come into play. That position in this regard is in my opinion fortified by the provisions of subs. (4)(b) of s. 24 which makes it clear that all of the rights set forth in subs. (3) must, where there is more than one class of shares, be attached to at least one class of shares.

In the result for the reasons aforesaid the answer to the preliminary point of law put before the Court is that the defendant's By-law No. 6 which provides that no person shall be entitled to vote more than 1,000 shares of the defendant notwithstanding the number of shares actually held by him does, in fact, contravene the provisions of the *Canada Business Corporations Act* and is invalid. . . .

Order accordingly.

Notes

1   Immediately before the decision in *Jacobson* was released, United Canso was continued as a Nova Scotia company. See *Jacobsen v. United Canso Oil & Gas Ltd.* (1980), 12 B.L.R. 113, 40 N.S.R. (2d) 692, 1980 CarswellNS 28 (T.D.), where the Court declined to rule on the validity of the voting restriction.

2   Why do you think the company's managers wished to have the 1000 vote restriction? What do you expect would be the effect of the restriction on the value of the company's shares? Why do you suppose a majority of shareholders apparently supported the change?

Bowater Canadian Limited v. R.L. Crain Ltd.
(1987), 62 O.R. (2d) 752 (C.A.)

[The appellant, Bowater Canadian Limited ("Bowater") challenged a provision of the articles of incorporation of the respondent, R.L. Crain Inc. ("Crain") which provided that special common shares held by the respondent Craisec Ltd. ("Craisec") carry ten votes per share in the hands of Craisec, but only one vote per share in the hands of a potential transferee (a "step-down" provision). McRae J. at trail held the voting restriction to be invalid and held that the special common shares shall carry ten votes irrespective of who holds them. Bowater appealed.]

HOULDEN J.A.: In his reasons for judgment, McRae J. held that although there was no express prohibition in the CBCA against a step-down provision, s. 24(4) of the Act should be interpreted in accordance with the general principles of corporation law with the result that the rights which are attached to a class of shares must be provided equally to all shares of that class, this interpretation being founded on the principle that rights, including votes, attach to the share and not to the shareholder. Subsections (3) and (4) of s. 24 of the CBCA, as amended by S.C. 1978-79, c. 9, s. 9, provide:

> 24(3) Where a corporation has only one class of shares, the rights of the holders thereof are equal in all respects and include the rights
>
> (a) to vote at any meeting of shareholders of the corporation;
>
> (b) to receive any dividend declared by the corporation; and
>
> (c) to receive the remaining property of the corporation on dissolution.

(4) The articles may provide for more than one class of shares and, if they so provide,

(a) the rights, privileges, restrictions and conditions attaching to the shares of each class shall be set out therein; and

(b) the rights set out in subsection (3) shall be attached to at least one class of shares but all such rights are not required to be attached to one class.

... In our opinion if there was not equality of rights within a class of shareholders, there would be great opportunity for fraud, even though that is not a problem in this case. Section 24(5) of the Alberta *Business Corporations Act*, S.A. 1981, c. B-15, reflects what we take to be the applicable principle of corporate law, it provides:

24(5) Subject to section 27, if a corporation has more than one class of shares, the rights of the holders of the shares of any class are equal in all respects.

Mr. Garrow contended that even if the step-down provision violates the provision of the CBCA, it was saved by s. 181(8) of the Act which reads:

181(8) Subject to subsection 45(8),a share of an extra-provincial corporation issued before the extra-provincial corporation was continued under this Act is deemed to have been issued in compliance with this Act and with the provisions of the articles of continuance irrespective of whether the share is fully paid and irrespective of any designation, rights, privileges, restrictions or conditions set out on or referred to in the certificate representing the share, and continuance under this section does not deprive a holder of any right or privilege that he claims under, or relieve him of any liability in respect of, an issued share.

With respect, we do not agree with Mr. Garrow's submission. We do not think that the subsection was intended to protect "rights, privileges, restrictions or conditions" that are unlawful.

Having held that the step-down provision of the special common shares was invalid, McRae J. turned his attention to the issue of severability. After a careful review of the submissions of counsel, he concluded that the stepdown provision was severable, with the result, as we have stated, that special common shares now carry ten votes each regardless of whether they are held by Craisec or a transferee. Again, we agree with this ruling. In this connection, we are particularly impressed with the minutes of a meeting of shareholders of Crain held January 19, 1959. This is the meeting which authorized the creation of the special common shares. The portion of the minutes dealing with the special common shares reads as follows:

On motion duly made by Mr. MacTavish and seconded by Mr. Plummer, it was resolved that the shareholders sanction, ratify and confirm By-law number 80 being a By-law sub-dividing the present 100,000 Common Shares into 400,000 Common shares, creating an additional 400,000 Common shares ranking *pari passu* in all respects with the existing Common shares as sub-divided and creating 167,000 Special Common Shares which shall carry the right to ten votes per share, and authorizing an application to the Secretary of State of Canada for Supplementary Letters Patent confirming such changes.

It will be noted that no mention is made of the step-down provision, only that each special common share is to carry the right to ten votes per share.

When the special common shares were created, Crain was making a very advantageous purchase of a majority interest in a company known as Business Systems Limited ("BSL"). Under the purchase agreement the vendors were to receive either four common shares of Crain or $40 cash. At the time of the purchase Craisec had effective control of Crain. Craisec agreed to exchange 41,750 common shares of Crain for BSL common and Class "C" preferred shares in consideration for which it received 167,000 special common shares of Crain enabling it to maintain control of Crain.

The provisions for ten votes per share have now been in force for almost 30 years and, prior to this application, have not been questioned by shareholders, although the share capital of Crain has been rearranged on several occasions, the last being August, 1986.

Mr. Thomson contended that because the step-down provision was invalid, the whole of cl. 1 of the articles of amalgamation was also invalid so that the special common shares and the subordinate voting shares would all carry only one vote. We do not agree. Rather, as we have said, we agree with McRae J. that the step-down provision can be severed without affecting the validity of the provision for ten votes for each special common share. We believe that this accords with the intention of the parties at the time that the shares were created.

In the result, the appeal is dismissed with costs. The cross-appeals are also dismissed but in the circumstances without costs.

Appeal and cross-appeals dismissed.

Notes and Questions

1   Before the lower court, Craisec had proposed an amendment to the company's articles that it requested the court put in place under the authority given it in current CBCA s. 241. Under the proposed amendment, should Craisec desire to sell special common shares, it would be able to do so by means of first converting the shares into ordinary common shares, and then transferring the shares to the third party. This proposal was designed to get around the problems identified by the court in the holding, *supra*. Calling this proposal a

"conversion shuffle," McRae J. held that this was an impermissible attempt to do indirectly what it could not do directly. See *Bowater Canadian Ltd. v. R.L. Crain Ltd. and Craisec Ltd. (No. 2)*, unreported, Sup. Ct. Ont.

2   The plaintiff in the Bowater case proceeded by way of application under the oppression remedy, seeking relief under that provision. The lower court held that the step down did not violate the CBCA oppression provision, but nonetheless violated s. 24 of the Act (a finding affirmed in the appeal judgment, *supra*). Having determined that there was no oppression, what jurisdiction did the Court have to determine that there was a violation of another provision of the CBCA? In giving Bowater relief, did the Court also give substantive effect to the merely procedural rules of court (which it relied on, in addition to s. 24)?

3   Suppose that Crain had initially incorporated into its articles the conversion provision that it asked the Court to insert in Crain's articles in the lower court (see note 1, *supra*), rather than the step down. Do you think that the Court would have upheld the provision?

4   Many companies that trade publicly in Canada (and many that do not) are controlled by families, as in the Bowater case. It is very common in such enterprises to see two classes of shares; voting (or multiple voting) shares held or controlled by the family, and non-voting (or inferior voting) shares held by public shareholders. This enables the key shareholders to control the enterprise by holding a relatively small portion of the total equity in the company. For example, after a 1983 reorganization of the capital structure of Canadian Tire, the controlling family (the Billeses) were able to control the company by virtue of holding about 62% of the voting shares of the company, even though this constituted only about 2.5% of the total equity of the company. It is clear that this type of bifurcated share structure makes it very difficult, and in many cases impossible, for a potential acquiror to obtain control of the company through the mechanism of a "hostile" takeover bid (i.e., one not sanctioned by the existing controllers). Is this a good or a bad thing? Are there good reasons why we observe this kind of capital structure? In the same vein, what are the policy arguments for and against a step-down provision? Does it serve a useful estate planning function? See Stephanie Ben-Ishai and Poonam Puri, "Dual Class Shares in Canada: A Historical Analysis" (2006) 29 Dal LJ 117, and Anita I. Anand, "Offloading the Burden of Being Public: An Analysis of Multi-Voting Share Structures," Va L & Bus Rev forthcoming.

(e) Protection of Non-Voting Shares in Takeover Bids

When a takeover bid is made, it is usually made for the *voting* shares of a target corporation. This is because the acquiror can only exercise control if it has the power to replace the directors, and it is the voting class of shares that confers this power. Takeover bids are almost always made at a premium to the current market price to induce shareholders to tender; hence, those who hold the voting equity receive a premium for their shares, while non-voting shareholders do not. Since one of the important policies underlying modern takeover legislation is equality of treatment for all shareholders of the target company, it has been suggested by some that this "unequal treatment" is unfair. To overcome this, in 1984 the Ontario Securities Commission (OSC) included in Interim Policy 1.3 a requirement that non-voting or restricted voting shares carry "coattail" provisions. Such provisions are designed to ensure that the non-voting equity will share in the fruits of any takeover bid. One of the most common coattails, for example, automatically converts the non-voting shares into voting shares if any takeover bid is made for the company. This effectively forces the acquiror to bid for the non-voting equity as well as the voting in order to secure control. The OSC received a considerable amount of unfavourable comment on this feature of the Interim Policy, based (ostensibly) not on any objection to the principle of equal treatment, but on practical difficulties in implementing the Policy. Thus, the requirement for coattails was omitted from the final version of the policy. See "OSC Statement Concerning Restricted Shares" [12 Oct. 1984] O.S.C.B. 4295.

The argument about coattails was revived in 1987 with the takeover bid by the "independent dealers" of Canadian Tire for 49% of the voting shares of Canadian Tire. The non-voting Class A shares contained a coattail that converted the Class A shares into voting shares should there be a takeover bid for "a majority" of the voting shares. The bid was thus structured in a manner that would secure control for the dealers, but would avoid triggering the coattail. The Ontario Securities Commission issued a cease trade order to halt the transaction on the grounds that it was "grossly abusive" of the capital markets and the minority (Class A) shareholders. The OSC held that the transaction was "artificial" in that it would effect a change in control without triggering the coattail, when (in the OSC's view) investors had expected that any change in control would trigger the coattail. The OSC further held that the spirit, if not the letter of the coattail protection had been violated. See *Re Canadian Tire Corporation Limited and C.T.C. Dealer Holdings Limited* (1987), 35 B.L.R. 56. The Ontario Divisional Court affirmed; see (1987), 35 B.L.R. 117. The Ontario Court of Appeal declined to hear an appeal.

Following *Canadian Tire*, the Toronto Stock Exchange (TSE) decided to step in where the OSC had not. On July 30, 1987, the Exchange issued a "Notice to Members, Listed Companies and Securities

Lawyers" entitled "Exchange Policy on Take-over Protection for Holders of Non-voting and Subordinate Voting Shares." The TSE indicated that it would refuse to list any newly created restricted voting shares that lacked coattail protection.

As noted, a concern that shareholders be treated "equally" underlies the coattail requirement. Would permitting unequal treatment tend to foster more changes of control, and, if so, would both majority and minority shareholders be better off as a result? For differing views on this question, see Andrews, "The Shareholder's Right to Equal Opportunity in the Sale of Shares" (1965), 78 Harv. L. Rev. 505 and Easterbrook and Fischel, "Corporate Control Transactions" (1982), 91 Yale L.J. 698 and Edward M. Iacobucci, "Why Does Ontario Require Equal Treatment in Sales of Corporate Control?" (2008) 58 U. Toronto L.J. 123 (WLeC).

Note that determining what "equal treatment" entails may involve more than a simple mechanical exercise in instances where the classes of shares to be equally treated differ in more respects than simply voting rights. Establishing what equal treatment is may therefore involve a costly administrative and/or judicial proceeding, especially if the rule leads minority shareholders to litigate purely in order to grab a larger share of the pie. Is this another reason for dispensing with an "equal treatment" rule in some or all situations? See *Palmer v. Carling O'Keefe Breweries of Canada Ltd.*, 1987 CarswellOnt 140, [1987] O.J. No. 1005 (Ont. H.C.), reversed 1989 CarswellOnt 119, 67 O.R. (2d) 161 (Ont. Div. Ct.) (the Court of Appeal declined to hear the appeal).

(f) Cumulative Voting for Directors

Section 107 of the CBCA provides for cumulative voting and sets out detailed rules for how such voting is to be carried out. Section 120 of the OBCA and section 102 of the SBCA adopt the CBCA's approach to cumulative voting procedure. Section 65 of the NBBCA requires that cumulative voting be used in the election of directors. The BCBCA and NSCA do not expressly provide for cumulative voting.

For an explanation of the mechanics of cumulative voting, see MacKinnon, "The Protection of Dissenting Shareholders" in Ziegel (Ed), *Studies in Canadian Company Law*, Volume 1, p. 507, at pp. 540–43 (1967).

Report of the Ontario Select Committee on Company Law
pp. 71–73 (1967)

Discussion on whether cumulative voting provisions should be mandatory

8.2.5 Impressive arguments can be made for and against mandatory cumulative voting. Of the arguments in favour of the system, the most persuasive is that based on the "democratic necessity" or "fairness" concept, that is, that the cumulative voting system is equitable and consistent with acceptable democratic principles and therefore should be compulsory. However, this argument depends upon the aptness of the analogy drawn between the incorporated business organization and the political body, an analogy which is inherently defective. The most persuasive argument against cumulative voting is that it encourages the election of directors representing particular interest groups who, by virtue of their partisan role, encourage disharmony in the management of the affairs of the company. An American author who made a comprehensive study of cumulative voting established that cumulative voting, in the States in which it was available, was rarely used by shareholders. [Williams, *Cumulative Voting for Directors*.] The author attributed this disinterest to the fact that the typical shareholder, at least in publicly-held companies, has long since come to regard himself as an investor rather than a proprietor and is apparently content to leave management in the hands of the professional managers.

8.2.6 In view of the uncertainties which surround the true value of the cumulative voting system, the Committee does not recommend that cumulative voting be made mandatory for Ontario companies. The many recommended legislative changes outlined in this Report will significantly strengthen the position of the minority shareholder in Ontario and until those recommendations have been implemented and put into practice, it is difficult to know whether or not mandatory cumulative voting would be a necessary or desirable feature of Ontario law.

Proposals for a New Business Corporations Law for Canada
pp. 73-74 (1971)

207. The right to cumulate may be effectively defeated by a variety of devices such as rotating directorships and reduction in the number of directors. The former is precluded by paragraph (f) which requires the annual retirement of the entire body of directors, and the latter by paragraph (h) which limits the right to reduce the number of directors of corporations in which cumulation is permitted. Paragraphs (c) and (d) of s. [107] introduce a procedure for the election of directors that is novel in Canadian legislation. Under this provision, which is based upon comparable legislation in the United Kingdom — *Companies Act*, 1948, s. 183 — and South Africa — Act 46 of 1926, s. 96 — the election of every director must be the subject of a separate resolution, unless the shareholders first pass a resolution allowing more than one director to be elected by a single resolution. The purpose of this requirement is to prevent shareholders from being confronted with the necessity to vote upon an entire slate of nominees for office, of only some of whom they may approve. This is a necessary part of the cumulative voting provisions. Paragraph (e) is designed to deal with a problem that may arise under this system if there is a greater number of candidates than there are offices to be filled. The procedure prescribed here is simply that the candidates

receiving the lowest number of votes are eliminated, and the remaining candidates are declared elected.

Question

In view of the foregoing, what conclusion do you draw with respect to the matter of cumulative voting? Should it be required for all corporations? What factors should be considered in deciding the matter?

(g)   The Right to Appoint a Proxy

(i)   Background to Present Legislation

The case summarized below was decided before the enactment of the modern legislation on the subject of proxy voting and deals with some aspects of the common law regarding use of proxy. The common law is still important in the case of a corporation which is exempt from the proxy information requirements under the relevant statute.

In *Garvie v. Axmith*, [1962] O.R. 65, 31 D.L.R. (2d) 65, the directors of the defendant company gave notice of a special meeting of shareholders to approve an agreement by the company to purchase the assets and undertaking of a second company and an application for supplementary letters patent to permit refinancing of the company under a new name. The material sent out with the notice, including financial statements of the two companies, made it apparent that the net worth of the two companies as shown in their balance sheets did not form the basis of comparative valuation for the purposes of the proposed refinancing, but no information as to valuation was in fact given. In addition, since many shares were held by several brokers in the form of "street" certificates (that is, in the names of nominees on behalf of the beneficial share owners) some shareholders received no notice of the meeting.

The resolutions were passed by the shareholders with the directors casting a substantial number of proxy votes, many of which were declared invalid. Spence J. held that it was the right of each shareholder to receive sufficient information with notice of a meeting to permit him to come to an intelligent conclusion whether he should vote in favour of the proposal to be put to the meeting or against it. The court also held that, although the use of a proxy form with the names of the proxy printed therein and without the provision of a blank form of proxy is not good corporate practice, it does not vitiate the notice of a meeting.

The Report of the Attorney General's Committee on Securities Legislation in Ontario (the "Kimber Report" (1965)) noted the importance of proxies in large public companies with numerous shareholders and argued that, since management most always solicits proxies on its own behalf in a way which invites shareholders to appoint management nominees, it therefore tends to perpetuate itself in office.

The Committee adopted the US view concerning the importance of accompanying proxies. For this reason, the Report recommended that an "information circular," with prescribed contents, should accompany each proxy when mailed to the shareholders. The standard of disclosure in the information circular was aimed at ensuring that the circular would reveal as much information as would be revealed by attending the meeting in person.

Finally, the Committee recommended that solicitation of proxies by the management of all public companies be made mandatory, but that it not be required that the proxy or the information circular be filed with or reviewed by any governmental agency prior to mailing.

(ii)   The Proxy Legislation

Iacobucci, Pilkington, and Prichard
Canadian Business Corporations
pp. 181–183, (footnotes omitted)

The legislation dealing with proxies and proxy solicitation serves at least three important purposes. It provides a means of participation for shareholders in company decisions, disclosure of sufficient information in order that the shareholders may evaluate proposed company initiatives, and disclosure of information which adequately depicts the financial position of the company and which is vital to the investing public...

The *Kimber Report* emphasized the importance of disclosure to the investing public as it "provides the capital market with the information necessary" to achieve its principal economic functions which are "to assure the optimum allocation of financial resources in the economy, to permit maximum mobility and transferability of those resources, and to provide facilities for a continuing valuation of financial assets."

Canada has recently seen substantial reform of the proxy legislation. Following the recommendations of the *Kimber Report*, the Ontario, Alberta, British Columbia, and Federal Acts have all adopted similar proxy provisions which have resulted in a comprehensive and basically sound set of requirements recognizing the important purposes described above. The legislation was a response to the common law by which shareholders had no right to vote by proxy. The right to vote by proxy had to be granted by special authority in the corporate constitution and, in a memorandum jurisdiction, "there seemed to be no limit so the extent to which the right, if granted, could be contractually circumscribed." Moreover, since management determined the form and use of the proxy, various practices developed which favoured the directors' ability to accumulate voting support unfairly. Further, the only obligation upon those calling company meetings was to give adequate notice. . .

The statutory provisions that deal with proxies are found in the CBCA at sections 147 to 154, and sections 32 to 43 of the Regulations [currently, ss. 46-9 of the Regulations]; see also sections 175 to 181 of the BCCA [currently, ss.172-185 of the BCBCA] and sections 109 to 114 of the OBCA. The OBCA sections have been based on the CBCA provisions with some important variations. For example, section 110(2) [currently, s. 110(2.1)] of the OBCA provides that a proxy ceases to be valid one year from its date with respect to meetings of shareholders of offering corporations. The implication is that a proxy with respect to a non-offering corporation continues to be valid until duly revoked. In comparison, section 148(3) of the CBCA provides that a proxy is valid only at the meeting for which it is given or any adjournment thereof.

There have been some decisions which have emphasized the importance of adherence to the proxy legislative requirements. In *Charlebois et al. v. Bienvenu et al.*, [1967] 2 O.R. 635, 64 D.L.R. (2d) 683 (H.C.) [rev'd on another point, [1968] 2 O.R. 217, 68 D.L.R. (2d) 578 (C.A.)], Fraser, J. held that the management of a corporation committed a constructive fraud on the minority shareholders by soliciting proxies without complying with the provisions of the Corporations Act as to proper notice. In the result, an interlocutory injunction was ordered restraining the board of directors which had been purportedly elected from acting. In *Babic et al. v. Milinkovic* (1972), 22 D.L.R. (3d) 732 (B.C. S.C.), Kirke Smith, J. granted an interim injunction restraining the directors of a company from acting on resolutions because of the failure of the corporation's officers to provide each shareholder with proxies prior to or with each notice of the corporation's meeting as provided by the B.C. Companies Act, thereby rendering the decisions purportedly taken at that meeting incurable nullities. The decision was affirmed: (1972), 25 D.L.R. (3d) 752 (B.C. C.A.).

(iii)   The Concept of Solicitation

The concept of "solicitation" is central to the proxy system. For the definition of solicitation, see OBCA ss. 109-114; CBCA ss. 147-154. The BCBCA is silent on proxy solicitation, as well as form of proxy and information circular requirements, leaving the matter to the British Columbia *Securities Act*.

Brown v. Duby

1980 CarswellOnt 100, 28 O.R. (2d) 745, 11 B.L.R. 129 (Ont. H.C.)

[The plaintiff, United Canso Oil & Gas Ltd., brought a motion for an interlocutory injunction restraining the defendants, shareholders of United Canso, from soliciting proxies from shareholders of United Canso Oil & Gas Ltd. without the dissident proxy circular required by the *Canada Business Corporations Act*, S.A. 1974-75-76, c. 33.]

CRAIG J.: The plaintiffs claim that the individual defendants caused two letters to be sent by D.E King & Co. Inc. to certain shareholders and stockbrokers. The first letter was dated March 7th, 1980, and was sent only to the shareholders of Canso resident in the United States of America. The second letter was dated March 30th, 1980, and was sent to all shareholders. The plaintiffs claim that both letters constitute a solicitation of proxies within the meaning of s. 144(1) [now section 150(1)(b)] of, and in breach of, the Act . . .

In my opinion the letter of March 30th is not a solicitation for proxies within the meaning of s. 144(1) [now s. 150(1)(b)] but is directed to requesting the shareholders to sign a requisition requiring the calling of a meeting of shareholders "for the election of directors" pursuant to s. 137 [now s. 143(1)] . . .

Turning now to the letter of March 7th, I quote it in full (except for the 'proxy circular" attached to it giving the names, addresses, principal occupations and shareholdings of the Shareholders' Committee):

UNITED CANSO OIL & GAS LTD.	SHAREHOLDERS COMMITTEE
335-8th Avenue	2810 Glenda Avenue
Calgary, Alberta	Forth Worth, Texas
T2P 1C9	76117
(403) 269-8221	(817) 831-0761

March 7, 1980

DEAR FELLOW UNITED CANSO SHAREHOLDER:

We believe it's time for a change in the management of your Company.

As substantial shareholders of United Canso Oil & Gas Ltd. we have formed this Committee because of our serious concern about your Company's past operating record and its future prospects under a board of directors led by the incumbent president, John W. Buckley.

In our view, the Buckley-headed management has failed to achieve the Company's potential for growth. The history of your Company's management, as we see it, has been marked by conflicts of interest and little progress. Your Company lost $272,079 for the fiscal year ended September 30, 1979 and $1,056,533 for the quarter ended December 31, 1979. Instead of a record of earnings growth, the Buckley management as it has done in the past offers you promises for the future.

We intend to solicit proxies at the next meeting of shareholders for the election of an entirely new Board of Directors, committed to managing the Company for the benefit of all its shareholders.

The members of the Committee together own more than 394,000 shares over twenty times the amount owned by the present board, which together owns fewer than 18,000 shares, or less than one-third of 1% of your Company. We believe we share with you a common interest in the Company and its future.

We are writing to you now to introduce the Committee. We enclose a description of the Committee members, including their present principal occupations and their shareholders [sic] in United Canso.

We are not requesting proxies at this time. The Shareholders Committee will ask for your proxy only after we have prepared a definite proxy statement, which cannot be done for the next shareholders' meeting until the incumbents' materials have been sent out. At present, we do not know the date of the meeting, the incumbent slate, or, indeed, what matters are to be considered at the meeting.

If the experience of the past two shareholder meetings is any guide, the present management will mail their materials to you not more than 30 days before the meeting date. *We urge you not to send in any management proxy before you have received and considered our proxy materials.*

In their proxy materials, management may well attempt to win your vote by attacking the Committee and its members. We also expect that the incumbents will attempt to divert your attention from their record in recent years by promises of future growth. You should know that Mr. Buckley has already begun to make vague promises for the future: "record fiscal 1980 operating revenues" and a "turnaround in profitability". We ask you to consider what these promises really mean. Operating revenues are not necessarily any measure of profitability: remember fiscal 1979, a year in which, despite record operating revenues, your Company suffered a sizeable loss. Moreover, any profit - however small - would fulfill Mr. Buckley's promise of a "turnaround in profitability", after the loss the Company sustained last year.

Management may also attempt to point with pride to the recent rise in the price of United Canso stock-even though the stock has only recently sold at the levels it reached in 1974.

Do not be misled by these tactics. We ask you not to sign any proxy for the Buckley slate of directors, but to consider, in your own best interests, the information we will be reporting to you.

If you are undecided, we suggest you consult your broker, banker or investment advisor.

We Welcome Your Comments

We hope you, as an owner of United Canso, will share with us your concerns about the Company, and your hopes and thoughts for the Company's future. *Please write us at either of the addresses shown on our letterhead, or call us collect at the numbers shown there.*

For those of you whose stock is held of record by a broker, bank or other nominee, we enclose a postage prepaid card which will enable you to furnish your name, address and telephone number so that we may contact you directly should you so desire.

We look forward to hearing from you and to working together toward a new management for United Canso.

Sincerely yours

UNITED CANSO OIL & GAS LTD.
SHAREHOLDERS COMMITTEE

It is my view that, while this letter states that "we are not requesting proxies at this time", it appears to be a solicitation within the meaning of the definition of "solicit" or "solicitation" in s. 141(b) and (c) [now s. 147(a)(ii) and (iii)] in that it is a "request not to execute a form of proxy" for management and/or a "withholding" of proxies from management.

The proxy circular giving a description of the committee members, including occupations and their shareholders [sic] in Canso, does not meet the requirements of a "dissident's proxy circular" referred to in s. 144(b) [now s. 150(1)(b)].

The requirements of a dissident's proxy circular are provided for by s. 38 [now s. 57(1)] of the regulations, SOR/79-316 [now SOR/2001-512].

* * *

It is my opinion that the background information required by the above quoted regulation is obviously important material to be considered by shareholders along with other information in deciding whether to support management or the dissidents; and that the regulation was framed with that in mind.

Because the shares of Canso are listed for trading on certain U.S. exchanges, Canso is required to meet certain requirements of the *Securities Exchange Act* of 1934 (U.S.) (SEC), including its proxy provisions. The evidence before me indicates that the March 7th letter was also sent to the SEC and to the Boston and Pacific Stock Exchanges pursuant to the requirements of the SEC.

There is evidence before me that United States counsel for the Shareholders' Committee advises that the March 7th letter complied in full with the SEC requirements.

The letter of March 7th was sent from the United States and it was not sent to Canadian shareholders. It is suggested by counsel for the defendants that the provisions of the Act relating to proxy solicitation do not have extraterritorial effect in this situation. I disagree. The status of a corporation is to be determined by the law of the incorporating jurisdiction; see Cheshire's *Private International Law* (8th ed.), p. 191, and 20 C.J.S. 12, s. 1788. The general rules are stated in *Corpus Juris Secundum*.

1802. Every corporation necessarily carries its charter wherever it goes, for that is the law of its existence. Whatever disabilities are thereby placed upon the corporation at home it retains abroad, and whatever legislative control is it subject to at home must be recognized and submitted to by those who deal with it elsewhere with knowledge of such limitations . . .

Apart from burdens which may be imposed upon them by the laws of a state which a foreign corporation enters and in which it undertakes to do business . . . the rights and liabilities of stock-holders and directors are determined by the charter and governing laws of the state in which the corporation is created. (pp. 21, 22, 23)

* * *

In the instant case, as a condition of registration of its shares in the United States, Canso is obliged to comply with the trading rules and regulations of the SEC. These rules and regulations apply irrespective of the incorporating statute but these do not supplant the Canadian Act and its requirements. That is, the provisions of the Act relating the proxy solicitation apply to Canso and its shareholders wherever Canso carries on business; even though they are also required to comply with the laws of the host jurisdiction. Therefore if the letter of March 7th is interpreted as a solicitation of proxies then it was written in contravention of the Act and its regulations. In my opinion the plaintiffs have established a *prima facie* case of solicitation, or at least there is a serious question to be tried as to that issue: *Yule Inc. v. Atlantic Pizza Delight Franchise* (1968) Ltd. (1977), 17 O.R. (2d) 505, 35 C.P.R. (2d) 273, 80 D.L.R. (3d) 725 (Div. Ct.).

In my opinion the object of the Act and the provisions in question are for the benefit of the shareholders and to protect them from possible harm. The Act provides for offences and penalties for breach. It is my view that these penalties are not the sole remedies available; but that this legislation gives rise to rights enforceable by action: *Direct Tpt. Co. v. Cornell*, [1938] O.R. 365, [1938] 3 D.L.R. 456 (C.A.); also the comments of Duff J. in *Orpen v. Roberts*, [1925] S.C.R. 364, [1925] 1 D.L.R. 1101 at 1105-6; and *Cunningham v. Moore*, [1972] 3 O.R. 369, 28 D.L.R. (3d) 277, affirmed [1973] 1 O.R. 357, 31 D.L.R. (3d) 149 (H.C.). Also the action is based on the alleged tort of conspiracy; that is an agreement of two or more shareholders to breach the provisions of the statute: *Posluns v. Toronto Stock Exchange*, [1964] 2 O.R. 547, 46 D.L.R. (2d) 210, affirmed [1966] 1 O.R. 285, 53 D.L.R. (2d) 193, affirmed [1968] S.C.R. 330, 67 D.L.R. (2d) 165.

Upon the application in this action the question of the appropriateness of interlocutory injunction remains. There is very little Canadian jurisprudence in matters involving proxy solicitation disputes between shareholders of a corporation. Undoubtedly the next meeting of shareholders will be held before the trial of the action, so that an interlocutory injunction is almost tantamount to a final judgment after trial. The annual meeting is required by law to be held within 15 months of the last annual meeting — which now means that it must be held on or before June 28th, 1980; counsel for the plaintiffs advises me that an undertaking has been given to the Toronto Stock Exchange that it will be held on or before that date.

In my view damages in lieu of injunction would not be an adequate remedy to either side in this case, so that the question of balance of convenience arises. Also injunction is an extraordinary remedy and in my view it ought not to be ordered in this case solely because of the breach mentioned unless it can be said that is clearly required to protect the shareholders in the circumstances. I was referred to American authorities which indicate that United States Courts are generally unwilling to tip the scales toward one shareholders group or the other in a proxy contest: *Cook United Inc. v. Stockholders' Protective Committee of Cook United Inc.* (1979), Fed. Sec. L. Rep. (C.C.H.) 95,576 (S.D.N.Y); *McConnell v. Lucht* (1970), 320 F. Supp. 1162 (S.D.N.Y); and *Kennecott Copper Corpn. v. Curtiss-Wright Corpn.* (1978), 584 F.2d 1195 (U.S.C.A., 2nd Cir.).

In *Gen. Time Corpn. v. Talley Indust. Inc.* (1968), 403 F. 2d 159 the United States Court of Appeals, Second Circuit, dealt with a case involving use of proxies allegedly obtained in violation of the SEC regulations including allegations of false or misleading statements with respect "to any material fact, or which omits to state any material fact contrary to regulation." Judge Friendly stated at p. 162:

* * *

> The test, we suppose, is whether, taking a properly realistic view, there is a substantial likelihood that the misstatement or omission may have lead a stockholder to grant a proxy to the solicitor or to withhold one from the other side, whereas in the absence of this he would have taken a contrary course. This latter circumstance— that there is another side — has a bearing on materiality in a case where, as here, the facts have been disclosed to it in ample time for comment.

The case of *Twentieth Century Fox Film Corpn. v. Lewis* (1971), 334 F. Supp. 1398 (S.D.N.Y), dealt with an application, among other things, to a U.S. District Court, New York, for a preliminary injunction restraining the defendants from soliciting proxies until certain statements were filed in compliance with the SEC rules and until a written proxy statement also complying with the SEC rules was forwarded to the shareholders. In dismissing the application the Court stated at p. 1402:

> It may be that whatever defects alleged here may be cured by the final material submitted to the shareholders and no one may be mislead (sic). Additionally in view of the active nature of the contest here, it seems unlikely to this court that the shareholders will not be fully exposed to the issues involved.

In the instant case there is some (but not much) evidence that some shareholders have already decided to support the dissidents; but it is not shown that it would be otherwise but for the breach. In the light of my decision the defendants will be required to comply with the solicitation rules of the Act. Here the letter of March 7th, 1980, was critical of management; also the material before me alleges specific instances of mismanagement. The dissident shareholders are entitled to be critical and to communicate their criticisms to other shareholders. Here, however, their letter of March 7th, 1980, gives rise to a *prima facie* case that it solicits proxies contrary to s. 144. It might be said that the real breach was one of omission to provide the required background information as to the members of the committee by way of "dissidents proxy circular". It is apparent to me (as in the *Twentieth Century Fox Film* case, *supra*) that there will be an active proxy contest. Ample time remains with which to make full presentation of the relevant information and conflicting contentions of both sides; and the shareholders will have the particulars omitted from the March 7th letter. It seems unlikely to this Court that the shareholders will not be fully exposed to the issues involved.

Counsel for the defendants submits that the defendants will be seriously harmed by an interlocutory injunction far more than the plaintiffs will be aided. The balance of convenience element in a proxy battle was considered in *D-Z Invt. Co. v. Holloway* (1974), Fed. Sec. L. Rep. (C.C.H.) 96,057 (S.D.N.Y.), at p. 96,061:

> Additionally, and in balancing the hardships, the Court finds that the equities of the present situation tip decidedly in defendants' favor, rather than that of the plaintiff. If a preliminary injunction were to issue, no matter how such was explained to the shareholders by the present management, a substantial number of shareholders would regard its issuance as a determination of the alleged *Securities Act* violations on the merits and a finding that the incumbent management had acted improperly with regard to the Trust Again, as this Court had opportunity to state in *Sherman v. Posner, supra*:
>
> > Conversely, if the preliminary injunction were granted at this time, irreparable injury would accrue to the defendants. Beyond a peradventure, the issuance of an injunction would come to the attention of the stockholders . . . And no matter how clearly it was indicated otherwise, the issuance of the injunction undoubtedly

would be viewed by some as a favourable adjudication of the claims of the plaintiff. This would be tantamount to a determination of wrongdoing on the part of the [present] management.

Just how this result could be remedied in the event it was found at a full hearing that the claims of the plaintiff were unfounded is not readily perceptible to this Court. (The italics are mine.)

See also *Kass v. Arden-Mayfair Inc.* (1977), 431 F. Supp. 1037 (C.D. Calif.) where the Court stated (at p. 1041):

In addition, the issuance of a preliminary injunction now would undoubtedly come to the attention of all stockholders. No matter how clearly it was indicated that the issuance was in no way an adjudication on the merits, it would be inevitable that at least a substantial number of stockholders would reach the conclusion that such a holding was tantamount to final determination of wrongdoing on the part of management. *Kauder v. United Board and Carton Corp.*, 199 F. Supp. 420, 423 (S.D.N.Y., 1961).

For these reasons it is my opinion that the balance of convenience favours the defendants; the extraordinary remedy of injunction is not appropriate. The application is dismissed. Having reached this decision it is unnecessary for me to deal with any of the other interesting points raised by counsel on this application.

Both motions dismissed.

Note

For a comment on an unreported case involving the definition of "solicitation", namely, *Western Mines Ltd. v. Sheridan*, see Getz, "Proxies — The Meaning of Solicitation," 1 Can. Bus. L.J. 472 (1976).

(iv)   Critique of the Proxy Provisions

Much criticism has been heard of the proxy legislation. Recall that the motivating purpose behind the proxy rules is to foster shareholder democracy by ensuring that management's nominees for directors (and proposed fundamental changes) are exposed to scrutiny and that shareholders have an adequate opportunity to vote. It has been argued that the proxy rules have had exactly the opposite effect. In particular, as the *Duby* case makes clear, there is a risk that relatively informal communications between shareholders may be construed as proxy "solicitations" requiring the assembly (at great expense) of a dissidents' proxy circular. While the court in *Duby* took a very pragmatic view of the situation, and refused to penalize the dissident shareholders' conduct, how many shareholders would be willing to risk a lawsuit (and one with perhaps a less favourable outcome than *Duby*) by engaging in informal communications that might be construed to be solicitations?

This issue has drawn much more attention in the United States than in Canada. One of the largest US public pension funds (the California Public Employees Retirement System, often referred to as "CalPERS") was instrumental in bringing the issue to the attention of the Securities and Exchange Commission ("SEC," which administers the federal proxy legislation). A number of academic commentators have also been influential in bringing the issue to prominence. See, *e.g.*, Bernard S. Black, "Shareholder Passivity Reexamined" (1990), 89 Mich. L. Rev. 520; John Pound, "Proxy Voting and the SEC: Investor Protection Versus Market Efficiency" (1991) 29 J. Fin. Econ. 241. As a result, the SEC sought and received from Congress changes to the proxy legislation that are designed to exempt informal shareholder communications from the full rigours of the proxy rules. See also Jeffrey N. Gordon, "Proxy Contests in an Era of Increasing Shareholder Power" (2008) 61 Vanderbilt L. Rev. 475, online: SSRN < http://papers.ssrn.com/sol3/ papers.cfm?abstract id = 1085356# > .

In "The Role of Institutional and Retail Investors in Canadian Capital Markets" (1993), 32 Osgoode Hall L.J. 370, Jeffrey MacIntosh proposed similar changes to Canadian proxy legislation. In 2001, some of the risk of shareholder communications being construed as proxy "solicitations" has been mitigated by exceptions that were added to the requirement to assemble a dissident's proxy circular under s. 150 of the CBCA. A shareholder may now solicit proxies without a dissident's proxy circular in the case of a targeted solicitation to 15 or fewer shareholders (s. 150(1.1)), or if the solicitation is by public broadcast, speech or publication (s. 150(1.2)). See, e.g., *JLL Patheon Holdings, LLC v. Patheon Inc.*, 2009 CarswellOnt 7315, 64 B.L.R. (4th) 98 (Ont. S.C.J.). However, in Alberta, the 15 or fewer shareholders exception is not available. The Alberta exception only applies if the corporation has 15 or fewer shareholders entitled to vote at a shareholders' meeting (ABCA s. 150(2)), or through an exemption order from the Commission or the Court (s. 151(a)(b)).

In the CBCA, the definition of "solicitation" in s. 147(b)(v) has been narrowed to exclude a public announcement by a shareholder on how he or she intends to vote. Prior to the amendments to the CBCA, it is true that many institutional investors (pension funds, mutual funds, insurance companies, banks, trust companies, etc.) had made a fairly regular habit of informally discussing management initiatives amongst themselves; however, the targeted solicitation exception now expressly authorizes such activity. Taking advantage of the narrower definition of "solicitation," the Ontario Teachers' Pension Plan, for example, now makes publicly available on its website how it intends to vote at upcoming corporate meetings.

In *Polar Star Mining Corp. v. Willock*, 2009 CarswellOnt 1416, 96 O.R. (3d) 688 (Ont. S.C.J.), the Court seemed to leave open the possibility that a press release could be considered solicitation. However, in

Smoothwater Capital Partners LP I v. Equity Financial Holdings Inc., 2014 CarswellOnt 503, 2014 ONSC 324 (Ont. S.C.J.), Smoothwater, a shareholder of Equity Financial Holdings Inc., requisitioned a meeting, and issued a press release criticizing the current board of Equity. Equity responded with a press release. The press release did not request proxies, but defended the board's actions, and criticized dissidents, including Smoothwater, for initiating a costly and unnecessary proxy fight. The court held that a press release during a solicitation process does not automatically become a proxy solicitation. Based on the nature of the press release, the Court found that it did not constitute a solicitation, especially when it did not encourage shareholders to provide Equity with proxies.

(v)   Proxy Solicitation Expenses

There is very little statutory guidance relating to proxy solicitation expenses or expenses relating to the costs of holding shareholders' meetings. Both s. 105(6) of the OBCA and s. 143(6) of the CBCA deal with this to a certain extent by stating that a corporation shall reimburse shareholders with some exceptions. Looking at common law, there is not much Anglo-Canadian case law on the matter, although see *Peel v. London and North Western R.R. Co.*, [1907] 1 Ch. Div. 5 (C.A.), which held that management could expend funds to make its position known to shareholders. In *Goodwood Inc. v. Cathay Forest Products Corp.*, 2013 CarswellOnt 8321, 2013 ONSC 4242, Goodwood, a shareholder of Cathay, sought an order requiring Cathay to reimburse costs relating to Goodwood's dissident proxy circular in a court-directed meeting under s. 144(1) of the CBCA. The court acknowledged that the Goodwood's counsel was unable to find any cases discussing this issue. However, the court considered that the dissident proxy circular disclosed the intention to seek reimbursement from the corporation, the shareholders overwhelmingly supported the applicant's proposal, and that the applicant would have been entitled to reimbursement if it was a meeting called under s. 143(4) of the CBCA. As a result, the applicant was allowed to recover costs.

Also see *Pala Investments Holdings Ltd. v. Bristow*, 2009 CarswellBC 1480, 2009 BCSC 680 (B.C. S.C.), where shareholders were asked to vote on whether the company would reimburse the requisitioning shareholder.

In *Levin v. Metro-Goldwyn-Mayer Inc.*, 264 F. Supp. 797 (S.D.N.Y. 1967) the action arose from a conflict for corporate control of MGM between two groups, one of which included the plaintiff. The plaintiffs sought an injunction to stop the current management from soliciting proxies for an upcoming shareholders' meeting by means of public relations firms, proxy soliciting organizations and the like. The plaintiffs argued that the costs of such allegedly extravagant means of proxy solicitation should be borne by the directors themselves. The plaintiffs were contesting seats on the board of directors and undoubtedly felt that their own campaign resources could not stretch the company's funds which were being used for the management solicitation. The court held that the proper question to be determined was whether or not illegal or unfair means of communication were being employed by management, and contended that they were not and so denied the injunctive relief. The court also refused to enjoin the use of corporate employees for proxy solicitation, the use of more than one proxy solicitation firm by management, the use of persons in business relationships with MGM (actors, directors, etc.) in the solicitation of proxies for management, the employment by the corporation of a public relations firm, and the use of Louis Nizer's law firm in the solicitation process.

In *Rosenfeld v. Fairchild Engine & Airplane Corp.*, 309 N.Y. 168, 128 N.E. 2d 291 (N.Y.C.A. 1955), the plaintiff, a shareholder, sought to compel the defendant corporation to return money paid out to both sides in a proxy contest for their expenses. The court denied the plaintiff's request:

"The rule then which we adopt is simply this: In a contest over policy as compared to a purely personal power contest, corporate directors have the right to make reasonable and proper expenditures, subject to the scrutiny of the courts when duly challenged, from the corporate treasury for the purpose of persuading the stockholders of the correctness of their position and soliciting their support for policies which the directors believe, in all good faith, are in the best interests of the corporation. The stockholders, moreover, have the right to reimburse successful contestants for the reasonable and *bona fide* expenses incurred by them in any such policy contest, subject to like court scrutiny. . . . "

Van Voorhis J. dissented, preferring the expenses be submitted to trial court to ascertain whether they should be allowed or disallowed.

Questions

1   What considerations should be taken into account in deciding whether insurgent shareholders' expenses should be reimbursed? Is success determinative or relevant? Would it be a boon to shareholder democracy to routinely reimburse dissident shareholder proxy expenses and thus encourage shareholders to enter into proxy battles? Or would this simply tend to attract cranks and persons with an ax to grind with management? Is there some middle ground that would encourage meritorious proxy battles while weeding out the frivolous or vexatious proxy challenges?

2   Should the fact of shareholder approval or disapproval of the expenses be conclusive of the matter?

3   Should an insurgent group be required to disclose whether it will seek reimbursement? Should a stated intention not to seek reimbursement bar the insurgents from later seeking reimbursement?

4   Would it make sense to allow reimbursement of expenses on the basis of the proportion of shareholder votes obtained by the insurgents compared to the expenses and votes obtained by management?

(vi)   Remedies for Breach of Proxy Legislation

A right is only as effective as the remedies to secure enforcement of the right. Thus, a crucial question in relation to the rights created by proxy legislation is the means by which aggrieved parties may secure their enforcement. A number of bases for such enforcement are explored in this note.

(A)   Implied Civil Right of Action

Sometimes a statute will mandate, regulate or prohibit certain activity without indicating if any civil (or in some cases, either civil or criminal) consequences arise from breach of the statutory provisions. In these cases, the courts are sometimes willing to "imply" a private right of action arising in favour of at least some private parties. *Brown v. Duby*, *supra*, which involved a dissident's proxy circular that failed to comply with the CBCA regulations, is such a case. The court held that the criminal penalties that the CBCA prescribed for breach of the statute were not exclusive of civil liability, and that a private right of action arose for breach of the proxy legislation. The plaintiff in favour of whom the action arose was both an officer of United Canso as well as a shareholder, and it is not entirely clear in which of these capacities the right of action arose, although the court recognized such a right in the corporation as well.

The existence of an implied private right of action has also been recognized by the Ontario Court of Appeal in *Goldex Mines v. Revill*, *infra*. The statute under consideration (the forerunner to the current OBCA) contained nothing that would expressly allow the corporation or an aggrieved shareholder to sue for breach of the statutory provisions. Nevertheless, the court held that misleading or deficient disclosure to shareholders in connection with a proxy solicitation could give rise to both a derivative and a personal cause of action. Although we have not yet explored in detail the difference between these two types of actions, a derivative action arises where the corporation is the injured party, and shareholders are hurt only indirectly, as a consequence of the harm to the corporation. A personal action generally arises where the harm to the shareholder is not merely incidental to the harm to the corporation, but is particular to a shareholder or group of shareholders. Breaches of fiduciary duty owed to the corporation give rise to derivative actions; breaches of duties owed directly to shareholders give rise to personal actions. Can you articulate how an action for breach of proxy legislation (or in respect of any other matter) could give rise to both a personal and a derivative action? How can the injury be at once one that harms the corporation and grounds a derivative action (and therefore one in respect of which all shareholders suffer indirectly and in equal measure) and one in respect of which the complainant shareholders suffer special harm?

No discussion of an implied private right of action would be complete without reference to *Canada v. Saskatchewan Wheat Pool*, [1983] 1 S.C.R. 205, 143 D.L.R. (3d) 9. In *Saskatchewan*, the Supreme Court of Canada held that there was no independent tort of breach of a statutory provision. Rather, breach of a statutory provision might serve as evidence of the breach of a duty owed by the defendant. *Saskatchewan* thus appears to call into question all of those cases which have held that breach of a statute might by itself ground a civil action. Despite *Saskatchewan*, however, at least one court has implied a private right of action in the securities law context. In *Jones v. Deacon Hodgson* (1986), 34 B.L.R. 1 (Ont. H.C.), the court recognized the existence of an implied right of action for failure to prepare and file a prospectus as required by the Ontario *Securities Act*. More recently, however, see *Roman Corp. v. Peat Marwick Thorne* (1992), 8 B.L.R. (2d) 43, 11 O.R. (3d) 248, 1992 CarswellOnt 149 (Gen. Div. [Commercial List]), holding that breach of statute cannot by itself ground an action.

Would such a right of action (if it exists) support a claim for damages? In *Brown*, the Court suggested that damages would not be an adequate remedy. The difficulties associated with calculating damages are further explored below.

(B)   Statutory Liability

CBCA
Section 154 of the CBCA provides a statutory means for ensuring that the proxy legislation is complied with. An "interested person" or the director may apply to a court which may make "any order it thinks fit," including a restraining order, a mandatory injunction and an order enjoining the meeting. The section applies where "a form of proxy, management proxy circular or dissident's proxy circular contains an untrue statement of a material fact or omits to state a material fact required therein or necessary to make a statement contained therein not misleading in light of the circumstances in which it was made..." An interested person would certainly include a shareholder. Who else might the phrase include (*e.g.*, a director or officer of the company; an outside party)? Note that the Director's power to sue allows him to commence an action not unlike a class action in favour of minority shareholders: see *Sparling v. Royal Trustco Ltd.* (1984), 24 B.L.R. 145 (Ont. C.A.), affirmed [1986] 2 S.C.R. 537.

One curiosity surrounding the *Brown* case, *supra*, is that the Court felt compelled to recognize a private right of action to ground the suit. Can you think of a reason why s. 154 of the CBCA (the applicable statute) would not have been a sufficient basis upon which to ground the suit?

If the holding in *Goldex* (discussed, *supra*) applies to s. 154, then is it necessary to obtain leave of the court under CBCA s. 239 before suing under s. 154? Or is there perhaps some argument that s. 154 is restricted to personal causes of action? In *Goldhar v. Quebec Manitou Mines Ltd.*, 1975 CarswellOnt 478, 9 O.R. (2d) 740, 61 D.L.R. (3d) 612 (Ont. Div. Ct.), *infra*, the court held that the general compliance and restraining order provision of the former OBCA could not be used in relation to derivative causes of action. *Prima facie*, the holding applies to s. 154 as well.

S. 247 of the CBCA may also provide a somewhat limited statutory means for ensuring compliance with proxy legislation. In *Polar Star*, Polar Star sought a restraining order under s. 247 for a director's alleged breach of solicitation violating s. 150(1)(b). However, since the director acted in his position as a shareholder, and not as a director, the court held that s. 247 was not available as a remedy. Even if it were available, the court stated it would have discretion over whether to grant relief, and would likely grant it only if the conduct had substantial risk of harm to the corporation or the shareholders as a group or the conduct was patently clear to be illegal or abusive.

While we have not yet explored the statutory oppression remedy in detail, you should keep in mind the possibility of resorting to the oppression remedy in any case involving breach of the disclosure requirements. The question of whether the oppression provision can be used in relation to causes of action which are essentially derivative in nature is explored, *infra*.

OBCA

Section 253(2) of the OBCA is drafted in a manner broadly similar to s. 154 of the CBCA. However, notice that the provision allows only the Ontario Securities Commission to apply to a court for an order. Could a shareholder nonetheless apply under s. 253(1) for an order restraining a management solicitation where there has been a material misrepresentation in a management proxy circular? Could management apply to restrain a solicitation by a dissident shareholders' group in a case involving a misrepresentation in a dissident proxy circular? Look carefully at the statutory definition of "complainant" in s. 245(b). Respondent's counsel in *Polar Star* (discussed, *supra*) made this argument, pointing out that s. 253(1) of the OBCA includes non-compliance by any shareholder.

(C)   Injunctions

Whether the action arises by way of an implied right of action or statutory provision, one of the most effective remedies for breach of the proxy legislation is the injunction (or "restraining order"). Despite the reluctance to issue an injunction against dissident shareholders evident in *Brown v. Duby*, the courts have not been shy to use the injunction in a number of cases involving misleading or incomplete proxy materials sent to shareholders by management. For example, in *Garvie v. Axmith*, [1962] O.R. 65, 31 D.L.R. (2d) 65 (H.C.), the court issued an injunction to prevent the corporation from acting on resolutions where shareholders were sent a deficient notice of meeting. Similarly, in *Alexander v. Westeel Rosco Ltd.* (1978), 22 O.R. (2d) 80, 75 D.L.R. (3d) 16 (H.C.), the court issued an interim injunction to prevent the consummation of an amalgamation because of, *inter alia*, a deficient proxy circular mailed to shareholders under the CBCA. The injunction is a flexible tool that can be used to prevent a solicitation from occurring, a meeting from being held, or resolutions passed at a meeting from being acted upon. A mandatory injunction (or "compliance order") may also be issued requiring correction of deficient or misleading proxy material or other action.

You should note the functional similarity between the grant of an injunction and an order rescinding corporate action. See, e.g., *Babic v. Milinkovic* (1972), 22 D.L.R. (3d) 732 (B.C. S.C.), affirmed 25 D.L.R. (3d) 752 (B.C. C.A.).

(D)   Damages

It is conceivable that a shareholder or other aggrieved party may wish to pursue a claim for damages rather than injunctive relief in connection with a violation of proxy legislation. Such a claim may be relatively difficult to make. The courts have preferred injunctive relief; indeed, there is not a single case in Canada where damages have been awarded in connection with false, misleading or deficient proxy disclosure to shareholders. Given the difficulties associated with making an award of damages, this is perhaps not surprising. Suppose, for example, that shareholders elected the slate of directors nominated by management. If it could be shown that the management proxy circular was misleading in some material respect, what would the measure of damages be? If the action was constituted as a derivative action in favour of the corporation, then presumably the nature of the damage alleged would be the harm resulting to the company by reason of having an improperly elected (and perhaps incompetent or otherwise unsuitable) board of directors. By what metric could this damage be measured? Indeed, could it even be shown that the harm was actually caused by the misrepresentation? Without the misrepresentation, the same board of directors might have been elected anyway. Similar comments might be made in relation to the adoption of corporate fundamental changes by shareholders. Nor is there reason to believe that the calculation of damages in relation to personal actions commenced by shareholders would be any easier. On the issue of causation, see *Harris v. Universal Explorations Ltd.* (1982), 17 B.L.R. 135, 37 A.R. 35 (C.A.). See generally Crête, *The Proxy System in Canadian Corporations*, at 324–330, 348–349. Despite the fact that Canadian courts have not yet awarded damages in connection with a proxy violation, there may be cases where a court anxious to give relief is forced to award damages because it is too late to apply injunctive relief. See, for example, *Norcan Oils Ltd. v. Fogler*, [1965] S.C.R. 36, 49 W.W.R. 321, 46 D.L.R. (2d) 630, where the Supreme Court held that it was beyond the jurisdiction of the court under the legislation in question to unwind an already consummated amalgamation. In such a case, damages would be the only available remedy.

Another question worth pondering: would a court in fact have jurisdiction to award damages under s. 154? Are the words "any order it thinks fit" to be given a broad reading, or are these words limited *ejusdem generis* by the more specific enumerations which follow?

Question

We have already referred to a number of problems that imperil the efficacy of shareholder oversight of management, like shareholder "collective action" problems and the domination of the proxy machinery by management. The proxy rules are designed to ensure that shareholder oversight through the mechanism of the shareholder meeting is truly meaningful. Now that you know something about the design of these rules, we invite you to conduct your own evaluation of the effectiveness of these rules in achieving that objective.

4. SHAREHOLDER MEETINGS

(a) Introduction

The shareholder meeting is (or at least is intended to be) a key instrument of managerial accountability to shareholders. There are two types of shareholder meetings: annual and special. The company must have an annual meeting each year (within 15 months of the last annual meeting): CBCA s. 133(1)(b), OBCA s. 94(1)(a). At least three items of business must be transacted at an annual meeting. These are the election of directors (see CBCA s. 106(3), OBCA s. 119(4)) (although since directors may hold office for as long as three years, there may be no directors to elect in any given year), the appointment of auditors (see CBCA s. 162(1), OBCA s. 149(1)) and the presentation of financial statements and auditor's report to the shareholders (CBCA s. 155(1), OBCA s. 154(1)). Other specific items of business may be transacted as well.

Sometimes there may be important business that arises between annual meetings. In this case, the directors may call a special meeting of shareholders (CBCA s. 133(2), OBCA s. 94(1)(b)). Special meetings will typically be held when management is contemplating a fundamental change in the corporation that requires shareholder approval (*e.g.*, an amalgamation, continuance in another jurisdiction, etc.), although they may be held for other reasons as well.

The directors are not the only group with the power to call a shareholders' meeting. Both the CBCA and OBCA provide that the holders of not less than 5% of the issued shares that carry the right to vote at a meeting sought to be held may "requisition" a shareholders' meeting (CBCA s. 143, OBCA s. 105) to transact the business stated in the requisition. See *Concept Capital Management Ltd. v. Oremex Silver Inc.*, 2013 CarswellOnt 17951, 2013 ONSC 7820 (Ont. S.C.J. [Commercial List]).

You should also note that the CBCA and OBCA both have provisions relating (*inter alia*) to the place where meetings may be held (CBCA s. 132, OBCA s. 93), notice of meetings (CBCA s. 135, OBCA s. 96) and the requisite quorum to hold a meeting (CBCA s. 139, OBCA s. 101).

Aside from allowing shareholders to vote on such important matters as the election of directors and fundamental corporate changes, the shareholders' meeting is designed, at least in theory, to provide a forum for shareholders to discuss matters relating to the business and affairs of the corporation. Thus, shareholders have a right of discussion and a right to submit proposals to be discussed at shareholders' meetings. These rights are explored further, *infra*.

For an international comparison of the impact of the legal framework on shareholders' abilities to monitor management, consequently the impact on shareholder meetings, see Dirk A. Zetzsche, "Shareholder Interaction Preceding Shareholder Meetings — A Six Country Comparison" (2005) 2 ECFR 107.

(b) Unanimous Shareholders' Resolutions

Eisenberg v. Bank of Nova Scotia
1965 CarswellOnt 580, [1965] S.C.R. 681, (sub nom. *Walton v. Bank of Nova Scotia & Ridout*) 7 C.B.R. (N.S.) 264 (S.C.C.)

SPENCE J.: This is an appeal from the judgment of the Court of Appeal for Ontario pronounced on March 16, 1964, affirming the judgment at trial pronounced on March 15, 1963.

The action was brought by the appellant as trustee in bankruptcy of Ridout Real Estate Limited to recover from the respondent bank certain sums realized by the bank from assets which the said company had pledged to the bank as security for a loan to one George H. Ridout and his brother Ernest Ridout.

George Ridout was a director and president and was the sole beneficial owner of all the issued shares in the said Ridout Real Estate Limited. Ernest Ridout had been such sole beneficial owner but had transferred his shares to George Ridout and at all relevant times was neither a director nor shareholder of the Ridout Real Estate company.

On July 18, 1955, the said Ernest Ridout arranged with an officer of the defendant bank that it should loan to George Ridout and to him the sum of $100,000 for the purpose of permitting the said Ernest Ridout to obtain a release of his guarantee of the bonds of Taylor Forbes Limited which were then in default. As security for the loan, the bank was given a hypothecation of eleven promissory notes made by the Irmac Construction Company Limited in favour of Ridout Real Estate Limited and an assignment of the interest of Ridout Real Estate Limited in a partnership known as the Town and Country Development. One McIntosh, the supervisor of the Toronto branches of the respondent bank, was directed to carry out the transaction on behalf of the bank.

On the next day, July 19, 1955. . . Miss M.E. MacDonald. . .delivered to him an envelope containing the following documents:

(1) Note for $95,000 signed by George Ridout and Ernest Ridout.

(2) Assignment of the interest of Ridout Real Estate Limited in Town and Country Development, executed on behalf of the Ridout company by George Ridout and bearing the corporate seal.

(3) Copy of a resolution authorizing the Ridout company to assign its interest in Town and Country Development as security and authorizing George Ridout to sign the assignment, certified by Miss M.E. MacDonald under the Ridout company's seal, to be a true copy of a resolution of the board of directors of the Ridout company, passed at a meeting of directors on July 19, 1955.

(4) Hypothecation Agreement executed on behalf of the Ridout company by George Ridout and Miss M.E. MacDonald under the seal of the Ridout company, by which hypothecation agreement Ridout Real Estate Limited hypothecated "all notes, cheques, drafts and other bills of exchange now lodged and/or which may hereafter be lodged with the bank and any resultant proceeds".

(5) Copy of a resolution authorizing the Ridout company to pledge the eleven Irmac notes of $10,000 each, and authorizing George Ridout to sign such hypothecation, certified by Miss MacDonald under the seal of the Ridout company to be a true copy of a resolution of the board of directors of the Ridout company, passed at a meeting of the directors.

(6) Direction from George Ridout requesting the bank to issue the cheque for $100,000 to M.H. Roebuck.

(7) The eleven notes of the Irmac company.

(8) Cheque of the Ridout company in favour of the Bank of Nova Scotia for $5,000 signed by George Ridout and Miss M.E. MacDonald.

Mr. McIntosh was familiar with the signatures of George Ridout and Ernest Ridout and was satisfied with their signatures on the document. Miss MacDonald represented that she was the secretary of Ridout Real Estate and was entitled under the by-laws to execute the said documents. She was not such secretary but she was the head office manager and was a signing officer of the Ridout company in connection with its business with its ordinary bank which was not the respondent. The secretary-treasurer of the company was one Mr. Muir who was then absent on holidays.

. . . The loan . . . was discharged . . . and the final payment was on June 5, 1956.

. . . The appellant was appointed trustee in bankruptcy of Ridout Real Estate Limited.

* * *

At trial, the action was dismissed by King J. and the appeal from the judgment of the learned trial judge was dismissed in the unanimous judgment of the Court of Appeal.

* * *

[In this court i]t is admitted that no resolution of directors was passed and that no meeting of directors took place. However, the "inside management rule" enunciated *inter alia* in *The Royal British Bank v. Turquand*, would apply to protect an innocent third party dealing with Ridout Real Estate Ltd., without notice of those facts and that Miss MacDonald was not the secretary of the company.

In the Court of Appeal for Ontario, Schroeder J.A. said:

Since I have come to the decision that the doctrine of estoppel operates in favour of the defendant it follows that I also take the view that the defendant comes within the protection of the principle of *The Royal British Bank v. Turquand* (1856), 6 El. & Bl. 327, and *William Augustus Mahony v. The East Holyford Mining Company (Limited)* (1875), L. R. 7 H.L. 869.

I have come to the conclusion that, in this Court, it is not necessary to investigate whether the respondent bank is entitled to rely on the "inside management rule". Whether or not it were able to do so it is plain that the transactions were not only approved by the sole beneficial owner but he was the chief instigator of the transactions and directed them throughout. It is true that no meeting of shareholders was ever held to approve the transactions. If there had been a directors' meeting, fully attended, the directors were George Ridout, Mr. Muir and two other employees. None of the latter three held any shares beneficially, and all were mere nominees of George Ridout. Therefore, the result of either the shareholders' meeting or the directors' meeting would have been a foregone conclusion. If any director had seen fit to oppose George Ridout's wishes, he could be removed from his position as director with the utmost celerity and, of course, George Ridout was the sole beneficial owner of all the shares and his wishes would have been the unanimous decision of the shareholders' meeting.

Under these circumstances, the problem of what kind of unanimous authorization of shareholders is sufficient becomes important. . . . [Mr. Justice Spence then reviewed several authorities and concluded:]

Therefore, upon a consideration of the above authorities, I have been led to the conclusion that a corporation, when a matter is ultra vires of the corporation, cannot be heard to deny a transaction to which all the shareholders have given their assent even when such assent be given in an informal manner or by conduct as distinguished from a formal resolution at a duly convened meeting. Since, of course, George Ridout not only assented to the transaction but instigated it, his assent being, as admitted, that of the sole beneficial shareholder therefore binds the company...

Appeal dismissed with costs.

Notes and Questions

1   Both the CBCA and OBCA now provide that the shareholders may dispense with shareholders' meetings and do all those matters normally required to be dealt with at a shareholders' meeting (or other business) by unanimous shareholder resolutions (CBCA s. 142, OBCA s. 104); be careful to distinguish these from unanimous shareholder agreements, discussed, *infra*. Since shareholders' meetings are both expensive and time consuming, these provisions are especially useful for smaller private corporations with few shareholders (particularly family corporations), at least where little disagreement arises about the conduct of the business. Such shareholder resolutions are also very useful where the shareholders reside in widely disparate locations, or if there is but a single shareholder in the corporation. Note that the holding in *Eisenberg v. Bank of Nova Scotia* goes further in that it validates corporate actions "to which all the shareholders have given their assent even where such assent be given in an informal manner or by conduct . . ." Given that the statutory provisions cited above post-date *Eisenberg*, do they replace the common law by virtue of the principle of *expressio unius exclusio alterius*? Or does the Eisenberg decision continue to have force?

2 Note that not only was there no shareholders' meeting to authorize the transaction in *Eisenberg*, there was no directors' meeting either (although the company submitted documents to the bank which purported to be true copies of directors' resolutions). Was it necessary for the Supreme Court to hold as they did in order to protect the bank? More specifically, could the court have simply invoked principles of agency law (explored in Chapter 4) to achieve the same result? What does the *Eisenberg* decision add to these principles of agency law?

(c)   The Use of Directors' Powers in Relation to Meetings

Schnell v. Chris-Craft Industries Inc.
285 A.2d 430 (Del. Ch. 1971), rev'd. 437 (S.C. Del.)

[The plaintiffs were dissatisfied with Chris-Craft's recent performance, and along with other dissident shareholders of Chris-Craft formed a shareholders' committee. On October 16, 1971, the committee filed with the SEC their intention to wage a proxy contest for the purpose of electing new directors. Two days later at a directors' meeting, the company's bylaws in respect of its annual meeting were amended. Previously, the annual meeting was to be held on the second Tuesday in January; the new bylaw allowed the directors to hold the meeting any day in December or January. That year's meeting was then rescheduled for December 8, 1971. The plaintiffs sought a preliminary injunction against the corporation carrying out the change in date, and an order reinstating the former meeting date. They argued that the change in meeting date was to handicap the efforts of the shareholders' committee to adequately prepare for the proxy battle. The defendants claimed that the new meeting date was chosen to take advantage of better weather conditions and to avoid the necessity of mailing notices to shareholders during the rush of Christmas mail. The Delaware Court of Chancery found that management's intention was to hamper the efforts of the shareholder committee. However, as management's actions were legal under Delaware law, and because the plaintiffs had already had adequate time to present their views to other shareholders, a preliminary injunction was deemed to not be warranted. The plaintiffs appealed.]

HERRMANN J. (for the majority of the Court):
. . . I am satisfied, however, in a situation in which present management has disingenuously resisted the production of a list of its stockholders to plaintiffs or their confederates and has otherwise turned a deaf ear to plaintiffs' demands about a change in management designed to lift defendant from its present business doldrums, management has seized on a relatively new section of the Delaware Corporation Law for the purpose of cutting down on the amount of time which would otherwise have been available to plaintiffs and others for the waging of a

proxy battle. Management thus enlarged the scope of its scheduled October 18 directors' meeting to include the by-law amendment in controversy after the stockholders committee had filed with the S.E.C. its intention to wage a proxy fight on October 16.

Thus plaintiffs reasonably contend that because of the tactics employed by management (which involve the hiring of two established proxy solicitors as well as a refusal to produce a list of its stockholders, coupled with its use of an amendment to the Delaware Corporation Law to limit the time for contest), they are given little chance, because of the exigencies of time, including that required to clear material at the S.E.C., to wage a successful proxy fight between now and December 8. . . .

In our view, those conclusions amount to a finding that management has attempted to utilize the corporate machinery and the Delaware Law for the purpose of perpetuating itself in office; and, to that end, for the purpose of obstructing the legitimate efforts of dissident stockholders in the exercise of their rights to undertake a proxy contest against management. These are inequitable purposes, contrary to established principles of corporate democracy.

The advancement by directors of the by-law date of a stockholders' meeting, for such purposes, may not be permitted to stand. Compare *Condec Corporation v. Lunkenheimer Company*, 43 Del.Ch. 353, 230 A.2d 769 (1967).

When the by-laws of a corporation designate the date of the annual meeting of stockholders, it is to be expected that those who intend to contest the reelection of incumbent management will gear their campaign to the by-law date. It is not to be expected that management will attempt to advance that date in order to obtain an inequitable advantage in the contest.

Management contends that it has complied strictly with the provisions of the new Delaware Corporation Law in changing the by-law date. The answer to that contention, of course, is that inequitable action does not become permissible simply because it is legally possible.

Management relies upon *American Hardwater Corp. v. Savage Arms Corp.*, 37 Del.Ch. 10, 135 A.2d 725, aff'd 37 Del.Ch. 59, 136 A.2d 690 (1957). That case is inapposite for two reasons: it involved an effort by stockholders, engaged in a proxy contest, to have the stockholders' meeting adjourned and the period for the proxy contest enlarged; and there was no finding there of inequitable action on the part of management. We agree with the rule of American Hardware that, in the absence of fraud or inequitable conduct, the date for a stockholders' meeting and notice thereof, duly established under the by-laws, will not be enlarged by judicial interference at the request of dissident stockholders solely because of the circumstances of a proxy contest. That, of course, is not the case before us.

We are unable to agree with the conclusion of the Chancery Court that the stockholders' application for injunctive relief here was tardy and came too late. The stockholders learned of the action of management unofficially on Wednesday, October 27, 1971; they filed this action on Monday, November 1, 1971. Until management changed the date of the meeting, the stockholders had no need of judicial assistance in that connection. There is no indication of any prior warning of management's intent to take such action; indeed, it appears that an attempt was made by management to conceal its action as long as possible. Moreover, stockholders may not be charged with the duty of anticipating inequitable action by management, and of seeking anticipatory injunctive relief to foreclose such action, simply because the new Delaware Corporation Law makes such inequitable action legally possible.

Accordingly, the judgment below must be reversed and the cause remanded, with instructions to nullify the December 8 date as a meeting date for stockholders; to reinstate January 11, 1972 as the sole date of the next annual meeting of the stockholders of the corporation; and to take such other proceedings and action as may be consistent herewith regarding the stock record closing date and any other related matters.

WOLCOTT C.J. (dissenting): I do not agree with the majority of the Court in its disposition of this appeal. The plaintiff stockholders concerned in this litigation have, for a considerable period of time, sought to obtain control of the defendant corporation. These attempts took various forms.

In view of the length of time leading up to the immediate events which caused the filing of this action, I agree with the Vice Chancellor that the application for injunctive relief came too late.

I would affirm the judgment below on the basis of the Vice Chancellor's opinion.

Appeal allowed.

Notes and Questions

1   Note that the majority of the Supreme Court of Delaware suggested that the Delaware statute made the conduct undertaken by management "legally possible," but nonetheless held that the court could intervene (as it did in this case) to enjoin "fraud or inequitable conduct." An important question for you to consider is by what legal theory a Canadian court might intervene to achieve the same result. Consider the "improper purpose" cases explored in Chapter 6. Could these be applied to "read down" the authority given the directors to set the meeting date? (You should also consider if these cases are still good law, given their fate in the *Teck, Hiram Walker* and *Olson* cases considered earlier (see Chapter 6).) If not, could a court simply invoke principles of fiduciary duty now given statutory force (see, *e.g.*, CBCA s. 122) or the statutory oppression remedy? What other decisions might the directors make in relation to meetings which would be subject to the same judicial oversight?

2   Note also that the majority in *Schnell* held that "[i]t is not to be expected that management will attempt to advance the date [of the meeting] in order to obtain an inequitable advantage in the contest." To what extent do the cases explored thus far suggest that a Canadian court would feel free to invoke an expectations principle in order to limit the authority given the directors? You should keep this question in mind when reading cases on the oppression remedy and winding up in Chapter 10.

(d)   The Conduct of Meetings and the Right of Discussion

Wall v. London and Northern Assets Corp.
[1898] 2 Ch. 469 (C.A.)

[The London and Northern Assets Corporation (referred to in the excerpt from the report's statement of facts below as "the Assets Company") was registered as a limited company. This action arose from, among other things, a meeting convened by the company in order to approve of a sale of assets.

An extraordinary general meeting of the Assets Company was held on February 22, 1898, at which a resolution approving of the agreement of the 11th was moved and seconded. The meeting was adjourned to March 22, when, after the chairman had addressed the meeting Mr. Wall entered into an explanation of his objections to the scheme. Mr. Parker pointed out the advantages of the scheme, and the objections to the schemes outlined in a circular of Mr. Wall. A Mr. Rowley was speaking against the schemes, both of the directors and of Mr. Wall, but was interrupted by cries of "Vote." The chairman then, supported by others, put a motion that the debate should then close, and there voted 24 in favour of the motion and 2 against it. The chairman then put the resolution, which was carried by 35 to 3. Mr. Wall expressed his wish for a poll, but could not obtain the support of four other members present for demanding it, and the chairman declared the meeting closed. The above is the substance of what appears in the minutes of the meeting. Mr. Wall deposed that, "Shortly after the discussion of the scheme had begun, and while I and other shareholders were desirous of addressing the meeting, the chairman put a resolution to the meeting that the discussion should be terminated. This resolution was carried, and those shareholders who were desirous of speaking were thus prevented from so doing."

On April 6 an extraordinary general meeting was held for the purpose of confirming the resolution. The chairman referred to a notice of amendment received from Mr. Wall, which was as follows: "That the following be added to the resolution confirming contract — 'Subject to the purchaser agreeing to allow any individual or any body of dissentient shareholders to have their share of the assets agreed to be sold in lieu of the London and Northern debenture shares due to them.'" The chairman ruled that the amendment could not be put, and moved that the resolution of March 22 should be confirmed. This motion was seconded.

* * *

On April 15 Mr. Wall commenced an action, on behalf of himself and all other shareholders in the Assets Company except those who had voted for the resolution, against the Assets Company and its directors, asking a declaration that the special resolution which the company purported to pass on March 22, 1898, and to confirm on April 13, 1898, and the agreement therein referred to, were *ultra vires*, void, and invalid, and an injunction to restrain the defendants from acting upon the resolution. The plaintiff moved for an injunction.

The trial Judge, Stirling J., held, *inter alia*, that there had been no such irregularities in the meeting as to vitiate the resolution. The plaintiff appealed to the Court of Appeal.]

SIR NATHANIEL LINDLEY M.R.: . . . Then Mr. Cozens-Hardy raised various points of irregularity, which I shall dispose of very shortly, because I think they mostly are not points with which this Court has anything to do. The only new one is the point about the closure. It appears that there was a discussion about this matter at a meeting of shareholders of the Assets Company, and, after having heard the views — I do not say of all those who opposed, but of one or two of them — the meeting came to the conclusion that they had heard enough, and did not want to hear any more, and there-upon the chairman declared the discussion closed. That is said to be a matter calling for the interference of this Court. I do not think so. I think it would be a very bad precedent that we should interfere in such a case. I am aware of the importance of the observations made by Lord Eldon in *Const v. Harris*, in which he said, "I call that the act of all" (he was speaking of the meeting of large companies), "which is the act of the majority, provided all are consulted, and the majority are acting *bona fide*, meeting, not for the purpose of negativing, what any one may have to offer, but for the purpose of negativing, what, when they are met together, they may, after due consideration, think proper to negative: For a majority of partners to say, We do not care what one partner may say, we, being the majority, will do what we please, is, I apprehend, what this Court will not allow." I think that principle is as important, and, perhaps, more important, to bear in mind now than it was sixty or seventy years ago; but Lord Eldon does not mean that a minority who are bent on obstructing business and resolved on talking for ever should not be put down. He means that the majority are not to be tyrannical. After hearing what is to be said, they may say, "We have heard enough. We are not bound to listen till everybody is tired of talking and has sat down." There is no reason for supposing that there was any terrorism in this matter, and this appeal must be dismissed with costs.

CHITTY L.J.: As to the closure, I think if we laid down that the chairman, supported by a majority, could not put a termination to the speeches of those who were desirous of addressing the meeting, we should allow a small minority, or even a member or two, to tyrannize over the majority. The case has been put by Mr. Cozens-Hardy as the terrorism of the majority. If we accepted his proposition we should put his weapon into the hands of the minority, which might involve the company in all-night sittings. That seems to me to be an extravagant proposition, and in this particular case there seems to have been nothing arbitrary or vexatious on the part of the chairman or of the majority. I am not, of course, saying that the majority must not listen to reasonable arguments for a reasonable time. I will advert only to one other point, and must be excused for not going into the other "irregularities" which Mr. Cozens-Hardy has mentioned. He said that it was wrong of the chairman to refuse to put to the meeting, merely held for the confirmation of the original resolution passed by three-fourths of the proprietors, another resolution by way of amendment. His refusal, in my opinion, was right, because that meeting was called for one purpose only, and that was to confirm or reject the original resolution which had been passed, and any amendment would be wholly irrelevant, because the single purpose of the meeting was to say Aye or Nay, is the original resolution to stand or fall?

COLLINS L.J.: . . . I am of the same opinion.

Appeal dismissed.

National Dwellings Society v. Sykes
[1894] 3 Ch. 159

[By the articles of the National Dwellings Society, the business of the society was to be managed by a council invested with all the usual powers of directors. The articles of the society provided that every general meeting would be led by a member of the council, but if one was not present, the members present could choose one of their own rank to preside. The articles also allowed any ordinary meeting to, without notice, receive the accounts, balance sheets, and reports of council and the auditors, and accept or reject them.

At the annual general meeting on April 12, 1894, the chair was taken by Sykes, a council member, who moved a resolution that the report and accounts be received. The resolution was put to a vote and defeated with six votes in favour and 28 against. Sykes declared the resolution lost, declared the meeting dissolved, and left the room with his supporters, though the election of directors and auditors had not been disposed of. The remaining members elected another chairman and passed a resolution to adjourn the meeting for six weeks. At that meeting, unattended by Sykes, an investigation committee was appointed to look into the society's affairs. The committee commenced an action against the council. At issue in the case was the legality of Sykes' conduct as chairman of the April 12 meeting.]

CHITTY J.: A question of some importance has been mooted in this case, with regard to the powers of the chairman over a meeting. Unquestionably it is the duty of the chairman, and his function, to preserve order, and to take care that the proceedings are conducted in a proper manner, and that the sense of the meeting is properly ascertained with regard to any question which is properly before the meeting. But, in my opinion, the power which has been contended for is not within the scope of the authority of the chairman — namely, to stop the meeting at his own will and pleasure. The meeting is called for the particular purposes of the company. According to the constitution of the company, a certain officer has to preside. He presides with reference to the business which is there to be transacted. In my opinion, he cannot say, after that business has been opened, "I will have no more to do with it; I will not let this meeting proceed; I will stop it; I declare the meeting dissolved, and I leave the chair." In my opinion, that is not within his power. The meeting by itself (and these articles certainly apply to what I have said) can resolve to go on with the business for which it has been convened, and appoint a chairman to conduct the business which the other chairman, forgetful of his duty or violating his duty, has tried to stop because the proceedings have taken a turn which he himself does not like. I think perhaps what I have said is sufficient for the present purpose, and I need say no more except that the other questions raised by this application will stand adjourned till after the general meeting has been held as arranged.

Notes

1 Subsection 137(1)(b) of the CBCA and s. 99(1)(b) of the OBCA now provide for a shareholder right of discussion. The CBCA provides that: "A shareholder entitled to vote at an annual meeting of shareholders may (b) discuss at the meeting any matter in respect of which the person would have been entitled to submit a proposal." This section thus statutorily enshrines a right of discussion only at annual meetings. By contrast, the OBCA extends such right to every shareholder "entitled to vote at a meeting of shareholders," thus including special as well as annual meetings. Does the CBCA provision exclude by implication a right of discussion at special meetings? Or is there a common law right of discussion? If so, does the common law right allow the shareholder to discuss the same range of matters as the statute provides in respect of an annual meeting?

2 Note that the CBCA and OBCA extend the right of discussion to any shareholder entitled to vote at an annual meeting, and at a meeting, respectively. A shareholder may be so entitled because the shareholder holds voting shares. As we saw in the preceding section, the statutes may also create an entitlement to vote, either in a group with

other classes of shareholders or separately as a class, whether or not the shares normally carry the right to vote. If these statutory provisions are not called into play, however, there is nothing in the corporate legislation that gives the non-voting shareholders a right either to attend shareholders' meetings or to ask questions. Out of a concern that the voice of non-voting (or restricted voting) shareholders should be heard, the Ontario Securities Commission has issued Rule 56-501 and the TSX's Company Manual Sec. 604 requires that "reporting issuers" (public corporations) send non-voting shareholders all material sent to voting shareholders in connection with meetings, to allow these shareholders to attend shareholders' meetings and to ask questions.

3   An Ontario case arising under the CBCA followed the holding in the *National Dwellings Society* case and reaffirmed the right of shareholders to be heard at an annual shareholders' meeting, without discussion of s. 137. In *Re Bomac Batten Ltd. and Pozhke* (1983), 43 O.R. (2d) 344 (Ont. H.C.) the chairman (Pozhke) had ruled that a proxy deposited with the company was invalid because the shareholder, a partnership, had not complied with the corporate by-law requiring that a proxy be "authorized by a resolution of the board of directors or governing body of the body corporate or association . . ." He then ruled that, because of the invalidity of the proxy, there was no quorum present at the shareholders' meeting and declared the meeting adjourned. The proxyholder whose proxies were declared invalid immediately protested, requesting that the validity of the proxies be discussed, asserting that the partnership was not an "association" within the by-laws, and representing that if a resolution was necessary it had in fact been passed. The chairman refused to entertain any discussion and left the meeting. The remaining shareholders present elected a new chairman who accepted the proxies in question; the meeting then proceeded to elect a new board of directors. The newly elected board of directors sought (*inter alia*) a declaration from the court that the meeting had been improperly adjourned, that the proxies were valid, and that the new board was validly elected. Cromarty J. found that a partnership of the character in question was not a "body corporate" or "association," and hence the by-law in question did not apply, and the proxies were valid. He also held that the meeting had been improperly adjourned, that the shareholders had properly continued the meeting, and that the new board of directors was validly elected. In the course of his judgment, he stated:

> In *Gray v. Yellowknife Gold Mines Ltd. et al.*, [1946] O.W.N. 938, Mr. Lennox, the learned Assistant Master of the Supreme Court who had been directed by the Court of Appeal to ascertain "who

are the duly elected directors of Yellowknife Gold Mines Ltd. at present holding office", said of the chairman of a meeting at p. 942:

> Mr. Gale classifies the position of chairman as quasi-judicial. That may be placing the standard too high when matters in which the chairman is actually interested are being debated but in the exercise of the discretion vested in him, and in making rulings in the course of his conduct of the meeting, the position at least approximates that of a person occupying a quasi-judicial position. Due, no doubt, to the high standard required of a chairman, he is afforded some protection in the performance of his duty.

4   The Ontario courts were given a chance to revisit these issues in a series of cases involving litigation between Michael Blair and Canadian Express Limited (a member of the Bronfman group of companies). The facts were as follows. Blair was a director, chief executive officer and substantial shareholder in Consolidated Enfield Corporation ("Enfield"). Canadian Express was the largest shareholder in Enfield, and in the months leading up to the annual shareholders' meeting, considerable tension had developed between Blair and Canadian Express. Nonetheless, Canadian Express had indicated that it would support management's slate of nominees for director, including Blair, at the meeting. Fearing that Canadian Express might change its mind, Blair consulted Enfield's lawyers on the night before the meeting with a view to determining what he should do if a nomination for directors was made from the floor. He was told that Canadian Express had used the form of proxy sent to shareholders by management, and that because of a note on the back of the form of proxy, the form of proxy gave the proxyholders no discretion to vote for candidates other than the management slate. Just before the annual meeting, Canadian Express did indeed change its mind and decided to nominate Timothy Price as a director, rather than Blair. The Canadian Express proxyholders voted for Price. Had their votes been counted, there would have been enough votes to elect Price in Blair's stead. As Chairman of the meeting, however, Blair again consulted with Enfield's lawyers, who again advised him that the proxies could only be voted for the management slate of directors. Blair then returned to the floor, indicated that a number of proxies had been held invalid, and declared the management slate of directors elected. When a representative of Canadian Express indicated that he wished to be heard, Blair declined to give him the floor. Canadian Express subsequently sued both Blair and Enfield seeking a declaration that Price, and not Blair, had been validly elected as a director.

In *Canadian Express Ltd. v. Blair* (1989), 46 B.L.R. 92 (Ont. H.C.), Holland J. held that on the proper construction of the proxies, they had been properly voted for Price. In so holding, he stated that:

> In coming to this conclusion, I have accepted the evidence of Professor Crête, recognized by both sides as a leading authority in this country on proxies, which evidence dealt with the policies underlying the proxy solicitation process and particularly the importance of enabling shareholders to freely exercise their voting rights in accordance with their intentions. I have also accepted the evidence of King, DaCosta and Norris as establishing a generally accepted industry practice and particularly their evidence that shareholder designees who hold blank proxies as here submitted are recognized as having full discretion to vote as they see fit, just as the shareholders in person at the meeting could vote . . . There is no doubt on the evidence that the proxyholders intended to and did cast their votes for Price and not for Blair.

Holland J. also held that Canadian Express's challenge succeeded because Blair had failed to meet the quasi-judicial standard of behavior expected of the Chair of the meeting. He held that Blair had failed to accord dissenting shareholders the right to be heard following his ruling on the validity of the proxies:

> At the very least, he had an obligation to allow those affected by his ruling on the disputed ballots an opportunity to be heard. He chose to act as judge in his own cause and it is properly inferred from the evidence that he had determined to act in this way, at least at the time of the July 19th meeting, and, until the announcement of the voting results. In view of Blair's conduct alone and quite apart from the true construction of the proxies, his ruling cannot stand.

He held that reliance on legal advice was no excuse, holding that "it was his responsibility to conduct himself quasi-judicially throughout the proceedings. Holland J. awarded costs jointly and severally against Blair and Enfield. Canadian Express, however, now had control of Enfield, and decided to collect the costs (of about $165,000) solely from Blair.

Blair then requested Enfield to indemnify him as to costs. When Enfield refused, Blair sued. In *Blair v. Consolidated Enfield Corp.*, unreported, Ont. Gen. Div., October 28, 1992, Carruthers J. held that Blair was not entitled to an indemnity under s.136 of the OBCA (nor under the similarly worded by-law of Enfield). He held that, whether or not Blair had acted in good faith, he had not acted in the best interests of Enfield in defending the litigation begun by Canadian Express.

The following is the appeal from that judgment. Although the central issue is Blair's entitlement to an indemnity, this turns on the propriety of his conduct as Chairman of the shareholders' meeting. Consolidated Enfield subsequently appealed to the Supreme Court, which upheld the Court of Appeal decision.

Blair v. Consolidated Enfield Corp.
1993 CarswellOnt 165, 15 O.R. (3d) 783 (Ont. C.A.), affirmed 1995 CarswellOnt 1393, 1995 CarswellOnt 1179, [1995] 4 S.C.R.5 (S.C.C.)

CARTHY J.A.: [Carthy J.A. reviewed the facts, as recounted above, and continued:]

The single issue before this court is the proper application to the facts of the company by-law which grants rights of indemnity in the terms authorized by s. 136(1) of the Ontario *Business Corporations Act*. I will refer throughout to the Act because the by-law of the company reads to the same effect.

[Carthy J.A. then quoted s. 136 of the OBCA. He also noted that the trial judge in this proceeding, Carruthers J., had concluded that Blair could not be acting in the best interests of Enfield in defending the litigation against him unless it could be shown that he was a better director than the director who replaced him. Addressing this last point, Carthy J.A. stated:]

> There are implicit errors in this reasoning. First, the best interest of the corporation in this case centres not upon the choice of particular directors, but upon the integrity of the voting procedure and the validity of corporate acts of the directors following the vote. . . Second, it is in the interest of a corporation to defend its corporate acts, if defence is justified, for the same reason that it is concerned with the validity of those acts when performed. Finally, I read s. 136(1)(a) and the language "acted . . . with a view to the best interests of the corporation" as referring back to, in this case, the conduct of the vote for directors — not to the conduct of the litigation. The litigation that is contemplated by s. 136(1)(a) is against the director personally and the indemnity is against personal liability. There is no purpose in a requirement that personal litigation be conducted in the best interests of the corporation".

[T]he respondent says that if Blair had been acting in a *bona fide* fashion in keeping with his quasi-judicial duties as chairman he would, once it was recognized that a "mistake" had been made, have given Walt and Boultbee [two representatives of Canadian Express with proxies from shareholders who between them, held the majority of the votes] an opportunity to correct the proxies or, at least, give them an opportunity to make representations concerning the interpretation with another disinterested chairperson appointed to make a ruling. Blair's answer is that he asked indisputably competent lawyers to advise him in the broadest of terms, and he followed their advice. Further, he argues that the vote had been taken and the chairman owed a duty to all shareholders to rule upon its legal effect. Nor could he simply accept the word of the proxyholder that the shareholder intended to proffer an open discretion and that a mistake had been made in filling out the proxies. While Walt, as president of Canadian Express, could speak for the company, Boultbee could not speak for the shareholders he represented and thus, given the legal opinion, he would be countermanding their written instructions.

Issue

Should Carruthers J. have held that Blair satisfied the onus of bringing himself within the language of s. 136 of the Ontario *Business Corporations Act*? Has he demonstrated that on July 20 he acted honestly and in good faith with a view to the best interests of the corporation?

Good Faith Reliance on Legal Advice

At issue is his ruling on the overall balloting, and to conclude that his ruling was *male fide* because the result favoured him is to conclude that he was compelled to rule the other way, or give up the chair, no matter what advice he received. Aside from the question of giving up the chair, the real test should be whether the ruling was made with the *bona fide* intent that the company have a lawfully elected board of directors.

. . . I have already concluded that, on a proper reading of ss. 130 to 136 of the Ontario *Business Corporations Act*, legal advice does not automatically sanctify conduct based upon it as honest and in good faith for purposes of claiming indemnity under s. 136. It is, however, an ingredient to be considered and one should not be dismissive of it simply because it favours the election of the chairperson or, as in many such situations, because it comes from a law firm whose own retainer is at stake. It must be considered in the context in which it was given and alongside the duty of the chairperson to act fairly.

The authorities referred to above generally describe the chairperson's duty as quasi-judicial without defining what that means in this context. It is confusing to me to use, and seek to define, the word judicial or quasi-judicial in this context because an adjudicator or judge can never have a personal interest in the issue. A chairperson who is more than a nominal shareholder of a public company, on the other hand, always has a personal interest in everything that affects the company, which includes all of the rulings of the chair. If that distinction is not recognized the reflex reaction is to assume that a decision which benefits the chair personally is non-judicial and thus not *bona fide*. In my view, it is preferable to describe the duty as one of honesty and fairness to all individual interests, and directed generally toward the best interests of the company.

* * *

The ballots cast were in accordance with the instructions in the proxies or they were not. An experienced team of lawyers gave an opinion the evening before and, broadening their inquiries to even more lawyers when the event occurred, they remained of the same view. They also told Blair that it was his duty to make the ruling despite his interest in the outcome . . . If lawyers for Canadian Express had expressed a contrary view, he would then have two opinions on a complicated legal problem. Given the necessity of determining who the legal directors of the company were, so that business could be carried on in a regular fashion, some decision had to be made . . .

Counsel for Canadian Express focused on the lack of fairness shown by Blair in knowing that a mistake had been made and giving no opportunity to correct it. They argue that when the nomination of Price was made from the floor that Blair, in fairness, should have alerted Walt and Boultbee that they would not be able to vote for Price. Presumably, Walt would then have executed a new proxy on behalf of Canadian Express but Boultbee would have had to return to the shareholders he represented to obtain new proxies, on the assumption that it would be their desire to change them. It must be remembered that there is another faction deserving fairness from the chairman — the 15 per cent of shareholders who decided not to be represented on the basis of what they read in the management information circular, or for whatever other reason. If the meeting was to be adjourned to accommodate Walt and Boultbee, should these shareholders not be informed that a battle for control was on and that their votes could determine the result? In my view it goes too far to say that the duty of fairness means that Blair must selectively assist those who attend to vote in the process leading to the vote. His duty of fairness relates to the decision-making process and the conduct of a proper corporate meeting . . .

The Conduct of the Litigation

* * *

As I said earlier when dealing with the reasons of Carruthers J., on my reading of the Ontario *Business Corporations Act*, good faith is related to the ruling on July 20 and the expenses of the litigation are limited by s. 136(1) to those which are reasonably incurred . . . Litigation that is pursued in bad faith is not likely to involve "reasonably incurred" expenses. My analysis will be as to whether Blair acted reasonably in his defence of the litigation.

[Carthy J.A. found that Blair J. had acted reasonably in defending the litigation. Indeed, on July 24 he had requisitioned a shareholders' meeting to conduct a fresh election for directors.]

Blair added nothing to the costs of the proceedings, his requisition of an annual meeting made it possible for the board to hold one before the litigation reached the courtroom . . .

In conclusion, I would allow the appeal, set aside the dismissal of the application, and in its place grant judgment against Enfield requiring it to indemnify Blair for any costs payable by Blair to Canadian Express arising out of application No. RE1730/89 and requiring it to pay Blair the amount of costs he incurred in contesting the assessment of costs in that litigation. If the amount is contested those costs are to be assessed.

The costs of this appeal and of the application before Carruthers J. should be paid by the respondent to the appellant forthwith after assessment.

Appeal allowed.

Questions

1   Given that the Court of Appeal did not overrule Holland J.'s judgment that Price was elected director rather than Blair, what is the status of Holland J.'s finding that Blair had failed to meet the quasi-judicial standard of behavior expected of him?

2   Whose reasoning do you prefer on the issue of Blair's conduct? That of Holland J. and Carruthers J. or that of the Court of Appeal?

3   In *Catalyst Fund General Partner I Inc. v. Hollinger Inc.*, 2006 CarswellOnt 1416, 79 O.R. (3d) 288 (Ont. C.A.), the Ontario Court of Appeal denied the indemnity claim of a director who, although he subjectively believed he was acting in the best interests of the corporation, was found to objectively not have acted in good faith. Does this alter the test in *Blair*? See *Bennett v. Bennett Environmental Inc.*, 2009 CarswellOnt 1132, [2009] O.J. No. 853 (Ont. C.A.).

4   In *Wells v. Melnyk*, 2008 CarswellOnt 4438, [2008] O.J. No. 2845 (Ont. S.C.J.), there was a proxy battle for the board of directors of Biovail Corporation. Prior to the annual general meeting, the respondents revoked their proxies, reducing the number of out-standing shares at the meeting to less than the 51% required for quorum. The Board then amended the by-laws of Biovail to reduce the quorum for a meeting to two shareholders holding at least 25 per cent of the outstanding shares, and a new management slate was elected. The applicant argued that the meeting was validly con-stituted, or, if not, that the court should retroactively validate the meeting. Wilton-Siegel J. denied the application. He held that the by-law amendment was not effective, as there had been a lack of notice and shareholder approval. Further, an order to retroactively validate the meeting could not be justified as an exercise of the Court's inherent jurisdiction under the *CBCA*.

5   Is bad-faith of a director the same as bad-faith of an administrative agent? See *Entreprises Sibeca inc. c. Frelighsburg (Municipalité)*, 2004 CarswellQue 2404, 2004 CarswellQue 2405, [2004] 3 S.C.R. 304 (S.C.C.).

(e)   Shareholder Proposals

Normally, matters like nominations for directors, proposed changes to the company's articles and by-laws, and proposals relating to other matters (like the adoption of fundamental changes) originate with the managers of the corporation. Certainly in larger public companies, most shareholders are entirely divorced from the management of the company and are content to leave matters in the hands of the professional managers.

To foster shareholder democracy, however (see *Proposals for a New Business Corporations Law for Canada*, Vol. 1, Ottawa, 1971, paras. 273–279), the CBCA (and provincial acts, see below) allows shareholders to make proposals to be considered at shareholders' meetings (CBCA s. 137, OBCA s. 99, BCBCA s. 188).

There are four categories of proposals that a shareholder might make. First, shareholders may make a proposal that the articles be amended (CBCA s. 175(1), OBCA s. 169(1)); second, that a by-law be made, amended or repealed (CBCA s. 103(5), OBCA s. 116(5)); third, shareholders holding at least 5% of the shares or 5% of a class of voting shares may make nominations for the election of directors (CBCA s. 137(4), OBCA s. 99(4)). The last category is a residual category of somewhat uncertain dimensions. Broadly speaking, if the proposal does not relate to the business or affairs of the corporation, the managers may refuse to circulate it; thus, the fourth category consists of those proposals that fall outside of this limit (and that do not run afoul of the more technical limitations in CBCA s. 137(5), OBCA s. 99(5)). The proposal is circulated at the corporation's expense with the management proxy circular; the shareholder may also request that management circulate a supporting statement that in combination with the proposal does not exceed 500 words under the OBCA (Regulations s. 23(4)), 500 words under the CBCA (Regulations s. 48), and 1000 words under the BCBCA (s. 188(3)).

The CBCA's shareholder proposals provisions were reformed in 2001. The changes were influenced by two major cases arising out of the similar shareholder proposals sections of the *Bank Act*: *Verdun v. Toronto Dominion Bank*, [1996] 3 S.C.R. 550; and *Michaud c. Banque Nationale du Canada*, [1997] R.J.Q. 547 (Que.S.C.), both of which will be discussed below. Proposals may be made by registered or beneficial shareholders. To be eligible to submit a proposal, a shareholder must continuously hold a prescribed minimum number of shares for a prescribed amount of time before submitting a proposal. The current requirement is a six-month hold period on shares worth $2,000 or comprising 1% of the total number of outstanding voting shares, whichever is less (CBCR s. 46). Support from other shareholders can be counted toward meeting these eligibility requirements (CBCA s. 137(1.1)(b)). The corporation has the right to demand proof that the shareholder meets the eligibility requirements (s.

137(1.4)), which may be necessary if a beneficial shareholder is making the proposal. In Ontario, OBCA s. 169(1) was amended (and came into force on December 31, 2015) to clarify that shareholders included both registered and beneficial owners.

Management must circulate a shareholder proposal to shareholders, except in certain circumstances where they may refuse to do so. While the CBCA previously allowed management to refuse to circulate a proposal that was "primarily for the purpose of promoting general economic, political, racial, religious, social or similar causes" (old s. 137(5)(b)), the CBCA now uses much more general wording, allowing management to omit a proposal that "does not relate in a significant way to the business or affairs of the corporation" (CBCA s. 137(5)(b.1)). Does the latter formulation give management and/or the court a freer hand in defining what shareholders may include in a proposal, given the comparative vagueness of the "business or affairs of the corporation"? If the phrase is defined narrowly to mean only those matters relating to corporate profitability (in conformity with cases like *Dodge v. Ford* and *Parke v. Daily News*, considered earlier in Chapter 4), then perhaps there is little difference in the scope of the exception between the old CBCA provision and the new one. But if a broader meaning is accepted (as per Berger J. in *obiter* in the *Teck* case, *supra*, Chapter 6) then might the new CBCA provision permit shareholder proposals that the prior CBCA provision would not have?

One question that arises in connection with shareholder proposals is the effect of the proposal. Is it binding on management? Is it merely a recommendation to management? This question must be examined separately in relation to the four categories of shareholder proposals. The answer is straightforward in relation to nominations for the election of directors. A nomination for the election of directors is simply that — nothing more and nothing less.

In relation to a proposal to change the by-laws, the OBCA explicitly answers the question of the effect of the proposal in s. 116(5), by indicating that: "If a shareholder proposal to make, amend or repeal a by-law is made in accordance with section 99 and is adopted by shareholders at a meeting, the by-law, amendment or repeal is effective from the date of its adoption and requires no further confirmation." The OBCA contains no such provision in relation to a shareholder proposal to change the articles (see s. 169(1)). The reason for the difference in drafting appears to be because s. 116(3) requires shareholder confirmation of a by-law where initiated by a director. In other words, the wording of s. 116(5) is designed merely to emphasize that no shareholder confirmation of a by-law is necessary where the by-law initiates with shareholders as a proposal (rather than with the directors) and the proposal is passed by the shareholders. This emphasis is not necessary for s. 169(1). Moreover, s. 169(2) suggests by implication that if the proposal is passed, it is effective; otherwise, no dissent right would arise, and notice about such right would be unnecessary.

The CBCA does not deal explicitly with the effect of a shareholder proposal relating to the articles either. Again, however, it would seem rather curious if the proposal, duly passed by a resolution of shareholders, were merely a recommendation to management rather than a completed act. You might note that the predecessor statute to the CBCA (the *Canada Corporations Act*, R.S.C. 1970, c. C-32, s. 13(6)) required all amendments to the articles to begin with a directors' resolution. The CBCA omits this requirement (as does the OBCA) suggesting the no directors' resolution is necessary to complete a change in the articles. Further, in the case of an amendment to the articles, s. 175(2) of the CBCA suggests by clear implication that a properly passed proposal to amend the articles is binding.

Perhaps the greatest difficulties arise in connection with determining the effect of a proposal in the fourth category. Both the CBCA (s. 102(1)) and the OBCA (s. 115(1)) give the directors the power to manage or supervise the management of the corporation. If a shareholder made a proposal to amalgamate the corporation with another corporation, and this was passed by a special resolution (as required to effect an amalgamation), would that trench on the authority of the directors to manage the corporation if it were considered binding? Or, if a shareholder made a proposal to discontinue the manufacture of a certain product (as in the *Medical Committee* case, briefly recounted, *infra*), would that be an impermissible interference with the power to manage and would the proposal therefore assume the status of a recommendation only? What it is that is encompassed within the power to manage is not entirely self-defining. In the normal course of events, the directors (and their appointed managers) will make a decision to amalgamate, and will then submit this decision to shareholders for approval. Thus, the decision to amalgamate will involve activity that would normally be considered to fall within management's prerogative to manage as well as the exercise of shareholder powers of approval. A decision to abandon a particular product would appear to fall more clearly within the exclusive domain of management decision-making.

What in your view is the effect of a shareholder proposal in each of these cases? Could it perhaps even be argued that, because these matters fall within management's domain, management would be justified in refusing to entertain the proposal? And is there any benefit to having non-binding shareholder proposals? See Doron Levitt and Nadya Malenko, "Non-Binding Voting for Shareholder Proposals" (2011) 66:5 J. Fin. 1579.

Should there be a requirement for management to report on any follow-up action it has taken in relation to a proposal that was approved by a majority of shareholders?

Notes

1   Some empirical research suggests that shareholder proposals are an
effective corporate governance mechanism in the US. See Bonnie
Buchanan, Jeffrey Netter and Tina Yang "Are Shareholder Proposals
an Important Corporate Governance Device? Evidence from US and
UK Shareholder Proposals" (2010) Working Research Paper, update
online, ResearchGate: < https://www.researchgate.net/publication/
228239694_Are_Shareholder_Proposals_an_Important_Corporate_-
Governance_Device_Evidence_from_US_and_UK_Shareholder_-
Proposals >. The American framework governing shareholder
proposals in publicly traded companies is set out in Rule 14-a8 of
the *Securities Exchange Act* of 1934. As in Canada, a shareholder
may deliver a proposal and request that management circulate it in
the corporation's proxy materials. There are 13 grounds under which
management may refuse to circulate a shareholder proposal. A
proposal can be refused, for example, on procedural grounds, for
dealing with the ordinary business operations of the corporation, for
relating to the election to an office or for being motivated by general
political and moral concerns. If management refuses a shareholder
proposal, it must notify the shareholder and the SEC and provide
reasons for the refusal. If the SEC rules that the refusal is unjustified,
it will send a letter recommending that the proposal be included in the
proxy materials. To obtain a legally binding ruling, a shareholder
must commence an action in the courts or appeal to the SEC for a
decision binding the corporation.

Medical Committee *for Human Rights v. SEC*, 139 U.S. App. D.C.
226, 432 F.2d 659 (D.C., 1970), deals with management's right to
refuse to circulate a shareholder proposal on the ground that it deals
with the ordinary business of the corporation. The Medical
Committee for Human Rights wrote to the Board of Dow Chemical
Company requesting that it include a proposal in the corporation's
proxy materials. The proposal was to the effect that Dow stop selling
napalm to buyers who could not give reasonable assurance that it
would not be used on human beings. Dow refused to include this
proposal in the 1968 proxy statement on the ground that it had
arrived too late, and again refused to include it in the 1969 proxy
statement, on the grounds that it was motivated by general political
and moral concerns and not related to the conduct of Dow's ordinary
business operations. The SEC agreed with Dow's position, and the
Medical Committee initiated an action to force the SEC to reconsider
its claim and furnish adequate reasons for its decision. Tamm C.J.,
said:

> The management of Dow Chemical Company is repeatedly quoted
> in sources which include the company's own publications as

proclaiming that the decision to continue manufacturing and marketing napalm was made not because of business considerations but in spite of them; that management in essence decided to pursue a course of activity which generated little profit for the shareholders and actively impaired the company's public relations and recruitment activities because management considered this action morally and politically desirable. (App. 40a-43a; see also *id.* at 33.) The proper political and social role of modern corporations is, of course, a matter of philosophical argument extending far beyond the scope of our present concern; the substantive wisdom or propriety of particular corporate political decisions is also completely irrelevant to the resolution of the present controversy. What is of immediate concern, however, is the question of whether the corporate proxy rules can be employed as a shield to isolate such managerial decisions from shareholder control. After all, it must be remembered that "[t]he control of great corporations by a very few persons was the abuse at which Congress struck in enacting Section 14(a)." *SEC v. Transamerica Corp., supra.* We think that there is a clear and compelling distinction between management's legitimate need for freedom to apply its expertise in matters of day-to-day business judgment, and management's patently illegitimate claim of power to treat modern corporations with their vast resources as personal satrapies implementing personal political or moral predilections. It could scarcely be argued that management is more qualified or more entitled to make these kinds of decisions than the shareholders who are the true beneficial owners of the corporation; and it seems equally implausible that an application of the proxy rules which permitted such a result could be harmonized with the philosophy of corporate democracy which Congress embodied in section 14(a) of the *Securities Exchange Act* of 1934.

Note that the result of this case was not an order that the company circulate the proposal, but rather that the SEC reconsider the petitioner's claim and furnish adequate reasons for its decision. As such, the holding in the Medical Committee case can be interpreted as somewhat less far reaching than might at first appear.

Is the holding consistent with holdings in cases like *Dodge v. Ford* (*supra*, Chapter 4)? Is it consistent with the purpose and intention of the SEC regulation in question?

Varity Corp. v. Jesuit Fathers of Upper Canada
1987 CarswellOnt 145, 59 O.R. (2d) 459 (Ont. H.C.), affirmed 1987
CarswellOnt 2264, 60 O.R. (2d) 640 (Ont. C.A.)

AUSTIN J.: This is an application by Varity Corporation, formerly Massey-Ferguson, for an order permitting Varity not to include in its mailing to shareholders for the annual general meeting, a proposal that the company end its investments in South Africa . . .

* * *

The proposal reads [in part] as follows:

WHEREAS the Commonwealth Eminent Persons Group concluded in June 1986 that the South African government was not prepared to negotiate the dismantling of apartheid, and that economic measures to compel change "may offer the last opportunity to avert what could be the worst bloodbath since the Second World War";

* * *

WHEREAS present conditions in South Africa make continued viable economic investments risky;

WHEREAS Varity Corporation has an 18.95% investment in Fedmech Holdings Limited, a South African corporation, which produces farm implements, tractors and accessories, harvesting machinery, trailers, industrial loaders and transport systems;

WHEREAS Varity, through its subsidiary Perkins Diesel Engines (UK), has a license agreement for the production of diesel engines with Atlantis Diesel Engines Co. (ADE), established by the South African government to ensure South African self-sufficiency in diesel engines for agricultural, commercial and military needs;

WHEREAS Varity recently argued before the Parliamentary Standing Committee on Human Rights that it is "a positive force for peaceful progress" in South Africa, but at the same time

— cited its lack of decision-making power as a minority shareholder in responding to questions about sub-standard wages paid for a period of time at Fedmech;

— revealed that it had terminated donations to assist black South African development in 1983 because of "hard times",

— reported that the declared policy of Atlantis Diesel Engines (ADE) is 'completely nondiscriminatory', when in fact ADE is located in a 'coloured only' area and employs no blacks;

[. . .]

WHEREAS Varity's license agreement with Atlantis Diesel Engines (ADE) involves it in an industry of sufficient strategic importance to the South African government that ADE has been declared a Key Point Industry, which by order of the Minister of Defence must establish a private plant-based militia, subject to government takeover in the event of civil unrest;

THEREFORE BE IT RESOLVED that the shareholders ask the Board of Directors to:

— take immediate steps to terminate Varity's investments in South Africa;

— take immediate steps to terminate Varity's license agreement with Atlantis Diesel Engines, and if there are legal obstacles, provide a report and a plan of action to the shareholders within ninety days;

— announce publicly to the South African government Varity's plans to leave South Africa as soon as possible.

In support of that proposal is a "supporting statement" which reads as follows:

"Varity Corporation is among Canada's largest transnational corporations. As a result of refinancing assistance to the company, the Government of Canada and the Government of Ontario are among its shareholders. Thus, the presence of Varity in South Africa is of particular significance, since it represents an investment by Canadian taxpayers in South Africa.

We believe that a meaningful process of disinvestment involves the termination of all business which might provide support to the South African government, including sales and technology transfers. A meaningful process of disinvestment should also include the provision of full information to representatives of black workers, and consultation with them about the terms of withdrawal. In addition, in consultation with the workers and other anti-apartheid groups, the Company should establish, or continue, corporate financial contributions to projects for the enhancement of black welfare and in support of anti-apartheid activities."

Section 131(5)(b) of the Act provides that a corporation is not required to comply with a shareholder's request if

(b) it clearly appears that the proposal is submitted by the shareholder primarily for the purpose of enforcing a personal claim or redressing a personal grievance against the corporation or its directors, officers or security holders, or primarily for the purpose of promoting general economic, political, racial, religious, social or similar causes . . .

Varity applies for exemption from the mailing requirement upon the basis that the proposal has been submitted primarily for the purpose of promoting general economic, political, racial, religious, social, or similar causes and in particular the abolition of apartheid in South Africa.

The application was opposed by the Jesuit Fathers and the Ursuline Religious. Their position was that:

(a) the onus was on the applicant;

(b) apartheid is not only socially and morally wrong, it contributes to the maintenance of an unstable and undesirable business climate from which Varity should withdraw;

(c) most shareholders of companies such as Varity do not attend company meetings, so one of the obstacles to reaching and activating shareholders is the cost of communication;

(d) s. 131 was designed to permit shareholders to communicate with other shareholders on matters concerning the company at the company's expense;

(e) to succeed, the applicant has to persuade the court that the proposal was submitted primarily for the purpose of promoting general economic, political, racial, religious, social, or similar causes;

(f) the present proposal relates not to any such general purpose but to the specific business affairs of Varity in South Africa.

I agree with propositions (a) through (e). In so far as (f) is concerned, the respondents point out that their resolution is directed at Varity's involvement in South Africa and that their desire is to have Varity terminate that involvement. They argue that this is a specific goal or purpose and that while it may be an economic, political, racial, religious, or social purpose, it remains specific and accordingly does not fall within the reach of s. 131(5)(b).

I agree that the proposal has a specific purpose and that that purpose is directly relevant to Varity. It is argued that because of this, s. 131(5)(b) has no application even if the respondents have as their general over-all goal the abolition of apartheid in South Africa. It is argued that if s. 131(5)(b) were to apply, it would prevent the taking of the first step towards that goal.

The language of the proposal and the supporting statement leave me in no doubt that the primary purpose of the proposal is the abolition of apartheid in South Africa. As I read the legislation, the fact that there may be a more specific purpose or target does not save the proposal. That more specific purpose here is the withdrawal of Varity. The legislation makes it clear that if the primary purpose is one of those listed, however commendable either the specific or the general purpose may be, the company cannot be compelled to pay for taking the first step towards achieving it. In other words, the company cannot be compelled to distribute the proposal.

In my view, the applicant is entitled to the order asked for. It indicated at the outset that it would not ask for costs in any event so I make no order as to costs.

Order accordingly.

Notes and Questions

1   Did the Court pay adequate attention to the assertion in the Jesuit Fathers' proposal (an assertion accepted as fact by the Court) that apartheid results in an "unstable and undesirable business climate . . ."? Would the result be any different under the new CBCA provision?

2   Note that the Court puts the onus of proof on the "applicant" to make out its case. In this case, the company was applying for an order to omit the proposal from the management proxy circular, pursuant to what is now CBCA s. 137(9). But suppose the company had simply decided to omit the proposal and the Jesuit Fathers had sought an order under s. 137(8) that the proposal be included in the management proxy circular. Would the onus of proof still be on the "applicant" (i.e., the Jesuit Fathers)? Would (or should) it be on the company? Does it make any sense to shift the onus of proof depending on who makes the application?

3   In *Greenpeace Foundation of Canada v. Inco Ltd.* (February 23, 1984), [1984] O.J. No. 274 (H.C.), a proposal was submitted to limit sulphur dioxide emissions at Inco's Sudbury operations to 274 tonnes per day. Inco refused to circulate the proposal, leading Greenpeace to apply to the court. The court rejected Greenpeace's application, in part because a proposal to reduce emissions to 43 tonnes per day had been voted on the previous year and had only received 1.6% of the votes cast. The court found these proposals to be substantially the same, thus running afoul of OBCA section 99(5)(d). The earlier proposal involved a much more drastic reduction in sulphur dioxide emissions, which would likely be much more costly for the company to implement. If you were a shareholder voting on these proposals, would you regard them as interchangeable, especially considering this potentially significant difference in cost?

4   An important shareholder proposal case in Canada is *Michaud c. Banque nationale du Canada*, [1997] R.J.Q. 547, 1997 CarswellQue 3831 (S.C.). Mr. Michaud was a registered shareholder of National Bank and the Royal Bank of Canada ("RBC") who, since he owned one share of each bank, was qualified to make proposals under the shareholder proposal provisions in the *Bank Act*, which are equivalent to those under the CBCA. The proposals related to various aspect of corporate governance, including: capping the

overall compensation of the highest-ranking bank executives to twenty times the average salary of bank employees; separating the role of the chair of the board of directors from the CEO of the bank; prohibiting providers of services to the bank from serving as directors; and increasing the number of women nominated for election as directors. The banks declined to submit Michaud's resolutions, and Michaud sought an order that the banks circulate the proposals under section 144(2) of the *Bank Act*.

The banks argued in court that since Michaud had only a small amount invested in each bank, he was not sufficiently aggrieved to have standing. They also argued that Michaud's proposals could be excluded under the *Bank Act* for being submitted primarily to redress a personal grievance; to secure publicity; and to promote general economic, political and social causes. Rayle J. rejected all of these arguments, finding that, by virtue of his share ownership, Michaud had standing and was not abusing the shareholder proposal right. She found that the inclusion of his proposals in the documentation was his only way of communicating with other shareholders; preventing this communication gave rise to the prejudice against him. She stated that a civilized discussion of Michaud's proposals would benefit the banks and their shareholders. The banks were ordered to include Michaud's proposals in their proxy materials and allow his proposals to go to a vote at the annual general meetings. Ultimately, the resolutions were defeated at the meetings.

Another noteworthy case is *Verdun v. Toronto Dominion Bank*, [1996] 3 S.C.R. 550, 1996 CarswellOnt 3943, 1996 CarswellOnt 3944. Verdun, with his wife, was the beneficial owner of over 2000 shares of Toronto-Dominion Bank. He submitted 11 proposals relating to the structure and make-up of the board of directors and procedures at the annual shareholders' meetings. Management refused to circulate the proposals, arguing that they were submitted to address a personal grievance and that Verdun was seeking to gain publicity, running afoul of section 143(5) of the *Bank Act*. As well, they argued that since Verdun was not a registered shareholder, he was not a "shareholder entitled to vote" under the meaning of section 143 of the *Bank Act* and therefore not entitled to submit proposals. The Ontario Court (General Division) dismissed Verdun's application, finding his proposals to have been submitted to secure publicity. The Court of Appeal found that it was unnecessary to consider section 143(5), as Verdun was not a "shareholder entitled to vote" under s. 93(1) of the Bank Act. The Supreme Court agreed with the Court of Appeal.

Compare the facts of *Michaud* and *Verdun*. Michaud was the registered owner of a single share of Royal Bank, purchased only in order to qualify to make a proposal, and was entitled to do so. Verdun was beneficial co-owner of over 2000 shares of Toronto-Dominion Bank, but was not entitled to make a proposal. Note that both *Verdun* and *Michaud* would have been treated differently under the post-2001 CBCA: Michaud would not have met the ownership requirement to make a proposal, while Verdun would not have been barred from making a proposal on the basis of being a beneficial shareholder. Are the new ownership requirements fairer in restricting the right to make proposals to those shareholders with a significant investment in the corporation?

5 Suppose a shareholders' meeting is requisitioned and a shareholder proposal sought to make a fundamental change in the corporation (e.g., removal of the present board, as authorized by removal of the present board or an amalgamation). What, if anything, can the current board do to frustrate the purpose for which the meeting is called? *Cf. Shield Development Co. v. Snyder* (1975), [1976] 3 W.W.R. 44, 1975 CarswellBC 227 (S.C.) and *Carrington Viyella Overseas (Holdings) Ltd. v. Taran* (February 24, 1983), Doc. Montreal 500-05-022164-824, 500-022164-824, Applications 2–4 (Que. S.C.).

6 Are shareholder proposals truly useful in promoting corporate democracy? Schwartz, "The Public Interest Proxy Contest: Reflections on Campaign G.M." (1970-71), 69 Michigan L.R. 419 recounts the efforts undertaken by the Project on Corporate Responsibility, a Washington-based non-profit corporation formed to "promote corporate responsibility and to educate management and the public about the social role of corporations." The goals of the Project were to carry on a proxy contest to gain public attention and obtain support for several resolutions, including enlarging the GM Board of Directors so that public interest directors might be elected, and creating a Shareholders' Committee for Corporate Responsibility to act as a commission and report on the corporation and its role in modern society. The campaign succeeded in that the Courts ordered the inclusion of two of its resolutions in the circular mailed by GM to all its shareholders with the management proxy solicitation package. In the final result, however, the two Campaign proposals were overwhelmingly defeated, receiving under 3% of the votes cast. Even so, the leader of the Campaign announced victory for having created a national debate on the subject of corporate responsibility.

In a mid-1980s survey of Canadian corporations conducted by Raymonde Crête, 84 of 93 firms (or 90.3%) indicated that they had never received a request to include a shareholder proposal in the management proxy materials. Of the nine companies that did, only three had included the proposal in the proxy materials. Of the votes cast, only 0.1%, 1.3%, and 6.7% of shareholders voted in favour of the proposal. See Raymonde Crête, *The Proxy System in Canadian Corporations* (1986), at 387.

Do shareholder proposals thus serve no useful function? Perhaps they do, even though they routinely fail. Consider the following passage from Jeffrey G. MacIntosh, "The Role of Institutional and Retail Investors in Canadian Capital Markets" (1993), 31 Osgoode Hall L.J. 371, at 411-412:

> [T]he shareholder proposal provisions have not been extensively used in Canada. It has been suggested that a practical reason for this non-use is the fact that most public corporations have a controlling shareholder, and the prospects of success are typically not great. . . . . While the prospects for success may be poor in an individual case, shareholder proposals can nonetheless serve an educative function by putting issues of concern to . . . investors on the public agenda. This can have the salutary effect of creating pressure on corporate managers not to adopt wealth-reducing measures. By generating public debate, shareholder proposals can also cause normally passive shareholders to rethink their some-times unthinking support of management.

While shareholder proposals are becoming more frequently used in Canada, most of them have little chance of being successfully passed. The majority of publicly traded Canadian companies are controlled either legally or effectively by an individual or small group, making it impossible for a minority shareholder to secure enough votes to pass a proposal. The most likely avenue for success for a shareholder proposal is in winning enough support that management decides to make the changes to avoid alienating investors. For more discussion on this subject and the *Michaud* case, see Brian R. Cheffins, "Michaud v. National Bank of Canada and Canadian Corporate Governance: A 'Victory' for Shareholder Rights?" [1998] 30 C.B.L.J. 20–72.

A number of Canadian banks (and other companies) saw a series of shareholder proposals by MEDAC (Movement for the Education and Protection of Shareholders, founded in 1995 by Yves Michaud) in 2009, requesting 50% female representation on boards. Share-holders of the following voted down these proposals: Bank of Montreal, CIBC, Laurentian Bank, RBC, Scotiabank, and TD Bank. National Bank agreed in advance of its annual meeting to continue to recruit more women to its board of directors.

Another series of shareholder proposals in 2009, brought by Meritas Mutual Funds, resulted in four banks (Bank of Montreal, CIBC, RBC and Scotiabank) passing shareholder resolutions to adopt an advisory shareholder vote on executive compensation. These same resolutions were withdrawn by Meritas at TD Bank, Sun Life Financial, TMX Group, and Potash Corporation of Saskatchewan, after each of these corporations agreed, in advance of their annual meeting, to implement the proposal. Note that in the United States, these advisory votes on executive compensation are mandatory per the Dodd-Frank Act.

For an analysis of the role of shareholder proposals in respect of human rights and social policy considerations, see Aaron A. Dhir, "Realigning the Corporate Building Blocks: Shareholder Proposals as a Vehicle for Achieving Corporate Social and Human Rights Accountability" (2006) 43 Am.Bus.L.J. 365, Carol Hansell "The Quality of the Shareholder Vote in Canada," *supra*, and Poonam Puri, "The Future of Stakeholder Interests in Corporate Govern-ance" (2010) 48 Can Bus LJ 427.

(f) Judicially Ordered Meetings

The corporation statutes also contain provisions which enable the court to order a meeting of shareholders where it is "impracticable" to convene a meeting. See, *e.g.*, CBCA, section 144; OBCA, section 106.

The case law on these provisions falls into two categories. First, there are cases in which the "impracticability" arises from some technical cause, such as the impossibility of obtaining a quorum. As an example, in *Re Edinburgh Workmen's Houses Improvement Co. Ltd.*, [1934] S.L.T 513, the articles required a quorum of 13 members personally present. When an application was made to court to confirm certain resolutions, it was discovered that only 14 of the 54 members lived in or near Edinburgh, the site of the head office. It was concluded that great difficulty would be experienced in obtaining the personal attendance of the necessary quorum, and the court ordered a meeting to be held with a quorum of five members personally present.

On the other hand, in *Ebrahim v. Continental Precious Minerals Inc.*, 2012 CarswellOnt 6348, 2012 ONSC 2918 (Ont. S.C.J. [Commercial List]), although Continental's by-laws had a special quorum requirement that required "not less than 50% of the company's shareholders at any meeting considering resolutions to remove, replace or appoint directors", the court found that there was nothing that made it impracticable. Shareholders voted for such a requirement, and the board did not act in any way to frustrate attaining quorum. The court stated that the dissident shareholders could have used the available proxy fight devices or requisitioned a special meeting to elect new directors, but the dissident shareholders did neither. Therefore, the circumstances were not enough to make convening a meeting impracticable.

There is another category of cases, however, in which the impracticability, while superficially technical in character, is in fact a reflection of an underlying dispute over policy or control. The leading cases are discussed in Getz, "Court Ordered Company Meetings" (1969), 33 The Conveyancer and Property Lawyer (N.S.) 399. Getz states that the applicants for a court ordered meeting need not show that the directors have breached their duties to the corporation, but rather that the shareholders have been deprived of their rights "to have an account of the conduct of the company's affairs and an opportunity to express their views on Corporate policy". He concludes:

> If this view is correct, then, in principle, and contrary to the impression that may be gained from a reading of the decided cases, the provision for a court-ordered meeting is not simply a majority shareholders' remedy. If there is any opportunity to which a minority shareholder is entitled, it is the opportunity to persuade his fellows of the wisdom of his view, and the unwisdom of their view of corporate policy. The only chance he gets to do this is at company meetings, and for them to deprive him of it by exercising their undoubted right as shareholders not to attend must be a sufficient ground for invoking the section. While they have the right, they must pay the price of its exercise.

There is one important limitation upon the scope of section 135 [empowering the court to order a meeting]: the purpose for which the meeting is sought to be ordered must be one that is constitutionally proper having regard to the powers of the general meeting under the *Companies Act* and the articles. This proposition is clearly illustrated by the decision of the Ontario Court of Appeal in *Re British International Finance (Canada) Ltd., Charlebois v. Bienvenu*. Two factions were fighting for control of a company, and each claimed to be the duly elected board. The matters in dispute between the parties were the subject of a pending court action, but the practical difficulty was that until the issues in that action were decided, "no one would know who was entitled to control the affairs of the company." An application was made seeking a court-ordered meeting "for the purpose of electing directors." The trial judge granted the order, and on appeal, the Court of Appeal agreed that the impracticability of calling or conducting a meeting had been made out.

But the real issues on appeal were, first, whether the court could order a meeting "to achieve some purpose thereat beyond the power of shareholders at a meeting called in any other manner," and secondly, whether the election of directors was, in the circumstances, such a lawful purpose. On the first question Aylesworth J., delivering the opinion of the court, held that:

> the section is aimed at and limited to the removal of difficulties militating against the conduct of business which may lawfully come before the meeting. Once such difficulties have been removed by the provisions of the order, however, it is open to the

shareholders present at the meeting to conduct only such business thereat which could have been conducted at a meeting legally called in any other manner.

As to the second question, the court held that under the Ontario *Corporations Act* the election of directors was an annual affair. If, in the pending action, it was decided that the insurgent board had been improperly elected, the original board would remain in office. If, on the other hand, the contested election had resulted in the valid election of a new board, that would be the duly constituted board of directors. In either event, however, it was not competent for the company "to hold what in effect amounts to a second election of an entire board of directors within one year." Consequently, the appeal was allowed and the application dismissed.

If the view advanced above as to the true scope of s. 135 is sound, then what provision may represent a significant weapon in the armoury available to shareholders to secure accountability for managerial conduct. It is a view, moreover, that is especially attractive in the light of the limitations that seem to have become encrusted upon s. 210 [the former English oppression provision]. So long as English company law remains committed to the chimera of shareholder rights as a vehicle for the enforcement of managerial responsibilities, the wider interpretation suggested for s. 135 seems desirable.

Canadian Javelin Ltd. v. Boon-Strachan Coal Co.,
1976 CarswellQue 103, 69 D.L.R. (3d) 439 (Que. S.C.)

[This case arose out of a dispute between two factions in management of Canadian Javelin Ltd. John Doyle was the beneficial owner, directly and indirectly, of 18% of the stock of Canadian Javelin. He had been a director of the company, and its driving force in management, since its inception in 1951. One of the factions contended that at a directors' meeting on January 29, 1976, Doyle had offered to resign as director if the directors decided his presence was detrimental to the company.

A directors' meeting was held on March 6, and although four directors, including Doyle, were not in the Montreal area, the meeting was not postponed. At the meeting, the directors present accepted Doyle's earlier offer of resignation, elected and appointed new officers, changed the signing authority at the company's banks, and appointed new legal counsel. On March 15, another meeting was held with five directors present, including those who had been unable to attend the Montreal meeting. Those directors found that the directors of the March 6 meeting were no longer directors, and appointed their own directors and officers. As a result of the dispute, the company's line of credit with the Banque Nationale de Paris was terminated, putting the company's financial outlook in doubt. Boon Strachan Coal Co. Ltd., a shareholder of

Canadian Javelin, and owned by Doyle, requested that the court order a general special meeting of shareholders.]

COLAS J.: There is no doubt from the evidence that the situation is not only abnormal but detrimental to the best interests of the Company and of its shareholders. The role of directors is to act in a fiduciary capacity for the benefit of the Company... Directors should not try to take over the control of the Company for their own personal advantage and with the hope that they will consolidate their power by creating a climate of uncertainty that places the Company in a suspicious position.

On April 22, 1976, a letter (ex. P-7) was sent by petitioner Boon-Strachan asking that a special general meeting of the shareholders be called. No response has been given to said petitioner. An explanation was given at the hearing for not calling the said general meeting of the shareholders in that the financial statements were not ready. The Court is of the opinion that the mere fact of the financial statements not being ready is not a valid reason to preclude the holding of a special meeting of the shareholders . . .

[I]t is quite evident that the March 6th board and management of the *mis-en-cause* does not feel ready to ask the shareholders for a renewal of their mandate.

* * *

The Court has examined thoroughly the jurisprudence cited by the attorneys of both parties and has studied the relevant doctrines and like Mr. Justice Bell, in *Re Zimmerman and Commonwealth Int'l Leverage Fund Ltd. et al.* (1966), 56 D.L.R. (2d) 709, 52 M.P.R. 87, along with Chief Justice Campbell, who heard the appeal of said case reported in 58 D.L.R. (2d) 160, M.P.R. *loc. cit.*, the Court has found out that there is a meagre number of cases that may apply to this motion. Mr. Justice Bell in his said judgment quotes [at p. 714] Mr. Justice Wynn-Parry in the English case of *Re El Sombrero Ltd.*, [[1958] Ch. 990 at pp. 906-7], that is:

It is to be observed that the section opens with the words "If for any reason," and therefore it follows that the section is intended to have, and, indeed, has by reason of its language, a necessarily wide scope. The next words are ". . . it is impracticable to call a meeting of the company . . ." The question then arises, what is the scope of the word "impracticable"? It is conceded that the word "impracticable" is not synonymous with the word "impossible"; and it appears to me that the question necessarily raised by the introduction of that word "impracticable" is merely this: examine the circumstances of the particular case and answer the question whether, as a practical matter, the desired meeting of the company can be conducted, there being no doubt, of course, that it can be convened and held. Upon the face of the section there is no express limitation which would operate to give those words "is impracticable" any less meaning than that which I have stated . . .

In *Dumart Packaging Co. Ltd. v. Dumart*, [1928] 1 D.L.R. 640 at p. 641, 61 O.L.R. 478, Mr. Justice Middleton states:

Motions of this kind are somewhat frequent in company cases in which there is some internecine warfare between factions in the company, each claiming to be entitled to represent the company. In these cases the practice of the Court is to direct that the proceedings be stayed until a meeting of the shareholders of the company can be called so as to enable the will of the shareholders, or of the majority, to be ascertained. These cases are collected in *Buckley's Companies Acts*, 9th ed., p. 614, and in *1928 Yearly Practice*, p. 46.

CONSIDERING that the evidence has shown that it is urgent that a general meeting of the shareholders be called and held in order to stop the damage that may be caused to the assets of the Company at the detriment of the shareholders, on account of the contradictory decisions that are taken by the two parallel boards of directors presently purporting to act on behalf of the company and on account of the uncertainty as to the control of the management of the company;

CONSIDERING that the Company will be in default of holding an annual general meeting after June 30, 1976, and the Company has not prepared and is not in preparation of any notice and proxy statements and other relevant documents for such an annual meeting and it is obvious that the present management does not intend to call a meeting in the near future;

CONSIDERING that in view of the tactics adopted by certain of the directors of the Company and the evident animosities existing, certain shareholders and directors of the company cannot hope to be fairly treated if the meeting is conducted by any one of the present officers and directors of the Company and thus the Court is of the opinion that in the present case it is obvious that there are no means available to the petitioners which will provide any assurance that the business of the meeting will be properly conducted except under an order of this Court (*cf. Re Routley's Holdings Ltd.* (1960), 22 D.L.R. (2d) 410 at p. 415, [1960] O.W.N. 160);

CONSIDERING that it is in the best interest of the Company that a special general meeting of the shareholders be called as soon as possible for the purpose of giving a clear mandate to those persons whom the shareholders wish to manage the Company;

CONSIDERING that in order to put an end to the litigations presently pending and any future litigation and to have the decision of the shareholders accepted by all factions, it is necessary that the meeting be conducted by a disinterested person of high repute;

CONSIDERING that Mr. Michel Robert, the past Bâtonnier Général of the Province of Quebec, being a disinterested person of high repute has manifested his readiness to act as chairman of such meeting and to cause notices to be sent to the shareholders;

CONSIDERING that the Court, when ordering the calling of the meeting or directing the conduct of the meeting, has to be careful to do as little violence as possible to the corporate articles or regulations and should in fact be careful to see that any meeting ordered to be held should be called and conducted in conformity with such articles or regulations as far as practicable;

CONSIDERING that the attorneys of petitioners have mentioned that if a date is chosen for the holding of the meeting, it should be at the end of the month of July so as to give sufficient time for the preparation of the required documentation and of the meeting;

FOR THESE REASONS, THE COURT:

(i) DOTH ORDER that a special general meeting of the shareholders of the *mis-en-cause*, Canadian Javelin Limited be held ... at the cost of the Company, and order Mr. Michel Robert to cause notice of such meeting of the shareholders to be sent to all shareholders of record . . .;

(ii) DOTH ORDER that all shareholders of record on the books of the transfer agent and Registrar of the Company as of July 2, 1976, be conclusive evidence of eligibility to vote at said meeting;

* * *

(viii) DOTH ORDER and appoint the said Michel Robert, to preside over the special general meeting of shareholders and doth order that his decisions be final and binding over all parties concerned;

(ix) DOTH ORDER and authorize Michel Robert, to appoint two independent scrutineers for the purpose of counting and preparing proxies for voting and the further counting of votes of shareholders appearing in person at the meeting;

(x) DOTH ORDER that the directors elected at the special general meeting of shareholders hold office until the next annual general meeting of shareholders of the Company and their qualification and duties be governed by the by-laws of the Company;

(xi) DOTH ORDER that no additional new shares or convertible debentures or share options of the company be issued or allotted or transacted by the Company until after the next annual general meeting of shareholders . . .

Order accordingly.

Notes

1   Did the Court have jurisdiction to order a meeting in the *Javelin* case, given that one or the other of the contending boards was likely a properly elected board? Should the Court have instead simply determined who the properly elected board was, making it unnecessary for the company to go to the trouble and expense of calling a new shareholders' meeting? *Cf. Re British International Finance*

(Canada) Ltd., Charebois v. Bienvenu, referred to in the excerpt from the Getz article, *supra*.

2   See also *FTS Worldwide Corp v. Unique Broadband Systems Inc.*, [2001] O.T.C. 938, 2001 CarswellOnt 4557 (S.C.J.); *Atkinson, Re*, 2002 CarswellAlta 1549, [2002] A.J. No. 1306 (Alta. Q.B.); *Croation Peasant Party of Ontario, Canada v. Zorkin* (1981), 38 O.R. (2d) 659, 1981 CarswellOnt 725 (H.C.); and *Athabaska Holdings Ltd. v. ENA Data-systems Inc.* (1980), 30 O.R. (2d) 527, 1980 CarswellOnt 1391 (H.C).

See, generally, on shareholders' meetings, Getz "The Structure of Shareholder Democracy," in Ziegel (Ed.), *Studies in Canadian Company Law*, Vol. 2, p. 239 (1973); *Athabaska Holdings Ltd. v. ENA Datasystems Inc.* (1980), 30 O.R. (2d) 527, 116 D.L.R. (3d) 318 (H.C.).

Barsh v. Feldman
1986 CarswellOnt 2172, 54 O.R. (2d) 340 (Ont. H.C.)

VAN CAMP J.: This is an application under s. 106(1) of the *Business Corporations Act*, 1982 (Ont.), c. 4, for the following:

1.   an order requiring a meeting of the shareholders of the corporation;

2.   an order to vary the requirements of a quorum as set out in By-law I so that only two shareholders, holding at least 51% of the issued shares, are required to be present instead of the present requirement of the three shareholders who each hold one share.

Section 106 of the *Business Corporations Act*, 1982 is as follows:

106(1) If for any reason it is impracticable to call a meeting of shareholders of a corporation in the manner in which meetings of those shareholders may be called or to conduct the meeting in the manner prescribed by the by-laws, the articles and this Act, or if for any other reason the court thinks fit, the court, upon the application of a director or a shareholder entitled to vote at the meeting, may order a meeting to be called, held and conducted in such manner as the court directs and upon such terms as to security for the costs of holding the meeting or otherwise as the court deems fit.

(2) Without restricting the generality of subsection (1), the court may order that the quorum required by the by-laws, the articles or this Act be varied or dispensed with at a meeting called, held and conducted under this section.

(3) A meeting called, held and conducted under this section is for all purposes a meeting of shareholders of the corporation duly called, held and conducted.

Under s. 94 of the *Business Corporations Act, 1982* the directors are required to call an annual meeting of shareholders not later than 15 months after holding the last preceding annual meeting and may, at any time, call a special meeting of shareholders. The last meeting of shareholders and of directors was held on April 8, 1966. On May 27, 1985, Barsh, holding one of the three shares, requisitioned the directors under s. 105 of the *Business Corporations Act, 1982* to call a meeting of shareholders for the certain purposes stated. Under s. 105, the directors were required to call the meeting of shareholders. No such meeting has been called.

* * *

Benjamin Barsh died in 1983. His son, Harvey Samuel, exercised an option under the will to purchase his father's share . . .

Since 1983, Harvey Samuel Barsh has wished to see the two tracts of land developed and has formed certain plans to this effect. Mr. Feldman had shown little, if any, interest in these plans until at least August, 1985. In late 1984, Barsh proposed buying out Feldman's interest. Feldman did not return to Barsh the resolutions to effect the transfer of the share of the deceased or the resolution of the shareholders electing the corporate solicitor as a director. It was at this time that Barsh requisitioned the special meeting of shareholders. Negotiations continued for the purchase of Feldman's interest and for the amendment of By-law 1 which would have the effect of eliminating the need for his attendance or vote at a meeting of shareholders and directors and his removal as a signing officer. A new general by-law is required to conform with the requirements of the *Business Corporations Act, 1982*. Although Feldman states that he is now willing to meet with the applicants to formulate a joint policy for the development or disposition of these properties, the prior delay makes it doubtful that the parties can agree. However, Feldman has given an undertaking through his counsel to sign a resolution for the annual meeting, approving the annual financial statements, electing the officers, appointing a director to replace the deceased and to approve the transfer of the share of the deceased to Barsh, in trust. This obviates the necessity of the meeting of shareholders.

I am of the opinion that the facts do not support the exercise of discretion to change the quorum. The result would be that one of three equal shareholders was effectively locked into a company in which he had no control. The quorum here was not to permit attendance of a shareholder, but to ensure that there would be no corporate action, except on the consent of all. Each shareholder has an equal interest. If there is no such consent obtainable, then there are provisions for the winding-up of the Corporation. None of the shareholders wish a winding-up, but unless they can agree it is the only alternative. The corporation was carefully structured so that no shareholder could control it. The affidavit of Feldman shows that because the other two shares were held by father and son, to give Feldman protection all decisions of directors and shareholders would require his consent and all cheques drawn on the corporate account would require his signature . . . The letters patent give one vote for each share held, but there can be no meetings unless all are present, that is, unless all agree. The obligation to have a general meeting can be met by an agreed agenda.

The answer to the problem of disagreement among the shareholders is not to compel a meeting whereby two of the three equal shareholders may outvote the third. The answer is the winding-up of the corporation. When none of them wish that winding-up, they can find a compromise.

I find the respondent, Feldman, not unreasonable in refusing to call or to attend a meeting which would have resulted in loss of sharing of control for him and effective transfer of complete control to Barsh . . .

The corporation in this application was carefully structured to require agreement of the three equal shareholders. This court should not intervene to effectively remove the need for agreement by the third shareholder. The application is dismissed. In the circumstances, there should be no costs.

Application dismissed.

Note

For a contrasting holding on the issue of quorum variation, see *Re Pizza Pizza Limited*, unreported, Sept. 14, 1987, Ont. S.C., per Sutherland J.

Goodwood Inc. v. Cathay Forest Products Corp.
2012 CarswellOnt 7590, 2012 ONSC 3548 (Ont. S.C.J. [Commercial List]), additional reasons 2012 CarswellOnt 7587 (Ont. S.C.J. [Commercial List]), additional reasons 2013 CarswellOnt 8321 (Ont. S.C.J. [Commercial List])

[In this case, the directors of Cathay failed to call an annual meeting, and failed to comply with the *Ontario Securities Act*'s continuous disclosure requirements. There was also a lack of quorum on the board of directors, and an insufficient number of resident Canadian directors. At the previous annual general meeting, there were seven directors, but at the time of the suit, there were only three. Cathay's by-laws also stated a majority of the directors shall be resident Canadians, but none of the current directors were Canadian residents. As a result, ten of the largest shareholders called a shareholder meeting to reconstitute the board of directors, but the current board took no action. As a result, the ten shareholders sought a court order directing the holding of a shareholder meeting. The case speaks to the circumstances that will permit a judicially ordered meeting to be called.]

* * *

The evidence discloses that the applicant is entitled to call a shareholder meeting for two reasons. First, the current directors have failed to call "without delay" a special meeting of shareholders to meet the board quorum requirements as required by *CBCA* s. 111(2). Second, shareholders have lodged a requisition with the board under *CBCA* s. 143(1) and it is clear that the board has no intention of responding to that requisition by calling a meeting. Whatever uncertainty might exist about the ability of the "rump board" to respond to a section 143 requisition, no doubt exists regarding the board's power to call a shareholder meeting under section 111(2). The board has refused to exercise that power.

Under sections 111(2) and 143(4) it is open to the shareholders to call a meeting where the board refuses or neglects to act. Should this court order a shareholder meeting under section 144 of the *CBCA*, or leave it to the shareholders to exercise their corporate remedies under section 111(2) or 143(4)? In the circumstances of this case I conclude that it is appropriate for the court to call the shareholder meeting; this is one of those "extraordinary" circumstances justifying a court order. First, Cathay lacks a board with authority to manage or supervise the management of the business and affairs of the corporation. As identified above, its board has failed to discharge numerous corporate and securities obligations since the summer of 2010. Such a dysfunctional state of affairs calls for some degree of court supervision.

Second, Mr. Chan, Cathay's Chair, characterized the efforts by the shareholders to call a meeting as bad faith conduct. The remaining directors also sought to take steps to fill the vacancy preventing a quorum without resorting to a shareholder meeting. Such a profound misunderstanding by the incumbent directors of their corporate governance duties points to the need for court supervision of the process of holding a shareholder meeting.

Third, Mr. Chan's communications also raise significant concerns about whether the past affairs of Cathay have been subject to mismanagement and whether the company is approaching insolvency. Given that state of affairs, court supervision of the shareholder meeting process is appropriate.

Accordingly, for those reasons I conclude that an order should go calling a meeting of the shareholders of Cathay to elect up to seven (7) directors of the Company, the present size set for the Cathay board of directors. I say "up to" seven directors because I accept the submission of the applicant that at the meeting the shareholders should be permitted to consider whether the current directors of Cathay should be removed from office and whether size of the Board should be changed, items which were included in the applicant's requisition under *CBCA* s. 143(1).

(g) Shareholder-Requisitioned Meetings

Shareholders may requisition directors to call meetings under CBCA section 143 (see also, *e.g.*, OBCA s. 105). This right is limited to shareholders of 5% or more of the issued voting shares of a corporation. When a proper requisition is received, directors must, subject to certain exemptions, call a shareholders' meeting (s. 143(3)) as soon as possible (s. 143(5)). If directors do not call a meeting within 21 days of receipt of a requisition, any shareholder who signed the requisition may call the meeting. While the OBCA specifically makes this subject to the listed exemptions, the CBCA does not (*cf.* OBCA s. 105(4) with CBCA s. 143(4)). Does this mean that under the CBCA a shareholder may call a requisitioned meeting regardless of whether the proposed meeting runs afoul of the exemptions?

The business that can be conducted at shareholder-requisitioned meetings is limited in the same way that shareholder proposals are (CBCA s. 102). However, these meetings are often used to remove current directors and elect new ones, and because directors may be reluctant to call a meeting designed to remove them from power (as seen in the cases above), shareholder-requisitioned meetings make it easier to remove directors before their terms end. Shareholder requisitioning of meetings can be particularly significant in the context of a takeover bid. As an acquirer often cannot afford to wait until the annual meeting, and the board of directors will often be reluctant to call a special meeting, it may be necessary for the acquirer, through its shares in the target, to call the meeting.

Airline Industry Revitalization Co. v. Air Canada
1999 CarswellOnt 3020, 45 O.R. (3d) 370 (Ont. S.C.J. [Commercial List])
(footnotes omitted)

[Airline Industry Revitalization Co. ("AirCo") was a corporation used by Onex Corp. and American Airlines to acquire and merge Air Canada and Canadian Airlines. To this end, AirCo sought to take over Air Canada. AirCo acquired 3.1% of Air Canada's common shares and 6.6% of Air Canada's Class A non-voting shares. In order to put the takeover into effect, AirCo considered it necessary for Air Canada to implement changes to its articles. On August 30, 1999, the Air Canada Board called a special shareholders meeting for January 7, 2000. On August 31, AirCo and other shareholders comprising over 5% of Air Canada's voting shares requisitioned the Board to call a special meeting between November 4 and November 8 to approve the takeover bid, implement the suggested changes to the articles, and alter control of the Board. The Board rejected the requisition, and AirCo brought an application for an order requiring the directors to call the meeting, or for the court to call the meeting. It should be noted that the federal government, by making an order under the *Canada Transportation Act*, had created a 90 day window for Air Canada, Canadian, and other parties to negotiate a merger without violating the *Competition Act* and that the 90 day period was to end on November 10, 1999.]

R.A. Blair J.: The narrow issue on this application, however, is whether or not Air Canada should be required to hold a meeting in response to the AirCo requisition and, if so, when that meeting should be held. While the foregoing background helps provide an understanding of the context in which this issue must be determined, not all of the rhetoric which has accompanied the battle as a whole is pertinent to the resolution of what is presently before this court.

As I see it, the application stands to be determined upon a consideration of the following matters:

1. Whether Air Canada's Board of Directors is required by s. 143(3) of the *Canada Business Corporations Act*, R.S.C. 1985, c. C-44, as amended (the "CBCA") to call and hold a special meeting of shareholders pursuant to the requisition;

2. If not, does the applicant nonetheless have the right to call such a meeting on its own, by virtue of the provisions of s. 143(4) of the CBCA, and should it be left to do so without court intervention if such is the case?

3. If the answer is "No" in either case, should the court exercise its discretion under s. 144 of the CBCA to order that a meeting of the type requested by the applicant be held, and fix the date for such a meeting within the time parameters sought by the applicant?

On behalf of AirCo, Mr. Finkelstein submits that, in spite of all "the sound and fury", these considerations revolve around a simple issue. He defines that issue as whether the shareholders of Air Canada should be deprived of their opportunity to consider the AirCo offers before they expire on November 9 and before the s. 47 order expires on November 10. The shareholders cannot consider the AirCo offers effectively without a special meeting prior to those dates, he contends, because one of the conditions of the offers is that such a meeting be held and that the steps contemplated to be taken at that meeting be taken. The Air Canada Board has arrogated to itself the right to say "No" to the AirCo bid by refusing to hold a meeting until after the bid expires and the s. 47 order lapses, and they are not entitled to do so, the argument concludes. He relies upon the decision of this court in *RioCan Real Estate v. Realfund*, [1999] O.J. No, 1349 (Gen. Div.).

On behalf of Air Canada, on the other hand, Mr. Dunphy submits that s. 143 of the CBCA does not apply at all in the circumstances of this case because:

(a) "a record date" had been set for a meeting by the Air Canada Board and, accordingly, the Board is not required to respond to the requisition because of the exception provided for in s. 143(3)(a) of the CBCA;

(b) a shareholder is not entitled to call a meeting for the amendment of articles of incorporation by way of requisition and, accordingly, the business to be transacted at the requisitioned meeting is not business that can validly be considered by the shareholders at such a meeting; and

(c) the 10 per cent ownership restraint imposed by the *Air Canada Act* — which remains the law of Canada — insulates Air Canada from a take-over bid attempt and the AirCo proposal, including the business to be transacted at the meeting to give effect to it, is simply a cleverly contrived mechanism to circumvent that law, and is, accordingly, not something which can validly be considered by the shareholders at such a meeting.

If there is no right on the part of AirCo to resort to s. 143, Mr. Dunphy submits, and the applicant is left to rely upon the exercise of the court's discretion under s. 144, such discretion should be exercised very sparingly and only with great deference to the exercise of business judgment on the part of the Board of Directors. There is no basis for the exercise of such discretion on the facts of this case, he contends.

Law and Analysis

I have come to the conclusion that the AirCo requisition is a valid requisition in the proper form, for the purposes of this application, and that the Air Canada directors were obliged to call a meeting of the shareholders to transact the business stated in the requisition in accordance with s. 143 of the CBCA. In my opinion, the "record date" exception of s. 143(3)(a) does not apply on the facts of this case, and it cannot be said for the purposes of this application that the subject matter of the requisition is not the proper subject matter of such a meeting. Accordingly, it is open for AirCo to call the requisitioned meeting of the shareholders, pursuant to s. 143(4) of the CBCA, and they are at liberty to do so. That being the case, and AirCo having a corporate remedy of its own, it would not be wise in my view for the court to intervene at this stage and exercise its discretion under s. 144 of the CBCA to call the meeting itself.

My reasons for coming to this conclusion are the following.

[R.A. Blair J. examined the statutory framework of shareholder-requisitioned meetings and continued:]

The Record Date

At the directors' meeting held on August 30, 1999, Air Canada set a record date for a special meeting of shareholders to be held on January 7, 2000. The record date is November 18, 1999. Notice of the record date was given early the next morning, August 31, and published in the *National Post* of that date. It is conceded that the AirCo requisition was not made until later that day. Thus, it is clear on the facts that Air Canada had fixed "a record date" and given notice thereof, prior to receipt of the requisition.

In my opinion, however, the record date which was fixed is not a "record date" which qualifies as an exception under s. 143(3)(a) of the CBCA. Air Canada announced in its press release dated August 31, 1999, that the January 7 meeting was called, amongst other things, "to consider valid proposals, including the proposal of Onex Corporation and American Airlines, that may be presented". However, Air Canada now appears to have resiled from that position. In its factum, filed in response to this application, Air Canada states that "the [Air Canada] Board has not to date agreed to place the proposed AirCo amendments on the January 7 agenda" (para. 24), and that "the Air Canada Board has never agreed to hold a meeting to transact the business set out in the requisition" (para. 37). In argument, Mr. Dunphy made it clear that Air Canada does not consider the January 7 meeting to be a meeting called to deal with the business stated in the AirCo requisition.

That being the case, I do not see how the "record date" which was fixed by Air Canada can be a "record date" that qualifies as an exception under s. 143(3)(a). Section 143 contemplates that shareholders who meet the 5 per cent threshold are entitled to requisition a meeting. The directors shall call the meeting, unless the circumstances meet one of the exceptions articulated in s. 143(3). Although there appears to be no jurisprudence on the point, it seems to me that a "record date" as contemplated in s. 143(3)(a) must be a "record date" for a meeting at which there is some reasonable chance that the business stated in the requisition will be considered. It is one thing to say that if a meeting is requisitioned, and there is already a meeting pending at which the matters in question can be considered, then the directors are not obliged to call another meeting. .. It is quite another thing, however, to say that even though the required percentage of shareholders have requisitioned a meeting, their statutory right to have their business considered at a meeting may be thwarted by the simple expedient of the directors having already fixed a record date for a meeting on other matters. I interpret "record date" in para. 143(3)(a) of the CBCA to refer to a record date for a meeting having been fixed prior to receipt of the requisition but at which the requisitioners' business may nonetheless be considered. Likewise, I interpret "meeting of shareholders" in para. 143(3)(b) in the same way: the directors are obligated to call a validly requisitioned meeting, unless the directors have called a meeting of shareholders, and given notice thereof, and the requisitioners' business may be considered at that meeting.

Such is not the case here . . .

By adopting its stance that the pending January 7 shareholders' meeting is not a meeting to deal with the business stated in the AirCo requisition, Air Canada has removed from this application the argument that this is simply a case of determining whether the timing set by the Board for the meeting is reasonable or whether it should be interfered with because it has rendered consideration of the imminent business opportunity academic. On Air Canada's own view of the landscape, the AirCo proposal is not to be considered at all . . .

The Right to Requisition a Meeting to Amend Articles

Mr. Dunphy submits that deficiencies in the AirCo requisition made it "a dead letter" upon its delivery and, therefore, that the directors had no obligation to call the meeting sought. This submission is premised upon the argument that amendments to articles of incorporation may only be initiated by shareholders at an annual meeting of shareholders and that such amendments cannot be put forward by a shareholder at a special meeting.

I do not accept this submission.

Section 175 of the CBCA states:

175(1) Subject to subsection (2), a director or a shareholder who is entitled to vote at an annual meeting of shareholders may, in accordance with s. 137, make a proposal to amend the articles.

(2) Notice of a meeting of shareholders at which a proposal to amend the articles is to be considered shall set out the proposed amendment and, where applicable, shall state that a dissenting shareholder is entitled to be paid the fair value of his shares . . .

Section 137 is the provision which enables a shareholder entitled to vote at an annual meeting to submit notice of any matter the shareholder proposes to raise at the meeting. It requires that such a proposal be included in a management proxy circular, subject to certain legislative exceptions, and establishes a procedural remedy in the form of an application to court for shareholders claiming to be aggrieved by a refusal of the corporation to include the proposal.

I do not read the foregoing provisions as limiting to an annual meeting of shareholders the right of a shareholder to propose an amendment to articles of the corporation. The reference in s. 175(1) of the CBCA to a shareholder "who is entitled to vote at an annual general meeting of shareholders" is in my view descriptive of the type of share held rather than of the occasion on which the right to vote may be exercised. I observe that ss. (2) refers to notice of a meeting of shareholders at which a proposal to amend the articles is to be considered. It does not specify that the meeting is to be an annual meeting. Moreover, there is nothing whatsoever in the language of s. 143, which gives rise to the power to requisition a meeting, that in any way purports to limit the scope of matters which may properly be the subject matter of the requisition.

I can see no reason why proposed amendments to articles cannot be the subject matter of a requisitioned meeting. Mr. Dunphy argues that the implications of amendments to articles can be very significant — not the least of which is the creation of dissenting shareholder rights — and, accordingly, that such important considerations should not be ousted from the directors' general authority to govern the affairs of the corporation, including the question of determining the timing of such consideration. I have difficulty in understanding the substantive difference between dealing with amendments to articles at an annual meeting and doing so at a special meeting called by requisition, however . . . It was held in *Austin Mining Co. v. Gemmel* (1886), 10 O.R. 697 at p. 703, that a special meeting may be called to perform the work of a general meeting if the work to be done or object of the meeting is clearly defined and specified in the notice calling the meeting. Furthermore, as I have indicated, there is nothing in the language of s. 175, or s. 137 or, more particularly, s. 143, which precludes the requisitioning of a meeting to amend articles.

Accordingly, I am not prepared to give effect to the argument that AirCo has no right to requisition the meeting in question because it is not open for such a meeting of shareholders to consider an amendment to articles of incorporation.

[R.A. Blair J. then analyzed whether AirCo's proposal ran afoul of the *Air Canada Public Participation Act*, finding that there were arguments for and against the proposal. As it did not clearly violate the Act, it should be available for shareholders to decide whether or not to accept it.]

Conclusions Respecting Section 143

I am therefore of the view that the AirCo requisition is a valid requisition pursuant to s. 143 of the CBCA, in the sense that the requisition is signed by the holders of at least 5 per cent of the voting shares of Air Canada and is in the proper form, and that the business to be transacted, as stated in the requisition, is business which may properly be put before a requisitioned meeting of the shareholders. Further, I am satisfied that the only exception under s. 143(3) which was relied upon by Air Canada in argument, namely the fact that Air Canada had set a record date for a meeting to be held on January 7, 2000, has no application on the facts of the case as they were put to the court. It follows, then, that the Air Canada directors were obliged to call a meeting of the shareholders to transact the business stated in the requisition. They have chosen not to do so . . .

AirCo, however, is not without a remedy in the circumstances. Section 143(4) of the CBCA provides that if the directors do not call a meeting within 21 days of receipt of the requisition, any shareholder who signed the requisition may call the meeting . . . Having regard to the purpose of s. 143 — which, as I see it, is to ensure that shareholders who can garner sufficient support to meet the 5 per cent threshold are able to get the business which they wish to have transacted before a meeting of shareholders, notwithstanding their minority position and an actual or potentially unwilling board of directors — I am satisfied that the right of the requisitioning shareholder to call the meeting under s. 143(4), where the directors have declined to do so, applies even where the directors have correctly concluded that one of the exceptions of s. 143(3) applies. The difference is that the onus is on the shareholder and not on management to call the meeting "as nearly as possible in the manner in which meetings are to be called pursuant to the by-laws [and Parts XII and XIII of the CBCA]."

The language of s. 143(4) is straightforward. If the directors do not call the meeting within 21 days, "any shareholder who signed the requisition may call the meeting". Nothing indicates that if the directors have properly exercised their right not to call a meeting because of the applicability of one of the s. 143(3) exceptions, the meeting may not be held. Interestingly, the comparable provision of the Ontario *Business Corporations Act*, R.S.O. 1990, c. B.16, as amended (the "OBCA") — s. 105(4) — is identical in wording to that of s. 143(4) of the CBCA, except that it is prefaced with the words "subject to subsection (3)". This difference in wording suggests that under the OBCA regime, a requisitioned meeting which the directors are properly exempted from calling may not be called by the requisitioning shareholder, whereas under the CBCA regime the opposite is the case.

In any event, for the reasons I have articulated above, I do not think the Air Canada directors were entitled to rely on one of the exceptions of s. 143(3) of the CBCA on the facts of this case. I am therefore of the view that AirCo is entitled to rely upon the provisions of s. 143(4) and that it may, accordingly, "call the meeting". Moreover, I am of the view that it should be left to exercise its own statutory remedy to that effect, if it should choose to do so . . .

The Section 144 Discretion

Section 144 of the CBCA — which is cited in full earlier in these reasons — provides that if for any reason it is impracticable to call a meeting in the normal way or if for any other reason a court thinks fit, the court may order that a meeting be held. This provision gives the court a broad discretion to order that a shareholders' meeting be called and held, and to determine the manner in which the meeting shall be conducted. In my opinion, it is a discretion which should be exercised cautiously, however, given the general scheme of the CBCA, which is to repose in the directors of a corporation the general power to manage its business and affairs, including the primary responsibility for determining when shareholders will be consulted and asked to act at meetings. I agree with Mr. Dunphy that corporations are not run by plebiscite and that shareholders do not have a general power to call shareholders' meetings as and when they feel like it. The requisition provisions of s. 143 and the jurisdiction given to the court under s. 144 are exceptions to the primary role of directors in this regard.

Where there is a "corporate" remedy still open to a shareholder under the legislative scheme — as there is here for AirCo, by virtue of s. 143(4) of the CBCA — the court should be reluctant to step into the fray and impose its own solution to the "meeting" problem by exercising its discretion under s. 144, in my view: see, *Streit v. Swanson*, [1946] O.R. 565, [1946] 4 D.L.R. 107 per McRuer C.J.H.C., at p. 572. The bare-knuckled skirmishes of corporate restructuring warfare are best resolved by the combatants themselves to the extent possible, in their own boardrooms and meeting rooms and — where, as is the case here, there are political dimensions as well — in the public domain, rather than in the courtroom. The court's role is to decide issues of a procedural or substantive nature which need to be determined to enable the process to proceed in a proper and timely fashion, but otherwise to remain apart from the battle.

For these reasons, I am unwilling in the circumstances presented here to exercise the court's discretion to impose its own meeting with its own format and its own timing on the parties. This is not a case where it is "impracticable" to call the meeting in the manner in which meetings of the Air Canada shareholders may be called: s. 144. AirCo may call the requisitioned meeting of the shareholders itself. It should do that, if so advised.

Conclusion

I am not prepared, therefore, to grant the main relief sought by the applicant, namely an order requiring the Air Canada directors to call a meeting of the corporation's shareholders on a date between November 4 and November 8, 1999, for the purpose of transacting the business stated in the AirCo requisition. I am satisfied and declare, however, that the AirCo requisition is a valid one in the proper form under s. 143 of the CBCA and that AirCo is entitled, if so advised, to call the requisitioned meeting itself, having regard to the failure of the Air Canada directors to do so within 21 days of receipt of the requisition by virtue of the provisions of s. 143(4) of that Act. In doing so, AirCo will call the meeting, as nearly as possible, in the manner in which meetings of Air

Canada shareholders are to be called pursuant to the by-laws of the corporation and Parts XII and XIII of the CBCA.

Application dismissed.

Notes

1. For a comment on whether the court's interpretation of s. 143 was deficient, see Anita I. Anand, "Crash Landing: Comment on *Airline Industry Revitalization Co. v. Air Canada*" (2000) 25 Queen's L.J. 659.

2. A recent case, *Wells v. Bioniche Life Sciences Inc.*, 2013 CarswellOnt 10186, 2013 ONSC 4871 (Ont. S.C.J. [Commercial List]), reaches the same conclusion as *AirCo*. Bioniche's shareholders, William Wells and Greg Gubitz, made two requisitions for shareholders meetings. The board rejected the first requisition because Wells was not a registered owner of the shares, and because the requisition lacked adequate information for shareholders to make a decision concerning the business stated in the requisition. The court agreed. The court held that the meaning of "holders" in s. 143(1) is registered holder, and the names and qualifications of the new directors proposed by the requisitioning shareholders are required to permit shareholders sufficient detail to form a reasoned judgment.

    In response, Wells registered most of his shares, identified his proposed director nominees, and requisitioned a second meeting. Bioniche's board determined it was not under any legal obligation to call a meeting, because a November meeting and record date had already been fixed, and proceeding with a special meeting would be against the best interest of the company. Similar to the *AirCo* analysis, the court held that Bioniche fixed and gave notice of the record date for its November meeting, so it fell within the exception in s. 143(3)(a), and was not required to call a meeting.

    This case also highlighted the dissidents' conduct in analyzing the urgency of calling a shareholders meeting. The court pointed to the dissidents' lack of clarity in specifying a meeting date for their special meeting, even though they argued the board was not acting in a timely manner. Furthermore, after Bioniche's board refused the second requisition, the dissidents waited an entire month, without explanation, before invoking their rights to call a meeting under s. 143(4). Ultimately, the court held that dissidents have the right under s. 143(4) to call a meeting, but the delay until the November meeting was not prejudicial, so the dissidents could not proceed with their earlier proposed meeting.

5. RIGHT TO CORPORATE INFORMATION: ACCESS TO CORPORATE RECORDS

Corporate statutes require corporations to maintain specified records and to allow access to these records by shareholders and other designated persons. See ss. 19 to 22 and 138 of the CBCA and ss. 139 to 147 of the OBCA. In addition to corporate records, the statutes also require the preparation of and accessibility to prescribed financial information relating to the corporation and this will be briefly referred to in the next section dealing with the appointment of auditors.

Iacobucci, Pilkington, and Prichard
Canadian Business Corporations
(1977), pp. 178–181 (footnotes omitted)

The shareholders' access to corporate information has long been held to be of great importance; indeed Gower has described disclosure as the "fundamental principle underlying the *Companies Act*." But the *Kimber Report* found that despite this early recognition of the importance of disclosure, "what was considered adequate disclosure at one given time has proven to be inadequate in a subsequent period." Information is important for at least two basic reasons. First, it allows the shareholders and the securities market as a whole to evaluate the relative strengths and weaknesses of the enterprise so that they can make informed decisions as to whether or not to invest or continue to invest in the company. Second, only with adequate information are the shareholders able to evaluate effectively the performance of the corporation's directors and officers and to exercise their rights to hold the directors and officers accountable for their actions. In a dispute between a dissenting shareholder and those in control, the accessibility of information becomes a key factor as management's ready access to the records of the company and other inside information gives it a distinct advantage over the individual shareholder who may be unable to substantiate his suspicions of wrongdoing with documentary proof.

The statutory response has been on four fronts, the last three of which have been dealt with elsewhere in this book: (i) provisions giving shareholders the right to inspect company records, (ii) provisions allowing specified numbers of shareholders to requisition general meetings and circulate proposals, (iii) provisions requiring disclosure of financial and insider trading information, and (iv) provisions giving the right to have inspectors and auditors appointed to investigate the affairs of the corporation . . .

The provisions giving the shareholders the right to inspect company records are similar in all Canadian companies' legislation. Each shareholder is entitled to copies of the memorandum, articles and any ordinary or special resolutions at a nominal charge. He is also entitled to inspect the register of members and may obtain copies of the register or any part thereof at a nominal charge. A shareholder has similar rights with regard to the register of mortgages, and the minutes of general meetings of the company.

Each of these provisions is important and worthy of retention. It may be useful, however, to specify in the statute that shareholder lists obtained from the register must only be used for purposes connected with the corporation. Such a provision will help to avoid any potential misuse of the lists for the purposes of sending a shareholder advertising for other securities or unrelated matters. Also, the memorandum and articles should be available without charge to the shareholders rather than at the present fee since the statute should encourage shareholders to be aware of their rights and to participate in the corporation's affairs and such a provision, although perhaps largely symbolic, would be a small step in this direction.

The combined impact of the various mechanisms in each of the four classes of response to the need for information appears to be adequate in relation to specific transactions. However, they do not cover the case of the shareholder who wants information about the company's affairs when no specific transaction is contemplated. For example, should shareholders have the right to demand the identity of customers and suppliers and the volume of business with each, if they feel, and have some grounds to suspect, that one particular ethnic or racial group is being privileged or discriminated against? Although obviously an unlimited right to demand information cannot be provided since it could be damaging to the firm's competitive position and lead to harassment of corporate management, it may be that more information than is available at present could be provided without reaching these damaging limits. Serious consideration should be given to designing a mechanism with the appropriate safeguards . . .

Notes

The company's directors also have both common law and statutory rights to inspect the books of the company. In *Conway v. Petronius Clothing Co. Ltd.*, [1978] 1 All E.R. 185, [1978] 1 W.L.R. 72 (Ch. D.), the Court held that the U.K. *Companies Act* did not confer a statutory right on a director to inspect the company's books of account but that there was a common law right to do so. In *Healy v. Healy Homes Ltd.*, [1973] I.R. 308, it was held that a director is entitled to the assistance of an accountant in exercising his right of inspection.

Under the CBCA and OBCA, directors have a statutory entitlement to inspect certain records. CBCA s. 20(2) requires the corporation to "prepare and maintain adequate accounting records and records containing minutes of meetings and resolutions of the directors and any committee thereof." Section 20(4) requires that such records "at all reasonable times be open to inspection by the directors." In *Leggat v.*

Jennings, 2013 CarswellOnt 1501, 2013 ONSC 903 (Ont. S.C.J.), the court held that the applicant, as a director, has a statutory right to inspect the books of the company at any time under s. 20(4) of the CBCA. Look carefully at ss. 20(4) and 20(2); do the directors have a statutory right to inspect those records referred to in s. 20(1) (i.e., are these records described in subsections (1) or (2))? The court in *Leggat* seems to think so, the court stated that "Pursuant to s. 20(4) of the CBCA, such records prescribed by subsections 20(1) and 20(2) shall at all reasonable times be open to inspection by the directors." Why do you suppose the shareholders are not entitled to look at the accounting records and records of directors' meetings?

With respect to the shareholder's rights of inspection, see *EnCana Corp. v. Douglas*, 2005 ABCA 439, 2005 CarswellAlta 1872 (Alta. C.A.), where the Court granted the shareholder the right under the *CBCA* to inspect the corporate records regardless of an alleged improper purpose in getting the information. The Court also held that non-voting shareholder should have equal access to corporate records as voting shareholders.

In *Leggat*, the court held that although the applicant is a director, he could nonetheless access records based on his position as a shareholder. The first route is through s. 21(1) of the CBCA. It provides that shareholders and their personal representatives may examine the records in s. 20(1). Directors can access records under this route as well. However, the court emphasized that the documents are limited to those listed under s. 20(1) under this route. The second route is under s. 155(c) of the CBCA, which prescribes that directors shall place before shareholders at every annual meeting, "any further information respecting the financial position of the corporation and the results of its operations required by the articles, the by-laws or any unanimous shareholder agreement." However, this route is only available for information to be placed before the shareholders as required by the articles, by-laws, or unanimous shareholder agreement.

6.   RIGHT TO APPOINT AN AUDITOR: FINANCIAL DISCLOSURE, AUDITOR'S LIABILITY, AND THE AUDIT COMMITTEE

(a)   Introduction

Corporation statutes uniformly confer upon the shareholders the right to appoint and to remove an auditor. See OBCA s. 149 and CBCA ss. 162, 165. Aside from the exception discussed below, if the corporation fails to allow shareholders to appoint an auditor, shareholders can apply to the court to appoint an auditor regardless of the corporation's financial circumstances, as it is a mandatory provision. See *Merrill v. Afab Security*, 2007 CarswellOnt 1765, [2007] O.J. No. 1133 (Ont. S.C.J.),

Li v. Global Chinese Press Inc., 2014 CarswellBC 373, 2014 BCCA 53 (B.C. C.A.). The function of the auditor is to assess the financial statements which the corporation proposes to place before the shareholders and to report on the preparation and accuracy of those statements. Since the availability and reliability of financial information is vital to the efficiency and integrity of the corporation, the auditor, to be useful, must be guaranteed appropriate access to records, must be independent, and must be properly qualified. The legislation attempts to ensure that these requirements are met.

Of direct relevance to the role of the auditor is the nature and extent of the financial disclosure required by the particular corporation statute. The provisions of the corporation statutes dealing with financial statements are extremely important and reference should be made generally to ss. 155 to 172 of the CBCA, ss. 148 to 160 of the OBCA and s. 212 of the BCBCA. It is beyond the scope of this book to discuss these requirements in any detail but what will be highlighted are some specific issues relating to auditors.

Not all corporations require the appointment of an auditor. The various sections dealing with exemption and waiver (CBCA s. 163; OBCA s. 148; BCBCA s. 203) speak mainly of non-reporting companies or those whose gross revenues do not exceed certain limits or may, in the case of s. 148 of the OBCA, combine both criteria. The propriety of exempting companies other than those which are small and closely held and where none of the shareholders believes such safeguard is necessary has been questioned by Iacobucci, Pilkington, and Prichard in *Canadian Business Corporations* (1977), at page 396:

> The exemption should not be available to a wide range of companies. The requirement of an audit not only helps to ensure the reliability of financial statements but also has the effect of encouraging compliance with statutory requirements, checking corporate mismanagement, and developing standardized financial reporting. The costs involved are justified by these benefits, and therefore only small closely held corporations should be exempted from auditor requirements.

(b) Qualifications and Independence

The statutes uniformly impose qualifications upon eligibility for appointment as auditor. The BCBCA, for example, prescribes certain professional qualifications (s. 205). All the statutes disqualify persons from acting as auditors who are not "independent" (CBCA, s. 161; BCBCA, s. 206; and OBCA, s. 152) and, directly or indirectly, provide definitions of what does and does not constitute "independence."

(c) Functions

The OBCA, CBCA, BCBCA, and other provincial acts all require that the auditor make such examination as will enable him to report on the financial statements on an annual basis. The CBCA, for instance, in s. 170 gives the auditor a right to demand information and explanation from the directors, officers, employees or agents of the corporation and he is also given access to records, documents, books, accounts, and vouchers of the corporation or any of its subsidiaries that are, in his opinion, necessary to enable him to make the examination and give the report that is required by statute. The auditor also has a right to attend meetings (OBCA, s. 151(1); CBCA, s. 168(1)) and has qualified privilege to any written statement or report which the auditor makes pursuant to his duties under the act (CBCA s.172; OBCA s.151(7)).

The financial statements must be prepared in accordance with generally accepted accounting principles (see OBCA s. 155; CBCR s. 71). Generally accepted accounting principles are set by the Canadian Accounting Standards Board (AcSB) and published in the CPA Canada Handbook—Accounting. Since 2011, the AcSB has transitioned from the Canadian Generally Accepted Accounting Principles system to the International Financial Reporting Standard for publicly accountable enterprises. The auditor must state whether the statement is in accordance with generally accepted auditing standards consistent with that period (see OBCA s.153; CBCR s. 71.1). Generally accepted auditing standards are set by the Canadian Auditing and Assurance Standards Board. Does compliance with generally accepted accounting principles necessarily mean that the financial statements fairly present the financial position of a company? See generally Janne Chung, Jonathan Farrar, Poonam Puri, and Linda Thorne, "Auditor Liability to Third Parties after Sarbanes-Oxley: An International Comparison of Regulatory and Legal Reforms" (2010) 19:1 Journal of International Accounting, Auditing and Taxation 66.

In addition to his or her reporting duties, the auditor, as part of his general function of informing and reporting to shareholders, is under a duty to attend certain shareholders' meetings and answer any questions. It is worth noting that under s. 168(2) of the CBCA, a director, as well as a shareholder, has the right to require the auditor to attend a shareholders' meeting (see also OBCA s. 151(2)).One final point with regard to the duties of the auditor is significant. Under s. 247 of the CBCA, s. 253 of the OBCA and s. 228 of the BCBCA, the duties of the auditor, as set out in the statute, regulations, articles, by-laws or unanimous shareholder agreement can be enforced by application to the court. A present or former security holder, director, officer, the Director (under the CBCA), creditor and any other person to whom the court grants standing may apply to the court for an order directing the auditor to comply with, or restraining him or her from acting in breach of, his or her duties.

(d) Removal

There are two ways in which an auditor may be removed under the corporate law statues. An "interested party" may apply to the court for an order to disqualify or remove the auditor, or the shareholders may pass an ordinary resolution at a special or general meeting which has been called for the purpose of removing the auditor (CBCA ss. 161(4), 165(1); OBCA ss. 149(4), 152(4)). If the corporation is a reporting company, notice of removal must be given in the information circular, with the name of the management's new nominee placed on the proxy form (see CBCA ss. 168(5), (6); OBCA ss. 149(5), (6)). This is done in order to protect the independence of the auditor by providing him or her with an opportunity to place before the shareholders any explanation he feels they should have in order to evaluate a proposal to replace him. Consequently, management would not continuously seek to replace a questioning auditor with one who is more amenable to management interests.

(e) Oversight

Under National Instrument 52-108, there is an external oversight of auditors by the Canadian Public Accountability Board (CPAB). Every public accounting firm that issues auditors' reports with respect to the financial statements of reporting issuers must enter into an agreement with the CPAB. If CPAB is not satisfied with the audit firm's quality, the firm may cease to be a "participant in good standing," thus being prohibited from issuing auditor's reports. As you read the section on auditors' liability, keep in mind that there is now an oversight system in place to help ensure the quality of auditor's reports.

(f) Liability of Auditors

Iacobucci, Pilkington, and Prichard
Canadian Business Corporations
(1977), pp. 410–414 (footnotes omitted)

Although the Alberta, British Columbia, Ontario, and Federal Acts impose several duties on an auditor, many of which depend upon his exercising professional judgment, they do not specify any standard of care and skill according to which those duties must be fulfilled, nor do they specify to whom the duties are owed. Case law on the nature and extent of an auditor's liability to third parties for negligent mis-statement is still developing as the principle in *Hedley Byrne v. Heller* is elaborated and applied. It may be that this common law development should not be cut short by premature codification. However, the question of an auditor's liability to third parties who rely on his report may be left open without precluding the establishment of standards which an auditor must meet in performing his duties.

Though Anglo-Canadian companies' statutes specify the auditor's general duties, they do not, as Lord Justice Warrington pointed out in *Re City Equitable Fire Insurance Co., Ltd.*:

> . . . lay down any rule at all as to the amount of care, or skill, or investigation, or anything of that kind, which is to be brought to bear by the auditors in performing the duties which are imposed upon them.
>
> . . . That is left to be determined by the general rules which, in point of law, are held to govern the duties of the auditors, whether those rules are to be derived from the ordinary law, or from the terms under which the auditors are to be employed.

The standard of care which an auditor must meet may be specified in the company's articles, or in his contract, otherwise, the common law governs.

It can be argued that the judicial decisions governing an auditor's standard of care do not go far enough to ensure that an auditor provides shareholders with the kind of independent assessment which alone is useful to them. The traditional judicial formulation of an auditor's duty was propounded prior to the establishment of statutory requirements of corporate financial disclosure and prior to the requirement that companies appoint auditors. Even though in modern times the corporate context has changed and there has been improvement in accounting standards and increased concern about the need for accurate and full disclosure of financial information to shareholders, the traditional formulation of auditor's duties is still applied. The issue is whether the auditor is bound only to verify information presented by management or whether he is also under a duty to investigate and ensure that the information is reliable — that is, in the traditional catch-phrase, whether he must be a watchdog or a bloodhound.

Traditionally the auditor has been required to be merely a watchdog, as Lord Justice Lopes stated in the oft-quoted case of *Re Kingston Cotton Mill Co. (No. 2)*:

> It is the duty of an auditor to bring to bear on the work he has to perform that skill, care, and caution which a reasonably competent, careful, and cautious auditor would use. What is reasonable skill, care and caution must depend on the particular circumstances of each case. An auditor is not bound to be a detective, or, as was said, to approach his work with suspicion or with a foregone conclusion that there is something wrong. He is watch dog, but not a bloodhound. He is justified in believing tried servants of the company in whom confidence is placed by the company. He is

entitled to assume that they are honest, and to rely upon their representations, provided he takes reasonable care. If there is anything calculated to excite suspicion he should probe it to the bottom; but in the absence of anything of that kind he is only bound to be reasonably cautious and careful.

It would appear from this test and its application in subsequent cases, that unless an auditor comes across something which arouses his suspicion, he is not obliged to undertake investigations to substantiate whether the information before him is in fact reliable. In an obiter statement in *Fomento (Sterling Area), Ltd. v. Selsdon Fountain Pen Co. Ltd.*, Lord Denning challenged this traditional formulation of an auditor's responsibility:

> What is the proper function of an auditor? It is said that he is bound only to verify the sum, the arithmetical conclusion, by reference to the books and all necessary vouching material and oral explanations; and that it is no part of his function to inquire whether an article is covered by patents or not. I think this is too narrow a view. An auditor is not to be confined to the mechanics of checking vouchers and making arithmetical computations. He is not to be written off as a professional "adder-upper and subtractor". His vital task is to take care to see that errors are not made, be they errors of computation, or errors of omission or commission, or downright untruths. To perform this task property, he must come to it with an inquiring mind — not suspicious of dishonesty, I agree — but suspecting that someone may have made a mistake somewhere and that a check must be made to ensure that there has been none.

Lord Denning's formulation of the auditor's responsibility gives effect to the modern purpose of the audit requirement and the report of the auditor to the shareholders. As one commentator asks:

> . . . why should this discretion be limited to cases where the clues appear before his eyes? What great burdens would be thrown on him if his duties included those Lord Denning suggested flow from his appointment? In what sense does he fulfil his obligation of conducting an independent check if he is to rely "blindly" (or subject to a formal check) on the word and work of those in control of the company? A shareholder must expect and receive an unbiased and uninfluenced assessment by his expert of the financial position of his company. It is only the auditor who can fulfil the role expected of him.

In the recent Supreme Court of Canada case of *Haig v. Bamford*, Dickson J. in an *obiter* statement emphasized the importance of the auditor's responsibility:

The increasing growth and changing role of corporations in modern society has been attended by a new perception of the societal role of the profession of accounting. The day when the accountant served only the owner-manager of a company and was answerable to him alone has passed. The complexities of modern industry combined with effects of specialization, the impact of taxation, urbanization, the separation of ownership from management, the rise of professional corporate managers, and a host of other factors, have led to marked changes in the role and responsibilities of the accountant, and in the reliance which the public must place upon his work. The financial statements of the corporations upon which his reports can effect the economic interests of the general public as well as of shareholders and potential shareholders.

With the added prestige and value of his services has come, as the leaders of the profession have recognized, a concomitant and commensurately increased responsibility to the public. It seems unrealistic to be oblivious to these developments.

However, it has not yet been established in the case law that, in the absence of suspicious circumstances, an auditor is under any obligation to examine into the reliability of the statements on which he reports.

Since it is arguable that the case law has not established adequate standards for auditors, and since the duties of other corporate personnel, namely directors, officers and trustees under indentures, are specified in reformed corporations legislation, it may well be that the standards required of auditors should also be delineated. The fact that standards of care and skill are not specified is the more significant in light of the fact that directors may be relieved of liability if they rely and act in good faith on statements contained in an auditor's report. If the shareholders are expected to rely on auditors' reports and the directors are exempted from liability if they have relied upon them, then auditors ought to be under a duty to conduct their work in a manner which can be relied upon with confidence.

In addition to establishing a standard according to which an auditor must exercise his duty, it would also be useful if corporations' legislation specified to whom the duty is owed. Though an auditor's contractual relationship is with the corporation, his duty is to report not to the corporation but to the shareholders. Whether it can be implied from this that the auditor owes a duty of care to the shareholder, a breach of which would give the shareholder a cause of action in his own right, is far from clear.

Notes and Questions

1   The issue of the liability of auditors has been addressed in different ways throughout the commonwealth. In *Scott Group Ltd. v. McFarlane*, [1978] 1 N.Z.L.R. 553 (C.A.), the New Zealand Court of Appeal found that the auditors of a corporation owed a duty of

care to a plaintiff who had acquired the corporation through a takeover bid. In his majority judgment, Woodhouse J. found that there was a sufficient relationship to ground liability for four reasons. 1. The auditors were professionals who were in the business of providing expert advice for a reward. 2. Auditors of a public company must be taken to have accepted not only a duty to shareholders but also to those whom they can "reasonably forsee . . . will need to use and rely upon [the accounts] when dealing with the company or its members in significant matters affecting the Company assets and business." 3. The auditors had no direct knowledge that a takeover bid was contemplated, but they knew that the accounts would become a matter of public record under the *Companies Act* of 1955 and that concerned persons, such as the Scott Group, would have direct access to them. 4. There is no opportunity in the ordinary case for any intermediate examination of the underlying authenticity of a company's accounts.

In *Caparo Industries plc v. Dickman*, [1990] 2 W.L.R. 358 (U.K. H.L.), the House of Lords held that any cause of action against the auditors for breach of duty belonged to the company. Thus, if auditors were negligent, only the company could sue the auditors, and not an individual shareholder. For a comment on *Caparo*, see Brian R. Cheffins, "Auditors' Liability in the House of Lords: A Signal Canadian Courts Should Follow" (1991), 18 Can. Bus. L. J. 118.

2   In *Hercules Management Ltd. v. Ernst & Young*, [1997] 2 S.C.R. 165, 1997 CarswellMan 198, 1997 CarswellMan 1999, Ernst & Young was hired in 1971 by Northguard Acceptance Ltd. (NGA) and Northguard Holdings Ltd. (NGH) to audit their financial statements and to provide audit reports to the companies' shareholders. In 1984 NGA and NGH went into receivership. In 1988 shareholders and investors in NGA and NGH brought an action against Ernst & Young, claiming the audit reports for 1980, 1981, and 1982 were negligently prepared and seeking damages in tort and contract. Ernst & Young brought a motion in the Manitoba Court of Queen's Bench seeking to have the plaintiffs' claims dismissed. The motions judge granted the motion with respect to four plaintiffs. An appeal to the Manitoba Court of Appeal was dismissed. La Forest J., in addressing whether the appellants were owed a duty of care by the respondents, reiterated the two-part test for determining such a duty and stated that the test applies to negligent misrepresentation:

> In Kamloops, *supra*, at pp. 10-11, Wilson J. restated Lord Wilberforce's test in the following terms:

> (1) is there a sufficiently close relationship between the parties (the [defendant] and the person who has suffered the damage) so that,

in the reasonable contemplation of the [defendant] carelessness on its part might cause damage to that person? If so,

(2) are there any considerations which ought to negative or limit (a) the scope of the duty and (b) the class of persons to whom it is owed or (c) the damages to which a breach of it may give rise?

As will be clear from the cases earlier cited, this two-stage approach has been applied by this Court in the context of various types of negligence actions, including actions involving claims for different forms of economic loss. Indeed, it was implicitly endorsed in the context of an action in negligent misrepresentation in *Edgeworth Construction Ltd. v. N. D. Lea & Associates Ltd.*, [1993] 3 S.C.R. 206, at pp. 218-19. The same approach to defining duties of care in negligent misrepresentation cases has also been taken in other Commonwealth courts. In *Scott Group Ltd. v. McFarlane*, [1978] 1 N.Z.L.R. 553, for example, a case that dealt specifically with auditors' liability for negligently prepared audit reports, the *Anns* test was adopted and applied by a majority of the New Zealand Court of Appeal.

I see no reason in principle why the same approach should not be taken in the present case. Indeed, to create a "pocket" of negligent misrepresentation cases (to use Professor Stapleton's term) in which the existence of a duty of care is determined differently from other negligence cases would, in my view, be incorrect; see: Jane Stapleton, "Duty of Care and Economic Loss: a Wider Agenda" (1991), 107 L.Q. Rev. 249. This is not to say, of course, that negligent misrepresentation cases do not involve special considerations stemming from the fact that recovery is allowed for pure economic loss as opposed to physical damage. Rather, it is simply to posit that the same general framework ought to be used in approaching the duty of care question in both types of case.

La Forest J. held that the first branch of the test depends upon whether there is a close enough relationship between the plaintiff and defendant to constitute a relationship of proximity. He then examined how proximity would be found in a negligent misrepresentation case:

To my mind, proximity can be seen to inhere between a defendant representor and a plaintiff-representee when two criteria relating to reliance may be said to exist on the facts: (a) the defendant ought reasonably to foresee that the plaintiff will rely on his or her representation; and (b) reliance by the plaintiff would, in the particular circumstances of the case, be reasonable. To use the term employed by my colleague, Iacobucci J., in *Cognos, supra*, at p. 110, the plaintiff and the defendant can be said to be in a "special relationship" whenever these two factors inhere.

As well, the plaintiff's reliance on the defendant's statements must be reasonable. However, La Forest J. rejected the additional requirements that the House of Lords apply in cases of negligent misrepresentation, as not being relevant to the existence of a *prima facie* duty of care:

> As should be evident from its very terms, the reasonable foreseeability/reasonable reliance test for determining a *prima facie* duty of care is somewhat what broader than the tests used both in the cases decided before *Anns, supra,* and in those that have rejected the *Anns* approach. Rather than stipulating simply that a duty of care will be found in any case where reasonable foreseeability and reasonable reliance inhere, those cases typically require (a) that the defendant know the identity of either the plaintiff or the class of plaintiffs who will rely on the statement, and (b) that the reliance losses claimed by the plaintiff stem from the particular transaction in respect of which the statement at issue was made. This narrower approach to defining the duty can be seen in a number of the more prominent English decisions dealing either with auditors' liability specifically or with liability for negligent misstatements generally. (See, *e.g.: Candler v. Crane, Christmas & Co.,* [1951] 2 K.B. 164 (C.A.), at pp. 181-82 and p. 184, per Denning L.J. (dissenting); *Hedley Byrne & Co. v. Heller & Partners Ltd.,* [1964] A.C. 465; *Caparo, supra,* per Lord Bridge, at p. 576, and per Lord Oliver, at pp. 589.) It is also evident in the approach taken by this Court in *Haig v. Bamford,* [1977] 1 S.C.R. 466.

While I would not question the conclusions reached in any of these judgments, I am of the view that inquiring into such matters as whether the defendant had knowledge of the plaintiff (or class of plaintiffs) and whether the plaintiff used the statements at issue for the particular transaction for which they were provided is, in reality, nothing more than a means by which to circumscribe — for reasons of policy — the scope of a representor's potentially infinite liability. As I have already tried to explain, determining whether "proximity" exists on a given set of facts consists in an attempt to discern whether, as a matter of simple justice, the defendant may be said to have had an obligation to be mindful of the plaintiff's interests in going about his or her business. Requiring, in addition to proximity, that the defendant know the identity of the plaintiff (or class of plaintiffs) and that the plaintiff use the statements in question for the specific purpose for which they were prepared amounts, in my opinion, to a tacit recognition that considerations of basic fairness may sometimes give way to other pressing concerns. Plainly stated, adding further requirements to the duty of care test provides a means by which policy concerns that are extrinsic to simple justice — but that are, nevertheless, fundamentally important — may be taken into account in assessing whether the defendant should be compelled to compensate the plaintiff for losses suffered. In other words, these further requirements serve a policy-based limiting function with respect to the ambit of the duty of care in negligent misrepresentation actions.

These policy-based requirements are, La Forest J. held, more appropriately considered under the second branch of the test. Regarding policy, La Forest examined the concerns that exposing auditors to negligent misrepresentation claims would lead to indeterminate liability and much higher costs faced by auditors in the form of insurance premiums, resources expended on avoiding liability and litigation:

> In applying the two-stage *Anns/Kamloops* test to negligent misrepresentation actions against auditors, therefore, policy considerations reflecting those repercussions should be taken into account. In the general run of auditors' cases, concerns over indeterminate liability will serve to negate a *prima facie* duty of care. But while such concerns may exist in most such cases, there may be particular situations where they do not. In other words, the specific factual matrix of a given case may render it an "exception" to the general class of cases in that while (as in most auditors' liability cases) considerations of proximity under the first branch of the *Anns/Kamloops* test might militate in favour of finding that a duty of care inheres, the typical concerns surrounding indeterminate liability do not arise. This needs to be explained.

> As discussed earlier, looking to factors such as "knowledge of the plaintiff (or an identifiable class of plaintiffs) on the part of the defendant" and "use of the statements at issue for the precise purpose or transaction for which they were prepared" really amounts to an attempt to limit or constrain the scope of the duty of care owed by the defendants. It the purpose of the *Anns/Kamloops* test is to determine (a) whether or not a *prima facie* duty of care exists and then (b) whether or not that duty ought to be negated or limited, then factors such as these ought properly to be considered in the second branch of the test once the first branch concerning "proximity" has been found to be satisfied. To my mind, the presence of such factors in a given situation will mean that worries stemming from indeterminacy should not arise, since the scope of potential liability is sufficiently delimited. In other words, in cases where the defendant knows the identity of the plaintiff (or of a class of plaintiffs) and where the defendant's statements are used for the specific purpose or transaction for which they were made, policy considerations surrounding indeterminate liability will not be of any concern since the scope of

liability can readily be circumscribed. Consequently, such considerations will not override a positive finding on the first branch of the *Anns/Kamloops* test and a duty of care may quite properly be found to exist . . .

The foregoing analysis should render the following points clear. A *prima facie* duty of care will arise on the part of a defendant in a negligent misrepresentation action when it can be said (a) that the defendant ought reasonably to have foreseen that the plaintiff would rely on his representation and (b) that reliance by the plaintiff, in the circumstances, would be reasonable. Even though, in the context of auditors' liability cases, such a duty will often (even if not always) be found to exist, the problem of indeterminate liability will frequently result in the duty being negated by the kinds of policy considerations already discussed. Where, however, indeterminate liability can be shown not to be a concern on the facts of a particular case, a duty of care will be found to exist.

Turning to the facts of the case, La Forest J. found that while the respondent owed the plaintiffs a *prima facie* duty of care, the second part of the test was not met. While the respondent had knowledge of the plaintiffs, the purpose of the auditor's report is to assist the shareholders as a group in scrutinizing the conduct of the company's affairs and to protect the company from the consequences of incorrect financial statements. The purpose is not to assist individual shareholders in making investment decisions. He rejected the appellants' claims that the respondents had agreed to prepare reports aimed at aiding them in protecting their individual investments, and dismissed the appeal.

3   The narrowing of auditor liability brought about by *Hercules* was closely followed by an amendment to the CBCA from joint and several liability of defendants to proportionate liability in situations where there is a financial loss that arises out of an error, omission or misstatement in financial information (CBCA s. 237.3(1)). Under the old scheme of joint and several liability, if the auditors were responsible for, e.g., 5% of the plaintiff's losses, with the company and any other defendants being 95% responsible, the auditor could still be liable for 100% of the plaintiff's losses. Under the new scheme, with some exceptions, the auditors would be liable only to the extent that they were responsible for the losses. See P. Puri and S. Ben-Ishai, "Proportionate Liability under the CBCA in the Context of Recent Corporate Governance Reform: Canadian Auditors in the Wrong Place at the Wrong Time?" (2003) 39 C.B.L.J. 1. Professors Puri and Ben-Ishai argue that the threat of shareholder litigation acts as an incentive for auditors to perform their function effectively, and in light of recent corporate governance and accounting scandals that

have reduced investor confidence in auditors, the reduction in the scope of auditor's liability is not a favourable development.

Under the OBCA, the liability of auditors remains joint and several. In October 2010, the Law Commission of Ontario held a roundtable discussion to review the joint and several liability of professionals under the OBCA. Based on this discussion, the Law Commission of Ontario made recommendations for reform to the OBCA. See Law Commission of Ontario "Joint and Several Liability Final Report" online < http://www.lco-cdo.org/en/content/joint-several-liability > .

Livent Inc. (Receiver of) v. Deloitte & Touche
2016 CarswellOnt 122, 2016 ONCA 11, 31 C.B.R. (6th) 205 (Ont. C.A.)

[Garth Drabinsky and Myron Gottlieb created and developed Live Entertainment Corporation of Canada Inc., (Livent). Livent was a developer of high-profile theatre. Livent fell apart in 1998 when new management discovered that Drabinsky and Gottlieb had been fraudulently manipulating the company's financial books and records over a number of years in order to inflate the earnings and profitability of the operation so they could attract over US$200 million and $77.5 million through the capital markets. As a result, Livent filed for insolvency protection in Canada and the United States and was placed in receivership. Its assets were subsequently sold for a realization value of approximately US$144 million. Drabinsky and Gottlieb were convicted of fraud and forgery and sent to jail. Deloitte & Touche and its predecessor ("Deloitte") was the auditor for Livent from 1989 through to 1998, when the fraud was discovered. Deloitte issued clean audited financial statements throughout this period. In this action, Livent — through a Special Receiver appointed in the insolvency proceedings — sues Deloitte for damages in contract and negligence arising out of Deloitte's failure to follow generally accepted auditing standards and discover material misstatements in Livent's books, records, and financial reporting. Similar to *Sino-Forest,* the court found that auditors may be subject to a higher standard of care than that of a "reasonably cautious and competent accountant" particularly in relation to high risk or complex audits. Again, the court focused on the importance of professional skepticism. The court found that Deloitte had failed to exercise the level of "professional skepticism" required in the circumstances, choosing instead to accommodate the needs of management when red flags were uncovered, rather than dig deeper into the evidence.]

* * *

(b) The CICA Handbook

Deloitte's role as Livent's auditor was also subject to the professional standards applicable to auditors as set out in the CICA Handbook and the ICAO Handbook at the time.

The Supreme Court of Canada has said that rules set by a self-governing professional body are "of guiding importance in determining the nature of the duties flowing from a particular professional relationship": *Hodgkinson v. Simms*, [1994] 3 S.C.R. 377 (S.C.C.), at p. 425. Further, "[t]hese rules must be taken as expressing the collective views of the profession as to the appropriate standards to which the profession should adhere": *MacDonald Estate v. Martin*, [1990] 3 S.C.R. 1235 (S.C.C.), at p. 1244.

In the auditing context, this Court has held that the CICA Handbook "is of great assistance" to courts in determining the requisite standard and "a persuasive guide to the applicable standard of care": *Bloor Italian Gifts Ltd. v. Dixon* (2000), 48 O.R. (3d) 760 (Ont. C.A.), at paras. 27, 31; and *Sherman v. Orenstein & Partners* (2005), 11 B.L.R. (4th) 233 (Ont. C.A.), at para. 33.

* * *

(iii) Management's Good Faith and Professional Skepticism

The CICA Handbook dealt with the concept of management's good faith and the related concept of professional skepticism, which are particularly significant in this case given the trial judge's finding that one of Deloitte' shortcomings was its failure to exercise sufficient professional skepticism.

The Handbook recognized at s. 5000.05 that "the assumption of management's good faith [was] a fundamental auditing postulate", which meant that "*in the absence of evidence to the contrary*, the auditor [could] accept accounting records and documentation as genuine and representations as complete and truthful" (emphasis added). At the same time, "[t]he assumption of management's good faith [was] not a source of audit evidence nor a substitute for the requirement to obtain sufficient appropriate audit evidence to afford a reasonable basis to support the content of the auditor's report."

Sections 5000.06 and 5135.05 dealt with the need to approach the audit with an attitude of professional skepticism. . .

* * *

(iv) The Detection of Material Misstatements

The CICA Handbook affirmed that the auditor was responsible for detecting material misstatements in financial statements or other financial information. It defined misstatements as either "errors" (i.e., unintentional misstatements) or "fraud and other irregularities" (i.e., intentional misstatements): ss. 5135.01-5135.02.

The CICA Handbook recognized — as did the trial judge — that fraud may be very difficult to detect. However, given the difficulty in detecting fraud, the Handbook stressed the need to have proper auditing procedures in place to reduce the risk of not detecting material misstatements to an appropriately low level, and, in particular, the need to adapt the auditing plan where circumstances made the auditor suspect the financial statements were materially misstated: ss. 5135.07-5135.17.

For instance, in circumstances involving "higher risk assessment" — as Deloitte recognized the Livent environment to be — the CICA Handbook imposed an obligation to perform heightened audit procedures providing more reliable evidence: s. 5135.07. This included recognizing the need for more extensive supervision and the use of personnel with more experience and training: s. 5135.08. The CICA Handbook also stipulated that where there was a reason to suspect the financial statements were materially misstated, the auditor was required to perform procedures to confirm or dispel that suspicion: s. 5135.14.

These provisions were consistent with the common law, which affirmed that until a suspicion is dispelled — until the auditor has "probe[d] it to the bottom" — the auditor cannot make an unqualified auditor's report. Even where the auditor may be following or attempting to follow GAAS, it may not be excused from liability where the auditor "has an opportunity to acquire or is exposed to knowledge or information which might affect [its] opinion but [it] fails to recognize and act on that information": *Revelstoke Credit Union v. Miller*, [1984] 2 W.W.R. 297 (B.C. S.C.), at p. 303.

Subsequent authorities considering the same applicable standards have confirmed that where the auditor uncovers "significant weaknesses" during the course of the audit, it has a duty to inform the directors of the client company: BDO Dunwoody, at paras. 231-32. See also *Pineridge Capital Group Inc. v. Dunwoody & Co.* [1999 CarswellBC 58 (B.C. S.C.)], 1999 CanLII 5925, at paras. 26-27; and *Sydney Cooperative Society Ltd. v. Coopers & Lybrand* (2002), 2003 NSSC 35, 213 N.S.R. (2d) 115 (N.S. S.C.), at paras. 148-49.

* * *

(a) 1996 Audit — The PPC

The trial judge observed that the "PPC should have been front and center in the Deloitte collective mindset when it came to the completion of the 1996 audit": para. 143. He concluded that "Deloitte's approach to the 1996 PPC audit cannot be said to have been in accordance with GAAS by any measure": para. 152. Indeed, it did not even comply with Deloitte's own undertaking in its audit plan for the year to "[o]btain operating projections for each production" and to "compare projected results with historical results where data available": paras. 146-48. Deloitte was aware that the Livent productions had performed poorly in 1996, and that "after amortization of PPC, the Livent shows lost, in the aggregate, $22.9 million, while they were projected to earn a net income of $20.6 million, a variance or swing of 218%": para. 148. Nonetheless, except for isolated instances, Deloitte failed: (i) to obtain and review the 1996 budgets; (ii) to do more than accept management's estimates as to potential revenue for any one show (which led it into the realm of "audit by conversation"); (iii) to test the accuracy of those estimates against recently experienced results (which were available and which would have cast doubt on the accuracy of the estimates); or, (iv) to test the reasonableness of Livent's forecasting by looking at past forecasts against actual results. In the end, when Deloitte did its after-the-fact corrective audit, an $11 million charge was taken against 1996 net income in respect of the PPC not sufficiently amortized in the year, in addition to a $3.1 million adjustment for the PPC improperly recorded or moved from account to account between various productions.

* * *

(b) 1996 Audit — Musicians' Pension Surplus Receivables

Under New York law, Livent was required to use musicians represented by a local union for its performances in New York, and to remit a percentage of box office revenues to the union on account of the musicians' pension entitlements. Livent told Deloitte, however, that the union was entitled to receive less under its collective agreement than what Livent had remitted and so Livent was entitled to record the difference as a credit and a receivable. Livent did not disclose that the union disputed this interpretation.

The trial judge concluded that it was acceptable for Deloitte to have accepted Livent's representation for the 1995 audit, but not for the 1996 audit. Instead of decreasing, which one would have expected had Livent's representation been accurate, the receivable remained the same for one show (the *Kiss* tour in New York) and increased for the other (*Show Boat* New York). Deloitte ignored this evidence, which the trial judge found "was a red flag and should have been recognized as such, especially considering that the audit risk for the 1996 audit was set as 'high'": para. 162. Deloitte's expert acknowledged in cross-examination at trial that this aspect of the audit did not conform to GAAS.

(c) 1996 Audit — Revenue Transactions

I described the Revenue Transactions in general terms above. As explained, they were designed to enhance the veneer of Livent's profitability in order to attract much-needed cash funding and involved the "sale" to third parties of various Livent assets. A common feature of these transactions was that the income they generated was to be received over a period of time and so there was a continuing tension about when and in what amounts these income streams could be counted for the purposes of financial accounting. Many of the transactions also had another theme in common: they were not true sales of assets, but were more in the nature of loans or financing agreements.

* * *

The criticisms of the 1996 audit treatment of the Revenue Transactions are significant, however, because they signal a flaw that would ultimately prove to be Deloitte's undoing: Deloitte was becoming too accommodating to its client — something driven by the threat of losing its high-profile and high-flying client — and in the process had lost its professional objectivity and its required attitude of professional skepticism. As I will explain, Deloitte yielded to Livent pressures and lent its name to the Q2 1997 financial statements that did not comply with Canadian GAAP and provided a clean audit opinion for the 1997 audit year that did not comply with GAAS. Had Deloitte not done so, the trial judge found that the fraud would have been uncovered in August/September 1997 or, at the very latest, in April 1998.

* * *

In other words, Deloitte's thinking about the substantive issues was, at least to some degree, influenced by strong pressure from Gottlieb.

(3) 1997 Engagements

In 1997, the seeds of trouble took root. Unfortunately, Deloitte continued to mistake the weeds for flowers when a little digging in the exercise of its professional skepticism obligation and the application of its accumulated audit knowledge would have revealed the underlying rot.

* * *

As explained above, the Pantages Air Rights Agreement purported to transfer Livent's air rights above the Pantages Theatre and adjoining lands to Dundee for a price of $7.4 million. The parties initially entered into a letter agreement dated May 22, 1997. Attached to the letter agreement was a term sheet, which included the Put in favour of Dundee enabling Dundee to withdraw from the arrangement in certain circumstances. The parties subsequently entered into a more formal "Master Agreement", which was said to be effective as of June 30, 1997, although the transaction did not close until August 15, 1997.

* * *

Deloitte had a number of concerns about the Pantages Air Rights Agreement, including that the Put effectively allowed Dundee to exit the Agreement without paying the balance of $4.9 million on the transfer price. On August 1st, Wardell and Peter Chant, who were Advisory Partners on the Livent file, met with Gottlieb, Messina and Gord Eckstein, Livent's Senior Vice-President of Finance. Wardell and Chant advised them that it would not be appropriate to recognize the gain from the transfer of the air rights in Q2 1997 — something that Livent was intent on accomplishing in order to shore up its Q2 financial statements for the purposes of a planned debenture offering in fall 1997.

On August 6th, Messina informed Wardell that Gottlieb was pushing to have $6 million included in Q2 and to have no public disclosure of its inclusion. That same day, Wardell called Gottlieb to express concern that Gottlieb would even consider that course of action. He warned Gottlieb that if Livent were to include a material gain on the air rights transaction in Q2, Deloitte would not be able to provide the comfort letters needed for the debenture offering in the fall.

Gottlieb ignored Wardell's warning. Instead, he went to the Livent Audit Committee and tabled draft consolidated financial statements for Q2 and the six months ending June 30, 1997, which included a $6 million gain on the sale of the air rights. Deceitfully, he did not inform the Audit Committee about Deloitte's concerns, and the Audit Committee approved the financial statements. No one from Deloitte was present at the meeting.

When Wardell and Chant learned what had happened shortly thereafter, they were understandably upset. Gottlieb was advised that Deloitte was going to exercise its statutory right as an auditor to insist that an Audit Committee meeting be convened. Deloitte sent Gottlieb a letter on August 25th formally advising that, in its view, the Q2 results as reported were materially misstated.

Gottlieb responded, before the Audit Committee met, by purporting to eliminate at least some of Deloitte's concerns by having Livent's lawyer delete any reference to the Put in the Master Agreement. Livent's solicitors and Dundee provided misleading information that the Put had been removed and that there was a firm deal for the sale of the air rights as at June 30, 1997. In spite of these assurances, Deloitte remained concerned.

As it turned out, Deloitte's concerns were justified. Assurances from Livent's external counsel and from Dundee aside, and unbeknownst to Deloitte, Livent and Dundee had entered into a covert side agreement on August 15th that contained the Put that Deloitte had been advised was "intentionally deleted" from the Master Agreement.

There were intense discussions over this period of time, but in the end Deloitte's opposition was overcome.

* * *

In the end, the trial judge took Deloitte to task at para. 196 for being too accommodating to Livent:

Whatever might have been Deloitte's motivation to continue as auditor, I have concluded that it was too accommodating at this point and put itself in a most curious if not fatal position by changing the audit team, virtually from top to bottom.

In addition, the trial judge found that "Deloitte should have remained firm in its resolve to sever its relationship with Livent at the end of August 1997 at the earliest, but no later than the end of Q3, or September 30th, at the latest": para. 201. In his view, the "red flags were certainly aflutter by that time": para. 201. However, while Deloitte, "even with the change of audit teams, was clearly aware that Livent's management was more than merely pushing the envelope from a GAAP perspective, it seemed to turn a blind eye to the warning signs": para. 201.

In reaching those conclusions, he made a number of key findings:

- there was a complete breakdown in the Deloitte/Livent relationship when Gottlieb placed the Q2 statements before the Audit Committee in early August 1997 without advising the Committee of Deloitte's concerns, an inexcusable action that could not — once discovered — simply be negotiated away: para. 202;

- with this knowledge, and with or without knowledge of the other Revenue Transactions, Deloitte's "collective professional skepticism should have been elevated at this point when they had reason to question the integrity of Gottlieb": para. 204;

- someone at Deloitte should have questioned Dundee's president and Deloitte's external counsel about why the Put was apparently "intentionally deleted": para. 204;

- the situation deteriorated even further when Deloitte agreed to the September 2nd press release when it knew or ought to have known that it was misleading: para. 205; and

- to make matters worse, Gottlieb subsequently sought to include the present value of a new Revenue Transaction involving AT&T in the Q3 results: para. 206.

Notes and Questions

1. In *Hercules,* the SCC held that auditors do not generally owe a duty of care to shareholders, and therefore cannot generally be sued by shareholders directly. It is the corporation that has the cause of action if it suffers a loss attributable to its auditor's negligence. In *Livent,* the receiver sued on behalf of the corporation, and while the claim for breach of contract and negligence was the corporation's, shareholders and creditors of *Livent* might nonetheless benefit from the judgment. This means that despite *Hercules,* shareholders, creditors, and other stakeholders may still indirectly recover losses caused by an auditor's negligence.

2. There are other routes available to hold auditors accountable, including through a securities regulator. In *Ernst & Young LLP, Re,* 2014 CarswellOnt 13350, 37 O.S.C.B. 9107 (Ont. Securities Comm.), the staff of the Ontario Securities Commission (OSC) brought a

proceeding against Ernst & Young regarding its audits for failure to adhere to generally accepted auditing standards.

Although Ernst & Young was Sino-Forest's auditor, fraudulent financial statements still emerged. During the auditing process, there were multiple red flags that Ernst & Young failed to address. For example, important documents verifying the ownership and existence of the important timber assets were often unavailable, yet Ernst & Young failed to inquire about these deficiencies nor record in the audit files that they were missing. They also failed to choose the sites for visits, but instead made limited visits to sites chosen by Sino-Forest. The OSC stated that the red flags should have caused Ernst & Young to treat Sino-Forest's representation with greater caution, perform additional audit procedures, and obtain additional evidence from independent sources. Ernst & Young failed to do so, and therefore failed to exercise a sufficient level of professional skepticism. In the end, Ernst & Young agreed to a settlement with the OSC. Ernst & Young did not confirm or deny the allegations, but agreed to make a voluntary payment of $8 million to the OSC.

3. Do you think the above decisions in *Livent*, and *Ernst & Young* impose too high a standard for auditors? Does the standard rise to the level of indeterminate liability contemplated in *Hercules*? In *Livent*, the court even went to great lengths discussing the duty of an auditor to resign. The trial judge found that Deloitte should have done so in *Livent*, and the Court of Appeal held that the trial judge did not err in this finding. By raising the standard for auditors to such a level, do you think the decisions will limit the type of work auditors are willing to take on? Will that affect the efficiency of the market considering the limited number of auditing firms available?

(g) Evaluation

Poonam Puri, in her article "Converging Numbers: Harmonization of Accounting Standards in the Context of the Role of the Auditor in Corporate Governance" (in A. Anand and W. Flanagan, Eds., *Responding to Globalization: Queen's Annual Business Law Symposium 2001* (Toronto: Carswell, 2001)), raises some serious questions about the credibility of the auditor's role in the corporate governance of public corporations, in light of the financial collapse of Enron and the demise of accounting firm Arthur Andersen. Puri notes that accounting standards provide broad principles and argues that they allow management the ability to posture and afford auditors too much discretion in determining whether management's financial statements fairly present the financial picture of the company. While some may consider the flexibility in GAAP a strength, Puri argues that the wide scope of discretion afforded to auditors assists in creating an environment where auditors are more likely to succumb to pressure by management to report financial data in ways favourable to management. If an accounting principle is generally accepted in that sense, and if it has been used in past financial statements, then an auditor may certify a company's financial statements notwithstanding that the particular principle chosen might not result in the fairest presentation of the company's results for the past year.

Puri is also concerned about the manner in which accountants are appointed and dismissed. Notwithstanding that the corporations statutes may require that this is to be done by shareholders, the reality is that management controls who the accountant is to be and also decides when an accountant is to be dismissed. As we have seen, the accountant is given independent rights of audience and explanation before the shareholders if he is dismissed. But it may be queried how often one of the major national accounting firms will take advantage of these statutory rights with respect to the audit of a large public corporation.

Responding to the financial collapse of Enron and Worldcom and the demise of accounting firm Arthur Andersen, US Congress passed the *Sarbanes-Oxley Act* of 2002 (SOX) which required the US Securities and Exchange Commission (SEC) to, *inter alia*, strengthen its rules on auditor independence and clarify the relationship between the auditor and a company's audit committee. SOX and related SEC rules clarify auditor independence requirements by creating bright line prohibitions against certain non-audit activities, by requiring audit partner rotation and by playing restrictions on audit partner compensation and employment relationships. As required by SOX, the SEC also promulgated Rule 10A-3 which makes it clear that the audit committee, not management, is responsible for appointing, compensating and overseeing the company's relationship with its auditors. The audit committee is also charged with resolving any disputes between the auditors and management over financial statement reporting. Finally, SOX created the Public Companies Accountability Oversight Board (PCAOB), which regulates public accounting firms, including non-US accounting firms, that audit the financial statements of SEC reporting companies.

In light of the competition and convergence in corporate governance and global capital markets, Canadian regulatory reform largely mirrored the US changes. The Canadian Institute of Chartered Accountants created new independence standards for auditors in 2003. Canadian securities regulators released Multi-lateral Instrument 52-110, discussed below, which defines the audit committee's role and composition. As noted earlier, the Canadian Public Companies Accountability Board has been created, with similar functions as PCAOB, its US counterpart. In May 2004, proposals were also released to strengthen the corporate governance provisions in the CBCA. It is interesting to note that while in the US reform has come from government regulation, while Canada largely relies on self-regulatory model. See Adam Pritchard and Poonam

Puri "The Regulation of Public Auditing in Canada and the United States: Self-Regulation or Government Regulation?" (2006) Fraser Institute Digital Publication, 1.

(h)   The Audit Committee

The CBCA, s. 171, and the OBCA, s. 158, require the appointment of an audit committee in large or widely held corporations. In each case, the audit committee is to be composed of not fewer than three directors, a majority of whom shall not be officers or employees of the company. The essential task of this "independent" audit committee is to review the company's financial statements before they are signed by the directors and presented to the shareholders. In each case the auditor is given the right to appear before any meeting of the audit committee and may be required to appear before the audit committee when it so requests. The auditor is also given an independent right to call a meeting of the audit committee to consider any matter that the auditor believes should be brought to the attention of the directors or the shareholders.

Stricter rules regarding audit committee independence are prescribed by securities law. Multilateral Instrument 52-110, adopted in 2004 by all Canadian securities jurisdictions save British Columbia, requires every member of the audit committee of an issuer to be independent (with some exceptions). MI 52-110 applies a more restrictive definition of "independence" than corporate statutes. At the time of publication of this book, corporate statutes only require that the majority of audit committee members not be officers or employees of the company, while Multilateral Instrument 52-110 disallows any "material relationship" which could interfere with a member's independent judgment (s. 1.4). The Instrument also requires that audit committee members be "financially literate," a requirement not currently present in the corporate statutes (s. 3.1(4)). Under MI 52-110, audit committees are now responsible for overseeing the work of the external auditor, for preapproving all non-audit services to be conducted by the auditor for the company or its subsidiaries and for reviewing the financial reporting documents before they are publicly released. For a comment on the audit committee's composition and responsibilities, see Poonam Puri and Stephanie Ben-Ishai, "Proportionate Liability under the CBCA in the Context of Recent Corporate Governance Reform: Canadian Auditors in the Wrong Place at the Wrong Time?" (2003) 39 C.B.L.J. 1.

Chapter 9

Special Aspects of the Closely Held or Private Corporation

1. INTRODUCTION

Although the vast majority of Canadian corporations are closely held or private corporations, there has been relatively little attention paid by the courts or the legislatures to devising special legal rules for their treatment. It is not easy to point to a widely accepted definition of the closely held corporation, but there are some features of such corporations that are generally discernible. Shareholders of such corporations are few in number and usually take an active part in the corporation's business. The shares of the corporation are not publicly traded and generally the resources of the corporation, both in terms of its invested capital and ability to attract additional capital, are limited. However, there are notable exceptions such as the Jim Pattison Group, the PCL Construction Group and Ellis-Don Inc. The growth of private equity also poses an alternative to public equity markets.

In many respects the closely held corporation can be viewed as an incorporated partnership which, *inter alia*, emphasizes the consensual relationship among the shareholders. As such, they will want to determine who will become a shareholder to ensure they can get along with the individual and will often insist on unanimity of decisions, thereby rejecting the majority rule of corporation law. Because they often depend on the corporation for their livelihood, shareholders of closely held corporations will normally want to play an effective role in management and may reinforce this, if necessary or desirable, by seeking a veto power over major decisions.

Before dealing with some of the ways that shareholders of such corporations arrange their affairs and deal with control of the corporation, we will take a brief look at the historical development of the closely held or private corporation.

Nicholls, Corporate Law
(Emond-Montgomery, 2005) pp. 91–98 (footnotes omitted)

In the lexicon of social democrats and free-trade protesters, the word "corporation" has come to be associated with "big business." This association is neither new nor entirely without some historical justification. At least one academic commentator has suggested that there may be a link between the development of the modem legal conception of the corporation, and apologies for the growth of very large businesses, especially in the period beginning after the First World War.

Certainly the corporate form does facilitate the accumulation of pools of capital that would be too large for even the wealthiest of individuals and families to purchase with their personal assets. Defying the logic of Adam Smith (who saw little future for corporations in all but a handful of industries), these modem corporate behemoths and leviathans appear to have provided the opportunity for wealthy capitalists to lever already large fortunes to achieve economic control over enterprises of almost incomprehensible size. Their growth is surely one of the most important economic phenomena of the past century.

Of the economic, social, and political implications of such corporate giantism, no more will be said here. From the necessarily more narrow and pragmatic lawyer's perspective, it is of principal importance to offer this gentle reminder, Although large public corporations are certainly the most visible manifestations of the corporate form, they are not the most common, Most Canadian corporations are actually small enterprises with few shareholders.

Corporations that have never sold their shares or other securities to the public are often referred to as "private," "closely held," or "close" corporations — all terms that are discussed in more detail below. To be sure, not all of these ostensibly "small," private corporations are running corner grocery stores and video shops. Many are merely subsidiaries of (much larger) corporate entities — their corporate "parents" — and have been established to accommodate some specific corporate transaction, to hold particular corporate assets, or to fulfill some other tax or operational purpose.

But a considerable number of private corporations are not merely the instruments of big business. They are the vehicles of closely held, often family owned, businesses. They have been incorporated to gain the corporate benefits of limited liability, estate planning, and often certain favourable income tax treatment.

The Distinction between Private and Public Companies

Commentators and business people have long recognized the absurdity of purporting to treat alike, for corporate law purposes, widely held billion-dollar, multinational businesses, on the one hand, and small, family owned corner stores, on the other. Accordingly, corporate legislation, in Canada and elsewhere, occasionally distinguishes between public and private corporations for various purposes. Historically, one of the most important legal consequences of such a distinction related to the different rules to which corporations of each sort were subject concerning public disclosure of financial statements: public corporations were required to make such disclosure; private corporations were not. Recognizing that some private corporations are in truth, however, merely part of larger corporate enterprises, the special exemption from such public filing requirements was frequently denied to these offspring of public corporations. So, for example, company legislation in the United Kingdom once categorized private companies as either "exempt" (that is, exempt from the requirement to file financial information) or "non-exempt." And although this same terminology was not adopted in Canada, Canadian corporate statutes in the past have also drawn distinctions between private corporations based on the aggregate size of those corporations when considered together with their affiliates.

Times have changed. The requirement to file financial and other information publicly has increasingly come within the ambit of Canadian securities regulation, rather than corporate law; so the need for corporate statutes to draw distinctions between corporations for this particular purpose has diminished. In the meantime, business practice and investor concerns have brought to light other policy reasons to differentiate between widely held (that is, public) and closely held (or private) corporations.

Private and Public Companies: Early English and Canadian Origins

The legal distinction between "private" and "public" companies has an interesting and illuminating history. Gower notes, for example, that in the 18th century, unincorporated companies were often referred to as "private" companies, while the term "public" companies was reserved for incorporated business entities. This distinction was significant at the time because the infamous *Bubble Act* of 1720 had made it illegal for certain kinds of unincorporated companies to operate. The *Bubble Act* was rather ambiguous, however, on the question of *which* unincorporated companies would be considered illegal. Evidently, the view emerged that one of the key features characterizing the illegal sort of unincorporated company was free transferability of such a company's shares. Promoters of unincorporated businesses were wary of prosecution under the Act, and so took care to ensure that shares of the firms they were promoting were subject to transfer restrictions.

Thus, the earliest use of the public company/private company distinction in English law was closely connected to the free transferability of shares, a distinction that survives to this day in Canadian securities laws.

As explained in Chapter 1, English and Canadian corporate statutes in the 19th century began to regularize and formalize corporate law. The earliest English corporate law statutes had no particular reason to draw any distinction between public and private companies because they really were not concerned with private companies. They were primarily aimed only at larger public-type companies in any event — namely, companies with a minimum number of members (more than 25 in the 1844 legislation) or companies with freely transferable shares. Smaller business enterprises would not, in those days, have been incorporated. Indeed, when the privilege of shareholder limited liability was first introduced in 1855, enjoyment of that privilege was made conditional, among other things, on companies having a certain minimum size. The subject had been debated in England, and the "dangers" of extending limited liability to small partnerships was specifically adverted to.

Gradually, however, through a process that began with the *Companies Act, 1862*, and culminated in *Salomon's* case in 1896, it became clear that the full benefits of incorporation — including the benefits of limited liability - were available even to corporations with but a single beneficial shareholder.

At this critical point in its history, corporate law could readily have moved in either of two directions. Legislators might have decided to clamp down on *Salomon-type* sole shareholder companies, and so restore the registered corporation to its original intended purpose: to provide a means for larger enterprises to be formed in order to pool capital from passive investors for large-scale indivisible enterprise. Many would argue that this would have been a sensible approach. Kahn-Freund, for example, wrote in 1944 that "it is open to doubt whether there is a case for the continued existence of private companies." He did not mean by this that there would be any lack of demand for such vehicles on the part of entrepreneurs. Rather, his point was that such vehicles could be justified only in the rarest circumstances because, for the most part, they were something of an abuse of the corporate form.

However, corporate law took a second path. Rather than seeking to reverse the House of Lords' decision in *Salomon*, legislators essentially institutionalized it (without immediately permitting, however — at least explicitly — incorporation by a single owner). And so, the first legislative distinction between "public" and "private" companies appeared in the English corporate statute in 1907. Indeed, the origin of the term "private company" that now appears in many Canadian securities law statutes (and one Canadian corporate statute) may be traced to that English legislation, the English *Companies Act*, 1907. The phrase was defined in s. 37 of that statute in this way:

"private company" means a company which by its articles:

(a) Restricts the right to transfer its shares; and

(b) Limits the number of its members (exclusive of persons who are in the employment of the company) to fifty; and

(c) Prohibits any invitation to the public to subscribe for any shares or debentures of the company.

Private companies were permitted to have as few as two members; but although the statute was passed some 10 years after the House of Lords landmark decision in *Salomon's* case, single-shareholder companies were not expressly provided for.

The significance of the new private company definition was summarized in a contemporary annotated version of the 1907 statute:

A private company enjoys all the privileges and is exempt from many of the obligations imposed on public companies; it need not file a statement in lieu of prospectus . . . ; it can commence business as soon as it is incorporated . . . ; and the restrictions on the appointment of directors and allotment of shares do not apply to it. It need not include in its annual summary a statement in the form of a balance sheet . . . ; it need not file or forward to its members the report required by Section 12 of the Act of 1900 to be forwarded to every member at least seven days before the statutory meeting . . . ; nor need it give to its preference shareholders and debenture holders the same right of inspecting and receiving the balance sheets and reports as are possessed by the ordinary shareholders.

Ziegel et al. report that this public/private distinction was emulated by the drafters of Ontario's corporation law in 1912, and thereafter by Canada's federal statute and most other provincial corporate statutes as well. Writing in 1931, Wegenast notes that "the sole purpose of the distinction [between public and private companies] is to relieve private companies from the necessity of filing either a prospectus or a 'notice in lieu of prospectus.'"

The link between the requirement to file a prospectus and a company's characterization as either "public" or "private" underlies the inclusion of "private company" as a defined term in many Canadian provincial securities law statutes. The Ontario *Securities Act*, for example, includes a definition of private company that clearly shows its English ancestry:

"private company" means a company in whose constating document,

(a) the right to transfer its shares is restricted,

(b) the number of its shareholders, exclusive of persons who are in its employment and exclusive of persons who, having been formerly in the employment of the company, were, while in that employment, and have continued after termination of that employment to be, shareholders of the company, is limited to not more than fifty, two or more persons who are the joint registered owners of one or more shares being counted as one shareholder,

(c) any invitation to the public to subscribe for its securities is prohibited;

This definition was originally included in the legislation to support specific exemptions from the registration and prospectus requirements otherwise imposed by the statute upon a corporation (or other issuer of shares or other securities) when it sells (or, more technically, "trades" and "distributes") any of its securities. Trades and distributions of the securities of private companies, as defined in the provision reproduced above, were, at one time, exempt from the registration and prospectus requirements, respectively. In other words, such companies were permitted to raise money by selling their securities to a modest number of people — all of whom were connected to the company in some way — without having to incur fees to registered securities dealers, and without having to undertake the expensive and time-consuming process of complying with the statutory procedures that accompany a public offering of securities.

Companies that did not satisfy the "private company" definition enjoyed no such exemption; so, unless some alternative exemption from the registration and prospectus rules were available to them, these companies would be required to produce a prospectus each time they sold shares or other securities.

Recent changes to securities law in Ontario have now made the private company definition something of a dead letter in that province. Elsewhere in Canada, for securities law purposes, the similar term "private issuer" has supplanted the term "private company" in importance. The term "private company" is still found in the PEI *Companies Act*, and companies incorporated under that statute must indicate in their application for letters patent whether the company to be incorporated is to be a private company. However, the corporate statute itself does not otherwise appear to deal significantly with private companies.

In the United Kingdom, private companies can be readily distinguished from public companies by the nature of the legal element (or cautionary suffix) in their corporate name. All public companies must include "public limited company" or "Plc" in their corporate names, while the names of private companies must include the word "limited" or "ltd." No such distinction is made in Canada, where all corporations — public or private — may use the same suffixes, as chosen by the incorporators from those permitted by the incorporating statute.

Canadian Reforms

When the Dickerson committee undertook its comprehensive review of the federal corporate statute in 1971, it specifically eschewed the "traditional private-public corporation dichotomy." Instead, as the committee explained,

We have defined "corporation" in different ways in different parts of the Draft Act where it seemed necessary or desirable to create a distinction. Corporations are therefore distinguished on functional rather than on doctrinal grounds.

Thus, for example, statutory requirements concerning the minimum number of a corporation's directors and the obligation of a corporation's management to solicit proxies in connection with a shareholder meeting differed depending on the numbers of the corporation's shareholders or on the question of whether the corporation had ever issued securities to the public (some of which were still outstanding in the hands of more than one shareholder).

That same approach is found in the current version of the *Canada Business Corporations Act* (CBCA) as well. But, although the CBCA still contains no definition of, or references to, "private companies," it has, since November 2001, formally classified certain corporations as "distributing corporations." This statutorily defined term denotes what many practitioners would describe informally as "public companies," or what are known for most provincial securities law purposes as "reporting issuers."

Distributing corporations are subject to a number of additional requirements under the CBCA, discussed more fully in the section entitled "The Public Corporation," below. With the express adoption of this general "distributing corporation" definition," the federal statute has now come full circle. Early corporate statutes included only a definition of "private company"; all other corporations were considered public corporations by default. The modern CBCA now includes only a definition of "distributing corporation"; all other corporations are, in effect, private companies, by default.

The Ontario *Business Corporations Act* provides a similar taxonomy, but adopts the term "offering corporation" rather than "distributing corporation," to describe corporations that have issued their securities publicly. The new British Columbia *Business Corporations Act* uses the term "public company" to mean a "reporting issuer" for Canadian securities law purposes, a company with securities registered under the US *Securities Exchange Act of 1934*, or a company with securities that trade on an exchange or are reported through a quotation and trade reporting system. The term "distributing corporation" is also found in the Alberta *Business Corporations Act, The Business Corporations Act* (Saskatchewan), and the Newfoundland and Labrador *Corporations Act*. The *Corporations Act* (Manitoba) uses the cumbersome phrase formerly found in the CBCA (discussed further below). The New Brunswick *Business Corporations Act* occasionally refers to corporations that have "shares listed on a prescribed stock exchange." The term "public company" is used in the PEI *Companies Act*.

One final note on corporation taxonomy. The CBCA does include a special definition of "personal body corporate." A personal body corporate is, essentially, an individual or family holding company. However, the use of this definition in the CBCA is very narrow. It is included only for the purposes of the proportionate liability provisions.

* * *

Newer types of corporate forms, some particularly well-suited to closely-held corporations, are rapidly evolving, particularly in the UK and the US.

Among the UK forms are Community Interest Companies and European Private Companies. Community Interest Companies (CICs), a new form of limited company created pursuant to the *Companies Act* 2004 and the *Community Interest Company Regulations* 2005, came into existence in July 2005. This new corporate form can be seen as sitting between a traditional company and a registered charity: CICs are intended to serve the needs of the growing sector of social enterprise organizations: businesses whose primary objectives are social or community benefit or advancement, and whose funds are reinvested primarily in pursuit of those objectives in the community. This is similar to the *Not-for-Profit Corporations Act* in Ontario, *supra*, Chapter 3.

The EU has created *Societas Privata Europaea* (SPEs) pursuant to the *Small Business Act for Europe* to facilitate small and medium sized enterprises (SMEs) conducting inter-state business among EU member states. The *Act* is intended to enhance the competitiveness of SMEs by reducing compliance costs associated with the creation and operation of cross-border companies, stemming from differences in Member States' companies law.

Limited Liability Corporations (LLCs) were introduced to the US in the early 1990s, and between 1995 and1998 grew enormously popular among small business entities. They are a hybrid between a corporation and a partnership: they offer the benefits of a partnership tax structure, as well as limited liability, and default rules more suited to small business than a corporate structure. In states offering 'full-shield LLPs' — LLPs that offer protection from both contract and tort liability, LLPs are still used to a certain extent; however, in states not offering full shield LLPs, the LLC has taken over in popularity among small businesses. For a detailed analysis of LLCs and their history, see Howard M. Friedman "The Silent LLC Revolution — The Social Cost of Academic Neglect" (2004) 38 Creighton L.Rev.35 (Q.L.).

In 1996, Series Limited Liability Companies (Series LLCs) — also known as Cell LLCs — were introduced by Delaware (DEL. CODE ANN. tit. 6, § 18-215 (2008)) and adopted, in various forms, by six other states by 2009. The Series LLC is a form of a Limited Liability Company and acts as an umbrella entity, under which a number of businesses or operations — potentially with different purposes and objectives — can be shielded from every other business under that umbrella in respect of assets and liabilities. Essentially, the same protections for the respective businesses could be achieved using a number of LLCs; however, the Series LLC structure is intended to be more efficient for the business owner(s), as the business owner must file registration documents only once, pay only one filing fee, and submit only one income tax return annually (provided that each series member is also a founding member). The Series LLC is not dissimilar in structure to a corporation with a number of subsidiaries.

2. RESTRICTIONS ON THE TRANSFER OF SHARES

(a) Statutory and Contractual Provisions

The major provisions concerning restrictions on the transfer of shares are found in CBCA ss. 6(1)(d), 49(8) and (9) and OBCA ss. 5(1), 42 and 56(8) and (9).

Coates, "Share Transfer and Transmission Restrictions in the Close Corporation"
(1968), 3 U.B.C.L. Rev. 96 at pp. 98–104 (footnotes omitted)

Why Restrictive Provisions Are Needed

Share transfer and transmission restrictions are needed for many reasons, some of the main ones being: (i) to prevent intrusion of undesirable business associations; (ii) to preserve the relative interests of the owners; (iii) to resolve deadlock (or as a control device); (iv) to comply with the definition of private company in legislation; (v) to anticipate and prevent unnecessary conflict; (vi) to ensure continuity of the business; (vii) to provide a market at an acceptable price for the shares. The emphasis to be placed on any one of the above reasons will of course depend on the specific corporation.

In a public company or a private company other than a close corporation the transfer of shares in the company will normally have no effect on the operation or management of the business. In a close corporation, however, a transfer of shares may result in financial loss to the shareholders and to the company. If the new shareholder wishes to participate actively in the business it is often found that his personality, business skills, honesty, and energy do not correspond to those of the retiring shareholder and are not compatible with those of the remaining shareholders. Participants in a partnership or close corporation often associate originally because of their complementing skills and talents. If the new shareholder wishes merely to invest and not work in the business, friction will almost inevitably arise as to the mode and amount of distribution of income. In a close corporation profits are normally distributed by means of salaries. The active shareholders would normally be unwilling to pay an inactive shareholder a salary. Also, they would feel that they were entitled to take up the amount of the salary formerly paid to the shareholder who has just left because they have probably assumed most of his responsibilities and work. The problems become more acute if the new shareholder has purchased a controlling interest.

It is undesirable that the proportionate shareholders be altered except by unanimous consent. When the enterprise is initiated the owners agree on the control and profit division and it is usually desirable that this initial arrangement is not altered. This could be done by one shareholder buying all or a part of the holdings of another. This problem is especially serious in the United States where stock redemption plans (i.e., the corporation purchases the stock from the retiring shareholder) are used. For example, if A holds forty per cent (40%), B thirty per cent (30%) and C thirty per cent (30%), and B's stock is redeemed, A would then have complete control.

The use of share transfer restrictions as control devices and as a means of resolving deadlocks is a very important but often forgotten reason for the use of comprehensive transfer restrictions. Transfer restrictions are considered to be the basis of an effective control system. Variations of the buy-out agreement such as a "Russian Roulette" arrangement is an example of this. One shareholder should not be able to threaten to sell his shares to an undesirable person or to a competitor in order to force his will on other members. Since corporate assets are often not capable of being divided up and have little liquidation value, dissolution may not be the most desirable method of resolving deadlock . . .

[Certain statutes] require that the right to transfer shares be restricted as a condition of being a private company, however, there is no minimum restriction specified which will satisfy the requirements of the Acts. For example, would a stipulation that shares could not be transferred to anyone with blue eyes be sufficient and satisfactory? Most of the restrictions which are adopted in the articles are a simple consent restriction.

Often the only potential purchasers for shares in a close corporation are the other shareholders and so in the absence of a binding buy-out agreement, stipulating a valuation price or formula, the selling shareholder is at the mercy of the remaining ones. Transfer restrictions in the form of buy-out agreements provide a market in the event of certain contingencies. Closely related to the problem of marketability of shares is the necessity of the minority preventing squeeze-outs by the majority, a situation which is becoming more frequent.

Transfer restrictions may even be desirable on preferred shares and on shareholders' loans or debentures, depending on the various rights attached such as voting, dividends or interest. In a joint venture corporation involving equal shareholders, a transfer restriction is essential because the purchaser of either party's fifty per cent (50%) obtains an automatic veto over the entire affairs of the corporation.

Comprehensive and sophisticated transfer and transmission restrictions are a necessity in a close corporation.

Nature of the Restriction and Some Preliminary Considerations

There are some things of importance which should be noted generally now even though they are discussed in more detail later in the paper. First, it is generally recognized that there is a difference between a transfer and transmission. A transfer is a voluntary change of ownership of the shares, *e.g.*, a normal sale. A transmission is a non-voluntary change of ownership by operation of law. A transfer or transmission restriction could be defined as any condition or limitation which qualifies the right of a shareholder or anyone acting through or on behalf of him to alienate his interest in a corporation. There is no limit as to the variety of restrictions which may be employed, and the events upon which they may be contingent. The rationale of restrictive provisions was succinctly stated by Mr. Justice Holmes in the case of *Barret v. King*.

> Stock in a corporation is not merely property. It also creates a personal relation analogous otherwise than technically to a partnership. [Hence] . . . there seems no greater objection to retaining the right of choosing one's associates in a corporation than in a firm.

The basic drafting problem is to anticipate all possible contingencies, not just the normal ones. The basic legal problem is whether by careful drafting one can block all transfers and transmissions.

Planning and preparing share transfer and transmission restrictions involves many general considerations such as the legality of the proposed restrictions, under what law the legality is determined, the efficacy of the restrictions in achieving the desired results, the instruments in which the restrictions should be placed, tax considerations, and the specific needs of each corporation and each shareholder. Examples of the latter are the number of shareholders, whether all of them participate in the affairs of the company, health, estate, and family of each of the shareholders, the kind of business they are involved in, the value of the business and its annual income. When preparing that part of the corporate paper which involves transfer restrictions, the lawyer must keep all these considerations in mind and not be enticed into accepting a standard form buy-sell or combined buy-sell and first option agreement which may be offered by the client's insurance advisor or a precedent text. It is an area where he must be imaginative and flexible.

Types of Restrictions, Their Advantages, Disadvantages and Validity

Variations of the main types of restrictions are almost infinite, but the main types utilized are: absolute prohibitions on share transfer limited in time, consent restraints requiring up to one hundred per cent (100%) approval of the directors or the shareholders; a first option provision or some variation such as a Russian Roulette arrangement; special time or event buy-out arrangements or options; and the buy-sell agreement contingent on death. There are many contingencies upon which a transfer or transmission restriction may be operative, and so the specific provision must be chosen carefully.

Absolute restrictions. In certain enterprises an absolute prohibition on share transfer unlimited in time would be the most advantageous but this has always been held invalid. However, it would seem that an absolute restraint limited in time may be valid but the time limit must be reasonable and necessary in the circumstances. Five years would probably be the longest period available regardless of the circumstances. Such a restriction may be necessary to ensure that certain skills or assets are guaranteed during the formative stages. Again, the joint venture corporation would be the most likely and frequent user of the absolute restriction. In any event an absolute restraint can be virtually ensured indirectly. A shareholders' agreement may provide that each party provide certain assets for a specific period of time, or the capital structure may be devised with a minimum amount in share capital and a maximum number of dollars in the form of a loan or debentures which are not repayable for a specified number of years. In either case a shareholder would be reluctant to sell his shares and leave all his original investment tied up in a business in which he is not a member and over which he has no control. An effectively drafted consent restriction will achieve almost the same result.

Consent restrictions. In practice, the consent restriction is adopted almost universally, probably because it appears in the Table A articles [a standard form set of articles appended to legislation in memorandum jurisdictions]. The mechanics of it are that no transfer is valid or effective until it has been approved by the directors, or the shareholders, or both, or a certain proportion of either or both. The main advantage of it is that the remaining shareholders can prevent the sale of shares to an undesirable outsider without tying up their own capital to purchase such shares. But this advantage would seem to be more than outweighed by the disadvantage that anyone wishing to sell is virtually at the mercy of the remaining shareholders and is very vulnerable to a "squeeze-out". The parties having the right of refusal do not have to give reasons for their refusal to transfer, the only requirement being that the refusal must be *bona fide* in the best interests of the company. The court will assume that the directors have acted *bona fide* even when reasons are not given. The directors do not have to give reasons and an examination for discovery to determine the reasons or grounds will be refused. Occasionally the court will infer *mala fides* from the circumstances or from the refusal to give reasons. If reasons are given, however, they can be examined by the court and declared wrong. Consent may be inferred from an entry in the share register and where the restriction is such that the directors have a power to refuse a transfer, inability to exercise this power of refusal due to deadlock will entitle the transferee to demand registration of the transfer. As is obvious, the consent restriction has always been accepted as valid in Canadian and English jurisdictions and has been held to bind an executor, a sheriff seizing under a writ of execution, and a trustee in bankruptcy.

First option restrictions. This is probably the best and most equitable *inter vivos* restriction. The mechanics of it are that any shareholder desiring to sell his shares must offer them to the other shareholders by a specified procedure and at a specified price before he can sell them to an outsider. There is no express or implied covenant that the remaining shareholders will purchase the shares so offered and no obligation to do so. Preciseness in drafting such a restriction is particularly vital. It must be stated whether the whole block has to be taken and if not what procedure of allocation is to be adopted. It also must be stated whether the restriction applies to transfers to both shareholders and outsiders obviously it must be in most cases. The first option overcomes the main disadvantage of the consent restriction in that it balances the relative positions of the buying and selling shareholders since the seller is no longer at the mercy of the remaining shareholders. But this may not solve his problems in that there may be no outside market for the shares, a situation which is not abnormal when dealing with a close corporation, especially if his interest is a minority one. The disadvantage to the remaining shareholders is that they have to produce the necessary cash to purchase the shares within, normally, ninety days. If they do not have the funds available they may find themselves forced to accept as a fellow shareholder an undesirable outsider. Again, this is even more crucial if the interest being sold is a majority one. This could be overcome to a certain extent by providing that the purchase price is to be paid off in either fixed annual installments or as a percentage of gross or net profit. There are many useful variations of the normal first option provision such as the Russian Roulette arrangement or the similar restricted auction. The mechanics of the Russian Roulette arrangement are as follows: X offers to buy Y's shares for a certain price. Y then has the choice of accepting the offer or buying X's shares at the same price. The restricted auction eliminates some of the risk inherent in such a plan by providing that all the shares shall be sold at an auction with the present shareholders being the only allowable bidders. The advantage of both of these schemes is that they have a built in valuation mechanism eliminating one of the most difficult problems.

Event options. These are actually only an extension of the first option arrangement. They merely provide that at a special time or on the happening of a special event one party shall offer his shares to the other by a certain procedure and at a specified price. The following are examples of the special times or events which may trigger such an option: if one corporation isn't able to provide essential services, if one shareholder does not contribute a specified minimum amount of capital within a certain time period, bankruptcy, seizure of shares by writ of execution, termination of employment and retirement.

Buy-out arrangements. These provisions are usually made contingent on the same events as the ones listed above. The fact that there is a binding obligation on the remaining shareholders to purchase may make them more appropriate in certain circumstances such as retirement from employment or from the board of directors. There is a problem which will be discussed later of whether such provisions can bind a trustee in bankruptcy, a sheriff acting under a writ of execution, and any person taking from either of them. It is often desirable in connection with such provisions to provide for some kind of funding, possibly by arrangements that the price be paid off in installments.

Buy-sell agreement. This is an agreement between all shareholders which provides that on the death of a shareholder his executors are obligated to sell his shares to the remaining shareholders at a specified price and the remaining shareholders are likewise obligated to purchase such shares when offered. There appears to be no question as to the validity of such an agreement, it being accepted that such is not a testamentary disposition and that each shareholder has an insurable interest in the life of the others. The advantages of such an agreement are obvious — ready cash is provided to the estate for estate taxes, succession duties, and normal living expenses, and, as suggested earlier, it being essential in a close corporation that the membership be selected and restricted, this agreement ensures continuity of the business and harmony among the shareholders. The arrangement may become unwieldy, however, if there are more than four shareholders or if there are significant differences in age, health and financial resources of the shareholders. It is essential that the buy-sell agreement be funded with life insurance.

(b)   Judicial Interpretation of Restrictions

Smith & Fawcett Ltd., Re
[1942] 1 All E.R. 542, [1942] 1 Ch. 304 (C.A.)

[The articles of association of Smith & Fawcett Ltd. provided that "the directors may at any time in their absolute and uncontrolled discretion refuse to register any transfer of shares." The appellant, as executor of his father, claimed to be registered in respect of 4,001 shares. The directors refused to register a transfer unless he was willing to sell 2,000 of the shares to a named director at a certain price, in which case they would register a transfer of the remainder.]

LORD GREENE M.R.: The principles to be applied in cases where the articles of association of a company confer a discretion on directors with regard to the acceptance of transfers of shares are, for the present purposes, free from doubt. They must exercise their discretion *bona fide* in what they consider — not what a court may consider — to be in the interests of the company, and not for any collateral purpose. They must have regard to those considerations, and those considerations only, which the articles upon their true construction permit them to take into consideration. In construing the relevant provisions in the articles, it is to be borne in mind that one of the normal rights of a shareholder is the right to deal freely with his property and to transfer it to whomsoever he pleases. When it is said, as it has been said more than once, that regard must be had to this last consideration, it means, I apprehend, nothing more than this: that the shareholder has such a *prima facie* right, and that right is not to be cut down by uncertain language or doubtful implications. The right, if it is to be cut down, must be cut down with satisfactory clarity. It certainly does not mean that articles, if appropriately framed, cannot be allowed to cut down the right of transfer to any extent which the articles on their true construction permit.

There is also another consideration which I think is worth bearing in mind when one comes to examine the construction of any article that falls for consideration, and that is that this type of article is one which is for the most part confined to private companies. Private companies are, of course, separate entities in law just as much as are public companies, but from the business and personal point of view they are much more analogous to partnerships than to public corporations. Accordingly, it is to be expected that, in the articles of such a company, the control of the directors over the membership may be very strict indeed. There are very good business reasons, or there may be very good business reasons, why those who bring such companies into existence should give them a constitution which gives to the directors powers of the widest description.

In the present case the article is as follows:

> The directors may at any time in their absolute and uncontrolled discretion refuse to register any transfer of shares.

As I have said, it is beyond question that that is a fiduciary power, and the directors must exercise it *bona fide* in what they consider to be the interests of the company. The language of the article does not point to any particular matter as being the only matter to which the directors are to pay attention in deciding whether or not they will allow the transfer to be registered. The article does not, for instance, say, as is to be found in some articles, that they may refuse to register any transfer of shares to a person not already a member of the company, nor does it say that they may refuse to register any transfer of shares to a transferee of whom they do not approve. In cases where articles are framed with some such limitation on the discretionary power of refusal as I have mentioned in the two examples which I have given, it follows on plain principle that, if they go outside the matters which the articles say are to be the only matters to which they are to have regard, the directors will have exceeded their powers.

Counsel for the appellant maintained that, whatever language was used in the articles, the power of the directors to refuse to register a transfer must always be limited to matters personal to the transferee, and he points out that in the present case there can be no personal objection to his client becoming a member of the company, for the simple reason that the directors are prepared to accept him as the holder of 2,000 of the shares which have come to him as legal personal representative of his father. Counsel therefore says that there is no personal objection to the transferee here, and that is the only matter which directors are entitled to take into account. He relies for that proposition upon observations in several authorities where that is laid down, but on examination of those authorities it becomes quite clear that the judges who delivered the judgments in them were dealing with the particular form of article which happened to be before them, and the form of article was one which by its express language confined the directors to the consideration of the desirability of admitting the proposed transferee to membership on grounds personal to him.

I cannot put the point, which I am endeavouring to make, with greater clearness than it is put by Warrington L.J., in *Re Bede Steam Shipping Co.* In that case the articles empowered the directors:

> . . . in their discretion and without assigning any reasons therefor [to] refuse to register the transfer of any shares (not being a fully paid up share) to any person of whom they do not approve as transferee and may decline to register the transfer of any fully paid up share or shares on certifying that in their opinion it is contrary to the interests of the company that the proposed transferee should be a member thereof.

That was the precise limitation on the directors' power to refuse the transfer which was in issue in that case. Warrington L.J., says this at p. 136:

> The article gives them one ground, and one ground only, for refusing to register the transfer of a fully-paid share, namely, that in their opinion it is contrary to the interests of the company that the proposed transferee should be a member.

It is perfectly clear from that observation that the court was not laying down some general rule to be applied to all forms of article, but was coming to a decision upon the particular article before it, the nature of which was such as to confine the directors to the consideration of one particular matter.

There is nothing, in my opinion, in principle or in authority to make it impossible to draft such a wide and comprehensive power to directors to refuse to transfer as to enable them to take into account any matter which they conceive to be in the interests of the company, and thereby to admit or not to admit a particular person and to allow or not to allow a particular transfer for reasons not personal to the transferee but bearing on the general interests of the company as a whole — such matters, for instance, as whether by passing a particular transfer the transferee would obtain too great a weight in the affairs of the company or might even perhaps obtain control. The question, therefore, is simply whether, on the true construction of the particular article, the directors are limited by anything except their *bona fide* view as to the interests of the company. In the present case the article is drafted in the widest possible terms, and I decline to write into that clear language any limitation other than a limitation, which is implicit by law, that a fiduciary power of this kind must be exercised *bona fide* in the interests of the company. Subject to that qualification, an article in this form appears to me to give the directors what it says, namely, an absolute and uncontrolled discretion.

That being my view on the question of law in this case, it only remains to consider the issue of fact which has been raised. It is said that on the evidence before us we ought to infer that the directors here were purporting to exercise their power to refuse a transfer, not *bona fide* in the interests of the company, but for some collateral purpose-namely, the desire of the leading director to acquire part of the shares for himself at an under-value. Speaking for myself, I strongly dislike being asked on affidavit evidence alone to draw inferences as to the *bona fides* or *mala fides* of the actors. In the present case the principal director has sworn an affidavit which, if accepted, makes it clear that, whether rightly or wrongly, the directors have *bona fide* considered the interests of the company and come to the conclusion that it would be undesirable to register the transfer of the totality of these shares.

We are invited to say that that does not represent the fact and that the real motive which influenced the deponent was not a consideration for the interests of the company but a consideration for his own personal interests. I for one, except in a clear case, am strongly opposed to drawing an inference of that kind from mere affidavit evidence. If it is desired to charge a deponent with having given an account of his motives and his reasons which is not the true account, then the person on whom the burden of proof lies should, in my judgment, take the ordinary and obvious course of requiring the deponent to submit himself to cross-examination. That does not, of course, mean that it is illegitimate to draw such inferences in a proper case. There may be on the face of the affidavit sufficient justification for doing so, but where you have the oath of the deponent, as we have it here, and the only grounds on which the court is asked to disbelieve it are matters of inference, many of them of a doubtful character, I for one must decline to give to those suggestions the weight which it is desired to give to them.

Accordingly, on the evidence I am satisfied, as the judge was satisfied, that there is no ground shown here for saying that the directors' refusal has been due to anything but a *bona fide* consideration of the interests of the company as the directors see them. That being so, and that being on the true construction of the article the only matter to which the directors have to pay regard, I am of opinion that the judge was perfectly right in the conclusion to which he came, and that this appeal fails and must be dismissed with costs.

Luxmoore L.J.: I agree.

Asquith J.: I agree.

Appeal dismissed.

Note

Smith & Fawcett Ltd., Re remains one of the leading cases on the scope of directors' discretion. For other cases, see *Lyle Scott Ltd. v. Scott's Trustees & British Invt. Trust Ltd.*, [1959] A.C. 763, [1959] 2 All E.R. 661 (H.L.); *Re Shoal Harbour Marine Service Ltd.* (1956), 19 W.W.R. (N.S.) 670, (1956), 20 W.W.R. (N.S.) 312, 448 (B.C. S.C.); *Charles Forte Invt. Ltd. v. Amanda*, [1963] 2 All E.R. 940 (C.A.); and *Re Swaledale Cleaners, Ltd.*, [1968] 3 All E.R. 619, [1968] 1 W.L.R. 1710 (C.A.).

Case v. Edmonton Country Club Ltd.
1974 CarswellAlta 67, 1974 CarswellAlta 187, [1975] 1 S.C.R. 534
(S.C.C.)

[The appellant company was incorporated under the Alberta *Companies Act* in 1945. In 1963 the articles of association were altered to impose a minimum annual fee and to give a right of forfeiture or forced sale of shares in the event of default. In 1969 further changes in the articles of association were approved by which the owner of a common or preferred share of the company was required to pay to the company an "annual minimum fee to be established by the Directors" unless he or his nominee exercised playing privileges and paid the playing fee, failing which his common and preferred shares became subject to a lien or charge in favour of the company enforceable by sale of the shares. Also in that year article 17 was altered to permit the directors to set the amount of a transfer fee for the registration of share transfers. In 1970 a special resolution was passed stipulating that "each shareholder, whether playing or non-playing, shall be required to pay the annual club fees as levied by the Board for the then current year."

A challenge to the validity of the 1963, 1969 and 1970 resolutions was brought by the respondent, who in 1966 inherited one common and one preferred share of the company from his father. The trial judge found that the resolutions were *ultra vires* the company and void *ab initio*. He also found that article 20A, which gave the directors the right to refuse to register any transfer of shares, was *intra vires* and valid. An appeal and cross-appeal were dismissed by the Appellate Division of the Supreme Court of Alberta. With leave, the company then appealed to the Supreme Court of Canada and the shareholder cross-appealed. The Supreme

Court of Canada dismissed the appeal and the cross-appeal. On the major issue relating to the levying of an annual fee, the Supreme Court held the resolutions *ultra vires* because they offended the basic principle of limited liability, namely, that a shareholder who has paid for his shares is thereafter free from further pecuniary obligations with respect to those shares. The Supreme Court split on the issue relating to article 20A with Dickson J. speaking for the majority upholding the validity of the provision and Laskin J. for the minority denying the validity of the provision. The excerpts from the judgment deal with this issue.]

DICKSON J.: . . . The other aspect of the transferability problem concerns the validity of art. 20A of the articles of association. This provision appeared in the articles as originally drafted and has remained unaltered:

> 20A. No shares in the Company whether or not paid up shall be transferred to any person without the consent of a majority of the Directors, who may refuse such consent whether such shares are or are not paid up, in their unfettered discretion.

The effect is to vest in the directors a power, exercisable without stated criteria, to restrict or even veto the transfer of a fully paid share of the company. The question which must be answered is whether a company incorporated under *The Companies Act* of Alberta can give its directors such a power. The trial judge and the Court of Appeal answered this question in the affirmative and Mr. Case has cross-appealed.

A private company must, by its memorandum or articles, restrict or prohibit the right to transfer any of its shares, and a public company, other than one whose shares are listed for trading on a stock exchange, may include in its articles restrictions on the right of transfer. In *Canada National Fire Insurance Co. v. Hutchings*, the Privy Council held that a company incorporated by letters patent under the *Companies Act*, R.S.C. 1906, c. 79, could not validly make a by-law giving the directors an unrestricted power to disapprove transfers but Sir Walter Phillimore said in the course of the judgment, p. 456:

> There is . . . for the present purpose no analogy between companies in the United Kingdom which are formed by contract, whether it be under deed of settlement or under memorandum and articles of association to which the Registrar of Joint-Stock Companies necessarily assents if the documents are regular in form, and Canadian companies which are formed under the Canadian *Companies Act*, either by letters patent or by special Act.

and at p. 459, referring to the power of veto given the directors, he said:

> There are decided cases in the English Courts which show that such a power may be lawfully reserved on the occasion of the constitution

of the company, and a sufficient number of such cases to show that the power has been found convenient in use.

Re Gresham Life Assur. Society; Ex p. Penney; Re Bell Bros, Ltd.; Ex p. Hodgson; Re Coalport China Company; and *Re Smith and Fawcett, Limited* might be cited as examples.

The right of a shareholder to transfer his shares is undoubtedly one of the incidents of share ownership, assured by *The Companies Act* of Alberta, s. 61, "The shares or other interest of any member in a company are personal estate, transferable in the manner provided by the articles of the company . . .", as it is by the *Companies Act*, 1948 (U.K.), s. 73, but the right is not absolute. We find in 6 Halsbury, 3rd ed., p. 252, the statement:

> A restriction on the right to transfer shares is not repugnant to absolute ownership of the shares, but is one of the original incidents of the shares attached to them by the contract contained in the articles.

and:

> There is apparently no limit to the restriction on transfer which may be so imposed . . .

The same thought is expressed, more positively, in Palmer's *Company Law*, 21st ed., p. 340:

> It is common for articles to provide that the directors shall have the power of declining to register a transfer without assigning any reason therefor; or in their absolute and uncontrolled discretion; or in some equally sweeping terms . . .

and in Gower's *Modern Company Law*, 3rd ed., p. 392:

> These restrictions may take any form, but in practice they normally either give the existing members a right of pre-emption or first refusal, or confer a discretion on the directors to refuse to pass transfers.

This footnote follows:

> The latter restriction is commonly found in conjunction with the former. In the U.S.A. it is generally held that restrictions, being restraints on the alienability of personal property, must be reasonable. In England it is clear that there is no such rule except, perhaps, when the restrictions are imposed after the shares have been issued.

I have concluded that art. 20A is not *ultra vires* the company and that the cross-appeal must fail. The power to refuse to consent to a transfer of shares was reserved to the directors upon incorporation of the company, by the contract contained in the articles, and is not something now sought to be imposed upon unwilling shareholders. Before we move to strike down such a power on the ground that it is unreasonable, we should, in my view, have some factual support for that conclusion. There is no evidence before us, nor is it alleged, that the directors have at any time in the almost 30-year history of the company acted in bad faith or arbitrarily or otherwise abused the power.

I would accordingly dismiss the appeal with costs and dismiss the cross-appeal without costs.

The judgment of Spence and Laskin JJ. was delivered by

LASKIN J.(*dissenting in part*): I am in agreement with my brother Dickson that the appeal fails for the reasons that he has given. The cross-appeal respecting the validity of art. 20A of the articles of association gives me more pause, but, on balance, I am of the opinion that the article should be struck out.

My brother Dickson has fairly assessed it as vesting in the directors "a power exercisable, without stated criteria, to restrict or even veto the transfer of a fully paid share of the company". The difference between us is whether this arbitrary power, not related to any standard for the exercise of an unfettered discretion, should be controlled only in the context of a particular case requiring its exercise (as he would have it), or whether it should be struck out simply because it is on its face utterly arbitrary (as I would have it).

The considerations which move me to strike it out are easily stated. What the company has in effect done is to turn itself into a private club, despite the fact of its incorporation as a public company. I am not persuaded that persons, knowing of the arbitrary power of the directors to control shareholdings, would, or should be expected to submit themselves to whatever obloquy may be involved in the possible rejection of their application for a transfer of shares. If the company is unwilling to establish criteria upon which to enable a measure of reasonable exercise of discretion to be considered in advance, it ought not to be permitted to have the cover of incorporation as a public company.

The relevant *Companies Act* of Alberta, R.S.A. 1942, c. 240, does not confer any express power upon a public company to restrict the transfer of fully paid shares. Any such power must be drawn inferentially from s. 65 which provides that "the shares . . . of any member in a company shall be personal estate, transferable in the manner provided by the articles of the company . . .". In so far as this may be thought to confer some authority to restrict transfer, I would read it, as I would read a similar power in a municipal Act or in legislation establishing a statutory agency, as requiring some standard which would be amenable to judicial control, if need be. The standard articles of association set out in Table A of the First Schedule of the Act include s. 17 which provides that "the directors may decline to register any transfer of shares, not being fully paid shares, to a person of whom they do not approve, and may also decline to register any transfer of shares on which the Company has a lien". This is hardly a telling provision one way or another, but, so far as it is indicative of policy, it militates against a conclusion that an absolute restriction of the transfer of fully paid shares may be introduced into the articles of association of a public company. Restrictions on transfer are, of course, part of the very being of a private company, as is evident from s. 2(z) of the Act.

It is said, however, and certainly there is case law to support this view, that in memorandum and articles of association companies, albeit incorporated as public companies, the contractual aspect of the memorandum and articles supports the power to include drastic restrictions on transfer. This has been also referred to as part of the general law governing such companies.

There are two comments that I would make on this submission. The first is that, although originating in contract, shares in a public company are a species of property and as such are entitled to the advantage of alienability free from unreasonable restrictions unless there is statutory warrant otherwise. The second comment concerns the so-called contractual aspect of memorandum of association companies. The memorandum of association is but a method of incorporation, under which its contractual aspect is submerged in a statutory regime subjecting the company to public regulation. I cannot, in such circumstances, and in the absence of express power in the memorandum, subscribe to the proposition that there is a contractual warrant for adopting an article of association which confers an unlimited discretion to refuse a transfer of shares.

My brother Dickson has referred to the judgment of the Judicial Committee in *Canada National Fire Insurance Co. v. Hutchings*, where a distinction was drawn, in respect of the matter under consideration, between a letters patent company or one incorporated under a special Act and a memorandum of association company. I cannot be persuaded that the form of incorporation can have such a remarkable effect upon the permissible scope of a power to regulate or prescribe conditions for the transfer of stock in a public company.

I am not concerned here to examine how far restrictions on transfer may go in a public company before courting invalidity. In *Ontario Jockey Club Ltd. v. McBride*, the Judicial Committee, dealing with a letters patent company, said that it is permissible to give a right of pre-emption but that "a restriction which precludes a shareholder altogether from transferring may be invalid" (at p. 923). I would not be so equivocal and, certainly, the Judicial Committee was not equivocal on this very point in the *Hutchings* case.

The pre-emption or first option type of restriction is a common one in the United States and it has generally been held valid. But the position there is otherwise in respect of restrictions of the kind found in art, 20A, particularly where there is no limitation of time on the restriction. The law in the United States appears to have sought reconciliation of the contractual and property aspects of shares, so far as restrictions on transfers are concerned, by applying a test of reasonableness. *Ballantine on Corporations*, rev. ed., 1946, at p. 778, states the position as follows:

> It has been held in numerous cases that restrictions which prohibit transfers except upon the approval and consent of the directors or other shareholders are invalid as contrary to public policy and as imposing undue restraints upon the alienation of property. But a requirement of consent by directors or shareholders has sometimes been upheld, especially when imposed by charter or by an agreement of the shareholders of a closed corporation.

I should note that the closed corporation is similar to the private company in Canadian law: see Gower: "Some Contrasts Between British and American Corporation Law" (1955), 69 Harv. L. Rev. 1369, at pp. 1375-6. Oleck, *Modern Corporation Law*, vol. 3, 1959, deals with the same point in a more modified way than Ballantine in two passages at pp. 286 and 300 respectively, as follows:

> Take a restriction, not uncommon, which declares that a shareholder shall not transfer his shares unless he first obtains the consent of the directors, or of the shareholders, or of a certain proportion of the directors or the shareholders. Generally speaking, this type of restriction is considered an unreasonable one and is thought to contravene public policy, and it is held, on this ground, that a mere by-law restriction of this character is "void" and unenforceable. On the other hand, a restriction of this kind inserted in the original articles of incorporation has been sustained in two cases.
>
> A less common restraint is the "consent" restriction, whereunder the consent of the board of directors or of the remaining shareholders is a prerequisite to the transfer of the stock. While these restrictions have been upheld they operate virtually to bar the alienation of the shares and are more likely to be considered unreasonable and therefore void.

A test of reasonableness commends itself to me, especially in view of the emphasis on the property aspect of shares indicated by s. 65 of the Alberta *Companies Act* already referred to. On this view, it is my opinion that art. 20A is bad. I am reinforced in this view by the fact that it would *ex facie* preclude even involuntary transfers, although it appears in the present case that the plaintiff who acquired the shares under his father's will did get the approval of the directors for their effective transfer to him.

I would, accordingly, allow the cross-appeal with costs.

Appeal dismissed.

Note

For some cases dealing with questions arising from restrictions on the transfer of shares, see *Assoc. Finance Co. Ltd. v. Webber and Dixon,*

[1972] 4 W.W.R. 131, 28 D.L.R. (3d) 673 (B.C. S.C.); *Nadeau v. Nadeau and Nadeau Ltd.* (1973), 6 N.B.R. (2d) 512 (N.B. S.C.); *Harvey v. Harvey*, [1979] 2 W.W.R. 661 (B.C. C.A.); and *Carter v. Roy M. Lawson Ltd.* (1982), 36 N.B.R. (2d) 353, 129 D.L.R. (3d) 214 (Q.B.).

3. SHAREHOLDERS' AGREEMENTS

(a) Introductory Note

One of the most important rights of a shareholder is the right to vote. Just as important can be the right to join with other shareholders to combine voting rights. Such combinations can be effected by separate agreements which may also contain many other provisions, for example, a right of first refusal or other restriction on the transfer of shares. These agreements are usually found in closely held companies reflecting a partnership approach to the corporation, but they can also be useful for those large corporations that have one or two dominant shareholders who wish to combine their voting power in some way. As will be discussed below, this objective can be achieved by a variety of means: voting agreements, voting trusts or, pursuant to the CBCA or OBCA, by a unanimous shareholder agreement.

At common law, agreements among shareholders as to the manner in which they will vote their shares are lawful (*Ringuet v. Bergeron*, [1960] S.C.R. 672, 24 D.L.R. (2d) 449; *Greenwell v. Porter*, [1902] 1 Ch. 530). See, generally, Pickering, "Shareholders' Voting Rights and Company Control" (1965), 81 L.Q.R. 248.

CBCA s. 145.1 and OBCA s. 108(1) provide that agreements among two or more shareholders as to how shares shall be voted are permitted.

However, this rule is generally stated as subject to the qualification that the agreements must be for a lawful purpose (*Motherwell v. Schoof*, [1949] 2 W.W.R. 529, [1949] 4 D.L.R. 812 (Alta. S.C.)). This is an important qualification where the agreement purports to bind the shareholders *qua* directors since such an agreement is unlawful as an invalid attempt to fetter the exercise of the directors' discretion. There is authority that this limitation applies even to unanimous shareholder agreements (*Atlas Dev. Co. Ltd. v. Calof and Gold* (1963), 41 W.W.R. 575 (Man. Q.B.) and *Alder v. Dobie* (1999), [1999] B.C.J. No. 808, 1999 CarswellBC 758 (S.C.)). Another potential qualification on shareholders' agreements may be created by the recent decision in *Bhasin v. Hrynew*, 2014 CarswellAlta 2046, 2014 SCC 71 (S.C.C.). The Supreme Court of Canada's emphasis on the duty of good faith in contractual relations may further affect how courts interpret provisions in shareholders' agreements.

(b) Voting Agreements

Clark v. Dodge
269 N.Y. 410; 199 N.E. 641 (1936) (citations omitted)

CROUCH J.: The action is for the specific performance of a contract between the plaintiff Clark and the defendant Dodge, relating to the affairs of the two defendant corporations. To the complaint a joint answer by the three defendants was interposed, consisting of denials and a separate defense and counterclaim. To the separate defense and counterclaim a reply was made. The defendant then moved under rule 112 of the Rules of Civil Practice, and under sections 476, 96 and 279 of the *Civil Practice Act*, to dismiss the complaint. The motion was made "on the pleadings in this action and the admissions of the plaintiff" in two affidavits submitted by him on a prior motion in the action. The alleged admissions are equivocal at best, and clearly were not "intended to be treated as a part of a pleading or made to avoid some question arising on the pleadings." . . .

We shall deal, therefore, with the questions here presented in the light of the facts most favorable to plaintiff appearing in the pleadings only.

Those facts, briefly stated, are as follows: The two corporate defendants are New Jersey corporations manufacturing medicinal preparations by secret formulae. The main office, factory and assets of both corporations are located in the State of New York. In 1921, and at all times since, Clark owned twenty-five per cent and Dodge seventy-five per cent of the stock of each Corporation. Dodge took no active part in the business, although he was a director and, through ownership of their qualifying shares, controlled the other directors of both corporations. He was the president of Bell & Company, Inc., and nominally general manager of Hollings-Smith Company, Inc. The Plaintiff Clark was a director and held the offices of treasurer and general manager of Bell & Company, Inc., and also had charge of the major portion of the business of Hollings-Smith Company, Inc. The formulae and methods of manufacture of the medicinal preparations were known to him alone. Under date of February 15, 1921, Dodge and Clark, the sole owners of the stock of both corporations, entered into a written agreement under seal, which after reciting the stock ownership of both parties, the desire of Dodge that Clark should continue in the efficient management and control of the business of Bell & Company, Inc., so long as he should "remain faithful, efficient and competent to so manage and control the said business;" and his further desire that Clark should not be the sole custodian of a specified formula but should share his knowledge thereof and of the method of manufacture with a son of Dodge, provided, in substance, as follows: That Dodge during his lifetime and, after his death, a trustee to be appointed by his will, would so vote his stock and so vote as a director that the plaintiff (a) should continue to be a director of Bell & Company, Inc. and (b) should continue as its general manager so long as he should be "faithful, efficient and competent;" (c) should during his life receive one-fourth of the net income of the corporations either by way of salary or dividends; and (d) that no unreasonable or incommensurate salaries should be paid to other officers or agents which would so reduce the net income as materially to affect Clark's profits. Clark on his part agreed to disclose the specified formula to the son and to instruct him in the details and methods of manufacture; and further, at the end of his life to bequeath his stock-if no issue survived him to the wife and children of Dodge.

It was further provided that the provisions in regard to the division of net profits and the regulation of salaries should also apply to the Hollings-Smith Company.

The complaint alleges due performance of the contract by Clark and breach thereof by Dodge in that he has failed to use his stock control to continue Clark as a director and as general manager, and has prevented Clark from receiving his proportion of the income, while taking his own, by causing the employment of incompetent persons at excessive salaries, and otherwise.

The relief sought is reinstatement as director and general manager and an accounting by Dodge and by the corporations for waste and for the proportion of net income due plaintiff, with an injunction against further violations.

The only question which need be discussed is whether the contract is illegal as against public policy within the decision in *McQuade v. Stoneham* (263 N.Y. 323), upon the authority of which the complaint was dismissed by the Appellate Division.

"The business of a corporation shall be managed by its board of directors" (General Corporation Law [Cons. Laws, Ch. 23], 27). That is the statutory norm. Are we committed by the *McQuade* case to the doctrine that there may be no variation, however slight or innocuous, from that norm, where salaries or policies or the retention of individuals in office are concerned? There is ample authority supporting that doctrine . . . and something may be said for it, since it furnishes a simple, if arbitrary, test. Apart from its practical administrative convenience, the reasons upon which it is said to rest are more or less nebulous. Public policy, the intention of the Legislature, detriment to the corporation, are phrases which in this connection mean little. Possible harm to *bona fide* purchasers of stock or to creditors or to stockholding minorities have more substance; but such harms are absent in many instances. If the enforcement of a particular contract damages nobody-not even, in any perceptible degree, the public-one sees no reason for holding it illegal, even though it impinges slightly upon the broad provision of section 27. Damage suffered or threatened is a logical and practical-test, and has come to be the one generally adopted by the courts.

Where the directors are the sole stockholders, there seems to be no objection to enforcing an agreement among them to vote for certain people as officers. There is no direct decision to that effect in this court, yet there are strong indications that such a rule has long been recognized. The opinion in *Manson v. Curtis* closed its discussion by saying: "The rule that all the stockholders by their universal consent may do as they choose with the corporate concerns and assets, provided the interests of creditors are not affected, because they are the complete owners of the corporation, cannot be invoked here." That was because all the stockholders were not parties to the agreement there in question. So, where the public was not affected, "the parties in interest, might, by their original agreement of incorporation, limit their respective rights and powers," even where there was a conflicting statutory standard. (*Ripin v. U.S. Woven Label Co.*) Such corporations were little more than (though not quite the same as) chartered partnerships.

In *Lorillard v. Clyde* (86 N.Y. 384) and again in *Drucklieb v. Harris* (200 N.Y. 211), where the questioned agreements were entered into by all the stockholders of small corporations about to be organized, the fact that the agreements conflicted to some extent with the statutory duty of the directors to manage the corporate affairs was thought not to render the agreements illegal as against public policy, though it was said they might not be binding upon the directors of the corporation when organized. (*Cf.* Lehman J., dissenting opinion in the *McQuade* case.) The rule recognized in *Manson v. Curtis*, and quoted above, was thus stated by Blackmar J., in *Kassel v. Empire Tinware Co.*:

> As the parties to the action are the complete owners of the corporation, there is no reason why the exercise of the power and discretion of the directors cannot be controlled by valid agreement between themselves, provided that the interests of creditors are not affected.

Fells v. Katz, where all the stockholders were parties to the agreement, is no authority to the contrary. The decision there merely construed the agreement and found that plaintiff had breached it, thereby justifying his removal. "The agreement of the stockholders to continue a man in the directorate must be construed as an obligation to retain him only so long as he keeps the agreement on his part faithfully to act as a trustee for the stockholders". Indeed, the case may be regarded as applying the test of damage above referred to. Any other construction would have caused damage to the corporation and its stockholders and would have been illegal.

Except for the broad dicta in the *McQuade* opinion, we think there can be no doubt that the agreement here in question was legal and that the complaint states a cause of action. There was no attempt to sterilize the board of directors, as in the *Manson* and *McQuade* cases. The only restrictions on Dodge were (a) that as a stockholder he should vote for

Clark as a director — a perfectly legal contract; (b) that as director he should continue Clark as general manager, so long as he proved faithful, efficient and competent — an agreement which could harm nobody; (c) that Clark should always receive as salary or dividends one-fourth of the "net income." For the purposes of this motion, it is only just to construe that phrase as meaning whatever was left for distribution after the directors had in good faith set aside whatever they deemed wise; (d) that no salaries to other officers should be paid unreasonable in amount or incommensurate with services rendered — a beneficial and not a harmful agreement.

If there was any invasion of the powers of the directorate under that agreement, it is so slight as to be negligible; and certainly there is no damage suffered by or threatened to anybody. The broad statements in the *McQuade* opinion, applicable to the facts there, should be confined to those facts.

The judgment of the Appellate Division should be reserved and the order of the Special Term affirmed, with costs in this court and in the Appellate Division.

Crane C.J., Lehman, O'Brien, Hubbs, Loughran, and Finch JJ., concur.

Judgment accordingly.

Ringuet v. Bergeron
[1960] S.C.R. 672, 24 D.L.R. (2d) 449

Abbott and Ritchie JJ. concur with Judson J.
Taschereau J. concurs with Fauteux J. (dissenting)

JUDSON J.: The respondent sued the appellants for a declaration that against each of them, he was entitled to certain shares of the St. Maurice Knitting Mills Ltd. registered in their names. In the Superior Court the learned trial Judge dismissed the action. The Court of Queen's Bench (Appeal Side) [[1958] Que. Q.B. 222] allowed the appeal and maintained the action. The two unsuccessful shareholders now appeal to this Court.

The action was brought on an agreement dated August 3, 1949, between the respondent and the appellants. At that time these parties and four other persons each held 50 shares of the St. Maurice Knitting Mills Ltd., a company incorporated by letters patent under Part I of the Quebec *Companies Act*, R.S.Q. 1941, c. 276. These shares constituted all the issued capital stock of the company. The purpose of the agreement was to provide for the acquisition of 50 shares from one Frank Spain and the division of these shares among the parties. With these 50 shares divided among them the parties then had control of the company and they agreed, among other matters, to vote for their election to the Board of Directors; to ensure the election of the appellant Ringuet as president of the company, of the appellant Pagé as vice-president and general manager, and of the respondent Bergeron as secretary-treasurer and assistant general manager of the company, all at stated and agreed salaries. They also agreed to vote unanimously at all meetings of the company and provided for a penalty for breach of the contract . . .

The point of the appeal is therefore whether an agreement among a group of shareholders providing for the direction and control of a company in the circumstances of this case is contrary to public order, and whether it is open to the parties to establish whatever sanction they choose for a breach of such agreement.

Did the parties to this agreement tie their hands in their capacity as directors of the company so as to contravene the requirements of the Quebec *Companies Act*, which provides (s. 80) that "the affairs of the company shall be managed by a board of not less than three directors"? I agree with the reasons of the learned Chief Justice that this agreement does not contravene this or any other section of the Quebec *Companies Act*. It is no more than an agreement among shareholders owning or proposing to own the majority of the issued shares of a company to unite upon a course of policy or action and upon the officers whom they will elect. There is nothing illegal or contrary to public order in an agreement for achieving these purposes. Shareholders have the right to combine their interests and voting powers to secure such control of a company and to ensure that the company will be managed by certain persons in a certain manner. This is a well-known, normal and legal contract and one which is frequently encountered in current practice and it makes no difference whether the objects sought are to be achieved by means of an agreement such as this or a voting trust. Such an arrangement is not prohibited either by law, by good morals or public order.

It is important to distinguish the present action, which is between contracting parties to an agreement for the voting of shares, from one brought by a minority shareholder demanding a certain standard of conduct from directors and majority shareholders. Nothing that can arise from this litigation and nothing that can be said about it can touch on that problem. The fact that this agreement may potentially involve detriment to the minority does not render it illegal and contrary to public order. If there is such injury, there is a remedy available to the minority shareholder who alleges a departure from the standards required of the majority shareholders and the directors. The possibility of such injurious effect on the minority is not a ground for illegality.

* * *

I have the greatest difficulty in seeing how any question of public order can arise in a private arrangement of this kind. The possibility of injury to a minority interest cannot raise it. If this were not so, every arrangement of this kind would involve judicial enquiry. Minority rights have the protection of the law without the necessity of invoking public order. This litigation is between shareholders of a closely held company.

The agreement which the plaintiff seeks to enforce damages nobody except the unsuccessful party to the agreement. No public interest or illegality is involved . . .

Appeal dismissed.

Notes

1   For a discussion of this decision, see K.S. Howard, (1959), 37 Can. Bar Rev. 490; and R.A. Harris, "Note" (1961), U.T. Fac. L. Rev. 149. The concern about using a shareholder agreement to reallocate powers assigned to directors was subsequently addressed in CBCA s. 146(2).

2   What should happen when a unanimous shareholder agreement (USA) and a shareholder's last will and testament are in conflict? When a shareholder dies and leaves his shares to a beneficiary contrary to the USA's transfer restrictions, how should the courts resolve the matter? See *Frye v. Frye Estate*, 2008 ONCA 606, 2008 CarswellOnt 5207, 299 D.L.R. (4th) 184 (Ont. C.A.), leave to appeal refused 2009 CarswellOnt 615, 2009 CarswellOnt 616 (S.C.C.), and OBCA s. 67(2).

(c) Voting Trusts

Pickering, "Shareholders' Voting Rights and Company Control"
(1965), 81 L.Q.R. 248 at pp. 257–260 (footnotes omitted)

The voting trust. A voting trust is created when the voting rights of some or all of the shares in a company are settled upon trust. The trust in this context, as in others, can be a very flexible instrument. It may be comprised of all or only some of the shares with voting rights. The powers of the trust may give the trustees an absolute and unfettered discretion to act as they wish or their authority may be restricted. The objects which they are empowered to fulfill may be general or, usually in combination with capital structures conferring appropriate class rights, they may be confined to certain specific matters. In effect a voting trust confers a joint irrevocable proxy with general or restricted powers. It is a more formal device for concentrating control than the voting agreement and usually will have wider effect.

The voting trust in some ways has similar effects to the use of non-voting and "loaded" shares as a means of concentrating control in relatively few hands. Together with other inter-member devices it has been widely used in the United States of America, but relatively neglected in the United Kingdom where in general the constitutional devices have been preferred. In contrast to the extensive litigation which has taken place in the United States on problems arising from the use of voting trusts, and their regulation by statute in many cases, there is apparently no reported case in English law dealing expressly with issues arising from a corporate voting trust, nor are there statutory provisions specifically applicable to them.

There are perhaps three situations where voting trusts may have special usefulness. First, particular circumstances may make the intervention of outside or independent trustees desirable. For example, where there is a close association of members and directors each individually having a comparable status within the company the existence of independent trustees with powers to appoint or supervise the appointment of directors and managing directors may prevent undesirable internecine strife. Secondly, where a company is incorporated for objects which require for their proper implementation the continued control of persons holding certain beliefs or opinions a voting trust may be one way of achieving this. Thirdly, in very large companies where the membership is both great in number and dispersed in area the interests of the shareholders may be more effectively and continuously safeguarded by trustees acting on their behalf than by the efforts of individual members in general meeting. In addition, it can be argued forcefully that such trustees could more appropriately exercise the power of appointing directors than what are, in effect, often self-perpetuating boards of directors, and similarly that they might exercise a valuable independent role in deciding such questions as directors' remuneration and terms of appointment. These are very contentious points and in practice voting trusts established for this latter purpose are extremely rare or non-existent among larger companies in England.

Apart from such specific functions voting trusts may be employed as a straightforward device by which a relatively small group of individuals within a company can acquire majority control. Under it shareholders may surrender more of their legal rights and remedies than under almost any other means of concentrating control, except perhaps the management contract, but the questions raised by its use have not yet been decided by the courts in England. Ballantine has described the issues of principle involved in the following terms:

> In general, the power to control the election of directors and so to manage and control the property, business and patronage of a great corporation, to direct its policies and the expenditure of vast sums of money, indirectly to appoint and fix the compensation of its officials and executives, is a power of great value, even if the corporation is not in a position to pay dividends on its shares. But this power of control is not properly regarded as a species of property which may be reserved or split off, and bought and sold, apart from the beneficial interests in the shares of stock. Voting power is an ancillary or protective right, not an independent species of property which may be used to give dominion over the investments of others.

Note on US Position

The United States has developed extensive case and statute law to deal with the problem of abuse of control by trustees. Among the devices used by American courts are limitation periods (the most common being 10 years); cancellation provisions requiring the agreement either of all beneficiaries or of a simple majority of them; notice provisions whereby the voting trust, to be valid, must be registered on the company books so that it becomes subject to the general notice provisions; and the requirement of "proper purpose" for the existence of the trust (the securing of control as an end in itself may not be a proper purpose). See *Painter on Close Corporations* (3d ed. 1998), s. 3.2.

(d)   Unanimous Shareholder Agreements

The use of unanimous shareholder agreements is the most radical instrument for altering the relationship between shareholders and directors. While relatively obscure, the potential for usage is great (including, arguably, in the public company context). A 1996 Industry Canada discussion paper entitled "Unanimous Shareholders Agreements" identified at least fifteen areas in respect of which the current statutory provision could be clarified. To date, only three of those issues have been addressed by statutory amendments. The rest (and others) remain unclear and may account for the fact that such agreements are not more widely employed.

Nicholls, Corporate Law
(Emond-Montgomery. 2005) pp.113-119 (footnotes omitted)

In Canada, it might be more accurate to describe cases such as *Ringuet v. Bergeron* as antiques, rather than fossils. As will be seen, however, modem unanimous shareholder agreement provisions in Canadian corporate statutes now do away with the sometimes murky distinction between valid agreements to exercise shareholder voting power and invalid fettering of director discretion.

The Dickerson committee recommended the inclusion in the CBCA of a statutory provision that would expressly permit all shareholders to enter into a "unanimous shareholder agreement," and in such agreement to restrict in whole or in part the directors' powers. The committee included such a statutory provision to effectively reverse the "unnecessarily rigid" effect of judicial decisions that held that even where the shareholders acted unanimously, a shareholder agreement could not operate to fetter director discretion. (It was assumed that the parties to these agreements were both shareholders and directors.)

However, the statutory language originally proposed by the Dickerson committee differed somewhat from the wording actually adopted by Parliament. The committee's proposed provision read, in part, as follows:

> An otherwise lawful agreement among all the shareholders of a corporation . . . is valid, notwithstanding that the agreement restricts in whole or in part the *discretion or* powers of the directors to manage the business and affairs of the corporation.

When the CBCA was finally enacted, in addition to specifying that such an agreement must be in writing, the drafters chose to omit the phrase "discretion or." Thus, what appeared to be among the most critical reasons for proposing this provision in the first place was not explicitly addressed by the statutory language. This technical deficiency prevailed for more than a quarter century. It was at last corrected in 2001, and s. 146 of the current version of the CBCA now explicitly confers power on a corporation's shareholders to fetter directors' discretion by way of a unanimous shareholder agreement.

A unanimous shareholder agreement, as defined in the CBCA, is quite different from an ordinary shareholder agreement. In fact, even if a shareholder agreement is signed by all of a corporation's shareholders, that agreement is not necessarily a unanimous shareholder agreement within the meaning of the statute. This is so because the definition of unanimous shareholder agreement, in s. 2(1), refers to "an agreement described in subsection 146(1) or a declaration of a shareholder described in subsection 146(2)." To come within the meaning of either of these subsections, an agreement (or a resolution signed by a sole shareholder) must be one that restricts, in whole or in part, the powers of the directors to manage, or supervise the management of, the business and affairs of the corporation.

It may be very important to determine whether a particular agreement is or is not a unanimous shareholder agreement as defined. Only a statutorily defined unanimous shareholder agreement can have the effect of shifting what would otherwise be directors' liabilities onto the shareholders who are parties to such an agreement. This is why it is not uncommon for agreements to which all shareholders are parties to contain a provision expressly declaring that such agreements are *not* unanimous shareholder agreements within the meaning of the legislation.

Moreover, a unanimous shareholder agreement has greater corporate constitutional significance than an ordinary shareholder agreement. The Supreme Court of Canada in *Duha Printers (Western) Ltd. v. Canada* equated such agreements with a corporation's constating documents — ranking on a par, in other words, with the corporation's articles and bylaws. Directors and officers are statutorily obliged to comply with a unanimous shareholder agreement. Compliance with a unanimous shareholder agreement may be enforced, not only through a conventional breach of contract claim, but by way of a statutory compliance order, as in the case of a breach of the corporation's articles.

A unanimous shareholder agreement may impose additional shareholder voting thresholds (beyond those required by the CBCA itself); it may require the directors to place additional information before the annual meeting, limit the directors' power to manage the corporation's affairs, and, specifically (among other things), limit the directors' authority under the statute to issue shares, authorize the corporation to borrow money, deal with corporate bylaws, appoint officers, and determine director, officer, and employee remuneration.

Its constitutional significance is reinforced by the fact that a unanimous shareholder agreement, unlike an ordinary shareholder agreement, can become binding on shareholders who were not among the original signatories. The CBCA provides that "a purchaser or transferee of shares subject to a unanimous shareholder agreement is deemed to be a party to the agreement." Such a provision could work considerable unfairness on a transferee of shares who was not aware that a unanimous shareholder agreement existed at the time that he or she acquired the shares. To relieve against this unfairness, the Act provides that if a purchaser or transferee was not made aware that the shares he or she was acquiring were subject to a unanimous shareholder agreement, either by a legend placed on the share certificates themselves, or otherwise, he or she may rescind the transaction by which he or she acquired the shares within 30 days of becoming aware of the existence of the agreement.

Note that the CBCA states that a transferee *and a purchaser* of shares will be bound by the terms of a unanimous shareholder agreement. Some other Canadian corporate statutes, including the Ontario *Business Corporations Act*, refer only to transferees. This difference is not trivial. The addition of the word "purchaser" to the CBCA provision in 2001 was intended to ensure that subscribers of new shares from the corporate treasury as well as transferees of previously issued shares would equally be bound by the provisions of a unanimous shareholder agreement.

In *Sportscope Television Network Ltd. v. Shaw Communications Inc.*, a shareholder of a corporation incorporated under the Ontario *Business Corporations Act* who had acquired its shares in the corporation by converting a previously issued debenture and as the result of an amalgamation was held not to be bound by a unanimous shareholder agreement because it was not a "transferee" of the shares. *Sportscope* would presumably have been decided differently under the current CBCA provision.

Although the CBCA's unanimous shareholder agreement provisions are rarely litigated, a number of theoretical questions have arisen surrounding the concept of such an agreement. For instance, it has occasionally been asked whether a unanimous shareholder agreement could, by its terms, provide for subsequent amendments to be effected with less-than-unanimous approval. If so, would this not potentially undermine the policy rationale on which such agreements are based? In some jurisdictions, this issue is dealt with expressly by statute. For example, under the Alberta *Business Corporations Act*, a unanimous shareholder agreement cannot be amended except with the written consent of all shareholders at the effective date of the agreement. In contrast, the Ontario *Business Corporations Act* states that a unanimous shareholder agreement may indeed provide that "any amendment . . . may be effected in the manner specified therein," clearly anticipating the possibility of amendments by less-than-unanimous consent.

Where a statute is silent on the issue, however, on what basis can it be said that shareholders — who have been expressly permitted to enter into such contracts — ought to be disallowed from contracting with respect to such a conventional matter as a contractual amending procedure? Although the courts have not provided definitive guidance on this matter, it is interesting to note the early views of Robert Dickerson, who chaired the committee upon whose recommendations the unanimous shareholder agreement provision was introduced into the federal incorporation statute. Dickerson suggested that "[p]resumably . . . the original agreement could itself provide for amendment by fewer than all the parties."

A second issue raised by unanimous shareholder agreements is their impact on the role of corporate directors. It is problematic that a corporation must always have at least one director, even in cases where the directors may have no power to act, owing to the existence of a comprehensive unanimous shareholder agreement that strips their powers away. Dickerson noted that his committee would in fact have preferred that no directors be required in such a case, but "this idea ran aground on the shoals of nationalism. The rule. . . requiring every corporation to have a majority of 'resident Canadians' on its board of directors was thought to be more important." This statement suggests that the drafters were especially concerned about corporations incorporated by foreign nationals. The presence on the board of foreign-controlled corporations of totally powerless resident Canadian directors would seem to offer cold comfort to fervent Canadian nationalists. Indeed, it has long been recognized that the CBCA's resident Canadian director requirements are rather easily circumvented in the case of CBCA corporations incorporated as subsidiaries of foreign corporations. Such corporations need only execute unanimous shareholder agreements, then appoint to their boards Canadian nominees who are no more than placeholders. It is clear, however, that the residency requirement is of political importance, not practical importance. A 1996 Industry Canada discussion paper canvassed this issue in some detail. This paper noted that any attempt to eliminate corporate directors would likely be "quite controversial, as it would represent a departure from convention and tradition."

The above discussion has focused upon the unanimous shareholder agreement provisions found in the CBCA. Similar provisions are found in many other Canadian statutes as well. However, there are two other flexible variations of unanimous shareholder agreement legislation in place in Alberta and British Columbia.

First, under the Alberta *Business Corporations Act*, there is no requirement that an agreement restrict the directors' powers in some ways in order to constitute a unanimous shareholder agreement within the meaning of the Act — although, of course, the agreement may have this effect.

Second, under the Alberta statute, a unanimous shareholder agreement may *exclude* all (but not less than all) of the special rules applicable to unanimous shareholder agreements.

Third, the Alberta statute provides that a unanimous shareholder agreement may be binding not only on transferees of existing shares, but also on new shareholders to whom the corporation has issued shares directly. This provision, like the similar language added to the CBCA in 2001, is aimed at addressing the sort of issue raised in *Sportscope v. Shaw*, discussed above.

Fourth, the rights of a shareholder who has acquired shares without knowledge of the existence of the unanimous shareholder agreement are unique. As discussed above, under the CBCA, a purchaser or transferee of shares without knowledge of a unanimous shareholder agreement may rescind the transaction by which he or she became a shareholder within 30 days of becoming aware of the agreement. Under the Ontario Act, a purchaser who had no knowledge of the unanimous shareholder agreement is not bound by it, unless reference to the agreement had been noted conspicuously on the transferred share certificate. Under the Alberta *Business Corporations Act*, however, purchasers of newly issued shares and transferees of previously issued shares are given slightly different remedies in the event that they have acquired their shares without knowledge that they are subject to a unanimous shareholder agreement. A purchaser of new shares from the corporation — provided he or she was not an existing shareholder — may rescind the purchase by giving notice within a "reasonable time" after becoming aware of the existence of the unanimous shareholder agreement. A transferee of shares, on the other hand, may, within 30 days of acquiring actual knowledge of the existence of the agreement, send a notice of objection to the corporation, and demand that the corporation purchase the shares at fair value. If the transferee had paid more than fair value for the shares, he or she then has the right to recover the difference from the transferor.

The approach toward unanimous shareholder agreements found in the BC *Business Corporations Act* has other distinct features. First, the BC Act does not explicitly refer to unanimous shareholder agreements at all, but instead provides a functional equivalent. Section 137 of the statute states that "the articles of a company may transfer, in whole or in part, the powers of the directors to manage or supervise the management of the business and affairs of the company." Such a provision may be included in the articles at the time of incorporation (or, equivalently, when the company is "recognized" under the Act) or may be added later if so authorized by special resolution. Unlike the unanimous shareholder agreement provisions of the CBCA and other similar legislation the BC Act allows for powers of management to be transferred not only to a corporation's shareholders, but also to any other person or persons. Any such transferee acquires the rights, powers, duties, and liabilities of the directors "whether arising under the *[Business Corporations Act]* or otherwise" to the extent of the transfer, and the directors, in turn, are relieved of such rights, duties, powers, and liabilities.

Notes and Questions

1   A key difference between public and private corporations relates to the process of incorporation and constitutional structure. Both because of the small number of participants involved, and the often idiosyncratic needs of particular capital contributors, the structure of the corporation is established by elaborate bargaining between prospective shareholders. As a consequence of this bargaining process, a significant part of the relationship of the parties is embodied in shareholder agreements, and not merely the articles and by-laws. Through a shareholder agreement, the parties will frequently wish to allocate day-to-day powers of control by designating which of their number will serve as directors and officers of the corporation. A shareholder agreement will also very often indicate how the profits of the corporation shall be paid out. The choice between paying out profits as salary and directors' fees or as dividends can have profound and often differential tax consequences for the participants and will be something the shareholders will wish to settle in advance. Other important matters may be dealt with in shareholders' agreements. It is far from infrequent that disputes arise between shareholders of private corporations relating to the means and ends to be pursued by the corporation; thus, an important feature of many shareholder agreements will be elaborate dispute resolution mechanisms. Similarly, because of the close working relationship between the corporate constituents and the need for trust and mutual compatibility, restrictions on the transferability of shares are a common feature of shareholder agreements (note that CBCA s. 6(1)(d) requires that any restrictions on transfer be put into the articles; these will often be replicated in the shareholders' agreement). Shareholder agreements also very often require a demanding super-majority voting approval for the undertaking of fundamental changes like an amalgamation, a sale of the corporation's assets, *etc.* Sometimes, unanimity will be required, effectively giving each shareholder a power of veto.

As noted above, the enactment of the statutory unanimous shareholder agreement was a response to difficulties at common law associated with fettering the powers of the directors. Since the passage of these provisions, unanimous shareholder agreements have become the most important planning tool available to participants in private corporations in arranging mutual rights and entitlements. Such agreements will often embody contractual provisions of the variety discussed in Coates, "Share Transfer and Transmission Restrictions in the Close Corporation", *supra.*

2   The statutory provisions relating to unanimous shareholder agreements are found in ss. 2(1) and 146 of the CBCA, and ss. 1(1) and 108 of the OBCA. Note that the distinguishing feature of a "unanimous shareholder agreement" in the statutes is that it "restricts, in whole or in part, the powers of the directors to manage or [to supervise the management of] the business and affairs of the corporation". Suppose an agreement between all the shareholders of the corporation restricts the authority of the directors, but also contains other agreements, relating to such matters as buy-sell arrangements, requisite shareholder votes on the undertaking of fundamental changes, shareholder voting agreements, *etc.* Is the whole agreement a "unanimous shareholder agreement", or only that part that relates to the authority of the directors? Do the words "in whole or in part" in CBCA s. 146(1) and (2) and OBCA s. 108(2) refer to the "written agreement", or do they refer to the restriction of the powers of directors? The distinction may be important. For example, a transferee of shares with notice of a common law voting agreement is not bound by the agreement (because of the absence of privity of contract); see *Greenhalgh v. Mallard*, [1943] 2 All E.R. 234 (C.A.). However, a transferee of shares subject to a unanimous shareholder agreement (USA) is bound by the USA; see CBCA s. 146(3), OBCA s. 108(4) (although note the limitation contained in CBCA s. 49(8), OBCA s. 56(3)).

3   Unanimous shareholder agreements have been held to be considered constating documents of a corporation (*Duha Printers (Western) Ltd. v. R.*, 1998 CarswellNat 750, 1998 CarswellNat 751, (sub nom. *Duha Printers (Western) Ltd. v. Canada*) [1998] 1 S.C.R. 795 (S.C.C.)). A unanimous shareholder agreement — which by its nature governs the exercise of directors' powers — does not survive an amalgamation (provided the recipient of the shares is neither a purchaser nor transferee of the share), unless it is stipulated in the amalgamation agreement. (*Sportscope Television Network Ltd. v. Shaw Communications Inc.*, 1999 CarswellOnt 630, 46 B.L.R. (2d) 87 (Ont. Gen. Div. [Commercial List]).)

4   The status of a USA as a constating document of a corporation also plays an important role in determining whether shareholders have "de jure" control of a corporation. *Duha Printers (Western) Ltd. v. R.*, 1998 CarswellNat 750, 1998 CarswellNat 751, *sub nom.* Duha Printers (Western) Ltd. v. Canada), [1998] 1 S.C.R. 795 (S.C.C.),

explores how unanimous shareholder agreements (USAs) can have an effect in a "de jure" control analysis. *Bioartificial Gel Technologies (Bagtech) Inc. (Syndic de) c. R.*, 2013 CarswellNat 2049, 2013 CarswellNat 3309, 2013 FCA 164 (F.C.A.), expands on this issue. The cases suggest that if a USA offers a shareholder the ability to appoint a majority of the board of directors, even if the shareholder does not own 50% plus 1 of the votes, the shareholder may be considered to have de jure control.

5   Suppose that shares subject to a USA were transferred to a third party in circumstances under which that third party is not bound by the USA (see CBCA s. 49(8), OBCA s. 56(3)). What happens to the USA, since it is no longer an agreement between all the shareholders of the corporation? Does it cease to have effect (at least in relation to those parts restricting the authority of the directors)?

6   Note that where there is a USA, CBCA s. 146(5) and OBCA s. 108(5) give each shareholder the "rights, powers, duties and liabilities of a director of the corporation, whether they arise under this Act or otherwise". What is the scope of the "or otherwise"? It would appear that this phrase was intended to ensure that common law liabilities would be transferred from directors to shareholders. But what else? For example, the *Income Tax Act* fixes each director of the corporation with liability for failure of the corporation to remit employee source deductions to the government. Can a provincial enactment transfer to shareholders a federal liability specifically attaching to the directors of the corporation? If it cannot, then the directors might find themselves in the unenviable position of not actually managing the company, but being liable for the managerial dereliction of the shareholders.

7   What is the function and status of directors where the USA remits all authority to manage to the shareholders? Is there any point in retaining the requirement to have directors in such circumstances?

8   Note that the CBCA fails to specifically provide how a USA may be amended, while OBCA s. 108(6)(a) provides that "any amendment of the unanimous shareholder agreement may be effected in the manner specified therein". Would it be possible under the CBCA for a USA to specify a non-unanimous amendment procedure? Note also that there is common law authority that directors may not refer disputes amongst themselves to arbitration, as this would constitute a fettering of their discretion; see *Atlas Developments v. Calof and Gold* (1963), 41 W.W.R. 575 (Man. Q.B.). This limitation may apply to shareholders as well under a USA. This is why OBCA s. 108(6)(b) specifically provides that disputes arising under the USA may be referred to arbitration.

9 Note that it is standard practice for the corporation to be made a party to a USA, even where the agreement imposes no specific obligations upon the corporation. Can you think of why this might be done?

10 The court has authority under the oppression remedy to make an order "creating or amending a unanimous shareholder agreement". See CBCA s. 241(3)(c), OBCA s. 248(3)(c). The following case illustrates that the broad discretion given to the court under the oppression remedy may also be used to constrain the exercise of powers granted under a USA. As you read the case, you might pause to reflect on the manner in which the oppression remedy allows a court to import notions of contractual "unconscionability" into the law of corporations. Is this a good or a bad development?

Bury v. Bell Gouinlock Ltd.
(1984), 48 O.R. (2d) 57 (H.C.), affirmed (1985), 49 O.R. (2d) 91 (Div. Ct.)

EBERLE J.: The applicant was a shareholder and employee of the respondent. He left the employ of the respondent on May 9, 1984, in order to better himself and almost immediately began working for another brokerage house in Toronto. The shareholders of the respondent had a shareholders' agreement which provided that a shareholder who left the employ of the company was required to sell his shares to the company at prices and on terms spelled out in the agreement. It is the interaction of the terms of that agreement concerning the sale of the shares and s. 247 [now 248] of the Ontario *Business Corporations Act, 1982* S.O. 1982, c. 4, which gives rise to this application.

There seem to be three areas of difficulty. The first is whether s. 247 [248] of the Act may be utilized to give relief in face of a valid contract between the parties dealing with the very matters in issue. The second area is whether it is shown that the actions of the respondent fall within the type of conduct described in s. 247(2) [248(2)]. The third area is what relief may properly be given within the bounds of an originating motion and without the trial of an issue.

As to the first area, no case has been cited where the activities giving rise to the litigation were also the subject-matter of a written contract between the parties — a written contract the validity of which has not been questioned in the argument in this case. However, the reported cases cited to me do not contain any language suggesting that relief cannot be given in a case such as the present.

Indeed, s. 247(3)(c) [248(3)(c)] expressly provides that the court may make any order it thinks fit including, without limiting the generality of the foregoing:

    (c) an order to regulate a corporation's affairs by amending the
        articles or by-laws or creating or amending a unanimous
        shareholder agreement;

This is a far-reaching provision. Since the court has been given power to
remodel a shareholders' agreement, it seems to me that the court must
also have authority under the section to set limits to the exercise of a
power given by a shareholders' agreement, if the court finds that a
particular exercise of such power has the effect aimed at by s. 274(2)
[248(2)]. The appropriate canon of interpretation has been stated in *Re
Ferguson and Imax Systems Corp.* (1983), 43 O.R. (2d) 128 at p. 137, 150
D.L.R. (3d) 718 at p. 727, as follows, ". . . and the section should be
interpreted broadly to carry out its purpose". Those words were said in
relation to a section of the *Canada Business Corporations Act*, S.C. 1974-
75-76, c. 33 [s. 241], which is to substantially the same effect as s. 247 [248]
of the Ontario Act.

    Accordingly, I am of the view that s. 247 [248] may give relief in fact
of a provision in a contract valid between the parties.

    That is particularly so in the present case where the applicant seeks
not to invalidate any provision in the shareholders' agreement, but takes
the position that the exercise by the company of the right given to it by
para. 16 of the agreement to extend from six months to twelve months the
period within which the company will pay for the applicant's shares is
oppressive or unfairly prejudicial or unfairly disregards the interests of
the applicant in the circumstances of this case.

    This brings me to the second area of problem: is that decision of the
company in the circumstances of this case oppressive to the applicant or
otherwise within the concluding words of s. 247(2) [248(2)]?

    The relevant facts are these. The company and the other
shareholders were, as was the applicant, fully aware of the fact that in
the securities business, because of by-laws of the Investment Dealers
Association and of the Toronto Stock Exchange, an individual cannot be
a shareholder of two brokerage houses at the same time. Accordingly, the
invocation by the company of the 12 months provision in para. 16 of the
agreement has the effect of preventing the applicant from becoming a
shareholder in his new employer and thus prevents him from obtaining
dividend income or other income accruing only to a shareholder. It is
evident that since the applicant was a shareholder of the respondent
company it would be expected that he would likely become, or wish to
become, a shareholder in any new employer. His status in the securities
business is evidently one in which that would be expected.

    For what reason has the respondent chosen so to penalize the
applicant? None whatever has been advanced. The respondent argued
that the onus is on the applicant to show that the respondent's decision is
not properly based. In my view, since the basis for the respondent's action
lies peculiarly within the knowledge of the respondent, any onus on the

applicant is met where, as here, no ground is advanced to justify the decision. The deprivation to the applicant is sufficient to raise a *prima facie* case of oppression or unfairness. It is particularly striking that the respondent does not advance the ground that a requirement that it pay the applicant within six months would cause the respondent any financial difficulty.

If a payment within the initial six months period will not cause the respondent any financial difficulty, why has it chosen to rely on the provision in para. 16 to extend the payment period to 12 months? The only reasonable inference that comes to mind is that it is designed merely to punish the applicant. I do not mean to suggest that financial hardship would be the only justifiable ground for a 12-month payment period under the terms of the shareholders' agreement. There may be many other good grounds relevant in other cases. In the present case, no other justification is advanced, nor even suggested, beyond the bare legal right contained in para. 16.

There are, in my view, other relevant circumstances. For instance, the agreement provides that no interest shall be paid on the purchase price; accordingly, the company has the free use of the applicant's money for 12 months. Yet the applicant is deprived of his status as shareholder in the respondent company as and from the date of his departure from that company; and he is further deprived of any dividends paid on those shares during the 12-month period; yet, as observed above, he is unable to become a shareholder in his new employer. In the absence of some good reason for so acting, it seems to me that the result of the respondent's action is oppressive to the applicant. In addition, para. 12 of the agreement requires the company to notify the departing shareholder of the share price which the company will pay "forthwith" after the determination of the price. The price is to be determined according to a formula set out in the agreement and ought to have been done by the company as soon as it received the audited financial statements for the previous year. These were received, I am told, in February, 1984. Apparently no determination was made at that time but, more importantly, the company did not comply with the combined effect of paras. 11(3) and 12 of the agreement by notifying the applicant forthwith after his termination of the price at which the company would buy his shares according to the formula. Although on several occasions, the applicant sought this information from the president of the company, the company did nothing until July 20th, when it responded to a letter from the applicant's solicitors. On that occasion, for the first time, the company notified the applicant of the prices at which he was required to sell his shares. In my view, that is not "forthwith" after his departure from the company.

* * *

It is to be noted that it was not until September 6, 1984, the last day allowed for filing affidavit material pursuant to the order of McKinley J. of August 1, 1984, that an affidavit was filed by the company. In this affidavit is to be found the only evidence that the company made any decision to invoke the 12-month provision in para. 16 of the agreement.

While that agreement does not establish any time-limit for the company to give notification of such a decision, nevertheless, in my view, the actions of the company throughout exhibit a consistent policy of delaying the applicant at every step. This course of conduct, when viewed with the unexplained decision of the company to avail itself of the 12-month period for payment to the plaintiff for his shares, leads me to the conclusion that it would be contrary to the provisions of s. 247(2) [248(2)] of the Ontario *Business Corporations Act, 1982* to permit the company to invoke that 12-month period.

I have now reached the third problem area, namely, what relief may properly be granted.

* * *

The company could easily have notified the applicant on May 9th of the prices of his shares in accordance with the financial statement of December 31, 1983, and was required to do so "forthwith". Accordingly, I think the appropriate relief to be given is that the company be required to pay the applicant on November 9, 1984, the appropriate amount for his shares and, of course, the applicant must deliver his shares duly endorsed in blank for transfer on that date. The amount to be paid is $60,000 for the B shares plus $70,600 for the A shares. This is arrived at based on a price of $35.30 for each of 2,000 A shares. The total is $130,600.

Judgment for Plaintiff.

An appeal to the Ontario Divisional Court was dismissed. The Court concluded that s. 247(1) [248(1)] of the OBCA gives the Court a wide discretion and that Eberle J. had not improperly exercised his discretion. (49 O.R. (2d) 91.)

Notes and Questions

1   Consider and evaluate the following arguments:

A.   The Court in *Bury* overstepped the acceptable limits of judicial intervention by effectively re-making a contract freely entered into by two consenting and fully informed parties. Bury was under no compulsion to work for Bell Gouinlock. By voluntarily entering into the contract (the USA) with full knowledge of all its terms, he thereby agreed to accept the exercise of powers vested in Bell even where the consequences of such exercise might place him in a disadvantageous position. There was no requirement in the contract for Bell to give any reason for exercising its option to extend the payout period to 12 months. Had the parties wished to constrain Bell's ability to exercise this contractual power, and/or to require Bell to state reasons for exercise of the power, then terms to this effect could easily have been included in the agreement. The absence of such constraint strongly suggests that the choice of whether or not to extend the payout period was left by the parties to Bell's unfettered discretion. The result of the case is to confer an unearned windfall on Bury.

B.   There are good economic reasons for a contractual provision that allows the employer to inflict a hardship on departing employees. The employer (Bell) may invest a substantial amount of time, effort and money in training its employees. The skills acquired by its employees are highly transferable, however, and there is a significant danger that once the employee has acquired these skills another employer will steal the employee away with a more attractive offer. The firm's investment in the employee will be irretrievably lost. The result will be that brokerage firms will be very reluctant to hire and train "new blood", to the detriment not only of the industry and the investing public, but aspiring brokers as well. The clause in question is therefore simply a rational and reasonable response to a very real problem, and one that ultimately operates in favour of both the employer and employee.

C.   The Court reached the right result. Contractual silence regarding the limits of the exercise of an apparently unconstrained power does not incontestably confirm that such power was intended to be totally without boundaries. The parties might well have, and probably did expect that the power conferred upon Bell would only be exercised for some good reason. Such good reason might include the inability of Bell to raise the necessary funds, or the financial hardship caused Bell in paying out Bury immediately. It is not reasonable to expect the parties to formulate complete contracts that spell out what is to happen in every possible eventuality; greater economy of drafting (and not a great deal less certainty) will result from according broadly drafted contractual provisions the meaning that the parties would reasonably have expected. On these facts, it is probable that Bell extended the payout period for one reason only: to punish Bury for leaving the firm. That is not a good reason, and not one to which the Court ought to lend its *imprimatur*.

2   It is fair to say that the oppression remedy has revolutionized the law of private companies. Majority/minority relations (both in relation to public and private companies) were once characterized by the following quotation from *Re Jury Gold Mine Dev. Co.*, [1928] 4 D.L.R. 735 (Ont. C.A.):

> [The plaintiff] is a minority shareholder and must endure the unpleasantness incident to that situation. If he choose to risk his

money by subscribing for shares, it is part of his bargain that he will submit to the will of the majority. In the absence of fraud or transactions ultra vires, the majority must govern, and there should be no appeal to the Courts for redress.

The oppression remedy is designed to give minority shareholders significantly more power to challenge the actions of majority or controlling shareholders than they have at common law. Indeed, most of the cases decided under the statutory oppression remedy have involved private companies, although this is now starting to change.

3 It is difficult to argue the business judgment rule in the face of the express terms on the issue in a USA. Why do you think that is? In *2082825 Ontario Inc. v. Platinum Wood Finishing Inc.*, 2009 CarswellOnt 1808, 96 O.R. (3d) 467 (Ont. Div. Ct.), the court stated:

If the business judgment rule were held to override the express terms of a unanimous shareholder agreement, such agreements would be of negligible value to a minority shareholder who becomes an equity owner in reliance on the protection contained in terms of a unanimous shareholder agreement. Instead of providing protection, such agreements could easily become the instruments of a "bait and switch" if controlling shareholders were permitted to shelter under the business judgment rule when violating the terms of a unanimous shareholder agreement to the prejudice of a minority.

While the business judgment rule applies to confer deference upon business decisions made in good faith in the interests of the company, there is no rationale for conferring the same deference where the parties have at the outset made express agreements as to particular business matters.

As a result, the business judgment rule cannot be used as a defence if breach of the USA is oppressive. Breaching the terms of the USA is oppressive if the conduct is "burdensome, harsh and wrongful". In this case, the court found the act of freezing wages was oppressive, and also highlighted that the breach was contrary to the shareholder's reasonable expectations.

Chapter 10

Shareholder Remedies

1. INTRODUCTION

In Chapter 8, we examined various methods by which a shareholder may participate in the governance of the corporation through the bundle of rights that the corporation statute generally assigns to shareholders. These rights can be contractually embellished or supplemented, especially in the context of the private or closely held corporation as was briefly explored in Chapter 9. It is obvious that if the rights given to shareholders, whether by the statute or by contract, are to be worthwhile, correspondingly effective remedies must also be available to cure their breach.

The broad distinction between a right and a remedy can be stated easily enough. Remedies, generally speaking, are the means for ensuring that shareholders are given the rights to which they are entitled. For example, a shareholder may have the right to vote her shares, either by statute or under the articles of the company. Should the company deny this right, then some means must exist to protect the right. The shareholder might commence a personal action, a derivative action, or an oppression action. A court could then order that the company accord the shareholder the right to which she is entitled.

The distinction between a right and a remedy is not always crystal clear in practice, however. Consider the oppression provision; although commonly referred to as the oppression "remedy", it is clear that this provision augments the substantive rights of shareholders by expanding upon the range of matters that would be actionable at common law (or under CBCA s. 122, OBCA s. 134) for breach of fiduciary duties, especially after *BCE Inc., Re*. It is also clear that the oppression remedy provides a new, more expeditious procedure for defending rights the denial of which would have been actionable at common law. Thus, it has the characteristics of both a right and a remedy. See, *Sparling v. Javelin International Ltd. et al.*, [1986] R.J.Q. 1073, *infra*.

Our main task in this chapter is to understand the differences between derivative actions, personal actions, and oppression actions. As we have already indicated, shareholder remedies, including a derivative action may be commenced where all shareholders are affected equally by the impugned conduct. The plaintiff is the corporation and any remedy will be given in favour of the corporation, rather than an individual shareholder or shareholders. A personal action may be commenced where certain shareholders (or a single shareholder) have some grievance that is peculiar to themselves, and not shared by all other shareholders. In such an action, the remedy would issue in favour of the shareholder(s). The oppression remedy, once again, straddles the line.

As you read the following materials, which focus on the descriptive aspects of shareholder remedies, you should not lose sight of the normative questions. For example, how far-reaching are the rights and remedies that the legislation ought to accord shareholders? Shareholders' rights and remedies have both costs and benefits. The oppression remedy may be beneficial if it protects shareholders against conduct that constitutes little more than redistributions of wealth in favour of managers or a constituency of shareholders. As we have seen, there are many ways in which this can occur, and the common law of fiduciary duties will not always prove adequate to the task of thwarting such unproductive redistributions. The oppression remedy also is potentially costly in that it may invite meritless shareholder claims ("nuisance suits", or in the US, "strike suits") launched solely with the intention of extorting a costly settlement from the company. A widely drawn oppression remedy (or other shareholder rights or remedies) also creates uncertainty about legal rights which we can predict will result in a greater amount of litigation. Litigation is costly in a number of ways. Most obviously, there is the direct cost to the participants. There is also a cost to the state, which provides courtrooms, pays judges' salaries, *etc.* In many cases, there is a cost to the company as well, even should it ultimately prevail. Executives of the company may have to spend time with company lawyers planning strategy, collecting evidence, or testifying in court. An oppression suit may delay or even abort a value-generating transaction, to the ultimate detriment of all corporate constituents.

Other arguments, however, can be marshalled in favour of widely drawn shareholder remedies. All shareholder-initiated litigation suffers from a "free rider" problem. Litigation alleging breach of fiduciary duty or oppression is potentially costly to the litigants (particularly so with the "costs follow the event" rule). However, the benefits of a successful suit (particularly if the action is derivative in character) are likely to be realized by some or all of the shareholders. Thus, the incentive of each shareholder is to lie in the grass hoping someone else will expend the time and expense and take the risk of suing. This is particularly true where the shares are widely held and most shareholders have small holdings and stand to gain relatively little from successful litigation. Where the substantive rights of shareholders are broadly drawn, there is a greater incentive to sue, overcoming to a degree the free rider problem. There are more direct solutions to the free rider problem, however, which involve an appropriate casting of the rules on costs. These are discussed, *infra* (can you think of what they might be?).

Another key question is that of standing to sue. Is there a principled basis upon which we can decide who should be able to sue, and for what wrongs? We turn our attention first to the derivative action.

2.   THE DERIVATIVE ACTION

(a)   Introduction

Where a corporation has been injured by some wrongdoing, a shareholder of the corporation arguably also has been injured through the diminution in value of his or her shares that is traceable to the corporate injury. As we will examine, the courts followed by legislatures developed a remedy whereby a shareholder was permitted to bring an action to rectify a wrong committed against the corporation for which management did not seek redress, often because they or one of their members were the alleged wrongdoers. Under the derivative action, a shareholder on behalf of the corporation brings an action which derives from the corporation's cause of action. This indirect or derivative action is in contrast to the personal or direct action whereby a shareholder enforces his or her own rights as distinct from those of the corporation.

The positive aspects of the derivative action are that it can be an effective private remedial instrument to ensure and enhance management accountability. On the other hand, the US "strike suit" action — litigation having little merit that seeks to extract gains from the nuisance value of claims for high damages — provides ample evidence of potential abuse. This abuse has led to procedural reforms and responses in the US and Canada to prevent or minimize the adverse aspects of derivative actions. As will be seen, the derivative action has been subject to debate about its utility.

A brief examination will first be made of the situation that existed in Anglo-Canadian common law. We then will turn to the special legislative provisions that create a statutory derivative action which has received a number of interpretations by Canadian courts. Some of these cases will also be briefly studied. Finally we will consider how recent case law, and in particular the decision of the Supreme Court of Canada in *BCE Inc., Re* has modified the traditional interpretation of the statutory derivative action.

(b)   At Common Law: The Rule in *Foss v. Harbottle* and the Need for the Derivative Action

Beck, "The Shareholders' Derivative Action"
(1974), 52 C.B.R. 159 at 164–168 (footnotes omitted)

A Recapitulation of Foss v. Harbottle

In order to understand and evaluate the reform of the derivative suit it is necessary to set out briefly the substantive and procedural problems spawned by the rule. The decision in *Foss v. Harbottle* was premised on the separate legal personality of the corporation and on majority rule in internal corporate affairs. If the corporation is a legal person separate from its members, it follows that for a wrong done to it the corporation itself is the only proper plaintiff. The two shareholders who appeared as plaintiffs in *Foss v. Harbottle* alleged, *inter alia*, a sale by the directors of their own property at inflated values to the company. The wrong alleged was thus a wrong to the company and the Vice-Chancellor ruled that the plaintiffs had no standing to sue on behalf of the corporation.

As to the transaction itself and bringing suit for damages for the injury caused by it, those were both matters to be decided upon by the company in general meeting. The purchase of their own lands for the corporation by the directors was a transaction that was voidable at the option of the corporation. The corporate pleasure was to be determined by the shareholders in general meeting and as the plaintiffs did not represent a majority, or allege that the will of the majority had been determined, they had no standing to sue in the name of the company. The court was not going to be put in the position of ruling on a breach of trust that the principal might elect to confirm. Moreover, the decision whether or not to bring suit in the company name belongs at common law to the general meeting where, once again, the majority rules. In short, the will of the majority had not been ascertained and the plaintiffs were non-suited. Thus in 1843, one year before the first modern companies Act, the Court of Chancery applied its rule of noninterference in the internal affairs of a partnership to the incorporated company. Internal affairs were a matter for the majority and the majority was thus firmly established in a pivotal position and has remained there ever since.

* * *

Taken in its purest form, these rules would allow the directors — and/or majority shareholders to ride roughshod over the majority. Although the common law developed a number of exceptions to the rules in an attempt to give shareholders who are aggrieved by an unremedied wrong to the company access to the courts to sue on behalf of the company, these exceptions gave rise to their own sets of problems. It was in response to these problems, and the restrictive effects of the rule on minority shareholders' rights, that the derivative action (and the oppression remedy) were introduced by legislators. The derivative action in particular, granted by section 246 in the Ontario Act and section 239 in the federal Act, opened the door to a wider range of derivative actions than what the common law had historically allowed.

Note

The common law derivative action remains in use in the U.K., though it has been somewhat overshadowed by the creation of a statutory "unfair prejudice" remedy similar to the Canadian oppression remedy. For U.K. cases that have discussed the exceptions to the rule in *Foss v. Harbottle*, see *Prudential Assurance Co. v. Newman Industries Ltd. (No. 2)* (1981), [1982] 1 All E.R. 354 (C.A.); *Smith v. Croft (No. 2)*, [1988] Ch. 114; and *Barrett v. Duckett*, [1995] 1 B.C.L.C. 243.

(c)   The Statutory Derivative Action

The Federal Act

The CBCA creates a statutory derivative action in s. 239. Section 239(1) allows a complainant to "apply to a court for leave to bring an action in the name and on behalf of a corporation or any of its subsidiaries, or intervene in an action to which any such body corporate is a party, for the purpose of prosecuting, defending or discontinuing the action on behalf of the body corporate". "Complainant" is defined in s. 238 as (a) a current or former registered holder or beneficial owner of a security of a corporation or any of its affiliates, (b) a current or former director or officer of a corporation or any of its affiliates, (c) the Director or (d) anyone else who the court considers a proper person to make an application.

Section 239(2) provides that several conditions that must be satisfied for the court to allow a derivative action to be brought. First, the complainant must give the directors notice of intent to apply to the court at least fourteen days before the application is made, and therefore allow the directors of the corporation to bring the action. Second, the complainant must be acting in good faith. Third, the bringing of the action must appear to be in the interests of the corporation.

Section 240 sets out specific orders that a court may make in connection with a derivative action. These include, but are not limited to: (a) an order allowing a person to control the action, (b) an order directing the conduct of the action, (c) an order that payment to a defendant go to security holders rather than the corporation and (d) an order requiring the corporation to pay the complainant's legal fees.

Section 242(1) indicates that shareholder approval of an alleged wrongdoing is not conclusive, but may be taken into account. Section 242(2) requires the court's approval of any settlement or discontinuation of an action. Section 242(4) allows the court to order the corporation to pay the interim costs of the complainant.

A striking feature of the statutory derivative action is the importance of the court. Leave of the court is required to commence the action, and the grounds on which leave may be granted lend themselves to a large degree of judicial discretion. As noted by Iacobucci, Pilkington and Prichard in *Canadian Business Corporations*:

> a paramount role is given to the court [in respect of statutory derivative actions]. This approach has no doubt been influenced by largely unregulated (to Canadian observers) shareholder actions in the United States about which Canadian draftsmen were most apprehensive. Leave of the court appears to be the compromise struck by the draftsman to allay the fears of those who thought imminent tragedy was approaching by the conferral of a derivative action right.

The Provincial Acts

Most of the provincial acts have statutory derivative action legislation similar to that in the CBCA. Sections 245-7 of the OBCA do not differ significantly from their CBCA counterparts. The statutory derivative actions of Manitoba (MCA ss. 231-3), Newfoundland (NCA, ss. 368-70), Saskatchewan (SBCA ss. 231-3), and Nova Scotia (NSCA, Third Schedule s. 4) differ from that of the CBCA only in that their notice requirements do not set a time limit but instead require "reasonable notice". Unlike other acts, Alberta (ABCA ss. 239-41) and New Brunswick (NBBCA ss. 163-5) also specifically include "a creditor of the corporation" in their definitions of "complainant".

In 2004, the *Company Act* in British Columbia was replaced by the *Business Corporations Act*. Sections 232 and 233 of the new BCBCA deal with the derivative action. While the old BCCA granted the right to seek leave to a "member or director", the BCBCA grants the right to a shareholder or director. The criteria for leave to commence a derivative action are listed in section 233(1) of the BCBCA, and include reasonable efforts by the complainant to cause the directors to commence the action, notice, good faith and the requirement that the legal proceeding appears to the court to be in the best interests of the company. The old BCCA had required that the action be "*prima facie* in the interests of the company". The BCBCA does not contain an equivalent to CBCA s. 240(c), which specifically allows the court to make an order such that damages be paid to shareholders rather than the corporation. However, a court could fashion such an order under the BCBCA s. 233(4) because the court may make any order it deems appropriate.

(d) Judicial Interpretation of the Derivative Action

Re Northwest Forest Products Ltd.
[1975] 4 W.W.R. 724 (B.C. S.C.)

[Northwest was 51% owner of Fraser Valley Pulp and Timber Ltd. Assets of Fraser Valley were sold to another company at what appeared to be a great undervaluation. The directors of Northwest were petitioned by its shareholders to vote the company's shares of Fraser Valley to set aside the sale, but did not respond. The complainants sought leave to commence a derivative action.]

CASHMAN L.J.S.C.: Mr. McConnell submits that when viewed as a whole the affidavit and material in support of the motion does not disclose a *prima facie* case and furthermore that the directors were never informed of the specific action they were requested to take prior to this motion and indeed he questions whether the motion itself discloses an action.

As I understand his submission it appears that while he does not necessarily agree that the applicants are acting in good faith as required by subs. (3)(b) or that both were members of the company within the meaning of subs. (3)(d) he does not seriously contend that these things are not so.

Accordingly I find that the applicants have satisfied the requirements of s. 222(3)(b) and (d).

He does however submit that while the applicants did make a reasonable effort to cause the directors to commence an action the applicants failed to specify the precise nature of the action. In making this submission he relies upon the United States case of *Halprin v. Babbit* (1962), 303 E 2nd 138 at 14 1. He submits that there is no evidence that the directors had full knowledge of the basis of the claim.

It is my view that this is the correct interpretation of the requirement of s. 222(3)(a). The directors could hardly bring any action whether by their own initiative or on the requisition of a minority shareholder without knowing the specific cause of action. However I would think that no more would be required than that sufficient to found an endorsement on a generally endorsed writ of summons.

Mr. McConnell submits that there is difference between the relief sought in the motion and that set out in the requisition, the two paragraphs of which read as follows:

1. To pass a resolution that the Company take action against the persons who were directors of the Company during the time when certain shares of Fraser Valley Pulp & Timber Ltd. owned by the Company were voted for a special resolution to sell the assets of Fraser Valley Pulp & Timber Ltd. to Green River Log Sales Ltd., and against the person who held the proxy for the said shares and cast them for such special resolution.

2. To pass a resolution that the directors of the Company cause the shares of Fraser Valley Pulp & Timber Ltd., held by the Company be voted at a meeting of Fraser Valley Pulp & Timber Ltd., to bring action to set aside the sale by Fraser Valley Pulp & Timber Ltd., to Green River Log Sales Ltd., on the ground that the assets of Fraser Valley Pulp & Timber Ltd., in such sale were so grossly undervalued to the knowledge of the directors of both Fraser Valley Pulp & Timber Ltd. and Green River Log Sales Ltd., as to amount to a fraud on the shareholders of Fraser Valley Pulp & Timber Ltd.

In my view that notice sufficiently specifies the cause of action and contains sufficient information to found an endorsement on a writ.

While there are some differences between the wording of the requisition and that relief sought in the motion, which is conceded by Miss Southin, I do note that Mr. Ross's letter of 3rd April 1974 sets out the relief sought in substantially the same words as contained in the motion. Those words I have set out heretofore in this judgment.

Furthermore the relief sought is in the nature of equitable relief and there is in my view no substantial difference between the requisition and the motion as both refer to fraud. Furthermore there is no evidence that the directors refused to commence the action in the terms specifically set out in either the letter or the requisition. All the directors did was defeat the motion.

Accordingly I find that the applicants have satisfied the requirements of s. 222(3)(a).

The real question here is whether in the circumstances of this case "it is *prima facie* in the interests of the company that the action be brought" (s. 222(3)(c)). It will be noted that the Legislature has said that it is sufficient to show that the action sought is *prima facie* in the interests of the company and does not appear to require that the applicants prove a *prima facie* case. Presumably the authors of that legislation had in mind that a minority shareholder being in a real sense on the outside is often not in a position to obtain evidence such as that the Crown would be expected to put forward to found a *prima facie* case in a criminal matter.

In a criminal case the Crown is not required to do more than produce evidence which if unanswered and believed is sufficient to raise a *prima facie* case upon which the jury might be justified in finding a verdict: *Girvin v. The King* (1911), 45 S.C.R. 167, 20 W.L. R. 130; *Rex v. Scott*, [1919] 2 W.W.R. 227, 14 Alta. L.R. 439, 31 C.C.C. 399 (C.A.).

The words "*prima facie*" are not defined in any statute of which I am aware.

"*Prima facie*" is defined as "at first sight", "on the face of" in *Jowitt's Dictionary of English Law* and *Black's Law Dictionary*. The latter volume also contains the definition "so far as can be judged from the first disclosure".

It should be borne in mind that an application such as this is in the nature of an interlocutory application because it decides nothing more than that an action may or may not be commenced.

That being so then the various civil cases set out in *Cross on Evidence*, 2nd ed., at pp. 24–26, and *Phipson on Evidence*, 11th ed., p. 103, are of small assistance. The cases set out in these volumes are concerned with "*prima facie* evidence" upon the trial of an issue. The definition of "*prima facie* evidence" when used in English statutes usually has that meaning attributed to it by Statford J. A. in *Regina v. Jacobson and Levy*, [1931] App. D. 466 at 478 (South Africa), where he said this:

> . . . "*prima facie* evidence" in its usual sense is used to mean *prima facie* proof of an issue, the burden of proving which is upon the party giving that evidence. In the absence of further evidence from the other side, the *prima facie* proof becomes conclusive proof and the party giving it discharges his onus.

It will be seen that that definition is not particularly helpful because such a criterion must be for proof upon trial. This application decides nothing more than whether the applicant has adduced sufficient evidence which on the face of that evidence discloses that it is, so far as can be judged from the first disclosure, in the interests of the company to pursue the action.

Adopting that definition one must then consider what disclosures are contained in the evidence which might warrant a Court exercising its discretion to allow the minority shareholders here to commence an action against the directors for fraud in the name of and on behalf of the company.

The principal matters relied upon by the applicants are:

1. The sale to Green Valley of the entire undertaking of Fraser Valley for a price of approximately $91,700 less than its apparent value for lending purposes, both transactions having been concluded on the same day.

2. The apparent failure of the directors to seek out any bids from other persons, bearing in mind that Louis Clarke as a director of both companies appears on the face of the documents to have derived a benefit from this transaction.

3. The apparent failure of the directors to find out the current market value of the lands sold as it appears in the notes of Mr. Ross that the directors did not rely upon the appraisal made 31st December 1971 when consummating the sale to Green River.

4. The possible loss of diminution of the water lot.

5. The question as to the authority of the directors to make the sale to Green River in the absence of any evidence as to voting authority or the presence or absence of sufficient members to pass the resolutions.

6. The acceptance of a promissory note in substitution for a debenture and an account receivable.

In my view these are matters which concern the interests of the company as the major shareholders of Fraser Valley within the meanings of s. 222(3)(c). These may also be matters of moment and concern to the individual shareholders of the company, but that, in my view, does not detract from the derivative nature of the action sought to be commenced.

Miss Southin submits that the question is whether there is evidence that discloses a case that should be dealt with. Mr. McConnell who relies in his argument essentially on majority rule points out that a court must give careful consideration to the possible consequences of such an order. There can be no question but that that is an important consideration.

The standard of care required of a director of a company is that set out in 6 Hals. (3d) 309, para. 619:

> A director is liable for negligence if he fails to exercise such degree of care as a reasonable man might be expected to take in the circumstances on his own behalf, and the company in consequence suffers loss.

Bearing that standard in mind it is my view that the applicants have put forward sufficient evidence which on the face of it discloses a failure on the part of the directors to take that degree of care required of them and accordingly I grant leave to the applicants to bring the action set out in the motion in the name of and on behalf of Northwest Forest Products Ltd. against the five persons named in the motion.

The motion also claims security for costs and disbursements. It is conceded that that application is premature and cannot as appears by s. 222(4) be brought until the action is commenced.

The costs of the motion will be costs in the cause.

Application granted.

Re Marc-Jay Investments Inc. and Levy
(1974), 5 O.R. (2d) 235, 50 D.L.R. (3d) 45 (H.C.)

O'LEARY J.: This is an application under s. 99(2) of the *Business Corporations Act*, R.S.O. 1970, c. 53, for an order permitting a shareholder to commence a representative action under s. 99(1) of the said Act.

I understand it to be agreed that the applicant was the beneficial owner of approximately 12.9% of the shares of Levy Industries Limited at the time of the purchase by it on November 15, 1972, of Premium Forest Products Limited, which transaction the intended action is designed to set aside. The applicant was not at the time the registered owner of any shares in Levy Industries Limited. I am satisfied on the reasoning to be found in *Re Great West Permanent Loan Co. and Winding-up Act*, [1927] 2 W.W.R. 15, and *Goodbun v. Mitchell et al.*,

[1928] 1 W.W.R. 495, that the beneficial owner of a share has the status to bring an action under s. 99(1) even though he is not the registered owner of the share.

I am also satisfied that the applicant has made reasonable efforts to cause Levy Industries Limited to commence such an action and that Levy Industries Limited refused to do so.

I am likewise satisfied that the shareholder, in bringing this application and in regard to his expressed intention to commence that contemplated action, is acting in good faith. Levy Industries Limited purchased Premium from Seaway Multi-Corp Limited. At the time of the purchase, Levy's board of directors and Seaway's board of directors were identical, that is to say the 12 directors of Seaway were also the 12 directors of Levy.

On the contemplated action the applicant intends to allege, *inter alia*, that the purchase by Levy of Premium was an improvident transaction to the knowledge of Levy's directors and was therefore fraudulent, at least in so far as it affected the minority shareholders, and that in any event the material provided to the shareholders under Item No. 10 of Form 15 of the Regulations, R.R.O. 1970, Reg. 78, under the *Business Corporations Act* was so deficient, that it did not permit the shareholders to form a reasoned judgment concerning the transaction in question, when a meeting was called to approve of the purchase under s. 134(5) of the said Act.

Since the transaction involving the purchase of the shares of Premium was between companies with the same directors it is argued that a constructive fraud occurred and the purchase would be set aside even without proof that the transaction was in fact improvident. It is not my function to decide whether such contemplated action will succeed at trial, but simply to decide whether there is *prima facie* merit to it. It is argued by the applicant that if the transaction was in fact fraudulent on the shareholders it would be in the interest of the shareholders that it be set aside and I accept that proposition.

While Levy has tendered evidence in opposition to the allegations made against it, it appears that some information was not disclosed in the material sent to the shareholders which may have been essential for them to make a reasoned judgment in deciding whether or not to confirm the action of the directors in buying Premium.

It further appears that the applicant is of the belief that Levy paid far too much for Premium and the appellant points to some evidence in support of that belief.

It is obvious that a Judge hearing an application for leave to commence an action, cannot try the action. I believe it is my function to deny the application if it appears that the intended action is frivolous or vexatious or is bound to be unsuccessful. Where the applicant is acting in good faith and otherwise has the status to commence the action, and where the intended action does not appear frivolous or vexatious and could reasonably succeed; and where such action is in the interest of the shareholders, then leave to bring the action should be given.

The respondent has not shown that the intended action would be either frivolous or vexatious. It is beyond question that if the allegations of the applicant are correct it would be in the interest of the minority shareholders that the action be brought. The main position of the respondent was that the material filed by it should convince me that the purchase of Premium was not improvident for the shareholders of Levy. To reach that conclusion I would have to weigh the affidavit material filed on this application. I agree that I have to weigh it to determine whether it shows that the intended action is without merit or is frivolous or vexatious. Having weighed the evidence I am not of the opinion that the contemplated action is without merit or is frivolous or vexatious. I believe, however, that is the extent to which I am entitled to weigh the evidence. I am not to deny leave to bring an action simply because on a weighing of the evidence I should decide it is unlikely that the action will be successful. I might say I have not reached any such conclusion in this case.

I feel, therefore, that I must give the applicant leave to bring its intended action. Such leave is granted with costs to the applicant in the cause.

Application granted.

Note

For a case following *Marc-Jay*, see *Armstrong v. Gardner* (1978), 20 O.R. (2d) 648 (Ont. H.C.). Cory J., in granting leave to commence an action under s. 99 of the predecessor to the present OBCA, made some useful observations on the requirements for getting leave. For example, he stated that an application for leave under the section could be based on the information and belief of others since first-hand evidence would not usually be available.

Re Bellman and Western Approaches Ltd.
(1981), 33 B.C.L.R. 45, 130 D.L.R. (3d) 193 (C.A.).

[This case arose from a dispute between two groups of shareholders of Western Approaches Ltd., a CBCA corporation. The petitioners, the Bellman group, were minority shareholders, whose control of the "investors' common shares" allowed them to select three of the corporation's eight directors. The Duke group controlled the "founders' common shares", entitling them to select the other five directors. They also held 25% of the investors' common shares. The Duke group and their controlled companies entered into a loan agreement with a bank, which enabled them to purchase the majority of the investors' common shares and control the election of all of Western's directors. The loan agreement included a provision providing for disclosure of confidential information about Western to the bank, and a requirement that the directors use their powers to cause Western to go public. The complainants sent a letter to the company, alleging wrongdoing on the part of the directors, and requesting that the corporation seek relief. The board sought outside advice from a law firm and an accounting firm, and was advised that the corporation should not take any action. Western was advised to execute a supplemental agreement reinforcing the overriding obligation of the directors to act in the best interests of the corporation. The complainants sought leave to bring a derivative action, which was granted by the lower court.]

NEMETZ C.J.B.C.: Mr. Goldie's submission may be summarized by saying that the alleged error relating to each of the three conditions precedent set out in s. 232(2) of the federal Act. I will deal with these subsections *seriatim*:

(a)   Notice

This subsection requires that reasonable notice be given to the directors of the corporation, in this case, Western. It was pointed out to us that one of the grounds in the petition (para. l(b)) concerning take-over bids was not contained in the notice letter. Price Waterhouse and Bull Housser proceeded with their investigations as set out in the notice letter. Accordingly, it is said that the directors decided not to sue without having an opportunity of considering this allegation. It is to be noted that the Federal Act only requires the giving of "reasonable notice" of intention to apply to commence a derivative action. A perusal of the notice letter of June 26, 1980, when read together with the response of January 16, 1981, leads me to conclude that the directors were reasonably notified of the Bellman group's intention to apply to commence a derivative action. Failure to specify each and every cause of action in a notice does not, in my opinion, invalidate the notice as a whole.

(b)   Good faith

Mr. Goldie agreed that it is possible for both a personal and a derivative action to proceed on the same set of facts: *cf. Goldex Mines Ltd. v. Revill et al.* (1974), 54 D.L.R. (3d) 672, 7 O.R. (2d) 216 (Ont. C.A.); *Borak v. J.I. Case Co.* (1963), 317 F. Supp. 2d 838; *Johnson v. American General Ins. Co.* (1969), 296 F. Supp. 802 at p. 808. However, he argued, where the relief requested in both actions is substantially the same, that is evidence of a lack of good faith since it is vexatious to seek the same relief in two actions. However, after examining the relief sought in each action, I conclude that the relief is not the same. Damages for breach of fiduciary duty are not available in the personal action, nor have such damages in that action been sought. Damages are being sought in the derivative action. That distinction, among others, is sufficient to justify the initiation of the derivative action under this heading.

(c)   Interests of the corporation

In my view this is the key section for consideration in this case. The section does not say that the Court must be satisfied that it is in the interests of the corporation. It says that no action may be brought unless the Court is satisfied that it appears to be in the interests of the corporation to bring the suit. I take that to mean that what is sufficient at this stage is that an arguable case be shown to subsist. This is quite different from the rules established at common law. [Nemetz C.J.B.C. examined the common law rule in *Foss v. Harbottle* and its exceptions, the state of the American common law, and the American statutory derivative action.] Presumably it was the intention of the drafters of our federal Act to remove the common law barriers which I have described. Section 235(i) clearly eliminates the ratification procedure. An alleged breach of duty, ratification of which is approved by the shareholders, no longer provides a sole reason to dismiss an application for leave to proceed derivatively. Sections 232 and 233 set out a summary procedure by way of an application before a Chambers Judge to have a quick determination of where a complainant may institute a derivative suit. The conditions precedent, although bearing a resemblance to the prerequisites of the common law, have significant differences.

Because of my views in relation to (a) and (b), I will allude only to (c) regarding which we are informed no Canadian case law exists.

How is a Court to exercise its discretion in coming to a determination that it is satisfied that "it appears to be in the interests of the corporation" to allow the derivative action to be brought? The discretion is a wide one. However, despite its breadth, nowhere does Parliament say, nor, in my opinion, was it intended, that the logic of the common law in cases of this kind be disregarded. One must first look to the decision of the directors who, having been given reasonable notice by a complainant in good faith, decide not to assert a corporate right of action. In this case they refused. Can it be said that this refusal was given impartially? It was submitted that the resolution not to sue was passed by four independent directors since the Duke group and Asper did not vote. It was also submitted that the decision of these "independent" directors was based upon the reports of their accountants and outside lawyers and that in any event they could reasonably conclude that the disadvantages to the company outweighed the advantages. How do I conclude that these four directors were not independent? Messrs. Milroy, Dewar, Shier and Atkinson were nominated by the Investors Group on January 16, 1980, at a time when the Duke group held a majority of the investors' shares. More important is the effect upon their independence of cls. 3.03 and 3.04 of the guarantor's agreement where the borrowers covenanted to use their powers as directors to assert control over the directors nominated by the investors group to act and vote in ways favorable to the lender.

It is also curious that the instructions of the directors to the investigators, i.e., Price Waterhouse, were limited to certain periods of time in respect only of legal expenses, expenses charged to the company and contra account settlements. Since the legal opinion of January 15, 1981, was based on this limited report it can hardly be said to have been conclusive of the substantive issues raised by the complainants, namely, the breach of fiduciary duty.

Considering the whole of the evidence before the Chambers Judge, she could have come to the conclusion that at the time when they came to the decision not to sue, the directors did stand in a dual relation which prevented them from exercising an unprejudiced judgment. While it is true that a quantifiable loss was not proven, nevertheless, it was sufficient to have adumbrated a potential loss resulting from the covenant in the guarantor's agreement requiring the borrowers to pay a fee to the guarantor in the event that they were not able to cause the company to go public. Since the fee was based on gross revenue, it might place the directors in a position of conflict in deciding whether it is in their interest to keep revenues down in order to reduce the potential fee or to maximize revenues in the interest of all of the shareholders. However, this would be a matter for the trial Court to consider. It is sufficient that it appears to be in the interest of the company that the action be brought.

I would, accordingly, dismiss the appeal.

Appeal dismissed.

Notes

1   There is much American jurisprudence on the effect of the directors of the defendant corporation seeking outside advice with respect to the substance of the grieving shareholder's complaints, and the desirability of an action being brought by the corporation against the wrongdoers. There are two lines of authority on the question of how much deference to give to a litigation committee's findings. Courts in some jurisdictions refuse to question the business judgment of a litigation committee, so long as it is disinterested and performed an adequate investigation. Therefore, the use of an independent litigation committee acts as a defence to derivative actions in these jurisdictions. See *Auerbach v. Bennett*, 419 N.Y.S.2d 920 (1979); *Hirsch v. Jones Intercable, Inc.*, 984 P.2d 629 (Colo., 1999); and *Cuker v. Mikalauskas*, 692 A.2d 1042 (Pa., 1997). In other jurisdictions, the litigation committee must be independent and conduct a fair investigation in order for its decision to be considered, but the court may also question whether or not the committee's decision was reasonable. See *Zapata v. Maldonado*, 430 A.2d 779 (Del., 1981); *Abramowitz v. Posner*, 672 F.2d 1025 (2nd Cir. N.Y., 1982); and

Strougo ex rel. Brazilian Equity Fund, Inc. v. Bassini, 112 F.Supp.2d 355 (S.D.N.Y., 2000).

For a detailed set of guidelines on the question of independent committee recommendations in the context of derivative actions, see *Principles of Corporate Governance* (American Law Institute, 1994). The recommendations attempt to balance the right of the corporation, as seen by the drafters, to seek termination of an action for business reasons and the need for careful judicial review of the reasons so offered because those in control of the corporation may wish to justify dismissal for self-serving motives.

What importance should a Canadian court attach to such an independent review in a derivative action? For a discussion of independent reviews in the context of a hostile takeover bidder allegeing oppression, see *Pente Investment Management Ltd. v. Schneider Corp.* (1998), 42 O.R. (3d) 177; and *C.W. Shareholding Ltd. v. WIC Western International Communications Ltd.* (1998), 39 O.R. (3d) 755 (Gen. Div.). Do you think special statutory provisions should be enacted to deal with the issue?

2   Shareholder approval of an alleged breach of a right or duty does not automatically disallow a derivative action. The CBCA provides:

> 242 (1) An application made or an action brought or intervened in under this part shall not be stayed or dismissed by reason only that it is shown that an alleged breach of a right or a duty owed to the corporation or its subsidiary has been or may be approved by the shareholders of such body corporate, but evidence of approval by the shareholders may be taken into account by the court in making an order under section 214, 240, or 241.

See *Schadegg v. Alaska Apollo Resources Inc.* (1994), [1994] B.C.J. No. 1100, 1994 CarswellBC 2132 (S.C.), where a financing scheme of a widely held company was approved of by over 80% of the shareholders. This overwhelming approval and corresponding scant support for the complainant's petition, while not a bar to an action, was taken as evidence that a derivative action would not be in the company's interests. What evidence should a court examine beyond shareholder approval in assessing the merits of a derivative action?

3   The good faith of the applicant is one of the criteria for leave to bring a derivative action. To what extent must good faith be demonstrated and to what extent may it be assumed? See *Tremblett v. S.C.B. Fisheries Ltd.* (1993), 116 Nfld. & P.E.I.R. 139, 1993 CarswellNfld 52 (T.D.); *Primex Investments Ltd. v. Northwest Sports Enterprises Ltd.* (1995), 13 B.C.L.R. (3d) 300, 1995 CarswellBC 958 (S.C. [In Chambers]), reversed (1996), 26 B.C.L.R. (3d) 357, 1996 CarswellBC

2505 (C.A.), leave to appeal to S.C.C. dismissed [1998] S.C.C.A. No. 406; and *Discovery Enterprises Inc. v. Ebco Industries Ltd.* (1997), 40 B.C.L.R. (3d) 43, 1997 CarswellBC 1586 (S.C.), affirmed (1998), 50 B.C.L.R. (3d) 195, 1998 CarswellBC 1225 (C.A.), leave to appeal to S.C.C. dismissed [1997] S.C.C.A. No. 4. In *Discovery*, Williams C.J.S.C. said (at 59):

> The test for good faith in this type of case was dealt with in Primex, where the court considered the requirement under s. 225 of the B.C. *Company Act*. Mr. Justice Tysoe in finding the applicant acted in good faith appears to tie the requirement of "good faith" to the test of the "interest of the company". He states that where there is an arguable case, the applicant cannot be said to be acting in bad faith because he wants the company to pursue what he genuinely considers to be a valid claim. In that case, there was no evidence the applicant was using the prospect of a derivative action as a threat in order to extract some advantage from the company. Tysoe J. also indicates that an applicant advancing self-interest is not necessarily acting in bad faith.

The onus of showing good faith rests upon the applicant, but it appears that it will be assumed if the applicant seems to have a good claim. The result is that the fate of the good faith requirement may depend upon whether the action is in the best interests of the corporation.

4   Can a creditor be granted leave to bring a derivative action? A creditor may be a "proper person" to bring an action under s. 238 of the CBCA or an equivalent. See *First Edmonton Place Ltd. v. 315888 Alberta Ltd.* (1988), 40 B.L.R. 28, 1988 CarswellAlta 103 (Q.B.) [appeal adjourned (1989), 45 B.L.R. 110, 1989 CarswellAlta 181 (C.A.)] (at 63):

> In the case of a creditor who claims to be a "proper person" to make a s. 232 application, in my view the criterion would be whether, even if the applicant did not come within s. 231(b)(i) or (ii), he or it would nevertheless be a person who could reasonably be entrusted with the responsibility of advancing the interests of the corporation by seeking a remedy to right the wrong allegedly done to the corporation. The applicant would not have to be a security holder (as I have defined that notion), director or officer of the corporation.

Note, however, that *First Edmonton* examined this issue in the context of an oppression claim. See also *Daon Development Corp., Re* (1984), 10 D.L.R. (4th) 216, 1984 CarswellBC 175 (S.C.); and *Royal Trust Corp. of Canada v. Hordo* (1993), 10 B.L.R. (2d) 86, 1993 CarswellOnt 147 (Gen. Div. [Commercial List]). Are there valid reasons for a broader characterization of a "proper person" to be a complainant in the context of an oppression action as compared to a derivative action? Does it make a difference to the analysis that the New Brunswick and Alberta Acts specifically include a creditor in their definitions of a complainant? The Supreme Court of Canada in *BCE Inc., Re*, 2008 CarswellQue 12595, 2008 CarswellQue 12596, (sub nom. *BCE Inc. v. 1976 Debentureholders*) [2008] 3 S.C.R. 560 (S.C.C.) considered to whom the fiduciary duties are owed. The following excerpt suggests that it might be possible for stakeholders other than shareholders (such as a creditor) to bring an action on behalf of the corporation in a derivative action:

> Normally only the beneficiary of a fiduciary duty can enforce the duty. In the corporate context, however, this may offer little comfort. The directors who control the corporation are unlikely to bring an action against themselves for breach of their own fiduciary duty. The shareholders cannot act in the stead of the corporation; their only power is the right to oversee the conduct of the directors by way of votes at shareholder assemblies. Other stakeholders may not even have that.

> To meet these difficulties, the common law developed a number of special remedies to protect the interests of shareholders and stakeholders of the corporation. These remedies have been affirmed, modified and supplemented by the CBCA.

> The first remedy provided by the *CBCA* is the s. 239 derivative action, which allows stakeholders to enforce the directors' duty to the corporation when the directors are themselves unwilling to do so. With leave of the court, a complainant may bring (or intervene in) a derivative action in the name and on behalf of the corporation or one of its subsidiaries to enforce a right of the corporation, including the rights correlative with the directors' duties to the corporation. (The requirement of leave serves to prevent frivolous and vexatious actions, and other actions which, while possibly brought in good faith, are not in the interest of the corporation to litigate.)

5   Can a person who does not fall within the definition of "complainant" at the time of the wrongdoing buy shares of the corporation, thereby purchasing the right to bring a derivative action? See *Richardson Greenshields of Canada Ltd. v. Kalmacoff* (1995), 22 O.R. (3d) 577, 1995 CarswellOnt 324 (C.A.), leave to appeal to S.C.C. dismissed [1995] S.C.C.A. No. 260, which concerned an application for leave to commence a derivative action under the *Trust and Loan Companies Act*, S.C. 1991, c. 45. The definition of "complainant" under this Act is substantially similar to the CBCA. Robins J.A. found that the Act did not impose a condition of ownership

contemporaneous with the acts complained of. He held that it is sufficient that the complainant be a registered holder of a security of the company at the time he or she brings the application.

This raises the possibility of an entrepreneurial plaintiff "buying-in" to a right to recovery by purchasing stock in a wronged corporation and bringing a derivative action. How, if at all, does this differ from buying-in to any other form of litigation, which is generally not permitted? See Poonam Puri, "Financing of Litigation by Third Party Investors: A Share of Justice?" 36(3) (1998) O.H.L.J. 515.

6   Is the common law derivative action still available despite the existence of the statutory derivative action? In *Farnham v. Fingold*, [1973] 2 O.R. 132, 33 D.L.R. (3d) 156, 1973 CarswellOnt 840 (C.A.), *infra*, which dealt with Ontario's old derivative actions provisions, Jessup J.A. said for the court (at 135):

> Section 99 of the *Business Corporations Act*, R.S.O. 1970, c. 53 provides . . . All forms of derivative actions purporting to be brought on behalf of and for the benefit of the corporation come within it, and therefore s-s. (2) applies to all such actions.

The Supreme Court in *BCE Inc., Re*, 2008 CarswellQue 12595, 2008 CarswellQue 12596, (sub nom. *BCE Inc. v. 1976 Debentureholders*) [2008] 3 S.C.R. 560 (S.C.C.) at para. 44 recently considered the status of the derivative action and concluded that the duty of care under s. 122(1)(b) did not ground a private right of action, suggesting that perhaps the common law derivative action may still be available:

> A second remedy lies against the directors in a civil action for breach of duty of care. As noted, s. 122(1)(b) of the *CBCA* requires directors and officers of a corporation to "exercise the care, diligence and skill that a reasonably prudent person would exercise in comparable circumstances". This duty, unlike the s. 122(1)(a) fiduciary duty, is not owed solely to the corporation, and thus may be the basis for liability to other stakeholders in accordance with principles governing the law of tort and extracontractual liability: *Peoples Department Stores*. Section 122(1)(b) does not provide an independent foundation for claims. However, applying the principles of *Saskatchewan Wheat Pool v. Canada*, [1983] 1 S.C.R. 205 (S.C.C.), courts may take this statutory provision into account as to the standard of behaviour that should reasonably be expected.

(e)   Costs in Derivative Actions

As previously mentioned, the prevailing costs rules are absolutely pivotal to an assessment of the efficacy of shareholder rights and remedies. Costs can be staggering in complex corporate-commercial litigation, and the average shareholder with a small stake will have neither the resources nor appropriate incentives (due both to the free rider problem and small stake) to commence litigation. Larger shareholders may have both the resources and the incentives, but too often these shareholders will be part of the control group accused of wrongdoing. Although institutional shareholders, like pension funds, banks, trust and insurance companies and the like might also sue, these shareholders will frequently be loath to sue rather than simply sell their holdings if dissatisfied with management. Fortunately, this attitude (sometimes referred to as the "Wall Street Rule") is rapidly changing, and institutional shareholders are now willing to adopt a more confrontational stance *viz* management and controlling shareholders. In any case, there are ways in which costs rules can be cast that will greatly attenuate the free rider problem facing shareholders. One of these is to allow recovery of costs by the plaintiff from all those who stand to benefit from a favourable judgment. Where the action is derivative in character, and the award is made in favour of the corporation, a convenient way of avoiding costly collection problems while indirectly distributing the costs of litigation amongst all those who benefit is to have the corporation pay the costs of the litigation. While this seems an ideal solution to the free rider problem, it unfortunately creates another, equally vexing problem. Where the corporation automatically pays all the costs of the action, shareholders may be encouraged to commence nuisance or "strike" suits lacking any merit. Even when commencing an action in good faith, shareholders have an incentive to sue if there is any possibility, however remote, of success. This is almost certain to result in excessive litigation. One balancing mechanism is to presumptively require the corporation to pay the costs of the litigation, subject to a demonstration that the plaintiff has not commenced the action in good faith and/or the action has some reasonable possibility of success. *Cf.* OBCA s. 105(6). Are there any other solutions? Note that a number of provisions in the CBCA deal with the issue of costs. The Act provides that a complainant is not required to give any security for costs (s. 242(3)), that the court may make an interim order as to costs (s. 242(4)), and that the court may also order an indemnity as to costs (s. 240(d) and s. 242(4)). Similar provisions may be found in the OBCA (see ss. 249(3), 249(4), 247(d)).

The following case considers the question of when an indemnity for costs will be ordered.

Turner et al. v. Mailhot et al.
(1985), 28 B.L.R. 222 (Ont. H.C.)

[The Plaintiff and his wife owned 30% of the common shares of the corporation; the balance of the shares were owned by the defendant and his wife. A disagreement arose between the parties, which led to the plaintiff and his wife being locked out of the company's premises and the termination of their employment and of Turner's position as director and officer of the company. The plaintiff sought and obtained leave to bring a derivative action seeking return to the company of lost income diverted to the defendant. He then applied for indemnity for the costs of the action, under s. 246 [now 242(4)] of the CBCA.]

REID J.: . . . The situation here may be compared with that before the English Court of Appeal in *Wallersteiner v. Moir (No. 2)*. That was a carefully considered decision which justifies close scrutiny and extensive reference. Each of the Judges, Denning M.R. and Buckley and Scarman L.JJ, wrote separate reasons which although not entirely in agreement with each other produced a common agreed result.

In that case Moir was acting as the representative of the minority shareholders in litigation equivalent to a derivative action under the *Business Corporations Act*. An order was made indemnifying him against his fees and costs. The gist of the Court's decision was that the order rested upon equity and the Court's discretion, the Court having concluded that the action was reasonable and prudent in the company's interest, was brought in good faith and, as well, in Denning M.R.'s view was also in the public interest.

It was observed that Moir had exhausted his own funds in fighting the litigation for over ten years and contributions from other minority shareholders had as well been exhausted. As Denning M.R. said Moir had "come to the end of his tether" (p. 856 [All E.R.]) yet the litigation was not finished. Moir had "not any money left with which to pay the costs in further matters" and was fearful of the prospect of having to pay personally costs if he should lose (pp. 856-57). On that basis there is a clear distinction between that case and this for I have already observed that Turner make no such claim.

Another distinction exists. The company on whose behalf Moir was suing was "a substantial public company of long standing" (p. 853) (sometimes referred to in the judgments as "the companies"). Moir was a minority shareholder holding only a few shares. We are not told how many, or what relation their number bore to the number of issued shares of the company but comments made in the judgments are revealing. Denning M. R. referred at p. 857 to Moir's "few shares which might appreciate a little in value" if he were successful in the litigation. At p. 860 he observed further:

> It would appear that any advantage to Mr. Moir himself would be trivial, seeing that he holds so few shares . . .

In contrast, Turner and his wife, are the only minority shareholders, in the defendant company. It is not realistic here to say, as was said in *Wallersteiner*, that if Turner "wins all the way through no part will redound to his own benefit" (p. 860). If Turner is successful in this litigation the monetary benefit to the company could be in the millions. That, in turn, would greatly increase the book value of Turner's shares. Whether he would be capable of forcing the reluctant majority to turn that into a realizable benefit for him and his wife is certainly open to question at this point. Yet, that aside, this action more closely resembles a struggle between Turner and Mailhot over their own advantage with the company used as a vehicle than an attack by an almost lone altruist (Moir) upon an entrenched and devious miscreant (Wallersteiner) for the advantage of the company involved.

[Reid J. quoted from the *Wallersteiner* case and continued:]

If that reasoning were applied here it would suggest strongly that Turner, having obtained leave of this Court to bring the action, had established a *prima facie* claim to indemnity. There is nothing in the *Business Corporations Act* which would indicate to me that the views expressed in *Wallersteiner* would not form a reasonable basis for the interpretation of the sections of the Act governing the application before me. The section of our Act that governs applications for leave to bring a derivative action simply states in statutory language the gist of what the Judges of the Court of Appeal said in *Wallersteiner*. Thus, it must be established that directors of the relevant company refused to bring the action, that the complainant is acting in good faith, and that the action appears to be in the interests of the company. Section 245 is the relevant provision. It states: [s. 245 omitted] Since an applicant, in order to obtain leave under s. 245 must, in effect, fulfil the conditions laid down in *Wallersteiner*, he or she could reasonably be taken to have established a *prima facie* right to indemnity.

Yet the right is merely *prima facie*. There may, in my opinion, be considerations arising out of the circumstances of particular cases that might affect the question whether that *prima facie* right should be turned into a proven right. I would think, for instance, that financial inability to carry on an action would weigh heavily in favour of a grant of indemnity and may well overbear any considerations raised by a respondent.

In the absence of such an element, however, other factors might predominate. I have already said that Turner makes no claim of financial inability and the beneficiaries of a successful outcome would not so much be the company as the two minority shareholders. I do not think that the financial ability to carry on an action should necessarily deprive a plaintiff in a derivative action of indemnification: that would be contrary to the principle that the plaintiff is the agent of the company for the purposes of the action. Yet the fact that the benefit sought is more for plaintiff than the company is a consideration that weighs with me.

In the result I do not think that, at this stage anyway, an order for complete indemnity should be made. I therefore direct that Turner is entitled to indemnity to the extent of one-half of his incurred and reasonable future fees and costs. That direction is made without prejudice to any future application that Turner might be advised to make for more complete indemnification as would be the case, for instance, if the day arrived when he was financially incapable of sustaining the litigation.

[The court noted that $40,000 had been paid by the company towards Mailhot's costs of defending the action.]

In my opinion it was inappropriate to pay out company funds for the defence of Mailhot. Similarly, it would be inappropriate to pay out further funds for that purpose. Since the funds were paid out essentially for Mailhot's benefit and at his direction an order shall go directing Mailhot to pay into court the sum of $40,000 for the purpose of furnishing indemnification for Turner in accordance with the order that I have made or with any future order of this Court.

Notes and Questions

1 Note that to the extent that the corporation is ordered to pay all or part of the costs of the action, then the costs are indirectly spread to all the shareholders in the proportion of their shareholdings (at least, assuming there are no significant creditors; see note 2, *infra*). If the corporation is ordered to pay half the costs of the action, and the plaintiffs own approximately half the shares (as in *Turner*) then the indemnity is, in effect, as to only one-quarter of the costs of the action. A full indemnity from the corporation is still only an indemnity as to half the costs, from the plaintiff shareholder's point of view. Is there any reason for awarding an indemnity as to only half the costs in the *Turner* case? Should the court be able to award a partial or full indemnity against the accused wrongdoers, rather than the corporation?

2 Where a costs award is made against the corporation, at least part of the burden of the award is shouldered by the corporation's fixed claimants, including creditors, trade creditors and employees. This is because any depletion of the assets of the corporation jeopardizes, to at least some degree, the corporation's ability to meet its fixed claims as they come due. Does this strengthen the case in favour of an indemnity against the accused wrongdoers, rather than the corporation?

3 Should the rules regarding the awarding of an indemnity be different in relation to private corporations and public corporations? If so, why?

4 The relevant corporate legislation, unlike the CBCA and OBCA, may not provide for an indemnity as to costs. In such a case a court may still be able to draw upon relatively recent common law to order an indemnity. In *Wallersteiner v. Moir (No. 2)*, [1975] 1 All E.R. 849, [1975] Q.B. 373 (C.A.), Lord Denning ordered such an indemnity in a case involving apparently meritorious litigation by an impecunious plaintiff, basing his award on principles of equity. The circumstances in which such an award will be made have most recently been discussed by the English Chancery Court in *Watts v. Midland Bank*

PLC., [1986] B.C. L.C. 15, and by the English Court of Appeal in
Smith v. Croft, [1986] 2 All E.R. 551.

In the United States, there has been considerable controversy
surrounding the payment of plaintiff's counsel fees and expenses in
derivative actions. See Douglas G. Cole, "Counsel Fees in Stockholders' Derivative and Class Actions – Hornstein Revisited" (1972),
6 U. Rich. L. Rev. 259; Robert T. Mowrey, "Attorney Fees in
Securities Class Action and Derivative Suits" (1978), 3 J. Corp. Law
267; Leo Herzel and Robert K. Hagan, "Plaintiffs' Attorneys' Fees in
Derivative and Class Actions" [Winter, 1981] Litigation 25. For
detailed recommendations on the topic, see s. 7.17 of *Principles of
Corporate Governance: Analysis and Recommendations*, Discussion
Draft No. 1 (American Law Institute, 1985).

5   For a case considering the issue of an award of interim costs (rather
than an indemnity) under the oppression remedy, see *Alles v.
Maurice*, *infra*.

(f)   The Relationship Between the Complainant and the Corporation

While a derivative action is brought "in the name of and on behalf of
a corporation", the representative nature of the action raises the question:
What is the relationship between the complainant, who is acting in the
name of the corporation, and the corporation? Is the complainant
required to look after all of the corporation's interests in the derivative
action? In *Discovery Enterprises Inc. v. Ebco Industries Ltd.* (1998), 41
B.L.R. (2d) 207, 1998 CarswellBC 2539 (C.A.), Discovery was pursuing
an oppression action against Ebco and had obtained leave to bring a
derivative action in Ebco's name against its creditors. Ebco sought to
enjoin Discovery's law firm, which was representing it in both actions,
from participating in the derivative action, arguing that it was a conflict
of interest to have it acting both on Ebco's behalf and against it. Newbury
J.A. held that while Discovery was acting in Ebco's name, this did not
mean that Discovery was acting *for* Ebco (at 212):

> The fact that the company's name is used as plaintiff, presumably to
> ensure that it receives any damages or other sums ultimately awarded
> to it, should not obscure the substance of the litigation, which is a
> contest between the Class D and majority shareholders. Since
> Discovery has conduct of the action, it will be instructing its counsel
> as plaintiff's counsel — they will not take instructions from Ebco,
> and Ebco should not seek advice from them.

Ebco also argued that the representative acting on behalf of a company in
a derivative action assumes a fiduciary duty to that company, and that it
is the representative's duty to look after that company's interests.
Newbury J.A. disagreed with this, saying that the relationship between

the parties could not be simultaneously adversarial and fiduciary. Ebco's interests in the litigation process in matters such as document discovery and privilege were not to be looked after by Discovery but by Ebco's board. Further protection would be offered by the court's overall supervisory powers in a derivative suit.

(g) The Statutory Derivative Action after *BCE*

The Supreme Court of Canada recently considered the derivative action in the pivotal case of *BCE Inc., Re* discussed in Chapter 6 relating to fiduciary duties. For a review of the facts of *BCE Inc., Re*, see Chapter 4.

BCE Inc., Re
2008 CarswellQue 12595, 2008 CarswellQue 12596, (sub nom. *BCE Inc. v. 1976 Debentureholders*) [2008] 3 S.C.R. 560 (S.C.C.)

In *Peoples Department Stores*, this Court found that although directors *must* consider the best interests of the corporation, it may also be appropriate, although *not mandatory*, to consider the impact of corporate decisions on shareholders or particular groups of stakeholders. As stated by Major and Deschamps JJ., at para. 42:

> We accept as an accurate statement of law that in determining whether they are acting with a view to the best interests of the corporation it may be legitimate, given all the circumstances of a given case, for the board of directors to consider, *inter alia*, the interests of shareholders, employees, suppliers, creditors, consumers, governments and the environment.

As will be discussed, cases dealing with claims of oppression have further clarified the content of the fiduciary duty of directors with respect to the range of interests that should be considered in determining what is in the best interests of the corporation, acting fairly and responsibly.

In considering what is in the best interests of the corporation, directors may look to the interests of, *inter alia*, shareholders, employees, creditors, consumers, governments and the environment to inform their decisions. Courts should give appropriate deference to the business judgment of directors who take into account these ancillary interests, as reflected by the business judgment rule. The "business judgment rule" accords deference to a business decision, so long as it lies within a range of reasonable alternatives: see *Pente Investment Management Ltd. v. Schneider Corp.*, 1998 CarswellOnt 4035, (sub nom. *Maple Leaf Foods Inc. v. Schneider Corp.*) 42 O.R. (3d) 177 (Ont. C.A.); *Kerr v. Danier Leather Inc.*, 2007 SCC 44, 2007 CarswellOnt 6445, 2007 CarswellOnt 6446, [2007] 2 S.C.R. 331 (S.C.C.). It reflects the reality that directors, who are mandated under s. 102(1) of the *CBCA* to manage the corporation's business and affairs, are often better suited to determine what is in the best interests of the corporation. This applies to decisions on stakeholders' interests, as much as other directorial decisions.

Normally only the beneficiary of a fiduciary duty can enforce the duty. In the corporate context, however, this may offer little comfort. The directors who control the corporation are unlikely to bring an action against themselves for breach of their own fiduciary duty. The shareholders cannot act in the stead of the corporation; their only power is the right to oversee the conduct of the directors by way of votes at shareholder assemblies. Other stakeholders may not even have that.

To meet these difficulties, the common law developed a number of special remedies to protect the interests of shareholders and stakeholders of the corporation. These remedies have been affirmed, modified and supplemented by the *CBCA*.

The first remedy provided by the *CBCA* is the s. 239 derivative action, which allows stakeholders to enforce the directors' duty to the corporation when the directors are themselves unwilling to do so. With leave of the court, a complainant may bring (or intervene in) a derivative action in the name and on behalf of the corporation or one of its subsidiaries to enforce a right of the corporation, including the rights correlative with the directors' duties to the corporation. (The requirement of leave serves to prevent frivolous and vexatious actions, and other actions which, while possibly brought in good faith, are not in the interest of the corporation to litigate.) A second remedy lies against the directors in a civil action for breach of duty of care. As noted, s. 122(1)(b) of the *CBCA* requires directors and officers of a corporation to "exercise the care, diligence and skill that a reasonably prudent person would exercise in comparable circumstances". This duty, unlike the s. 122(1)(a) fiduciary duty, is not owed solely to the corporation, and thus may be the basis for liability to other stakeholders in accordance with principles governing the law of tort and extracontractual liability: *Peoples Department Stores*. Section 122(1)(b) does not provide an independent foundation for claims. However, applying the principles of *Saskatchewan Wheat Pool v. Canada*, 1983 CarswellNat 521, 1983 CarswellNat 92, (sub nom. *Saskatchewan v. R.*) [1983] 1 S.C.R. 205 (S.C.C.), courts may take this statutory provision into account as to the standard of behaviour that should reasonably be expected.

A third remedy, grounded in the common law and endorsed by the *CBCA*, is a s. 241 action for oppression. Unlike the derivative action, which is aimed at enforcing a right of the corporation itself, the oppression remedy focuses on harm to the legal and equitable interests of stakeholders affected by oppressive acts of a corporation or its directors. This remedy is available to a wide range of stakeholders — security holders, creditors, directors and officers.

* * *

The following two excerpts discuss the implications of the *BCE* decision on corporate law remedies and particularly the derivative action.

Jeffrey G. MacIntosh, "BCE and the Peoples' Corporate Law: Learning to Live on Quicksand"
(2009) 48 C.B.L.J. 255

What is a Derivative Action? What Evidence Must be Adduced to Succeed?

Until *Peoples* and *BCE*, it has been customary in law schools to distinguish between personal and derivative actions on the basis that a derivative action is one which shareholders are hurt indirectly, but co-equally. By contrast, a personal action arises when a single shareholder, or a subset of shareholders are hurt. Because a derivative action is one in which the complainant brings "an action in the name and on behalf of a corporation," this distinction is obviously reflective of the widely held understanding that "the corporation" means the shareholders.

After *Peoples* and *BCE* however, it would seem to be impossible to distinguish between the derivative and the personal action in any intelligible way. If "[t]he interests of the corporation are not to be confused with the interests of creditors or those of any other stakeholders", then how does one demonstrate harm to the corporation? It is obviously not enough to show that one constituency's ox was gored. But what evidence must be adduced, and relating to which constituencies? The facts of *BCE* itself are illustrative. The debentureholders could easily show that the contemplated leveraged buyout would materially reduce the value of the debentures. But since that falls short of demonstrating harm to the corporation, it is unlikely, on that basis alone, that the debentureholders could secure leave to bring a derivative action, let alone succeed in that action. But what evidence is necessary, either to secure leave, or to succeed? Must they show that shareholders, or employees, or the public at large are likely to be harmed? All of these groups? That the net effect on all corporate constituents was likely to be negative? Ultimately, these questions are unanswerable in any intellectually coherent fashion. Consequently, to the extent that *Peoples* and *BCE* are indeed followed by lower court judges, they are likely to lead to different and contradictory readings in different courts, at different times, and by different judges. While Justice Brandeis once remarked that "[i]t is usually more important that rule of law be settled, that it be settled right," the Supreme Court appears to have failed on both counts.

Ed Iacobucci, "Indeterminacy and the Canadian Supreme Court's Approach to Corporate Fiduciary Duties"
(2009), 48 Can. Bus. L.J. 232

Support for the conclusion that the procedure should follow substance is found in the Supreme Court's approach to procedure for the duty of care in *Peoples* and *BCE*. In *Peoples*, the court noted that the statutory duty of care in s. 122(1)(b) does not explicitly name a beneficiary of the duty. In determining that the creditors had a cause of action for breach of the duty, the court turned to provincial procedure, in that case art. 1457 of the Civil Code of Quebec, which create a cause of action where one person does not abide by the "rules of conduct" and causes damages to another. Given that the substance of the statutory duty of care does not exclude a duty to creditors, and given that they could be harmed by negligence, the court concluded that the procedure and substance together imply that creditors do have the right to bring a duty of care suit.

Peoples did not address the cause of action that may or may not be available to creditors in other jurisdictions that do not have Art. 1457 of the C.C.Q. This was, and continues to be, unfortunate. In *BCE*, the court returned to this question and in passing, noting that s. 122(1)(b) does not itself provide a foundation for claims, while also suggesting that *Canada v. Saskatchewan Wheat Pool* implies that "courts may take [s. 122(1)(b)] into account as to the standard of behavior that should be reasonably expected". It is unfortunate that the court was not definitive on the matter, but two points are reasonably inferred from the court's discussion. First, since *Peoples* seems to suggest that the duty of care is likely in substance owed to creditors, the court is likely to find that a procedural right to enforce this duty follows. This is certainly true in Quebec — the only residual confusion elsewhere arises to the extent that the C.C.Q. was used not just for procedure, but also in part to ground the substantive duty owed to creditors. The second point from *Peoples* is of greater relevance to this article: since the fiduciary duty to the corporation comprehends attention to the interests of a range of stakeholders, derivative action and oppression remedy procedures ought to be receptive to claims by a range of stakeholders.

3. THE PERSONAL ACTION

Beck, "The Shareholders' Derivative Action"
(1974), 52 C.B.R. 159 at 169–179 (footnotes omitted)

A. The Personal Action

The ownership of stock in a corporation carries with it a number of personal rights. A partial list of the most common are the right to receive timely and informative notice of company meetings, the right to vote at such meetings, the right to have a properly executed proxy accepted and the right to inspect certain of the corporation's records. Some of these rights arise out of the companies Acts (the right to inspect books), some out of the articles or bylaws (number of days before meeting by which notice must be given) and some out of judicial legislation to make the requirements of the statute or corporation contract meaningful (truly informative notice). As to a right that can be truly classified as personal, the individual shareholders may have had similar rights infringed and may join in the action for redress in which case the action will be representative in form, but the substance remains the assertion of a personal right by each shareholder. The *locus classicus* is the judgment of Jessel M.R., in *Pender v. Lushington*:

> This is an action by Mr. Pender for himself. He is a member of the company, and whether he votes with the majority or the minority he is entitled to have his vote recorded — an individual right in respect of which he has a right to sue. That has nothing to do with the question like that raised in *Foss v. Harbottle* and that line of cases.

It might be thought that the line between personal rights and corporate rights would be well and clearly drawn. There is after all not much confusion between being denied the right to vote and a taking of property which depletes the corporate treasury. Between those two poles, however, there is uncertain ground and it is suggested that the personal rights category is in fact much broader than has been thought to be the case.

The reason for the confusion and for limiting personal actions stems from the idea that all wrongs committed by corporate directors and officers, and all duties owed by them, run exclusively to the corporation. The fictional legal entity is viewed by the courts as an unbreachable barrier behind which the directors are safe from personal shareholder attack. Moreover, acts by the directors which could readily be construed as their own personal acts are invariably seen as corporate acts. All of which is a natural result of the fact that a company acts only through its board of directors and, occasionally, its shareholders. But a director acts in a variety of capacities — as an agent of the company, as the company itself, and as an appointed officer to carry out such formal functions as running the proxy machinery and calling and conducting meetings. If a functional analysis were given to the directors'actions in each case it is suggested that it would lead to a result that would accord more with reality while widening the ambit of the shareholders' personal action. The matter was well stated by Judge Fuld in *Gordon v. Elliman*. At issue in the Gordon case was the alleged failure of the corporation to pay dividends in fraud of the minority shareholders in order to squeeze them out. It was argued, successfully, that the action was derivative and that New York's security for expenses provision applied. Fuld J. dissented:

> The action, is, in short, brought against the corporation as a legal entity and, if successful, will require the corporation to part with some of its assets in favour of its stockholders. I am, therefore, unable to follow the legal alchemy by which a breach of duty by the

corporation — a corporate wrong is transmitted into a corporate right.

The vice of the test [is the action open to compel the performance of corporate acts which good faith requires the directors to take in order to perform a duty which they owe to the corporation?] is that it presupposes that every duty owed by corporate directors runs exclusively to the corporation as such and never directly to the stockholders in their personal and individual right. The law is otherwise . . . In a very real sense all suits against corporation — which must of necessity act through directors and officers — involve the action of the directors or of officers responsible to the directors . . . . In short, it simply is not the law that an attack on directors' conduct is, *ipso facto*, the assertion of a corporate right of action. The mere fact that the power to declare dividends resides in the directors and that a suit to compel a dividend payment challenges directors' action has no bearing on the question of whose right is involved in such a suit. We must seek elsewhere to ascertain the manner of the "right" that a court enforces when it overrules the decision of corporate directors . . .

The confusion in Anglo-Canadian company law over whether a personal action is possible when the directors act for an improper purpose, other than taking corporate property, would be cleared up by the type of functional analysis that Judge Fuld advocated. Directors' fiduciary duties are said to be "owed to the company and to the company alone", and "to redress a wrong done to the company . . . the action should *prima facie* be brought by the company itself". In issuing shares, for example, the directors are exercising a fiduciary power which must be performed *bona fide* for the general advantage of the company. If they use the power to keep themselves in control, or to turn a minority into a majority, or to defeat the wishes of the majority, or to discriminate between groups of shareholders, they will have breached their fiduciary duty and an action will lie. But an action by whom? The answer to that question is best approached by asking who, in reality, is the aggrieved party and not by the mechanistic application of the formula that the director is an agent, the company is the principal and therefore action for fraud, negligence or irregularity lies only at the suit of the company. Most cases of fraud will clearly involve a taking by the director to the detriment of the company and the company is the only proper complainant. But a variety of other cases in which the directors act improperly involve not a breach of duty by the agent but a causing of the company to perform a corporate act in an improper or irregular manner to the direct detriment of the shareholders and for which they ought personally to be able to sue.

No doubt a company may be said to have a vital interest in having its affairs conducted in a proper manner and in accordance with the law and its internal regulations. But how, to ask Judge Fuld's question, is a wrongful issuance of shares by the company truly turned into a wrong to the company for which only the company may seek redress? Only in the most theoretical sense may the company be said to have been injured by its directors' misuse of the power granted to them. A more realistic analysis is that by the misuse of their powers the directors have caused the company to issue shares to the detriment of one group of shareholders and to the advantage of another — including, most likely, themselves. It should follow, therefore, that the shareholders that have been injured have a personal right of action against the company and the directors for a declaration that the issue and allotment is void and for an injunction to restrain the voting of such shares if they are about to be used at a general meeting. This is the American position and it is suggested that it is in fact what has occurred in similar cases in England and in Canada.

In *Condec Corporation v. Lunkenheimer* the directors of the defendant company caused it to enter into a merger agreement with a third company that involved the issuance of a large block of defendant's shares to the third company. The issue was large enough to prevent the plaintiff from exerting the voting control which it had just acquired through a cash tender offer. In declaring the issue void, the Delaware court observed:

> Finally, we are not here concerned with the need of proving corporate injury as has been held to be the case when a stockholder attacks derivatively the spending of corporate funds for the purchase of his corporation's own stock. This rather is a case of a stockholder with a contractual right being deprived of such control by what is virtually a corporate legerdemain.

There was no doubt in the Vice-Chancellor's mind that the directors had breached their fiduciary duty which they owed "to the company and to the shareholders". But breach of fiduciary duty did not necessarily mean that a corporate right was being asserted. There is no need for the Anglo-Canadian courts to take the step that the American courts have long since taken and hold that the directors owe a fiduciary duty to the shareholders (and the majority shareholders, on occasion, to the minority) to allow a personal right of action in such cases. The reference above by the Vice-Chancellor to the shareholder's "contractual right" is presumably a reference to the right to vote that goes with each share. A tainted allotment to shift control deprives the shareholder of his votes which, in the aggregate, give him control. Seen in this light, the reasoning is the same as in *Pender v. Lushington* — the shareholder's personal rights have been interfered with.

The line of cases from *Piercy v. Mills* and *Punt v. Symons* deal with an invalid issuance of shares do not give any clear guide as to whether they were considered to be personal or derivative actions. The form of the action was usually representative (as it may be when personal rights are being asserted, and as it must be in a derivative suit) and the company and the wrong doing directors were joined as defendants, so an argument for either cause of action is plausible. With one exception, however, there is no discussion in all these cases of the procedural necessities of the derivative action, or indeed any mention of the derivative action as there invariably is in the true derivative suit. In fact, *Piercy v. Mills* was an individual shareholder's action and it is submitted that each of the other cases were also personal actions brought in representative form. Moreover, analogous leading cases in which the directors were alleged to have breached their fiduciary duty by exercising their powers for an improper purpose have also been personal actions. *Smith v. Fawcett* was a personal action by the executor of a deceased shareholder alleging that the directors were exercising their unrestricted power to refuse transfers in bad faith. As there was no showing of bad faith the action failed, but there was no question of the standing of the individual plaintiff to challenge the directors' action. Similarly in *Galloway v. Hale Concerts Society*, two individual shareholders successfully alleged that the directors had breached their fiduciary duty in causing the company to levy calls on their shares to the exclusion of the other shareholders.

What is occurring in these cases is an interference by the company with the rights of certain of the shareholders and is the same type of conduct that occurs in similar cases where the right of a shareholder to take personal action is firmly established. These cases involve such matters as varying or abrogating class rights, depriving a member of some right conferred upon him by the articles or by-laws, altering the internal corporate structure in a manner that amounts to a fraud on the minority, and depriving a member of his right to vote. A personal action may be more readily granted in such cases because one group of shareholders is more clearly seen to be taking action that deprives another of their rights. But this is also the case where the directors, while acting for a collateral purpose, cause the corporation to act in a manner that deprives a group of shareholders of their rights. In such cases as *Piercy, Smith and Galloway*, the judicial reasoning, although it is not clearly expressed as such, is that in causing the company to do certain acts which are primarily of an internal nature and which primarily affect the shareholders (issue shares, make calls, refuse transfers, solicit proxies) the directors assume a fiduciary obligation toward the company as a whole, that is to the shareholders as a general body, to act with an even hand and in good faith. If they breach that duty the shareholders may sue in their individual capacities for a declaration of their rights or to restrain the company from acting. Some observations of Russell L.J., in *Bamford v. Bamford* may seem to clash with this argument. *Bamford* was, once again, an allotment of shares to fend off a takeover bid. The articles of association of the Bamford Company vested the power to issue shares in the directors. The question in the case was not whether the directors had exceeded their powers, (it was assumed by Plowman J. that they had), but whether the shareholders might ratify such directorial excess and thus validate the issue. That was the point of law set down for argument, and on that basis Plowman J. treated the action as a personal one by the two individual plaintiffs to enforce the contract in the articles between the members and the company created by section 20(1) of the English *Companies Act, 1948*. In short, the plaintiffs argued that the terms of their contract required that only the directors could issue shares and to allow the shareholders to ratify an unlawful issue would be, in effect, to allow them a power of issuance.

In the Court of Appeal, in the course of discussing the ratification point, Russell J.A. said:

> The point before us is not an objection to the proceedings on *Foss v. Harbottle* grounds. But it seems to me to march in step with the principles that underlie the rule in that case.

After thus implicitly recognizing that the action was personal and not derivative, but expressing the opinion that some of the same principles applied, His Lordship then observed:

> None of the factors that admit exceptions to that rule appear to exist here. The harm done by the assumed improperly motivated allotment is a harm done to the company, of which only the company can complain. It would be for the company by ordinary resolution to decide whether or not to proceed against the directors. Russell L.J. then expressed the opinion that the decision whether or not to litigate was the equivalent of a decision on ratification. It is suggested that the analogy, and that was clearly all that it was, to *Foss v. Harbottle* for the purpose of deciding the ratification point was unfortunate. There is little, if any precedent for his Lordship's dictum that only the company can complain of an improper allotment. For the reasons advanced above it is suggested that an individual shareholder has standing to complain of such an allotment, or of any other corporate act which the directors cause the company to take for a collateral purpose.

The Australian courts have clearly treated an improper allotment of shares as giving rise to a personal action, although the reasoning in the leading cases is rather confused. In *Ngurli v. McCann* the High Court held that in failing to consider the interests of the company as a whole in issuing new shares the directors had breached their fiduciary duty and ". . . the plaintiffs have a clear right to sue in their own names to remedy the breach of trust". In so holding, the High Court relied on the decisions of the Privy Council in *Burland v. Earle* and *Cook v. Deeks* to the effect that where the acts complained of are of a fraudulent character the minority can sue when the wrongdoers are in control. The High Court then reasoned that the right to issue new capital is an advantage which belongs to the company and the appropriation of a corporate advantage for the benefit of the majority to the exclusion of the minority is a fraudulent act.

The difficulty with applying this reasoning to *Ngurli* (apart from the novel idea that the right to issue new shares is a corporate asset) is that both *Burland* and *Cook* were shareholders' derivative actions and what was clearly being referred to was the right of the minority to personally bring suit or, behalf of the company when the wrongdoers are in control — the fraud exception to *Foss v. Harbottle*.

In *Provident International Corporation v. International Leasing Corporation*, Helsham J. relied on *Ngurli* and held that the rule ". . . does not apply in the case of a fraud on the powers of directors, at any rate where the abuse of power concerns a purported issue of shares, and I am of the opinion that this is so where the fraud consists of no dishonesty but a mere attempt to use the power for purposes other than that for which it is given". But here again the non-applicability of the rule has reference to the ability of the minority to sue in a derivative and not a personal capacity. However, Heisham J. went on to use language that could be taken to be a holding that the directors owe fiduciary duties directly to the shareholders.

> The reason why the rule in *Foss v. Harbottle* does not apply in a case of fraud on a power such as the present no doubt resides in the fiduciary nature of the duty owed and the fact that it is owed to all the corporators of the company. A breach of duty owed to an individual shareholder as one of the corporators could not be ratified by a majority of shareholders; any attempt by a majority to ratify a breach of fiduciary duty by directors would be no less a fraud qua that shareholder than was the case in the acts of the directors.

It is certainly the accepted position in the United States that directors, and majority shareholders in certain cases, stand in direct fiduciary relationship to the shareholders. But there is no case in the Commonwealth that so holds and as much as such a development is desirable and inevitable, it is not clear that that is what Heisham J. meant. *Provident International Corp.* is simply based on the proposition, elaborated above, that it is the shareholders who are directly affected when an improper allotment of shares is made and they therefore have a personal right to sue, have the corporate act declared void and to have the share register rectified. The directors who authorized the allotment may, but need not be, joined as co-defendants with the company. Heisham J. also relied on the more recent High Court judgment in *Harlowe's Nominees Pty. Ltd. v. Woodside Oil Co.* which was a personal action to set aside an improper allotment and for rectification of the share register. There was no question either at trial or in the High Court of the plaintiff's right to maintain a personal action.

It may be, as in threatened *ultra vires* or illegal acts, that there is both a personal and corporate right of action. The shareholder may properly sue to restrain the company, or the company may proceed against the directors to restrain them from taking the proposed action. "But the fact that this second alternative is a possible one is no reason for refusing to allow a member to sue the company if he has an independent right to do so". So too in collateral purpose cases; the shareholders are the ones most directly concerned, and injured, in such cases and the fact that the corporation, in an indirect way, may also be injured by the failure of the directors to stay within their powers should not prevent the shareholders from asserting their personal rights.

Securities legislation provides the clearest example of both personal and corporate rights of action arising from the same wrongful act. Both the Ontario *Securities Act* and the Ontario *Business Corporations Act* provide for individual and corporate recovery when an insider trades in a company's securities with knowledge of material, confidential information. Such a statutory provision is necessary for a personal action because of the holding in *Percival v. Wright*. But even if the statute were silent as to a corporate right of action it is suggested that one would exist, in addition to the personal right, by extension of the principles in *Regal (Hastings) Ltd. v. Gulliver*, particularly as recently elaborated by the Supreme Court of Canada in *Canadian Aero Services Ltd. v. Terra Surveys Ltd.* This result was reached recently in the United States where a common law derivative action was allowed both in cases of insider trading by directors and by directors and "tippees".

The courts in the United States have recognized, particularly in the context of securities legislation, that the same allegations of fact can support both a derivative and personal action. The leading case is *J.I. Case Co. v. Borak* in which the Supreme Court indicated that violation of the proxy solicitation requirements of the *Securities Exchange Act* of 1934 gave rise to a private as well as a derivative action. In the Court of Appeals the plaintiff had, *inter alia*, appealed from a trial holding that the cause of action in the first count in the complaint, which related to a denial of pre-emptive rights, was derivative and that Wisconsin's security for expenses statute applied. In reversing, the court held that the security for expenses statute was not applicable, saying:

> . . . we think the trial court failed to recognize the principle that the same allegations of fact might support either a derivative suit or an individual cause of action by shareholders.

It is fairly clear that breaches of the proxy solicitation legislation in Canada give rise to a personal action. The analogy is to the notice cases in which it has consistently been held that every shareholder is entitled to truly informative notice of matters proposed for decision. Mandatory proxy solicitation and the information circular that must accompany it, is an attempt to provide fuller corporate disclosure on a continuing, consistent basis — it is simply notice in the modern form. If the statutory provisions have not been complied with, or if the material is inadequate or misleading, a shareholder has a personal right to sue for a declaration that the meeting and all acts done at it are void. It may also be, as the

United States Supreme Court thought in Borak, that deceptive proxy solicitation also give rise to a derivative action. It tells nothing against the right to bring a personal action for a declaration to agree with Justice Clark that: [(1964), 377 U.S. at 432.]

> The injury which a stockholder suffers from a corporate action pursuant to a deceptive proxy solicitation ordinarily flows from the damage done to the corporation, rather than from the damage inflicted directly upon the stockholder. The damage suffered results not from the deceit practiced on him alone but rather from the deceit practiced in the stockholders as a group.

In *Charlebois v. Bienvenu*, Fraser J. also seemed to be of the opinion that the sending of a misleading proxy statement could support a derivative suit but on somewhat different grounds than those expressed in Borak: [(1967), 64 D.L.R. (2d) 683 at 694]

> The defendants were also in breach of duty owed to the company quite apart from the requirements of the *Corporations Act*. The relationship of directors to a company is fiduciary and to hold an annual meeting and election of directors after sending out a misleading information circular . . . would seem *prima facie* to be a breach of that duty.

Farnham v. Fingold
[1973] 2 O.R. 132, 33 D.L.R. (3d) 156 (C.A.)

JESSUP J.A. (for the Court): This is an appeal from the order of Morand J. dismissing, *inter alia* three motions of various of the defendants to strike out the statement of claim on the grounds that the claims therein set forth disclose no reasonable cause of action and that the plaintiff has no status to maintain the claims in a class action. The appellants ask for an order dismissing the plaintiff's action without prejudice to the plaintiff's right to commence a fresh and properly constituted action, alternatively for an order striking out the statement of claim with leave to amend the writ of summons and to deliver a fresh statement of claim, and, alternatively for an order striking out specific paragraphs of the statement of claim.

The judgment of Morand, J., is reported in [1972] 3 O.R. 688, 29 D.L.R. (3d) 279, and it sets forth the facts alleged to give rise to the action and its nature so that it is unnecessary to repeat them. The prayer for relief reads:

37. The plaintiff therefore claims:

  (a) damages in the amount of $25 million against the defendant for conspiracy to injure the plaintiff and other shareholders and former shareholders of Slater Steel Industries Limited;

(b) damages in the amount of $25 million as against the defendants J. Paul Fingold, David B. Fingold, Ralph W. Cooper, Harvey Fingold, Marvin Gerstein, Sidney Fingold, Fobasco Limited, for breach of their fiduciary duty as directors and/or officers and/or insiders of Slater Steel Industries Limited to the plaintiff and other shareholders of Slater Steel Industries Limited in the sale of shares of Slater Steel Industries Limited to Stanton Pipes Limited;

(c) damages in the amount of $25 million against all the defendants for breach of the provisions of The Securities Act and The Business Corporations Act of Ontario in the sale of shares of Slater Steel Industries Limited to Stanton Pipes Limited;

(d) damages in the amount of $25 million against the defendant Stanton Pipes Limited for inducing a breach by the other defendants of their fiduciary duties to the shareholders of Slater Steel Industries Limited and breach of The Securities Act and The Business Corporations Act of Ontario, in the sale of shares of Slater Steel Industries Limited to Stanton Pipes Limited;

(e) a declaration that the controlling shareholders hold any premium obtained upon the sale of their shares in Slater Steel Industries Limited to Stanton Pipes Limited over the market price of those shares for the benefit of Slater Steel Industries Limited and/or its general shareholders and/or the vendors of such shares to them;

(f) an accounting of all sums paid or to be paid by Stanton Pipes Limited to the other defendants except Slater Steel Industries Limited and McDonald Currie & Co. on account of the sale of shares of Slater Steel Industries Limited to Stanton Pipes Limited by such defendants, a reference to the Master at Toronto for the taking of such accounting and directions for the payment of any such sums as may have been or may be received by such defendants;

(g) damages in the amount of $25 million against the defendants Henderson and Morris;

(h) an interlocutory and permanent injunction restraining the defendants and each of them from entering into or completing any sale of shares or purported sale of shares of Slater Steel Industries Limited to Stanton Pipes Limited;

(i) his costs of this action;

(j) such further and other relief as to this Court may seem just.

The claims made in the statement of claim are completely novel. Their success may depend on the trial Court applying or extending the principle followed in *Perlman v. Feldmann* (1955), 219 F. 2d 173, and *Brown v. Halbert* (1969), 76 Cal. Rptr. 781, or on the trial Court holding that a breach of the provisions of Part IX of the *Securities Act*, R.S.O. 1970, c. 426, constitutes an actionable civil wrong. As I appreciate the appellants' argument, they do not now challenge Morand, J.'s decision that the difficult question of law raised by the novelty of the plaintiff's claims should not be determined in interlocutory proceedings, and their attack on the form of the action and the statement of claim is confined to matters not specifically dealt with in the judgment below.

The defendants Barney Morris and Ralph Henderson are claimed to be members of the alleged conspiracy. However, in addition, it is separately alleged with respect to them alone:

30. With regard to the defendants Ralph Henderson and Barney Morris, the plaintiff states the Bache & Co. and in particular the defendants Ralph Henderson and Barney Morris recommended the shares of Slater Steel Industries Limited to their customers for a long period of time and encouraged the plaintiff and other persons to invest in such shares. Relying upon the recommendations of the defendants Henderson and Morris, the plaintiff and other shareholders purchased shares in Slater Steel Industries Limited. The plaintiff states that the defendants Henderson and Morris, in concert with and/or upon the inducement of the controlling shareholders, have acted in breach of their obligations to the plaintiff and to other shareholders of Slater Steel Industries Limited who have purchased shares through or upon the recommendations of such defendants and/or Bache & Co., in arranging for the sale of shares owned by the defendants Henderson and Morris, and their friends and relations to the exclusion of other shareholders of Slater Steel Industries Limited including the plaintiff and at a premium price not available to such shareholders.

In my view, the relief claimed against Morris and Henderson based on this para. 30 is not, in the words of Rule 66, "in respect of or arising out of the same transaction or occurrence, or series of transactions or occurrences", as those which may give rise to liability of the other defendants. In the result, I think the claims so made against them are not properly joined in the action. In addition, the shareholders who dealt with Morris and Henderson or Bache & Co. constitute a separate class whose interest would seem to be antagonistic to those of some other members of the class on whose behalf the plaintiff brings the action.

Certain parts of the statement of claim and in particular all or parts of paras. 22, 23, 29, 32, 34, 36 and 37E are concerned with rights, duties or obligations owed to the defendant Slater Steel Industries Limited or with damage alleged to be suffered by that corporation as a result of the actions of the other defendants. Such matters are properly the subject of a derivative action rather than a class action. Morand, J., said it was "crucial" to distinguish between the two types of action, but found this action to be entirely a class action. I respectfully disagree.

Section 99 of the *Business Corporations Act*, R.S.O. 1970, c. 53, provides in part:

99(1) Subject to subsection 2,a shareholder of a corporation may maintain an action in a representative capacity for himself and all other shareholders of the corporation suing for and on behalf of the corporation to enforce any right, duty or obligation owed to the corporation under this Act or under any other statute or rule of law or equity that could be enforced by the corporation itself, or to obtain damages for any breach of any such right, duty or obligation.

(2) An action under subsection 1 shall not be commenced until the shareholder has obtained an order of the court permitting the shareholder to commence the action.

Counsel for the respondent argues that the type of derivative action exemplified by *Foss v. Harbottle* (1843), 2 Hare 461, 67 E.R. 189, and succeeding cases continues to be maintainable in this Province apart from s. 99 and that the section only applies to plaintiffs who wish to take advantage of ss. (4) and (5) which provide:

(4) At any time or from time to time while an action commenced under this section is pending, the plaintiff may apply to the court for an order for the payment to the plaintiff by the corporation of reasonable interim costs, including solicitor's and counsel fees and disbursements, for which interim costs the plaintiff shall be accountable to the corporation if the action is dismissed with costs on final disposition at the trial or on appeal.

(5) An action commenced under this section shall be tried by the court and its judgement or order in the cause, unless the action is dismissed with costs, may include a provision that the reasonable costs of the action are payable to the plaintiff by the corporation or other defendants taxed as between a solicitor and his own client.

However, in my opinion, the very broad language of s. 99(1) embraces all causes of action under any statute or law or in equity, that a shareholder may sue for on behalf of a corporation. All forms of derivative actions purporting to be brought on behalf of and for the benefit of the corporation come within it, and therefore s-s. (2) applies to all such actions. Furthermore, I think it is clear that the interests of the corporation would be antagonistic to at least a part of the class the plaintiff represents with respect to the other claims in the action, i.e., to the sub-class of former shareholders. . .

[Jessup J.A. discussed the law surrounding class actions under the old Rule 75.]

In so far as the action is founded upon s. 150 of the *Business Corporations Act*, Mr. Garrow submitted that such a claim, if not brought by the corporation, could be brought only by the Ontario Securities Commission "in the name of and on behalf of the corporation", by virtue of s. 151. Section 150 creates a liability to "any person" who suffers a direct loss as a result of a transaction by insiders that falls within the section. it also creates an obligation on the insider to account to the corporation. Section 151, in my view, relates only to the obligation to the corporation and does not affect the cause of action of "any person who suffered any direct loss". The same conclusion must be reached with respect to ss. 113 and 114 of the *Securities Act*.

It was also argued that in so far as the plaintiff's cause of action is founded upon s. 113 of the *Securities Act* and s. 150 of the *Business Corporations Act* it cannot be maintained because the loss claimed is not "direct loss" within the meaning of those sections. I agree with Morand J., that this is not a question that should be decided in interlocutory proceedings.

Besides those mentioned, the statement of claim is prejudicial or embarrassing in the following respects:

(1) Special damages and not the conspiracy is the gist of an action for conspiracy and the special damages of each member of the class should be pleaded. As I understand the respondent's argument, those special damages will be pleaded as the pro rata share of each member of the class of the gross premium I have mentioned.

(2) The class on behalf of which the action is maintained is not clearly and specifically defined and facts are not alleged to show the plaintiff is a member of that class. As I understand the respondent's factum, the class comprises all shareholders and former shareholders of Slater Steel Industries Limited who were shareholders at the time of the sale of control to Stanton Pipes Limited. I see no antagonism between the interests of the members of such a class but it should be so defined in the statement of claim.

(3) Paragraphs 34 and 35 are embarrassing in that they do not allege facts but rather possible future wrongs.

(4) Paragraphs 37(b) to (e) both inclusive are evidently alterative claims and should be pleaded as such. Moreover, the plaintiff's claim is not for 25 million dollars but rather for whatever is shown to be the amount of the gross premium I have mentioned.

In the result, I would allow the appeal with costs here and below, set aside the order of Morand, J., and in its place direct an order:

A. Dismissing the action with costs against the defendants Morris and Henderson in so far as the action against them is based on the allegations of fact made in para. 30 of the statement of claim, without prejudice to the right to commence a separate action against such defendants;

B. Dismissing the action with costs against all defendants in so far as the action is derivative in nature, without prejudice to the right to commence such separate action for which leave may be granted in the future under s. 99(2) of the *Business Corporations Act*;

C. Striking out the statement of claim with liberty to amend the writ of summons and deliver a fresh amended statement of claim within 20 days.

Appeal allowed.

Note

Do you agree that where a minority shareholder brings an action alleging that the majority has appropriated a control premium on the sale of its shares that the action is derivative rather than personal? Both the OBCA, s. 247(c), and the CBCA, s. 240(c), expressly allow such a "personal" remedy in a derivative action, but s. 233 of the BCBCA does not. See *Perlman v. Feldman*, 219 R.2d 173.

Goldex Mines Ltd. v. Revill
(1975), 7 O.R. (2d) 216, 54 D.L.R. (3d) 672 (C.A.)

[Goldex Mines was a shareholder of Probe Mines Ltd. This decision culminated from the fifth round of proceedings stemming from a dispute among Probe's directors and over a proposed purchase of gypsum claims from a company controlled by a former Probe director. Goldex alleged breaches of duties by directors and defendant shareholders, but did not specify whether these duties were owed to Probe or to its shareholders.]

BY THE COURT: The right to sue.

With the foregoing questions dealt with, there remains the real and important issue: does Goldex have the right to maintain this (second) action without first obtaining the leave of the Court under s. 99 of the Act? Haines J., would have left this question to the trial Judge, as he suggested was done by Morand, J. in *Farnham v. Fingold et al.*, [1972] 3 O.R. 688, 29 D.L.R. (3d) 279.

His decision was given before the judgment of this Court in that case, reported in [1973] 2 O.R. 132, 33 D.L.R. (3d) 156. Our judgment was not only considered by the Divisional Court but in the end formed the basis on which the writs were set aside, since that Court concluded that the action was "wholly derivative in nature" and no leave to bring it had been obtained under s. 99. Its judgment sets out the entire endorsement of the writ ([1973] 3 O.R. at pp. 880-4, 38 D.L.R. (3d) at pp. 524-8) and we need not repeat it.

In broad terms the issue is whether the Divisional Court was right in its conclusion. We think the issue can be confined in narrower terms. It is this: Where the same acts of directors or of shareholders cause damage to the company and also to shareholders or a class of them, is a shareholder's cause of action for the wrong done to him derivative?

It is well to draw attention to the appropriate terminology which should be employed. The point is well taken by Professor Stanley M. Beck in his thorough and useful article "The Shareholders' Derivative Action", 52 Can. Bar Rev. 159 (1974) (see pp. 185-6). Where a legal wrong is done to shareholders by directors or other shareholders, the injured shareholders suffer a personal wrong, and may seek redress for it in a personal action. That personal action may be by one shareholder alone, or (as will usually be the case) by a class action in which he sues on behalf of himself and all other shareholders in the same interest (usually, all other shareholders save the wrongdoers). Such a class action is nevertheless a personal action.

A derivative action, on the other hand, is one in which the wrong is done to the company. It is always a class action, brought in representative form, thereby binding all the shareholders. This was so at common law, as s. 99 recognizes (see Beck, *op. cit.*, at p. 185).

The distinction, therefore, as Professor Beck points out, is not between a class action and a derivative action, but between a personal action (whether or not a class action) and a derivative action. The action here is a class action. No one suggests that on that ground alone it is open to objection. The objection is that it is derivative, and cannot be brought without leave.

In *Farnham v. Fingold, supra,* this Court was not required, on the facts of that case, to consider a situation where the same wrongful act is both a wrong to the company and a wrong to each individual shareholder. In one sense every injury to a company is indirectly an injury to its shareholders. On the other hand, if one applies the test: "Is this wrongful act one in respect of which the company could sue?", a shareholder who is personally and directly injured must surely be entitled to say, as a matter of logic, "the company cannot sue for my injury; it can only sue for its own".

These distinctions have been considered in several American cases, usually in States where a shareholder bringing a derivative action may be required to put up security for costs. Some of these cases are discussed by Professor Beck, *op. cit.* It has not been necessary in Ontario heretofore to draw such a fine dividing line, but the enactment of s. 99 makes some distinction essential, because leave of the Court is required for all those parts of a claim that are derivative. (Once leave is obtained, personal and derivative claims may be joined, subject to the Rules, i.e., if the claims arise out of the same transaction or occurrence.)

It would not be difficult to reach the conclusion that a shareholder's action is personal where one group of shareholders, by their own nonrepresentative activities (i.e. not as directors) acts in such a way as to deprive another group of shareholders of their rights, where those rights are derived from the letters patent (or articles of incorporation), the company's by-laws, or from statutory provisions enacted for the protection of shareholders as such. The more difficult case arises where the directors, whose shareholdings are controlling or merely substantial, for a collateral purpose of their own, cause the company to act in a manner that deprives a group of shareholders of their rights (Beck, *op. cit.*, at p. 174). To cause the company to act to serve personal objectives of directors would clearly be a breach of the directors' fiduciary duty to the company. Beck suggests that it is also a breach of the directors' fiduciary duty to shareholders as a whole — the duty "to act with an even hand and in good faith"; he also asserts that this principle has been indicated (if not always clearly expressed) in the decided cases.

The line of demarcation between a derivative action and a personal action was discussed by Traynor C.J., in *Jones v. H.F. Ahmanson & Co. et al.* (1969), 460 Pac. Rep. 2d 464 at p. 470 *et seq.*, 81 Cal. Rptr. 592. The argument that the directors, officers and controlling shareholders owe a duty only to the corporation was rejected. The plaintiff was held entitled to bring her action without complying with s. 7616 of the California Financial Code, requiring a prior determination by a commissioner that a proposed derivative action complied with certain statutory prerequisites.

One phrase used in the judgment of Traynor C.J., requires comment. At pp. 470-1, referring to *Shaw v. Empire Savings & Loan Ass'n*, 186 Cal. App. 2d 401 at p. 407, he said:

> the court [in *Shaw*] noted the "well established general rule that a stockholder of a corporation has no personal or individual right of action against third persons, including the corporation's officers and directors, for a wrong or injury to the corporation which results in the destruction or depreciation of the value of his stock, since the wrong thus suffered by the stockholder is merely incidental to the wrong suffered by the corporation and affects all stockholders alike." From this the court reasoned that a minority shareholder could not maintain an individual action unless he could demonstrate the injury to him was somehow different from that suffered by other minority shareholders. In so concluding the court erred. The individual wrong necessary to support a suit by a shareholder need not be unique to that plaintiff. The same injury may affect a substantial number of shareholders. If the injury is not incidental to an injury to the corporation, an individual cause of action exists.

What limitation on the general principle is intended by the words in the last sentence: ". . . not incidental to an injury to the corporation"?

In the context of the whole judgment, we believe Traynor, C.J. meant by this phrase: ". . . not arising simply because the corporation itself has been damaged, and as a consequence of the damage to it, its shareholders have been injured".

In *Charlebois et al. v. Bienvenu. et al.*, [1967] 2 O.R. 635 at p. 644, 64 D.L.R. (2d) 683 at p. 692, Fraser J., held that the holding of an annual meeting and election of directors after the sending out of a misleading information circular by the directors was a breach of the directors' fiduciary duty to the company. We hold that such an act is also a breach of duty to the other shareholders. If the directors of a company choose, or are compelled by statute, to send information to shareholders, those shareholders have a right to expect that the information sent to them is fairly presented, reasonably accurate, and not misleading.

The proposition that a shareholder is entitled to adequate information from which he can form an intelligent judgment on the matters he is entitled to vote on was enunciated by Spence J., in *Garvie v. Axmith et al.*, [1962] O.R. 65 at pp. 82-7, 31 D.L.R. (2d) 65 at pp. 82-7. It was supported by quotations of opinion by Roach J., in *Re National Grocers Co. Ltd.*, [1938] O.R. 142 at p. 154, [1938] 3 D.L.R. 106 at p. 116, and LeBel J., in *Re N. Slater Co. Ltd.*, [1947] O.W.N. 226 at p. 227, [1947] 2 D.L.R. 311 at pp. 313-4, 28 C.B.R. 31. We accept the proposition and hold that it is not confined to cases under s. 33 of the *Corporations Act*, R.S.O. 1960, c. 71 [now R.S.O. 1970, c. 89, s. 35] (special resolutions; see now s. 189(2) of the Act).

Examples of statutory directions respecting the sending of information to shareholders are found in ss. 106(i)(a), 115 to 120, 134(5)(b), 169, 184 and 194(2) and (3) of the Act. Section 256 provides that every person who makes or assists in making a statement in any document required by or for the purposes of the Act or the Regulations that, at the time and in the light of the circumstances under which it was made, is false or misleading in respect of any material fact or that omits to state a material fact the omission of which makes the statement false or misleading, is guilty of an offence.

It has long been the law that minority shareholders can sue, even where there is a clear wrong to the company, where there has been "an oppressive and unjust exercise of the powers of the majority shareholders for the promotion of an advantage to themselves to the peculiar detriment of the minority": *Henderson v. Strang et al.* (1919), 60 S.C.R. 201 at p. 202, 54 D.L.R. 674 at p. 675, [1920] 1 W.W.R. 982, followed in *Gray v. Yellowknife Gold Mines Ltd. et al. (No. 1)*, [1947] O.R. 928 at p. 963, [1948] 1 D.L.R. 473 at p. 498. With the legislative trend obviously towards greater protection of shareholders by seeing that they receive certain information, truthfully and fairly presented, we see no difficulty in holding that shareholders are injured if they do not receive it, apart altogether from any breach of duty owed to the company itself. Where information is sent to shareholders that is untrue or misleading, the duty to shareholders is breached, whether the senders were required by statute to send out that class of information, or whether they simply chose to do so.

The principle that the majority governs in corporate affairs is fundamental to corporation law, but its corollary is also important — that the majority must act fairly and honestly. Fairness is the touchstone of equitable justice, and when the test of fairness is not met, the equitable jurisdiction of the Court can be invoked to prevent or remedy the injustice which misrepresentation or other dishonesty has caused. The category of cases in which fiduciary duties and obligations arise is not a closed one: *Laskin v. Bache & Co. Inc.*, [1972] 1 O.R. 465 at p. 472, 23 D.L.R. (3d) 385 at p. 392.

Turning to the way the plaintiff's case is pleaded in the extensive endorsement on the writ, set out in full in the reasons of Hughes J., there is no clear allegation anywhere that that plaintiff sues in respect of wrongs to shareholders personally. On the contrary — as Hughes J., pointed out: [1973] 3 O.R. at p. 885, 38 D.L.R. (3d) at p. 529 — cls. E, G and I all give grounds for the injunctions sought therein, and in each case the concluding ground is that "the Defendant Directors are in breach of their fiduciary duty to Probe" (giving reasons for the allegation). The grounds are expressed cumulatively and not in the alternative. Thus, on their face, these three clauses assert claims to relief which are founded on a breach of duty to Probe and which Probe itself could assert.

Clause E(1) asserts that the defendants

> . . . circulated to all shareholders of the corporation a communication dated the 29th day of September, 1972 which was calculated to result in the procurement of proxies in favour of the personal defendants and the withholding of proxies in favour of the plaintiff, thereby effecting a solicitation without appendixing thereto or delivering as a separate document accompanying such solicitation an information circular as prescribed by section 118 of The *Business Corporations Act* . . .

If this passage stood alone, it could be interpreted as a pleading of wrongful acts causing damage to the plaintiff and other shareholders, and thus disclosing a cause of action which we have earlier said is not derivative, and which is therefore outside s. 99.

Similarly, cl. E(2) alleges that the information circular dated October 5, 1972, approved by the defendant directors and sent out with the notice calling the annual meeting of Probe for October 31, 1972, in conjunction with a solicitation of proxies by the defendant directors, was false and misleading in three respects. This subcl. (2), while not framed as an allegation of wrongful acts causing damage to the plaintiff and other shareholders, as shareholders, could also be interpreted as meaning that in substance.

The allegations with respect to the annual report of Probe to its shareholders dated September 25, 1972, pose more difficult problems. They occur:

(1) in clause C. of the endorsement, claiming that the resolution of the directors approving the annual report is a nullity;

(2) in clause D., claiming that all proxies obtained by the defendant directors "in response to the solicitation of proxies accompanied by the Information Circular . . . and the Annual Report . . ." are null and void;

(3) in clause E(3), which, in support of the claim for an injunction restraining the personal defendants from

voting their proxies, alleges that the Annual Report is false and misleading.

There is also an oblique reference to the annual report in cl. L, which seeks to prevent the defendant directors from engaging in any renewed solicitation of proxies "until a corrected and complete Information Circular and Annual Report are provided to shareholders".

While the preparation, approval and circulation to shareholders of a "false and misleading" annual report is undoubtedly a wrong to the company, the circulation of such a report to shareholders, accompanied by a solicitation on behalf of the directors of the shareholders' proxies, is in our view also a wrong to shareholders as such, affecting their own personal rights. An action attacking such a report, seeking a declaration or an injunction, or both, is not derivative, and leave of the Court to bring it is not required.

The allegations in the endorsement respecting the Mountain Gypsum agreement with Probe, as now framed, all raise causes of action which are really Probe's, although the carrying out of them could affect shareholders of Probe and possibly solidify or change the control of Probe's shares. This portion of the claim, referred to in cls. E(2)(a), (3), (4), F, G, H,I and K, is in substance derivative. The same applies to the underwriting agreement of June 21, 1972, with W.D. Latimer Co. Ltd. which is tied to cl. E(2)(b) and (c).

The trouble with the endorsement is that it discloses no attempt to differentiate between claims personal to shareholders and claims which are derivative. As already indicated, the subclauses of claims E and G intermingle "grounds" that are clearly derivative in nature with some that are not. We do not think it is our function to suggest a redraft of the endorsement so as to bring it into conformity with the principles enunciated herein.

The Divisional Court decided that all of the claims made were derivative, and set aside the writ and interlocutory orders made on the basis of it. We have concluded that the facts set out in the material would support an endorsement making some claims for relief that are personal and not derivative, if properly pleaded, but they are inextricably woven in to the derivative claims, in the present endorsement.

We considered whether it would be appropriate merely to strike out the endorsement on the writ, with leave to amend, rather than strike out the writ itself, as the Divisional Court did. We have decided against doing so, for two reasons. No limitation period is involved, and a new writ can be issued. In addition, the plaintiff may decide to apply for leave under s. 99, and if it obtains leave, it can add to the derivative claims thus permitted such personal claims as it sees fit (subject, of course, to the Rules).

The Divisional Court was asked to grant leave *nunc pro tunc* under s. 99(2), if it concluded that the claims made were derivative. It declined to do so: [1973] 3 O.R. at pp. 886-7, 38 D.L.R. (3d) at pp. 530-1. The same request was made to this Court. We agree with the reasons for refusing leave given by the Divisional Court, which apply with even greater force to the application for leave made to us. We refuse leave also.

There was considerable discussion before us as to our directing the calling of an annual meeting, with a neutral chairman. With the writ struck out, there is nothing left on which we can act.

Section 111 of the Act empowers the Court to order a meeting to be called if it is "impracticable" to call a meeting in the regular way. If it is not impracticable for the present directors to call a new meeting, which is now long overdue.

Clause M of the endorsement seeks "an order removing the Defendant Directors as officers and directors of Probe". We have no jurisdiction to order this. It is a matter for the shareholders, either under s. 140 [am. 1972, c. 138, s. 37(2)] of the Act, or at an annual meeting.

Appeal dismissed.

Hercules Management Ltd. v. Ernst & Young
[1997] 2 S.C.R. 165, 1997 CarswellMan 198, 1997 CarswellMan 199

[The appellants were shareholders of two related corporations. The respondent was an accounting firm that was hired by the two corporations to perform annual audits of their financial statements and provide audit reports to their shareholders. After the corporations went into receivership, the appellants brought an action claiming that the audit reports were negligently prepared, and that they had lost money in reliance on them. Much of the judgment focused on procedural matters and the issue of whether the respondents owed a duty of care under the law of negligence to the appellants.]

LA FOREST J.: . . . All the participants in this appeal — the appellants, the respondents, and the intervener — raised the issue of whether the appellants' claims in respect of the losses they suffered in their existing shareholdings through their alleged inability to oversee management of the corporations ought to have been brought as a derivative action in conformity with the rule in *Foss v. Harbottle* rather than as a series of individual actions. The issue was also raised and discussed in the courts below. In my opinion, a derivative action — commenced, as required, by an application under s. 232 of the Manitoba *Corporations Act* — would have been the proper method of proceeding with respect to this claim. Indeed, I would regard this simply as a corollary of the idea that the audited reports are provided to the shareholders as a group in order to allow them to take collective (as opposed to individual) decisions. Let me explain.

The rule [in *Foss v. Harbottle*] provides that individual shareholders have no cause of action in law for any wrongs done to the corporation and that if an action is to be brought in respect of such losses, it must be brought either by the corporation itself (through management) or by way of a derivative action. The legal rationale behind the rule was eloquently set out by the English Court of Appeal in *Prudential Assurance Co. v. Newman Industries Ltd. (No. 2)*, [1982] 1 All E.R. 354, at p. 367, as follows:

> The rule [in *Foss v. Harbottle*] is the consequence of the fact that a corporation is a separate legal entity. Other consequences are limited liability and limited rights. The company is liable for its contracts and torts; the shareholder has no such liability. The company acquires causes of action for breaches of contract and for torts which damage the company. No cause of action vests in the shareholder. When the shareholder acquires a share he accepts the fact that the value of his investment follows the fortunes of the company and that he can only exercise his influence over the fortunes of the company by the exercise of his voting rights in general meeting. The law confers on him the right to ensure that the company observes the limitations of its memorandum of association and the right to ensure that other shareholders observe the rule, imposed on them by the articles of association. If it is right that the law has conferred or should in certain restricted circumstances confer further rights on a shareholder the scope and consequences of such further rights require careful consideration.

To these lucid comments, I would respectfully add that the rule is also sound from a policy perspective, inasmuch as it avoids the procedural hassle of a multiplicity of actions.

The manner in which the rule in *Foss v. Harbottle, supra*, operates with respect to the appellants' claims can thus be demonstrated. As I have already explained, the appellants allege that they were prevented from properly overseeing the management of the audited corporations because the respondents' audit reports painted a misleading picture of their financial state. They allege further that had they known the true situation, they would have intervened to avoid the eventuality of the corporations' going into receivership and the consequent loss of their equity. The difficulty with this submission, I have suggested, is that it fails to recognize that in supervising management, the shareholders must be seen to be acting as a body in respect of the corporation's interests rather than as individuals in respect of their own ends. In a manner of speaking, the shareholders assume what may be seen to be a "managerial role" when, as a collectivity, they oversee the activities of the directors and officers through resolutions adopted at shareholder meetings. In this capacity, they cannot properly be understood to be acting simply as individual holders of equity. Rather, their collective decisions are made in respect of the corporation itself. Any duty owed by auditors in respect of this aspect of the shareholders' functions, then, would be owed not to shareholders *qua* individuals, but rather to all shareholders as a group, acting in the interests of the corporation. And if the decisions taken by the collectivity of shareholders are in respect of the corporation's affairs, then the shareholders' reliance on negligently prepared audit reports in taking such decisions will result in a wrong to the corporation for which the shareholders cannot, as individuals, recover.

This line of reasoning finds support in Lord Bridge's comments in *Caparo, supra*, at p. 580:

> The shareholders of a company have a collective interest in the company's proper management and in so far as a negligent failure of the auditor to report accurately on the state of the company's finances deprives the shareholders of the opportunity to exercise their powers in general meeting to call the directors to book and to ensure that errors in management are corrected, the shareholders ought to be entitled to a remedy. But in practice no problem arises in this regard since the interest of the shareholders in the proper management of the company's affairs is indistinguishable from the interest of the company itself and any loss suffered by the shareholders . . . will be recouped by a claim against the auditor in the name of the company, not by individual shareholders. [Emphasis added.]

It is also reflected in the decision of Farley J. in *Roman I, supra*, the facts of which were similar to those of the case at bar. In that case, the plaintiff shareholders brought an action against the defendant auditors alleging, *inter alia*, that the defendant's audit reports were negligently prepared. That negligence, the shareholders contended, prevented them from properly overseeing management which, in turn, led to the winding up of the corporation and a loss to the shareholders of their equity therein. Farley J. discussed the rule in *Foss v. Harbottle* and concluded that it operated so as to preclude the shareholders from bringing personal actions based on an alleged inability to supervise the conduct of management.

One final point should be made here. Referring to the case of *Goldex Mines Ltd. v. Revill* (1974), 7 O.R. (2d) 216 (C.A.), the appellants submit that where a shareholder has been directly and individually harmed, that shareholder may have a personal cause of action even though the corporation may also have a separate and distinct cause of action. Nothing in the foregoing paragraphs should be understood to detract from this principle. In finding that claims in respect of losses stemming from an alleged inability to oversee or supervise management are really derivative and not personal in nature, I have found only that shareholders cannot raise individual claims in respect of a wrong done to the corporation. Indeed, this is the limit of the rule in *Foss v. Harbottle*. Where, however, a separate and distinct claim (say, in tort) can be raised with respect to a wrong done to a shareholder *qua* individual, a personal action may well lie, assuming that all the requisite elements of a cause of action can be made out.

The facts of *Haig, supra,* provide the basis for an example of where such a claim might arise. Had the investors in that case been shareholders of the corporation, and had a similarly negligent report knowingly been provided to them by the auditors for a specified purpose, a duty of care separate and distinct from any duty owed to the audited corporation would have arisen in their favour, just as one arose in favour of Mr. Haig. While the corporation would have been entitled to claim damages in respect of any losses it might have suffered through reliance on the report (assuming, of course, that the report was also provided for the corporation's use), the shareholders in question would also have been able to seek personal compensation for the losses they suffered *qua* individuals through their personal reliance and investment. On the facts of this case, however, no claims of this sort can be established.

Appeal dismissed with costs.

Notes

1   In *Kraus v. J.G. Lloyd Pty. Ltd.,* [1965] V.R. 232 (Vict. S.C.), the plaintiff shareholder asked for an injunction to restrain the first defendant from acting as a director after being called upon by a majority of shareholders of a closely held company to retire. The plaintiff complained that the defendants were running the affairs of the company without a proper quorum of directors and that they had refused to allow the plaintiff and other shareholders to appoint other directors. The court held that the individual rights of the plaintiff as a member of the company had been invaded and that the rule in *Foss v. Harbottle* presented no obstacle to her claim for relief. The court declared the first defendant no longer entitled to serve as a director and granted the injunction. The court also ordered the one remaining director to convene a general meeting within 21 days for the election of directors.

2   In *Jones v. H.F Ahmanson & Co.,* 460 P. 2d 464 (Cal. 1969); 81 Ca. 3d 592, Traynor C.J. said (at pp. 598-9):

> Analysis of the nature and purpose of a shareholders' derivative suit will demonstrate that the test adopted in the Shaw case does not properly distinguish the cases in which an individual cause of action lies.

> A shareholder's derivative suit seeks to recover for the benefit of the corporation and its whole body of shareholders when injury is caused to the corporation that may not otherwise be redressed because of failure of the corporation to act. Thus, "the action is derivative, i.e., in the corporate right, if the gravamen of the complaint is injury to the corporation, or to the whole body of its

stock or property without any severance or distribution among individual holders, or if it seeks to recover assets for the corporation or to prevent the dissipation of its assets."

A stockholder's derivative suit is brought to enforce a cause of action which the corporation itself possesses against some third party, a suit to recompense the corporation for injuries which it has suffered as a result of the acts of third parties. The management owes to the stockholders a duty to take proper steps to enforce all claims which the corporation may have. When it fails to perform this duty, the stockholders have a right to do so. Thus, although the corporation is made a defendant in a derivative suit, the corporation nevertheless is the real plaintiff and it alone benefits from the decree; the stockholders derive no benefit therefrom except the indirect benefit resulting from a realization upon the corporation's assets. The stockholder's individual suit, on the other hand, is a suit to enforce a right against the corporation which the stockholder possesses as an individual.

It is clear from the stipulated facts and plaintiff's allegations that she does not seek to recover on behalf of the corporation for injury done to the corporation by defendants. Although she does allege that the value of her stock has been diminished by defendants' actions, she does not contend that the diminished value reflects an injury to the corporation and resultant depreciation in the value of the stock. Thus the gravamen of her cause of action is injury to herself and the other minority stockholders.

In *Shaw v. Empire Savings & Loan Assn.*, the court noted the "well established general rule that a stockholder of a corporation has no personal or individual right of action against third persons, including the corporation's officers and directors, for a wrong or injury to the corporation which results in the destruction of depreciation of the value of his stock, since the wrong thus suffered by the stockholder is merely incidental to the wrong suffered by the corporation and affects all stockholders alike."

From this the court reasoned that a minority shareholder could not maintain an individual action unless he could demonstrate the injury to him was somehow different from that suffered by other minority shareholders.

In so concluding the court erred. The individual wrong necessary to support a suit by a shareholder need not be unique to that plaintiff. The same injury may affect a substantial number of shareholders. If the injury is not incidental to an injury to the corporation, an individual cause of action exists. To the extent that

Shaw v. Empire Savings & Loan Assn. is inconsistent with the opinion expressed herein, it is disapproved.

3   Assuming certain wrongs can give rise to both derivative and personal actions, what rules should be followed? Should the rules on, and distinctions between, derivative and personal actions apply where a small closely held corporation is involved? See *Watson v. Button*, 235 F. 2d 235 (9th Cir. 1956) and *Thomas v. Dickson*, 250 Ga. 772 (S.C., 1983). In *Thomas*, the plaintiff, the sole shareholder of a corporation, was allowed to bring a personal action for a wrong done to the corporation. Bell J. said (at 774-5):

> The general rule is that a shareholder seeking to recover misappropriated corporate funds may only bring a derivative suit . . . However, exceptions to this rule have been recognized, including an exception which looks to the reasons requiring derivative actions to determine if they are applicable . . .

> In the instant case, the reasons requiring derivative suits do not exist. The reasons underlying the general rule are that 1) it prevents a multiplicity of lawsuits by shareholders; 2) it protects corporate creditors by putting the proceeds of the recovery back in the corporation; 3) it protects the interests of all shareholders by increasing the value of their shares, instead of allowing a recovery by one shareholder to prejudice the rights of others not a party to the suit; and 4) it adequately compensates the injured shareholder by increasing the value of his shares . . .

> We will now examine this case to see if these reasons are applicable. First, Mrs. Dickson is the *only* injured shareholder; consequently, there can be no multiplicity of lawsuits, and there is no concern that a recovery by her will prejudice the rights of other shareholders. In addition, Mrs. Dickson would not be adequately compensated by a corporate recovery. For a shareholder, the potential benefit of a corporate recovery in such cases is the increase in the value of his or her shares. See, Note, "Distinguishing Between Direct and Derivative Shareholder Suits", 110 U. of Penn. L. Rev. 1147 (1962). There would be no such benefit to Mrs. Dickson, however, since, in a closely held corporation, there is no ready market for her shares.

> The final consideration underlying the general rule, the protection of creditors, is also not present in this case. The audit reports of Trio introduced below indicate that for the fiscal years 1976 through 1980, Trio was paying its debts as they came due, and that there was no outstanding or dissatisfied creditor. Additionally, neither Thomas nor Akin offered evidence of any creditor in need of protection . . .

Because Mrs. Dickson was *the sole injured* shareholder and because the reasons underlying the general rule calling for corporate recovery do not exist in this case, we find that Mrs. Dickson was properly allowed to bring this direct action.

Should this line of reasoning be followed in Canada?

4.   RELIEF FROM OPPRESSION

(a)   Introduction: The Mischief and Response

As we have seen a basic principle of corporation law is majority rule, a concept which has many ramifications. At one level, it means that the majority shareholders decide who will be the directors of the corporation who in turn determine how the corporation will be run. At another level, the majority shareholders will also determine the outcome of questions that are required to be referred to shareholders for approval. In each case, whether a decision by the directors or approval by shareholders, the interests of minority shareholders are recognized through the duties owed by directors, and the equitable restraints imposed on majority shareholder action to ensure fair treatment of the minority.

However, notwithstanding these restraints on directors and majority shareholder action, the case law offers a number of examples where shareholders were being unfairly or improperly treated and courts were reluctant to interfere. This was especially the case in private or closely held corporations. Many U.K. cases, however, are also cited as examples where the court ought to have recognized more effectively the plight of minority shareholders: see e.g., *Greenhalgh v. Arderne Cinemas Ltd.*, [1951] 1 Ch. 286, [1950] 2 All E.R. 1120 (C.A.), which is discussed briefly, *infra*.

One immediate response to this minority shareholder problem was to resort to the court for a winding-up order. However, this remedy could well result in a disadvantage to the minority shareholder who wished to continue his or her investment and maintain the business enterprise as a viable entity. Moreover, the proceeds from dissolution might not in any way reflect the damage already allegedly inflicted upon the shareholder's investment; and the proceeds could also be small compared to the earnings potential of the business especially where the only buyers for the shares are the alleged oppressors.

Against this background, the 1945 U.K. Cohen Committee recommended giving the court power to put an end to an act of oppression and this was enacted in section 210 of the U.K. *Companies Act*, 1948. In 1962, the U.K. Jenkins Committee recommended substantial amendments to overcome what turned out to be a number of judicially constructed limitations on the scope and application of the remedy. In particular, these committees highlighted four situations where the remedy would be appropriate: (1) where controlling directors unreasonably refuse to register transfers of the minority's holdings to force a reduced sale price for them to take advantage of; (2) where directors award themselves excessive remuneration that diminishes the funds available for distribution as dividends; (3) to prevent the issuing of shares to directors and others on special or advantageous terms; and (4) to prevent the refusal to declare non-cumulative preference dividends on shares held by the minority. It does not take an abundance of imagination to envision many other circumstances in which the oppression remedy would be an appropriate response.

The Canadian jurisdictions slowly adopted and improved on the U.K. provision, which in turn was significantly altered by section 75 of the 1980 U.K. *Companies Act* (now s. 994 of the U.K. *Companies Act*, 2006). An increasing number of decisions have been rendered by Canadian courts that already indicate that the oppression remedy may be the most significant one in the shareholder arsenal.

(b) The Canadian Statutory Provisions

Iacobucci, Pilkington, and Prichard,
Canadian Business Corporations
(1977) pp. 204–208 (footnotes omitted)

Federal

Section 234 [now s. 241] is the Federal Act's equivalent of the United Kingdom section 210 [now s. 994 of U.K. *Companies Act*, 2006]. It is supplemented by the provisions of section 235 [s. 242] and is in essence section 210 [s. 994] plus the changes recommended by the Jenkins Committee.

A "complainant" may apply to a court for an order and where the court is satisfied that (a) any act or omission of the corporation or its affiliates effects a result, or (b) the business or affairs of the corporation or its affiliates are or have been carried on or conducted in a manner, or (c) the powers of the directors of the corporation or any of its affiliates are or have been exercised in a manner that is "oppressive or unfairly prejudicial to or that unfairly disregards the interests of any security holder, creditor, director or officer", the court may make an interim or final order it thinks fit and subsection 234(3) [s. 241(3)] without limiting the generality of this power, gives examples including: orders (i) restraining the conduct complained of, (ii) appointing a receiver or receiver-manager, (iii) amending the articles or by-laws or a unanimous shareholder agreement, (iv) directing an issue or exchange of securities, (v) directing changes in directors, (vi) directing the purchase of the securities of a security holder, (vii) directing payment to a security holder, (viii) varying or setting aside a transaction to which the corporation is a party and compensating any other parties, (ix) directing production of any financial statement or accounting, (x) compensating any aggrieved person, (xi) directing rectification of the corporate records or registry, (xii) liquidating or dissolving the corporation, (xiii) directing an investigation, or (xiv) requiring the trial of any matter. If the order directs amendments of the articles or by-laws, the directors shall comply forthwith and paragraph 234(4)(b) [s. 241(4)(b)] prevents any further amendments without the court's approval. Any such amendments ordered by the court do not give rise to a dissenting shareholders' right of appraisal under section 184 [s. 190]. Subsection 234(6) [s. 241(6)] prevents the court from ordering the corporation to purchase securities of a security holder or pay to a security holder any part of the moneys paid by him for securities if there are reasonable grounds for believing that after the payment the corporation would be unable to meet its liabilities or the realizable value of its assets would thereby be less than the aggregate of its liabilities.

Section 235 [s. 242] adds four procedural and evidentiary qualifications to a section 234 [s. 241] application. First, the fact that the complained of conduct has been approved by the shareholders of the corporation is not sufficient grounds to stay or dismiss the application for relief; it is merely a factor that the court may take into account in making an order. Second, court approval is required for any stay, discontinuance or dismissal under section 234 [s. 241], and if the court determines that any complainant may be substantially affected by such stay, discontinuance or dismissal, it may order any party to the application to give notice to the complainant. Third, a complainant is not required to give security or costs when making his application. Fourth, the court may order the corporation to pay the complainant's interim costs, including legal fees and disbursements, but the complainant is accountable for these costs upon the final disposition of the application.

Section 234 [s. 241] has incorporated the six major recommendations of the Jenkins Report, each of which was designed to strip away the self-imposed judicial qualifications that have limited the application of section 210 [s. 994]. First, under section 210 [s. 994] the petitioner was required to show that the corporation's conduct was sufficiently poor so as to provide just and equitable grounds to wind-up the corporation. This requirement has now been omitted by section 459 of the 1985 U.K. *Companies Act*. This duty, which often prevented successful actions, has been criticized as too difficult an onus:

> It was the view of the Northern Ireland Committee on Company Law Reform that the section imposed too heavy an onus on the petitioner because the requirement that the company should be wound-up necessitated proof of a lack of probity akin to fraud. Shareholders, it is said, are entitled to relief long before this point is reached.

Section 234 [s. 241] abrogates this standard. It merely requires that the applicant show that the conduct is "oppressive or unfairly prejudicial to" or that it "unfairly disregards the interests of any security holder, creditor, director, or officer". It is not necessary to establish that grounds for winding-up the corporation exist.

Second, the courts have interpreted section 210 [s. 994] as requiring the petitioner to show a "course of conduct" which is oppressive, and it therefore does not cover isolated acts of the corporate body. The wording of section 234 [s. 241] clearly applies to isolated acts and does not require a continuing course of conduct. [Note that s. 994 of the U.K. *Companies Act*, 2006 no longer requires a "course of conduct".]

Third, the sole criterion in the original section 210 [s. 994] was "in a manner oppressive". The Jenkins Committee felt that this was too narrow a basis for protection and that the section should be expanded to include affairs which were being conducted "in a manner unfairly prejudicial to the interests of those members". Section 234 [s. 241] incorporated these broader grounds.

Fourth, the Jenkins Committee recommended that "section 210 [s. 994] should be amended to make clear that legal personal representatives and others to whom shares are transmitted by process of law, but who are not registered as members, are entitled to present a petition or seek an injunction under that section". Section 234 [s. 241] not only incorporated this recommendation but goes considerably further. By extending the availability of the section to "complainants", the section gives discretion to the court to entertain applications by the registered or beneficial owners, present and former, the Minister's representative and "any other persons who, in the discretion of a court, is a proper person to make an application".

Fifth, the Jenkins Committee recommended that the court have an express power to restrain the continuation or commission of any act which would suffice to support a petition under section 210. Paragraph 243(3)(a) [s. 241(3)(a)] includes this as a particular power of the court: "an order restraining the conduct complained of".

Sixth, section 234 [s. 241] incorporates the recommendation that the court be given the express power to authorize the bringing of proceedings in the name of the company against a third party on such terms as the court may direct. This power must be seen as complementary to the derivative action under section 233 [now s. 240].

Note

The oppression remedies of the corporate Acts of Alberta (ABCA s. 242), Saskatchewan (SBCA s. 234), Manitoba (MCA s. 234), New Brunswick (NBBCA s. 166), Nova Scotia (NSCA Third Schedule, s. 5) and Newfoundland (NCA s. 371) are substantially similar to that of the CBCA. Ontario's s. 248 differs in that it allows the applicant to seek relief from "threatened" acts of the company, and thus has a prospective aspect. In addition, in the case of an offering corporation, the Ontario Securities Commission may apply to the court for a remedy. British Columbia's s. 227 also offers protection from threatened acts, but does not list the ground of "unfairly disregards" and is arguably narrower in scope than the other oppression remedies.

(c) Overlap Between Oppression Remedy and Fiduciary Duties

What is the distinction between conduct that constitutes a breach of a director or officer's fiduciary duty, and conduct that is oppressive, unfairly prejudicial, or that unfairly disregards (collectively referred to below simply as conduct that is "oppressive")? The answer is that there is a significant overlap between common law and statutory fiduciary duties and the oppression remedy. For example, the oppression provision explicitly makes actionable any conduct that results in the powers of the directors having been exercised in an oppressive manner. The substantive ground for invoking the oppression section is "unfairness", and this substantive trigger is almost always broader than the substantive trigger for the invocation of fiduciary duties. What this means in practice is that the courts have routinely characterized directorial conduct that is a breach of fiduciary duty as oppressive.

What if an officer who is not a director acts in breach of fiduciary duty? Although the conduct of officers is not explicitly countenanced by the oppression provision, the provision does embrace any conduct of the corporation that is oppressive. The acts of senior officers are, in effect, acts of the corporation. Thus, acts of officers that are breaches of fiduciary duty are also drawn into the oppression remedy.

It may have occurred to you that a breach of a director's or officer's fiduciary duty will normally give rise to a derivative action, since the fiduciary duty is owed to the company. What about the oppression remedy? Does it embrace derivative actions? This question is explored further below. For now it will suffice to say that, although the drafters of the oppression remedy appear to have intended that oppression actions have a personal character, most courts have allowed actions of a derivative character to go forward under the oppression remedy. This development has further confounded the action for breach of fiduciary duty and the action alleging oppression.

It is not therefore surprising that it has become common in any action alleging breach of fiduciary duty to also allege oppression. Indeed, it is probably easiest to think of the oppression remedy as simply creating an expanded fiduciary duty (keeping in mind that the oppression remedy does in fact embrace some actions that will be purely personal in character) — although for some reason the courts have shied away from characterizing the substantive duties created by the oppression remedy as fiduciary in nature. In fact, as noted above, the oppression provision was designed precisely to circumvent limitations in the common law of fiduciary duties that denied minority shareholders a remedy where it was thought just that one should be available. This makes all the more curious the courts' continuing reluctance to characterize the oppression remedy as creating duties of a fiduciary character, although one explanation for why the courts have done so is offered in Jeffrey G. MacIntosh, Janet Holmes, and Steve Thompson, "The Puzzle of Shareholder Fiduciary Duties" (1991), 19 Can. Bus. L.J. 86. MacIntosh *et al.* argue that the conservative precedent-bound Anglo-Canadian legal tradition resulted in a situation in which judges could offer minority shareholder few remedies against abuse by majority or controlling shareholders. It was widely felt, however, that the common law was excessively restrictive. The oppression remedy has served the function of allowing judges wedded to a doctrine of precedent (and hence unable without legislative intervention to subvert the old paradigm of virtually unchecked majority rule) to fashion a new definition of majority-minority relations in corporation law. If this theory is correct, then it makes some sense that the courts have continued to treat fiduciary duties and the oppression remedy as two related but distinct legal doctrines. Confounding the oppression remedy with fiduciary duties might result in judges feeling that they could do no more under the oppression remedy than under the law of fiduciary duties. This would defeat the very reason for having an oppression remedy that is designed to allow judges to voyage into hitherto unchartered territory.

Because (i) any breach of fiduciary duty (by a director or officer, or even, as explored below, by a controlling shareholder) is almost certain to be characterized as oppression, (ii) the oppression remedy offers a broader substantive cause of action ("fairness", and no requirement that *mala fides* be shown: see *infra*) than does the law of fiduciary duties, (iii) the remedies available under the oppression remedy are broader than those available in an action for breach of fiduciary duty, (iv) the courts have allowed derivative-type actions to proceed under the oppression provision, the oppression remedy is, little by little, swallowing up the law of fiduciary duties. The danger that this creates is that the broad fairness standard for intervention under the oppression remedy creates so much judicial discretion that it undermines the comparatively greater certainty created by the law of fiduciary duties. Perhaps this danger is self-correcting; as new cases are decided under the oppression remedy, new paradigms will be fashioned and a new jurisprudence will emerge that will channel judicial decision-making much as the older fiduciary cases did. What do you think?

In any case, the important lesson to keep in mind is that the oppression provision is probably the most important innovation in corporate law in the twentieth century, and one that stands to transform the relationship between corporate directors, officers, and shareholders. Having said this, you should also keep in mind that the majority of cases decided under the oppression provision involve private companies; fewer cases apply the remedy to public companies. As you read through the materials in this section, you should ask yourself whether the broad judicial discretion that is given to judges under the oppression remedy is as appropriate for public corporations as it is for private corporations.

We turn first to consider the BCE case again, given that it substantially melds the oppression remedy with the fiduciary duty under section 122(1)(a).

BCE Inc., Re

2008 CarswellQue 12595, 2008 CarswellQue 12596, (sub nom. *BCE Inc. v. 1976 Debentureholders*) [2008] 3 S.C.R. 560 (S.C.C.)

B. *The Section 241 Oppression Remedy*

The debenture holders in these appeals claim that the directors acted in an oppressive manner in approving the sale of BCE, contrary to s. 241 of the *CBCA*. Security holders of a corporation or its affiliates fall within the class of persons who may be permitted to bring a claim for oppression under s. 241 of the *CBCA*. The trial judge permitted the debenture holders to do so, although in the end he found the claim had not been established. The question is whether the trial judge erred in dismissing the claim.

We will first set out what must be shown to establish the right to a remedy under s. 241, and then review the conduct complained of in the light of those requirements.

(1) The Law

Section 241(2) provides that a court may make an order to rectify the matters complained of where

(a) any act or omission of the corporation or any of its affiliates effects a result,

(b) the business or affairs of the corporation or any of its affiliates are or have been carried on or conducted in a manner, or

(c) the powers of the directors of the corporation or any of its affiliates are or have been exercised in a manner that is oppressive or unfairly prejudicial to or that unfairly disregards the interests of any security holder, creditor, director or officer. . . .

Section 241 jurisprudence reveals two possible approaches to the interpretation of the oppression provisions of the *CBCA*: M. Koehnen, *Oppression and Related Remedies* (2004), at pp. 79-80 and 84. One approach emphasizes a strict reading of the three types of conduct enumerated in s. 241 (oppression, unfair prejudice and unfair disregard): see *Scottish Cooperative Wholesale Society Ltd. v. Meyer* (1958), [1959] A.C. 324 (U.K. H.L.); *Diligenti v. RWMD Operations Kelowna Ltd.*, 1976 CarswellBC 3, 1 B.C.L.R. 36 (B.C. S.C.), additional reasons at 1977

CarswellBC 139 (B.C. S.C.); *Stech v. Davies*, 1987 CarswellAlta 175, [1987] 5 W.W.R. 563 (Alta. Q.B.). Cases following this approach focus on the precise content of the categories "oppression", "unfair prejudice" and "unfair disregard". While these cases may provide valuable insight into what constitutes oppression in particular circumstances, a categorical approach to oppression is problematic because the terms used cannot be put into watertight compartments or conclusively defined. As Koehnen puts it (at p. 84), "[t]he three statutory components of oppression are really adjectives that try to describe inappropriate conduct. . . . The difficulty with adjectives is they provide no assistance in formulating principles that should underline court intervention."

Other cases have focused on the broader principles underlying and uniting the various aspects of oppression: see *First Edmonton Place Ltd. v. 315888 Alberta Ltd.*, 1988 CarswellAlta 103, 40 B.L.R. 28 (Alta. Q.B.), varied 1989 CarswellAlta 181, 45 B.L.R. 110 (Alta. C.A.); *820099 Ontario Inc. v. Harold E. Ballard Ltd.*, 1991 CarswellOnt 141, 3 B.L.R. (2d) 113 (Ont. Div. Ct.); *Westfair Foods Ltd. v. Watt*, 1991 CarswellAlta 63, 79 D.L.R. (4th) 48 (Alta. C.A.), leave to appeal refused (1991), 85 D.L.R. (4th) viii (note) (S.C.C.).

In our view, the best approach to the interpretation of s. 241(2) is one that combines the two approaches developed in the cases. One should look first to the principles underlying the oppression remedy, and in particular the concept of reasonable expectations. If a breach of a reasonable expectation is established, one must go on to consider whether the conduct complained of amounts to "oppression", "unfair prejudice" or "unfair disregard" as set out in s. 241(2) of the *CBCA*.

We preface our discussion of the twin prongs of the oppression inquiry by two preliminary observations that run throughout all the jurisprudence.

First, oppression is an equitable remedy. It seeks to ensure fairness — what is "just and equitable". It gives a court broad, equitable jurisdiction to enforce not just what is legal but what is fair: *Wright v. Donald S. Montgomery Holdings Ltd.*, 1998 CarswellOnt 370, 39 B.L.R. (2d) 266 (Ont. Gen. Div.), at p. 273 [B.L.R.]; *Keho Holdings Ltd. v. Noble*, 1987 CarswellAlta 107, 38 D.L.R. (4th) 368 (Alta. C.A.), at p. 374; see, more generally, Koehnen, at pp. 78-79. It follows that courts considering claims for oppression should look at business realities, not merely narrow legalities: *Scottish Co-operative Wholesale Society*, at p. 343.

Second, like many equitable remedies, oppression is fact-specific. What is just and equitable is judged by the reasonable expectations of the stakeholders in the context and in regard to the relationships at play. Conduct that may be oppressive in one situation may not be in another.

Against this background, we turn to the first prong of the inquiry, the principles underlying the remedy of oppression. In *Ebrahimi v. Westbourne Galleries Ltd.* (1972), [1973] A.C. 360 (U.K. H.L.), at p. 379,

Lord Wilberforce, interpreting s. 222 of the U.K. *Companies Act, 1948*, described the remedy of oppression in the following seminal terms:

> The words ["just and equitable"] are a recognition of the fact that a limited company is more than a mere legal entity, with a personality in law of its own: that there is room in company law for recognition of the fact that behind it, or amongst it, there are individuals, with rights, expectations and obligations inter se which are not necessarily submerged in the company structure.

Lord Wilberforce spoke of the equitable remedy in terms of the "rights, expectations and obligations" of individuals. "Rights" and "obligations" connote interests enforceable at law without recourse to special remedies, for example, through a contractual suit or a derivative action under s. 239 of the *CBCA*. It is left for the oppression remedy to deal with the "expectations" of affected stakeholders. The reasonable expectations of these stakeholders is the cornerstone of the oppression remedy.

As denoted by "reasonable", the concept of reasonable expectations is objective and contextual. The actual expectation of a particular stakeholder is not conclusive. In the context of whether it would be "just and equitable" to grant a remedy, the question is whether the expectation is reasonable having regard to the facts of the specific case, the relationships at issue, and the entire context, including the fact that there may be conflicting claims and expectations.

Particular circumstances give rise to particular expectations. Stakeholders enter into relationships, with and within corporations, on the basis of understandings and expectations, upon which they are entitled to rely, provided they are reasonable in the context: see *Main v. Delcan Group Inc.*, 1999 CarswellOnt 1605, 47 B.L.R. (2d) 200 (Ont. S.C.J. [Commercial List]). These expectations are what the remedy of oppression seeks to uphold.

Determining whether a particular expectation is reasonable is complicated by the fact that the interests and expectations of different stakeholders may conflict. The oppression remedy recognizes that a corporation is an entity that encompasses and affects various individuals and groups, some of whose interests may conflict with others. Directors or other corporate actors may make corporate decisions or seek to resolve conflicts in a way that abusively or unfairly maximizes a particular group's interest at the expense of other stakeholders. The corporation and shareholders are entitled to maximize profit and share value, to be sure, but not by treating individual stakeholders unfairly. Fair treatment — the central theme running through the oppression jurisprudence — is most fundamentally what stakeholders are entitled to "reasonably expect".

Section 241(2) speaks of the "act or omission" of the corporation or any of its affiliates, the conduct of "business or affairs" of the corporation and the "powers of the directors of the corporation or any of its affiliates". Often, the conduct complained of is the conduct of the corporation or of its directors, who are responsible for the governance of the corporation. However, the conduct of other actors, such as shareholders, may also support a claim for oppression: see Koehnen, at pp. 109-10; *GATX Corp. v. Hawker Siddeley Canada Inc.*, 1996 CarswellOnt 1434, 27 B.L.R. (2d) 251 (Ont. Gen. Div. [Commercial List]). In the appeals before us, the claims for oppression are based on allegations that the directors of BCE and Bell Canada failed to comply with the reasonable expectations of the debenture holders, and it is unnecessary to go beyond this.

The fact that the conduct of the directors is often at the centre of oppression actions might seem to suggest that directors are under a direct duty to individual stakeholders who may be affected by a corporate decision. Directors, acting in the best interests of the corporation, may be obliged to consider the impact of their decisions on corporate stakeholders, such as the debenture holders in these appeals. This is what we mean when we speak of a director being required to act in the best interests of the corporation viewed as a good corporate citizen. However, the directors owe a fiduciary duty to the corporation, and only to the corporation. People sometimes speak in terms of directors owing a duty to both the corporation and to stakeholders. Usually this is harmless, since the reasonable expectations of the stakeholder in a particular outcome often coincides with what is in the best interests of the corporation. However, cases (such as these appeals) may arise where these interests do not coincide. In such cases, it is important to be clear that the directors owe their duty to the corporation, not to stakeholders, and that the reasonable expectation of stakeholders is simply that the directors act in the best interests of the corporation.

Having discussed the concept of reasonable expectations that underlies the oppression remedy, we arrive at the second prong of the s. 241 oppression remedy. Even if reasonable, not every unmet expectation gives rise to claim under s. 241. The section requires that the conduct complained of amount to "oppression", "unfair prejudice" or "unfair disregard" of relevant interests. "Oppression" carries the sense of conduct that is coercive and abusive, and suggests bad faith. "Unfair prejudice" may admit of a less culpable state of mind, that nevertheless has unfair consequences. Finally, "unfair disregard" of interests extends the remedy to ignoring an interest as being of no importance, contrary to the stakeholders' reasonable expectations: see Koehnen, at pp. 81-88. The phrases describe, in adjectival terms, ways in which corporate actors may fail to meet the reasonable expectations of stakeholders.

In summary, the foregoing discussion suggests conducting two related inquiries in a claim for oppression: (1) Does the evidence support the reasonable expectation asserted by the claimant? and (2) Does the evidence establish that the reasonable expectation was violated by conduct falling within the terms "oppression", "unfair prejudice" or "unfair disregard" of a relevant interest?

* * *

Jeffrey G. MacIntosh, "BCE and the Peoples' Corporate Law: Learning to Live on Quicksand"
(2009) 48 C.B.L.J. 255

Conflating the Oppression Remedy and the Duty of Loyalty

In exploring the content of the directors' duty of loyalty (the fiduciary duty), the court conflates the duty of loyalty and the oppression remedy. For example:

> However, this case does involve the fiduciary duty of the directors to the corporation, and particularly the "fair treatment" component of this duty, which, as will be seen, is fundamental to the reasonable expectations of stakeholders claiming an oppression remedy.

The court also seems to suggest that "reasonable expectations" is now part of the duty of loyalty. In like fashion, the concept of acting "in the best interests of the corporation" is imported from s. 122(1)(a) into the oppression remedy. In net, two independent liabilities are surgically merged into Siamese twins of apparently identical mien.

There are a number of difficulties with this position. First, the duty of loyalty and the oppression remedy are independent statutory provisions. They have independent purposes (a fact explicitly acknowledged by the court). While the duty of loyalty specifically seeks to hold directors accountable to shareholders, the oppression remedy was enacted to address shortcomings in the law relating to the treatment of minority shareholders. It is drafted quite differently from the duty of loyalty, and (in respect of its own substantive territory) has always been regarded as establishing a different and lower threshold for liability than s.122(1)(a). While there may be good substantive reasons for finding a coherent way to unite the two into a single liability, that is for Parliament, and not the courts to do. It simply is not appropriate as a matter of statutory interpretation to conflate the meaning of one with another, particularly given the stark differences in both drafting and function.

Second, to the extent that courts have propounded a "fair treatment" doctrine under the duty of loyalty, it is one that operates solely in the interest of different classes of *shareholders*. To assert that it is co-extensive with the "fairness" doctrine under the oppression remedy is simply incorrect.

Third, the notion that the directors must act "in the best interests of the corporation" is a livery that ill-fits the oppression remedy. The Dickerson Committee (which drafted the CBCA) anticipated that the oppression remedy would be used primarily to redress *personal* wrongs, with some admixture of actions of a formally derivative character (mostly arising in private corporations) where the true nature of the *lis* is a dispute between majority and minority shareholders. The Supreme Court seems to recognize this in stating:

> Unlike the derivative action, which is aimed at enforcing a right of the corporation itself, the oppression remedy focuses on harm to the legal and equitable interests of stakeholders affected by oppressive acts of a corporation or its directors.

The predominantly personal flavor of the oppression remedy is why it requires that the complainant show harm to a "security holders, creditor, director or officer".

A number of observations are in order. First, the drafting of the oppression remedy does not permit a complainant to succeed by showing harm to *the corporation*; only harm to a security holder, creditor, director or officer will do. And as we have been told in *Peoples* and *BCE*, none of these should be "confused" with "the corporation". Thus, the importation of acting in "the best interests of the corporation" into the oppression remedy mixes apples and oranges.

Second, this same drafting expressly forbids a court from taking into account the full range of interests that the Supreme Court hints might be "considered" by directors in prosecuting their duty to the corporation. This further emphasizes the ill-fit between the oppression remedy and the admonition that the directors must act in the "best interests of the corporation".

Third, acting in the best interests of "the corporation" could easily entail running roughshod over the reasonable expectations of particular constituencies, driving a wedge between the jurisprudential foundations of the oppression remedy and the duty of loyalty. This may in fact underlie the Supreme Court's introduction of a novel two-step process for determining whether oppressive conduct has occurred. If, under the oppression remedy, directors are expected to act in the best interests of the corporation, then reasonable expectations can ground only defeasible rights. While (given the premises) this logic is inexorable, it leads to the unfortunate result of materially diminishing the ability of the oppression remedy to redress wrongs to its client constituencies.

Finally, the shotgun marriage of the duty of loyalty and oppression remedy creates yet further uncertainty regarding *both*. Are all oppression cases to be mapped into the duty of loyalty, and vice-versa? Again, this uncertainty cries out for a legislative solution.

(d) Judicial Interpretation of the Action

(i)   Standing to Bring an Oppression Action

The statutory definition of "complainant" for an oppression action is the same as in an application for leave to commence a derivative action. They are both defined under s. 238 of the CBCA. The action is open to shareholders, directors and officers of the corporation, as well as those the court considers "proper persons". The next case is an important one for the meaning of "proper person" within the context of an oppression action, and the issue of whether a creditor may bring an oppression action.

First Edmonton Place Ltd. v. 315888 Alberta Ltd.
(1988), 40 B.L.R. 28, 1988 CarswellAlta 103 (Q.B.)

D.C. McDonald J.: In order to obtain leave to bring an action under either of these sections, the applicant must be found to be a "complainant" as defined in s. 231. As the applicant is clearly not within s. 231(b)(ii), First Edmonton Place can satisfy this requirement only if it can come within s. 231(b)(i) or (iii).

Is the applicant a "complainant" within the meaning of s. 231(b)(i)?

It will be recalled that s. 231(b)(i) defines a "complainant" as "a registered holder or beneficial owner, or a former registered holder or beneficial owner, of a security of a corporation or any of its affiliates". On behalf of First Edmonton Place it is contended that the lease is a security of the corporation and that the lessor is the beneficial owner of the security. To repeat the definition of "security" as found in s. 1(u), that word includes a "debt obligation of a corporation and includes the certificate evidence in such a share or debt obligation". We have seen also that under s. 1(g.1) "debt obligation," is defined as meaning "a bond, debenture, note or other evidence of indebtedness or guarantee of a corporation, whether secured or unsecured". The report of the Institute of Law Research and Reform of Alberta, made the following observations concerning this definition of "complainant" (at p, 149): The definition of "complainant" in CBCA s. 231 includes a present and former registered holder of a "security" of a company or its affiliates. The definition of "security" in CBCA s. 2 includes a "debt obligation of a corporation," and, a certificate evidencing such a . . . debt obligation." The reference to the certificate in CBCA s. 2 and the reference to a registered holder in CBCA s. 231 Probably restricts the definition of "complainant" to those creditors who are entitled to have certificates and who are to be entered in the securities register.

In my opinion, that is a correct interpretation of CBCA s. 231 and of the definition of "complainant" found in s. 231(b)(i) of the ABCA. In other words, a creditor can be a "complainant" under s. 231(b)(i) only if it holds or is the beneficial owner of a security of the corporation, and if the security is of a type which is capable of being registered under s. 88.2(2) or (5) with the Registrar of Corporations, and in the register of mortgages specifically affecting property of the corporation, which is to be kept by the corporation pursuant to s. 88.5(1). Those provisions apply, according to the definitions contained in s. 88.1 to any "mortgage", and the word "mortgage" includes a "charge", so that the provisions in s. 88.2 relating to the filing of "debentures containing any charge" require the registration of such debentures as well as mortgages. Section 88.2 thus creates a scheme for the registration of mortgages and debentures. Such written evidence of a debt obligation is in my view a certificate evidencing . . . a . . . debt obligation".

Thus, it is clear that, by reference to the clear implication on the face of s. 231(b)(i), the word "complainant" includes only the registered holders or beneficial owners of a mortgage issued by the corporation or a debenture creating a charge, issued by the corporation. It is therefore not necessary to turn to the Institute's report to justify that result, but it is nonetheless worth quoting the rationale which was given by the Institute for the inclusion of holders of debt security as complainants (at p. 150):

> the holders of debt securities are in much the same position as, and virtually indistinguishable from, the holders of non-voting preference shares, and should have similar treatment in the interests of fairness and of maintaining the attractiveness of debt securities as investments.

That rationale could, however, apply equally to lessors and to creditors who have extended credit to the corporation, for it could be argued that they too, like the holders of non-voting preference shares, should be treated fairly, and that there is an interest in encouraging the commercial liability of corporations by making it attractive to extend credit to them. Whether such a logical extension of the rationale would be justified is, however, a matter that need not be considered further because of the plain meaning of the statute.

This plain meaning reflects the meaning of "bonds, debentures and notes" in the world of corporate financing. In *Securities Law and Practice* (Vol. 1, 1984) by V.P. Alboini, bonds and debentures are stated to be the "traditional debt instruments issued by corporations" while notes are "issued by any issuer including individuals" (at pp. 0-33, 0-34).

Is the applicant a "complainant" under s. 231(b)(iii)?

Under s. 231(b)(iii),a person may be a complainant" if he is a person "who, in the discretion of the court, is a proper person to make an application under this Part".

This is not so much a definition as a grant to the court of a broad power to do justice and equity in the circumstances of a particular case, where a person, who otherwise would not be a "complainant", ought to be permitted to bring an action under either s. 232 or s. 234 to right a wrong done to the corporation which would not otherwise be righted, or to obtain compensation himself or itself where his or its interests have suffered from oppression by the majority controlling the corporation or have been unfairly prejudiced or unfairly disregarded, and the applicant is a "security holder, creditor, director or officer".

The report of the Institute of Law Research and Reform of Alberta had some reservations about the inclusion of such a broad power to permit a person to complain. It is stated, at p. 150: "We have some reservations about legislation which confers broad statutory discretions without guidelines". Here, however, we think such a discretion appropriate. The specific listed classes appear to us to cover all cases in which the derivative and personal remedies should be available, but foresight is necessarily imperfect, and the general discretion would allow the courts to make up for the imperfections of foresight. We think also that the courts can be relied upon to allow only proper applications. Section 231(b)(iv) of the *Draft Act* therefore follows CBCA s. 231(d).

(It should be noted that what was s. 231(b)(iv) in the *Draft Act* became s. 231(b)(iii) in the ABCA.) The Institute's report thus recommended that the question of who is a "proper person" be left to the discretion of the court. Even accepting that the s. 232 and s. 234 remedies should be given a liberal interpretation, the circumstances in which a person who is not a security holder (as I have interpreted that phrase), or a director or officer should be recognized as a proper person to make an application must show that justice and equity clearly dictate such a result.

In the case of a creditor who claims to be a "proper person," to make a s. 232 application, in my view the criterion to be applied would be whether, even if the applicant did not come within s. 231(b)(i) or (ii), he or it would nevertheless be a person who could reasonably be entrusted with the responsibility of advancing the interests of the corporation by seeking a remedy to right the wrong allegedly done to the corporation. The applicant would not have to be a security holder (as I have defined that notion), director or officer of the corporation. The applicant could be a creditor. The applicant might even be a person who at the time of the act or conduct complained of was not a creditor but was a person toward whom the corporation might have a contingent liability. No good purpose would be served in saying more than that now.

I turn now to an application by a person who claims to be a "proper person" to make an application under s. 234. As in the case of an application made under s. 232, an applicant for leave to bring an action under s. 234 does not have to be a security holder, director or officer. The applicant could be a creditor, or even a person toward whom the corporation had only a contingent liability at the time of the act or conduct complained of. However, it is important to note that he would not be held to be a "proper person" to make the application under s. 234

unless he satisfied the court that there was some evidence of oppression or unfair prejudice or unfair disregard for the interests of a security holder, creditor, director or officer.

Having said that, assuming that the applicant was a creditor of the corporation at the time of the act or conduct complained of, what criterion should be applied in determining whether the applicant is, a "proper person" to make the application? Once again, in my view, the applicant must show that in the circumstances of the case justice and equity require him or it to be given an opportunity to have the claim tried.

There are two circumstances in which justice and equity would entitle a creditor to be regarded as "a proper person". (There may be other circumstances; these two are not intended to exhaust the possibilities.) The first is if the act or conduct of the directors or management of the corporation, which is complained of, constituted using the corporation as a vehicle for committing a fraud upon the applicant. (In the present case there is no evidence suggesting such fraud, although there is some evidence of the directors having used the money paid as a cash inducement for their own personal investment purposes, and that, as I shall later explain, may constitute fraud against the corporation: see *infra* where *R. v. Olan, Hudson and Hartnett* is cited.)

Second, the court might hold that the applicant is a "proper person to make an application," for an order under s. 234 if the act or conduct of the directors or management of the corporation, which is complained of, constituted a breach of the underlying expectation of the applicant arising from the circumstances in which the applicant's relationship, with the corporation arose. For example, where the applicant is a creditor of the corporation, did the circumstances, which gave rise to the granting of credit, include some element which prevented the creditor from taking adequate steps when he or it entered into the agreement, to protect his or its interests against the occurrence of which he or it now complains? Did the creditor entertain an expectation that, assuming fair dealing, its chances of repayment would not be frustrated by the kind of conduct which subsequently was engaged in by the management of the corporation? Assuming that the evidence established the existence of such an expectation, the next question would be whether that expectation was, objectively, a reasonable one . . .

In the case of the application under s. 234, leave to bring an action in regard to either claim is denied because the applicant was not a creditor at the time of the act or conduct complained of.

Notes

1   Professors Ben-Ishai and Puri's empirical study of the oppression remedy in Canada found that while the remedy's wording suggests that it is not exclusively for shareholders, shareholders constituted the largest class of complainants, accounting for 80% of all complainants, with a 53% success rate. Creditors accounted for only 8% of

all complainants in Professors Ben-Ishai and Puri's study but had a tremendously high success rate of 83%. Given the high rate of success for actions that were brought by creditors, combined with recent jurisprudence and commentary and the current economic climate, Professors Puri and Ben-Ishai predict that of all non-shareholder complainants, we will see more claims and a higher success rate for creditors against both widely held and closely held corporations. See Stephanie Ben-Ishai and Poonam Puri, "The Canadian Oppression Remedy Judicially Considered: 1995–2001" (2004), 30 Queen's Law Review 79.

In the trial decision of *Peoples Department Stores Inc. v. Wise*, (1998), 23 C.B.R. (4th) 2000 (Que. S.C.), Justice Greenberg held that because only creditors have a meaningful stake in the assets of an insolvent corporation, directors have an obligation to ensure that an insolvent corporation is properly administered and its assets are not dissipated in a manner that is prejudicial to the creditors. Justice Pelletier, writing for the Quebec Court of Appeal, overturned Justice Greenberg's decision holding that "by importing this theory into Canadian law the trial judge was usurping the intervention role of the legislator by establishing a general regime for liability of directors favouring third parties who find themselves prejudiced by the management acts of directors . . .". See 2003 CarswellQue 145, 41 C.B.R. (4th) 225 (Que. C.A.). Leave to appeal from the Quebec Court of Appeal's decision has been granted to the Supreme Court of Canada 2003 CarswellQue 3487, 2003 CarswellQue 3488, [2003] S.C.C.A. No. 133 (S.C.C.), affirmed 2004 CarswellQue 2862, 2004 CarswellQue 2863 (S.C.C.).

Following the lower court decision in *Peoples*, many commentators were swift in pointing out the difficulties of extending a fiduciary duty to creditors and expressed a preference for the development of the oppression remedy to deal with the treatment of creditor stakeholders: see, for example, Edward A. Sellers, Natasha J. MacParland, and F. James Hoffner, "Governance of the Financially Distressed Corporation in Global Capital Markets: Selected Aspects of the Financing and Governance of Canadian Enterprises in Cross-Border Workouts" in Janis Sarra, Ed., *Corporate Governance in Global Capital Markets* (Vancouver: UBC Press, 2003) 297 at 307. See also Edward M. Iacobucci and Kevin E. Davis, "Reconciling Derivative Claims and the Oppression Remedy" (2000) 12 Sup. Ct. L. Rev. (2d) 86.

2 Is a wrongfully dismissed employee a "proper person" who can bring an oppression action under statute? If, for example, an employee-shareholder is dismissed, the oppression remedy may be available if the loss of employment is intrinsically linked to his or her status as a shareholder. See *Naneff v. Con-Crete Holdings Ltd.* (1993), 11 B.L.R.

(2d) 218, 1993 CarswellOnt 157 (Gen. Div. [Commercial List]), varied (1994), 19 O.R. (3d) 691, reversed (1995), 23 O.R. (3d) 481, 1995 CarswellOnt 1207 (C.A.); *Flatley v. Algy Corp.* (2000), [2000] O.J. No. 3787, 2000 CarswellOnt 3734 (S.C.J. [Commercial List]); and *Krynen v. Bugg*, 2003 CarswellOnt 1138 (Ont. S.C.J.), additional reasons at 2003 CarswellOnt 2197 (Ont. S.C.J.). Free-standing employees have not been successful in bringing oppression actions. Why do you think that is? See Stephanie Ben-Ishai and Poonam Puri, "The Canadian Oppression Remedy Judicially Considered: 1995–2001", (2004), 30 Queen's Law Review 79.

3   Other applicants who have been deemed "proper persons" to bring an oppression action include the widow of a deceased shareholder (see *Lenstra v. Lenstra* (1995), 1995 CarswellOnt 2678 (Gen. Div.)), a trustee in bankruptcy (see *Olympia & York Developments Ltd. (Trustee of) v. Olympia & York Realty Corp.*, [2001] O.T.C. 646, 2001 CarswellOnt 2954 (S.C.J. [Commercial List])), additional reasons at (2001), 2001 CarswellOnt 4739 (S.C.J. [Commercial List]) and a custodian of funds set up for immigrant investors (see *HSBC Capital Canada Inc. v. First Mortgage Alberta Fund (V) Inc.* (1999), 47 B.L.R. (2d) 180, 1999 CarswellAlta 458 (Q.B.)). Also of interest is *Gainers Inc. v. Pocklington* (1992), 7 B.L.R. (2d) 87, 1992 CarswellAlta 277 (Q.B.), in which the court held that in special circumstances the corporation itself may be a proper person to bring an oppression action. Finally, some cases have held that an applicant need not have actually been affected by the alleged oppression to have standing, but may have standing in the interests of righting a wrong done to others. When might this be the case? See *PMSM Investments Ltd. v. Bureau* (1995), 24 B.L.R. (2d) 295, 1995 CarswellOnt 1394 (Gen. Div. [Commercial List]); and *Joncas v. Spruce Falls Power & Paper Co.*, [2000] O.T.C. 339, 6 B.L.R. (3d) 109, 2000 CarswellOnt 1689 (S.C.J.), affirmed by 15 B.L.R. (3d) 1 (O.C.A.).

4   As a practical matter, why might an aggrieved party who is not a shareholder prefer commencing an oppression action over an ordinary civil claim? Professors Ben-Ishai and Puri suggest that from the litigation strategy perspective of an advocate initiating an action, the oppression remedy may be preferable to the ordinary civil action for three reasons. First, the oppression remedy may be commenced by way of application, without pleadings or discovery, and as a result it may proceed more quickly if there are no significant factual issues in dispute. Second, the relief that a court can provide under the oppression remedy is broader and more flexible than can be provided under an ordinary civil action. Third, the blurry state of Canadian law on the nature and type of fiduciary duties owed to non-shareholder stakeholders has created the need for an alternative flexible remedial option. See S. Ben-Ishai and P. Puri, "The Canadian

Oppression Remedy Judicially Considered: 1995–2001", (2004), 30 Queen's Law Review 79.

5   As a matter of corporate law theory, should non-shareholder stakeholders who may have recourse against the corporation under common law, statutory and/or contract law remedies be allowed to utilize the oppression action? What implications does an expansionary interpretation of the definition of "complainant" have for the purposes for which a corporation is said to exist?

(ii)   The Substantive Scope of the Oppression Remedy

The English Act of 1948 that introduced the oppression remedy to Anglo-Canadian jurisprudence made actionable corporate conduct that was "oppressive". Thus, in defining the substantive scope of the oppression remedy, the early English jurisprudence dealt solely with the meaning of "oppressive" conduct, rather than the broader formulation found in the CBCA and OBCA. The word "oppression" has a common law lineage that predates the oppression remedy; see, e.g., *Northwest Transportation Company, Limited v. Beatty.* However, what was "oppressive" or a "fraud on the minority" at common law was essentially restricted to takings of property or other clearly egregious interferences with minority shareholder rights or expectations. See Beck, "The Shareholders' Derivative Action", *supra*, this chapter. The English courts accorded the statutory concept of "oppression" a much wider ambit than at common law. Two definitions are widely cited. In *Elder v. Elder & Watson Ltd.*, [1952] S.C. 49, Lord Cooper said that "the essence of the matter seems to be that the conduct complained of should at the lowest involve a visible departure from the standards of the fair dealing and a violation of the conditions of fair play on which every shareholder who entrusts his money to a company is entitled to rely." In *Scottish Cooperative Wholesale Society Ltd. v. Meyer*, [1959] A.C. 324, [1958] 3 All E.R. 66 (H.L.), a number of the judgments considered the meaning of "oppressive" conduct. Lord Simmonds adopted the dictionary meaning of "burdensome, harsh and wrongful" and the outcome of the case indicates that "wrongful" includes conduct that falls short of actual illegality or invasion of legal rights but that can nonetheless be described as reprehensible.

In the CBCA and the OBCA, the oppression remedy is triggered not only by actions that are "oppressive", but also by any action that is "unfairly prejudicial or that unfairly disregards the interests of any security holder, creditor, director or officer". As can be seen from the following cases, the Canadian courts have used this expanded definition to widen the scope of conduct covered by the original English provision, moving towards a broadly based definition of "fairness" as the substantive standard. The first case, *Ferguson v. Imax*, is also helpful in exploring the relationship between the oppression remedy and the common law of fiduciary duties.

Ferguson v. Imax Systems Corp.
(1983), 150 D.L.R. (3d) 718, 1983 CarswellOnt 926 (C.A.), leave to appeal refused (1983), 2 O.A.C. 158 (note), 52 N.R. 317 (note) (S.C.C.)

[Imax Systems Corp. was incorporated to exploit a film projection system. The founding shareholders were the appellant, her then-husband, and two other couples. Upon incorporation the husbands each received seven hundred shares of the common shares of the company, while the wives each received 700 shares of the class B shares. The class B shares were non-voting and paid a dividend of five cents per share in priority to the common shares, sharing equally in dividends and liquidation thereafter. The appellant had knowledge of the film business and participated in the management and administration of the company. Following Ferguson's separation and subsequent divorce, the company, acting under pressure from her ex-husband, tried to squeeze her out. She was discharged by Imax, and the company refused to declare dividends beyond those required by the class B shares. The company also proposed to cancel and convert all class B shares to non-voting, limited-dividend shares. Ferguson sought relief under s. 234 of the CBCA alleging that the company and its directors were acting in a manner that was oppressive, unfairly prejudicial, or that unfairly disregarded her interests as a security holder.]

BROOKE J.A.: . . . The policy of the law to ensure just and equitable treatment of minorities can be traced back to early cases. In *Allen v. Gold Reefs of West Africa, Ltd.*, [1900] 1 Ch. 656 at p. 671, Lindley M.R., speaking of the powers of a corporation to amend its articles, said:

> it must, like all other powers, be exercised subject to those general principles of law and equity which are applicable to all powers conferred on majorities and enabling them to bind minorities. It must be exercised, not only in the manner required by law, but also *bona fide* for the benefit of the company as a whole, and it must not be exceeded.

In *Goldex Mines Ltd. v. Revill et al.* (1974), 7 O.R. (2d) 216 at p. 224, 54 D.L.R. (3d) 672 at p. 680, Arnup J.A. for this court, after considering the earlier cases, said:

> The principle that the majority governs in corporate affairs is fundamental to corporation law, but its corollary is also important — that the majority must act fairly and honestly. Fairness is the touchstone of equitable justice and when the test of fairness is not met, the equitable jurisdiction of the court can be invoked to prevent

or remedy the injustice which misrepresentation or other dishonesty has caused.

But s. 234 must not be regarded as being simply a codification of the common law. Today one looks to the section when considering the interests of the minority shareholders and the section should be interpreted broadly to carry out its purpose: see the *Interpretation Act*, R.S.C. 1970, c. I-23, s. 11. Accordingly, when dealing with a close corporation, the court may consider the relationship between the shareholders and not simply legal rights as such. In addition, the court must consider the *bona fides* of the corporate transaction in question to determine whether the act of the corporation or directors effects a result which is oppressive or unfairly prejudicial to the minority shareholder. Counsel has referred us to a number of decisions. They establish primarily that each case turns on its own facts. What is oppressive or unfairly prejudicial in one case may not necessarily be so in the slightly different setting of another.

Here we have a small close corporation that was promoted and is still controlled by the same small related group of individuals. The appellant's part in that group and her work for the corporation is important. Further, the attempt to force her to sell her shares through non-payment of dividends was not simply the act of Mr. Ferguson, but was also the act of the others in the group including the present director, in concert with him. Having regard to the intention of that group to deny the appellant any participation in the growth of the company I think the resolution authorizing the change in the capital of the company is the culminating event in a lengthy course of oppressive and unfairly prejudicial conduct to the appellant. In my opinion the company has not acted *bona fides* in exercising its powers to amend. By the payment of moneys now as a capital payment, which moneys on the evidence ought to have been by way of dividends over the years the appellant's non-redeemable shares are now to be redeemed and those in control of the company will be rid of her. She is the only one so affected. All of the other class B shareholders hold an equal number of common shares personally or through their spouses. The appellant cannot be considered like someone who came to the company lately and took a minority position in one of several classes of stock. Like the Kroiters and the Kerrs, her investment must be regarded as being in the shares which she and her husband held. The agreements as to the disposition of family shares in the event of the death of the husband or the wife confirm that this was really a family venture not only in the case of the Fergusons, but for each of the three couples.

Viewed in this way, and as all of the other class B shareholders held an equal number of common shares either personally or with their spouses, it is idle to suggest that the vote on the resolution would be anything other than a means to get moneys which they had eagerly sought by way of dividends but were denied because of the appellant's presence and as a means to end her presence as an obstacle to further payment. I doubt if any corporate purpose would enter the minds of the class B shareholders when the resolution was put to them to vote on. The resolution was a final solution to the problem of the ex-wife shareholder.

In my opinion the appellant satisfied the onus upon her when relying on s. 234 of the Act and she was entitled to the relief sought in the first instance. We have been advised that a motion to prohibit the company from proceeding with the meeting of shareholders to vote on the resolution was dismissed by Holland J. and accordingly the vote was held and its outcome was as predicted. In the circumstances the appeal is allowed. The order of Hollingworth J. dismissing the appellant's claim and appointing an assessor pursuant to s. 184(4) of the Act is set aside and an order will go forever prohibiting the company from implementing the resolution.

The appellant will have her costs in this court and in all of the proceedings below.

Appeal allowed.

Note

Reread *Ebrahimi v. Westbourne Galleries Ltd.* (1972), [1972] 2 All E.R. 492, [1973] A.C. 360 (H.L.), which is set out in Chapter 7, *supra*. It is not, in fact, an oppression case at all. It arises pursuant to a motion to wind up the corporation, on the ground that it is "just and equitable" to do so (such actions are dealt with, *infra*, this chapter). And indeed, you will notice that Lord Wilberforce is careful to confine the scope of the decision to actions seeking a winding up on the just and equitable ground. Why is the decision important to consider in the context of the oppression remedy? The answer is that the Canadian courts have ignored Lord Wilberforce's attempt to confine the scope of the "equitable rights" enunciated in the case. There are now literally scores of cases applying the concept of equitable rights in the context of suits arising under the oppression remedy. In other words, *Ebrahimi* has had a huge impact on the way in which the Canadian courts have applied the oppression remedy.

Ebrahimi is arguably one of the most important company law cases decided in the twentieth century. It evinces an attitude to resolving corporate disputes that is very different from prior cases. Instead of confining minority interests to the rights they had explicitly "contracted" for (whether pursuant to the articles, by-laws, or any shareholder agreement), *Ebrahimi* indicates that shareholder expectations may be a source of rights as well. This greatly broadens the grounds upon which a disgruntled minority may challenge the actions of majority or controlling shareholders.

One of the first cases in which a Canadian judge called upon Lord Wilberforce's "equitable rights" to resolve an oppression suit was *Diligenti v. RWMD Operations Kelowna Ltd.* (1976), 1 B.C.L.R. 36,

1976 CarswellBC 3 (S.C.). In *Diligenti*, Diligenti was one of four "partners" (owning equal 25% shareholdings) in a business that was formed to operate a Keg and Cleaver restaurant in Kelowna; they later acquired a second franchise in Prince George. As in *Ebrahimi*, Diligenti was entitled to remuneration for his managerial duties; he claimed to have done the main work in obtaining the franchises and getting them going. Disagreements arose between the shareholders and Diligenti was ousted from management. He was removed as a manager and also, at a shareholders' meeting, as a director. The other three shareholders then formed a management company and charged the restaurants a 2 1/2% management fee for managing the business. Diligenti sued under the oppression remedy in the B.C. legislation, which created a cause of action in relation both to conduct that is "oppressive" and to conduct that is "unfairly prejudicial". While Diligenti alleged oppressive acts other than his removal from management, the court dealt mainly with the issue of his ouster from management. The court held that "unfairly prejudicial" is broader in its meaning than that which is "oppressive". Conduct that is oppressive would include only an interference with the strict legal rights of the petitioner. However, the "unfairly prejudicial" ground allows the court to import Lord Wilberforce's notion of equitable rights into the oppression remedy and thus to inquire into whether the petitioner's equitable rights have been violated. On the facts, the court held that Diligenti's equitable rights had indeed been interfered with in his removal as a director, and that this constituted unfair prejudice. In the course of his judgment, Fulton J. stated that:

> On the face of it it would appear to me that, particularly in a company of the nature of those involved here — private companies, closely held, formed to take over the operations of four individuals who have been equal founders and proprietors of a venture and in which companies each of the four holds the same number of shares — each of its members has a very real interest and concern in the management of the affairs of the company.

However, it was Diligenti's removal as a director, rather than simply as a manager, which constituted the unfair prejudice:

> I am referring here to management generally in the sense that management of the affairs of the company is in the hands of the directors and policy decisions and general business decisions affecting the future of the companies are made by them, as distinct from a particular managerial position to which a director — or a member — may be appointed. In my view, as such shareholder he would have a very real interest in being and remaining a director so as to have a voice and a vote in the shaping of the policies and the general business decisions which the board, in its over-all responsibilities, will make on behalf of the company. This is not solely a

matter of protection of his interest in the narrow sense — for being one of four he can always be out-voted: it is a matter of whether or not he has a right, in the circumstances, to the opportunity for a continued voice and vote in shaping policies.

Importantly, there was no explicit agreement for all the shareholders to participate in management. Indeed, there was no longstanding partnership between the shareholders (one of the facts referred to by Lord Wilberforce in *Ebrahimi* as giving rise equitable rights). Fulton J. was prepared to infer the existence of an agreement to participate in management from the circumstances of the partnership and the nature of the relationship between the parties:

> [I]t is clear from the material I have reviewed that the whole concept commenced on a joint venture-partnership basis, with each of the four partners sharing equally in the continuing management and direction of affairs. This is borne out by the fact that the properties in question where the operations were to be carried on were acquired in the names of the four partners jointly, and that the shares in the companies formed to take over the operations were held in equal proportions, and that each of the partners became a director of those companies.

Thus, his removal as a director constituted unfair prejudice:

> First, in circumstances such as exist here there are "rights, expectations and obligations *inter se*" which are not submerged in the company structure, and these rights are enjoyed by a member as part of his status as a shareholder in the company which has been formed to carry on the enterprise: amongst these rights are the rights to continue to participate in the direction of that company's affairs. Second, although his fellow members may be entitled as a matter of strict law to remove him as a director, for them to do so in fact is unjust and inequitable, and is a breach of equitable rights which he in fact possesses as a member. And third, although such breach may not "oppress" him in respect of his proprietary rights as a shareholder, such unjust and inequitable denial of his rights and expectations is undoubtedly "unfairly prejudicial" to him in his status as member.

Fulton J. also held that complaints of diversion of profits might also fit within the oppression provision:

> [T]here is evidence that substantial sums were and are still being so diverted to a company owned by the three majority shareholders, and in my view in the circumstances here— the exclusion of the applicant from all enjoyment of such moneys and the diversion of them to those three shareholders — there is thus *prima facie* evidence

of an act at least unfairly prejudicial to the applicant, if not indeed of conduct oppressive to him.

The end result of the case was to refuse a motion to dismiss for failure to state a cause of action.

The concept of reasonable expectations has been extremely important to the judicial consideration of the oppression remedy. The next case deals with this concept.

Westfair Foods Ltd. v. Watt
(1991), 79 D.L.R. (4th) 48, 1991 CarswellAlta 63 (C.A.)

[The appellant was a public corporation that had two classes of shares. The class A shares carried a $2 dividend in priority to the common shares, and all dividends beyond those going to the class A shares went to the common shares. In the event of liquidation, the class A shares shared equally with the common shares. The corporation had a long-standing policy of paying a regular dividend to its shareholders while retaining much of its earnings. In 1985 the corporation adopted a policy of distributing its net annual earnings as dividends. At trial the new policy was found to be oppressive to holders of class A shares, who had an interest in retained earnings. It was also found to be oppressive on the basis of procedural shortcomings surrounding the change in policy. The trial judge ordered that the corporation purchase the class A shares.]

KERANS J.A.: I turn then to the substantial rights conferred by the provision. Obviously, they turn on effect not intent. Equally obviously, they govern all the activities of the corporation. The rights conferred upon shareholders are that they, at any time and in any way during their relationship with the company, are to be insulated from anything oppressive, unfairly prejudicial, or that unfairly disregards their interests. For the relations among shareholders, this is a major modification of majority rule.

In my view, the provisions were and remain a compendious way for Parliament to say to the courts that the classes mentioned in the Act are to be treated fairly in the sense of justly by corporations. For example, both parties cite and rely on *Ebrahimi v. Westbourne Galleries*, [1973] A.C. 360. Lord Wilberforce there said at p. 379:

[T]here is room in company law for recognition of the fact that behind it, or amongst it, there are individuals with rights, expectations and obligations *inter se* which are not necessarily submerged in the company structure.

I agree with a similar sentiment by McDonald J. in *First Edmonton Place v. 315888 Alberta Ltd.* (1988), 40 B.L.R. 28 at pp. 59-60, 60 Alta. L.R. (2d) 122, 10 A.C.W.S. (3d) 268 (Q.B.).

I cannot put elastic adjectives like "unfair", "oppressive", or "prejudicial" into watertight compartments. In my view, this repetition of overlapping ideas is only an expression of anxiety by Parliament that one or the other might be given a restrictive meaning. I am grateful for the history in the *First Edmonton Place* case. Recent changes adding words like "unfairly disregard" reflect just that concern: see Dickerson *et al.*, *Proposals for a New Business Corporations Law for Canada* (Ottawa: Information Canada, 1971), p. 163, where the mischief was reported to be:

> the self-imposed judicial qualifications that have limited the applica-
> tion. . . . and. . . . cast considerable doubt upon the effectiveness of
> the original provisions.

The irony is that too much repetition encourages rather than eliminates narrowing arguments. For example, in Peterson, *Shareholder Remedies in Canada* (Butterworths, 1989), para. 18.60, the author contends that "unfairly disregards" implies that some "disregarding" is fair! I reject that kind of parsing. The original words, like the new additions, command the courts to exercise their duty "broadly and liberally", as this court has already said about the nearly identical Alberta law in *Keho Holdings Ltd. v. Noble* (1987), 38 D.L.R. (4th) 368, 52 Alta. L.R. (2d) 195, 78 A.R. 131 (C.A.).

Having concluded that the words charge the courts to impose the obligation of fairness on the parties, I must admit that the admonition offers little guidance to the public, and Parliament has left elucidation to us. I have elsewhere said that I take this sort of indirection as legislative delegation: see *Transalta Utilities Corp. v. Alberta Public Utilities Board* (1986), 43 Alta. L.R. (2d) 171 at p. 180, 68 A.R. 171, 36 A.C.W.S. (2d) 376 (C.A.).

We fail in that duty of elucidation, I think, if we merely say "this is fair" or "that is not fair" without ever explaining why we think this or that is fair. Thus I, and I dare say others, am not much helped by cases and comments that simply announce that I am to enforce "fair play" or "fair dealing": see, for example, Dickerson, *op. cit.*, para. 48.

On the other hand, I do not understand that the delegation of this duty permits a judge to impose personal standards of fairness. Let me illustrate what is probably obvious by two extreme examples. A judge who firmly believes in the virtues of unrestricted private enterprise might say that fairness requires that people protect themselves to their best capacity and that the courts not protect those who fail to protect themselves. On the other hand, a judge who firmly believes that private property is a trust held for the benefit of society as a whole might say that what is fair is what best benefits society.

The role of a judge in our society limits the impulses of both my mythical judges. We must not make rules unless we can tie them to values that seem to have gained wide acceptance. We do that largely by testing any proposed rule against other legal rules, which by long tradition seem accepted. In short, we seek precedent, or we seek to argue from what we consider to be principles adopted in precedent. So, in *Keho*, this court relied upon precedent in other situations where courts were asked to decide what was "just and equitable".

I will not attempt to catalogue all the rules generated by the words in the statute. For example, the courts have imposed the duty on directors to protect the interests of all shareholders, not just those who elect them. I will later deal with that rule. The authorities also impose upon the majority interest the obligation not to use their electoral power to profit themselves at the expense of minority shareholders. The principal complaint here does not engage that rule. The complaint is not by a minority who has been outvoted. It is by an entire class of shares in competition with another class of shares.

It is said for the shareholders that yet another rule exists. This is that the directors must have due regard for, and deal fairly with, the "interests" of all shareholders. I have concern about over-use of the word interests. This example serves to express it: a thief is very interested in my watch, and will get it if he can. A law about fairness will not, however, show any respect for his interest. The real question is whether the law should accept his obvious interest in financial gain as, in all the circumstances, one that deserves protection. I do not accept that all ambition to acquire property deserves protection. I do accept that our tradition is that a hope for profit, as opposed to a mere desire, sometimes deserves protection.

One deserving case is where the person to whom the profit will go has nourished that hope. The company and the shareholders entered voluntarily, not by duty or chance, into a relationship. Our guides are the rules in other contexts, such as contract law, equity, and partnership law, where the courts have also considered just rules to govern voluntary relationships. In very general terms, one clear principle that emerges is that we regulate voluntary relationships by regard to the expectations raised in the mind of a party by the word or deed of the other, and which the first party ordinarily would realize it was encouraging by its words and deeds. This is what we call reasonable expectations, or expectations deserving of protection. Regard for them is a constant theme, albeit variously expressed, running through the cases on this section or its like elsewhere. I emphasize that all the words and deeds of the parties are relevant to an assessment of reasonable expectations, not necessarily only those consigned to paper, and not necessarily only those made when the relationship first arose.

I do not for a moment suggest that that analysis about expectations deserving protection is the sole basis for rules under the statute. I think, for example, of totally unforeseen windfalls or calamities. This is not such a case, but I dare say that even in those cases the expectations of the parties are a sound starting point. And the test will always be helpful in cases where mere interests collide.

The test then is always facts-specific, and cases decided on other facts offer only a limited guide. Unfortunately, no other reported case offers the same facts as this. The closest is *International Power Co. v. McMaster University*, [1946] 2 D.L.R. 81, [1946] S.C.R. 178, 27 C.B.R. 75. That case is about the distribution of a surplus from the winding-up of a company. Even after reimbursement of the par value of both common and preferred shares, a large surplus remained. The court decided that the by-laws, properly interpreted, awarded that exclusively to the common shares. No "fairness" rule was invoked, but the court strayed into those areas. In a dissent, the Chief Justice proposed that both classes share equally after an adjustment for the capitalized value of preferential dividends. In response, Kerwin J., for the majority, quoted this statement from *Will v. United Lanket Plantations*, [1914] A.C. 11 (H.L.), at p. 19:

> [T]he people who took the preference shares . . . knew perfectly well that they were taking shares with a preferential dividend of 10 per cent. I think they would have been rather surprised, although no doubt they would have been gratified, if they had been told that they are about to receive the almost boundless additional advantages which have been held out to them in the arguments we have been hearing.

During argument before us, both parties dwelt at length with two US cases: *Burton v. Exxon Corp.*, 583 F. Supp. 405 (1984) (U.S.D.C.), and *Jedwab v. MGM Grand Hotels Inc.*, 509 A. 2d 584 (1986) (Delaware Chancery Court). Both are trial level decisions. Both consider and apply the rule earlier established in *Sinclair Oil Corp. v. Levien*, 280 A.2d 717 (1971) (Del. Supr.), that decisions by the board of directors about matters of conflict between shareholders may, if the board is dominated by one party to the conflict, be vacated unless the board shows that the decision was "inherently fair".

In *Burton*, the court pronounced upon the distribution as dividends of funds suddenly available to a moribund company that had operated in Hungary, but had been caught first by World War II and then by the Iron Curtain. In a slight twist on this case, the controlling interests caused the entire amount to be paid on outstanding and unpaid dividends to one class of shares, the first preferred shares, which were held by them. The holders of second preferred shares protested that this was unfair because the funds could be reinvested, and some day produce a return to all shareholders. The court disagreed, saying that the result "may be unfortunate" (p. 418) but not unfair. I do not find either the decision or the discussion very helpful.

In *Jedwab* the common shareholders proposed a corporate merger that would convert all the assets of the corporation to cash and distribute them. The preferred shares protested that the distribution proposal was unfair, and sought interim injunctive relief. On the application the judge had to assess the chance of success. This turned in part on whether there was an arguable conflict and in part on what possible claims a preferred share might make. On that latter point, he concluded that the relations between classes of shares were "essentially contractual" but the right of equal distribution raised "may be measured by equitable as well as legal standards" (p. 594). I do not disagree with either statement, but find neither of much help.

I conclude that what is appropriate in this case is to assess the facts found by the learned Chief Justice on the scales of "reasonable expectations" to see if that offers a fair solution. In my view, it does but not one of assistance to the shareholders here on the principal issue.

The learned Chief Justice held that the new dividend policy [48 B.L.R. at p. 75]:

> already diminishes the value of the Class A Shares in relation to the common shares and alters the relationship between them in the marketplace. There can be little doubt that this unfairly prejudices the interests of the class A shareholders who purchased the shares with the expectation that they would share in the business success or failure of the corporation.

Moreover, he observed sternly that the company did not take a broad view of the issue [at p. 78]:

> Throughout these proceedings, counsel for Westfair made no argument with respect to the interests of the class A shareholders, relying solely on a definition and interpretation of their rights as expressed in the shareholders agreement of 1946. Repeatedly, in written argument, the language of rights, not interests, is utilized, further reinforcing this impression. On the basis of the evidence presented before me, I am satisfied that the directors of Westfair and, specifically the sole common shareholder, Kelly Douglas, relied upon the narrowest definition of the rights of the class A shareholders to achieve, by means of the trailing dividend and borrowing policies, what they were unable to achieve with the consent of the class A shareholders in the 1980 proxy resolution.

If it did not do so before, the company through its counsel certainly took a different view before us. It accepted that the current law requires a company to respect both rights and interests. But, it contended that respect for the interests of both common and preferred shareholders produces the same result here as would having regard merely for their rights. The need for fairness to both remains, and can only be resolved fairly by the traditional means.

My disagreement with the learned Chief Justice, while of great significance, can be simply stated. In the passage quoted, he said that the right to share in distribution of the assets on liquidation created an expectation by class A shareholders that they would share in the "success or failure" of the company. In my view, any expectation that they would share in the future success (as opposed to failure) of the company in a measure beyond the dividend promised them was not a reasonable expectation . . .

Counsel also said that the board of directors of the company, even if it did not make a decision adverse to the legitimate interests of the shareholders, did not adequately address the issue. The submissions were that they did not consult or inform the shareholders, did not arrange independent review, did not do a careful study, and did not even address their minds to the position of the shareholders. These were what Mr. Haigh called "procedural" complaints, as opposed to the "substantial" complaint about the new dividend policy.

The burden of the argument is that, if they correctly decided the "substantial" issue as I have held they did, they did so from good luck, not good and fair management. In fairness to them, I should add that the directors did take counsel on that point.

The shareholders complained that the directors also paid them insufficient heed in other respects. It must have been particularly galling to see the auditors describe the company in the financial statements as a "wholly owned subsidiary", thus expunging the shareholders from the face of the globe with the stroke of an accountant's pen. Like the learned Chief Justice, I am not impressed with the explanation that the reference is about control, not ownership. A non-fact remains so whatever an accountant says. But I cannot see what harm this did, other than to give understandable offence.

Other examples exist. The Toronto Stock Exchange wrote to the company to propose a de-listing of the class A shares. The company did not even trouble to respond to the letter. I cannot, with respect, raise this event to class higher than insensitivity. The number of outstanding class A shares falls well below the latest TSX standards. When this court proposed an injunction to use best efforts to relist, Mr. Crawford expressed no interest, and one reason was that there was no hope of success.

I acknowledge that the learned Chief Justice judged some "procedural" complaints as well-founded. I will accept that the company viewed the shareholders as a nuisance. No doubt the failure of the management to agree with the shareholders about retained earnings is the main reason for a loss of confidence, but other events exacerbated this. These other matters exemplify an unfair disregard for the shareholders.

Also, forced purchase is an appropriate remedy. No doubt it would be best for all if the shares were to be sold. I therefore would let the order of the learned Chief Justice stand.

Appeal dismissed.

Notes

1   For a summary of the role of reasonable expectations in the oppression remedy, see *820099 Ontario Inc. v. Harold E. Ballard Ltd.* (1991), 3 B.L.R. (2d) 113, 1991 CarswellOnt 141 (Div. Ct.). See also *Naneff v. Con-Crete Holdings Ltd.* (1993), 11 B.L.R. (2d) 218, 1993 CarswellOnt 157 (Gen. Div. [Commercial List]), reversed (1995), 23 O.R. (3d) 481, 1995 CarswellOnt 1207 (C.A.); *C.I. Covington Fund Inc. v. White* (2000), 10 C.P.R. (4th) 49, 2000 CarswellOnt 4680 (S.C.J.), affirmed (2001), 15 C.P.R. (4th) 144, 2001 CarswellOnt 3527; and *BCE Inc., Re*, 2008 CarswellQue 12595, 2008 CarswellQue 12596, (*sub nom.* BCE Inc. v. 1976 Debentureholders) [2008] 3 S.C.R. 560 (S.C.C.).

2   The English House of Lords has recently reviewed the role of reasonable expectations, referred to as "legitimate expectations", in the oppression remedy. See *O'Neill v. Phillips*, [1999] 1 W.L.R. 1092, [1999] 2 All E.R. 961 (H.L.). The court advocated using two ways to define the scope of legitimate expectations. The first is to base intervention in company affairs on equitable principles that have evolved from the law of partnership. The second is to interpret the contract between the parties in light of their real intentions, including promises that arose later in the relationship. How different is this equity/contract approach from the approach of the Canadian courts?

(iii)   Does the Oppression Remedy Require a Showing of Bad Faith?

A very important issue arising under the oppression provision is whether success requires a showing that the defendant acted without *bona fides*. Are bad intentions essential, or can a court find that well-intentioned conduct is nonetheless actionable if it effects a result that is oppressive?

This issue is particularly important because breach of the statutory fiduciary duty would appear to require an absence of *bona fides*. For example, the CBCA states that every director and officer must "act honestly and in good faith with a view to the best interests of the corporation". See CBCA s.122(1)(a). Thus, if the oppression remedy is based on the results of conduct rather than motive or intentions, its substantive scope is that much broader than the law of fiduciary duties.

As demonstrated in Jeffrey G. MacIntosh, "Bad Faith and the Oppression Remedy: Uneasy Marriage or Amicable Divorce?" (1990), 69 Can. Bar Rev. 276, the courts have given remarkably inconsistent answers to this question. Professor MacIntosh argues that bad faith might be seen either as a necessary condition for finding liability, or as a sufficient condition. Under the former, there can be no liability without a showing of bad faith. Under the latter, an unfair result might by itself ground liability, but a showing of bad faith will also ground liability. Conversely, it might be the case that bad faith is neither necessary nor sufficient to ground liability: i.e., the issue is only whether an unfair result has been effected. Or, one could take the view that both bad faith and unfair result are necessary to ground liability. Professor MacIntosh classifies the cases and finds that cases can be found to support all four views of the role of bad faith in the oppression remedy.

Professor MacIntosh argues, however, that the origins and construction of the oppression provision suggest that it was never intended that bad faith be a necessary part of the cause of action. He argues that the question of unfair result should be at the centre of the inquiry (although cases in which there is bad faith but no unfair result should probably also be actionable in order that the plaintiff be able to prevent future conduct that achieves an unfair result):

> If the jurisprudential foundation of the "bad faith" school is exceedingly weak, the fundament upon which the "unfair result" school rests is correspondingly strong. In this section I will argue that statutory interpretation points strongly to the absence of a bad faith requirement. I will also suggest that a bad faith requirement would be inconsistent with the general drift of corporate law towards protection of the reasonable expectations of shareholders.
>
> Subsection 122(1) of the CBCA and similar provisions of cognate statutes require that "[e]very director and officer of a corporation in exercising his powers and discharging his duties shall (a) act honestly and in good faith with a view to the best interests of the corporation . . .". This is a subjective test that makes bad faith the central element of a breach of fiduciary duty. By contrast, the . . . oppression provision makes no reference at all to acting in "good faith", "honestly", or "*with a view* to the best interests of the corporation" (emphasis added). Rather, it creates liability for conduct that is "oppressive" or unfairly prejudicial to or that unfairly disregards the interests of "the complainant." This suggests that, while bad faith may be a key element of breach of the statutory fiduciary duty, it forms no part of the oppression action. This conclusion is fortified by reference to the Dickerson Report [which gave rise to the current federal legislation]. In drafting the fiduciary duty provision of the CBCA, the Dickerson Committee left no doubt of its intention to eliminate the proper purpose doctrine (which required no showing of bad faith) and substitute a single test for liability with "an emphasis on good faith". Having done so in a conscious and deliberate manner, it does not seem tenable that the Committee would forget to include a requirement to show bad faith in the oppression provision if it was their intention that such a requirement be an intrinsic and indispensable part of the cause of action. Moreover, the Committee adopted Lord Cooper's definition of oppression (*supra*, focusing on the question of fairness), rather

than Lord Keith's definition (*supra*, requiring "lack of probity" to make out a cause of action). All of these facts point to the omission of a bad faith requirement under the oppression provision.

One of the most significant recent trends in Canadian corporate law is the recognition that legal rights may derive from the reasonable expectations of shareholders regarding their relationship to other corporate constituents. This trend can, in no small measure, be traced to the [judgment of Lord Wilberforce in the signal case *Ebrahimi v. Westbourne Galleries Ltd.*].

This reasoning was largely adopted by the Ontario Court of Appeal in *Brant Investments Ltd. v. KeepRite Inc.* (1991), 80 D.L.R. (4th) 161, 45 O.A.C. 320, 1 B.L.R. (2d) 225, 1991 CarswellOnt 133 (C.A.), in which Madame Justice McKinlay stated:

> I have concluded that evidence of bad faith or want of probity in the actions complained of is unnecessary in an application under s. 234. I should have been content to arrive at that conclusion merely on the basis of a literal reading of the provision coupled with an application of the statutory objective articulated in s. 4, "to revise and reform the law applicable to business corporations incorporated to carry on business throughout Canada", had it not been for the substantial body of conflicting opinion on this issue cited to us, involving the application of s. 234 or similarly worded provisions in provincial or Commonwealth statutes.
>
> In considering whether conduct is "oppressive" one can appropriately look to the English cases decided before 1980 which defined that word in a similar context. Adopting the definition applied by Lord Simonds in the *Scottish Co-Operative* case — namely, "burdensome, harsh and wrongful" — it is unlikely that an act could be found to be oppressive without there being an element of bad faith involved. However, in considering the alternative question of whether any act is unfairly prejudicial to, or unfairly disregards the interests of one of the protected persons or groups, I am of the view that a requirement of lack of *bona fides* would unnecessarily complicate the application of the provision and add a judicial gloss that is inappropriate given the clarity of the words used. Of course, there may be many situations where the rights of minority shareholders have been prejudiced or their interests disregarded, without any remedy being appropriate. The difficult question is whether or not their rights have been prejudiced or their interests disregarded "unfairly". In testing the facts in a given case against the word "unfairly", evidence of bad faith as to motive could be relevant, but there may be other cases where particular acts effect an unfair result, but where there has been no bad faith whatsoever on the part of the actors.

For cases following this aspect of *Brant*, see *Sidaplex-Plastic Suppliers Inc. v. Elta Group Inc.* (1998), 40 O.R. (3d) 563, 1998 CarswellOnt 2819 (C.A.); and *Krynen v. Bugg*, 2003 CarswellOnt 1138 (Ont. S.C.J.), additional reasons at 2003 CarswellOnt 2197 (Ont. S.C.J.). Note, however, that some British Columbia cases have held that in the absence of some illegal act, bad faith is required: see *Mahoney v. Taylor* (1996), [1996] B.C.J. No. 1479, 1996 CarswellBC 1441 (S.C.); and *Saarnok-Vuus v. Teng*, 2003 CarswellBC 342, [2003] B.C.J. No. 353 (B.C. S.C.). Can this difference be explained by the absence of protection against unfair disregard of interests in the BC Act?

(iv)   Is the Oppression Remedy Personal or Derivative?

A question of even greater importance than whether a showing of bad faith is required is the question of whether the oppression remedy embraces actions of a derivative character. As noted above, if it does, then the overlap between the action for breach of fiduciary duty and the oppression remedy becomes virtually complete, since breaches of fiduciary duty will almost always involve derivative actions. As noted further below, the cases have not been consistent on this issue. The case which follows, however, expresses the point of view which appears now to be the dominant one.

Sparling v. Javelin International Ltd.
[1986] R.J.Q. 1073

[The following facts are condensed from a 72-page judgment that followed a 66-day trial. John C. Doyle was the moving force behind Javelin, a company started in 1949 and continued under the CBCA on March 10, 1980. He was originally the controlling (but not majority) shareholder and, until 1976, a director as well. The company had been public since 1951; it became widely held; of record, about 10,000 were US residents or citizens. Doyle became a fugitive in Canada based on criminal fraud charges laid by the R.C.M.P. He also became a fugitive in the United States after failing to present himself to the authorities to serve a three-year term for securities fraud. He lived outside Canada (in Panama, which has no extradition treaty with either Canada or the United States) from 1964 onwards. From Panama, Doyle incorporated a subsidiary of Javelin called Pavonia, although the share certificates representing Javelin's sole ownership of Pavonia were never sent to the parent, Javelin. Doyle had control of the company, through ownership of a control block of shares, since the company was founded, with the sole exception of about 4 months during which a group of dissident directors attempted to seize power (an event referred to in the report as the "palace revolt"); see *Re Canadian Javelin Ltd. and Boon-Strachan Coal Co. Ltd.*, *supra*, Chapter 8. Following the palace revolt, and the judicially-ordered meeting of shareholders that followed, Doyle resumed control of the company by means of using his control block to elect a sympathetic board of directors. He appears to have had an absolute grip on the company, appointing directors who were neither inquisitive about his actions nor reluctant to do his bidding. An earlier oppression action commenced by the Director of the CBCA, Frederic Sparling, resulted in a finding that certain actions of Doyle were oppressive towards the minority shareholders. Rothman J. of the Quebec Superior Court (in a judgment rendered April 7, 1982) ordered the suspension of the powers of the board of directors and the appointment of a receiver-manager to run the company.

In this follow-up case, the Director commenced an oppression action on behalf of the minority shareholders of Javelin seeking additional findings of oppression relating to past conduct and alleging that Doyle had continued to act oppressively towards the interests of the minority shareholders. The Director also sought a new remedy — namely, a winding-up of the company. The action alleged that Doyle had, *inter alia*, arranged phony transactions paid for by Javelin the benefit of which flowed back to Doyle personally. Doyle had also been paid hefty "consulting" fees that the Director alleged were unearned. Javelin had paid Doyle's personal legal expenses to fight about a dozen and a half shareholder suits that had been commenced against him (mostly in the US). He had also arranged the affairs of the company so that the subsidiary, Pavonia, effectively acquired control of the parent, disenabling the receiver-manager from removing the oppressive effects of Doyle's control. The Court found in favor of the Director in respect of all substantial allegations.

Doyle nonetheless argued that the wrongs alleged by the Director and found by the Court to have occurred were all derivative in character, and not a suitable matter for an oppression application. The Court ruled as follows]

GOMERY J.: . . . Counsel for Mr. Doyle submit that the Court has no jurisdiction to adjudicate upon a claim directed against their client for restitution of money since such a claim is of the nature of a derivative action and may only be exercised in conformity with the rules and procedure provided in section 232 C.B.C.A.; since no preliminary permission to bring such an action was granted by the Court, conclusions of the nature being requested by the Director are illegal.

It is not contested that the claims brought by the Director could have been exercised by way of derivative action under section 232. The question is whether or not they may also be made by way of an application under section 234.

A series of decided cases seems at first glance to support the proposition made on behalf of Mr. Doyle, but care must be taken in reading these Judgments because they were decided before the relevant provincial and federal laws enacted the oppression remedy as it is now expressed in section 234. Thus *Re Goldhar and Quebec Manitou Mines Ltd., Goldex Mines Ltd. v. Revill*, and *Farnham v. Fingold* should be read with caution: in none of these decisions is the question the same as what must be decided here.

Be that as it may, the headnote in the *Goldex Mines Ltd.* case states flatly:

> Any action by a shareholder seeking relief against a wrong done to a corporation is a derivative action . . . leave of the Court is required for its commencement. Where an action is commenced without leave it is improperly constituted . . .

Similar decisions have been rendered in two British Columbia cases but the fact situation in each instance is distinguishable from the circumstances here.

The only reported case where the issue is addressed directly is *Re Peterson and Kanata Investments Ltd.*, a decision of the British Columbia Supreme Court. Under B.C. legislation very similar if not identical to the C.B.C.A., minority shareholders applied to the court for relief on the ground that the affairs of the company were being conducted in a manner oppressive to them, in that the controlling shareholder had abused his control in order to profit at the company's expense. Counsel for the controlling shareholder argued that the applicants should have proceeded by way of derivative action. This submission was not accepted, Mr. Justice Toy stating:

> In my view, the new rights created by s. 222 (the B.C. equivalent of s. 234 C.B.C.A.) are in addition to whatever other rights or remedies the three members have either by statute or at common law.

Some distinguished scholars are of the same opinion. In *Canadian Business Corporations* the authors state:

> There will be no clear dividing line between cases where this remedy for relief from oppression will be available and cases where the derivative action will be available and appropriate. Actually, there will be some middle ground where both will be available and the aggrieved person will be able to select the remedy which best resolved his problem. The object of a derivative action is to remedy a wrong done to the corporation. The usual object of a section 234 application is to remedy a wrong done to a minority shareholder or other aggrieved person. For example, diversion of corporate profits is clearly a wrong done to the corporation and would normally be remedied by a derivative action. On the other hand, a refusal to declare dividends in order to squeeze out minority shareholders would be remedied by an application for relief from oppression of that minority. But the payment of excessive salaries to

dominant shareholders who appoint themselves as officers is a borderline case; it may constitute a wrong to the corporation and at the same time it may have as its specific goal the squeezing out of a minority group. In this case the aggrieved persons would be free to select either remedy. We do not foresee any difficulty with this overlap, particularly since the court maintains full discretion over both of them.

And Professor Mary Anne Waldron, in an article entitled "Corporate Theory and the Oppression Remedy" says:

> All corporate statutes in Canada that provide for oppression remedies also provide for corporate derivative actions brought by shareholders with the consent of the court on behalf of their corporation for wrongs done to the corporation. However, if an oppression application rather than a derivative action is used to seek relief from directors' misconduct, no court approval is needed to commence the action.

The Court is of the same view. The intent of Parliament in enacting section 234 was to include in its ambit all shareholders' recourses, on the condition that a finding of oppression or unfairness first opens the door to the exercise of the Court's jurisdiction. Nothing in the wording of section 234 suggests that the recourses foreseen in section 232 may not be included in a section 234 application. Indeed, some of the orders suggested by section 234(3) encompass derivative recourses; in particular subsection (h) foresees an order compensating the corporation and subsection (j) foresees an order compensating an aggrieved person; the corporation itself may be the aggrieved person.

To decide that any right belonging to the corporation may only be exercised by way of derivative action would be to deny the fundamental nature of the reform which enactment of section 234 represents. Such an interpretation would also require a multiplicity of proceedings in a case such as this. There is a decided advantage to a simplified procedure whereby all demands to enforce the rights of minority shareholders can be dealt with in one application.

The derivative action will continue to apply in cases where the applicant does not choose to scale the barrier that section 234(2) represents, but in our view it may be combined with other recourses if the applicant is able to overcome that obstacle.

Malata Group (HK) Ltd. v. Jung
2008 ONCA 111, 2008 CarswellOnt 699 (Ont. C.A.)

R.P. Armstrong J.A.: This appeal concerns the relationship between derivative actions and oppression complaints under the *Business Corporations Act*, R.S.O. 1990, c. B.16 ("the Act"), and the impact on that relationship of the rule in *Foss v. Harbottle* that a shareholder has no personal cause of action for harm done to the corporation.

The appellant moved before Justice Ground of the Superior Court of Justice to dismiss certain paragraphs of the statement of claim pursuant to rule 21.01(3)(b) of the *Rules of Civil Procedure* on the ground that the claims advanced were derivative in nature and required leave of the court as provided in s. 246 of the Act. The motion judge declined the relief sought and held that the claims were appropriately advanced in an oppression action. In doing so, the motion judge observed that, "the rule in Foss v. Harbottle has been substantially diluted by the enactment of the derivative and oppression action provisions of the [Act]".

The appellant also appeals the judge's order declining to dismiss two other paragraphs of the statement of claim pursuant to rule 21.01(3)(b) on the ground that they breach the notice provisions of a unanimous shareholder agreement.

I would dismiss the appeal.

Facts

The respondent, Malata Group (HK) Limited ("Malata HK"), commenced an action against the appellant, Henry Chi Hang Jung. According to the allegations in the statement of claim, Malata HK, Mr. Jung and Jimmy Jian Yuan Chen are the three shareholders of Malata Canada Ltd. Jung and Chen each own approximately 41 per cent of the common shares of Malata Canada. Malata HK owns approximately 18 per cent of the common shares of Malata Canada. Malata HK is also a creditor of Malata Canada. Jung, Chen and Malata HK are parties to a unanimous shareholder agreement. Messrs. Chen and Jung are also directors and officers of Malata Canada.

Malata Canada is an Ontario corporation that imported and sold consumer electronic products manufactured in China. Malata Canada operated in the wholesale market in Canada and sold its products to customers such as Home Depot, Canadian Tire, Best Buy, and Philips Electronics.

Malata HK alleges in its statement of claim that Mr. Jung misappropriated corporate funds, breached his fiduciary duty to Malata Canada, and failed to act honestly and in the best interests of Malata Canada and Malata HK. It is alleged that such conduct has threatened the business life of the company and rendered Malata Canada incapable of paying its debt to Malata HK. Malata HK also alleges that Jung breached the shareholder agreement.

* * *

Laskin J.A. in *Meditrust Healthcare Inc. v. Shoppers Drug Mart*, 2002 CarswellOnt 3380, 61 O.R. (3d) 786 (Ont. C.A.), additional reasons at 2003 CarswellOnt 1729 (Ont. C.A.) succinctly stated the rule in Foss v. Harbottle as follows at para. 12:

> The rule in *Foss v. Harbottle* provides simply that a shareholder of a corporation — even a controlling shareholder or the sole shareholder — does not have a personal cause of action for a wrong done to the corporation. The rule respects a basic principle of corporate law: a corporation has a legal existence separate from that of its shareholders. See *Salomon v. Salomon*, [1897] A.C. 22, 66 L.J. Ch. 35 (H.L.). A shareholder cannot be sued for the liabilities of the corporation and, equally, a shareholder cannot sue for the losses suffered by the corporation.

In *Meditrust* at para. 16, Laskin J.A. also considered the limits to the rule in Foss v. Harbottle as described by the Supreme Court of Canada in *Hercules Management Ltd. v. Ernst & Young*, 1997 CarswellMan 198, 1997 CarswellMan 199, [1997] 2 S.C.R. 165 (S.C.C.) at para. 62:

> The rule in *Foss v. Harbottle* does not, of course, preclude an individual shareholder from maintaining a claim for harm done directly to it. Again, in *Hercules*, LaForest J. explained the limit of the rule at p. 214 S.C.R.:
>
> > One final point should be made here. Referring to the case of *Goldex Mines Ltd. v. Revill* (1974), 7 O.R. (2d) 216 (C.A.), the appellants submit that where a shareholder has been directly and individually harmed, that shareholder may have a personal cause of action even though the corporation may also have a separate and distinct cause of action. Nothing in the foregoing paragraphs should be understood to detract from this principle. In finding that claims in respect of losses stemming from an alleged inability to oversee or supervise management are really derivative and not personal in nature, I have found only that shareholders cannot raise individual claims in respect of a wrong done *to the corporation.*
>
> Indeed, this is the limit of the rule in *Foss v. Harbottle*. [Emphasis in original.]

(ii)   Can the claims advanced in subparagraphs 1(c), (d) and (e) be advanced under the oppression remedy of the Act?

The answer to this question raises the distinction between derivative actions and oppression claims. One author has described this distinction as "murky": see Markus Keohnen, *Oppression and Related Remedies* (Toronto: Thomson Carswell, 2004) at 443. Another author observed in 1991 that, "for every holding that the oppression remedy may not be enlisted in a derivative cause, there is an opposite holding": see Jeffrey G.

MacIntosh. "The Oppression Remedy: Personal or Derivative?" (1991) 70 Can. Bar Rev. 29 at 49.

It appears from my reading of the case law that there is not a brightline distinction between the claims that may be advanced under the derivative action section of the Act and those that may be advanced under the oppression remedy provisions.

Owing to this overlap between the oppression remedy and the derivative action, a court cannot determine which is the appropriate avenue for a claim to proceed through the simple application of a rule such as the rule in *Foss v. Harbottle*. Instead, a court must examine the relevant statutory text and the facts of the claim at issue. I now turn to the language of s. 248.

Subsection 248(2) of Act defines the nature of the conduct which is covered by the oppression remedy:

> Where, upon an application under subsection (1), the court is satisfied that in respect of a corporation or any of its affiliates,
>
> (a) any act or omission of the corporation or any of its affiliates effects or threatens to effect a result;
>
> (b) the business or affairs of the corporation or any of its affiliates are, have been or are threatened to be carried on or conducted in a manner; or
>
> (c) the powers of the directors of the corporation or any of its affiliates are, have been or are threatened to be exercised in a manner,
>
> that is oppressive or unfairly prejudicial to or that unfairly disregards the interests of any security holder, creditor, director or officer of the corporation, the court may make an order to rectify the matters complained of.

Subsection 248(3) sets out a non-exhaustive list of remedial orders available to the court. In its preamble, s. 248(3) states that, "the court may make any interim or final order it thinks fit".

It is stating the obvious to say that s. 248 of the Act is drawn in broad language, both in terms of the harms it addresses and the non-exhaustive list of remedies it contemplates. Included in the list of remedies in s. 248(3) is a provision for "an order varying or setting aside a transaction or contract to which a corporation is a party and *compensating the corporation* or any other party to the transaction or contract": see s. 248(3)(h). [Emphasis added.] This provision contemplates a remedy under s. 248 that benefits the company itself even though the claim made by the complainant could also have been pursued by way of a derivative action.

As already noted, this court recognized in Jabalee, *supra*, that there is a degree of overlap between the claims that could be made out as derivative actions and those that could fall under the oppression remedy. As this court said at para.5 of the endorsement, "[t]he two are not mutually exclusive." One situation in which the overlap between the oppression remedy and the derivative action can be found is where directors in closely held corporations engage in self-dealing to the detriment of the corporation and other shareholders or creditors. A relevant case in this respect is *C.I. Covington Fund Inc. v. White*, 2000 CarswellOnt 4680, [2000] O.J. No. 4589 (Ont. S.C.J.), affirmed 2001 CarswellOnt 3527 (Ont. Div. Ct.), in which Swinton J. observed at para. 41:

> A number of oppression cases turn on the fact that there has been conduct by directors or majority shareholders that amounts to self-dealing at the expense of the corporation or other corporate stakeholders (*SCI Systems Inc. v. Gornitzki Thompson & Little Co.* (1997), 36 B.L.R. (2d) 207 (Ont. Ct. (Gen. Div.)), aff'd (1998), 110 O.A.C. 160 (Div. Ct.)); *Neri v. Finch Hardware* (1976) Ltd. (1995), 20 B.L.R. (2d) 216 (Ont. Ct. (Gen. Div.)); *Loveridge Holdings Ltd. v. King-Pin Ltd.* (1991), 5 B.L.R. (2d) 195 (Ont. Ct. (Gen. Div.)). For example, in SCI, there was oppression because the directors unfairly removed assets from the corporation so as to prevent the payment of a corporate debt and to benefit themselves.

In *Covington*, the complainant purchased shares in and loaned money to a closely held company. The respondent, the CEO and majority shareholder of the company (presumably also a director), misappropriated intellectual property (patents) belonging to the company, resulting in the company's inability to pay its creditors. Invoking s. 248(3) of the Act, the court ordered the respondent to cease using the technology related to the patents and assigned the patents and patent applications to the company. In reaching this conclusion, Swinton J. said at paras. 46 and 47:

> Section 248(3) of the OBCA confers a broad discretion on the Court in determining an appropriate remedy, including "any interim or final order it thinks fit". The purpose of the remedy is to rectify the oppression. The provision has been used to make compensation orders against individual directors where their conduct has been found oppressive in small, closely held corporations such as Delta, and they have personally benefited — for example, by the removal of assets from the corporation (see, for example, SCI; Sidaplex, *supra*).

> In this case, Delta has represented that the patents and patent applications for the Snowfluent technology are the property of the corporation, and White, as a principal of the corporation, was behind those representations. The corporation has a right to claim beneficial ownership at common law. This is not a case where a monetary award against White will adequately protect the interests

of the stakeholders, especially given his evidence that he faces financial difficulties personally. If Delta's proprietary interest is not protected, the corporation will be denied the value of the patents, both in terms of possible licensing fees for their use and their value if they can be sold. Clearly, the creditors will be in a better position to recoup some of their funds if the patents are assets of the corporation which can be sold.

I find Swinton J.'s analysis persuasive and useful. Although not identical, the circumstances in *Covington* are not dissimilar from the circumstances alleged in the statement of claim in this case. The complainant in each case is a shareholder and creditor of a closely held corporation. In both cases, the complainant alleges misappropriation of corporate property by another shareholder and director. In both cases, a loss to the company results in a derivative loss to the complainant.

This analysis begs the question of whether there is any meaningful distinction between the oppression remedy under s. 248 of the Act and the derivative action under s. 246 of the Act. In my view, allowing s. 248 oppression claims to proceed where there is harm to the corporation would not nullify s. 246, because the two sections involve different threshold tests. Section 246 simply requires a violation of the corporation's legal rights. On the other hand, s. 248 requires, in the case of harm to the corporation, a violation of corporate legal rights that is oppressive or unfairly prejudicial, or that unfairly disregards the complainant's interests.

It is perhaps worth noting that another relevant difference between the derivative action and the oppression remedy relates to costs. Subsection 247(d) explicitly allows a court to order the corporation to pay the legal fees or other costs reasonably incurred in connection with a derivative action. The oppression remedy section of the Act, though it invests courts with broad remedial authority, contains no such provision.

On the appeal of the *Ford* case, *supra*, Rosenberg J.A., in a much different fact situation, considered the distinction between personal causes of action and derivative actions in the context of the oppression remedy under the *Canada Business Corporations Act*, R.S.C. 1985, c. C-44. He observed at paras. 111 and 112:

> It seems to me that it would be a serious mistake to attempt to confine the broad discretion granted courts by the oppression remedy within a formal construct of causes of action. To do so could bring with it all the complexities of the common law as to when a shareholder might, notwithstanding the rule in *Foss v. Harbottle*. . . maintain a personal action and thrust those complexities into the oppression remedy. Parliament could not have intended such a result. The breadth of the remedy to which these shareholders are entitled must turn on the wording of the statutory provisions.

While s. 241 contemplates remedies that benefit the corporation or shareholders as a whole, it is nevertheless founded on the principle of a wrong done to a shareholder or identifiable group of shareholders. Section 241(2)(a) (the provision relied upon in this case) is drawn in broad terms but it depends upon a finding that the complained of act or omission by the corporation or any of its affiliates "is oppressive or unfairly prejudicial to or that unfairly disregards the interests of any security holder, creditor, director or officer".

See *Ford Motor Co. of Canada v. Ontario (Municipal Employees Retirement Board)*, 2006 CarswellOnt 13, 79 O.R. (3d) 81 (Ont. C.A.), additional reasons at 2006 CarswellOnt 1526 (Ont. C.A.), leave to appeal refused 2006 CarswellOnt 5134, 2006 CarswellOnt 5135 (S.C.C.).

While Rosenberg J.A. makes it clear in *Ford* that the minority shareholder in that case was seeking a personal remedy, i.e., damages, I find that his reasoning in the above paragraphs informs the approach to be taken to the issue raised in this case.

It is important in my view that in this case, we have a closely held corporation. It seems to me that if the alleged oppressive conduct is made out when Malata HK is one of three shareholders and, more particularly, is a major creditor of Malata Canada, it is appropriate for Malata HK to seek a return of the monies to Malata Canada under s. 248 of the Act. Malata HK could have proceeded by way of a derivative action. However, given the overlap between ss. 246 and 248 of the Act and the particular circumstances of this case, I do not believe that it was required to do so.

In disputes involving closely held companies with relatively few shareholders, such as the case at bar and *Covington*, there is less reason to require the plaintiff to seek leave of the court. The small number of shareholders minimizes the risk of frivolous lawsuits against the corporation, thus weakening the main rationale for requiring a claim to proceed as a derivative action.

In the result, I am satisfied that the claims in subparagraphs 1(c), (d) and (e) of the statement of claim are properly advanced under the oppression remedy section of the Act.

Counsel for the appellant also submits that the oppression remedy cannot be invoked against an individual in his personal capacity. He argues that Mr. Jung was acting personally and not as a director of Malata Canada when he is alleged to have misappropriated the company's funds. This is a matter better left to the trial judge who will have the benefit of argument made on a full trial record. I would not give effect to this ground of appeal.

Rea v. Wildeboer
2015 ONCA 373, 2015 CarswellOnt 7602 (Ont. C.A.) (footnotes omitted)

[The appellant, Rea Holdings Inc., alleged that certain insiders of the corporation — including the founders, some of the directors, and one executive officer of Martinrae International Inc. — undertook a series of improper actions in breach of their fiduciary duties that resulted in the misappropriation of Martinrae's corporate funds in the range of $50 to $100 million. The appellant brought an oppression remedy in respect of the allegedly misappropriated corporate property. The motion judge struck the oppression claim as against the respondents on a motion to strike.]

R.A.   Blair J.A.: "Oppression remedy" or "derivative action"? What is the nature of these proceedings? The appellants have asserted an oppression claim under s. 248 of the *Business Corporations Act* alleging misappropriation of funds from Martinrea International Inc. and seeking to recover those funds for the corporation. They submit that they are entitled to proceed on that basis, arguing that the "somewhat murky" line between oppression remedies and derivative actions has all but disappeared. The respondents argue, on the other hand, that the claim is solely Martinrea's claim and that it must be pursued as a derivative action on behalf of the corporation, with leave of the court.

R.B.   The motion judge agreed with the respondents and struck the claim as against them. In the context of this claim as against these respondents, I too agree, and for the following reasons would dismiss the appeal.

* * *

Analysis

The general issue raised on this appeal is whether a complainant may assert, by way of an oppression remedy proceeding, a claim that is by nature a derivative action for a wrong done solely to the corporation, thereby circumventing the requirement to obtain leave to commence a derivative action.

Some understanding of how and why these two forms of statutory redress evolved will help in addressing this issue.

History

At common law, minority shareholders in corporations had very little protection in the face of conduct by the majority (or by directors controlled by the majority) that negatively affected either the corporation itself or their interests as minority shareholders. This handicap was due to two well-entrenched common law principles of corporate law: the notion of a "corporate personality" and the "indoor management rule". Both of these principles can be traced back to a decision of now almost mythical stature — that of Vice-Chancellor Wigram in *Foss v. Harbottle* (1843), 67 E.R. 189, 2 Hare 461 (Eng. V.C.).

In law, a corporation is a legal entity distinct from its shareholders. It followed from this that shareholders were precluded from bringing their own action in respect of a wrong done to the corporation. Except as modified by the derivative action, the oppression remedy, and winding-up proceedings, this remains a governing principle in Canadian corporate law: see *Hercules Management Ltd. v. Ernst & Young*, [1997] 2 S.C.R. 165 (S.C.C.), at para. 59; *Meditrust Healthcare Inc. v. Shoppers Drug Mart* (2002), 61 O.R. (3d) 786 (Ont. C.A.). As Laskin J.A. put it, in *Meditrust*, at paras. 12-14:

> The rule in *Foss v. Harbottle* provides simply that a shareholder of a corporation — even a controlling shareholder or the sole shareholder — does not have a personal cause of action for a wrong done to the corporation. The rule respects a basic principle of corporate law: a corporation has a legal existence separate from that of its shareholders. See *Salomon v. Salomon & Co.* (1896), [1897] A.C. 22, 66 L.J. Ch. 35 (U.K. H.L.) A shareholder cannot be sued for the liabilities of the corporation and, equally, a shareholder cannot sue for the losses suffered by the corporation.

> The rule in *Foss v. Harbottle* also avoids multiple lawsuits. Indeed, without the rule, a shareholder would always be able to sue for harm to the corporation because any harm to the corporation indirectly harms the shareholders.

> *Foss v. Harbottle* was decided nearly 160 years ago but its continuing validity in Canada has recently been affirmed by the Supreme Court of Canada in Hercules *Management Ltd. v. Ernst & Young*, [1997] 2 S.C.R. 165 (S.C.C.) and by this court in *Martin v. Goldfarb* (1998), 163 D.L.R. (4th) 639 (Ont. C.A.).

The companion indoor management rule has also played a significant role in restricting minority shareholders' rights to redress. At common law, if an act that was claimed to be wrongful could be ratified by the majority at a general meeting of shareholders, neither the corporation nor an individual shareholder could sue to redress the wrong. The rationale for this was that courts were reluctant to interfere in the internal management affairs of the corporation.

It took over a century for legislative reforms to be put in place to temper the restrictive effect of these principles on minority shareholder rights. In the latter part of the 20th century, however, the two statutory forms of relief that are at the heart of this appeal — the derivative action and the oppression remedy — were created for this purpose. It is noteworthy that they approached the problem in two different, although potentially overlapping, ways.

The derivative action was designed to counteract the impact of *Foss v. Harbottle* by providing a "complainant" — broadly defined to include more than minority shareholders — with the right to apply to the court for leave to bring an action "in the name of or on behalf of a corporation . . . for the purpose of prosecuting, defending or discontinuing the action on behalf of the body corporate": *Business Corporations Act*, R.S.O. 1990, c. B.16, s. 246 ("OBCA"). It is an action for "corporate" relief, in the sense that the goal is to recover for wrongs done to the company itself. As Professor Welling has colourfully put it in his text, *Corporate Law in Canada: The Governing Principles*, 3rd ed. (Mudgeeraba: Scribblers Publishing, 2006), at p. 509, "[a] statutory representative action is the minority shareholder's sword to the majority's twin shields of corporate personality and majority rule."

The oppression remedy, on the other hand, is designed to counteract the impact of *Foss v. Harbottle* by providing a "complainant" — the same definition — with the right to apply to the court, without obtaining leave, in order to recover for wrongs done to the individual complainant by the company or as a result of the affairs of the company being conducted in a manner that is oppressive or unfairly prejudicial to or that unfairly disregards the interests of the complainant. The oppression remedy is a personal claim: *Ford Motor Co. of Canada v. Ontario (Municipal Employees Retirement Board)* (2006), 79 O.R. (3d) 81 (Ont. C.A.), at para. 112, leave to appeal refused, [2006] S.C.C.A. No. 77 (S.C.C.); *Hoet v. Vogel*, [1995] B.C.J. No. 621 (B.C. S.C.), at paras. 18-19.

These two forms of redress frequently intersect, as might be expected. A wrongful act may be harmful to both the corporation and the personal interests of a complainant and, as a result, there has been considerable debate in the authorities and amongst legal commentators about the nature and utility of the distinction between the two. In the words of one commentator, "the distinction between derivative actions and oppression remedy claims remains murky": Markus Koehnen, *Oppression and Related Remedies* (Toronto: Thomson Canada Limited, 2004), at p. 443.

Yet the statutory distinctions remain in effect.

The Parties' Positions

The appellants submit that the distinction between the remedies has been significantly moderated and that a complainant is entitled to pursue an oppression remedy even where the wrong in question is a wrong in respect of the corporation, provided that the shareholders' reasonable expectations have been violated by means of conduct caught by the terms "oppression", "unfair prejudice" or "unfair disregard". They rely on the decision of the Supreme Court of Canada in *BCE Inc., Re*, 2008 SCC 69, [2008] 3 S.C.R. 560 (S.C.C.), at para. 68, for this proposition. The rationale, they say, is that the oppression remedy provisions provide stakeholders with "a personal, statutory right" not to have their reasonable expectations violated in this manner.

The appellants stress that in *Malata Group (HK) Ltd. v. Jung*, 2008 ONCA 111, 89 O.R. (3d) 36 (Ont. C.A.), and *Jabalee v. Abalmark Inc.*, [1996] O.J. No. 2609 (Ont. C.A.), this Court acknowledged that there could be a degree of overlap between claims that could be made out as a derivative action and those that could fall under the oppression remedy, and that "the two are not mutually exclusive": *Malata*, at para 30; *Jabalee*, at para. 5.

The respondents submit, on the other hand, that the distinction between the two remedies remains, and for good reason. They accept — as did the motion judge — that there has been some relaxation in the approach to the commencement of oppression remedy actions in cases where the factual circumstances create an overlap between the two remedies, particularly in the case of small closely held corporations. But they contend that the distinction remains important — because of the leave requirement for derivative actions — in the case of publicly-held corporations such as Martinrea.

In such cases, they argue, the leave requirement fulfills its important threefold purpose of (i) preventing strike suits, (ii) preventing meritless suits, and (iii) avoiding a multiplicity of proceedings — all of which may lead to the corporation incurring significant and unwarranted costs, concerns that are less acute for closely-held corporations. Relying on *Malata* themselves, the respondents point to the importance Armstrong J.A. placed in that case on the fact that Malata was a closely held corporation (para. 38) and to his observation, at para. 39, that:

> [i]n disputes involving closely held corporations with relatively few shareholders . . . there is less reason to require the plaintiff to seek leave of the court. The small number of shareholders minimizes the risk of frivolous lawsuits against the corporation, thus weakening the main rationale for requiring a claim to proceed as a derivative action.

Discussion

I accept that the derivative action and the oppression remedy are not mutually exclusive. Cases like *Malata* and *Jabalee* make it clear that there are circumstances where the factual underpinning will give rise to both types of redress and in which a complainant will nonetheless be entitled to proceed by way of oppression remedy. Other examples include: *Ontario (Securities Commission) v. McLaughlin*, [1987] O.J. No. 1247 (Ont. H.C.); *Deluce Holdings Inc. v. Air Canada* (1992), 12 O.R. (3d) 131 (Ont. Gen. Div. [Commercial List]); *C.I. Covington Fund Inc. v. White*, [2000] O.J. No. 4589 (Ont. S.C.J.), aff'd [2001] O.J. No. 3918 (Ont. Div. Ct.); *Waxman v. Waxman*, [2004] O.J. No. 1765 (Ont. C.A.), at para. 526, leave to appeal refused, (2005), [2004] S.C.C.A. No. 291 (S.C.C.).

However, I agree with the respondents that claims must be pursued by way of a derivative action after obtaining leave of the court where, as here, the claim asserted seeks to recover solely for wrongs done to a public corporation, the thrust of the relief sought is solely for the benefit of that corporation, and there is no allegation that the complainant's individualized personal interests have been affected by the wrongful conduct.

It is true that the jurisprudence is inconsistent about how to treat cases where there is an overlap and that there has been considerable discussion amongst legal commentators about this and whether the distinction should be maintained. See, for example, the following texts and articles and the jurisprudence referred to therein: Koehnen, at pp. 440-448; Jeffrey G. MacIntosh, "The Oppression Remedy: Personal or Derivative?" (1991) 70 Can. Bar. Rev. 29; Edward M. Iacobucci and Kevin E. Davis, "Reconciling Derivative Claims and the Oppression Remedy" (2000) 12 S.C.L.R. 87.

While this debate is interesting, it is not necessary to resolve it here. On my reading of the authorities, in the cases where an oppression claim has been permitted to proceed even though the wrongs asserted were wrongs to the corporation, those same wrongful acts have, for the most part, also directly affected the complainant in a manner that was different from the indirect effect of the conduct on similarly placed complainants. And most, if not all, involve small closely-held corporations not public companies.

Waxman is a good example. The company was a family scrap metal business. Some of the acts complained of, including the wrongful distribution of bonuses, could have been the subject of a derivative action, but it was not disputed on appeal that the complainant "was personally aggrieved by the distribution" and that it "was done at the expense of his interest in the company": para. 526.

Malata — a case involving another closely-held company — is also a good example. The misappropriation of funds in that case affected not only the company (and therefore the indirect interests of all shareholders), but the direct interests of the minority shareholder as a creditor of the company.

Here, however, on the facts pleaded, there is no overlap between the derivative action and the oppression remedy (once one goes beyond the boiler plate repetition of the statutory language from the OBCA describing the oppression remedy). The appellants are not asserting that their personal interests as shareholders have been adversely affected in any way other than the type of harm that has been suffered by all shareholders as a collectivity. Mr. Rea — the only director plaintiff — does not plead that the Improper Transactions have impacted his interest *qua* director.

Since the creation of the oppression remedy, courts have taken a broad and flexible approach to its application, in keeping with the broad and flexible form of relief it is intended to provide. However, the appellants' open-ended approach to the oppression remedy in circumstances where the facts support a derivative action on behalf of the corporation misses a significant point: the impugned conduct must harm the complainant personally, not just the body corporate, *i.e.*, the collectivity of shareholders as a whole.

The oppression remedy is not available — as the appellants contend — simply because a complainant asserts a "reasonable expectation" (for example, that directors will conduct themselves with honesty and probity and in the best interests of the corporation) and the evidence supports that the reasonable expectation has been violated by conduct falling within the terms "oppression", "unfair prejudice" or "unfair disregard". The impugned conduct must be "oppressive" of or "unfairly prejudicial" to, or "unfairly disregard" *the interests of the complainant*: OBCA, s. 248(2). No such conduct is pled here.

That the harm must impact the interests of the complainant personally — giving rise to a personal action — and not simply the complainant's interests as a part of the collectivity of stakeholders as a whole — is consistent with the reforms put in place to attenuate the rigours of the rule in *Foss v. Harbottle*. The legislative response was to create *two* remedies, with two different rationales and two separate statutory foundations, not just one: a corporate remedy, and a personal or individual remedy.

The derivative action provides aggrieved minority stakeholders with the ability to pursue a cause of action on behalf of the corporation to redress wrongs done in respect of the corporation, provided leave is obtained from the court to do so. As Professor MacIntosh has observed:

> The corporation will be injured when all shareholders are affected equally, with none experiencing any special harm. By contrast, in a personal (or "direct") action, the harm has a differential impact on shareholders, whether the difference arises amongst members of different classes of shareholders or as between members of a single class. It has also been said that in a derivative action, the injury to shareholders is only *indirect*, that is, it arises only because the corporation is injured, and not otherwise. [See, for example, *Farnham v. Fingold*, [1973] 2 O.R. 132 (C.A.); *Goldex Mines Ltd. v. Revill* (1974), 7 O.R. (2d) 216 (C.A.)].

The requirements for leave are straightforward and are set out in s. 246(2) of the OBCA: the directors must be given 15 days' notice of the intention to bring the application, and the court must be satisfied: (i) that the directors will not pursue the claim; (ii) that the complainant is acting in good faith; and (iii) that it appears to be in the best interests of the corporation that the action be brought. In this way the legislative goals of avoiding strike suits, meritless actions and a multiplicity of proceedings against the corporation — and the potentially unwarranted costs that accompany them — are strengthened. Although they have been the subject of some academic criticism, these remain valid legislative objectives and concerns, in my view, particularly in the context of actions against publicly-traded corporations.

Indeed, in para. 28 of their statement of claim the appellants themselves flagged Martinrea's potential exposure "to legal proceedings by each person or company that acquired or disposed of shares of Martinrea during the period in which the Improper Transactions took place." A judgment in a derivative action, however, if proceeded with and ultimately successful, will be binding on all shareholders.

Much of the debate here focussed on *Malata* — this Court's most recent consideration of the relationship between derivative actions and the oppression remedy. Does it stand for the proposition, as the appellants assert, that oppression remedy claims and derivative action claims may be collapsed into an oppression remedy claim? Or, as the respondents say, does it stand for the proposition that the remedies may not be conflated when it is a public corporation that is involved? In my view, *Malata* stands for neither of these broad propositions and, in any event, is distinguishable from the present appeal.

Like this case, *Malata* involved the alleged misappropriation of funds from the corporation — there, by a director, officer and major shareholder. Unlike this case, however, *Malata* involved a small closely-held corporation. The aggrieved minority shareholder was one of only three shareholders of the corporation and, significantly, was also a major creditor of the corporation. On those facts, there was clearly an overlap and coexistence between the wrong caused by the alleged misappropriation to the corporate collectivity and the wrong caused by it to the minority shareholder in its capacity as creditor because the misappropriation threatened the corporation's ability to pay its debt to the minority shareholder/creditor. Martinrea, however, is a large, widely-held public corporation and no type of personal wrong is evident.

To be sure, there are bald allegations in the statement of claim that the Improper Transactions "caused significant damage to [Martinrea] *and its shareholders*" (para. 28, emphasis added) and that the defendants "have acted and continue to act in a manner that is oppressive, unfairly prejudicial to, and that unfairly disregards *the interests of the Plaintiffs and other Martinrea shareholders*" (para. 33, emphasis added). However, there is no particularized allegation of any wrong done to the interests of the plaintiffs themselves, *qua* shareholders or otherwise, as opposed to a wrong affecting the "corporate body", *i.e.*, the collectivity of shareholders as a whole.

In their written and oral arguments, although not in their pleadings, the appellants make three submissions in an attempt to particularize the alleged harm to them individually, and thus bring the claim within the rubric of an oppression remedy. They assert first that the alleged misappropriations "precluded [them] from managing [their] investment[s] or exercising [their] voting rights in an informed manner"; secondly, that the failure to provide adequate disclosure of material information to shareholders has been recognized as oppressive conduct; and thirdly, that by reason of the director defendants' lack of candour with their fellow directors, "Mr. Rea lacked the full information needed to genuinely exercise his role in governing Martinrea." None of these allegations is specifically pleaded and none suffices to permit the appellants to cross the line — however "murky" that line may be — between the derivative reality of this action and its proposed oppression remedy illusion, in my opinion.

"[M]anaging [their] investments and exercising [their] voting rights" in this context means exercising their role as shareholders in supervising management. The Supreme Court of Canada has held that "claims in respect of losses stemming from an alleged inability to oversee or supervise management are really derivative and not personal in nature": *Hercules Management*, at para. 62.

It may be that, in some circumstances, the failure to provide proper disclosure of material information to shareholders can constitute oppressive conduct and, similarly, that in some circumstances wrongfully withholding information from a director may be "oppressive" to the director's ability to carry out his or her role in that capacity. However, no such pleading is asserted here. To the extent that the preparation of inaccurate financial statements and the lack of candour *vis-à-vis* fellow directors are asserted as facts in the statement of claim, they are pleaded as examples of the Insider Defendants' breach of fiduciary duty to the corporation, not as something that impacts the interests of the appellants in any individual manner other than what might affect the collectivity of the shareholders. Mr. Rea is the only plaintiff who was a director and he asserts no claim that his interests have been affected in that capacity. As pleaded, these wrongs are relevant as tools used to perpetrate the fraud against Martinrea, not as acts that have any particularized impact on any of the plaintiffs individually.

At its heart, the appellants' allegation involves the misappropriation of corporate property by the Insider Defendants, assisted in some cases by the respondents here (IM and Pashak) and others. The substantive remedy claimed is the disgorgement of the ill-gotten gains back to Martinrea.

The misappropriation of corporate property was effected through the alleged Improper Transactions which in essence consisted of: (i) payment to the Insider Defendants of secret kickbacks and improper commissions in relation to services provided and equipment sold to Martinrea, as a result, at inflated prices; (ii) payments by Martinrea to third parties for construction, renovation and other services (including in one case the settlement of potential legal exposure) for the personal benefit of the Insider Defendants; and (iii) in the case of the respondents IM and Pashak, the purchase of used equipment by Martinrea at inflated prices (feeding kickbacks to the Insider Defendants) and the purchase of real estate in Kitchener by Martinrea from a related Pashak company, on terms unfavourable to Martinrea. All of these allegations, if proved, will establish losses sustained by the corporation to its financial bottom line — *i.e.*, to the collectivity of shareholders as a whole — and not to any particular shareholder, including the appellants, individually.

For these reasons, I do not accept that the wrongs as pleaded in the statement of claim are wrongs other than wrongs done to the corporation that form the basis of a derivative action. As noted earlier, I do not see this as a case involving overlap between the oppression remedy and the derivative action.

Conclusion and Disposition

I recognize that a party seeking to strike out a pleading under Rule 21.01(1)(b) must demonstrate that it is plain and obvious the claim discloses no reasonable cause of action. For these purposes, the facts as pleaded must be accepted as true, the pleading should be given a large and liberal interpretation and courts should not, at this stage of the proceedings, strike out claims that are novel or dispose of matters of law that are not fully settled in the jurisprudence: see *Hunt v. T & N plc*, [1990] 2 S.C.R. 959 (S.C.C.), at pp. 971, 973 and 990-991; *Falloncrest Financial Corp. v. Ontario* (1995), 27 O.R. (3d) 1 (Ont. C.A.), at pp. 5-6.

For the reasons outlined above, I am satisfied that the appellants' statement of claim does not disclose a reasonable cause of action based upon the oppression remedy. Nor do I think it is a novel or unsettled principle of law that wrongs done solely to a corporation, for which remedies are sought on behalf of the corporation, give rise to a derivative action and require leave of the court before an action can be commenced to assert those claims. Where the facts may give rise to both a "corporate claim" and a "personal" oppression remedy claim — as *Malata* and the other cases referred to above illustrate — the question of whether an oppression remedy proceeding is available will have to be sorted out on a case by case basis. This task does not arise on the facts as pleaded here, however.

Accordingly, I would dismiss the appeal.

Notes and Questions

1   One thing that seems absolutely clear about the oppression remedy is that it achieves one aim envisioned by the drafters and expands the range of actionable wrongs as compared to the common law of fiduciary duties. See generally MacIntosh, "Minority Shareholder Rights in Canada and England, 1860–1987" (1988), 27 O.H.L.J. 1. The derivative action provision in the statute is purely procedural in nature; in order to succeed in a derivative action, the plaintiff must show that there has been a breach of a fiduciary duty owed to the

corporation. Thus, the substantive hurdle in s. 241(2) is easier, not more difficult to scale than the substantive hurdle required to commence a derivative action. However, compare this view to the *Malata* decision above in which Armstrong JA states, "In my view, allowing s. 248 oppression claims to proceed where there is harm to the corporation would not nullify s. 246, because the two sections involve different threshold tests. Section 246 simply requires a violation of the corporation's legal rights. On the other hand, s. 248 requires, in the case of harm to the corporation, a violation of corporate legal rights that is oppressive or unfairly prejudicial, or that unfairly disregards the complainant's interests."

If the oppression remedy can be resorted to in any case involving a derivative type of action, this appears, as a practical matter, to render the derivative action completely obsolete. Who would risk failing to comply with the procedural strictures applying in the case of a derivative action when they can be entirely circumvented by commencing an oppression action? One might argue that a derivative action affords procedural protections not found in an oppression action. However, although the oppression action is commenced by summary procedure (i.e., by application rather than an action), without pleadings and discoveries, the court will almost routinely order the trial of complex issues involving factual disputes, converting the oppression application into a regular action with pleadings and discoveries, and putting it on a par to the type of action that results when the suit is brought derivatively. If the oppression action can be used in this way, then why did the drafters of the CBCA (and OBCA) not simply remove the provisions relating to derivative actions? Also, why should they be so solicitous to prevent abuses connected with derivative actions by requiring leave of the court to commence the action (and to discontinue it), but provide such an easy way around this requirement (and the other procedural hurdles)? Perhaps the problem was that the drafters simply failed to adequately consider the relationship between the two provisions. Interestingly enough, the situations cited by the Cohen and Jenkins committees in England as showing the need for an oppression remedy consist of conduct that would give rise to both personal and derivative actions at common law. How do you think this dilemma should be resolved? For an argument that derivative actions should be allowed to proceed only with leave of the court under the statutory derivative action provisions, see Jeffrey G. MacIntosh, "The Oppression Remedy: Personal or Derivative?" (1991), 70 Can. Bar Rev. 29. However, see also Edward M. Iacobucci and Kevin E. Davis, "Reconciling Derivative Claims and the Oppression Remedy" (2000), 12 S.C.L.R. (2d).

2   Very often in a private corporation, a wrong that is formally a wrong
to "the company" is in fact simply symptomatic of a dispute between
various parties in the corporation. The *Diligenti* case, discussed *supra*,
falls into this camp. Diligenti, you will recall, went into business with
three other shareholders, and when there was a falling out the other
three ganged up on him and diverted profits to a corporation that
they controlled. Formally, this is a derivative wrong, since the wrong
was done to the corporation. In substance, however, the wrong was
symptomatic of a dispute between the shareholders. This argument
has sometimes been used to justify allowing derivative types of
actions to proceed under the oppression remedy. Note, however, that
this argument only applies to private corporations, and not public.
Further, what if not all shareholders are part of the dispute? If the
action does not proceed derivatively, then these other parties will be
forced to become parties to the litigation. Moreover, where the
remedy is one of favour of the company (as it will normally be in a
derivative proceeding) the interest of these shareholders is protected
whether or not they are parties to the litigation. Indeed, where all
shareholders are similarly harmed by the impugned conduct (*e.g.*, by
the taking of excessive remuneration), there is no easy or fair way to
institute a personal remedy in favour of some shareholders but not
others. Thus, even in the case of the private corporation where the
wrong to the corporation is symptomatic of an underlying dispute
between shareholders, there are good arguments for forcing the
action to proceed derivatively.

This is to say nothing of the interests of creditors. A personal remedy
in a derivative type of suit (*e.g.*, an award of damages directly to
aggrieved shareholders in a case in which there is excessive managerial compensation) trumps the interests of creditors in the corporation's assets and earnings stream. This is another reason for forcing
all derivative types of proceedings to go forward only as properly
constituted derivative actions. These are other arguments made by
MacIntosh, *supra*.

Yet another complication that arises where derivative types of actions
are allowed to proceed under the oppression provision is highlighted
by *Alles v. Maurice* (1992), 9 C.P.C. (3d) 49, 5 B.L.R. (2d) 154 (Ont.
Gen. Div.), per Austin J. In *Alles*, the plaintiff sued under the
oppression remedy claiming, *inter alia*, payment of excessive remuneration and other derivative-type wrongs by other shareholder/
director/managers in a number of related corporations. The corporations in question, as well as the individual managers were named as
defendants. The issue arose, however, of who would instruct the
lawyers for the corporation. On the facts, the alleged wrongdoers had
hired and instructed lawyers. The dangers of this are obvious.
Assuming that real harms had been perpetrated on the corporation,

the wrongdoers were hardly the best people to instruct the corporation's lawyers as to how they should best defend the corporation's interests. On the other hand, assuming that there has not been any harm to the corporation, the plaintiff is no better a person to instruct the lawyers for the corporation. The difficulty is that there is no unbiased person to instruct the lawyers acting for the corporation, and we therefore should have little confidence that the corporation's best interests (and thus the interests of all of those who have some claim on the corporation but are not represented in the proceeding) will be properly represented. By contrast, where the action proceeds derivatively, the plaintiff appointed by the court to prosecute the action in the name of and on behalf of the corporation must demonstrate to a court that the action is *prima facie* in the best interests of the corporation.

In *Alles*, Austin J. granted the plaintiff's motion that the solicitors appointed (by the defendants) to represent the corporation be removed. He further ordered that the parties agree upon a solicitor, and indicated that if they could not agree, the court would select one.

(v) Can the Oppression Action be Applied to the Conduct of Shareholders of the Corporation?

Whether the oppression remedy applies to the conduct of shareholders is one of the most difficult, but important, questions that arise under the oppression remedy. One must of course start out by looking at the statute. Section 241(2) indicates that the oppression remedy will apply in cases where:

> (a) any act or omission of the corporation or any of its affiliates are or have been carried on or conducted in a manner, or
> (b) the business or affairs of the corporation or any of its affiliates are or have been carried on or conducted in a manner, or
> (c) the powers of the directors of the corporation or any of its affiliates are or have been exercised in a manner that is oppressive . . .

At first glance, this formulation seems to allow little room to attack the conduct of a shareholder. However, you will note that the remedy applies not only to conduct of the corporation, but also to that of any "affiliate" of the corporation. Look at the definition of "affiliate" in CBCA s. 2(2), and the definition of "control" in s. 2(3). These definitions include a parent corporation that owns at least 50% of the shares of the subsidiary (and see *Sparling v. Javelin International Ltd. et al.*, [1986] R.J.Q. 1073 at 1130, suggesting that it is possible to "control" within the meaning of the statute with fewer than 50% of the shares).

Recall the case of *Scottish Co-operative Wholesale Society Ltd. v. Meyer, supra*, Chapter 7. In that case, Lord Denning found the conduct of the controlling parent company to be oppressive, noting the crucial importance of the interlocking directorships. You should review *Ferguson v. Imax, supra,* with an eye to how carefully the Ontario Court of Appeal distinguished (or failed to distinguish between) "the corporation" and those shareholders who controlled the corporation. Is *Ferguson* in the same mould as *Scottish Co-operative Wholesale,* and the subsequent cases of *Harmer* and *Jermyn, supra* Chapter 7? In many cases, it is not necessary to characterize the acts of shareholders as oppressive, unfairly prejudicial etc. in order to bring oneself within the oppression remedy. For example, if an oppressive shareholder resolution is passed and the company acts on the resolution, then it can be said that the corporation has committed the act of oppression. Having found oppression, it is clear that the court may then make orders that have affect or are directed against shareholders. For example, it is common for the court to order that a majority or controlling shareholder buy the shares of the complainant minority shareholder. See, *e.g., Wind Ridge Farms Ltd. v. Quandra Group Investments Ltd.* (1999), 178 D.L.R. (4th) 603, 1999 CarswellSask 592 (C.A.); *Miller v. F. Mendel Holdings Ltd.* (1984), 26 B.L.R. 85 (Sask. Q.B.). This is another way of, in effect, bringing shareholder conduct within the purview of the oppression remedy. See generally MacIntosh, "Minority Shareholder Rights in Canada and England, 1860-1987" (1988), 27 O.H.L.J. 1.

(vi)   The Oppression Remedy and the Duties of Directors in the Context of Corporate Transactions

Illustrating the sprawling nature of the oppression remedy, shareholders and defeated take-over bidders have attempted to utilize the oppression action against the target company in the context of hostile take-over bids. However, the use of the oppression remedy against public companies has not been met with much success in Canada. Professor Puri and Ben-Ishai's empirical study, *supra,* found that of the 8% of cases that dealt with public companies, the success rate was 33% as compared to a success rate of 54% for closely held corporations. See for example *Pente Investment Management Ltd. v. Schneider Corp.* (1998), 42 O.R. (3d) 177, 1998 CarswellOnt 4035 (C.A.); and *CW Shareholdings Inc. v. WIC Western International Communications Ltd.* (1998), 39 O.R. (3d) 755, 1998 CarswellOnt 1891 (Gen. Div. [Commercial List]). In both *Pente* and *WIC,* the judges determined whether the case for oppression had been made out on the basis of whether the directors discharged their fiduciary duties to the corporation. In this regard, the business judgment rule has become very important. In cases involving alleged oppression in the context of a takeover bid, it has become standard practice for the target company to form a committee of independent directors to judge the merits of the bid and to attempt to solicit other bids. Courts have generally deferred to the judgments of such committees. Also reread *Brant Investments Ltd. v. KeepRite Inc., supra,* Chapter 7, in which the court was faced with the application of the oppression remedy in the context of a related party transaction. What is the appropriate level of review by the courts in an oppression action given the deference generally afforded to corporate decisions under the business judgment rule?

(vii)   Costs Orders Under the Oppression Remedy

The costs provisions relevant to oppression actions are dealt with in part (a), *supra*. One of the powers granted to the court is the power to award interim costs (payable by the corporation). See, *e.g.*, CBCA s.242(4). *Alles v. Maurice* (1992), 9 C.P.C. (3d) 42, 5 B.L.R. (2d) 146 (Ont. Gen. Div.), per Blair J., deals with the issue of when an award of interim costs will be made. The plaintiff in the oppression action accused a number of participants in a number of related corporations of taking excessive remuneration, charging personal expenses to the companies, and making incomplete disclosure to shareholders. She had spent a great deal of money on valuators and lawyers in attempting to fulfill her obligations as director of two of the companies in question, and in determining the financial position of these companies. Some $45,000 had already been spent, and some $68,000 worth of work remained unbilled. The plaintiff indicated that she could not continue with the action if the company did not pay her interim costs. Blair J. noted that in *Wilson v. Conley* (1990)1 B.L.R. (2d) 220, 46 C.P.C. (2d) 85 (Ont. Gen. Div.) it had been held that there were three requisites to the award of interim costs: 1) that the Applicant be in financial difficulty; 2) that the financial difficulty arise out of the alleged oppressive actions of the Respondents; and 3) that the Applicant has made out a strong *prima facie* case. Blair J. expressly declined to follow the second and third of these criteria, stating that:

> [The plaintiff's] inability to finance lawsuit is every bit as real, [even where the cause is not the alleged oppressive conduct]. In my view it is this inability to fund an otherwise meritorious lawsuit and the advantage which such a situation gives to an "oppressive" majority that the power given under s. 248(4) [of the OBCA] to order costs is directed. There is nothing in the language of the statute or in its purpose which, to my mind, requires that the applicant demonstrate a cause and effect relationship between the conduct of the respondents and the need for funding . . .

> In the end, I would prefer to say simply that an applicant for relief under s. 248(4) need establish that there is a case of sufficient merit to warrant pursuit and that the applicant is genuinely in financial circumstances which but for an order under s. 284(4) would preclude the claim from being pursued.

(e) **Remedy**

Professors Ben-Ishai and Puri's empirical study on the oppression remedy, *supra*, found that the Canadian judiciary has shown a willingness to be innovative in granting remedies for a successful oppression application. The most common remedy granted by the court was a share purchase, at 32% of all remedies granted. A share purchase involves an order directing the corporation (or any other person) to purchase securities from a security holder. This remedy was most commonly granted in the context of a closely held corporation where a minority shareholder was successful in showing oppression by the majority shareholder. The Canadian judiciary had found the share purchase remedy appropriate where shareholders have lost confidence in each other and accordingly could not continue to work together. On the other hand, their results indicate that the Canadian judiciary did not find the share purchase remedy appropriate where the corporation or the majority shareholders did not have sufficient funds to make a share purchase. In such situations, the Canadian judiciary found it more appropriate to grant a winding-up order. Six per cent of the remedies granted involved a winding-up order. Their results indicate that Canadian courts are open to using this remedy but do so in limited cases and reluctantly. This reluctance can be traced back to the reluctance of the English courts to impose the winding-up remedy because of the drastic consequence of terminating the existence of a company, which as discussed in an earlier section of this article, ultimately pushed the English legislature to develop the oppression remedy.

After the share purchase remedy, their results indicate that the most common remedy in 17% of the remedies granted was the residual remedy, which included remedies such as specific performance, constructive trusts, ordering a directors' meeting, and valuation of assets. In 21% of the remedies granted compensation of an aggrieved person was ordered, which included current and former shareholders, employee-shareholders, but more often, creditors as complainants.

The following case is a good example of oppression arising in the context of a smaller, closely held corporation. It is in this context that the oppression remedy has had significant impact.

Naneff v. Con-Crete Holdings Ltd.
(1995), 23 O.R. (3d) 481, 1995 CarswellOnt 1207 (C.A.)

[Mr. Naneff built a successful family business. In 1977 he made his two sons, Alex and Boris, equal holders of all of the equity in the business, while retaining control through redeemable voting preference shares. In 1990, angry about his lifestyle, Alex's family threw him out of the family home. They also removed him as an officer of all of the companies of the family business, excluded him from participation in the management of the business and cut off most of his income from the business. At trial, the family's conduct was found to be oppressive to Alex, and the trial judge ordered that the family business be sold publicly with any of (or a combination of) Alex, Boris and Mr. Naneff entitled to purchase it.]

GALLIGAN J.A.: The judgment at trial contained a number of specific remedies. The fundamental and most important remedy, contained in para. 9, was that the business, i.e., those corporations which comprise it, be sold publicly as a going concern with each of or any combination of Mr. Naneff, Alex and Boris being entitled to purchase it. There were remedies contained in paras. 4 to 7, inclusive, of the judgment which set aside certain changes in corporate structure and other corporate arrangements which were made after Alex was ejected. Those remedies were ordered in an effort to restore the corporate arrangements to the state which they were in at the time of Alex's ejection. One remedy ordered the payment to Alex of his outstanding shareholder's loans to two of the corporations together with interest. There were two other ancillary remedies which I will mention later. I propose to discuss those remedies and give my opinion with respect to their validity.

1. Public Sale of the Companies Forming the Business as a Going Concern

Before discussing the merits of the challenge to this remedy, I wish to make brief reference to the principles which guide an appellate court in its review of a remedy ordered under s. 248(3) of the O.B.C.A. Section 248(3) empowers a court upon a finding of oppression to make any order "it thinks fit". When that broad discretion is given to a court of first instance, the law is clear that an appellate court's power of review is quite limited. In *Mason v. Intercity Properties Ltd.* (1987), 59 O.R. (2d) 631 at p. 636, 38 D.L.R. (4th) 681 (C.A.), Blair J.A. set out the governing principle:

> The governing principle is that such a discretion must be exercised judicially and that an appellate court is only entitled to interfere where it has been established that the lower court has erred in principle or its decision is otherwise unjust.

I approach this issue, therefore, keeping in mind that this court can only interfere with the remedy if it concludes that there was an error in principle on the part of Blair J. or if the remedy in all of the circumstances is an unjust one. It cannot be interfered with, as Carruthers J. said (at p. 701) when giving the judgment of the Divisional Court, "simply because someone else might prefer a different way of going about things". With great deference to Blair J., who is a distinguished jurist with extensive commercial law experience, I regret to say that I have concluded, in the circumstances of this case, that the remedy of public sale of this business amounts to an error in principle and is unjust to Mr. Naneff.

At the outset I think it is important to keep in mind that this is not a normal commercial operation where partners make contributions and share the equity according to their contributions or where persons invest in a business by the purchase of shares. This is a family business where the dynamics of the relationship between the principals are very different from those between the principals in a normal commercial business. As the courts below have correctly held, the fact that this is a family business cannot oust the provisions of s. 248 of the O.B.C.A. Nevertheless, I am convinced that the fact that this is a family matter must be kept very much in mind when fashioning a remedy under s. 248(3), as it bears directly upon the reasonable expectations of the principals.

I have come to that conclusion after considering certain observations made by Lord Wilberforce during the course of his speech in *Ebrahimi v. Westbourne Galleries Ltd.*, [1973] A.C. 360, [1972] 2 All E.R. 492 (H.L.). The statute under consideration, the *Companies Act, 1948*, s. 222, authorized the court to wind up a company if it was "just and equitable" to do so. In my opinion, the words "just and equitable" convey the same meaning as the word "fit" in s. 248(3) of the O.B.C.A. Lord Wilberforce explained that when this jurisdiction is being exercised, the relationship between the principals should not be looked at from a technical legal point of view; rather the court should examine and act upon the real rights, expectations and obligations which actually exist between the principals. He said at p. 379:

> The words are a recognition of the fact that a limited company is more than a mere legal entity, with a personality in law of its own: that *there is room in company law for recognition of the fact that behind it, or amongst it, there are individuals, with rights, expectations and obligations inter se which are not necessarily submerged in the company structure.* That structure is defined by the *Companies Act* and by the articles of association by which shareholders agree to be bound. In most companies and in most contexts, this definition is sufficient and exhaustive, equally so whether the company is large or small. The "just and equitable" provision does not, as the respondents suggest, entitle one party to disregard the obligation he assumes by entering a company, nor the court to dispense him from it. *It does, as equity always does, enable the court to subject the exercise of legal rights to equitable considerations; considerations, that is, of a personal character arising between one individual and another,* which may make it unjust, or inequitable, to insist on legal rights, or to exercise them in a particular way. (Emphasis added.)

Thus, I think any remedy granted under s. 248(3) in this case had to be fashioned so that it was just, having regard to the considerations of a personal character which existed among Mr. Naneff, Alex, and Boris.

The provisions of s. 248(3) give the court a very broad discretion in the manner in which it can fashion a remedy. Broad as that discretion is, however, it can only be exercised for a very specific purpose; that is, to rectify the oppression. This qualification is found in the wording of s. 248(2) which gives the court the power, if it finds oppression or certain other unfair conduct, to "make an order to rectify the matters complained of". Therefore, the result of the exercise of the discretion contained in s. 248(3) must be the rectification of the oppressive conduct. If it has some other result, the remedy would be one which is not authorized by law. I agree with the opinion expressed by Professor J.G. MacIntosh in his paper "The Retrospectivity of the Oppression Remedy" (1987-88), 13 Can. Bus. L.J. 219 at p. 225:

> The private law character of the enactment strengthens the argument, for in seeking to redress equity between private parties the provision *does not seek to punish but to apply a measure of corrective justice.* (Emphasis added.)

That opinion was referred to with approval by Glube C.J.T.D. in *Mathers v. Mathers* (1992), 113 N.S.R. (2d) 284 (N.S.T.D.) at p. 304, 309 A.P.R. 284, reversed on other grounds (1993), 123 N.S.R. (2d) 14, 340 A.P.R. 14 (C.A.).

My analysis of s. 248(2) indicates that there is another limit imposed by law upon the apparently unlimited discretionary powers contained in s. 248(3). Section 248(2) provides that when the court is satisfied that in respect of a corporation there is certain specified conduct "that is oppressive, or unfairly prejudicial to or that unfairly disregards the interest of any security holder, creditor, director, or officer of the corporation, the court may make an order to rectify the matters complained of". The expression "security holder" includes a shareholder. Thus, the provision only deals with the interest of a shareholder, creditor, director or officer. It follows from a plain reading of the provision that any rectification of a matter complained of can only be made with respect to the person's interest as a shareholder, creditor, director or officer.

In *Stone v. Stonehurst Enterprises Ltd.* (1987), 80 N.B.R. (2d) 290, 202 A.P.R. 290 (Q.B.), Landry J. was called upon to interpret s. 166(2) of the New Brunswick *Business Corporations Act*, S.N.B. 1981, c. B-9.1, whose provisions are the same as s. 248(2) of the O.B.C.A. The company in question was a family company run as a family business. The company decided to sell its assets. A minority shareholder in his personal capacity wanted to buy the assets and bid for them. When the majority shareholder exercised her controlling interest and sold the assets to someone else, the minority shareholder attacked the transaction as being oppressive to him as a shareholder. Landry J. held that the Act protected a person's interest as a shareholder "as such". Basing his opinion on the judgment of Jenkins L.J. in *Re H.R. Harmer Ltd.*, [1958] 3 All E.R. 689 at p. 698, [1959] 1 W.L.R. 62 (C.A.), Landry J. said at p. 305:

It must be remembered, and it is very important in this case, that it is only the interest of a shareholder *as such*, or of a director or officer *as such* that is protected by this section.

The applicant must establish that his interest *as a shareholder* has been affected. He may of course have other interests, such as being a prospective purchaser of the assets of the company. But it is only the applicant's interest as a shareholder which we must be concerned with in applying s. 166. (Emphasis in original.)

I agree with and adopt Landry J.'s analysis as a correct statement of the law. Persons who are shareholders, officers and directors of companies may have other personal interests which are intimately connected to a transaction. However, it is only their interests as shareholder, officer or director as such which are protected by s. 248 of the O.B.C.A. The provisions of that section cannot be used to protect or to advance directly or indirectly their other personal interests

I conclude, therefore, that the discretionary powers in s. 248(3) O.B.C.A. must be exercised within two important limitations:

(i) they must only rectify oppressive conduct;

(ii) they may protect only the person's interest as a shareholder, director or officer as such.

The law is clear that when determining whether there has been oppression of a minority shareholder, the court must determine what the reasonable expectations of that person were according to the arrangements which existed between the principals. The cases on this issue are collected and analyzed by Farley J. in *820099 Ontario Inc. v. Harold E. Ballard Ltd.* (1991), 3 B.L.R. (2d) 113 at p. 123 (Ont. Gen. Div.), affirmed (1991), 3 B.L.R. (2d) 113 (Ont. Div. Ct.). I agree with his comment at pp. 185-86:

Shareholder interests would appear to be intertwined with shareholder expectations. It does not appear to me that the shareholder expectations which are to be considered are those that a shareholder has as his own individual "wish list". They must be expectations which could be said to have been (or ought to have been considered as) part of the compact of the shareholders.

The determination of reasonable expectations will also, in my view, have an important bearing upon the decision as to what is a just remedy in a particular case.

The finding made by Blair J. that Alex expected ultimately to be an equal co-owner of the business with his brother cannot be challenged. However, it must be interpreted in the light of two other important and intertwined considerations. The first consideration is that Alex fully understood that until death or voluntary retirement his father retained ultimate control over the business even to the extent of deciding what dividends would be paid and what would be done with any of those dividends. The second consideration is that this was a family business which had been built by his father.

The importance of the first of those considerations is that Alex knew that until his father died or retired he could under no circumstances have any right to have or even to share absolute control of the business. Therefore, under no circumstances could Alex's reasonable expectations include the right to control the family business while his father was alive and active. The second consideration is important because, while Alex expected that his father would give him an equal share in the control of the business upon his death or retirement, that expectation was based upon his belief that his father would continue to be bountiful to him in the future. It should have been apparent to Alex that he could not expect that paternal bounty to continue if his father for good reason or bad no longer considered him to be a dutiful son. It would have been quite unrealistic of Alex to expect that his father would continue to be bountiful to him if his family ties were severed. Alex knew that the reason for his father giving him one-half of the equity in the family business was his father's desire for his sons to work with him in his business. He must also have known that it would be impossible for him, Mr. Naneff, and Boris to work together in the business as a family if the family bonds ceased to exist. It is for those reasons that Alex's reasonable expectation must be looked at in the light of the family relationship.

It is my view that the first error in principle in this remedy is that it did more than simply rectify oppression. As I noted above, the O.B.C.A. authorizes a court to rectify oppressive conduct. I think the words of Farley J. in Ballard, *supra*, at p. 197 are very appropriate in this respect:

> The court should not interfere with the affairs of a corporation lightly. I think that where relief is justified to correct an oppressive type of situation, the surgery should be done with a scalpel, and not a battle axe. I would think that this principle would hold true even if the past conduct of the oppressor were found to be scandalous. *The job for the court is to even up the balance, not tip it in favour of the hurt party*. I note that in *Explo Syndicate v. Explo Inc.*, a decision of the Ontario High Court, released June 29, 1989, Gravely L.J.S.C. stated at p. 20:
>
> > In approaching a remedy the court, in my view, should interfere as little as possible and *only to the extent necessary to redress the unfairness*. (Emphasis added.)

The order of Blair J. gave Alex something which he knew he could never have while his father was alive and active — the opportunity to obtain full control of the family business. A remedy that rectifies cannot be a remedy which gives a shareholder something that even he never could have reasonably expected.

Moreover, I am unable to view the remedy as anything other than a punitive one towards Mr. Naneff. There was never any doubt among the three men that Mr. Naneff would exercise ultimate control of the family business until he died or retired. Mr. Naneff solidified his right of complete control by the corporate arrangements he put in place at the time of the estate freeze and which he kept in place to the knowledge of his sons throughout the time that the three of them worked together. It is not the task of any court of law to judge the family dispute or to rule upon the justice of the expulsion of Alex from the family. However, I am unable to accept as anything other than punitive a remedy which puts at risk the very condition upon which Mr. Naneff exercised his bounty in favour of his sons — his total control of the business during his active life. The O.B.C.A. authorizes a court to rectify oppression; it does not authorize the court to punish for it.

The second error in this remedy is that it attempts to protect Alex's interest in the family business as a son and family member, in addition to protecting his interest as a shareholder as such. As I mentioned above, it is my view that Alex's expectation of ultimately obtaining an equal share of the control of the business with Boris was based upon his expectation of being the continuing object of his father's bounty. That in turn depended upon him remaining in his father's favour and remaining in his father's eyes a member of the family. The remedy of public sale, which gives Alex the opportunity to buy the company, enables him to obtain that control while out of his father's favour. This appears to protect much more than his interest as a shareholder as such; it protects, indeed it advances, his interest as a son.

It is my view, therefore, that the remedy imposed in this case constituted an error in principle in that it did more than rectify oppression, and it did more than protect Alex's interest as a shareholder as such in the companies.

As well as concluding that the remedy granted to Alex was wrong in principle, it is my view that the remedy was unjust to Mr. Naneff. By the time of Alex's ouster from the business, Mr. Naneff had devoted almost 40 years of his life to creating, nurturing and building the business into a very significant enterprise. Instead of using profits from the business to acquire other personal assets, he used them to finance the growth and expansion of the business. There was never any doubt in the minds of his sons that their father gave them their equity positions upon the understanding that he would retain ultimate control as long as he wanted to exercise it. No one can disparage the productive and devoted work which Alex put into the business. But his nine years of contribution pales to almost insignificance when compared with that of his father's contribution.

The effect of the relief granted to Alex is to put Mr. Naneff in the position where he is just another person, equal to Alex, who is entitled to buy the business which he had himself founded and built from nothing.

The remedy jeopardizes something which Alex knew was always to be his father's, the right to ultimate control of the business. The remedy gives to Alex the possibility of taking control of the business, something he knew he could never have during his father's lifetime. Having regard to the circumstances of this case this remedy, which jeopardizes the right which everyone knew belonged to Mr. Naneff and which gives Alex the opportunity to take away that right, strikes me as unjust.

At trial there were three possible fundamental remedies suggested to the trial judge. One of them was properly rejected out of hand. No more need be said about it. The alternative remedy to public sale of the business as a going concern was that Mr. Naneff and Boris acquire Alex's shares of the companies at fair market value, without minority discount. In my view that was the just remedy in this case. While I find that Mr. Naneff's oppressive conduct should not endanger his right to control the business, neither should he be able to take away what he had given to Alex, or to take away what Alex had contributed to the business. This remedy, together with certain of the other remedies ordered by Blair J., would have had the effect of fully compensating Alex for the value of the equity given to him by his father and for his own contributions to the business. The value of his shares would reflect the success of the business and Alex's contribution toward that success, as well as the value of the gift of equity which he had received from his father. When I discuss the remedy respecting the shareholders' loans, it will be seen that when the business was ordered to repay Alex the amounts of his loans, in fact he was receiving his share of the operating profits of the business over previous years.

This remedy would be just because it will put Alex, in so far as money can, in the position which he would have been in had he not been ejected. It would not give him an opportunity to which he had no reasonable expectation. It would not put at risk Mr. Naneff's right to ultimate control which Alex knew was a condition of his father's gift of equity. The remedy would protect Alex's interest as a shareholder as such.

It is my opinion that para. 9 of the trial judgment, which provides for the sale of the appellant companies on the open market as a going concern, cannot be sustained. In its place, I would order that the appellants acquire Alex's shares of the companies at fair market value fixed as of the date of his ouster, December 25, 1990. It is conceded on behalf of the appellants that it would not be fair to apply a minority discount to the market value of Alex's shares. I agree and would order that there be no minority discount when fixing the fair market value of his shares. Alex is also entitled to prejudgment interest on the value of his shares as provided in the *Courts of Justice Act*, R.S.O. 1990, c. C.43, from December 25, 1990.

In the event that the parties cannot agree upon the value of the shares or to having the value of them fixed in some other way, I would direct a new trial restricted to fixing the value of Alex's shares in the appellant companies as of December 25, 1990. In my view the costs of such a new trial ought to be in the discretion of the judge presiding at it.

Appeal allowed.

Note

Disputes of the Naneff variety do not always end up in court if counsel for each of the parties has planned appropriately for the possibility of irreconcilable differences. Contractual devices like buyout arrangements, arbitration clauses and the like can go a long way to resolving difficulties without resort to the courts, if only by allowing one disputant to buy out the other(s). The courts are often asked to intervene in cases where adequate buyout arrangements would have ended the difficulties. As noted above, the most common remedy dispensed by the courts under the oppression remedy is an order that one party (or parties) buy out the other (or others). Such a court-ordered buyout accomplishes the same result as a privately negotiated buyout provision. Unfortunately, the lawyer as planner will frequently confront two pressing difficulties. First, a number of parties commencing a small business — very likely members of the same family, or close friends — will not seek separate legal advice upon incorporating and capitalizing the business. Rather, even when apprised of the conflict of interest, they will insist that one lawyer act for all. A lawyer asked to do so should reflect very carefully both on the rules of ethics governing his conduct in acting in the face of a clear conflict of interest and the further possibility of civil liability should the relationship fall apart (which it will do in a non-trivial number of cases) and one or more of the parties claim that their interests were not adequately provided for. A second difficulty is client resistance. Family members and good friends will not always be terribly receptive to the idea of incorporating dispute resolution procedures in a unanimous shareholder agreement. They would prefer to believe that disharmony is an impossibility, and will want to avoid communicating to the other participants even the suggestion that they think a falling out is a likelihood. As a solicitor, however, you omit such arrangements only at your peril (and that of your clients).

5. APPRAISAL REMEDY

Iacobucci, Pilkington, and Prichard
Canadian Business Corporations
(1977), pp. 168–171 (footnotes omitted)

Introduction

An appraisal right is the right of a shareholder to require the company to purchase his shares at an appraised price if the company takes certain "triggering" actions from which he dissents. The right works as a device to reconcile the majority's need to adjust to changing economic conditions with the right of the members of the minority to refuse to participate in ventures beyond their initial contemplation. Such a right of appraisal is intended to avoid the common law difficulties of trying to restrict an abuse of power detrimental to minority shareholders by the directors or by majority shareholders where shareholder approval is required. As a rule, it will arise only in situations involving major structural changes, often described as "fundamental changes", and while the enterprise is continuing. Next to dissolution it is the most drastic step for the shareholder to take and will therefore likely be used sparingly but, as we argue below, its existence is essential and may lead not only to minority relief but also to more diligent efforts by management and the controlling shareholders.

The appraisal remedy exists in some form in all of the states of the United States except West Virginia. The Ontario, British Columbia, and Federal Acts all grant appraisal rights as do the proposed statutes for New Brunswick and Prince Edward Island. There is an extensive body of literature on the appraisal right in the United States which surveys the arguments for and against and the *Select Committee Merger Report* recently examined these same issues.

The leading critic of the appraisal right is Manning, who makes a twofold criticism. First, he says that it ill-serves the shareholder who uses it since the legal technique is laborious, slow, technical and expensive and the awards are unpredictable. Each of these criticisms is valid to some extent but they are equally applicable to many types of litigation. They do not assess the validity of the concept as an integral part of the protection of the minority. Second, Manning argues that the corporation is ill-served by an appraisal right because it creates a drain on cash flow at a critical time (but if the remedy is slow then the award will likely be made after the enterprise survives its critical period), it frightens creditors and suppliers (no evidence is offered to support this), and uncertainty is created by the unknown number of dissenters.

Some writers suggest that the appraisal right should be limited to the private company because of the alternative means available for dissent in the public company. In a private company there may be no or only very limited opportunities for the dissenter to sell his shares to anyone except the majority. In a publicly-held corporation, the market offers a potentially viable alternative. Further, shareholder expectations in the publicly-held firm may be more closely related to the market rather than the enterprise itself. The viability of the market alternative is directly related to the depth and transactions costs of the market. If the market is thin the dissenter's sale, particularly if he owns a large block of stock, may have a depressing effect on the available price. Further, the news of the structural change from which the shareholder dissents may have a depressing effect on the price before he has an opportunity to sell if securities analysts agree that the change is unwise.

There is, however, another consideration which makes a strong case for maintaining the appraisal right even in the publicly-held corporation. This is the function which the appraisal right serves as a check on management:

> Appraisal rights . . . have, in the past, served as a countervailing power to force the insiders to tailor their plans to minimize the number of dissenters by getting the best deal possible . . . when [the appraisal right] is removed, the insiders lack the real self-interest to fashion a plan acceptable to a sufficient number of shareholders.

By retaining his check, a check to be used only as a last resort by the dissenting shareholders who feel the decision was so improvident that the market no longer offers a fair alternative, it may be that it will produce extra care on the part of management and the majority when making such a decision.

Once the appraisal right is adopted in principle, the most difficult remaining task is to define the appropriate class of triggering events in a manner that is consistent with the normative model discussed above and which recognizes the competing interests of the majority and minority. . . .

Each of the B.C., Ontario, and Federal corporation statutes provide for a dissenting shareholder's appraisal right: see section 238 of the BCBCA, section 185 of the OBCA, and section 190 of the CBCA. Review the above sections with respect to:

(a) the events giving rise to the appraisal right;the procedure to be followed;

(b) the exclusiveness or non-exclusiveness of the right;

(c) the treatment of costs arising from exercising the appraisal rights; and

(d) the conditions under which the appraisal right can be withheld (see section 185(29) of the OBCA), withdrawn, or deferred.

One of the most important questions arising under these sections is the determination of the value of the dissenting shareholder's shares. A discussion of the various approaches adopted by the courts follows (See generally, Campbell, *The Principles and Practice of Business Valuation* (1975).)

Notes

1   In *Domglas Inc. v. Jarislowsky, Fraser & Co.*, 1980 CarswellQue 51, 13 B.L.R. 135 (C.S. Que.), affirmed 1982 CarswellQue 32, 138 D.L.R. (3d) 521 (C.A. Que.), the Quebec Superior Court discussed four different accepted and recognized approaches to the valuation of corporate shares. Under the first approach, using the market value, the quoted market price of each share on the stock exchange is used as the basis of valuation. The second approach is the assets approach. This approach analyzes the fair market value of the net assets of the

corporation to provide a valuation of shares. The third approach is the earnings or investment value approach. This method uses the expected earnings of the corporation to asses share value. Finally, some combination of each of the other three approaches can be used for valuation. What are the advantages and disadvantages of each of the four approaches?

2   *Smeenk v. Dexleigh Corp.* (1990), 74 O.R. (2d) 385, 1990 CarswellOnt 130 (H.C.), additional reasons 1990 CarswellOnt 2728, 72 D.L.R. (4th) 609 at 651 (Ont. H.C.), affirmed 1993 CarswellOnt 154, 105 D.L.R. (4th) 193 (Ont. C.A.), is another appraisal remedy case that discusses valuation principles.

In the course of his judgment, Henry J. set out several principles which flow from the statute and judicial decisions by which he was guided in making the valuation:

> 1. There is no onus on the applicants to demonstrate that the value represented by the company's offer is too low. The court must itself value the shares of the dissenting shareholders; however, any party who asserts a proposition must prove it by a preponderance of the evidence on the balance of probabilities. This case, however, does not necessarily depend upon onus unless the balance or scale needs to be tipped in favour of one party over the other (the usual rule).

> 2. The court must proceed on the basis of evidence offered by the parties. Where expert evidence is offered the court should be cautious in exercising its discretion to reject it. Where the court has offered the evidence of one expert only whose opinion is uncontroverted in any material respect the court cannot ignore it.

> 3. Valuation of shares under s. 190 of the Act is a matter of assessment in accordance with the facts of the particular case. It is not proper for the court to adopt a rigid formula and to view the matter as one of seeking mathematical precision. Whatever the decision, there is an important element of judgment involved and particular attention must be given to seeking a value that is fair having regard to all the circumstances; this invokes the equitable jurisdiction of the court.

> 4. The advantages of hindsight are not available either to the applicants or to the court. It is the policy of the Act to divorce the value of the shares on the valuation date from the effects of the amalgamation whether anticipated or *ex post facto*. Events that were not known on the valuation date or which occurred thereafter are therefore, in ordinary circumstances, not relevant to the issue which is to determine fair value on the valuation date; where they may nevertheless have some relevance or probative value they should on the basis of the same principle be given little weight.

5. The applicants are not entitled to obtain the benefits of the amalgamation, having dissented from the transaction. By dissenting the applicants elected to participate in neither the benefits nor the perceived detriments and risks of the amalgamation; they chose not to invest in the proposed arrangements and the resulting enterprise. The applicants in this case were not "squeezed out" or expropriated but were offered, with the other shareholders, a continuing interest in the amalgamated corporation. This interest and any benefits or risks flowing from it, the applicants declined in favour of referring the matter of their compensation to the court.

3   The court has discretion to select a valuation method to use. What method is selected depends upon the facts of the case. Factors include: whether the corporation is publicly traded and at what volume, the ease of asset valuation, and the likelihood of liquidation. For cases utilizing market value, see *Montgomery v. Shell Canada Ltd.* (1980), 111 D.L.R. (3d) 116, 3 Sask. R. 19, 1980 CarswellSask 113 (Sask. Q.B.) and *Lough v. Canadian Natural Resources Ltd.* (1983), 45 B.C.L.R. 335, 1983 CarswellBC 161 (B.C. S.C.), where market value was favoured because the corporations involved were highly traded. See also *Silber v. BGR Precious Metals Inc.* (1998), 41 O.R. (3d) 147, 1998 CarswellOnt 2994 (Ont. Gen. Div.), affirmed 2000 CarswellOnt 94, 46 O.R. (3d) 255 (Ont. C.A.), where market value was favoured because the corporation was a closed-end investment fund, where shares could not be redeemed but had to be traded on the open market.

4   If the events behind the need for a valuation amount to a forcible taking of the shares (for example, a transaction that "squeezes out" some shareholders), should this be taken into account in the valuation of those shares? While *Domglas Inc. v. Jarislowsky, Fraser & Co.* (1980), 13 B.L.R. 135, [1980] C.S. 925, 1980 CarswellQue 51 (C.S. Que.), affirmed (1982), 138 D.L.R. (3d) 521, 1982 CarswellQue 32 (C.A. Que.), held that a forcible taking premium applied, this decision appears to have been reversed. See *Locicero v. B.A.C.M. Industries Ltd.* (1984), 28 B.L.R. 172, 31 Man. R. (2d) 208, 1984 CarswellMan 18 (Man. Q.B.), reversed 1986 CarswellMan 305 (Man. C.A.), reversed 1988 CarswellMan 138, 1988 CarswellMan 256 (S.C.C.), which was reversed on appeal but ultimately restored by the Supreme Court, [1988] 1 S.C.R. 399, 1988 CarswellMan 138, 1988 CarswellMan 256 (S.C.C.), and *Brant Investments Ltd. v. KeepRite Inc.* (1991), 3 O.R. (3d) 289, 1991 CarswellOnt 133 (Ont. C.A.).

5   On the appraisal right generally, see Krishna, "Determining the 'Fair Value' of Corporate Shares" (1988), 13 C.B.L.J. 132, and MacIntosh, "The Shareholders' Appraisal Right in Canada: A Critical Reappraisal" (1986), 24 Osgoode Hall L.J. 201.

6.   OTHER REMEDIES

(a)   Compliance and Restraining Orders

As is pointed out in Chapter 3, s. 19 of the BCBCA provides that the memorandum and articles, when registered, shall bind the company and its members as though they had respectively been signed and sealed by each member and had contained covenants on the part of each member to observe all of them.

There is some authority in memorandum jurisdictions to the effect that each shareholder has a general contractual right to have the company's affairs managed in accordance with the terms of the memorandum of association and articles of association (*Re H.R. Harmer Ltd.*, [1959] 1 W.L.R. 62, [1958] 3 All E.R. 689 (C.A.)). Shareholders have been allowed to challenge the wrongful appointment of directors and conduct of the company's affairs by an improperly constituted board of directors (*Catesby v. Burnett*, [1916] 2 Ch. 325; *The Theatre Amusement Co. v. Stone* (1915), 50 S.C.R. 32, at 36-7, 6 W.W.R. 1438). Somewhat of an obstacle, however, is the principle from *Foss v. Harbottle* (1843), 2 Hare 461, 67 E.R. 189, stating that the corporation is the proper plaintiff to bring an action to rectify irregularities in the conduct of the corporation's affairs.

Several of the Canadian corporation statutes have distinct sections enforcing compliance with the rules governing the corporation. Section 247 of the CBCA allows a complainant (as defined in s. 238) or creditor to seek a compliance or restraining order against a variety of persons relating to abrogations of the statute, regulations, articles, by-laws, or a unanimous shareholder agreement. To similar effect is s. 253 of the OBCA, but noteworthy is the addition of "shareholder" to the list of persons against whom a compliance or restraining order may be obtained. See also ABCA s. 248, MCA s. 240, NBBCA s. 172, NCA s. 378, NSCA Third Schedule, s. 6 and SBCA s. 240. Of these, only the Alberta Act includes "shareholder" in the list of persons against whom such an order may be obtained.

The BCBCA has a most interesting compliance provision in s. 229 that allows for the correction of a "corporate mistake". On the motion of the court itself or the application of any interested person, the court may make an order to correct an omission, defect, error or irregularity in the conduct of the company that leads to a breach of the Act, causes non-compliance with the memoranda or articles or renders ineffective a shareholders' or directors' meeting. The court is given wide powers to rectify such a mistake.

Notes and Questions

1   In *Goldhar v. Quebec Manitou Mines Ltd.*, 1975 CarswellOnt 478, 9 O.R. (2d) 740, 61 D.L.R. (3d) 612 (Ont. Div. Ct.), Reid J. held that s. 261 [now s. 253] gave rise to a personal right that was not relevant to the pursuit of a derivative action; rather, the provision was more appropriate for rectifications of a "mechanical" nature. McIntyre J., in interpreting s. 248 of the ABCA (then s. 240), departed from *Goldhar*. See *Caleron Properties Ltd. v. 510207 Alberta Ltd.* (2000), 9 B.L.R. (3d) 218, 2000 CarswellAlta 1155 (Alta. Q.B.) (at p.225 [B.L.R.]), additional reasons 2000 CarswellAlta 1557 (Alta. Q.B.):

> [B]ased on the plain meaning of s. 240 in the context of the ABCA as a whole, I can see no justification for restricting its application to the rectification of simple mechanical omissions. Furthermore, because the right conferred on a complainant by s. 240 is in addition to any other right the complainant may have, I can see no justification for restricting its application based on whatever other standing that person may have. A complainant is not precluded from relying on s. 240 merely because that complainant may have concurrent standing pursuant to other sections of the ABCA. Indeed, as D.H. Peterson comments at para. 10.14, [*Shareholder Remedies in Canada* (Markam: Butterworths, 2000, 2nd edition)]: "[t]o strictly require that the wrongdoing be remedied through the traditional remedies, such as the oppression remedy and derivative and personal actions, can be overkill in many cases."

Which line of reasoning do you agree with?

2   There is also a compliance order provision in the Ontario *Securities Act*, R.S.O. 1990, c. S.5. Section 128 reads:

> 128.(1) The Commission may apply to the Ontario Court (General Division) for a declaration that a person or company has not complied with or is not complying with Ontario securities law. 1994, c. 11, s. 375.

> (3) If the court makes a declaration under subsection (1), the court may, despite the imposition of any penalty under section 122 and despite any order made by the Commission under section 127, make any order that the court considers appropriate against the person or company, including, without limiting the generality of the foregoing, one or more of the following orders:

> > 1.   An order that the person or company comply with Ontario securities law.

3   The statutory restraining and compliance order provisions allow the court to make not only a restraining order, but "any further order it thinks fit". Could this conceivably involve an award of damages? An

order that the articles of the corporation be changed, or that directors be removed? Any other remedy that a court might grant under the oppression remedy? If not, what would be the warrant for reading down the apparently clear words of the statute?

4   As an exercise, you should determine which statutory provisions bear on the question of awarding costs in connection with an application for a compliance and restraining order. Is the category of persons who are covered by the relevant costs provisions the same as those who may apply for a restraining order?

5   Note that the CBCA and OBCA both contain other restraining order provisions relating to specific subject matters. See, e.g., CBCA ss. 154 (proxy solicitations), 243(3)(b) (holding of shareholder meetings). Cf. OBCA ss. 253(2), 250(2)(b). See generally Dennis H. Peterson, Shareholder Remedies in Canada (Markham: Butterworths, 2000).

(b)   Rectification Orders

Under the CBCA, if the name of a person is alleged to be or has been wrongly entered or retained in, or wrongly deleted or omitted from, the register or other records of a corporation, the corporation, a security holder of the corporation or any aggrieved person may apply to a court for an order that the register or record be rectified (s. 243). The Director must be given notice of any application under this section and he is entitled to appear to be heard. The court may make any order it thinks fit including, without limiting the generality of the foregoing, an order (a) requiring the register or record to be rectified, (b) restraining the corporation from calling or holding a meeting of shareholders or paying a dividend before such rectification, (c) determining the right of a party to the proceedings to have his name entered or retained in, or deleted or omitted from the register or record whether the issue arises between two or more security holders or alleged security holders, or between the corporation and any security holders or alleged security holders and (d) compensating a party who has incurred a loss. To a similar effect is s. 250 of the OBCA which is based on s. 243 of the CBCA, but the Ontario section does not require notice to the Director of an application. See Iacobucci, Pilkington, and Prichard, *Canadian Business Corporations* (1977), pp. 219–223.

(c)   Investigations

The effective exercise of shareholder remedies will frequently depend on possessing the relevant information. An important statutory aid for shareholders in this respect is the court-ordered investigation of the corporation's affairs where the shareholder-applicant can satisfy the court that there are circumstances that warrant the court order. These court-ordered investigations should be distinguished from the shareholder-appointed investigations which are mounted by a shareholders' resolution appointing an inspector who has the same powers as one appointed by the court (see s. 250 of the BCBCA).

The provisions in the BCBCA, OBCA. and CBCA relating to investigations vary as to the terms and conditions under which an application for an investigation may be brought, by whom, and against whom. The powers of the court also vary.

Notes and Questions

1   The main role of an inspector is to discover facts. Does the inspector also have the power to determine that the law has been violated? The question arose in *Re First Investors Corp. (No. 1)*, unreported, Alta. Q.B., March 19, 1988, No. 8703-16333, in which Berger J. held that:

> the inspector shall report his opinion as to whether any individual, corporation or government agency has committed fraud or any other illegal act or is liable for acts of negligence, wrongdoing or illegality. As a necessary corollary of his fact-finding role, he shall consider and apply existing law in reporting to the court whether he has discovered evidence "tending to show" [that the legal grounds for commencing the investigation are supported]; he will set out his findings of fact together with the evidence in support of those findings: he will delineate the legal framework that guided his investigation.

The legal status of the investigator's report in subsequent proceedings is not entirely clear. In *Re Pergamon Press Ltd.*, [1970] 3 All E.R. 535 (C.A.), the English Court of Appeal held that the report cannot form the foundation of subsequent proceedings. As succinctly put by Middleton J.A. in *Re Shell Castle Fire Place Ltd.* (1927), 33 O.W.N. 195 (C.A.):

> The report merely gives the minority shareholders information of greater or less value. It may not be accurate, binds no one, and determines nothing.

However, in *Abraham v. Inter Wide Investments Ltd.* (1985), 51 O.R. (2d) 460 (H.C.), an inspector's report supplied the key facts relied upon by the Court in finding oppressive conduct under the oppression remedy (see also *Re Ferguson and Imax Systems Corporation* (1984), 44 C.P.C. 17 (Ont. Div. Ct.), in which an inspector's report was also admitted as evidence in an oppression action).

2   The courts have traditionally been reluctant to order an investigation, especially where it appears that some other source of information is available. For example, in *Re Baker and Paddock Inn Peterborough Ltd.* (1977), 16 O.R. (2d) 38, 2 B.L.R. 101 (H.C.), Galligan J. stated

that the power of the court to intervene in the affairs of a private corporation should be exercised with caution and held that the shareholders desirous of the court order did not establish that they could not get the information privately and hence an investigation was not ordered. Another example is *Royal Trustco Ltd. (No. 3), Re* (1981), 14 B.L.R. 307, 1981 CarswellOnt 120 (H.C.), which refused an investigation because there was already enough material information available. Eberle J. said (at p. 314 [B.L.R.]):

> However I am unable to conclude that any substantial area of factual investigation is now required. There is already on the table ample material on which any shareholder or other aggrieved party may decide whether or not take legal proceedings. If there were not, that might be sufficient justification to order an investigation, i.e., to ascertain facts in a manner and to an extent that might be beyond the capabilities of an ordinary shareholder to do. There may well be other grounds of justification, for I do not mean to suggest that the one I have indicated is the only one. The turning point in the present case is that the issues raised in this case, which are legal ones, or mixed legal and factual ones, are better disposed of in litigation between parties, where rights can be determined, than in an investigation which cannot determine rights.

See also *Budd v. Gentra Inc.* (1997), 53 O.T.C. 154, 1997 CarswellOnt 5226 (Gen. Div. [Commercial List]).

3   Note that there is no requirement in the statutory provisions noted above (re investigations) for the applicant to be acting in good faith. Nonetheless, at least one court has imposed such a requirement. In *Hendin v. Cadillac Fairview*, unreported, Jan. 31, 1983, S.C.D., No. 18-0206, the applicant was a real estate agent who alleged that he had not been paid his commission on the controversial sale of over 10,000 apartment units in Toronto. The Court held that the applicant's true purpose in bringing the application was to assist him in his claim to collect the real estate commission. Finding that he was not acting in good faith, the Court therefore denied the request for an investigation. See also *Balestreri v. Robert (receiver-manager)*; *Sparling et al. (mis-en-cause)* (1985), 30 B.L.R. 283. Is there any warrant for this super-added condition, given that there is no such requirement in the statute (contrast the derivative action provisions, which expressly require that the applicant be acting in good faith)?

4   An investigation may be authorized in connection with an oppression action. See CBCA s. 241(3)(m); OBCA s. 248(3)(m).

5   Note that an investigation may also be authorized under the Ontario *Securities Act*, R.S.O. 1980, c. 466, Part VI. You might have a look at these provisions and compare them to those in the CBCA and OBCA.

6   A case of potentially great impact is *Consolidated Enfield Corp. v. Blair* (1994), 19 B.L.R. (2d) 9, 1994 CarswellOnt 249 (Gen. Div.), per Logan J. In *Blair*, Blair applied to the Ontario court for an order of investigation order under s.161 of the OBCA respecting Consolidated Enfield ("Enfield"), a company of which he had formerly been a director and the Chief Executive Officer. When Enfield was taken over by Canadian Express (and Blair resigned as CEO and was removed as director), Blair alleged that Enfield had made insufficient disclosure to shareholders of transactions with related corporations for shareholders.

He pointed out that the financial statements and other disclosed material by Enfield did not accurately describe its relationship with its parent and related corporations.

Blair and another shareholder of Enfield (Algonquin, of which Blair was then CEO) sued, alleging that the failure to disclose was oppressive or unfairly prejudicial to shareholders, and that this justified an investigation. He also alleged that the manner in which related party transactions were approved was oppressive.

Logan J. held that, although it was not necessary that all related party transactions be approved by shareholders, inadequate disclosure to the auditor about related party dealings might nonetheless constitute unfair prejudice to a shareholder. (Note, however, that Logan J. deliberately refrained from saying anything about whether Ontario Securities Commission Policy 9.1 had been complied with.) Noting the "tremendous financial haemorrhage that has taken place in Enfield after the month of July 1989", he further held that there must be some special approval mechanism for related party transactions, and that the procedure adopted by Enfield was not adequate (at para. 87):

> It appears to myself that a structural deficiency exists in Enfield when it comes to the approval process for related party security transactions. The system used does not appear to be adequate. Even though directors may act honestly, the approval process does not operate in a fashion which allows the directors to act at all times in the best interests of the corporation. It is not fair and just. In my view it appears to unfairly disregard the interests of Blair and Algonquin as minority security holders in Enfield.

> It further appears that the inadequate approval system for related party transactions causes a lack of proper or sufficient communication of information by the officers of Enfield to the auditors about the nature and extent of related party transactions, the description of the relationship in all such transactions along with an accurate break down of amounts involved. The lack of communication that eventually results causes inappropriate dis-

closure to security holders about the proportion of Enfield's activities which involve related parties. It appears that the insufficiency of such information is unfairly prejudicial to Blair and Algonquin. It appears that the form of the existing structure means that partiality and deception may exist.

I order an investigation to be made by a person to be named by myself after receiving the submissions of counsel and Blair. The person so named shall investigate and report on the actual system employed by the current management of Enfield to independently review related party security transactions and the manner and method by which the approval process functions with individual settlements.

The *Blair* case has far-reaching implications, given that there are many Canadian corporations that are part of extended corporate empires and which frequently enter into related party transactions with other corporations in the same group.

7   As in the case with all shareholder rights and remedies, the issue of costs is crucially important in determining the efficacy of the right. Note that as in the case of derivative actions and oppression actions, the applicant is not required to give security for costs (CBCA s. 229(4); OBCA s. 161(4)). Other than this, the statutes say nothing about costs except that the court may order the corporation to pay the costs of the investigation (CBCA s. 230(1)(1); OBCA. s. 162(1)(1)). In *Re Ferguson and Imax Systems Corp.* (1984), 47 O.R. (2d) 225 (Ont. D.C.) (a follow-up case to *Re Ferguson and Imax Systems Corp.* (1983), 150 D.L.R. (3d) 718 (Ont. C.A.), *supra*), the plaintiff sought an investigation into alleged continuing acts of oppression. The trial judge had ordered that the investigation proceed without permitting cross-examination on the plaintiff's affidavits, apparently taking the earlier Court of Appeal finding of oppression as *res judicata* of the issue of ongoing oppression. Further, the inspector appointed by the Court (Laventhol and Horwath) had sworn an affidavit in favor of the plaintiff before the motions court judge, raising the appearance of bias. The District Court held that the trial judge had erred in two ways: first, he could not know if the statutory standard for an investigation ("it appears that" there is oppressive behavior) had been satisfied, owing to the absence of cross-examination and the incorrect taking of the earlier holding as *res judicata*. Second, an inspector other than Laventhol and Horwath should have been appointed in order to avoid the appearance of partiality. Nonetheless, the Court ordered that the company pay the costs of the already completed investigation, holding that the inspector had a right to be able to expect payment from somebody who would be able to pay. The Court nonetheless gave the trial judge

in the further oppression proceedings that were to follow the authority to allow the company a claim over against Mrs. Ferguson for the costs of the investigation.

In *Re Teperman & Sons Ltd.* (1984), 29 B.L.R.1 (Ont. H.C.J.) the Court held that it had a wide discretion under the statute to order costs in connection with an investigation. An order was made that the company pay the costs of the investigation, because (*inter alia*) the investigation had been of benefit to the company and stockholders in the company. An order also issued that the directors (whose conduct in paying generous and apparently unjustified remuneration had been called into question) should be jointly and severally liable should the company have insufficient funds to pay the costs. In *Consolidated Enfield Corp. v. Blair* (1996), 28 O.R. (3d) 714, 1996 CarswellOnt 455 (Div. Ct.), leave to appeal refused by 63 A.C.W.S. (3d) 1271, 1996 CarswellOnt 2291 (C.A.), the Court held that costs of an investigation were to be paid in most cases by the corporation. There could be cases where costs would be ordered a different way, but this would depend upon material before the judge other than the investigator's report.

(d) Winding-Up

The corporation statutes provide for liquidation and winding-up to take place voluntarily by shareholders' resolution or involuntarily by court order (*e.g.*, see, generally, ss. 207–228 of the CBCA, ss. 312–353 of the BCBCA and ss. 191–244 of the OBCA).

In the context of shareholder remedies, the dissolution order is the most drastic form of shareholder relief. Most statutes provide for a shareholder application to the court for such an order on the grounds that it is "just and equitable" to do so. See subparagraph 214(1)(b)(ii) of the CBCA, s. 324(1)(b) of the BCBCA and s. 207(1)(b)(iv) of the OBCA.

Huberman, "Winding-up of Business Corporations"
Ziegel, *Studies in Canadian Company Law* Vol. II (1973)
at p. 281 (footnotes omitted)

2. *The General Nature of the Relief*

The courts have, in the exercise of their powers under the "just and equitable" rule, made it abundantly clear that there are no fixed outside limits to the rule but rather that each case must be decided on its own facts. Indeed, where appropriate, the courts have, over the years, expanded the rule into new areas as fresh circumstances and situations have arisen and as the courts' reformulation of standards of intra-corporate conduct have developed. Thus, parallel to, and underlying, the expansion of the "just and equitable" rule there has been a corresponding imposition of stricter standards of behavior on the directors and majority shareholders in their treatment of minority shareholders. Similarly, there has been a growing recognition by the courts of the special nature and needs of the close corporation or, as some courts prefer to call it, the partnership in the guise of a company.

The power of the court to make a winding-up order is within the realm of its equitable jurisdiction and, as is traditional in courts of equity, the jurisdiction is construed liberally. Thus it has been said:

> The words "just and equitable" are words of the widest significance, and do not limit the jurisdiction of the Court to any case. It is a question of fact, and each case must depend upon its own circumstances.

And further:

> Nor . . . can any general rule be laid down as to the nature of the circumstances which have to be borne in mind in considering whether the case comes within the phrase.

In addition, it is clear from the legislation that the courts have been granted a broad discretion under the "just and equitable" rule. This is not to say that such discretion is unbounded, for, as was pointed out by Lord Clyde in *Baird v. Lees*:

> This discretion must, however, be judicially exercised. It is not enough for the Court in exercising it to have, in the familiar phrase of a decreearbitral, "God and a good conscience" before its eyes; grounds must be given which can be examined and justified.

As to the general approach that the court should take in any given case, Lord Shaw stated in *Loch v. John Blackwood Ltd.* that, in considering whether it was "just and equitable" to make a winding-up order, the court's consideration:

> . . . ought to proceed upon a sound induction of all the facts of the case, and should not exclude, but should include circumstances which bear upon the problem of continuing or stopping courses of conduct which substantially impair those rights and protections to which shareholders, both under statute and contract, are entitled.

It should be pointed out, however, that running through the cases under the "just and equitable" rule, and under each of the categories herein discussed, are several fundamental propositions. The most basic of these is that there is a well-recognized reluctance on the part of the courts to interfere in the internal affairs of a corporation. As one judge put it:

> While the words "just and equitable" are clearly intended to be elastic in their application in order that as the case arises injustice and inequity may be prevented, it is a common ground that a very

strong case must be made to justify the interference of the Court in the internal management of a company's affairs.

To the same effect, a leading Canadian judge has stated that: "The remedy is drastic, and hence must be addressed to a serious condition affecting the proper conduct or management of the company's affairs." This reluctance to interfere is based on several-known "rules", variously called the "internal management" rule, the "business judgment" rule, and the principal of "majority rule". Simply put, these rules come down to nothing more than this — the courts believe strongly that the majority of a corporation is entitled to govern the corporation as it, and not the court, sees fit and the majority will be allowed to do so free from court interference, unless its conduct is so gross as to shock the conscience of the court.

Not all courts are as reluctant as others to grant winding-up orders. Those that are reluctant tend invariably to fall back on the standard principles of majority rule and the like. The less reluctant courts manage skillfully to avoid reference to these time-worn clichés.

Notes and Questions

1 What circumstances constitute "just and equitable" grounds for winding up a corporation? From the case law, four principle grounds emerge:

1. Loss of Substratum: In *In re German Date Coffee Company* (1882), 20 Ch. D. 169 (C.A.), a corporation was formed for the purpose of acquiring a German patent to manufacture coffee from dates. The company was unable to acquire the patent but acquired instead a Swedish patent which was equally suitable. The company established a plant in Hamburg that operated at a profit. A petition was filed by two shareholders to have the company wound-up on the grounds that there was a complete failure of the corporate objects. On appeal from an order to wind-down the company, Baggallay L.J. upheld the trial judge's decision, finding that there was an impossibility of carrying on the business of the company, as the objective contemplated in the formation of the company was to use the German patent.

2. Justifiable Lack of Confidence: In *Loch v. John Blackwood* (1924) A.C. 783 (P.C.), Lord Shaw discussed this principle as follows:

   "It is undoubtedly true that at the foundation of applications for winding up, on the 'just and equitable' rule, there must lie a justifiable lack of confidence in the conduct and management of the company's affairs. But this lack of confidence must be grounded on conduct of the directors, not in regard to their private life or affairs, but in regard to the company's business. Furthermore the lack of confidence must spring not from dissatisfaction at being outvoted on the business affairs or on what is called the domestic policy of the company. On the other hand, wherever the lack of confidence is rested on a lack of probity in the conduct of the company's affairs, then the former is justified by the latter, and it is under the statute just and equitable that the company be wound up".

3. Deadlock: In *In Re Yenidje Tobacco Co. Ltd.* [1916] 2 Ch. 426 (C.A.), a corporation was formed between two tobacco manufacturers, Rothman and Weinberg, each with an equal number of shares and equal voting rights. There was a dispute between the two parties and Rothman brought an action alleging fraud against Weinberg. Evidence was provided that the two directors refused to speak to each other, that the meetings of the board of directors had become almost a farce or comedy, and that a third person had to convey communications between them. Lord Cozens-Hardy found that there was a complete deadlock between the two parties, that the corporation could not continue to function, and ordered that the company be wound-down.

4. The Partnership Analogy: This principle was also discussed in In *Re Yenidje Tobacco Co. Ltd.*, *supra*. Warrington L.J. held that, where the relationship between the parties to a corporation is essentially that of a partnership, the principles for dissolution of a partnership should apply. He found that Rothman and Weinberg were in substance partners, were at an impasse and therefore ordered the winding-down of the company.

2 *Ebrahimi v. Westbourne Galleries Ltd.*, [1972] 2 All E.R. 492, [1973] A.C. 360 (H.L.), which deals with the just and equitable winding up on the so-called "partnership analogy", may be found in Chapter 7 and is also discussed in the section of this chapter dealing with the oppression remedy.

3 Section 214 of the CBCA is not limited to the "just and equitable" ground for a court ordered dissolution. Paragraph 214(1)(a) mentions grounds for a dissolution which are similar to those for granting an oppression order under s. 241. The draftsmen of the CBCA explained the section as follows:

> Paragraph (a) of that subsection [ss.(1)] takes account of the strict limits which the courts have imposed on the "just and equitable" rule in paragraph (b)(ii). It is unlikely that the courts will be able to free themselves from the weight of the established precedents without statutory assistance. Paragraph (a) therefore contains a set of more relaxed criteria which, we hope, the courts may find useful in those cases where dissolution appears to be the most equitable solution, but which would be excluded under the "just and

equitable" rule. As long as the "just and equitable" rule is not the only basis upon which dissolution may be sought — and the other criteria in s. 17.07(1) [214] prevent this — then the established precedents are worth keeping. Paragraph (b)(ii) of s. 17.07(1) is therefore a residual provision, retained so that a useful fund of case law is not discarded. (Proposals for a New Business Corporations Law for Canada.)

Also, it should be noted that the wide powers available to the court in granting relief from oppression under s. 241 include an order liquidating and dissolving the corporation. (See also ss. 207 and 248 of the OBCA, which are comparable to the CBCA provisions in this respect.)

4   In a company that is analogous to a partnership, a lack of trust and cooperation between "partners" may act to incapacitate the company in the same sense that actual voting deadlock could. Winding-up may be ordered in such a situation. In *Bondi Better Bananas Ltd., Re,* [1951] O.R. 845, 1951 CarswellOnt 115 (C.A.), Aylesworth J.A. said (at p.855 [O.R.]):

> We think the principles governing the dissolution of partnerships apply to the circumstances in which these two gentlemen find themselves as equal owners of the capital stock and in equal control of this private company, and if this be so authority is not required for the proposition that "continued quarrelling, and such a state of animosity as precludes all reasonable hope of reconciliation and friendly co-operation" is sufficient to justify the order . . .

See also *Rogers v. Agincourt Holdings Ltd.* (1976), 1 B.L.R. 102, 1976 CarswellOnt 35 (C.A.); *Kapeluck v. Professional Industries Ltd.* (1983), 25 Sask. R. 58, 1983 CarswellSask 279 (Q.B.); and *King City Holdings Ltd. v. Preston Springs Gardens Inc.* (2001), 14 B.L.R. (3d) 277, 2001 CarswellOnt 1364 (S.C.J.).

5   On a winding-up application, the court is not limited to a decision between winding-up and doing nothing. The court may make an order for relief as under the applicable oppression remedy section. See, *e.g.,* CBCA s.214(2). The courts have also stated that winding-up is an extreme remedy and should sometimes not be granted if other remedies would suffice. See *Witlin v. Bergman* (1995), 25 O.R. (3d) 761, 1995 CarswellOnt 1204 (C.A.); and *Gold v. Rose* (2001), 2001 CarswellOnt 5 (S.C.J. [Commercial List]). The result is that while it may be "just and equitable" to order winding-up, another remedy may be ordered.